CHRIST

IN THE

OLD TESTAMENT

CHRIST

IN THE

OLD TESTAMENT

Sermons on The Foreshadowings of our Lord in
Old Testament History, Ceremony & Prophecy

By
C. H. Spurgeon

AMG *Publishers*
Chattanooga, TN 37422

Christ in the Old Testament

Originally published by
Passmore & Alabaster in London, 1899.

ISBN 0-89957-187-5

Printed in Canada
08 07 06 05 04 03 –T– 8 7 6 5 4 3 2

CONTENTS

II. CEREMONIAL

III. Prophetical

FOREWORD

Christ in the Old Testament was originally the sixth volume in a series of Spurgeon's sermons published by Passmore and Alabaster in the late 1800s, and it was published as a companion volume to *The Messiah: Sermons on Our Lord's Names, Titles, and Attributes.*

In this new edition we have sought to bring the power of Spurgeon's sermons to modern readers, and in doing so, we have updated the spelling in accordance with how our language has changed over the years. Readers should also note that the points of current history mentioned by Spurgeon are from the latter half of the nineteenth century.

Christ in the Old Testament contains sixty sermons, most of which were delivered between the years 1863 and 1897. Unless otherwise noted, all sermons were preached at the Metropolitan Tabernacle, Newington.

Preceding each sermon are the sermon number(s) in the complete Spurgeon series, the date on which it was read or intended to be read, portion(s) of Scripture read before the sermon, and where known, hymn numbers sung during the service from *Our Own Hymn Book*, a collection compiled by Spurgeon for the Metropolitan Tabernacle congregation.

PREFACE TO THE
ORIGINAL EDITION

When *The Messiah: Sermons on Our Lord's Names, Titles, and Attributes* was issued, a promise was given of a companion compilation to be entitled *Christ in the Old Testament*. Here it is; the sixth volume of a series which includes sermons on the Parables, the Miracles, the Canticles, and the Titles of Christ.

To the two disciples on the moonlit road, the Master, beginning at Moses and all the prophets, expounded the things concerning Himself. He is everywhere in Scripture; patriarchs and kings are types of Him who is the Ancient of Days and the Prince of Peace: the law was but a shadow of good things to come, and the testimony of Jesus is the spirit of prophecy. The Old Testament was Christ's Bible, and it is a Bible full of Christ. He is as surely in it as in the New Testament, albeit the revelation is not as vivid nor as full. Of course, when Spurgeon preached, he poured the content of the New Testament revelation into the mold of the Old Testament type and prophecy; expounding, in the blaze of the gospel light, that which was hidden from the prophets when they inquired and searched diligently what manner of time the Spirit of Christ which was in them did signify, when it testified beforehand of the sufferings of Christ and of the glory that should follow: interpreting, perhaps, more than the prophet or lawgiver understood, but not more than the Spirit intended and revealed.

There are sixty discourses within these covers. They fall naturally into three groups—Historical, Ceremonial, and Prophetical—each merging into the other. [In the table of contents, a historical reference relating Christ to Old Testament figures has been given to each sermon in part one in the form of a subject heading.] Twenty sermons are given under each heading; this number might easily have been doubled; on many of the subjects Mr. Spurgeon has preached several times, and sermons on other topics were available; but enough has been chosen to set forth the fair and glorious image of Him who is fairer than the children of men, who fulfills all the law and the prophets, who is the theme of Scripture as He is the joy of heaven.

May the glory of Christ in the Old Testament lead some to receive Christ into the heart as the hope of glory, and lend a new value to that Scripture which, though unsparingly assailed, is ever its own best witness!

I. HISTORICAL

HONEY FROM A LION

SERMON NO. 1,591
DELIVERED ON LORD'S DAY MORNING, APRIL 3, 1881.
PORTION OF SCRIPTURE READ BEFORE SERMON—ROMANS 5.

But not as the offense, so also is the free gift. For if through the offense of one many be dead, much more the grace of God, and the gift by grace, which is by one man, Jesus Christ, hath abounded unto many—Romans 5:15.

THIS text affords many openings for controversy. It can be made to bristle with difficulties. For instance—there might be a long discussion as to the manner in which the fall of Adam can justly be made to affect the condition of his posterity. When this is settled there might arise a question as to the exact way in which Adam's fault is connected with ourselves—whether by imputation of its sin, or in what other form; and then there might be further dispute as to the limit of evil resulting from our first parents' offense, and the full meaning of the fall, original sin, natural depravity, and so forth. There would be another splendid opportunity for a great battle over the question of the extent of the redeeming work of the Lord Jesus Christ; whether it covers, as to persons, the whole area of the ruin of the Fall; whether, in fact, full atonement has been made for all mankind or only for the elect. It would be easy in this way to set up a thornhedge, and keep the sheep out of the pasture; or to use another metaphor, to take up so much time in pelting each other with the stones as to leave the fruit untasted. I have, at this time, neither the inclination nor the mental strength either to suggest or to remove the difficulties, which are so often the amusement of unpractical minds. I feel more inclined to chime in with that ancient father of the church who declined controversy in a wise and explicit manner. He had been speaking concerning the things of God and found himself at length confounded by a certain clamorous disputant, who shouted again and again, "Hear me! Hear me!" "No," said the father, "I will not hear you, nor shall you hear me; but we will both be quiet and hear what our Lord Jesus Christ has to say." So we will not at this time listen to this side or that; but we will bow our ear to hear what the Scripture itself has to say apart from all the noise of sect and party. My object shall be to find out in the text that which is practically of use to us, that which may save the unconverted, that which may

3

comfort and build up those of us who are brought into a state of reconciliation with God; for I have of late been so often shut up in my sick chamber that when I do come forth I must be more than ever eager for fruit to the glory of God. We shall not, therefore, dive into the deeps with the hope of finding pearls, for these could not feed hungry men; but we will navigate the surface of the sea, and hope that some favoring wind will bear us to the desired haven with a freight of corn wherewith to supply the famishing. May the Holy Spirit bless the teaching of this hour to the creation and nourishment of saving faith.

I. The first observation from the text is this—THE APPOINTED WAY OF OUR SALVATION IS BY THE FREE GIFT OF GOD. We were ruined by the fall, but we are saved by a free gift. The text tells us that "the grace of God, and the gift by grace, which is by one man, Jesus Christ, hath abounded unto many." "Where sin abounded, grace did much more abound." "Grace reigns through righteousness unto eternal life by Jesus Christ our Lord." Although this doctrine is well known, and is taught in our synagogues every Sabbath day, yet this grand essential truth is often enough forgotten or ignored, so that it had need be repeated again and again. I could wish that every time the clock struck it said, "By grace are ye saved." I could wish that there were a trumpet voice ringing out at daybreak both on sea and land, over the whole round globe the words, "By grace are ye saved." As Martin Luther said of a certain other truth so say I of this, "You so constantly forget it that I feel inclined to take the Bible and beat it about your head, that you may feel it and keep it in remembrance." Men do not naturally love the doctrine of grace, and therefore they cast it out of their minds as much as possible. The larger portion of mankind do not believe that salvation is of grace: another part of them profess to believe it, but do not understand its meaning; and many who do understand it have never yielded to it or embraced it. Happy are they who belong to the remnant according to the election of grace, for they know right well the joyful sound, and they walk in the light of the glory of the grace of God which is in Christ Jesus.

Observe, that salvation is a free gift, that is to say, it is bestowed upon men by God *without regard to any merit, supposed or real.* Grace has to do with the guilty. Mercy in the very nature of things is not a fit gift for the righteous and deserving, but for the undeserving and sinful. When God deals out to men his gracious salvation they are regarded by him as lost and condemned, and he treats them as persons who have no claim upon him whatsoever, to whom nothing but his free favor and infinite love. It is according to the nature of God to pity the miserable and forgive the guilty, "for he is good, and his mercy endureth forever." God has a reason for saving men; but that reason does not lie in man's merit in any degree whatever. This is clear from the fact that he often begins his work of grace upon those who can least of all be credited with goodness. It was said of our Lord, "This man receiveth sinners," and the saying was most emphatically true. Sovereign grace selects such as Rahab the harlot, and Manasseh the persecutor, and Saul of Tarsus, the mad zealot against Christ: such as these have been seized upon by grace, and arrested in infinite love, that in them, the Lord might manifest the power and plentitude of his mercy. Salvation is a work which is begun by the pure, unpurchased, free favor of God, and in the same spirit it is carried on and perfected. Pure grace, which lays the foundation, also brings forth the capstone.

Salvation is also brought to men *irrespective of any merit which God foresees will be in man.* Foresight of the existence of grace cannot be the cause of grace. God Himself does not foresee that there will be any good thing in any man, except what He foresees that he will put there. What is the reason, then, why he determines that he will put it there? That reason, so far as we are informed, is this, "He will have mercy on whom he will have mercy." The Lord determines to display His love, and set on active work His attribute of grace, therefore does He save men according to the good pleasure of His will. If there be salvation given to men upon the foresight of what they are yet to be, it is clear it is a matter of works and debt, and not of grace; but the Scripture is most decided that it is not of works, but of unmingled grace, for saith the apostle, "If by grace, then is it no more of works: otherwise grace is no more grace. But if it be of works, then is it no more grace: otherwise work is no more work." Our text is express that salvation is "the free gift," and that it comes to us by "the grace of God, and the gift of grace, which is by one man, Jesus Christ."

I go a little further in trying to explain how salvation is a free gift, by saying that it is given *without reference to conditions which imply any desert.* But I hear one murmur, "God will not give grace to men who do not repent." I answer, God gives men grace to repent, and no man ever repents till first grace is given him by which he is led to repentance. "God will not give His grace to those who do not believe," says one. I reply, God gives grace to men by which they are moved to believe, and it is through the grace of God that they are brought into the faith of Jesus Christ. You may say, if you please, that repentance and faith are conditions of salvation, and I will not quarrel with you; but please remember that they are not conditions in the sense of deserving anything of God. They may be conditions of receiving, but they are not conditions of purchasing, for salvation is without money and without price. We are expressly told that salvation "is of faith, that it might be by grace": for faith is not to be numbered with works of the law, to which the idea of merit may be attached. Faith is far as the poles asunder from claiming anything of God by way of debt. Faith comes as a poor, undeserving thing, and simply trusts the free mercy of God. It never attempts to wear the crown, or grasp a particle of praise. The believer never can be a boaster, for boasting is excluded by the law, of faith. If a Christian should begin to boast, it would be because his believing is failing, and his evil nature is coming to the front; for faith is of all graces most self-denying; her song is always, *Non nobis Domine,* "Not unto us, but unto thy name give praise." While, therefore, the Word of God assures us that except we repent we shall all likewise perish, and that if we believe not in Jesus Christ we shall die in our sins, it would have us at the same time know that there is no merit in repenting or believing, but grace reigns in God's acceptance of these graces. We are not to regard the requirement of faith, repentance, and confession of sin as at all militating against the fullness and freeness of divine grace, since, in the first place, both repentance, faith, and true confession of sin are all gifts of grace, and, in the next place, they have no merit in themselves, being only such things as honest men should render when they know that they have erred and are promised forgiveness. To be sorry for my sin is no recompense for having sinned; and to believe God to be true is no work for which I may demand a reward; if, then, I am saved through faith, it is of the pure mercy of God, and of that alone that pardon comes to me.

Beloved, so far is God from giving salvation to men as a matter of reward and debt, and therefore bestowing it only upon the good and excellent, that *He is pleased to bestow that salvation over the head of sin and in the teeth of rebellion.* As I said before, mercy and grace are for the sinful, for none others need them; and God's grace comes to us when we are far off by wicked works. "God commendeth his love toward us, in that, while we were yet sinners, Christ died for us." Free grace breaks forth like a mighty flood, and sweeps in torrents over the hills of our transgressions, rising above the high Alps of our presumptuous sins. Twenty cubits upward doth this sea of grace prevail till the tops of the mountains of iniquity are covered. The Lord passeth by transgression, iniquity, and sin, and remembereth not the iniquity of His people, because He delighteth in mercy. Almsgiving needs a pauper, and grace needs a sinner. There is no opportunity for forgiveness where there is no offense. If men are meritorious how can God be gracious to them? In such a case it will be enough for Him to be just. When good works can put in a valid claim peace and heaven can be obtained by the rules of debt; but since it is clear that eternal life is the gift of pure favor, you need not marvel when I say that grace comes to men leaping over the mountains of their iniquities. Abounding mercy delights to blot out abounding sin, and it will never lack for opportunity to do its pleasure. There is no lack of occasions for grace in this poor fallen world, and of all the places where there is most room I know of one spot not far from here where there is a grand opportunity for infinite mercy and superabounding grace to exercise their power. Here is the spot—it is this treacherous, guilty heart of mine. I think, my brother, you know of another spot that is very like it; and you, my sister, too, can say, "Wondrous mercy! Sure there is room for all its heights and depths to be shown in this sinful soul of mine." Aye, and it will be shown, too, if you can but look for it through Christ Jesus; for it is the delight of God's grace to flow into unlikely places: mercy is the glory of God, and He loves to bestow it on those who least deserve it.

We are saved by grace, free grace, pure grace, grace without regard to merit or to the possibility of such a thing, and *many of us have been saved by grace of the most abounding and extraordinary sort.* Some of us will be prodigies of divine love, miracles of mercy, to be wondered at throughout eternity: we shall be set up in heaven as monuments for angels to gaze at, in which they shall see a display of the amazing goodness of the Lord. *Some of us*, I said; but I suppose that in each one of the redeemed there is some particular development of grace which will make him especially remarkable, so that the whole body of us, as one glorified church, shall be made known unto angels, and principalities, and powers, the manifold wisdom of God. Oh, what a revelation of grace and mercy will be seen when all the blood-washed race shall gather safely around the eternal throne, and sing their hallelujahs unto Him that loved them and washed them from their sins in His own blood.

Note one thing more concerning this plan of salvation, that *all this grace comes to us through the one man Jesus Christ.* I sometimes hear people talking about a "one man ministry." I know what they mean, but I know also that I am saved by a one man ministry, even by one who trod the winepress alone, and of the people there was none with Him. I was lost by a one man ministry, when father Adam fell in Eden; but I was saved by a one man ministry, when the blessed Lord Jesus Christ bore my sin in His own body on the tree. O matchless ministry of love, when the Lord from heaven came into the world and took upon Himself our nature, and became in all respects human, and being found in fashion as a man, was obedient to death, even the death of the cross! It is through the one man, Christ Jesus, that all the grace of God comes streaming down to all the chosen. Mercy flows to no man save through the one appointed channel, Jesus the Son of man. Get away from Christ, and you leave the highway of God's everlasting love; pass this door, and you shall find no entrance into life. You must drink from this conduit-pipe, or you must thirst forever, and ask in vain for a drop of water to cool your parched tongue. "In him dwelleth all the fullness of the Godhead bodily." All the infinite mercy of God and love of God—and God Himself is love—is concentrated in the person of the well-beloved Son of the Highest, and unto Him be glory forever. Sing unto Him, ye angels! Chant His praise, ye redeemed! For by the one man Christ Jesus the whole company of the elect have been delivered from the wrath to come, to the praise of the glory of the grace of God.

Thus I have tried to set before you God's way of salvation.

II. Starting aside, as it may seem, from the current of our thoughts, but only with the view of coming back to it with a forcible argument, we next note that IT IS CERTAIN THAT GREAT EVILS HAVE COME TO US BY THE FALL. Paul speaks in this text of ours of the "offense," which word may be read the "Fall," which was caused by the stumbling of our father Adam. Our fall in Adam is a type of the salvation which is in Christ Jesus, but the type is not able completely to set forth all the work of Christ: hence the apostle says, "But not as the offense, so also is the free gift. For if through the offense of one many be dead, much more the grace of God, and the gift by grace, which is by one man, Jesus Christ, hath abounded unto many." It is certain, then, that we were heavy losers by the offense of the first father and head of our race. I am not going into details and particulars, but it is clear that we have *lost the garden of Eden* and all its delights, privileges, and immunities, its communion with God, and its freedom from death. We have lost our first honor and health, and we have become the subjects of pain and weakness, suffering and death: this is the effect of the Fall. A desert now howls where otherwise a garden would have smiled.

Through the sin of Adam we have been born under conditions which are far from being desirable, heirs to *a heritage of sorrow*. Our griefs have been alleviated by the bounty of God, but still we are not born under such conditions as might have been ours had Adam remained in his integrity and kept his first estate. We came into the world with *a bias towards evil*. Those of us who have any knowledge of our own nature must confess that there is in us a strong tendency towards sin, which is mixed up with our very being. This is not derived solely from faults of education, or from the imitation of others; but there is a bent within us in the wrong direction, and this has been there from our birth. Alas! that it should be so; but so it is. In addition to having this tendency to sin, we are made *liable to death*—nay, not liable alone, but we are sure in due time to bow our heads beneath the fatal stroke. Two only of the human race have escaped death, but the rest have left their bodies here to molder back into mother earth, and unless the Lord cometh speedily, we expect that the same thing will happen to these bodies of ours. While we live we know that the *sweat of our brow* must pay the price of our bread; we know that our children must be born with pangs and travail; we know that we ourselves must return to the dust from whence we are taken; for dust we are, and unto dust must we return. O Adam, thou didst a sad day's work for us when thou didst hearken to the voice of thy wife and eat of the forbidden tree. The world has no more a Paradise anywhere, but everywhere it has the place of wailing and the field of the dead. Where can you go and not find traces of the first transgression in the sepulchre and its moldering bones? Every field is fattened with the dust of the departed: every wave of the sea is tainted with atoms of the dead. Scarcely blows a March wind down our streets but it sweeps aloft the dust either of Caesar or his slave, of ancient Briton, or modern Saxon; for the globe is worm-eaten by death. Sin has scarred, and marred, and spoiled this creation by making it subject to vanity through its offense. Thus terrible evils have come to us by an act in which we had no hand: we were not in the Garden of Eden, we did not incite Adam to rebellion, and yet we have become sufferers through no deed of ours. Say what you will about it, the fact remains, and cannot be escaped from.

This sad truth leads me on to the one which is the essence of the text, and constitutes my third observation.

III. FROM THE FALL WE INFER THE MORE ABUNDANT CERTAINTY THAT SALVATION BY GRACE THROUGH CHRIST JESUS SHALL COME TO BELIEVERS. If all this mischief has happened to us through the fall of Adam why should not immense blessing flow to us by the work of Christ? Through Adam's transgression we lost Paradise, that is certain; but if anything can be more certain we may with greater positiveness declare that the second Adam will restore the ruin of the first. If through the offense of one man many be dead, much more the grace of God and the gift by grace, which is by one man, Jesus Christ, shall abound and has abounded unto many. Settle in your minds, then, that the fall of Adam has wrought us great damage, and then be as much assured that the life, death and resurrection of Christ, in which we had no hand whatever, must do us great service. Believing in Christ Jesus, it becomes beyond all measure sure to us that we are blessed in Him, seeing that it is already certain through the fall of Adam we have become subject to sorrow and death.

For, first, *this appears to be more delightful to the heart of God.* It must be fully according to His gracious nature that salvation should come to us through His Son. I can understand that God, having so arranged it that the human race should be regarded as one, and should stand or fall before him in one man, should carry out the arrangement to its righteous end, and allow the consequences of sin to fall upon succeeding generations of men: but yet I know that he takes no pleasure in the death of any, and finds no delight in afflicting mankind. When the first Adam transgressed it was inevitable that the consequences of his transgression should descend to his posterity, and yet I can imagine a perfectly holy mind questioning whether the arrangement would be carried out. I can conceive of angels saying one to another, "Will all men die through this entrance of sin into the world? Can it be that the innumerable sons of Adam will all suffer from his disobedience?" But I cannot imagine any question being raised about the other point, namely, the result of the work of our Lord Jesus. If God has so arranged it that in the second Adam men rise and live, it seems to me most gloriously consistent with His gracious nature and infinite love that it should come to pass that all who believe in Jesus should be saved through Him. I cannot imagine angels hesitating and saying, "Christ has been born; Christ has lived; Christ has died; these men have had nothing to do with that: will God save them for the sake of His Son?" Oh, no, they must have felt, as they saw the babe born at Bethlehem, as they saw Him living His perfect life and dying His atoning death, "God will bless those who are in Christ; God will save Christ's people for Christ's sake." As for ourselves, we are sure that if the Lord executes judgment, which is His strange work, He will certainly carry out mercy, which is His delight. If He kept to the representative principle when it involved consequences which gave Him no pleasure, we may be abundantly assured that He will keep to it now that it will involve nothing but good to those concerned in it. Here, then, is the argument—"For if through the offense of one many be dead, much more the grace of God, and the gift by grace, which is by one man, Jesus Christ, hath abounded unto many."

This assurance becomes stronger still when we think that *it seems more inevitable that men should be saved by the death of Christ than that men should be lost by the sin of Adam.* It might seem possible that, after Adam had sinned, God might have said, "Notwithstanding this covenant of works, I will not lay this burden upon the children of Adam"; but it is not possible that after the eternal Son of God has become man, and has bowed His head to death, God should say, "Yet after all I will not save men for Christ's sake." Stand and look at the Christ upon the cross, and mark those wounds of His, and you will become absolutely certain that sin can be pardoned, nay, must be pardoned to those who are in Christ Jesus. Those flowing drops of blood demand with a voice that cannot be gainsaid that iniquity should be put away. If the voice of Abel crying from the ground was prevalent, how much more the blood of the Only-begotten Son of God, who through the eternal Spirit offered

Himself without spot? It cannot be, O God, that thou shouldest despise or forget the sacrifice on Calvary. Grace must flow to sinners through the bleeding Savior, seeing that death came to men through their transgressing progenitor.

I do not know whether I shall get into the very soul of this argument as I desire, but to me it is very sweet to look at *the difference as to the causes of the two effects*. Look now at the occasion of our ruin—"the offense of one." The one man transgresses, and you and I and all of us come under sin, sorrow, and death. What are we told is the fountain of these streams of woe? The one action of our first parents. Far be it from me to say a word to depreciate the greatness of their crime, or to raise a question as to the justice of its consequences. I think no one can have a more decided opinion upon that point than I have; for the offense was very great, and the principle which led to our participation in its results is a just one, and, what is more, is fraught with the most blessed after-consequences to fallen men, since it has left them a door of hope of their rising by the same method which led to their fall. Yet the sin which destroyed us was the transgression of a finite being, and cannot be compared in power with the grace of the infinite God; it was the sin of a moment, and therefore cannot be compared for force and energy with the everlasting purpose of divine love. If, then, the comparatively feeble fount of Adam's sin sends forth a flood which drowns the world in sorrow and death, what must be the boundless blessing poured forth from the infinite source of divine grace? The grace of God is like his nature, omnipotent and unlimited. God hath not a measure of love, but He is love; love to the uttermost dwells in Him. God is not only gracious to this degree or to that, but He is gracious beyond measure; we read of "the exceeding riches of his grace." He is "the God of all grace," and His mercy is great above the heavens. Our largest conceptions fall far short of the lovingkindness and pity of God, for "His merciful kindness is great towards us." As high as the heavens are above the earth, so are His thoughts above our thoughts in the direction of grace. If, then, my brethren, the narrow fount which yielded bitter and poisonous waters has sufficed to slay the myriads of the human race, how much more shall the river of God which is full of water, even the river of the water of life, which proceedeth out of the throne of God and of the Lamb, supply life and bliss to every man that believeth in Christ Jesus? Thus saith Paul, "For if by one man's offense death reigned by one; much more they which receive abundance of grace and of the gift of righteousness shall reign in life by one, Jesus Christ." That is the argument of the text, and to me it seems to be a very powerful one, sufficient to dash out the very life of unbelief and enable every penitent man to say, "I see what I have lost in Adam, but I also see how much I obtain through Christ Jesus, my Lord, when I humbly yield myself to Him."

Furthermore, I would have you note *the difference of the channels* by which the evil and the good were severally communicated to us. In each case it was "by one," but what a difference in the persons! We fell through Adam, a name not to be pronounced without reverence, seeing he is the chief patriarch of the race, and the children should honor the parent: let us not think too little of the head of the human family. Yet what is the first Adam as compared with the second Adam? He is but of the earth, earthy, but the second man is the Lord from heaven. He was at best a mere man, but our Redeemer counts it not robbery to be equal with God. Surely, then, if Adam with that puny hand of his could pull down the house of our humanity, and hurl this ruin on our first estate, that greater man, who is also the Son of God, can fully restore us and bring us back to our race the golden age. If one man could ruin by his fault, surely an infinitely greater man in whom dwelleth all the fullness of the Godhead bodily can restore us by the abounding grace of God.

And look, my brethren, what this man did. Adam commits *one* fault and spoils us; but Christ's works and achievements are not one, but many as the stars of heaven. Look at that life of obedience: it is like a crown set with all manner of priceless jewels: all the virtues are in it, and it is without flaw in any point. If one sinful action of our first covenant head destroys, shall not a whole life of holiness, on the part of our second covenant representative be accepted for us?

But what is more, Adam did but eat of the forbidden fruit, but our Lord Jesus died, pouring out His soul unto death, bearing the sin of His people upon Himself. Such a death must have more force in it than the sad deed of Adam. Shall it not save us? Is there any comparison between the one act of rebellion in the garden and the matchless deed of superlative obedience upon the cross of Calvary which crowned a life of service? Am I sure that the act of disobedience has done me damage? Then I am much more certain that the glorious act of self-sacrifice must be able to save me, and I cast myself upon it without question or misgiving. The passion of God's Only-begotten must have in it infallible virtue for the remission of sin. Upon the perfect work of Jesus my soul hangs at this moment, without a suspicion of possible failure, and without the addition of the shadow of a confidence anywhere else. The good which may be supposed to be in man, his best words and holiest actions, are all to me as the small dust of the balance as to any title to the favor of God. My sole claim for salvation lies in atonement for my sin, but that one Man, Christ Jesus, is a sure foundation, and nail upon which we may hang all the weight of our eternal interests. I feel the more confidence in the certainty of salvation by Christ because of my firm persuasion of the dreadful efficacy of Adam's fall. Think awhile and it will seem strange, yet strangely true, that the hope of Paradise regained should be argued and justified by the fact of Paradise lost, that the absolute certainty that one man ruined us should give us an abounding guarantee that one glorious Man has in very deed effectually saved all those who by faith accept the efficacy of his work.

Now, if you have grasped my thought, and have drunk into the truth of the text, you may derive a great deal of comfort from it, and it may suggest to you many painful things which will henceforth yield you pleasure. A babe is born into the world amid great anxiety because of its mother's pains, but while these go to prove how the consequences of the Fall are still with us, according to the word of the Lord to Eve, "in sorrow shalt thou bring forth children," they also assure us that the second Adam can abundantly bring us bliss through a second birth, by which we are begotten again unto a lively hope. You go into the arable field and mark the thistle, and tear your garments with a thorn: these prove the curse, but also preach the gospel. Did not the Lord God say, "Cursed is the ground for thy sake; thorns also and thistles shall it bring forth to thee." Through no fault of ours, for we were not present when the first man offended, our fields reluctantly yield their harvests. Well, inasmuch as we have seen the thorn and the thistle produced by the ground because of one Adam, we may expect to see a blessing on the earth because of the second and greater Adam. Therefore with unabounded confidence do I believe the promise—"Ye shall go out with joy, and be led forth with peace: the mountains and the hills shall break forth before you into singing, and all the trees of the field shall clap their hands. Instead of the thorn shall come up the fir tree, and instead of the brier shall come up the myrtle tree: and it shall be to the Lord for a name, for an everlasting sign that shall not be cut off."

Do you wipe the sweat from your brow as you toil for your livelihood? Did not the Lord say, "In the sweat of thy face shalt thou eat bread"? Ought not your labor to be an argument by which your faith shall prove that in Christ Jesus there remaineth a rest for the people of God. In toiling unto weariness you feel that Adam's fall is at work upon you; he has turned you into a tiller of the ground, or a keeper of sheep, or a worker in metals, but in any case he has made you wear a yoke; say you then to the Lord Jesus, "Blessed second Adam, as I see and feel what the first man did, I am abundantly certified as to what thou canst accomplish. I will therefore rest in thee with all my heart."

When you observe a funeral passing slowly along the street, or enter the church-yard, and notice hillock after hillock above the lowly beds of the departed, you see set forth evidently before your eyes the result of the Fall. You ask,—Who slew all these? and at what gate did the fell destroyer enter this world? Did the first Adam through his disobedience lift the latch for death? It is surely so. Therefore I believe with the greater assurance that the second Adam can give life to these dry bones, can awake all these sleepers, and raise them in newness of life. If so weak a man as Adam by one sin has brought in death, to pile the carcasses of men heaps upon heaps, and make the earth reek with corruption, much more shall the glorious Son of God at His coming call them again to life and immortality, and renew them in the image of God. How blessed are those words,—"Now is Christ risen from the dead, and become the firstfruits of them that slept. For since by man came death, by man came also the resurrection of the dead. For as in Adam all die, even so in Christ shall all be made alive. The first man is of the earth, earthy: the second man is the Lord from heaven. As is the earthy, such are they also that are earthy: and as is the heavenly, such are they also that are heavenly. And as we have borne the image of the earthy, we shall also bear the image of the heavenly." Is not this killing a lion, and finding honey in its carcass? "Out of the eater cometh forth meat, and out of the strong cometh forth sweetness," when from the fact of the Fall we derive a strong assurance of our restoration by Christ Jesus.

Time fails me; otherwise I meant to have dwelt somewhat at length upon the last head which can now only be cursorily noticed.

IV. It seems certain that if from the fall of Adam such great results flow, GREATER RESULTS MUST FLOW FROM THE GRACE OF GOD, AND THE GIFT BY GRACE, WHICH IS BY ONE MAN, JESUS CHRIST. Brethren, suppose that Adam had never sinned, and we were at this moment unfallen beings, yet our standing would have remained in jeopardy, seeing that at any moment he might have transgressed and so have pulled us down. Thousands of years of obedience might not have ended the probation, seeing there is no such stipulation in the original covenant. You and I therefore would be holding our happiness by a very precarious tenure; we could never glory in absolute security and eternal life as we now do in Christ Jesus. We have now lost everything in Adam, and so the uncertain tenure has come to an end, our lease of Eden and its joys has altogether expired; but we that believed, have obtained an inheritance which we hold by an indisputable and never-failing title which Satan himself cannot dispute; "All things are yours, and ye are Christ's, and Christ is God's." The Lord Jesus Christ has finished the work by which His people are saved, and that work has been certified by His resurrection from the dead. There are no "ifs" in the covenant now; there is not a "peradventure" in it from beginning to end; no chances of failure caused by unfinished conditions can be found in it. "He that believeth and is baptized *shall be saved.*" Do you say, "I believe he shall be saved if he—"? Do not dare to an place "if" where God has placed none. Remember what will happen to you if you add anything to the book of God's testimony. No, it is written, "He that believeth and is baptized *shall be* saved": "He that believeth in him hath *everlasting* life." "There is therefore now no condemnation to them that are in Christ Jesus." Thus we have obtained a surer standing than we could have had under the first Adam, and our hymn is true to the letter when it sings—

> He raised me from the deeps of sin,
>   The gate of gaping hell,
> And fix'd my standing more secure
>   Than 'twas before I fell.

Our Lord has not only undone the mischief of the Fall, but He has given us more than we have lost: even as the Psalmist said, "Then I restored that which I took not away."

By the great transgression of Adam we lost our life in him, for so ran the threatening— "In the day that thou eatest thereof thou shalt surely die"; but in Christ Jesus we live again with a higher and nobler life, for the new life being the direct work of the Spirit, and being sustained by feeding upon the person of the Lord Jesus, is higher than the life of innocence in the garden of Eden. It is of a higher kind in many respects, of which we cannot now speak particularly, but this much we may say, "The first Adam was made a living soul, the second Adam is a quickening Spirit."

The Lord Jesus has also brought us into a nearer relationship to God than we could have possessed by any other means. We were God's creatures by creation, but now we are His sons by adoption; in a certain narrow sense we were the offspring of God, but now by the exaltation of the man Christ Jesus, the representative of us all, we are brought into the nearest possible relationship to God. Jesus sits upon the throne of God, and manhood is thus uplifted next to deity: the nearest akin to the Eternal is a man, Christ Jesus, the Son of the Highest. We are members of His body, of His flesh, and of His bones, and therefore we share His honors and participate in His triumphs. In Christ Jesus man is made to have dominion over all the works of God's hands, and the redeemed are raised up together with Christ and made to sit in the heavenly places with Him, above all principalities and powers, and all things else that be; for these are the favorites of heaven, the beloved of the great King. No creatures can equal perfected men; they rise superior even to the angels who never have sinned; for in them the riches of the glory of God's grace is more fully seen than in pure, unfallen spirits.

O beloved, hath not the Lord Jesus Christ done much for us, and ought we not to expect that it should be so, for the grace of God, and the gift by grace by the man Christ Jesus, are infinitely stronger forces than Adam's sin. There must be much more sap in the man, the Branch, than in that poor plant, the one man who was made from the dust of the earth. Oh the bliss which opens up before us now. We have lost Paradise, but we shall possess that of which the earthly garden was but a lowly type: we might have eaten of the luscious fruits of Eden, but now we eat of the bread which came down from heaven; we might have heard the voice of the Lord God walking in the garden in the cool of the day, but now, like Enoch, we may walk with God after a nobler and closer fashion. We are now capable of a joy which unfallen spirits could not have known: the bliss of pardoned sin, the heaven of deep conscious obligation to eternal mercy. The bonds which bind redeemed ones to their God are the strongest which exist. What a joy it will be to love the Lord more than any other of His creatures, and assuredly we shall do so. Do not think that this is an unwarrantable assertion, for I feel sure that it is the truth. Do you not read in the gospels of a woman who washed the Savior's feet with tears and wiped them with the hairs of her head, and anointed them with ointment? Did not the Savior say that she loved much because she had much forgiven. I take it that the same general principle will apply to all places, to eternity as well as to time, and therefore I believe that forgiven sinners will have a love to God and to His Christ such as cherubim and seraphim never felt; Gabriel cannot love Jesus as a forgiven man will do. Those who have washed their robes and made them white in the blood of the Lamb will be nearer and dearer to Him, and He will be nearer and dearer to them, than all the ministering spirits before the throne, for He took upon Him our nature and not theirs. Glory be unto Thee, O Christ! As I look into the awful deeps of Adam's fall, I tremble, but when I lift up my eyes again to the eternal heights whither Thou hast raised me by Thy passion and Thy resurrection I feel strengthened by the former vision. I magnify the infinite grace of God, and believe in it unstaggeringly. Oh, that I had power to magnify it with fit words and proper speech, but these are not with me. Accept the feeling of the heart when the language of the lip confesses its failure. Accept it, Lord, through the Well-beloved. Amen.

THE BLOOD OF ABEL AND THE BLOOD OF JESUS

Sermon No. 708
Delivered on Lord's day Morning, September 2, 1866.

And he said, What hast thou done? the voice of thy brother's blood crieth unto me from the ground—Genesis 4:10.

And to Jesus the mediator of the new covenant, and to the blood of sprinkling, that speaketh better things than that of Abel—Hebrews 12:24.

THE first shedding of human blood was a very terrible experiment. Whether Cain's murderous blow was premeditated or not, the sight of a bleeding human corpse must have been a terrible novelty to him. He had not been hardened by reading details of warfare, or listening to tales of murder; killing and slaying were new terrors to mankind, and he who was the ringleader in such violence must have been filled with mingled astonishment at the result of his blow, and apprehension as to its consequences. I think I see him standing there by the corpse, for a moment stiff with affright, awe-struck at the sight of blood. Will the skies dart malignant fires upon him? Will the sodden earth produce speedy avengers from her astonished soil? What questions must have flashed through the murderer's mind! But lo! the warm lifeblood flows in a crimson stream upon the earth, and some ghastly comfort arises to the mind of the guilty wretch as he observes the earth soak in the blood. It stands not in a pool, but the earth opens her mouth to receive and to conceal his brother's blood. Sad memorials bespatter the herbage and crimson the soil, but still the dreadful flood is drying up, and the murderer feels a momentary joy. Perhaps Cain went his way dreaming that the terrible matter was all over. He had done the deed, and it could not be undone; he had smitten the blow, ridden himself of the presence of one who was obnoxious to him; the blood had been swallowed up by the earth, and there was an end to the business which need cause no further thought. There was no machinery in those days of police, and law, and judges, and gallows, and therefore Cain had little or nothing to fear; strong and hale man, with no one to punish him, and nobody to accuse or upbraid him, except his father and his mother, and those, possibly, too bowed with grief and

15

too mindful of their own offense to show much resentment toward their first-born. He may therefore have imagined that the deed was speechless and silent, and that now oblivion would cover his crime, so that he might go his way as though the deed were never done. It was not so, however, for though that blood was silent in the seared conscience of Cain, it had a voice elsewhere. A mysterious voice went up beyond the skies; it reached the ear of the Invisible, and moved the heart of Eternal Justice, so that breaking through the veil which conceals the Infinite from man, God revealed Himself and spoke to Cain: "What hast thou done? The voice of thy brother's blood crieth unto me from the ground." Then Cain knew that blood could not be idly spilt, that murder would be avenged, for there was a tongue in every drop of the vital essence which flowed from murdered manhood, which prevailed with God, so that he would interpose and hold a solemn inquest thereon.

Brethren, that was a more terrible experiment still which was tried at Calvary, when not the first man was slaughtered but the Son of God Himself; He who was man but yet was more than man, God manifest in the flesh; it was a dread experiment when having dragged Him before the judgment seat and falsely condemned Him, having shouted, "Away with him, away with him," they actually dared to take the nails and fasten the Son of God to the accursed tree, to lift up His body between earth and heaven, and there to watch its griefs till they ended in His death, when they pierced His side, and forthwith flowed thereout blood and water. No doubt Pilate, who had washed his hands in water, thought that no mischief would come of it. The Scribes and Pharisees went their way, and said, "We have silenced the accusing voice. There will no more be heard in our streets of Him who said, 'Woe unto you, Scribes and Pharisees, hypocrites.' We shall no longer be disturbed in our hypocrisy and formality by the presence of a pure and holy being, whose simple honesty shall be a stern rebuke to us. We have murdered Him, we have put Him to death without just reason, but there is an end of it. There will be no voice to that blood." Little did they know that up to heaven the cry of Jerusalem had already gone, "His blood be on us, and on our children," was registered in the tablets of justice, and before long Jerusalem became the treasure house of woe and a den of misery, so that the like to her destruction hath not been, neither ever shall be, upon the face of the earth. Far more delightful is the fact that another and more melodious cry went up to heaven from the cross of Calvary. "Father, forgive them," resounded from the wounds of Immanuel. The blood of Abel was not voiceless, and the blood of Jesus was not dumb; it cried so as to be heard amid the thrones of heaven, and blessed be God, it spoke *for us* and not against us; it spoke not worse things, as it might well have done, but better things than that of Abel. It did not demand fiercer vengeance than that which fell upon Cain, it did not ask that we might be driven vagabonds and fugitives upon the face of the earth, and to be at last banished from God into hell forever, but it cried, "Father, forgive them," and it prevailed, and the curse was taken away, and a blessing came to the sons of men.

This morning we propose to keep our discourse to the subject of the voice of the blood of Abel and the voice of the blood of Jesus, as standing in comparison the one with the other. They both spoke. That is evident. Abel being dead yet speaketh, saith the apostle, and we know to our abiding comfort that the blood of Jesus pleads before the eternal throne. All blood has a voice, for God is jealous of its preservation, the blood of excellent and just men has a more heavenly speech still, but the voice of the blood of Jesus far surpasses all, and among ten thousand voices it bears the palm.

I. In the first place, JESUS' BLOOD SPEAKS BETTER THINGS IN GENERAL.

What did the blood of Abel say? Was it not the blood of *testimony*? When Abel fell to the ground beneath his brother's club, he bore witness to spiritual religion. Cain was the lover of a merely outward worship, in which faith had no place. He loved a worship of show and pomp, he garnished the altar with fruits and decked it with flowers; his was a religion of taste and elegance, a religion of his own devising; but it was devoid of a humble, believing, spiritual reference to the promised Deliverer. Abel stood there the professor of an ungarnished religion of faith in the promised sacrifice. On the altar was a lamb, bleeding from its death wound, and laid in order for burning; a ghastly spectacle not to be delighted in by taste, a thing from which the lovers of the beautiful would turn away. Abel had chosen such an offering because God had chosen it, and because it was the fit means for leading his faith to its true object, the Lord Jesus. He saw by faith in the bleeding lamb the memorial of the Lord's great propitiation for sin, which could not be seen in Cain's offering of the fruits of the earth, however tasteful that offering might be. Abel stands forth before us as the first in a cloud of witnesses, bearing brave testimony, and prepared to seal it with their lives. He died a martyr for the truth, the grandly God-like truth that God accepteth men according to their faith. All honor to the martyr's blood which speaks so effectually for precious truth. Our Lord Jesus Christ, being also a testifier and witness for the faith of God, spoke better things than Abel, because He had more to speak, and spoke from more intimate acquaintance with God. He was a fuller witness of divine truth than Abel could be, for He brought life and immortality to light, and told His people clearly of the Father. Our Lord Jesus Christ had been in the bosom of the Father, and knew the divine secret; this secret He revealed to the sons of men in His ministry, and then He sealed it by His blood. It is not to be forgotten that though the death of Christ was in chief an atonement for sin, yet it was also a testimony to the truth, for He is said to be a witness to the people, a leader and commander to the people, and as a dying, bleeding martyr, it will be clear to you that this blood testifies to fuller, brighter, and more glorious truth than did the blood of Abel.

Moreover, the blood of Abel spoke good things in that it was the *proof of faithfulness*. This dear servant of the Great Master was faithful under his brother's opposition; yea, faithful unto death. It could not be said of him as the apostle said of certain others, "Ye have not yet resisted unto blood, striving against sin." He resisted sin even unto blood; he was faithful in all his house as a servant; he turned not from his integrity, but counted not his life dear unto him. His blood as it fell to the ground spoke this good thing; it said, "Great God, Abel is faithful to thee." But the blood of Jesus Christ testifies to yet greater faithfulness still, for it was the sequel of a spotlessly perfect life, which no act of sin had ever defiled; whereas Abel's death furnished, it is true, a life of faith, but not a life of perfection. The faithfulness of Jesus was complete from the day of His birth to the hour of His death; and inasmuch as He needed not otherwise to die, His voluntary yielding up of life was all the more an act of obedience, and the better proof of His fidelity to His trust.

Moreover, we must never forget that all that Abel's blood could say as it fell to the ground was but *the shadow* of that more glorious substance to which Jesus' death assures us. Jesus did not typify atonement, but offered it; He was not the representative of sacrifice; He was the great Sacrifice itself, and inasmuch as the substance must ever excel the shadow, the blood of Jesus Christ speaketh better things than that of Abel.

It is well to add that our Lord's person was infinitely more worthy and glorious than that of Abel, and consequently His death must yield to us a more golden-mouthed discourse than the death of a mere man like Abel. He who dies at the hand of Cain is but one of our race, testifying to truth and righteousness, testifying by faith to a sacrifice to come; but He who died at the hand of Herod and of Pilate was divine, and came upon no common errand, with no ordinary message to deliver. When the glorious Son of God bowed His head and gave up the ghost, the voice that arose from His blood must necessarily have been louder, sweeter, more full, and more God-like than the voice of the martyred Abel's gore. We understand then, before coming to details, that on general principles we may be pretty clear that the blood of Jesus would speak better things than that of Abel.

II. Now we will enter the very heart of our text, while we remember that THE BLOOD OF JESUS SPEAKS BETTER THINGS TO GOD than the blood of Abel did. The blood of Abel cried in the ears of the Lord, for thus He said to Cain, "The voice of thy brother's blood crieth unto *me* from the ground." That cry did not go round to seek a mediator, but went directly to the judgment seat of God, and laid an accusation against the murderer. Now what did Abel's blood say to God? Standing by the spot where Abel fell, and marking the ground all crimson with clotted gore, what would the blood seem to you to say? What would be your own reflection? What would you conceive that the blood said to God? It said just this, "O God, one of thine own creatures, the product of thy matchless skill, has been dashed in pieces, and barbarously destroyed. A living, sensitive body formed by art and skill, such as only Thou couldst show, has been wantonly broken. The potter will not bear, that the vessel which has been fashioned upon the wheel with much cost and labor should be wantonly broken, but here is a body far more costly, far more wonderful than anything which human art could create, and this has been destroyed. Great God, the Creator of all things, wilt Thou look on this with patience, wilt Thou bear to see the work of thine own hands most cruelly destroyed?" Was there not much in this cry? Then that blood would plead still further, "O God, thy creature has been destroyed without cause. No just reason of provocation has been given, no offense has been committed which could deserve so terrible a stroke; but one of thy feeble creatures who has a claim upon thy kind protection has been wantonly and needlessly slain: his blood appeals to Thee! Thou Judge of all the earth, wilt Thou let the weak be trodden down by the strong, and wilt Thou suffer the innocent to be smitten by the fierce hand of the wicked?" You see the cry gathers force. At first it is, "O God, thy creature has been destroyed"; next it is, "O God, thy subject has been maltreated by one of his fellow-subjects, by one who has become thine enemy: wilt Thou not interfere?" Yet the blood of Abel said more than this; it said, "O God, the blood shed here was shed for Thee." It seemed to say, "If it were not for love of thee this blood had not been shed! If these drops had not been consecrated by devotion, if this blood had not flowed in the veins of man who loved God with all his heart it had not been poured out upon the ground. O God," cries every drop, "I fell upon the ground for Thee—wilt Thou endure this? Shall a creature that Thou hast made yield up its life with pain and anguish for Thee, and wilt Thou be like a cold, motionless, unmoved, immovable statue, and look on without emotion? Wilt Thou not bestir thyself, O God? Shall blood be shed on thine own behalf, shed unjustly too, the blood of thine own loving, righteous creature, and wilt Thou not interfere?" What force there is in such a voice! Yet the blood added to this, "O God, I have been shed in defiance of Thee," for the stroke which came from Cain's hand was not aimed merely at Abel, it was in spirit aimed at God, for if Cain could have done the same to God as he did to his brother, Abel, he doubtless would have done it. He was of that wicked one, and therefore slew his brother, and the wickedness which was in him was *deicidal*; he would have slain God Himself if it had been in his power, and so the blood cried, "O God, here is the gauntlet of defiance thrown down to Thyself. Cain defies Thee. He has struck the first blow at Thyself, he has smitten down the vanguard of the army of thine elect. Wilt Thou look on in quiet? Wilt Thou take no vengeance? Wilt Thou have no regard? Shall there be silence in heaven when there are groans and cries on earth? Shall heaven's heart be cold when the heart of the enemy is hot with rage and fierce with rebellion? O God, wilt Thou not interpose?" Surely this is a heaven-piercing cry, but this is not all. The blood of the proto-martyr added to all this such an appeal as the following: "O God, this is the first of human blood that has been murderously shed, and shed by an unnatural brother's hand. Wilt Thou pass this by? Then how canst Thou be just? Did not this blood challenge the very existence of justice in God? O God, if Thou do not punish this first barbarous man-slayer, who kills his brother, then all down the ages men will riot in blood and wanton in murder, and they will say, 'How doth God know?' He that sitteth in the heavens regardeth not, He will not so much as speak?" It were as though God should issue a license for man to shed each other's blood, and give permission for red-handed murder to lord it over the whole creation, if the first murder should pass unnoticed by the great Judge of all. Do you hear, my brethren, what a cry the blood of Abel must have had, and with what power it arose to heaven? But we are not left to conjecture as to the power of that cry, for we are told that God heard, and when He heard it *He* came to reckoning with Cain, and He said, "What hast thou done? The voice of thy brother's blood crieth to me from the ground." Then came the withering sentence of it. The ground which had drank in the blood became accursed to Cain, so that delve it as he might it could not yield him a bounteous harvest, plow it as he would, with all his skill and craft, it never could yield its strength to him. The original curse of the thorn and the thistle, which had fallen upon it when Adam survived, was now doubled to Cain, so that he reaped but handfuls and gathered scanty sheaves. This would be a constant bitter mingled with his daily bread, while over and above that, he received unto his heart a curse which made him the slave of his own dreads. He served fear and trembling as his gods, and went about the earth with darkness within him and darkness round about him, never more rejoicing, but wearing the mark of reprobation fixed upon his brow. He life was doubtless hell upon earth, and at last he was driven forever from the presence of the Most High God. Blood has a voice in it, and when it is heard against a man it brings upon him a curse untold.

Well now, brethren, it is a very sweet task to ask you to turn your minds away from the blood of Abel to the blood of Jesus. I feel persuaded that you did just now recognize the voice of Abel's blood, and I want your minds to hear with equal distinctness the voice of Jesus Christ's blood, for there are the same reasons for its loudness, but they are all far more emphatic. Can you stand at Calvary now and view the flowing of the Savior's blood from hands, and feet, and side? What are your own reflections as to what that blood says to God? Think now at the cross-foot. That blood crieth with a loud voice to God, and what doth it say? Does it not say this? "O God, this time it is not merely a creature which bleeds, but though the body that hangs upon the cross is the creature of Thy Holy Spirit, it is Thine own Son who now pours out His soul unto death. O God, it is Thine only-begotten One, dear to Thyself, essentially One with Thee, One in whom Thou art well pleased, One whose obedience is perfect, whose love to Thee has been unwavering, it is he who dies. O God, wilt Thou despise the cries and the tears, the groans, the moans, the blood of Thine own Son? Most tender Father, in whose bosom Jesus lay from the foundations of the earth, *He* dies, and wilt Thou not regard *Him*? Shall His blood fall to the ground in vain?" Then, moreover, the voice would plead, "It is not only Thy Son, but Thy perfectly innocent Son, in whom was no necessity for dying, because He had no original sin which would have brought corruption on Him, who had moreover no actual sin, who throughout life had done nothing worthy of death or of bonds. O God, it is Thine only-begotten, who, without a fault, is led as a lamb to the slaughter, and stands like a sheep before her shearers. Canst Thou see it, Thou God of all, canst Thou see the infinitely holy and just Son of Thy heart led here to die—canst Thou see it, and not feel the force of the blood as it cries to Thee?" Was there not added to this fact that our Lord died to vindicate the honor of His Father? "For Thee, O God, for Thee He dies! He who hangs on Calvary hangs there in deference to

Thine own decree, in fulfillment of Thine own purpose, in vindication of the honor of Thy law, that Thou mayest Thyself be glorified, that Thy justice may have full scope, and Thy mercy may have illimitable sway. O God, the sufferer, pal in death, whose wounds are torn open with the cruel nails, and whose soul is racked with pain unutterable, dies for Thee. If there had been no God He need not die. If there were no law to vindicate, no truth to defend, no honor, and majesty, and justice to which to pay homage, it need not that He died. If Thou wert content to stain thine honor or to restrain thy mercy, there were no need that He should give Himself. But it is for Thee, for Thee with each pang, for Thee with each groan, for Thee each drop of blood, and wilt Thou not be moved thereby?" Brethren, is there not power in this voice? Yet over and above this the blood must have pleaded thus with God: "O God, the blood which is now being shed, thus honorable and glorious in itself, is being poured out with a motive which is divinely gracious. He who dies on this cross dies for His enemy, groans for those who make Him groan, suffers for those who thrust the dart into His soul, and then mock at the agony which they themselves have caused. O God, it is a chain for God in heaven which binds the victim to the horns of the altar, a chain of everlasting love, of illimitable goodness." Now, dear friends, you and I could not see a man suffer out of pure benevolence without being moved by his sufferings, and shall God be unmoved? the perfectly holy and gracious God, shall He be indifferent where you and I are stirred to deep emotion? The sight of blood makes some of us shudder; the sight of blood shed from an innocent person—shed by the hand of violence—would make our very souls chill within us; but the thought of that blood being shed with a motive so marvelous, because of a disinterested affection towards undeserving criminals—this would move us indeed; and do you dream that it did not move the heart of God? Blessed be His name, we are not left to conjecture here; it so moved our heavenly Father that to this day God has come to man, and speaking to us through that blood He has said, "What hast thou done? Whatever thou hast done, however black and filthy thy sin may have been, the voice of My Son's blood crieth unto Me from the ground, and now from this day forth I have taken off the curse from the earth for His sake, neither will I curse it any more. Ye shall be blessed in your basket and in your store, in your going out and in your coming in. I have forgiven you your iniquities; I have set a mark upon you, and no man shall hurt you, neither shall justice smite you, for in the person of my dear Son I have received and accepted you, guilty as you are. Go your way, and live happily and peaceably, for I have taken away your iniquities and cast your sins behind my back, and the day has come in the which if thy sins be searched, for they shall not be found, yea, if they be sought out they shall not be, saith the Lord, for I have pardoned them whom I have reserved." Abel's blood had mighty prevalence to curse, but Jesus' blood has prevalence to bless the sons of men.

I want you to stay a little over this thought to digest it. I wish I had the power to send it home; only the Holy Ghost, however, can do that. I want, however, just to dwell on it, that you may get into the soul of it. Observe that the blood of Abel spoke to God long before Cain spoke. Cain was deaf to the voice of his brother's blood, but God heard it. Sinner, long before you hear the blood of Jesus, God hears it, and spares your guilty soul. Long before that blood comes into your soul to melt you to repentance, it pleads for you with God. It was not the voice of Cain that brought down vengeance, but the voice of Abel's blood; and it is not the cry of the sinner seeking mercy that is the cause of mercy, it is the cry of that blood of Jesus. I know you will tell me you cannot pray; oh what a mercy it is that the blood can, and that when you cannot plead so as to prevail, the blood pleads. If you are to win mercy from God and get forgiveness, it will not be by the efficacy of your prayers and tears, but through the efficacy of that blood of God's dear Son. Cain did not ask for vengeance, but it came unsought through the blood; and you, though you feel as if you hardly dare look for mercy, yet shall find it if you can trust the blood of Jesus which speaks for you. The blood does not need your voice to increase its power with God; He will hear your voice, but it is because He hears the blood of Jesus first of all. It is a mercy for us that the blood of Abel spoke against the guilty. Jesus' blood pleads not for the innocent, if such there be, they need no plea from an atoning sacrifice. Jesus pleads for the rebellious that the Lord God may dwell among them; for you that have broken His laws, and despised His love, and fought against His power; the blood of Jesus pleads for such as you, for He came into the world to save sinners. "The Son of Man is come to seek and to save that which was lost."

The precious book speaks constantly. Did you notice that word in the text? "Which *speaketh*," not "which did speak," but "which speaketh." The blood of Jesus pleaded for the thief upon the cross, but it

> Shall never lose its power,
> Till all the ransom'd church of God
> Be saved to sin no more.

Brother, when prevailing sin oppresses the conscience, it is a thousand mercies to know that we have even now a prevailing Savior. Years ago some of us came to Christ, and we found pardon; but our faith occasionally faints, and our doubts grow strong. Come, let us go afresh to the fountain, let us look anew to the cross, for the blood speaks still. Still in effect our Lord Jesus bleeds today as much as He did 1800 years ago, for the blood is just as certain in its power with God at the present moment as when the thief said, "Lord, remember me." Let us think of this and rejoice in this. My soul, when thou canst not plead with God, when thou darest not, when thy tongue is silent, and despair gags thy mouth, even then Jesus pleads. Now lay thou hold upon the intercession; come and cast thyself upon Him; rest wholly in Him, He must prevail though thou canst not, He must succeed though thou hast no power whatsoever. Come then, and link thyself with the infallible prevalent plea of the precious blood, and it is all well with thee, all safe with thee, and safe forever. God grant us grace to do this, each one of us, and His be the praise!

III. Furthermore, Jesus' blood speaks better things to us in our own hearts than did the blood of Abel.

I suppose most of you read the account written by the newspaper correspondents who have passed over the battlefields of Königgratz or Sadowa. How it thrilled one to read of ditches filled with blood, and of the smell from putrid corpses being so intolerable that the travelers were fain to leave the battle-field in haste. I would not like to be Bismarck, nor the Crown Prince of Prussia, nor the King, nor anyone who had a hand in a war so sanguinary and so unjustifiable. I suppose that wholesale assassins grow used to such things; I suppose that they can read of thousands mangled by shot and shell without emotion, and even see the heaps of corpses without a shudder, but I am certain of this, that it would drive me mad. Ah! to have the blood of one person knowingly laid at my door would be enough to dash all comfort from my life; but to have the blood of tens of thousands poured out to gratify my ambition, I think must make reason reel at once. It must be an absence of conscience which makes reason to keep her throne when men have been wading through their fellows' blood for mere purposes of selfish gain. Seeing that there had been no wars in Cain's day, and that the human heart had not been brutalized as it now is, so as to speak of war as we now do in such gentle terms, surely if he had had any conscience at all, it must have been a horrible thought to him that he had killed his brother. "I have killed a man, I have shed his blood." Surely it made him start in his sleep. How could he be quiet upon his lonely couch? That red-handed man! Guilt, a grim chamberlain, with fingers bloody red would surely draw the curtains of his bed. Would not the spectacle all come up before his mind? The talk in the field, the sudden impulse, the blow, the blood, the look of his victim as he cried for pity as one cruel stroke succeeded another; and then the sight of the ghastly body and the streaming blood, and the crimson marks on the sodden earth. Oh, it must have been a remembrance clinging like a viper around the murderer wherever he might be! He might well build a city, as we are told he did, in order to quench these fiery remembrances. Then would the thought come upon him, "You slew him though he was your brother." "Am I my brother's keeper?" said he, but men can talk sometimes more braggingly than their heart talks in secret. The horror of brother-killing must have haunted Cain: "I slew my brother, I, the first that was born of woman slew the second born." And then it would be suggested, "And wherefore did I slay him? What evil had he done me? What if he did offer a different sacrifice from mine, and what if God did accept *him* and not me, yet what hurt had he done me?" The innocence of his victim, if Cain had any conscience, must have increased his uneasiness, for he would recollect how inoffensively he had kept those sheep of his, and had been like one among them, so lamblike, that shepherd man himself, a true sheep of God's pasture. "Yet," would Cain say, "I slew him because I hated God, the God before whose bar I am soon to stand, the God who set this mark on me." Can you picture the man who had thus to be daily schooled and upbraided by his brother's blood? It needs a poet's mind to teach him. Think how you would feel if you had killed your own brother, how the guilt would hang over you like a black cloud, and drop horror into your very soul.

Now, brethren, there is more than equal force in the cry of the blood of Jesus, only it acts differently, and it speaketh better things. Let it be remembered, however, that it speaks those better things with the same force. Comforts arise from the blood of Jesus as powerful as the horrors which arose from the blood of Abel. When the sinner looks to Jesus slain, he may well say, "If I did not know that all this blood was shed for me as well as by me, my fears would multiply a thousandfold; but when I think that that precious blood is blood shed instead of mine, that it is blood which God planned and ordained should be shed for me from before the foundation of the world, when I think that that is the blood of God's own dear Son, whom He has smitten instead of smiting me, making Him bear the whole of His wrath that I might not bear it, O my God, what comforts come streaming from this blessed fountain?" Just in proportion as thought of murder would make Cain wretched, in the same proportion ought faith to make you happy as you think upon Jesus Christ slain; for the blood of Christ, as I said at the beginning of the sermon, cannot have a less powerful voice; it must have a more powerful voice than that of Abel, and it cries therefore more powerfully for you than the blood of Abel cried against his brother Cain. Oh, then, my clamoring sins, I can hear you, but I am not afraid of you, for the blood of Jesus speaks louder than you all. Oh, then, conscience, I can hear thine accusation, but I am not alarmed, for my Savior died. I come before God with perfect confidence, because I am sprinkled with the blood of my Substitute. If the horror of Cain with an awakened conscience might be unendurable, so the peace which comes to me through the precious blood of Jesus is indescribable and unutterable, a peace like a river, a righteousness like the waves of the sea. Sweet peace have all they who hear the blood speaking in their souls, telling them that sin is forgiven, that God is reconciled, that we are accepted in the Beloved, and that now we are preserved in Christ Jesus, and shall never perish, neither shall any pluck us out of His hand. I trust you know, I know many of you do, the sweet power of this peace-speaking blood. Such innocent blood, ordained on purpose to give peace, is precious beyond all price. O my soul! never look for peace elsewhere, and never be afraid of finding peace here. If today, O Christian, you have lost your confidence, if today you are conscious of having been false to your Lord, and of having done despite to His Spirit, if today you feel ashamed of the very name of a Christian because you have dishonored it, if today despair is ready to strangle your hope, and you are tempted to give it all up, yet come now, even now, to this precious blood. Do not think that my Savior can save merely the little sinners; He is a great Savior—mighty to save. I know your sins speak very loudly—ah! well they may; I hope you will hear their voice and hate them in the future—but they cannot speak so loudly as the blood of Jesus does. It says, "Father, Father, shall I die in vain? Father, I paid my blood for sinners, shall not sinners be saved? I was smitten for the guilty, shall the guilty be smitten too?" The blood says, "O God, I have vindicated thy law, what more dost Thou demand? I have honored thy justice, why shouldst Thou cast the sinner into hell? O thou Divine Benignity! canst Thou take two exactions for one offense, and punish those for whom Jesus suffered? O Justice! wilt thou here avenge? O Mercy! when the way is cleared, wilt thou not run to guilty sinners? O Love Divine, when the pathway is opened for Thee, wilt Thou not show Thyself to the rebellious and the vile?" The blood shall not plead in vain; sinners shall be saved, and you and I, I hope, among them to the praise and glory of His grace.

IV. Two or three words to close with. Jesus' blood, even in my text, speaks better things than that of Abel.

It speaks the same things but in a better sense. Did you notice the first text? God said unto Cain, "What has thou done?" Now that is what Christ's blood says to you: "What hast thou done?" My dear hearer, dost thou not know that thy sins slew the Savior? If we have been playing with sin, and fancied it to be a very little thing, a trifle to play with and laugh at, let us correct the mistake. Our Savior hangs on the cross, and was nailed there by those sins of ours; shall we think little of them? Looking from the cross, Jesus says to us, "What hast thou done?" O my hearer, what hast thou done? Thou hast slain thy best friend and ruined thyself! Let me come home personally to every one. Make an inventory now of your sins. Go over the black list from your childhood till now. What hast thou done? Ah! Lord, done enough to make me weep forever if it were not that Thou hast wept for me. Drops of grief can never repay the debt which is due to thy blood. Alas! I have done evil, Lord, but Thou hast done good to me. "What hast thou done? What hast thou done?" was a dreadful accusation to Cain, it might have gone through him like a dart; but to you and to me it is the soft inquiring voice of a Father's love bringing us to repentance. May it bring us now!

What I want mainly to indicate is this. If you notice in the second text, this blood is called "*the blood of sprinkling.*" Whether Abel's blood sprinkled Cain or not I cannot say, but if it did it must have added to his horror to have had the blood actually upon him. But this adds to the joy in our case, for the blood of Jesus is of little value to us until it is sprinkled upon us. Faith dips the hyssop in the atoning blood and sprinkles it upon the soul, and the soul is clean. The application of the blood of Jesus is the true ground of joy, and the sure source of Christian comfort; the application of the blood of Abel must have been horror, but the application of the blood of Jesus is the root and ground of all delight.

There is another matter in the text with which I conclude. The apostle says, "We are *come* to the blood of sprinkling." He mentions that among other things to which we are *come*. Now, from the blood of Abel every reasonable man would flee away. He that has murdered his fellow desires to put a wide distance between himself and the accusing corpse. But we come to the blood of Jesus. It is a topic in which we delight as our contemplations bring us nearer and nearer to it. I ask you, dear Christian friends, to come nearer to it this morning than ever you have been. Think over the great truth of substitution. Portray to yourselves the sufferings of the Savior. Dwell in His sight, sit at the foot of Calvary, abide in the presence of His cross, and never turn away from that great spectacle of mercy and of misery. *Come* to it; be not afraid. Ho, ye sinner, who have never trusted Jesus, look ye hither and live! May you come to Him now!

> Come, guilty souls, and flee away,
> Like doves to Jesus' wounds.

Nay, do not run away from the wounds which you have made, but find shelter in them; forget the sufferings of Christ, but rest in them! Your only hope lies in trusting in Jesus, resting wholly upon Him. Think much of the griefs of your Lord, and if I might suggest to some of you who will not be coming out this afternoon, perhaps if you could spend an hour or two between services in considering the sufferings of the Savior, those considerations might be the means of bringing faith to you. Faith cometh by hearing, but it is a thoughtful hearing; and hearing comes by the Word of God, but the Word must be thought over. Open the Word, read the story of the cross, ask the Master to bless it to you, and who knoweth but through the Divine Spirit some of you may yet hear the voice of that blood which speaketh better things than that of Abel. The Lord bless every one of you for His name's sake. Amen.

SHUT IN OR SHUT OUT

SERMON NO. 1,613

DELIVERED ON LORD'S DAY MORNING, AUGUST 14, 1881.

The LORD shut him in—Genesis 7:16.

NOAH was a very different man from the rest of those who lived in his time, for the grace of God had set a division between him and them. *They* forgot God, and *he* feared Him; they lived for things seen and temporal, and he lived in sight of the invisible. When he was building his ark he was in a miserable minority, as men count heads; and, even after 120 years of ministry, when his ark was built and his family entered it, they were eight against many millions, an insignificant few, as men would say; a pitiful sect among mankind. Who could imagine that the eight would be right and all the millions wrong? Where God is, there is the majority. But very clearly there was a very marked distinction between Noah and his household, and all the rest of mankind. Yet, great as that distinction was, throughout 120 years there was no impassable gulf between the two parties. Although Noah could not, would not go to them, yet they that would might pass to him; if they would hear, believe, and obey, they, too, might be amongst the company whom God has blessed, and whom He would surely preserve from destruction. Yea, when the 120 years were over, and God's Spirit would no longer strive with men, there stood the great ark with its vast door wide open, and still Noah continued to preach and to declare that all who would pass within that open portal into the ark of safety should be preserved from the coming destruction. Outside that door death would reign universally, but all would be peace within.

When the last seven days of grace had come to a close the Lord began His work of justice by separating Noah, and "the Lord shut him in." Then there was a more marked difference between Noah and the rest of mankind. He that openeth and no man shutteth, He that shutteth and no man openeth, even He had interposed a barrier impassable between Noah and those that believed not. Mercy's gate was shut, the time of longsuffering had come to a close.

Brethren, the Church of God stands at the present moment in the world very much in the same condition as Noah and his family. Still is the door of the ark wide open, and it is our business with all our might to persuade, constrain, compel men

27

to come in. Not without success have our entreaties been; for many have entered the ark of salvation which is found in the Person of our divine Lord Jesus. These make up with us the chosen family of God who shall be safe when the world is deluged with the last devouring fire. But the time cometh, it comes to each man in death, and it will come to the whole company of the ungodly in the day when the Lord Jesus shall descend from heaven with a shout, that the door shall be shut, and it shall be said, "Between us and you there is a great gulf fixed; so that they which would pass from hence to you cannot; neither can they pass to us, that would come from thence." Character will become unchangeable; he that is unjust will be unjust still, and he that is filthy will be filthy still.

My heart trembles as I think of this matter. There is a joy in being shut in with the saints, but a great grief in knowing that many will be shut out. I shall labor so to set forth this truth that, mayhap, before the door closes a goodly company may cry, "We will come with you, for we perceive that the Lord is with you." Surely in the floods of great waters they shall not come nigh unto the Lord; but until those waterfloods break forth they may come, and they shall find a glad welcome; for it is written, "Him that cometh to me I will in no wise cast out."

Our meditation will be arranged under two heads, which may readily be remembered: *shut in* and *shut out*. They stand in very distinct contrast, and admit of no third condition.

I. First, let us think of truths which range themselves under the head of SHUT IN. This is a blessed text. Oh that the Spirit of God may help me to preach from it, and you to enjoy it.

Observe, then, that Noah was *shut in*—shut in the ark. Noah's condition as to an evil world was now one of permanent separation. He was severed from the world, and his separation was beyond recall. There is a time in the human character when it has some good thing in it towards the Lord God of Israel, and yet that good thing may be lost; but there is another and happier time when the truly converted have stepped over the boundary, and shall never go back again unto corruption. They are dead, and their life is hid with Christ in God; hidden beyond further damage or death. They are henceforth kept by the power of God unto salvation; crucified unto the world and the world unto them. There was a time when, speaking after the manner of men, Noah might have given up his testimony and sided with the ungodly mass; but that possibility is all over; for the door is shut, the Lord hath shut him in. There was no wish in Noah's heart to come out, and he could not come out. The deed was done, and could not be undone: the bolt was turned and could not be withdrawn. Noah was shut in by a hand which is not given to undo its own work. I believe that this fixity of character and condition has happened to all believers who can truly say that they are dead unto the world. Dying unto the world is our way of salvation; by this process we pass into newness of life. I dare say when that door was shut the men of the world said, "Look at old Noah! He has gone into his coffin. He is as good as dead and buried." Yes, that was exactly what they were meant to see and to say; and Peter says, "The like figure whereunto also baptism doth now save us." He does not say that baptism saves us; but that it is a "like figure" of the way of salvation. The ark and immersion set forth the same truth. The man is "buried in baptism," to signify that he is dead to the world; wherein also he rises again to show his fellowship with Christ in resurrection, and the fact that he has risen to newness of life. Baptism is a picture of the way of salvation, just as Noah's ark was. Entrance into the ark and submergence beneath forty days' deluge of rain, was a fit type of death and burial; and the rising of the ark above the waters fitly sets forth resurrection to a new life. Noah underwent burial to all the old things that he might come out into a new world, and even so we die in Christ that we may live with Him. This is the doctrine, but the experience is grand. Beloved, it is a great mercy when a man can feel in his own soul that God has fixed forever his condition towards the ungodly. We have come out, my brethren, from among men just as Abraham did when he left his fatherland and went into the land of which he knew nothing but that God had said that He would give it to him and to his seed. It is written concerning Abraham and the other patriarchs that "doubtless if they had been mindful of the place whence they came out, they had opportunity to return," but they did not return, it entered not into their minds and hearts to do so. They had as fully left Padanaram behind them as if they had been dead and buried to it, and their life showed each one of them to be a pilgrim and a sojourner with God. Even so with believers, the Lord has called us out and set us apart unto Himself. Henceforth a door is shut behind us, and we cannot go back. We are like Bunyan's Pilgrim, we must go forward, for we have no armor for our backs. There is no inducement to go back if we fairly consider the matter. The City of Destruction which we have left is to be burnt with fire—shall we go back to that? The enemies we have fought with and encountered are left behind; shall we seek them to fight with them again, or to become their friends? Sin is bitter to us, it hath already broken our teeth as with gravel stones—shall we go back to it again? What inducement have we to return to the house of bondage? No; by God's grace "Forward" is out motto till we come to "the city which hath foundations, whose builder and maker is God."

Brethren, I am always glad when I can feel concerning any of you that you have finally done with the world, and may be numbered with the irreconcileables: for, alas, I fear there are too many who have so questionably come out of Sodom that their hearts are there still, and they are apt to cast lingering looks towards the accursed city. Ah me! What if any of you should become pillars of salt! "Remember Lot's wife!" But when, like Noah, you are divided from the world's pursuits by God's own act, then is it well with you. Noah was shut in, and could not follow after the festivities and worldliness of men. They were eating and drinking, marrying and given in marriage, but to Noah the dance and the viol, the feast and the revel, called in vain. He could not now hoard up wealth, nor seek for fame among the sons of men. He was utterly exiled and excluded from all those things which charmed the minds of his contemporaries; he was out of the fashion, yea, out of the world. He was shut out, too, from all their possessions; even from his own farm he was now expatriated. Blessed is that man who, whatsoever he hath, hath it as though he had it not; he sets no store by earthly things, and does not lock up his soul in his iron safe. He is shut out from the things which rust and corrupt, so that they are not his God, nor his treasure. Noah was divided from the evil generation among which he dwelt by the act of God: here was his safety. Adam was put in Paradise by God, but he was never shut in by God, and therefore very soon he left his first estate and wandered among thorns and thistles. But Noah was both put in the ark and shut in the ark, and therefore he never left his shelter until the Lord bade him come forth to possess the new world. Blessed are the men of whom the Lord Jesus can say, "They are not of the world." Such have passed by death into life, and are members of a new race, who shall go forth with joy, and be led forth with peace; for they shall inherit the earth. Blessed is that man who has crossed the Rubicon, deciding to be on the Lord's side whatever others may do. Blessed is the man who has burnt his boats behind him, having landed in a country from which he will never retreat. I would fain be one who can cease to be, but cannot cease to be a Christian; who can die, but cannot deny his Lord; who will, if needful, go with Him to prison and to death, and can do no otherwise, for the love of Christ constraineth him. Then is the will most truly free when it is under the sweet dominion of infinite love; this is true liberty—to be led about in triumph in every place, bound with the silken cords of gratitude, a captive to the power of grace. O happy man who can truly say that henceforth he is "shut in," because he is born again, and thus entirely changed. In the olden time a newly-converted man who became an eminent saint was met in the street by a woman who had at other times tempted him to sin. He took no notice of her, and at last she cried out, "Do you not know me? It is I." "Ah," said the new man, "but it is not I." No, he was not the man who could take pleasure in uncleanness; he could no longer sin, for he was born of God. Our inner life shuts us in to holiness, and the wounds of Jesus seal the door. The goodness of God interposes a barrier between us and evil; for we say with Joseph, "How can we that are dead to sin live any longer therein?" Hence our prayer is that of Toplady—

> Oh nail me to the sacred wood,
> There tie me with thy Spirit's chain;
> There seal me with thy fastening blood,
> Nor ever let me loose again;
> There let me bow my suppliant knee,
> And own no other Lord but thee!

We must now remark, secondly, that Noah was not only shut in, but he was *shut in by God*. There was the excellence of it—"The Lord shut him in." No man can shut in as the Lord can. I cannot shut professors in to the ways of godliness as I could wish; alas, with all my preaching, many wander, and try to be members of the church and citizens of the world, too. We have among us avowed lovers of Christ, who act too much like "lovers of pleasure." I have preached no liberty to sin, as some do, but I have declared that "strait is the gate and narrow is the way"; but yet these men make excursions into the broad road. I would still hammer at the door of the ark, in hope of shutting it close and keeping it so; but it is little that I can do. If Noah had shut himself in he might have come out again; and if any of the world outside had shut him in, he would, probably, have burst open the door; but "the Lord shut him in," and thus sure work was made of it. Oh to be enclosed by Almighty grace! The Lord has shut His people in unto Himself by His choice of them in Christ Jesus, by His redemption of them from among men, and by His sanctifying them to be a peculiar people unto Himself. Yes, the Lord has done it—"The Lord shut him in."

Take notice that this was a very *close* shutting, so as to keep out the water. I fancy that if you saw a huge vessel lying upon the dry land where the floods would come to float it, you would be very anxious about that great opening in its side. It was evidently a huge doorway, for a pair of elephants passed through it; so that it was a gaping lead which would take in enough water in an hour to sink the ark to the bottom. How could the great door be closed? All the timbers are stanch, and the ship is well caulked, and pitched within and without with pitch; but all will go for nothing unless we can secure the big door. Merely to shut the door will be of no use. When the rain begins to fall in torrents from above, and the waters leap up from below, and the ship commences to rise, she will take in any quantity of water at the points where the door fits into the wood. Shipwrights will be wanted, and the caulkers must come, and the men with the pitch. No shipwright could manage to shut so huge a door close enough for safety unless you give him time, and call in the help of other workers. Hence "the Lord shut him in" because nobody else could be safely trusted to shut such a door, against which a forty days' tempest was to beat most furiously. What a mercy it is that when we get into Christ by faith, and are shut in from the world with Him, that we are perfectly safe, because the Lord Himself has shut us in. We are not only brought to Christ Jesus by divine power, but we are preserved in Christ Jesus unto eternal life by the same divine might.

Beloved, there is no doubt about the salvation of those who are in Christ, for none can separate us from the love of God which is in Christ Jesus our Lord. Never has a soul perished trusting in Jesus, and never shall a soul so perish; for though salvation be so difficult that the righteous scarcely are saved, yet when the Lord Jehovah puts His hand to the work, it is well done, and done forever. In Noah's case the huge chasm that would have let in the water-floods was perfectly closed up. Even so all the yawning leaks and openings of our fall and sin are closed by the grace of God, and in Christ Jesus we are secure: the Lord has shut us in.

That door was also shut *very fast*, to prevent the entrance of enemies from the outside. For who can tell? I should fancy that when the waters began to rise, when they were up to the ankles, or knee deep, those who had hitherto ridiculed the patriarch's barge would assemble around that door and clamorously demand to be admitted, resolved, if refused, to force their way. In vain. God had shut the door, and no violence could force it open, by push of crowd, or leverage of strength. Even so it is with us, we are protected against every onslaught of the enemies of our soul. Come life, come death, things present or things to come, salvation hath God appointed for walls and bulwarks. Come temptations of every sort, come craft or assault of devils, none can force the doorway and come at us for our destruction. "At evening let them return; and let them make a noise like a dog, and go round about the city. But I will sing of thy power; yea, I will sing aloud of thy mercy in the morning: for thou hast been my defense and refuge in the day of my trouble. Unto thee, O my strength, will I sing."

This divine shutting in of Noah was *very necessary*: for I suppose that no one else could have moved the gigantic door upon its enormous hinges. It was probably too massive to have been stirred by Noah, or his united family. It must have been a moment of wonder and awe when that stupendous door began silently to move of its own accord, as though an invisible hand was carefully closing it, so that not a crevice should be made through which water could penetrate. The ark was soon as entire as if it had never exhibited an opening from stem to stern. You and I need shutting into Christ by a divine hand, or it never will be done securely. When a soul is brought to Christ, it is by divine grace, but the whole is not done then; the grand difficulty is to keep us in Christ; for without continued grace we shall still perish despite all the arrangements of redeeming love. How many have ventured to sea in the galleys of their own resolve and have perished there! How many have hoped to shut themselves in with Christ by the mere force of personal determination, and the leakage of their own depraved heart has drowned them. But, oh, when God has brought us into union with Jesus He shuts us in, and we are saved in the Lord with an everlasting salvation. The great door of covenant faithfulness is shut behind the believer, and he is surrounded with the power and grace of God, even as Noah was housed within the strong timbers of the ark. There is no crack or cranny through which the floods of wrath can penetrate; omnipotent love hath shut us in.

And the Lord did this not only necessarily, but *graciously*. I call your attention to the change of the names in the text, a very significant change indeed: "They that went in, went in male and female of all flesh: as *God* had commanded him: and *the Lord*"—that is, Jehovah—"shut him in." Elohim, as the Creator and Preserver, takes care of living things to preserve them; but the Lord, even Jehovah, the covenanting God interposes in great mercy to protect His chosen servant. It was Jehovah who entered into solemn league and covenant with His servant Noah that He would preserve him in the ark, and float him into the new world in it; and as Jehovah the covenanting One He shut him in. There is no security like that which is given us by the covenant of grace. The hand which was lifted to swear our safety has also been outstretched to effect it. The everlasting covenant ordered in all things and sure guarantees salvation to all who are represented by the great Head and Surety of that covenant, even our Lord Jesus. Love and power cooperate with faithfulness and truth to keep the chosen from all danger. Dwell much upon the covenant, and note the immutable pledges by which it is secured and the immortal principles upon which it is founded. Try to suck out the delicious sweetness which is to be found in the hive of the covenant; for if you are an advanced child of God no form of truth can be more nourishing or refreshing to your mind. The doctrines which spring out of the covenant are peculiarly comforting to believing minds. The promises of God are yea and amen in Christ Jesus, and can never fail nor change, since the covenant standeth fast forever and ever. Its tenure is free and sovereign grace, and it cannot be disanulled. Here is a line of it, "I will put my fear in their hearts, that they shall not depart from me." With such a promise doth Jehovah shut us in with Christ Jesus in matchless kindness and unspeakable love.

Notice, once again, that this deed was very *instructive* to Noah, it must have been so. Noah had ceased to live according to the mere senses of the body, and had come to perceive his absolute dependence upon God; but he was made by the opened door to see that dependence most clearly. By divine orders he had built an ark on dry land, and when it was built Noah might have said, "Now I feel safe": but he could not say so, for there was a gaping gash in the side of the ark, a vast aperture which he could not close up. It was an occasion of mercy to mankind, and Noah was probably glad to see it open that he might still preach righteousness and warn men to escape, saying, "The door is open! Come, ye great sinners! Enter, ye sons of Anak. Come and be saved."

> Come to the ark, ere yet the flood
>   Your lingering steps oppose;
> Come, for the door which open stood
>   Is now about to close.

Yet when he had done his sermon and went home perhaps he said to his wife, "Beloved, how can this ark save us? That door, if ever the floods come, will be a dreadful danger to us. We cannot shut it, what is to be done? We must leave it with God. We are still dependent upon a divine interposition, and Jehovah will stretch out His hand and shut the door effectually so that we shall float above the deluge." In this condition of daily dependence the Lord would have His people abide, conscious to the very last that in Him only do they live. "Without Me ye can do nothing." We are entirely dependent upon our faithful, loving God for everything. If I were to get up to heaven's wall and gaze in through the pearly gateway, I know that if God did not give me grace to take the last step I should die upon the threshold of the celestial city. We rest upon God at the first for hope and pardon, and the like is the case to the last. "My soul, wait thou only upon God, for my expectation is from him." You will never be able to throw your cap up and say, "I have done with further prayer and watchfulness, for I need no longer depend on God." Never will you cease to look unto the Lord for your salvation till you shall be safely housed in heaven—

> Far from a world of grief and sin,
>   With God eternally shut in.

Then joyfully will you confess that salvation is of the Lord, and glorify your great God and Savior.

Thus, then, the text tells us that Noah was shut in, and that he was shut in by God; but now let us remember that *he was shut in with God*; for in the first verse of the chapter we read, "The Lord said unto Noah, Come thou and all thy house into the ark"; and this clearly shows that the Lord was in the ark already. O what a joy it is to know that when a soul is buried to the world it lives with Christ. "For if we have been planted together in the likeness of his death, we shall also be in the likeness of his resurrection." God is in Christ Jesus, and we are in Christ Jesus, and thus we have fellowship with the Father and with His Son Jesus. The tabernacle of God among men is the Person of Christ, and when we are joined unto the Lord and become members of His body, we are alive unto God and have fellowship with Him. It is a blissful privilege to be hidden away in the person of Christ, for "in him dwelleth all the fullness of the Godhead bodily, and ye are complete in him." You are in Him, that is true, joined unto the Lord in one spirit. Oh the fellowship the saved have with God! How cheering! How near! How elevating! How strengthening! God has left all the world to its own destruction; but in the ark, Christ Jesus, there is joy, and peace, and fellowship; for God is there, and all His redeemed family are shut in with Him. Happy man, to be enclosed in the secret place of the tabernacle of the Most High, he shall abide under the shadow of the Almighty.

Next, notice that Noah's happiness was all the greater because *he was shut in the ark with all his family*. This is a great joy, to have all your household brought unto the faith of Christ. Some among us have one or two of their family still without Christ, and strangers to His salvation. This is a great grief. I will not enlarge upon a subject so painful, but I know instances in which godly women have all their children with them in Christ, but the husband is still a stranger to the covenant of promise.

There is a brother among us who joys to dwell in Christ, but his father and mother are still without God and without Christ. How often have we heard that dear brother's prayer for his relatives. Perhaps his parents are here, and if so I would tell them how much their son's prayers affect me; he cries as for his very life that God would save his father. Some among us never pray in the prayer meeting without strong crying and tears for their kinsmen according to the flesh; they cannot get through a prayer without mentioning their children, or their brothers, or others of their house; I hope they never will; I hope God will lay their kindred on their heart as a heavy burden till they are all saved in answer to prayer. Noah would have been an unhappy man that day if his wife had been outside the ark, or if Shem or Ham had been outside, or if Japheth's wife, or any other had been left to perish. How joyful are they who can say that all theirs are God's. You are very pleased, some of you, to see your sons and daughters respectably settled in life, thank God for His gracious providence, but, mark you, if they were all poor, and you saw them all saved, there would still be the highest cause for gratitude. Better to see them regenerate than rich, better married to Christ than to a fortune. Give your God no rest till it is so; and if there is one who seems quite outside of spiritual things, pray for him as Abraham prayed for Ishmael, "Oh that Ishmael might live before thee!" It is better you should pray hard for them while they live, than that you should mourn bitterly over them when dead, as David did when he lamented aloud, "O Absalom, my son; would God I had died for thee, O Absalom, my son, my son!" May the Lord, when He blesses us as He did Jacob, extend that blessing to all our tribes, and cause all that are born unto us to be born again unto Himself.

Noah and his household were *shut in*, dear friend, *to be perfectly preserved, and then to come forth into a new world.* The rains descended, the water-springs poured forth their fountains, the waters rose, and the huge vessel began to quit the ground, and to walk the waters like a thing of life. Methinks the little company might well have sung a hymn; but if they did, it is probable that the hymn was brought to a pause as they heard the cries of the drowning men and women outside. I cannot attempt to picture the scene: they must have come clustering in great multitudes round the ark when they saw that in very deed the flood was descending and uprising. As the fast-closed ark began to move the inmates must have heard a chorus of cries, and groans, and shrieks of men and women as they perished in the insatiable waters. Down poured the incessant showers, beating on the roof with perpetual thunder. The hidden eight were in solitude, shut in from the all-enveloping sheet of rain. The waters continued to gather, and still up rose the ark; though they could scarce tell where they were amid the watery solitude, they knew that they were safe. When they looked out and saw no living thing, not even the top of a mountain, and they were floating on a sea that knew no shore, how strange must have been their sensations! But the Lord had shut Noah in, so he was perfectly safe. He knew that the Lord High Admiral of the seas was at the helm to steer the lonely bark aright. Then came a strong wind to assuage the waters; and how the ark must have sped before the gale, none knew whither: it was tossed about, doubtless, for it is the nature of winds to raise waves, and where there was no shore to give the slightest shelter the vessel must have felt all their force. Yet the favored family was safe.

> Without deep calleth unto deep,
> But all is peace within.

The waters were assuaged, and by-and-by the ark owned to a strange sensation, for its keel was touching the earth, the ark was coming to its rest. God remembered Noah, and brought the ark to rest on the mountains of Ararat. But will the ark ground safely? Perhaps she will break her back on a rock, or slide down the side of a hill, or over the brink of a precipice. No, no. He who was her Architect will be her Preserver. God has found an anchorage for the stars, and He can surely berth a ship. He found the ark a safe resting place, and brought out all her passengers safe and sound. He is berthing many a vessel now in the everlasting harbors, and He hath such skill in navigation that no vessel which belongs to Him shall ever come to an ill end. So far Noah fared well and felt solid ground beneath him once again. Now the waters quickly assuage; but what a mass of mud—shall the rescued family run the risk of fever and miasma? They shall not be let out till the land is dry, and then when the earth has been fertilized by its own destruction and is ready to receive seed from the sower's hand, and the grass has begun to grow for the cattle, then shall they come out into a new world. How fair the face of nature so newly washed! How like a bride decked for her marriage day! God sets open wide the door, and out they come, camels, elephants, sheep, lions, Noah and all his family, rejoicing to range at liberty. A sacrifice is offered and God smells a savor of rest. So shall it be with us: shut in with Christ away from this world, to which we are not conformed, we shall ride in safety as exiled beings out of this old world into another. A day cometh when the new heaven and the new earth shall be seen, and then the meek shall inherit the earth and shall delight themselves in the abundance of peace; then shall our sacrifice of praise be accepted of the Lord. Blessed are they who enter into the ark of Jesus Christ, and so die to the old life that they may live in newness of life, rejoicing in Him who sitteth upon the throne and saith, "Behold, I make all things new!" This be your lot and mine forever and ever.

II. I have purposely reserved a very few minutes only for the second and much more painful point of my discourse, which comes out of the words, SHUT OUT.

To have the door shut is well enough for Noah and those who are with him, but as for all the rest, that big door when it closed on its hinges shut them all *out!* Shut them all out to perish with a swift and sure destruction. *Who were they?* I wonder if any of the sort are here!

Well, they were a people that had been preached to. Noah was a "preacher of righteousness," and fulfilled his office perseveringly. The men of his generation were not left to perish without light; they had been warned, they had been instructed, they had been entreated. They were such as you are who have been habitual hearers of the Word, but hearers only. Of course, you have none of you heard the gospel for 120 years from one man; but many of you have heard it quite often enough to have incurred great guilt in having rejected it so often.

They were a people who had been prayed for. You will ask me how I come to know that. I answer that Ezekiel speaks of three men notable as intercessors, Noah, Daniel, and Job; and I feel sure he would not have mentioned Noah in that company if he had not been a man of great prayer. I believe that he prayed much for his generation, and yet they were not saved. Sure I am, dear hearers, that some of you are daily the objects of earnest supplication. On Monday nights I have had notes about some of you, and hundreds, even thousands of us have joined together in praying for you. Beside that, you know the dear ones at home are earnestly interceding for you, and some who are now in heaven pleaded hard for you before they departed; yet you will be shut out as sure as you are alive unless you fly to Christ, and enter into His salvation very soon.

They were a people who had many of them been associated with Noah in his work. It is hardly likely that Noah built the ark with his own hands all alone; he must have hired fellers of trees, and carpenters, and caulkers, and shipwrights of various kinds. None of these were saved. It is a sad thing that those who helped to build the ark were shut out of it! Remember, however, that they shut themselves out! They chose their own destruction. Do I speak to any who have subscribed to build the house in which they worship? Who contribute their share to the expenses of the church and to the help of the poor, and to the education of the young; and yet to have no part in Christ? I do not understand those of you who are zealous in promoting religion, and yet have no share in the great salvation? Why will you resolve to be shut out? As sure as ever you sit on that seat, you will be shut out of heaven, and shut out of Christ forever, unless you arise and go unto your Father confessing your sins and seeking His mercy. May God arouse you to flee from the wrath to come!

These people had seen great wonders. Half the world must have gathered to see the camels and elephants, eagles and peacocks, snails and worms, all come running, or flying, or creeping to the ark. Such a sight never could have been before. There they come in pairs: four wild beasts, two and two; and clean beasts by sevens! Voluntarily entering the ark! What a sight it must have been! Many saw it and confessed that God's Hand was in it, and yet they did not enter the ark themselves. Oh, my hearers, some of you have been here in times of revival; you have seen drunkards saved, you have seen the most unlikely ones converted, and yet you have not turned unto the Lord. Be ye sure of this—you will be shut out of hope forever! May God grant it may never be so; but except you repent it must be the case. Let me read you a passage from the gospel of Luke, and as I read it, think of it and tremble:

> When once the master of the house is risen up, and hath shut to the door, and ye begin to stand without, and to knock at the door saying, Lord, Lord, open unto us; and he shall answer and say unto you, I know you not whence ye are: then shall ye begin to say, We have eaten and drunk in thy presence, and thou hast taught in our streets. But he shall say, I tell you, I know you not whence ye are; depart from me, all ye workers of iniquity. There shall be weeping and gnashing of teeth, when ye shall see Abraham, and Isaac, and Jacob, and all the prophets, in the kingdom of God, and you yourselves thrust out.

Thrust out—pushed out, not permitted to enter—the great door interposing between you and all hope of mercy.

Next, notice *what they did*. What they did was this: they were a people who took all their delight in worldly things. We are told in the New Testament that they "ate and drank, they married and were given in marriage, till the day that Noah entered into the ark." They were altogether taken up with this world—like some of you, who have no regard for the world to come, but live as if this life would be everything. Prayer and praise, and looking into eternal things are all a weariness to you; you look after the shop and the farm and the house, and forget God. I do not blame you for diligence in business any more than I blame these people for eating and drinking and marrying; but to make this the main thing in life is to despise God and heaven and eternity. O my hearer, remember your God! your Savior! your soul! death! heaven! hell! How little do you think of these things! Be not like those ungodly ones who gave their hearts to worldly things.

And then they did not believe, there was the point. Whatever Noah might say they replied, "Poor old man, you have entered on a second childhood. Perhaps when we are 500 years old we shall talk nonsense too." When the patriarch came to be 600 years old they said, "That graybeard is always telling us these stories," and they jested at the old man's fable. Alas, some of you do not believe the gospel, and therefore do not seek its salvation; but it is true, and you will own it to be so when you get breast deep in the fire-flood, as you will be before long. Oh that you would believe, and escape from the wrath to come! They despised the longsuffering of God. They said, "Here has Noah been telling us these 120 years that a flood is coming, and where is it?" Among ourselves it is a common proverb, "Christmas is coming," but in Noah's day there must have been more sting in that proverb, "The deluge is coming." They would not believe that such a thing could ever be. Some say, "I have gone on very well, I have had no religion and yet I have always prospered. I have seen godly people getting poor, but I have always added field to field and house to house. I do not want religion. I am comfortable enough without it." If we say we pity them, they reply, "We do not want your pity." Just so! But the tables will be turned before long, and then you will demand our pity, though it will avail you nothing, for the door will be shut. Once let God shut the door, and there will be an eternal separation between the ungodly and all hope and happiness.

What came of it then? The door of hope was shut and the multitude perished without hope.

When I was thinking this over I fancied that I could preach about it; but I cannot. When I realize the fact that any one of my dear hearers should be shut out of heaven I cannot bear myself. I want to find a secret place wherein to weep. If an angel should say to me this morning, "All your hearers shall be saved but one, and you must pick out the one who shall be shut out of heaven," I should run my eye anxiously up and down these lines of pews, and I should take up many an hour, and at last cry, "No, I cannot take the responsibility of marking out the doomed man." I should keep you here, I think, till I expired before I could make the horrible death-choice. I would say, "Lord, save every one." And as for the marked man, I would cry, "Spare him! Do spare him!" Oh, my hearers, will you do for yourselves what I could not dare to do for you? Will any man choose for himself to be lost? Will he count himself unworthy of eternal life, and put it from him? Then I must shake off the dust of my feet against him. I will have none of the responsibility. If you will be damned you must do it yourselves. I will not be a partaker in the crime. Your blood be on your own heads. Go down to the pit if you will deliberately choose to do so; but this know, that Christ was preached to you, and you would not have him; you were invited to come to him, but turned your backs upon him; you chose for yourselves your own eternal destruction! God grant you may repent of such a choice, for Jesus Christ's sake. Amen.

THE GOSPEL OF ABRAHAM'S SACRIFICE OF ISAAC

SERMON NO. 869
DELIVERED ON SUNDAY EVENING, MAY 2, 1869.
PORTION OF SCRIPTURE READ BEFORE SERMON—HEBREWS 6.

He that spared not his own Son, but delivered him up for us all—
Romans 8:32.

WE have selected this verse as our theme, but our true text you will find in the twenty-second chapter of Genesis, the narrative which we read to you this morning at full length, and upon which we spoke in detail in our discourse. I thought it meet to keep to one point this morning, on the ground that one thing at a time is best, and therefore I endeavored to lead your undivided contemplations to the peerless example of holy, believing obedience, which the father of the faithful presented to us when he offered up his son.

But it would be a very unfair way of handling Holy Scriptures to leave such a subject as this, so full of Christ, without dwelling upon the typical character of the whole narrative. If the Messiah be anywhere symbolized in the Old Testament, He is certainly to be seen upon Mount Moriah, where the beloved Isaac, willingly bound and laid upon the altar, is a lively foreshadowing of the Well-beloved of heaven yielding His life as a ransom. We doubt not that one great intent of the whole transaction was to afford Abraham a clearer view of Christ's day; the trial was covertly a great privilege, unveiling as it did, to the patriarch, the heart of the great Father, in His great deed of love to men, and displaying at the same time, the willing obedience of the great Son, who cheerfully became a burnt offering unto God. The gospel of Moriah, which is but another name for Calvary, was far clearer than the revelation made at the gate of Paradise, or to Noah in the ark, or to Abraham himself on any former occasion. Let us pray for a share in the privilege of the renowned friend of God, as we study redemption in the light which made Abraham glad.

Without detaining you with any lengthened preface, for which we have neither time nor inclination, we shall first, *draw the parallel between the offering of Christ and the offering of Isaac;* and secondly, we shall show *wherein the sacrifice of Christ goes far beyond even this most edifying type.* O blessed Spirit of God, take of the things of Christ at this hour, and show them unto us.

39

I. first, the parallel.

You know the story before you; we need not repeat it, except as we weave it into our meditation. As Abraham offered up Isaac, and so it might be said of him that he "spared not his own son," so the ever blessed God offered up His Son Jesus Christ, and spared him not.

There is a likeness in the person offered. Isaac was Abraham's son, and in that emphatic sense, his only son; hence the anguish of resigning him to sacrifice. There is a depth of meaning in the word "only" when it is applied to a child. Dear as life to a parent's heart is his only child; no gold of Ophir nor sparkling gems of Inde can be compared therewith. Those of you blessed with the full quiver, having many children, would yet find it extremely difficult, if one had to be taken from you, to say which it should be. A thousand pangs would rend your hearts in making choice of one out of the seven or the ten, upon whose claycold brow you must imprint a last fond kiss; but what would be your grief if you had but one! What agony to have torn from you the only token of your mutual love, the only representative of your race! Cruel is the wind which uproots the only scion of the ancient tree; rude is the hand which dashes the only blossom from the rose. Ruthless spoiler, to deprive you of your sole heir, the cornerstone of your love, the polished pillar of your hope. Judge you then the sadness which pierced the heart of Abraham when God bade him to take his son, his only son, and offer him as a burnt offering! But I have no language with which to speak of the heart of God when He gave up His only begotten Son. Instead of attempting the impossible, I must content myself with repeating the word of Holy Writ: "God *so* loved the world, that he gave his only begotten Son, that whosoever believeth in him should not perish, but have everlasting life." Nothing but infinite love to man could have led the God of love to bruise His Son and put Him to grief. Christ Jesus, the Son of God, is, in His divine nature, One with God, coequal and coeternal with Him, His only begotten Son in a manner mysterious and unknown to us. As the divine Son the Father gave Him to us: "Unto us a Son is given, and his name shall be called the Mighty God." Our Lord, as man, is the Son of the Highest, according to the angel's salutation of the Virgin: "The Holy Ghost shall come upon thee, and the power of the Highest shall overshadow thee: therefore also that holy thing which shall be born of thee shall be called the Son of God." In His human nature Jesus was not spared, but was made to suffer, bleed, and die for us. God and man in one person, two natures being wondrously combined, He was not spared but delivered up for all His chosen. Herein is love! Behold it and admire! Consider it and wonder! The beloved Son is made a sacrifice! He, the Only-begotten is smitten of God and afflicted, and cried, "My God, my God, why hast thou forsaken me?"

Remember that in Abraham's case *Isaac was the child of his heart.* I need not enlarge on that, you can readily imagine how Abraham loved him; but in the case of our Lord what mind can conceive how near and dear our Redeemer was to the Father? Remember those marvelous words of the Incarnate Wisdom, "I was by him as one brought up with him: and I was daily his delight, rejoicing always before him."

Our glorious Savior was more the Son of God's love than Isaac could be the darling of Abraham. Eternity and infinity entered into the love which existed between the Father and the Son. Christ in human nature was matchlessly pure and holy, and in Him dwelt the fullness of the Godhead bodily; therefore was He highly delightful to the Father, and that delight was publicly attested in audible declarations, "This is my beloved Son in whom I am well pleased." Yet He spared Him not, but made Him to be the substitute for us sinners, made Him as a curse for us, and to be hanged on a tree. Have you a favorite child? Have you one who nestles in your bosom? Have you one dearer than all other? Then should you be called to part with him, you will be able to have fellowship with the great Father in delivering up His Son.

Remember, too, that *Isaac was a most lovely and obedient son*. We have proof of that in the fact that he was willing to be sacrificed, for being a vigorous young man, he might have resisted his aged father, but he willingly surrendered himself to be bound, and submitted to be laid on the altar. How few there are of such sons! Could Abraham give him up? Few, did I say, of such sons? I cannot apply that term to Christ the Son of God, for there was never another such as He. If I speak of His humanity, who ever obeyed his father as Christ obeyed His God? "Though he were a Son yet learned he obedience." It was his meat and his drink to do the will of him that sent him. "Wist ye not," said He, "that I must be about my Father's business?" And yet this obedient Son, this Son of sons, God spared not, but unsheathed His sword against Him, and gave Him to the agony and bloody sweat, the cross and death itself. What mighty love must have led the Father to this! Impossible is it to measure it.

> So strange, so boundless was the love
> Which pitied dying men,
> The Father sent His equal Son,
> To give them life again.

It must not be forgotten, too, that *around Isaac there clustered mysterious prophecies*. Isaac was to be the promised seed through which Abraham should live down to posterity and evermore be a blessing to all nations. But what prophecies gathered about the head of Christ! What glorious things were spoken of Him before His coming! He was the conquering seed destined to break the dragon's head. He was the messenger of the covenant, yea, the covenant itself. He was foretold as the Prince of Peace, the King of kings, and Lord of lords. In Him was more of God revealed than in all the works of creation and providence. Yet this august Person, this heir of all things, the Wonderful, the Counselor, the Mighty God, the Everlasting Father, the Prince of Peace, must bow His head to the stroke of sacred vengeance, being given up as the scapegoat for all believers; the Lamb of our passover, the victim for our sin. Brethren, I have left the shallows, and am far out to sea tonight; I am swimming in a great deep, I find no bottom, and I see no shore; I sink in deeps of wonder. My soul would rather meditate than attempt to utter herself by word of mouth. Indeed, the theme of God's unspeakable gift, if we would comprehend its breadth and length, is rather for the closet than for the pulpit, rather to be meditated upon when you muse alone at eventide than to be spoken of in the great assembly. Though we speak with the tongues of men and of angels, we cannot attain to the height of this great argument. God gave such a One to us that the world could not find His fellow nor heaven reveal His equal. He gave to us a treasure so priceless that if heaven and earth were weighed like the merchant's golden wedge, they could not buy the like thereof. For us was given up the chiefest among ten thousand, and the altogether lovely. For us the head of most fine gold was laid in the dust, and the raven locks bestained with gore. For us those eyes which are soft as the eyes of doves, were red with weeping, and washed with tears instead of milk. For us the cheeks which were as a bed of spices were defiled with spittle, and the countenance like Lebanon, excellent as the cedars, marred more than the sons of men. And all this was by the Father's appointment and ordaining; according to the eternal purpose written in the volume of the Book.

The parallel is very clear in *the preface of the sacrifice*. Let us show you in a few words. Abraham had three days in which to think upon and consider the death of his son; three days in which to look into that beloved face and to anticipate the hour in which it would wear the icy pallor of death. But the Eternal Father foreknew and foreordained the sacrifice of His only begotten Son, not three days nor three years, nor 3,000 years, but or ever the earth was Jesus was to His Father "the Lamb slain from the foundation of the world." Long before His birth at Bethlehem it was foretold, "All we like sheep have gone astray; we have turned every one to his own way; and the Lord hath laid on him the iniquity of us all." It was an eternal decree that from the travail of the Redeemer there should arise a seed that should serve Him, being purchased by His blood. What perseverance of disinterested love was here! Brethren, suffer me to pause and worship, for I fail to preach. I am abashed in the presence of such wondrous love. I cannot understand Thee, O great God. I know Thou art not moved by passions, nor affected by grief as men are; therefore dare I not say that Thou didst sorrow over the death of thy Son. But oh! I know that Thou art not a God of stone, impassable, unmoved. Thou art God, and therefore we cannot conceive Thee; but yet Thou dost compare Thyself to a father having compassion on a prodigal; do we err, then if we think of Thee as yearning over thy Well-beloved when He was given up to the pangs of death? Forgive me if I transgress in so conceiving of thy heart of love, but surely it was a costly sacrifice which Thou didst make, costly even to Thee! I will not speak of Thee in this matter, O my God, for I cannot, but I will reverently think of Thee, and wonder how Thou couldst have looked so steadily through the long ages, and resolved so unwaveringly upon the mighty sacrifice, the immeasurable generosity of resigning thy dear Son to be slaughtered for us.

Remember, that *Abraham prepared with sacred forethought everything for the sacrifice*. As I showed you this morning, he became a Gibeonite for God, acting as a hewer of wood, while he prepared the fuel for his son's burning. He carried the fire, and built the altar, providing everything needful for the painful service. But what shall

I say of the great God who, through the ages, was constantly preparing this world for the grandest event in its history, the death of the Incarnate God? All history converged to this point. I venture to say it, that every transaction, whether great or small, that ever disturbed Assyria, or aroused Chaldea, or troubled Egypt, or chastened Jewry, had for its ultimate object the preparing of the world for the birth and the sacrifice of Christ. The cross is the center of all history. To it, from ancient ages, everything is pointing; forward from it everything in this age proceeds, and backward to it everything may be traced. How deep is this subject, yet how true! God was always preparing for the giving up of the Well-beloved for the salvation of the sons of men!

We will not tarry, however, on the preface of the sacrifice, but advance in lowly worship to behold *the act itself*. When Abraham came at last to Mount Moriah, *he bade his servants remain at the foot of the hill*. Now, gather up your thoughts, and come with me to Calvary, to the true Moriah. At the foot of that hill God bade all men stop. The Twelve have been with Christ in His life-journey, but they must not be with Him in his death throes. Eleven go with Him to Gethsemane: only three may draw near to Him in His passion; but when it comes to the climax of all, they forsake Him and flee; He fights the battle singly. "I have trodden the wine-press alone," said He, "and of the people there was none with me." Although around Calvary there gathered a great crowd to behold the Redeemer die, yet spiritually Jesus was there alone with the avenging God. The wonderful transaction of Calvary as to its real essence and spirit, was performed in solemn secrecy between the Father and the Son. Abraham and Isaac were alone. The Father and the Son were equally alone when His soul was made a sacrifice for sin.

Do you observe also that *Isaac carried the wood!*—a true picture of Jesus carrying His cross. It was not every malefactor who had to bear the tree which was afterwards to bear him, but, in our Lord's case, and by an excess of cruelty, wicked men made Him carry His cross. With felicity of exactness to the prophetic type, God had so ordered it, that as Isaac bore the wood up to the altar, so Christ should carry His cross to the place of doom.

A point worthy of notice is, that it is said, as you will find if you read the chapter of Abraham and Isaac, "that they went both of them together." He who was to smite with the knife, and the other who was to be the victim, walked in peaceful converse to the altar. "They went both together," agreeing in heart. It is to me delightful to reflect that Christ Jesus and His Father went both together in the work of redeeming love. In that great work by which we are saved, the Father gave us Christ, but Christ equally gave us Himself. The Father went forth to vengeance dressed in robes of love to man, and the Son went forth to be the victim of that vengeance with the same love in His heart.

They proceeded together, and at last, *Isaac was bound*, bound by his father. So Christ was bound, and He saith, "Ye could have no power against me unless it were given to you of my Father." Christ could not have been bound by Judas, nor Pilate, nor Herod, if the Eternal Father had not virtually bound Him and delivered Him into the hands of the executioner. My soul, stand and wonder! The Father binds his Son; 'tis God thy Father who binds thine Elder Brother, and gives him up to cruel men that he may be reviled, spit upon, and nailed to the tree to die.

The parallel goes still further, for while the father binds the victim, *the victim is willing to be bound.* As we have already said, Isaac might have resisted, but he did not; there are no traces of struggling, no signs of so much as a murmur. Even so with Jesus; He went cheerfully up to the slaughter-place, willing to give himself for us. Said He, "No man taketh my life from me, but I lay it down of myself. I have power to lay it down, and I have power to take it up again."

You see how the parallel holds, and as you behold the earthly parent, with anguish in his face, about to drive the knife into the heart of his dear child, you have before you, as nearly as earthly pictures can paint heavenly things, the mirror of the divine Father about to give up the Well-beloved, the just, for the unjust, that He may bring us to God. I pause there. What further can I say? It is not, as I have said before, a theme for words, but for your heart's emotions, for the kisses of your lips, and the tears of your soul.

Yet the parallel runs a little further, after having been suspended for a moment, *Isaac was restored again.* He was bound and laid upon the altar, the knife was drawn, and he was in spirit given up to death, but he was delivered. Leaving that gap, wherein Christ is not typified fully by Isaac, but by the ram, yet was Jesus also delivered. He came again, the living and triumphant Son, after He had been dead. Isaac was for three days looked upon by Abraham as dead, on the third day the father rejoiced to descend the mountain with his son. Jesus was dead, but on the third day He rose again. Oh! the joy on that mountain summit, the joy of the two as they returned to the waiting servants, both delivered out of a great trial. But, ah! I cannot tell you what joy there was in the heart of Jesus and the great Father when the tremendous sacrifice was finished, and Jesus had risen from the dead; but, brethren, we shall know some day, for we shall enter into the joy of our Lord.

It is a bold thing to speak of God as moved by joy or affected by grief, but still, since He is no God of wood and stone, no insensible block, we may, speaking after the manner of men, declare that God rejoiced over His risen Son with exceeding joy, while the Son rejoiced also because His great work was accomplished. Remembering that passage in the prophet, where God speaks of His saints, and declares that He will rejoice over them with singing, what if I say that much more He did this with His Son, and, resting in His love, He rejoiced over the risen One, even with joy and singing.

What followed the deliverance of Jesus? You heard, this morning, that from the moment *the covenant was ratified.* Just at the base of that altar the angel declared the oath wherein God swore by Himself. Brethren, the risen Savior, once slain, has confirmed the covenant of grace, which now stands fast forever upon the two immutable things wherein it is impossible for God to lie.

Isaac, also, *had that day been the means of showing to Abraham the great provision of God.* That name, Jehovah-jireh, was new to the world; it was given forth to men that day from Mount Moriah; and in the death of Christ men see what they never could have seen else, and in His resurrection they behold the deepest of mysteries solved. God has provided what men wanted. The problem was, How can sinners be forgiven? How can the mischief of sin be taken away? How can sinners become saints, and those who were only fit to burn in hell be made to sing in heaven? The answer is yonder, where God gives up His only-begotten to bleed and die instead of sinners, and then bids that Only-begotten return in glory from the grave. "Jehovah-jireh," is to be read by the light which streams from the cross. "The Lord will provide" is beheld on the Mount of Calvary as nowhere else in heaven or earth.

Thus have I tried to show the parallel, but I am sadly conscious of my want of power. I feel as if I were only giving you mere sketches, such as schoolboys draw with chalk or charcoal. You must fill them in; there is abundance of room—Abraham and Isaac, the Father and Christ. In proportion to the tenderness and love with which you can enter into the human wonder, so, methinks, by the loving and affectionate teaching of the Holy Spirit, you may enter into the transcendent wonder of the divine sacrifice for men.

II. But now, in the second place, I have to HINT AT SOME POINTS IN WHICH THE PARALLEL FALLS SHORT.

The first is this, that *Isaac would have died in the course of nature*. When offered up by his father, it was only a little in anticipation of the death which eventually must have occurred. But Jesus is He "who only hath immortality," and who never needed to die. Neither as God nor man had He anything about Him that rendered Him subject to the bands of death. To Him Hades was a place He need never enter, and the sepulchre and the grave were locked and barred fast to Him, for there were no seeds of corruption within His sacred frame. Without the taint of original sin, there was no need that His body should yield to the mortal stroke. Indeed, though He died, yet did not His body see corruption; God had shielded Him from that. So Isaac must die, but Jesus need not. His death was purely voluntary, and herein stands by itself, not to be numbered with the deaths of other men.

Moreover, *there was a constraint upon Abraham to give Isaac*. I admit the cheerfulness of the gift, but still the highest law to which his spiritual nature was subject, rendered it incumbent upon believing Abraham to do as God commanded. But no stress could be laid upon the Most High. If He delivered up His Son, it must be with the greatest freeness. Who could deserve that Christ should die for him? Had we been perfection itself, and like the sinless angels, we could not have deserved such a gift as this. But, my brethren and sisters, we were full of evil; we hated God; we continued to transgress against Him; and yet out of pure love to us He performed this miracle of grace—He gave His Son to die for us. Oh! constrained love—a fountain welling up from the depth of the divine nature, unasked for and undeserved! What shall I say of it? O God, be Thou ever blessed! Even the songs of heaven cannot express the obligations of our guilty race to thy free love in the gift of thy Son!

Furthermore, remember that *Isaac did not die after all, but Jesus did*. The pictures were as nearly exact as might be, for the ram was caught in the thicket, and the animal was slaughtered instead of the man; in our Lord's case He was the substitute for us, but there was no substitute for Him. He took our sins and bore them in His own body upon the tree. He was personally the sufferer. Not by proxy did He redeem us, but He Himself suffered for us; in *propria persona* He yielded up His life for us.

And here comes in one other point of difference, namely that *Isaac, if he had died, could not have died for us.* He might have died for us as an example of how we should resign life, but that would have been a small boon; it would have been no greater blessing than the Unitarian gospel offers when it sets forth Christ as dying as our exemption. Oh, but beloved, the death of Christ stands altogether alone and apart, because it is a death altogether for others, and endured solely and only from disinterested affection to the fallen. There is not a pang that rends the Savior's heart that needed to have been there if not for love to us; not a drop of blood that trickled from that thorn-crowned head or from those pierced hands that needed to be spilled if it were not for affection to such undeserving ones as we. And see what He has done for us! He has procured our pardon; we who have believed in Him are forgiven. He has procured our adoption; we are sons of God in Christ Jesus. He has shut the gates of hell for us; we cannot perish, nor can any pluck us out of His hands. He has opened the gates of heaven for us; we shall be with Him where He is. Our very bodies shall feel the power of His death, for they shall rise again at the sound of the trumpet at the last day. He was delivered for us His people, "for us all"; He endured all for all His people, for all who trust Him, for every son of Adam that casts himself upon Him; for every son and daughter of man that will rely alone upon Him for salvation. Was He delivered for you, dear hearer? Have you a part in His death? If so, shall I need to press upon you as you come to this table to think of the Father's gift and of the Father Himself? Do I need to urge you with tearful eye and melting heart as you receive the emblems of our Redeemer's passion, to look to His Father and to Him, and with humble adoration to admire that love which I have failed to depict, and which you will fail to measure? I have never felt, I think, in all my life, more utterly ashamed of words, and more ready to abandon speech, for the thoughts of God's love are too heavy for the shoulders of my words; they burden all my sentences, and crush them down; even thought itself cannot bear the stupendous load. Here is a deep, a great deep, and our bark knows not how to sail thereon. Here deep calleth unto deep, and our mind is swallowed up in the vastness and immensity of the billows of love that roll around us. But what reason cannot measure faith can grasp, and what our understanding cannot comprehend our hearts can love, and what we cannot tell to others we will whisper out in the silence of our spirits to ourselves, until our souls bow with lowliest reverence before the God whose name is Love.

As I close, I feel bound to say that there may be some here to whom this is but an idle tale. Ah! my heart breaketh as I think of you, that you should continue to sin against your Maker, and forget Him from day to day as most of you do. Your Maker gives His own Son to redeem His enemies, and He comes to you tonight and tells you that if you will repent of your sins, and trust yourselves in the hands of His dear Son, who died for sinners, you shall be saved, but, alas! you will not do so; so evil is your heart, that you turn against your God, and you turn against His mercy. Oh! do you say, "I will not turn against Him any more"? Are your relentings kindled? Do you desire to be reconciled to the God you have offended? You may be reconciled; you shall be reconciled tonight, if you do now but give yourselves up to God your Father, and to Christ your Savior. Whosoever believeth in Him shall not perish, but have everlasting life, for this is His gospel, "He that believeth and is baptized shall be saved; but he that believeth not shall be damned." What that damnation is may you never know, but may His grace be yours. Amen.

JEHOVAH-JIREH

SERMON NO. 1,803

DELIVERED ON LORD'S DAY MORNING, OCTOBER 12, 1884.

PORTION OF SCRIPTURE READ BEFORE SERMON—GENESIS 22:1–19.

HYMNS FROM *Our Own Hymn Book*—426, 226, 199.

And Abraham called the name of that place Jerhovah-jireh: as it is said to this day, In the mount of the Lord it shall be seen—Genesis 22:14.

"ABRAHAM called the name of that place Jehovah-jireh," or "Jehovah will see it," or "Jehovah will provide," or "Jehovah will be seen." We are offered a variety of interpretations, but the exact idea is that of seeing and being seen. For God to see is to provide. Our own word "provide," is only Latin for "to see." You know how we say that we will *see* to a matter. Possibly this expression hits the nail on the head. Our heavenly Father sees our need, and with divine foresight of love prepares the supply. He sees to a need to supply it; and in the seeing He is seen, in the providing He manifests Himself.

I believe that the truth contained in the expression "Jehovah-jireh" was ruling Abraham's thought long before he uttered it and appointed it to be the memorial name of the place where the Lord had provided a substitute for Isaac. It was this thought, I think, which enabled him to act as promptly as he did under the trying circumstances. His reason whispered within him, "If you slay your son, how can God keep His promise to you that your seed shall be as many as the stars of heaven?" He answered that suggestion by saying to himself, "Jehovah will see to it!" As he went upon that painful journey, with his dearly beloved son at his side, the suggestion may have come to him, "How will you meet Sarah when you return home, having inbrued your hands in the blood of her son? How will you meet your neighbors when they hear that Abraham, who professed to be such a holy man, has killed his son?" That answer still sustained his heart—"Jehovah will see to it! Jehovah will see to it! He will not fail in His word. Perhaps He will raise my son from the dead; but in some way or other He will justify my obedience to Him and vindicate His own command. Jehovah will see to it!" This was a quietus to every mistrustful thought. I pray that we may drink into this truth, and be refreshed by it. If we follow the Lord's bidding, He will see to it that we shall not be ashamed or confounded. If we come into great need by following His command, He will see to it that the loss shall be recompensed. If our difficulties multiply and increase so that our way seems completely blocked up, Jehovah will see to it that the road shall be cleared. The Lord will see us through in the way of holiness if we are only willing to be thorough in it, and dare to follow wheresoever He leads the way. We need not wonder that Abraham should utter this truth, and attach it to the spot which was to be forever famous: for his whole heart was saturated with it, and had been sustained by it. Wisely he makes an altar and a mountain to be memorials of the truth which had so greatly helped him. His trials had taught him more of God—had, in fact, given him a new name for his God; and this he would not have forgotten, but he would keep it before the minds of the generations following by naming the place Jehovah-jireh.

Observe as you read this chapter that this was not the first time that Abraham had thus spoken. When he called the name of the place Jehovah-jireh he had seen it to be true—the ram caught in the thicket had been provided as a substitute for Isaac: Jehovah had provided. But he had before declared that truth when as yet he knew nothing of the Divine action, when he could not even guess how his extraordinary trial would end. His son Isaac had said to him, "Behold the fire and the wood, but where is the lamb for a burnt offering?" and the afflicted father had bravely answered, "My son, God will provide." In due time God did provide, and then Abraham honored him by saying the same words, only instead of the ordinary for God he used the special covenant title—Jehovah. That is the only alteration; otherwise in the same terms he repeats the assurance that "the Lord will provide."

That first utterance was most remarkable: it was simple enough, but how prophetic! It teaches us this truth, that *the confident speech of a believer is akin to the language of a prophet.* The man who accepts the promise of God unstaggeringly, and is sure that it is true, will speak like the seers of old: he will see that God sees, and will declare the fact, and the holy inference which comes of it. The believer's childlike assurance will anticipate the future, and his plain statement—"God will provide"—will turn out to be literal truth. If you want to come near to prophesying, hold you hard to the promise of God and you shall "prophesy according to the measure of faith." He that can say, "I know and am sure that God will not fail me in this mine hour of tribulation," will, before long, drop pearls of divine confidence and diamonds of prediction from his lips. Choice sayings which become proverbs in the church of God are not the offspring of a mistrust, but of firm confidence in the living God. To this day many a saying of a man of God is quoted among us, even as Abraham's word was quoted. Moses puts it, "As it is said to this day, In the mount of the Lord it shall be seen"; and we might mention many a sentence which is said unto this day which first fell from the mouth of a faithful spirit in the hour of the manifestation of the Lord. The speech of the father of the faithful became the speech of his spiritual seed for many a year afterwards, and it abides in the family of faith unto this day. If we have full faith in God, we shall teach succeeding generations to expect Jehovah's hand to be stretched out still.

True faith not only speaks the language of prophecy, but, *when she sees her prophecy fulfilled, faith is always delighted to raise memorials in the God of truth.* The stones which were set up of old were not to the memory of dead men, but they were memorials of the deeds of the living God: they abundantly uttered the memory of God's great goodness. Abraham on this occasion did not choose a name which recorded what *he* had done, but a name which spoke of what *Jehovah* had done. It is true Abraham's faith was worthy to be remembered throughout all generations, for there he believed God and it was counted unto him for righteousness, and the Lord said to him, "And in thy seed shall all the nations of the earth be blessed; because thou hast obeyed my voice." There the patriarch had endured the extreme test: no gold was ever passed through a hotter furnace. But true faith is always modest; from her gate boasting is excluded by law. Abraham says nothing about himself at all, but the praise is unto God, who sees and is seen; the record is, "Jehovah will provide." I like that self-ignoring; I pray that we, also, may have so much strength of faith that self may go to the wall. Little faith is very apt to grow proud when, to its own astonishment, it has wrought righteousness; but strong faith so completely empties itself, and so entirely depends upon the all-sufficiency of God, that when anything is achieved it remembers nothing but the divine hand, and lays the crown where it ought to be laid. Growing in experimental acquaintance with the God of the covenant, faith has a new song and a new name for her God, and takes care that His wonderful works shall be remembered.

Note yet further, that when faith has uttered a prophecy, and has set up her memorial, *the record of mercy received becomes itself a new prophecy.* Abraham says, "Jehovah-jireh—God will see to it"; what was he doing then but prophesying for a second time for future ages? He bids us know that, as God had provided for him in the time of his extremity, so He will provide for all them that put their trust in Him. The God of Abraham liveth, and let His name be praised, and let us rest assured that, as certainly as in the patriarch's distress, when there seemed no way of escape, the Lord appeared for him and was seen in the mount, even so shall it be with all the believing seed while time endureth. We shall all be tried and tested, but in our utmost need God will see us, and see to our deliverance, if we will but let faith have her perfect work, and will hope and quietly wait the moment when the Lord shall be seen working salvation. The Lord is the Preserver of men and the Provider for men. I long for all of us to get this truth firmly fixed in our hearts, and therefore I shall try to show that God's provision for Abraham and Isaac typified the far greater provision by which all the faithful are delivered from death; and that God, in providing in the mount, has given us therein a sure guarantee that all our necessities shall be provided for henceforth even forever.

Consider, then, that the provision which God made for Abraham was symbolic of the greater provision which He has made for all His chosen in Christ Jesus. "Jehovah-jireh" is a text from which to preach concerning providence, and many have been the sermons which have been distilled from it; but I take the liberty of saying that providence, in the ordinary sense of the term, is not the first thought of the passage, which should be read with some sort of reference to its connection, and the more so because that connection is exceedingly remarkable.

I. When Abraham said "Jehovah will provide," he meant us, first of all, to learn that THE PROVISION WILL COME IN THE TIME OF OUR EXTREMITY. The provision of the ram instead of Isaac was the significant type which was before Abraham's mind; but our Lord tells us, "Abraham rejoiced to see my day, and he saw it, and was glad"; and surely if ever Abraham saw the day of Christ, and was beyond measure glad, it was at that same moment when he beheld the Lord providing a substitute for Isaac. At any rate, whether Abraham understood the full meaning of what he said or not, he spoke not for himself, but for us. Every word he uttered is for our teaching, and the teaching is this: that God, in the gift of His Son, Jesus Christ, made the fullest provision for our greatest needs; and from that we may infer that whatever need shall ever occur to us, God will certainly provide for it; but He may delay the actual manifestation thereof till our darkest hour has come.

> Just in the last distressing hour
> 　　The Lord displays delivering power;
> The mount of danger is the place
> 　　Where we shall see surprising grace.

The Lord gave our Lord Jesus Christ to be the Substitute for men in view of the utmost need of our race. Isaac was hard pressed when God interfered in his behalf. The knife was lifted up by a resolute hand; he was within a second of death when the angelic voice said, "Lay not thine hand upon the lad." God provided instantly when the need pressed urgently. Beloved, was Isaac nearer to death than sinful man was near to hell? Was that knife closer to the throat of the beloved Isaac than the axe of the executioner was near to the neck of every sinner, aye, to the neck of the whole race of man? We have so sinned and gone astray that it was not possible for God to wink at our transgressions; He must visit our iniquities with the just punishment, which is nothing less than death eternal. I constantly meet with persons under the convincing power of the Spirit of God, and I always find that in their apprehension the punishment of sin is something terrible and overwhelming. When God deals with men by His convincing Spirit, they feel that their sin deserves nothing less than the wrath of God in hell. So it was with our race; we had altogether destroyed ourselves, and were shut up under condemnation by the law, and it was in that dread hour that God interposed and proclaimed a Savior for men. "While we were yet sinners, Christ died for us." I would to God we all felt what a dreadful thing it is to be lost; for then we should value the provision of the Savior much more than we do now. Oh, sirs, if no Redeemer had been provided, we might have gathered here this morning, and if you could have had patience to hear me, all I should have been able to say would have been, "Brethren, let us weep together and sigh in chorus; for we shall all die, and dying, we shall sink into the bottomless pit, and shall abide forever under the righteous anger of God." It must have been so with us all if a substitute had not been found.

If the gift of the loving Father had not been bestowed, if Jesus had not condescended to die in our place, we must have been left for execution by that law which will by no means spare the guilty. We talk about our salvation as if it were nothing very particular: we have heard of the plan of substitution so often that it becomes commonplace. It should not be so; I believe that it still thrills the angels with astonishment that man, when he had fallen from his high estate, and had been banished from Eden, and had become a rebel against God, should be redeemed by the blood of the Heir of all things, by whom the Divine Father made the worlds. When death and hell opened their jaws to devour, then was this miracle completed, and Jesus taken among the thorns was offered up a sacrifice for us.

God not only interposed when the death of Isaac was imminent, but also when the anguish of Abraham had reached its highest pitch. The patriarch's faith never wavered; but we must not forget that he was a man like ourselves, and no father could see his child offered up without an inward agony which surpasses all description. The anguish of so perfect a man as Abraham, a man who felt all the domestic affections intensely, as every truly godly father must feel them, and who loved his son as much as he loved his own life, must have been unspeakably great. What must have been the force of faith which enabled the man of God to master himself, to go contrary to the current of human nature, and deliberately to stand ready to sacrifice his Isaac! He must have been wound up to a fearful pitch of anguish when he lifted up the knife to slay his son; but just then the angel arrested his hand, and God provided the ram as the substitute in the moment of his utmost misery.

Surely the world had come to a great state of misery when at last God sent forth His Son, born of a woman, that He might become the sacrifice for sin. At any rate, this I know, that as a rule men do not see Christ to be their substitute nor accept Him as their Redeemer till they feel that they lie at hell's door, and till their anguish on account of sin has become exceeding great. I remember well when I first beheld the lamb of God who suffered in my stead. I had often heard the story of His death; I could have told it out to others very correctly; but then I did not know my own pressing need, I had not come to feel the knife at my throat, nor was I about to die; and therefore my knowledge was a cold, inoperative thing. But when the law had bound me, and given me over to death, and my heart within me was crushed with fear, then the sight of the glorious Substitute was as bright to me as a vision of heaven. Did Jesus suffer in my stead without the gate? Were my transgressions laid on Him? Then I received Him with joy unspeakable, my whole nature accepting the good news. At this moment I accept the Lord Jesus as my Substitute with a deep, peaceful delight. Blessed be the name of Jehovah-jireh for having taken thought of me, a beggar, a wretch, a condemned criminal, and for having provided the Lamb of God whose precious blood was shed instead of mine.

II. Secondly, upon the mount THE PROVISION WAS SPONTANEOUSLY MADE for Abraham, and so was the provision which the Lord displayed in the fullness of time when He gave up His Son to die. The ram caught in the thicket was a provision which on Abraham's part was quite *unsought*. He did not fall down and pray, "O Lord, in thy tenderness provide another victim instead of my son, Isaac." Probably it never entered his mind. But God spontaneously, from the free grace of His own heart, put the ram where Abraham found it. You and I did not pray for Christ to die. He died for us before we were born, and if He had not done so it would never have entered into our mind to ask for so great a gift. Until the Lord sought us we did not even seek to be saved by Christ, of the fact of whose death we had been made aware. Oh, no; it is not in man by nature to seek a Savior: it is in God to give a Savior, and then the Spirit of God sweetly inclines the heart to seek Him; but this seeking comes not of man. "When we were yet without strength, in due time Christ died for the ungodly." It is ours to sin, it is God's to save. "We have turned every one to his own way, and *the Lord* hath laid on him the iniquity of us all." Ours is the wandering, but the laying of those wanderings upon Jesus is of the Lord alone: we neither bought it, nor sought it, nor thought it.

In Abraham's case I believe it was an *unexpected* thing. He did not reckon upon any substitute for his son; he judged that he would have to die, and viewed him as already dead. As for ourselves, if God had not revealed the plan of salvation by the substitution of His only-begotten Son we should never have dreamed it. Remember that the Son of God is one with the Father; and if the Holy Ghost had not revealed the fact that the offended God would Himself bear the penalty due for the offense, it would never have occurred to the human mind. The brightest of the spirits before God's throne would never have devised the plan of salvation by the sacrifice of Jesus. It was unexpected. Let us bless the Lord, who has done for us exceeding abundantly above what we asked or even thought in giving to us redemption through the death of our Lord Jesus Christ.

I may say of Christ what I could not have said of Abraham's ram, that not only was He unsought for by us and unexpected, but now that He is given He is *not perfectly comprehended*.

> Much we talk of Jesus' blood,
> But how little's understood!
> Of His sufferings, so intense,
> Angels have no perfect sense.

I am often ready to beat upon my own breast as I study the wondrous mystery of atoning love; for it seems to me so mean a thing to be so little affected by such boundless grace. If we fully felt what God has done for us in the great deed of Jesus' death, it might not be wonderful if we were to die under the amazing discovery. "Such knowledge is too wonderful for me; it is high, I cannot attain unto it." The immortal God undertakes to bear death for man! The immaculate stands in the sinner's place. The well-pleasing Son is made accursed for those who else had been accursed forever. He who was above all shame and sorrow laid aside His glory and became the "Man of Sorrows," "despised and rejected of men." "Though he was rich, yet for your sakes he became poor." It is more extraordinary than romance! Poets may sing their loftiest stanzas, but they shall never reach the height of this great argument. *Paradise Lost* a Milton may compose, and fascinate a world with his majestic lines; but Paradise Restored by the divine substitution is not to be fully sung by mortal mind. God only knows the love of God. All the harps of redeemed men and all the hymns of adoring angels can never set forth the splendor of the love of Jehovah in providing for our need, providing for our salvation, providing His only-begotten Son, and providing Him of His own free love, unsought, and undesired of men.

III. But thirdly, we ought to dwell very long and earnestly upon the fact that for man's need THE PROVISION WAS MADE BY GOD HIMSELF. The text says, "Jehovah-jireh," the *Lord* will see to it, the *Lord* will provide. None else could have provided a ransom. Neither on earth nor in heaven was there found any helper for lost humanity. What sacrifice could be presented to God if a sacrifice could be accepted? Behold Lebanon, as it rises majestically toward heaven, white with its snows; see the forests which adorn its sides! Set these all on fire, and see them blaze as the wood of the altar of God. Yet "Lebanon is not sufficient to burn, nor the beasts thereof sufficient for a burnt offering." Take the myriads of cattle that roam the hills, and shed their blood till you have made a sea of gore, but what of that? "It is not possible that the blood of bulls and of goats should take away sins." Men may themselves die, but in death each man who dies only pays his own debt to nature; there is nothing left for another. "None can by any means redeem his brother, nor give to God a ransom for him." Where shall a redemption be found by which it shall be possible that the multitude of the elect shall be effectually redeemed from death and hell? Such a ransom could only be found by God, and He could only find it in Himself—in Him who was One with Himself, who lay in the bosom of the Father from old eternity. The provision was made by God Himself, since none other could provide. God alone could say, "Deliver him from going down to the pit: I have found a ransom."

But was it not singular that the Lord Jehovah should provide it? When law has been broken, and its honor has to be retrieved, it would not be judged likely that the aggrieved party should make the sacrifice. That God, against whom all the blasphemy and sin and wickedness of a ribald world was aimed, shall He Himself make expiation? Shall the Judge bear the penalty due to the criminal? "Lay it on the sinner; for it is his due"; so justice cries aloud—"Lay the penalty on the transgressor"; but if a substitute can be permitted, where can one be found able and willing to become surety for the guilty? Found upon the throne! Found in the Majesty that is offended! Brethren, I am beaten down by my subject; forgive me that I cannot speak of it as I would desire. There is no room here for words; it is a matter for silent thought. We want the fact of substitution to strike us, and then the cross will grow sublimely great. In vision I behold it! Its two arms are extended right and left till they touch the east and west and overshadow all races of men; the foot of it descends lower than the grave, till it goes down even to the gates of hell; while upward the cross mounts with a halo round about it of unutterable glory, till it rises above the stars, and sheds its light upon the throne of the Most High. Atonement is a divine business; its sacrifice is infinite, even as the God who conceived it. Glory be to His name forever! It is all that I can say. It was nothing less than a stretch of divine love for Jesus to give Himself for our sins. It was gracious for the Infinite to conceive of such a thing; but for Him to carry it out was glorious beyond all. What shall I say of it?

I will only interject this thought here—let none of us ever interfere with the provisions of God. If in our dire distress He alone was our Jehovah-jireh, and provided for us a Substitute, let us not think that there is anything left for us to provide. O sinner, do you cry, "Lord, I must have a broken heart"? He will provide for thee. Do you cry, "Lord, I cannot master sin, I have not the power to conquer my passions"? He will provide strength for thee. Do you mourn, "Lord, I shall never hold on and hold out to the end. I am so fickle"? Then He will provide perseverance for thee. Dost thou think that after having given His own dear Son to purchase thee He will let that work fail because *thou* canst not provide some little odds and ends to complete the work? Oh, dream not so; dote not on such a folly. Whatever thou wantest, poor sinner, if thou believest in Christ the Lord's provision of a Savior in Christ warrants thy believing that God will provide it. Salvation begins with Jehovah-jireh, the cross and the bleeding Savior; dost thou think it will afterwards drivel down into thy providing this and that? Oh, thy pride! Thy insane pride! Thou art to do something, art thou? What! and yoke thy little something with the Eternal God? Didst thou ever hear of an angel failing to perform a duty until he was assisted by an ant? Hast thou ever heard of God's great laws of nature breaking down till some child's finger could supplement their force? Thou to help thy God to provide! Get thee out of the way, and be nothing; then shall God come in and be everything. Sink! It is the Lord that must rise. *He* shall be seen in the mount and not in thyself. Hide thyself, and let the glory of the Lord be manifested in thee. I wish that every troubled one here could catch this idea, and hold it fast. Whatever you want to put away your sin, whatever you want to make you a new creature, whatever you want to carry you to heaven, Jehovah-jireh, the Lord will provide it. He will see to it. Trust thou in Him and before long thou shalt see the divine provision and Jehovah shall be glorious in thine eyes.

IV. But I must pass on. That which God prepares for poor sinners is A PROVISION MOST GLORIOUSLY MADE. God provided a ram instead of Isaac. This was sufficient for the occasion as a type; but that which was typified by the ram is infinitely more glorious. In order to save us God provided *God*. I cannot put it more simply. He did not provide an angel, nor a mere man, but God Himself. Come, sinner, with all thy load of sin: God can bear it; the shoulders that bear up the universe can well sustain thy load of guilt. God gave thee His Godhead to be thy Savior when He gave thee His Son.

But He also gave in the person of Christ *perfect manhood*—such a man as never lived before, eclipsing even the perfection of the first Adam in the garden by the majestic innocence of His nature. When Jesus has been viewed as man, even unconverted men have so admired His excellence that they have almost adored Him.

Jesus is God and man, and the Father has given that man, that God, to be thy Redeemer. For thy redemption the Lord God has given thee the death of Christ; and
what a death it was! I would that troubled hearts would oftener study the story of the
Great Sacrifice, the agony and bloody sweat, the betrayal in the garden, the binding
of the hands, the accusation of the innocent, the scourging, the thorn-crowning, the
spitting in the face, the mockery, the nailing to the tree, the lifting up of the cross,
the burning fever, the parching thirst, and, above all, the overpowering anguish of
being forsaken of His God. Consider, O soul, that to save thee the Son of God must
cry, "*Lama sabachthani!*" Consider that to save thee He must hang naked to His shame
between heaven and earth, rejected of both; must cry, "I thirst," and receive nothing but vinegar wherewith to moisten His burning lips. Jesus must "pour out his soul
unto death" that we might live. He must be "numbered with the transgressors," that
we might be numbered with His saints in glory everlasting. Was this not a glorious
provision? What greater gift could be bestowed than one in whom God and man are
blended in one?

When Abraham on the mount offered a sacrifice it was called a "burnt offering";
but when the Lord Jesus Christ on Calvary died it was not only a burnt offering, but
a sin offering, a meat offering, and a peace offering, and every other kind of sacrifice
in one. Under the oldest of all dispensations, before the mosaic economy, God had
not taught to men the distinctions of sacrifice, but an offering unto the Lord meant
all that was afterwards set forth by many types. When the venerable patriarch offered
a sacrifice, it was an offering for sin, and a sweet smelling savor besides. So was it with
our Lord Jesus Christ. When He died He made His soul an offering for sin, and "put
away sin by the sacrifice of himself." When He died, He *also* offered unto God a burnt
offering, for we read, "And walk in love, as Christ also hath loved us, and hath given
himself for us an offering and a sacrifice to God for a sweet smelling savor." When
Jesus died He gave to us a peace offering; for we come to feast upon Him with God,
and to us "His flesh is meat indeed, his blood is drink indeed." One would need many
a day in which to expatiate upon the infinite virtues and excellencies of Christ, in
whom all perfections are sweetly hived. Blessed be His name, God has most gloriously provided for us in the day of our need. Jehovah-jireh!

V. Fifthly, THE PROVISION WAS MADE EFFECTIVELY. Isaac did not die; the laughter in Abraham's house was not stifled; there was no grief for the patriarch; he went
home with his son in happy companionship, because Jehovah had provided himself
a lamb for a burnt offering. The ram which was provided did not bleed in vain; Isaac
did not die as well as the ram; Abraham did not have to slay the God-provided victim and his own son also. No, the sacrifice sufficed. Beloved, this is my comfort in
the death of Christ—I hope it is yours—that He did not die in vain. I have heard of
a theology which, in its attempt to extol the efficacy of Christ's death, virtually de-
prives it of any certain efficiency; the result of the atonement is made to depend entirely upon the will of man, and so is left to haphazard. Our Lord, according to certain
teachers, might or might not see of the travail of his soul. I confess that I do not be-

lieve in this random redemption, and I wonder that any persons can derive comfort from such teaching. I believe that the Son of God could not possibly have come into the world in the circumstances in which He did come, and could not have died as He did die, and yet be defeated and disappointed. He died for those who believe in Him, and these shall live, yea, they *do* live in Him.

I should think that Isaac, the child of laughter, was solemnly joyous as he descended the hill and went home with his father. Methinks both of them tripped along with happy step toward Sarah's house and their own loved home; and you and I this day may go home with like joyousness. We shall not die, for the Lamb of God has died for us. We shall never perish, for He has suffered in our stead. We were bound on the altar, we were laid on the wood, and the fire was ready for our consuming; but no knife shall touch us now, for the sacrifice is offered once for all. No fire shall consume us, for He who suffered in our stead has borne the heat of the flame on our behalf. We live, and we shall live. "There is therefore now no condemnation to them which are in Christ Jesus." This is an effectual and precious providing. I do not believe in a redemption which did not redeem or in an atonement which did not atone; but I do believe in Him who died in vain for none, but will effectually save His own church and His own sheep for whom He laid down His life. To Him we will all render praise, for He was slain, and He has redeemed us unto God by His blood out of every kindred and people and nation.

VI. Turn we then, sixthly, to this note, that we may well glorify Jehovah-jireh because THIS PROVISION WAS MADE FOR EVERY BELIEVER. The provision on the Mount of Moriah was made on behalf of Abraham: he was himself a man of faith, and he is styled the "father of the faithful"; and now every faithful or believing one may stand where Abraham stood, and say, "Jehovah-jireh, the Lord will provide." Remember, however, that our faith must be of the same nature as that of Abraham, or it will not be counted to us for righteousness. Abraham's faith worked by love; it so worked in him that he was willing to do all that the Lord bade him, even to the sacrifice of his own dear son. You must possess a living, working, self-sacrificing faith if you would be saved. If you have it, you may be as sure that you are saved as you are sure that you have sinned. "He that believeth on him is not condemned," because Christ was condemned for him. "He that believeth on him hath everlasting life": he cannot die, for Christ died for him. The great principle upon which our security is based is the righteousness of God, which assures us that He will not punish the substitute and then punish the person for whom the substitute endured the penalty. It were a matter of gross injustice if the sinner, having made atonement for his sin in the Person of his covenant Head, the Lord Jesus, should afterwards himself be called upon to account for the very sin which was atoned for. Sin, like anything else, cannot be in two places at once: if the great God took my sin, and laid it on His Son, then it is not on me any more. If Jesus bore the wrath of God for me, I cannot bear that wrath; it were contrary to every principle of a just moral government that the Judge should cast our Surety into prison and exact the penalty of Him, and then come upon those for whom the suretyship was undertaken. By this gospel I am prepared to stand or fall; yea, by it I will live or die: I know no other. Because I believe it, I this day cry from the bottom of my heart, "Jehovah-jireh," the Lord has provided an effectual redemption for all those who put their trust in Him whom God has set forth to be a propitiation. It is true, as it is written, "he that believeth and is baptized shall be saved." It is true that the faith which worketh by love brings justification to the soul.

VII. But now I close with a remark which will reveal the far-reaching character of my text. "Jehovah-jireh" is true concerning all necessary things. The instance given of Abraham being provided for shows us that the Lord will ever be a Provider for His people. As to the gift of the Lord Jesus, this is A PROVISION WHICH GUARANTEES ALL OTHER PROVISION. "He that spared not his own Son, but delivered him up for us all, how shall he not with him also freely give us all things?" Abraham learned that; for, as soon as he had slaughtered the ram, the covenant was repeated in his ears, and repeated as he had never heard it before—accompanied with an oath. God cannot swear by any greater than Himself, and so He said, "By myself have I sworn." Thus was the covenant ratified by blood and by the oath of God. Oh, that bleeding Sacrifice! The covenant of God is confirmed by it, and our faith is established. If you have seen Jesus die for you, your heart has heard God swear, "Surely in blessing I will bless thee!" By two immutable things, wherein it is impossible for God to lie, He hath given us strong consolation who have fled for refuge to the hope set before us in the gospel. Let us fall back on this eternal verity, that if God has provided His own Well-beloved Son to meet the most awful of all necessities, then He will provide for us in everything else.

Where will He provide? He will provide for us *in the mount*, that is to say, in the place of our trial. When we reach the place where the fatal deed of utmost obedience is to be wrought, then God will interpose. You desire Him to provide for you when you lift up your eyes and see the mount afar off. He does not choose so to do; but in the mount it shall be seen, in the place of the trial, in the heat of the furnace, in the last extremity Jehovah will be seen, for He will see to it, and it shall become a proverb with you—"In the mount Jehovah shall be seen." That is to say, when you cannot see, the Lord will see you and see to your need; for His eyes are upon the righteous, and His ears are open to their cry. You will not need to explain to God your difficulties and the intricacies of your position, He will see it all. Joyfully sing that revival ditty—

This my Father knows.

As soon as the Lord has seen our need, then His provision shall be seen. You need not climb to heaven or descend into the deep to find it: the Lord's provision is near at hand—the ram in the thicket is behind you though you see it not as yet. When you have heard God speak to you, you shall turn and see it, and wonder you never saw it before. You will heartily bless God for the abundant provision which He reveals in the moment of trial. Then shall the Lord Himself be seen. You will soon die, and perhaps in dying you will be troubled by the fear of death; but let that evil be removed by this knowledge—that the Lord will yet be seen, and when He shall appear you shall be manifested in His glory. In the day of the revelation of the Lord Jesus your body shall be raised from the dead, and then shall the divine provision yet more fully be discovered. "In the mount it shall be seen," and there shall God Himself be manifested to you, for your eyes shall behold Him and not another.

There is a rendering given to my text which we cannot quite pass over. Some read it that "in the mount the people shall be seen"—in that mount in years to come the multitude would gather to worship God. God's presence was in the temple which was built upon that spot, and thither the tribes went up, the tribes of the Lord to worship the Most High. I dwell in a house not made with hands, but piled by God of solid slabs of mercy. He is building for me a palace of crystal, pure and shining, transparent as the day. I see the house in which I am to abide forever gradually growing around me. Its foundation was laid of old, in eternal love—"in the mount it shall be seen." The Lord provided for me a Covenant Head, a Redeemer, and a Friend, and in Him I abide. Since then, course upon course of the precious stones of lovingkindness has been laid, and the jeweled walls are all around me. Has it not been so with you? By-and-by we shall be roofed in with glory everlasting, and then as we shall look to the foundations, and the walls, and to the arch above our head, we shall shout, "Jehovah-jireh"—God has provided all this for me! How shall we rejoice in every stone of the divine building! On such a day was that stone laid, I remember it right well: "I was sore sick and the Lord comforted me." On such a day was that other stone laid—I was in prison spiritually, and the heavenly visitor came unto me. On such another day was that bejeweled course completed, for my heart was glad in the Lord and my glory rejoiced in the God of my salvation. The walls of love are still rising, and when the building is finished and the capstone is brought out with shoutings of "Grace, grace, unto it!" we shall then sing this song unto the Lord—JEHOVAH-JIREH! The Lord has provided it. From the beginning to the end there is nothing of man and nothing of merit, nothing of self, but all of God in Christ Jesus, who hath loved us with an everlasting love, and therefore hath abounded towards us in blessing according to the fullness of His infinite heart. To Him be praise world without end. Amen, and amen.

FIRST KING OF RIGHTEOUSNESS, AND AFTER THAT KING OF PEACE

SERMON NO. 1,768
DELIVERED ON LORD'S DAY EVENING, FEBRUARY 3, 1884.
PORTION OF SCRIPTURE READ BEFORE SERMON—HEBREWS 7.
HYMNS FROM *Our Own Hymn Book*—397, 393.

First being by interpretation King of righteousness, and after that
also King of Salem, which is, King of peace—Hebrews 7:2.

WE will not enlarge upon the story of Melchizedek, nor discuss the question as to who he was. It is near enough for us to believe that he was one who worshiped God after the primitive fashion, a believer in God such as Job was in the land of Uz, one of the world's gray fathers who had kept faithful to the Most High God. He combined in his own person the kingship and the priesthood; a conjunction by no means unusual in the first ages. Of this man we know very little; and it is partly because we know so little of him that he is all the better type of our Lord, of whom we may inquire, "Who shall declare his generation?" The very mystery which hangs about Melchizedek serves to set forth the mystery of the person of our divine Lord. "Without father, without mother, without descent, having neither beginning of days, nor end of life; but made like unto the Son of God; he abideth a priest continually. Now consider how great this man was, unto whom even the patriarch Abraham gave the tenth of the spoils."

Melchizedek seems to have been, first by name, and then by place of office, doubly designated a king. First, his name is *Malchi-tsedek*, which signifies by interpretation, "king of righteousness." His personal name is "king of righteousness." As a matter of fact, he was also the monarch of some town called Salem; it is not at all likely to have been Jerusalem, although that may have been the case. The interpretation of his official name is "king of peace." A teaching was intended by the Holy Spirit in the names: so the apostle instructs us in the passage before us. I believe in the verbal inspiration of Scripture; hence, I can see how there can be instruction for us even in the proper names of persons and places. Those who reject verbal inspiration must in effect condemn the great apostle of the Gentiles, whose teaching is so frequently based upon a word. He makes more of words and names than any of us should have thought of doing, and he was guided therein by the Spirit of the Lord, and therefore he was right. For my part, I am far more afraid of making too little of the Word than of seeing too much in it.

This man, is, first, named "*Malchi-tsedek*"—"king of righteousness" by *interpretation*; and herein he is like our divine Lord, whose name and character can only come to us by interpretation. What he is and who he is and all his character, no angel's tongue could tell. No human language can ever describe to the full what Jesus is. He is King, but that is a poor word for such royalty as His. He reigns, but that word "reigns" is but a slender description of that supreme empire which He continually exercises. He is said to be King of righteousness, but that is by interpretation, by the toning down of His character to our comprehension. Scripture might have called Him King of holiness, for He is "glorious in holiness." His character, better known to spirits before the throne than to us, is not to be comprehended in that one word "righteousness": it is but an interpretation, and most things lose by translation, and so the perfect character of the Son of God, as it stands before the Eternal Mind, cannot be fully expressed in human language. In fact, when our faculties are enlarged, and our spirits raised to the highest platform, they can never reach the eternity of our Lord's sonship, and the glory of His kingdom: the equity of His character, and the loveliness of His mind, both as God and man, must still be far beyond us. But this much is translated to us into our own tongue—that He is a King, and that He is a righteous King—yea, the very King of righteousness—the Sovereign of the realm of equity, the supreme Lord of everything that is good and holy. That, you see, is wrapped up in His name and nature. Jesus is righteousness, and every righteous thing gathers beneath the right scepter of His kingdom.

But the second word, *Salem*, which, brought down to our tongue, signifies "peace," is in reference to a place rather than a person. You see our Lord Jesus is essentially righteousness, that is interwoven with His name and person; but He gives, bestows, deposits, pours forth peace in a place which He has chosen, and upon a people whom He has ordained, and whom He has brought near unto Himself: so that His kingdom of peace links Him with His redeemed, to whom He has given the peace of God.

"First, King of righteousness." How early that "*first*" is I cannot tell you. "In the beginning was the Word," but when that beginning was, who knows?—for is He not, indeed without beginning? First and firstborn, from everlasting Thou art God, O mighty Son of Jehovah! First King of righteousness, and then afterwards when men fell, when rebellion, and strife, and war had sprung up—then He came to heal the mischief and become "King of peace." He comes Himself as the divine Ambassador, our Peacemaker and Peace; He comes here into this place even into the midst of His Salem, into the midst of His people, and gives us now, as He has long given, the vision of peace; opening up before the eye of faith the completeness, the sureness, and the delight of perfect peace in Himself.

The one matter which I am going to set forth at this time is just this—"First King of righteousness, and after that also King of peace." Note well the order of these two, and the dependence of the one upon the other; for there could be no true peace that was not grounded upon righteousness; and out of righteousness peace is sure to spring up. Righteousness is essential to peace; if it were not first, peace could not be second. If there could be a king of peace apart from righteousness, it would be dank, dark, deadly, a horrible peace, ending in a worse misery than war itself could inflict. It is needful where an unrighteous peace exists that it should be broken up, that a better peace should be established upon a true foundation which will last forever.

I shall ask you—and may the Spirit of God help us to do it—first, *to admire the King*, and, secondly, *to enjoy Him*—to enter with holy delight into the full meaning of his name and character as King of Righteousness and King of peace.

I. First, I ask you to ADMIRE THIS KING.

This Melchizedek, whom we exhibit as a type, is *such a king as God is*. He is according to divine model. He is priest of the Most High God, and He is like the Most High God, for the Lord Jehovah Himself is, first, King of righteousness, and after that also King of peace. The great Creator entered the garden of Eden in that sorrowful hour when our parents had rebelled, and were hiding among the trees to escape His call; and He bade them answer for their fault. When they stood trembling before Him in the nakedness of their conscious guilt, they knew him as their King and their Judge. At that moment He was not first the King of peace to them, but first the King of righteousness. He pronounced sentence upon the serpent, upon the woman, and upon the man, gently making much of the punishment to fall aslant upon the ground; but yet vindicating justice before He spoke a word of peace. After that discourse, yea, in the midst of His sentences, He spoke of peace when He mentioned the woman's seed that should bruise the serpent's head. Then also there happened the slaying of a victim, for the Lord God made unto them coats of skins, of beasts which had, no doubt, been slain in sacrifice, and with these they were covered. In beginning to deal with an apostate race the Lord observed the fitting order of our text: He began with righteousness, and afterwards went on to peace. At the gate of the garden commenced the dispensation of mercy and peace, but first of all there was the pronouncing of the sentence that man should eat bread in the sweat of his face, and that unto dust he should return. Substantial righteousness was dealt out to the guilty, and then peace was provided for the troubled. At the fall God first set up a Judgment-seat, and right speedily a Mercy-seat. Righteousness must ever lead the van.

Well, the times went on, and men began to sin with a high hand. There were giants in those days, and the people of God were mixed up with the men of the world. This is the worst sign of the world's depravity when there ceases to be a division between the people of God and the sons of men. There was an unholy alliance between sin and righteousness; and then the King came forth again, and displayed His countenance, and began to judge, and correct, and call to repentance. Men perceived that the countenance of God towards them was the face of one who is first King of righteousness. Noah's teaching taught men to return unto the Lord, or He would surely deal with them in righteousness, and make a full end. Space most ample was given for repentance, but men were made upon their follies. He is first King of righteousness, and afterwards King of peace; and so he dealt with that guilty world. He pulled up the sluices of the great deep which lieth under; He let loose all the cataracts of heaven from above, and He swept men from off the face of the earth. Then afterwards He hung the rainbow in the sky, and He smelled a sweet savor of rest; and there was peace once more between God and a race that had to begin again with father Noah instead of father Adam. Righteousness ruled first, and washed out with a flood the traces of ungodliness, and then peace set up her gentle reign upon a new world.

All along, in the history of God's dealings with men, He kept to this unvarying rule. God has never forsaken righteousness, not even for the sake of love. He selected a people for Himself; He called His Son out of Egypt; He brought His chosen people through the Red Sea into the wilderness, and there He communed with them. But they went astray after graven images; they defiled themselves with the vices of the surrounding heathen. They became degraded and polluted, and then He came again among them as the King of righteousness, setting Sinai on a blaze, making even Moses to fear and quake, compelling the earth to open and swallow up rebels, causing the fire to break out among them, or fiery serpents to inflame their veins with death: for, though to them He was a King of peace, and walked among them in tenderness, and by the fiery cloudy pillar led their band, and in the midst of the tabernacle by His Shekinah unveiled His glory, yet it was then true, as it is now true, "The Lord thy God is a jealous God." He would not bear iniquity. He could not look upon sin without indignation. His anger smoked against it, for He is and ever must be "first King of righteousness, and after that also King of peace." That wonderful wilderness journey is bright with mercy, but it is equally dark with justice. Remember the graves of lusting and its burnings. Israel's God was ever sternly righteous though glorious in grace. It is a high but terrible privilege to dwell near to God, for His holiness burns like a consuming fire, and will not endure evil.

Aye, and when He had brought His people into the promised land, and had given them their heritage by lot, we must remember how they sinned against Him; and it was not long before He brought upon them the Midianites, or the Philistines, or foes of one race or another, so that they were grievously oppressed, and afflicted, and brought low. When they cried to Him, then He delivered them; but He took vengeance upon their inventions. He would not bear their sin: He took it exceedingly ill from them that a people so highly favored should so constantly rebel. He said, "You only have I known of all the families of the earth: therefore I will punish you for all your iniquities." He was to His own elect nation, first, King of righteousness, and then King of peace.

And so it went on until, at last, Israel provoked the Lord beyond measure, and the chosen people went astray to their own confusion, and then with the besom of destruction He swept them off from the face of their land. He scattered them as a man scattereth dung upon the field. Are they not divided to this day among all the people, a by-word and a proverb still, for men everywhere say, "These are the people that forgot their God, and He banished them from their own land, and will keep them in banishment till they return unto their God in spirit and in truth?" Every Jew whom we see pacing our streets, far off from the city of his fathers, is a proof that the Lord of heaven is, first, King of righteousness.

All over the world, and everywhere, this is God's way of dealing with men. Do not imagine that God will ever lay aside His righteousness for the sake of saving a sinner—that He will ever deal with men unrighteously in order that they may escape the penalty due to their transgression. He has never done so, and He never will. Glorious in holiness is He forever and ever. That blazing throne must consume iniquity; transgression cannot stand before it; there can be no exceptions to this rule. The Judge of all the earth must do right. Whatever things may change, the law of God cannot alter, and the character of God cannot deteriorate. High as the great mountains, deep as the abyss, eternal as His being, is the righteousness of the Most High. Peace can never come to men from the Lord God Almighty except by righteousness. The two can never be separated without the most fearful consequences. Peace without righteousness is like the smooth surface of the stream before it takes its awful Niagara plunge. If there is to be peace between God and man, God must still be a righteous God, and by some means or other the transgression of man must be *justly* put away; for God cannot wink at it, or permit it to go unpunished. Salvation must first of all provide for righteousness, or peace will never lodge within its chambers. The Lord of heaven is first King of righteousness, and then King of peace, so that Melchizedek was such a king as God is.

And now, next, the type is especially meant to teach us that he was *such a king as Christ is*; for when the Lord Jesus Christ came into the world, He came with His everlasting and unchangeable rule girt about him—that, though He should be a King, yet He would be first King of righteousness, and after that also King of peace. Why did He not set up a kingdom here below among the Jews? Many spirits would have welcomed Him. If He had only set Himself up to be a king, promising them sure conquest and abundant plunder, the zealots of the Jewish nation would have fought like tigers at His side. But, no; He came first to be a King of righteousness, and that was a topic for which they cared nothing. He went into His own Father's house like a king into His palace; but it was with a scourge of small cords, crying, "Take these things hence!" The temple was no abode for Him while greed, and self, and mammon defiled its courts. In that temple He looked round about Him with indignation, for He saw no trace of righteousness there, but every indication that up to the very veil of the temple all was given over to human unrighteousness.

They wanted an unrighteous kingdom, but He would not have it. His fan was in His hand, and He would thoroughly purge His floor. His laws were not to be like those of Caesar; His soldiers were not to fight with carnal weapons. He came not to set up a kingdom of power and force, but a kingdom of love and truth and righteousness; and hence His own people knew Him not, and rendered Him no homage. His holiness stood in the way of such a kingdom as the Jews desired, and hence they turned upon Him and cried, "Let him be crucified." Though they would not acknowledge His sovereignty, he was their King; and at His death He bore above His head the superscription, "This is Jesus, the King of the Jews." He would not set up a carnal kingdom of their sort; Church and State, truth and force united in some form or other, must have been suggested to Him; but no; He must be first King of righteousness, and then King of peace. He preached no peace apart from purity. He never made little of vice or error; He was the deadly foe of all evil. He said, "I came not to bring peace, but a sword." Until there is righteousness there must be conflict, and peace can only enter when righteousness has won the field. Oh, my brethren, I wish I had power to describe to you how our divine Master in all His lowliness began to be the King of righteousness by His superlative, unrivaled character. Here among us there was never such righteousness as His—such royal righteousness throughout all His career in all the details of life. I see an imperial righteousness in the character of my divine Lord—a righteousness that is master and superior of all other. Even those that hate Jesus cannot find fault with Him. Books written to disprove His divine mission are nevertheless full of almost fulsome adulation of Him: I call it by no better word, because I think that the praises which infidels have given to our Lord are no more acceptable to Him than were the praises of devils when they said, "This is the Son of God!" Then He bade them hold their peace, and I think He has the same wish at this moment touching His Unitarian and Infidel admirers. All sorts of men have been compelled to do homage to this kingly One who has passed across the page of history, the very sovereign of all that is right and good.

But ah, methinks he was most King of righteousness when He said unto Himself, "My Father's law has been broken: I will restore its honor. Men have defiled it and trampled on it: I will pay to it the highest homage." With this strong desire upon Him He went up to the cross, and gave His hands and feet to the nails, and His side to the spear, and with a thorn crown upon His dying brow He became in very deed the King of righteousness. As the Son of God, He rendered unto the divine majesty all the honor due to the law by reason of the many insults which sin had heaped thereon. The transgressions of His people were laid upon their Great Shepherd, they were made to meet upon Him in one dreadful storm, and that hurricane spent itself upon Him. Our Great Substitute endured the consequences of human guilt on our behalf, and thus He is able to pacify the troubled conscience. He is, first, King of righteousness. He knew that He could not be King of peace to us till, first of all, He had woven a perfect righteousness in the loom of His life, and dyed it in His own heart's blood in His death: but when He had achieved this, then He became King of righteousness, demonstrated to be so before the eyes of all, and then to you and to me He became henceforth the King of peace. How glorious is His name! Oh, for a voice of thunder with which to praise Him!

Today our Lord and Master has gone His way up to the eternal hills where He reigns; but His kingdom, for which we daily pray, is coming; and, mark you, it will come by righteousness. I say no word against those who endeavor to bring peace to the nations by the extension of commerce, facilities for travel, and so forth; but it is not thus that the sword of war shall be broken. Would God the sword of the Lord were quiet in its scabbard forever; but I never anticipate the reign of universal peace on earth till first the King of righteousness is acknowledged in every place. I do not think that we shall ever see the fruits without the tree, or the stream without the source, or peace without the enthronement of the principle of righteousness from which it springs. There shall come a day when the lion shall eat straw like the ox, and the wolf shall lie down with the lamb—when they shall hang the useless helmet in the hall, and study war no more; but that reign of the joyous King, that era of plenty, love, and joy, can only commence as a reign of righteousness. It cannot be anything else; and until sin is dethroned, till iniquity is banished, we shall not see the divine fruit of peace upon the face of the earth. Wherever Jesus is King He must be first King of righteousness, and after that King of peace.

So, then, Melchizedek is such a king as God is, and such a king as Jesus is.

Note, next, that *he is such a king as right-hearted minds desire.* I say "right-hearted minds." I mean not only those who are saved, but those in whom there is some good thing towards the Lord God of Israel. There is an honest and good ground not yet sown, and we know what that soil waiteth for. I remember what my thoughts used to be when I was seeking the Lord; I longed to be saved; I desired to escape from my sin; but with it there always went this thought—"God must be just." I had ever a certain trembling sense of guilt, but at the same time a deep reverence for righteousness. In my heart of hearts I said, "Let not the Lord even for my sake do an unrighteous thing. I am nothing; but God and His righteousness are all in all. It were a greater calamity for God to be unjust than for me to be lost. It were a dark day for all the aspirations of noble minds if it were possible for God to swerve from the strict rule of His integrity. Though He slay me, yet let His name be honored, and let His righteousness remain untarnished." I remember distinctly being the subject of that feeling. Sinner as I was I had a care for the perfect law of the Lord, and would by no means have agreed to its being dishonored in order to my own personal salvation. I wanted this question answered—"How can God be just and yet the Justifier of him that believeth?" I did not know at that time the sweet secret of substitution; but when I did know it, no music ever sounded so sweetly in the human ear as that sounded in my heart. When I saw that, by the interposition of the Son of God, and His bearing my guilt, God could be sternly, strictly, severely just, to the letter, in every jot and tittle, and yet could put all my sin away, and take me to His bosom, and let me be His child, then I said, "This must be of God. This divine secret bears upon its own face its own warranty of truthfulness, for no man could have invented a system at once so just to God, so safe to man." To be able to look for mercy as just, and receive pardon on the ground of righteousness, is certainly a high ground to reach; and yet every believer stands there before God. I say that every right-minded man feels a deep concern for the righteousness of God, when he is soberly in his senses, and thinking the matter over. He longs to be saved, that is more than natural; but he does not wish to be saved in a way that would derogate from the supreme splendor of the righteousness of God. Let the Lord God be glorious in justice, and then, if I can be saved, well and good. Blessed be God, we can be thus saved. Our entrance to heaven can be as justly secured as our banishment to hell was righteously deserved. How justice and peace have kissed each other is now made known. That secret is told us in the Word of God. Is it not written on the cross of our Lord Jesus Christ?

And I am sure, again, that no right-hearted man wants Christ to come and be to him the King of peace, and then to let him live in sin. Brothers, I want no peace in my heart concerning any fault. If I know myself before God, my heart's inmost prayer is that I may never be able to rest till I am rid of every relic of evil. I do not want to make myself happy and yet to live in a single known sin. If I could have the offer of heaven, and be a drunkard, I wish not for a drunkard's heaven. What could it be but a scene of riot, strife, and obscenity? If I could have heaven and be a liar, I want not a liar's heaven. What could the heaven of falsehood be but hell in truth? Nay, I would not wish for a heaven in which I might freely indulge some minor sin, or be jovial in the commission of some unconsidered transgression. Nay, there can be no heaven for me till evil in very form is expelled from my nature. My God, my longing is not for happiness first, but for purity first, and happiness afterwards; and hence it is my delight to read that my King is first the King of righteousness, and then the King of peace. My heart rejoices in a sin-killing King, and then a peace-bestowing King, sweeping out the buyers and the sellers from the temple, and then manifesting Himself there in all His majesty to His waiting people.

Melchizedek, therefore, sets forth such a king as all right-minded people desire.

Again, this wonderful Melchizedek *is such a king as Jesus must be to every one of you who have not yet known Him, if you are ever to receive Him as your Savior.* Let me not sew pillows to all armholes by preaching salvation to those who do not repent of their evil ways. I do not come here to chant in dulcet tones sweet lullabies to men who sleep in unrighteousness. If you would have peace with God, you must repent of sin. If you love evil you cannot love God. There must be a divorce between you and sin, or there can be no marriage between you and Christ. When Jesus comes to a soul, He comes as King of righteousness first, and after that as King of peace. We must have a positive righteousness of life, a cleanness of heart and hand, or we shall not be found at the right hand of the Judge. Let no man deceive himself. "Whatsoever a man soweth, that shall he also reap." He that comes to Christ, and takes Christ to be his Savior, must take Christ also to be his Ruler; and Christ ruling him, there must be in that man's heart an active, energetic pursuit of everything that is good and holy, for "without holiness no man shall see the Lord." He that liveth in sin is dead while he liveth, and knows nothing of the life of God in his soul. Righteousness must hold the scepter, or peace will not attend the court.

I know that I speak to many who long to be saved; but will you give up your sin? For Christ has come to save His people from their sins. If you do not wish to be saved from sinning, you will never be saved from damning. Do you hug your Delilah? Then shall you lose your eyes like Samson. Do you hold to the viper, and press the asp to your bosom? Then shall the poison boil within your veins. Christ cannot save you while sin is loved and followed after, and has a reigning power in you; for it is an essential of His salvation that He should deliver you from the mastery of evil. I would to God that many here would cry, "That is the very thing I want. I long for it. Can I be helped to renounce sin?" O poor heart, if thou hungerest after righteousness, thou shalt be filled! Thou shalt be helped to conquer evil: thou art being helped by the very desire which has been breathed into thee. "Oh," says one, "can I break off the iron yoke, and come out of the Egyptian bondage of my lust?" Thou canst; for Christ has come to set thee free. Trust thou in Him, the great Emancipator. But if thou sayest, "I will live in sin, and yet go to heaven," thou shalt never do so. There shall by no means enter into the celestial city anything that defileth. He that takes men to heaven is first King of righteousness, and after that he is King of peace.

I have closed this first head when I noticed that *that is the kind of king that God would have every one of us to be.* We ought all to be, first, kings of righteousness, and then kings of peace. The Lord has appointed each man his kingdom: let us see to it that we reign for good and not for evil. On all sides we hear voices inviting us to peace apart from righteousness. "Oh," they say to us, "a confederacy, a confederacy." What mean you? You are to preach a lie, and we are to preach the truth, and yet we are to call each other brothers. We are *no* brothers, and we will not by our silence aid the fraud. "Oh, but," say they, "be charitable." Charitable with what? Charitable with God's truth, flinging it down into the mire of error? Charitable by deceiving our fellowmen? That we cannot be. Brethren, we must so hold and love the truth as to hate every false way; for the way of error is ruinous to the souls of men, and it will go hard with us if even by our silence we lead men to run therein. If any man shall say to you, "Come and let us sin together," reply to him, "I cannot enter into association with you, for I must first be pure and then peaceable, since I serve a Lord who is first King of righteousness, and after that King of peace." "Hold your tongue," says the world. "Do not fight against error. Why need you speak so loudly against a wrong thing?" We must speak, and speak sharply too, for souls are in danger. We must uplift the banner of truth, or we shall be meanest of all cowards. God has made us kings, and we must be first kings of righteousness, and after that kings of peace.

God's people are tempted sometimes to be a little too peaceable. Remember that our Lord Jesus has not come to make us live at peace with sin. He has come to set a man against his brother—to divide a household where iniquity holds sway. There can be no peace between the child of God and wrongdoing or wrong thinking of any kind. We must have "war to the knife" with that which would rob God of His glory and men of their salvation. Our peace is on the footing of righteousness, and on no other ground. We are for all that is good and right; but we dare not cry, "Peace, peace, where there is no peace."

II. Now my time has fled, but I must occupy a little upon the best part of my subject. I have asked you to admire the King. I now beg you to ENJOY HIM.

Our Lord Jesus Christ is first King of *righteousness*. You know what it means. Shall I tell you what it includes? All who are in Him, and one with Him in His kingdom, are righteous in His righteousness. His is a righteous kingdom, and those who obey it will be found to have done rightly. If we follow Christ's rule we need never be afraid that it will mislead us. We are righteous, certainly, when we are doing His bidding. If any cavil and say, "Why doest thou this?" quote the King's authority. Do not thou be afraid if thou doest the King's bidding. He is a King of righteousness, and thou art righteous in obeying His righteous ordinances. He who religiously obeys Mohammed may yet be doing grievous moral wrong; but it is never so with the disciple of Jesus: obedience to Jesus is holiness.

Notice, next, that if we trust this King of righteousness we are righteous in His merit. I want you to believe this. If you had always kept God's law and had never sinned, you would have been conscious of righteousness. Now, by faith, as many of you as believe in the Lord Jesus Christ are as righteous as He is righteous in the sight of God—as righteous as if you had never sinned. Oh, I want you to feel this. "Being justified by faith we have peace with God"; but there must first be this justifying righteousness before there can be peace. What Christ did He did for His people. I say not that what Christ did is imputed to His people, though I believe that it is so; but it belongs to His people, for they are part and parcel of Him, and so are partakers with Him. They are in Him as in their Federal Head, and whatsoever Christ is, or has, or does, belongs in itself, in the very nature of things, to all that are in Him and in that covenant whereof He is the Head. Stand up straight, then, before thy God, and though in thyself the publican's humble demeanor suits thee well, yet in thy Lord thou mayest take another stand and say, "Who shall lay anything to the charge of God's elect? It is God that justifieth. Who is He that condemneth? It is Christ that died; yea, rather, that is risen again." The Lord Jesus is "made of God unto us wisdom and righteousness." "This is His name whereby He shall be called, The Lord our Righteousness"; for "as by one man's disobedience many were made sinners," as you and I know to our cost, "so by the obedience of one shall many be made righteous." "By his knowledge"— by the knowledge of Him—"shall my righteous servant justify many, for he shall bear their iniquities."

Now, then, dost thou believe in Christ? Then thou hast no sin. Thy sin was laid upon Christ of old, and He bore the punishment of it, and thou canst not be punished for it. Divine righteousness cannot exact a double penalty for the same offense. Dost thou believe in Jesus? Then He hath made an end of all the sin which was once written against thee. He has buried thy transgressions forever in His own sepulcher. If thou art in Christ, His perfect righteousness is wrapped about thy loins, and thou standest this day "accepted in the beloved." Oh, it is a glorious standing, Jesus the King of righteousness, and we in our King made righteous. We are comely through the comeliness of Christ which is put upon us.

Now this I want you to think of. Whenever you are enjoying the salvation of the Lord Jesus Christ, please to recollect that He never gives you any part of salvation without giving it to you righteously. My sins are pardoned. Yes, and righteously pardoned. Oh, is not this a wonder? Righteousness and peace have kissed each other. If I pray, I have naturally no right to be heard as a sinner; but, using the name of Christ, I expect to be heard as righteously as if I were the new-created Adam fresh from the hand of Deity. When I come before God and ask His protection, I look for it as righteously as Christ looked for it when He was here below, for He has put upon me, a poor unworthy believer, all His regal rights; and all His righteousness is mine, so that I may use His name at the foot of my prayers, and stamp my petitions with His Christly authority. I may take the blessings of the covenant as freely as he may take them who bought them with His blood; for He bought them for all His people, and He has made transfer of all the covenant estate to all who are in Him. Oh, brothers, it is a dreadful thing to be under a sense of sin, but it is an equally blessed thing to be under a sense of righteousness. We are righteous even as He is righteous. Let us never forget this.

And then, next, he is after that King of *peace*. I want you to try tonight—nay, I do not want you to try, I want the Holy Spirit to do it for you—I want you to enjoy the King of Salem, the King of peace. Do you know that at this moment, if you are a believer, you have peace with God through Jesus Christ our Lord? There is no quarrel between you and God tonight. You are one with Him, your delight is in Him. I know not now in my own soul of anything whatever that I could say against the Lord's dealings with me throughout the whole of my life; nor, let Him deal with me as He will, do I feel any repugnance to putting myself entirely into His hands. For weal or woe, for wealth or poverty, for life or death, I am content to hand myself over to the Lord absolutely. And now, there being peace on the poor creature's side, it is such a joy to think that there is peace from God's side, only still more perfect and enduring. He looks at you through His dear Son, and He sees no sin in you—no iniquity in you. He loves you with a perfect love at this moment, and He knows of no just cause or impediment why He should not love you. "Why," says one, "I have not been a believer more than a week." I do not care if you have not been a believer more than ten minutes: he that believeth hath everlasting life and everlasting love. As soon as the prodigal son was home, what did his father do? Upbraid him? No, he kissed him. Had his father no fault to find? No, not any. He said, "Bring forth the best robe, and put it on him. Put a ring on his hand and shoes on his feet. Let us eat and be merry." Why did he not say, "Come, my dear son, I must have a little sharp talk with you, for your good. You know you have behaved very badly to me. I must chide with you and upbraid you"? No, no. Not a word of the sort. Not a syllable or even a look after that fashion. He giveth liberally, and upbraideth not. He puts his dear child at perfect ease with himself, and says, "Be at home. Be happy. Eat, drink, and be merry with me; for you are my child, and though you were lost, you are found. You were dead, but you are alive again. Let us rejoice together in this blessed salvation which glorifies my Son."

I want you to sit in those pews—you that really believe in Jesus, and receive this bread and wine in perfect contentment, saying within yourselves, "It is well. It is all well. It is well from beginning to end—from top to bottom. Being justified by faith, I have peace with God. The peace of God that passeth all understanding doth keep my heart and soul by Jesus Christ." Come. If you have never enjoyed it before, enjoy it tonight, and do not be afraid. If you go to the devil's feasts, put a knife to your throat if you are a man given to appetite, for you may soon eat and drink and be drunken. Solomon is the author of this prudent advice. But when you come to the feasts of love, drink, yea, drink abundantly, O beloved. There never was a Christian man that was too happy in God. There never was a believer that was too peaceful, too serene, too confident, too hopeful. You cannot drink too much of this heavenly nectar. Oh, that you would but have grace to take in all that you *may* have! I know what you will do. You will come tonight into my Lord's treasury, and He will say, "Take what you will." There will be mints of gold and silver before you, and you will look all round and take up some brass farthing or other and say, "Bless the Lord for this!" Such gratitude is right enough. Bless the Lord for anything. At the same time, why not take something better? "Oh, I have been a mourner," you say, "all my days." Whose fault is that? "Oh, but I have never had any great light or any great joy." Whose fault is that? Is it not your own? The Lord seems to me to say tonight even to the elder brothers here, "Rejoice and be glad." I do not think that many grumblers come to the Tabernacle, but there are certain grumpy elder brothers that are apt to say, "Neither at any time transgressed I thy commandments, and yet thou never gavest me a kid that I might make merry with my friends. I never have any joy. I am a regular seat-holder and a member. I go to the communion; I do all I can; but I never get any of these holy raptures and spiritual delights. These reformed thieves and converted rascals when they are converted seem to monopolize all the music and the dancing. I have never a dance to myself at all." But the father was in such a blessed humor that night that he did not even upbraid the elder brother; but said, "Son, thou art ever with me, and all that I have is thine. If you have had not kid wherewith to make a supper for your friends, why did you not take it? All that I have is thine." Come in, dear elder brother, as well as you younger ones, and let us eat and drink and be merry this night in the name of Him who, having been the King of righteousness upon the bloody tree, is now tonight the King of peace upon His glorious throne; who upon this table shows you how He wrought out perfect righteousness, breaking His body and pouring out His blood for you, and now bids you come and see how all this is wrought for your peace, for His flesh and blood are now your bread and wine to make you glad. Wherefore, rejoice in the Lord! and again I say, Rejoice! Amen.

JESUS MEETING HIS WARRIORS

SERMON No. 589
DELIVERED ON LORD'S DAY MORNING, SEPTEMBER 11, 1864.

And Melchizedek king of Salem brought forth bread and wine: and he was the priest of the Most High God. And he blessed him, and said, Blessed be Abram of the Most High God, possessor of heaven and earth: and blessed be the Most High God, which hath delivered thine enemies into thy hand. And he gave him tithes of all—Genesis 14:18–20.

WHAT a splendid type is Abram, in the narrative before us, of our Lord Jesus Christ! Let us read this story of Abram in connection with our Savior, and see how full of meaning it is. Our Lord Jesus Christ, in the abundance of His love, had taken us to be His brothers; but we, through our sin, had removed into the land of Sodom, and Jesus Christ dwelt alone in His safety and His happiness, enjoying the presence of God. The hosts of our enemies, with terrible force and cruel fury, carried us away captives. We were violently borne away with all the goods which we possessed, into a land of forgetfulness and captivity forever. Christ, who had lost nothing by this, nevertheless being a "brother born for adversity," pursued our haughty foes. He overtook them; He smote them with His mighty hand—He took their spoil, and returned with crimsoned vesture, leading captivity captive. He restored that which He took not away. Methinks as I see Abram returning from the slaughter of the four kings, I see in him a picture of a greater than Abram, returning "from Edom, with dyed garments from Bozrah, traveling in the greatness of his strength." Who answers to my inquiry who he is? "I that speak in righteousness, mighty to save." Abram was that righteous man raised in the East, to whom God gave his enemies as driven stubble to his bow; and so the Lord Jesus has driven our enemies like chaff over to the wind, for they fled at the presence of Jehovah Jesus; and by the valor of the atoning Lamb they have been utterly broken in pieces forever. Let that thought dwell with you, it may furnish you with matter for meditation at your leisure.

We shall this morning rather consider Abram as the type and picture of all the faithful. He was the father of the faithful; and in his history you have condensed—as I think—the history of all faithful men. You will scarcely find a trial which will befall you, which has not in some respect happened unto Abraham. I will not say that he was tempted in all points like as we are, but he was tempted in so many points that he well deserves to be called the father of the faithful, being partaker of flesh and blood even as all the children *are* who belong to his faithful family.

Observe then, in handling our subject in this manner, *that believers are frequently engaged in warfare.* Notice, secondly, *that when they are thus engaged, they may expect to be met by their Lord, the great Melchizedek;* and remember, thirdly, *that when they are favored with an interview with Him, and are refreshed by Him as with bread and wine, then, like Abram, they consecrate themselves anew, and as Abram gave tithes of all, even so do they.*

I. We mention then, what you must all know right well by experience—you who are God's people—THAT THE BELIEVER IS OFTEN ENGAGED IN WARFARE.

This warfare will be both within and without—within with the innumerable natural corruptions which remain, with the temptations of Satan, with the suggestions of his own wicked heart; and without, he will frequently be engaged in warfare, wrestling "not against flesh and blood, but against principalities, against powers, against the rulers of the darkness of this world, against spiritual wickedness in high places." The peculiar case of Abram leads me to remark that sometimes the believer will be engaged in warfare, not so much on his own account as on the account of erring brethren, who, having gone into ill company, are by-and-by carried away captive. It was no quarrel of Abram's, it was Lot's matter. Lot had gone to Sodom. Instead of standing in the separated path of the true believer, he had joined himself unto the world, and when evil days came, Lot was carried away captive with the rest. Abram cared little enough for the king of Sodom: I do not suppose he would have taken his sword from the sheath for all the men who dwelt in Admah or Zeboiim; but for Lot's sake, seeing him in ill company and in danger, he draws the sword. And sometimes, brethren, when we see those who are God's servants putting themselves into alliance with evil systems, we find them carried away captive, and taken where we believe their hearts would never go, and we feel compelled to come out and draw the sword against the common enemy of Christ and of all His people; and though they may heartily wish that we would let them alone in their sin, and let them be quiet in their evil union, we see into what spiritual capacity it leadeth them, and we cannot be silent, but must draw the sword when conscience and when God demand it, and never sheath it until God's work is done. However, this rarely occurs; for the most part the Christian spends his sword's edge upon his own spiritual foes: and truly we have enough of these. What with pride, sloth, lust; what with the arch enemy of souls, and his insinuations and blasphemies; what with the lust of the eye, the pleasures of this world, and the pride of life; what with enemies who come upon us even from providence in the shape of temptations, arising out of our trials and our vocations, we ought to carry our sword always drawn; and, above all, we should ever carry the shield of faith and take the weapon of all-prayer. The Christian is never to feel himself at ease so long as he is on this side or Jordan. This is an enemy's land. Expect a foe behind every bush, look to hear the shot come whistling by, and each night adore almighty grace that you have not fallen a prey to your cruel and remorseless foes. The Christian is engaged throughout his whole life as a soldier—he is so called in Scripture—"A good soldier of Jesus Christ"; and if any of you take the trouble to write out the passages of Scripture in which the Christian is described as a soldier, and provision is made for his being armed, and directions given for his warfare, you will be surprised to find there are more of this character than concerning any other metaphor by which the Christian is described in the Word of God. His chief and main business seems to be, like his Master, to bear witness for the truth; "For this purpose was I born and sent into the world"; and though in himself a man of peace, yet he can say with his Master, "I came not to send peace but a sword"; for wherever he goes, he finds that his presence is the signal for war—war within him and war without him: he is a man of peace, and yet a man of war because a man of peace. The Christian is engaged in warfare with sin, Satan, error, and falsehood, and sometimes he is called to fight for erring friends.

Observe that this war is one *against powerful odds*. The four kings mentioned in this chapter were all great sovereigns. From what little we can glean from profane history, they appear to have been very mighty monarchs, and they must have been assisted by very valiant armies to have smitten the giants whose names are mentioned in the opening verses. They appear to have carried away the five kings of the plain with the greatest possible ease; yet here is Abram, who has little more than three hundred of his own armed servants at his call, and yet he ventures against the embattled thousands of the kings of nations. Such is the warfare of the Christian: he has to contend against foes far too many for him—he is like the worm that is to arise and thrash the mountain. He is little and despised, and if he measures his own strength he will find it to be perfect weakness; and yet, for all this, he anticipates a victory, and like Abram, hastens to the holy war.

Carefully notice, that as it is a battle of fearful odds, it is one *which is carried on in faith*. Abram did not venture to this fight with confidence in his own strength, or reliance upon his own bow, but he went in the name of the Lord of Hosts. Faith was Abram's continual comfort. Sometimes his faith failed, as it will in the best, but still the spirit of the man's life was a simple confidence upon God, whom he had not seen, but whose voice he cheerfully obeyed. The Christian is to carry on his warfare in faith. You will be vanquished, indeed, if you attempt it by any other method. Brethren, there is not a sin in your heart which will not master you if you seek to fight it by resolutions of your own; faith in the precious blood of Christ must win you the victory, and the world will laugh you to scorn if you assail it with any other weapons than such as Calvary will furnish you. "This is the victory which overcometh the world, even our faith"; and if you ask faith what weapon she uses, her reply is, "They overcame through the blood of the Lamb." Live near to Jesus Christ, rest upon the power of His atonement and the prevalence of His plea, and then go forward against every enemy without and every foe within, and you shall be more than a conqueror.

In this great battle, carried on by faith, Abram *had a right given him from God*, and the promise of God's presence virtually in that right. What business had Chedorlaomer to come unto Canaan? Had not Jehovah said to Abram, "All this land will I give unto thee"? Therefore he and his confederate monarchs were neither more nor less than intruders. For thirteen years they might have exercised sovereignty over the cities of the plain, but those cities and everything around them belonged virtually to Abram. It is true they would have laughed at the very idea of Abram's claiming the whole land of Canaan, but that claim was nevertheless valid in the court of heaven, and the patriarch by right divine was heir of all the land. Christian, you are, by virtue of a covenant made with you to drive out every sin, as an intruder. "Sin shall not have dominion over you: for ye are not under the law, but under grace." You are to drive out every error, for you are a servant of the truth and the truth alone has a right to live and a right to exist; and in fighting this lawful warfare, you may expect that the right arm of the Most High God, the possessor of heaven and earth will be bared that he may show himself strong on behalf of all those who are valiant for His truth and for His name. Fear not; the battle is not yours, but God's. You go not a warfare at your own charges; and though hell may roar as it will, and earth be all in arms, and your own heart may fail you, and your flesh when you take counsel with it may make you feel a coward, yet say, "In the name of God will I destroy them," go forward and conquer. "They compass me about like bees," said David, "yea, like bees they compass me about: but in the name of God will I destroy them"; and what David did you shall do through David's God.

Yet more, the Christian is engaged in a conflict in which he walks by faith and leans upon God; but yet it is a conflict in which *he uses all means*, calls in all lawful assistance, and exerts himself with all vigor and speed. Abram did not sit still and say, "Well, God will deliver Lot; He has promised to keep His servants as the apple of His eye"—Oh! no, that is not faith; that is foolish presumption. Abram did not take his time about it, and go marching leisurely after the foe, nor did he go without the assistance of his friends, Aner, and Eshcol, and Mamre. So the Christian, if he sees any method by which he may be assisted in overcoming sin or promoting truth, uses it with wisdom and discretion. He trusts in God as though he did nothing himself, and yet he does everything as if all depended upon him. He knows that good works cannot save him, and he equally knows that he is not saved unless there be some fruits of good works. He understands that the means of grace cannot of themselves convey grace to him, and yet at the same time he never despises them, but looks to find a blessing in the use of them. He understands that the ministry, and private prayer, and the searching of the Scriptures cannot save him, but he also understands that thus using helps which God has given him, and diligently pressing forward and setting a bold face before the foe, he is in the path of God's ordinances, and may expect to have God's help.

And do observe, dear friends, yet again, that Abram marching on thus with activity, and using discretion, by attacking his enemies at night rather than by day, *did not cease until he had gained a complete victory over them*. It was not enough to smite them at one corner of their host, nor merely to deliver Lot, but now he is come out against them he will win a sure and decisive victory. O beloved, you and I are never to sit still and say, "It is enough." Have I smitten my drunkenness? Have I overcome by blaspheming habits? Am I delivered from Sabbath breaking? Have I become honest and chaste? Yet this is not where I should stop. Have I sought to bring down my self-conceit, my pride, my sloth? It is well and good, but let me never be satisfied with any attainment short of absolute perfection. We do not believe we shall be perfect in this life, but we will never be satisfied until we are. "Onward," is the Christian's motto. As long as there is one sin which is not removed we will fight, and cry, and groan, and go to the cross concerning it. As long as there is one soul in this world unsaved, we will wrestle with the mighty One of Jacob to stretch out His hand to save it. So long as there remains one error upon earth, so long as we have a tongue to speak and God gives us grace, we will bear our witness against it. In this battle there is no holding our hand till the victory is wholly won; we must bring back the goods, and the men, and the women, and Lot, and the whole company; for the victory must be complete. More than conquerors must we be through him who hath loved us. Let us anticipate the time when it shall be so. O brethren, methinks I see the victors ascending in triumphal state the starry steeps, Christ at their head rides gloriously; he who loved them leads the van; the gates open to him as the great Conqueror who has led their captivity captive. Methinks I see the glad faces of all those soldiers of the cross as they enter the portals of eternal peace.

> I ask them whence their vict'ry came—
> They with united breath,
> Ascribe their conquest to the Lamb,
> Their triumph to his death.

See, then, beloved, here you are this morning soldiers; you are to fight by faith in God. However tremendous the power of your adversaries, you are not to fear since God is with you. You are to fight, using discretion as your armorbearer, but you are also to couple this with perseverance, continuing faithful to the end, for only those who overcome shall sit upon the throne of God forever.

We have thus perhaps said enough concerning this first point, and now, may the Holy Spirit bedew with His holy influences while we talk of the second, for otherwise it will be only talk.

II. While engaged in such earnest spiritual contention, the believer may expect to SEE HIS LORD.

When Shadrach, Meshach, and Abed-nego were fighting Christ's battles in the fiery furnace, then the Son of Man appeared unto them. As in the building of Jerusalem in troublous times, they had the sword in one hand and the trowel in the other; so our Lord Jesus Christ, while He teaches us to use the sword, takes care to edify and build us up in the faith at the same time. He understands that warriors require strengthening meat, and that especially when they are under stern conflict they need extraordinary comforts that their souls may be stayed and refreshed. *Why does Jesus Christ, as set forth here under the type of Melchizedek, appear unto His children in times of conflict?* Answer—He comes to them *first, because they are weary.* In every conflict which the child of God has to wage, it is not the private person who goeth to the warfare, it virtually is Christ fighting—Christ contending. It is a member of Christ's body laboring against Christ's enemy for the glory of the Head. Christ the Head as an intense feeling of sympathy with every member, no matter how humble. Since there is a vital union between Christ and every member, there is also an undying sympathy; and whenever, brother, thou contendest for the faith till thou growest weary, Jesus Christ will be sure to give thee some proof of His close communion with thee. The martyrs protest that they never had such communion with God anywhere as among the caverns of the hills, or the swamps of the woods, to which they were exiled for Christ; and that even on the rack, in extremity of torture, or even upon the gridiron in the heat of the fire—even there the sweet presence of Christ has been overpoweringly delightful to them, so that they almost lost the sense of pain. Thou, Lord, dost send a plenteous rain, whereby thou dost refresh thine heritage when it is weary! Spend your strength for God, brother, for when fainting seems inevitable, then shall come such a sweet renewing of your strength, that, like an eagle, you shall stretch your wings and mount aloft to commune with God in solitary joys. Christ, your Melchizedek, will meet you in your conflicts, if He never did before.

The King of Peace met the returning warrior for another reason. *Abram was probably flushed with victory,* and this is a very dangerous feeling to any child of God. When the seventy disciples returned to Christ they said, with evident exultation, "Lord, even the devils are subject unto us": but Jesus Christ sweetly and gently rebuked them by saying, "Nevertheless, rejoice not in this, but rather rejoice because your names are written in heaven." The true secret of a Christian's joy is not to be his conquest over sin or over error, but the person of his Lord Jesus Christ. The Lord knows that His people, if they are successful, even in spiritual warfare, when they have used the best of means and felt the best of motives, are nevertheless very liable to the intoxication of pride, and therefore He either sends "a thorn in the flesh," or else, what is better still, He comes Himself. I am persuaded, beloved, that the best cure for pride is a sight of Christ. Oh! when your eyes see *him,* then your own loathsomeness, blackness, and deformity, are clearly revealed. I am fair until the sun ariseth—then am I black indeed. I think myself pure until I see *Him* whiter than any fuller could make him, and then I fall down and cry, "Unclean, unclean, unclean!" "Now mine eye seeth thee," said Job, "wherefore I abhor myself, and repent in dust and ashes." Down go your flaunting pennons and your lofty plumes, when you have a sight of Christ. No humbler man than George Herbert—no humbler man than Samuel Rutherford—and these were men who lived close to Christ. Christ's presence is a cure-all. When Melchizedek comes, every spiritual disease flies before him. The Church at Laodicea was very far gone, but how did the Master propose to cure it? Here it is— "Behold, I stand at the door, and knock: if any man hear my voice, and open the door, I will come into him, and will sup with him." What, Lord, is this thy delightful treatment of thy sick Church? "Yes, my communion with thee, poor lukewarm Laodicea, will revive thee." Truly that is a most suggestive figure by which John describes the countenance of Christ; he says, "His countenance was as the sun shining in his strength." So, Lord, it does not matter how dark I am, the moment Thou dost show thy face, all must be light. This, I think, was the reason why the King of Righteousness met Abram, to turn away his thoughts from the tempting joys of victory, to his sure portion in the Most High God, possessor of heaven and earth.

Yet again, was not this visit bestowed because Abram was *about to be tried in a yet more subtle manner than he had been before?* It is easier to fight Chedorlaomer, than to resist the King of Sodom. Joshua down in the plain never grew weary when he was fighting the Amalekites, but Moses on the mountain felt his hands grow heavy. Why? Because the more spiritual the exercise, the more aptness is there in us to grow weary in it; and so the more spiritual the temptation the more likelihood of our becoming a prey to it, and the more strength do we need to overcome it. That was a very subtle temptation to Lot, by the King of Sodom. Why it looked so right—perfectly right. Abram has brought back these captives: he has a right to the spoil; he ought, therefore, to take it. If he had done so, no one could blame him on ordinary rules, but then there is a higher rule for believers than for other men. Brethren, I contend that the common rules of morality are binding upon all, but that a supernaturally high rule of morality should regulate the Christian; that the Christian is not allowed to wink at an evil because he has educated his conscience not to think it so, but he shall so act that there shall not be any wrong in the action, upon the common judgment of any unbiased spectator. He who is of the King's Council, must walk very daintily, lest he offend his Master. I tell you, from experience, that the nearer you come to Christ, and the more you have of communion with him, the more jealous you must be of yourself, or else, if other men escape the rod, you will not: you will have to smart for it behind the door, where another may not see nor understand your grief. Beloved, it is well to have communion with Christ, to prepare us against subtle temptations, for to feed us upon Melchizedek's bread and wine, is to make us more than a match for the King of Sodom. O Jesus! when I have seen thy face, my soul beholds not the dazzling beauties of earthly excellence. Brother, if ever thou hast seen Christ's face, that painted harlot, the world, will never win thy love again. Didst thou ever eat the pure white bread of heaven? Then the brown, gritty bread of earth will never suit you, but will break your teeth with gravel stones. You will never care to drink earth's sour and watery wine, if you have once been made to drink of the wines on the lees well refined—the spiced wine of Christ's pomegranate. If you want to be strengthened against the most subtle worldly temptations, cry, "Let him kiss me with the kisses of his mouth: for thy love is better than wine"; and you may go forth to conflicts of every kind, more than a conqueror, through Him that hath loved you.

Thus we have spoken upon the fact that Melchizedek met Abram, and the reasons. Now, let us look a little more closely at what he did. *In what character did he meet Abram?* The reply is easy—he met him as one possessed of a royal priesthood.

Christ meets us, brethren, as a priest and a king in all our battles. What a mercy it is that Christ visits us as *a priest*, for we never fight against sin without being in some measure partakers of it. I do not believe there ever was a controversy for truth upon which any gracious man, though engaged upon the right side, could look back without some regrets and some tears. I much believe that even Martin Luther or John Knox, when upon their dying beds, though never regretting that they contended earnestly for the faith, yet felt that while they were in the flesh, something of flesh mingled with all that they did. Thus it will be to the end, and even, when contending against our own sins and lusts, yet, beloved, our very repentance has something in it to be repented of, and our very flying to the cross has something in it of a lingering *from* the cross, and therefore something of evil. Jesus, all hail! How much I need to meet Thee as a priest! And you, beloved, do you not feel that you need Him too? Do you not, as you look upon Calvary and the flowing blood, confess that you need, in all spiritual conflicts, to meet Christ?

But Melchizedek was also *a king*, and truly thus we want to view our Lord whenever we are fighting His battles. "The Lord reigneth," is perhaps one of the most comforting texts in the compass of God's Word to the contending Christian. "Ah!" says the poor soul, "I am trodden under foot of Satan, but rejoice not over me, O mine enemy: though I fall, yet shall I rise again, for the Lord reigneth." Oh! that is our consolation when at any time we think we are routed, when we see our Church dismayed and our banner trailed in the mire, then we remember Jesus, for Him hath God the Father exalted, "and given him a name which is above every name: that at the name of Jesus every knee should bow, of things in heaven, and things in earth, and things under the earth." Hail! King of Righteousness and Peace, much do we need to meet thee! Come, mount thy glorious chariot, ride forth conquering and to conquer drawn by thy three white horses, meekness, truth, and righteousness! Heaven adores Thee, earth obeys Thee, hell trembles at thy presence, gates of brass must burst at thy touch, and bars of iron snap at thy word! O King immortal, ride gloriously and let thy people behold Thee and rejoice in Thee. But we must *see* Christ, see Him, by close communion with Him. You cannot see Him by my description. Melchizedek met Abram, and Jesus Christ must meet you; He must stop you on a sudden, when you least expect it, and reveal Himself unto you as He doth not unto the world. Jacob before wrestling was met by hosts of angels at Mahanaim, but what are these when compared with the Lord Himself? There is a high blessing in being met by angels—do not mistake me there—but oh! to be met by *the angel* of the covenant, the Michael the archangel, to be met by Him, ah! what comfort is here! And will He meet *me*? Will He meet *you*? Yes, we can answer, He will, for we *have* met with Him. "Mine eyes have seen the King in His beauty," many of us can say, and our souls are exceedingly comforted and full of holy joy because we have beheld Him as Priest and King.

The next inquiry is, *what did he do for him?* He brought him bread and wine, precisely setting forth what Jesus does, who brings us His flesh and His blood.

Carnal people say, in order to understand Christ's words, that when you eat bread and drink wine at the Lord's table, there is His flesh in the bread, or that the bread is transubstantiated into flesh, and the same with the wine; but the spiritual mind understands that these emblems awaken the spiritual powers, and that then the spiritual powers—not the lips and the stomach, but the spiritual powers—do really and spiritually feed upon the flesh and blood of Jesus Christ, and so the Word is fulfilled: "Except ye eat my flesh and drink my blood, there is no life in you." I do not know that Christian people feed altogether on doctrine. I know that the truth of God is food, but believers get richer nourishment than even this affords. When I am very gloomy, I like to take down some work upon the high doctrines, God's sovereignty, election, perseverance, and I get comforted; but there are other times when I am brought very low, and that kind of food will not suit me. I am obliged then to turn to my Lord Himself. There is, I believe, in times of conflict no food which can be the stay of an immortal soul except the Master Himself—communion with Him, a putting of the fingers into the print of the nails, and a thrusting of the hand into the side—this is the sovereign remedy for unbelief, and the best food for faith. His manifest presence is our noblest nutriment. When Christ reveals Himself, then all grows calm and peaceful; but until we can get *Him*, we still abide in darkness, and we see no light. The worshiper who came up to the temple could not live upon the brazen laver, nor the golden snuffers, nor even upon the cherubic emblems, he must need partake with the priests of the lamb offered in sacrifice; and so the true food of the child of God is Jesus Christ Himself—not so much ordinances and doctrines, which are only the utensils and the vestments, but Christ Himself, the very Christ, made flesh for us, received with joy into our soul, and fed upon until, like Abram, we go on our way rejoicing. That is what the royal priest did for the patriarch.

Bear with me patiently while I remark *what Melchizedek said to him.* First he blessed him, and then he blessed God, and that is just what we need our Lord to do for us. We want our Lord Jesus Christ first *to bless us.* "Blessed be Abram of the Most High God, possessor of heaven and earth." We need a blessing upon our own persons and especially upon our own works. What are our works when we have done them all but futile vanity, until God comes to strengthen us? Beloved, you and I may contend for Christ until we are dumb, but not a soul that will see the light or know the truth by our witness of itself; we may go with tender hearts and seek to bring sinners to the cross of Christ, but we shall never bring a sinner unless God's own arm is revealed. We shall come back like the prophet, saying, "Who hath believed our report," and feeling that the arm of God hath not been revealed unto men. But when, on the other hand, the possessor of heaven and earth has blessed us, then our earthly substance is blessed and our earthly words are blessed, and then we get a heavenly blessing; heaven's rest and peace, heaven's omnipotence rests upon us, and in the glory of a heaven-given strength we go forth confident of victory. We want a blessing from Christ. Ask it now, beloved, ask it now you who are weary with last week's fighting, you who can scarcely endure any longer by reason of your trials and troubles, say to him now, "Melchizedek, bless me! O Jesus, bless me now." Possessor of heaven and earth, forget not one of us, thy beloved ones, but give us a blessing.

Beloved brethren, Melchizedek did not stop there, but he fulfilled another part of his priestly office—*he blessed God*. Whenever we are singing here, when I am in right order, my soul takes wing and wants to fly to heaven; when we all sing with power and force there is a sweetness and grandeur about the song which we do not often meet with; yet I am always conscious that we cannot praise God as He deserves to be, and herein I bless the great Melchizedek that though *we* cannot bless God as He should be blessed, yet *He* can. Jesus Christ presents the praises of his saints before God as well as their prayers. He is the Intercessor, and while He has the vials full of odors sweet to present, he also presents the music of our harps; both our offerings come up accepted in the beloved. Now what say you, brethren, have you done anything this week that is of good repute? Has God given you any success? Dear sister, have you won any souls for Christ? I know you have. Dear brother, has God blessed you in any witness-bearing? Have you felt that God has been with you? Well now, come and lay your honors down at His feet, whatever they may be, put them *there*, and pray the great Melchizedek to take out of your heart every particle of self-glory and every atom of self-exaltation, and ask him to say for you in a higher sense than ever you can say it, "Blessed be the Most High God, possessor of heaven and earth, who hath delivered mine enemies into mine hand." Thus you shall be glad that the great Melchizedek has met you.

I have talked thus, but truly one word from the lip of Christ will be worth ten thousand of mine; and if you ever have seen Him, you will think me a very dauber when I try to paint Him. If you get this day so much as ten minutes real fellowship with Jesus, you will wonder how it is, that I, if I know anything about Him, could talk in this cold way. Go your way, brethren, and pray Melchizedek to meet you.

III. Lastly, and very briefly indeed, since our time is gone, when a wrestling believer is favored with a sight of the great Melchizedek, voluntarily and yet necessarily he makes a new dedication of himself to God. You see Abram does not appear to delay a moment, but he gives to Melchizedek a tithe of all, by which he seemed to say, "I own the authority of my superior liege lord, to all that I am, and all that I have." There is one of our hymns which says—

> Hail, Melchizedek divine;
> Thou, great High-Priest, shalt be mine;
> All my powers before thee fall—
> Take not tithe, but take them all.

And truly our holy faith deserves of us that we should give all to Christ. I would that some Christians, however, practiced the rule of giving a tenth of their substance to the Lord's cause. The Lord's Church need never lack if you had a bag in which you stored up for Christ: when you gave anything, you would not feel it was giving of your own; your left hand would not know what your right hand did, for you would be taking out of the Lord's stock which you had already consecrated to the Lord's cause. Not less than one-tenth should be the Lord's portion, especially with those who have a competence; and more than this, methinks, should be expected of those who have wealth. But there is no rule binding with iron force upon you, for we are not under law in Christ's Church, but under grace, and grace will prompt you to do more than law might suggest; but certainly the Christian should reckon himself to be not his own, and that he has nothing to retain for his own private account. I pray God if I have a drop of blood in my body which is not His, to let it bleed away; and if there be one hair in my head which is not consecrated to Him, I would have it plucked out, for it must be the devil's drop of blood and the devil's hair. It belongs to either one or the other: if not to God, then to Satan. No, we must, brethren, have no division of ourselves, no living unto this world and unto God too. Mark Anthony yoked two lions together, and drove them through the streets of Rome: they do strange things at Rome, and there are many people who can yoke two lions together, and drive towards Rome; but you will never be able to yoke the lion of the tribe of Judah and the lion of the pit together—they are at deadly antagonism, and Christ will not have you for His servants if you seek to serve two masters. I know that any talk of mine here will be in vain, but if, beloved, you should see Christ, and have communion with Him, your consecration to Him will be a matter of course. I will suppose that this afternoon one of you should sit down in your armchair, and, as you are sitting there, you will be thinking, "How little I have been giving of late to the cause of Christ! How seldom I have opened my mouth for Him!" Perhaps you will think, "I have got on in the world too, but I really cannot afford it! My expenses are so great!" Suppose the Lord Jesus Christ should come into the room with those pierced hands and bleeding feet—suppose He were to remind you of what He has done for you, how He visited you in your low estate, when your heart was breaking under a sense of sin, you would not then tell Him you could not afford to give to His cause. Suppose our Lord Jesus Christ should look you in the face and say to you, "I have done all this for you. What wilt thou do for Me?" What would be your answer? Why you would say, "Take it all, my Master, take it all, all that I am, and all that I have shall be forever thine." Or, if you felt niggardly—supposing He should say to you, "If you will never ask anything of Me, I will never take anything from you." Would you agree to that? No, but as you still will have immense demands to make upon His liberality, cease not still to give your whole spirit, soul and body, as a whole burnt-offering unto God. As Abram did before Melchizedek so do you in the presence of Christ, own that you are His, and give yourself to Him.

My dear brethren, I pray God that this may stir you up to seek a high grade of piety and to live in daily communion with a living Savior, and He will bless and keep you.

But there are some of you who are not like Abram. You need not hope yet to see Melchizedek. There are some of you strangers, far off. Ah! I may rather compare you to the men of Sodom. Christ has done something for you as Abram did for Sodom. You know it was only for the sake of Lot that He brought them back, but He did bring them all back, and for the sake of Lot gave a respite to them all; although a few years after they had grown so wicked that they were all destroyed. My Master has given a respite to free you all. While His great work was the salvation of His own chosen, yet He has spared you all in the land of the living. Take heed lest you do as did the men of Sodom, for then a hail more fiery, a destruction more terrible must come upon you, seeing that you turn not aside from your evil ways, nor seek His face. Trust Christ, and you are saved; believe in Him and your sins are forgiven; but if you refuse, beware, lest that come upon you which is written in the prophets, "Behold, ye despisers, and wonder, and perish!" The Master now send us away with His benediction. Amen.

JESUS AND HIS BRETHREN

Sermon No. 2,516
Delivered on Lord's day Evening, October 4, 1885.

Then Joseph could not refrain himself before all them that stood by him; and he cried, Cause every man to go out from me. And there stood no man with him, while Joseph made himself known unto his brethren. And he wept aloud: and the Egyptians and the house of Pharaoh heard. And Joseph said unto his brethren, I am Joseph; doth my father yet live? And his brethren could not answer him; for they were troubled at his presence. And Joseph said unto his brethren, Come near to me, I pray you. And they came near. And he said, I am Joseph your brother, whom ye sold into Egypt. Now therefore be not grieved, nor angry with yourselves, that ye sold me hither: for God did send me before you to preserve life—Genesis 45:1–5.

I NEED not say to you, beloved, who are conversant with Scripture, that there is scarcely any personal type in the Old Testament which is more clearly and fully a portrait of our Lord Jesus Christ than is the type of Joseph. You may run the parallel between Joseph and Jesus in very many directions, yet you need never strain the narrative even so much as once. I am not about to attempt that task on the present occasion; but I am going to take this memorable portion of the biography of Joseph, and to show you how, in making himself known to his brethren, he was a type of our Lord revealing himself to us.

It seems that, at last, Joseph could bear the suspense no longer. He knew who his brethren were, he knew which was Benjamin, and which was Reuben, Simeon, Levi, Judah, and the rest, and he recollected all the story of their early days together; but they did not know him. They thought him some mysterious potentate, some great ruler of the land of Egypt—as indeed he was, but they did not know so much about him as he knew about them. Consequently, there was a distance between him and them, and his loving heart ached to bridge that gulf by manifesting himself to them. It is the way of love to desire to make itself known.

Now, in a still higher sense, the Lord Jesus Christ knows all about those in this place whom He has redeemed with His precious blood. The Father gave them to Him from before the foundation of the world, and He took them into covenant rela-

84

tionship with Himself or ever the earth was. Often has He thought of these His beloved ones; His delights have been with the sons of men, and He has looked forward, and foreseen all that would happen to them. Ever since these redeemed and chosen ones have been born into the world, He has watched them so carefully that He has counted the very hairs on their heads. They are so precious to Him, as the purchase of His heart's blood, that they have never taken a single wandering step but His eye has tracked the mazes of their life. He knows them altogether—knows their sins, knows their sorrows, knows their ignorance of Him, knows how sometimes that ignorance has been willful, and they have continued in the dark when they might have walked in the light; and now, at this moment, speaking after the manner of men, the heart of Christ aches to manifest Himself to some of them, He wants to be known, He thirsts to be known, He can only be loved as He is known, and He pines for love, and so He pines to manifest Himself to His loved ones. Aye, and there are some of them who do know Him already in a measure, but their measure is a very little one; it is but as a drop compared with the great deep sea. I have been praying, and am praying still, and I am not alone in the prayer, that this very hour, the Lord Jesus may be pleased to manifest Himself to His own blood-bought ones. To all who have been called by His grace already, and to many not yet called to Him, may He come in the fullness of His own glorious revelation, and make Himself known; for know ye not this—that the revelation of Christ in the Word will not save you unless Christ be revealed in you and to you personally? Nay, more than that; the Christ born at Bethlehem will not save you unless that Christ be formed in you the hope of glory, He must Himself come to *you*, and make himself known to *you*. It will not suffice you to read about his healing the sick, He must touch *you* with His hand, or you must touch the hem of His garment with your hand; but somehow there must be personal contact between yourself and the Lord Jesus Christ, or else all that He did will avail nothing to you. Let this be our prayer now—that to each man and woman and child here the Lord may graciously make himself known.

I. Notice, first, that THE LORD JESUS CHRIST, LIKE JOSEPH, REVEALS HIMSELF IN PRIVATE FOR THE MOST PART.

Joseph cried, "Cause every man to go out from me. And there stood no man with him, while Joseph made himself known unto his brethren." It would not have been seemly for this great ruler to lose all command of himself in the presence of the Egyptians. His heart was carried away with love to his brothers, and the cry that he lifted up was so loud that the people in other parts of the palace could hear that something strange was going on; but he could not bear that they should all stand around, and gaze with curious eyes upon their ruler as he unbosomed himself to his brothers. They would not have understood it, they might have misrepresented it; at any rate, he could not bear that the scene of affection which was now to be enacted should be witnessed by strangers, so he cried, "Cause every man to go out from me."

My dear friends, do you really want savingly to see and know the Lord Jesus Christ? Have you never yet beheld Him by the eye of faith? Then, permit me to exhort you to be *literally much alone*—much alone in searching the Scriptures, and much alone in private, secret prayer. That gracious revelation of Himself to you as bearing your sins, and putting away your guilt, will not be likely to come to you until you get a little time in private, where you can quietly meditate upon your Lord and His great atoning work. The mischief of this busy London is that we are fretted and worn with incessant occupations; we should all of us be much stronger and better if we saw less of the faces of men and more of the face of God. But for a penitent sinner, who desires to behold his pardon written in the smiling countenance of Christ, there must be solitude. You must rise earlier in the morning, and get a half-hour to yourself then, or you must sit up later at night, or you must steal out of bed at the dead of night, or you must even resolve that you will not go to your business until the first business of finding Christ is ended once for all. I feel persuaded that, with some of you at least, there will be no peace to your heart, and no comfortable sight of Christ, until you have gone up-stairs, and said, "Here, alone, with every man put out and every wandering thought excluded, will I bow the knee, and cry, and look, and hope, and believe, until I can say, 'I have seen the Lord; I have looked to Him whom I have pierced, and I have seen my sin put away by His death upon the tree.' "

Further, I want you to notice, not only the excellence of solitude in general, but *the benefit of a kind of mental solitude*. Brethren, if in the house of God, in the midst of the assembly, the Lord Jesus Christ is ever to manifest Himself personally to us, it must be in a kind of mental and spiritual solitude. I believe that the preacher will never succeed in winning a soul if he tries to make himself prominent in his own preaching. An old man, who was accustomed to catching trout in a certain stream, was asked by one who had been fishing in vain, "Have you caught any fish today?" "Yes, sir," he said, "I have a little basketful." "Oh!" said the other, "I have been fishing all day long, and I have taken none." "No," said the man, "but there are three rules about catching trout, which, perhaps you have not observed. The first is—Get quite out of sight; and the second is—Get still more out of sight, and the third is—Get still more out of sight than that; and you will catch them so." And I believe that it is just so in preaching. If the preacher can get quite out of sight, and still more out of sight, and yet still more out of sight, then he will be the means of bringing souls to Christ. And you, dear friends, will only see Him well in any kind of preaching when you try to forget the man. I mean that remark to apply in two ways. Perhaps the preacher is one whom you dearly love, and you expect much from him. Well then, forget him, expect nothing from him, but look away from him to your Lord. Or perhaps the preacher's voice has no particular charm for you, the man is not very bright in his ut-terances; well, forget him, and try to see his Master. Forget the preacher for good and for bad, for better and for worse, and get to the Lord Himself.

There is a story told of Mr. Erskine having preached on one occasion before the communion, and a good woman, a child of God, heard him with such delight, and was so much fed and satisfied, that she left her own pastor, and went some miles on the next Lord's day to go and hear him again. That morning, he was dreadfully dry and barren, or at least she thought that he was. There was no food for her whatever; and being not a very wise woman, she went in to tell him so. She said, "Oh, Mr. Erskine, I heard you at the communion with such delight; you seemed to take me to the very gates of heaven, and I was fed with the finest of the wheat; so I have come this morning on purpose to hear you, and I confess that I have got nothing out of you!" So he said, "My good woman, what did you go for last Sabbath-day?" "I went to the communion, sir." "Yes, you went to the communion; that was to have communion with the Lord?" "Yes," she said, "I did." "Well," said Mr. Erskine, "that is what you went for, and you got it; and the Lord blessed my word to you, and you had communion with Him. Now, what did you come here for this morning?" "I came to hear you, sir." "And you have got what you came for, there is nothing in me." Think of this story when you are remembering the Lord's servants, and forgetting their Master Himself. I do believe that, as you are sitting here, you whose eyes have already been opened by the Spirit of God, if you will but say, "Cause every man to go out from me; shut to the door, I have entered into my closet even while in the pew; I am alone now, and I desire to see no man save Jesus only," you shall see Him, for He manifests Himself to His people all alone. Oh, that each one here would say, "There is nothing but Christ that I desire to see, there is nothing else I wish to remember, I would think only of my Lord Jesus; may He be pleased to reveal Himself to me!"

II. The second remark I have to make is this—when the Lord Jesus Christ reveals Himself to any man for the first time, it is usually in the midst of terror, and THAT FIRST REVELATION OFTEN CREATES MUCH SADNESS.

When Joseph made himself known to his brethren, and said to them, "I am Joseph," "they were troubled at his presence." Judah had made a very plaintive speech when it was threatened that Benjamin should be detained in Egypt, and all the brothers were in deep trouble; so that, when the great ruler said to them, "I am Joseph," they were not filled with joy by his words, so we read, "His brethren could not answer him; for they were troubled at his presence." He was Joseph, their brother, and he loved every one of them; yet "they were troubled at his presence." It was the best thing that could have happened to them to be in the presence of him who was sent of God to save their lives with a great deliverance; yet "they were troubled at his presence."

And you and I recollect, perhaps, when, under a deep sense of sin and sorrow, we had our first perception of Christ's salvation, instead of being glad at it, we were "troubled at his presence." "Why!" we said to ourselves, "this Christ is He whom we have despised, and rejected, and crucified." There did not seem, at first, much comfort for us in the manifestation of Christ. One said, in order to cheer us, "He died for sinners." "But," we answered, "surely not for such sinners as we are." Even the very sound of that blessed word "salvation" grated on our ears, because we thought we should be like the fabled Tantalus, up to our neck in water which we could not drink, or surrounded by fruit which we could not pluck. "He may have died for others," we seemed to say, "but scarcely for us." We "were troubled at his presence." Even the house of God, to which we continued to go, was a place of terror to us, and we cried, like Jacob did at Bethel, "How dreadful is this place!" In the worst sense of that word, it really was "dreadful" to us, full of dread, although we believed it to be "none other but the house of God, and the gate of heaven." We said, "What right have we to be in the house of God? How can we expect to enter heaven even though its gate is so near to us?" We heard that Jesus of Nazareth was passing by, but we sorrowfully exclaimed, "Ah, that is only too true! He will pass by, He will never stop to look at us." We heard that precious text, "God so loved the world, that he gave his only begotten Son, that whosoever believeth in him shall not perish, but have everlasting life"; yet we said, "What is it to believe in Him? How can we believe in Him?" The light seemed shining all around us, but our eyes were blind to it; the music of heaven was sounding in all its sweetness, but our ears were closed to its melody; everlasting love was coming near to us, yet our hearts did not open to receive it; and therefore we could not answer Christ, for we "were troubled at his presence."

Dear friends, if any of you are in this sad state, do not therefore be driven away from our Jesus, our greater Joseph; but still stand in His presence, even though you are troubled at it, for that experience, though it be bitter, is a bitter sweet. There may be trouble in Christ's presence, but there is a far greater trouble in being driven from His presence, and from the glory of His power. So keep standing just where you are, even though you stand trembling, for by-and-by, and perhaps this very hour, He will graciously reveal Himself to you, and you shall no longer tremble at His presence, but, on the contrary, you shall rejoice with joy unspeakable and full of glory, as you perceive that this Joseph, this Jesus, is your Brother, your Savior, your Friend, your all in all.

III. Now, thirdly, though the first appearance of Jesus, like that of Joseph, may cause sadness, THE FURTHER REVELATION OF THE LORD JESUS CHRIST TO HIS BRETHREN, BRINGS THEM THE GREATEST POSSIBLE JOY.

If you look at this passage when you are at home, you will perhaps say to yourself, "The second time that Joseph spoke to his brethren, he had not much more to say than he said the fist time," for then he said, "I am Joseph; doth my father yet live?" And the second time there was much the same burden in his language: "I am Joseph, your brother, whom ye sold into Egypt." So, when Christ reveals Himself in grace to any poor heart, *the revelation, for substance, is much the same as at the first, yet there is a great difference.* When, for the first time, I heard the gospel to my soul's salvation, I thought that I had never really heard the gospel before, and I began to think that the preachers to whom I had listened had not truly preached it. But, on looking back, I am inclined to believe that I had heard the gospel fully preached many hundreds of times before, and that this was the difference—that I then heard it as though I heard it not; and when I did hear it, the message may not have been any more clear in itself than it had been at former times, but the power of the Holy Spirit was present to open my ear, and to guide the message to my heart. O dear friend, if you have heard me preach Christ crucified, and you have not yet seen Christ to your soul's salvation, I pray that you may do so now! I do not suppose that there will be any difference in the sermon, or in the truth proclaimed; the difference will be that, in the one case, it has not reached your heart, and in the other case it will. O blessed Master, speak comfortably to the hearts of sinners, and to the hearts of thy people, too. Make the old, old gospel to be new to us by clothing it with a new power within our hears and consciences, and throughout our lives!

Yet, there were some differences in the words which Joseph uttered to his brethren. If you turn again to the narrative, you will see that he began his second speech by saying to them, "Come near to me, I pray you." *There was a longing for nearness to those he loved,* and that is the point of my sermon at this time. I want you, who do not believe in the Lord Jesus Christ, but who are, nevertheless, His elect, His redeemed ones, to come near to Him now by an act of faith, and trust Him with yourselves, your souls, your sins, and everything else. Stand not back through shame or fear, ye chief of sinners, for He says, "Come near to me, I pray you. 'Come unto me, all ye that labor and are heavy laden, and I will give you rest.' " As for you who are His brethren already, come you near to Him, for to you also he says, "Come near to me, I pray you." Oh, if our Lord were actually here in bodily presence—and I can almost picture Him in the loveliness and glory of Divine Majesty—if He were to stand here, and say to us, "Come near to me, I pray you," we would, with solemn reverence, bow before Him, but we would with joyful obedience come near to Him, and try to hold Him by the feet and worship Him. Would not each one of you press forward to come near unto Him? I am sure that you would; well, that is what you have to do in a spiritual fashion. We know not Christ after the flesh, but we do know Him after the Spirit. So, come near to Him, dear brethren in Christ; believe in Him again as you did at the first, look to Him again as if you have never looked before. Worship Him as your Lord and your Redeemer, prostrate yourselves before Him, and adore Him as the Son of God revealed in our midst; come near to Him. Then talk to Him; tell Him all that is in your inmost heart. Unburden to Him your cares and your doubts; aye, and come near to Him with your fondest affection, and say to Him now, in the silence of your spirit, "Lord, Thou knowest all things; Thou knowest that I love Thee." Come near to Christ with all your tears of penitence, come near with your alabaster box of gratitude, come near with the kisses of your lips of love, come near with your whole heart's purest affection, and come now, for that is what He invites you to do. It is a part of His manifestation of Himself to you that you should endeavor to come near to Him. Cry, "Stand back, O self! Stand back, O devil! Stand back, all care for the world! Stand back, even care for the church just now! My heart must come near unto her Lord, and sit like a dove on His finger, and be satisfied to look with her gentle eyes at the beauties of His countenance." God help us so to do, in response to our Lord's gracious invitation, "Come near to me, I pray you."

Then, as if to help us to come near, *our Lord, in this revelation, declares His relationship to us.* The speaker in the type says, "I am Joseph your brother"; and the Lord

Jesus Christ, though He is Head over all things to His Church, and King and Lord of death and hell, yet says to everyone who believes in Him, "I am your Brother; I am of your kith and kin; Head of the family, but still of the family; and touched with the feeling of your infirmities, for I was in all points tempted like as you are." Do not imagine, concerning the Lord Jesus, that there is only a fanciful or sentimental brotherhood between Him and you. It is a real brotherhood; there is no such brotherhood under heaven, so complete and true, as that which exists between Christ and every blood-washed soul, for it is not a brotherhood according to the flesh, but an everlasting, spiritual brotherhood. An eternal union of the closest and most vital kind is established between Christ and every one who believes in Him.

We do not reckon it hard, do we, to win a brother's heart? If we have been a little cold towards a brother, his heart soon warms to us again; and as for our Lord, if we have not seen Him of late, if any of us have not loved Him as we should, if we are saying, "We are troubled at His presence, we hardly dare come to His table," may He say to us, "Come near to me, I pray you; I am your Brother. Come near, come nearer, nearer still. I am pleased when you are near." Come with your sin and your lukewarmness; come just as you are, as you came to Him at the first; and He will receive you, and will manifest Himself unto you as He does not unto the world.

In addition to revealing his relationship, which was a great motive for inviting his brethren to come near, *he also told them a secret*. He said, "I am Joseph your brother, whom ye sold into Egypt." I think he mentioned that to show them that he must be Joseph their brother, for who else in all the world knew of that shameful action on their part? I do not suppose that the Midianite merchants, who bought Joseph, knew that he was sold by his own brethren; or if they did know, there were none of them in Pharaoh's palace, for they were Ishmaelites, and they had gone their way to traffic somewhere else. All who knew of that wicked transaction were Joseph and his brothers, so by this password he lets them know that there was a sort of freemasonry between them. This was the sign, "I am Joseph your brother, whom ye sold into Egypt." It made them blush, I dare say; and it must have made them mourn; but it also made them feel, "Yes, that is our brother; nobody but Joseph would know that we sold him into slavery." And, dear friends, have you never seen your Well-beloved as He reads your heart? I have known Him read mine from the first thought in it to the last, and I have thanked Him as He has read it, for I have said, "Lord, Thou hast read that book right through, and now Thou knowest all things, Thou knowest that I love thee. Alas! I did sell thee into Egypt; there was a day when I chose Egypt and its pleasures rather than Thyself; and there have been days since when I have sold Thee again into Egypt by treating Thee with lukewarmness, and giving myself up to other lovers. Yes, Lord, I have sold Thee to the Ishmaelites by doubting Thee and mistrusting Thee; and by my sins I have stripped Thee of thy many-colored garment, and by my own folly I have let Thee go away from thy Father's house, and from the chamber of her that bore Thee. Thou knowest all this, my Lord, but I know Thee, too, because Thou knowest me so well."

Then notice that, when Joseph thus revealed himself to his brethren, he did not say more till he had *sweetly put away all their offenses against him*. They had been troubled because they knew that they had sold him into Egypt, but he said to them, "Now therefore be not grieved, nor angry with yourselves, that ye sold me hither." So Jesus says to His loved ones, who have grieved Him by their evil deeds, "Be not grieved, for, 'I have blotted out, as a thick cloud, thy transgressions, and, as a cloud, thy sins.' Be not angry with yourselves, for I will receive you graciously, and love you freely. Be not angry with yourselves, for your sins, which are many, are all forgiven; go, and sin no more. For my name's sake, will I defer mine anger; wherefore, 'Come now, and let us reason together: though your sins be as scarlet, they shall be as white as snow; though they be red like crimson, they shall be as wool.' " Many of you know the way our Savior talks; I pray that He may just now make every believer sure that there is not a sin against him in God's Book of remembrance. May you, dear friends, be clear in your conscience from all dead works! May you have the peace of God, which passeth all understanding, to keep your hearts and minds through Christ Jesus, and in the clear white light of your Savior's glorious presence, may you see the wounds He endured when suffering for your sins! Then will you sing with the disciple whom Jesus loved, "Unto him that loved us, and washed us from our sins in his own blood, and hath made us kings and priests unto God and His Father; to him be glory and dominion forever and ever. Amen."

Last of all, Joseph was not satisfied with thus revealing himself to his brethren, and assuring them of his free forgiveness, but he promised them rich supplies for the future. To my mind, this was the next best news to his message of forgiveness. He said to them, in effect, "You have had two years of famine. It is only through me that you have been preserved alive; you have come down to Egypt with your asses and your sacks, and you have taken home provender to my father and to your households; but there are yet five more years in which there will be no plowing and no harvest. What will become of you? What little you had in store, is already all consumed. God has sent me here that, through those five years, I may nourish you. You shall come down, and live in Goshen, on the fat of the land of Egypt, and you shall never have any want, for all the treasures of the land of Egypt are mine, and I will take care of you, you shall never know any lack." In like manner, beloved, your Lord stands, and says to you, "You will have many more troubles yet." Some of my dear brothers and sisters in Christ, who are here, will be in heaven before five more years have expired; they have good reason to be very grateful to God. But to some of us who are younger, it may be that God has appointed many a year to abide here; but our Savior lives.

> He is at the Father's side,
> The Man of love, the Crucified;

and the arrangements of providence are in His hand, and all that providence shall be over-ruled for us. "No good thing will he withhold from them that walk uprightly." You will be in Egypt for a while longer, dear friend, but you will be in the Goshen of Egypt, and the good of all the land is yours. Oh, what a blessing it is to think that we have a Brother who reveals Himself to us as the Universal Provider, who will not let us have a want, but will take care that, before our need comes, the supply shall be ready, and we shall have nothing to do but to rejoice in Him who careth for us!

Let not that sweet thought take away from your minds what I want to be the center of all the meditation, namely, that you should come near to your Lord. We never use a crucifix; we should think it sinful to do so. Neither do I want to have an imaginary crucifix, by trying to set Christ before you so that you should picture Him mentally; but I want your faith to do much more than imagination can. The Lord Jesus Christ is spiritually here in the midst of us, according to His gracious promise, "Lo, I am with you alway, even unto the end of the world"; and He hears me speaking these words at this moment, I am as sure of it as if I saw that mystic presence with my natural eyes. If I did see Him, I know that I should fall at His feet as dead, and the rest of this service would have to be spent in awe-struck silence by everyone that did behold Him. But, O thou Son of God and Son of Mary, Jesus Christ our Savior, we trust Thee wholly and alone to save us, and we love Thee with all our heart, and mind, and soul, and strength; and as we live *by* Thee, we pray Thee to help us to live *for* Thee, to live *to* Thee, to live *like* Thee, and by-and-by to live *with* Thee! We could almost wish that we might now fall down and kiss thy dear feet, but Thou art not here in visible presence; for Thou hast gone up into the glory; but Thou art here spiritually, and we come to Thee, and say, "Lord, Thou art ours, and we are thine; we will hold to Thee, and will not let Thee go."

> Sun of my soul, thou Savior dear,
> It is not night if thou be near.

Come, stay with me while yet the evening shade shall linger, till death's dark night comes on, and then, instead of night, let the morning break upon my gladdened eyes because it is Thyself that has come, the life, the resurrection, and not death at all! Come, beloved, can you not get nearer to your Lord? Can you not speak familiarly with Him? Can you not whisper into His ear the story of your love?

> Come, Holy Spirit, heavenly Dove,

and help us now to come near to Jesus! Amen and Amen.

THE PROPHET LIKE UNTO MOSES

SERMON NO. 1,487
DELIVERED ON LORD'S DAY MORNING, AUGUST 3, 1879.
PORTIONS OF SCRIPTURE READ BEFORE SERMON—DEUTERONOMY 5; 18:15–22.
HYMNS FROM *Our Own Hymn Book*—240, 229, 21.

> *The LORD thy God will raise up unto thee a Prophet from the midst of thee, of thy brethren, like unto me; unto him ye shall hearken; according to all that thou desiredst of the LORD thy God in Horeb in the day of the assembly, saying, Let me not hear again the voice of the LORD my God, neither let me see this great fire any more, that I die not. And the LORD said unto me, They have well spoken that which they have spoken. I will raise them up a Prophet from among their brethren, like unto thee, and will put my words in his mouth; and he shall speak unto them all that I shall command him. And it shall come to pass, that whosoever will not hearken unto my words which he shall speak in my name, I will require it of him*—Deuteronomy 18:15–19.

MAN, the creature, may well desire intercourse with his Creator. When we are right-minded we cannot bear to be like fatherless children, born into the world by a parent of whom we know nothing whatever. We long to hear our father's voice. Of old time, or ever sin had entered into the world, the Lord God was on the most intimate terms with His creature man. He communed with Adam in the garden; in the cool of the day He made the evening to be seven-fold refreshing by the shadow of His own presence. There was no cloud between unfallen man and the ever-blessed One: they could commune together, for no sin had set up a middle wall of partition. Alas, man being in honor continued not, but broke the law of his God, and not only forfeited his own inheritance, but entailed upon his descendants a character with which the holy God can hold no converse. By nature we love that which is evil, and within us there is an evil heart of unbelief in departing from the living God, and consequently intercourse between God and man has had to be upon quite another footing from that which commenced and ended in the glades of Eden. It was condescension at the first which made the Lord speak with man the creature; it is mercy, unutterable mercy, now if God deigns to speak with man the sinner.

Through His divine grace the Lord did not leave our fathers altogether without a word from Himself even after the Fall, for between the days of Adam and Moses there were occasional voices heard as of God speaking with man. "Enoch walked with God," which implies that God walked with him and had communion with him, and we may rest assured it was no silent walk which Enoch had with the Most High. The Lord also spoke to Noah, once and again, and made a covenant with him: and then He, at still greater length and with greater frequency, spoke with Abraham, whom He graciously called His friend. Voices also came to Isaac, and Jacob, and Joseph, and celestial beings flitted to and fro between earth and heaven. Then there was a long pause and a dreary silence. No prophet spoke in Jehovah's name, no voice of God in priestly oracle was heard, but all was silent while Israel dwelt in Egypt, and sojourned in the land of Ham. So completely hushed was the spiritual voice among men that it seemed as if God had utterly forsaken His people and left the world without a witness to His name; yet there was a prophecy of His return, and the Lord had great designs, which only waited till the full time was come. He purposed to try man in a very special manner, to see whether he could bear the presence of the Lord or no. He resolved to take a family, multiply it into a nation, and set it apart for Himself, and to that nation He would make a revelation of Himself of the most extraordinary character. So He took the people who had slaved amongst the brick kilns of Egypt, and made them His elect, the nation of His choice, ordained to be a nation of priests, a people near unto Him, if they had but grace to bear the honor. Though they had lain among the pots, with a high hand and an outstretched arm He delivered them, and with gracious love He favored them, so that they became for beauty and excellence as the wings of a dove that are covered with silver and her feathers with yellow gold. He divided the Red Sea and made them a way of escape, and afterwards set that sea as a barrier between them and their former masters. He took them into the wilderness, and there fed them with manna which dropped from heaven, and with water out of the rock did He sustain them. After a while He began to speak to them, as He had never spoken to any nation before. He spoke with them from the top of Sinai, so that they heard His voice out of the midst of the fire, and in astonishment they cried, "We have seen this day that God doth talk with man, and he liveth." But the experiment failed. Man was not in a condition to hear the direct voice of God. On the very first day the people were in such terror and alarm that they cried out, "This great fire will consume us: if we hear the voice of the Lord our God any more we shall die." As they stood still at a distance to hear the words of God's perfect law they were filled with great fear, and so terrible was the sight that even Moses said, "I exceedingly fear and quake." The people could not endure that which was commanded, and entreated that the word should not be spoken to them any more. They felt the need of someone to interpose—a daysman, an interpreter, one of a thousand was needed to come between them and God. Even those among them that were the most spiritual, and understood and loved God better than the rest, yet confessed that they could not endure the thunder of His dreadful voice, and their elders and the heads of their tribes came unto Moses and said, "Go thou near, and hear all that the Lord our God shall say: and speak thou unto us all that the Lord our God shall speak unto thee; and we will hear it, and do it."

The Lord knew that man would always be unable to hear his Maker's voice, and He therefore determined not only to speak by Moses, but, ever and anon, to speak by His servants the prophets, raising up here one and there another; and then He determined, as the consummation of His condescending mercy, that at the last He would put all the word He had to say to man into one heart, and that word should be spoken by one mouth to men, furnishing a full, complete, and unchangeable revelation of Himself to the human race. This He resolved to give by one of whom Moses had learned something when the Lord said to him in the words of our text, "I will raise them up a Prophet from among their brethren, like unto thee, and will put my words in his mouth; and he shall speak unto them all that I shall command him." We know assuredly that our Lord Jesus Christ is that prophet like unto Moses by whom in these last days He has spoken unto us. See Peter's testimony in the third chapter of the Acts of the Apostles, and Stephen's in the seventh chapter of the same book. "This man was counted worthy of more glory than Moses, inasmuch as he who hath built the house hath more honor than the house," yet did He bear a gracious likeness to Moses, and therein His apostles found a sure argument of His being indeed the Messiah, sent of God.

The subject of this morning's discourse is the Lord's speaking to us by Jesus Christ, the one Mediator between God and man, and our earnest aim is that all of us may reverently hear the voice of God by this greatest of all prophets. Men and brethren, this is the Word of God unto you this morning, that very Word which He spoke on the holy Mount, when the Lord was transfigured and there appeared with Him Moses and Elijah speaking to Him, and out of the excellent glory there came the word, "This is my beloved Son, hear ye him." This is my message at this hour—"Hear ye him." He saith to you all this day, "Incline your ear and come unto me: hear, and your soul shall live. Hearken diligently unto me, and eat ye that which is good, and let your soul delight itself in fatness." "See that ye refuse not him that speaketh. For if they escaped not who refused him that spoke on earth, much more shall not we escape, if we turn away from him that speaketh from heaven."

Our meditation will run in this line: first, we will think for a moment upon *the necessity* for a Mediator; secondly, upon *the person* of the Prophet-Mediator whom God hath chosen; and, thirdly, upon *the authority* with which this Mediator is invested, by which authority He calleth upon us this day to hearken to God's voice which is heard in him.

I. We begin by considering how urgently there existed THE NECESSITY for a Mediator. I need but very short time to set this forth. There was a necessity for a Mediator in the case of the Israelites, first, *because of the unutterable glory of God*, and their own inability to endure that glory, either with their eye, their ear, or their mind. We cannot suppose that the revelation of God upon Sinai was the display of all His greatness: nay, we know that it could not be such, for it would have been impossible for man to have lived at all in the presence of the infinite glory. Habakkuk, speaking of this manifestation, says, "God came from Teman, and the Holy One from Mount Paran. His glory covered the heavens, and the earth was full of his praise. And his brightness was as the light; he had horns coming out of his hand"; but he adds, "there was the hiding of his power." Despite its exceeding glory, the manifestation upon the mount of God at Horeb was a subdued manifestation, and yet, though it was thus toned down to human weakness, it could not be borne. The unveilings of Jehovah's face no mortal eye could bear. The voice with which God spoke at Sinai is by Moses compared to the voice of a trumpet waxing exceeding loud and long, and also to the roll of thunder; and we all know the awe-inspiring sound of thunder when it is heard near at hand, its volleys rolling overhead. How the crash of peal on peal makes the bravest heart, if not to quail, yet still to bow in reverent awe before God! Yet this is not the full voice of God: it is but His whisper. Jehovah hath hushed His voice in the thunder, for were that voice heard in its fullness it would shake not only the earth, but also heaven. If He were for once to unveil His face the lightning's flame would pale to darkness in comparison. The voice of the Lord God is inconceivably majestic, and it is not possible that we, poor creatures, worms of the dust, insects of a day, should ever be able to hear it and live. We could not bear the full revelation of God apart from mediatorial interposition. Perhaps when He has made us to be pure spirit, or when our bodies shall have been "raised in power," made like unto the body of our Lord Jesus, we may then be able to behold the glorious Jehovah, but as yet we must accept the kindly warning of the Lord in answer to the request of Moses, "thou canst not see my face, for there shall no man see me and live." The strings of life are too weak for the strain of the unveiled presence; it is not possible for such a gossamer, spider-like thread as our existence to survive the breath of Deity, if He should actually and in very deed draw nigh to us. It appeared clearly at Sinai, that even when the Lord did accommodate Himself, as much as was consistent with His honor, to the infirmity of human nature, man was so alarmed and afraid at His presence that He could not bear it, and it was absolutely necessary that instead of speaking with His own voice, even though He whispered what He had to say, He should speak to another apart, and afterwards that other should come from the mount and repeat the Lord's words to the people.

This sufficient reason is supported by another most weighty fact, namely, that *God cannot commune with men because of their sin.* God was pleased to regard His people Israel at the foot of Sinai as pure. "Moses went down from the mount unto the people, and sanctified the people; and they washed their clothes." They had abstained for awhile from defiling actions, and as they stood outside the bounds they were ceremonially clean; but it was only a ceremonial purity. Before long they were really unclean before the Lord, and in heart defiled and polluted. The Lord said of them, "O that there were such a heart in them, that they would fear me, and keep all my commandments always, that it might be well with them, and with their children forever!"

He knew that their heart was not right even when they spoke obediently. Not many days after the people had trembled at Sinai they made a golden calf, and set it up and bowed before it, and provoked the Lord to jealousy so that He sent plagues among them. It is quite clear that after such a rebellion, after a deliberate breach of His covenant, and daring violation of His commands, it would have been quite impossible for God to speak to them, or for them to listen to the voice of God, in a direct manner. They would have fled before Him because of His holiness, which shamed their unholiness; and because of their sin, which provoked His indignation, because of the wandering, and instability, and treachery of their hearts, the Lord could not have endured them in His presence. The holy angels forever adore with that threefold cry, "Holy, holy, holy Lord God of Sabaoth"; and He could not permit men of unclean lips to profane His throne with their unholy utterances. Oh no, my brethren, with such a sense of sin as some of us have, and as all of us ought to have, we should have to cover our faces, and cower down in terror, if Jehovah Himself were to appear. He cannot look upon iniquity, neither can evil dwell with Him, for He is a consuming fire. While we are compassed with infirmity we cannot behold Him, for our eyes are dimmed with the smoke of our iniquities. If we would see even the skirts of His garments we must first be pure in heart, and He must put us in the cleft of the rock, and cover us with His hand. If we were to behold His stern justice, His awful holiness, and His boundless power, apart from our ever-blessed Mediator, we should dissolve at the sight, and utterly melt away, for we have sinned.

This double reason of the weakness of our nature, and the sinfulness of our character, is a forcible one, for I close this part of the discourse by observing that the argument was so forcible that *the Lord Himself allowed it*. He said, "They have well spoken, that which they have spoken." It was no morbid apprehension which made them afraid, it was no foolish dread which made them start, for wisdom's own self in the person of Moses, said, "I do exceedingly fear and quake." The calmest and meekest of men had real cause for fear.

God's face is not to be seen. An occasional glimpse may come to spirits raised above their own natural level, so that they can for awhile behold the King, the Lord of hosts; but even to them it is a terrible strain upon all their powers, the wine is too strong for the bottles. What said John, when he saw, not so much absolute Deity, but the divine side of the Mediator? "When I saw him I fell at his feet as dead." Daniel, the man greatly beloved, confesses that there remained no strength in Him and His comeliness was turned into corruption when he heard the voice of God; and Job said, "I have heard of thee by the hearing of the ear, but now mine eye seeth thee; therefore I abhor myself in dust and ashes." No, God knoweth it is not silly fright nor unbelieving fear; it is a most seemly awe and a most natural dread which takes hold of finite and fallible creatures in the presence of the Infinite and Perfect One. These frail tabernacles, like the tents of Cushan, are in affliction when the Lord marches by in the greatness of His power. We need a Mediator. The Lord knows right well that our sinfulness provokes Him, and that there is in us, in the best here present, that which would make Him to break out against us to destroy us if we were to come to Him without a covering and a propitiation.

We must approach the Lord through a Mediator: it is absolutely necessary. God Himself witnesses it is, and therefore in His mercy He ordains a Mediator, that by Him we may be able to approach His throne of grace. May the Holy Spirit make this truth very plain to the consciousness of all of us, and cause us to sing with the poet:

> Till God in human flesh I see,
>   My thoughts no comfort find;
> The holy, just, and sacred Three
>   Are terrors to my mind.
>
> But if Immanuel's face appear,
>   My hope, my joy begins;
> His name forbids my slavish fear,
>   His grace removes my sins.

II. This brings us to consider THE PERSON of the appointed Mediator, and in my text we obtain a liberal measure of information upon this point. Read these blessed words, "The Lord thy God will raise up unto thee a Prophet from the midst of thee, of thy brethren." Dwell with sweetness upon this fact, that our Lord Jesus was raised up from the midst of us, from among our brethren. In Him is fulfilled that glorious prophecy, "I have exalted one chosen out of the people." He is one of ourselves, a brother born for adversity. He was born at Bethlehem, not in fiction, but in fact: where the horned oxen fed He in a manger lay, as any other babe might do, wrapped in swaddling bands, and dependent on a woman's loving care as any other babe might be. He was like ourselves in His growth from infancy to manhood, increasing in stature as we do from our childhood to our riper age. Though the holy child Jesus He was yet a child; and therefore He was subject to His parents. And when He came forth as a man, His was no phantom manhood, but true flesh and blood; He was tempted and He was betrayed: He hungered and He thirsted; He was weary and He was sore amazed; He took out sicknesses, and He carried our sorrows; He was made in all points like unto His brethren. He did not set Himself apart as though He were of an exclusive caste or of a superior rank, but He dwelt among us; the brother of the race, eating with publicans and sinners, mingling ever with the common people. He was not one who boasted His descent, or gloried in the so-called blue blood, or placed himself among the *Porphyro-geniti*, who must not see the light except in marble halls. He was born in a common house of entertainment where all might come to Him, and He died with His arms extended as a pledge that He continued to receive all who came to Him. He never spoke of men as the common multitude, the vulgar herd, but He made Himself at home among them. He was dressed like a peasant, in the ordinary smock of the country, a garment without seam, woven from the top throughout; and He mixed with the multitude, went to their marriage feasts, attended their funerals, and was so much among them, a man among men, that slander called Him a gluttonous man and a winebibber, a friend of publicans and sinners. In all respects our Lord was raised up from the midst of us, one of our own kith and kin. "For this cause he is not ashamed to call us brethren." He was our brother in living, our brother in death, and our brother in resurrection; for after His resurrection He said, "Go, tell my brethren"; and He also said, "My Father, and your Father; my God, and your God." Though now exalted in the highest heavens He pleads for us and acts as a High Priest who can be touched with a feeling of our infirmities. God has graciously raised up such a Mediator, and now He speaks to us through Him. O sons of men, will ye not hearken when such an One as Jesus of Nazareth, the Son of man, is ordained to speak of the eternal God? Ye might be unable to hear if He should speak again in thunder, but now He speaketh by those dear lips of love, now He speaketh by that gracious tongue which has wrought such miracles of grace by its words, now He speaketh out of that great heart of His, which never beats except with love to the sons of men—will ye not hear Him? Surely we ought to give the most earnest heed and obey His every word.

Moses was truly one of the people, for he loved them intensely, and all his sympathies were with them. They provoked him terribly, but still he loved them. We can never admire that man of God too much when we think of his disinterested love to that guilty nation. See him on the mountain there as Israel's advocate. The Lord said, "Let me alone that I may destroy them, and I will make of thee a great nation." That proposal opened up before Moses' eye a glittering destiny. It was within his grasp that he himself should become the founder of a race, in whom the promises made to Abraham should be fulfilled. Would not the most of men have greedily snatched at it? But Moses will not have it. He loves Israel too well to see the people die if he can save them. He has not an atom of selfish ambition about him; but with cries and tears he exclaims, "Wherefore should the Egyptians speak and say, For mischief did he bring them out, to slay them in the mountains, and to consume them from the face of the earth? Turn from thy fierce wrath, and repent of this evil against thy people." He prevailed with God by his pleading, for he identified himself with Israel. Moses did, as it were, gather up all their griefs and sorrows unto himself, even as did our Lord. True Israelite was he, for he refused to be called the son of Pharaoh's daughter, and cast in his lot with the people of God. This is just what our blessed Lord has done. He will not have honor apart from His people, nor even life, unless they live also. He saved others, himself he could not save. He would not be in heaven, and leave His saints behind. He loved the people and so proved Himself to be one chosen out of their midst, a brother among brethren.

Mark well that, while thus our Lord is our brother, the great God has in His person sent us One who is lifted up above us all in the knowledge of His mind. Thus saith the Lord (v. 18), "I will put my words in his mouth." Our Lord Jesus Christ comes to us inspired by God. Not alone cometh He, nor of His own mind; but saith He, "The Father is with me: I do always the things which please him: the Father that dwelleth in me, he doeth the works." Both in word and work He acted for His Father, and under His Father's inspiration. Men and brethren, I beseech you not to reject the message which Jesus brings, seeing it is not his own, but the sure message of God. Trifle not with a single word which Jesus speaks, for it is the word of the Eternal One: despise not one single deed which He did, or precept which He commanded, or blessing which He brought, for upon all these there is the stamp of deity. God chose one who is our brother that He might come near to us; but He put His own royal imprimatur upon Him, that we might not have an ambassador of second rank, but One who counts it not robbery to be equal with God, who nevertheless for our sake has taken upon Himself the form of a servant that He might speak home to our hearts. For all these reasons, I beseech you despise not Him that speaketh, seeing He speaketh from heaven.

The main point, however, upon which I want to dwell is, that Jesus is like to Moses. There had been no better mediator found than Moses up to Moses' day; the Lord God, therefore, determined to work upon that model with the great prophet of His race, and He has done so in sending forth the Lord Jesus. It would be a very interesting task for the young people to work out all the points in which Moses is a personal type of the Lord Jesus. The points of resemblance are very many, for there is hardly a single incident in the life of the great Lawgiver which is not symbolical of the promised Savior. You may begin from the beginning at the waters of the Nile, and go to the close upon the brow of Pisgah, and you will see Christ in Moses as a man sees his face in a glass. I can only mention in what respects, as a Mediator, Jesus is like to Moses, and surely one is found in the fact that Moses beyond all that went before him was *peculiarly the depository of the mind of God*. Once and again we find him closeted with God for 40 days at a time. He went right away from men to the lone mountain-top, and there he was 40 days and 40 nights, and did neither eat nor drink, but lived in high communion with his God. In those times of seclusion he received the pattern of the tabernacle, the laws of the priesthood, of the sacrifices of the holy days, and of the civil estate of Israel, and perhaps the early records which compose the book of Genesis. To whom else had God ever spoken for that length of time, as a man speaketh with his friend? He was the peculiar favorite of God. From the first day of his call, when he was keeping his father's flock at the back of the desert, right to the day when God kissed away his soul on the top of Nebo, he was a man greatly beloved, to whom God manifested Himself as to no other. Hear the Lord's own words to Aaron and Miriam. "And he said, Hear now my words: If there be a prophet among you, I the Lord will make myself known unto him in a vision, and will speak unto him in a dream. My servant Moses is not so, who is faithful in all mine house. With him will I speak mouth to mouth, even apparently, and not in dark speeches: and the similitude of the Lord shall he behold: wherefore then were ye not afraid to speak against my servant Moses?" In this our Lord Jesus is like to Moses, only He far surpasses him, for the intercourse between Christ and the Father was very much more intimate, seeing that Jesus is Himself essential deity, and "in him dwelleth all the fullness of the Godhead bodily." Cold mountains and the midnight air continually witnessed to His communion with the Father. Nor these alone, for He abode with the Father. His language was always spoken out as God was speaking within Him; He lived in God, and with God. "I know," said He, "that thou hearest me always." Instead of having to point out when Christ was in communion with the Father, we have rather, with astonishment, to point out the solitary moment when he was left of the Father, even that dread hour when He cried, "My God, my God, why hast thou forsaken me?" Only for that once the Father had left Him, and even then it was inexplicable, and He asked the reason for it; though He knew Himself to be then suffering as the Substitute for man, yet did His desertion by God come upon Him as a novelty which utterly overwhelmed Him, so that He asked in agony why He was forsaken.

Moses, to take another point, is the first of the prophets *with whom God kept up continuous revelation.* To other men He spoke in dreams and visions, but to Moses by plain and perpetual testimony. His Spirit rested on him, and he took of it to give thereof to Joshua, and to the 70 elders, even as Jesus gave of His Spirit to the apostles. Sometimes God spoke to Noah, or to Abraham and others; but it was upon occasions only; and even then, as in the case of Abraham and Jacob, they must fall asleep to see and hear Him best: but with Moses the Lord abode perpetually; whensoever he willed he consulted the Most High, and at once God spoke with him, and directed his way. So was it with Christ Jesus. He needed not to behold a vision: the spirit of prophecy did not occasionally come upon Him, and bear Him out of Himself, for the Spirit was given him without measure, and He knew the very mind and heart of God perpetually. He was always a prophet; not sometimes a prophet, like him of old, of whom we read, "The Spirit of God came upon him in the camp of Dan"; or like others of whom it is written, "the word of the Lord came to them." At all times the Spirit rested upon Him: He spoke in the abiding power of the Holy Ghost, even more so than did Moses.

Moses is described as a prophet *mighty in word and deed,* and it is singular that there never was another prophet mighty in word and deed till Jesus came. Moses not only spoke with matchless power, but wrought miracles. You shall find no other prophet who did both. Other prophets who spoke well wrought no miracles, or only here and there; whilst those who wrought miracles, such as Elijah and Elisha, have left us but few words that they spoke: indeed, their prophecies were but lightning flashes, and not as the bright shining of a sun. When you come to our Lord Jesus you find lip and heart working together, with equal perfectness of witness. You cannot tell in which He is the more marvelous, in His speech or in His act. "Never man spoke like this man," but certainly never man wrought such marvels of mercy as Jesus did. He far exceeds Moses and all the prophets put together in the variety and the multitude and the wonderful character of the miracles which He did. If men bow before prophets who can cast down their rods, and they become serpents, if they yield homage to prophets who call fire from heaven, how much more should they accept Him whose words are matchless music, and whose miracles of love were felt even beyond the boundaries of this visible world; for the angels of God flew from heaven to minister to Him, the devils of the pit fled before His voice, and the caverns of death heard His call and yielded up their prey. Who would not accept this prophet like unto Moses, to whom the Holy Ghost bore witness by mighty signs and wonders?

Moses, again, was *the founder of a great system of religious law*, and this was not the case with any other but the Lord Jesus. He founded the whole system of the Aaronic priesthood and the law that went with it. Moses was a lawgiver: he gave the ten commandments in the name of God, and all the other statutes of the Jewish polity were ordained through him. Now, till you come to Christ you find no such lawgiver; but Jesus institutes the new covenant as Moses introduced the old, the Sermon on the Mount was an utterance from a happier Sinai, and whereas Moses gives this and that command, Jesus gives the like in sweeter form and in diviner fashion, and embodies it in His own sacred person. He is the great legislator of our dispensation, the King in the midst of Jeshurun, giving forth His command which runneth very swiftly, and they that fear the Lord are obedient thereunto.

Time will fail us, or we would mention to you that *Moses was faithful before God* as a servant over all his house, and so was Jesus as a Son over His own house. He was never unfaithful to His charge in any respect, but in all things ruled and served to perfection as the anointed of the Father. He is the faithful and true Witness, the Prince of the kings of the earth. Moses, too, was *zealous for God* and for His honor. Remember how the zeal of God's house did eat him up. When he saw grievous sin among the people, he said, "Who is on the Lord's side?" and there came to him the tribe of Levi, and he said, "Go in and out, and slay ye every one his men that were joined to Baal-peor." Herein he was the stern type of Jesus, who took the scourge of small cords, and drove out the buyers and sellers, and said, "Take these things hence: it is written, My Father's house shall be a house of prayer, but ye have made it a den of thieves"; for the zeal of God's house had eaten him up.

Moses, by divine grace, was *very meek*, and perhaps this is the chief parallel between him and Jesus. I have said, "by divine grace," for I suppose by nature he was strongly passionate. There are many indications that Moses was not meek, but very far from it until the Spirit of God rested upon him. He slew the Egyptian hastily, and in after years he went out from the presence of Pharaoh "in great anger." Once and again you find him very wroth: he took the tables of stone and dashed them in pieces in his indignation, for "Moses' anger waxed hot"; and that unhappy action which occasioned his being shut out of Canaan was caused by his "being provoked in spirit so that he spoke unadvisedly with his lips," and said, "Hear now, ye rebels; must I fetch you water out of this rock?" Divine grace had so cooled and calmed him that in general he was the gentlest of men, and when his brother and sister thrust themselves into his place and questioned his authority, it is written, "Now the man Moses was very meek, above all the men which were upon the face of the earth." In his own quarrel he has never anything to say: it is only for the people and for God that his anger waxeth hot. Even about his last act of hastiness he says, "God was angry with me for your sake," not for his own sake. He was so meek and gentle that for 40 years he bore with the most rebellious and provoking nation that ever existed. But what shall I say of my Master? Let Him speak for Himself. "Come unto me, all ye that labor and are heavy laden, and I will give you rest: take my yoke upon you, and learn of me; for I am meek and lowly in heart: and ye shall find rest unto your souls."

Our children call Him "Gentle Jesus, meek and mild." The man Jesus is very meek above all men that are upon the face of the earth. He has His indignation—

> Like glowing oven is His wrath,
> As flame by furious blast upblown,

for He can be angry, and the wrath of the Lamb is the most awful wrath beneath the sun; but still to us, in this gospel day, He is all love and tenderness; and when He bids us come to Him, can we refuse to hear? So meek is the Mediator that He is love itself incarnate love; so loving, that when He died His only crime was that He was "found guilty of excess of love"; can we be so cruel as to reject Him? O brothers and sisters, do not refuse to listen to the voice of this Tender One by whom God speaketh to you.

Our Lord was like to Moses in meekness, and then to sum up all—Moses was *the Mediator for God with the people*, and so is our blessed Lord. Moses came in God's name to set Israel free from Pharaoh's bondage, and he did it: Jesus came to set us free from a worse bondage still, and He has achieved our freedom. Moses led the people through the Red Sea, and Jesus has led us where all the hosts of hell were overthrown, and sin was drowned in His own most precious blood. Moses led the tribes through the wilderness, and Jesus leads us through the weary ways of this life to the rest which remaineth for the people of God. Moses spoke to the people for God, and Jesus hath done the same. Moses spoke to God for the people, and Jesus ever liveth to make intercession for us. Moses proposed himself as a sacrifice when he said, "If not, blot my name out of the book of life"; but Jesus was an actual sacrifice, and was taken away from the land of the living for our sakes, being made a curse for us. Moses, in a certain sense, died for the people, for he could not enter into the land, but must needs close his eyes on Nebo. Those are touching words, "The Lord was angry with me for your sakes"; words which in a diviner sense may be fitly applied to Jesus, for God was angry with Him for our sakes. Right through to the very end our blessed Lord Jesus Christ, our Savior, is a prophet like unto Moses, raised up from the midst of His brethren. O my hearers, hear ye Him. Turn not your ear away from this Prophet of prophets, but hear and live.

III. I close with that point, and if my words are very few let them be weighty. Let us think of THE AUTHORITY of our great Mediator, and let this be the practical lesson—Hear ye Him. Men and brethren, if our hearts were right, the moment it was announced that God would speak to us through Jesus Christ there would be a rush to hear Him. If sin had not maddened men they would listen eagerly to every word of God through such a Mediator as Jesus is; they would write each golden sentence on their tablets, they would hoard His word in their memories, they would wear it between their eyes, they would yield their hearts to it. Alas, it is not so; and the saddest thing of all is that some talk of Jesus for gain, and others hear of Him as if His story were a mere tale or an old Jewish ballad of 1800 years ago. Yet, remember, God speaks by Jesus still, and every word of His that is left on record is as solemnly alive today as when it first leaped from His blessed lips. I beseech you remember

Christ cometh not as an amateur, but He hath authority with Him: this ambassador to men wears the authority of the King of kings. If ye despise Him ye despise Him that sent Him: if ye turn away from Him that speaketh from heaven ye turn away from the eternal God, and ye do despite to His love. Oh, do not so.

Note how my text puts it. It saith here, "Whosoever shall not hearken unto my words which he shall speak in my name, *I will require it of him.*" My heart trembles while I repeat to you the words, "I will require it of him." Today God graciously requires it of some of you, and asks why you have not listened to Christ's voice. Why is this? You have not accepted His salvation. Why is this? You know all about Jesus, and you say it is true, but you have never believed in Him: why is this? God requires it of you. Many years has He waited patiently, and He has sent His servant again and again to invite you. The men of Nineveh sought mercy in their day, and yet you have not repented. God requires it of you. Why is this? Give your Maker a reason for your rejection of His mercy if you can: fashion some sort of excuse, O ye rebellious one. Do you despise your God? Do you dare His wrath? Do you defy His anger? Are you so mad as this?

The day will come when He will require it of you in a much more violent sense than He does today; when you shall have passed beyond the region of mercy He will say, "I called you and you refused, why is this? I did not speak to you in thunder. I spoke to you with the gentle voice of the Only Begotten who bled and died for men: why did you not hear Him? Every Sabbath day my servant tried to repeat the language of His master to you: why did you refuse it? You are cast into hell, but why did not you ac- cept the pardon which would have delivered you from it?" You were too busy. Too busy to remember your God? What could you have been busy about that was worth a thought as compared with Him? You were too fond of pleasure. And do you dare in- sult your God by saying that trifling amusements which were not worth the mentioning could stand in comparison with His love and His good pleasure? Oh, how you deserve His wrath. I pray you consider what this meaneth, "I will require it of him." You who still harden your hearts, and refuse my Master, go away with this ringing in your ears, "I will require it of him! I will require it of him." "When he lieth dying alone in that sick chamber I will require it of him: when he hath taken the last plunge, and left this world, and finds himself in eternity, I will require it of him: and when the thunder wakes the dead, and the great Prophet like unto Moses shall sit on the great white throne to judge the quick and the dead, I will require it of him, I will require it of him."

My Master will require of me how I have preached to you, and I sincerely wish it were in my power to put these things in better form, and plead with you more earnestly; but, after all, what can I do? If you have no care for your own souls, how can I help it? If you will rush upon eternal woe, if you will despise the altogether lovely One through whom God speaks to you, if you will live day after day carelessly and wantonly, throwing away your souls, oh, then mine eyes shall weep in secret places for you; but what more can I do but leave you to God? At the last I shall be compelled to say "Amen" to the verdict which condemns you forever. God grant that such a reluctant task may not fall to my lot in reference to any one of you, but may you now hear and obey the Lord Jesus, and find eternal salvation at once, for His dear name's sake. Amen.

THE MEDIATOR—THE INTERPRETER

Sermon No. 2,097
Delivered on Lord's day Morning, July 28, 1889.
Portions of Scripture read before Sermon—Exodus 20:18–21;
Deuteronomy 5.
Hymns from *Our Own Hymn Book*—92 (Part 1), 433, 281.

And all the people saw the thunderings, and the lightnings, and the noise of the trumpet, and the mountain smoking: and when the people saw it, they removed, and stood afar off. And they said unto Moses, Speak thou with us, and we will hear: but let not God speak with us, lest we die. And Moses said unto the people, Fear not: for God is come to prove you, and that his fear may be before your faces, that ye sin not—Exodus 20:18–20.

The giving of the law was glorious with pomp of power. The blaze of splendor was intended to impress the people with a sense of the authority of the law, by letting them see the greatness of the Lawgiver. It was meet that with great solemnity the law of the Most High should be proclaimed, that Israel might have a holy reverence for its commands. This terrible grandeur may also have been intended to suggest to the people the condemning force of the law. Not with sweet sound of harp, nor with the song of angels, was the law given; but with an awful voice from amid a terrible burning. Not in itself is the law condemnatory; for if there could have been life by any law, it would have been by this law: but by reason of man's sinfulness, the law worketh wrath; and to indicate this, it was made public with accompaniments of fear and death: the battalions of Omnipotence marshaled upon the scene; the dread artillery of God, with awful salvos, adding emphasis to every syllable. The tremendous scene at Sinai was also in some respects a prophecy, if not a rehearsal, of the Day of Judgment. If the giving of the law, while it was yet unbroken, was attended with such a display of awe-inspiring power, what will that day be when the Lord shall, with flaming fire, take vengeance on those who have willfully broken His law?

To us, that day at Horeb is a type of the action of the law in our nature: thus doth the law deal with our consciences and hearts. If you have ever felt the law spoken home to you by the Spirit of God, you have heard great thunderings within. You have been forced to cry with Habakkuk, "When I heard, my belly trembled; my lips quivered at the voice: rottenness entered into my bones." And God intended it to be so, that you might look to the flames which Moses saw, and abandon forever all hope of acceptance by the works of the law.

The glorious majesty which surrounded the institution of the law is not, however, our subject at this time. I shall handle the text in another manner. The Lord God, in this instance, came as near to man as was possible; yea, He came nearer than man could bear. Until a Mediator was found, the approach of God brought to man nothing but terror. Although under no great apprehension of guilt at the time—for they had only then heard the law for the first time—yet the people removed, and stood afar off, and cried out, "If we hear the voice of the Lord our God any more, then we shall die." God was near them in special condescension; for Moses said, "Did ever people hear the voice of God speaking out of the midst of the fire, as thou hast heard, and live?" Yet this memorable manifestation caused them alarm. Does it ever happen now that the Lord comes to His people in a way which dismays them? I think so. It is not really so, that God will fight against His people; but, to our apprehension, so it seems at certain times. Of these tempestuous manifestations of the Lord to our hearts I am going to speak at this time; and may the heavenly Comforter use it to the spiritual profit of His tried family!

Our first head is this: *the Lord has ways of communing with His people which fill them with fear*; but, secondly *this endears the Mediator to them*; and thirdly, *this Mediator teaches them to interpret wisely the Lord's darker dealings with them*. When we have thought upon these things, we shall close by saying to you that *this sacred art of interpretation should be practiced by us now*.

I. First, let me remind you that THE LORD HAS WAYS OF COMMUNING WITH HIS PEOPLE WHICH FILL THEM WITH FEAR. You must not think that the Lord always appears to His people in robes of light: sometimes He enrobes Himself in clouds and darkness. His paths drop fatness, and yet He often hath His way in the whirlwind. True, He manifests Himself to us as He doth not unto the world; but in the brightest of those manifestations He may make us fear as we enter into the cloud. It is not every revelation of God which inspires the saints with joy; for in many cases it is far otherwise, even as with Daniel, who said, "I saw this great vision, and there remained no strength in me: for my comeliness was turned in me into corruption, and I retained no strength." This experience may not have occurred to some of you; it is, however, known to many of the people of God, who have had long dealings with Him. If any of you do not understand this matter, lay the sermon by till you do.

Sometimes the near approach of the Lord fills His people with apprehension and alarm; and this sure to be the case when His coming includes *a close application of the law* to their hearts. We used to talk of "law-work" in days which are now past, and are by moderns looked upon with contempt; and, my brethren, our talk was not without good reason, for there is such a work, and it ministers greatly to our good. Certain servants of God, who had experienced this law-work to a very deep degree, fell into the error of regarding a marked measure of it as absolutely necessary to every child of God. We will avoid that evil, for it was a grievous cause of uncharitableness; but we will not conceal the fact that many souls, in coming to God, and in God's coming to them, have been made to feel a hewing and burning work from the law of God. The law has rent them in pieces, because they themselves have rent it in pieces. The law has wrought in them a sense of bondage, burden, and despair. Even after we have fled for refuge to the hope set before us in the gospel, after we have a full assurance that our iniquities are put away, the Lord sometimes works in us a further work of the law, in which He makes us to see its exactness, its spirituality, strictness, and infinite compass. It is no little thing to see how the law judges the thoughts, desires, and imaginations of the heart. As the plummet of the holy law is held up, we see how out of the perpendicular we are, and we are therefore distressed. Brethren, when I have carefully considered, and inwardly perceived, the holiness of God's law, I have felt as though the sharp edge of a saber had been drawn across my heart, and I have shivered and trembled. Though the law did not actually cut or wound, yet its very presence, in all the keenness of its two edges, has made me shudder. So pure, so just, so uncompromising is the law of God, that when it is really understood, it makes us quail, and brings us to our knees. The law searches to the dividing asunder of joints and marrow, and it is a discerner of the thoughts and intents of the heart. Its excessive light strikes us, like Saul of Tarsus, to the earth, and makes us cry for mercy. When you begin to judge yourself, and estimate your actions by its infallible rule, you cease from boasting, and are filled with self-abhorrence. I believe it to be one of the best means to growth in humility, to be well instructed in the law, in the force and power of it. No man knows the brightness of the gospel till he understands the blackness of those clouds which surround the law of the Lord. Much of the shallowness of current religion is the result of a failure to apprehend the demands of divine justice, and a want of clear perception of the heinousness of disobedience. Let but God set up the throne of His law in your heart, and make you feel the power of that law in any one item of your daily conduct, much more in the whole circle of your life, and you will feel as the Israelites did when they could not abide the presence of the Most High.

The Lord also may most truly and profitably come to a man, and in His coming may *unveil to him the depravity of his nature*. If any man could see his own heart as it is by nature, he would be driven mad: the sight of our disease is not to be borne unless we also see the remedy. When the Lord permits the fountains of the great deep of our depravity to be broken up, then are the tops of the hills of our self-sufficiency drowned in fear. When we see what we are capable of being, apart from divine grace, our spirit sinks. When believers are allowed to see how much there is still about them that is akin to hell, when sin becomes exceeding sinful, and we feel that the taint of it has defiled our whole nature, then it is that we are horrified and appalled. What an abyss of evil is within our bosoms! Probably some of you know very little about it. I pray that you may never discover it by its painful results; but I desire that you may believe it, so as to take a firmer grip upon the doctrines of grace, and exercise greater watchfulness over your hearts. Sin which dwelleth in us is no enemy that we can safely despise. Even in one single member of our fallen nature, namely, the tongue, there dwells a world of iniquity: "It defileth the whole body, and setteth on fire the course of nature; and it is set on fire of hell." What poor creatures we are! The best of men are men at the best; and, apart from the work of the Holy Spirit, and the power of divine grace, hell itself does not contain greater monsters of iniquity than you and I might become. Within the magazine of our hearts there is powder enough to destroy us in an instant, if omnipotent grace did not prevent. When this is distinctly perceived, we are troubled before the presence of the thrice holy God. Standing before the Lord, we cry with the prophet, "Woe is me! for I am undone; because I am a man of unclean lips." This is a true manifestation of God; but it is by no means a cause of comfort to us.

The Lord may also come to us, and lead us, by His light, to *a discovery of actual sin in our life*. We may sit here, and think ourselves very good; but if so, we are in the dark. If a beam of divine light is now entering our mind, our apprehension of our own character will be changed. The sins of a single day, if fully known in all their bearings, would drive us to despair, apart from the infinite grace of God. Apart from the divine plan of justifying the ungodly in Christ Jesus, any one hour would shut us up in hell. Beloved, think a minute of your omissions during the past week, how much you might have done, and ought to have done, which you have not done. It is on the side of omission that some of us are most vulnerable. Honestly looking down upon our lives, we may be able to say that we do not know of any overt offense against God, and for this we bless the divine grace; but when we come to think of what we have left undone, we feel like a traveler who, when crossing a glacier, suddenly sees an unfathomable crevasse opening just before him, and widening fast as he looks down into its blue depths of frozen death. Oh the sadness of that confession, "We have left undone the things which we ought to have done!" There is as much of lamentation in it as in the cry which precedes it—"We have done those things which we ought not to have done." When we think of all our omissions, how can we stand before the Lord?

Think again of your failure in what you have done. Brethren, you have prayed this week. I only refer to this week; for seven days are more than enough for my purpose. You have prayed: you have kept your regular times for devotion. But how have your prayed? With fervency? With careful consideration? With concentrated mind? Brethren, have you prayed with faith? With importunity? Surely, each of these questions must cut into you like a whip of wire. If you are as I am, you cannot answer to this examination without wincing. Why, even in the one matter of prayer, the sins of our holy things may shrivel us up before the burning eye of the Lord, who searcheth the heart. Your Bible also: you have read your Bible, of course you have; but with what attention? with what intention? with what devout belief? with what resolve to feel its force, and obey its commands? Have we not sinned against this Book enough to cast us into the lowest hell in the space of four-and-twenty hours?

When the Lord begins to take a man to pieces by coming near to him, another matter will often trouble him, and that is his falseness, even where, in a measure, he is sincere. You prayed in public, and expressed most proper emotions and desires; but were they really your own emotions and desires, or did you steal the expressions of another man? You preached about the things of God; did your testimony come from your heart? Do you act in accordance therewith? You, my Christian friend, expressed yourself strongly, but, in your heart of hearts, can you justify the expression? Do we not often go further with our lips than we go with our hearts? Is not this, to some degree, hypocrisy? Must it not be very displeasing to God that we should use words towards Him which we have not weighed, and which are not fully true, as we use them? O brethren, if the Lord sets our secret sins in the light of His countenance, we too, like Israel, shall start and shrink from the presence of the Lord.

If we add to these apprehensions of our own unworthiness *a sense of the divine glory*, then we cower down and hide ourselves in the dust. When a peal of thunder rends the heavens, and is followed up by a crash, as if the house would fall about your ears, while flames of fire blind you with their excessive brilliance, you feel that the Lord is terrible out of His holy places. God's nearness has inspired you with an awe which has been shaded with dread. The one attribute of power suffices to make the strongest believer feel that Jehovah is to be feared above all gods. But, my brethren, if properly apprehended, God's omniscience inspires an equal awe, while His goodness, His love, and His holiness are even more overwhelming when fully realized. One might possibly stand with unblanched cheek in the presence of divine power; but when the Lord reveals His holiness, a man might far sooner gaze into the sun than look into the face of God. Even His love is as the fire of a furnace to our unloveliness. At the sight of our God we say with Job, "I have heard of thee by the hearing of the ear: but now mine eye seeth thee. Wherefore I abhor myself, and repent in dust and ashes." The nearness of God to sinful man is a killing thing, and those who have known it will confess that it is so.

What, my brethren, if, in addition to this, there should come to you *a succession of alarming providences*? These Israelites not only knew that God was near, but they heard the thunder, they saw the lightning, they looked into the thick darkness, they marked the mountain altogether on a smoke, and by all this they were horror-stricken. Has it come to pass that the Lord has laid many blows upon His servant? Has He taken away the desire of thine eye with a stroke? What if there be one, two, three little graves in yonder cemetery? What if love and friend have forsaken thee? What if thy business fail thee, and if thy health fail thee also? What if thy spirits sink? Oh, then, indeed I marvel not that thou art scared with forebodings of still worse calamities, and art ready to give up the ghost! Now art thou afraid because of the nearness of the great God, who is trying thee.

If to this be added *an apprehension of speedy death*, as in the case of the Israelites, who cried, "This great fire will consume us"; then, indeed, it is difficult to remain calm and hopeful. It will be no trifle to stand before the face of the Eternal. Since heaven and earth shall flee from thy face, and rocks shall melt, and stars shall fall, and the moon shall be turned black as sackcloth of hair, who shall stand before Thee, thou great and glorious One!

Thus have I spoken to you upon the fact that our God does sometimes commune with His people in a way that fills them with overwhelming dread; let us advance to our next theme.

II. Secondly, ALL THIS ENDEARS TO US THE MEDIATOR. The Israelites turned at once to Moses. They had already murmured against him: they afterwards said, "As for this Moses, the man that brought us up out of the land of Egypt, we know not what is become of him"; once they took up stones to stone him; but now they are of another mind. Terrified by the presence of God, they cry to Moses, "Go thou near, and hear all that the Lord our God shall say: and speak thou unto us all that the Lord Our God shall speak unto thee." The Mediator is everything to them now. They had found out by experience the necessity for an interposer; and they had not made a mistake either, for God Himself said they had well spoken what they had said. There is in God's esteem an urgent need for a Mediator. When we sang just now—

> Till God in human flesh I see,
> My thoughts no comfort find;
> The holy, just, and sacred Three
> Are terrors to my mind,

we did not give utterance to morbid or ungrounded fear. It is so in truth; and the next verse is accurate also:

> But if Immanuel's face appear,
> My hope, my joy begins;
> His name forbids my slavish fear,
> His grace removes my sins.

It is a matter of fact that we need a Mediator; and these people were driven to see it. Brethren, be sensible of your sin, and you will no more attempt to approach an absolute Deity than you would walk into a volcano's mouth. You will feel that you need a sacrifice, a propitiation, a Savior, a Mediator. Perceive the infinite difference between your nothingness and the divine infinity, and you will feel that there is no drawing nigh to the Eternal but by Jesus Christ. How can we, of ourselves, draw nigh unto God? It is wisdom to say unto the Well-beloved, "We pray thee, stand between the Lord and us." When your trembling is upon you, when your heart faints with awe, then you perceive how much you need an Advocate. Bless God that He has appointed one to be High Priest for you, who can safely go into the thick darkness, and stand in the presence of the Thrice Holy Majesty, and represent you without fail.

Moses was well fitted to be the type of the true Mediator of the gospel covenant. He was himself in great favor with God, so that the Lord hearkened to his voice. Behold his dauntless courage in the presence of God, and, at the same time, his intense tenderness towards the people. Mark his faithfulness Godward as a servant over all his Master's house, and then note his self-sacrifice for Israel, so that he once said, "Blot me, I pray thee, out of thy book which thou hast written." He offered himself to be a sacrifice for them. But, O beloved, consider Jesus Christ our Mediator. Where is the like of Him? He is man, like ourselves; in all respects a sufferer, poor, needy, knowing even the pangs of death; and therefore He can lay His hand upon us with a warm, brotherly love. But then He is "God over all, blessed forever," equal with the Most High, the Well-beloved of the Father; and thus He can give His hand to the eternal God, and so link our humanity with God. I feel most safe in trusting all my concerns with that dear Advocate, that Interpreter, one of a thousand. O Jesus, who can rival thee?

> God, and yet man, thou art,
>   True God, true man, art thou;
> Of man, and of man's earth a part,
>   One with us thou art now.

Into the thick darkness our Mediator went. Forth from it He came. He interprets to us the language of the Eternal, and He takes our petitions up to heaven, and translates them into the tongue of the Holy One, so that God hears us and accepts us in the Well-beloved.

I know that some of you imagine that you would believe the gospel if God were to speak to you out of the skies. Do not wish for it. The terror of His voice would overwhelm you, but it would not convert you. The Israelites were happy with a Mediator, and so will you be. If you hear not Jesus, neither would you hear though God should thunder. A Mediator is provided. Could you, with all your wit, suggest a better Mediator than Christ? I entreat you, accept the gospel in Christ, and come to God through Him. As there is no other way, so assuredly there could be no better way. If you had all wisdom and all power in your hands with which to make a way of acceptance with God, could you devise one more pleasant, more simple, more perfect, more adequate, more exactly what you need? Come, then, dear heart, come at once to God in Christ; and remember, Jesus says, "Him that cometh to me I will in no wise cast out"; "No man cometh unto the Father, but by me."

III. Now I come to my third point, upon which I would lay stress: THE MEDIATOR TEACHES US TO INTERPRET WISELY THE LORD'S DEALINGS. Moses became an interpreter of the Lord's terrible appearance to the trembling people, and he put a cheering construction upon it. You, to whom God has been speaking in a way of terror, and I know there are such here, for I have had to comfort them; you have a Mediator to explain to you the ways of the Lord. Be ready to learn the lesson which He teaches you: it is this—"Fear not: for God is come to prove you, and that his fear may be before your faces, that ye sin not." These rough dealings of God with your conscience, with your body, with your family, and with your estate, are not for your destruction, but for *your instruction*: not for your killing, but for your healing. As He came in tempest and thunder to teach the children of Israel, so has He come to you. If God is teaching you, He cannot mean to destroy you: the law does not provide a schoolmaster for a convict who is to be hanged tomorrow. The discipline in God's house, however severe it may be, is a sure proof of love. We educate sons, and not enemies. The Lord is teaching you what you are, and what He is. If He had meant to destroy you, He would not have showed you such things as these. If a criminal must needs die, we do not put him through a rehearsal of the pains of death. No, no, there would be no use in such a course—it would be sheer cruelty; and depend upon it, the Lord will not show you His own greatness merely to make you miserable, nor reveal to you your own ruin merely to drive you to despair. He does not afflict willingly. Infinite love dictates the apparent severity with which He afflicts your conscience. You are being judged here, that you may not be judged hereafter with the ungodly; you are now made to abhor yourself, that the Lord may not abhor you in the day of the judgment of the wicked.

The Mediator here explains to trembling Israel that God had come *to test them.* We all need testing, do we not? Would you like to cross a railway bridge if it was reported to you that it had never been tested by a train? When the first Exhibition was built, I remember how they marched troops along the galleries to test them. Do you not desire to have your hope for eternity tested? The Lord draws near to us in ways which inspire our fears because He would test us. What is the result of the test? Do you not feel your own weakness? Does not this drive you to the strong for strength? You feel your own sinfulness; and you fly to the Lord Jesus for righteousness. Testing has a practically good effect in slaying self-confidence, and driving you to put your confidence where God would have it rest.

When God came to these people in cloud and storm, it was *to impress them*, to put depth into their thought and feeling. We are filled with fear at times on purpose that our religion may not be a flimsy, superficial thing. Our tendency is to slur spiritual work. We easily get to be trifling and careless. Levity in religion is an easily-besetting sin with many; but when we are made to see the plague of our heart, and the awful majesty of God, that fear of the Lord which endureth forever soon drives out the triflers from the temple. Fear plows deep, and then faith sows, and love reaps; but godly fear must lead the way. Godly fear makes prayer to be fervent prayer; it makes the hearing of the word to be quite another thing from listening to the chatter of the world's vanity. Holy awe of God makes preaching to me to be the burden of the Lord. It may be light work to your men of genius and learning; but to me it is life and death work. Often have I thought that I would rather take a whipping with a cat-o'-nine-tails than preach again. How can I answer for it at the last great day unless I am faithful? "Who is sufficient for these things?" When I have felt the dread responsibility of souls which may be lost or saved by the word they hear, the fact that God is so near has made my flesh creep, and made me wish that I had never ventured on so bold a life-work. How shall I give in an honorable account of my commission at last? Beloved, God, by such apprehensions as these, is deepening in us the work of His grace, making us more alive to our position, and better fitting us for it. It is all in love that He allows our awe of Him to darken into dread, our sense of weakness to deepen into faintness of heart.

Above all, it is explained to us that the dealings of the Lord are meant *to keep us from sin*. What does David say? "Before I was afflicted, I went astray: but now have I kept thy word." Does not Hezekiah tell us that by these things men live, and in all these things is the life of our spirit? We are so worldly, that we need our nest to be stirred to keep us on the wing. Six days we are taken up with business, mixing with those who despise heavenly things; and *we* should come to think lightly of them too, were it not that God comes to us in His dread majesty and makes us think, consider, and fear. This holy trembling drives off the shams which else would grow over us like mold on decaying matter. Our inward tempests clear the air, and keep us from stagnation and the pestilence which breeds in it. God's love will not suffer us to settle down in mere pretenses, and so glide into gross sins: He empties us from vessel to vessel, and thus discovers our evil sediment, and cleanses us from it. Many people, when they hear a sermon, say, "How did you enjoy it?" If you always *enjoy* sermons, the minister is not a good steward. He is not acting wisely who deals out nothing but sweets. God's people need that the word should at times be medicine to them, and we do not enjoy medicine. The word is as fire, and the iron does not like the fire; yet it is needful to its melting. It is as a hammer, and the rock does not love the hammer; yet it is needful to its breaking. Experiences which are painful may be therefore all the more profitable. That which makes us hate sin is a thing to be valued. I pray you, after this manner read the dispensations of God with you. When He chides He loves; when He chastens He shows fatherly affection; and when He scourges He receives into peculiar familiarity. Do not therefore run away from a chastening God. If fear drives thee away, let faith draw thee near. He means thy highest good. Never doubt it. Steadfastly believe that His heart loves even if His face frowns.

IV. I close by asking you to PRACTICE THIS ART OF SACRED INTERPRETATION. Whensoever thy Lord speaketh with thee in thunder and writeth bitter things against thee, by faith read between the lines, and after the example of Moses, the mediator, put a comfortable construction upon rough words.

Faith sees many reasons for refusing to read as fear would suggest: here is one of them. When the Lord spoke to these people with the voice of trumpet and thunder, He did not speak in anger after all, but in love; for His first words set the keynote. Here they are: "I am the Lord thy God, which have brought thee out of the land of Egypt, out of the house of bondage." What gracious words! What happy memories they arouse! What lovingkindnesses they record! It is true that your Lord has taken your wife or your child away, or has made you sick, or has tried your soul by the hidings of His face; but it is not an enemy who has done this. It is your God who has done it, even the same God that delivered you from the power of sin, and made you free in Christ

Jesus. The Lord of love has chastened you, and chastened you in love. Learn Job's philosophy, and say from your heart, "The Lord gave, and the Lord hath taken away; blessed be the name of the Lord." Think of His former lovingkindness. Consider what He has done for you through the Lord Jesus and His death on your behalf. He brought you out of the bondage of your natural depravity, and He set you free from the Pharaoh of your evil passions. He has washed you from your sins, and brought you through the Red Sea of your fears by His own right hand. Can you not believe that He means well to you? What if He does speak roughly; may He not do so without being distrusted? He is the same God: He changeth not, and therefore you are not consumed: can you not rely on His faithful love? Will you take good from His hand, and will you not also take evil? He who humbles us is our covenant God, bound to us by His promise and His oath. He gave His Son to redeem us, He cannot now do us a displeasure: let Him do as seemeth Him good. We give Him *carte blanche* to do what He wills, for His love is beyond dispute. He died that I might live, and now it is impossible for Him to mean anything other than good towards me. I sometimes think that if I never had a gleam of love from His face again, I would live on that one text: "God so loved the world, that He gave His only begotten Son, that whosoever believeth in Him should not perish, but have everlasting life." Salvation from sin and death and hell should make us interpret every trying revelation, and every afflicting providence, and every painful experience, by the key of His ancient love; and so interpreted, every sorrowful line is sweetened.

Notice next, dear friends, in your process of interpretation, that God cannot mean to destroy us, since this would be contrary to His word. He hath said, "He that believeth in him hath everlasting life." Can "everlasting life" be destroyed or die? How, then, could it be "everlasting life"? Can God declare it everlasting, and yet end it? Yes, He has given us everlasting life in His dear Son; and, what is more, He has laid up that life in Christ; for "your life is hid with Christ in God." Can He destroy the life which He has hid in His own immortal Son? Does not Jesus say, "Because I live ye shall live also?" What are you afraid of, then? God cannot destroy you. He has said, "I will never leave thee, nor forsake thee." What if He speaks severely to thee, it is that He may deliver thee from sinning. Wilt thou not bless Him? He will not curse thee, for He hath blessed thee in His Son, and "there is therefore now no condemnation to them which are in Christ Jesus." Bow thyself, and take from thy Father's hand whatever He appoints.

Remember, that you are not, after all, in the same condition as Israel at the foot of Horeb. Though I have drawn a sort of parallel this morning, yet there remains a wonderful difference. "Ye are not come unto the mount that burned with fire, nor unto blackness, and darkness, and tempest." Ye are not come to a terrible voice which mortal ears could not endure. "But ye are come unto mount Zion, and unto the city of the living God, the heavenly Jerusalem, and to an innumerable company of angels. And to Jesus the Mediator of the new covenant, and to the blood of sprinkling, that speaketh better things than that of Abel." You are come to the land of pardon, peace, and promise: you are in the home of life, love and liberty. You have come to the Lord of adoption, acceptance and glory. Wherefore, do not, I pray you, construe the acts and dealings of God with your soul after the mean and slavish manner which unbelief suggests to you, but believe your God in the teeth of all you hear, or see, or feel. The Lord hath come to prove thee, to put His fear before thy face, and to keep thee from sin; wherefore look for sweet fruit from the bitter tree of thy present grief, and flee not from thy God.

Again, dear friend, here is our great comfort: *we have a Mediator.* When God dealeth with thee by the law, or by His rod, or by His searching Spirit, thou art apt to say, "How can I endure His hand?" Hide behind the Mediator. Let Jesus be thy shield, even as He is the Lord's Anointed. Beseech the Lord God not to look on thee as thou art in thyself, but to see thee in Christ Jesus. Say

> Him, and then the sinner see,
> Look through Jesus' wounds on me.

Take care that thou lookest through Jesus' wounds on God; and if thou dost, thou wilt see in Him infinite love and boundless kindness. The glory of God in the face of Jesus Christ is unutterable love. "Like as a father pitieth his children, so the Lord pitieth them that fear him"; and when they fear Him most, His pity goes out to them in streams of tenderness. If thy God use the knife on thee, it is to cut out a deadly cancer. If thy God break thee, and grind thee, it is to get away thy bran, and make thee as the fine flour of the meat-offering. He may seem to slay thee, but by this He makes thee live. Though He slay thee, still trust thou in Him. Never believe anything which would militate against the truth of His love, or the wisdom or the tenderness of it. Cling to Him when He frowns. The closer thou canst cling the less thou wilt feel the blows of His hand when He chastens. A faith which believes when it smarts will soon have done with the rod. If thou wilt have nothing but good to say of God, He will take thee out of the fire, for it is evident that thou dost not need more of it. A full and firm belief in God when He seems to be against us, is a grand mark of sanctification. To be able to spell out "love" when it is written in cruciform characters, shows a high state of spiritual education.

And now, beloved, if you can take the Lord in this way, henceforth and forever believing in His love, and never staggering through unbelief, thou wilt glorify thy God and get good to thyself in every way. If thou believest, then thou wilt be strong; for faith is the backbone of the spiritual man. If thou believest, thou wilt love, and love is the very heart of the spiritual man. Believing and loving, thou wilt endure with patience, and thy patience shall be a crown to thee. Believing, loving, and enduring, thou shalt become equipped for every holy service, and in that service thou shalt acquire more and more of likeness to thy Lord, till when thou hast endured to the full, thou shalt be in all points a brother of Him who is the Firstborn. Like Him, thou shalt be able to go into the thick darkness, and have that communion with God which only they can know who have felt the consuming fire passing through them again and again, and burning up that corruption of the flesh which makes God to be a terror to men. Like our Mediator, may we be made to plead with God for men, and with men for God. May we go up into the mount and see God and eat and drink; and then come down with faces shining with the heavenly light. God give us thus to have a Mediator, to interpret our God through a Mediator, and then to grow like our Mediator by the work of his own Spirit.

I have said a great deal that must be very terrible to ungodly men, since it even tries the holiest. O my hearers, if you are unconverted, I do not suppose that the terrors of the Lord, even though they make you fear, will work any lasting good in you; for I remember that those very people who trembled at Sinai were found, in a very few weeks, madly dancing before a golden calf, and saying, "These be thy gods, O Israel, that brought thee up out of Egypt." Fear alone will work no saving or sanctifying effect on the heart. It plows, but it does not sow. In the child of God, mixed with faith, fear becomes a holy tonic, a salutary medicine; but, as for you who have cause for fear, there is something else for you. Flee to the Mediator, trust in Christ Jesus, who stands between man and God, look unto Him at once, and looking you shall live. To our adorable Mediator be glory forever and ever. Amen, and Amen.

THE HIGH PRIEST STANDING BETWEEN THE DEAD AND THE LIVING

SERMON NOS. 341, 342
DELIVERED ON LORD'S DAY MORNING, OCTOBER 21, 1860
AT EXETER HALL, STRAND.

And Aaron took as Moses commanded, and ran into the midst of the congregation; and behold, the plague was begun among the people: and he put on incense, and made an atonement for the people. And he stood between the dead and the living; and the plague was stayed—Numbers 16:47, 48.

WE have attentively read the passage which contains the account of this transaction. The authority of Moses and Aaron had been disputed by an ambitious man belonging to an elder branch of the family of Levi, who had craftily joined with himself certain factious spirits of the tribe of Reuben, who themselves also sought to attain to power by their supposed rights through Reuben the first-born. By a singular judgment from heaven, God had proved that rebellion against Moses was a mortal sin. He had bidden the earth open its mouth and swallow up all the traitors, and both Levites and Reubenites had disappeared, covered in a living grave. One would have imagined that from this time the murmurings of the children of Israel would have ceased, or that at least even should they have daring enough to gather in little mutinous knots, yet their traitorous spirit never would have come to so great a height as to develop itself in the whole body openly before the Lord's tabernacle. Yet so was it. On the very morrow after that solemn transaction, the whole of the people of Israel gathered themselves together, and with unholy clamors surrounded Moses and Aaron, charging them with having put to death the people of the Lord. Doubtless they hinged this accusation upon the fact, that whenever Moses prayed God heard him; then would they say, "Had he prayed upon this occasion the people would not have been destroyed; the earth would not have opened her mouth, and they would not have been swallowed up." They would thus attempt to prove the charge which they brought against these two great men of God. Can you picture the scene now in your mind's eye. There is the infuriated mass of people; the spectacle of such a crowd as I see before me in this hall is overpowering, and were all this multitude in tumult against two men, the two might have sufficient cause for trembling; but this would be but as a grain of sand compared with that inconceivable number who were then gathered. A large part of those three millions would come up in one vast tumultuous host; whatever was proposed by any leader of the mob would no doubt have instantly been carried into effect, and had it not been for the awful majesty which surrounded the person of Moses, no doubt they would have torn him to pieces on the spot. But just as they are rushing up like the waves of the sea, the cloudy pillar which hung above the tabernacle descends, and envelopes in its fold, as with a protecting baptism, the whole of the sacred place. Then in the center of this cloud there blazed out that marvelous light called the Shekinah, which was the indication of the presence of Him who cannot be seen, but whose glory may be manifest. The people stand back a little; Moses and Aaron fall upon their faces in prayer; they beg of God that He would spare the people, for they have heard a voice coming out of the excellent glory, saying, "Get thee up from this people, that I may destroy them in a moment." This time God's blow goes forth with His word, for the destroying angel begins to mow down the outer ranks of the vast tumultuous host, there they fall one upon another; Moses with his undimmed vision, looking over the heads of the people, can see them begin to fall beneath the scythe of death. "Up," saith he, "up Aaron, up, and take with thee thy censer; snatch fire from off the holy altar, and run among the people, for the plague has begun." Aaron, a man of a hundred years of age, fills his censer, runs along as if he were a youth, and begins to swing it towards heaven with holy energy, feeling that in his hand was the life of the people; and when the incense is accepted in heaven, death stops in his work. On this side are heaps upon heaps of corpses slain by God's avenging angel; and there stand the crowd of living people, living only because of Aaron's intercession; living simply because he had waved that censer and burned that incense for them; otherwise, had the angel smitten them all, they would all have lain together as the leaves of the forest lie in autumn—dead and sear.

I think you can now in your imaginations picture the scene. I desire to use the picture before us as a great spiritual type of what the Lord Jesus Christ has done for that erring multitude of the sons of men, who "like sheep have gone astray, and have turned every one to his own way." We shall look at Aaron this morning in a five-fold character. The whole scene is typical of Christ; and Aaron, as he appears before us in each character is a most magnificent picture of the Lord Jesus.

I. First, let us look at Aaron as the LOVER of the people. You know who it is to whom *we* give that name of "Lover of my Soul." You will be able to see in Aaron the lover of Israel; in Jesus the lover of His people.

Aaron deserves to be very highly praised for his patriotic affection for a people who were the most rebellious and stiffnecked that ever grieved the heart of a good man. You must remember that in this case *he* was the aggrieved party. The clamor was made against Moses and against Aaron, yet it was Moses and Aaron who interceded and saved the people. They were the offended ones, yet were they the saving ones. Aaron had a special part in the matter, for no doubt the conflict of Korah especially was rather against the priesthood, which belonged exclusively to Aaron, than against the prophetical dispensation which God had granted to Moses. Aaron must have felt when he saw Korah there and the two hundred and fifty men, all of them with their censers, that the plot was against *him*; that they wished to strip from him his miter, to take from him his embroidered vest, and the glittering stones that shone upon his breast; that they wished to reduce him to the position of a common Levite, and take to themselves his office and his dignity. Yet, forgetting himself, he doth not say, "Let them die; I will wait awhile till they have been sufficiently smitten." But the old man with generous love hastened into the midst of the people, though he was himself the aggrieved person. Is not this the very picture of our sweet Lord Jesus? Had not sin dishonored Him? Was He not the Eternal God, and did not sin therefore conspire against Him as well as against the Eternal Father and the Holy Spirit? Was He not, I say, the One against whom the nations of the earth stood up and said, "Let us break his bands asunder, and cast his cords from us." Yet He, our Jesus, laying aside all thought of avenging Himself, becomes the Savior of His people.

> Down from the shining seats above,
> *With joyful haste he fled*;
> Entered the grave in mortal flesh,
> And dwelt among the dead.

Oh! generous Christ, forgetting the offenses which we have committed against Thee, and making atonement by thine own blood for sins which were perpetrated against thine own glory!

Well, you note again, that Aaron in thus coming forward as the deliverer and lover of his people, must have remembered that he was abhorred by this very people. They were seeking his blood; they were desiring to put him and Moses to death, and yet all thoughtless of danger, he snatches up his censer and runs into their midst with a divine enthusiasm in his heart. He might have stood back, and said, "No, they will slay me if I go into their ranks; furious as they are, they will charge this new death upon me and lay me low." But he never considers it. Into the midst of their crowd he boldly springs. Most blessed Jesus, Thou mightest not only think thus, but indeed Thou didst feel it to be true. Thou didst come unto thine own, and thine own received Thee not. Thou didst come into the world to save a race that hated Thee, and oh, how they proved their hatred to Thee, for they did spit upon thy cheeks; they did cast calumny and slander upon thy person; they did take the Heir, and said, "Come, let us kill him that the inheritance may be ours." Jesus Thou wast willing to die a martyr, that Thou mightest be made a sacrifice for those by whom thy blood was spilt. Jesus transcends Aaron; Aaron might have feared death at the hands of the people; Jesus Christ did actually meet it, and yet there he stood even in the hour of death, waving his censer, staying the plague, and dividing the living from the dead.

Again, you will see the love and kindness of Aaron, if you look again; Aaron might have said, "But *the Lord* will surely destroy *me* also with the people; if I go where the shafts of death are flying they will reach me." He never thinks of it; he exposes his own person in the very forefront of the destroying one. There comes the angel of death, smiting all before him, and here stands Aaron in his very path, as much as to say, "Get thee back! get thee back! I will wave my incense in thy face; destroyer of men, thou canst not pass the censer of God's high priest." Oh thou glorious High Priest of our profession, thou mightest not only had feared this which Aaron might have dreaded, but thou did actually endure the plague of God; for when thou didst come among the people to save them from Jehovah's wrath, Jehovah's wrath fell upon thee. Thou was forsaken of thy Father. The plague which Jesus kept from us slew Him, "The Lord hath laid on him the iniquity of us all." The sheep escaped, but "His life and blood the Shepherd pays, a ransom for the flock."

Oh, Thou lover of thy church, immortal honors be unto Thee! Aaron deserves to be beloved by the tribes of Israel, because he stood in the gap and exposed himself for their sins; but Thou, most mighty Savior, Thou shalt have eternal songs, because, forgetful of Thyself, Thou didst bleed and die, that man might be saved!

I would again for one moment, draw your attention to that other thought which I have already hinted at, namely, that Aaron as a lover of the people of Israel deserves much commendation, from the fact that it is expressly said, he *ran* into the host. I am not just now sure about Aaron's age, but being older than Moses, who must have been at this time about 90 years of age, Aaron must have been more than a hundred, and probably, a hundred and twenty, or more. It is no little thing to say that such a man, clad no doubt in his priestly robes, ran, and that for a people who had never shown any activity to do him service, but much zeal in opposing his authority. That little fact of his running is highly significant, for it shows the greatness and swiftness of the divine impulse of love that was within. Ah! and was it not so with Christ? Did He not haste to be our Savior? Were not His delights with the sons of men? Did He not often say, "I have a baptism to be baptized with, and how am I straitened till it be accomplished." His dying for us was not a thing which He dreaded. "With desire have I desired to eat this passover." He had panted for the moment when He should redeem His people. He had looked forward through eternity for that hour when He should glorify His Father and His Father might glorify Him. He came voluntarily, bound by no constraint, except His own covenant engagements; and He cheerfully and joyfully laid down His life—a life which no man could take from Him, but which He laid down of Himself. While I look with admiration upon Aaron, I must look with adoration upon Christ. While I write Aaron down as the lover of his race, I write down Jesus Christ as being the best of lovers—the friend that sticketh closer than a brother.

II. But I now pass on to take a second view of Aaron as he stands in another character. Let us now view Aaron as THE GREAT PROPITIATOR.

Wrath had gone out from God against the people on account of their sin, and it is God's law that His wrath shall never stay unless a propitiation be offered. The incense which Aaron carried in his hand *was* the propitiation before God, from the fact that God saw in that perfume the type of that richer offering which our Great High Priest is this very day offering before the throne.

Aaron as the propitiator, is to be looked at first as bearing in his censer that which was necessary for the propitiation. He did not come empty-handed. Even though God's high priest; he must take the censer; he must fill it with the ordained incense, made with the ordained materials; and then he must light it with the sacred fire from off the altar, and with that alone. With the censer in his hand he is safe, without it Aaron might have died as well as the rest of the people. The qualification of Aaron partly lay in the fact that he had the censer, and that that censer was full of sweet odors which were acceptable to God. Behold, then, Christ Jesus as the propitiator for His people. He stands this day before God with His censer smoking up towards heaven. Behold the Great High Priest! See Him this day with His pierced hands, and head that once was crowned with thorns. Mark how the marvelous smoke of His merits goeth up forever and ever before the eternal throne. 'Tis he, 'tis he alone who puts away the sins of His people. His incense, as we know, consists first of all of His positive obedience to the divine law. He kept His Father's commands; He did everything that man should have done; He kept to the full the whole law of God, and made it honorable. Then mixed with this is His blood—an equally rich and precious ingredient. That bloody sweat—the blood from His head, pierced with the crown of thorns; the blood of His hands as they were nailed to the tree; the blood of His feet as they were fixed to the wood; and the blood of His very heart—richest of them all— all mixed together with His merits—these make up the incense—an incense incomparable—an incense peerless and surpassing all others. Not all the odors that ever rose from tabernacle or temple could for a moment stand in rivalry with these. The blood alone speaketh better things than that of Abel, and if Abel's blood prevailed to bring vengeance, how much more shall the blood of Christ prevail to bring down pardon and mercy! Our faith is fixed on perfect righteousness and complete atonement, which are as sweet frankincense before the Father's face.

Besides that, it was not enough for Aaron to have the proper incense. Korah might have that too, and he might have the censer also. That would not suffice— he must be the ordained priest; for mark, two hundred and fifty men fell in doing the act which Aaron did. Aaron's act saved others; their act destroyed themselves. So Jesus, the propitiator, is to be looked upon as the ordained One—called of God as was Aaron. Settled in eternity as being the predestinated propitiation for sin, He came into the world as an ordained priest of God; receiving His ordination not from man, neither by man; but like Melchizedek, the priest of the Most High God, without father, without mother, without descent, having neither beginning of days nor end of life, He is a priest forever after the order of Melchizedek. Stand back, sons of Korah, all of you who call yourselves priests. I can scarce imagine that any man in this world who takes to himself the title of a priest, except he take it in the sense in which all God's people are priests—I cannot imagine that a priest can enter heaven. I would not say a thing too stern or too severe; but I do most thoroughly believe that an assumption of the office of priest is so base an usurpation of the priestly office of Christ, that I could as well conceive of a man being saved who called himself *God*, as conceive of a man being saved who called himself a priest; if he really means what he says, he has so trenched upon the priestly prerogative of Christ, that it seems to me he has touched the very crown jewels, and is guilty of a blasphemy, which, unless it be repented of, shall surely bring damnation on his head. Shake your garments, ye ministers of Christ, from all priestly assumption; come out from among them; touch not the unclean thing. There are no priests now specially to minister among men. Jesus Christ, and He only is the priest of His Church, and He hath made all of us priests and kings unto our God, and we shall reign forever and ever. If I should have any person here so weak as to depend for his salvation upon the offerings of another man, I conjure him to forego his deception. I care not who your priest may be. He may belong to the Anglican or to the Romish church. Aye, and to any church under heaven. If he claimeth to be anything of a priest more than you can claim yourself—away with him—he imposes upon you; he speaks to you that which God abhors, and that which the Church of Christ should abhor and would detest, were she truly alive to her Master's glory. None but Jesus, none but Jesus; all other priests and offerings we disdain. Cast dirt upon their garments, they are not and they cannot be priests; they usurp the special dignity of Jesus.

But let us note once more in considering Aaron as the great propitiator, that we must look upon him as being ready for his work. He was ready with his incense, and ran to the work at the moment the plague broke out. We do not find that he had need to go and put on his priestly garments; we do not find that he had to prepare for performing the propitiatory work; but he went there and then as soon as the plague broke out. The people were ready to perish and he was ready to save. Oh, my hearer, listen to this, Jesus Christ stands ready to save thee now; there is not need of preparation; He hath slain the victim; He hath offered the sacrifice; He hath filled the censer; He hath put to it the glowing coals. His breastplate is on His breast; His miter is on His head; He is ready to save thee now. Trust Him, and thou shalt not find need for delay. Rely upon Him, and thou shalt not find that He hath to go a day's journey to save thee; "He is able to save unto the uttermost them that come unto God by Him, seeing He ever liveth to make intercession for them." Ye who know not Christ, hear this! Ye are lost and ruined by the fall. Wrath is gone out from God against you. That wrath must consume you to the lowest hell, unless someone can propitiate God on your behalf. You cannot do it. No man can do it; no prayers of yours; no sacraments, nay, though you could sweat a bloody sweat, it would not avail; but Christ is able to make propitiation. He can do it, and He alone; He can stand between you and God, and turn away Jehovah's wrath, and he can put into your heart a sense of His love. Oh, I pray you, trust Him, trust Him. You may not be ready for

Him, but He is always ready to save, and indeed I must correct myself in that last sentence, *you are* ready for him. If you be never so vile, and never so ruined by your sin, their needs no preparation and no readiness. It was not the merit of the people that saved them, nor any preparation on their part; it was the preparedness of the high priest that saved them. *He* is prepared. He stands on the behalf of those who believe on Him. Would that thou wouldst now believe on Him and trust thy soul in His hands; and oh, believe me, thy sins which are many shall be all forgiven; the plague shall be stayed, nor shall God's wrath go out against thee, but thou shalt be saved.

III. Let me now view Aaron as THE INTERPOSER.

Let me explain what I mean. As the old Westminster Annotations say upon this passage, "The plague was moving among the people as the fire moveth along a field of corn." There it came; it began in the extremity; the faces of men grew pale, and swiftly on, on it came, and in vast heaps they fell till some 14,000 had been destroyed. Aaron wisely puts himself just in the pathway of the plague. It came on, cutting down all before it, and there stood Aaron the interposer with arms outstretched and censer swinging towards heaven, interposing himself between the darts of death and the people. "If there be darts that must fly," he seemed to say, "let them pierce me; or let the incense shield both me and the people. Death," saith he, "art thou coming on thy pale horse? I arrest thee, I throw back thy steed upon his haunches. Art thou coming, thou skeleton king? With my censer in my hand I stand before thee; thou must march over my body; thou must empty my censer; thou must destroy God's High Priest, ere thou canst destroy this people." Just so was it with Christ. Wrath had gone out against us. The law was about to smite us; the whole human race must be destroyed. Christ stands in the forefront of the battle. "The stripes must fall on me," he cries; "the arrows shall find a target in my breast. On me, Jehovah, let thy vengeance fall." And he receives that vengeance, and afterwards upspringing from the grave he waves the censer full of the merit of His blood, and bids this wrath and fury stand back. On which side are you today, sinner? Is God angry with thee, sinner? Are thy sins unforgiven? Say, art thou unpardoned? Art thou abiding still an heir of wrath and an inheritor of death? Ah! then would that thou wert on the other side of Christ. If thou doest believe on Christ, then let me ask thee, dost thou know that thou art completely saved? No wrath can ever reach thee, no spiritual death can ever destroy thee, no hell can ever consume thee, and why? What is thy guard, what thy protection? I see the tear glistening in thine eye as thou sayest, "There is nothing between me and hell save Christ? There is nothing between me and Jehovah's wrath save Christ? There is nothing between me and instant destruction save Christ? But He is enough. He with the censer in His hand—God's great ordained Priest—He is enough." Ah, brothers and sisters, if you have put between you and God, baptisms and communions, fastings, prayers, tears and vows, Jehovah shall break through your refuges as the fire devours the stubble. But if, my soul, Christ stands between thee and Jehovah, Jehovah cannot smite thee; His thunderbolt must first pierce through the Divine Redeemer before it can reach thee, and that can never be.

My dear hearers, do you perceive this great truth, that there is nothing which can save the soul of man, save Jesus Christ standing between that soul and the just judgment of God? And oh, I put again the personal inquiry to you, are you sheltered behind Christ? Sinner, are you standing today beneath the cross? Is that thy shelter? Is the purple robe of Jesus' atonement covered over you?

Are you like the dove which hides in the clefts of the rock? Have you hidden in the wounds of Christ? Say, have you crept into His side, and do you feel that He must be your shelter till the tempest be overpast? Oh, be of good cheer; he for whom Christ is the intercessor, is a rescued man. Oh, soul, if thou art not in Christ, what wilt thou do when the destroying angel comes? Careless sinner, what will become of thee when death arrests thee? Where wilt thou be when the judgment trumpet rings in thine ears, and sounds an alarm that shall wake the dead? Sleepy sinner, sleeping today under God's Word, will you sleep then, when Jehovah's thunders are let loose, and all His lightnings set the heavens in a blaze? I know where then you shall seek a shelter! You shall seek it where you cannot find it; you shall bid the rocks fall upon you, and ask the mountains to hide you, but their stony bowels shall know of no compassion, their hearts of adamant shall yield you no pity, and you shall stand exposed to the blast of vengeance and the shower of the hot hail of God's fury, and nothing shall protect you; but as Sodom and Gomorrah were destroyed from off the face of the earth, so must you be destroyed, and that forever and ever, because ye believed not on Jesus Christ, the Son of God.

IV. But we cannot tarry longer here; we must again pass to another point. We have viewed Aaron in three characters—as the lover, the propitiator, and the intercessor; now fourthly, let me view him as THE SAVIOR.

It was Aaron, Aaron's censer, that saved the lives of that great multitude. If he had not prayed the plague had not stayed, and the Lord would have consumed the whole company in a moment. As it was, you perceive there were some fourteen thousand and seven hundred that died before the Lord. The plague had begun its dreadful work, and only Aaron could stay it. And now I want you to notice with regard to Aaron, that Aaron, and especially the Lord Jesus, must be looked upon as a gracious Savior. It was nothing but love that moved Aaron to wave his censer. The people could not demand it of him. Had they not brought a false accusation against him? And yet he saves them. It must have been love and nothing but love. Say, was there anything in the voices of that infuriated multitude which could have moved Aaron to stay the plague from before them? Nothing! nothing in their character! nothing in their looks! nothing in their treatment of God's High Priest! and yet he graciously stands in the breach, and saves them from the devouring judgment of God! Oh! brothers and sisters—if Christ hath saved us He is a gracious Savior indeed. Often as we think of the fact that we are saved, the tear falls down our cheek; for we never can tell why Jesus hath saved *us*.

What was there in you that could merit esteem?
Or give the Creator delight?
'Twas "Even so, Father!" you ever must sing
"Because it seem'd good in thy sight."

There is no difference between the glorified in heaven and the doomed in hell, except the difference that God made of His own sovereign grace. Whatever difference there may be between Saul the apostle and Elymas the sorcerer, has been made by infinite sovereignty and undeserved love. Paul might still have remained Saul of Tarsus, and might have become a damned fiend in the bottomless pit, had it not been for free sovereign grace, which came out to snatch him as a brand from the burning. Oh, sinner, thou sayest "There is no reason in me why God should save me"; but there is no reason in any man. Thou hast no good point, nor hath any man. There is nothing in any man to commend him to God. We are all such sinners, that hell is our deserved portion; and if any of us be saved from going down into the pit, it is God's undeserved sovereign bounty that doth it, and not any merits of ours. Jesus Christ is a most gracious Savior.

And then again, Aaron was an unaided Savior. Even Moses did not come with Aaron to help him. He stood alone in the gap with that censer—that one solitary stream of smoke dividing between the living and the dead. Why did not the princes of Israel come with him? Alas! they could have done nothing; they must have died themselves. Why did not all the Levites come with him? They must have been smitten if they had dared to stand in the place of God's High Priest. He stands alone, alone, alone! and herein was he a great type of Christ, who could say, "I have trodden the winepress alone, and of the people there was none with me." Do not think, then, that when Christ prevails with God, it is because of any of your prayers, or tears, or good works. He never puts your tears and prayers into His censer. They would mar the incense. There is nothing but His own prayers, and His own tears, and His own merits there. Do not think that you are saved because of anything that you have ever done or can ever do for Christ. We may preach, and we may be made in God's hand the spiritual fathers of thousands of souls, but our preaching doth in no way help to turn away the wrath of God from us. Christ doth it all, entirely and alone, and no man must dare to stand as His helper. Sinner, dost thou hear this; thou art saying, "I cannot do this or that." He asks thee not to do anything; thou sayest, "I have no merits." Man, He does not want any, if thou wouldst help Christ thou wilt be lost, but if thou wilt leave Christ to do it all, thou shalt be saved. Come now, the very plan of salvation is this, to take Christ to be thine all in all; He will never be a part-Savior; He never came to patch our ragged garments; He will give us a new robe, but He will never mend the old one. He did not come to *help* build the palace of God, He will quarry every stone and lay it on its fellow; He will have no sound of hammer, or any mortal help in that great work. Oh that this voice could ring through the world while I proclaim again those words, the deathblow of all Popery, legality, and carnal merit, "Jesus only, Jesus only." "There is none other name under heaven given among men, whereby we must be saved." Nor doth He need a helper; "He came not to call the righteous but sinners to repentance." "He is able to save unto the uttermost them that come unto God by him."

He was, then, you will perceive, a gracious Savior, and an unaided one; and, once more, Aaron as a Savior was all-sufficient. Death came up to the very feet of Aaron; there lay a dead man, there lay a mother, a child, a prince, a hewer of wood, a drawer of water—there they lay. There stood a strong man in his agony, and implored that he might not die, but he fell backward a corpse. There stood up a prince of Israel and must he die? Yes, he must fall. All-devouring death, like a hungry lion, came howling onward, amidst the screams and shrieks of the people, but there he stood; that censer seemed to say, "Hitherto shalt thou come, but no further." What a miracle that the censer should stop the reign of death. Up to this mark the waves of that shoreless sea are flowing; *there* men stand on the *terra firma* of life. Aaron stands, and as God's High Priest with that censer alone, he puts back grim death; the whole host of Israel, if they had been armed and had carried bows, could not have driven back the pestilence; nay, all the hosts of armed men that ever stained the earth with blood could not have driven back God's plagues. Death would have laughed at them, yea, he would have trodden in among their ranks and cut them in pieces, but Aaron alone is enough, fully sufficient, and that through the burning of the incense. Oh sinner, Christ is an all-sufficient Savior, *able* to save; you cannot save yourself, but He *can* save you. Oh sinner, all sin and blasphemy shall be forgiven unto men; it mattereth not how base and vile you may have been, "Believe in the Lord Jesus Christ and thou shalt be saved." Though the remembrance of thy sin bring scarlet into thy face; dost thou blush to think what a wretch thou hast been, has thy life been foul adultery, has it been blasphemy, lying, hatred of God's people, and what not—I add to this another, if thou wilt—or lasciviousness, debauchery, murder—if all these crimes were there, the blood of Jesus Christ, God's Son, would be able still to cleanse thee from all sin. Though thou had committed every crime in the catalogue of iniquity, sins which we cannot mention, yet "Though thy sins be as scarlet, they shall be as wool; though they be red like crimson, they shall be as white as snow." And thou sayest, "How can I partake of this?" Simply by trusting Christ with thy soul. "He that believeth on the Lord Jesus Christ shall be saved, he that believeth not shall be damned." This was Christ's commission to the apostles, He bid them go forth and preach this great truth, and again I proclaim it, "He that believeth and is baptized shall be saved, but he that believeth not must be damned." He that believeth not shall be damned, be his sins never so few, he that believeth shall never be lost, though his sins may have been never so many. Trust thou thy soul with Christ, and thy sins are at once forgiven, at once blotted out.

V. And now I come to my last point, and that is, Aaron as THE DIVIDER—the picture of Christ.

Aaron the anointed one stands here; on that side is death, on this side life; the boundary between life and death is that one man. Where his incense smokes the air is purified, where it smokes not the plague reigns with unmitigated fury. There are two sorts of people here this morning, we forget the distinction of rich and poor, we know it not here; there are two sorts of people, we forego the distinction of the learned and unlearned, we care not for that here; there are two sorts here, and these are the living and the dead, the pardoned, the unpardoned, the saved, and the lost. What divides the true Christian from the unbeliever? Some think it is that the Christian takes the Sacrament, the other not. It is no division; there be men who have gone to hell with sacramental bread in their mouths; others may imagine that Baptism makes the difference, and indeed it is the outward token, the baptismal pool is the means by which we show to the world that we are buried in Christ's grave, in type that we are dead to the world and buried in Christ; we rise up from it in testimony that we desire to live in newness of life by the resurrection of Jesus Christ from the dead. He who is baptized does in that way cross the Rubicon, he draws the sword and throws away the scabbard, he is the baptized one, and has a sign that can never be eradicated from him. He is dedicated through that baptism to Christ, but it is but an outward sign, for many have there been who have been baptized with water, who not having the baptism of the Holy Ghost, have afterwards been baptized in the fiery sufferings of eternal torment. No! no! the one division, the one great division between those who are God's people and those who are not, is *Christ*. A man in Christ is a Christian: a man out of Christ is dead in trespasses and sins. "He that believeth on the Lord Jesus Christ is saved, he that believeth not is lost." Christ is the only divider between His people and the world. On which side, then, art thou today, my hearer? Come, let the question go individually to you. Young man, on which side are you? Are you Christ's friend and servant, or are you his enemy? Old man, thou with the gray head, yonder, thou hast but a little while to live, on which side art thou? Art thou my Master's blood-bought one, or art thou still a lost sheep? And thou matron, thou who are busied, perhaps, even now in thy thoughts upon thy children, think not of them for a moment, on which side art thou? Hast thou believed, hast thou been born again, or art thou still in the gall of bitterness and the bonds of iniquity? Ye that stand yonder, let the question penetrate your thick rank now, where are you? Can you take the name of Christ upon your lips, and say, "Jesus, I am thine, and Thou art mine, thy blood and righteousness are my hope and trust"; for if not, my hearer, thou art among the spiritually dead, and thou shalt soon be among the damned unless divine grace prevent, and change, and renew thee.

Please remember, brothers and sisters, that as Christ is the great divider now, so will He be in the day of judgment. Do you never think of that, *He* shall divide them the one from the other, as the shepherd divideth the sheep from the goats. It is the Shepherd's person that divideth the sheep from the goats. He stands between them, and in that last day of days for which all other days were made, Christ shall be the great divider. There the righteous clad in white, in songs triumphant glorified with Him; and there the lost, the unbelieving, the fearful, the abominable. What divides them from you bright host? Nothing but the person of the Son of Man, on whom they look, and weep, and mourn, and wail because of Him. That is the impenetrable barrier that shall shut out the damned from eternal bliss. The gate which may let you in now will be the fiery gate which shall shut you out hereafter. Christ is the door of heaven; oh, dreadful day when that door shall be shut, when that door shall stand before you, and prevent you entering into the felicity which you shall then long for, when you cannot enter it.

Oh! on which side shall I be, when all these transitory things are done away with, when the dead have risen from their graves, when the great congregation shall stand upon the land, and upon the sea, when every valley, and every mountain, and every river, and every sea, shall be crowded with multitudes standing in thick array! Oh! when He shall say, "Separate my people, thrust in the sickle, for the harvest of the world is ripe"; my soul, where shalt thou be? Shalt thou be found among the lost? Shall the dread trumpet send thee down to hell, while a voice that rends thine ear, shall call after thee, "Depart from me, depart from me, ye workers of iniquity into everlasting fire in hell, prepared for the devil and his angels." Oh, grant that I may not be there, but among thy people may I stand. So may it be; may we be on the right hand of the Judge to all eternity, and remember that forever and ever Christ will be the divider; He shall stand between the lost and the saved, He shall interpose forever between the damned and the glorified. Again, I put it to you, give me your ears just for one moment while I speak. What say you, sirs, shall this congregation be rent in twain? The hour is coming when our wills and wishes shall have no force. God *will* divide the righteous from the wicked then, and Christ shall be the dread division; I say, are we prepared to be separated eternally? Husband, are you prepared to renounce today your wife forever; are you prepared when the clammy sweat gathers on her brow to give her the last kiss, and say, "Adieu, adieu, I shall never meet with thee again." Child, son, daughter, are you ready to go home and sit down at the table of your mother, and before you eat, say, "Mother, I now forswear you once for all, I am determined to be lost, and as thou art on the side of Christ, and I will never love him, I will part with you forever." Surely the ties of kinship make us long to meet in another world, and do we wish to meet in hell? Do you wish all of you to meet there—a grim company to lie in the midst of the flames. Will you abide in the devouring fire, and dwell in everlasting burning? No, your wishes are that you may meet in heaven, but you cannot unless you meet in Christ, you cannot meet in Paradise unless you meet in Him. Oh that now the grace of God were poured upon you, that you might come unto Jesus.

JOSHUA'S VISION

SERMON NOS. 795, 796
DELIVERED ON LORD'S DAY MORNING, FEBRUARY 16, 1868.
PORTION OF SCRIPTURE READ BEFORE SERMON—JOSHUA 6:10–27.

And it came to pass, when Joshua was by Jericho, that he lifted up his eyes and looked, and behold, there stood a man over against him with his sword drawn in his hand: and Joshua went unto him, and said unto him, Art thou for us, or for our adversaries? and he said, Nay; but as captain of the host of the LORD am I now come. And Joshua fell on his face to the earth, and did worship, and said unto him, What saith my lord unto his servant? and the captain of the LORD's host said unto Joshua, Loose thy shoe from off thy foot; for the place whereon thou standest is holy. And Joshua did so—Joshua 5:13–15.

THE Lord divided the Jordan that His people might pass through dry-shod. This miracle greatly dispirited the Canaanites, and so prepared the way for an easy triumph for the invading Israelites. You would have naturally expected that the Lord would have bidden His people avail themselves immediately of this terror to strike a heavy blow at once, and press on with might and main before the enemy could take breath, and so sweep the land clear of the adversaries in a single campaign. But it was not so. Instead of immediate activity, the children of Israel pitched their tents at Gilgal, and there tarried for a considerable season. For God is in no hurry. His purposes can be accomplished without haste, and though He would have us redeem the time because our days are evil, yet in His eternity He can afford to wait, and by His wisdom He so orders His delays, that they prove to be far better than our hurries. Wherefore, were the people to delay? That they might be obedient to commands which had been forgotten. In the desert, for diverse reasons, circumcision and the passover had been neglected. They were not visited with any chastisement on account of this neglect, for the Lord considered their position and condition, and winked at their error, but before He would use them He would have them fully obedient to His will. It cannot be expected that God should tolerate disobedient servants, and therefore they must stay awhile, till they had been attentive to the two great precepts of the Mosaic covenant. Dear friends, let us pause and ask ourselves, as believers, whether we have been in all respects conscientiously attentive to our Master's commands? If not, we may not expect Him to send a blessing to the church or to the world through us, until first of all we have yielded our willing obedience to that which He has prescribed for us. Are any of you living in the neglect of a known part of the divine will? or are you undesirous of knowing some portions of God's will, and therefore willfully blind to them? My dear brother, you are cutting the Achilles' tendon of your strength. You can never overthrow your enemies like Samson while your locks are thus shorn. You cannot expect that God should send you forth to conquer and to bring to Him renown, when you have not as yet conquered your own personal indolence and disobedience. He that is unfaithful in that which is least will be unfaithful in that which is greater; and if you have not kept the Master's saying in the little vineyard of your personal history, how much less shall you be able to do it if He should entrust you with a greater field of service! Here then is the reason for Israel's delay, and it is a reason why at the commencement of our special services we should make diligent search for neglected duties, and promptly fulfill them.

The two precepts which had been overlooked were very suggestive. The one was *circumcision*. Every man throughout the whole camp of Israel must be circumcised before God would begin to speak about Jericho. Not a word about the walls falling flat to the ground; not a syllable concerning compassing the accursed city seven days, until, first of all, the reproach of Egypt had been put away, and His people had received the token of the covenant. Now, we are told in the New Testament that Christians must partake in a circumcision without hands, not of the flesh, but of the spirit. "He is not a Jew which is one outwardly . . . but he is a Jew which is one inwardly." In the Colossians the apostle tells us that the true circumcision is the putting away of the body of death by the circumcision of Christ, by which I understand that the Christian must purge himself, in the power of the Spirit and in the name of Christ, of every fleshly defilement, of every sinful thought, of every wrong ambition, of every carnal desire: if he is to be used by his Master it is imperative that this be done, and be done at once, in the name of the Most High. "Be ye clean that bear the vessels of the Lord." God will not fight His battles by the uncircumcised. He will have His people clean from the sin that doth so easily beset them, or else He will not use them. Stop, then, my brethren, and let me beseech you to search your own hearts, and see what there may be within that might render you unfit to be blessed. If I, as God's minister, have no conversion, I dare not attribute the fact to divine sovereignty. It may be so, but I am always afraid to make divine sovereignty the scapegoat for my iniquities. I rather think that if God withholds the blessing, there is a cause; and may not the cause be in myself, that I do not live as near to God as I should, or am indulging in something which His holy eyes cannot look upon? I speak to you who are church members, if in the Sabbath-school, if in your tract distribution, or if in any other work you are doing, you do not win souls to God, cry unto Him, "Search me, O God, and know my heart: try me, and know my thoughts: and see if there be any wicked way in me, and lead me in the way everlasting." Sin blocks up the channel of mercy; the stream is strong enough, but you restrain its flow; your sins separate between you and your God; and, therefore, I conjure each one of you, if you be the Lord's, now shake yourselves from the dust, sanctify a fast unto the Most High, and come before Him with supplication. Sit before Him in sackcloth and ashes, in the silent dejection of your abashed spirits, and confess before Him all your sins. Arise, pour out your hearts like water before the Lord, acknowledge your sins and offenses, and then, being purged from these by the water and the blood which flowed from the riven side of Jesus, you may arise to service and expect to be made a blessing.

But circumcision was not enough, they must also keep *the passover*. This it appears they had only celebrated twice, once in Egypt, and once at the foot of Sinai; but they were now to begin a passover which was to be kept every year without cessation. Brethren, ye know the meaning the passover has to us; it represents feeding upon Christ. He is the Paschal Lamb; we must put away the old leaven of sin, and we must come with pure hearts to feed upon our Lord. You will never be able to fight the Canaanites till you have fed on Christ. A spiritual man who tries to live without feeding upon Jesus, soon becomes weak; he who has but slight communion with Christ, he who day after day has no sight of the King in His beauty, who is never taken to the banqueting house, and sees not the love banner waving over his head, is not likely to be a hero. If you do not eat the bread of heaven, how can you do the work of heaven? The husbandman that laboreth must be first partaker of the fruits; and if we would labor for God with success, we must first of all feed upon the Christ of God, and gather strength from Him. "Son of man," said the voice from heaven to the prophet, "eat this roll": he must first eat it, and then speak concerning what he has handled and tasted. We must enjoy true religion in our own souls before we can be fit exponents of it to others. How shall ye be heralds of a message which has never been spoken into your inner ear by the voice of the Lord? How can you expect to bring others to life when your own soul is all but dead? How shall you scatter the live coals of eternal grace when the flame upon the hearth of your heart has almost expired? Brethren, let us keep the feast, let us draw nigh unto our Lord Jesus with pure hearts, let us renew our first faith and early love, taking the great Son of God to be once more the ground of our hope, the source of our joy, the object of our desires. Let us come near, yea, nearer and nearer still to Him, pressing to His embrace; so shall we be prepared to brave the conflict, and earn the victory.

After the ordinances had been kept, you will suppose that at once the trumpet sounded for an assault, and the valiant men of Israel with their scaling ladders, and their battering rams, gathered round the devoted city to attack and carry it by storm. Patience! patience! you are always in a hurry, but God is not. Joshua himself, that bold, brave, spirit is in some haste, and therefore, he goes forth by night, meditating and patrolling; and as he is meditating upon God, and gazing every now and then at that huge city, and wondering where would be the best point of attack, and how it would be captured, he is astonished by the appearance of a stately personage who bears a sword in his hand. Brave Joshua, unconscious of anything like fear, advances at once to the apparent interloper and demands of him, "Art thou for us, or for our adversaries?" He little guessed in what august presence he was standing until a majestic voice said, "Nay, but as captain of the host of the Lord am I now come." Then Joshua discerning the divinity of the celestial warrior bowed and worshiped and humbly inquired what he should do; and then after he had been instructed, he rose and went according to the Lord's directions to the capture of the city of palm-trees.

The children of Israel may be likened to yonder gallant vessel, prepared for a long voyage. All the cargo is on board that is needed, all the stores are there, and every man in his place. In all respects, the good ship is fully equipped, but why does she linger? Why do not the sailors weigh the anchor? If you ask the man at the helm, he will tell you, "We are waiting for the captain." A good and sufficient reason indeed, for till the captain has come on board, it is idle for the vessel to put out to sea. So here Israel had been circumcised, and the blessed feast of the paschal lamb had been celebrated, but still they must not go to the conflict until the captain himself had arrived; and here, to Joshua's joy, the angel of the presence of the Most High appeared to claim the presidency of the war, and lead forth the hosts of God to certain victory. Brethren, this is precisely the condition of this church at the present moment; we have endeavored, I think, to draw near unto God and to abide in His love; we have sought to purge ourselves from sin, and to be holy even as He is holy; but still this will not suffice, we want the divine presence, and we are now bidden to pause awhile and to seek it, prayerfully, that in its matchless power, we may go forward successfully.

I. I shall ask your earnest attention, this morning, to two or three brief rules for our present solemn engagements. *First*, REALIZE THE FACT OF THE DIVINE PRESENCE.

Jesus Himself comes to this holy war. Joshua saw a *man* clad in armor, equipped for war. Cannot the eyes of your faith see the same? There He stands, Jesus, God over all, blessed forever, yet a man. Most surely God, but with equal certainty bone of our bone, and flesh of our flesh. He is in the midst of His church; He walketh amongst the golden candlesticks. His promise is, "Lo, I am with you alway, even unto the end of the world." I do not wish to talk, but I desire rather that you should exercise your own minds, your faith, your spiritual powers, and vividly believe that Jesus is here; so believe it, that your inner eye beholds what you believe. The Son of Man is here, as surely here as He was with the disciples at the lake, when they saw coals of fire, and fish laid thereon, and bread; He is here to talk with us by His Spirit, as He did to Peter and to the rest of the disciples on that memorable day. Not carnally, but still in real truth, Jesus is where His people meet together. Joshua saw Him *with His sword in His hand.* O that Christ might come in our midst with the sword of the Spirit in His hand; come to effect deeds of love but yet deeds of power; come with His two-edged sword to smite our sins, to cut to the heart His adversaries, to slay their unbelief, to lay their iniquities dead before Him. The sword is drawn, not scabbarded, as alas! it has been so long in many churches, but made bare for present active use. It is *in His*

Hand, not in the minister's hand, not even in an angel's hand, but the sword drawn is in *His* hand. Oh, what power there is in the gospel when Jesus holds the hilt, and what gashes it makes into hearts that were hard as adamant, when Jesus cuts right and left at the hearts and consciences of men! Brethren, seek this presence, and seeking it, believe it; and when you hear the gospel preached, or when you meet together for prayer, think you see in the center of the assembly the Champion of Israel, with up-lifted sword, prepared to do great exploits, as in days of old.

The glorious man whom Joshua saw, was *on his side*. The day shall come when the ungodly shall see this man with His sword drawn; but in answer to their question, "Art thou for us, or for our adversaries?" they shall find Him to be the fiercest of their foes. In the midst of His church, Christ carries a sword only for the purposes of love to them. Oh, how blessed it will be if you can know that out of His mouth there goeth a two-edged sword, like unto a flame of fire; and if you dare to bring your heart near to that sword, that it may cut and kill in you everything obnoxious to the divine will, and then can bring your children and kinsfolk, and those that sit in these pews side by side with you, and say, "O Master, let thy sword of fire go through them according to thy word, 'I kill and make alive, I wound and I heal,' O kill, that they may live; O wound, that they may be healed."

> Thine arrows sharply pierce the heart
> Of foemen of the King;
> And under thy dominion's rule
> The people down do bring.
>
> O thou that art the mighty One,
> Thy sword gird on thy thigh,
> Ev'n with thy glory excellent,
> And with thy majesty.

The divine presence then is what we desire, and if we have it, brethren, *faith at once is encouraged*. It was enough for the army of Cromwell to know that he was there, the ever victorious, the irresistible, to lead on his Ironsides to the fray. Many a time the presence of an old Roman general was equal to another legion; as soon as the cohorts perceived that he was come whose eagle eye watched every motion of the enemy, and whose practiced hand led his battalions upon the most salient points of attack, each man's blood leaped within him, and he grasped his sword and rushed forward secure of success. My brethren, our King is in the midst of us, and our faith should be in active exercise. "The shout of a King is in the midst of us," it is said, for where the King is there the people shout for joy, and because of confidence of victory. The preacher may preach, but what is that? but if the King be there, then it is preaching in very deed. The congregations may have met, and they may have gone again. "The panoramic view which has dissolved," you say. Ah, so it may seem to you, but if the Spirit of God was there, all that has been done will abide, and remain even to that day of judgment, when the fire shall try every man's work of what sort it is. "Nothing but a simple girl sitting down to talk to a few little children about their souls." Just so, but if the Lord be there, what awe gathers round that spot! If the King Himself sit in that class, what deeds are done that shall make the angels of heaven sing anew for joy! "Nothing but a humble man, unlettered, earnest, but not eloquent, standing in the corner of a street, addressing a few hundred people. His talk will soon be forgotten." Precisely so, but if the King be there it shall never be forgotten. The footprints of every true servant of the Lord shall not be in the sand, but in the enduring brass, the record of which shall outlast the wreck of matter. When the King is with us, faith is confident, because God girds faith as with a golden girdle, and from head to foot clothes her with a panoply of armor, and puts a sword into her hand which is all destroying, and with which she cuts through coats of mail, "If God be for us, who can be against us?"

When the King is with His people, then *hope is greatly encouraged*, for saith she, "Who can stand against the Lord of Hosts?" There must be conversions; it is no longer a question of trust and expectation, but of absolute certainty when Jesus is at the preaching. My brethren, if by earnest prayer we shall really bring the King into our midst today, as I am persuaded we shall, and if we keep Him here, holding Him by our entreaties, and by our tears, which are the golden chains that bind Christ to His people, then we need not think that there shall be good done, nor hope so, but it *must* be so, it *shall* be so, for where Christ is, there is the manifestation of the omnipotence of deity, and the hardest of hearts feel the influence thereof.

Where Jesus is, *love becomes inflamed*, for oh! of all the things in the world that can set the heart burning, there is nothing like the presence of Jesus. A glimpse of Him will overcome us, so that we shall be almost ready to say, "Turn away thine eyes from me, for they have overcome me." Oh, but a smell of the aloes, and the myrrh, and the cassia which drop from His perfumed garments, but a smell of these I say, and the sick and the faint among us shall grow strong. Oh, but a moment's leaning of the head upon that gracious bosom, and a reception of His divine love into our poor cold hearts, and we shall be cold no longer, but shall glow like seraphs, being made equal to every labor, and capable of every suffering. Then shall the Spirit of the Lord be upon us, and our old men shall see visions, and our young men shall dream dreams, and upon the servants and the handmaidens will God pour out His Spirit. If we do but know that Jesus is here, every power will be developed, and every grace will be strengthened, and we shall cast ourselves into the Lord's battle with heart, and soul, and strength. There is not a single part of our inner man which will not be bettered by the presence of Christ; therefore is this to be desired above all things.

Brethren, suppose that Christ is here, this morning, *His presence will be most clearly ascertained by those who are most like Him.* Joshua was favored with this sight because he alone had eyes that could bear it. I do not read that even Caleb saw this man with his sword drawn; only Joshua saw him, because Joshua was the most spiritual and the most active. If you desire to see Christ you must grow to be like Him, and labor to serve Him with heart, and soul, and strength. Christ comes not in the visions of the night to those who toss upon the bed of indolence, but He reveals Himself in the night watches to those who learn to watch and war. Bring yourselves, by the power of the Spirit, into union with Christ's desires, and motives, and plans of action, and you are likely to see Him. I would that all of you were Joshuas; but if not, if but some shall perceive Him, we shall still receive a blessing.

I am sure this presence of Christ *will be needed by us all*. All of you who love Jesus intend to do Him service during this next month, and indeed, I hope as long as you live. Now, there is nothing good which you can do without Christ. "Without me ye can do nothing," is a great and undoubted fact. If you meet to pray, you shall not pray acceptably unless He be with you. If you teach, or preach, or whatever you do, however small the labor, you shall accomplish nothing unless it be through His power, and through His manifested presence with you. Go not to warfare at your own charges, but wait upon your Master, tarrying at Jerusalem until ye be endued with power from on high.

But, brethren, *Jesus Christ's presence may be had*. Do not despond and say that in the olden times the Master revealed Himself, but He will not do so now. He will, He will, He will. His promise is as good as ever. He delights to be with us even as with our fathers. If He doth not come it is because we hinder Him—we are not straitened in Him, but straitened in our own bowels. Let me persuade you that all the great things which were done at Pentecost can be done again in this Tabernacle. Let me persuade you that all the wondrous conversions which were wrought in any of the ages of the church may be repeated at this hour.

Do not say that Luther, or Calvin, or Whitefield, or Wesley were great men, and therefore around them great things gathered; my brethren, the weakest of men may be more honored than the greatest, if God so wills it. Our weakness, want of learning, want of eloquence, and what not—I look upon these as advantages rather than not, for if we were eminent, we might perhaps claim some of the glory, but if we be "less than nothing and vanity," then is there a clear stage for the divine operations. And why should we not so see in this place such a revival as shall shake all England, and stir the dry bones in the valley of vision at this day as they never were stirred since apostolic times. We have but to expect it, to believe it, to pray for it, to work for it, and we shall have it. God's clouds still pour down the water floods as plenteously as when Elisha went up to the top of Carmel. The Lord thundereth mightily against His enemies at this day, as when He went forth with His people in the days of yore. Think not that the Almighty has ceased to do marvels—the Lord of Hosts is still the king eternal, immortal, and invisible, with an arm which doeth wonders. You have still only to plead the power of the precious blood and the meritorious death of Christ, to see wonders in this year of grace which shall even eclipse any that your fathers saw, or heard of in the old time before them. May God grant to each believer among us the vision of the godlike man with the sword drawn in his hand, and then may we go forth in the strength which He alone confers.

II. In the second place, UNDERSTAND THE LORD'S POSITION IN THE MIDST OF HIS PEOPLE. "As captain of the host of the Lord am I now come."

What a relief this must have been for Joshua. Perhaps he thought himself the captain; but now the responsibility was taken from him; he was to be the lieutenant, but the King Himself would marshal His hosts. I feel it no small relief to my own mind to feel that though I have been at your head these 14 years, leading you on in God's name to Christian service, yet I am not your captain, but there is a greater one, the presence angel of the Most High, the Lord Jesus—He is in our midst as Commander-in-chief. Though my responsibilities are heavy, yet the leadership is not with me. He is a leader and commander for the people. Brethren, wherever Christ is, we must recollect that *He is Commander-in-chief to us all.* We must never tolerate in the church any great man to domineer over us; we must have no one to be Lord and Master save Jesus. Christ is the Field marshal, the Captain of our salvation; and if you are a member of the church of God, you must own this, not as a general fact only, but as a fact particularly in your case. Christ is *your* Master. You are not to say, "I prefer this or that doctrine." What have you to do with likes or dislikes? Believe what He tells you. You are not to say, "I prefer a certain form of worship." What have you to do with preferences? Worship as the Master bids you. Alas! for the day when whims and tastes and fancies come into the Christian church to lead the people. All this Puseyism which we hear so much outcry about, is simply the putting up of taste into the place of simple obedience to Christ. If we would but just keep close to Christ's word, we should be right enough. I pray each believer here to recollect that he is in no respect his own master in the things of God, but that Christ is Commander-in-chief. "Is it of any use to send missionaries to India?" said someone to the Duke of Wellington. "What are your marching orders?" said the Duke. "Go ye into all the world and preach the gospel to every creature." Those are our marching orders. We have nothing to do with whether they are prudent orders or not; they are sure to be good if they come from *Him*! Our duty is to do as our Commander bids us to do. Every word of Christ, if we would see Him do wonders in our midst, must be obeyed. Not the great precepts only, but the little ones, too. It behooves Christians to have done with that cant about nonessentials. My brethren, every command of Christ is essential to us as servants. Not essential to our salvation—we *are* saved; that is not the question for us to raise; but being saved, and being servants of Christ, every command which comes from the great Captain it is essential for every soldier to keep. It matters not though it be simply a ceremonial, yet still we have no right to alter it. What would the court-martial say to any of the private soldiers, who, having received an order from a captain, should say, "Well, I did not consider it to be exceedingly important?" "Drum him out of the regiment, sir, there is an end to all discipline in the army when soldiers criticize their orders." So is it with Christ's law. We have no right to say, for instance about believers' baptism, "Well, it is a nonessential." Who told you so? If Jesus commands it, obey it, and if it be the Lord's law, make haste and delay not to keep the Master's statute. I single out that one precept, but there are many others which are perhaps of greater importance, if we are allowed to say greater or less about anything which Christ has bidden us do. My brethren, do let us seek now to put our minds into the hands of the Holy Spirit to be taught what the great Captain's will is, and when we know it, let our souls bend under it, as the osier bends in the breath of the wind, and as the boat upon the sea is driven to and fro in the gale. Down with thee, self, down with thee! Carnal judgment and foolish reason, lie still! Let the Word of God be paramount within the soul, all opposition being hushed.

Brethren, if we do not act with the Captain, *disappointment will be sure to follow*. The Lord had issued orders that none of the tribes should take of the accursed spoil of Jericho. Achan did so. I have often wondered that only Achan did it, but that one Achan brought defeat upon Israel at the gates of Ai. I wonder how many Achans there are here this morning. I should feel myself very much at ease if I thought there were only one, but I am afraid that there are many who have the accursed thing hidden within them, the love of money, or wrong ways of doing business, or unforgiving tempers, or an envious spirit towards their fellow Christians. Now, if the possession of these bad things by one will stop the blessing, we are in a very evil plight, but he is in a worse plight by far who is the occasion of the evil. Where are you, Achan? God will find you out even if we do not. He will bring us all by our tribes, by our families, by our households, and then man by man, and woe unto the son of Carmi if he be taken. Brethren, the violation of the law of the captain may bring defeat upon the whole company.

And where the law is not obstinately and willfully violated, yet its neglect will cause much trouble. They were commanded to make no covenant with the Canaanites, but in a thoughtless hour, the Gibeonites came like persons from a far country, they believed their deceitful story, and made a covenant with them; and this became a trouble to Israel long afterwards. If as a church we forget the law of Christ, even though we do not contemptuously break it, if we ignorantly forget it, we may expect no small amount of evil to flow from it. Do not tolerate the idea that God punishes His people for sin in the sense of punitive justice, but always hold it for certain, that the Lord chastises His people for sin as a father chastises his children, and that the great Head of the church will not suffer His laws to be broken with impunity by His own people. I wish I could speak to you with the earnestness which I feel boiling up within my soul. I would, my brethren, that we should keep our Master's commands in every jot and tittle, depending upon His presence, feeling it to be here, not daring in His presence to offend, but yielding up to Him the reins of government in all respects, that we might then have His blessing. I want that we should all keep to the Word of God, minding each precept as far as we understand it. I want, moreover, that we should be attentive to that mind of Christ which is often expressed by the Holy Spirit in divine monitions in our minds, that the law of the book may be with us, and the law of the Spirit within us. If we are obedient to both these, we shall be prepared like Joshua to advance to the war.

III. Thirdly, and very briefly. Our third rule is WORSHIP HIM WHO IS PRESENT WITH US.

Joshua, it is said, fell on his face to the earth. Worship is the highest elevation of the spirit, and yet the lowliest prostration of the soul. If Christ be here, brethren, when you reach your homes get a little time of quiet and worship, and when you come up again, this evening, in your songs and prayers truly worship the ever present God, bow down in the lowliest reverence of your subdued spirit as though you actually were in heaven. If you have no wings with which to veil your face, still cover it with shame; if you have no crown to cast, yet such talent as you have, lay it all down reverentially before Him. Worship the Son of God! Then, when you have so done, *give up yourself to His command*: say to him, "What saith my Lord unto his servant?" I wish you could spend this afternoon, those of you who are not actively engaged, in trying to get an answer to this question: "What saith my Lord unto his servant? What is there for me to learn, for me to feel, for me to do? and as I would help my brethren during this month, Lord, what part of the work am I to take?" When you have done this, dear friends, I want you to imitate Joshua in the third things, namely, *put off your shoes from off your feet*. Joshua, perhaps, had not felt what a solemn thing it was to fight for God, to fight as God's executioner against condemned men. He must put his shoes off, therefore. We never can expect a blessing if we go about God's work flippantly. I shudder when I see any sitting at the Lord's table who can indulge in light remarks or in wandering thoughts, on so solemn an occasion. What hast thou to do here, not having on a wedding garment? There are some of us whose besetting sin is levity of spirit. Cheerfulness we are to cultivate, but we must beware lest levity become a cankerworm to our graces. Brethren, this next month must be a holy month unto us. I ask our young and our old friends alike to seek a quiet and sober spirit. To seek to save souls from going down to the pit is no pastime: to talk of Jesus is no trifle. We do not meet to pray in sport; we do not gather together in supplication as a mere matter of form. Angels are in our midst observing us, the King Himself is here. How would you behave if you actually saw Jesus with your eyes? If I were to vacate this pulpit and the crucified One stood here, stretching out His pierced hands and looking down upon you with the mild radiance of His sovereign love, how would you feel? Ask to feel just so, for He is here. Faith can perceive Him. Ask to feel just so at this present moment, and so to go out to your work this afternoon and all the remaining days of your life, as a servant of God who is standing in the presence of his Lord upon holy ground, and cannot therefore afford to trifle, since he has solemn work to do, and means to do it in his Master's name.

IV. To conclude, let us now even before we separate, ADVANCE TO ACTION, according to the Master's command.

Unconverted men and women, you are in our Jericho, we wish to conquer you for Christ. Our desire is to win you to Jesus for your own good and for His glory. Now, what are we to do with you? Joshua was bidden to go round the city seven times. We would preach to you the gospel of Christ, not seven times, but seventy times seven. They were to blow the rams' horns. The rams' horn was most mean as to matter, most dull as to sound, and the least showy as to appearance. So, not with enticing words of man's wisdom, but in simplicity do we warn you with the rough sound of our ram's horn, that unless you repent, you must perish. Sin must be punished. Sin is upon you, and God must punish you. Heaven and earth may pass away, but not one jot or tittle of His law can fail; and this is one part of his law, "The soul that sinneth, it shall die." You have sinned, you are always sinning, and die you must. Some of you are going from bad to worse. If you do not live in outward sin, yet the sins of thought and heart will condemn you. You will die before long, and when you die the Lord will cast you into the place which He has prepared for the devil and his angels. Be not deceived, there may be but a step between you and death; or if your life be prolonged for a little season, yet how soon will it *be over*. Eternity! eternity! how dread to you if you plunge into it unprepared, to face an angry Judge, no righteousness of Christ to plead, and no blood in which to wash your guilty soul. You are standing, some of you, between the jaws of perdition. The gospel has been preached to you and you have neglected it. You have been brought up by godly parents, and you have despised their admonitions. Therefore wrath will come upon you to the uttermost. As sure as you live you shall be driven from Jehovah's presence into the place where hope cannot follow you, and where mercy will never seek you. We must sound this ram's horn; we only pray that God may bless our warning voice to you.

After the rams' horns came the ark, which the priests carried round and round the city. That ark was the type of Christ. We beg to bring Christ before you, ye unconverted ones. Jesus Christ came into this world to seek and to save that which was lost. God smote Him instead of us. He took the sins of His people, and God punished Him for our sins instead of punishing us. Christ is the great Substitute for sin. If you trust Him you shall live. If you will take Him this day to be your Savior, and to be your Master and your Lord, you shall never perish, for God has pledged His word for it, that if you believe in Him you shall be saved. O that you would look to Christ, and live! Your good works are nothing, your tears and prayers all go for nothing as to merit, but if you look to Jesus hanging from yonder cross, you shall live. If you will trust yourself with Him who is now at the right hand of the eternal Father, crowned with many crowns, sooner shall heaven's high throne be shaken than your soul be suffered to perish. Only believe in Jesus, and thou shalt live; for this is the gospel, "He that believeth and is baptised shall be saved, he that believeth not shall be damned." We seek not to mince matters with you—damned you will be unless you trust Christ, damned you never shall be if you will come and cast yourself before Him. "Kiss the Son lest he be angry, and ye perish by the way, when his wrath is kindled but a little." Suppose that in the visions of the night, this night when you are on your bed you should suddenly see in your chamber the man with a sword drawn in his hand! You would not need to ask the question, "Art thou for us or for our adversaries?" for your own conscience would soon tell you. Suppose you should hear a solemn voice declare, "The harvest is past, and the summer is ended, and you are not saved." "Because I have called and ye refused; I have stretched out my hand, and no man regarded . . . I also will laugh at your calamity; I will mock when your fear cometh."

Suppose you saw that sword uplifted, and about to smite you, would you not start in your dream, and your face be covered with a clammy sweat, feeling horrors indescribable? Yet such is your case today; except you repent, such will be your case eternally. I bless God that now our Lord Jesus has no sword drawn in His hand, but He comes to you with open hands, and saith, "Come unto me all ye that labor, and are heavy laden, and I will give you rest." With tears He invites you to come to Him, persuades you to come. O wherefore do ye tarry, wherefore do you turn your backs upon your own mercy, and seal your own death warrant? God grant that you may come to Jesus, and before He grasps that sharp destroying sword.

Lastly, brethren, we are not only to sound the ram's horn of warning, and to bear round and round the sinner's conscience the ark of Christ's grace, but *all the host must engage in the work.* Did you notice that the whole of the people were to compass the city! It would not fall else; and they were to shout, too, at the last. I want you, my fellow members, to unite in our earnest efforts to win souls for Christ. I have a right to claim it, and now I entreat you to fulfill the claim. You profess to have been bought with the Lord's blood, and to be His disciples. I ask you all, if you be sincere in your professions, come with us round about this Jericho, every one of you. If ye cannot all come up to the public prayer-meetings, yet send us your hearts, pray for sinners, plead for the unconverted, give the eternal Leader no rest till He be pleased to use His great power for their conversion. I am almost inclined to fall on my knees to ask you church members to rally round us at this hour. If you owe your conversion to me under God, as many of you do, I charge you by every filial tie you feel, desert me not just now. If you have ever been comforted, as I know some of you have, if I have ever been God's voice to your souls, I beseech you return to me this kindness by drawing very near to God in prayer for the souls of others. For your own children's souls be very earnest; for the souls of your servants, and kinsfolk, and neighbors, wrestle with God even unto tears; and if you will not do it, I had almost said I had sooner you were not with us. If you will not pray, if you will not join in the common supplication, wherefore do ye cumber us? O Meroz, take care lest thou be accused if thou come not up to the help of the Lord, to the help of the Lord against the mighty! But you will come, God will be with us, and show us His bare right hand resplendent in our midst, and unto Him shall be the praise forever and ever.

DAGON'S UPS AND DOWNS

SERMON No. 1,342
PORTIONS OF SCRIPTURE READ BEFORE SERMON—ROMANS 7:18–25;
ROMANS 8:1–14.
HYMNS FROM *Our Own Hymn Book*—377, 648, 631.

> *When the Philistines took the ark of God, they brought it into the house of Dagon, and set it by Dagon. And when they of Ashdod arose early on the morrow, behold, Dagon was fallen upon his face to the earth before the ark of the LORD. And they took Dagon, and set him in his place again. And when they arose early on the morrow morning, behold, Dagon was fallen upon his face to the ground before the ark of the LORD; and the head of Dagon and both the palms of his hands were cut off upon the threshold; only the stump of Dagon was left to him—*1 Samuel 5:2–4.

THE ark of the Lord was captured by the Philistines though it was guarded by all the men of arms that Israel could muster for the battle. It came to no hurt when it was surrounded by unarmed priests: although the times were exceedingly disturbed and perilous all through the dreary period of the Judges, yet never was the ark a captive till it was protected by the carnal weapon. When those whom God had ordained to take care of the ark of the covenant had it in charge it was safe enough; but when the proud banners of the State and the warlike array of the nation formed the bodyguard of the sacred shrine the ark of God was taken. When the civil power was joined with the spiritual, and the arm of flesh came in to patronize and to take into connection with itself the arm of God's strength, then it was that the ark was borne away in triumph by its foes. All through human history you will find the explanation of this instructive fact: let God's truth alone, and it will take care of itself without the aid of kings and princes, laws or establishments, endowments or privileges. Only state the pure truth of revelation and it will force its own way, but garnish and adorn it by your eloquent language, or protect and guard it by your carnal wisdom and prudence, and the truth goes into captivity. Leave the church alone, O ye kings and princes, or persecute it if ye will, for it will laugh your opposition to scorn; but pretend not to propagate its doctrines by the civil power, for this is the worst curse that can befall it. Take it under your patronage, and the mere touch of your royal hands will create disease within it. Almost to the death has the so-called "church" come down when her ministers like Hophni and Phinehas, have allied themselves with the temporal power; for God will do His work by His own instruments, and in His own way; He will not be indebted to the might of the flesh, but will defend His own glory by His own mysterious power. He uses for His instruments His consecrated ones who wear the white linen, which is the righteousness of saints, and not the blood-stained men of war arrayed in coat of mail and glittering breastplate of steel.

Another lesson may be learned from the incident before us. When the Philistines had beaten the Israelites in battle, and captured the sacred chest called the ark, they boasted and gloried as though they had defeated God Himself. They evidently regarded the golden casket as the very choicest part of the spoil, and they placed it as a trophy in the chief temple of their god Dagon, to show that he was mightier than the God Jehovah, who was unable, as they thought, to protect His people. This touched at once the honor of Jehovah, and because He is a jealous God this boded good for Israel. The fact that God is a jealous God has often a terrible side to us, for it leads to our chastisement when we grieve Him: this, indeed, led to the defeat of Israel. But it has also a bright side towards us, for His jealousy flames against His foes even more terribly than against His friends; and when His name is blasphemed, and honors that are due to Him are ascribed to a mere idol, or He is declared to have been defeated by a false god, then His jealousy burns like coals of juniper, and He makes bare His right arm to smite His adversaries, as He did on this occasion. He thinks it meet to punish His offending people, but when Philistia saith, "Dagon has defeated Jehovah," then the Lord will no longer suffer Philistia to triumph. Jehovah's answer to His foes was Dagon broken to shivers before His ark, and the Philistines plagued with emerods till, in their desperate pain and dire disgrace, they set free the ark, being no longer able to endure its presence in any of their towns; so that the Jews ever afterwards used to exasperate the Philistines by reminding them of the disease which so sorely tried them; and there is a dash of this in the psalm which saith of the Lord, "He smote his enemies in the hinder part; he put them to a perpetual reproach." Never did a boastful nation undergo a deeper dishonor in the eyes of their neighbors, to whom they became a laughingstock, and never did an image suffer a worse disgrace than that which befell their god Dagon.

Now, then, whenever at any time infidelity or superstition shall so prevail as to discourage your minds, take you comfort out of this—that in all these God's honor is compromised. Have they blasphemed His name? Then He will protect that name. Have they gone further than they used to do in foul utterances against Him? Then they will provoke Him, and He will make bare His holy arm. I pray that, they may so provoke Him! All His church will say "Amen!" to that, so that He may arise and perform the glorious works of His strength and of His love among the sons of men, and put the adversary to confusion by proving that He is still with His people, and still the same mighty God as He was in the days of yore. Say you to yourselves, then, "Our Lord will not always endure this idolatrous popery, which is multiplying its priests within our national church. His people cannot bear it; much less will He. He will not always tolerate these blasphemous theories, by which self-conceited, learned men and vainglorious skeptics seek to get rid of God out of the world. They will provoke Him. He will bestir Himself; He will show Himself strong on the behalf of His truth, He will roll back the waves of sin, and let the ages know that He is still the great I AM, the victorious God over all, blessed forever." Those two truths seem to me to lie upon the surface of this passage.

And now, though it would be very wrong to make out the word of God to be a mere set of allegories, and so to deny that it records facts—and this, I trust, we shall never do—yet, as the Apostle Paul has shown us that many of the events in the Old Testament are an allegory, and as, indeed, these things are evidently types, and must be regarded as emblems and patterns of things that still occur—we shall use this passage in a spiritual way, and make it the channel of experimental teachings. Where the living God comes into the soul, Dagon, or the idol god of sin and worldliness, must go down. This is the one thought which we shall hammer out at this time.

I. To begin, then: THE COMING OF THE ARK INTO DAGON'S TEMPLE WAS AN APT SIMILE OF THE COMING OF CHRIST INTO THE SOUL.

Dagon, according to the best information, was the fish-god of Philistia; perhaps borrowed from the Sidonians and the men of Tyre, whose main business was upon the sea, and who therefore invented a marine deity. The upper part of Dagon was a man or woman, and the lower part of the idol was carved like a fish. We get a very good idea of it from the common notion of the fictitious, fabulous creature called a mermaid. Dagon was just a merman or mermaid; only, of course, there was no pretense of his being alive. He was a carved image, like that which the papists worship and call the Blessed Virgin, or Saint Peter, or Saint Remy. The temple at Ashdod was, perhaps, the cathedral of Dagon, the chief shrine of his worship; and there he sat erect upon the high altar with pompous surroundings. The ark of the covenant of the Lord of hosts was a small wooden box overlaid with gold, by no means a very cumbersome or bulky matter, but nevertheless very sacred, because it had a representative character, and symbolized the covenant of God: its capture was grievous indeed to pious Israelites, for they felt that the glory was departed when the ark was taken. The sacred chest was carried in triumph by the Philistines, and brought into the temple where Dagon stood. In your mind's eye you can see the fish-god high upon his throne, and the incense burning before him as the priests gather around, and the princes of Philistia with triumphant banners bow before his shrine. We hear the shouts of the Philistine lords as they bring in the golden coffer with the golden staves, and set it down at the foot of Dagon, and sing their exultant songs. Hear them as they sound their trumpets and chant their blasphemous hymns:

"Glory be unto thee, O Dagon! Thou hast triumphed this day, O mighty god of the land and the sea! Glorious fish-god, thou hast vanquished those who vanquished the Canaanites; and though their God slew the Egyptians of old, thou hast smitten them by their thousands. Glory be unto thee, thou mighty god!" Thus would they extol their deity and pour contempt upon the captured ark, which they placed at the foot of the image. Then, when the service was over, and they had worshiped Dagon to their heart's content, they shut up the temple, and there was darkness in the holy place, or unholy place—which shall I call it? Not long did the ark remain where it was, with Dagon still supreme, but the mere incoming of the ark *into the idol temple was a fair picture of the introduction of the grace of God into the human heart.* The Philistines brought in the ark of the Lord, but only an act of divine power can bring the grace of God into the soul. By diverse instrumentalities the truth as it is in Jesus is read, is heard, is brought to the recollection, is seen printed in the lives of men, and so enters into the temple of the inner manhood. When it first comes into the heart it finds sin enthroned there; and the Prince of Darkness reigning supreme. The first grace that enters into the soul finds it in darkness and in death, under the dominion of sin. Brethren, we have not to deliver ourselves from sin and death and darkness, and then obtain grace; but, while we are yet dead, grace visits us; while we are yet slaves the liberator comes; on our blackest midnight the sun of righteousness arises. While the Dagon of sin sits firmly on his throne, as if he never could be stirred, and his horrid form is alone to be seen lording it over all the thoughts and imaginations of the heart, even then it is that "God, who is rich in mercy, for his great love wherewith he loved us, even when we were dead in trespasses and sins," sends His almighty grace to dwell within us. When that grace enters the soul it comes not with observation, and sin at the first does not know any more about the incoming of grace than Dagon knew about the ark. The grace, the light, the truth, the love of God come into the soul, and the man does not know as yet what the Lord has done for him. He is only conscious of some impression, of a thoughtfulness he had never known before, of a calm frame of mind, of a desire to consider eternal things; and that is all that he perceives of the Lord's work within him. His Dagon seems to be there in as supreme a majesty as ever, only something strange is also within the mind, the man knows not what it is. It is the beginning of the end—of a blessed and glorious end.

We have now Dagon and the ark in the same temple, sin and grace in the same heart, *but this state of things cannot long abide.* No man can serve two masters, and even if he could then two masters would not agree to be so served. The two great principles of sin and grace will not abide in peace with each other, they are as opposite as fire and water. There will be conflict and a victory, and we know which will conquer, for as surely as ever the grace of God comes into the soul sin receives notice to quit. That night, when the Philistines had finished their exulting ceremonies, they thought they had left Dagon robed in glory, reigning and triumphing over the ark of the Lord. They had scarcely shut the doors and gone before Dagon fell on his face to the ground before the ark. Down he went. He did not lean over, but *he fell,* nor did he drop upon his side, but he was made to do obeisance before the ark, for he fell *on his face;* and he did not fall part of the way merely, but fell on his face *to the ground* before the ark: a change of positions very significant to his worshipers! The ark was set at the foot of Dagon, and now Dagon lies before the ark as if he were prostrating himself in worship before the great and mighty God. Even thus grace in the soul is not long before it overthrows sin. What a turning of things upside down grace always makes! The watchword is, "Overturn, overturn, overturn." The Breaker is come up, and the images of man's invention must be dashed to shivers.

Very likely your Dagon is in the shape of *self-righteousness.* I shall call it Dagon, for it is nothing better: one of the worst idols in the whole world is the idol of self. The self-righteous man boasts that he is as good as other people, if not rather better, although he is not a Christian. He does not know that he has ever done anything very wrong, and he feels that in him there is a great deal that is very good and excellent, and therefore he expects that things will go well with him at last. He has a very fine figure-head for his god, and though there may be a rather "fishy" tail to his character, he keeps that as much out of sight as possible, and conceals it with excuses. The god of his self-confidence is a very pretty thing, take it for all in all; it is beautiful as a mermaid, and he is fascinated with its beauty. He bows before his idol and sings before it that ancient canticle of the Philistines—I mean the Pharisees—which begins, "God, I thank thee that I am not as other men are!" When grace enters the soul the dominion of self-confidence comes to an end, down goes the fish-god on its face to the ground before the ark of the Lord, and the man discovers that he has no such righteousness as that wherein he trusted. He begins to bemoan his sins and to lament his shortcomings. A perfect change of feeling has come over him. He loathes himself as much as he once admired himself; and now, instead of taking the highest seat in the synagogue, he is willing to be a doorkeeper in the house of the Lord. "Ah, me!" says he, "what a sinner I am! How vile in the sight of God!" See you not how this brave Dagon has gone down on his face to the ground before the ark.

Perhaps the man never had much of this vainglorious self-righteousness, but he served the Dagon of *besetting and beloved sin.* The man was a drunkard, Bacchus ruled him: but as soon as the grace of God is brought into his soul he has done with the drink-god. The horrible Dagon of drunkenness is hurled from its throne by grace. The man cannot bear to think that he should have so disgraced himself as to be fond of wantonness, and chambering, and surfeiting, and drunkenness, and such-like abominable sins, which bring manhood below the level of the best. He who is truly penitent hates the very name of these filthy sins. If a man has been guilty of using bad language and profane swearing, the grace of God generally cures him of that at once. I have heard men who had lived in the practice of swearing for many years say that, from the time they were converted, they never had a temptation to it; that black sin went off bag and baggage at once. Some sins are slow in dying, but profanity generally gives up the ghost without a struggle. John Bunyan says that a stone from the battering-ram slew Mr. Profane by cracking his skull, so that he died early in the siege of Mansoul; it were well if more deceptive sins did the like. The grosser outward offenses, like Dagon, are soon down before the ark.

Sin of every sort is bowed low before triumphant grace. Yea, and the man who receives the grace of God feels that the love of any and every sin is cast out of its place in his heart. Now he desires to be quit of it all, and anxiously cries, "Lord, what wouldst thou have me to do?" He will no more go and live in sin, as he did before, than Paul will continue to be a persecutor after the Lord, even Jesus, has appeared to him by the way. What a Dagon-fall there was in the apostle's pride just outside the Damascus gate! Such a fall takes place in the heart of every man to whom the grace of God comes with power.

Now the parallel may be run a little further. *This fall of Dagon very soon began to be perceived*, for "When they of Ashdod arose early on the morrow, behold, Dagon was fallen on his face to the earth." Very soon after the entrance of grace this sign follows, and before long it is seen and known. Let no man conceive that there is grace in his soul if Dagon sits on the throne still. This is one of the earliest tokens of the entrance of the life of God into the soul—that sin falls down from its high place, and is no more had in honor.

At the same time, observe that Dagon was not broken. He had fallen on his face, but that was all; so that the next day his foolish worshipers could set him up again. Sometimes at the first entrance of grace there is a downfall of sin, but nothing like such a breaking and destroying of sin in the soul as there will be afterwards. When the divine life has entered sin is dethroned, it no longer sits up there in the place of God; but yet, for all that, there is an awful power remaining in the corrupt nature, a deadly tendency to sin, a powerful law in the members bringing the soul into captivity. Still, down the idol goes, even if it be not broken: it cannot reign, though it may remain to trouble us.

Now, what happened on the night mentioned in the text? *Dagon fell before the ark when it was all quiet and still in the temple.* While the worshipers were there, during the day, there was noise, and shouting, the false god sat aloft and you could not tell that there was any mysterious power about the ark. It was in the quiet of the night that this deed was done, and thus often in the hearing of the word grace is introduced into the heart, but you would not know that any change was wrought, for it is only when the man gets away from the world's business—gets alone and begins to consider—that a divinely-mysterious might is displayed by the inward grace, so as to sink sin, and lay the power of evil low. Would to God our hearers took more opportunities for quietly considering the word of God! How much more blessing might often be gotten out of sermons and books if there were more meditation! You get the grapes, but you do not tread them in the wine-vat. There is more trouble taken to collect the sheaves of the sermon than is afterwards expended in threshing them out. The power which smote Dagon was displayed in the quiet of the night; and when the grace of God has entered into your souls it is probable that the downcoming of sin will be better effected in times of quiet thought and searching of heart than at any other period. Thought is the channel of immense benefit to the soul. Shut the temple doors and let all be still, and then will the Holy Ghost work wonders in the soul.

II. Now, secondly, THE SETTING UP OF DAGON THE SECOND TIME, AND HIS SECOND FALL, VERY WELL REPRESENT THE BATTLE GOING ON IN THE SOUL BETWEEN SIN AND GRACE.

What fools these Philistines were to continue worshiping a god which when it tumbled down could not get up again. To worship a god which fell on its face was bad enough, but to worship one that could not rise when he fell, but needed to be set in his place by human hands, was certainly vile infatuation: but they took up their precious deity, and they put him in his place again, and no doubt sang a special "high mass" to him, and then went their way quietly to their homes, little dreaming that their pretty fish-god would want their help again so soon. Even thus *Satan and the flesh come into our souls and try to set our fallen Dagon up again, with some measure of success.* It often happens that in young converts there comes a period when it looks as if they had altogether apostatized and gone back to their former ways. It seems as if the work of God were not real in their souls, and grace was not triumphant. Do you wonder at it? I have ceased to wonder. The gospel is preached, and the man accepts it, and there is a marvelous difference in him; but when he goes among his old companions, although he is resolved not to fall into his former sins, they try him very severely. He is assailed in a thousand ways! Some of our young people, if they were to tell their story, would harrow up your feelings by mentioning the way in which all sorts of jests, and insinuations, and taunts are hurled at them, and that by influential persons—their parents, their elder brothers and sisters, and those who oversee their work; they are beset behind and before, so that if they do not transgress in one way, it is very likely that the devil craftily trips them up in another. I have known a man when he has been tempted to go into evil company refuse again, and again, and again. His tempters have laughed at him, and he has borne it all, but at last he has lost his temper; and as soon as the enemies have seen his passion boiling up they have cried out, "Ah, there you are! We have got you." At such a time as that the poor man is apt to cry, "Alas, I cannot be a believer, or else I should not have done this." Now, all this is a violent attempt of Satan and the flesh to set Dagon up again. They know that the Lord has thrown him down and they cannot bear it, but would fain set the fish-god again on his throne. Sometimes they do for a time set Dagon up again and cause great sorrow in the soul. I have known a poor lost lamb to be found and brought into the fold; but it has miserably wandered for a time, and the devil has thought that, surely, he had got that lamb, and would tear him into pieces, and yet he has been deceived after all. Dagon was only set up for a time, and he had to come down again; and so it happens wherever grace enters the heart. The wanderers have come back, weeping and sighing, to own that they have dishonored their profession: and what has been the result in the long run? Why, they have had more humility, more tenderness of heart, more love to Christ, more gratitude, than they had before; and I have been glad (not glad that they wandered, but glad) that the grace of God, when He has brought them back again more fully, has given them a deeper conversion and a more lasting and substantial work of grace, so that afterwards they have continued by the grace of God honorable, useful Christians even to the end. Often and often is that the case, and I speak at this time to any young convert who can say in his heart, "O sir, I do love the Lord, but I have been such a backslider. I do trust Jesus. I wish to be a Christian, but I have been overthrown by enemies, I fear I must not join a Christian church, because if I could not resist temptation for six weeks how could I expect to stand fast all my life. I am such a poor, weak creature, so apt to be led astray, what is to become of me?" Dear friend, grieve to think you were so foolish, but do not doubt the power of God's Holy Spirit to help you, and to break in pieces the enemy, who seems to have resumed his power over you.

Now, notice that *although they again set Dagon up, he had to go down again with a worse fall.* I have no doubt it took them a long pull and a great heave to haul the uncomely lump of marble into its place again. Many strong limbs were tired, and muscles strained, to lift up the huge god, and set him on his pedestal; but it was no trouble to the Lord to upset the ugly stone. No rope was wanted, and no straining or pulling, "Bel boweth down and Nebo stoopeth" when Jehovah uplifts Himself. Only shut the temple gates, and leave the ark and Dagon to have it out between them, and Dagon gets the worst of it. Only, mark this, Dagon has not gained much by being reinstated, for this time, when he comes down, behold he was fallen on his face to the ground before the ark of Jehovah, "and the head of Dagon and both the palms of his hands were cut off upon the threshold." The idol's *head* was gone, and even so the reigning power of sin is utterly broken and destroyed, its beauty, its cunning, its glory are all dashed to atoms. This is the result of the grace of God, and the sure result of it, if it once comes into the soul, however long the conflict may continue, and however desperate the efforts of Satan to regain his empire. O believer, sin may trouble thee, but it shall not tyrannize over thee. "Sin shall not have dominion over you," saith the Holy Spirit, "for ye are not under the law, but under grace." If the power of evil be set up for awhile it shall only come down with the greater force, and its head shall be cut off.

Then, too, the *hands* of Dagon were broken off and even thus the active power, the working power of sin is taken away. Both the palms of the idols' hands were cut off upon the threshold, so that he had not a hand left. Neither right-handed sin or left-handed sin shall remain in the believer when God's sanctifying grace fetches Dagon down. The secret reigning power is broken, and so is the manifest working power. The Christian is kept from putting forth his hand into iniquity. He is crucified with Christ, and so both hands are nailed to the cross and fastened up from performing those deeds of ill towards which the lustings of the flesh would urge him.

This happened, too, if you notice, *very speedily;* for we are told a second time that, when they arose early on the morrow, behold, Dagon was fallen upon his face. It does not take grace long, when it is once in the soul, to overturn the reigning power and the active energy of sin, when these for a while appear to get the upper hand.

Brothers and sisters, I hope you know this. I hope that the Spirit of God which is in you, and the love of Christ which reigns in you, have destroyed the power which sin once had in your souls. If it be not so, then question yourselves whether the Spirit of God be in you at all. It is not possible that the ark should be in the temple and that Dagon should be standing there unbroken. Not till the morrow morning shall evil remain unchallenged and unmoved upon the throne. It is not possible that you, dear friend, could live and delight in sin, and yet be a child of God. If your heart is set upon iniquity, where your heart is there your treasure is, and if sin be your treasure you are no heir of heaven. That which governs your heart is your lord and your god; what your heart loves, by that you shall be judged, and if you love evil you shall be condemned. We may sin—ah, would God we did not!—but to love sin is not in the believer. There is a deadly antagonism between grace and sin; and where the gracious life comes the evil life must fall. There cannot be an alliance between Dagon and the ark, between God and the world, or between Christ and sin.

III. And now, thirdly, the parallel still holds good in one more point, namely, that THOUGH THE FISH-GOD WAS THUS MAIMED AND BROKEN, YET THE STUMP OF DAGON WAS LEFT TO HIM.

The original Hebrew is, "Only Dagon was left to him," or "only the fish": only the fishy part remained. The head and the upper portions were broken away, there remained only the fishy tail of Dagon, and that was all; but that was not broken. Now, *this is the business which brings us so much sorrow*—that the stump of Dagon is left to him. I wish it were not. I have heard some say that they have no sin remaining in them. Well, dear brother, the Lord convert you! I shall say no more than that, for if there were in you enough light for you to perceive your darkness, it were better than to talk as you do. Every child of God who knows anything about himself and the experience of a real believer, knows that there is indwelling sin in him, and that to a most fearful extent, so as to make his very soul cry out in agony, "O wretched man that I am, who shall deliver me from the body of this death?" I could not go the length of singing, with Ralph Erskine, as a description of myself, the lines written by him in his "Believer's Sonnets"—

> To good and evil equal bent—
> And both a devil and a saint.

But yet, taken with a large lump of salt, there is a good deal of truth even in that unguarded expression. There is the old corruption within us, and there is no use denying it, because denying it will put us off our guard, will make many of the puzzles of life to be quite unanswerable, and often bring upon us great confusion of soul. The other law is within us as well as the law of grace. Canst thou draw near to God, my brother, and not see that He can justly charge thee with folly? Canst thou stand in His presence, as Job did, and behold His glory, and not say, "I abhor myself in dust and ashes?" Canst thou have dealings with perfection, and not perceive thy faultiness? Canst thou come near unto the innermost court of the temple, and stand in that excessive light of fellowship which is the portion of the Lord's chosen, and not see within thyself spots and wrinkles, yea, thousands of them, so as to make thee cover thy face for shame, and adore the amazing grace which loves thee still? Canst thou not see in thy daily life enough to condemn thee, and cast thee into hell, were it not that God still sees thee in Christ, and imputes not thy iniquity to thee, but accepts thee in the Beloved? Oh, it is so—it is so, indeed! The stump of Dagon is still left; and because it is left, dear friend, *it is a thing to be watched against*, for though that stony stump of Dagon would not grow in the Philistine temple; yet they would make a new image, and exalt it again, and bow before it as others. Alas, the stump of sin within us is not a slab of stone, but full of vitality, like the tree cut down, of which Job said, "At the scent of water it will bud." Leave the sin that is in you to itself, and let temptation come in the way, and you shall see that which will blind your eyes with weeping. It is a good thing to look at your face in a glass, but your face is not yourself; no mirror can show you yourself. There is a certain temptation which has an affinity to the evil within you; and should Satan bring that temptation near you will see yourself to your horror and shame. There shall then look out of the window of your countenance a man whom you did not see when you looked in the glass, for you only saw the house he lived in. So ugly is he that he makes the very house he lives in look horrible. When the angry man comes up, and is visible to the naked eye, how he deforms the countenance! When obstinate old Adam comes to the window, what a dark forbidding face he wears! When that envious spirit comes up, what an evil glance there is in the eye! When the unbelieving spirit peers through the lattice, what a miserable countenance he shows compared with the face of faith and childlike confidence in God! There is nobody in this world, dear brother, that you have so much cause to be afraid of as yourself. Augustine used to pray, "Lord, deliver me from that evil man, myself." A very appropriate prayer for a woman, too—"Lord, save me from myself." If you are saved from yourself you will be saved from the devil; for what can the devil do unless self joins hands with him in unholy league? But, oh, what watchfulness it will need! Here is room for faith indeed! Faith does not decline the conflict, nor puff us up with the notion that the fight is over; on the contrary, it takes to itself the whole armor of God, because it sees the battle to be still raging. Faith is wanted to be the shield to keep off the fiery darts, and the sword with which to smite the foe. Here is the sphere in which faith is to work; it does not talk of ended warfare, but carries on the lifelong campaign to ultimate victory. Faith does not say, "I have ceased the conflict": she knows better: faith says, "I am in the midst of it, warring with a thousand foes, and looking for the victory through Jesus Christ my Lord." O brothers and sisters, be strong in faith by the power of the Holy Spirit, for you have need to be so, since the stump of Dagon still remaineth. The lusting of the flesh abideth still in the regenerate.

Look at this matter again. That stump of Dagon which remained was a vile thing: it was a piece of an idol, a fragment of a monstrous image which had been worshiped instead of God. Now, the sin which dwelleth in you is never to be regarded by you as anything else than a horrible, loathsome, and detestable thing. That after such love as you and I have known there should be in us even the power to be ungrateful ought to shock us; that after such proof of His truth as God has shown to us, after such faithfulness and such abundant evidences of faithfulness, we should still be capable of unbelief ought to be a sorrow to us. Oh, I wish I could never sin again throughout time or eternity. Oh, that every particle of the tinder of depravity into which the devil could let a spark fall was gone from my nature. It is a mercy to have the sparks put out, but it is a pity to have even the tinder left; and there is plenty of this tinder about us all. Tinder? Aye, gunpowder, so quick is it to take the light which Satan is ever ready to bring. We carry a bombshell heart about with us, and we had better keep clear of all the devil's candles lest there should be an explosion of actual sin. These candles are common enough in the form of some plausible but skeptical friend, or in the form of amusements which are questionable. Keep you clear of Lucifer's matches. You have got enough mischief in your heart without going where you will get more. If anybody here feels that he is so very gracious and good that he can safely enter into temptation, I am sure that he is laboring under a very great mistake. I would say to him, Brother, there is devil enough in you without your sending out invitation cards to seven more. Go you to him that casteth out devils. Go you into company where the powers of evil will be held in chains and bound; but do not go where other devils as wicked as himself will call to the demon who now besets you, and stir him up to work mischief. The stump of Dagon is left. Be careful, watchful, prayerful, and loathe sin with all your soul.

IV. But now, lastly, here is mercy that THOUGH THE STUMP OF DAGON WAS NOT TAKEN OUT OF THE PHILISTINE TEMPLE, WE MAY GO BEYOND THE HISTORY AND REJOICE THAT IT WILL BE TAKEN FROM OUR HEARTS. The day is coming, brother, sister, in which there will be no more inclination in you to sin than there is in an angel. The day is coming in which your nature shall be so established in truth and righteousness and holiness that all the devils in hell will not be able to make you think a wrong thought. "Oh," says one, "I wish that time would come soon." It will come, brother. The Lord will keep you fighting yet and warring yet; but there will come a day when a messenger will wait at your door, and he will say, "The pitcher is broken at the fountain, and the wheel broken at the cistern. Thy flesh must return to the dust, and thy spirit to God that made it," and then your spirit shall open its eyes with glad surprise and find itself delivered from the body, and at the same time delivered from all sin. There shall also come by-and-by the sound of the trumpet of resurrection, and the body shall rise; and one of the chief characteristics of the risen body will be that as it rises it will be free from the bondage of corruption, and it will have no tendency to lead us into sin. When our perfected spirit shall enter into our perfect body, then our complete manhood, body, soul, and spirit shall have no stain, or spot, or flaw. All its past sin will be washed away—nay, *is* washed away—in the blood of the Lamb, and all its propensities, tendencies and inclinations to sin shall all be gone forever, and the very possibilities of sinning shall be eternally taken away.

> No cloud those blissful regions know,
>   Forever bright and fair;
> For sin, the source of mortal woe,
>   Can never enter there.

John Bunyan represents Mercy as laughing in her sleep. She had a dream, she said; and she laughed because of the great favors which were yet to be bestowed upon her. Well, if some of you were to dream tonight that the great thing which I have spoken of had actually happened to you, so that you were completely free from all tendency to sin, would not you also be as them that dream and laugh for very joy. Think of it—no more cause for watchfulness, no more need of weeping over the day's sin before you fall asleep at night; no more sin to confess, no devil to tempt you, no worldly care, no lusting, no envy, no depression of spirit, no unbelief, nothing of the kind—will not this be a very large part of the joy of heaven? Why, I am ready to cry for joy to think that this will happen to me, unworthy though I be. "Bless the Lord, O my soul, and all that is within me bless His holy name." It will be so, brother, both to you and to me. As surely as we have trusted Christ He will perfect that which concerneth us.

> The feeblest saint shall win the day,
>   Though death and hell obstruct the way.

The Lord has undertaken our perfect sanctification, and He will accomplish it. He has brought old Dagon down, and broken his head and his hands, and He will break him to shivers before long. Yea, He will take the ark of the Lord away where Dagon shall never come into contact with it any more. He will take you— the gracious part of you, your truest and best self—away into the glory, to abide with Him forever. Think of this and sing. Yea, brother, sing with all your might, for all this may happen within a week. A week! It may happen within a day. It may happen before you reach home tonight. We are so near to heaven that if we were not very dull, and our ears very heavy, we might at once hear the angels chanting their ceaseless hallelujahs. Some of God's saints—some here, perhaps— have almost got their foot upon the threshold of the eternal city, and do not know it. They are closer than they think to the harp and the palm branch. They would not fret about what they will do next year, they would not be worrying about next quarter-day if they knew that they would be amongst the royalties of heaven by then. They would not even think about tomorrow did they know how soon it will all be over, and how soon the eternal joy will begin.

God bless you, dear friends. May the Lord's grace reign over all in the power of the Holy Ghost; and even to sinners in whom sin is triumphant may Jesus Christ come, and His grace enter, and then their beloved sins must fall. To the only living and true God be glory forever and ever. Amen.

THE LOVE OF JONATHAN, AND
THE LOVE OF JESUS

Sermon No. 2,336
Intended for Reading on Lord's day, November 26, 1983;
Delivered On Lord's day Evening, September 29, 1889.

Thy love to me was wonderful, passing the love of women—
2 Samuel 1:26.

David was a poet; and when he found that his best-beloved friend had fallen by the arrows of the Philistines, he wept greatly, and then he cheered his heart by writing the very fine elegy, which in after years was called "The Song of the Bow." Even if David's lamentation is judged according to the canons of literary taste, it must be placed among the first of poetical compositions. Thus David tried to keep his friend's memory green; the song was meant to be a memorial of him. Such friends as Jonathan are not common; and when we have had them, we must not forget them.

It is sad that, in these days, friendship is proverbially a frail thing. Friends are like swallows, that are with us in our summertime, and gone when the damps of autumn begin to gather. When a man has a faithful friend, let him grapple him to his side with hooks of steel; and when he loses him, let him know that he has lost what will be very hard to replace, and let him not forget his friend though he be buried beneath the sod. True friendship likes to fashion memorials of the departed. We keep mementos of the loved ones we have lost, we like to think of the happy days of communion we have had together, and we will not allow the cherished name to be blotted out from the memory of men.

When I thought of this subject, I said to myself, "I shall see many tonight who are lovers of the Lord Jesus Christ; I shall be face to face with thousands who love Him as they love their own soul." I believe that is my happiness now. Well then, beloved friends, let us who love Christ keep Him ever in memory. If you can speak of His name, be not silent. If you can make melody, in honor of Jesus, in the great congregation, take down the minstrel's harp, and lay your fingers among the strings, and bring out sweetest music to His dear name that thousands may hear; but if you have a feebler instrument, sing or play to the two or three, and let those who love you know that you love your Lord best of all. Or if thy tongue fail thee, use thy pen to let men know who Jesus is. Say, with the psalmist, "My heart is indicting a good matter: I speak of the things which I have made touching the King."

What shall *we* do to keep Christ's name before the sons of men? Let us be inventive, and often make the winds and waves to bear the story of His life and love to those who know it not. I would whisper in the ear of someone, "If thou lovest Jesus, how is it that thou art never at His table?" If there be any way of keeping Him in memory, which is better than every other, it is the one which He has Himself chosen, "This do in remembrance of me." How do you excuse yourselves, ye lovers of Christ, who have never kept up this feast of love? This is one of His dying requests, "Meet and remember me"; and yet, though you say that you love Him, and I will not challenge the truth of what you say, you have never yielded obedience to His loving request, and come to eat the bread and drink of the cup which are the memorials of His broken body and His poured-out blood. David, thou couldst sing of Jonathan, though there was no law that thou shouldst do so; what wilt thou say of some who love the Christ of God better than thou didst love Jonathan, and yet have never remembered Him in the way in which He asked to be remembered, but have cast behind their back the sweet forget-me-not of the table of communion?

Let that stand as a preface. May the Lord put our hearts in tune now while we think upon two things! The first is the small type, *Jonathan's love to David*; the second is the infinite anti-type, *Christ's love to men*. Perhaps it will be sweetest tonight if we can each one say, "*Christ's love to me*. He loved *me*, and gave Himself for *me*." That expression will be in harmony with the words of the text, "Thy love to me was wonderful."

I. First, then, we have to think a little about JONATHAN'S LOVE TO DAVID.

Jonathan's was a singular love, because of *the pureness of its origin*. Jonathan loved David out of great admiration of him. When he saw him come back with the head of Goliath in his hand, he loved him as a soldier loves a soldier, as a brave man loves another brave man. He felt that there was the right kind of metal in that young man; and though Jonathan was the king's son, and heir-apparent to the throne, we find that he "stripped himself of the robe that was upon him, and gave it to David, and his garments, even to his sword, and to his bow, and to his girdle." He felt that such a hero, who could so trust his God, and so expose his life, and come off so victorious, deserved his utmost love. It did not begin in self-interest, it did not begin in relationship; but it began in the likeness that Jonathan saw between his own nature, and that of David. It was one brave man loving another brave man.

Jonathan's love proved also to be *most intense*. It is said that "he loved him as his own soul." He would at any moment have sacrificed his life to preserve the life of David; in fact, I do not doubt that Jonathan thought David's life much more valuable than his own, and that he was quite willing to expose himself to peril that David might be preserved. Jonathan's was a very intense love. May we see more of this kind of love among Christian men! May they love each other for Christ's sake, and because of the love of God which they see in one another, and may they be intense in their affection!

Jonathan's love was *very disinterested*; because, as I have said, Jonathan was heir-apparent to the throne, but David had been anointed king by Samuel. The kingdom was to be taken from the house of Saul, and given to the house of David. Very naturally, the young prince Jonathan might have felt first envy, and then hatred of David, who was to supplant him; but instead of that, he said to him one day, very touchingly, "Thou shalt be king over Israel, and I shall be next unto thee." He meant to be his friend, and his helper, taking joy in seeing David wear the crown which might have adorned his own brow. Happy Jonathan, to be able to put himself in the background like that, and to feel that, if David was first, it was what he himself desired. That friendship, in which a man can set himself on one side for the sake of another, is not yet so common that we can hawk it in the streets.

Jonathan's was a love which *bore up under all opposition*, for he soon found that Saul, his father, in his black heart, hated David. He could not bear the thought that another man should take the place which he coveted for himself, though he did not himself deserve to keep it. He wished to see David dead; and because Jonathan took David's part, Saul was exceedingly angry, and made Jonathan's lot hard to bear; yet Jonathan did not cast off his friend, he clung to David through good report and through evil report. Jonathan was faithful to his father, and very obedient to him; but still he would not give up his friend David, and he would sooner be in jeopardy of the javelin of Saul than end the friendship that existed between himself and God's chosen servant.

And this love was *very active*, for you know how he pleaded for David with his father. He went out into the field, and took counsel with David. He arranged plans and methods for David's preservation; and, on one occasion, we find that he "went to David in the wood, and strengthened his hand in God." Yes, his love was not a matter of mere talk, it was real, practical, active; it was a love which never failed. When the arrow of the Philistine went through the heart of Jonathan on Mount Gilboa, it struck the name of David that was engraven there.

> He loved him long, and loved him well,
> And loved him to the death;

so that David could truly say, "Thy love to me was wonderful, passing the love of women."

Now, dear friends, do you not think that when we read a story like that of Jonathan and David, it should stir up in us the desire, not so much to have such a friend, as to be such a friend as Jonathan was to David? Any man can selfishly desire to have a Jonathan; but he is on the right track who desires to find out a David to whom he can be a Jonathan. There is great joy in life with real friendship on both sides. Some people expect friendship to be always heaping its treasures upon them; but true friendship has two hands, and two feet, and two eyes. You cannot have a real friendship that is all for taking, and never for giving. David loved Jonathan as Jonathan loved David. May that blessed Spirit of God, who teaches us to love even our enemies, help us to cultivate sanctified friendships, and to be willing to help those who are our brethren in Christ in time of need!

I shall say no more upon that part of my subject; but I hope it will rebuke some who are no friends at all. Oh, how often have we met with such! They are very friendly when their legs are under your mahogany; but they are not so friendly when you have no mahogany, and have hardly a deal table left. They think all the world of you while you can be a ladder by which they climb the wall of prosperity; but when they are on the top of the wall, they too often say that they never saw that ladder in all their lives, and you may take it away. We continually see that kind of thing among men of the world. May it not be so among Christians! May we be true to all who are our friends, as we would be generous even to any who are our foes, if such persons are in existence!

II. But I want now to talk of something more sweet, and more sure. THE LOVE OF CHRIST TO ME, using the first personal pronoun, because it is in the text: "Thy love to *me* was wonderful."

I hope that many here will be helped to use that same pronoun each one for himself or for herself. I do not wish to preach tonight; I want rather to be a sort of leader, just to go through the exercise that others may do the same. I am to speak of love which I trust many feel, which I hope they may feel even more than the speaker does; and let it be the ambition of every one of us to love Christ more and more. Let us think of Christ as present here tonight, for so He is, according to His promise, "Lo, I am with you alway, even unto the end of the world." There He stands. With closed eyes, faith perceives Him, and she cries, "Thy love to me was wonderful."

I think that we feel this most *when we see our Savior die.* Sit down at the foot of the cross, and look up. Behold that sacred brow with the thorny wreath upon it. See those blessed eyes, red with weeping; mark those nailed hands, that once scattered benedictions; gaze on those bleeding feet, which hurried on errands of mercy; watch till you can peer into that gaping side, how deep the gash, how wide the breach, see how the water and the blood come streaming forth! This is the Lord of life and glory, who thus dies amid derision and scorn, suffering the Just for the unjust, to bring us to God. Oh, if you can picture Christ on the cross, and believe that He died for you, you will be led to cry, "Thy love to me was wonderful, passing the love of mothers or of wives. Thy love to me was—I cannot describe what it was— it was wonder-full—as full of wonders as the heavens are full of stars, or as a forest is full of leaves. Thy love, as I see it in thy death, was wonderful." Do you picture David saying this as he thinks of the body of Jonathan pierced with the arrows of his enemies, "Thy love to me was wonderful?" Will you not stand tonight, in imagination, over your Savior's body, as you see it wrapped in spices, and laid in the tomb of Joseph of Arimathea?" Ere yet the stone is rolled to the cave's mouth, will you not look on that mangled form, and say, "In very truth, thy love to me was wonderful"?

Beloved friends, sometimes we feel as if our love to our departed ones would know another great floodtide if they could come back again. You have lost—no, I will not harrow up your feelings,—you have all lost those most dear, and your sorrow was great as you laid them in the grave; but if tonight, when you reached your home, you should find, sitting in that room of yours, the beloved one come back, I think that your love would suddenly leap up into an ecstasy, and it would be greater than ever it was before. "Has my husband returned to me? Has my spouse come back to me? Has my mother, my child, been restored to me?" Oh, what a feast of love our souls would have if there could be such a reunion in our bereaved households! Well, remember that *He who died for us rose again.*

He lives, the great Redeemer lives,

lives with our love still within His heart, lives to love us as much in His eternal glory as He did in the shame and spitting, while He was on earth. Come, give your love room and space tonight, as you remember Him as dead, but rejoice in Him as living.

I think, also, that we sometimes feel the greatest love to dear friends when we find others doing them despite. When David found that Jonathan's body had been dishonored by the Philistines, that they had taken away the bodies of King Saul and his sons to hang them on the wall of Beth-shan, then was he sorely troubled, and his love broke forth again in sighs, and cries, and tears. And I must say tonight that *I love my Lord all the more because of the insults others heap upon Him.* When I have lately seen books written against His atoning sacrifice, when I meet with men, calling themselves Christians, who speak lightly of the sacred expiation, and even of the divine Person of the great sacrifice, my heart first burns with indignation against the traitors,—true successors of Judas,—and then my soul cries, "My Savior, by the dishonor that they put on Thee, I love Thee all the more. By the shame that they again cast on Thee, as though Thou wert a hundred times crucified, I vow to serve Thee with a hundredfold energy and force of concentrated love, for thy love to *me* was wonderful." Some can speak lightly of Christ; mayhap they never knew such love as He has shown to me. Some can despise His blood; possibly they were never washed from such sins as mine. Some think lightly of His faith; perhaps they have never had such communion with Him as my heart has known; but I must say of Him, "Thy love to *me* was, is, and ever shall be, wonderful, passing all loves supposable in heaven or earth besides."

Now let me briefly tell the story of that love,—it is a long story,—the love of Christ to me. Part of its wonder lies in *the object of this love*, that it should be bestowed upon me: "Thy love to *me*." Dear brother, dear sister, will you only talk about it just now to yourself? "It is a wonder that Christ should love anybody; but is it not the greatest wonder of all that He should love me? Who am I, and what is my father's house, that Christ should love me?"

What was there in you that could merit esteem,
Or give the Creator delight?

Thy love to *me*! There was special undesert; there were many reasons why love should have passed me by; but thy love to me was wonderful that Thou shouldst single out me. Tell it in heaven that there is no greater wonder there than that Christ should love me; and when you get there, say to all the bright spirits before the throne, "There is no greater wonder in the salvation of you all than there is in my salvation. Thy love to me, my Lord," and you will bow adoringly at Christ's feet as you say it, "Thy love to me was wonderful."

Then throw the emphasis on the first word, "*Thy* love to me," and you have another part of the wonder, that is, in *the Giver of this love*. For a man to love me, well, should not men love their kind? But for God to love me, for the Infinite, for the inconceivably lovely One, whose ideal of that which is loveable must be far beyond human conception, for Him to love me, this is a miracle indeed. Can you imagine it, that God who is greater than immensity, whose life is longer than time, that God the all-boundless One, should love you? That He should think of you, pity you, consider you, this is all very well; but that He should *love* you, that His heart should go out to you, that He should choose you, that He should have graven you on the palms of His hands, that He should not rest in heaven without you, that He should not think heaven complete until He brings you there, that you should be the bride, and Christ the Bridegroom, that there should be eternal love between Him and you, oh, as you think of it, lift up your hands with adoring wonder, and say, "Thy love to me was wonderful."

Now begin, if you can, to *consider the commencement of this love*. When did God begin to love His own elect? There was a time when He began to make the worlds; but from eternity He has loved His chosen. Before the first flash of light illumined the primeval darkness, God loved His people. Before the first pulsation of life came into human bodies, long ere there were such beings as men and women, He loved His own. He saw them in the glass of predestination and foreknowledge, and He loved them then; His delights even then were with the sons of men. His love had no beginning, it was like Himself, self-existent, starting from itself, and there never was a time when God did not love His own people. Think of that wonder of grace, that such a speck of dust as you are should have been loved from eternity, that such a handful of ashes as I am should have been loved from before all worlds! Tell it as with voice of trumpet, for God hath said it, "I have loved thee with an everlasting love: therefore with lovingkindness have I drawn thee."

Christ's love, then, is wonderful in its beginning; and *when it began to work on me*, it was still wonderful, for what did I do? I refused it. When Christ came in robes of love to me, and presented Himself as a candidate for my heart's acceptance, I told Him that I would not have Him. There was a wanton world that had my heart. There was the devil himself, in all manner of sinful shapes; and he had my hand, and I was his. Was it not so with some of you, that Christ wooed you many a year, and you would not have Him? He came to you sometimes threatening, and sometimes inviting; He came to you by providences, by preachers, by books, by His good Spirit; yet though you turned your back on Him, He never turned His back on you; He would not take "No" for an answer.

> Determined to save, He watched o'er my path
> When, Satan's blind slave, I sported with death.

Think of a man, who used to come staggering out of a public-house late at night, yet He is loved of God! Or of a thief, whose hair was cut short in prison, yet He was loved of God, and here He is tonight sitting at Jesus' feet, rejoicing in that love! Oh, what songs there will be in heaven concerning the love of Christ to His own, and the rebuffs which the dear Lover of our souls received by the sad, sad usage of ungodly, willful men! "Thy love to me was wonderful."

And when *Christ's love led Him to come here, and take our nature,* was it not wonderful? He reigned enthroned in heaven; seraphim and cherubim gladly did His bidding. He was God, and yet He came down from yonder royal palace to that stable at Bethlehem, and to the manger where the horned oxen fed. 'Tis He! 'Tis He! But as George Herbert reminds us, He hath unrobed Himself, and hung His azure mantle on the sky, and all His rings upon the stars; and there He lies, a babe in swaddling bands, taking human nature into union with His divinity because He loved us. Truly, thou blessed Child, whom I would take into mine arms as Simeon did, and say, "Lord, now lettest thou thy servant depart in peace, according to thy word: for mine eyes have seen thy salvation"; Thy love to me was wonderful! Behold Christ with the scepter of heaven in His hand, and then see Him sitting on the edge of a well, talking to an adulterous woman. Gaze on Him with the harps of angels ringing out His praise, and then see Him with all the riff-raff of Jerusalem scoffing at Him, and bidding Him come down from the cross. If He stooped to become a man like ourselves, and stopped lower still, even unto death, truly may each saved one cry to Him, "Thy love to me was wonderful."

There is one thing that makes the love of Christ more wonderful than anything else, and that is, that He not only took our nature, but *He took our sin.* There, scrape it up together, the filthy stuff that has made God Himself to sicken at the thought of man, I mean, the sin and the pollution of our lives. Behold, the Lord hath gathered it up together in one foul heap, enough to putrefy the universe, and He hath laid it all on Christ, and the great Sin-bearer takes it upon Himself as though it were His own, though it was not. He suffers for it, He bears the sentence of justice on account of it, and then He hurls it all away into the abyss of oblivion, where it shall never be found again. My Savior, didst Thou bear my sin in thine own body on the tree? Wast Thou condemned for my condemnation? Then, in very deed, thy love to me was wonderful.

I do not know how to break my text up so as to bring it home to each believer; I wish that everyone here, who really has known Christ's love, would help me by a personal thought upon *the brotherly and condescending character of this love.* Times have been when we, who love Christ's name, have been in trouble, and He has been very near to us. Times have been when we have been misrepresented, and abused, and He has smiled, oh, so sweetly on us! Times have been when bodily pain has made us very faint, and He has put underneath us the everlasting arms. Speak as you find, beloved; how have you found the Lord Jesus in your dark days, in your heavy days, in your weary days? Have you not found Him a matchless Friend? I can bear my own witness that there is no comfort like His comfort, there is no smile like His smile, there is no touch of help like His delivering hand. "Thy love to me was wonderful." Sometimes, when I have told the story of God's goodness to me, a Christian friend has said, "Have you not written all that down?" "No, I have not," I have replied. "Will you not take care, before you die, that it is all written down?" I have said, "No, I do not know that I shall." Now perhaps your life's story will die out with yourself, yet have there not been very marvelous touches of Christ's love in it? Have there not been windows of agates, and gates of carbuncle, through which you have seen your Lord's face; and can you not say tonight, looking over your pilgrim path from the first day until now, "Lord, Thou hast been ever with me; Thy love to me was wonderful in condescending, helpful fellowship in the time of my need"?

Think, also, of *the comforting and thoughtful provisions of Christ's love*. Sometimes you have been well-nigh slipping, not merely as to trouble, but as to sin. Our lives are not all to our credit; there have been sad moments, when unbelief has crept in on the back of thoughtlessness, and you have been almost a skeptic. There have been evil moments, when sin has insinuated itself into the imagination, and you have almost done that which would have been your ruin. Have there not been times in your life when you have been smitten, and, if there had not been some One to uphold you, you would have fallen, almost unconsciously fallen, and there have lain down to die? But oh, how Jesus has watched over you, and cared for you! Never mother nursed her babe with such care as Christ has given to you. When you look back, sometimes, and see the pit from which you have been preserved, into which you might have fallen; when you meet with some old friend, who used, years ago, to be singing at your side, but is now a drunkard or profane, and you say, "Why should he be like that any more than I should? Who hath made me to differ? What but the grace of God has kept me until now?" ah, then you see how Christ's love to you has been wonderful, passing the love of women!

But the love of Christ to us is most of all wonderful in *its plans for the future*. You know not, and you cannot conceive, what He will yet do for you. You are in trouble, are you? Well, joy cometh in the morning. Just now, you have to drink the bitter cup, and God gives you pills that you do not like. Take them at His hand, for they are meant for your good. 'Tis but a little while, and then sorrow and sighing shall forever flee away. Has any redeemed man here any notion of what God has prepared for them that love Him? You shall stand among the perfected, and go in and out amongst the holy. You shall be where no trouble shall ever reach you, or even the noise and dash of a wave of sorrow ever reach your ears. You shall be where it shall be your felicity to serve God without mistake, without transgression, and without omission. You shall behold the face of the King in His beauty, not now and then, but forever without a cloud or a veil between. You shall find it your delight to praise Him; and your voice shall be heard amid the choirs of the glorified as you adore the Lamb whose love to you has been so wonderful. And what will be your employments in heaven? Ah, that I cannot tell you; but they shall be employments that shall be equally honorable and delightful!

I have told you before what I sometimes dream shall be my lot in glory, to stand not here, and preach to a handful of people, though it be verily a large handful; but to stand upon some starry orb, and preach of Christ to whole constellations at once, and thunder out my remembrances of His sweet love to myriads of beings who have never heard of Him as yet, for they have never sinned, but who will drink in all the tidings of what Jesus did for sinful men. And each of you, according to your training for it, shall make known to angels, and principalities, and powers, the manifold wisdom of God. There is plenty of room for you all, for God's universe will need millions upon millions of messengers to go through it all, and tell out the story of redeeming love. And we, I believe, are here in training for that eternal work of making known to illimitable regions of space, and countless myriads of intelligent beings whom God has created, but who have never fallen, the story of this little planet, and of the God who loved it so that He came here, and died that He might save His people from their sins.

Get ready, brethren, for the eternity which is so near. Within about a hand's breadth, you and I shall be in eternity. Even if we live to be 80 or 90, or fulfill the tale of 100 years, it is but a little while, and we shall have quitted these dark shores, and landed in the everlasting brightness of endless glory, that is, if we know the love of Christ today, and trust in Christ today. We shall go on and on forever and forever experiencing more and more of this great truth, "Thy love to me was wonderful."

Now let each one answer this question—Can you say, "He loved me, and gave Himself for me?" If not, you are an unhappy man. God make you even more unhappy until you come and look to Jesus Christ, as men looked to the brazen serpent; and as by their looking they were healed, so by your looking may you be made to live tonight! Remember that—

> There is life for a look at the Crucified One;
> There is life at this moment for thee;
> Then look, sinner—look unto him, and be saved—
> Unto him who was nail'd to the tree.

RECRUITS FOR KING JESUS

SERMON NO. 1,770

DELIVERED ON LORD'S DAY EVENING, FEBRUARY 17, 1884.

PORTION OF SCRIPTURE READ BEFORE SERMON—JOHN 1:29–51.

HYMNS FROM *Our Own Hymn Book*—639, 670, 674.

And there came of the children of Benjamin and Judah to the hold unto David. And David went out to meet them, and answered and said unto them, If ye be come peaceably unto me to help me, mine heart shall be knit unto you: but if ye be come to betray me to mine enemies, seeing there is no wrong in mine hands, the God of our fathers look thereon, and rebuke it. Then the spirit came upon Amasai, who was chief of the captains, and he said, Thine are we, David, and on thy side, thou son of Jesse: peace, peace be unto thee, and peace be to thine helpers; for thy God helpeth thee. Then David received them, and made them captains of the band—1 Chronicles 12:16–18.

AT this time David was in the hold—I suppose in the stronghold of Ziklag, which the king of the Philistines had given to him. It was in that fortress town that he received a welcome addition to his band. David was an exile; and it is not every man who cares to cast in his lot with a banished nobleman. He was outlawed, and his sovereign would have slain him with his own hand if he had found opportunity: few care to stake their all with a man in such a condition. The many who were on Saul's side spoke very bitterly of David, and, wishing to curry favor with the king, they slandered him to the blackest degree, few respectable people care to associate themselves with a person who is in ill repute. Many to whom he had done no ill were eager to betray David, and sell him into the hand of his enemy; for men sought their own gain, and cared not whom they sold, so long as they clutched the price: it was no small thing for a band of men to unite with a man upon whose head a price was set. David had to stand upon his guard, for traitors were all around: the men of Keilah would have delivered him up when he went in all simplicity of heart within their gates. The fortunes of David were at a low ebb, and hence when these men came to David they did a valorous action—an action which he would be sure to remember in the after-days of his triumph.

I want to run a parallel between the case of David and that of our Lord Jesus Christ. At the present moment our Lord Jesus, the Son of David, is still in the hold. Among the men of this world He is not yet enthroned: their hearts go after another prince, and as yet the kingdom has not come to the Son of David. I know that He reigns in heaven, and that He is in very deed King of kings and Lord of lords; but before the eyes of the mass of men He is still despised and rejected. His people, as yet, are but a feeble folk, and often hard put to it; while His kingdom is ridiculed, His claims are derided, and His yoke is scorned. The doctrines which He preached are tossed to and fro like a ball; and men at the present time are glorying in science or tradition, in reason or in speculation; yea, they speak as if human wisdom would soon wipe out the very name of Christianity. It is not so in truth before God; but it is so in appearance before men. This is an age of blasphemy and of rebuke for our Lord the King. Brave are they who will stand to Christ in this, the day of His exile. They shall be right royally rewarded who will now take up His cause, and will go forth to Him without the camp, bearing His reproach. He is the man for the Lord Jesus who can now run the gauntlet of miles of scoffers, and be willing to be called a fool, a madman, or an idiot for His name's sake. Blessed are they who are not ashamed this day to bear the name of Christ written out large; and to confess that, after the way which men call "orthodoxy," so worship they the Lord God of their fathers. The philosophic Christian may escape if he will drown the Christian in the philosopher; but this is not to stand out square for Christ. It does our heart good nowadays to meet with a few brethren who are not ashamed still to believe in the merit of the Redeemer's precious blood, and in the power of His Spirit to regenerate. We feel at home when we drop in with a few who believe in prayer, and expect the Lord to interpose on the behalf of His people. I say, blessed are they who, like these men of Benjamin and Judah, are willing to go to the King in the hold, and take up His cause though it be at a low ebb, and stand up for Him when the many are ready to trample Him down, and are ridiculing His work and His cause. For my own part, I never loved my Lord better than now that He is defamed; and His truth is all the dearer to me because it is flouted by the worldly-wise.

It is to those who will volunteer for Jesus that I am about to speak; and our first head is, that using the text as a parable we have here *a commendable example*. It is a commendable example for men to join themselves with Christ while He is at a discount. Secondly, here is *a cautious inquiry*. When David sees these men come he does not at once receive them with open arms, but there is a reserve about him till he has asked them a question or two. He wants to know who they are before he writes down their names in his muster-roll. And, thirdly, here is *a very cordial enlistment* as they answer to his question, and say, "Thine are we, David, and on thy side, thou son of Jesse; for thy God helpeth thee."

I. First, then, here is A VERY COMMENDABLE EXAMPLE. May the Holy Spirit lead many of my dear hearers to follow it.

Many of these men of Benjamin and Judah, in the first place, went to join themselves to David because *they had heard that he was the Lord's anointed*. They understood that Samuel had gone down to Ramah, and, in the days of David's youth, had anointed him in the name of the Lord to be king instead of Saul. Therefore they said, "Whom God anoints we will follow," and they came after David. It was fit that they should be loyal to David if they would be obedient to God.

Now, it is within the belief, I trust, of all assembled here, that the Lord God Almighty has anointed "one chosen out of the people" to be His King in Zion—the King of His church forever and ever; and that One chosen out of the people is Jesus of Nazareth, of the house of David, who is Himself, as man, the servant of God, but who is also divine, and counts it not robbery to be equal with God. We have, I trust, all of us drunk in this doctrine, that the Lord Jesus is the Anointed of God, the very Word of God, in whom dwelleth all the fullness of the Godhead bodily. Now, it seems to me that if it be so, the next inevitable step for men who fear God is to go forth and follow the Lord's Anointed. If Jesus be the Messiah, the sent One of God, in the name of everything that is gracious and right let us follow Him. God has given Him to be a leader and a commander to the people; let us rally to His banner without delay. If the Lord has anointed Jesus to be a prince and a Savior, let Him be our prince and our Savior at once. Let us render Him obedience and confidence, and openly avow the same. Our Lord puts it thus—"If I tell you the truth, why do ye not believe me?" The argument is irresistible with true-hearted men. If any of you believe that Jesus is anointed to be the Savior of men, I say that you are unreasonable if you do not practically accept Him as such. But if you are willing to come right straight out, and say, "Let others do as they will; as for me, I will be the loving servant of the Anointed of the Lord"; then you act rightly, and render a reasonable service. What better argument can I find with just and reasonable persons than this? You believe that God has anointed Jesus, therefore accept Him for yourself. If these men followed David because God had anointed him, infinitely more binding is it upon you and upon me, believing that God has anointed Jesus of Nazareth to be the King, for us to follow *Him*, that we may be found faithful to His cause and kingdom. Oh, my dear hearers, I am perplexed about some of you: you call Jesus Lord, and yet you do not obey Him; you own that He is the Savior, and yet you do not trust in Him for salvation. Do think this over, and may the Holy Ghost lead you to a sensible decision. If Jesus be God's Anointed, let Him be your Beloved.

Next, these men, no doubt many of them, followed David because of *his personal excellencies*. They had heard of him—of what he was in his youth, what he had been at home, and at court, and in the army, and in the day of battle. He had behaved admirably everywhere, and these warriors had heard of it. I should not wonder if some of them remembered that, when he was a youth and ruddy, he came forth with his sling and stone and smote the giant foe of Israel on the forehead. Perhaps they had heard of all his mighty acts that he did when, as Saul's captain, he went in and out before the host and did valiantly in the name of the Most High. And when they heard of his gentleness, and of his courtesy, and of all the many virtues which adorned him, making him so greatly different from those leaders of freebooting bands who were so common in that land, I do not wonder if they enthusiastically gave themselves up to be the loyal followers of this David the son of Jesse. A good soldier should have a good captain: a good captain deserves good soldiers. These men of war argued well when they enlisted under David. But how shall I commend the Lord Jesus Christ to you that are of a noble spirit? Was there ever any like unto Him? Who among the good, the great, the brave, the beautiful, can be likened unto Him? He left the courts of heaven that He might save men. Love brought Him from glory to be the Redeemer of His enemies! Being found in fashion as a man, He gave Himself up to death, even the death of the cross for love of men. All His life long He did valiantly for the Lord His God, in all holiness and righteousness, defeating every temptation and over-coming all evil, and He ended His labor by going up to the cross to enter into per-sonal duel with death and hell, therein overthrowing all the powers of evil on the behalf of His people. Oh, could I paint His face, and could you see it as it is beheld by the eyes of God, you would all be enamored of Him! Oh, could all men know how good He is, how gracious He is, as some of us do know; even if they only went to that partial extent, surely no men would stand out, but the Prince Immanuel would win all hearts! All these young men and all the vast multitude who gather to this Taber-nacle would gladly take up their cross, and follow after Jesus at once, if they had any idea of His surpassing excellence. O my soul, how wouldst thou rejoice if men would come at once to Jesus! Oh to hear you all say, "We also will be with Jesus in the day of His derision and His scorn; for we see what He is, and there is none like Him. He shall be our King and our Captain, for He is the Chief among ten thousand, and the altogether lovely." He, being such a One, and so worthy of the anointing which He has received of God, I do as His recruiting sergeant commend Him to every one here. Oh, that you would all become His true followers at once; for He deserves the love and loyalty of every one of you. If ye would be safe and happy, come to my Lord, and be henceforth His servants. If ye would fight a good fight, enlist beneath this glorious "Captain of our salvation."

There was a third reason why brave spirits resolved to enlist under David, and that was, that he was so cruelly persecuted by Saul—*so misrepresented and abused by his enemies.* There are some cringing, fawning spirits in this world, who must always go with the majority. What everybody says they say: they take their cue from those who lead the fashion of the hour. They ask leave of common custom to breathe or eat. They dare not swallow down their spittle till they have obtained permission so to do. Cringing, fawning, sycophants of all that is great, and all that is fashionable, scarcely could a soul be found in them if they were searched through and through with a microscope. These will never come to David when he is in the hold, nor need he wish that they would. On the other hand, there are brave spirits who rather pre-fer to be in the minority. They do not even care if they have to stand alone for truth and righteousness. They could have ventured to say with Athanasius, "I, Athanasius, against the world"; for they know the right and they cling to it; and it is not to them a question whether truth walks in silver slippers or whether she plods barefoot through the mire. It is the truth they care for, and not the habiliments with which she may be adorned or disfigured. Such men took up David's side chivalrously because it was the right side, and the despised side; and they liked it none the less because so many spoke evil of it. Sadly true is it that the Lord Jesus Christ is still of so little account in this world. His name, ah, I am sick of the way in which they use His name today! Shame on some that are called Christian ministers! They believe in Christ, but it is a Christ without His crown, His atonement, His judgment seat, or even His Godhead. They mock us with orthodox phrases, from which the essential truth is gone. They pretend that they believe in the atonement, and when we listen to their atonement we find that it does not effectually atone for anyone. It is a mere fiction, and not a fact. It saves nobody, but is a mere sham. They have viscerated the gospel, and then they hold up the empty carcass, and claim that they are Christians still. Christians who have murdered Christianity! Believers who doubt whether there is anything to be believed! Yet we are entreated in our charity to hug such traitors to our bosom. We shall do nothing of the kind. We would sooner believe in infidels outright than in those who pretend to be Christians and are infidels at heart. "Modern thought" is a more evil thing than downright atheism; even as a wolf in a sheep's skin is worse than a wolf in his natural form. There are pretty things said of our Lord Jesus by those who deny the faith which are sickening to me. I loathe to hear our true Lord praised by false lips. They deny the doctrines which He taught, and yet prate about believing *Him*. It is a shallow trick, but yet it deceives shallow souls. Poor, weak minds say, "The man speaks so beautifully of Jesus, surely he cannot be in error." I tell you it is the old Judas trick—the Son of man is betrayed with a kiss. How nauseating their praises must be to Him whom they are betraying. Think not that they are honest; their designs are far other than appear upon the surface. They laud Him as man that they may dishonor Him as God: they cry up His life, and His example, that they may cast His atoning sacrifice into the ditch. They lift up one part of the divine revelation with no other intention than that they may dash down the other: they crouch at His feet that they may stab at His heart.

I avow myself at this hour the partisan of Christ, and of the whole truth of Christ, in its old-fashioned form: the more old-fashioned the better for me. I am for Jesus Christ, the same yesterday, today, and forever. I am for the gospel of martyrs and confessors who gave their hearts' blood as the seal of their faith. New gospels and new theologies I abhor. I am for that same ancient gospel which today is said to be absolutely defunct. Science has wiped out the evangelicals: we are dead: we are gone. So they say of us. Yet in our graves we turn: even in our ashes live our wonted fires: we expect a resurrection. Truth may be crushed down, but it cannot be crushed out. If there survived but one love of the doctrines of grace he would suffice by God's Spirit to sow the world again with the verities of our holy faith. The eternal truth which

Christ and His apostles taught is not dead but sleepeth; at a touch of the Lord's hand she shall rise in all her ancient power and look round for her adversaries, and they shall not be: yea, she shall diligently consider their place and they shall not be. Blessed are they who at this time are not afraid to be on the side that is ridiculed and laughed at. Truth will have its turn, and though it now grind the dust it shall be at the top before long, and they who are loyal to it shall share its fortunes. Let us be bold enough to say, "Put down my name among the fools who believe, and not among those whose wisdom lies in doubting everything." God save us from the wisdom which believes in itself, and give us more of the wisdom which believes in *Him*!

Once more. These men came to David because *they believed that David had a great future before him.* He was very poor when they came to him, an exile, as we have said, an outlaw, one who could not return to his land because the king himself had a personal feud with him. But they said, "It doth not yet appear what he shall be. This son of Jesse will be king yet, and his enemies shall beg their lives of him." So, looking to the great future that awaited him, they determined to take shares with him in his present low estate that they might be raised with him in his exaltation. Now, I think that I can say to every one here, "I would that ye would come over to David's side—to Jesus' side—for there is a future awaiting Him, a glory, a triumph, even here on earth, such as shall make those men gnash their teeth who throw away this opportunity of enlisting in His host." How will souls lament forever their neglect of joining themselves to Jesus! It shall be their everlasting regret that they lost the opportunity of standing straight out for truth, and right, and love, as they are seen in the person of the Son of God. Oh, it will be an endless loss to have refused to stand upon the pillory of scorn, and avow Jesus of Nazareth as the Son of God, and the Savior of men. "Behold he cometh with clouds, and every eye shall see him." Woe to those who pierced Him by refusing to believe in Him. The Lord shall reign forever and ever, and the shout of "Hallelujah, hallelujah," shall come up from earth and descend from heaven. He shall sit upon the throne of his father David, and of his kingdom there shall be no end. Who does not desire to be with Him and to behold His glory? Cast in your lot with him, then, O ye undecided! Let His cause be as it may in the eyes of worldlings, espouse it at once right heartily; for they that are with Him in His humiliation shall be with Him in His triumph.

Those are the reasons why, at this time, I stand here, and exhort, beg, beseech, entreat every one among you to be on the side of Jesus Christ our Lord. Woe unto you if you turn your backs upon Him! Woe unto you if you attempt to be neutrals! Woe unto you if you are lukewarm followers! Remember, He that is not with Him is against Him. He that takes not up his cross and follows after Him is not worthy of Him, and shall not be counted among His disciples. Oh, that this whole company here tonight were distinctly and avowedly, perfectly and continuously, on the side of Jesus Christ, the Prince of peace, the coming King! O my friend, yonder, I speak to you personally, I would to God that you would at once put on the livery of my Lord Jesus, and become His sworn servant forever!

II. Now, I have just a few words to say upon the second head. A CAUTIOUS INQUIRY.

These men of Benjamin and of Judah came to David, and David met them as a warrior standing upon his guard. The times were not such as to allow of a negligent confidence in all who professed friendship. The Benjamites were of the same tribe as Saul, and it was singular that they should come and join with David, the rival of their own leader. The men of Judah belonged to the same tribe as those men of Keilah who had betrayed David: therefore the hero was cautious and made careful inquiry. My Lord Jesus Christ is never so eager after disciples as to enroll those who cannot bear to be questioned. He did not go abroad sweeping up a heap of nominal followers who would increase His apparent strength and prove a real weakness to Him. He said to those who offered themselves, "Count the cost." "Lord, I will follow thee whithersoever thou goest," says one. Jesus does not there and then enlist him, but calmly replies, "Foxes have holes, and the birds of the air have nests; but the Son of man hath not where to lay his head." He wants followers, but He wants them to be of the right kind; therefore He does not delude them and excite them to enter suddenly upon a course which they will, before long, renounce. He does not act as, I am afraid, the recruiting sergeant does when he tells the brave boys of all the glories they will enjoy, and crosses their hands with a shilling, so that they may take Her Majesty's money and become her servants. The sergeant does not say much about the wounds of battle and the pains of hospital: he does not dwell very long upon wooden legs, and broken arms, and lost eyes, and all that. No; he dwells on pleasure, victory, pension, glory. Our great Captain does not in this manner entrap allies, but He sets the worst part of His service first, and bids men consider whether they will be able to carry out that which they propose to do. I would in this matter imitate my Lord: I have pressed you to come to His banner, but at the same time I would cautiously inquire of you.

Now, see what David said to them: he set before them *the right way*. He said, "If ye be come peaceably *unto me* to help me, mine heart shall be knit unto you." If you wish to join with Christ's people, and have your name numbered with them, one main question is—Do you come unto *Him*? Do you first give yourselves to the Lord and afterwards unto His people? "If ye be come *unto me*," says David. It would have been useless for them to answer, "We have come because we are fond of some of the people that are with you." "No," he says, "if ye be come *to me*, then my heart shall be knit to you. Not else." Do you come to Christ, dear friend? Are you sure that Jesus is your Leader? Do not profess to be a Christian if you have not come to Christ, for Christ is the soul of Christianity. To come to Christ is this: confessing your sin, look to Him as the sin-bearer, trust Him with your future, trust Him with your soul altogether. By a sincere, simple, undivided faith, you do really come to Jesus: have you such a faith? Let Jesus Christ be first and last with you. Take Him to be your Savior altogether. Do not be your own Savior even in part. Let Him save you from beginning to end, from top to bottom, in all ways and respects. If it be so, come along with you, for our host will be glad to have its number increased by your coming. If you do not thus come to our Lord, pray do not come to us, for you will neither do good, nor get good thereby.

Then David puts the question, "If ye be come *peaceably* unto me," and this was needful, for some are captious and quarrelsome. Some profess to come to Christ, but they quarrel with Christ at the very first. They would make terms with Him and they come intending to dispute with His people. From the first they are discontented and fault-finding, rather patronizing Christ and His cause than humbly uniting with Him and His people. They do not think half as much of God's people as God thinks of them. When I hear people say, "Oh, there is So-and-So, who is not what he ought to be, and he is a member of the church," and then they begin finding fault with this and with that, I say to myself, "That critic is no true friend." The church is not perfect, but woe to the man who finds pleasure in pointing out her imperfections. Christ loved His church, and let us do the same. I have no doubt that the Lord can see more fault in His church than I can; and I have equal confidence that He sees no fault at all, because He covers her faults with His own love—that love which hides a multitude of sins; and He removed all her defilement with that precious blood which washes away all the transgressions of His people. I dare not find fault with those whom the Lord has loved from before the foundation of the world; more especially since I find that I need all my time to find out my own faults and to get rid of them. If you are a faultless man I do not ask you to join the Christian Church, because I am sure that you would not find anybody else there like yourself. It is true that if you do not join a church till you find a perfect one you will not be a church member this side of heaven; but I may add, that if there were such a church, the moment your name was written in the list it would leave off being a perfect church, for your presence would have destroyed its perfection. If you are coming to pick holes, and quiz, and question, and find fault, and talk about inconsistencies and so forth, then you may pass on and join some other army; but if you be come peaceably to our Lord and to us, then I offer you a hearty welcome. We are not anxious to enlist men who love to have the pre-eminence, nor men of fierce temper, nor unforgiving spirits, nor proud, envious, lovers of strife; we want only those who have the mind of Christ. Come peaceably, or come not at all.

Again David puts the question, "If ye be come peaceably to me *to help me.*" Mind this and mark it well: they that join with Christ must join in His battles, join in His labors, join in His self-sacrifice. We must come to His church not only to be helped, but to help. It is of no use your entering the army if you do not mean to fight; and it is of no use your uniting with the host of God unless you mean to take your share in the holy warfare. Many forget this, and look upon a religious life as one of sanctified selfishness. A great many stop the gospel plow. "Hi!" say they; "stop!" They want to ride on one of the horses. Yes, but the plowman has no opinion of such friends. Let them lead the horses or hold the plow-handles, or do something, or else let them take themselves off. Of course, I do not mean the sick and faint; but all fit for war must go to the war. There is something for every church member to do as well as to receive. They that join the Church of Christ must come to pull as well as to be pulled—come to work as well as to eat; and usually the rule is true in Christ's house as it ought to be in everybody else's, "He that will not work, neither shall he eat." They that do not labor in the cause of Christ will very soon find that they are not fed in the house of God. Why should they be? I count it no office of mine to carry bread and meat to sluggards and lie-a-beds: I would sooner feed swine. They who never do a hand's turn among us ought to be turned out from us. If ye be come peaceable to help us, then I speak for my Captain, and bid you welcome; but if you do not mean real service, please to march on.

There are the three questions, then. Do you come to Christ and accept Him? If so, come along. Do you come with a desire to maintain peace among your Christian brethren? If so, come! Do you come with the intent of helping the Lord Jesus Christ to spread abroad His truth? Then come, and welcome, and the Lord be with you and with us!

Do you know what Jesus says to you who come to Him aright? "My heart shall be knit unto you." Oh, I think that if I had been Amasai, I should have felt the spirit come upon me to speak just as Amasai did when he so heartily declared that he and his brethren came to join heart and soul with David. With all that loving warmth which was so natural to him, David said, "My heart shall be knit to you." Now when the Lord Jesus Christ says, "Will you espouse my cause? Will you accept me for leader? Will you come and join with my people? Then my heart shall be knit unto you"—do not your hearts leap within you? What a charming promise it is! What union of soul it sets forth! I do not know much about knitting; but some of you do. Things knit together are not merely joined in one, but they are one. They are not merely sewn together by a machine, so that you can draw out a thread and the pieces divide; but they are knit together and are of one piece, one fabric, one substance. Come, then, ye truly faithful, you shall be knit together with Christ, His heart with your heart; you shall never be separated from Him any more. It is a great thing when the hearts of God's people are knit together; but it is greatest of all when their hearts are knit with Christ's heart, and His heart is knit with theirs. Come hither, ye true-hearted: cast in your lot with your Lord. Is it not reward enough for coming into His host, that His heart shall be knit to you? I count this my heaven upon earth, to have my Lord's love; do you not agree with me?

Notice how David put the other side of it, and set before them *the wrong way*;—"But if ye be come to betray me to my enemies, seeing there is no wrong in mine hands, the God of our fathers look thereon, and rebuke it." Will persons ever join the church to betray the Lord Christ to His enemies? I say not that such is their present purpose; but a great many have acted as if they were from the beginning traitors to Him and to His truth. They have come into the church, and yet they have betrayed Christ to His enemies; yea, they have been aided in their treachery by having been admitted within our ranks. Some have done this by giving up the doctrines of the gospel. Falling into this error and that, they have denied the gospel, overthrown the weak, and shaken the strong. Some have proved themselves the enemies of the cross of Christ by their inconsistent lives. People have pointed at them, and said, "Those are followers of Christ, you see. They can lie, and cheat, and get gain as the basest rogues do." They say that they are Christians, and yet you cannot trust them in trade. They are just as gay, and worldly, and false as if they were not Christians at all. Why, then I suspect that they are not Christians at all; but like Judas Iscariot, they are children of perdition. Then there are some in all ages who betray the Lord Jesus by apostasy. They run well for a time, and then they are hindered. Being armed and carrying bows, they turn back in the day of battle. They are trees twice dead, plucked up by the roots. Such sorrowful heart-breaking cases do occur in all churches, where men come to the very front, and appear to do great service for Christ, and yet forsake Him, and walk no more with His people, nor in His ways; even denying that they ever were associated with Him and with His cause. They open His wounds! They put Him to an open shame! Woe unto them! Sorrowfully, yet sternly would I say, If there should be one here who will in some future day willfully betray the Savior on any account whatever, the Lord have mercy upon such, and prevent His joining with our church lest we be overwhelmed with shame and sorrow. True-hearted men, we invite you! Half-hearted, fickle men, we would avoid you! Yet such do come, and will come, and what can we say of them? "The God of our fathers look thereon and rebuke it,"—aye, rebuke it so as to prevent it, that they may not be as thorns in our side.

III. But time fails me, and therefore I must finish up, thirdly, by describing from the text A CORDIAL ENLISTMENT. The captain of these brave men felt the Spirit come upon him, and he spoke up as warm-heartedly as David had spoken, saying, "Thine are we, David, and on thy side, thou son of Jesse: peace, peace, be unto thee, and peace be to thine helpers; for thy God helpeth thee."

He began thus:—"Thine are we, David." Now, that is the first thing I want of those who are going to join the church—"Thine are we, Jesus. We are not our own; we are bought with a price." Well may that man avow himself to belong to Christ who has been bought with the blood of Christ: "For ye were not redeemed with corruptible things, as with silver and gold, but with the precious blood of Christ." Now, if ye be indeed redeemed by Him, I pray you confess that you are altogether and absolutely your Lord's. Sing with your whole heart—

> All that I am, and all I have
> Shall be forever thine.

Do not sing it alone, but practice it. Let your lives say—Thine are we, Jesus. Neither count we anything that we possess to be our own; but all is dedicated to thy royal use.

Then Amasai added, "and on thy side, thou son of Jesse": for, if we belong to Christ, of course we are on Christ's side, whatever that side may be. In religion, morals, politics, we are on Christ's side. Here is the side of the learned; there is the side of the ignorant: we are on neither the one, nor the other: we are on Christ's side. In every political question we desire to be and ought to be on Christ's side: we are neither of this party nor of that, but on the side of justice, peace, righteousness. In every moral question we are bound to be on Christ's side. In every religious question we are not on the side of predominant thought, nor on the side of fashionable views, nor on the side of lucre, but on the side of Christ. Make this your oracle—"What would Jesus do?" Go and do *that*. How would Jesus think? Go and think *that*. What would Jesus have you to be? Ask God to make you just *that*. "Thine are we, David, and on thy side, thou son of Jesse."

Then he added, "Peace be to thee." "Peace, peace, be to thee." Double peace to thee. So say we to our Lord Jesus Christ: our heart salutes Him and invokes peace upon Him. Blessed Master, we are at peace with Thee so completely as to be at one with Thee. What Thou sayest we believe; what Thou doest we admire, what Thou commandest we obey; what Thou claimest we resign; what Thou forbiddest we forego. We yield ourselves up to Thee wholly, and are at perfect peace with Thee in all thy purposes, and designs and acts. Peace, peace to thee.

"And peace be to thy helpers." We desire all good for all good men. We pray for the peace of the peaceful. The day that we were converted we felt that we loved every Christian. I used to say of the little village where I first preached, that I had such an attachment to every inhabitant in it that if I had seen a dog that came from Waterbeach I would have given him a bone. Do you not feel the same towards all the Lord's people? The proverb hath it, "Love me, love my dog"; and when you love Christ you love the very lowest of His people. Aye, if Jesus had a dog, you would love that dog for Christ's sake. I am sure that it is so. When a man is always caviling, I fear he has not the spirit of Christ, and is none of His. We know some people who might be compared to hedgehogs, they cannot be touched by anybody, they are all spines and prickles; such people may think well of themselves, but it is to be feared that the loving Jesus does not think well of them. The man with a hot head and a bitter heart, is he a friend of Jesus? I cannot imagine that such a head as that will lie in Jesus Christ's bosom. Oh, no, dear friends, he that loveth is born of God but not the man of hate and spite. Give me the eyes of the dove, and not those of a carrion crow. When the dove soars aloft into the air, what does she look for? Why, for her dovecote, and when she discovers the beloved abode she uses her wings with lightning speed, for there is her delight. If you were to throw a raven or a carrion-crow into the air, it would be looking for something foul which it could feed upon; and there are men and women in every Christian church who are always trying with far-reaching and greatly-magnifying eyes to find out some wretched scandal or another. If you want to go to your bed uncomfortable, and to lie awake all night, if your are a pastor of a church, have a few minutes' talk with a friend of this order. These are the folks who have just sniffed out a matter that ought to be inquired into. When it is inquired into there is nothing to discover, and great heart-burning is caused in the process of investigation. These same scandal-mongers will have something fresh tomorrow morning wherewith to keep their dear tongues going. May we be favored with very few of these irritating beings.

May those that come among us always be those that can say, "Peace be to thy helpers." Whatever helps Christ I would help. Wherever I see anything of Christ there my heart shall rest. Oh, to have a large increase to this church and all the churches of hearty, loving, peace-making people!

The last word that they said to David was, "For thy God helpeth thee"; and I shall keep that last sentence very much to myself: I want to feed upon it as my portion of meat: you must not muzzle the mouth of the ox that treadeth out the corn, and I am that ox at this time. "Thy God helpeth thee." How I do rejoice to think that God is helping the Great Son of David. All the powers of the God of nature and providence are working to aid the Lord of grace. The stars in their courses are fighting for our Immanuel. Everything is being overruled for the advance of Christ's kingdom. We are all on the tremble as to the Sudan and Egypt; but could we see all things we should rejoice. None of us knows what is coming. I am no prophet, nor the son of a prophet, but I venture to foretell that mountains will be leveled for the coming of our Lord even by calamities and disasters. There will be a speedier dissolution of the empire of the false prophet and of the false prophet's imitator because of all this mixing up of the west and the east in an unwilling conjunction. I say not how or when, but the Lord's purpose shall stand, and He will do all His pleasure. When the ocean roars at its utmost fury, the Lord puts a bit into the mouth of the tempest and reins up the storm. Jehovah maketh a way for Himself amid the tumult of great waters. When confusion and uproar predominate everywhere, and old chaos seems to be coming back again, all this is but a phase of unbroken order. How swift and sure are the revolutions of the wheels which are bringing nearer the chariot of the Son of God!

Cast in your lot with "the Leader and Commander of the people," who has God with him. It is the glory of Christ's cause that the Lord God is involved in it. Mr. Wesley's dying words were, "The best of all is, God is with us!" As I repeat the truth my heart cries, "Hallelujah! Blessed be the name of the Lord!" The Lord thy God helpeth thee, O Christ of God! The pleasure of the Lord shall prosper in thy hand. Thou must reign: thy Father swears it to thee. Thou shalt divide a portion with the great, and Thou shalt share the spoil with the strong, for Thou hast given up thy soul unto death, and permitted thy glory to be rolled in the dust; and Thou hast risen and gone into the glory; therefore Thou must reign. O Anointed of the Lord, thy throne shall endure forever! Tonight, thy servants salute Thee again, Thou Son of David. Wounded Christ, we lay our fingers in the print of the nails, and say, "My Lord and my God." Risen Christ, we look upward as the heavens receive Thee, and we adore. Ascended Christ, we fall at thy dear feet, and say, "Thine are we, O Son of David, anointed to be a Prince and a Savior." Coming Christ, we wait and watch for thine appearing! Come quickly to thine own! Amen and amen.

LOYAL TO THE CORE

Sermon No. 1,512
Portions of Scripture read before Sermon—2 Samuel 15:13–23;
Matthew 10:24–33.
Hymns from *Our Own Hymn Book*—670, 658, 666.

And Ittai answered the king, and said, As the LORD liveth, and as my lord the king liveth, surely in what place my lord the king shall be, whether in death or life, even there also will thy servant be—2 Samuel 15:21.

ALTHOUGH the courage of David appears to have failed him when he fled from his son Absalom, yet certain other noble characteristics came out in brilliant relief, and among the rest, his large-heartedness and his thoughtfulness for others. A man in such a desperate condition as he was must have earnestly coveted many friends and have been anxious to retain them all, but yet he would not exact their services if they were too costly to themselves, and so he said to Ittai, who appears to have been a Philistine—a proselyte to Israel, who had lately come to join himself to David—"Wherefore I goest thou also with us? Thou hast newly come to me, and should I make thee wander with me in my sorrows? Return to thy place and abide with the new king, for thou art a stranger and an exile. May every blessing be upon thee. May mercy and truth be with thee." He did not send him away because he doubted him, but because he felt that he had no claim to the great sacrifices which Ittai might have to make in attending his checkered fortunes. "I do not know what may become of me," he seems to say, "but I do not want to drag you down with myself. Should my cause become desperate, I have no wish to involve you in it, and therefore with the best of motives I wish you farewell." I admire this generosity of spirit. Some men have great expectations: they live upon their friends, and yet complain that charity is cold. These people expect more from their friends than they ought to give. A man's best friends on earth ought to be his own strong arms. Loafers are parasitical plants, they have no root of their own, but like the mistletoe they strike root into some other tree, and suck the very soul out of it for their own nourishment. Sad that men should ever degrade themselves to such despicable meanness! While you can help yourselves, do so and while you have a right to expect help in times of dire necessity, do not be everlastingly expecting everybody else to be waiting upon you. Feel as David did towards Ittai—that you would by no means wish for services to which you have no claim. Independence of spirit used to be characteristic of Englishmen. I hope it will always continue to be so; and especially among children of God.

On the other hand, look at Ittai, perfectly free to go, but in order to end the controversy once for all, and to make David know that he does not mean to leave him, he takes a solemn oath before Jehovah his God, and he doubles it by swearing by the life of David that he will never leave him; in life, in death, he will be with him. He has cast in his lot with him for better and for worse, and he means to be faithful to the end. Old Master Trapp says, "All faithful friends went on a pilgrimage years ago, and none of them have ever come back." I scarcely credit that, but I am afraid that friends quite so faithful as Ittai are as scarce as two moons in the sky at once, and you might travel over the edge of the world before you found them. I think, however, that one reason why faithful Ittais have become so scarce may be because large-hearted Davids are so rare. When you tell a man that you expect a good deal of him, he does not see it. Why should you look for so much? He is not your debtor. You have closed at once the valves of his generosity. But when you tell him honestly that you do not expect more than is right, and that you do not wish to be a tax upon him, when he sees that you consult his welfare more than your own, that is the very reason why he feels attached to you, and counts it a pleasure to serve such a generous-hearted man. You will generally find that when two people fall out there are faults on both sides: if generous spirits be few, it may be because faithful friends are rare, and if faithful friends are scarce it may be because generous spirits are scarce too. Be it ours as Christians to live to serve rather than to be served, remembering that we are the followers of a Master who said, "The Son of man came not to be ministered unto, but to minister." We are not to expect others to serve us, but our life is to be spent in endeavoring to serve them.

I am going to use Ittai's language for a further purpose. If Ittai, charmed with David's person and character, though a foreigner and a stranger, felt that he could enlist beneath his banner for life—yea, and declared that he would do so there and then—how much more may you and I, if we know what Christ has done for us, and who He is and what He deserves at our hands, at this good hour plight our troth to Him and vow, "As the Lord liveth, surely in whatsoever place my Lord and Savior shall be, whether in death or life, even there also shall His servant be."

And so, I shall begin by noticing first *in what form this declaration was made*, that we may learn from it how to make the same declaration.

I. IN WHAT FORM AND MANNER WAS THIS DECLARATION MADE?

It was made, first, at a time *when David's fortunes were at their lowest ebb*, and consequently it was made unselfishly, without the slightest idea of gain from it. David was now forsaken of everybody. His faithful bodyguard was all that he had on earth to depend upon, and then it was that Ittai cast in his lot with David. Now, beloved, it is very easy to follow religion when she goes abroad in her silver slippers, but the true man follows her when she is in rags, and goes through the mire and the slough. To take up with Christ when everybody cries up his name is what a hypocrite would do, but to take up with Christ when they are shouting, "Away with him! away with him!" is another matter. There are times in which the simple faith of Christ is at a great discount. At one time imposing ceremonies are all the rage, and everybody loves decorated worship, and the pure simplicity of the gospel is overloaded and encumbered with meretricious ornaments; it is such a season that we must stand out for God's more simple plan, and reject the symbolism which verges on idolatry and hides the simplicity of the gospel.

At another time the gospel is assailed by learned criticisms and by insinuations against the authenticity and inspiration of the books of Scripture, while fundamental doctrines are undermined one by one, and he who keeps to the old faith is said to be behind the age, and so on. But happy is that man who takes up with Christ, and with the gospel, and with the truth when it is in its worst estate, crying, "If this be foolery, I am a fool, for where Christ is there will I be; I love Him better at His worst than others at their best, and even if He be dead and buried in a sepulchre I will go with Mary and with Magdalene and sit over against the sepulchre and watch until He rise again, for rise again He will; but whether He live or die, where He is there shall his servant be." Ho, then, brave spirits, will ye enlist for Christ when His banner is tattered? Will you enlist under Him when His armor is stained with blood? Will you rally to Him even when they report Him slain? Happy shall ye be! Your loyalty shall be proven to your own eternal glory. Ye are soldiers such as He loves to honor.

Ittai gave himself up wholly to David *when he was but newly come to him*. David says, "Whereas thou camest but yesterday, should I this day make thee go up and down with us? But Ittai does not care whether he came yesterday or twenty years ago, but he declares, "Surely in what place my lord the king shall be, whether in death or life, even there also will thy servant be." It is best to begin the Christian life with thorough consecration. Have any of you professed to be Christians, and have you never given yourselves entirely to Christ? It is time that you began again. This should be one of the earliest forms of our worship of our Master—this total resignation of ourselves to Him. According to His Word, the first announcement of our faith should be by baptism, and the meaning of baptism, or immersion in water, is death, burial, and resurrection. As far as this point is concerned, the avowal is just this: "I am henceforth dead to all but Christ, whose servant I now am. Henceforth let no man trouble me, for I bear in my body the marks of the Lord Jesus. The watermark is on me from head to foot. I have been buried with Him in baptism unto death to show that henceforth I belong to Him." Now, whether you have been baptized or not I leave to yourselves, but in any case this must be true—that henceforth you are dead, and your life is hid with Christ in God. As soon as ever Christ is yours you ought to be Christ's. "I am my Beloved's" should be linked with "My Beloved is mine," in the dawn of the day in which you yield to the Lord.

Again, Ittai surrendered himself to David *in the most voluntary manner*. No one persuaded Ittai to do this; in fact, David seems to have persuaded him the other way. David tested and tried him, but he voluntarily out of the fullness of his heart said, "Where, my lord, the king, is, there also shall his servant be." Now, dear young people, if you believe that the Lord Jesus Christ is yours, give yourselves up to Him by a distinct act and deed. Feel that one grand impulse without needing pressure or argument—"The love of Christ constraineth me"; but do not wait to have your duty urged upon you, for the more free the dedication the more acceptable it will be. I am told that there is no wine so delicious as that which flows from the grape at the first gentle pressure. The longer you squeeze the harsher is the juice. We do not like that service which is pressed out of a man: and certainly the Lord of love will not accept forced labor. No; let your willingness show itself. Say—

> Take myself, and I will be
> Ever, *only*, ALL for thee.

My heart pants after the service of her Lord. With the same spontaneity which Ittai displayed make a solemn consecration of yourselves to David's Lord.

I used a word then which suggests another point, namely, that *Ittai did this very solemnly*. He took an oath which we Christians may not do, and may not wish to do, but still we should make the surrender with quite as much solemnity. In Dr. Doddridge's "Rise and Progress of Religion in the Soul" there is a very solemn form of consecration, which he recommends young men to sign when they give themselves to Christ. I cannot say that I can recommend it, though I practiced it, for I fear that there is something of legality about it, and that it may bring the soul into bondage. I have known some write out a deed of dedication to Christ and sign it with their blood. I will neither commend nor censure, but I will say that a complete dedication must be made in some manner, and that it should be done deliberately and with grave thought. You have been bought with a price, and you should, therefore, in a distinct manner own your Lord's property in you, and transfer to Him the title-deeds of your body, spirit, and soul.

And this, I think, *Ittai did publicly*. At any rate, he so acted that everybody saw him when David said, "Go over," and he marched in front—the first man to pass the brook. Oh yes, dear friend, you must publicly own yourself a Christian. If you are a Christian you must not try to sneak to heaven round the back alleys, but march up the narrow way like a man and like your Master. He was never ashamed of you, though He might have been: how can you be ashamed of Him when there is nothing in Him to be ashamed of? Some Christians seem to think that they shall lead an easier life if they never make a profession. Like a rat behind the wainscot they come out after candlelight and get a crumb, and then slip back again. I would not lead such a life. Surely, there is nothing to be ashamed of. A Christian—let us glory in the name! A believer in the Lord Jesus Christ—let them write it on our door plates, if they will. Why should we blush at that? "But," says one, "I would rather be a very quiet one." I will now place a torpedo under this cowardly quietness. What saith the Lord Jesus?

"Whosoever shall deny me before men, him will I also deny before my Father which is in heaven; but he that shall confess me before men, him will I confess also before my Father which is in heaven." Take up your cross and follow Him, for "with the heart man believeth unto righteousness, and with the mouth confession is made unto salvation." When our Master ascended up on high He told us to preach the gospel to every creature; and how did He put it? "He that believeth and is baptized shall be saved." There must be, therefore, the believing and the acknowledgment of believing. "But cannot I be saved as a believer if I do not openly confess Christ?" Dear friend, you have no business to tamper with your Master's command, and then say, "Will He not graciously forgive this omission?" Do not neglect one of the two commands, but obey all His will. If you have the spirit of Ittai you will say, "Wheresoever my lord the king is, there also shall thy servant be."

I leave the matter with the consciences of those who may be like Nicodemus, coming to Jesus by night, or may be like Joseph of Arimathea, who was a disciple, but secretly, for fear of the Jews. May they come out and own their Master, believing that then He will own them.

II. Secondly, WHAT DID THIS DECLARATION INVOLVE? As to Ittai, what did it involve?

First, that *he was henceforth to be David's servant*. Of course, as his soldier, he was to fight for him, and to do his bidding. What sayest thou, man? Canst thou lift thy hand to Christ, and say, "Henceforth I will live as thy servant, not doing my own will, but thy will. Thy command is henceforth my rule?" Canst thou say that? If not, do not mock Him, but stand back. May the Holy Ghost give thee grace thus to begin, thus to persevere, and thus to end.

It involved, next, for Ittai that *he was to do his utmost for David's cause*, not to be his servant in name, but his soldier, ready for scars and wounds and death, if need be, on the king's behalf. That is what Ittai meant as, in rough soldier-tones, he took the solemn oath that it should be so. Now, if thou wouldst be Christ's disciple, determine henceforth by His grace that thou wilt defend His cause; that if there be rough fighting thou wilt be in it; and if there be a forlorn hope needed thou wilt lead it, and go through floods and flames if thy Master's cause shall call thee. Blessed is the man who will follow the Lamb whithersoever He goeth, giving himself wholly up to his Lord to serve Him with all His heart.

But Ittai in *his promise declared that he would give a personal attendance upon the person of his master*. That was, indeed, the pith of it, "In what place my lord, the king, shall be, even there also will thy servant be." Brethren, let us make the same resolve in our hearts, that wherever Christ is, there we will be. Where is Christ? In heaven. We will be there by-and-by. Where is He here, spiritually? Answer: in His church. The church is a body of faithful men; and where these are met together, there is Jesus in the midst of them. Very well, then, we will join the church, for wherever our Lord, the King, is, there also shall His servants be. When the list of the redeemed is read we will be found in the register, for our Lord's name is there.

Where else did Jesus go? In the commencement of His ministry He descended into the waters of baptism. Let us follow the Lamb whithersoever He goeth. At the close of His ministry He brake bread, and said, "This do ye in remembrance of me." Be often at His table, for if there is a place on the earth where He manifests Himself to His children it is where bread is broken in His name. Let me now tell a secret. Some of you may have heard it before, but you have forgotten it. Here it is—my Lord is generally here at prayer-meetings on Monday nights, and, indeed, whenever His people come together for prayer, there He is. So I will read you my text, and see whether you will come up to it—"Surely in what place my Lord the King shall be, whether it be in a prayer-meeting or at a sermon, even there also will thy servant be." If you love your Lord, you know where His haunts are; take care that you follow hard after Him there.

Where is the Lord Jesus Christ? Well, brethren, He is wherever the truth is, and I pray God that He may raise up a race of men and women in England who are determined to be wherever the truth of God is. We have a host of molluscous creatures about who will always be where the congregation is the most respectable: respectability being measured by clothes and cash. Time was in the church of God when they most esteemed the most pious men; has it come to this that gold takes precedence of grace? Our fathers considered whether a ministry was sound, but now the question is—Is the man clever? Words are preferred to truth, and oratory takes the lead of the gospel. Shame on such an age. O you who have not altogether sold your birthrights, I charge you keep out of this wretched declension.

The man who loves Christ thoroughly will say, "Wheresoever the Lord the King is, there also shall His servant be, if it be with half a dozen poor Baptists or Methodists, or among the most despised people in the town." I charge you, beloved, in whatever town or country your lot is cast, be true to your colors, and never forsake your principles. Wherever the truth is, there go, and where there is anything contrary to truth, do not go, for there your Master is not to be found.

What next? Well, our Master is to be found wherever there is anything to be done for the good of our fellow-men. The Lord Jesus Christ is to be found wherever there is work to be done in seeking after His lost sheep. Some people say that they have very little communion with Christ, and when I look at them, I do not wonder. Two persons cannot walk together if they will not walk at the same pace. Now, my Lord walks an earnest pace whenever He goes through the world, for the King's business requires haste; and if His disciples crawl after a snail's fashion they will lose His company. If some of our groaning brethren would go to the Sunday-school, and there begin to look after the little children, they would meet with their Lord who used to say, "Suffer the little children to come unto me." If others were to get together a little meeting, and teach the ignorant, they would there find Him who had compassion on the ignorant and on those that are out of the way. Our Master is where there are fetters to be broken, burdens to be removed, and hearts to be comforted, and if you wish to keep with Him you must aid in such service.

Where is our Master? Well, He is always on the side of truth and right. And, O, you Christian people, mind that in everything—politics, business, and everything— you keep to that which is right, not to that which is popular. Do not bow the knee to that which for a little day may be cried up, but stand fast in that which is consistent with rectitude, with humanity, with the cause and honor of God, and with the freedom and progress of men. It can never be wise to do wrong. It can never be foolish to be right. It can never be according to the mind of Christ to tyrannize and to oppress. Keep you ever to whatsoever things are pure and lovely and of good report, and you will so far keep with Christ. Temperance, purity, justice—these are favorites with Him; do your best to advance them for His sake.

Above all, remember how Jesus loved secret prayer, and if you resolve to keep with Him you must be much at the throne of grace.

I will not detain you over each of these points, but simply say that Ittai's declaration meant also this—that *he intended to share David's condition.* If David was great, Ittai would rejoice. If David was exiled, Ittai would attend his wanderings. Our point must be to resolve in God's strength to keep to Christ in all weathers and in all companies, and that whether in life or death. Ah that word "death" makes it sweet, because then we reap the blessed result of having lived with Christ. We shall go up-stairs for the last time and bid good-bye to all, and then we shall feel that in death He is still with us as in life we have been with Him. Though our good works can never be a ground of confidence when we are dying, yet if the Lord enables us to follow the Lamb whithersoever He goeth, and so to lead a decided, positive, downright, upright Christian life, our death pillow will not be stuffed with thorns of regret, but we shall have to bless God that we bore a faithful witness as far as were able to do so. In such a case we shall not when we are dying wish to go back again to rectify the mistakes and insincerities of our lives. No, beloved, it will be very, very sweet to be alone with Jesus in death. He will make all our bed in our sickness; He will make our dying pillow soft, and our soul shall vanish, kissed away by His dear lips, and we shall be with Him forever and forever. Of those that are nearest to Him it is said, "These are they that follow the Lamb whithersoever he goeth. They shall walk with him in white, for they are worthy."

I conclude with this observation. Will our Lord Jesus Christ accept at our hands tonight such a consecrating word? If we are trusting in Him for salvation will He permit us to say that we will keep with Him as long as we live?

We reply, He will not permit us to say it in our own strength. There was a young man who said, "Lord, I will follow thee whithersoever thou goest," but Christ gave him a cool reception: and there was an older man who said, "Though all men shall forsake thee yet will not I," and in reply his Master prayed for Him that his faith should not fail. Now, you must not promise as Peter did, or you will make a greater failure. But, beloved, this self-devotion is what Christ expects of us if we are His disciples. He will not have us love father or mother more than Him; we must be ready to give up all for His sake. This is not only what our Master expects from us, but what He deserves from us.

Love so amazing, so divine,
Demands my soul, my life, my all.

This, also, is what the Lord will help us to do, for He will give us grace if we will but seek it at His hands: and this it is which He will graciously reward, and has already rewarded, in that choice word of His in the twelfth of John, where He says of His disciples in the twenty-sixth verse, "If any man serve me, let him follow me; and where I am, there shall also my servant be: if any man serve me, him will my Father honor." Oh, to be honored of God in eternity when He shall say, "Stand back, angels; make way, seraphim and cherubim; here comes a man that suffered for the sake of my dear Son. Here comes one that was not ashamed of my Only-begotten when his face was smeared with the spittle. Here comes one that stood in the pillory with Jesus, and was called ill names for His sake. Stand back, ye angels, these have greater honor than you." Surely the angels of heaven as they traverse the streets of gold and meet the martyrs will ask them about their sufferings, and say, "You are more favored than we, for you have had the privilege of suffering and dying for the Lord." O brothers and sisters, snatch at the privilege of living for Jesus; consecrate yourselves this day unto Him; live from this hour forward, not to enrich yourselves, nor to gain honor and esteem, but for Jesus, for Jesus alone. Oh, if I could set Him before you here; if I could cause Him to stand on this platform just as He came from Gethsemane with His bloody sweat about Him, or as He came down from the cross with wounds so bright with glory and so fresh with bleeding out our redemption, I think I should hear you say, each one of you, "Lord Jesus, we are thine, and in what place Thou shalt be, whether in death or life, even there also will thy servants be." So may the Lord help us by His most gracious Spirit who hath wrought all our works in us, for Jesus' sake. Amen.

"DAVID'S SPOIL"

Sermon No. 2,017
Intended for reading on Lord's day, April 15, 1888.
Portions of Scripture read before Sermon—Matthew 25:31–46; 26:6–13.
Hymns from *Our Own Hymn Book*—416, 802.

This is David's spoil—1 Samuel 30:20.

We have aforetime gathered spoil for ourselves out of David's behavior in the hour of his sorrow at Ziklag, and we will now turn to the other side of this leaf in his history, and receive instruction from the time of his victory. But we must not do this till we have refreshed our memories with the story of his conduct under distress. When he came to the city he found it burned, with fire, the property of himself and his comrades carried away, and, what was worse, all their wives, and their sons, and their daughters, gone into captivity. In the madness of their grief the people turned upon their leader, as if he had led them into this calamity. He was the only calm person among them, for he "encouraged himself in the Lord his God." With due deliberation he waited upon the Lord, and consulted the oracle through the appointed priest, and then, under divine guidance, he pursued the banditti, took them at unawares, recovered all of his people's goods, and captured a large booty which the Amalekites had collected elsewhere. David, who had been the chief object of the people's mutiny, and the leader of the successful pursuit of the robbers, most properly received a special portion of the spoil, and concerning it the words of our text were spoken, "This is David's spoil."

We shall now look into this victorious act on the part of David with the view of finding spiritual teaching in it. David may be regarded as a very special type of our Lord Jesus Christ. Among the personal types David holds a leading place, for in so many points he is the prophetic foreshadowing of the great and glorious Son of David. Whenever David acts as the man after God's own heart, he is the picture and emblem of the One who is still more after God's own heart, even the Christ of God. David, under divine guidance, pursued the Amalekites, who had come as thieves to smite and to burn, and carry away captive. The marauders were overtaken and slaughtered, and a great spoil was the result. David recovered all that the Amalekites had taken. "And there was nothing lacking to them, neither small nor great, neither sons nor daughters, neither spoil, nor anything that they had taken to them: David recovered all." We are told several times over in the chapter that nothing was lacking: "David recovered all." When our Lord Jesus wrought out our redemption, He recovered all, and left nothing in the enemy's hand. All glory to His name! But over and above, David took great store of cattle, and jewels, and gold, and silver, and so forth, which belonged to the Amalekites, and out of this a bountiful portion was taken which was set apart as David's spoil. David's men, in the moment of their despair, had spoken of stoning him; but now, in the morning of their victory, with general acclamations, they determine that David shall have, as his portion of the spoil, all the cattle which belong to the Amalekites themselves; and so, driving these in front, as they return to Ziklag, they say, "This is David's spoil." I think I hear them, as they drive the bullocks and the sheep before them, shouting right lustily, "This is David's spoil."

Now, using David as the type of Christ, I want, if I can, to set all David's men —all Christ's men—shouting with all their hearts. "This is Jesus' spoil!" He it is of whom Jehovah saith, "I will divide him a portion with the great, and he shall divide the spoil with the strong." He has a grand reward as the result of the great battle of His life and death. We will even now award to Him the spoil, and cry, "This is David's spoil"; feeling, all the while, as the Psalmist did, when he said, "Thou art more glorious and excellent than the mountains of prey."

I. We begin with the first observation that, practically, all the spoil of that day was David's spoil, and in truth, ALL THE GOOD THAT WE ENJOY COMES TO US THROUGH OUR LORD JESUS. He has been given as a Leader and a Commander to the people, and every victory they win is due to Him, and to Him alone. Without Him we can *do* nothing, and without Him we can *obtain* nothing. All that we once possessed by nature, and under the law, the spoiler has taken away. By our own efforts we can never regain what we have lost; only through our great Leader can be we restored and made happy. We ascribe unto Jesus all our gains, even as David's men honored their captain.

For, first, David's men defeated the Amalekites, and took their spoil, but *it was for David's sake that God gave success to the band.* God's eye rested upon His chosen servant, the Lord's anointed, and it was not for the warrior's own sakes, but for David's sake, that God guided them to the hosts of Amalek, and gave them like driven stubble to their sword. How much more true it is to us that every blessing, every pardoning mercy, every delivering mercy, is given to us through Him who is our shield and God's anointed! It is for the sake of Jesus that we are pardoned, justified, accepted, preserved, sanctified. Only through this channel does the mercy of God come to us. The Lord God saith, "Not for your sakes do I this, O house of Israel! Be ashamed and confounded for your own ways"; and we, in response to that, can answer, "Not unto us, not unto us, but unto the name of the Well-beloved be praise, and honor, and glory, forever and ever!" Since everything comes to us because of Christ Jesus, we may say of every covenant mercy, "This is David's spoil." On this blessing, and on that favor, yea, on them all, we see the mark of the cross. These are all fruits of our

Redeemer's passion, the purchase of His blood. Again we say with gratitude, "This is David's spoil."

Moreover, *David's men gained the victory over Amalek because of David's leadership.* If he had not been there to lead them to the fight, in the moment of their despair they would have lost all heart, and would have remained amidst the burning walls of Ziklag a discomfited company. But David encouraged himself in the Lord, and so encouraged all his desponding followers. Drawing his sword, and marching in front, he put spirit into them: they all followed with eager step because their gallant leader so courageously led the way. This is exactly our case, beloved, only we are even more indebted to our Lord Jesus than these men were to David. The Lord Jesus Christ has been among us, and has fought our battle for us, and recovered all that we had lost by Adam's fall and by our own sin. It is written of Him, "He shall not fail nor be discouraged." You know how He sets His face like a flint, how stout-hearted He was to accomplish the work of our redemption, and how He ceased not till He could cry victoriously, "It is finished."

> Our glorious Leader claims our praise
> For his own pattern given.

Following at His feet, we, too, fight with sin. Treading in His footsteps, we, too, overcome the world, the flesh, and the devil. Have you never heard Him say, "Be of good cheer, I have overcome the world"? And you, dear brothers and sisters, whatever victories you win, whatever spoils you divide, will own that it is through Jesus that you have conquered. They said of Waterloo that it was a soldier's battle, and the victory was due to the men; but ours is our Commander's battle, and every victory won by us is due to the great Captain of our salvation. Let the crown be set upon His head, even on the battlefield, and let us say of every sin that we have overcome, every evil habit that we have destroyed, "This is David's spoil." We had never won this victory if Jesus had not led us: we have it for His sake. We have it under His leadership. Without exception, all the saints on earth and in heaven confess this to be true.

> I ask them whence their victory came?
> They, with united breath,
> Ascribe their conquest to the Lamb,
> Their triumph to his death.
>
> They mark'd the footsteps that He trod,
> His zeal inspired their breast,
> And, following their incarnate God,
> Possess the promised rest.

I will not say more upon this point, but only ask you to remember that by nature we had all lost everything. We lost the garden with all its Paradisiacal joys; lost this world, the very earth bringing forth thorns and thistles to us; lost life, lost hope, lost peace, lost the favor of God. But Jesus has recovered all. All that the first Adam lost the second Adam has restored. David recovered all, and Jesus has recovered all. We ourselves were lost; but Jesus has brought us back from the hand of the enemy. He has given us ourselves, if I may use such an expression, and now we who were dead are alive again, the lost are found. Once, every faculty of ours was being used for our own destruction, but now, sanctified by the grace of God, all is being used for God's glory, and for our own ripening and perfecting. Jesus has recovered us for ourselves and for our God: the prey has been taken from the mighty, and the lawful captive has been delivered.

Yes, and our Lord Jesus has recovered for us the future as well as the past. Our outlook was grim and dark indeed till Jesus came; but oh, how bright it is now that He has completed His glorious work! Death is no more the dreaded grave of all our hopes. Hell exists no longer for believers. Heaven, whose gates were closed, is now set wide open to every soul that believeth. We have recovered life and immortal bliss. We are snatched like brands from the burning, and made to shine like lamps of the palace of the great King. We are set up to be forever trophies of the conquering power of Jesus, our glorious David. Look at all the saints in heaven in their serried ranks, and say of them all, "This is David's spoil." Look at the blood-bought church of God on earth—the ten thousands that are already washed in His blood, and following at His feet—we may say of all this ransomed flock, "This is David's spoil." Each one of us, looking at himself, and all his past, and all his future, may say, "This, too, is David's spoil." Christ has done it, done it all, and unto His name let the whole host shout the victory.

I feel as if I could stop the sermon, and ask you to sing, but it will be better if I content myself with repeating the hymn—

> Rejoice, ye shining worlds on high,
> Behold the King of glory nigh!
> He comes adorned with victory,
> He made our foes before him flee.
>
> Ye heavenly gates, your leaves display,
> To make the Lord the Savior way!
> Laden with spoils from earth and hell,
> The Conqueror comes with God to dwell.
>
> Raised from the dead, he goes before;
> He opens heaven's eternal door:
> To give his saints a blest abode,
> Near their Redeemer and their God.

II. But the most interesting part of our subject is this: all the booty was practically David's spoil, but there was a part of it which was not recovered, but was a clear gain. They recovered all they had lost, and over and above there was a surplus of spoil from the defeated foe. Now, in the great battle of Christ on our behalf, He has not only given us back what we lost, but He has given us what Adam in his perfection never had. And I want you to dwell upon that, because this part of it is peculiarly our Lord's spoil. THOSE GOOD THINGS WHICH WE NOW POSSESS, OVER AND ABOVE WHAT

WE LOST BY SIN, COME TO US BY THE LORD JESUS. Now that the Son of God has come into the field, He is not content with restoration, He turns the loss into a gain, the fall into a greater rising.

And first, dear friends, think: *In Christ Jesus human nature is lifted up where it never could have been before.* Man was made in his innocence to occupy a very lofty place. "Thou madest him to have dominion over all the works of thy hands; thou hast put all things under his feet." Man would have enjoyed that dominion had he never fallen, but he never could have obtained what he has now gained, for, "we see Jesus, who was made a little lower than the angels for the suffering of death, crowned with glory and honor." And we see in Jesus human nature joined in mysterious union with the Godhead. I never know how to speak about this miracle of the divine incarnation. We are men and women, poor creatures at our very best; yet in Christ Jesus our dignity is perfectly amazing. Angels excel in strength and beauty, but no angel was ever joined to the Godhead as manhood is now united to God. The nearest being to God is a man. The noblest existence—how shall I word it?—the noblest of all beings is God, and the God-man Christ Jesus, in whom dwelleth all the fullness of the Godhead bodily, is with Him upon His throne. It is a wondrous honor this—that manhood should be taken into intimate connection, yea, absolute union with God! For listen: through Jesus Christ we are this day made the sons of God, which angels never were. "Unto which of the angels said he at any time, Thou art my Son?" But He has said this to us. Christ took not up angels, but He took up the seed of Abraham, and He has made the believing seed of Abraham to be the sons of God. Listen again: "And if children, then heirs; heirs of God." God's heirs! What a word is this! How simple, but how sublime! I know how to say it, but not how to expound it! It does not want explanation, and yet its depths are fathomless. Every believer is God's heir—the heir of God. Could this have been, and there been no fall and no redemption? Children and heirs are more than was ever spoken of in Eden. Aye, listen yet again. Now we are one with God in Christ Jesus; for it is written concerning our Lord, "We are members of his body, of his flesh, and of his bones." Close as the marriage-union is, yet Paul declared, when he spoke of it, "This is a great mystery: but I speak concerning Christ and the church." Unfallen manhood was never declared to be one with the Son of God, and yet through the covenant of grace this is our position. We are joined by vital, real, conjugal union to Jesus Christ the Son of the Highest, very God of very God; and this is an elevation so transcendent that I feel bowed down beneath the weight of glory which is revealed in us. The most glorious being next to God is man. A sinner most shameful once, but now in Christ a child accepted and honored! What can I say of this but "This is David's spoil"? This is what Jesus brought us. It came to us by no other way or method. Neither do we know in what way or method it could have been given to us, but by the will of God through our Lord Jesus Christ. It is given to us through Jesus Christ, our elder Brother and our covenant Head, and unto Him let the glory of it be ascribed world without end.

Another blessing which was not ours before the fall, and therefore never was lost, but comes to us as a surplusage, is *the fact that we are redeemed*. You sang just now that verse,

> Never did angels taste above
> Redeeming grace and dying love.

It is clear that you could never have known free grace and dying love if Jesus had not come to redeem you. Unfallen intelligent spirits will say in eternity, "Do you see those beings bowing nearest to the eternal throne? Do you see those well-beloved creatures? Who are they?" Spirits that have lived in other worlds will come crowding up to the great metropolis, and will say one to another, "Who are those courtiers—those that dwell nearest to God? Who are they?" And one spirit will say to another, "They are beings whom God not only made as he made us, but whom the eternal Son of God redeemed by blood." And one shining one will say to his fellow, "What is that? Tell me that strange story." Then will his companion delight to say, "They were saved because the Son of God took their nature, and in that nature died." "Wonderful! Wonderful!" his friend will answer, "How could it be? Was there suffering for them, and pain for them, and bloody sweat for them, and death for them on the part of the ever-blessed Son of God?" The answer "It was even so," will be news full of astonishment even to the best instructed celestial mind. Spirits will look at us with wonder, and say, "What strange beings are these? Others are the work of God's hands, but these are the fruit of the travail of His soul. On others we see the marks of divine skill and power, but here we see the tokens of a divine sacrifice—a divine blood-shedding." Truly, we may say of our redemption, "This is David's spoil." That you and I should be such wonders as we must be in being redeemed beings, is indeed something given to us by Jesus over and above what Adam lost; and throughout eternity all the sacred brotherhood of the redeemed by blood will be princes in the courts of God—the aristocracy of heaven, for "He hath made us kings and priests unto God."

We shall be creatures who have known sin, and have been recovered from its pollution. There will be no fear of our being exalted with pride, or drawn away by ambition as the now-apostate angels were; for we shall constantly remember what sin did for us, and how grievous was our fault. We shall forever remember the price at which we were redeemed; and we shall have ties upon us that will bind us to an undeviating loyalty to Him who exalted us to so glorious a condition. It seems to me wonderful beyond expression: the more I consider, the more I am astonished. A spirit that has never fallen cannot be trusted in the same way as one that has fallen and has been delivered, and has been new-created and blood-washed, and has been gifted with an abiding and eternal character. Such a being shall never fall, because forever held by cords of love eternal, and bonds of gratitude infinitely strong, which will never let it waver in holy service. It is a work worthy of a God to create such beings as we shall be, since we shall be securely bound to voluntary holiness; and our wills, though always free, shall be immutably loyal to our Lord. As the twice-born, we shall be the noblest of God's works; we shall be the first-fruits of His creatures; we shall be accounted as the royal treasure of Jehovah. Then shall we sit with Christ upon His throne, and reign with Him forever. "This is David's spoil."

We receive blessings unknown to beings who have never fallen. I sometimes murmur to myself—and sweet music it has been as I have quietly murmured it—we are the elect of God. Election is a privilege most high and precious, what can exceed it in delight? This also is David's spoil. We are also redeemed from among men: the redemption of the soul is precious. "This is David's spoil." We are covenanted ones, with whom God has entered into bonds of promise, swearing by an oath to keep His word: this, too, is David's spoil. Where had you ever heard of redemption, election, covenant, and such-like words, if it had not been for the blessed Christ of God, who hath redeemed us by His blood? Sing ye, then, who have received back your lost inheritance: and sing more sweetly still, ye who have been blessed with all spiritual blessings, in the heavenlies according as the Father hath chosen you in Christ Jesus. Sing ye aloud unto His holy name; and say of your special privileges, "This is David's spoil."

Again, to my mind it is a very blessed fact that you and I will partake of a privilege which would have been certainly unnecessary to Adam, and could not by Adam have been known, and that is, *the privilege of resurrection.* We shall die unless the Lord should suddenly appear. I would not have you, brothers and sisters, look upon the prospect of death with any sort of dread. I know that death is associated with pain; but nothing can be more absurd. There is no pain in death: pain belongs to life; death, even naturally, puts an end to pain. But death to the believer is undressing as His Lord undressed—putting off garments of which, I think, we need not be so very fond, for they do fit us ill; and oftentimes, when our spirit is willing, it is hampered by these garments of clay, for the flesh is weak. Some look with intense delight to the prospect of the Savior's coming, as a means of escape from death. I confess I have but slender sympathy with them. If I might have my choice, I would prefer, of the two, to die. Let it be as the Lord wills; but there is a point of fellowship with Christ in death which they will miss who shall not sleep; and it seems to me to have some sweetness in it to follow the Lamb whithersoever He goeth, even though He descend into the sepulchre. "Where should the dying members rest but with their dying Head?" That grave of our blessed Lord, if He had not meant us to enter it, would have been left an empty tenement when He came away; but when He came out of it, He left it furnished for those that should come after Him. See there the graveclothes folded up for us to use! The bed is prepared for our slumber.

The napkin is laid by itself, because it is not for the sleeper, but for those who have lost His company. Those who remain behind may dry their eyes with the napkin, but the graveclothes are reserved for others who will occupy the royal bedchamber. When great men removed in the olden time, their servants took away the arras or hangings of their chambers; but if those hangings remained, it was for the convenience of guests who were invited to occupy my lord's rooms. See, then, our Lord expects us to lie in His royal bedchamber, for He has left the hangings behind Him! To the retiring-room of the tomb we shall go in due time. And why should we be grieved to go? For we shall come forth again: we shall rise from the dead. "Thy brother shall rise again," was Mary's consolation from the Master's lips. It is yours. We are not going to a prison, but to a bath, wherein the body, like Esther, shall be purified to behold the King. It is our joy to be sure that "as the Lord our Savior rose, so all His followers must." We do not know much about the resurrection of the body, and therefore we will not attempt to describe it; but surely it will be a delightful thing to be able to dwell forever in a body that has been in the grave, and has had fulfilled in it the sentence, "Dust thou art, and unto dust shalt thou return," but which has been raised again by that same power which raised our Lord Jesus Christ from the dead. We shall inhabit a body which shall no more see corruption, or be subject to weakness, or pain, or decay, but shall be like the glorified person of our Lord. Oh, there is sweetness in the thought that we shall in this forever have fellowship with our risen Lord! Children of the resurrection, dread not death! Your faces are turned to the sun. Press forward to the light eternal, and fear not to pass through the death-shadow: it is no more than a shadow. If you cannot leap over the grave, you can pass through it. It shall be your joy to rise when the morning breaketh, and to be satisfied; for you shall wake up in His likeness. As for the resurrection, "this is David's spoil," this is Christ's gift and boon. The resurrection from the dead is the peculiar glory of Christianity. The immortality of the soul had been taught and known before, for it is a truth which even reason itself teaches; but the resurrection of the body comes in as the last and crowning effort of our spirits: and "this is David's spoil."

Let me not weary you. The topic might well interest us on several occasions; it is too large to be confined to one discourse. *Our singular relation to God, and yet to materialism,* is another rare gift of Jesus. God intended, by the salvation of man, and the lifting up of man into union with himself, to link together in one the lowest and the highest—His creation and Himself. Shall I make it very plain? These poor substances—earth, water, and the like—they seem far down in the scale. God makes a being that shall be, as an old Puritan used to say, half soul and half soil; even man who is both spirit and dust of the earth. We find in him water, salts, acids, all sorts of substances combined to make up a body, and married to this is a soul, which is brother to the angels, and akin to Deity. Materialism is somewhat exalted in being connected with spirit at all. When spirit becomes connected with God, and refined materialism becomes connected with a purified spirit, by the resurrection from the dead, then shall be brought to pass the uplifting of clay, and its junction with the celestial. Do you not see how God, in the perfecting of His gracious purpose through the resurrection of the dead, causes His glory to be reflected even upon what we regard as poor material substances, gross and mean?

Try and get at my meaning again. Quakers, whom I greatly respect, get rid of the two ordinances, by denying that they are of perpetual obligation. They banish baptism: they put away the Lord's supper. I have sometimes wished that I were able to agree with them, because my whole spirit and tendency are towards the spiritual rather than the ritual; but if anything be plain to me in Scripture, it is that Jesus Christ did command us to be baptized in water in the Triune name, and that He bade His disciples remember Him in the breaking of bread and in the drinking of the cup. The danger of men's making too much of outward forms was encountered for some wise purpose. It was, I think, because God would have us know that even the material, though it can only enter the outer court, is still to be sanctified unto Himself. Therefore, water, bread, and wine, all material substances, are used not only as symbols, but as tokens that all created things shall be ennobled and sanctified. Look ye, sirs, "Creation was made subject to vanity, not willingly, but by reason of Him who hath subjected the same in hope." Through man's sin this outward world became blackened, darkened, and degraded; but God intends, through man, to lift up the nethermost extremities of His creation into a greater nearness to Himself than they ever could have reached by any other means. And this is how it comes about. We are taking up with us, as it were, the earth which makes a part of ourselves. We are drawing up with ourselves the earth in those simple symbols with which we worship God. We are ourselves lifted up as spirits, and we are soon to be lifted up as spirits enshrined in purified bodies, and thus we bring the whole creation of God into nearer contact with Himself. Hence it is that we are called "kings and priests." What can the dead earth do in worship till there comes one who worships God as the world's priest? What can the fields and woods and hills say in the worship of God? They are dumb till a tongue attempts the holy task of uttering their praise. You and I are made of such stuff as the world around us, and yet we are the compeers of angels. We are brothers to the worm; and this body of ours is but a child of mother earth on which it lives. See then how mother earth worships God through us, and dull, dead matter finds life and song. Behold the mists and the clouds become a steaming incense of praise to God through men like ourselves, who, because Christ was slain, have been made kings and priests unto God.

I wish you would, rather than listen to me, try and muse upon the wonderful position which redeemed men do now occupy, and will occupy forever and ever. For my own part, I would not change places with the angel Gabriel, nay, not if he gave me his swift wing to boot, for I believe that an infinitely greater honor belongs to the least of God's children than to the very highest of God's servants. To be a child of God—oh, bliss!—there is no glory that can excel it. But all this is a special gift to our humanity through our Lord Jesus. "This is David's spoil."

Our manifestation of the full glory of God is another of the choice gifts which the pierced hands of Jesus alone bestow. Principalities and powers shall see in the mystical body of Christ more of God than in all the universe besides. They will study in the saints the eternal purposes of God, and see therein His love, His wisdom, His power, His justice, His mercy blended in an amazing way. They will admire forever those whom God loves and delights in, those whom He keeps as the apple of His eye, those whom He rejoices over, and of whom He hath said that He will rest in His love, and He will rejoice over them with singing. Truly it hath not entered into the heart of man to guess at the glory of God in the saints, the exceeding glory which shall be revealed in us through Jesus Christ our Lord. "This is David's spoil." Oh, come, let us sing unto the Lord, let us magnify the name of Jesus Christ!

III. I close with the most practical part of my sermon: THAT WHICH WE WILL-INGLY GIVE TO JESUS MAY BE CALLED HIS SPOIL. There is a spoil for Christ which every true-hearted follower of His votes to Him enthusiastically. We have already seen that all things which we have are of Christ, and that there are certain special gifts which are peculiarly of Christ; and now, what shall be David's spoil from you and from me?

First, *our hearts are His alone forever.*

> Here's my heart, Lord, take and seal it,
> Seal it for thy courts above.

Of every believing heart it may be said, "This is David's spoil." You and I must give ourselves tomorrow to earning our daily bread, and our thoughts must go, to a large extent, after earthly things in the common pursuits of everyday life. But our hearts, our hearts, are as fountains sealed for our Well-beloved. O mammon, thou shalt not have them! O pleasure, thou shalt not have them! These are David's spoil. Our hearts belong to Jesus only. "My son, give me thine heart," is an Old Testament command, but under the New Testament manifestation of love we ful-fill it; "for the love of Christ constraineth us; because we thus judge, that if one died for all, then were all dead: and that He died for all, that they which live should not henceforth live unto themselves, but unto Him which died for them, and rose again." Let it be so that our whole heart is the sole possession of Jesus! We will neither rend it, nor cast lots whose it shall be, for "this is David's spoil."

Now, there is another property I should like King Jesus to have, and that is, *our special gifts.* I know one who, before his conversion, was wont to sing, and he often charmed the ears of men with the sweet music which he poured forth; but when he was converted he said, "Henceforth my tongue shall sing nothing but the praises of God." He devoted himself to proclaiming the gospel by this song, for he said, "This is David's spoil." Have you not some gift or other, dear friend, of which you could say, "Henceforth this shall be sacred to my bleeding Lord?" Some peculiar faculty? Some choice piece of acquirement not generally possessed? Something in which you excel? I would that you had at least some little garden of flowers or herbs which you could so reserve that therein only Jesus should pluck the fruits. Say of the best gift you pos-sess, "This is David's spoil." Is it not well to consecrate some part of the day, and say, "This hour is Christ's. I have my work to do, my business must be seen to; all is Christ's. But, still I will reserve a special season, and wall it in, like a private garden, in which, with prayer, and praise, and meditation, I will commune with my Lord; or else in actual service I will honor His name"? Say, "This is David's spoil." Come dear heart, what do you mean to give Him? Surely you have some natural faculty or acquired skill which you can lay at His feet.

Moreover, while our whole selves must be yielded to the Lord Jesus, there is one thing that must always be Christ's, and that is *our religious homage as a church.* Somebody says that the Queen is head of the church. God bless her; but she is no head of the church of Christ! The idea is blasphemous: headship "is David's spoil." Jesus Christ is Head over all things to His church, and nobody else can take that position. No one may dare to take the title of "head of the church" without a usurpation of our Lord's royal right. Certain teachers of the church claim authority over conscience, and assert that they are infallible. I have heard it said that they are supreme guides, but I do not believe it, because "This is David's spoil." We have one infallible Teacher, and that is Jesus Christ our Savior. We yield obedience to His every word, and demand that others should do the same. Whatsoever *He* says to us by His Spirit in the Word of God is to us infallible truth, and we cease to dispute when Jesus speaks; but no man else shall dictate doctrine to us, for "This is David's spoil." He must be sole Rabbi in the midst of His church. We call Him Master and Lord, for so He is. I would have you keep your conscience for Christ alone. Take care that no book ever overlaps the Bible; that no creed ever contradicts the form of sound words contained in God's own Word; that no influence of minister or writer supplants the guidance of the Holy Ghost. Your soul's obedience and faith belong to Jesus only: "This is David's spoil."

Lastly, have you not something of *your own proper substance* that shall be David's spoil just now? That was a blessed act when the woman broke the most precious thing she had—her box of alabaster, and let the perfumed nard stream down the Savior, anointing Him for His burial. She felt that the precious perfume was "David's spoil." There was no waste; in fact, no other gift ever went so completely to its purpose without being taxed on the road, for Jesus had it all. Kindly did He observe the loving honor which she paid Him. What if the ointment were sold, and given to the poor? Yet it could never be so economically used as when it was all devoted to Him. I do think it so pleasant sometimes to give Jesus Christ distinctly a gift from yourself of somewhat that you will miss. It is good to give to the poor, but it has a daintier sweetness in it to do somewhat distinctly for Him, for the spread of His own glory, and the making known of His own fame. "The poor ye have always with you": abound towards them in your charity whenever you will; but to your Lord at special seasons dedicate a choice gift, and say, "This is David's spoil." There was a poor woman once, whose little fortune could be carried between her finger and her thumb,—her fortune I said, for it was all she had. Two mites, I am told, was all it came to. She took it, it was her all, and she put it in the treasury; for this was "David's spoil." It belonged to the Lord her God, and she gave it cheerfully. I do not know whether since the days of the apostles anybody has ever given so much as that woman. I have not. Have you? She gave all her living. Not all her savings, but all her living. She had nothing left when she gave her farthing: she loved so much that she consecrated all her living. We sometimes sing—

Yet if I might make some reserve,
   And duty did not call,
I love my God with zeal so great
   That I would give him all.

But do we mean it? If not, why do we sing falsehoods? There was a man who, in the providence of God, had been enabled to lay by many thousands. He was a very rich and respected man. I have heard it said that he owned at least half-a-million; and at one collection, when he felt especially grateful and generous, he found a well-worn sixpence for the plate, for that was David's spoil! That was David's spoil! Out of all that he possessed, that sixpence was David's spoil! This was the measure of his gratitude! Judge by this how much he owed, or at least how much he desired to pay. Are there not many persons who, on that despicable scale, reward the Savior for the travail of His soul? I shall not upbraid them. I shall not urge them to do more, lest I spoil the voluntariness of the large gifts they mean to bring. Let a hint suffice. For us, who are deep in the Redeemer's debt, who have had much forgiven, who every day are bankrupt debtors to the measureless mercy of infinite love—for us, no paltriness will suffice. We must give something which, if it be not worthy of Him, shall, at least, express the truth and warmth of the gratitude we feel. God help us to be often setting aside this, and that, and the other choice thing, and saying, "This is David's spoil, and it shall be a joy to my heart to give it!" We shall find much sweetness in buying our sweet-cane with money, and filling our Lord with the fat of our sacrifices. It is heaven for a true heart to give largely to Jesus.

God bless you, dear friends. May we come to the table of communion, and meet with our glorious David there, and feel His praises making music in our hearts! Amen.

THE THRESHING-FLOOR OF ORNAN

SERMON NO. 1,808
DELIVERED ON LORD'S DAY MORNING, NOVEMBER 9, 1884.
Portion of Scripture read before Sermon—1 Chronicles 21; 22:1–5.
HYMNS FROM *Our Own Hymn Book*—302, 553, 551.

At that time when David saw that the LORD had answered him in the threshingfloor of Ornan the Jebusite, then he sacrificed there—
1 Chronicles 21:28.

Then David said, This is the house of the LORD God, and this is the altar of the burnt offering for Israel—1 Chronicles 22:1.

DAVID was for many years searching for a site for the great temple which he purposed to build for Jehovah his God. It had been ordained that the sacrifices offered to the one God should be offered by all Israel upon one altar; but as yet the ark of the Lord was within curtains, near to David's palace, and the altar of burnt offering was situated at Gibeon. Where should the one altar be erected? Where should the ark find its permanent dwelling-place? David said, "Surely I will not come into the tabernacle of my house, nor go up into my bed; I will not give sleep to mine eyes, or slumber to mine eyelids, until I find out a place for the Lord, a habitation for the mighty God of Jacob." Yet for a long time he received no indication as to the exact spot whereon the Lord's altar should be reared, save only that he was told the Lord had chosen Zion and desired it for His habitation.

David watched, and waited, and prayed, and in due time he received the sign. God knew the spot, and had consecrated it long before by His appearance unto Abraham. The other Sabbath-day, you remember, our text was "Jehovah-jireh," [No. 1803, p. 48], and we then learned that in the mount the Lord would be seen. Upon Mount Moriah, on or near that particular spot which had been named Jehovah-jireh, was the temple to be built. Abraham had there unsheathed the knife to slay his son. Wondrous type of the great Father offering up his Only-begotten for the sins of men! The scene of that grand transaction was to be the center of worship for the chosen people. Where Abraham made the supreme sacrifice, there should his descendants present their offerings. Or if we look into the type and see God there presenting Jesus as a sacrifice for men, it was most suitable that man should forever sacrifice to God where God made a sacrifice for him. As yet it was not known to David that this was the chosen place. Now it is indicated by memorable signs: the angel of justice stands above the spot; and his sword is sheathed there in answer to the cries of the afflicted king, according to the longsuffering mercy of God. Then David clearly saw the mind of the Lord, and said, "This is the house of Jehovah my God, and this is the altar of the burnt-offering for Israel." Then he commenced at once with double speed to prepare the materials for the temple. Though he knew that he might not build it, since his hands had been stained with blood, yet he would do all that he could to help his son Solomon in the great enterprise.

This problem which David had at last worked out by the good hand of God upon him, is one which in a deep spiritual sense exercises our hearts full often. Where is it that man may meet with God? How is it that man may speak with his offended Lord and be reconciled to Him? Is there not some meeting-place where the sinner may express his repentance, and where mercy may grant full absolution? Many are saying, "Oh, that I knew where I might find Him!" Hearts touched by the Spirit of God are still seeking after God if haply they may find Him. In what condition, and by what means may man be at peace with God, and dread no longer the sword of His justice?

For the heart of some of us that problem takes a further shape: we know where man may meet with God but we want to know how the careless, proud, rebellious heart shall be induced to come to God in His appointed way. We know it is by the power of the Holy Ghost, through the preaching of the Word, and the uplifting of the all-attracting cross; but we would fain know the state of mind which will lead up to reconciliation; for now we often have to go back to Him that sent us, and to cry, "Who hath believed our report? and to whom is the arm of the Lord revealed?" We would lead men to God by Jesus Christ if we could; we stretch out the finger, and we point the way, but they will not see; we stretch out both hands, and entreat them to come, but they will not yield; our heart breaketh for the longing that it hath to present every man in Christ reconciled unto the living God; but how shall it be? How shall the sinner come unto God?

We may get some light from the type before us upon that question—Where shall God's temple be? How shall we be brought to it? We speak not at this time upon natural things, but upon the things of the Spirit; therefore let us pray the Holy Spirit to enlighten and instruct us, for only by His aid shall spiritual truth enter our hearts!

And, first, I remark that *externally there was, and there is nothing in any place why it should be the peculiar meeting-place of God with man;* but, secondly, that *spiritually the place which God did choose was most suitable*; for in it we read the true ground upon which God does actually meet with men in a way of grace. When we have lingered over these two subjects, we shall then have to exhort you after this fashion,—*heartily let us use the place which God hath set apart to be our meeting-place with himself.* "O come, let us worship and bow down: let us kneel before the Lord our Maker."

I. First, then, this truth is believed by you, though, alas! not by all men, that EX-TERNALLY THERE IS NOTHING IN ANY PLACE WHY GOD SHOULD THERE MEET WITH MEN.

The Lord chose the threshing-floor of Ornan the Jebusite as the spot whereupon for many a day His holy worship should be openly celebrated according to the outward ceremonies of a typical dispensation. There the Temple was built, and for a thousand years it stood as the center of Divine worship, so far as it was visibly presented according to His ordinance. What that mount may yet become we will not at this time consider. Prophets give us bright hints of what shall yet be even on Mount Zion, which has so long been trodden under foot of the adversary. But why was the threshing-floor of Ornan to be the meeting place of David with his God, and the spot where prayer was to be heard?

Certainly it was a *very simple, unadorned, unecclesiastical place.* The threshing-floor of Ornan boasted no magnificence of size, or beauty of construction. There was just the rock, and I suppose a composition spread upon it of hard clay or cement, that the feet of the oxen might the better tread out the corn. That was all it was; yet when the Temple with all its glory crowned the spot, God was never more conspicuously present than on that bare, ungarnished threshing-floor. "Meet God in a barn!" saith one. Why not? Does that astonish you? God met Adam in a garden, Abraham under a tree, and Noah in an ark. There is less of man in the open field than in the cathedral, and where there is least of man there is at least an opportunity to find most of God. "Meet God on a threshing-floor!" Why not? It may be a thousand times more sacred than many a chancel; for there simple minds are likely to pay their homage in hearty truthfulness, while in the other the artificialness of the place may foster formality. God has met with man in a dungeon, in a cave, in a whale's belly. When you have displayed all your skill in architecture, can you secure any more of the Divine presence than the disciples had in the upper room? Can you get as much of it? A tasteful building may be a way of showing your pious regard for the Lord, and so far it may be justifiable and acceptable; but take care that you do not regard it as essential, or even important, or you will make an idol of it. If the church or chapel be esteemed for its form or tastefulness, it will become a mere exhibition of skill and industry, and so be no more sacred than the house of a greedy merchant, or the palace of a profligate prince. No chisel of mason, or hammer of carpenter can build a holy place. Without either of these a spot may be none other than the house of God, and the gate of heaven. God chose a threshing-floor for His audience with David, just as aforetime He had chosen to reveal Himself in a bush to Moses. His presence had been glorious on the sandy floor of the wilderness, in the midst of the curtains of goats' hair; and now it was gracious among the sheaves and the oxen. How can He that filleth all things care about a house which is made with hands? You know how curtly Stephen dismisses even Solomon's Temple with a word—"but Solomon built him a house. Howbeit, the Most High dwelleth not in temples made with hands." What was that golden fane to the Infinite Majesty? Is not His own Creation sublimer far?

No arch can compare with the azure of heaven, no lamps can rival the sun and moon, no masonry can equal that city whose twelve foundations are of precious stones. Thus saith the Lord by the prophet: "Heaven is my throne, and the earth is my footstool: where is the house that ye build unto me? and where is the place of my rest? For all those things hath mine hand made." Wherefore, then, should He not choose the hill whereon Ornan had made a hardened floor whereon to thresh his corn? At any rate that was the Lord's meeting-place with David, His audience chamber with the suppliant king; as if to show that He careth not for tabernacles or temples, but by His own presence makes that place glorious wherein He reveals Himself.

Moreover, it was *a place of ordinary toil*—not merely a floor, but a threshing-floor in present use, with oxen present, and all the implements of husbandry ready to hand. It was so ordinary, and so everyday a place that none could have been more so: as if the Lord would say to us, "I will meet you anywhere; I will be with you in the house and in the field; I will speak with you when you till the ground, when you thresh your corn, when you eat your bread." Every place is holy where a holy heart is found. This ought to gladden the solitude of godly men. God is with you, therefore be of good cheer. If you are on board ship, or if you are wandering in the woods, or are banished to the ends of the earth, or are shut out from the Sabbath assemblies of God's house, yet

> Where'er you seek him he is found,
> And every place is hallowed ground.

On the threshing-floor of Ornan the Jebusite did God meet with David, and in your workroom, at your bench, or upon your bed, or behind the hedge, or in the corner of a railway carriage, the Lord will hear you, and commune with you.

My heart rejoices when I think that this was not only a very unadorned place, and one that was given up to common uses, but it was also *in the possession of a Jebusite.* The Jebusites were among the nations doomed for their iniquities; they were aliens from the commonwealth of Israel, and strangers to the covenants of promise; and this vast rock on which the Temple is to stand, beautiful for situation, the joy of the whole earth, belongs at first to one of the accursed seed of Canaan. Herein the Lord showeth that He is no respecter of persons; He would meet the king, not on the land of an Israelite, but on the threshing-floor of a Jebusite. The Jews wrapped themselves up within themselves, and said, "The temple of the Lord; the temple of the Lord are we": but the Lord seemed to rebuke their national pride by saying, "And your Temple is built upon the threshing-floor of a Jebusite." If they would but have remembered this, the Jews might in our Lord's day have been more tolerant of the conversion of the Gentiles to God. Moreover, Gentile blood flowed in the veins of that very king who established their empire, and who was now prostrate before his God, interceding for Jerusalem. Remember Ruth, and whence she came. She put her trust under the wings of Jehovah, God of Israel, and became the great-grandmother of David. David never seemed to forget that fact, for his psalms are full of far-reaching desires and good wishes for all the peoples of the earth. Remember his words: "Let the whole earth be filled with his glory; Amen, and Amen. The prayers of David the son of Jesse are ended." He looks back upon his birth, as the son of Jesse and the great-grandson of Ruth, and a large heart beats within his breast, desiring that Jehovah may be the God of the whole earth. Let us, therefore, not consider our own peculiar nationality or condition, or rank among men, as if salvation came by natural descent. The blood of fallen Adam is in the veins of every man, and there is neither Jew nor Gentile in Christ Jesus. If you happen to have been born of parents who did not train you in the fear of God, yet do not despond; for as the Temple was built upon the threshing-floor of Ornan the Jebusite, so shall the great God dwell in your heart though your fathers knew Him not. Say thou in thy soul, "The Lord shall have a dwelling within my heart, Jebusite though I be."

Once more, there was one matter in reference to Ornan's threshing-floor which it would be well to mention: before it could be used *it had to be bought with money*. I frequently meet with impossibly spiritual people who hate the mention of money in connection with the worship of God. The clatter of a collection jars upon their sublime feelings. The mention of money in connection with the worship of God is more dreadful to them than it is to God Himself; for He saith, "Thou hast bought me no sweet cane with money"; and again, "None shall appear before me empty." To these pious persons money saved and hoarded is abundantly pleasant; their only objection is to giving it. In this they somewhat differ from David, who paid to Ornan for the place 600 shekels of gold by weight. Before he would offer a sacrifice he paid down 50 shekels of earnest money; for he said, "I will not offer burnt offerings unto Jehovah my God of that which doth cost me nothing." It is a very curious thing, is it not? that one man should show his spirituality by his liberality, and another should pretend to do it by the reverse method. In connection with all true worship of God in the olden times there was always the offertory, and frequently the sound of gold or silver. Beneath the drawn sword of the avenging angel money is given, and land is bought. The solemnity of the transaction is not marred thereby. Yet there was no absolute need for money, since Ornan said, "Take it to thee, and let my lord the king do that which is good in his eyes: lo, I give thee the oxen also for burnt offerings, and the threshing instruments for wood, and the wheat for the meat offering; I give it all." David cannot endure to worship at another man's expense, and he answers, "Nay; but I will verily buy it for the full price." That religion which costs a man nothing is usually worth nothing. Under the old dispensation, when men went up to worship God, it was with a bullock or with a lamb; even the poorest brought at least a pair of turtle doves, or two young pigeons. Do you think that this bringing of cattle and birds into the sanctuary would spoil your spirituality? It would do so if you have no spirituality; but if you have grace in your heart, your spirituality will choose just such a practical way in which to show itself. Some men's godliness is a thin, misty, ghostly, ghastly nothing: true adoration is a thing of substance, and of truth. The highest act of adoration that was ever paid on earth was when that woman, whose name is to be mentioned wherever this gospel is preached, emptied upon the head of our blessed

Lord an alabaster box of precious nard. That gift was known to have cost her at least 500 pence. It might have been sold for much, but the costliness of the perfume entered into the very essence of the act in the mind of the holy and grateful woman. The Lord Jesus Christ when He sat over against the treasury not only read the hearts of the givers, but He noticed the actual offering of the woman who dropped into the box two mites that made a farthing, which were all her living. Some people would sneeringly allude to the two dirty half-farthings, and condemn the collection as spoiled by Alexander the coppersmith; but the Lord is not so dainty as His servants, for He accepts the poor gifts of his people. The rattle of the coins did not take away from the heavenliness and the spirituality of that woman's worship. Far otherwise. The top of Moriah, where God appoints that His Temple should be built, saw the weighing out of gold and silver, and was all the fitter for Divine communion because thereof.

From the whole learn that it is not needful for meeting with God that you should be aided by persons arrayed in special robes, oxen will do as well; neither do you require a holy pavement, a threshing-floor may be holiness unto the Lord; neither do you need stained glass and vaulted roofs, the open air is better still. Do not believe for a moment that visible grandeur is necessary to the place where God will meet with you. Go to your threshing-floor and pray; aye, while the unmuzzled oxen take their rest, bow your knee and cry to the Lord of the harvest, and you shall meet with God there amongst the straw and the grain. Fear not to draw nigh to God in these streets, but consecrate all space to the Lord your God. Study simplicity and plainness of worship. Remember how the Lord hated altars of brick, and how He would have His people build an altar of earth or of unhewn stone, to keep His worship simple and natural. "If thou lift up thy tool upon it, thou hast polluted it."

II. But now, secondly, SPIRITUALLY THIS THRESHING-FLOOR OF ORNAN WAS AN ADMIRABLE TYPE OF HOW GOD MEETS WITH MEN.

I think, first, *its extreme simplicity enters into the essence of the type.* So far from thinking that a threshing-floor was a bad place to pray in, if I look a little beneath the surface I think I can see the reason for it. Golden grain is being separated from the straw by the corn drag—whence came this corn? From Him who openeth His hand and supplieth the want of every living thing. Here, then, God meets me in the kindest way. Where can I meet Him better than where He gives me food? Where can we better adore than in the midst of His rich gifts by which He doth sustain my life? Why, I think if I had gone out to gather manna every morning with my omer, I should have kept on praising God every moment as I collected the heavenly bread. Never could spot be more propitious than where the gracious Preserver of men spread out needful food for His children. We cannot do better than praise God when we are in our daily service earning our daily bread, or gathered at our meals refreshing our bodies. At the gate of God's almonry let us wait with worship. Where better a temple out of which the bread of eternal life shall come, than on a threshing-floor where the bread of the first life is to be gathered? The two things seem to meet right well together. The temporal and the eternal join hands in common consecration. That same prayer which teaches us to say, "Our Father, which art in heaven, hallowed be thy name, thy kingdom come, thy will be done on earth as it is in heaven," leads us on to cry, "Give us day by day our daily bread." There is a spiritual significance in the type.

Would it be fanciful if with a glance I indicated that the *threshing-floor is the exact type of affliction*? Tribulation signifies threshing in the Latin, and the saints through much tribulation enter the kingdom. One of the titles of the people of God is "my threshing and the corn of my floor." Now it is well known that the Lord is with His people in their trials. When He smites with one hand He holds with the other. In the lion of trial we find the honey of communion. The temple of glory is built on the threshing-floor of affliction. I do not thrust forward this observation as though it were of great weight; but even if it be a fancy so far as the type is concerned, the thought conveys a truth in a pleasing manner.

But much more, *this was the place where justice was most clearly manifest*. Above Ornan's threshing-floor, in mid-air, stood a dreadful apparition. A bright and terrible figure, a mysterious servant of God, was beheld with a drawn sword in his hand, which he brandished over the guilty city of Jerusalem. Deaths were constant. The people fell as forest leaves in autumn. Then was it that David went out to meet with his God, and make confession before Him. Oh, sirs, the lack of many of you is that you have never yet beheld sin in its consequences, sin in its guilt, sin in its doom. God is angry with the sinner every day. Men do not fly to God till fear puts wings upon their feet. Take away the dread of the wrath to come, and you have removed the great impulse which makes men seek for mercy. Men will not meet God till they see the angel with the drawn sword. They will trifle and play with sin, and neglect the invitation of God, and even doubt His existence, till conviction comes home to them, and they are made to feel that sin is an exceeding evil and bitter thing. Conviction of sin wrought by the Spirit of God is more powerful than argument. I had religiousness, but I never drew near to God in spirit and in truth till I had seen and almost felt that drawn sword. To feel that God must punish sin, that God will by no means clear the guilty, is the best thing to drive a man Godward. To feel that sword as it were with its point at your own breast, its edge ready to descend upon your own being, this it is that makes the guilty plead for pardon in real earnest. Men cry not "Lord save" till they are forced to add "or I perish." I could wish for certain preachers that I hear of, that they were made more vividly to realize the terror of the Lord in their own souls. He who has felt the hot drops of despair scald his throat, has had it cleared for the utterance of free grace doctrine. If some men had more fully felt that they were sinners, they would have made better saints. David meets with God at the place where he sees that sin necessitates condign punishment, and I do not believe that any man can be in fellowship with God and be blind to that truth. David saw the result of his own sin, and dreaded what would further come if, day after day, the Lord should visit him and his people with judgment. He had grown proud of the number of his subjects, and had begun to act the independent potentate, instead of loyally remaining the viceroy of Jehovah; but now he sees that he has been guilty of high treason, and beholds the sword at his back. There he bows himself, and there the God of all grace meets with him.

Perhaps the point which brought David out into complete brokenness of heart was a clear view of the deadly effect of his sin upon others. Seventy thousand people had died of the black death already through his sin, and still the pestilence raged: this brought the matter home to his heart. Every ungodly man ought to reflect upon the mischief which he has caused to others by his evil life: his wife has been hindered from good things, his children have grown up without the fear of God, his companions with whom he has worked and traded are hardened in their wickedness by a sight of his wickedness: youthful minds have been seduced from virtue by his vice, simple hearts have been led into infidelity by his unbelief. O men, you know not what you do. You let fly sparks, but what the conflagration may have already been none of you can tell. Carelessly, O man, hast thou cast the thistledown to the wind; but what harvests of the ill weed have come, and may yet come, from thy single handful, who can tell? Are there not some in hell through thine influence? Are not others going there through thine unhallowed teaching? O thou whose hair is snow-white with 60 or 70 winters, how much of ruin hast thou wrought already! How much more is still to come! This came home to David, and he stood aghast at it, crying to God about it, and pleading as for his life that the evil might be stayed.

Thus, you see, when the deadly fruit of sin is clearly perceived, then the soul turns to God, and the Lord meets that soul. The cross is the place of doom: under its shadow we admit our guilt, and vividly see it, and thus put ourselves into a truthful position, where the God of truth will meet with us. God will meet with sinners when they come to Him as sinners; but he will not hearken to them while they refuse to see their sin, and will not believe in the vengeance due to it.

Furthermore, that place where God met with David and made it to be His temple forever, was the place *where sin was confessed*. David's confession is very frank and full. David says, "Is it not I? Even I it is that have sinned." Go thou, sinner, to the Lord with thine own personal confession. Shut thine eye to thy fellow-man, and say, "Father, I have sinned." Cry with the publican, "God be merciful to me a sinner." Make private personal confession, without comparing thyself with thy fellow-men, and the Lord has promised to forgive thee, and all those who confess their transgressions.

Set forth in thy confession the aggravated nature of thy sin. David said, "I it is that have sinned and done evil *indeed*." He emphasizes the evil, "I have done evil *indeed*." You will not find God in a way of grace till you begin to put an "indeed" at the end of the evil which you confess. Have you not sinned against light, sinned against knowledge, sinned against love, sinned against warnings, sinned against entreaties? Then go and tell the Lord that you have sinned with grievous aggravations. "Father," said the prodigal, "I have sinned against heaven, and before thee, and am no more worthy to be called thy son." Where such a confession as this is offered, God will meet the sinner.

That confession also had within itself an admission of the justice of the punishment; for he says, "Let thine hand be on me, and on my father's house." He does not cavil against the sword of the Lord and its deadly blows. That sinner truly repents who feels—

> My lips, with shame, my sins confess
> Against thy law, against thy grace:
> Lord, should thy judgment grow severe,
> I am condemn'd, but thou art clear.
>
> Should sudden vengeance seize my breath,
> I must pronounce thee just in death;
> And, if my soul were sent to hell,
> Thy righteous law approves it well.

That repentance which questions the justice of God in the punishment of sin is a repentance that needs to be repented of; but when the penitent doth, as it were, lay his head upon the block, yield his neck to the rope, and give himself up to God, saying, "I have sinned," then mercy feels free to display itself. As long as a man quarrels with justice he cannot be at peace with mercy. We must accept God as king, even though He beareth not the sword in vain, or else He will never put up that sword into its sheath. Condemn thyself, and God will acquit thee. Come penitently and submissively, and the just God will be a Savior unto thee.

But this is only the beginning of it; for Ornan's threshing-floor was then the place *where sacrifice was offered and accepted.* Hastily they piled the altar of unhewn stones; they brought up to it ox after ox that had been lately threshing out the corn: the blood flowed in plentiful streams, and the sacrifice was laid upon the wood. God meets with men not where the blood of bulls and of goats flows in rivers, but where the glorious person of His own dear incarnate Son is offered up once for all for guilty men. Calvary is the trysting-place between God and penitents. Now we have reached it. This is the site of the temple: this is the temple "not made with hands," once destroyed, but built up in three days. The person of the Lord Jesus, crucified and raised from the dead, is that place where God meeteth guilty, confessing men, and striketh hands with him; aye, eats and drinks with him in peace, as was indicated by the peace offering which David presented, and the Lord accepted. Oh, souls, you need to see this, for if you do not see it you will never see God. A reconciled God is only to be seen through the smoke of the great sacrifice. The wounds of Christ are the windows of the heart of God. If thou canst believe in Jesus Christ, by faith presenting Him again to God as thy sacrifice, then God will meet with thee.

But what did David see ere long when he had laid his bullock on the altar? A flame descended from the Lord. Like a flash of lightning it came, and the sacrifice was consumed; sure token that the Lord had accepted it, and was well pleased because of it. Even thus has the Lord accepted the one great sacrifice for sin. When our Lord

Jesus offered Himself He came under the judicial sentence, and cried, "My God, my God, why hast thou forsaken me?" He was consumed with sorrow. "It pleased the Lord to bruise him." The Lord Himself put Him to grief, and made His soul a sacrifice for sin. "He was made a curse for us, as it is written, Cursed is every one that hangeth on a tree." And now the Lord has placed His mercy seat where the blood is sprinkled. He accepts us in the Beloved whose sacrifice He accepted long ago when He raised Him from the dead. We have access by the blood of Jesus. Come, poor trembling sinner; come with thine eye on Jesus crucified and thou shalt be welcome of the Lord.

As soon as David had seen the sacrifice he had only one more sight to see, and that made the threshing-floor of Ornan more glorious than ever. *He beheld the sign of peace.* Above the threshing-floor stood the angel of the Lord; but what a change! The drawn sword, which threatened death to the city and to the nation, was suddenly thrust into its scabbard, and all was still. Not a soul more in Jerusalem should die of the pestilence. The sword of the Lord rested and was quiet. Oh, the joy of David's spirit when he saw this! What a solemn but joyous melting of heart he felt as his soul gushed forth in streams of gratitude. Learn from this that the point of full communion with God today is the place where we see the angel with the sheathed sword. Oh, how sweet to know that God hath nothing against us! He hath blotted out our transgressions, and will never remember them. He cannot smite us, for He has justified us in His Son. How shall He destroy those for whom Christ hath shed His blood? He hath a sword, but it is for those who are the adversaries of our souls, even for the arch-fiend who would destroy us. Its edge is not for us who are sprinkled with the blood of Jesus. Many of you cannot draw near to God, and I do not wonder at it, because you have not yet seen that sin was in very deed put away by the sacrifice of Jesus. You have seen the drawn sword, and that is something; but you have not yet beheld that sword sheathed, nor heard the voice of Jehovah saying, "It is enough." The place where love meets love, where your little tiny stream melts into the great river of God's love, is where we sing, "O Lord, I will praise thee; for though thou wast angry with me, thine anger is turned away, and thou comfortedst me." Henceforth our life flows with the life of Jesus in one deep, peaceful stream, onward and onward forever. You cannot rest in the Lord and live in Him till you have seen the Sacrifice and its eternal results in peace with God. May God bring you there! Atonement is the basis of worship. The sacrifice of Christ and His righteousness, these are the Jachin and the Boaz, the two sublime pillars of the temple gate. God communes with men where Jesus becomes man's rest. You cannot pass to the mercy seat to speak with God except through the veil of the Savior's body which was rent on our behalf.

Thus I think I have made you familiar with the threshing-floor of Ornan the Jebusite, and showed you wherein it was felt to be a place of divine manifestation and a fit site for the permanent temple of God.

III. And now I am going to close by HEARTILY EXHORTING YOU TO USE THIS PLACE. Brethren and sisters, if we have found out where to meet with God, then let us meet with Him continually. Do you feel guilty this morning? Is your sin heavy upon you? Do you see the sworded angel? Well, you have to meet God even there! Therefore, gird up your loins! "What garments shall I put on?" Put on sackcloth. I mean not literally; but while there is any guilt upon you come to God with lowliest penitence, mourning for sin, as David did, and the elders that were with him. You may not come now in the silken garments of your luxury, nor in the purple robes of your pride, nor in the mail of your hate. Put these away from you, and come with sackcloth and ashes, weeping for your transgressions, and God will meet with you; for He will meet with sinners who come to Him mourning because of their sin.

When you thus come, I want you to be quiet a while. Stand still! Listen! Suppose you had been with those elders of Israel; what would you have heard? You would have heard your shepherd-king pleading for His flock: "These sheep, what have they done? Let thine hand be on me and on my father's house." But now David is dead and buried, and his sepulchre is in his own land; but another King of the house of David, one Jesus, is standing before the Lord pleading for mercy. While you are clothed in the sackcloth of your repentance, you may hear Him cry, "As for these sheep, let them live. Thou hast awakened the sword against me, their shepherd, therefore let my sheep be spared! Thine hand has been on me, therefore let these go their way!" Do you hear that intercession? Jesus is pleading in that fashion now. He is "able to save them to the uttermost that come unto God by him, seeing he ever liveth to make intercession for them." Oh it is blessed to come to God that way—with the sackcloth on your loins, but with the prevalent intercession in your ears; confidently believing that Jesus maketh intercession for the transgressors, and that He must and will so prevail that by His knowledge He shall justify many.

Further, when you are coming to God, dear hearts, always take care that you come to the sacrifice. We frequently miss communion with God, I am persuaded, because we do not remember enough that precious blood which gives us access to God. When you go upstairs to pray, and you cannot get near to God, then do not speak, but sit in silence, and muse upon the agony and bloody sweat, the cross and passion of the Lord, and all the circumstances of His wondrous death, and say, "He loved me and gave Himself for me." There is matchless power in the Lord's sacrifice to remove the stone out of the heart, and pluck away selfishness from the affections. Come, come, come, come to the sacrifice! There shall you dwell with God in sweet delight.

If you would come still nearer to God, do not forget the effect of the sacrifice and intercession in the sheathing of the sword of justice. I have already set forth this truth; now I entreat you to turn it to practical use by enjoying it.

> Oh how sweet to view the flowing
>   Of my Savior's precious blood,
> With divine assurance knowing
>   He has made my peace with God.

Do not say, "I hope that the sword is sheathed"; it either is so, or it is not so. Do not be content with questionable hopes, but aim at certainties. Rest not till you obtain a solid assurance of your peace with God. If Jesus Christ was punished for your sin you cannot be punished for it; if He did bear your sin He did bear it, and there is an end of it; and if you have believed on Him you have the full proof in the Word of God that you are justified before God. What more do you want than God's own Word for it? and that Word declares that you, as a believer, have eternal life and shall never perish, neither shall you come into condemnation. Do not continue to mutter, "Well, I hope I may yet realize it." Why these debates? It is so: "he that believeth in him is justified from all things, from which we could not be justified by the law of Moses": God has turned away His wrath from the believer, and the sword is sheathed; therefore, being justified by faith, we have peace with God through Jesus Christ our Lord.

And lastly, if this be so, and you realize it, go away and begin to build a temple. You say, "Do you want us to build a new place of worship?" No, I speak only of a spiritual house. Of course, build as many meeting-places as you can where people may come together to hear the Word, for many are needed in this growing city, but the peculiar sort of building which I urge upon you is of the heart and spirit. Make your entire being a living temple for the living God. Begin now: the foundations are laid, you would not dream of building on any other; for "other foundation can no man lay than that which is laid." The Divine Moriah of Christ's person, the sacred place of His sacrifice is the mount wherein God shall be seen. Jesus Christ has Himself become the foundation of your hope; go and build on Him. Set up the pillars of earnest supplication, and arch them over with lofty praises. Remember, your God "inhabiteth the praises of Israel." Build Him a house of praise, that He may dwell in you, make your bodies to be the temples of the Holy Ghost, and your spirits the priests that sacrifice therein. In acts of holiness, piety, charity, and love spend all your days. Let your houses be churches dedicated to His fear and love; and let their chambers be holy as the courts of the tabernacle in the wilderness. Let each morning and evening have its sacrifice. Be yourself a priest at the altar. Let the garments of your daily toil be as vestments, your meals as sacraments; let your thoughts be psalms, your prayers incense, and your breath praise. Let every action be a priestly function, bringing glory unto the Lord from this day forth and forever. He that died for you reckons you to be dead to all things but Himself; and so it becometh you to be. "Ye are not your own, for ye are bought with a price," and from this day forward your motto should be—"Thine entirely. Thine entirely, O my God, I am." Begin to build this living temple, and the Lord help you to complete it to His praise. A poor edifice it will be when you have finished it, compared with the Lord your God; but yet if you have labored sincerely and earnestly it will turn out to be compacted of gold and silver and precious stones, and it will be found in the day of Christ to honor and glory. So may the Lord bless you, beloved, now and forever. Amen, and amen.

A GREATER THAN SOLOMON

A Sermon Delivered on Lord's day Evening, February 6, 1881.
Portion of Scripture read before Sermon—Colossians 1.
Hymns from *Our Own Hymn Book*—390, 389, 416.

Behold, a greater than Solomon is here—Luke 11:31.

Our first thought is that no mere man would have said this concerning himself unless he had been altogether eaten up with vanity; for Solomon was among the Jews the very ideal of greatness and wisdom. It would be an instance of the utmost self-conceit if any mere man were to say of himself—"A greater than Solomon is here." Any person who was really greater and wiser than Solomon would be the last man to claim such pre-eminence. A wise man would never think of it; a prudent man would never say it. The Lord Jesus Christ, if we regard Him as a mere man, would have never uttered such an expression, for a more modest, self-forgetting man was never found in all our race. View it on the supposition that the Christ of Nazareth was a mere man, and I say that His whole conduct was totally different from the spirit which would have suggested an utterance like this—"A greater Solomon is here." For men to compare themselves with one another is not wise, and Christ was wise; it is not humble, and Christ was humble. He would not have thus spoken if there had not been cause and reason in His infinitely glorious nature. It was because the divinity within Him must speak out. For God to say that He is greater than all His creatures is no boasting; for what are they in His sight? All worlds are but sparks from the anvil of His omnipotence. Space, time, eternity, all these are as nothing before Him; and for Him to compare or even to contrast Himself with one of His own creatures is supreme condescension, let Him word the comparison how He may. It was the divine within our Lord which made Him say—and not even then with a view to exalt Himself, but with a view to point the moral that He was trying to bring before the people—"A greater than Solomon is here." He did as good as say, "The queen of the south came from a distance to hear the wisdom of Solomon, but you refuse to hear *Me*. She gave attention to a man, but you will not regard your God. You will not listen to the incarnate Deity who tells you words of infinite, infallible wisdom." Our Lord Jesus is aiming at His hearers' good, and where the motive is so disinterested there remains no room for criticism. He tells them that He is greater than Solomon, to convince them of the greatness of their crime in refusing to listen to the messages of love with which His lips were loaded. Foreigners came from afar to Solomon; but I, says He, have come to your door, and brought infinite wisdom into your very gates, and yet you refuse Me. Therefore the queen of the south shall rise up in judgment against you, for, in rejecting Me, you reject a greater than Solomon.

The second thought that comes to one's mind is this: notice the self-consciousness of the Lord Jesus Christ.

He knows who He is, and what He is, and He is not lowly in spirit because He is ignorant of His own greatness. He was meek and lowly in heart—"*Servus servorum*," as the Latins were wont to call Him, "Servant of servants," but all the while He knew that He was *Rex regum*, or King of kings. He takes a towel and He washes His disciples' feet; but all the while He knows that He is their Master and their Lord. He associates with publicans and harlots, and dwells with the common people; but all the while He knows that He is the only begotten of the Father. He sits as a child in the temple hearing and asking questions of the rabbis; He stands among His disciples as though He were one of themselves, conversing with the ignorant and foolish of the day, seeking their good; but He knows that He is not one of them; He knows that He has nothing to learn from them: He knows that he is able to teach senates and to instruct kings and philosophers, for he is greater than Solomon. He wears a peasant's garb, and has not where to lay His head; but He knows that, whatever the lowliness of His condition, He is greater than Solomon; He lets us perceive that he knows it, that all may understand the love which brought Him down so low. It is grand humility on Christ's part that He condescends to be our servant, our Savior, when He is so great that the greatest of men are as nothing before Him. "He counted it not robbery to be equal with God": mark that; and yet "He made himself of no reputation." Some people do not know their own worth, and so, when they stoop to a lowly office it is no stoop to their minds, for they do not know their own abilities. They do not know to what they are equal; but Christ did know: He knew all about His own Deity, and His own wisdom and greatness as man. I admire, therefore, the clear understanding which sparkles in His deep humiliation, like a gem in a dark mine. He is not one who stoops down according to the old rhyme—

As needs he must who cannot sit upright;

but He is One who comes down wittingly from His throne of glory, marking each step and fully estimating the descent which He is making. The cost of our redemption was known to Him, and He endured the cross, despising the shame. Watts well sings—

This was compassion like a God,
    That *when the Savior knew*
The price of pardon was his blood,
    His pity ne'er withdrew.

Brethren, if our Savior Himself said that He was greater than Solomon, you and I must fully believe it, enthusiastically own it, and prepare to proclaim it. If others will not own it, let us be the more prompt to confess it. If He Himself had to say, before they would own it, "A greater than Solomon is here," let it not be necessary that the encomium should be repeated, but let us all confess that He is indeed greater than Solomon. Let us go home with this resolve in our minds, that we will speak greater things of Christ than we have done, that we will try to love Him more and serve Him better, and make Him in our own estimation and in the world's greater than He has ever been. Oh for a glorious high throne to set Him on, and a crown of stars to place upon His head! Oh to bring nations to His feet! I know my words cannot honor Him according to His merits: I wish they could. I am quite sure to fail in my own judgment when telling out His excellence; indeed, I grow less and less satisfied with my thoughts and language concerning Him. He is too glorious for my feeble language to describe Him. If I could speak with the tongues of men and of angels, I could not speak worthily of Him. If I could borrow all the harmonies of heaven, and enlist every harp and song of the glorified, yet were not the music sweet enough for His praises. Our glorious Redeemer is ever blessed: let us bless Him. He is to be extolled above the highest heavens: let us sound forth His praises. Oh for a well-tuned harp! May the Spirit of God help both heart and lip to extol Him at this hour.

First, then, we shall try to *draw a parallel between Jesus and Solomon*; and, secondly, we will break away from all comparisons, and show where *there cannot be any parallel between Christ and Solomon at all*.

I. First, then, BETWEEN CHRIST AND SOLOMON there are some points of likeness.

When the Savior Himself gives us a comparison it is a clear proof that a likeness was originally intended by the Holy Spirit, and therefore we may say without hesitation that Solomon was meant to be a type of Christ. I am not going into detail, nor am I about to refine upon small matters; but I shall give you five points in which Solomon was conspicuously like to Christ, and in which our Lord was greater than Solomon. O for help in the great task before me.

And, first, in *wisdom*. Whenever you talked about Solomon to a Jew his eyes began to flash with exultation; his blood leaped in his veins with national pride. Solomon—that name brought to mind the proudest time of David's dynasty, the age of gold. Solomon, the magnificent, why, surely, his name crowns Jewish history with glory, and the brightest beam of that glory is his wisdom. In the east, and I think I may say in the west, it still remains a proverb, "To be as wise as Solomon." No modern philosopher or learned monarch has ever divided the fame of the son of David, whose name abides as the synonym of wisdom. Of no man since could it be said as of him, "And all the kings of the earth sought the presence of Solomon, to hear his wisdom, that God had put in his heart." *He intermeddled with all knowledge,* and was a master in all sciences. He was a naturalist: "and he spoke of trees from the cedar trees that are in Lebanon even unto the hyssop that springeth out of the wall: he spoke also of beasts, and of fowl, and of creeping things, and of fishes." He was an engineer and architect, for he wrote: "I made me great works; I built me houses; I planted me vine-yards: I made me gardens and orchards, and I planted trees in them of all kind of fruits: I made me pools of water, to water therewith the wood that bringeth forth trees." He was one who understood the science of government—a politician of the highest order. He was everything, in fact. God gave him wisdom and largeness of heart, says the Scripture, like the sand of the sea: "and Solomon's wisdom excelled the wisdom of all the children of the east country, and all the wisdom of Egypt. For he was wiser than all men; than Ethan the Ezrahite, and Heman, and Chalcol, and Darda, the sons of Mahol: and his fame was in all nations round about." Yes; but our Savior knows infinitely more than Solomon. I want you tonight to come to Him just as the Queen of Sheba came to Solomon, only for weightier reasons. You do not want to learn anything concerning architecture or navigation, agriculture or anatomy. You want to know only how you shall be built up a spiritual house, and how you shall cross those dangerous seas which lie between this land and the celestial city. Well, you may come to Jesus and He will teach you all that you need to know, for all wisdom is in Christ. Our divine Savior knows things past and present and future: the secrets of God are with Him. He knows the inmost heart of God, for no one knoweth the Father save the Son and He to whom the Son shall reveal Him. To Him it is given to take the book of prophetic decree and loose the seven seals thereof. Come, then, to Christ Jesus if you want to know the mind of God, for it is written that He "is made unto us wisdom." Solomon might *have* wisdom, but he could not *be* wisdom to others; Christ Jesus is that to the full. In the multifarious knowledge which He pos-sesses—the universal knowledge which is stored up in Him—there is enough for your guidance and instruction even to the end of life, however intricate and overshadowed your path may be.

Solomon proved his wisdom in part by his *remarkable inventions*. We cannot tell what Solomon did not know. At any rate, no man knows at this present moment how those huge stones, which have lately been discovered, which were the basis of the as-cent by which Solomon went up to the house of the Lord, were ever put into their places. Many of the stones of Solomon's masonry are so enormous that scarcely could any modern machinery move them; and without the slightest cement they are put together so exactly that the blade of a knife could not be inserted between them. It is marvelous how the thing was done. How such great stones were brought from their original bed in the quarry—how the whole building of the temple was executed—nobody knows. The castings in brass and silver are scarcely less remarkable. No doubt many inventions have passed away from the knowledge of modern times, inventions as remarkable as those of our own age. We are a set of savages that are beginning to learn something, but Solomon knew and invented things which we shall, perhaps, rediscover in 500 years time. By vehement exertion this boastful nineteenth century, wretched century as it is, will crawl towards the wisdom which Solomon possessed ages ago. Yet is Jesus greater than Solomon. As for inventions, Solomon is no inventor at all compared with Him who said, "Deliver him from going down into the pit, for

I have found a ransom." O Savior, didst thou find out the way of our salvation? Didst thou bring into the world and carry out and execute the way by which hell-gate should be closed, and heaven-gate, once barred, should be set wide open? Then, indeed, art thou wiser than Solomon. Thou art the deviser of salvation, the architect of the church, the author and finisher of our faith.

Solomon has left us some very *valuable books*—the Proverbs, Ecclesiastes, and the matchless Song. But, oh, the words of Solomon fall far short of the words of Jesus Christ, for they are spirit and life. The power of the word of Jesus is infinitely greater than all the deep sayings of the sage. Proverbial wisdom cannot match His sayings, nor can "The Preacher" rival His sermons, and even the divine Song itself would remain without a meaning—an allegory never to be explained—if it were not that Christ Himself is the sum and substance of it. Solomon may sing of Christ, but Christ is the substance of the song. He is greater than Solomon in His teachings, for His wisdom is from above, and leads men up to heaven. Blessed are they that sit at His feet.

Again, Solomon showed His wisdom in *difficult judgments*. You know how he settled the question between the two women concerning the child; many other puzzles Solomon solved, and many other knots Solomon was able to untie. He was a great ruler and governor—a man wise in politics, in social economy, and in commerce—wise in all human respects. But a greater than Solomon is present where Christ is. There is no difficulty which Christ cannot remove, no knot which He cannot untie, no question which He cannot answer. You may bring your hard questions to Him, and He will answer them; and if you have any difficulty on your heart tonight, do but resort to the Lord Jesus Christ in prayer, and search His word, and you shall hear a voice as from the sacred oracle, which shall lead you in the path of safety.

My point at this time, especially as we are coming to the Communion table, is this. I want you that love the Lord Jesus Christ to believe in His infinite wisdom, and come to Him for direction. I fear that when you are in trouble, you half suppose that the great keeper of Israel must have made a mistake. You get into such an intricate path that you say, "Surely, my Shepherd has not guided me aright." Never think so. When you are poor and needy still say, "This my poverty was ordained by a greater than Solomon." What if you seem to be deprived of every comfort, and you are brought into a strange and solitary way, where you find no city to dwell in? Yet a guide is near, and that guide is not foolish; but a greater than Solomon is here. I think I look tonight into a great furnace. It is so fierce that I cannot bear to gaze into its terrible blaze. For fear my eyeballs should utterly fail me and lose the power of sight through the glare of that tremendous flame, I turn aside, for the fury of its flame overpowers me. But when I am strengthened to look again I see ingots of silver refining in the white heat, and I note that the heat is tempered to the last degree of nicety. I watch the process to the end, and I say, as I behold those ingots brought out all clear and pure, refined from all dross, and ready for the heavenly treasury, "Behold, a greater than Solomon was in that furnace work." So you will find it, O sufferer. Infinite wisdom is in your lot. Come, poor child, do not begin to interfere with your Savior's better judgment, but let it order all things. Do not let your little "Know" ever rise up against the great knowledge of your dear Redeemer. Think of this when you wade in deep waters and comfortably whisper to yourself—"A greater than Solomon is here."

I have not time to enlarge, and therefore I would have you notice, next, that our Lord Jesus Christ is greater than Solomon in *wealth*. This was one of the things for which Solomon was noted. He had great treasures: he "made gold to be as stones, and as for silver it was little accounted of," so rich did he become. He had multitudes of servants. I think he had 60,000 hewers in the mountains hewing out stones and wood, so numerous were the workmen he employed. His court was magnificent to the last degree. When you read of the victuals that were prepared to feed the court, and of the stately way in which everything was arranged from the stables of the horses upwards to the ivory throne, you feel, like the queen of Sheba, utterly astonished, and say, "The half was not told me." But, oh, when you consider all the wealth of Solomon, what poor stuff it is compared with the riches that are treasured up in Christ Jesus. Beloved, He who died upon the cross, and was indebted to a friend for a grave; He who was stripped even to the last rag ere He died; He who possessed no wealth but that of sorrow and sympathy, yet had about Him the power to make many rich, and He has made multitudes rich—rich to all the intents of everlasting bliss; and therefore He must be rich Himself. Is He not rich who enriches millions? Why, our Lord Jesus Christ, even by a word, comforted those that were bowed down. When He stretched out His hand He healed the sick with a touch. There was a wealth about His every movement. He was a full man, full of all that man could desire to be full of; and now, seeing that He has died and risen again, there is in Him a wealth of pardoning love, a wealth of saving power, a wealth of intercessory might before the Father's throne, a wealth of all things by which He enriches the sons of men, and shall enrich them to all eternity.

I want this truth to come home to you: I want you to recognize the riches of Christ, you that are His people; and, in addition, to remember the truth of our hymn—

> Since Christ is rich can I be poor?
> What can I want besides?

I wish we could learn to reckon what we are by what Christ is. An old man said, "I am very old; I have lost my only son; I am penniless; and, worst of all, I am blind. But," added he, "this does not matter, for Christ is not infirm; Christ is not aged; Christ has all riches; and Christ is not blind; and Christ is mine; and I have all things in Him." Could you not get hold of that somehow, brothers and sisters? Will not the Holy Spirit teach you the art of appropriating the Lord Jesus and all that He is and has. If Christ be your representative, why, then you are rich in Him. Go to Him to be enriched. Suppose I were to meet a woman, and I knew her husband to be a very wealthy man, and that he loved her very much, and she were to say to me, "I am dreadfully poor; I do not know where to get raiment and food." "Oh," I should say,

"That woman is out of her mind." If she has such a husband, surely she has only to go to him for all that she needs. And what if nothing is invested in her name, yet it is in his name, and they are one, and he will deny her nothing." I should say, "My good woman, you must not talk in that fashion, or I will tell your husband of you." Well, I think that I shall have to say the same of you who are so very poor and cast down, and yet are married to Jesus Christ. I shall have to tell your Husband of you, that you bring such complaints against Him, for all things are yours, for ye are Christ's and Christ is God's; wherefore, "lift up the hands that hang down, and confirm the feeble knees"; use the knees of prayer and the hand of faith, and your estate will well content you. Do not think that you are married to Rehoboam, who will beat you with scorpions, for you are joined to a greater than Solomon. Do not fancy that your heavenly Bridegroom is a beggar. All the wealth of eternity and infinity is His; how can you say that you are poor while all that He has is yours?

Now, thirdly, and very briefly indeed. There was one point about Solomon in which every Israelite rejoiced, namely that he was *the prince of peace*. His name signifies peace. His father, David, was a great warrior, but Solomon had not to carry on war. His power was such that no one dared to venture upon a conflict with so great and potent a monarch. Every man throughout Israel sat under his vine and fig tree, and no man was afraid. No trumpet of invader was heard in the land. Those were halcyon days for Israel when Solomon reigned. Ah, but in that matter a greater than Solomon is here; for Solomon could not give his subjects peace of mind, he could not bestow upon them rest of heart, he could not ease them of their burden of guilt, or draw the arrow of conviction from their breast and heal its smart. But I preach to you tonight that blessed divine Man of Sorrows who has wrought out our redemption, and who is greater than Solomon in His peace-giving power. Oh, come and trust Him. Then shall your "peace be as a river, and your righteousness like the waves of the sea." Am I addressing one of God's people who is sorely troubled, tumbled up and down in his thoughts? Brother or sister, do not think that you must wait a week or two before you can recover your peace. You can become restful in a moment, for "He is our peace"—even He Himself, and He alone. And, oh, if you will but take Him at once, laying hold upon Him by the hand of faith as your Savior, this Man shall be the peace even when the Assyrian shall come into the land. There is no peace like the peace which Jesus gives; it is like a river, deep, profound, renewed, ever flowing, overflowing, increasing and widening into an ocean of bliss. "The peace of God, which passeth all understanding, shall keep your heart and mind, through Jesus Christ." Oh, come to Him. Come to Him at this moment. Do not remain an hour away from your Noah, or rest, for with Him in the ark your weary wing shall be tired no longer. You shall be safe and restful the moment you return to Him. The fruit of the Spirit is joy. I want you to get that joy and to enter into this peace. Blessed combination, joy and peace! Peace, peace, there is music in the very word: get it from Him who is the Word, and whose voice can still a storm into a calm. A greater than Solomon is here to give you that peace; beat the sword of your inward warfare, into the plowshare of holy service; no longer sound an alarm, but blow up the trumpet of peace in this day of peace.

A fourth thing for which Solomon was noted was his *great works*. Solomon built the temple; which was one of the seven wonders of the world in its time. A very marvelous building it must have been, but I will not stay to describe it, for time fails us. In addition to this he erected for himself palaces, constructed fortifications, and made aqueducts and great pools to bring streams from the mountains to the various towns. He also founded Palmyra and Baalbed—those cities of the desert—to facilitate his commerce with India, Arabia, and other remote regions. He was a marvelous man. Earth has not seen his like. And yet a greater than Solomon is here, for Christ has brought the living water from the throne of God right down to thirsty men, being Himself the eternal aqueduct through which the heavenly current streams. Christ has built fortresses and munitions of defense, behind which His children stand secure against the wrath of hell; and He has founded and is daily finishing a wondrous temple, His church, of which His people are the living stones, fashioned, polished, rendered beautiful—a temple which God Himself shall inhabit, for He "dwelleth not in temples made with hands, that is to say, of this building"; but He dwells in a temple which He Himself doth pile, of which Christ is architect and builder, foundation, and chief cornerstone. But Jesus builds for eternity, an everlasting temple, and, when all visible things pass away, and the very ruins of Solomon's temple and Solomon's aqueduct are scarcely to be discerned, what a sight will be seen in that New Jerusalem! The twelve courses of its foundations are of precious stones, its walls bedight with diamonds rare, its streets are paved with gold, and its glory surpasses that of the sun. I am but talking figures, poor figures, too; for the glory of the city of God is spiritual, and where shall I find words with which to depict it? There, where the Lamb Himself is the light, and the Lord God Himself doth dwell—there the whole edifice, the entire New Jerusalem—shall be to the praise and the glory of His grace who gave Jesus Christ to be the builder of the house of His glory, of which I hope we shall form a part forever and ever.

Now, if Christ does such great works, I want you to come to Him, that He may work in you the work of God. That is the point. Come and trust Him at once. Trust Him to build you up. Come and trust Him to bring the living water to your lips. Come and trust Him to make you a temple of the living God. Come, dear child of God, if you have great works to do, come and ask for the power of Christ with which to perform them. Come, you that would leave some memorial to the honor of the divine name, come to Him to teach and strengthen you. He is the wise master-builder; come and be workers together with Christ. Baptize your weakness into His infinite strength, and you shall be strong in the Lord, and in the power of His mind. God help you to do so.

Once more. I draw the parallel upon the fifth point, and I have done with it. Solomon was great as to *dominion*. The kingdom of the Jews was never anything like the size before or after that Solomon made it. It appears to have extended from the river of Egypt right across the wilderness far up to the Persian Gulf. We can scarcely tell how far Solomon's dominions reached; they are said to have been "from sea to sea, and from the river even unto the ends of the earth." By one mode or another he managed to bring various kings into subjection to him, and he was the greatest monarch that ever swayed the scepter of Judah. It has all gone now. Poor, feeble Rehoboam dropped from his foolish hands the reins his father held. The kingdom was rent in pieces, the tributary princes found their liberty, and the palmy days of Israel were over. On the contrary, our Lord Jesus Christ at this moment has dominion over all things. God has set Him over all the works of His hands. Aye, tell it out among the heathen that the Lord reigneth. The feet that were nailed to the tree are set upon the necks of His enemies. The hands that bore the nails sway at this moment the scepter of all words: Jesus is King of kings, and Lord of lords! Hallelujah! Let universal sovereignty be ascribed to the Son of man: to Him who was "despised and rejected of men, a man of sorrows and acquainted with grief." Tell it out, ye saints, for your own comfort. The Lord reigneth, let the earth rejoice, let the multitude of the isles be glad thereof. Everything that happens in providence is under His sway still, and the time is coming when a moral and spiritual kingdom will be set up by Him which shall encompass the whole world. It does not look like it, does it? All these centuries have passed away, and little progress has been made. Ah, but He cometh; and when He cometh, or ere He cometh, He shall overturn, overturn, overturn, for His right it is, and God will give it Him. And, as surely as God lives, unto Him shall every man bow the knee, "and every tongue shall confess that Jesus Christ is Lord, to the glory of God the Father." Do not be afraid about it. Do not measure difficulties, much less tremble at them. What is faith made for but to believe that which seems impossible? To expect universal dominion for Christ when everything goes well is but the expectation of reason; but to expect it when everything goes ill, is the triumph of Abrahamic confidence. Look upon the great mountain and say, "Who art thou, O great mountain? Before the true Zerubbabel thou shalt become a plain." In the blackest midnight, when the ebon darkness stands thick and hard as granite before you, believe that, at the mystic touch of Christ, the whole of it shall pass away, and at the brightness of His rising the eternal light shall dawn, never to be quenched. This is to act the part of a believer; and I ask you to act that part, and believe to the full in Christ the Omnipotent. What means this stinted faith in an almighty arm? What a fidget we are in and what a worry seizes us if a little delay arises! Everything has to be done in the next ten minutes, or we count our Lord to be slack. Is this the part of wisdom? The Eternal has infinite leisure, who are we that we should hasten Him?

> His purposes will ripen fast,
> Unfolding every hour.

A day is long to us: but a thousand years to Him are but the twinkling of a star. Oh, rest in the Lord, and wait patiently for Him, for the time shall come when the God of Israel shall put to rout His adversaries, and the Christ of the cross shall be the Christ of the crown. We shall one day hear it said—The great Shepherd reigns; and

His unsuffering kingdom now hath come. Then rocks and hills, and vales and islands of the sea shall all be vocal with the one song, "Worthy is the Lamb that was slain to receive honor and glory and power and dominion and might forever and ever!"

Thus have I tried to draw the parallel, but I pray you to see the Lord Jesus for yourself, and know whether I have spoken the truth about Him. You have heard the report; now, like the Queen of Sheba, go and see for yourself. Get to Christ, as to His dominion, come under His sway and own His scepter. Go and trust your King; love your King; praise your King; delight in your King. How courtiers delight to be summoned to court! How glad they are to see the queen's face. How pleased they are if she gives them but a kindly word! Surely, their fortune is made, or at least their hopes are raised and their spirits lifted up. Shall we not sun ourselves in the presence of the blessed and only Potentate? Let us come into the presence of our King tonight, or else let us sit here and weep. Let us come to His table to feed upon Himself. Let us live on His Word. Let us delight in His love; and we shall surely say, "A greater than Solomon is here."

II. I shall not detain you longer than a minute or two while I remark that we must rise beyond all parallels, if we would reach the height of this great argument, for BETWEEN CHRIST AND SOLOMON THERE IS MUCH MORE CONTRAST THAN COMPARISON—much more difference than likeness.

In His *nature* the Lord Jesus is greater than Solomon. Alas, poor Solomon! The strongest man that ever lived, namely, Samson, was the weakest of men; and the wisest man that ever lived, was, perhaps, the greatest, certainly the most conspicuous, fool. How different is our Lord! There is no infirmity in Christ, no folly in the incarnate God. The backsliding of Solomon finds no parallel in Jesus, in whom the prince of this world found nothing though he searched Him through and through.

Our Lord is greater than Solomon because He is not mere man. He is man, perfect man, man to the utmost of manhood, sin excepted; but still He is more, and infinitely more, than man. "In him dwelleth all the fullness of the Godhead bodily." He is God Himself. "The Word was God." God dwells in Him, and He Himself is God.

As in nature He was infinitely superior to Solomon, and not to be compared with him for a moment, so was He in *character*. Look at Christ and Solomon for a minute as to real greatness of character, and you can hardly see Solomon with a microscope, while Christ rises grandly before you, growing every moment till He fills the whole horizon of your admiration. Principally let me note the point of self-sacrifice. Jesus lived entirely for other people; He had never a thought about Himself. Solomon was, to a great extent, wise unto himself, rich unto himself, strong unto himself; and you see in those great palaces, and in all their arrangements, that he seeks his own pleasure, honor, and emolument; and, alas! that seeking of pleasure leads him into sin, that sin into a still greater one. Solomon, wonderful as he is, only compels you to admire him for his greatness, but you do not admire him for his goodness. You see nothing that makes you love him, you rather tremble before him than feel gladdened by him. Oh, but look at Christ. He does not have a thought for Himself. He lives for others. How grandly magnificent He is in disinterested love. He "loved his church and gave himself for it." He pours out even His heart's blood for the good of men: and hence, dear friends, at this moment our blessed Lord is infinitely superior to Solomon in His *influence.* Solomon has little or no influence today. Even in his own time he never commanded the influence that Christ had in His deepest humiliation. I do not hear of any that were willing to die for Solomon; certainly nobody would do so now. But how perpetually is enthusiasm kindled in 10,000 breasts for Christ! They say that if again there were stakes in Smithfield we should not find men to burn at them for Christ. I tell you, it is not so. The Lord Jesus Christ has at this moment a remnant according to the election of His grace who would fling themselves into a pit of fire for Him, and joy to do it. "Who shall separate us"—even us poor pygmies—"from the love of God which is in Christ Jesus our Lord?" "Oh," says one, "I do not think I could suffer martyrdom." You are not yet called to do so, my brother, and God has not given you the strength to do it before the need arises; but you will have strength enough if ever it comes to your lot to die for Jesus. Did you never hear of the martyr who, the night before he was to be burnt, sat opposite the fire, and, taking his shoe off, he held his foot close to the flame till he began to feel the burning of it? He drew it back and said, "I see God does not give me power to bear such suffering as I put upon myself, but I make none the less doubt," said he, "that I shall very well stand the stake tomorrow morning, and burn quick to the death for Christ without starting back." And so he did, for he was noticed never to stir at all while the flames were consuming him. There is a great deal of difference between your strength today and what your strength would be if you were called to some tremendous work or suffering. My Lord and Master, let me tell you, wakes more enthusiasm in human breasts at this moment than any other name in the universe. Napoleon once said, "I founded a kingdom upon force, and it will pass away"; but "Christ founded a kingdom upon love, and it will last forever and ever." And so it will. Blot out the name of Christ from the hearts of His people? Strike you sun from the firmament, and quench the stars; and when you have achieved that easy task, yet have you not begun to remove the glory of the indwelling Christ from the hearts of His people. Some of us delight to think that we bear in our body the marks of the Lord Jesus. "Where?" says one. I answer, it is all over us. We have been buried into His name, and we belong to Him, in spirit, soul, and body. That watermark, which denotes that we are His, can never be taken out of us. We are dead with Him, wherein also we were buried with Him and are risen again with Him; and there is nothing at this moment that stirs our soul like the name of Jesus. Speak for yourselves. Is it not so? Have you never heard of one who lay dying, his mind wandering, and his wife said to him, "My dear, do you not know me?" He shook his head; and they brought near his favorite child. "Do you not know me?" He shook his head. One whispered, "Do you know the Lord Jesus Christ?" and he said, "He is all my salvation and all my desire." Oh, blessed name! Blessed name! Some years ago I was away from this place for a little rest, and I was thinking to myself, "Now, I wonder whether I really respond to the power of the gospel as I should like to do? I will go and hear a sermon and see." I would like to sit down with you, in the pews sometimes and hear somebody else preach—not everybody, mark you, for when I hear a good many I want to be doing it myself. I get tired of them if they do not glow and burn. But that morning I thought I would drop into a place of worship such as there might be in the little town. A poor, plain man, a countryman, began preaching about Jesus Christ. He praised my Master in very humble language, but he praised Him most sincerely. Oh, but the tears began to flow. I soon laid the dust all round me where I sat, and I thought, "Bless the Lord! I do love Him." It only wants somebody else to play the harp instead of me, and my soul is ready to dance to the heavenly tune. Only let the music be Christ's sweet, dear, precious name, and my heart leaps at the sound. Oh, my brethren, sound out the praises of Jesus Christ! Sound out that precious name! There is none like it under heaven to stir my heart. I hope you can all say the same. I know you can if you love Him; for all renewed hearts are enamored of the sweet Lord Jesus. "A greater than Solomon is here." Solomon has no power over your hearts, but Jesus has. His influence is infinitely greater; *his power to bless* is infinitely greater; and so let us magnify and adore Him with all our hearts.

Oh, that all loved Him! Alas that so many do not! What strange monsters! Why, if you do not love Christ, what are you at? You hearts of stone, will you not break? If His dying love does not break them, what will? If you cannot see the beauties of Jesus, what can you see? You blind bats! O you that know not the music of His name, you are deaf. O you that do not rejoice in Him, you are dead. What are you at, that you are spared through the pleadings of His love, and yet do not love Him? God have mercy upon you, and bring you to delight yourselves in Christ, and trust him! As for us who do trust Him, we mean to love Him and delight in Him more and more, world without end. Amen.

THE DROMEDARIES

SERMON NO. 1,504

WE will read a few verses first, and at the close of them you will find the text.

> Judah and Israel were many, as the sand which is by the sea in multitude, eating and drinking, and making merry. And Solomon reigned over all kingdoms from the river unto the land of the Philistines, and unto the border of Egypt: they brought presents, and served Solomon all the days of his life. And Solomon's provision for one day was thirty measures of fine flour, and threescore measures of meal, ten fat oxen, and twenty oxen out of the pastures, and a hundred sheep beside harts, and roebucks, and fallow deer, and fatted fowl. For he had dominion over all the region on this side the river, from Tiphsah even to Azzah, over all the kings on this side the river: and he had peace on all sides round him. And Judah and Israel dwelt safely, every man under his vine and under his fig tree, from Dan even to Beersheba, all the days of Solomon. And Solomon had forty thousand stalls of horses for his chariots, and twelve thousand horsemen. And those officers provided victual for King Solomon, and for all that came into King Solomon's table, every man in his month: they lacked nothing. Barley also and straw for the horses and dromedaries brought they unto the place where the officers were, every man according to his charge—1 Kings 4:20–28.

The last words are the text for this occasion.

From the whole passage you will see that the kingdom of Israel under the sway of Solomon was a fair type of the reign of our Lord Jesus Christ. Perhaps it most exactly describes His future dominion, in the long-expected glory of the latter days. The present state of the church may be compared to the reign of David, splendid with victories, but disturbed with battles; but there are better days to come, days in which the kingdom shall be extended and become more manifest; and then the Lord Jesus Christ shall be even more conspicuously seen as the Solomon of the kingdom, "who shall have dominion from sea to sea." Yet even now, as "we that have believed do enter into rest," so do we also enter into the richest provision which is made in the covenant of grace, even at this present; and I may say of all who have come under the sway of Christ, that we dwell in a region of *peace*, seated every man under his vine and figtree, and none making us afraid. "There is, therefore, now no condemnation to them which are in Christ Jesus," and, "therefore, being justified by faith, we have peace with God through our Lord Jesus Christ." "The peace of God which passeth all understanding" doth keep our heart and mind by Jesus Christ. Israel under Solomon had *abundance* as well as peace. What says the historian? They were "as the sand which is by the sea in multitude, eating and drinking, and making merry." It is said that there was such plenty in the land in Solomon's time that gold was of no more value than silver, and silver became of little more value than iron; and as for the other metals, they were little accounted of. So common had precious metals become that they were scarcely precious any longer, they were so plentiful. The whole land flowed with milk and honey, and the people rejoiced and were glad. Certainly the Lord Jesus Christ has brought His people into a state of the greatest plenty, for "all things are yours; whether things present, or things to come; or life, or death; all are yours; and ye are Christ's; and Christ is God's." What plenty must that man have to whom the Lord has said, "No good thing will I withhold from them that walk uprightly"! "Whatsoever ye shall ask in prayer, believing, ye shall receive." He has given us *carte blanche* in prayer. He has put into our hands the keys of his treasury, and has bidden us take what we will. He has said, "Delight thyself also in the Lord, and he shall give thee the desires of thine heart"; and He has added, "Open thy mouth wide and I will fill it." If we have not, it is "because we ask not, or because we ask amiss."

So, too, we dwell in a kingdom which is ruled with *wisdom*. It is said of Solomon in this chapter that he had wisdom and understanding exceeding much, and largeness of heart, even as the sand on the sea shore; and Solomon's wisdom excelled the wisdom of all the children of the east country, and all the wisdom of the Egyptians. Is not this also our honor and privilege? Behold, this day the Lord Jesus Christ is "made unto us wisdom." "We have an unction from the Holy One, and know all things" while we dwell in Him; for "the secret of the Lord is with them that fear him, and he will show them his covenant." "If any man will do his will he shall know of the doctrine." "All thy children shall be taught of the Lord, and great shall be the peace of thy children." Hence we dwell under a rule of wisdom, which wisdom imparts itself to each one of us according to his capacity to receive it, yea, even to those whose experience is but shallow: "to teach the young men wisdom, and the babes knowledge and discretion." "If any many lack wisdom, let him ask of God that giveth to all men liberally, and upbraideth not."

Israel had a king who was full of *power*. Solomon had squadrons of horses and chariots of war, and he was so strong that the kings of the earth dared not come into conflict with him, but paid him tribute. As for our King, He has better forces than horses and chariots of war, for He has but to speak to His Father, and He will presently send Him twenty legions of angels. All power is delivered unto Him in heaven and in earth. The fullness of the Godhead dwells in Him for the defense and help of His people, and if you will but open your eyes you shall see horses of fire and chariots of fire round about your Lord. Hosts of angels are ascending and descending upon the Son of man, and all heaven is in motion for the purposes of God in

Christ Jesus. Not an angel stands still beneath the sway of Christ, but each one either ascends or descends to do his Master's bidding. Talk of mighty princes—He is the Prince of the kings of the earth, the "blessed and only Potentate," to whom belongeth rule over all principalities and powers. I might go on with the parallel, but that is not the object of my discourse.

The great kingdom of Solomon was managed by a well-appointed body of officers, and certain persons were set over each province, who, amongst other duties, had to provide for king Solomon's table and stable. The table was very sumptuously furnished, as you saw in the reading; and in the stable stood horses of war, and also swift dromedaries, which were used in the same manner as our modern post-horses, to carry messages rapidly from one station to another. These swift horses and dromedaries were made to run from town to town with the royal mandates, and thus the whole country was kept in speedy communication with the capital. Appointed officers were bound to provide for these horses and dromedaries, and all else that concerned the king's business; and my subject at this time will illustrate the likeness between this arrangement and the methods of our Lord's kingdom.

I. First we shall note that EACH OF SOLOMON'S OFFICERS HAD A CHARGE. The text says, "Every man according to his charge." We have officers about modern courts who may be highly ornamental, but when you have said that, there is very little else to add. On high days and holidays they wear many decorations, and glitter in their stars and garters, and sumptuous garments, but what particular charge they fulfill it is beyond my power to say. *In Solomon's court all his officers had a service to carry out,* "every man according to his charge." It is exactly so in the kingdom of our Lord Jesus Christ. If we are truly His, He has called us to some work and office, and He wills us to discharge that office diligently. We are not to be gentlemen-at-ease, but men-at-arms; not loiterers, but laborers; not glittering spangles, but burning and shining lights.

It is an exceeding glory to be the lowest servant of King Jesus. It is more honor to be a scullion in Christ's kitchen than to be a peer of the realm. The meanest position that can be occupied in the kingdom of Jesus Christ, if any can be mean in such a service, has a touch of divine glory about it; and if we rightfully discharge it, though it be only to wash the saints' feet, we partake in the honor of our Master, who Himself did not disdain to do the like. But no man is put in any office in the church that he may be merely ornamental. We are set in our places with an end and design, every man according to his charge—every woman according to *her* charge. My dear brother, you do not occupy the post of a minister or a pastor that you may be respected, but that you may "adorn the doctrine of God your Savior in all things." You are not, my dear brother, ordained to be an elder or a deacon in a church that our Lord may put honor upon you, though He does put honor upon you in it, but that you may bring glory to God—that the people may see the grace of God in you, and may magnify God in you. Churches were not made for ministers, but ministers for churches. We who are officers in the church are not ordained for our own sakes, but for the people's sake, and we should always recollect that fact, and live with it in our eye. Dear friend, if you are called to teach in the school, if you are called to visit from house to house, or to act as a City Missionary, or a Bible woman, you have work to do, and you must do it well, or render a sorrowful account at the last. Office is not given to you that you may get credit by it, and have the honor of filling it, but that you may do real service to your Lord and Master Jesus Christ. No servant of Christ can be faithful if he regards that title as one of barren honor involving no responsibility. If we would be servants and officers under our great King we must bow our necks to the yoke, and not imagine that it will suffice to bind burdens upon other men's shoulders, and act as lookers-on ourselves. It is said of Job's cattle, that "the oxen were plowing, and the asses were feeding beside them"; but in our Lord's field we must all be oxen, and steadily keep to the furrow.

Those who served Solomon were officers under a strict king, for such was his wisdom that he would not tolerate unfaithfulness in any office. He chose the best men, and so long as he retained them he meant business and expected prompt attention. If they did not do their duty, he did his, and sent them packing. It is very much so in the church of Jesus Christ. I am not speaking as if the children of God could perish; but I do say this, that in the service of Christ if you are not a faithful servant you will soon have to make room for another. You may be laid aside by sickness, and then you will have suffering instead of serving, or you may be made to drop into the rear rank and go behind and weep in sorrow because you did not faithfully do your duty in the front. Recollect that text, "The Lord thy God is a jealous God," and rest assured that our Lord Jesus Christ is like His Father, He will have the diligent obedience of His servants, and their faithful zeal, or else He will cashier them, and take away their commissions. "Be ye clean," saith He, "that bear the vessels of the Lord," for He will be had in reverence of them that are about Him, and unholy servants and unfaithful servants shall soon find that their Master can do without them. Many a minister has had to come away from a place of vantage because he has not zealously used it to win souls and lead on the people to the holy war. I do not doubt that many rising officers have been sent back to the ranks because the Commander-in-Chief could not have patience with them any longer in their positions. They were removed because they discouraged their fellow-soldier and checked the progress of the campaign. Do not suppose that our Lord Jesus Christ is any less strict in His discipline than Moses, for love is always severe towards those it highly favors. I greatly question the love of that man who can tolerate unchastity in his wife; certainly the Husband of the church will not do so. The love of our Lord Jesus is of so fervent a character that He cannot bear a divided heart, or a negligent walk in any one of us. There is a text which some Christian people do not like, and so they cut the heart out of it: "Our God is a consuming fire." They say, "God, out of Christ, is a consuming fire." The text does not say so; it speaks of "*Our* God," and that means our covenant God, our God *in Christ,* and it is God in Christ Jesus who is a consuming fire. Beware how you deal with Him; for while His love is strong as death, His jealousy is cruel as the grave; and if our hearts and motives and aims in His service once become divided, it will be as great a crime as if one of Solomon's servants should have been playing into the hands of Pharaoh, the king of Egypt. Solomon would have taken care that a man who had two lords should not have him for one of them. None of us can serve two masters: certainly, if Christ be one of them He will be the only One. A divided heart is an abhorrence to the loving Savior, and we must not insult Him with it.

The officers of Solomon were also obliged to recollect that the *orderly working of the whole system* depended upon each one of them. That is to say, Solomon had so arranged it that there was a certain troop of horses in a certain town, and the appointed officer must see to their fodder: barley and straw were to be on the spot in full quantity for the horses at that particular depot. It would not have done to send it anywhere else; and if an officer had failed to supply his department, the horses must have starved and the system been thrown out of gear. Now, in any well-arranged Christian church a Christian who is not faithful to his charge little knows what mischief he does; but, as far as he can, he puts the whole machine out of gear, and, apart from the interposing mercy and supreme wisdom of Christ, he would throw the whole economy of the Lord's house into disorder. Brethren and sister, we think when we neglect a part of our service that it ends there, but it does not. A father neglects his duty to his children: there is mischief to the child, but it goes further; that child in after life spreads the evil by his example, and transmits it to his descendants; aye, to his children's children after him. A Christian man in a church keeps in the background when he should be in the front, or he comes to the front when he should be in the rear, and this is just the upsetting of the whole business, so that affairs cannot move smoothly. The little church cannot prosper because an influential member is where he ought not to be. In a great house the servants must keep their places, and if the cook will persist in doing the chambermaid's duties, and does not prepare the meals, everything is in a muddle; and if, on the other hand, the maid who has to clean the rooms neglects that duty, but must needs be in the kitchen, there will be no comfort either by day or by night. You can all see the bearing of this upon a Christian church.

To change the figure, a church is like a house, and if the windows are put where the doors should be; or if what should make the roof is laid on the floor, the house is out of order. To be "fitly framed together" is the true condition of the Lord's house. The church is also compared to the body. If the eye should transfer itself to the foot, or if the ear should move to the hand, or if the hand should take the place of the foot, or the foot should attempt to do the work of the mouth, our comely frames would become monstrosities. So it must be in the system of the church of Jesus Christ if His arrangements are broken through. Under God everything depends upon each child of God having his "charge," and looking well to it. If he does not look well to his own department the Christian man does damage to others as well as to himself.

In Solomon's kingdom it came to pass that *the spirit of the king infused itself into all his officers*, and therefore the country was well governed. Beloved, I pray that it may be so with this church, and with all the churches of Jesus Christ, that the Spirit of our great King may infuse itself into us all. Nothing makes men fight like having a hero for a leader. When Cromwell came to the front nobody was afraid. Away went the cavaliers like chaff before the wind, when once he was present. And, surely, when our glorious Master, the Captain of our salvation, the standard bearer among ten thousand, is seen to be in the midst of a church, then everything goes well, and we all fight with confidence and daring. One man sometimes seems to have the power of pervading thousands of other men; his spirit appears to govern, to move, to stir the hearts of his fellow men till the man lives in them all; and so is it supremely with the Lord Christ. We live in Him, and He lives in us. If we are all moved by the spirit which dwells in Jesus—the spirit of love, of self-denial, of consuming zeal, and of ardor, then all will be done gloriously. If we copy His consecration, His prayerfulness, His boldness and His gentleness, what a troop shall we make, and how well will our Solomon's kingdom be administered!

Only one more thought here. *When Solomon's kingdom came to mischief it was through one of his officers.* You recollect that, when Solomon died, Jeroboam split the kingdom in twain, and he was a runaway servant. Whenever a church comes to ruin, we grieve to confess that it is generally through its own officers. I fear it is oftener the ministers than any other persons. The great heresies which have infested the church have not sprung from the mass of the people, but from certain famous leaders; and at this day the heart of our churches, I believe, is infinitely more sound than the ministry. I wish it were not so, but I cannot conceal my fears. When our Lord was betrayed it was not by private followers, such as Mary Magdalene, Zaccheus, or Joseph of Arimathea, but Judas, the treasurer of the College of Apostles. It was an apostle who sold his Master for thirty pieces of silver. Still the fault is equally grievous if it be committed by the lowest officer. As I have already said, we are all servants: we are all clothed with responsibilities, and we can, if the Holy Spirit shall leave us to it, do grievous damage—more damage than the outside world can ever accomplish. Let the raging crowd surround Zion's wall, let them cast up their banks and seek to shoot their arrows there; but lo, the virgin daughter of Zion hath shaken her head at her foes and laughed them to scorn. But when the traitor comes within—when it is written that "Judas also which betrayed Him knew the place"—then is the Master betrayed in the garden where He resorted for prayer. When from the bowels of the church there springs a serpent, even her head must be stung thereby. Let the question go round, "Lord, is it I?" and may God of His grace grant that none of us may ever betray our charge, and so bring damage to the glorious cause and kingdom of our blessed King.

II. Our second head is somewhat like the first. We now note that EACH MAN WAS BOUND TO ACT ACCORDING TO HIS CHARGE—"Every man according to his charge." The officers were bound to obey their orders; first, as to *matter.* Certain of them had to provide fat oxen for Solomon's table, and others had to see that the roebucks were hunted and that the fowls were fatted for the same purpose; while others were commissioned to provide the barley and the straw for the horses and the dromedaries. As I have already said, if they had gone out of place—if the man who had to provide the barley for the horses had fed the chickens with it, and if the officer who was bound to hunt the roebucks had occupied himself with carting the straw, there would have been great confusion. And so, dear brother, when you will not do what you were evidently meant to do, and are quite able to do, but must needs attempt something quite out of your range, all goes amiss. Observe your own body: if your ear were to have a feeling that it ought to eat instead of hearing, the mouth would be interfered with, and the feeding of the frame would be very badly done. The eye is a very serviceable member, but if it persisted in refusing to see, and must needs take to hearing, we should be run over in the streets. Each member has its own office in the body, and must attend to its own work, and not to the office of another. Dear friend, have you found out what you can do—what the Lord has fitted you to do, and what He has blessed you in doing? Then keep to it, and do it better and better, and by no means complain of your vocation. Do not find fault with others whose work differs from your own. The eye would be very foolish if it should say, "Do not tell me about that frivolous member the ear; it is of no use, for it only knows what it is told, and it is so blind that it could not see a house if it were within a yard of it, nor even a mountain a mile high." Equally idle would it be if the ear should say, "Do not tell me about the mouth; it is a selfish organ, always wanting to be fed. It is good for nothing; for it cannot hear, and if a cannon were fired off close to it, it would not perceive it." Neither may the mouth say, "That roving foot is always running about. Why does it not work like the hand?" Nor may the hand find fault with the tongue because it boasts great things, and does nothing. There would be sad confusion in the body if such a spirit prevailed: but the hand keeps to its work, and even there there is a subdivision of service. The little finger plays a part which the thumb cannot fulfill, and there is something for the thumb which the forefinger cannot do. So should it be in the church of God: you should each find out what you can do, and then seek, God the Holy Spirit helping you, to do *that*, to the very best of your ability, out of love to Jesus.

Observe that with Solomon it was "every man according to his charge" as to *measure;* for if a man had charge of a barrack where there were 2,000 horses, he had to send in more barley and straw than the officer who superintended a smaller barrack of only 500 horses. The purveyor who was ordered to supply Solomon's table with fat bullocks had to send more than he who fed the tables of the inferior officers. Note this well, for certain of us are bound to do much more than others. Some of us bear heavy responsibilities, and if we were to say, "I shall do no more than anybody else, I need not overburden myself," we should be unfit to occupy the position to which God has called us. Dear friends, I am not afraid that any of you will do too much for Jesus Christ, but I would like you to try. Just see now whether you can be too ardent, too self-sacrificing, too zealous, or too consecrated. It were a pity that such a thing should not be attempted. I have never known anybody who could accuse himself of so rare a crime. Oh no; we all feel that all we can do, and more, is well deserved by our blessed Master who has given us our charge. Do not forget that you who are fathers ought to be better men than those single men who have no children, to look up to them, and to copy their example. You who are large employers ought to be better men, because your workmen will watch how you live. You who have talents and abilities ought to be more active than those who have none, for five talents call for more interest than one. Do remember the rule of proportion. If you have five talents, and your brother has only one, you may do twice as much as he does and yet fall short. He is faithful with his small capital, but your proportion is five times as much, and therefore twice as much falls short of what is expected from you. Many a servant girl gives her fourpenny-piece to the offering, and if the same proportion were carried out among those who are wealthy, gold would not be so rare a metal in the Lord's treasury. A tithe may be too much for some, but a half might not be enough for another. Let it be, "Every man according to his charge," as to measure as well as to matter.

"Every man according to his charge," applied to *place*; for if the servant who had to send in barley for the dromedaries to Jerusalem had sent it off to Joppa, or if the Joppa man had sent all his fodder to Jericho, there would have been considerable trouble and outcry in the stables, and if the fatted beef and the venison for Solomon's table when he stopped in the house of the forest of Lebanon had been sent over to his other house on Mount Zion, the king would have had his table ill supplied. Some men are not satisfied to serve God in their proper place; they must run fifty miles off, or a hundred, before they can work. Is this right? I remember a little text in the Proverbs,— "As a bird that wandereth from her nest, so is a man that wandereth from his place." There is a sphere for every star which decks the sky, and a blade of grass for every drop of dew which spangles the meadow. Oh that every one would keep his place. Very much depends on position. Statues upon a building may look magnificent, and seem to be in fine proportion, but if those statues were one night to say, "We do not like standing up here in this exposed place; we will walk down and stand in the public square," you would see at once that the artist never meant them to be there, for they would be out of proportion in their new position. So a man is a man when he keeps his niche, but he may be a nobody if he leaves it. Many a man have I known who has done nothing till he has found his place, and then he has astonished his friends. I find it so with young men entering the ministry: a brother has not succeeded, in fact, he has been an utter failure in his first position, and yet, when God has opened the proper door for him, he has done marvels. Why did he not succeed before? Because he was out of his place. The best thing applied to the purpose for which it is not suited is a mere waste, and the best man in an unsuitable position may unwittingly be a hindrance to the cause he loves. Solomon's officer would have been very foolish if he had sent his barley down to Dan when it was his duty to supply Beersheba. Find your place, good brother, and do not be in a hurry to move. He who keeps a shop in a dozen towns in a dozen years will at the end look in vain for a shop which will keep him. The spirit of roving tends to poverty. Those who are eager to move because they imagine that they will leave their troubles behind them are much deceived, for these are found everywhere. You may soon get into some such predicament as

Jonah, who thought that all would be well if he could avoid Nineveh trials, but he had forgotten the troubles of being aboard ship in a storm. I do not suppose he ever ran away to Tarshish again. That one experiment satisfied him, and I hope you will profit by his experience. Do not try running away on your own account, for if you do endeavor to escape your Lord's hard work, I would have you remember that the sea is quite as tempestuous now as ever, and whales are fewer now than in Jonah's day, and not at all so likely to carry a live man to shore. Keep your place: "every man according to his charge."

Once more, every man was to act according to his charge as to *time*, because the passage speaks of each one "in his month." If the January man had taken care to provide for Solomon's table in February, what would have happened? There was a man for February, and there would have been two supplies for one month, but none for the first weeks of the year. If the August officer had kept back till September the corn which was wanted by the horses and the dromedaries in August, what would the poor creatures have done during that month? While the barley was coming the steeds would have been starving. In serving Christ there is a great deal in being up to time, punctual in everything. Not tomorrow, brother: not tomorrow, that is somebody else's day: today is the day for you. Up and do the day's work. Some soul is to be won for Christ, some truth to be vindicated, some deed of kindly charity to be wrought, some holy prevalent prayer to be offered, and it is to be done *at once*. Or ever tomorrow's sun has risen, see that thou hast carried out thy charge, for time in reference to these solemn matters is life. Promptness we always admire in responsible persons. If they have any public duty to do, we cannot endure to see men leaving matters in arrears, to be done by-and-by, or never done at all. If Jesus Christ "straightway" did this and that, as Mark always takes care to tell us He did, let us imitate His promptitude, and serve God without the sluggard's delays.

III. I close with the third point, that EACH MAN WOULD RECEIVE SUPPLIES "ACCORDING TO HIS CHARGE." I do not quite understand the precise and definite bearing of my text. Surely it means, not only that one set of officers was to send in the barley, but that another set of officers was to receive the barley and the straw in proportion to the number of horses and dromedaries. "Barley also and straw for the horses and dromedaries brought they unto the place where the officers were, everyone according to his charge"; that is to say, according to the number of horses to be provided for, such was the amount of corn and of straw that was sent in for their food.

So I gather, first, that concerning the servants of our Lord Jesus Christ *a great charge from Him is a guarantee of great supplies*. There is something very comfortable about this as to temporals. Some declare that God sends mouths and does not send bread; or at least they say He sends the mouths to one house and the bread to another. If it be so, those who get too much bread should send it round to their neighbors. Yet I note that somehow where there are mouths bread does come. It often amazes me, I must confess, and it brings tears to my eyes when I see it, and indeed it is perfectly wonderful, that poor widows with a swarm of little children do feed them in some fashion. The poor woman comes to the Orphanage about a little boy, and she does not like to part with him, but want compels; and when we have said, "My good woman, how many children had you when your husband died?" she has replied, "Seven, sir, and none of them able to earn a penny." "You have been fighting your way alone these three or four years, how have you done it?" "Ah, sir," she answers, "God only knows. I cannot tell you." No, no; and there are many of God's dear children who could not tell you how they lived, but they have lived, and their children too. The Lord leaves them a great charge, and in His own way He sends a supply. Most of us have found that if our King sends us the dromedaries He sends us the barley. It has been so in my case in the matter of our 250 orphan children at Stockwell; our gracious God has always sent us enough, and the boys have known no lack; and when we receive another 250 children, and have girls as well as boys, I feel sure our heavenly Father will provide for them all. I hope you will all recollect that the provision must come instrumentally through the Lord's own people, and much of it through the readers and hearers of the sermons, but come it will. If my Lord puts more dromedaries into my stable I shall look for the corresponding increase in the barley and the straw, for I am quite sure He will send it. When I think of my dear friend, Mr. George Müller, with 2050 orphan children, and nothing to depend upon, as they say, but just prayer and faith, I rejoice greatly. He never has a fear or a want, and is as restful as if he were an incarnate Sabbath. If we had 20,000 orphans to feed, our Master is quite able to supply them all. He feeds the universe, and we may well trust Him. If we have a simple, childlike faith, we shall find that a great charge is a guarantee of a great supply: "Every man according to his charge."

As it is in temporals, so is it in grace. When God gives a man a few people to look after, He gives him grace enough; and when He gives him ten times that number, He gives him more of His Holy Spirit; and when He gives him a hundred times that number, He increases the divine anointing. If the Lord sends you a little trial, dear brother, you shall have grace enough, and if He send you a huge trial you shall still have grace enough. If He gives you some little work to do in the back settlements, your strength shall be as your day, and if He allots you a great charge in the front of the enemy's fire you shall not come short. "Every man according to his charge." You will not have a farthing's worth of grace over. You shall never have so much that you can boast about it, and talk of having lived for months without sinning, and the like kind of nonsense. You shall be forced to feel that, when you have done all, you are an unprofitable servant. Never in my life have I had in the morning, left from yesterday's manna, as much as would cover a threepenny-piece. I have always been so hungry that I have had to devour all I could get there and then. I have lived from hand to mouth; the hand has been that of my Lord, which is ever full, and the mouth has been mine, and it has been always gaping for more. When in my ministry I have had a double quantity of food, I have had a double number to feed upon it. The Lord's grace has been sufficient for my necessities, but it has never left me room for glorying in self. Still, take it as a sure fact that a great charge is a guarantee of a great supply.

Now we will turn the truth over, and say that *a great supply indicates a great charge*. O that some would think of this! A man has grown richer than he used to be. Brother, with more barley and more straw you ought to keep more dromedaries; I mean, that God did not send that corn for the mice to destroy, but He means it to be eaten. When God gives men money or means of any sort, they ought to feel that they are His stewards, and must use all they have for their Master. If you do not use it, but hoard it, it will happen to you as once befell a little brook. It had always been running, rippling along, rolling its gladsome stream down to the river, and thus ever emptying itself, but remaining ever full. This little brook became greedy, and said, "I have been too extravagant. I have made no provision for the hot summer weather. I always give all I get; it keeps running through me in one perpetual stream, and none of it stays. This must be altered. I will make a great store, and become full." So there came a bank across it: it was dammed up, and the waters kept on swelling and rising. After a little time the water turned green and foul. It became encumbered with all sorts of weeds, was the haunt of all manner of creeping things, and gave forth an offensive smell. It became a very great nuisance to the villagers, and they called in the sanitary commissioners to get rid of it, for it was breeding fever. How now, thou once sparkling brook! What an end has come to thy bright and cheerful life. Do you see the drift of the parable? Recollect that in Palestine there is one sea which always receives and never gives out. What is its name? The Dead Sea. It must always be the Dead Sea while this is its character. If they were to cut a channel into the great ocean, to let its waters run away, it might grow sweet, but otherwise it never can do so. The man who much receives but nothing gives is dead while he lives. He who has great receipts should reckon that he has a great charge, and act accordingly. When a brother has great talents, great possessions, great influence—when he is great at anything—by God's grace let him say, "God requireth great things of me; for to whom much is given, of him shall much be required." It is a law of the kingdom of Christ—a law which He will take care is always carried out.

So I finish up with this: somebody will say, "I could almost wish that I could escape from the responsibility of being a servant of Christ." Dear brother, take note of these two or three facts.

You cannot better your circumstances as a servant of Christ by diminishing your charge. If you say, "I shall not attempt quite so much," you will not improve your circumstances by that course; for if you diminish work, the Lord will diminish strength. Our great Solomon will stop some of the supplies if you have fewer dromedaries to feed, and so you will be no better off. If you have to keep six He will give you provision for six; if you take to keeping three He will only give you supplies for three, and you will be poorer rather than richer.

Neither can you improve your circumstances by entirely and only increasing the supply; for, if you receive more straw and barley, certainly our Solomon will send you more dromedaries. When you have more strength you will have more trials. When God's children do not discharge their service with the means which He entrusts to them, He frequently lets them take shares in a "limited liability company," which is the same thing as throwing your money into the river; or He leaves them to become shareholders in a breaking bank, with unlimited catastrophe as its capital, and this is more terrible still. It often happens to a man who has scraped and saved, and stinted the cause of Christ, that in his later years he is in straits, and he cries to himself, "It is all gone, and I wish I had used it better before it went. It would have been far better to give it to the Lord than to see the lawyers devour it." Ah, your sin has found you out. Your Master could not trust you, and so He has taken away His goods from you, and now you wish that you had behaved yourself. Let us take warning from such bad managers; and let us see that, as our charge is so we cry for supplies, and that as the supplies come we use them wisely.

Everything for Jesus, the glorious Solomon of our hearts, the Beloved of our souls! Life for Jesus! Death for Jesus! Time for Jesus! Eternity for Jesus! Hand and heart for Jesus! Brain and tongue for Jesus! Night and day for Jesus! Sickness or health for Jesus! Honor or dishonor for Jesus! Shame or glory for Jesus! Everything for Jesus, "every man according to his charge." So may it be! Amen.

II. CEREMONIAL

THE BEGINNING OF MONTHS

SERMON NO. 1,637
DELIVERED ON LORD'S DAY MORNING, JANUARY 1, 1882.
PORTION OF SCRIPTURE READ BEFORE SERMON—EXODUS 12.

And the LORD spoke unto Moses and Aaron in the land of Egypt, saying, this month shall be unto you the beginning of months: it shall be the first month of the year to you—Exodus 12:1, 2.

IN all probability up to that time the year had been supposed to begin in the autumn. The question has been raised at what season of the year did God create man, and it has been decided by many that it must have been in autumn, so that when Adam was placed in the garden he might at once find fruits ripe and ready for his use. It has not seemed probable that he would have begun his career while as yet all fruits were raw and green; therefore many have concluded that the first year of human history began in the time of harvest, when fruits were mellowed for man's food. For this reason, perhaps, in the old time the new year began when the feast of harvest had been celebrated. Here at the point of the Exodus, by a decree of God, the commencement of the year was altered, and so far as Israel was concerned the opening of the year was fixed for the time of our spring—in the month called Abib, or Nisan. We know that a little before the barley was in the ear (see Ex. 9:31), and on the Sabbath after the passover, the produce of the earth was so far advanced that the firstfruits were offered, and a sheaf of new barley was waved before the Lord. Of course, when I speak of spring, and then of ears of barley, you must remember the difference of climate, for in that warm region the seasons are far in advance of ours. You must pardon me if my ideas should become a little mixed; you can correct them easily at your leisure. From the time when the Lord saved His people from destruction by passing them over the ecclesiastical year began in the month of Abib, in which the passover was celebrated. The jubilee year was not altered, but began in the autumnal equinox. The Jews seem to have had two or three beginnings of the year in relation to different purposes; but the ecclesiastical year, the great year by which Israel reckoned its existence, commenced henceforth in the month Abib, when the Lord brought His people out with a high hand and an outstretched arm.

It is with God to change times and seasons as He pleases, and He has done so for great commemorative purposes. The change of the Sabbath is on the same manner, for whereas the day of rest was formerly the seventh, it is now merged in the Lord's day, which is the first day of the week. As Herbert says, "He did unhinge the day," and He set the Sabbath on golden hinges by consecrating the day of His resurrection. To every man God makes such a change of times and seasons when He deals with him in a way of grace; for all things are become new within him, and therefore he begins a new chronology. Some of us used to think our birthday fell at a certain time of the year; but now we regard with much more delight another day as our true birthday, since on that second natal day we began truly to live. Our calendar has been altered and amended by a deed of divine grace.

This morning I want to bring to your mind this fact, that, just as the people of Israel when God gave them the passover had a complete shifting and changing of all their dates, and began their year on quite a different day, so when God gives to His people to eat the spiritual passover there takes place in their chronology a very wonderful change. Saved men and women date from the dawn of their true life; not from their first birthday, but from the day wherein they were born again of the Spirit of God, and entered into the knowledge and enjoyment of spiritual things. The passover is, as we all know, a type of the great work of our redemption by the blood of Jesus, and it represents the personal application of it to each believer. When we perceive the Lord's act of passing us over because of Christ's atoning sacrifice, then it is that we begin to live, and from that day we date all future events.

So this morning we shall first *describe the event*; secondly, *mention varieties of its recurrence*; and thirdly, *consider in what light the day of this grand event is to be regarded* according to the law of the Lord.

I. First, then, let us DESCRIBE THIS REMARKABLE EVENT, which was henceforth to stand at the head of the Jewish year, and, indeed, at the commencement of all Israelitish chronology.

First, this event was *an act of salvation by blood.* You know how the elders and heads of families each one took the lamb and shut it up, that they might examine it carefully. Having chosen a lamb without blemish, in the prime of its life, they kept it by itself as a separated and consecrated creature, and after four days they slew it, and caught its blood in a basin. When this was done they took hyssop and dipped it in the blood, and therewith sprinkled the lintel and the two side posts of their houses. By this means the houses of Israel were preserved on that dark and dreadful night, when with unsheathed sword the angel of vengeance sped through every street of Pharaoh's domain and slew the firstborn of all the land, both of men and of cattle. You will remember, dear friends, the time when you yourselves perceived that God's vengeance was out against sin; you can even now recollect your terror and your trembling. Many of us can never forget the memorable time when we first discovered that there was a way of deliverance from the wrath of God. Memory may drop all else from her enfeebled grasp, but this is graven on the palms of her hands. The mode of our deliverance is before us in the type as Moses describes it. The angel could not be restrained, his wing could not be bound, and his sword could not be sheathed: he must go forth, and he must smite. He must smite us among the rest, for sin was upon us, and there must be no partiality: "the soul that sinneth it shall die." But do you remember when you discovered God's new way, His blessed ordinance by which, without abrogating the destroying law, He brought in a glorious saving clause by which we were delivered?

The clause was this—that if another could be found who could and would suffer instead of us, and if there could be clear evidence that this surety did so suffer, then the sight of that evidence should be enough for our deliverance. Do you remember your joy at that discovery? for, if so, you can enter into the feelings of the Israelites when they understood that God would accept an unblemished lamb in the place of their first-born; and if the blood was displayed upon the doorpost as the clear evidence that a sacrifice had died, and a substitute had suffered, then the angel should know that in that house his work was done, and he might therefore pass over that habitation. The avenger was to demand a life; but the life was already paid, for there was the blood-mark which proved it, and the exactor might go on his way. It was the night of God's passover, not because the execution of vengeance was left undone in the houses passed over, but for a reason of the opposite kind—because in those houses the deathblow had been struck, and the victim had died, and, as the penalty could not be exacted twice, that family was clear.

I do not know whether there is any truth in the statement of a correspondent that whatever part of the earth the lightning once strikes it never strikes it again: but whether it be so or not, it is certain that wherever the lightning of God's vengeance has once struck the sinner's substitute it will not strike the sinner. The best preservative for the Israelite's house was this—vengeance had struck there and could not strike again. There was the insurance mark, the blood-streak; death had been there, no matter though it had fallen on a harmless lamb, it had fallen on a victim of God's own appointment, and in His esteem it had fallen upon His Christ, the Lamb slain from before the foundation of the world. Because the claims of retribution had been fully met there was no further demand, and Israel was secure. This is my eternal confidence, and here is my soul's sweet hymn:—

> If thou hast my discharge procured,
>   And freely in my room endured
> The whole of wrath divine:
>   Payment God cannot twice demand,
> First at my bleeding Surety's hand,
>   And then again at mine.
>
> Turn then, my soul, unto thy rest;
>   The merits of thy great High Priest
> Have bought thy liberty:
>   Trust in his efficacious blood,
> Nor fear thy banishment from God,
>   Since Jesus died for thee.

It was to me the beginning of my life, that day in which I discovered that judgment was passed upon me in the person of my Lord, and that there is therefore now no condemnation to me. The law demands death—"The soul that sinneth it shall die." Lo, there is the death it asks, and more. Christ, my Lord, has died, died in my stead: as it is written, "Who his own self bore our sins in his own body on the tree." Such a sacrifice is more than even the most rigorous law could demand. "Christ our passover is sacrificed for us." "Christ hath redeemed us from the curse of the law, being made a curse for us." Therefore do we sit securely within doors, desiring no guard without to drive away the destroyer; for, when God sees the blood of Jesus He will pass over us. "In his days Judah shall be saved, and Israel shall dwell safely: and this is his name whereby he shall be called, the Lord our righteousness" (Jer. 23:6). I say again, it was the beginning of life to me when I saw Jesus as dying in my stead. I beheld the first sight that was worth beholding, let all the rest be darkness and as the shadow of death. Then did my soul rejoice when I understood and accepted the substitutionary sacrifice of the appointed Redeemer. That is the first view of this event—the blood of sprinkling made Israel secure.

Secondly, that night *they received refreshment from the lamb*. Being saved by its blood, the believing households sat down and fed upon the lamb. They never ate as they ate that night. Those who spiritually understood the symbol must have partaken of every morsel with a mysterious awe mingled with an unfathomable delight. I am sure there must have been a singular seriousness about the table as they stood there eating in haste; and especially if ever and anon they were startled with the shrieks that rose from every house in the land of Egypt, because of the slain of the Lord. It was a solemn feast, a meal of mingled hope and mystery. Do you remember, brothers and sisters, when first you fed upon Christ, when your hungry spirit enjoyed the first morsel of that food of the soul? It was dainty fare, was it not? It was better than an-gels' bread, for

> Never did angels taste above
> Redeeming grace and dying love.

I hope you have never risen from that table, but are daily feeding upon Jesus. It is a very instructive fact that we do not go to our Lord's table, like Israel, to eat in haste, with a staff in our hand, but we come there to recline at ease with our heads in His bosom, reposing in His love. Christ Jesus is the daily bread of our spirits.

Observe that the refreshment which Israel ate that night was the Lamb "roast with fire." The best refreshment to a troubled heart is the suffering Savior; the Lamb roast with fire. A poor sinner under a sense of sin goes to a place of worship, and he hears Christ preached as an example. This may be useful to the saint, but it is scant help to the poor sinner. He cries, "That is true; but it rather condemns than comforts me." It is not food for him: he wants the lamb roast with fire, Christ his substitute, Christ suffering in his place and stead. We hear a great deal about the beauty of Christ's moral character, and assuredly our blessed Lord deserves to be highly exalted on that score; but that is not the aspect under which He is food to a soul conscious of sin. The chief relish about our Lord Jesus to a penitent sinner is His sin-bearing, and His agonies in that capacity. We need the suffering Savior, the Christ of Gethsemane, the Christ of Golgotha and Calvary. Christ shedding His blood in the sinner's stead, and bearing for us the fire of God's wrath. Nothing short of this will suffice to be meat for a hungry heart. Keep this back and you starve the child of God.

We are told in the chapter that they were not to eat of the lamb raw. Alas! there are some who try to do this with Christ, for they preach a half-atoning sacrifice. They would make Him in His Person and in His character to be meat for their souls, but they have small liking for His Passion, and they cast His Atonement into the background, or represent it to be an ineffectual expiation which does not secure any soul from vengeance. What is this but to devour a raw Christ? I will not touch their half-roasted lamb; I will have nothing to do with their half substitution, their half-complete redemption. No, no; give me a Savior who has borne all my sins in His own body, and so has been roast with fire to the full. "It is finished," is the most charming note in all Calvary's music. "It is finished," the fire has passed upon the Lamb, He has borne the whole of the wrath that was due to His people: this is the royal dish of the feast of love.

What a multitude of teachers there are who must needs have the Lamb sodden with water, though the Scripture saith, "Eat not of it raw, nor sodden at all with water." I have heard it said that a great number of sermons are about Christ and about the gospel, but yet neither Christ nor His gospel are preached in them. If so, the preachers present the lamb sodden in the water of their own thoughts and speculations and notions. Now, the mischief of this boiling process is that the water takes away a good deal from the meat. Philosophical discoursings upon the Lord Jesus take away much of the essence and virtue of His person, offices, work, and glory. The real juice and vital nutriment of His glorious Word is carried off by interpretations which do not explain, but explain away. How many boil out the soul of the gospel by their carnal wisdom! What is worse still, when meat is sodden, it is not only that the meat gets into the water, but the water gets into the meat; and so, what truth these gospel-boilers do hand out to us is sodden with error, and you receive from them dishes made up partly of God's truth and partly of men's imaginings. We hear in some measure solid gospel and in larger measure mere watery reasoning. When certain divines preach atonement, it is not substitution pure and simple; one hardly knows what it is. Their atonement is not the vicarious sacrifice, but a performance of something they are long in defining. They have a theory which is like the relics of meat after months of boiling, all strings and fibers. All manner of schemes are tried to extract the marrow and fatness from the grand soul-satisfying doctrine of substitution, which to my mind is the choicest truth that can ever be brought forth for the food of souls. I cannot make out why so many divines are afraid of the shedding of blood for the remission of sin, and must needs stew down the most important of all the truths of revelation. No, no; as the type could only be correct when the lamb was roast with fire, so the gospel is not truly set forth unless we describe our Lord Jesus in His sufferings for His people, and those sufferings in the room, place, and stead of sinners, presenting absolutely and literally a substitution for them. I will have no dilution: it is substitution:—"He bore our sins." He was made sin for us. "The chastisement of our peace was upon him, and by his stripes we are healed." We must have no mystifying of this plain truth, it must not be "sodden at all with water," but we must have Christ in His sufferings fresh from the fire.

Now, this lamb they were to eat, and the whole of it. Not a morsel must be left. Oh that you and I would never cut and divide Christ so as to choose one part of Him and leave another. Let not a bone of Him be broken, but let us take in a whole Christ up to the full measure of our capacity. Prophet, Priest, and King, Christ divine and Christ human, Christ loving and living, Christ dying, Christ risen, Christ ascended, Christ coming again, Christ triumphant over all His foes—the whole Lord Jesus Christ is ours. We must not reject a single particle of what is revealed concerning Him, but must feed upon it all as we are able.

That night Israel had to feed upon the lamb there and then. They might not put by a portion for tomorrow: they must consume the whole in some way or other. Oh, my brother, we need a whole Christ at this very moment. Let us receive him in his entirety. Oh for a splendid appetite and fine powers of digestion, so as to receive into my inmost soul the Lord's Christ just as I find Him. May you and I never think lightly of our Lord under any light or in any one of His offices. All that you now know and all that you can find out concerning Christ you should now believe, appreciate, feed upon, and rejoice in. Make the most of all that is in the Word concerning your Lord. Let Him enter into your being to become part and parcel of yourself. If you do this the day in which you feed on Jesus will be the first day of your life, its day of days, the day from which you date all that follows. If once you have fed upon Christ Jesus you will never forget it in time or in eternity. That was the second event which was celebrated in each succeeding Passover.

The third event was *the purification of their houses from leaven,* for that was to go in a most important way side by side with the sprinkling of the blood and the eating of the lamb. They were told that they must not eat leaven for seven days, for whosoever did partake of leaven should be cut off from Israel. It shows the deep importance of this purification that it is put in equal position with the sprinkling of the blood; at any rate it might not be separated from it upon pain and penalty that he who divided the two should himself be divided from the congregation of Israel. Now, it is always a pity when we are preaching justification by faith so to bring in sanctification as to make it a part of justification; but it is also a horrible error when you are preaching justification so to preach it as to deny the absolute necessity of sanctification, for the two are joined together of the Lord. There must be eating of the lamb as well as the sprinkling of the blood; and there must be the purging out of the old leaven, as well as the sprinkling of the blood and the eating of the lamb. Very carefully the Jewish householder looked into every closet, corner, drawer, and cupboard to sweep out every crumb of stale bread; and if they had any bread in store, even if it was new and they intended to eat it, they must put it all away, for there must not be a particle of leaven in the same house with the lamb. When you and I first came to Christ what a sweep there was of the leaven. I know I was clean delivered from the leaven of the Pharisees, for all trust in my own good works went, even the last crumb of it. All confidence in rites and ceremonies must go too. I have not a crust left of either of these two sour and corrupt confidences at the present moment, and I wish never to taste that old leaven any more. Some are always chewing at that leaven, glorying in their own prayers, and alms, and ceremonies; but when Christ comes in, this leaven all goes out. Moreover, the leaven of the Pharisees, which is hypocrisy, must be cleared out. "Blessed is he whose transgression is forgiven, whose sin is covered. Blessed is the man unto whom the Lord imputeth not iniquity, and in whose spirit there is no guile." Guile must go, or guilt will not go. The Lord sweeps the cunning out of His people, the craftiness, the deceit: He makes them true before His face. They wish that they were as clear of every sin as they are clear from insincerity. They once tried to dwell before the Lord with double dealing, pretending to be what they were not; but as soon as ever they ate of Christ, and the blood was sprinkled, then they humbled themselves in truth, and laid bare their sinnership, and stood before God as they were, with their hypocrisy rent away. Christ has not saved the man who still trusts in falsehood. You cannot feed on Christ and at the same time hold a lie in your right hand by vain confidence in yourself, or by love of sin. Self and sin must go. But oh what a day it is when the old leaven is put out—we shall never forget it! This month is the beginning of months, the first month of the year to us, when the Spirit of truth purges out the spirit of falsehood.

A fourth point in the passover is not to be forgotten. On the passover night there came, as the result of the former things, *a wonderful, glorious, and mighty deliverance.* That night every Israelite received promise of immediate emancipation, and as soon as the morning dawned he quitted the house in which he had sheltered during the night, and quitting his home he quitted Egypt too. He left forever the brick kilns, washed the brick-earth for the last time from his hands, looked down on the yoke he used to carry when he worked amid the clay, and said, "I have done with you." He looked at every Egyptian taskmaster, remembered how often he had struck him with the stick, and he rejoiced that he would never strike him again, for there he was at his feet begging him to be gone lest all Egypt should die. Oh what joy! They marched out with their unleavened bread still on their backs, for they had some days in which they were still to eat it, and I think before the seventh day of unleavened bread was over they had reached the Red Sea. Still eating unleavened bread they went down into the depths of the Red Sea, and still with no flavor of leaven in their mouths they stood on its shore to sing unto the Lord the great Hallelujah, because He had triumphed gloriously, and the horse and his rider had been cast into the sea. Do you recollect when the Lord purged you from the love of sin, and from trust in self, and when He brought you clean out and set you free, and said, "Go on to the promised rest, go on to Canaan"? Do you remember when you saw your sins drowned forever, never to rise in judgment against you—not merely your destruction prevented, not merely your soul fed with the finest food, not merely your heart and your house cleansed of hypocrisy, but yourself delivered and emancipated, the Lord's free man? Oh, if so, I am sure you will grant the wisdom of the ordinance by which the Lord decreed—"this month shall be unto you the beginning of months, it shall be the first month of the year to you." Thus much, then, on describing the event.

II. Now, secondly, I want to MENTION THE VARIETIES OF ITS RECURRENCE among us at this day.

The first recurrence is of course on *the personal salvation of each one of us*. The whole of this chapter was transacted in your heart and mine when first we knew the Lord. Our venerable Brother and Elder White, when I saw him the other night, said to me, "Oh, sir, it is very precious to read the Bible, but it is infinitely more delightful to have it here in your own heart." Now I find it very profitable to read about the passover; but oh, how sweet to have a passover transacted in your own soul by the work of the Holy Spirit! Moses wrote of something that happened thousands of years ago, but the substance of it all has happened to me in all its details, and to thousands who are trusting in the Lord. Can we not read this story in Exodus, and say, "Yes, it is even so?" Every word of it is true, for it has all occurred to me, every atom of it, even to the eating of the bitter herbs; for I recollect right well that, at the very moment when I had the sweet flavor of my Lord's atonement in my mouth, I felt the bitterness of repentance on account of sin, and the bitterness of struggling against the temptation to sin again. Even the minute touches of that typical festival are all correct, as thousands know who have participated in its antitype. This passover record is not a story of olden times alone, it is the record of your life and mine—I hope it is. Thus by each separate saved man the paschal feast is kept.

But then it happens again in a certain sense *when the man's house is saved*. Remember, this was a family business. The father and mother were present when the lamb was slain. I dare say the eldest son helped to bring the lamb to the slaughter, another held the knife, a third held the basin, and the little boy fetched the bunch of hyssop, and they all united in the sacrifice. They all saw father strike the lintel and the side posts, and they all ate of the lamb that night. Everyone that was in the house, all that were really part of the family, partook of the meal: they were all protected by the blood, they were all refreshed by the feast, and they all started the next morning to go to Canaan. Did you ever hold a family supper of that kind? "Oh," some fathers might say, "it would be the beginning of family life to me if ever I might eat bread in the kingdom of God with all my sons and daughters. Oh that every chick and child around my table truly belonged to Christ." A family begins to live in the highest sense when as a family, without exception, it has all been redeemed, all sprinkled with the blood, all made to feed on Jesus, all purged from sin, and all set at liberty to go out of the domains of sin, bound for the Kingdom. Joy! joy! joy! "I have no greater joy than to hear that my children walk in truth." If any of you enjoy the privilege of family salvation, you may well set up a monument of praise, and make a generous offering to God, by whom you are thus favored. Engrave it upon marble, and set it up forever—This household is saved, and the day of its salvation is the beginning of its history in connection with the Lord's Israel.

Extend the thought—it was not only a family ordinance but *it was for all the tribes of Israel.* There were many families, but in every house the passover was sacrificed. Would it not be a grand thing if you that employ large numbers of men should ever be able to gather all together and hopefully say, "I trust that all these understand the sprinkling of the blood, and all feed upon Christ." Dear men and women that are placed in such responsible positions, you might indeed say, "This shall be the beginning of months to us." Labor for it, therefore, and make it your heart's desire. If you live to see a district in which you labor permeated with the gospel, what a joy! If we shall live to see London with every house sprinkled with the redeeming blood! If we should live to see all England feeding, not as many do at Christmas to excess on the delicacies of earth, but feasting spiritually, where there can be no excess, upon Christ. Oh, what a beginning of years it would be to our happy island! What a paradise it would be! If it should be so with France, if it should be so in any country, what a day to be remembered. Commence a nation's annals from its evangelization. Begin the chronicle of a people from the day when they bow at the feet of Jesus. There will come a day to this poor earth when all over it Jesus shall reign. It may be long yet, but the day shall come when Christ shall have dominion from sea to sea. The nations which are called Christians, although they so little deserve the title, do already date their chronology from the birth of Christ, and this is a sort of faint foreshadowing of the way in which men shall one day date all things from the reign of Jesus; for His unsuffering kingdom yet shall come. God hath decreed His triumph, and on all the wings of time it hastens. When He cometh that month shall be the beginning of months unto us. I say no more.

III. And now, in the last place, I come to SHOW IN WHAT LIGHT THIS DATE IS TO BE REGARDED, if it has occurred to us in the senses I have mentioned.

Primarily, if it has occurred in the first sense to us personally: what about it then? Why, first, the day in which we first knew the Savior as the Paschal Lamb should always be *the most honorable day* that has ever dawned upon us. The Israelites placed the month Abib in the first rank because it was the month of the passover: put down the date at which you knew the Lord as the premier day, the noblest hour you have ever known. It eclipses your natural birthday, for then you were born in sin, then you were "born to trouble as the sparks fly upward"; but now you are born into spiritual life, born unto eternal bliss. It eclipses your marriage day, for union to Christ shall bring you greater felicity than the happiest of conjugal bonds. If you have ever known a day in which you received the honors of the State, or gained distinction in learning, or attained to a position in society, or arrived at a larger wealth, all these were but dim, cloudy, foggy days compared with this "morning without clouds." On that day your sun rose never to go down again: the die was cast, your destiny for glory was

openly declared. I pray you never in your thoughts degrade that blessed day by thinking more of any pleasure, honor, or advancement than you do of the blessing of salvation by the blood of Jesus. I am afraid that some are striving and struggling after
other distinctions, and if they could once reach a certain event then they would be
satisfied: is not your salvation worth vastly more than this? They would feel that they
were made of life if a certain matter turned out right. Brother, you were made for life
when you were made anew in Christ Jesus. You came to your estate when you came
to Christ: you were promoted when He received you to His friendship. You gained
all that you need desire when you found Christ, for a saint of old said, "He is all my
salvation, and all my desire." Do not, therefore, if the Queen should knight you or
the people should send you to Parliament, think that the event would overshadow your
conversion and salvation. Think of that act of grace as the Lord thinks of it, for He
says, "Since thou wast precious in my sight thou hast been honorable, and I have loved
thee." Unto you that believe Jesus is honor; in Him you boast and glory, and well you
may. The blood-mark is a believer's chief adornment and decoration, and his being
cleansed and set free by grace is his noblest distinction. Glory in grace and in nothing else. Prize the work of grace beyond all the treasures of Egypt.

   This date is to be regarded as *the beginning of life*. The Israelites reckoned that all
their former existence as a nation had been death. The brick-kilns of Egypt, the lying
among the pots, the mixing up with idolaters, the hearing of a language which they
understood not—they looked on all Egyptian experience as death, and the month
which ended it was to them the beginning of months. On the other hand, they looked
upon all that followed after as being life. The passover was the beginning, and only
the beginning: a beginning implies something to follow it. Now then, Christian
men, whenever you speak about your existence before conversion always do it with
shamefacedness, as one risen from the dead might speak of the charnel-house and the
worm of corruption. I feel grieved when I hear or read of people who can stand up
and talk about what they used to do before they were converted very much in the way
in which an old seafaring man talks of his voyages and storms. No, no, be ashamed
of your former lusts in your ignorance; and if you must speak of them to the praise
and glory of Christ, speak with bated breath and tears and sighs. Death, rottenness,
corruption are all most fitly left in silence, or, if they demand a voice, let it be as
solemn and mournful as a knell. Let your sin-story be told in a way which shall show
that you wish it had never been true. Let your conversion be the burial of the old existence, and as for that which follows after, take care that you make it real life,
worthy of the grace which has quickened you.

   Suppose these Israelites had loitered about in Egypt: suppose one of them had
said, "Well, I did not finish that batch of bricks. I cannot go out just yet. I should like
to see them thoroughly well baked and prepared for the pyramid"—what a foolish fellow he would have been! No, but they left the bricks, and the clay, and the stuff behind, and went straight away, and let Egypt take care of itself. Now, child of God, quit
the ways of sin with determination, leave the world, leave its pleasure, leave its

cares and get right away to Jesus and His leadership. You are now the Lord's free man; shall the blood be sprinkled for nothing! Shall the lamb be eaten and mean nothing! Shall the leavened bread be purged out in vain! Shall the Red Sea be crossed, and the Egyptians drowned, and you remain a slave? The thought is abhorrent. That was the mischief about the Israelites, that they had still a hankering after the leeks and garlic of Egypt: these strong-smelling things had scented their garments, and it is hard to get such vile odors out of one's clothes. Alas, that Egyptian garlic clings to us, and the smell of it is not always so abominable to us as it ought to be. Besides, they pined for fish which they did eat in Egypt in plenty, muddy fish though it was. There were better fisheries for them in Jordan, and Gennesaret, and the Great Sea, if they had gone ahead; and sweeter herbs were on Canaan's hills than ever grew in Egypt's mire. Because of this evil lusting they were kept dodging about for 40 years in the wilderness. They might have marched into Canaan in 40 days if it had not been for that stinking garlic of theirs, and their Egyptian habits and memories. Oh, that God would cut us quite free, and enable us to forget those things whereof we are now ashamed.

I have nearly concluded when I have added this, that inasmuch as the passover was now the beginning of the year to them *it was the putting of all things right*. I told you that the year had formerly begun in autumn, according to most traditions: was this really the best season to pitch upon? Upon second thoughts, was autumn the best season in which to begin life, with winter all before you and everything declining? By the institution of the passover the year was made to begin in what is our spring. If I judge from the condition of our land I should ask—When could the year begin more fitly than in the springtide of early May? It seems to me that it actually does begin in spring. I do not see that the year naturally begins today, though it does so arbitrarily. We are in about the middle of winter, and the year as yet lies dead. When the birds sing and the flowers rise from their beds on earth, then the year begins. It seems to me a strange supposition that our first parents commenced life in autumn, amid lengthening nights and declining forces. No, we say, by all means let the date be fixed in spring, so that the salutations of the new year shall be sweet with fragrant flowers and rich with joyous songs. Nor would the time of our spring in the East be a season without supplies, for in April and May the first ears of corn are ready, and many other fruits are fit for food. It was good for the Israelites to have the feast of the firstfruits in the month Abib, to bring the first ears to the Lord, and not to wait till they were ripe before they blessed the Giver of all good. We ought to be grateful for green mercies, and not tarry till everything come to ripeness. In some parts of the East there is fruit all the year round, and why not in Eden? In the delightful country where I have sojourned, which bears a very close resemblance to the East, there are fruits still ripening upon the trees, and one tree or another will be found to bear fruit every month all the year round, so that if Adam had been created in the month of April there would have been food for him, followed by a succession of fruits which would have supplied all his wants. Then he would have had summer before him with all its ripening beauties, and this is a more paradisaical outlook than winter. It is right that the year should begin with the firstfruits, and I am sure it is quite right that the year should begin with you and with me when we come to Christ and receive the firstfruits of the Spirit. Everything is out of joint till a man knows Christ: everything is disorderly and bottom upwards till the gospel comes and turns him upside down, and then the right side is up again. Man is all wrong till the gospel puts him all right. Though grace is above nature it is not contrary to nature, but restores true nature. Our nature is never so truly the nature of a man as when it is no longer man's sinful nature. We become truly men, such as God meant men to be, when we cease to be men such as sin has made men to be.

Our life, beginning as it does at our spiritual passover, and at our feeding upon Christ, we ought always to regard our conversion as a festival and remember it with praise. Whenever we look back upon it the memory of it should excite delight in our hearts. I wonder how long a man ought to thank God for forgiving his sins? Is life long enough? Is time long enough? Is eternity too long? How long ought a man to thank God for saving him from going down to hell? Would 50 years suffice? Oh no, that would never do, the blessing is too great to be all sung of in a millennium. Suppose you and I never had a single mercy except this one, that we were made the children of God and co-heirs with Christ Jesus—suppose we had nothing else to enjoy! We ought to sing about that alone forever and ever. Aye, if we were sick, cast on the bed of pain with a hundred diseases, with the bone wearing through the skin, yet since God's everlasting mercy will sanctify every pain and every affliction, should we not still continue to lift up happy psalms to God and praise Him forever and ever? Therefore, be that your watchword all through the year—"Hallelujah, praise ye the Lord!" The Israelite always closed the passover with a hymn of praise, and therefore let us close our sermon this morning with holy joy, and continue our happy music till this year ends, aye, till time shall be no more. Amen.

THE BLOOD OF SPRINKLING AND THE CHILDREN

SERMON NO. 1,988
DELIVERED ON LORD'S DAY MORNING, OCTOBER 23, 1887.
PORTIONS OF SCRIPTURE READ BEFORE SERMON—EXODUS 12:21–36; 13:1–10, 14–16.
HYMNS FROM *Our Own Hymn Book*—414, 370, 281.

Then Moses called for all the elders of Israel, and said unto them, Draw out and take you a lamb according to your families, and kill the passover. And ye shall take a bunch of hyssop, and dip it in the blood that is in the basin, and strike the lintel and the two side posts with the blood that is in the basin; and none of you shall go out at the door of his house until the morning. For the LORD will pass through to smite the Egyptians; and when he seeth the blood upon the lintel, and on the two side posts, the LORD will pass over the door, and will not suffer the destroyer to come in unto your houses to smite you. And ye shall observe this thing for an ordinance to thee and to thy sons forever. And it shall come to pass, when ye be come to the land which the LORD will give you, according as he hath promised, that ye shall keep this service. And it shall come to pass, when your children shall say unto you, What mean ye by this service? that ye shall say, It is the sacrifice of the LORD'S passover, who passed over the houses of the children of Israel in Egypt, when he smote the Egyptians, and delivered our houses—Exodus 12:21–27.

I WANTED, dear friends, earnestly wanted, to continue the subject of last Lord's day morning; for I felt it important that we should bear again and again our witness to the doctrine of the vicarious sacrifice of Jesus Christ our Lord. But, at the same time, I promised that I would endeavor to keep "the feast of the children," and have a sermon which should be especially addressed to Sunday school teachers. I could not preach a school sermon at the appointed time, so as to open your children's week, but thought a discourse might come in none the less suitably if I brought up the rear by closing your meetings. How am I to fulfill both my purposes? I think the subject before us will enable me to do so. We shall preach of the sprinkled blood, and of Jesus

245

the great sacrifice for sin; and then we shall press upon all who know the value of the great redemption that they teach the young in their earliest days what is meant by the death of Jesus and salvation through His blood.

The Paschal lamb was a special type of our Lord Jesus Christ. We are not left to gather this from the general fact that all the ancient sacrifices were shadows of the one true and real Substance; but we are assured in the New Testament that "Christ our passover is sacrificed for us" (1 Cor. 5:7). As the Paschal lamb must be without blemish, so was our Lord, and its killing and roasting with fire were typical of His death and sufferings. Even as to time, our Lord fulfilled the type, for the time of His crucifixion was the passover. As the impression answers to the seal, so does the sacrifice of our Lord correspond with all the items of the passover ceremonial. We see Him "drawn out" from among men, and led as a lamb to the slaughter; we see His blood shed and sprinkled; we see Him roasted in the fire of anguish; by faith we eat of Him, and flavor the feast with the bitter herbs of penitence. We see Jesus and salvation where the carnal eye sees only a slaughtered lamb, and a people saved from death.

The Spirit of God in the passover ceremonial lays special emphasis upon *the sprinkling of the blood*. That which men so greatly oppose, He as diligently sets forth as the head and front of revelation. The blood of the chosen lamb was caught in a basin, and not spilled upon the ground in wastefulness; for the blood of Christ is most precious. Into this bowl of blood a bunch of hyssop was dipped. The sprays of that little shrub would hold the crimson drops, so that they could be easily sprinkled. Then the father of the family went outside, and struck with this hyssop the lintel and the two side posts of the door; and so the house was marked with three crimson streaks. No blood was put upon the threshold. Woe unto man that tramples upon the blood of Christ, and treats it as an unholy thing! Alas! I fear that many are doing so at this hour, not only among the outside world, but among those who profess and call themselves Christians.

I shall endeavor to bring forward two things. First, *the importance attached to the sprinkled blood*; and, secondly, *the institution connected with it*, namely, that the children should be instructed in the meaning of sacrifice, so that they also may teach their children, and keep alive the memory of the Lord's great deliverance.

I. First: THE IMPORTANCE ATTACHED TO THE BLOOD OF SACRIFICE is here made very plain. Pains are taken to make the sacrifice observable, yea, to force it upon the notice of all the people.

I note, first, that *it became and remained the national mark*. If you had traversed the streets of Memphis or Rameses on the night of the Passover, you could have told who were Israelites and who were Egyptians by one conspicuous token. There was no need to listen under the window to hear the speech of the people within the house, nor to wait till any came into the street so that you could observe their attire. This one thing alone would be a sufficient guide—the Israelite had the blood-mark upon his doorway, the Egyptian had it not. Mark you, this is still the great point of difference between the children of God and the children of the wicked one. There are, in truth, but two denominations upon this earth—the church and the world; those who are justified in Christ Jesus, and those who are condemned in their sins. This shall stand for a never-failing sign of the "Israelite indeed": he has come to the blood of sprinkling, which speaketh better things than that of Abel. He that believeth in the Son of God, as the one accepted Sacrifice for sin, hath salvation, and he that believeth not in Him will die in his sins. The true Israel are trusting in the sacrifice once offered for sin; it is their rest, their comfort, their hope. As for those who are not trusting in the atoning sacrifice, they have rejected the counsel of God against themselves, and thus have declared their true character and condition. Jesus said, "Ye believe not, because ye are not of my sheep, as I said unto you"; and want of faith in that shedding of blood, without which there is no remission of sin, is the damning mark of one who is a stranger to the commonwealth of Israel. Let us make no question about it: "Whosoever goeth onward and abideth not in the teaching of Christ, hath not God." (See 2 John 9, in the Revised Version.) He that will not accept the propitiation which God hath set forth must bear his own iniquity. Nothing more just, and yet nothing more terrible, can happen to such a man than that his iniquity should not be purged by sacrifice nor offering forever. I care not what your supposed righteousness may be, nor how you think to commend yourselves to God, if you reject His Son, He will reject *you*. If you come before God without the atoning blood, you have neither part nor lot in the matter of the covenant inheritance, and you are not numbered among the people of God. The sacrifice is the national mark of the spiritual Israel, and he that hath it not is an alien; he shall have no inheritance among them that are sanctified, neither shall he behold the Lord in glory.

Secondly, as this was the national mark, *it was also the saving token*. That night the Angel of Death spread his wings on the blast, and as he flew down the streets of Egypt he smote high and low, the first-born of princes and the first-born of beasts, so that in every house and in every stall there was one dead. Where he saw the blood-mark he entered not to smite; but everywhere else the vengeance of the Lord fell on the rebellious. The words are very remarkable: "The Lord will pass over the door, and will not suffer the destroyer to come in unto your houses to smite you." What holds back the sword? Nothing but the blood-stain on the door. The lamb has been slain, and they have sprinkled their houses with the blood, and therefore are they secure. The sons of Jacob were not richer, nor wiser, nor stronger, nor more skilled than the sons of Ham; but they were redeemed by the blood, and therefore they lived, while those who knew not the redeeming token died. When Jericho fell down, the one house that stood was that which had the scarlet line in the window; and when the Lord visits for sin, the man that shall escape is he who knows Jesus, "in whom we have redemption through his blood, the forgiveness of sin according to the riches of his grace."

I call your very special attention, however, to the words that are used in the twenty-third verse: "The Lord will pass through to smite the Egyptians; and when he seeth the blood upon the lintel, and on the two side posts, the Lord will pass over the door." What an instructive expression! "When *he* seeth the blood." It is a very comforting thing for you and for me to behold the atonement; for thus we gain peace and enter into rest; but, after all, the grand reason of our salvation is that the Lord Himself looks upon the atonement, and is well pleased for His righteousness' sake. In the thirteenth verse we hear the Lord Himself say: "When I see the blood I will pass over you." Think of the holy eye of God being turned to Him that taketh away the sin of the world, and so fixed on Him that He passes over us. He is of purer eyes than to behold iniquity, but He looks upon the face of His anointed and forgives the sin. He accepts us with our sacrifice. Well does our hymn-writer pray—

> Him and then the sinner see;
> Look through Jesus' wounds on me.

It is not *our* sight of the sprinkled blood which is the basis of salvation, but *God's* sight of it. God's acceptance of Christ is the sure guarantee of the salvation of those who accept His sacrifice. Beloved, when thine eye of faith is dim, when thine eye-balls swim in a flood of tears, when the darkness of sorrow hides much from thy vision, then Jehovah sees the blood of His Son, and spares thee. In the thick darkness, when thou canst not see at all, the Lord God never fails to see in Jesus that with which He is well pleased, and with which His law is honored. He will not suffer the destroyer to come near thee to harm thee, because He sees in Christ that which vindicates His justice and establishes the needful rule of law. The blood is the saving mark. At this moment this is the pressing question for each one in the company gathered in this house: Do you trust the divine propitiation or do you not? Bring to me what you will to prove your own personal excellence. I believe in no virtue which insults the Savior's blood, which alone cleanseth us from all sin. Rather confess your multiplied transgressions and shortcomings, and then take heart and hope; for there is forgiveness large and free for the very chief of sinners, through Him who has made peace by the blood of His cross.

O my hearer, guilty and self-condemned, if thou wilt now come and trust in Jesus Christ, thy sins, which are many, shall be all forgiven thee, and thou shalt love so much in return, that the whole bent and bias of thy mind shall be turned from sin to gracious obedience. The atonement applied to the conscience saves from despair, and then acting upon the heart it saves from the love of evil. But the atonement is the saving sign. The blood on the lintel and on the two side posts secured the house of the poorest Israelite; but the proudest Egyptian, yea, even Pharaoh on the throne, could not escape the destroyer's sword. Believe and live. Reject the atonement and perish!

Note, next, that *the mark of the blood was rendered as conspicuous as possible*. The Israelites, though they ate the Paschal lamb in the quiet of their own families, yet made no secret of the sacrifice. They did not make the distinctive mark upon the wall of some inner chamber, or in some place where they could cover it with hangings, that no man might perceive it; but they smote the upper part of the doorway and the two side posts of the door, so that all who passed by the house must see that it was marked in a peculiar manner, and marked with blood. The Lord's people were not ashamed to have the blood thus put in the forefront of every dwelling: and those that are saved by the great sacrifice are not to treat the doctrine of substitution as a hole-and-corner creed, to be secretly held, but not openly avowed. The death of Jesus in our room and place and stead is not a redemption of which we are ashamed to speak in any place. Call it old-fashioned and out of date, our critics may; but we are not ashamed to publish it to the four winds of heaven, and to avow our confidence in it. He that is ashamed of Christ in this generation, of him will Christ be ashamed when He comes in the glory of His Father, and all His holy angels with Him. There is a theology abroad in the world which admits the death of Christ to a certain indefinable place in its system, but that place is very much in the rear: I claim for the atonement the front and the center. The Lamb must be in the midst of the throne. Atonement is not a mystery scarcely to be spoken of, or if spoken of at all, to be whispered. No, no, it is a sublime simplicity, a fact for a child to know, a truth for the common people to rejoice in! We must preach Christ crucified whatever else we do not preach. Brethren, I do not think a man ought to hear a minister preach three sermons without learning the doctrine of atonement. I give wide latitude when I say this, for I would desire never to preach at all without setting forth salvation by faith in the blood of Jesus. Across my pulpit and my tabernacle shall be the mark of the blood; it will disgust the enemy, but it will delight the faithful. Substitution seems to me to be the soul of the gospel, the life of the gospel, the essence of the gospel; therefore must it be ever in the front. Jesus, as the Lamb of God, is the Alpha, and we must keep Him first and before all others. I charge you, Christian people, do not make this a secondary doctrine. Keep your perspective right, and have this always in the foreground. Other truths are valuable, and may most worthily be placed in the distance; but this is always to be in the foreground. The center of Christianity is the cross, and the meaning of the cross is substitution.

> We may not know, we cannot tell,
>   What pains our Jesus bare,
> But we believe it was for us
>   He hung and suffered there.

The great sacrifice is the place of gathering for the chosen seed: we meet at the cross, even as every family in Israel met around the table whereon was placed the lamb, and met within a house which was marked with blood. Instead of looking upon the vicarious sacrifice as placed somewhere in the remote distance, we find in it the center of the church. Nay, more; it is so much the vital, all-essential center, that to remove it is to tear out the heart of the church. A congregation which has rejected the sacrifice of Christ is not a church, but an assembly of unbelievers. Of the church I may truly say, "The blood is the life thereof." Like the doctrine of justification by faith, the doctrine of a vicarious sacrifice is the article of standing or falling to each church: atonement by the substitutionary sacrifice of Christ means spiritual life, and the rejection of it is the reverse. Wherefore, we must never be shamed of this all-important truth, but make it as conspicuous as possible. "For the preaching of the cross is to them that perish foolishness; but unto us which are saved it is the power of God."

Further, the sprinkled blood was not only most conspicuous, but *it was made very dear to the people themselves by the fact that they trusted in it in the most implicit manner.* After the doorposts had been smeared the people went inside into their houses, and they shut to the door, never to open it again till the morning. They were busy inside: there was the roasting of the lamb, the preparing of the bitter herbs, the girding of their loins, the getting ready for their march, and so forth; but this was done without fear of danger, though they knew that the destroyer was abroad. The command of the Lord was, "None of you shall go out at the door of his house until the morning." What is going on in the street? You must not go to see. The midnight hour has come. Did you not hear it? Hark, that dreadful cry! Again a piercing shriek! What is it? The anxious mother asks, "What can it be?" "There was a great cry in Egypt." The Israelites must not heed that cry so as to break the divine word which shut them in for a little moment, till the tempest was overpast. Perhaps persons of doubtful mind, during that dread night, may have said, "Something awful is happening. Hear those cries! Listen to the tramping of the people in the streets, as they hurry to and fro! It may be there is a conspiracy to slay us at dead of night." "None of you shall go out at the door of his house until the morning" was sufficient for all who truly believed. They were safe, and they knew it, and so, like the chicks beneath the wings of the hen, they rested in safety. Beloved, let us do the same. Let us honor the precious blood of Christ not only by speaking of it boldly to others, but by a calm and happy trust in it for ourselves. In full assurance let us rest. Do you believe that Jesus died for you? Then be at peace. Let no man's heart fail him now that he knows that Jesus died for our sins according to the Scriptures. Let the cross be the pillar of our confidence, unmoved and immovable. Do not be agitated about what has been or what is to be: we are housed in safety in Christ Jesus both from the sins of the past and the dangers of the future. All is well, since love's atoning work is done. In holy peacefulness let us proceed with our household work, purging out the old leaven and keeping the feast; but let no fear or doubt disturb us for an instant. We pity those who die without Christ, but we cannot quit our Lord under the pretense of saving them: that would be folly. I know there are terrible cries outside in the streets—who has not heard them? Oh, that the people would but shelter beneath the blood-mark! It pierces our heart to think of the doom of the ungodly when they perish in their sins; but, as Noah did not quit the ark, nor Israel leave her abode, so our hope is not larger than the cross will warrant. All who shelter beneath the blood of the atonement are secure, and as for those who reject this great salvation, how shall they escape? There are great and sad mysteries in this long night, but in the morning we shall know as much of God's dealings with men as it will be good for us to know. Meanwhile, let us labor to bring our fellows within the pale of safety, but yet let us be ourselves peaceful, composed, restful, and joyful. "There is therefore now no condemnation to them which are in Christ Jesus." "Therefore being justified by faith, we have peace with

God through our Lord Jesus Christ." "And not only so, but we also joy in God through our Lord Jesus Christ, by whom we have now received the atonement." Possess ye your souls in patience. Oh, rest in the Lord, and wait patiently for Him. Feed upon the Lamb, for His flesh is meat indeed. That same Jesus who has preserved your life from destruction will be the sustenance of that life evermore. Be happy beneath the saving blood-mark. Make a feast of your passover. Though there be death outside, let your joy within be undisturbed.

I cannot stay long on any one point, and therefore notice, next, that *the Paschal bloodshedding was to be had in perpetual remembrance.* "Ye shall observe this thing for an ordinance to thee and to thy sons forever." As long as Israel remained a people, they were to keep the passover: so long as there is a Christian upon earth the sacrificial death of the Lord Jesus must be kept in memory. No progress of years or advance of thought could take away the memory of the Paschal sacrifice from Israel. Truly it was a night to be remembered when the Lord brought out His people from under the iron yoke of Egypt. It was such a wonderful deliverance, as to the plagues which preceded it, and the miracle at the Red Sea which followed it, that no event could possibly excel it in interest and glory. It was such a triumph of God's power over the pride of Pharaoh, and such a manifestation of God's love to His own people, that they were not merely to be glad for one night, nor for one year, nor even for a century; but they were to remember it forever. Might there not come a time when Israel would have achieved further history? Might not some grander event eclipse the glory of Egypt's overthrow? Never! The death of Egypt's firstborn, and the song of Moses at the Red Sea must remain forever woven into the tapestry of Hebrew history. Evermore did Jehovah say, "I am the Lord thy God, which have brought thee out of the land of Egypt, out of the house of bondage." Beloved, the death of our Lord Jesus Christ is to be declared and showed by us until He come. No truth can ever be discovered which can put His sacrificial death into the shade. Whatever shall occur, even though He cometh in the clouds of heaven, yet our song shall be forever, "Unto him that loved us and washed us from our sins in his own blood." Amid the splendor of His endless reign He shall be "the Lamb in the midst of the throne." Christ as the sacrifice for sin shall ever be the subject of our hallelujahs: "For thou wast slain." Certain vainglorious minds are advancing—advancing from the rock to the abyss. They are making progress from truth to falsehood. They are thinking, but their thoughts are not God's thoughts, neither are their ways His ways. They are leaving the gospel, they are going away from Christ, and they know not whither. In quitting the substitutionary sacrifice they are quitting the sole hope of man. As for us, we hear the Lord saying to us, "Ye shall observe this thing for an ordinance to thee and to thy sons forever," and so will we do. "Jesus Christ, the same yesterday, today, and forever," is our boast and glory. Let others wander where they will, we abide with Him who bore our sins in His own body on the tree.

Notice next, dear friends, that when the people came into the land where no Egyptian ever entered, they were still to remember the passover. "It shall come to pass, when ye be come to the land which the Lord will give you, according as he hath promised, that ye shall keep this service." In the land that flowed with milk and honey there was still to be the memorial of the sprinkled blood. Our Lord Jesus is not for the first day of our repentance only, but for all the days of our lives: we remember Him as well amid our highest spiritual joys as in our deepest spiritual griefs. The Paschal lamb is for Canaan, as well as for Egypt, and the sacrifice for sin is for our full assurance as well as for our trembling hope. You and I will never attain to such a state of grace that we can do without the blood which cleanseth from sin. If we should ever reach perfection, then would Christ be even more precious than He is today; or, if we did not find Him so, we might be sure that our pretended attainment was a wretched delusion. If we walk in the light as God is in the light, and have constant fellowship with Him, yet still the blood of Jesus Christ His Son cleanseth us from all sin.

Moreover, brethren, I want you to notice carefully that *this sprinkling of the blood was to be an all-pervading memory.* Catch this thought: the children of Israel could not go out of their houses, and they could not come in, without the remembrance of the sprinkled blood. It was over their heads; they must come under it. It was on the right hand and on the left: they must be surrounded by it. They might almost say of it, "Whither shall we go from thy presence?" Whether they looked on their own doors, or on those of their neighbors, there was the same threefold streak, and it was there both by day and by night. Nor was this all; when two of Israel married, and the foundation of a family was laid, there was another memorial. The young husband and wife had the joy of looking upon their firstborn child, and then they called to mind that the Lord had said, "Sanctify to me all the firstborn." As an Israelite he explained this to his son, and said, "By strength of hand the Lord brought us out from Egypt, from the house of bondage: and it came to pass, when Pharaoh would hardly let us go, that the Lord slew all the firstborn in the land of Egypt, both the firstborn of man, and the firstborn of beast: therefore I sacrifice to the Lord all that openeth the matrix, being males; but all the firstborn of my children I redeem." The commencement of every family that made up the Israelitish nation was thus a time of special remembrance of the sprinkling of the blood; for then the redemption money must be paid, and thus an acknowledgment made that they were the Lord's, having been bought with a price. In ways many, and everywhere present, the people were reminded of the need of sacrifice. To the thoughtful, every going down of the sun reminded him of the night to be remembered; while the beginning of each year in the month Abib brought home to him the fact that the beginning of his nation dated from the time of the killing of the lamb. The Lord took means to keep this matter before the people; for they were wayward, and seemed bent upon forgetting, even like this present age.

In the thirteenth chapter, in verse 9, we read: "It shall be for a sign unto thee upon thine hand, and for a memorial between thine eyes." And again, in verse 16, we read: "And it shall be for a token upon thine hand, and for frontlets between thine eyes: for by strength of hand the Lord brought us forth out of Egypt." By this is meant that they were henceforth to see everything in connection with redemption. Redemption by blood was to consecrate each man's hand, so that he could not use it for evil, but must employ it for the Lord. He could not take his food, or his tool, in his hand, without remembrance of the sprinkled blood which had made his food and his labor a blessing. All his acts were to be under the influence of atoning blood. Oh, what service you and I would render if it was always redeemed labor that we gave! If we went to our Sunday-school class, for instance, feeling, "I am bought with a price," and if we preached with redeemed lips the gospel of our own salvation, how livingly and lovingly we should speak! What an effect this would have on our lives! You would not dare, some of you, to do what you now do, if you remembered that Jesus died for you. Many a thing which you have left undone would at once be minded if you had a clearer consciousness of redeeming love. The Jews became superstitious, and were content with the letter of their law, and so they wrote out certain verses upon little strips of parchment called "tephillin," which they enclosed in a box, and then strapped upon their wrists. The true meaning of the passage did not lie in any such childish action; but it taught them that they were to labor and to act with holy hands, as men under overwhelming obligations to the Lord's redeeming grace. Redemption is to be our impulse for holy service, our check when we are tempted in sin. They were also to wear the memory of the passover as frontlets between their eyes, and you know how certain Jews actually wore phylacteries upon their foreheads. That could be no more than the mere shell of the thing: the essence of the command was that they were to look on everything in reference to redemption by blood. Brethren, we should view everything in this world by the light of redemption, and then we shall view it aright. It makes a wonderful change whether you view providence from the standpoint of human merit or from the foot of the cross. We see nothing truly till Jesus is our light. Everything is seen in its reality when you look through the glass, the ruby glass of the atoning sacrifice. Use this telescope of the cross, and you shall see far and clear; look at sinners through the cross; look at saints through the cross; look at sin through the cross; look at the world's joys and sorrows through the cross; look at heaven and hell through the cross. See how conspicuous the blood of the passover was meant to be, and then learn from all this to make much of the sacrifice of Jesus, yea, to make everything of it, for Christ is all.

One thing more: we read in Deuteronomy, in the sixth chapter, and the eighth verse, concerning the commandments of the Lord, as follows: "And thou shalt bind them for a sign upon thine hand, and they shall be as frontlets between thine eyes. And thou shalt write them upon the posts of thy house, and on thy gates." See, then, that the law is to be written hard by the memorials of the blood. In Switzerland, in the Protestant villages, you have seen texts of Scripture upon the doorposts. I half wish we had that custom in England. How much of gospel might be preached to wayfarers if texts of Scripture were over Christian people's doors! It might be ridiculed as Pharisaical, but we could get over that. Few are liable to that charge in these days through being religious overmuch. I like to see texts of Scripture in our houses, in all the rooms, on the cornices, and on the walls; but outside on the door—what a capital advertisement the gospel might get at a cheap rate! But note, that when the Jew wrote upon his doorposts a promise, or a precept, or a doctrine, he had to write upon a surface stained with blood, and when the next year's passover came round he had to sprinkle the blood with the hyssop right over the writing. It seems to me so delightful to think of the law of God in connection with that atoning sacrifice which has magnified it and made it honorable. God's commands come to me as a redeemed man; His promises are to me as a blood-bought man; His teaching instructs me as one for whom atonement has been made. The law in the hand of Christ is not a sword to slay us, but a jewel to enrich us. All truth taken in connection with the cross is greatly enhanced in value. Holy Scripture itself becomes dear to a sevenfold degree when we see that it comes to us as the redeemed of the Lord, and bears upon its every page marks of those dear hands which were nailed to the tree for us.

Beloved, you now see how everything was done that could well be thought of to bring the blood of the Paschal lamb into a high position in the esteem of the people whom the Lord brought out of Egypt; and you and I must do everything we can think of to bring forward, and keep before men forever the precious doctrine of the atoning sacrifice of Christ. He was made sin for us though He knew no sin, that we might be made the righteousness of God in Him.

II. And now I will spend a short time in reminding you of THE INSTITUTION THAT WAS CONNECTED WITH THE REMEMBRANCE OF THE PASSOVER. "It shall come to pass, when your children shall say unto you, What mean ye by this service? that ye shall say, It is the sacrifice of the Lord's passover."

Inquiry should be excited in the minds of our children. Oh, that we could get them to ask questions about the things of God! Some of them inquire very early, others of them seem diseased with much the same indifference as older folks. With both orders of mind we have to deal. It is well to explain to children the ordinance of the Lord's Supper, for this shows forth the death of Christ in symbol. I regret that children do not oftener see this ordinance. Baptism and the Lord's Supper should both be placed in view of the rising generation, that they may then ask us, "What mean ye by this?" Now, the Lord's Supper is a perennial gospel sermon, and it turns mainly upon the sacrifice for sin. You may banish the doctrine of the atonement from the pulpit, but it will always live in the church through the Lord's Supper. You cannot explain that broken bread and that cup filled with the fruit of the vine, without reference to our Lord's atoning death. You cannot explain "the communion of the body of Christ" without bringing in, in some form or other, the death of Jesus in our place and stead. Let your little ones, then, see the Lord's Supper, and let them be told most clearly what it sets forth. And if not the Lord's Supper—for that is not the thing itself, but only the shadow of the glorious fact—dwell much and often in their presence upon the sufferings and death of our Redeemer. Let them think of Gethsemane, and Gabbatha, and Golgotha, and let them learn to sing in plaintive tones of Him who laid down His life for us. Tell them who it was that suffered, and why.

Yes, though the hymn is hardly to my taste in some of its expressions, I would have the children sing—

> There is a green hill far away,
> Without a city wall.

And I would have them learn such lines as these:

> He knew how wicked we had been,
> And knew that God must punish sin;
> So out of pity Jesus said,
> He'd bear the punishment instead.

And when attention is excited upon the best of themes, let us be ready to explain the great transaction by which God is just, and yet sinners are justified. Children can well understand the doctrine of the expiatory sacrifice; it was meant to be a gospel for the youngest. The gospel of substitution is a simplicity, though it is a mystery. We ought not to be content until our little ones know and trust in their finished sacrifice. This is essential knowledge, and the key to all other spiritual teaching. May our dear children know the cross, and they will have begun well. With all their gettings may they get an understanding of this, and they will have the foundation rightly laid.

This will necessitate your teaching the child his need of a Savior. You must not hold back from this needful task. Do not flatter the child with delusive rubbish about his nature being good and needing to be developed. Tell him he must be born again. Don't bolster him up with the fancy of his own innocence, but show him his sin. Mention the childish sins to which he is prone, and pray the Holy Spirit to work conviction in his heart and conscience. Deal with the young in much the same way as you would with the old. Be thorough and honest with them. Flimsy religion is neither good for young nor old. These boys and girls need pardon through the precious blood as surely as any of us. Do not hesitate to tell the child his ruin; he will not else desire the remedy. Tell him also of the punishment of sin, and warn him of its terror. Be tender, but be true. Do not hide from the youthful sinner the truth, however terrible it may be. Now that he has come to years of responsibility, if he believes not in Christ, it will go ill with him at the last great day. Set before him the judgment seat, and remind him that he will have to give an account of things done in the body. Labor to arouse the conscience; and pray God the Holy Spirit to work by you till the heart becomes tender and the mind perceives the need of the great salvation.

Children need to learn the doctrine of the cross that they may find immediate salvation. I thank God that in our Sabbath-school we believe in the salvation of children as children. How very many has it been my joy to see of boys and girls who have come forward to confess their faith in Christ! and I again wish to say that the best converts, the clearest converts, the most intelligent converts we have ever had have been the young ones; and, instead of there being any deficiency in their knowledge of the Word of God, and the doctrines of grace, we have usually found them to have a very delightful acquaintance with the great cardinal truths of Christ. Many of these dear children have been able to speak of the things of God with great pleasure of heart, and force of understanding. Go on, dear teachers, and believe that God will save your children. Be not content to sow principles in their minds which may possibly develop in after years; but be working for immediate conversion. Expect fruit in your children while they are children. Pray for them that they may not run into the world and fall into the evils of outward sin, and then come back with broken bones to the Good Shepherd; but that they may by God's rich grace be kept from the paths of the destroyer, and grow up in the fold of Christ, first as lambs of His flock, and then as sheep of His hand.

One thing I am sure of, and that is, that if we teach the children the doctrine of the atonement in the most unmistakable terms, we shall be doing ourselves good. I sometimes hope that God will revive His church and restore her to her ancient faith by a gracious work among children. If He would bring into our churches a large influx of young people, how it would tend to quicken the sluggish blood of the supine and sleepy! Child Christians tend to keep the house alive. Oh, for more of them! If the Lord will but help us to teach the children we shall be teaching ourselves. There is no way of learning like teaching, and you do not know a thing till you can teach it to another. You do not thoroughly know any truth till you can put it before a child so that he can see it. In trying to make a little child understand the doctrine of the atonement you will get clearer views of it yourselves, and therefore I commend the holy exercise to you.

What a mercy it will be if our children are thoroughly grounded in the doctrine of redemption by Christ! If they are warned against the false gospels of this evil age, and if they are taught to rest on the eternal rock of Christ's finished work, we may hope to have a generation following us which will maintain the faith, and will be better than their fathers. Your Sunday-schools are admirable; but what is their purpose if you do not teach the gospel in them? You get children together and keep them quiet for an hour-and-a-half, and then send them home; but what is the good of it? It may bring some quiet to their fathers and mothers, and that is, perhaps, why they send them to the school; but all the real good lies in what is taught the children. The most fundamental truth should be made most prominent; and what is this but the cross? Some talk to children about being good boys and girls, and so on; that is to say, they preach the law to the children, though they would preach the gospel to grown-up people! Is this honest? Is this wise? Children need the gospel, the whole gospel, the unadulterated gospel; they ought to have it, and if they are taught of the Spirit of God they are as capable of receiving it as persons of ripe years. Teach the little ones that Jesus died, the just for the unjust, to bring us to God. Very, very confidently do I leave this work in the hands of the teachers of this school. I never knew a nobler body of Christian men and women; for they are as earnest in their attachment to the old gospel as they are eager for the winning of souls. Be encouraged, my brothers and sisters: the God who has saved so many of your children is going to save very many more of them, and we shall have great joy in this Tabernacle as we see hundreds brought to Christ. God grant it, for His name's sake! Amen.

LIFTING UP THE BRAZEN SERPENT

SERMON NO. 1,500
DELIVERED ON LORD'S DAY MORNING, OCTOBER 19, 1879.

And Moses made a serpent of brass, and put it upon a pole, and it came to pass, that if a serpent had bitten any man, when he beheld the serpent of brass, he lived—Numbers 21:9.

THIS discourse when it shall be printed will make 1,500 of my sermons which have been published regularly week by week. This is certainly a remarkable fact. I do not know of any instance in modern times in which 1,500 sermons have thus followed each other from the press from one person, and have continued to command a large circle of readers. I desire to utter most hearty thanksgivings to God for divine help in thinking out and uttering these sermons—sermons which have not merely been printed, but have been *read* with eagerness, and have also been translated into foreign tongues; sermons which are publicly read on this very Sabbath day in hundreds of places where a minister cannot be found; sermons which God has blessed to the conversion of multitudes of souls. I may and I must joy and rejoice in this great blessing which I most heartily ascribe to the undeserved favor of the Lord.

I thought the best way in which I could express my thankfulness would be to preach Jesus Christ again, and set Him forth in a sermon in which the simple gospel should be made as clear as a child's alphabet. I hope that in closing the list of 1,500 discourses the Lord will give me a word which will be blessed more than any which have preceded it, to the conversion of those who hear it or read it. May those who sit in darkness because they do not understand the freeness of salvation and the easy method by which it may be obtained, be brought into the light by discovering the way of peace through believing in Christ Jesus. Forgive this prelude; my thankfulness would not permit me to withhold it.

Concerning our text and the serpent of brass. If you turn to John's gospel you will notice that its commencement contains a sort of orderly list of types taken from Holy Scripture. It begins with the Creation. God said, "Let there be light," and John begins by declaring that Jesus, the eternal Word, is "the true light, which lighteth every man that cometh into the world." Before he closes his first chapter John has introduced a type supplied by Abel, for when the Baptist saw Jesus coming to him he said, "Behold the Lamb of God which taketh away the sin of the world." Nor is the first chapter finished before we are reminded of Jacob's ladder, for we find our Lord declaring to Nathanael, "Hereafter ye shall see heaven open, and the angels of God ascending and descending upon the Son of man." By the time we have reached the third chapter we have come as far as Israel in the wilderness, and we read the joyful words, "As Moses lifted up the serpent in the wilderness, even so must the Son of man be lifted up, that whosoever believeth in him should not perish, but have everlasting life." We are going to speak of this act of Moses this morning, that we may all of us behold the brazen serpent and find the promise true, "every one that is bitten, when he looketh upon the brazen serpent, shall live." It may be that you who have looked before will derive fresh benefit from looking again, while some who have never turned their eyes in that direction may gaze upon the uplifted Savior, and this morning be saved from the burning venom of the serpent, that deadly poison of sin which now lurks in their nature, and breeds death to their souls. May the Holy Spirit make the word effectual to that gracious end.

I. I shall invite you to consider the subject first by noticing THE PERSON IN MORTAL PERIL for whom the brazen serpent was made and lifted up. Our text saith, "It came to pass that if a serpent had bitten any man, when he beheld the fiery serpent of brass, he lived."

Let us notice that the fiery serpents first of all came among the people because *they had despised God's way and God's bread*. "The soul of the people was much discouraged because of the way." It was God's way, He had chosen it for them, and He had chosen it in wisdom and mercy, but they murmured at it. An old divine says, "It was lonesome and longsome," but still it was God's way, and therefore it ought not to have been loathsome: His pillar of fire and cloud went before them, and His servants Moses and Aaron led them like a flock, and they ought to have followed cheerfully. Every step of their previous journey had been rightly ordered, and they ought to have been quite sure that this compassing of the land of Edom was rightly ordered, too. But, no; they quarreled with God's way, and wanted to have their own way. This is one of the great standing follies of men; they cannot be content to wait on the Lord and keep His way, but they prefer a will and way of their own.

The people, also, quarreled with God's food. He gave them the best of the best, for "men did eat angels' food"; but they called the manna by an opprobrious title, which in the Hebrew has a sound of ridicule about it, and even in our translation conveys the idea of contempt. They said, "Our soul loatheth this light bread," as if they thought it unsubstantial, and only fitted to puff them out, because it was easy of digestion, and did not breed in them that heat of blood and tendency to disease which a heavier diet would have brought with it. Being discontented with their God they quarreled with the bread which He set upon their table, though it surpassed any that mortal man has ever eaten before or since. This is another of man's follies; his heart refuses to feed upon God's Word or believe God's truth. He craves for the flesh-meat of carnal reason, the leeks and the garlic of superstitious tradition, and the cu-

cumbers of speculation; he cannot bring his mind down to believe the Word of God, or to accept truth so simple, so fitted to the capacity of a child. Many demand something deeper than the divine, more profound than the infinite, more liberal than free grace. They quarrel with God's way, and with God's bread, and hence there comes among them the fiery serpents of evil lusting, pride, and sin. I may be speaking to some who have up to this moment quarreled with the precepts and the doctrines of the Lord, and I would affectionately warn them that their disobedience and presumption will lead to sin and misery. Rebels against God are apt to wax worse and worse. The world's fashions and modes of thought lead on to the world's vices and crimes. If we long for the fruits of Egypt we shall soon feel the serpents of Egypt. The natural consequence of turning against God like serpents is to find serpents waylaying our path. If we forsake the Lord in spirit, or in doctrine, temptation will lurk in our path and sin will sting our feet.

I beg you carefully to observe concerning those persons for whom the brazen serpent was especially lifted up that *they had been actually bitten by the serpents*. The Lord sent fiery serpents among them, but it was not the serpents being *among* them that involved the lifting up of a brazen serpent, it was the serpents having actually poisoned them which led to the provision of a remedy. "It shall come to pass that *everyone that is bitten*, when he looketh upon it, shall live." The only people who did look and derive benefit from the wonderful cure uplifted in the midst of the camp, were those who had been stung by the vipers. The common notion is that salvation is for good people, salvation is for those who fight against temptation, salvation is for the spiritually healthy: but how different is God's Word. God's medicine is for the sick, and His healing is for the diseased. The grace of God through the atonement of our Lord Jesus Christ is for men who are actually and really guilty. We do not preach a sentimental salvation from fancied guilt, but real and true pardon for actual offenses. I care nothing for sham sinners: you who never did anything wrong, you who are so good in yourselves that you are all right—I leave you, for I am sent to preach Christ to those who are full of sin, and worthy of eternal wrath. The serpent of brass was a remedy for those who had been bitten.

What an awful thing it is to be bitten by a serpent! I dare say some of you recollect the case of Gurling, one of the keepers of the reptiles in the Zoological Gardens. It happened in October, 1852, and therefore some of you will remember it. This unhappy man was about to part with a friend who was going to Australia, and according to the wont of many he must needs drink with him. He drank considerable quantities of gin, and though he would probably have been in a great passion if anyone had called him drunk, yet reason and common-sense had evidently become overpowered. He went back to his post at the gardens in an excited state. He had some months before seen an exhibition of snake-charming, and this was on his poor muddled brain. He must emulate the Egyptians, and play with serpents. First he took out of its cage a Morocco venom-snake, put it round his neck, twisted it about, and whirled it round about him. Happily for him it did not arouse itself so as to bite. The assistant-keeper cried out, "For God's sake put back the snake," but the foolish man replied, "I am inspired." Putting back the venom-snake, he exclaimed, "Now for the cobra." This deadly serpent was somewhat torpid with the cold of the previous night, and therefore the rash man placed it in his bosom till it revived, and glided downward till its head appeared below the back of his waistcoat. He took it by the body, about a foot from the head, and then seized it lower down by the other hand, intending to hold it by the tail and swing it round his head. He held it for an instant opposite to his face, and like a flash of lightning the serpent struck him between the eyes. The blood streamed down his face, and he called for help, but his companion fled in horror; and, as he told the jury, he did not know how long he was gone, for he was "in a maze." When assistance arrived Gurling was sitting on a chair, having restored the cobra to its place. He said, "I am a dead man." They put him in a cab, and took him to the hospital. First his speech went, he could only point to his poor throat and moan; then his vision failed him, and lastly his hearing. His pulse gradually sank, and in one hour from the time at which he had been struck he was a corpse. There was only a little mark upon the bridge of his nose, but the poison spread over the body, and he was a dead man. I tell you that story that you may use it as a parable and learn never to play with sin, and also in order to bring vividly before you what it is to be bitten by a serpent. Suppose that Gurling could have been cured by looking at a piece of brass, would it not have been good news for him? There was no remedy for that poor infatuated creature, but there is remedy for you. For men who have been bitten by the fiery serpents of sin Jesus Christ is lifted up: not for you only who are as yet playing with the serpent, not for you only who have warmed it in your bosom, and felt it creeping over your flesh, but for you who are actually bitten, and are mortally wounded. If any man be bitten so that he has become diseased with sin, and feels the deadly venom in his blood, it is for him that Jesus is set forth today. Though he may think himself to be an extreme case, it is for such that sovereign grace provides a remedy.

The bite of the serpent was painful. We are told in the text that these serpents were "fiery" serpents, which may perhaps refer to their color, but more probably has the reference to the burning effects of their venom. It heated and inflamed the blood so that every vein became a boiling river, swollen with anguish. They write their own damnation, they are sure that they are lost, they refuse all tidings of hope. You cannot get them to give a cool and sober hearing to the message of grace. Sin works in them such terror that they give themselves over as dead men. They are in their own apprehension, as David says, "free among the dead, like the slain that lie in the grave, whom God remembers no more." It was for men bitten by the fiery serpents that the brazen serpent was lifted up, and it is for men actually envenomed by sin that Jesus is preached. Jesus died for such as are at their wits' end: for such as cannot think straight, for those who are tumbled up and down in their minds, for those who are condemned already—for such was the Son of man lifted up upon the cross. What a comfortable thing that we are able to tell you this.

The bite of these serpents was, as I have told you, mortal. The Israelites could have no question about that, because in their own presence "much people of Israel died." They saw their own friends die of the snakebite, and they helped to bury them. They knew why they died, and were sure that it was because the venom of the fiery serpents was in their veins. They were left without an excuse for imagining that they could be bitten and yet live. Now, we know that many have perished as the result of sin. We are not in doubt as to what sin will do, for we are told by the infallible Word, that "the wages of sin is death," and, yet again, "Sin, when it is finished bringeth forth death." We know, also, that this death is endless misery, for the Scripture describes the lost as being cast into outer darkness, "where their worm dieth not, and their fire is not quenched." Our Lord Jesus speaks of the condemned going away into everlasting punishment, where there shall be weeping, and wailing, and gnashing of teeth. We ought to have no doubt about this, and the most of those who profess to doubt it are those who fear that it will be their own portion, who know that they are going down to eternal woe themselves, and therefore try to shut their eyes to their inevitable doom. Alas, that they should find flatterers in the pulpit who pander to their love of sin by piping to the same tune. We are not of their order. We believe in what the Lord has said in all its solemnity of dread, and, knowing the terrors of the Lord, we persuade men to escape therefrom. But it was for men who had endured the mortal bite, for men upon whose pallid faces death began to set his seal, for men whose veins were burning with the awful poison of the serpent within them—for them it was that God said to Moses, "Make thee a fiery serpent, and set it upon a pole: and it shall come to pass, that every one that is bitten, when he looketh upon it, shall live."

There is no limit set to the stage of poisoning: however far gone, the remedy still had power. If a person had been bitten a moment before, though he only saw a few drops of blood oozing forth, and only felt a little smart, he might look and live, and if he had waited, unhappily waited, even for half an hour, and speech failed him, and the pulse grew feeble, yet if he could but look he would live at once. No bound was set to the virtue of this divinely ordained remedy, or to the freedom of its application to those who needed it. The promise had no qualifying clause—"It shall come to pass that everyone that is bitten, when he looketh upon it, shall live," and our text tells us that God's promise came to pass in every case, without exception, for we read—"It came to pass, that if a serpent had bitten *any man,* when he beheld the serpent of brass, he lived." Thus, then, I have described the person who was in mortal peril.

II. Secondly, let us consider THE REMEDY PROVIDED FOR HIM. This was as singular as it was effectual. *It was purely of divine origin,* and it is clear that the invention of it, and the putting of power into it, was entirely of God. Men have proscribed several fomentations, decoctions, and operations for serpent bites: I do not know how far any of them may be depended upon, but this I know—I would rather not be bitten in order to try any of them, even those that are most in vogue. For the bites of the fiery serpents in the wilderness there was no remedy whatever, except this which God had provided, and at first sight that remedy must have seemed to be a very unlikely one. A simple look to the figure of a serpent on a pole—how unlikely to avail! How and by what means could a cure be wrought through merely looking at twisted brass? It seemed, indeed, to be almost a mockery to bid men look at the very thing which had caused their misery. Shall the bite of a serpent be cured by looking at a serpent? Shall that which brings death also bring life? But herein lay the excellency of the remedy, that it was of divine origin; for when God ordains a cure He is by that very fact bound to put potency into it. He will not devise a failure, nor prescribe a mockery. It should always be enough for us to know that God ordains a way of blessing us, for if He ordains, it must accomplish the promised result. We need not know *how* it will work, it is quite sufficient for us that God's mighty grace is pledged to make it bring forth good to our souls.

This particular remedy of a serpent lifted on a pole was *exceedingly instructive*, though I do not suppose that Israel understood it. We have been taught by our Lord and know the meaning. It was a serpent impaled upon a pole. As you would take a sharp pole and drive it through a serpent's head to kill it, so this brazen serpent was exhibited as killed, and hung up as dead before all eyes. It was the image of a dead snake. Wonder of wonders that our Lord Jesus should condescend to be symbolized by a dead serpent. The instruction to us after reading John's gospel is this: our Lord Jesus Christ, in infinite humiliation, deigned to come into the world, and to be made a curse for us. The brazen serpent had no venom of itself, but it took the form of a fiery serpent. Christ is no sinner, and in Him is no sin. But the brazen serpent was in the form of a serpent; and so was Jesus sent forth by God "in the likeness of sinful flesh." He came under the law, and sin was imputed to Him, and therefore He came under the wrath and curse of God for our sakes. In Christ Jesus, if you will look at Him upon the cross, you will see that sin is slain and hung up as a dead serpent: there too is death put to death, for "He hath abolished death and brought life and immortality to light": and there also is the curse forever ended because He has endured it, being "made a curse for us, as it is written, cursed is every one that hangeth on a tree." Thus are these serpents hung up upon the cross as a spectacle to all beholders, all slain by our dying Lord. Sin, death, and the curse are as dead serpents now. Oh, what a sight! If you can see it what joy it will give you. Had the Hebrews understood it, that dead serpent, dangling from a pole, would have prophesied to them the glorious sight which this day our faith gazes upon—Jesus slain, and sin, death, and hell slain in Him. The remedy, then, to be looked to was exceedingly instructive, and we know the instruction it was intended to convey to us.

Please to recollect that in all the camp of Israel *there was but one remedy* for serpent-bite, and that was the brazen serpent; and there was but one brazen serpent, not two. Israel might not make another. If they had made a second it would have had no effect: there was one, and only one, and that was lifted high in the center of the camp, that if any man was bitten by a serpent he might look to it and live. There is one Savior, and only one. There is none other name given under heaven among men whereby we must be saved. All grace is concentrated in Jesus, of whom we read, "It pleased the

Father that in him should all fullness dwell." Christ's bearing the curse and ending the curse, Christ's being slain by sin and destroying sin, Christ bruised as to His heel by the old serpent, but breaking the serpent's head—it is Christ alone that we must look to if we would live. O sinner, look to Jesus on the cross, for He is the one remedy for all forms of sin's poisoned wounds.

There was but one healing serpent, and that one was *bright and lustrous*. It was a serpent of brass, and brass is a shining metal. This was newly-made brass, and therefore not dimmed, and whenever the sun shone, there flashed forth a brightness from this brazen serpent. It might have been a serpent of wood or of any other metal, if God had so ordained; but He commanded that it must be of brass, that it might have a brightness about it. What a brightness there is about our Lord Jesus Christ! If we do but exhibit Him in His own true metal He is lustrous in the eyes of men. If we will but preach the gospel simply, and never think to adorn it with our philosophical thought, there is enough brightness in Christ to catch a sinner's eye, aye, and it does catch the eyes of thousands. From afar the everlasting gospel gleams in the person of Christ. As the brazen standard reflected the beams of the sun, so Jesus reflects the love of God to sinners, and seeing it they look by faith and live.

Once more, this remedy was *an enduring one*. It was a serpent of brass, and I suppose it remained in the midst of the camp from that day forward. There was no use for it after Israel entered Canaan, but, as long as they were in the wilderness, it was probably exhibited in the center of the camp, hard by the tabernacle door, upon a lofty standard. Aloft and open to the gaze of all hung this image of a dead snake— the perpetual cure for serpent venom. Had it been made of other materials it might have been broken, or have decayed, but a serpent of brass would last as long as fiery serpents pestered the desert camp. As long as there was a man bitten there was the serpent of brass to heal him. What a comfort is this, that Jesus is still able to save to the uttermost all that come to God by Him, seeing He ever liveth to make intercession for them. The dying thief beheld the brightness of that serpent of brass as he saw Jesus hanging at his side, and it saved him; and so may you and I look and live, for He is "Jesus Christ, the same yesterday, today, and forever."

> Faint my head, and sick my heart,
> Wounded, bruis'd, in every part,
> Satan's fiery sting I feel
> Poison'd with the pride of hell:
> But if at the point to die,
> Upward I direct mine eye,
> Jesus lifted up I see,
> Live by him who died for me.

I hope I do not overlay my subject by these figures. I wish not to do so, but to make it very plain to you. All you that are really guilty, all you who are bitten by the serpent, the sure remedy for you is to look to Jesus Christ, who took our sin upon Himself, and died in the sinner's stead, "being made sin for us that we might be made the righteousness of God in him." Your only remedy lies in Christ, and nowhere else. Look unto Him and be ye saved.

III. This brings us, in the third place, to consider THE APPLICATION OF THE REM-EDY, or the link between the serpent-bitten man and the brass serpent which was to heal him. What was the link? It was of the most simple kind imaginable. The brazen serpent might have been, if God had so ordered it, carried into the house where the sick man was, but it was not so. It might have been applied to him by rubbing: he might have been expected to repeat a certain form of prayer, or to have a priest present to perform a ceremony, but there was nothing of the kind; he had only to look. It was well that the cure was so simple for the danger was so frequent. Bites of the serpent came in many ways; a man might be gathering sticks, or merely walking along, and be bitten. Even now in the desert serpents are a danger. Mr. Sibree says that on one occasion he saw what he thought to be a round stone, beautifully marked. He put forth his hand to take it up, when to his horror he discovered that it was a coiled-up living serpent. All the day long when fiery serpents were sent among them the Israelites must have been in danger. In their beds and at their meals, in their houses and when they went abroad, they were in danger. These serpents are called by Isaiah "flying serpents," not because they do fly, but because they contract themselves and then suddenly spring up, so as to reach to a considerable height, and a man might be well buskined and yet not be beyond the reach of one of these malignant reptiles. What was a man to do? He had nothing to do but to stand outside his tent door, and look to the place where gleamed afar the brightness of the serpent of brass, and the moment he looked he was healed. He had nothing to do but to look—no priest was wanted, no holy water, no hocus-pocus, no mass-book, nothing but a look. A Romish bishop said to one of the early Reformers, when he preached salvation by simple faith, "O Mr. Doctor, open that gap to the people and we are undone." And so indeed they are, for the business and trade of priestcraft are ended forever if men may simply trust Jesus and live. Yet it is even so. Believe in Him, ye sinners, for this is the spiritual meaning of looking, and at once your sin is forgiven, and what perhaps is more, its deadly power ceases to operate within your spirit. There is life in a look at Jesus; is not this simple enough?

But please to notice how *very personal* it was. A man could not be cured by anything anybody else could do for him. If he had been bitten by the serpent and had refused to look to the serpent of brass, and had gone to his bed, no physician could help him. A pious mother might kneel down and pray for him, but it would be of no use. Sisters might come in and plead, ministers might be called in to pray that the man might live; but he must die despite their prayers if he did not look. There was only one hope for his life—*he must look to that serpent of brass*. It is just so with you. Some of you have written to me begging me to pray for you: so I have, but it avails nothing unless you yourselves believe in Jesus Christ. There is not beneath the copes of heaven, nor in heaven, for any one of you unless you will believe in Jesus Christ.

Whoever you may be, however much bitten of the serpent, and however near to die, if you will look to the Savior you shall live; but if you will not do this you must be damned, as surely as you live. At the last great day I must bear witness against you that I have told you this straight out and plainly. "He that believeth and is baptized shall be saved: he that believeth not shall be damned." There is no help for it; you may do what you will, join what church you please, take the Lord's Supper, be baptized, go through severe penances, or give all your goods to feed the poor, but you are a lost man unless you look to Jesus, for this is the one remedy; and even Jesus Christ Himself cannot, will not, save you unless you look to Him. There is nothing in His death to save you, there is nothing in His life to save you, unless you will trust Him. It has come to this, *you must look*, and look for yourself.

And then, again, it is *very instructive*. This looking, what did it mean? It meant this—self-help must be abandoned, and God must be trusted. The wounded man would say, "I must not sit here and look at my wound, for that will not save me. See there where the serpent struck me, the blood is oozing forth, black with the venom! How it burns and swells! My very heart is failing. But all these reflections will not ease me. I must look away from this to the uplifted serpent of brass." It is idle to look anywhere except to God's one ordained remedy. The Israelites must have understood as much as this, that God requires us to trust Him, and to use His means of salvation. We must do as He bids us, and trust in Him to work our cure; and if we will not do this we shall die eternally.

This way of curing was intended that they might magnify the love of God, and attribute their healing entirely to divine grace. The brazen serpent was not merely a picture, as I have shown you, of God's putting away sin by spending His wrath upon His Son, but it was a display of divine love. And this I know because Jesus Himself said, "As Moses lifted up the serpent in the wilderness, even so must the Son of man be lifted up. For God so loved the world that he gave his only-begotten Son": plainly saying that the death of Christ upon the cross was an exhibition of God's love to men; and whosoever looks to that grandest display of God's love to man, namely, His giving His only-begotten Son to become a curse for us, shall surely live. Now, when a man was healed by looking at the serpent he could not say that he healed himself; for he only looked, and there is no virtue in a look. A believer never claims merit or honor on account of his faith. Faith is a self-denying grace, and never dares to boast. Where is the great credit of simply believing the truth, and humbly trusting Christ to save you? Faith glorifies God, and so our Lord has chosen it as the means of our salvation. If a priest had come and touched the bitten man he might have ascribed some honor to the priest; but when there was no priest in the case, when there was nothing except looking to that brazen serpent, the man was driven to the conclusion that God's love and power had healed him. I am not saved by anything that I have done, but by what the Lord has done. To that conclusion God will have us all come; we must all confess that if saved it is by His free, rich, sovereign, undeserved grace displayed in the person of His dear Son.

IV. Allow me one moment before the fourth head, which is THE CURE EF-
FECTED. We are told in the text that "if a serpent had bitten any man, *when* he beheld the serpent of brass, he lived"; that is to say, *he was healed at once*. He had not
to wait five minutes, nor five seconds. Dear hearer, did you ever hear this before? If
you have not, it may startle you, but it is true. If you have lived in the blackest sin
that is possible up to this very moment, yet if you will now believe in Jesus Christ you
shall be saved before the clock ticks another time. It is done like a flash of lightning;
pardon is not a work of time. Sanctification needs a lifetime, but justification
needs no more than a moment. Thou believest, thou livest. Thou dost trust to Christ,
thy sins are gone, thou art a saved man the instant thou believest. "Oh," saith one,
"that is a wonder." It is a wonder, and will remain a wonder to all eternity. Our Lord's
miracles when He was on earth were mostly instantaneous. He touched them and
the fevered ones were able to sit up and minister to Him. No doctor can cure a fever
in that fashion, for there is a resultant weakness left after the heat of the fever is
abated. Jesus works perfect cures, and whosoever believeth in Him, though he
hath only believed one minute, is justified from all his sins. Oh, the matchless
grace of God!

    This remedy healed again and again. Very possibly after a man had been healed
he might go back to his work, and be attacked by a second serpent, for there were
broods of them about. What had he to do? Why, to look again, and if he was
wounded a thousand times he must look a thousand times. You, dear child of God,
if you have sin on your conscience, look to Jesus, The healthiest way of living where
serpents swarm is never to take your eye off the brazen serpent at all. Ah, ye vipers,
ye may bite if ye will; as long as my eye is upon the brazen serpent I defy your fangs
and poison-bags, for I have a continual remedy at work within me. Temptation is
overcome by the blood of Jesus. "This is the victory which overcometh the world,
even our faith."

    This cure was of universal efficacy to all who used it. There was not one case in all
the camp of a man that looked to the serpent of brass and yet died, and there
never will be a case of a man that looks to Jesus who remains under condemnation.
The believer *must* be saved. Some of the people had to look from a long distance. The
pole could not be equally near to everybody, but so long as they could see the serpent
it healed those that were afar off as well as those who were nigh. Nor did it matter
if their eyes were feeble. All eyes were not alike keen; and some may have had a squint,
or a dimness of vision, or only one eye, but if they did but look they lived. Perhaps
the man could hardly make out the shape of the serpent as he looked. "Ah," he said
to himself, "I cannot discern the coils of the brazen snake, but I can see the shining
of the brass"; and he lived. Oh, poor soul, if thou canst not see the whole of Christ
nor all His beauties, nor all the riches of His grace, yet if thou canst but see Him who
was made sin for us thou shalt live. If thou sayest, "Lord, I believe; help thou mine
unbelief," thy faith will save thee; a little faith will give thee a great Christ, and thou
shalt find eternal life in Him.

Thus I have tried to describe the cure. Oh, that the Lord would work that cure in every sinner here at this moment. I do pray he may.

It is a pleasant thought that if they looked to that brazen serpent by any kind of life they lived. Many beheld it in the glare of noon, and saw its shining coils, and lived; but I should not wonder that some were bitten at night, and by the moonlight they drew near and looked up and lived. Perhaps it was a dark and stormy night, and not a star was visible. The tempest crashed overhead, and from the murky cloud out flashed the lightning, cleaving the rocks asunder. By the glare of that sudden flame the dying man made out the brazen serpent, and though he saw but for a moment yet he lived. So, sinner, if your soul is wrapped in tempest, and if from out the cloud there comes but one single flash of light, look to Jesus Christ by it and you shall live.

V. I close with this last matter of consideration: here is A LESSON FOR THOSE WHO LOVE THEIR LORD. What ought we to do? We should imitate Moses, whose business it was to set the brazen serpent upon a pole. It is your business and mine to lift up the gospel of Christ Jesus, so that all may see it. All Moses had to do was to hang up the brazen serpent in the sight of all. He did not say, "Aaron, bring your censer, and bring with you a score of priests, and make a perfumed cloud." Nor did he say, "I myself will go forth in my robes as lawgiver, and stand there." No, he had nothing to do that was pompous or ceremonial, he had but to exhibit the brass serpent and leave it naked and open to the gaze of all. He did not say, "Aaron, bring hither a cloth of gold, wrap up the serpent in blue and scarlet and fine linen." Such an act would have been clean contrary to his orders. He was to keep the serpent unveiled. Its power lay in itself, and not in its surroundings. The Lord did not tell him to paint the pole, or to deck it with the colors of the rainbow. Oh, no. Any pole would do. The dying ones did not want to see the pole, they only needed to behold the serpent. I dare say he would make a neat pole, for God's work should be done decently, but still the serpent was the sole thing to look at. This is what we have to do with our Lord. We must preach *Him*, teach *Him*, and make *Him* visible to all. We must not conceal Him by our attempts at eloquence and learning. We must have done with the polished lancewood pole of fine speech, and those bits of scarlet and blue, in the form of grand sentences and poetic periods. Everything must be done that Christ may be seen, and nothing must be allowed which hides Him. Moses may go home and go to bed when the serpent is once uplifted. All that is wanted is that the brazen serpent should be within view both by day and night. The preacher may hide himself, so that nobody may know who he is, for if he has set forth Christ he is best out of the way.

Now, you teachers, teach your children Jesus. Show them Christ crucified. Keep Christ before them. The young men that try to preach, do not attempt to do it grandly. The true grandeur of preaching is for Christ to be grandly displayed in it. No other grandeur is wanted. Keep self in the background, but set forth Jesus Christ among the people, evidently crucified among them. None but Jesus, none but Jesus. Let Him be the sum and substance of all your teaching.

Some of you have looked to the brazen serpent, I know, and you have been healed, but what have you done with the brazen serpent since? You have not come forward to confess your faith and join the church. You have not spoken to anyone about his soul. You put the brazen serpent into a chest and hide it away. Is this right? Bring it out, and set it on a pole. Publish Christ and His salvation. He was never meant to be treated as a curiosity in a museum; He is intended to be exhibited in the highways that those who are sin-bitten may look at Him. "But, I have no proper pole," says one. The best sort of pole to exhibit Christ upon is a high one, so that He may be seen the further. Exalt Jesus. Speak well of His name. I do not know any other virtue that there can be in the pole but its height. The more you can speak in your Lord's praise, the higher you can lift Him up the better, but for all other styles of speech there is nothing to be said. Do lift Christ up. "Oh," says one, "but I have not a long standard." Then lift Him up on such as you have, for there are short people about who will be able to see by your means. I think I told you once of a picture which I saw of the brazen serpent. I want the Sunday-school teachers to listen to this. The artist represented all sorts of people clustering round the pole, and as they looked the horrible snakes dropped off their arms, and they lived. There was such a crowd around the pole that a mother could not get near it. She carried a little babe, which a serpent had bitten. You could see the blue marks of the venom. As she could get no nearer, the mother held her child aloft, and turned its little head that it might gaze with its infant eye upon the brazen serpent and live. Do this with your little children, you Sunday-school teachers. Even while they are yet little, pray that they may look to Jesus Christ and live; for there is no bound set to their age. Old men snake-bitten came hobbling on their crutches. "Eighty years old am I," saith one, "but I have looked to the brazen serpent, and I am healed." Little boys were brought out by their mothers, though as yet they could hardly speak plainly, and they cried in child language, "I look at the great snake and it bless me." All ranks, and sexes, and characters, and dispositions looked and lived. Who will look to Jesus at this good hour? O dear souls, will you have life or no? Will you despise Christ and perish? If so, your blood be on your own skirts. I have told you God's way of salvation, lay hold on it. Look to Jesus at once. May His Spirit gently lead you so to do. Amen.

THE TRUE TABERNACLE, AND ITS GLORY OF GRACE AND PEACE

SERMON NO. 1,862
DELIVERED ON LORD'S DAY MORNING, SEPTEMBER 27, 1885.
PORTIONS OF SCRIPTURE READ BEFORE SERMON—EXODUS 34:1–8; 40:34–38;
JOHN 1:1–18.
HYMNS FROM *Our Own Hymn Book*—249, 256, 250.

And the Word was made flesh, and dwelt among us, (and we beheld his glory, the glory as of the only begotten of the Father,) full of grace and truth—John 1:14.

For the law was given by Moses, but grace and truth came by Jesus Christ—John 1:17.

THERE was a time when God freely communed with men. The voice of the Lord God was heard walking in the garden in the cool of the day. With unfallen Adam the great God dwelt in sweet and intimate fellowship; but sin came and not only destroyed the garden, but destroyed the intercourse of God with His creature man. A great gulf opened between man as evil, and God as infinitely pure; and had it not been for the amazing goodness of the most High, we must all of us forever have been banished from His presence, and from the glory of His power. The Lord God in infinite love resolved that He Himself would bridge the distance, and would again dwell with man; and in token of this He made Himself manifest to His chosen nation Israel when they were in the wilderness. He was pleased to dwell in type and symbol among His people, in the very center and heart of their camp. Do you see yonder tent with its curtains of goats' hair in the center of the canvas city? You cannot see within it; but it was all glorious within with precious wood, and pure gold, and tapestry of many colors. Within its most sacred shrine shone forth a bright light between the wings of cherubim, which light was the symbol of the presence of the Lord. But if you cannot see within, yet you can see above the sacred tent a cloud, which arises from the top of the Holy of Holies, and then expands like a vast tree so as to cover all the host, and protect the chosen of God from the intense heat of the sun, so apt to make the traveler faint when passing over the burning sand. If you will wait till the sun is down, that same cloud will become luminous, and light up the whole camp. Thus it was both shade and light; and by its means was enjoyed that safety which was afterwards set forth in the promise, "The sun shall not smite thee by day, nor the moon by night." Over all the glory was a defense and a comfort. The Lord dealt not so with any nation, save only His people Israel, of whom He said, "I will dwell in them, and walk in them; and I will be their God, and they shall be my people."

The day of the type is over; we see no more a nation secluded from all others and made to be as "the church in the wilderness." God doth not now confine His abode to one people; for "The God of the whole earth shall he be called." There is now no spot on earth where God dwells in preference to another. Did not our Lord say, at the well of Sychar, "Woman, believe me, the hour cometh, when ye shall neither in this mountain, nor yet at Jerusalem, worship the Father." "But . . . the true worshipers shall worship the Father in spirit and in truth"? Wherever true hearts seek the Lord, He is found of them. He is as much present on the lone mountain's side as in the aisles of yonder abbey, or in the galleries of this tabernacle. "Howbeit the most High dwelleth not in temples made with hands; as saith the prophet, Heaven is my throne, and earth is my footstool: what house will ye build me? saith the Lord: or what is the place of my rest?"

Yet there is a true house of God, a real temple of the Infinite, a living abode of the Godhead. The epistle to the Hebrews speaks of "the true tabernacle, which the Lord pitched, and not man." There is still a trysting-place where God doth still meet with man, and hold fellowship with him. That place is the person of the Lord Jesus Christ, "in whom dwelleth all the fullness of the Godhead bodily." The manhood of Christ is become to us the anti-type of that tent in the center of the camp. God is in Christ Jesus; Christ Jesus is God; and in His blessed person God dwells in the midst of us as in a tent; for such is the force of the original in our text. "The Word was made flesh, and tabernacled, or tented, among us." That is to say, in Christ Jesus the Lord dwelt among men, as God of old dwelt in His sanctuary in the midst of the tribes of Israel. This is very delightful and hopeful for us: the Lord God doth dwell among us through the incarnation of His Son.

But the substance far excels the shadow; for in the wilderness the Lord only dwelt in the abode of man, but now His approach to us is closer, for He dwells in the flesh of man. "The Word was made flesh, and dwelt among us." Note that word "flesh." It doth not say, "The Word was made *man*": it means that, but the use of the word "flesh" brings the Lord Jesus still closer to us, and shows that He took on Him the very nature and substance of manhood: He did not merely assume the name and notion, and appearance, of manhood, but the reality: the weakness, the suffering, the mortality of our manhood He actually took into union with Himself. He was no phantom, or apparition, but He had a human body and a human soul. "The Word was made flesh." When the Lord became bone of our bone, and flesh of our flesh, His incarnation in a human body brought Him far nearer to man than when He only abode within curtains, and occupied a tent in the midst of Israel.

Moreover, it is to be noted that God does in the person of Jesus not merely dwell among men; but He hath joined Himself unto men—the Word not only dwelt in flesh, but "was made flesh." It is impossible to use words which are exactly accurate to describe the wonderful incarnation of the Son of God in human flesh; but these words are used to show that our Lord is as truly and as really man as He is God. Not only does God dwell in the body of man; but our Lord Jesus is God and man in one person. He is not ashamed to speak of men as His brethren. "Forasmuch then as the children are partakers of flesh and blood, he also himself likewise took part of the same." So that the Lord Jesus is one with us. This approach to us is exceeding close. God was never one with the tabernacle, but in Christ Jesus He is one with us. This union hath in it a sweetness of sympathy, a tenderness of relationship, and a condescension of fellowship greatly to be admired. Now we listen to the music of that blessed name Emmanuel, "God with us." In the person of the only begotten, our Lord and Savior Jesus Christ, we see God reconciling the world unto Himself. Let us rejoice and be glad that we have in Jesus more than Israel had in the holy place of the tabernacles of the most High. The ancient believer gazed upon the sacred tent, he thought of the holy place of sacrifice, and the Holy of Holies, the inner shrine of the Lord's indwelling; but we have infinitely more, we have God in our nature, and in Him "truly our fellowship is with the Father, and with his Son Jesus Christ."

In and around the tent wherein the Lord dwelt in the center of the camp there was a manifestation of the presence of God. This was the glory of that house: but how scanty was the revelation! A bright light which I have already mentioned, the Shekinah, is said to have shone over the mercy seat; but the high priest only could see it, and he only saw it once in the year when he entered with blood within the veil. Outside, above the holy place, there was the manifest glory of the pillar of cloud by day, and of fire by night. This sufficed to bear witness that God was there; but still, cloud and fire are but physical appearances, and cannot convey a true appearance of God, who is a spirit. God cannot be perceived by the senses; and yet the fiery, cloudy pillar could appeal to the eyes only. The excellence of the indwelling of God in Christ is this—that there is in Him a glory as of the only begotten of the Father, the moral and spiritual glory of Godhead. This is to be seen, but not with the eyes; this is to be perceived, but not by the carnal senses: this is seen, and heard, and known, by spiritual men, whose mental perceptions are keener than those of sight and hearing. In the person of the Lord there is a glory which is seen by our faith, which is discerned of our renewed spirits, and is made to operate upon our hearts. The glory of God in the sanctuary was seen only by the priest of the house of Aaron; the glory of God in the face of Christ is seen by all believers, who are all priests unto God. That glory the priest beheld but once in the year; but we steadily behold that glory at all times, and are transformed by the sight. The glory of God in the face of Jesus Christ is not a thing of outward appearance, to be beheld with the eyes, like the pillar of cloud and fire; but there is an abiding, steady luster of holy, gracious, truthful character about our Lord Jesus Christ, which is best seen by those who by reason of sanctification are made fit to discern it. Blessed are the pure in heart, for they shall see God; yea, they do see Him in Christ Jesus. "No man hath seen God at any time; the only begotten Son, which is in the bosom of the Father, he hath declared him." Many of us besides the apostles can say, "We beheld his glory, the glory as of the only begotten of the Father, full of grace and truth." We have not seen Jesus raise the dead; we have not seen Him cast out devils; we have not seen Him hush the winds and calm the waves; but we do see, with our mind's eye, His spotless holiness, His boundless love, His superlative truth, His wondrous heavenliness; in a word, we have seen, and do see, His fullness of grace and truth; and we rejoice in the fact that the tabernacling of God among men in Christ Jesus is attended with a more real glory than the mere brilliance of light and the glow of flame. The condescension of Christ's love is to us more glorious than the pillar of cloud, and the zeal of our Lord's self-sacrifice is more excellent than the pillar of fire. As we think of the divine mysteries which meet in the person of our Lord, we do not envy Israel the gracious manifestations vouchsafed her when "a cloud covered the tent of the congregation, and the glory of the Lord covered the tabernacle"; for we have all this and more in our incarnate God, who is with us always, even to the end of the world.

As the Holy Spirit shall help me, I shall at this time say, first of all, *Let us behold this tabernacling of God*; and, secondly, *Let us avail ourselves of this tabernacling of God in all the ways for which it was intended.*

I. First, then, LET US BEHOLD THIS TABERNACLING OF GOD WITH US. "We beheld His glory, the glory as of the only begotten of the Father, full of grace and truth." In Jesus Christ all the attributes of God are to be seen; veiled, but yet verily there. You have only to read the gospels, and to look with willing eyes, and you shall behold in Christ all that can possibly be seen of God. It is veiled in human flesh, as it must be; for the glory of God is not to be seen by us absolutely; it is toned down to these dim eyes of ours; but the Godhead is there, the perfect Godhead in union with the perfect manhood of Christ Jesus our Lord, to whom be glory forever and ever.

Two divine things are more clearly seen in Jesus than aught else. Upon these I would speak at this time, considering the two together, and then each one separately—"Full of grace and truth."

Observe the two glorious qualities, joined inseparably—grace and truth—and observe that they are spoken of *in the concrete*. The apostle says that the only begotten is "full of grace and truth." He did not come to tell us about grace, but actually to bring us grace. He is not full of the news of grace and truth, but of grace and truth themselves. Others had been messengers of gracious tidings, but He came to bring grace. Others teach us truth, but Jesus is the truth. He is that grace and truth whereof others spoke. Jesus is not merely a teacher, an exhorter, a worker of grace and truth; but these heavenly things are in Him: He is full of them. I want you to note this. It raises such a difference between Christ and others: you go to others to hear of grace and truth, but you must go to Christ to see them. There may be, there is, grace in other men; but not as it is in Christ: they have it as water flowing through a pipe, but He has it as water in its fountain and source. He has grace to communicate to the sons of men, grace without measure, grace essential and abiding. There is truth in others where God has wrought it, by His Spirit; but it is not in them as it is in Christ. In Him dwell the depth, the substance, the essence of the fact. Grace and truth come to us by Him, and yet they evermore abide in Him. I say again, our Lord did not merely come to teach grace and truth, or to impress them upon us; but He came to exhibit in His own person, life, and work, all the grace and truth which we need. He has brought us grace in rivers and truth in streams: of these He has an infinite fullness; of that fullness all His saints receive.

This grace and truth are *blended*. The "and" between the two words I would treat as more than a common conjunction. The two rivers unite in one fullness—"Full of grace and truth": that is to say. The grace is truthful grace, grace not in fiction nor in fancy, grace not to be hoped for and to be dreamed of, but grace every atom of which is fact; redemption which does redeem, pardon which does blot out sin, renewal which actually regenerates, salvation which completely saves. We have not here blessings which charm the ear and cheat the soul; but real, substantial favors from God that cannot lie. Then blend these things the other way. "Grace and truth": the Lord has come to bring us truth, but it is not the kind of truth which censures, condemns, and punishes; it is gracious truth, truth steeped in love, truth saturated with mercy. The truth which Jesus brings to His people comes not from the judgment seat, but from the mercy seat; it hath a gracious drift and aim about it, and ever tends unto salvation. His light is the life of men. If thou art overshadowed with a dark truth which seems to deepen thy despair, look thou to it again and thou wilt perceive within it a hidden light which is sown for the righteous. The darkness of convincing and humbling truth maketh for light: by engendering despair of self, heart-searching truth is meant to drive thee to the true hope. There is grace to God's people in everything that falls from the lips of Jesus Christ. His lips are like lilies dropping sweet smelling myrrh; myrrh in itself is bitter, but such is the grace of our Lord Jesus that His lips impart sweetness to it. See how grace and truth thus blend, and qualify each other! The grace is all true, and the truth is all gracious. This is a wondrous compound made according to the art of the divine Apothecary. Where else is grace so true, or truth so gracious?

Furthermore, it is grace and truth *balanced*. I wish I were able to communicate my thoughts this morning as they came to me when I was meditating upon this passage; but this thought almost speaks for itself. The Lord Jesus Christ is full of grace; but then He has not neglected the other quality which is somewhat sterner, namely, that of truth. I have known many in this world very loving and affectionate, but they have not been faithful: on the other hand, I have known men to be sternly honest and truthful, but they have not been gentle and kind: but in the Lord Jesus Christ there is no defect either way. He is full of grace which doth invite the publican and the sinner to Himself; but He is full of truth which doth repel the hypocrite and Pharisee. He does not hide from man a truth however terrible it may be, but He plainly declares the wrath of God against all unrighteousness. But when He has spoken terrible truth, He has uttered it in such a gracious and tender manner, with so many tears of compassion for the ignorant and those that are out of the way, that you are much won by His grace as convinced by His truth. Our Lord's ministry is not truth alone, nor grace alone; but it is a balanced, well-ordered system of grace and truth. The Lord Himself is in His character "just and having salvation." He is both King of righteousness and King of peace. He does not even save unjustly, nor does He proclaim truth unlovingly. Grace and truth are equally conspicuous in Him.

Beloved, notice here that both these qualities in our Lord are *at the full.* He is "full of grace." Who could be more so? In the person of Jesus Christ the immeasurable grace of God is treasured up. God has done for us by Christ Jesus exceeding abundantly above all that we ask, or even think. It is not possible even for imagination to conceive of any person more gracious than God in Christ Jesus. You cannot desire, certainly you cannot require, anything that should exceed what is found of grace in the person, offices, work, and death of the only begotten. Come, ye that have large minds, and intellects that are creative, and see if ye can devise anything that should be mentioned in the same day with what God, in the infinite glory of His grace, has given us in the person of His Son. And there is an equal fullness of truth about our Lord. He Himself, as He comes to us as the revelation and manifestation of God, declares to us, not some truth, but all truth. All of God is in Christ; and all of God means all that is true, and all that is right, and all that is faithful, and all that is just, all that is according to righteousness and holiness. Christ Jesus has brought to us the justice, truth, and righteousness of God to the full: He is the Lord our righteousness. There are no reserves of disagreeable fact in Christ. There is nothing hidden from us of truth that might alarm us, nor anything that might have shaken our confidence; nor, on the other hand, is any truth kept back which might have increased our steadfastness. He says, "If it were not so I would have told you." Admire the full-orbed splendor of the Sun of Righteousness. Ask not with Pilate, "What is truth?" but behold it in God's dear Son. Oh, I know not how to speak to you upon themes so full and deep! How shall I, that am but as a twinkling dewdrop on a blade of grass, reflect the full glory of this Sun of Righteousness? But all truth and all grace dwell in Christ in all their fullness beyond conception, and the two lie in each other's bosoms forever, to bless us with boundless, endless joy and glory.

Thus have I taken the two together. Now I want to dwell briefly on each one by itself.

Grace is put first. "We beheld his glory, the glory as of the only begotten of the Father, full of grace." Jesus Christ is the Son of God; He is His only begotten Son. Others are begotten of God, but no other was ever begotten of God as Christ was; consequently, when He came into this world the glory that was about Him was a glory as of the only begotten. A very singular, and very special, and incommunicable glory abides in the person of our Lord. Part of this was the glory of His grace. Now, in the Old Testament, in that thirty-fourth chapter of Exodus, which we read in part this morning, you notice that the glory of God lay in His being "the Lord God, merciful and gracious, longsuffering, and abundant in goodness and truth." The glory of the only begotten of the Father must lie in the same things as the glory of the Father, namely, in longsuffering, goodness, and truth. In Christ there is a wonderful display of the gentleness, patience, pity, mercy, and love of God. Not merely did He teach the grace of God, and invite us to the grace of God, but in Himself He displayed the grace of God.

This is to be seen, first, in His incarnation. It is a wonderful instance of divine grace that the Word should be made flesh and dwell among us, and reveal His glory to us. Apart from anything that springs out of the incarnation of Christ, that incarnation itself is a wondrous act of grace. There must be hope for men now that man is next akin to God through Jesus Christ. The angels were not mistaken when they not only sang, "Glory to God in the highest," but also, "on earth peace, goodwill towards men," because in Bethlehem the Son of God was born of a virgin. God in our nature must mean God with gracious thoughts towards us. If the Lord had meant to destroy the race, He never would have espoused it and taken it into union with Himself. There is fullness of grace in the fact of the Word made flesh tabernacling among us.

More than this, there is fullness of grace in the life of Christ when we consider that He lived here in order to perfect Himself as our High Priest. Was He not made perfect through His sufferings, that He might sympathize with us in all our woes? He was compassed with infirmities, and bore our sorrows, and endured those crosses of the human life which press so heavily on our own shoulders; and all this to make Himself able to deal graciously with us in a tender and brotherly way. Apart from that which comes out of this wonderful brotherhood, there is a bottomless depth of grace about the fellowship itself. The Lord Jesus cannot curse me, for He has borne my curse: He cannot be unkind to me, for He has shared my sorrows. If every pang that rends my heart has also rent His heart, and if into all my woes He has descended even deeper than I have gone, it must mean love to me, it cannot mean anything else; and it must mean truth, for Jesus did not play at fellowship, His griefs were real. I say then that this manifestation of God in the person of Christ Jesus is seen in His sorrowing life to be full of grace and truth.

Then think for a minute of what He did. He was so full of grace that when He spoke His words dropped a fatness of grace, the dew of His own love was upon all His discourses; and when He moved about and touched men here and there, virtue went out of Him, because He was so full of it. At one time He spoke and pardoned a sinner, saying, "Thy sins be forgiven thee": at another moment He battled with the consequences of sin, raising men from sickness and from death: again He turned Himself and fought with the prince of darkness himself, and cast him out from those whom he tormented. He went about like a cloud which is big with rain, and therefore plentifully waters waste places. His life was boundless compassion. There was a power of grace about His garments, His voice, His look; and in all He was so true that none ever thought Him capable of subterfuge. Everywhere He went He scattered grace among the children of men; and He is just the same now; fullness of grace abides in Him still.

When it came to His death, which was the pouring out of His soul, then His fullness of grace was seen. He was full of grace indeed, forasmuch as He emptied Himself to save men. He was Himself not only man's Savior, but his salvation. He gave Himself for us. He was indeed full of grace when He bore our sins in His own body on the tree. His was love at its height, since He died on the cross, "the just for the unjust, to bring us to God." Pronounce the word "substitution," and you cannot help feeling that the Substitute for guilty man was full of grace; or use that other word, "representative," and remember that whatever Jesus did, He did as the covenant Head of His people. If He died, they died in Him; if He rose again, they rose in Him; if He ascended up on high, they ascended in Him; and if He sits at the right hand of God, they also sit in the heavenly places in Him. When He shall come a second time it shall be to claim the kingdom for His chosen as well as for Himself; and all the glory of the future ages is for them, and not for Himself alone. He saith, "Because I live, ye shall live also." Oh, the richness of the grace and truth that dwell in our Lord as the representative of His people! He will enjoy nothing unless His people enjoy it with Him. "Where I am, there also shall my servant be." "To him that overcometh will I grant to sit with me in my throne, even as I also overcame, and am set down with my Father in his throne."

There is yet another word higher than "substitution," higher than "representation," and that is "union." We are one with Christ, joined to Him by a union that never can be broken. Not only does He do what He does, representing us, but we are joined unto Him in one spirit, members of His body, and partakers of His glory. Is not this grace, grace unspeakable? Is it not a miracle of love that worms of earth should ever be one with incarnate Deity, and so one that they never can be separated throughout the ages?

Thus I have shown you that there is in our Lord a fullness of grace. Your own thoughts will dig deeper than mine.

But then it is said there is in Him also a fullness of *truth*, by which I understand that in Christ Himself, not merely in what He said, and did, and promised, there is a fullness of truth. And this is true, first, in the fact that He is the fulfillment of all the promises that went before concerning Him. God had promised great things by His prophets concerning the coming Messiah, but all those predictions are absolutely matters of fact in the person of the Well-beloved. "All the promises of God are yea and Amen in Christ Jesus." Verily He hath bruised the serpent's head. Verily He hath borne our griefs, and carried our sorrows. Verily He hath proclaimed liberty to the captives. Verily He hath proved Himself a prophet like unto Moses.

According to my second text, in verse 17, I understand our Lord Jesus to be "truth" in the sense of being the substance of all the types. The law that was given by Moses was but symbolical and emblematical; but Jesus is the truth. He is really that blood of sprinkling which speaketh better things than that of Abel; He is in very deed the Paschal lamb of God's passover: He is the burnt-offering, the sin-offering, and the peace-offering—all in one! He is the true scapegoat, the true morning and evening Lamb; in fact, He is in truth what all the types and figures were in pattern. Blessed be God, brethren, whenever you see great things in the Old Testament in the type, you see the real truth of those things in the person of the Lord Jesus Christ. The Jew had nothing that we have not: he had nothing even in outline and shadow which we have not obtained in substance. The covenant in its fullness is in Christ: the prophecy is in Moses, the fulfillment is in Jesus: the foreshadowing is in the law, the truth is in the Word made flesh.

Further than that, our Lord Jesus Christ is said to be grace and truth in this sense, that He truthfully deals with matters of fact in the case of our salvation. I know the notion of the world is that the salvation of Christ is a pretty dream, a handsome piece of sentiment. But there is nothing dreamy about it: it is no fiction; it is fact upon fact. The Lord Jesus Christ does not gloss over or conceal the condition of man in his salvation; He finds man condemned, and takes him as condemned in the very worst sense, condemned of a capital offense; and as man's substitute He endures the capital penalty, and dies in the sinner's stead. The Lord Jesus views the sinner as depraved, yea, as dead in trespasses and sins, and He quickens him by His resurrection life. He does not wink at the result of the fall and of actual sin; but He comes to the dead sinner and quickens him; He comes to the diseased heart and heals it. To me the gospel is a wonderful embodiment of omnipotent wisdom and truth. If the gospel had said to men, "The law of God is certainly righteous, but it is too stern, too exacting, and therefore God will wink at many sins, and make provision for salvation by omitting to punish much of human guilt," why, my brethren, we should always have been in jeopardy. If God could be unjust to save us, He could also be changeable, and cast us away. If there was anything rotten in the state of our salvation, we should fear that it would fail us at last. But our foundation is sure, for the Lord has excavated down to the rock; He has taken away every bit of mere sentiment and sham, and His salvation is real throughout. It is a glorious salvation of grace and truth, in which God takes the sinner as God is, on the principles of true righteousness; and yet saves him.

But it means more than that. The Lord deals with us in the way of grace, and that grace encourages a great many hopes, but those hopes are all realized, for He deals with us in truth. Our necessities demand great things, and grace actually supplies those great things. The old law could never make the comers thereunto perfect as pertaining to the conscience, but the grace of God makes believers perfect as pertaining to the conscience. If I were to sit down and try to imagine a flaw in the ground of my salvation by Christ, I could not do it. Believing as I do in Him who bore my sins in His own body on the tree, I feel that by no possibility can His atonement fail me. I have not imagination strong enough to feign a reason for distrust: I do not see hole or corner in which any charge could lurk against the man that believes in Jesus Christ. My conscience is satisfied, and more than satisfied. Sometimes it even seems to me that my sins could not have deserved that the Son of God should die. The atonement is greater than the sin. Speak of the vindication of the law!—is not the vindication even greater than the dishonor? Does not the law of God shine out more lustrous in its indescribable glory through the sacrifice of Christ as the penalty for sin, than it would have done had it never been broken, or had all the race of law-breakers been swept into endless destruction? O brothers, in the salvation of Jesus there is a truth of grace unrivaled! There is a deep verity, a substantiality, an inward soul-satisfaction in the sacrifice of Christ, which makes us feel that it is a full atonement—a fountain of "grace and truth."

Nor have I yet quite brought out all the meaning, even if I have succeeded so far. Christ has brought to us "grace and truth"; that is to say, He works in believers both grace and truth. We want grace to rescue us from sin; He has brought it: we need truth in the inward parts; He has wrought it. The system of salvation by atonement is calculated to produce truthful men. The habit of looking for salvation through the great sacrifice fosters the spirit of justice, begets in us a deep abhorrence of evil, and a love for that which is right and true. By nature we are all liars, and either love or make a lie: for this cause we are content with refuges of lies, and we compass ourselves with deceit. In our carnal state we are as full of guile as an egg is full of meat; but when the Lord comes to us in Christ, no longer imputing our trespasses to us, then He takes out of our heart that deceit and desperate wickedness which had else remained there. I say it, and dare avow it, that the system of salvation by the indwelling of God in Christ and the atonement offered by Him for men, has a tendency in it to infuse grace into the soul and to produce truth in the life. The Holy Ghost employs it to that end. I pray that you and I may prove it so by the grace which causes us to love both God and man, and the truthfulness with which we deal in all the affairs of life.

Thus has our Lord displayed the glory of God in the grace and truth with which He is filled. I am sorry I have spoken so feebly on a theme so grand. May the Spirit bless you even through the infirmities of my speech!

II. Now I want a few minutes to say to you, Come brothers and sisters, LET US AVAIL OURSELVES OF THIS TABERNACLING OF GOD AMONG US.

First, then, if God has come to dwell among men by the Word made flesh *let us pitch our tents around this central tabernacle*; do not let us live as if God were a long way off. To the Israelites God was equally near from every quarter of the camp. The tabernacle was in the center, and the center is equally near to every point of the circumference. No true Israelite could say, "I must go across the sea, or soar up into the air, or dive into the depths to find my God." Every Israelite could say "He dwelleth between the cherubim: I have but to go to His tabernacle to be in His presence and speak with Him." Our God is not far from any one of His people this day. We are made nigh by the blood of Christ. God is everywhere present, but there is a higher presence of effectual grace in the person of the only begotten. Do not let us live as if we worshiped a far-off God. Let us not repine as if we were deserted. Let us not feel alone, for the Father is with us.

God is near thee, therefore cheer thee, sad soul.

Open thy window towards Jerusalem, as Daniel did; pray with thine eye upon Christ, in whom dwelleth all the fullness of the Godhead bodily in the greatest nearness to us. God is never far away since Christ has come to dwell among men.

Next, *let us resort to this central tabernacle to obtain grace to help in time of need.* Let us come to Christ without fear, for He hath grace to give, and He will give it to us abundantly, whenever we need it. I like to think of the wording of my text. Leave out the parentheses, and it runs, "He dwelt among us full of grace." He could not have dwelt among such provoking ones if he had not been full of grace. But if He dwells among us full of grace, we need not fear that He will cast us away because of our sins and failings. I invite you, therefore, to come boldly to Him who is full of forgiving love. I beg you to come and receive of His fullness, for grace is truly grace when it is communicated: grace which is not distributed is grace in name only. "Alas!" you say, "I want so much grace." Brother, it is treasured up in Christ for you without measure. It is placed in Him that you may have it. Do we not try to persuade the sinner that there is life in a look? Shall I need to persuade saints that grace is equally free to them? Do we not tell the sinner that God is not to be sought for as far away, but that He is waiting to be gracious? Must I tell the believer the same? You may at this moment obtain all the grace you need. The door is open; enter and take what you will. Do not stop till you reach home and go through a set of religious exercises; but here, and now, believe in Jesus to the full. In the center of the camp is the incarnate God; Israel had but to go to the central tent to find present help in time of trouble. In the person of Christ, who hath said, "I am with you alway, even to the end of the world," there is, in truth, all the grace you can possibly need. Come to this well and drink. Receive of His fullness, and go on your way rejoicing.

What next shall we do? Brethren, since God in Christ is in the midst of us, *let us abide in joyful, peaceful confidence in Him who is grace and truth to us.* Do not let us wander to other sources. To whom should we go? Shall we leave our God? Shall we leave His grace, His truth? Do not let us dream that He is changed, for He is God. Do not imagine that He has removed, for He hath said, "This is my rest forever: here will I dwell, for I have desired it." Do not let us conceive that His grace and truth are exhausted; for His fullness is eternal. Let us receive strong consolation, and remain steadfast, unmovable. Let us quietly rest in the firm belief that all we can want between here and heaven, all that we need this moment and in all moments yet to come, is treasured up in Christ Jesus, who is abidingly the center of His church and the manifestations of God.

Once more: if this be so, and God does really in Christ dwell in the midst of His people "full of grace and truth," *let us tell everybody of it.* I am sure if I had been an Israelite in the wilderness, and had met an Amalekite or an Edomite, I should have gloried in my God, and in the privileges which His presence secured me. We know that Amalekites and Edomites could not have come into the house of the Lord; but nowadays, if we meet with one who is a stranger, we can tell him of our privilege, with sweet persuasion that the stranger can be brought nigh through the blood of the

Lamb. Therefore let us abundantly speak of the dwelling of God with men. Let us tell to all that the Lord has come to man, not in wrath, not in judgment, but "full of grace and truth." O my unconverted hearer, come to Jesus! He is able to save to the uttermost those that come unto God by Him. Draw nigh to the meek and lowly Jesus, and you draw nigh to God. He saith, "He that hath seen me hath seen the Father." Publish the invitation of grace to the four winds. Ring out your silver trumpets, or if you have them not, sound your rams' horns; but somehow let all people know that the tabernacle of God is with men, and He doth dwell among them. Tell out this news in the far country, that the wandering prodigal son may hear it, and cry, "I will arise, and go to my Father." God has come to men; will not men come to God? In Christ Jesus God invites men to come to Him; will you not come to receive grace and truth?

One more lesson remains, and that is—*what manner of people ought we to be among whom Jehovah dwells?* It must have been a very solemn thing to be a member of that great camp of two million in the wilderness of Sinai. God's presence in the midst of the camp must have made every tent sacred. As we walked through the streets of that canvas city, if we had been Israelites, and in our right minds, we should have said, "These tents are none other than the house of God and the very gate of heaven; for see, Jehovah is in the midst of us. Mark you not the bright light that shines about His sanctuary?" We should have felt that in such a camp all should be holy. The pollution of sin should be unknown there. In such a camp constant prayer and praise should be presented to Him whose presence was its glory and defense. Today let our congregation be a holy convocation; and as for ourselves, let us be holiness unto the Lord. We are consecrated men and women, seeing the Lord has come so very near to us. I spoke of solemnity; I meant not dread and sorrow, but a solemnity full of joy. It is a solemn thing to have God so near, but the joy is equal to the solemnity. Glory be unto God most high, for He is here! Let us spend our days and nights in gladness and delight. God is reconciled to us in the person of His dear Son, and we have fellowship with God in Christ Jesus; wherefore let us rejoice evermore. Amen and amen.

SILVER SOCKETS: *OR,* REDEMPTION THE FOUNDATION

SERMON No. 1,581

DELIVERED ON LORD'S DAY MORNING, JANUARY 30, 1881

PORTIONS OF SCRIPTURE READ BEFORE SERMON—1 PETER 2:1–10; EXODUS
26:15–25; 30:11–16; 38:25–28.

HYMNS FROM *Our Own Hymn Book*—84, 440, 549.

*And the LORD spoke unto Moses, saying, When thou takest the sum of the chil-
dren of Israel after their number, then shall they give every man a ransom for his
soul unto the LORD, when thou numberest them; that there be no plague among
them, when thou numberest them. This they shall give, every one that passeth
among them that are numbered, half a shekel after the shekel of the sanctuary:
(a shekel is twenty gerahs:) an half shekel shall be the offering of the LORD. Every
one that passeth among them that are numbered, from twenty years old and above,
shall give an offering unto the LORD. The rich shall not give more, and the poor
shall not give less than half a shekel, when they give an offering unto the LORD,
to make an atonement for your souls. And thou shalt take the atonement money
of the children of Israel, and shalt appoint it for the service of the tabernacle of
the congregation; that it may be a memorial unto the children of Israel before the
LORD, to make an atonement for your souls*—Exodus 30:11–16.

*A bekah for every man, that is, half a shekel, after the shekel of the sanctu-
ary, for every one that went to be numbered, from twenty years old and upward,
for six hundred thousand and three thousand and five hundred and fifty men.
And of the hundred talents of silver were cast the sockets of the sanctuary, and
the sockets of the veil; an hundred sockets of the hundred talents, a talent for a
socket*—Exodus 38:26, 27.

WILL you kindly first open your Bible at Exodus 30; for I must commence my discourse by expounding that passage. When the account was taken of the number of
the children of Israel the Lord commanded that every male over 20 years of age should
pay half a shekel as redemption money, confessing that he deserved to die, owning
that he was in debt to God, and bringing the sum demanded as a type of a great

281

redemption which would by-and-by be paid for the souls of the sons of men. The truth was thus taught that God's people are a redeemed people: they are elsewhere called "the redeemed of the Lord." If men reject the redemption which He ordains, then are they not His people; for of all His chosen it may be said—"The Lord hath redeemed Jacob, and ransomed him from the hand of him that was stronger than he." Whenever we attempt to number up the people of God it is absolutely needful that we count only those who at least profess to have brought the redemption price in their hands, and so to have taken part in the atonement of Christ Jesus. David, when he numbered the people, did not gather from them the redemption money, and hence a plague broke out amongst them. He had failed in obedience to the Lord's ordinance, and counted his subjects, not as redeemed people, but merely as so many heads. Let us always beware of estimating the number of Christians by the number of the population of the countries called Christian; for the only true Christians in the world are those who are redeemed from iniquity by the blood of the Lamb, and have personally accepted the ransom which the Lord has provided, personally brought their redemption money in their hands by taking Christ to be theirs and presenting Him by an act of faith to the great Father. God has upon earth as many people as believe in Jesus Christ, and we dare not count any others to be His but those who can say, "In whom we have redemption through his blood, the forgiveness of sins." We must not count heads which know about Christ, but hands which have received the redemption money and are presenting it unto God; not so much persons who are called Christians by courtesy as souls that are Christly in very fact, because they have accepted the atoning sacrifice, and live before God as "redeemed from among men."

Observe that this redemption, without which no man might rightly be numbered among the children of Israel lest a plague should break out among them, must be *personal and individual.* There was not a lump sum to be paid for the nation, or twelve amounts for the twelve tribes; but each man must bring his own half shekel for himself. So there is no redemption that will be of any use to any of you unless it is personally accepted and brought before God by faith. You must each one be able to say for yourself concerning the Lord Jesus, "He loved me, and gave Himself for me." The doctrine of general redemption, which teaches men to say, "Oh, yes; we are all sinners, you know; Christ died for us, for He died for us all," lays a very poor foundation for comfort. We need not so much a general as a personal redemption, a redemption which actually redeems, and redeems us as individuals. The great sacrifice for the sin of man must become to us a personal atonement, for only so can we realize its efficacy. You must each one bring Christ unto the Father, taking Him into your hands by simple faith. No other price must be there; but that price must be brought by every individual, or else there is no acceptable coming to God.

It was *absolutely essential* that each one should bring the half shekel of redemption money; for redemption is the only way in which you and I can be accepted of God. If birth could have done it, they had the privilege beyond all doubt; for they had Abraham to their father: they were lineally descended from the three great patriarchs, and they might have said, "We be Abraham's seed, and were never in bondage to any man." Nay, but salvation is not of blood, nor of birth, nor of the will of the flesh: salvation is by redemption, and even the true child of Abraham must bring his redemption money. So must you, you child of godly parents, find salvation by the redemption which is in Christ Jesus, or be lost forever. Do not believe the falsehood of certain modern divines, that you children of godly parents do not need to be converted because you are born so nobly and brought up so tenderly by your parents. You are by nature heirs of wrath even as others. "Ye must be born again," and ye must be personally redeemed as well as heathen children, or else you will perish, though the blood of ministers, martyrs, and apostles should be running in your veins. Redemption is the only ground of acceptance before God, and not godly birth, or pious education.

There were many, no doubt, in the camp of Israel who were men of station and substance; but *they* must bring the ransom money, or die amid their wealth. Others were wise-hearted and skillful in the arts, yet must they be redeemed or die. Rank could not save the princes, nor office spare the elders: every man of Israel must be redeemed; and no man could pass the muster-roll without his half shekel, whatever he might say, or do, or be. God was their God because He had redeemed them out of the house of bondage, and they were His people because He had "put a redemption between his people and the Egyptians." Well did David ask, "What one nation in the earth is like thy people, even like Israel, whom God went to redeem for a people to himself?"

Note well that every Israelitish man must be *alike redeemed*, and redeemed with the like, nay, with the same redemption. "The rich shall not give more, and the poor shall not give less than half a shekel." Every man requires redemption, the one as well as the other. Kings on their thrones must be redeemed as well as prisoners in their dungeons; the philosopher must be redeemed as well as the peasant; the preacher as much as the profligate, and the moralist as certainly as the prostitute or the thief. The redemption money for every person must be the same, for all have sinned and are in like condemnation.

And it must be *a redemption that meets the divine demand*, because, you see, the Lord not only says that they must each bring half a shekel, no more, no less, but it must be "the shekel of the sanctuary,"—not the shekel of commerce, which might be debased in quality or diminished by wear and tear, but the coin must be according to the standard shekel laid up in the holy place. To make sure of it Moses defines exactly how much a shekel was worth, and what its weight was—"A shekel is twenty gerahs." So you must bring to God the redemption which He has appointed—the blood and righteousness of Christ—nothing more, nothing less. The ransom of Christ is perfection, and from it there must be no varying. The price must satisfy the divine demand, and that to the full.

Note that the price appointed did effectually redeem so far as the type could go. Some rejoice in a redemption which does not redeem, for the general redemption by which all men are supposed to be redeemed leaves multitudes in bondage, and they go to hell despite this kind of redemption. Therefore we do preach a particular and special redemption of God's own chosen and believing people: these are effectually and really ransomed, and the precious price once paid for them has set them free, neither shall any plague of vengeance smite them, for the redemption money has procured them eternal deliverance.

This type is full of instruction: the more it is studied the richer will it appear. Every man that is numbered among the children of Israel, and permitted to serve God by going out to war, or to take upon him the duties of citizenship, must, as he is numbered, be redeemed. So must every one of us, if we are truly God's people and God's servants, find our right to be so in the fact of our redemption by Christ Jesus our Lord. This is the joy and glory of each one of us: "Thou hast redeemed me, O Lord God of truth."

Now we turn to the second of our texts, and there we learn a very remarkable fact. In the thirty-eighth chapter, verse twenty-five, we find that this mass of silver which was paid, whereby six hundred and three thousand five hundred and fifty men were redeemed, each one paying his half shekel, came to a great weight of silver. It must have weighed something over four tons, and this was dedicated to the use of the tabernacle: the special application of the precious metal was to make sockets into which the boards which made the walls of the tabernacle should be placed. The mass of silver made up one hundred talents, and these upheld the fifty boards of the holy place. They were in a wilderness, constantly moving, and continually shifting the tabernacle. Now, they might have dug out a foundation in the sand, or on coming to a piece of rock where they could not dig, they might have cut out foundations with great toil; but the Lord appointed that they should carry the foundation of the tabernacle with them. A talent of silver, weighing, I suppose, close upon one hundred pounds, was either formed into the shape of a wedge, so as to be driven into the soil, or else made into a solid square plate to lie upon it. In the wedge or plate were made mortises, into which the tenons of the boards could be readily fitted. These plates of silver fitted the one into the other, tenon and mortise wise, and thus they made a compact parallelogram, strengthened at the corners with double plates, and formed one foundation, movable when taken to pieces, yet very secure as a whole. *This foundation was made of the redemption money.* See the instructive emblem! The foundation of the worship of Israel was redemption. The dwelling-place of the Lord their God was founded on atonement. All the boards of incorruptible wood and precious gold stood upon the redemption price, and the curtains of fine linen, and the veil of matchless workmanship, and the whole structure rested on nothing else but the solid mass of silver which had been paid as the redemption money of the people. There was only one exception, and that was at the door where was the entrance to the holy place. There the pillars were set upon sockets of brass, perhaps because, as there was much going in and out of the priests, it was not meet that they should tread upon the token of redemption. The blood of the Paschal lamb, when Israel came out of Egypt, was sprinkled on the lintel and the two side posts; but out of reverence to that blood it was not be sprinkled on the threshold. Everything was done to show that atonement is to be the precious foundation of all holy things, and everything to prevent a slighting or disregard of it. Woe unto that man of whom it shall ever be said, "He hath trodden under foot the Son of God, and hath counted the blood of the covenant, wherewith he was sanctified, an unholy thing."

I do not for a moment bring before you the type of the text as a proof of doctrine; but I intend to use it simply as an illustration. It seems to me to be a very striking, full, and suggestive emblem, setting forth most clearly certain precious truths. I feel I am quite safe in using this illustration, because it is one among a group of acknowledged types, and could not have been given without a reason. I do not see why they could not have made the foundation sockets of iron, or why they could not have been content with tent pins and cords as in other cases of tent building: I see no reason in the necessity of the case why they must be sockets of silver; there must have been another reason. Why was that particular silver prescribed? Why must the redemption money be used, and nothing else? Surely there is a teaching here if we will but see it.

Moreover, this does not stand alone; for when the Tabernacle was succeeded by the Temple redemption was still conspicuous in the foundation. What was the foundation of the Temple? It was the rock of Mount Moriah. And what was the hill of Moriah but the place where in many lights redemption and atonement had been set forth. It was there that Abraham drew the knife to slay Isaac: a fair picture of the Father offering up His Son. It was there the ram was caught in the thicket and was killed instead of Isaac: fit emblem of the Substitute accepted instead of man. Later still, it was on Mount Moriah that the angel, when David attempted to number the people without redemption money, stood with his sword drawn. There David offered sacrifices and burnt offerings. The offering was accepted and the angel sheathed his sword—another picture of that power of redemption by which mercy rejoices against judgment. And there the Lord uttered the memorable sentence, "It is enough, stay now thine hand." This "enough" is the crown of redemption. Even as the Great Sacrifice Himself said, "It is finished," so does the Great Accepter of the sacrifice say, "enough." What a place of redemption was the hill of Zion! Now, if the temple was built on a mount which must have been specially selected because there the types of redemption were most plentiful, I feel that without an apology I may boldly take this first fact that the building of the tabernacle in the wilderness was based and grounded upon redemption money, and use it for our instruction. With this much of preface we will now fall to and feed upon the spiritual meal which is set before us. O for grace to feast upon the heavenly bread that we may grow thereby. Spirit of the living God, be pleased to help us in this matter.

I. First, I want you to view this illustration as teaching us something about God in relation to man. The tent in the wilderness was typical of God's coming down to man to hold intercourse with him: the fiery cloudy pillar visible outside, and the bright light of the shekinah, visible to him who was called to enter once a year into the innermost sanctuary, shining over the mercy seat—these were the tokens of the special presence of the Deity in the center of the camp of Israel. The Lord seems to teach us, in relation to His dealing with men, that *He will meet man in the way of grace only on the footing of redemption.* He treats with man concerning love and grace within His holy shrine; but the basis of that shrine must be atonement. Rest assured, dear friends, that there is no meeting with God on our part except through Jesus Christ our Redeemer. I am of Luther's mind when he said, "I will have nothing to do with an absolute God." God out of Christ is a terror to us. Even in Christ, remember, He is a consuming fire, for even "our God is a consuming fire"; but what He must be out of Christ, may none of us ever know.

> Till God in human flesh I see,
>   My thoughts no comfort find;
> The holy, just, and sacred Three
>   Are terrors to my mind.
>
> But if Immanuel's face appear,
>   My hope, my joy begins;
> His name forbids my slavish fear,
>   His grace removes my sins.

You must not attempt to have audience with God at first upon the footing of election. It were presumptuous to attempt to come to the electing Father except through the atoning Son. "No man," saith Christ, "cometh to the Father but by me." Never attempt to speak with God on the footing of your own sanctification; for very soon you will come to bringing your legal righteousness before Him, and that will provoke Him. Always enter the holy place with the thought, "I know that my Redeemer liveth." "Not without blood": recollect that! Into the holy place went the high priest once every year, "not without blood." There can be no coming of God to man on terms of peace except through the one great Sacrifice: that must be the foundation of it all.

Nay, and not only God's coming to us, but *God's abiding with us is upon the same foundation*; for the tabernacle was, so to speak, the house of God—the place where God especially dwelt among His people, as He said: "I will dwell in them, and walk in them." But He never dwelt among them in anything but in a tent that was based upon the silver of the redemption money; and you, dear friend, if you have ever walked with God, can only maintain your fellowship by resting where you did at first, as a poor sinner redeemed by your Savior. They have asked me to rise sometimes to a higher platform, and come to God as a sanctified person. Yes, but a rock, though it may be lower than the little wooden stage which some erect upon it, is safer to stand upon; and I do believe that those who walk with God, according to their attainments, and imaginary perfections, have climbed up to a rotten stage, which will fall under them ere long. I know no mode of standing before God today but that which I had at first. I am unworthy still in myself, but accepted in the Beloved! Guilty in myself, and lost and ruined; but still received, blessed, and loved, because of the person and work of Christ. The Lord cannot dwell with you, my dear friend, you will soon have broken fellowship and be in the dark, if you attempt to walk with Him because you feel sanctified, or because you have been active in His service, or because you know much, or because you are an experienced believer. No! no! no! The Lord will only abide with us in that tabernacle whose every board is resting upon the silver foundation of redemption by His own dear Son.

There can, beloved, be no sort of *communion* between God and us except through the atonement. Do you want to pray? You cannot speak with God except through Jesus Christ. Do you wish to praise? You cannot bring the censer full of smoking incense except through Christ. It is only within those foundations of silver that you can speak to God, or hear Him speak comfortably with you. Would you hear a voice out of the excellent glory? Do you pray that the great Father would speak with you as with His dear children? Expect it through Jesus Christ, for "through him we have access by one Spirit unto the Father." Even through Jesus. The tabernacle of communion even to him that lives nearest to God must be built upon the redemption price. Free grace and dying love must be the golden bells which ring upon our garments when we go into the holy place to speak with the Most High.

The tabernacle was the place of *holy service*, where the priest all day long offered sacrifice of one kind and another unto the Most High. And you and I serve God as priests, for He has made us a royal priesthood. But how and where can we exercise our priesthood? Everywhere as to this world; but before God, the foundation of the temple wherein we stand, and the ground of the acceptance of our priesthood, is redemption. The priests offered their sacrifice not in groves of man's planting, or on high hills, which were the natural strength of the land, but within the space marked out by the silver slabs of atonement money, and so must we worship and serve within redemption lines. If we come under the idea of legal merit, and suppose that there is a natural goodness in our prayers, or in our praises, in our observances of Christian ceremonies, or in almsgiving, or in zealous testimony, we make a great mistake, and we shall never be so accepted. We must bring our offerings unto that court which is fenced about by the foundation most precious which God has laid of old, even the merit of His dear Son. We are accepted in the Beloved, and in no other manner; we are shut in within the foundation which Christ has laid of old, not with corruptible things as with silver and gold, but with His own most precious blood.

Thus much, dear brethren, upon one view of this subject. May you learn much of God in His relation to man while you meditate thereon at your leisure and are taught of the Holy Ghost.

II. I think we may, in the second place, apply this illustration to CHRIST IN HIS DIVINE PERSON. The Tabernacle was the type of our Lord Jesus Christ, for God dwells among men in Christ. "He tabernacled among us, and we beheld his glory," says the apostle. God dwelleth not in temples made with hands, that is to say, of this building; but the Temple of God is Christ Jesus, "in whom dwelleth all the fullness of the Godhead bodily."

Our Lord is thus the Tabernacle which the Lord hath pitched and not man; and *our first and fundamental idea of Him must be in His character as Redeemer*. Our Lord does not come to us in other characters, and in them all He is right glorious; but unless we receive Him as Redeemer we have missed the essence of His character, the foundation idea of Him. As the tent in the wilderness was founded upon the redemption money, so our idea and conception of Christ must be first of all that "He is the propitiation for our sins"; and I say this, though it may seem unnecessary to say it, because Satan is very crafty, and He leads many from plain truth by subtle means. I remember a sister, who had been a member of a certain denomination, who was converted to God in this place, though she had been a professed Christian for years. She said to me, "I have hitherto believed only in Christ crucified: I worshiped Him as about to come in the second Advent to reign with His people, but I never had a sense of guilt, neither did I go to Him as putting away my sin; and hence I was not saved." When she began to see herself as a sinner she found her need of a Redeemer. Atonement must enter into our first and chief idea of the Lord Jesus. "We preach Christ *crucified*": we preach Him glorified, and delight to do so; but still the main point upon which the eye of a sinner must rest, if he would have peace with God, must be Christ crucified for sin. "God forbid that I should glory save in the cross of our Lord Jesus Christ." Do, then, my dear hearer, let the very foundation of your faith in Christ be your view of Him as ransoming you from the power of sin and Satan. Some say they admire Christ as an example, and well they may; they can never find a better: but Jesus Christ will never be truly known and followed if He be viewed only as an example, for He is infinitely more than that. Neither can any man carry out the project of being like Christ, unless he first knows Him as making atonement for sin, and as giving power to overcome sin through His blood. Some writers have looked upon Christ from one point of view and some from another, and there is no book that is more likely to sell than a *Life of Christ*, but the most essential view of Him is to be had from the cross foot. No complete life of Christ has been written yet. All the lives of Christ that have yet been written amount to about one drop of broth, while the four Evangelists are as a whole bullock. The pen of inspiration has accomplished what all the quills in the world will never be able to do again, and there is no need they should. However much we dwell upon the holiness of our Lord, we cannot complete His picture unless we describe Him as the sinner's ransom. He is white, but He is ruddy too. Rutherford said, "O then, come and see if he be not a red man. In His suffering for us He was wet with His own blood. Is He not well worthy of your love?" When he cometh forth in the vesture dipped in blood many shun Him, they cannot bear the atoning sacrifice; but He is never in our eyes so matchlessly lovely as when we see Him bearing our sins in His own body on the tree, and putting away transgression by making Himself the Substitute for His people.

Let this then be your basis idea of Christ—"He has redeemed us from the curse of the law." Indeed, in reference to Christ, we must regard His redemption as the basis of His triumphs and His glory—"the sufferings of Christ and the glory that shall follow." We cannot understand any work that He has performed unless we understand His vicarious sacrifice. Christ is a lock without a key, He is a labyrinth without a clue, until you know Him as the Redeemer. You have spilt the letters on the floor, and you cannot make out the character of the Wonderful till first you have learned to spell the words—atonement by blood. This is the deepest joy of earth and the grandest song in heaven. "For thou wast slain, and hast redeemed us unto God by thy blood."

I beg you to observe, in connection with our text, that as the foundation of the Tabernacle was very valuable, so our Lord Jesus as our Redeemer is *exceedingly precious to us*. His redemption is made with His precious blood. The redemption money was of pure and precious metal, a metal that does not lose weight in the fire. "The redemption of the soul is precious." What a redemption price hath Christ given for us; yea, what a redemption price He is! Well did Peter say, "Unto you that believe he is precious": silver and gold are not to be mentioned in comparison with Him. To me it is very instructive that the Israelites should have been redeemed with silver in the form of half-shekels, because there are many who say, "These old-fashioned divines believe in the mercantile idea of the atonement." Exactly so: we always did and always shall use a metaphor which is so expressive as to be abhorred by the enemies of the truth. The mercantile idea of the atonement is the Biblical idea of the atonement. These people were redeemed, not with lumps of uncoined silver, but with money used in commerce. Paul saith, "Ye are not your own: ye are bought"—listen—"*with a price*"—to give us the mercantile idea beyond all question. "Bought with a price" is double mercantile. What say you to this, ye wise refiners, who would refine the meaning out of the Word of the Lord? Such persons merely use this expression about the "mercantile idea" as a cheap price of mockery, because in their hearts they hate atonement altogether, and the idea of substitution and expiation by vicarious sacrifice is abhorrent to them. Therefore hath the Lord made it so plain, so manifest that they may stumble at this stumbling-stone, "whereunto also," methinks, as Peter saith, "they were appointed." To us, at any rate, the redemption price which is the foundation of all is exceedingly precious.

But there is one other thing to recollect in reference to Christ, namely, that *we must each one view Him as our own*, for out of all the grown up males that were in the camp of Israel, when they set up the tabernacle, there was not one but had a share in its foundation. We read in Exodus 35:25 and 26, "And all the women that were wise hearted did spin with their hands, and brought that which they had spun, both of blue, and of purple, and of scarlet, and of fine linen. And all the women whose heart stirred them up in wisdom spun goats' hair." The men could not spin, perhaps; they did not understand that art; but every man had his half a shekel in the foundation. I want you to think of that. Each believer has a share in Christ as his redemption: nay, I dare not say a share in Him, for He is all mine, and He is all yours. Brother and sister, have you by faith laid hold upon a whole Christ and said, "He has paid the price for me"? Then you have an interest in the very fundamental idea of

Christ. Perhaps you are not learned enough to have enjoyed your portion in certain other aspects of our Lord; but if you are a believer, however weak you are, though you are like the poor among the people of Israel, you have your half shekel in the foundation. I delight to think of that. I have my treasure in Christ; "my Beloved is mine." Do you say He is yours? I do not deny it. So He is, but "He is mine." If you deny that fact we will quarrel at once, for I do aver that "my Beloved is mine." Moreover, by His purchase, "I am His." "So am I," say you. Quite right: I am glad you are; but I know that "I am His." There is nothing like getting a firm, personal hold and grip of Christ: my half shekel is in the basis of the tabernacle; my redemption money is in the divinely glorious building of grace; my redemption is in the death of Christ, which is the foundation of all.

III. Time fails me, and yet I have now a third thought to lay before you very briefly. The tabernacle was a type of THE CHURCH OF GOD as the true place of divine indwelling. What and where is the church of God? The true church is founded upon redemption. Every board of shittim wood was tenoned and mortised into the sockets of silver made of the redemption money, and every man that is in the church of God is united to Christ, rests upon Christ, and cannot be separated from Him. If that is not true of you, my dear hearer, you are not in the church of God. You may be in the church of England or of Rome, you may be in this church or some other; but unless you are joined to Christ, and He is the sole foundation upon which you rest, you are not in the church of God. You may be in no visible church whatever, and yet, if you are resting upon Christ, you are a part of the true house of God on earth.

Christ is *a sure foundation for the church*: for the tabernacle was never blown down. It had no foundation but the talents of silver; and yet it braved every desert storm. The wilderness is a place of rough winds—it is called a howling wilderness; but the sockets of silver held the boards upright, and the holy tent defied the rage of the elements. To be united to Christ by faith is to be built on a sure foundation. His church will never be overthrown let the devil send what hurricanes he may.

And it was *an invariable foundation*, for the tabernacle always had the same basis wherever it was placed. One day it was pitched on the sand, another on a good piece of arable ground, a third time on a grass plot, and tomorrow on a bare rock; but it always had the same foundation. The bearers of the holy furniture never left the silver sockets behind. Those four tons of silver were carried in their wagons, and put out first as the one and only foundation of the holy place. Now, the learned tell us that the nineteenth century requires "advanced thought." I wish the nineteenth century was over; I have heard it bragged about so much that I am sick of the nineteenth century. We are told that this is too sensible a century to need or accept the same gospel as the first, second, and third centuries. Yet these were the centuries of martyrs, the centuries of heroes, the centuries that conquered all the gods of Greece and Rome, the centuries of holy glory, and all this because they were the centuries of the gospel; but now we are so enlightened that our ears ache for something fresh, and under the influence of another gospel, which is not another, our beliefs are dwindling down from alps to anthills, and we ourselves from giants to pygmies. You will want a microscope soon to see Christian faith in the land, it is getting to be so small and scarce. By God's grace some of us abide by the ark of the covenant, and mean to preach the same gospel which the saints received at the first. We shall imitate those who, having had a silver foundation at the first, had a silver foundation for the tabernacle, even till they came to the promised land. It is a foundation that we dare not change. It must be the same, world without end, for Jesus Christ is the same yesterday, today, and forever.

IV. Fourthly, and lastly, I think this tabernacle in the wilderness may be viewed as a type of THE GOSPEL, for the gospel is the revelation of God to man. The tent in the wilderness was the gospel according to Moses. Now, as that old gospel in the wilderness was, such must ours be, and I want to say just two or three things very plainly, and have done.

Redemption, atonement in the mercantile idea, must be *the foundation of our theology—doctrinal, practical, and experimental.* As to doctrine, they say a fish stinks first at the head, and men first go astray in their brains. When once there is anything wrong in your belief as to redemption you are wrong all through. I believe in the old rhyme—

> What think you of Christ? is the test
> To try both your state and your scheme,
> You cannot be right in the rest
> Unless you think rightly of HIM.

If you get wrong on atonement you have turned a switch which will run the whole train of your thoughts upon the wrong line. You must know Christ as the Redeemer of His people, and their substitute, or your teaching will give an uncertain sound. As redemption must be the foundation of doctrinal divinity, so it must of practical divinity. "Ye are not your own: ye are bought with a price," must be the source of holiness, and the reason for consecration. The man that does not feel himself to be specially "redeemed from among men" will see no reason for being different from other men. "Christ loved his Church and gave himself *for it*"; he who sees no special giving of Christ for His Church will see no special reason why the Church should give herself to Christ.

Certainly redemption must be the foundation of experimental theology; for what is an experience worth that does not make us every day prize more and more the redeeming blood? Oh, my dear friends, I never knew, though I had some idea of it, what a fool I was till of late years. I tell you that those dreadful pains, which may even make you long for death, will empty you right out, and not only empty you, but make you judge yourself to be a hollow sham, and cause you to loathe yourself, and then it is that you cling to Christ. Nothing but the atoning sacrifice will satisfy me. I have read plenty of books of modern theology, but none of them can heal so much as a pin's prick in the conscience. When a man gets sick in body and heavy in spirit he wants the old-fashioned puritanical theology, the gospel of Calvin, the gospel of Augustine, the gospel of Paul, the gospel of our Lord and Savior Jesus Christ. Our theology as a matter of experience must be based upon redemption.

Ah, brethren, and not only our theology but *our personal hope.* The only gospel that I have to preach is that which I rest upon myself—"Who his own self bore our sins in his own body on the tree." "For the chastisement of our peace was upon him, and with his stripes we are healed": "He bore the sin of many, and made intercession for the transgressors." Oh, dear hearers, build on that and you will never fail; but if you do not take Christ's redemption as the foundation of your hope—I do not care who you are—you may be very learned, but you know nothing at all. The Lord make you to know that you know nothing, and then you will know something: and when you have learned as much as that, may He teach you the redemption of His Son, and reveal Christ in you.

This, beloved, is henceforth *the burden of our service, and the glory of our life.* Those silver sockets were very precious, but very weighty. I dare say the men who had to move them sometimes thought so. Four tons and more of silver make up a great load. O blessed, blissful draught, to have to put the shoulder to the collar to draw the burden of the Lord—the glorious weight of redemption. My soul, blessed art thou to be made a laboring ox for Christ; ever to be bearing among this people the divinely precious load of the foundation which Christ has laid for His people. You, young brethren, that preach, mind you always carry your four tons of silver: preach a full and rich redemption all of you. You who go to the Sunday-school, do not let the children have a place to live in that has no foundation: the first wind will blow it over, and where will they be? Left naked under the ruins of that in which they had hoped. Lay Christ for a foundation. You cannot do better, for God Himself has said, "Behold, I lay in Zion a chief corner stone, elect, precious." Lay this silver foundation wherever you are.

Aye, but though the ingots were heavy to carry, every Israelite felt proud to think that that tabernacle had a foundation of silver. You Amalekites out there cannot see the silver footing of it all; you Moabites cannot perceive it. All you can see is the badger skins outside—the rough exterior of the tent. You say, "That tent is a poor place to be a temple: that gospel is a very simple affair." No doubt it is to you, but you never saw the silver sockets, you never saw the golden boards, you never saw the glory of the inside of the place lit up by the seven-branched candlesticks, and glorious with the presence of God. Brethren, redemption is our honor and delight.

> In the cross of Christ I glory
>   Towering o'er the wrecks of time:
> All the light of sacred story
>   Gathers round its head sublime.

This the first and this the last; the bleeding Lamb slain from before the foundation of the world, and yet living and reigning when the earth's foundations shall dissolve. That blessed Lamb of God is in the midst of the throne, and His people shall all be with Him, forever triumphant. He is the Alpha and Omega, the beginning and the ending, the foundation and the headstone. O Savior of sinners, glory be to thy name. Amen and amen.

THE ALTAR

SERMON NOS. 831, 832
DELIVERED ON LORD'S DAY MORNING, SEPTEMBER 20, 1868.
PORTION OF SCRIPTURE READ BEFORE SERMON—HEBREWS 10.

The altar that sanctifieth the gift—Matthew 23:19.

HAD man remained perfect, his communion with God would have been as unrestricted as that of an obedient child with an affectionate father. Adam might have worshiped his God acceptably anywhere, at any time, and in any mode he chose. Had there been literal offerings as well as sacrifices of praise, he might have brought before his God the delicious fruits of the garden, or poured forth libations from Eden's golden-sanded river; and these might have been presented on the high places of the earth, or in the shady groves, or amid the verdure of the plains—anywhere the Lord would have received the grateful offerings of men whose hearts were perfect towards Himself. But the fall intervened. Man became a rebel to his King. Man by his depravity of nature was placed far off from God, and his once unrestricted fellowship with heaven was brought to an end. Mercy gave tidings of renewed communion, but the good news came by slow degrees, and meanwhile if man would approach his God it must be under rules and regulations which should remind him of his changed estate. If he be permitted to draw near to his offended God at all it is a great favor, and he shall be made to learn by the way of coming how great that favor is. He shall, ere a fuller ceremonial is revealed, only be allowed to offer a bleeding sacrifice. He shall not present to God that which costeth him nothing—the growth of the soil—but he must bring a victim from his flock or herd, and by his own hand he must cause the victim to suffer and die, for God will accept only a life poured forth in blood as a sacrifice from man, whose own life was forfeited to justice. And while rules and regulations were laid down as to sacrifices, altars were also under commandment—they must be guilt of earth or unhewn stone; and at the last all altars of burnt-offering were suppressed save one only, the consecrated brazen altar of the tabernacle. All the rest of the world was left altarless. One spot was selected, and only one. First in the place where the tabernacle was pitched, and afterwards the temple of Jerusalem, the altar for bloody sacrifice was set up; and everywhere else when men offered to God on their high places, they did so in defiance of His command: prophets might make exceptions to the rule, but for the many the unbending rule was that all sacrifice must be made at the one holy altar.

Brethren, the outward truth clearly reveals to us its inner meaning. We must, had we remained innocent, have brought before God every day the thank-offerings of our hearts without a mediator, but we are guilty, and our holiest acts are the deeds of imperfect men, and our purest worship is the worship of fallen beings. Who can bring a clean thing out of an unclean? Not one. And before we can be accepted in our best things, there must be the shedding of the blood which taketh away sin. There is no door of acceptance for us except through the merit of the great Surety who solemnly laid down His life for His people; there is but one way by which we who have been washed in the blood of Jesus can offer unto God our humble service and our loving hearts, namely, through Jesus Christ who stands as the type of that one and only permitted altar; to Him we must bring ourselves as a living sacrifice, holy and acceptable unto God; for it is only by Jesus Christ that this reasonable service can be accepted of the Most High. In the one altar of the tabernacle or the temple we see a type of the person and merit of our glorious Lord Jesus, and learn that apart from Him there is no acceptable worship—for this is the truth which we desire this morning to teach.

Many mistakes have been made through applying the emblem of an altar to matters to which it has no correct reference. There was but one authorized altar of Jehovah, as we have already noted: that one altar finds its fulfillment in the person of our Lord Jesus Christ; but through loose talking, if not through doctrinal error, other things have come to be called altars which are not so, certainly not such altars as meet the requirements of my text, for they do not sanctify the gift, and are not greater than the gift. Frequently have we seen the *cross* spoken of as an altar. Upon the cross as upon an altar, our Lord is said to have been offered as the great Sacrifice for sin; but the expression is mere poetic flourish, and no more. As a man, Jesus died on the tree, and the wood to which He was nailed, was a gibbet, and not an altar; it was never appointed as such by God, nor is it ever so called in His Word. The cross of wood was simply the instrument of our Savior's torture and death, and is no more to be reverenced than the whips of Pilate or the spittle of the scoffers. The cross used at Calvary, and all other crosses, whether of wood, or stone, or gold, are no more to be esteemed than the same material shaped in circles or squares. Indeed, if we are to attach any kind of moral quality to the material and visible form of the cross, it is rather a thing accursed than a thing to be blessed, for the divine curse fell on every one that was hanged on a tree. Certainly this fancied altar of the cross in no way sanctified the victim. What honor did our Lord Jesus derive from the tree on which He hung? What virtue came from this so-called altar to make God's unspeakable gift acceptable? A piece of wood and nothing more was that cross. It could give no sanctity to Christ, and we ought never to use words concerning that piece of timber which would in any way lead men to associate its material substance with the meritorious work of Christ. It is to be feared that the constant use of the emblem of the cross, in itself as innocent as an oval or a square, often leads men into a species of idolatry. When I see a cross embossed on Bibles, wrought out in jewelry or fashioned gold, I cannot but think how contradictory it all seems: the cross, a thing of shame, the instrument of our Lord's execution by those who abhorred Him, and yet worn as an ornament! Surely men might as well wear at their girdles the dagger with which their friend was stabbed! Why do not the ladies wear a gibbet from their necks? For what more or less is a cross? Such was not the cross which Paul gloried in; he would have despised such idolatry. He gloried in the gospel, which is a spiritual cross, and he says of it, "By which the world is crucified to me, and I unto the world." Which of those cross wearers was ever crucified to the world by the cross which dangles on their bosoms? The sign of the cross when reverenced is much the same as the brazen serpent when Israel fell to adoring it: it must be broken, and Christian people should discountenance its use. Clearly it is no altar.

We occasionally read, and especially in poetry, of the "altar of the heart," but is not that also a misnomer, and may it not one day lead to doctrinal error? The heart an altar! It certainly does not sanctify the gift. If there be anything in the gift that is acceptable to God its sanctity must come from its being offered on a very different altar than that of our poor, corrupt, and depraved heart. I know the meaning is, that sincerity makes our service acceptable, but I doubt the truth of that assertion, for however sincere our devotions may be, apart from the atonement of Jesus, God accepteth them not. Sincerity there must be or there can be no offering made to God at all; but still all the sincerity that ever dwelt in human bosom could not make an offering to be received of God, unless faith found an altar in Jesus, and relied for acceptance upon the grand sacrifice and finished atonement of the Mediator. Talk not quite so loosely lest mischief come of it.

A more common and dangerous mistake, however, is to call the table which is used for the purpose of the Lord's Supper an altar. If it had been called a house, or a horse, or an angel, either title would have been quite as correct a name, for there is no likeness whatever between the table of communion and an altar. The mistake is egregious, and the mischief flowing from it is most terrible. All through Scripture we read of the communion table, but never find it either plainly, obscurely, directly, or indirectly called an altar. Jesus said, "The hand of him that betrayeth me is with me on the table"; he did not say, "The traitor is officiating with me at this altar," and yet surely that first celebration was quite as complete as any which have succeeded it! Paul saith, "Ye cannot be partakers of the Lord's table and of the table of the devil," and that too in a connection in which he would surely have said the Lord's altar had the term been allowable. Neither, except by the most violent straining, can there be found any passage of Scripture which represents this table, used to celebrate a feast, as an altar for the consumption of a sacrifice. Indeed, what sacrifice do the modern priests place upon their so-called altar? See, they bring forth bread and wine, fit furniture for a table, but where are the fire and the wood for a burnt-offering? If the table be an altar, then according to our Lord, it is better and holier than the bread and wine placed upon it, for the "altar sanctifieth the gift"; and yet our modern ritualists will hardly venture to say that their altars of wood and stone are really more holy than the body and blood of Jesus Christ, which they profess to offer thereon. I know not to what length folly may go, but one thing I marvel at, if these gentlemen must needs have a material altar, why do they not follow the scriptural form thereof? Why do they make a kind of sideboard or dresser of it, by setting it against a wall? a thing that was never heard of in all the world before, for everywhere altars are so placed as to be compassed about. David said, "So will I compass thine altar, O Lord." Elijah digged a trench about the altar. The altar of the Old Testament could be surrounded, but whence came these new-fashioned erections, which are not even according to the fashion of Judaism? From what heathenism did they borrow their steps to the altar, such things being forbidden of the Lord? Whence came their high altar? What means those ornaments on an altar? Strange intrusions these for an altar! Surely they must have taken their models from those altars of Baal, of which we read that there were images on high above them; for how commonly do we see either their pieces of plate with superstitious symbols, or their sumptuous common prayer books, adorned with silver crucifixes, for what is worse, pictures and images, and candles, and I know not what of trumpery besides? Let us never therefore use the term altar as synonymous with communion table, lest we countenance deadly error. Of all delusions that have ever happened to the human race, surely that of transubstantiation has been at once the most absurd and the most profane, and both that doctrine and all growing out of it should be protested against by every sincere Christian, especially at this dreary time when superstition is daily increasing. If ever we shall have Popery back in this land, it will owe much of its advance to the misuse of terms. Call not you a table an altar, lest ye come to bow before it as the Popish heathen do. Use it as a table of fellowship and communion, but never dream of it as an altar. The one altar which sanctifieth the gift is the person and merit of our Lord Jesus Christ, and nothing else.

Come we then to the consideration of this subject. I shall first refer you to the passage in the book of Exodus, in which the great brazen altar of the tabernacle was described, and try to *work out the type as it reveals our Lord;* and then, secondly, I shall *ask a few practical questions.*

I. In the twenty-seventh chapter of the book of Exodus you have the Lord's command: "And thou shall make an altar of shittim wood, five cubits long, and five cubits broad; the altar shall be four-square: and the height thereof shall be three cubits. And thou shalt make the horns of it upon the four corners thereof: his horns shall be of the same: and thou shalt overlay it with brass." Jesus Christ is the ANTITYPE OF THIS BRAZEN ALTAR. All that it signified typically we have in Him.

And first the altar typifies our Lord, if we consider *the use of it.* The altar had at least two uses. First, to sanctify that which was put upon it, and then, secondly, to sustain it or bear it up, while the fire was consuming it. Our Lord Jesus is Himself the Sacrifice as well as the Altar. Whatever is offered to God by Him or by us is accepted, because of the excellence of His person. As God and perfect man in one person, all that He does and all that He presents becomes acceptable because of the excellence that dwelleth in Him; and so, also, He bears and sustains all the violent heat both of the fire of divine wrath and the fire of divine presence, which consumeth the sacrifice put upon the altar. How our Lord Jesus Christ lifts up our gifts towards heaven! How of old did He lift up our sins! And when the holy flame descended and consumed Him, as the great victim for human guilt, what strength and power there was in Him, fitting Him like an altar of brass to endure all those furious flames! And how today does He sweetly lift up before God all the offerings of His people, and renders them acceptable in Himself! The old Puritans were wont to say that the altar represented the deity of Christ, because the deity of Christ lent power as well as virtue to the manhood of Christ; but may we not consider His entire person to be the sustaining and sanctifying altar of mediation? As the one appointed Mediator for mankind, He puts a value into the gifts of His people, and His own sacrifice derives efficacy from His person and character. In Him we are able to bear the presence of God when He accepts us, for our God is a consuming fire, and we can only meet Him in Jesus; it is only on the brazen altar that the heavenly fire can consume our sacrifice. The wrath which consumes Jesus has endured once for all; that glory of consuming love we are able to learn through our union with the incarnate God. Let it never then be forgotten by us all that if our souls and bodies, which we offer to God, are to be presented before the Lord, it must be by Christ as an altar; and if we are to be sanctified and rendered acceptable, it must still be by Christ as an altar. There never could be but this one altar for Israel—for all Israel, according to divine appointment, this was the alone altar; every victim must be slaughtered here; every acceptable burnt-offering must be brought here; and so with us. We cannot offer a prayer, much less ourselves, except by Him. There is one Christ for all the saints, one Jesus for you who are grown in grace, one Jesus for those who are but beginners in spiritual things, one Lord Jesus for the black and filthy sinner when he first seeks for mercy, one Lord Jesus for the Christian made perfect when he enters into his rest. One altar for all Israel, and that one altar for all times: for Israel in the days of Moses, for Israel in the days of Solomon, for Israel until the end of the dispensation. You and I come to God by the selfsame road which was traveled by David, and afterwards by the Lord's apostles. Never a believer accepted except in Jesus, in any age, never a word done that was acceptable to God in any period except through Jesus Christ. One altar, and only one for all ages, for the whole chosen seed. We hold this as a truth; let us prize it and defend it.

The place of the altar next deserves your consideration. You will remember that the moment you entered into the door of the tabernacle you saw this altar of burnt-offering, and before you could reach the veil which separated the holy from the most holy place, you must pass hard by the altar. So at the very beginning of the Christian life, the first thing we have to learn is that we approach God through Jesus Christ. Thou knowest nothing of Christianity unless the most prominent thought of thy soul is Jesus as the Mediator between thee and God. Talk not of Christian example or of Christian holy teaching, these things are but secondary; ye must know

Jesus Christ as suffering and pouring out His soul unto death as a propitiation for sin, or you do not know the inner sense of the divine religion of the cross. Nobody could help seeing that brazen altar. Walking with his eyes open through that court, every observer must see it. There was its perpetual smoke and smell—and this even one would perceive—while in itself it was so large and important, that it could not be overlooked. Even so, my hearer, thou canst not abide in the religion of Jesus, even for an hour, without beholding Him and without resting in Him. Thou knowest naught unless thou knowest Him as the Altar of God. The way to the most holy place was by this altar. "No man cometh to the Father but by me." We cannot enter into fellowship with God, nor understand the deep things of God, nor penetrate into the divine arcana or the highest of the doctrines of the truth, except by first passing where the atonement is offered and where Jesus stands, the only Mediator between God and man. How many have tried to learn the doctrines apart from Christ, and how many try to preach them! But they are unedifying, and even lead to mischief. The best of all preaching of doctrines is such as that which we had in Dr. Hawker's day, when he preached election, but it was always election in Christ; when the doctrine of predestination was clearly enough stated, but its sweet relationship to the Lamb of God was always dwelt upon. Let it be our desire when we enter into the deep things of God to view them in relation to Jesus, and pass by the altar to reach the veil.

The form of the altar deserves our attention, as it helps to bring out something more of Christ. The altar was four-square. Where shall we learn to measure the heights and depths, the lengths and breadths of the love of Christ that passeth knowledge? If we may not so measure them just yet, it is satisfactory to know that everything about Christ is well ordered and arranged by infinite wisdom; the altar is not made at haphazard, it is four-square. There is no excess in Him, there is no lack in Him, all that we can need to render our sacrifice acceptable to God we have in Him. Ainsworth saith that the form of four-square represents stability and endurance; and truly our Lord is the same yesterday, today, and forever. Other altars have been overturned, but this never. The saints came to Him thousands of years ago, and there He stood between the porch and the veil: we come to Him today, and He stands there still; and when the ages shall have passed by, and things that men have dreamed to be everlasting shall have melted like the morning's hoarfrost, there shall still be the self-same Savior fixed in His place to offer still the prayers and the praises of His people.

At each corner of the altar was *a horn*. The horn is always the emblem of power; and these horns indicated doubtless the power which lies in the person of Jesus Christ—the power with God on our behalf. We never need be afraid of acceptance in the Beloved when we see what might, what virtue, what sacred merit dwells in Him. God reject His Son! Impossible! The Adored of angels, the eternally Beloved, must be accepted of God. Having given His hands to the nails, and His heart to the spear, having suffered even unto death, it cannot be that the Lord should deny Him and disrespect His sacrifice. He must be forever prevalent with the Most High. Put thyself on the altar, Christian, God must accept thee, for He accepts the victim because of the altar which sanctifieth the gift; He must accept thee, feeble as thou art, for Jesus infuses merit into thee as the altar into the gift. Come with thy tears, come with thy sighs and thy groans, poor trembling one, there is no fear but what thou shalt speed; those four horns indicate how meritorious Jesus is, and He will render thee as acceptable as He is Himself.

The altar, too, while we are describing its form, we must remember, was built originally so low that it was reached by the priests without the use of steps, and, indeed, steps were expressly forbidden, the reason being given that, in going up to the altar, it might not be possible that the nakedness of the priest should be discovered. God would have nothing indecorous in His service. The spiritual meaning being, I suppose, that Jesus Christ, when we go to Him, is most accessible. We are not to climb to Him by steps of creature effort, merit, and preparation. Those preparations for Christ, of which so much is made by certain preachers, are all mischievous. Divines will tell you that you must feel this and feel the other, you must pass through that experience and the other, but truly—

> All the fitness he requireth,
> Is to feel your need of him.

And this He gives you. There are no steps up to the altar, there are no human preparations for Christ. You may come to Him just as you are, for He is waiting to be gracious. Solomon's altar in the temple was on a large scale, to show the greatness of our Lord's power and grace; and in order to maintain proportions, it was made much too high to be reached without some mode of ascent—and it is supposed, therefore, that the priests reached it by a gradual incline, since steps must not be made to it. And here we should be taught how, in coming to Christ, we ascend towards God. When we draw near unto Him with true hearts, we are elevated thereby. Man is never more truly exalted in spirit than when he bows lowest at the cross foot. Calvary, though it was no mountain, nor scarce a hill, outsoars the Hermons and Pisgahs; its top is nearer heaven than Carmel or Bashan.

> Here it is I find my heaven,
> While upon the cross I gaze.

Let me but tarry there, and if I am not in paradise, I should be, at least, in the suburbs of the New Jerusalem. No truth so dear as Jesus crucified: the altar of His atonement is so low, that a child may reach it, and yet it is so high, that by it we ascend to heaven.

It is notable, and you will kindly look this afternoon into your Bibles, and investigate the matter, that this altar was increased in size in the temple. It was far smaller in the tabernacle than in the temple; so may our conceptions of Christ be ever growing: if we know Him well enough to find that He is sufficient for our present needs, may we yet understand His all sufficiency; if we have discovered something of His excellence, and of the admirable way in which He secures our acceptance with God, may we know this more and more. May Jesus grow upon us, until unable to comprehend Him, we shall rejoice in His exceeding greatness and be filled with His fullness.

I must not forget, in speaking of the form of the altar, also that as the observed passed round it, he would be constantly struck with its bespattered appearance. Entertain not the notion the tabernacle and the temple must have been very pleasant places—we can scarcely imagine anything that must have been more awe inspiring, and even revolting to the mind of the observer, than the court of priests, when sacrificing was being carried on. It must on great occasions have resembled a butcher's shambles, with the addition of smoke and fire. And this brazen altar was so frequently besmeared with blood, and so constantly were bowl-fulls of warm gore thrown at its base, that it must have presented a very ghastly appearance. This was all to teach the observer what a dreadful thing sin is, and how it can only be put away through suffering and death. The Lord did not study attractive aesthetics, He did not prepare a tabernacle that should delight men's tastes; it was rich indeed, but so blood-stained as to be by no means beautiful. No staining of glass to charm the eye, but instead thereof the inwards of slaughtered bullocks. Such sights would disgust the delicate tastes of the fops of this present age. Blood, blood on every side; death, fire, smoke and ashes, varied with the bellowing of dying beasts, and the active exertions of men whose white garments were all crimson with the blood of victims. How clearly did the worshipers see the sternness and severity of the justice of God against human sin, and the intensity of the agony of the great Son of God who was in the fullness of time by His own death to put away all the sins and transgressions of His people! By faith come ye, my brethren, and walk round that blood-stained altar, and as you mark its four-square form and its horns of strength, and see the sacrifices smoking thereon acceptable to God, look down and mark the blood with which its foundations are so completely saturated, and understand how all salvation and all acceptance rests on the atonement of the dying Son of God.

We will pass on to observe, next, *the materials* of which the altar was made, for these also were instructive. It was made of shittim wood, overlaid with brass. The shittim wood is always understood to represent the incorruptible human character of our Lord Jesus, for this which was probably the acacia, was a wood which would not rot, even as Jesus when tempted, even in all points like as we are, yet remained without sin. The brass, of course, was necessary as an outer covering, lest the altar should be consumed by the flames. It had to bear perpetually the blazing and the burning fire; and so we in the brass see the endurance of Christ, how his loins were girt about with power, and how the divinity within sustained the perfect Man while He bore

> All that incarnate God could bear,
> With strength enough and none to spare.

Look on that brass, Christian, with admiring eye. Think how oftentimes it was heated by the fire, and then look upon your Lord, and think how in soul and body He was tortured and tormented for your sins, and reflect how strong He must have been to suffer so as to be able to bear the whole of wrath divine, and make a complete atonement for the transgressions of His elect!

The fire which burnt upon the altar also deserves to be noticed. It was doubtless no common fire of ordinary culinary use. It fell from heaven, and there may have been qualities about which it which rendered it different than any other. For instance, it may have left none of that residuum of ash, and smoke, and filth, that would be found in the use of ordinary fire; it may have been like lightning in its force and pureness. Complaints were always made of the old heathen temples of the abundance of flies and filth found there. Hence the Jews were accustomed in derision to call the idol god Baal, Baal-zebub, or the god of flies, because of the abundance of such noxious creatures found in his temples. Probably there were none such in God's temple, for the Lord's fire slew every unclean thing. This fire had noble and distinct qualities, consuming and blazing after a nobler and diviner sort than ordinary flames; and certainly our Lord Jesus Christ has burning upon His altar no impure flames; love burns there which sprang only from His own bosom; a holy zeal burns there without the slightest admixture of self-love; the Holy Ghost burns there, that purest and best of flames that can rest on mortal men, and there too burned the fire of divine wrath, which was a holy jealousy against sin: and when God Himself comes upon that altar to accept His people, it is a divine acceptance unutterably glorious.

But I must not detain you longer. If you will read the passage at home you will find abundance of matter suggestive of the person and the work of Jesus Christ. To Him must we always come in heart and soul. We know of no holy place now, nor holy days, nor holy implements. Our soul serves God in spirit, for He is a Spirit and seeketh those to worship Him who do so in spirit and in truth. Our soul gives to Jesus Christ pre-eminence in all her trusting, coming only to God through Him, and never thinking that she can either serve, or worship, or live aright, except as she dwells in Christ, and the merit of Christ commends her to the Father. That is the thought, the one thought I wish to bring forward; and though I cannot speak this morning as I would, yet if that abide with you, this hour shall not have been lost time.

II. Now a question or two.

My first inquiry is, *Have you and I always taken care to keep to the one spiritual altar?* The sin of this age is idolatry. The whole tendency of this generation is towards the setting up of other than spiritual altars. The only way to come to God is spiritually through Jesus Christ, but you will find yourself, dear friend, frequently tempted to make something else the vehicle of access to God, and to render homage to Him through some other vehicle. You may depend upon it, that the belief that this building or that any other building is a house of God, a place peculiarly suitable for worship, is idolatry; you are giving to bricks and mortar some little of the honor which is due only to Christ as an altar. If you suppose that there is any more acceptableness to God in a church or a cathedral than in any public hall or in the open air, you have made a material building into an altar, you have gone back to the types and have missed the Antitype, and so far have robbed Christ of a portion of His glory. If you will look upon any material substances as being holy, or, I will add, upon any postures, whether kneeling, standing, or sitting, as having in them any kind of holiness, or if, in fact, you get away from the spiritual in any manner—begin in any sort, or mode, or degree, to attach reverence to the physical and to the material—you have so far wandered away from the simplicity of Christ, you have set up an Antichrist, and you have robbed the Lord Jesus. God will never put away the sin of this land until the belief in material consecration is given up. Thus spoke Isaiah of old: "By this therefore shall the iniquity of Jacob be purged; and this is all the fruit to take away his sin; when he maketh all the stones of the altar as chalkstones that are beaten in sunder, the groves and images shall not stand up." We must down with idols, and learn that there is no more holiness in our parish steeple-houses, called churches, or in our chapels or cathedrals, than in barns and hovels. God abhors our idolatry, and will visit us for it unless we repent and turn from it. We cannot hope, in this England of ours, to see restored to us the purity of the gospel until Protestants cleanse themselves of this Antichristian, Popish belief and reverence for our postures, and places, and men, and days, and books, and I know not what beside. Worship God, men! Demean not yourselves by paying reverence to anything else. Worship God in Jesus Christ. That is the one only canon of worship; in the power of the eternal Spirit approach God through the merits of the Redeemer: and as for your so-called priests, and your churches, and your holy things, away with them! They are not to be borne by reason, much less by men of spiritual minds. Worship God in Jesus Christ, and give the glory due unto His name wholly to Him, but give none of it to things of human devising.

The next question is, *Are there not some among you who have been offering to God without an altar at all?* I mean this: you have been striving, you say, to do your duty; you are an honorable member of the state. You have sought to be religious too, and you have come up with the assembly of God's people. You never forget the Sabbath, nor the offering of your morning and evening prayer, and you believe yourself, therefore, to be among the good and the righteous, and you hope to be accepted at the bar of God. Yes, I see your sacrifice, but where is your altar? For be assured, God will not receive your sacrifice without an altar, and for altars there is but one. You have forgotten, my dear friend, the one great essential thing. According to our text, the altar sanctifies the gift: your gift is not sanctified at all then; it is an unsanctified, unacceptable gift. The whole of your life, though commendable in itself, and to be imitated by others in its outward development, is not accepted of God because you have never placed that life upon the appointed altar of Christ Jesus; you have not offered it to God, having first trusted in Christ and looked to His merit for its acceptance. You have been depending upon yourself, and therefore you are no more likely to be saved than Cain was when he went about to offer a sacrifice of his own, and could not submit to bring the lamb according to divine appointment. Oh, I could weep over some of you who have so much that is good about you, because you forget the Lord Jesus. Why, you have forgotten the One, the main, the essential thing. Those morning and evening prayers of yours, what are they? If you have not seen Jesus on the cross, if you have not looked to His wounds, you have not prayed at all. That helping of the poor which is so kind of you—aye, but if you have not done it for His sake, trusting in Him, who, though He was rich, yet for your sake became poor, you have not done it unto God at all. And if you have been working and going about to establish your own righteousness, and have not submitted yourself to the righteousness of Christ, it will all be a failure. You gentlemen who have brought up your families so well, you honest working men who fight the battle of life so valiantly, oh! it is grievous to think that you should labor in vain, and spend your strength for naught, and bring your bullocks and your rams and sacrifice to God, and they should all be an offense and an abomination, because you do not bring them to the one appointed altar. God help you to think of this and to repent of the folly, and henceforth live in consistency of character as you have done, but make not that your trust: come to Jesus first, and let the rest follow.

Next, my brethren and sisters, another inquiry, for those of us who have brought our offerings and ourselves to God through Jesus Christ. Let me ask whether *we have not often forgotten to attach the importance to the altar which we should have done.* I mean this: I pray, and when my prayer is done, I think within myself, will it prevail? And I remember that I did not plead the blood of Jesus as I ought to have done. I said, "for Jesus' sake"—I should be ashamed to pray except in His name—but did I realize that I could not be acceptable with God in myself? That it must be because of the Redeemer's perfections, sufferings, bloody sweat, passion, and resurrection, that I must be heard? Now my prayer has lost much power if I have not pleaded Christ's work, and Christ's merit, with all my heart, and soul, and strength. To plead the merit of Jesus is the marrow of prayer; good words are but the bone. This is the soul of prayer; this it is that takes heaven by storm: this moves the heart of God—the bringing before God the sacrifice of His dear Son, the making Gethsemane to ring again in the paternal ears, making the cross to shine again before the Father's face, pleading earnestly because Jesus deserves abundantly. Have we not often missed this? And if we have in our prayers, I am sure we have much more in our other engagements. I am afraid we preach without putting the sermon on the brazen altar, and that we distribute our tracts or teach in the Sabbath-school, or talk of Christ with the sick, and do it without presenting the service through the meritorious person of our Lord. Oh! it is blessed when one has preached, and felt, "Well, I have not succeeded as I could desire; I have felt heavy in my Master's service, shut up so that I could not come forth; but still I meant to honor Him, and now, my God, accept my poor service for my Redeemer's sake." This is the way to put our service right on the altar, and there it is sure to speed. Oh, then it is so blessed to know that Jesus sanctifies the gift! The gift was nothing—a poor speech for His name, a scanty gift to His poor saints, but still God receives it as He accepted the bullocks, not for the bullocks' sake, but for the altar's sake; and so will He receive our faulty services for the sake of Jesus, when we offer them through Him. Let your souls anchor themselves to the atonement of Jesus. Cast more cords about yourself, and bind your spirits fast to Him. You are never healthy, you are never strong, you are never happy, you are never lifted up towards heaven except when you abide close to the person of the Son of God made flesh for you. Never journey away from the cross. Seek other truths, and delight in other beauties if you will, but the first truth and the first beauty in heaven and earth is the crucified Redeemer: keep you to Him, and rejoice in Him.

I shall not detain you longer except to say this. Have we, dear friends, as believers, ever fed at this altar? For we have an altar of which they have no right to eat that serve the tabernacle. That is to say, those who trust in ceremonies have no right to Christ; those who think themselves priests above their fellow Christians cannot taste Christ; they are shut out by their own act and deed, they have no right there; but we who do not serve the outward tabernacle, but have come to spiritual worship, we have a right to eat at the altar of Christ. Here is a choice morsel for us, God has accepted us in Christ. Feed on that, Christian; you have condemned yourself but God has accepted you. Men have criticized and censured you, but in Christ God has accepted those imperfect works of yours. Why, is it enough for a courtier if his king smiles; is it not enough for you? Nay, lie not down and groan, and cry, because you have not acted perfectly, but having repented of every omission and transgression, rise up with courage to do better things, because even your worst things have been accepted. Feed on Christ who makes you accepted; feed on the acceptance itself, and so like the priest, commune with God at His table.

And if you have already laid yourself upon the altar of Christ as a reasonable sacrifice, come and do it again. It is very desirable frequently to renew our consecration to Jesus. "Thine are we, thou Son of David, and all that we have." You who have been bought with His blood, drawn nigh to Him, and yield yourselves anew to Him this morning. You own the soft impeachment that you are His in blessed marriage bonds, come, then, and anew declare, "My Lord, take me wholly! Use me, use me to the last ounce! Use me up! Grant that there may not be a hair of my head, nor a drop of my blood, nor a beating of my pulse, which is not thine! Lord, I make no reserve. I give thee my children, my house, my property, my time, my body, my soul, and I do not ask thee to spare me and give me an easy life. Do as thou wilt with me, only glorify thyself in me!" When the bullock was on the altar, the flesh-hook was used to aid in burning it completely—the priest desired that there should be nothing of the offering left. "So, Lord, if thou usest the flesh-hook of affliction to drag me into the fire, so let it be. I would that thou shouldst win as much glory out of me as thou canst extract from a mortal man by suffering, or by service; appoint me what thou wilt, only, Father, glorify thyself, and enable me to glorify thee!" If we shall thus consecrate ourselves, there will be better days in store for us than we have as yet known, and the church and the world will know that God has wrought wonders for us. May God give you a blessing, for His name's sake. Amen.

"THE ARK OF HIS COVENANT"

SERMON NO. 2,427
INTENDED FOR READING ON LORD'S DAY, AUGUST 25, 1895;
DELIVERED ON THURSDAY EVENING, AUGUST 18, 1887.

And the temple of God was opened in heaven, and there was seen in his temple the ark of his testament [covenant–R.V.]: *and there were lightnings, and voices, and thunderings, and an earthquake, and great hail*—Revelation 11:19.

I SHALL take the passage quite by itself. I do not fully understand its connection, whether it relates to that which goes before or to that which comes afterwards; and happily, it is not necessary for us to know this, for the passage stands complete in itself, and is full of valuable instruction.

Dear friends, even we who believe have as yet failed to see much of the truth of God. We know enough to save us, to comfort us, and to help us on our way to heaven; but oh, how much of the glory of divine truth has never yet been revealed to our eyes! Some of God's children do not fully know even the common truths as yet, and those who do not know them realize but little of their depth and height. From our text, it appears that there are certain things of God which as yet we have not seen; there is need that they should be opened up to us: "The temple of God was opened in heaven." When our Lord Jesus died, He rent the veil of the temple, and so He laid open the Holy of Holies; but such is our dimness of sight, that we need to have the temple opened, and we need to have the Holy of Holies opened, so that we may see what is not really concealed, but what we are not ready to perceive by reason of the slowness of our understandings. The two words for "temple" here may relate not only to the temple itself, but also to the Holy of Holies, the innermost shrine. Both of these, it seems, need to be opened, or else we shall not see what there is in them. Blessed be the Holy Spirit that He does open up one truth after another to us. Our Savior's promise to His disciples was, "When he, the Spirit of truth, is come, he will guide you into all truth." If we were more teachable, if we were more anxious to be taught, and waited upon Him more, He would, doubtless, lead us into many a truth which at the present moment we have not fully enjoyed. It is a happy thing for you and for me when at any time we can say, "The temple of God was opened in heaven, so that we saw even that which was in the innermost shrine of the holy temple."

The saints in heaven doubtless behold all the glory of God so far as it can be perceived by created beings; but we who are on the right way thither behold, as in a glass darkly, the glory of the Lord. We know only in part, but the part we do know is not so great as it might be, we might know far more than we do even here. Some suppose that they can know but little, because they say that it is written, "Eye hath not seen, nor ear heard, neither have entered into the heart of man, the things which God hath prepared for them that love him." Yes, but why do you stop there? Half a text is often not true; go on to the end of the passage: "But God hath revealed them unto us by his Spirit: for the Spirit searcheth all things, yea, the deep things of God"; and that which your eye cannot see, and your ear cannot hear, and the heart of man cannot imagine, can be revealed to you by the Spirit of the Lord. Oh, that we were more conscious of the power of the Spirit, and that we waited upon Him for yet fuller instruction! Then I am persuaded that, in our measure and degree, it would be true to us, even as to the perfected ones above, "The temple of God was opened in heaven," and they saw that which was in the holiest place.

What did they see when the temple was opened? When the secret place was laid bare to them, what did they see? That is to be my subject now. "There was seen in his temple the ark of his covenant." If we could look into heaven at this moment, this is what we should see, "the ark of his covenant." O sinner, thou thinkest that thou wouldst see an angry God, but thou wouldst see the ark of His covenant! O child of God, perhaps thou dreamest of many things that might distress thee in the glory of that sight; but rest thou content, this would be the main sight that thou wouldst see, Jesus, the incarnate God, the great covenant Surety! Thou wouldst see there, where the Godhead shines resplendent, the ark of His covenant.

I. I shall begin by noticing, first, that THE ARK OF HIS COVENANT IS ALWAYS NEAR TO GOD: "There was seen in his temple the ark of his covenant."

Of course, the outward symbol is gone; we are not now speaking of a temple made with hands, that is to say, of this building. We speak of the spiritual temple above; we speak of the spiritual Holy of Holies. If we could look in there, we should see the ark of the covenant; and we should see the covenant itself always near to God. The covenant is always there. God never forgets it; it is ever before Him: "There was seen in his temple the ark of his covenant."

Why is this? Is it not because the covenant is always standing? The Lord said concerning His people of old, "I will make with them an everlasting covenant," of which David said, "Yet hath he made with me an everlasting covenant, ordered in all things and sure." If God has made a covenant with you, it is not simply for today and tomorrow, nor merely for this life, but for the ages of ages, even forever and ever. If He has struck hands with you through the great Surety, and He has pledged Himself to you, remember, "If we believe not, yet he abideth faithful: he cannot deny himself." Jehovah hath said, "The mountains shall depart, and the hills be removed; but my kindness shall not depart from thee, neither shall the covenant of my peace be removed." What He hath said He will stand to forever. He will keep His Word. He said to His Son, "I will preserve thee, and give thee for a covenant of the people"; and He will never revoke the gift. This covenant stands secure. Though earth's old columns bow, and though my spirits sink, and flesh and heart fail me, yet this covenant shall bear me up even to the end.

The covenant of grace is forever the same, because, first, *the God who made it changes not.* There can be no change in God. The supposition is inconsistent with a belief in His deity. Hear what He says: "I am the Lord, I change not; therefore ye sons of Jacob are not consumed." The sun hath his changes, but the Father of lights is without variableness, or shadow of turning. "God is not a man, that he should lie; neither the son of man, that he should repent: hath he said, and shall he not do it? or hath he spoken, and shall he not make it good?" God has never to alter His purposes; why should He? Those purposes are always infinitely wise. He knoweth the end from the beginning; so His covenant, which He made with such deliberation in the councils of eternity, that covenant which is sealed with the most precious things He ever had, even with the blood of His only-begotten Son, that covenant upon which He stakes His eternal honor, for His glory and honor are wrapped up with the covenant of grace—that covenant cannot be changed because God Himself changeth not.

Then, next, *the Christ who is its Surety and Substance changes not.* Christ, the great Sacrifice by whose death the covenant was ratified, Christ, the Surety, who has sworn to carry out our part of the covenant, Christ, who is the very sum and substance of the covenant, never alters. "All the promises of God in him are yea, and in him Amen, unto the glory of God by us." If we had a variable Savior, brethren, we should have a changeable covenant. Look at Adam; he could change, and therefore he was a poor representative of the human race. Our first federal head soon fell because he was a mere man; but the Surety of the new covenant is the Son of God, who, like His Father, faileth not, and changeth not. Though He is of the substance of His mother, bone of our bone, and flesh of our flesh, and therefore can stand as man's Representative, yet is he Light of Light, very God of very God, and so He standeth fast and firm, like the unchanging God Himself. In this great truth we do and we will rejoice. The covenant is always before God, for Christ is always there. He, the Lamb in the midst of the throne, makes the covenant always to be close to the heart of God.

And, beloved, note you this. The covenant must always be near to God because *the love which suggested it changes not.* The Lord loves His people with a love which has no beginning, no end, no boundary, no change. He says, "I have loved thee with an everlasting love: therefore with lovingkindness have I drawn thee." When the love of God's heart goeth forth toward the believer, it is not changeful like the love of man, sometimes high and sometimes low, sometimes strong and sometimes weak; but, as it is said of our Savior, "having loved his own which were in the world, he loved them unto the end," so can it be said of the great Father that His love is evermore the same; and if the love which dictated the covenant is always in the heart of God, depend upon it that the covenant which comes of that love is always there in the secret place of the Most High.

Reflect also, beloved brethren, that *the promises contained in the covenant change not*. I quoted to you, just now, one passage about the promises, and that is enough: "All the promises of God in him are yea, and in him Amen." Not one single promise of God shall ever fall to the ground unfulfilled. His Word in the form of promises, as well as in the form of the gospel, shall not return unto Him void. O souls, you may hang your whole weight upon any promise of God! You need not fear that it will break. Though all the vessels of the King's house were hung on one nail made by Him, that nail would bear them all up, as well as the flagons as the vessels of smaller measure. Heaven and earth may hang upon a single promise of God. The voice that rolls the stars along, and keeps them all in their orbits, is that voice which spoke even the least of the promises, and therefore every promise of God stands secure forever.

And once more, not only the promises, but *the force and binding power of the covenant change not*. All God's acts are done with a reference to His covenant, and all His covenant has a reference to His covenanted ones. Remember what Moses said of old, "When the Most High divided to the nations their inheritance, when he separated the sons of Adam, he set the bounds of the people according to the number of the children of Israel." Everything that He does follows the line and rule of His covenant. If He chastens and afflicts, it is not in anger, but in His dear covenant love. When first that covenant came into full action with the redeemed, it was all powerful; but it is just as powerful still. All that God doeth is still guided and directed by His eternal purpose and His covenant pledges to His people. Stand still, then, and when thou lookest up, if thou canst not see that temple because thine eye of faith is dim, if thou scarcely darest to look within into the secret place which is the holiest of all, yet know thou of a surety that the covenant is still there, and always there, whether thou seest it or seest it not.

I will tell thee when, perhaps, thou wilt best know that the covenant is there; that is, when the storm-clouds gather the most thickly. When thou shalt see the black masses come rolling up, then remember that the Lord said to Noah, "I do set my bow in the cloud, and it shall be for a token of a covenant between me and the earth." Then shalt thou know that Jehovah remembereth His covenant; thou mayest even be half glad of a black cloud, that the sun of the divine love may paint upon it the many-colored bow, that God may look on it, and remember His covenant. It is good for thee to look on it; but what must it be for Him to look on it, and to remember His covenant? Be thou glad that the covenant is always near to God, as our text declares, "And the temple of God was opened in heaven, and there was seen in his temple the ark of his covenant."

II. Now, secondly, THE COVENANT IS SEEN OF SAINTS: "There was seen in his temple the ark of his covenant."

First, we see it when, by faith, *we believe in Jesus as our Covenant-head*.

By faith we know that God has entered into covenant with us. He that believeth in Christ Jesus is in covenant with God. "He that believeth on the Son hath everlasting life." "He that believeth on him is not condemned." He that believeth in Him is at peace with God, he has passed from death unto life, and shall never come into condemnation. Thou art in covenant with God, believer. Wipe thy weeping eyes, ask God to take the dust out of them, that thou mayest see that there is an unchanging covenant made with thee tonight and forever.

Next, we see this covenant when, by faith, *we perceive it in God's actions toward us*. Faith may see the covenant of God in all His actions. Do you not remember how the old Scotch woman blessed God for her porridge, but she blessed Him most of all because the porridge was in the covenant? God had promised bread and water, and therefore it was sure to come to her. God sent her bread to her in the form of porridge, and she blessed the Lord that it was in the covenant. Now, I thank God that food is in the covenant, and that raiment is in the covenant. It is written, "Thy shoes shall be iron and brass," so they are in the covenant. Life is in the covenant and death is in the covenant: "To die is gain." Everything that is to happen to us is in the covenant; and when faith sees it so, it makes like a happy one. Am I chastened? I say to myself, "Well, the rod was in the covenant, for the Lord said that, if His children disobeyed Him, He would chasten them with the rod of men. If I never had the rod, I should be afraid I was not in the covenant." Is it not written, "In the world ye shall have tribulation?" That is a part of the covenant, you see; so that, when you get it, say to yourself, "The God who is evidently keeping this part of His covenant will keep the rest of it to me, His child."

Brethren, we get, perhaps, the best sight of the covenant when *by prayer we plead it*. In that hour of our wrestling, in the time of our inward craving of mercies from the hand of God, we come at last to this, "Lord, thou hast promised; do as thou hast said." I love to put my finger on a promise, and then to plead it with the Lord, saying, "This is thy Word, my Father; and I know that thou wilt not run back from it. O God, I believe in the inspiration of this Book, and I take very word of it as coming from thy lips. Wilt thou not seal it to my conscience, my heart, my experience, by proving it to be true?" Have you ever found the Lord's promises fail you? I remember one who had put in the margin of her Bible in several places, "T and P"; and when she was asked what those letters meant, she said, "They mean, 'Tried and Proved.' As I go through life, I keep trying and proving the promises of God, and then I put a mark in the margin of my Bible against every one I have tested, that I may not forget it the next time I have to plead it." That is the way to see the covenant at the right hand of God, when you plead it in prayer.

And there are some of us, I think, who can say that *our experience up till now* proves that God does not forget His covenant. We have wandered, but we have been able to say, "He restoreth my soul," for He has restored us. We have needed many things, and we have gone to Him in prayer, and pleaded that word, "No good thing will he withhold from them that walk uprightly," and He has listened to the cries of His servants. He said He would do so: "Call upon me in the day of trouble: I will deliver thee, and thou shalt glorify me." He has remembered us in our low estate, for

His mercy endureth forever; and some of us who are no longer young can set to our seal that God is true because of many experiences of His faithfulness. If they tell us that there is nothing in the Bible, and nothing in God, and nothing in the gospel of Christ, we laugh them to scorn. We have now for many a year lived upon the faithfulness of God, and we cannot be driven into a distrust of Him. He is faithful, and His mercy endureth forever.

Do you not also think that, *when we arrive in heaven, we shall have a wonderful retrospect*, and that retrospect will all come to this: "The temple of God was opened in heaven, and there was seen in his temple the ark of his covenant"? Miss Hannah More very prettily puts it that, often, we do not see the right side of things here. She went into a carpet manufactory, and she looked at what the workmen were doing, and she could see nothing that looked like beauty of design. There were tags and ends hanging out, and she said to the men, "I cannot perceive any design here," and they answered, "No, madam, for you are on the wrong side of the carpet"; but when she went round to the other side, she saw the beauty of the workmanship. Alas! we are at present on the wrong side of God's work; we must get to heaven to see it perfectly, and when we get there, we shall—

> Sing, with wonder and surprise,
> His lovingkindness in the skies.

And we shall say, It was all right; it could not have been better.

> Every dark and bending line
> Meets in the center of his love.

God hath not erred. He has not gone about the longest way to do His work, but He has done in the wisest and most prudent manner all that was for the best and highest interests of His dear covenanted ones.

Thus, I have shown you that sometimes, and it should be always, God's people do see that glorious covenant of grace which is in the temple above.

III. Now I want to have your attention while I say briefly, in the third place, that THE COVENANT CONTAINS MUCH THAT IS WORTH SEEING.

Let us think of what was in the ancient ark of the covenant, for all that was in that ark as a type is to be seen in Christ our heavenly covenant ark above.

In that ark, if you and I could have gone into the holy place, and have had our eyes strengthened to look, we should have seen, first, *God dwelling among men.* What a wonderful thing! Over the top of the lid of that sacred coffer which was called the ark, there shone an amazing light which was the index of the presence of God. He was in the midst of the camp of Israel. He that filleth heaven and earth, the infinite Jehovah, deigned to make that place His special dwelling-place, so that He is addressed as, "Thou that dwellest between the cherubims." Here is a part of the new covenant: "I will dwell in them, and walk in them." It is marvelous that God does speak with men. He whom you heard thundering, last night, as He drove His chariot through the sky, that God in infinite condescension speaks with us, and has come down to us, and taken us into relationship with Himself in the person of the Lord Jesus Christ, who is at once the fellow of the Almighty, and the brother of the sons of men. O beloved, rejoice in the covenant, that God is no longer divided from men! The chasm made by sin is filled, the gulf is bridged, and God now dwells with me, and manifests Himself to them; and "the secret of the Lord is with them that fear him."

Next, in that ark you would have noticed, if you could have seen into it, *God reconciled and communing with men upon the mercy-seat.* Over the top of that ark, as I have told you, was a golden lid, which fitted it, and covered it exactly, and that golden lid was called the mercy seat, the throne of grace. There God spoke with men. He sat there, as it were, enthroned as the Friend of men. Now, it is a part of the covenant that God hears prayer, that God answers our petitions, that He meets us in a way of reconciled love, that He speaks to us in tones which the spirit can hear though the ear cannot. Thank God for a blood-besprinkled mercy seat. What should we do if we had not that as our meeting-place with the thrice-holy Jehovah?

Then, within the ark, underneath the lid, if we could have looked in, we should have seen the law, *the two tables of stone,* which represent *law fulfilled in Christ,* and henceforth laid up in His heart, and laid up in our hearts, too, if we delight in the law of God after the inward man. Now, this is our joy, that the law of God has nothing against the believer. It is fulfilled in Christ, and we see it laid up in Christ, not to be a stone to fall upon us to grind us to powder, but beautiful and fair to look upon as it is in the heart of Christ, and fulfilled in the life of Christ. I rejoice in the covenant which contains in it stipulations all fulfilled, and commands all executed, by our great Representative.

Together with those tables of the law there was laid up *a rod,* a rod which had originally been a dry stick in the hands of Aaron, but when it was laid up before the Lord it budded, and blossomed, and brought forth almonds. So, in the covenant of grace, we see *the kingdom established and flourishing in Christ,* and we rejoice in it. Oh how pleased we are to bow before His fruitful scepter! What wonderful fruit we gather from that blessed rod! Reign, reign, Jesus, reign! The more Thou dost rule us, the more Thou art absolute Sovereign of our hearts, the happier shall we be, and the more shall we delight ourselves in Thee. There is no liberty like complete subjection beneath the sway of Jesus who is our Prophet, Priest, and King.

Then, by the side of that rod there was laid up *the golden pot full of manna, the provision made for the wilderness.* Let us rejoice that there is in the covenant all the provision that we need. God has laid up for us in Christ all our spiritual meat, all the food that we shall ever need between here and heaven. "Feed me till I want no more," we cry to our blessed covenant Representative, and He will do so.

Then, over the top of the ark, sat *the cherubim with outstretched wings,* as, I think, *representing how the angels are in league with us, and with the angels all the forces and powers of the universe.* This day, the beasts of the field are our friends, and the stones of the field have ceased to be our foes. Child of God, you may travel by land or sea; you may go where you will; for everywhere you are in your Father's house. All that you see about you is a friend to you, since you are a friend to God. I often wonder that the earth bears up ungodly men. It must groan beneath the weight of a swearer; it must want to open and swallow him up. But with the gracious man, the man who fears God, all things are at peace, and we may know it to be so. "Ye shall go out with joy, and be led forth with peace; the mountains and the hills shall break forth before you into singing, and all the trees of the field shall clap their hands." We do not often enough realize, I think, the friendship of all God's creatures to those who are His children. St. Francis, though he was a Romish monk, yet had a true idea when he used to regard the sparrows and other birds of the air, and even the dogs in the street, as his friends and his brothers, and talked to them as such. And Luther was much of the same mind when he opened his window, and listened to the chirpings of the robins in the early spring, and felt that they had come to teach the theological doctor some lesson which he had not learned. Oh yes, oh yes, we are quite at home anywhere, now that God is our God! True, the earth travaileth, and is in pain, and the creation suffers and will suffer till Christ comes again; but still her travail is our travail, and we are in sympathy with her, and when she doth reflect the glory of her God she is our looking glass in which we see our Father's face.

Thus, I think, I have shown you that there is much to be seen in the ark of the covenant. God give us grace, like the angels, to fix our eyes upon it! "Which things the angels desire to look into." We have more to do with the ark of His covenant than they have; let us be more desirous even than they are to look therein.

IV. I close with this fourth point. The covenant has solemn surroundings. Listen: "There were lightnings, and voices, and thunderings, and an earthquake, and great hail."

When the people entered into covenant with God on Sinai, the Lord came down upon the top of the mount, and there were thunderings, and lightnings, and voices, and an earthquake. There were all these tokens of His presence, and *God will not leave the covenant of his grace without the sanctions of His power;* that thunder, that lightning, that storm—all these are engaged to keep His covenant. When they are wanted, the God who smote Egypt with great hailstones, the God who make the Kishon to sweep his enemies away, the God who made the stars in heaven to fight against Sisera, will bring all the overwhelming forces that are at His command to the help of His people, and the fulfilling of the covenant which He has made with them. O you who are His people, fall back in confidence upon the God who has treasures of snow, and hail, and the dread artillery of storm and tempest! Most of you, my hearers, have never seen a great storm yet, nor heard in its majesty the thunder of God's power. You must be in the tropics to know what these can be, and even then you would have to say, "These are but parts of His ways." Oh, how the Lord can shake the earth, and make it tremble even to its deep foundations when He pleases! He can make what we call "the solid earth" to be as weak as water when He doth but lift up His finger. But all the power that God hath—and it is boundless—is all in that right hand which has been lifted high to heaven in the solemn oath that He will save His people. Wherefore, lean upon

God without the shadow of a doubt. He may well put all your fears to rest even by the thunder of His power.

Then reflect that there is another side to this truth. You who are not in covenant with God, you who have not believed that Jesus is the Christ, you who have never fled for refuge to lay hold of the hope set before you, you who refuse the divine mercy which comes to you through the bleeding person of the suffering Christ, do remember that there will be for you the thunderings, and the lightnings, and the voices, and the earthquake, and the great hail, for these set forth *the terrors of eternal law, overthrowing God's adversaries.* You have no conception of what God will do with the ungodly. False teachers may smooth it down as much as they like, but that Book is full of thunderbolts to you who refuse God's mercy. Listen to this one text: "Consider this, ye that forget God, lest I tear you in pieces, and there be none to deliver." Can you sport with that? Listen to another: "Ah, I will ease me of mine adversaries, and avenge me of mine enemies!" What will you say to that, or to this? "And again they said Alleluia. And her smoke rose up forever and ever." "The same shall drink of the wine of the wrath of God, which is poured out without mixture into the cup of his indignation; and he shall be tormented with fire and brimstone in the presence of the holy angels, and in the presence of the Lamb. And the smoke of their torment ascendeth up forever and ever: and they have no rest day nor night, who worship the beast and his image, and whosoever receiveth the mark of his name." They talk as if we invented these terrible words, but we do not; we merely quote the Scriptures of truth, and they are terrible indeed to the wicked. They should make men start in their sleep, and never rest until they find a Savior. A Universalist once said to a Christian man that, whatever he did, God would not punish him, and the other replied, "If I spit on your god, I suppose he will not punish me. If I curse him, if I defy him, it will all come right at last?" "Yes," said the Universalist. "Well," answered the other, "that may be the character of your god; but don't you try that kind of thing with my God, the God of the Scriptures, or else you will find that because He is love He cannot, and He will not, suffer this world to be in anarchy, but he will rule it, and govern it, and He will punish those that refuse His infinite compassion." So I beseech you, my hearers, fly to Jesus at once; weary, and heavy-laden, look to Him, for He saith especially to you, "Come unto me, and I will give you rest." The Lord add His blessing to the truth I have tried to preach to you, the sweet and the terrible alike, for Jesus' sake! Amen.

Exposition by C. H. Spurgeon

Hebrews 9

Verse 1. *Then verily the first covenant had also ordinances of divine service, and a worldly sanctuary.*

That is to say, a material sanctuary, a sanctuary made out of such things as this world contains. Under the old covenant, there were certain outward symbols.

Under the new covenant, we have not the symbols, but we have the substance itself. The old law dealt with types and shadows, but the gospel deals with the spiritual realities themselves.

2, 3. For there was a tabernacle made; the first, wherein was the candlestick, and the table, and the shewbread; which is called the sanctuary. And after the second veil, the tabernacle which is called the Holiest of all;

All this was by divine appointment; the form of the rooms, the style of the furniture, everything was ordained of God; and that not merely for ornament, but for purposes of instruction. As we shall see farther on, the Holy Ghost intended a significance, a teaching, a meaning, about everything in the old tabernacle, whether it was a candlestick, or a table, or the shewbread.

4, 5. Which had the golden censer, and the ark of the covenant overlaid round about with gold, wherein was the golden pot that had manna, and Aaron's rod that budded, and the tables of the covenant; and over it the cherubims of glory shadowing the mercy seat; of which we cannot now speak particularly.

It would not have been to the point which the apostle had in hand, so he waived the explanation of those things for another time.

6–8. Now when these things were thus ordained, the priests went always into the first tabernacle, accomplishing the service of God. But into the second went the high priest alone once every year, not without blood, which he offered for himself, and for the errors of the people: the Holy Ghost this signifying,

It is from this sentence that I am sure that the Holy Ghost had a signification, a meaning, a teaching, for every item of the ancient tabernacle and temple; and we are not spinning fancies out of idle brains when we interpret these types, and learn from them important gospel lessons. "The Holy Ghost this signifying,"—

8. That the way into the holiest of all was not yet made manifest, while as the first tabernacle was yet standing:

It was necessary that you should take away the sacred tent, the tabernacle, aye, and take away the temple, too, before you could learn the spiritual meaning of them. You must break the shell to get at the kernel. So God had ordained. Hence, there is now no tabernacle, no temple, no holy court, no inner shrine, the holy of holies. The material worship is done away with, in order that we may render the spiritual worship of which the material was but the type.

9. Which was a figure for the time then present,

Only a figure, and only meant for "the time then present." It was the childhood of the Lord's people; it was a time when, as yet, the light had not fully broken in upon spiritual eyes, so they must be taught by picture-books. They must have a kind of

Kindergarten for the little children, that they might learn the elements of the faith by the symbols, types, and representations of a material worship. When we come into the true gospel light, all that is done away with; it was only "a figure for the time then present."

9. *In which were offered both gifts and sacrifices, that could not make him that did the service perfect, as pertaining to the conscience;*
All these rites could only give a fleshly purity, but they could not touch the conscience. If men saw what was meant by the outward type, then the conscience was appeased; but by the outward sign itself the conscience was never comforted, if it was a living and lowly conscience.

10. *Which stood only in meats and drinks, and divers washings, and carnal ordinances, imposed on them until the time of reformation.*
These ordinances were only laid upon the Jews—not upon any other people—and only laid upon them until the better and brighter days of reformation and fuller illumination.

11. *But Christ—*
Oh, how we seem to rise when we begin to get near to Him, away from the high priests of the Jews! "But Christ"—

11. *Being come an high priest of good things to come,*
Not of the shadows, but of the good things themselves: "an high priest of good things to come,"—

11. *By a greater and more perfect tabernacle, not made with hands, that is to say, not of this building;*
That tabernacle was His body, which was not made with hands, nor yet formed by carnal generation as our human tabernacle is. This greater and more perfect tabernacle was made according to the power of an endless life.

12. *Neither by the blood of goats and calves, but by his own blood he entered in once into the holy place, having obtained eternal redemption for us.*
The Jewish high priests went once a year into the Holy of Holies. Each year as it came round demanded that they should go again. Their work was never done; but "He entered in once," and only once, "into the holy place, having obtained eternal redemption for us." I love that expression, "eternal redemption"—a redemption which really does redeem, and redeems forever and ever. If you are redeemed by it, you cannot be lost; if this redemption be yours, it is not for a time, or for a season, but it is "eternal redemption." Oh, how you ought to rejoice in the one entrance within the veil by our great High Priest who has obtained eternal redemption for us!

13–15. For if the blood of bulls and of goats, and the ashes of an heifer sprinkling the unclean, sanctifieth to the purifying of the flesh: how much more shall the blood of Christ, who through the eternal Spirit offered himself without spot to God, purge your conscience from dead works to serve the living God? And for this cause he is the mediator of the new testament, that by means of death, for the redemption of the transgressions that were under the first testament, they which are called might receive the promise of eternal inheritance.

When you come to deal with Christ, you have to do with eternal things. There is nothing temporary about Him, or about His work. It is "eternal redemption" that He has obtained for us, it is an "eternal inheritance" that He has purchased for us.

16, 17. For where a testament is, there must also of necessity be the death of the testator. For a testament is of force after men are dead: otherwise it is of no strength at all while the testator liveth.

Or, "Where a covenant is, there must also be the death of him who covenants, or of that by which the covenant is established." Or read it as we have it in our version, for it seems as if it must be so, although we are loathe to give the meaning of "testament" to the word, since its natural meaning is evidently covenant: "Where a testament is, there must also of necessity be the death of the testator. For a testament is of force after men are dead; otherwise it is of no strength at all while the testator liveth"; or, if you will, while the victim that was to confirm the covenant lived, the covenant was not ratified; it must be slain before it could be thus effective.

18–22. Whereupon neither the first testament was dedicated without blood. For when Moses had spoken every precept to all the people according to the law, he took the blood of calves and of goats, with water, and scarlet wool, and hyssop, and sprinkled both the book, and all the people, saying, This is the blood of the testament which God hath enjoined unto you. Moreover he sprinkled with blood both the tabernacle, and all the vessels of the ministry. And almost all things are by the law purged with blood; and without shedding of blood is no remission.

There is no truth more plain than this in the whole of the Old Testament; and it must have within it a very weighty lesson to our souls. There are some who cannot endure the doctrine of a substitutionary atonement. Let them beware lest they be casting away the very soul and essence of the gospel. It is evident that the sacrifice of Christ was intended to give ease to the conscience, for we read that the blood of bulls and of goats could not do that. I fail to see how any doctrine of atonement except the doctrine of the vicarious sacrifice of Christ can give ease to the guilty conscience. Christ in my stead suffering the penalty of my sin—that pacifies my conscience, but nothing else does: "Without shedding of blood is no remission."

23. It was therefore necessary that the patterns of things in the heavens should be purified with these;

These things down below are only the patterns, the models, the symbols of the heavenly things; they could therefore be ceremonially purified with the blood which is the symbol of the atoning sacrifice of Christ.

23, 24. But the heavenly things themselves with better sacrifices than these. For Christ is not entered into the holy places made with hands, which are the figures of the true; but into heaven itself, now to appear in the presence of God for us:

He never went within the veil in the Jewish temple; that was but the symbol of the true holy of holies. He has gone "into heaven itself, now to appear in the presence of God for us."

25–28. Nor yet that he should offer himself often, as the high priest entereth into the holy place every year with blood of others; for then must he often have suffered since the foundation of the world: but now once in the end of the world hath he appeared to put away sin by the sacrifice of himself. And as it is appointed unto men once to die, but after this the judgment: so Christ was once offered to bear the sins of many;

There is no need that He should die again, His one offering has forever perfected all His people. There remains nothing but His final coming for the judgment of the ungodly, and the acquittal of His redeemed.

28. And unto them that look for him shall he appear the second time without sin unto salvation.

Christ's second coming will be "without sin," and without a sin offering, too, wholly apart from sin, unto the salvation of all His chosen. May we all be amongst those who are looking for Him! Amen.

THE RENT VEIL

Sermon No. 2,015
Delivered on Lord's day Morning, March 25, 1888.
Portion of Scripture read before Sermon—Hebrews 10.
Hymns from *Our Own Hymn Book*—318, 296, 395.

Jesus, when he had cried again with a loud voice, yielded up the ghost. And, behold, the veil of the temple was rent in twain from the top to the bottom—Matthew 27:50, 51.

Having therefore, brethren, boldness to enter into the holiest by the blood of Jesus, by a new and living way, which he hath consecrated for us, through the veil, that is to say, his flesh—Hebrews 10:19, 20.

The death of our Lord Jesus Christ was fitly surrounded by miracles; yet it is itself so much greater a wonder than all besides, that it as far exceeds them as the sun outshines the planets which surround it. It seems natural enough that the earth should quake, that tombs should be opened, and that the veil of the temple should be rent, when He who only hath immortality gives up the ghost. The more you think of the death of the Son of God, the more will you be amazed at it. As much as a miracle excels a common fact, so doth this wonder of wonders rise above all miracles of power. That the divine Lord, even though veiled in mortal flesh, should condescend to be subject to the power of death, so as to bow His head on the cross, and submit to be laid in the tomb, is among mysteries the greatest. The death of Jesus is the marvel of time and eternity, which, as Aaron's rod swallowed up all the rest, takes up into itself all lesser marvels.

Yet the rending of the veil of the temple is not a miracle to be lightly passed over. It was made of "fine twined linen, with cherubims of cunning work." This gives the idea of a substantial fabric, a piece of lasting tapestry, which would have endured the severest strain. No human hands could have torn that sacred covering; and it could not have been divided in the midst by any accidental cause; yet, strange to say, on the instant when the holy person of Jesus was rent by death, the great veil which concealed the holiest of all was "rent in twain from the top to the bottom." What did it mean? It meant much more than I can tell you now.

It is not fanciful to regard it as a solemn act of mourning on the part of the house of the Lord. In the East men express their sorrow by rending their garments; and the temple, when it beheld its Master die, seemed struck with horror, and rent its veil. Shocked at the sin of man, indignant at the murder of its Lord, in its sympathy with Him who is the true temple of God, the outward symbol tore its holy vestment from the top to the bottom. Did not the miracle also mean that from that hour the whole system of types, and shadows, and ceremonies had come to an end? The ordinances of an earthly priesthood were rent with that veil. In token of the death of the ceremonial law, the soul of it quitted its sacred shrine, and left its bodily tabernacle as a dead thing. The legal dispensation is over. The rent of the veil seemed to say—"Henceforth God dwells no longer in the thick darkness of the Holy of Holies, and shines forth no longer from between the cherubim. The special enclosure is broken up, and there is no inner sanctuary for the earthly high priest to enter: typical atonements and sacrifices are at an end."

According to the explanation given in our second text, the rending of the veil chiefly meant that the way into the holiest, which was not before made manifest, was now laid open to all believers. Once in the year the high priest solemnly lifted a corner of this veil with fear and trembling, and with blood and holy incense he passed into the immediate presence of Jehovah; but the tearing of the veil laid open the secret place. The rent from top to bottom gives ample space for all to enter who are called of God's grace, to approach the throne, and to commune with the Eternal One. Upon that subject I shall try to speak this morning, praying in my inmost soul that you and I, with all other believers, may have boldness actually to enter into that which is within the veil at this time of our assembling for worship. Oh, that the Spirit of God would lead us into the nearest fellowship which mortal men can have with the Infinite Jehovah!

First, this morning, I shall ask you to consider *what has been done*. The veil has been rent. Secondly, we will remember *what we therefore have*: we have "boldness to enter into the holiest by the blood of Jesus." Then, thirdly, we will consider *how we exercise this grace*: we "enter by the blood of Jesus, by a new and living way, which he hath consecrated for us, through the veil, that is to say, his flesh."

I. First, think of WHAT HAS BEEN DONE. In actual historical fact the glorious veil of the temple has been rent in twain from the top to the bottom: as a matter of spiritual fact, which is far more important to us, *the separating legal ordinance is abolished.* There was under the law this ordinance—that no man should ever go into the holiest of all, with the one exception of the high priest, and he but once in the year, and not without blood. If any man had attempted to enter there he must have died, as guilty of great presumption and of profane intrusion into the secret place of the Most High. Who could stand in the presence of Him who is a consuming fire? This ordinance of distance runs all through the law; for even the holy place, which was the vestibule of the Holy of Holies, was for the priests alone. The place of the people was one of distance. At the very first institution of the law when God descended upon Sinai, the ordinance was, "Thou shalt set bounds unto the people round about." There was no invitation to draw near. Not that they desired to do so, for the mountain was altogether on a smoke, and "even Moses said, I exceedingly fear and quake." "The Lord said unto Moses, Go down, charge the people, lest they break through unto the Lord to gaze, and many of them perish." If so much as a beast touch the mountain it must be stoned, or thrust through with a dart. The spirit of the old law was reverent distance. Moses, and here and there a man chosen by God, might come near to Jehovah; but as for the bulk of the people, the command was, "Draw not nigh hither." When the Lord revealed His glory at the giving of the law, we read—"When the people saw it, they removed, and stood afar off." All this is ended. The precept to keep back is abrogated, and the invitation is, "Come unto me, all ye that labor and are heavy laden." "Let us draw near" is now the filial spirit of the gospel. How thankful I am for this! What a joy it is to my soul! Some of God's people have not yet realized this gracious fact, for still they worship afar off. Very much of prayer is to be highly commended for its reverence; but it has in it a lack of childlike confidence. I can admire the solemn and stately language of worship which recognizes the greatness of God; but it will not warm my heart nor express my soul until it has also blended therewith the joyful nearness of that perfect love which casteth out fear, and ventures to speak with our Father in heaven as a child speaketh with its father on earth. My brother, no veil remains. Why dost thou stand afar off, and tremble like a slave? Draw near with full assurance of faith. The veil is rent: access is free. Come boldly to the throne of grace. Jesus has made thee nigh, as nigh to God as even He Himself is. Though we speak of the holiest of all, even the secret place of the Most High, yet it is of this place of awe, even of this sanctuary of Jehovah, that the veil is rent; therefore, let nothing hinder thine entrance. Assuredly no law forbids thee; but infinite love invites thee to draw nigh to God.

This rending of the veil signified, also, *the removal of the separating sin*. Sin is, after all, the great divider between God and man. That veil of blue and purple and fine twined linen could not really separate man from God: for He is, as to His omnipresence, not far from any one of us. Sin is a far more effectual wall of separation: it opens an abyss between the sinner and his Judge. Sin shuts out prayer, and praise, and every form of religious exercise. Sin makes God walk contrary to us, because we walk contrary to Him. Sin, by separating the soul from God, causes spiritual death, which is both the effect and the penalty of transgression. How can two walk together except they be agreed? How can a holy God have fellowship with unholy creatures? Shall justice dwell with injustice? Shall perfect purity abide with the abominations of evil? No, it cannot be. Our Lord Jesus Christ put away sin by the sacrifice of Himself. He taketh away the sin of the world, and so the veil is rent. By the shedding of His most precious blood we are cleansed from all sin, and that most gracious promise of the new covenant is fulfilled—"Their sins and their iniquities will I remember no more." When sin is gone, the barrier is broken down, the unfathomable gulf is filled. Pardon, which removes sin, and justification, which brings righteousness, make up a deed of clearance so real and so complete that nothing now divides the sinner from his reconciled God. The Judge is now the Father: He, who once must necessarily have condemned, is found justly absolving and accepting. In this double sense the veil is rent: the separating ordinance is abrogated, and the separating sin is forgiven.

Next, be it remembered that *the separating sinfulness is also taken away through our Lord Jesus*. It is not only what we have *done*, but what we *are* that keeps us apart from God. We have sin ingrained in us: even those who have grace dwelling in them have to complain, "When I would do good, evil is present with me." How can we commune with God with our eyes blinded, our ears stopped, our hearts hardened, and our senses deadened by sin? Our whole nature is tainted, poisoned, perverted by evil; how can we know the Lord? Beloved, through the death of our Lord Jesus the covenant of grace is established with us, and its gracious provisions are on this wise: "This is the covenant that I will make with them after those days, saith the Lord; I will put my laws into their mind, and write them in their hearts." When this is the case, when the will of God is inscribed on the heart, and the nature is entirely changed, then is the dividing veil which hides us from God taken away: "Blessed are the pure in heart: for they shall see God." Blessed are all they that love righteousness and follow after it, for they are in a way in which the Righteous One can walk in fellowship with them. Spirits that are like God are not divided from God. Difference of nature hangs up a veil; but the new birth, and the sanctification which follows upon it, through the precious death of Jesus, remove that veil. He that hates sin, strives after holiness, and labors to perfect it in the fear of God, is in fellowship with God. It is a blessed thing when we love what God loves, when we seek what God seeks, when we are in sympathy with divine aims, and are obedient to divine commands: for with such persons will the Lord dwell. When grace makes us partakers of the divine nature; then are we at one with the Lord, and the veil is taken away.

"Yes," saith one, "I see now how the veil is taken away in three different fashions; but still God is God, and we are but poor puny men: between God and man there must of necessity be a separating veil, caused by the great disparity between the Creator and the creature. How can the finite and the infinite commune? God is all in all, and more than all; we are nothing, and less than nothing; how can we meet?" When the Lord does come near to His favored ones, they own how incapable they are of enduring the excessive glory. Even the beloved John said, "When I saw him, I fell at his feet as dead." When we have been especially conscious of the presence and working of our Lord, we have felt our flesh creep, and our blood chill; and then we have understood what Jacob meant when he said, "How dreadful is this place! this is none other but the house of God, and this is the gate of heaven." All this is true; for the Lord saith, "Thou canst not see my face and live." Although this is a much thinner veil than those I have already mentioned, yet it is a veil; and it is hard for man to be at home with God. But *the Lord Jesus bridges the separating distance*. Behold the blessed Son of God has come into the world, and taken upon Himself our nature! "Forasmuch then as the children are partakers of flesh and blood, he also himself likewise took part of the same." Though He is God as God is God, yet is He as surely man as man is man. Mark well how in the person of the Lord Jesus we see God and man in the closest conceivable alliance; for they are united in one person forever. The gulf is completely filled by the fact that Jesus has gone through with us even to the bitter end, to death, even to the death of the cross. He has followed out the career of manhood even to the tomb; and thus we see that the veil, which hung between the nature of God and the nature of man, is rent in the person of our Lord Jesus Christ. We enter into the holiest of all through His flesh, which links manhood to Godhead.

Now, you see what it is to have the veil taken away. Solemnly note that this avails only for believers: those who refuse Jesus refuse the only way of access to God. God is not approachable, except through the rending of the veil by the death of Jesus. There was one typical way to the mercy seat of old, and that was through the turning aside of the veil; there was no other. And there is now no other way for any of you to come into fellowship with God, except through the rent veil, even the death of Jesus Christ, whom God has set forth to be the propitiation for sin. Come this way, and you may come freely. Refuse to come this way, and there hangs between you and God an impassable veil. Without Christ you are without God, and without hope. Jesus Himself assures you, "If ye believe not that I am he, ye shall die in your sins." God grant that this may not happen to any of you!

For believers the veil is not rolled up, but rent. The veil was not unhooked, and carefully folded up, and put away, so that it might be put in its place at some future time. Oh, no! But the divine hand took it and rent it from top to bottom. It can never be hung up again; that is impossible. Between those who are in Christ Jesus and the great God, there will never be another separation. "Who shall separate us from the love of God?" Only one veil was made, and as that is rent, the one and only separator is destroyed. I delight to think of this. The devil himself can never divide me from God now. He may and will attempt to shut me out from God; but the worst he could do would be to hang up a rent veil. What would that avail but to exhibit his impotence? God has rent the veil, and the devil cannot mend it. There is access between a believer and his God; and there must be such free access forever, since the veil is not rolled up, and put on one side to be hung up again in days to come; but it is rent, and rendered useless.

The rent is not in one corner, but in the midst, as Luke tells us. It is not a slight rent through which we may see a little; but it is rent from the top to the bottom. There is an entrance made for the greatest sinners. If there had only been a small hole cut through it, the lesser offenders might have crept through; but what an act of abounding mercy is this, that the veil is rent in the midst, and rent from top to bottom, so that the chief of sinners may find ample passage! This also shows that for believers there is no hindrance to the fullest and freest access to God. Oh, for much boldness, this morning, to come where God has not only set open the door, but has lifted the door from its hinges; yea, removed it, post, and bar, and all!

I want you to notice that this veil, when it was rent, was rent by God, not by man. It was not the act of an irreverent mob; it was not the midnight outrage of a set of profane priests: it was the act of God alone. Nobody stood within the veil; and on the outer side of it stood the priests only fulfilling their ordinary vocation of offering sacrifice. It must have astounded them when they saw that holy place laid bare in a moment. How they fled, as they saw that massive veil divided without human hand in a second of time! Who rent it? Who but God Himself? If another had done it, there might have been a mistake about it, and the mistake might need to be remedied by replacing the curtain; but if the Lord has done it, it is done rightly, it is done finally, it is done irreversibly. It is God Himself who has laid sin on Christ, and in Christ has put that sin away. God Himself has opened the gate of heaven to believers, and cast up a highway along which the souls of men may travel to Himself. God Himself has set the ladder between earth and heaven. Come to Him now, ye humble ones. Behold, He sets before you an open door!

II. And now I ask you to follow me, dear friends, in the second place, to an experimental realization of my subject. We now notice WHAT WE HAVE: "Having therefore, brethren, boldness to enter into the holiest." Observe the threefold "having" in the paragraph now before us, and be not content without the whole three. We have "boldness to enter in." There are degrees in boldness; but this is one of the highest. When the veil was rent it required some boldness to *look* within. I wonder whether the priests at the altar did have the courage to gaze upon the mercy seat. I suspect that they were so struck with amazement that they fled from the altar, fearing sudden death. It requires a measure of boldness steadily to look upon the mystery of God: "Which things the angels desire to look into." It is well not to look with a merely curious eye into the deep things of God. I question whether any man is able to pry into the mystery of the Trinity without great risk. Some, thinking to look there with the eyes of their natural intellect, have been blinded by the light of that sun, and have henceforth wandered in darkness. It needs boldness to look into the splendors of redeeming and electing love. If any did look into the holiest when the veil was rent, they were among the boldest of men; for others must have feared lest the fate of the men of Bethshemesh would be theirs. Beloved, the Holy Spirit invites you to look into the holy place, and view it all with reverent eye for it is full of teaching to you. Understand the mystery of the mercy-seat, and of the ark of the covenant overlaid with gold, and of the pot of manna, and of the tables of stone, and of Aaron's rod that budded. Look, look boldly through Jesus Christ: but do not content yourself with looking! Hear what the text says: "Having boldness to *enter in*." Blessed be God if He has taught us this sweet way of no longer looking from afar, but of entering into the inmost shrine with confidence! "Boldness to enter in" is what we ought to have.

Let us follow the example of the high priest, and, having entered, *let us perform the functions of one who enters in.* "Boldness to enter in" suggests that we act as men who are in their proper places. To stand within the veil filled the servant of God with an overpowering *sense of the divine presence.* If ever in his life he was near to God, he was certainly near to God then, when quite alone, shut in, and excluded from all the world, he had no one with him, except the glorious Jehovah. O my beloved, may we this morning enter into the holiest in this sense! Shut out from the world, both wicked and Christian, let us know that the Lord is here, most near and manifest. Oh that we may now cry out with Hagar, "Have I also here looked after him that seeth me?" Oh, how sweet to realize by personal enjoyment the presence of Jehovah! How cheering to feel that the Lord of hosts is with us! We know our God to be a very present help in trouble. It is one of the greatest joys out of heaven to be able to sing— Jehovah Shammah—the Lord is here. At first we tremble in the divine presence; but as we feel more of the spirit of adoption we draw near with sacred delight, and feel so fully at home with our God that we sing with Moses, "Lord, thou hast been our dwelling place in all generations." Do not live as if God were as far off from you as the east is from the west. Live not far below on the earth; but live on high, as if you were in heaven. In heaven you will be with God; but on earth He will be with you: is there much difference? He hath raised us up together, and made us sit together in heavenly places in Christ Jesus. Jesus hath made us nigh by His precious blood. Try day by day to live in as great nearness to God, as the high priest felt when he stood for awhile within the secret of Jehovah's tabernacle.

The high priest had *a sense of communion with God*; he was not only near, but he spoke with God. I cannot tell what he said, but I should think that on the special day the high priest unburdened himself of the load of Israel's sin and sorrow, and made known his requests unto the Lord. Aaron, standing there alone, must have been filled with memories of his own faultiness, and of the idolatries and backslidings of the people. God shone upon him, and he bowed before God. He may have heard things which it was not lawful for him to utter, and other things which he could not have uttered if they had been lawful. Beloved, do you know what it is to commune with God? Words are poor vehicles for this fellowship; but what a blessed thing it is! Proofs of the existence of God are altogether superfluous to those of us who are in the habit of conversing with the Eternal One. If anybody were to write an essay to prove the existence of my wife, or my son, I certainly should not read it, except for the amusement of the thing; and proofs of the existence of God to the man who communes with God are much the same. Many of you walk with God: what bliss! Fellowship with the Most High is elevating, purifying, strengthening. Enter into it boldly. Enter into His revealed thoughts, even as He graciously enters into yours: rise to His plans, as He condescends to yours; ask to be uplifted to Him, even as He deigns to dwell with you.

This is what the rent of the veil brings us when we have boldness to enter in; but, mark you, the rent veil brings us nothing until we have boldness to enter in. Why stand we without? Jesus brings us near, and truly our fellowship is with the Father, and with His Son Jesus Christ. Let us not be slow to take up our freedom, and come boldly to the throne. The high priest entered within the veil of blue, and purple, and scarlet, and fine twined linen, with blood, and with incense, that he might *pray for Israel*; and there he stood before the Most High, pleading with Him to bless the people. O beloved, prayer is a divine institution, and it belongs to us. But there are many sorts of prayers. There is the prayer of one who seems shut out from God's holy temple; there is the prayer of another who stands in the court of the Gentiles afar off, looking towards the temple; there is the prayer of one who gets where Israel stands and pleads with the God of the chosen; there is the prayer in the court of the priests, when the sanctified man of God makes intercession; but the best prayer of all is offered in the holiest of all. There is no fear about prayer being heard when it is offered in the holiest. The very position of the man proves that he is accepted with God. He is standing on the surest ground of acceptance, and he is so near to God that his every desire is heard. There the man is seen through and through; for he is very near to God. His thoughts are read, his tears are seen, his sighs are heard; for he has boldness to enter in. He may ask what he will, and it shall be done unto him. As the altar sanctifieth the gift, so the most holy place, entered by the blood of Jesus, secures a certain answer to the prayer that is offered therein. God give us such power in prayer! It is a wonderful thing that the Lord should hearken to the voice of a man; yet are there such men. Luther came out of his closet, and cried, *Vici*—"I have conquered." He had not yet met his adversaries; but as he had prevailed with God for men, he felt that he should prevail with men for God.

But the high priest, if you recollect, after he had communed and prayed with God, *came out and blessed the people.* He put on his garments of glory and beauty, which he had laid aside when he went into the holy place, for there he stood in simple white, and nothing else; and now he came out wearing the breast-plate and all his precious ornaments, and he blessed the people. That is what you will do if you have the boldness to enter into the holiest by the blood of Jesus: you will bless the people that surround you. The Lord has blessed you, and He will make you a blessing. Your ordinary conduct and conversation will be a blessed example; the words you speak for Jesus will be like a dew from the Lord: the sick will be comforted by your words; the despondent will be encouraged by your faith; the lukewarm will be recovered by your love. You will be, practically, saying to each one who knows you, "The Lord bless thee, and keep thee: the Lord make his face shine upon thee, and give thee peace." You will become a channel of blessing: "Out of your belly shall flow rivers of living water." May we each one have boldness to enter in, that we may come forth laden with benedictions!

If you will kindly look at the text, you will notice, what I shall merely hint at, that *this boldness is well grounded.* I always like to see the apostle using a "therefore": "Having *therefore* boldness." Paul is often a true poet, but he is always a correct logician; he is as logical as if he were dealing with mathematics rather than theology. Here he writes one of his "therefores."

Why is it that we have boldness? Is it not because of our relationship to Christ which makes us "brethren"? "Having therefore, *brethren*, boldness." The feeblest believer has as much right to enter into the holy places as Paul had; because he is one of the brotherhood. I remember a rhyme by John Ryland, in which he says of heaven—

They shall all be there, the great and the small;
Poor I shall shake hands with the blessed St. Paul.

I have no doubt we shall have such a position, and such fellowship. Meanwhile, we do shake hands with Him this morning as he calls us brethren. We are brethren to one another, because we are brethren to Jesus. Where we see the apostle go, we will go; yea, rather, where we see the Great Apostle and High Priest of our profession enter, we will follow. "Having therefore, boldness."

Beloved, we have now no fear of death in the most holy place. The high priest, whoever he might be, must always have dreaded that solemn day of atonement, when he had to pass into the silent and secluded place. I cannot tell whether it is true, but I have read that there is a tradition among the Jews, that a rope was fastened to the high priest's foot that they might draw out his corpse in case he died before the Lord. I should not wonder if their superstition devised such a thing, for it is an awful position for a man to enter into the secret dwelling of Jehovah. But we cannot die in the holy place now, since Jesus has died for us. The death of Jesus is the guarantee of the eternal life of all for whom He died. We have boldness to enter, for we shall not perish.

Our boldness arises from the perfection of His sacrifice. Read the fourteenth verse: "He hath perfected forever them that are sanctified." We rely upon the sacrifice of Christ, believing that He was such a perfect Substitute for us, that it is not possible for us to die after our Substitute has died; and we must be accepted, because He is accepted. We believe that the precious blood has so effectually and eternally put away sin from us, that we are no longer obnoxious to the wrath of God. We may safely stand where sin must be smitten, if there be any sin upon us; for we are so washed, so cleaned, and so fully justified that we are accepted in the Beloved. Sin is so completely lifted from us by the vicarious sacrifice of Christ, that we have boldness to enter where Jehovah Himself dwells.

Moreover, we have this for certain, that as a priest had a right to dwell near to God, we have that privilege; for Jesus hath made us kings and priests unto God, and all the privileges of the office come to us with the office itself. We have a mission within the holy place; we are called to enter there upon holy business, and so we have no fear of being intruders. A burglar may enter a house, but he does not enter with boldness; he is always afraid lest he should be surprised. You might enter a stranger's house, without an invitation, but you would feel no boldness there. We do not enter the holiest as housebreakers, nor as strangers; we come in obedience to a call, to fulfill our office. When once we accept the sacrifice of Christ, we are at home with God. Where should a child be bold but in his father's house? Where should a priest stand but in the temple of his God, for whose service he is set apart? Where should a blood-washed sinner live but with his God, to whom he is reconciled?

It is a heavenly joy to feel this boldness! We have now such a love for God, and such a delight in Him, that it never crosses our minds that we are trespassers when we draw near to Him. We never say, "God, my dread," but "God, my exceeding joy."

His name is the music to which our lives are set: though God be a consuming fire we love Him as such, for He will only consume our dross, and that we desire to lose. Under no aspect is God now distasteful to us. We delight in Him, be He what He may. So you see, beloved, we have good grounds for boldness when we enter into the holiest by the blood of Jesus.

I cannot leave this point until I have reminded you that *we may have this boldness of entering in at all times*, because the veil is always rent, and is never restored to its old place. "The Lord said unto Moses, Speak unto Aaron thy brother, that he come not at all times into the holy place within the veil before the mercy seat, which is upon the ark; that he die not"; but the Lord saith not so to us. Dear child of God, you may at all times have "boldness to enter in." The veil is rent both day and night. Yea, let me say it, even when thine eye of faith is dim, still enter in; when evidences are dark, still have "boldness to enter in"; and even if thou hast unhappily sinned, remember that access is open to thy penitent prayer. Come still through the rent veil, sinner as thou art. What though thou hast backslidden, what though thou art grieved with the sense of thy wanderings, come even now! "Today, if ye will hear his voice, harden not your heart," but enter at once; for the veil is not there to exclude thee, though doubt and unbelief may make you think it is so. The veil cannot be there, for it was rent in twain from the top to the bottom.

III. My time has fled, and I shall not have space to speak as I meant to do upon the last point—HOW WE EXERCISE THIS GRACE. Let me give you the notes of what I would have said.

Let us at this hour enter into the holiest. Behold the way! We come *by the way of atonement*: "Having therefore, brethren, boldness to enter into the holiest by the blood of Jesus." I have been made to feel really ill through the fierce and blasphemous words that have been used of late by gentlemen of the modern school concerning the precious blood. I will not defile my lips by a repetition of the thrice-accursed things which they have dared to utter while trampling on the blood of Jesus. Everywhere throughout this divine Book you meet with the precious blood. How can he call himself a Christian who speaks in flippant and profane language of the blood of atonement? My brothers, there is no way into the holiest, even though the veil be rent, without blood. You might suppose that the high priest of old brought the blood because the veil was there; but *you* have to bring it with you though the veil is gone. The way is open, and you have boldness to enter; but not without the blood of Jesus. It would be an unholy boldness which would think of drawing near to God without the blood of the great Sacrifice. We have always to plead the atonement. As without shedding of blood there is no remission of sin, so without that blood there is no access to God.

Next, the way by which we come is *an unfailing way*. Please notice that word— "by a *new* way"; this means by a way which is always fresh. The original Greek suggests the idea of "newly slain." Jesus died long ago, but His death is the same now as at the moment of its occurrence. We come to God, dear friends, by a way which is always effectual with God. It never, never loses one whit of its power and freshness.

> Dear dying lamb, thy precious blood
> Shall never lose its power.

The way is not worn away by long traffic: it is always new. If Jesus Christ had died yesterday, would you not feel that you could plead His merit today? Very well, you can plead that merit after these 19 centuries with as much confidence as at the first hour. The way to God is always newly laid. In effect, the wounds of Jesus incessantly bleed our expiation. The cross is as glorious as though He were still upon it. So far as the freshness, vigor, and force of the atoning death is concerned, we come by a new way. Let it be always new to our hearts. Let the doctrine of atonement never grow stale, but let it have dew upon it for our souls.

Then the apostle adds, it is a "living way." A wonderful word! The way by which the high priest went into the holy place was of course a material way, and so a dead way. We come by a spiritual way, suitable to our spirits. The way could not help the high priest, but our way helps us abundantly. Jesus says, "I am the way, the truth, *and the life*." When we come to God by this way, the way itself leads, guides, bears, brings us near. This way gives us life with which to come.

It is *a dedicated way*: "which he hath consecrated for us." When a new road is opened, it is set apart and dedicated for the public use. Sometimes a public building is opened by a king or a prince, and so is dedicated to its purpose. Beloved, the way to God through Jesus Christ is dedicated by Christ, and ordained by Christ for the use of poor believing sinners, such as we are. He has consecrated the way towards God, and dedicated it for us, that we may freely use it. Surely, if there is a road set apart for me, I may use it without fear; and the way to God and heaven through Jesus Christ is dedicated by the Savior for sinners; it is the King's highway for wayfaring men, who are bound for the City of God; therefore, let us use it. "Consecrated for us!" Blessed word!

Lastly, it is *a Christly way*; for when we come to God, we still come through His flesh. There is no coming to Jehovah, except by the incarnate God. God in human flesh is our way to God; the substitutionary death of the Word made flesh is also the way to the Father. There is no coming to God, except by representation. Jesus represents us before God, and we come to God through Him who is our covenant head, our representative and forerunner before the throne of the Most High. Let us never try to pray without Christ; never try to sing without Christ; never try to preach without Christ. Let us perform no holy function, nor attempt to have fellowship with God in any shape or way, except through that rent which He has made in the veil by His flesh, sanctified for us, and offered upon the cross on our behalf.

Beloved, I have done when I have just remarked upon the next two verses, which are necessary to complete the sense, but which I was obliged to omit this morning, since there would be no time to handle them. We are called to take holy freedoms with God. "Let us draw near," at once, "with a true heart in full assurance of faith."

Let us do so boldly, for we have a great high priest. The twenty-first verse reminds us of this. Jesus is the great Priest, and we are the sub-priests under Him, and since He bids us come near to God, and Himself leads the way, let us follow Him into the inner sanctuary. Because He lives, we shall live also. We shall not die in the holy place, unless He dies. God will not smite us unless He smites Him. So, "having a high priest over the house of God, let us draw near with a true heart in full assurance of faith."

And then the apostle tells us that we may not only come with boldness, because our high priest leads the way, but because we ourselves are prepared for entrance. Two things the high priest had to do before he might enter: one was, to be sprinkled with blood, and this we have; for "our hearts are sprinkled from an evil conscience."

The other requisite for the priests was to have their "bodies washed with pure water." This we have received in symbol in our baptism, and in reality in the spiritual cleansing of regeneration. To us has been fulfilled the prayer—

> Let the water and the blood,
> From thy riven side which flowed,
> Be of sin the double cure,
> Cleanse me from its guilt and power.

We have known the washing of water by the Word, and we have been sanctified by the Spirit of His grace; therefore let us enter into the holiest. Why should we stay away? Hearts sprinkled with blood, bodies washed with pure water—these are the ordained preparations for acceptable entrance. Come near, beloved! May the Holy Spirit be the spirit of access to you now. Come to your God, and then abide with Him! He is your Father, your all in all. Sit down and rejoice in Him; take your fill of love; and let not your communion be broken between here and heaven. Why should it be? Why not begin today that sweet enjoyment of perfect reconciliation and delight in God which shall go on increasing in intensity until you behold the Lord in open vision, and go no more out? Heaven will bring a great change in condition, but not in our standing, if even now we stand within the veil. It will be only such a change as there is between the perfect day and the daybreak; for we have the same sun, and the same light from the sun, and the same privilege of walking in the light. "Until the day break, and the shadows flee away, turn, my beloved, and be thou like a roe or a young hart upon the mountains of Division." Amen, and Amen.

THE CONSECRATION OF PRIESTS

Sermon Nos. 1,203, 1,204
Delivered on Lord's day Morning, November 15, 1874.
Portion of Scripture read before Sermon—Exodus 29:1–37.
Hymns from *Our Own Hymn Book*—411, 663, 878.

*This is the thing that thou shalt do unto them to hallow them, to
minister unto me in the priest's office*—Exodus 29:1.

UNDER the law, only one family could serve God in the priest's office, but under the gospel all the saints are "a chosen generation, a royal priesthood" (1 Pet. 2:9). In the Christian church no persons whatsoever are set apart to the priesthood above the rest of their brethren, for in us is fulfilled the promise which Israel by reason of her sin failed to obtain—"Ye shall be a kingdom of priests unto me." Paul, in addressing all the saints, bids them present their bodies a living sacrifice, holy, acceptable unto God, which is their reasonable service. It is the grand design of all the works of divine grace, both for us and in us, to fit us for the office of the spiritual priesthood, and it will be crown of our perfection when with all our brethren we shall sing unto the Lord Jesus the new song, "Unto him that loved us, and washed us from our sins in his own blood, and hath made us kings and priests unto God and his Father; to him be glory and dominion forever and ever." This honor have all the saints: according to Peter, in the second chapter of his first epistle, it belongs even to newborn babes in grace, for even such are spoken of as forming part of an holy priesthood, to offer up spiritual sacrifices. Nor is this confined to men as was the Aaronic priesthood, for in Christ Jesus there is neither male nor female. My subject today is the consecration of priests, but it does not refer exclusively or even specially to persons called clergymen, or minister, but to all of you who believe in Jesus, for ye are God's clergy, His *cleros*, that is, His inheritance, and ye should be all ministers, ministering according to the grace given to you.

The family of Aaron was *chosen* unto the priesthood, "for no man taketh this honor upon himself, but he that was called thereunto as was Aaron," and even thus all the Lord's people are chosen from before the foundation of the world. Being chosen, Aaron and his sons were at God's command *brought nigh* unto the door of the tabernacle. None ever come to God except they are brought to Him; even the spouse sings, "He brought me into the banqueting house." Jesus said, "No man can come unto me except the Father which hath sent me draw him." We are made nigh by the blood of Jesus and brought nigh by the drawings of the Holy Ghost.

Assuming that you and I have made our calling and election sure, let us further see what is needed to qualify us to serve as priests at the altar of the living God. Follow me carefully as I mention the ceremonies prescribed in the chapter before us, for they teach us necessary things: the outward ceremonies are abolished, but their inner meaning remains.

I. First, the priests were washed. We read in the fourth verse, "Aaron and his sons thou shalt bring unto the door of the tabernacle of the congregation, and shalt wash them with water." The pure and holy God cannot be served by men of unclean hands and impure hearts; He would not endure it under the law, nor will He tolerate it under the gospel. "Be ye clean that bear the vessels of the Lord," and, "Be ye holy for I am holy," are standing precepts of our priesthood. It was well said by the psalmist, "I will wash my hands in innocency, so will I compass thine altar, O Lord."

This washing is afforded us in two ways, answering to our double need. First, it is given to us in *regeneration*, wherein we are born of water and of the Spirit. By the power of the Holy Ghost we are made new creatures in Christ Jesus, and in us is fulfilled the type set forth in Naaman, who washed in Jordan, and his flesh came again unto him, even as a little child. Not in the waters of baptism, but in the living water of the Holy Spirit are we cleansed from nature's original defilement; He it is who causes old things to pass away, and makes all things new. Through His sanctifying operations we are cleansed from all filthiness of the flesh and of the spirit, and made vessels fit for the Master's use. This washing is in every case essential. You may say, "I desire to serve God," but you cannot do it till first you are born again. Your whole nature must be cleansed, or you will never be qualified to stand as a priest before the thrice holy God. I marvel how some who know nothing about regeneration can dare to call themselves priests. They are strangers to the renewing influences of the Spirit, and yet they style themselves God's ministers. Has God set blind men to be guides, and dead men to quicken souls? Unto such as these God saith, "What hast thou to do to declare my statutes?"

The need of another form of washing was indicated by the double stream which flowed from the pierced breast of Christ, for "forthwith came there out blood and water," We must be washed by *remission of sin*, of which David sang, "Purge me with hyssop and I shall be clean; wash me and I shall be whiter than snow." In the first moment of our faith in Jesus there is given to us a washing which makes us clean every whit in the sight of God, once for all. It is that washing to which the Lord Jesus referred when He said, "He that is washed needeth not save to wash his feet, for he is clean." The priests were washed once from head to foot, to make them ceremonially clean, and after that they needed only to wash their feet when they came into the holy place; and even thus our Lord told His disciples when He washed their feet that they had no need of another complete bathing, for they were clean every whit. Believers should not pray to their heavenly Father as if their sins still rested upon them and had never been forgiven, for the Lord has put away their sin, and as far as the east is from the west so far hath He removed their transgressions from them: yet as they continually accumulate some evil and stain by being in this body, and in this world, they have need to come each day with, "Forgive us our trespasses as we forgive them that trespass against us." Our first washing has removed all sin as before God the Judge; our daily washing cleanses us from offenses towards God as our Father. Even when we walk in the light as God is in the light, and have fellowship one with another, we yet need daily cleansing from all sin by the blood of Jesus Christ, His Son, and blessed be God we have it.

Now, my dear hearers, have you thus been cleansed from all sin? Do ye know today the power of that word, "Being made free from sin, ye became the servants of righteousness?" Have you the blessedness of that man unto whom the Lord imputeth not iniquity, and in whose spirit there is no guile? Do not try to stand as a priest before God till you have received this double washing. Remember the great aim of the gospel is to make us priests unto God, but the consecrating process must begin by our being cleansed as sinners from the guilt of sin and the defilement of our nature. He who would serve the Lord must first confess his iniquities and obtain remission, or he can no more approach the living God than a leper could enter into the holy place.

II. After being washed the priests were clothed. They might not wear one of the garments which belonged to themselves or to their former calling. Undergarments were provided for then, and outergarments too, within and without their raiment was new and appropriate. They put on what was given them, nothing more and nothing less. No man can serve God acceptably in his own righteousness, it is but filthy rags. We must have the fine linen of an inward sanctification, and the outer garment, for glory and for beauty, of the imputed righteousness of our Lord and Savior Jesus Christ. We must, in a word, sing with the hymn,

> Jesus, thy blood and righteousness,
> My beauty are, my glorious dress.

We cannot stand to worship God unless it be so; He will drive us from His presence.

Note, that *these garments were provided for them.* They were at no expense in buying them, nor labor in weaving them, nor skill in making them; they had simply to put them on. And you, dear child of God, are to put on the garments which Jesus Christ has provided for you, at His own cost, and freely bestows upon you out of boundless love. *These garments formed a complete apparel.* They had no shoes upon their feet, it is true, but they would have been superfluous, for the place whereon they stood was holy ground. They were sandalled with reverence. The child of God when he is bedecked in the righteousness of Christ still feels a solemn awe of the Lord, and comes into the presence of the Most High with lowliest adoration, for he remembers that he is but a creature at his best.

The garments were very comely to look upon. Though the common priests did not wear the breastplate of jewels, nor the bells and pomegranates, nor the girdle of blue and fine twined linen, yet, in their ordinary dress of pure white, they must have been very comely to look upon. Fine white linen is the emblem of the righteousness of the saints, and truly in God's eye, with the exception of His dear Son, there are no lovelier objects in the world than His own people when they are dressed in the garments of salvation.

The dress provided was absolutely necessary to be worn. No priest might offer sacrifice without the appointed garments, for we read in the forty-third verse of the twenty-eighth chapter, "They shall be upon Aaron, and upon his sons, when they come in unto the tabernacle of the congregation, or when they come near unto the altar to minister in the holy place; that they bear not iniquity, and die." They would have died had they attempted to sacrifice without being clothed according to the law. A man pretending to serve God without the divine righteousness upon him, puts himself in a most perilous position; he is where the flaming wrath of God burns terribly. Better for him to keep his own place in the distance, than to draw near unto the service of God, unless he is adorned with the glorious array which Christ has woven in the loom of His life and dyed in His own blood. Dear brethren, if you desire to worship God aright in holy labor, or prayer, or praise, you must go to your engagements dressed in the righteousness of Jesus, for you can only be "accepted in the Beloved."

III. Then, thirdly, THESE PRIESTS WERE ANOINTED. It does not appear that they were each one *personally* anointed so early in the ceremony, but they saw the fragrant oil poured upon Aaron on their behalf. So you find it written in the seventh verse, "Then shalt thou take the anointing oil, and pour it upon his head, and anoint him." So that in order to serve God aright, it is needful for us to see the anointing which has been given to our covenant Head, without measure. But you say to me, "Of what benefit can that be to us? We require the unction of the Holy Spirit upon ourselves." True, but the oil which was poured upon Aaron's head went down his beard, and its copious flow descended even to the skirts of his garments; and what you need to know if you are to be a true priest to God is, that the Holy Spirit comes to you through Christ and from Christ, and that it is because your Head is anointed, that you have an unction from the Holy One. You could not have been Christians if He had not first been the Christ. Be of good cheer concerning this, for though you may be one of the lowest members of the mystical body of Jesus Christ, you have an anointing from the Holy One, because Jesus has that anointing, and in the power of that anointing you may minister before the Lord. Further on in the discourse we shall have to show you the personal anointing which you must individually receive, but it is highly important for every worker to see where his fragrance before God must lie— never in himself, but always in his covenant Head. Be ye filled with the Spirit, but do not dream that the Spirit of God comes to you apart from your Lord. You are the branch, and the sap can only come to you through the stem. You are the member, and your life dwells in your head; divided from Jesus you are dead. Never forget this, for any attempt at independence will be fatal. A man in Christ is fragrant with a holy perfume before the Lord, but out of Christ he is an unclean thing, and cannot approach the altar.

IV. Fourthly, having been washed, clothed, and representatively anointed, they had next TO SHARE IN THE SIN OFFERING. They were sinful men, how could they approach a thrice holy God? You and I are sinful, as we know by bitter experience; how can we hope to stand before the mercy-seat, and present acceptable sacrifices unto such an One as God is? There is no way of approaching Him while our sin is seen, it must be covered, covered by a sin-offering. We are told that the sin-offering selected was a bullock without blemish, of the first year, strong, and vigorous, a perfect being as far as it could be. Lift your eyes to Jesus, in whom is no spot of sin, being undefiled in nature and immaculate in life. He it is who stands for you, even He who knew no sin, and yet was made sin for you that you might be made the righteousness of God in Him. He, in the fullness of His strength, and in the perfection of His manhood, gave Himself a ransom and a substitute for you. View Him with wondering gratitude.

The bullock of the sin-offering being brought to the altar, Aaron and his sons were to lay their hands upon it. Read the tenth verse—They "shall put their hands upon the head of the bullock." The Hebrew word means more than lightly placing the hand, it give the idea of pressing hard upon the bullock's head. They came each one and leaned upon the victim, loading him with their burden, signifying their acceptance of its substitution, their joy that the Lord would accept that victim in their stead. When they put their hands on the bullock, they made a confession of sin, and the Rabbis have preserved for us the form in which that confession was made, but time forbids our reading it to you. The act was evidently understood by all concerned as a typical transfer of guilt, and the placing of the bullock of the sin-offering in the place of the sinner. Come, brethren and sisters, though washed, though clothed, though anointed, come as penitents, and rejoice in the vicarious sacrifice of Jesus. Draw nigh unto the Lord with sincere hearts and acknowledge your transgressions, and again accept your Savior as your sin-bearer; for a sin-bearer who is not accepted by you can be of no service to you. The hands of faith must be laid upon the sacrifice: for my part, I like to lay them there every day, nay, I desire to keep them there always, believing without easing that my sin is imputed no more to me, but by a sacred act of God was laid upon Jesus, according to that sentence, "He hath laid on him the iniquity of us all."

The bullock was killed as a token that just as the poor beast was slain so they deserved to die for their sins, and that done, the blood was caught in bowls and taken to the altar, and there it was poured out, at the bottom of the altar, round about. Read the 17th verse. There must have been a pool of blood all round the altar, or at any rate a crimsoned line. What did it signify? Did it now show that our only access to God is by the blood? They were washed and robed and anointed, and yet they could not reach the altar till the way to it had been paved with atoning blood. Oh, my brother, there is no way for thee to God as His priest except through the precious blood. We cannot draw near to God, or serve Him aright, if we forget the blood of atonement. Our standing is upon and within the blood of sprinkling; we must bring our prayers, praises, preachings, almsgivings, and all other offerings, to the altar, around which the blood is poured. In vain are all good works which are not so presented. See ye well to this, my brethren. It is essential beyond all else.

This done, the choicer and more vital parts of the bullock were taken, and burned upon the altar, to show that even when our Lord Jesus is viewed as a sin of-fering, He is still a sweet savor unto God, and however He might hide His face from His Son because of our sin, yet He was always in Himself well pleasing unto the Fa-ther. Hence the inwards of the bullock were burned on the altar, where nothing could be presented but that which was a sweet savor to God. O thou Lamb of God, under whatever aspect we behold Thee, Thou art still precious to thy Father! Thou wert beloved by Him even when Thou hadst to cry, "My God, my God, why hast thou for-saken me!"

But because the bullock was a sin-offering, and therefore obnoxious to God, its flesh, and its skin, and all that remained were carried outside the camp, and burned with a quick, consuming fire, as a thing worthy to be destroyed, for sin was upon it, and it must be burned up. Believer, have you seen Jesus as the great Offering for sin, made a curse of us? You will never serve God in the priestly office aright unless you see sin is a hateful thing to God, so hateful that, even when it only lay upon His dear Son by imputation, He could not look upon Him, but bruised and smote Him until He cried in anguish, "*Eloi, Eloi, lama sabachthani.*" "Jesus also, that he might sanctify the people with His own blood, suffered without the camp," to show that not without His being treated as a transgressor could we be treated as righteous, and also that sin is in itself a deadly pest, which must not be endured in the camp of the chosen. Never let your joy concerning the atonement lessen your horror of transgression:—

> With your joy for pardoned guilt,
> Mourn that you pierced the Lord.

I am persuaded that no one will ever serve the Lord humbly and devotedly unless he obtains a clear view of the Lord Jesus as his sin-offering, and substitute. Some preachers either do not know that truth, or else they think too little of it to make it prominent in their sermons, hence their ministry does not save souls. The great saving truth is the doctrine of atonement by substitution. Without it ministers will keep souls in bondage year after year, because they do not proclaim the finished re-demption, nor let men know that sin was laid on Jesus that it might be forever re-moved from the believer. "He was made sin for us that we might be made the righteousness of God in him"; brethren, get that truth clearly into your heads, and intensely into your hearts, and you will become devoted to the Lord. Do not only believe that grand truth, but in the spirit of it serve ye the Lord without weariness, seeing ye have been redeemed with a price far more precious than silver and gold.

V. After the sin-offering the consecrated ones went on to TAKE THEIR SHARE IN THE BURNT-OFFERING. The burnt-offering differed widely from the sin-offering. The sin-offering indicated Christ as bearing our sin, but the burnt-offering sets Him forth as presenting an acceptable offering unto the Lord. God required of us perfect obedience, He demanded from us a pure and holy life, and the requirement was a just one: but among us all there is none righteous, no, not one; how then could we stand before the thrice Holy Lord? Beloved, Jesus stands in the gap. Before God His righteousness was perfect, acceptable, and delightful, and for us it is presented. He is made of God unto us righteousness. The burnt-offering does not bring to light the remembrance of sin except so far as it reminds us that we were in need of a perfect righteousness; it brings before us only the thought of Jesus offering Himself as a sweet savor unto God, and making us accepted in the Beloved. The priests were to bring a ram without blemish, and when killed, before it was laid on the altar, its inwards were to be washed, for otherwise the natural foulness of its body would prevent its being a fit type of that Savior who is pure within, in whom there is no taint of original sin. When this ram was brought the priests were to lay their hands upon it, as much as to say, "We accept this ram, that it may represent us as acceptable before God." Oh, beloved, lay your hands on Jesus now by faith, and say, "Jesus, I accept Thee as my righteousness before the Lord, and believe that as God sees in Thee all that is delightful, and smells a sweet savor of rest, so He will be will pleased with me for thy sake."

This offering when placed upon the altar was wholly burnt; not a fragment of it was put outside the camp, not a morsel of it was eaten by man, but the whole ram was utterly consumed with fire, for it was a burnt-offering unto the Lord. And thus, dear friends, it is very delightful to us to see that God received Jesus, the whole of Jesus; there was nothing in Him to reject, and nothing that could be done without. He satisfied the Lord; He asked no more, He would have no less. Jesus has rendered to the Father all that He could desire from men, and the Lord is well pleased for His righteousness' sake. A sense of acceptance is a very necessary thing to those who would worship God aright, for if you do not enjoy it the legal spirit will begin to work to win acceptance by merit, and that will spoil all. If men dream that they are to pray or preach their way to heaven, or to do this, and to do that, to be acceptable with God, they will offer strange fire on the Lord's altar and bring sacrifices with which He can never be pleased. Vain oblations He will call them, and frown on the offerers. How delightful it is to serve God with a sense that we are pleasant in the sight of God; for this fills us with gratitude, inspires us with zeal, creates boldness, and fosters every grace. With what joy will you stand to minister daily whatever your calling may be, whether it be as a mother in the family, a servant in the house, a minister in the pulpit, or a teacher in the class. You will not need driving like a slave to his toil, but like a dearly beloved child you will rejoice to please your Father in all things. Work in the prison-house of the law under the lash of conscience is a very different thing from holy work in the sunlight of the Lord's countenance and the liberty of full acceptance. He who knows that he is not now to be judged and condemned by the law, but stands forever justified because of what Christ has done for him, serves his God with a holy alacrity unknown to others.

VI. After the priests had seen for themselves the sin-offering and the burnt-offering, it was needful that they should partake of a third sacrifice, which was A PEACE OFFERING. Another ram was brought as unblemished and vigorous as the former, for Jesus is never to be typified by anything but the best of its kind. We are told in the nineteenth verse that Aaron and his sons were to put their hands upon it, for, whatever view of the great sacrifice they might gaze upon, it was imperatively necessary that they should have a personal interest in it; mere theory will never do, we must have personal acquaintance with the Lord, and we must have Him to be our own. So long as we have no part or lot in Jesus we are as much excluded from the service of the Lord as were the uncircumcised and the unclean. No man can run the heavenly race unless he is looking unto Jesus, he cannot be a soldier of the Lord unless he has Christ for his Captain, he cannot feed others until he has himself fed on Jesus, nor bring others to Jesus till he has come himself. "The husbandman that laboreth must first be partaker of the fruits"; this is one of the laws of spiritual husbandry, and cannot be set aside. Lay your hand upon the head of the substitute, before you venture to lay it upon the work of the Lord.

When this was done, the peace-offering was slain. A sin-offering was a thing obnoxious to God, and represented expiation made for sin, a burnt-offering was a sweet-savor offering unto God, and it was all burned on the altar, all being for the Lord alone—thus representing the Lord Jesus as rendering to the Lord a complete obedience, which magnified the law and made it honorable; but the peace offering was shared between the Lord and the priest or offerer. The Lord's part was consumed with fire upon the altar, and another portion was eaten by man in the holy place. The peace offering was thus an open declaration of the communion which had been established between God and man, so that they ate together, rejoicing in the same offering. Beloved brethren, when you have felt the sweets of seeing the Lord as a sin-offering, and then have tasted the high joys of acceptance as you have gazed upon Him as the burnt-offering, satisfying Jehovah's heart, it is surpassingly delightful to behold the Lamb of God as our peace-offering, making glad the heart of God and man, and bringing both in bonds of friendship to a common meeting-place. The eternal Father says, "This is my beloved Son, in whom I am well pleased," and we cry, "This is our beloved Lord, in whom our inmost soul rejoices."

In the peace-offering the communion between the priests and the Lord commenced outwardly by their being consecrated by the blood of the peace-offering. Moses dipped his finger in the blood, and smeared first the priest's right ear, then his thumb, and then his toe; as Matthew Henry says, as if they marked the boundaries and extremities of man's being, to show that all that was enclosed within the crimson lines was consecrated unto the Lord. We go not too far when we add that it signified the dedication of each faculty. The ear was henceforth to hear God's commands, to listen to divine teaching, and to drink in divine promises, and no more to regard falsehood, vanity, and vice. The hand was now henceforth to be engaged in the divine service with diligence and intelligence, for the right hand was thus marked, and the thumb, the most useful part of it: for holy work the hand must be reserved. The feet were to be equally holy, the priest, wherever he stood, or walked, or ran, was to be "holiness unto the Lord." He had no right to go anywhere if that blood-marked foot would be out of place. The whole man was thus consecrated by the blood of the everlasting covenant: a solemn seal indeed! Our personal share of the blood of Jesus has already done this for us, it has constrained us to yield unto God our whole manhood, spirit, soul, and body. My brother, you can never serve God as His priest unless you are wholly given up to God through the blood of Jesus. You must have this verse in your very soul, and must masticate it, digest it, assimilate it into your nature— "Ye are not your own, ye are bought with a price, therefore glorify God in your bodies and your spirits, which are his." This surrender of yourself unto the Lord commences your communion with the Lord; the peace-offering has begun.

The next thing was to sprinkle the priests all over with a mixture of oil and blood, and this is that anointing which I said we should see by-and-by. "Thou shalt take of the blood that is upon the altar, and of the anointing oil, and sprinkle it upon Aaron, and upon his garments, and upon his sons, and upon the garments of his sons with him: and he shall be hallowed, and his garments, and his sons, and his sons' garments with him." Yes, brethren, we need to know that double anointing, the blood of Jesus which cleanses, and the oil of the Holy Spirit which perfumes us. It is well to see how these two blend in one, Jesus and his atonement, the Spirit and His sanctification; the work for us and the work in us. Read the third of John, and there you find, "Ye must be born again"; but side by side with it you get, "Whosoever believeth in him is not condemned." It is not so easy for the preacher always to give these two doctrines with equal clearness and distinctness; he is very apt, when he is preaching up simple faith, and saying, "Only believe," to forget that equally important statement, "Ye must be born again." It is a terrible blunder to set the blood and the oil in opposition, they must always go together. Yet there are some who have even spoken depreciatingly of repentance, which is an essential part of the work of the Spirit of God; their zeal for holding up the righteousness of Christ by faith has driven them beyond the bounds of truth. Brethren, do not err in this matter, but abide in equal loyalty to these equally sure and important verities. If you would serve the Lord aright, you must have the blood and the oil sprinkled upon you, that is to say, you must know personally the influence of them both. What a strange sight these men in white garments must have presented, bespattered all over with blood and oil. Did that stain their garments? No, it adorned and perfumed them. Remember that saying, "They have washed their robes and made them white in the blood of the Lamb." No purity is comparable to that which comes by the Spirit and by the atoning blood: in God's sight these priests thus distained were more beautiful by far than they had been before. Oh, my soul, prize Jesus and His blood, and never forget that thou needest the gifts and graces of the Holy Spirit. Bless God for justification, but seek after sanctification. Praise Him for perfection in Christ Jesus, and go on to obtain the perfect work of the Holy Ghost. We have a cleansing and we also have an unction from the Holy One: as our experience is, so let our teaching be, for the priests' garments taught the people. We are to go forth as priests, and declare the virtue of the atoning sacrifice, but we must also manifest the sanctifying power of the Holy Spirit in our daily lives.

The next part of the ceremony was very singular. The priests had their hands filled. Certain parts of the ram were taken, and "one loaf of bread, and one cake of oiled bread, and one wafer out of the basket of unleavened bread, which is before the Lord," and all these were put into the hands of Aaron and his sons, so that they stood with their hands full before the Lord. See the beauty of this, pray for a complete realization of it yourself. The Lord intends to make you a priest, but your hands are full of sin. What have you to do? You must lay those guilty hands on the sin-offering, and make confession, and exercise faith: then the sin is gone, being transferred to another, and your hands are empty. What next? Will the Lord leave you empty-handed? No, He gives you somewhat to offer. He allows you a part of the peace-offering to fill your hands withal, and this you present before Him as a wave-offering. It is a blessed thing to stand before God with your hands full of Christ. The service which consists in holding forth Jesus is the most blessed. I love preaching when I have to preach Jesus only. Then I come before you, not empty-handed, but loaded with meat and bread for you. How idle it is for us to stand before God with nothing to offer, and if we have not Jesus we have nothing, or worse than nothing. We may also interpret the full hands of the priests as representing our being enriched with the truth. I believe it used to be a ceremony in the English church that, when the bishop ordained a minister, he always placed the Bible in his hands, to set forth what he was expected to deal out to the people. When the Lord ordains His people to be priests unto Him He puts the Bible into their hands, and fills their heads and hearts with the truth thereof. When you have the inspired word in your hands, you have both meat for strong men and bread for children; you have all sorts of spiritual food for all sorts of persons, and you need not fear that they will turn away dissatisfied, they cannot need more to feed upon than the bread of God's altar and the flesh of God's peace-offering.

When their hands were full, and they stood at the altar, it indicated the way in which they brought to the Lord all that they had. We cannot act as priests before God with empty hands. "None of you shall appear before me empty," is His command. Has He given us wealth? Let us give without grudging, devising liberal things. Never neglect weekly storing and weekly offering, these are fit parts of Sabbath worship. Have we time, talent, influence, let us consecrate them all, and come with those possessions which Jesus has lent us, and present them with the flesh of the peace-offering, and the sacred oil.

Holding this in their hands, the priests had to wave their pleasant burden to and fro. I scarcely know why, except that you who are God's priests have not had your hands filled that you may stand still; but that you may move them to and fro in the earth, that east, west, north, and south may know the benefit thereof, and that your brethren on either hand may commune with you in your ministering. Every now and then the priests stopped the horizontal motion, and heaved or lifted up their offering, as if to say, "It is all for Thee, O Jehovah. We lift it up into the presence of thine august Majesty, for it is thine, and we are about to lay it on thine altar." Believers, if you have had your hands filled by God, you must not be idle. Your fullness is meant for distribution to God's glory. If the clouds be full of rain they empty themselves upon the earth; if the rivers be full of water they run into the sea, and if God gives you a fullness, it is that you may communicate it to others and devote it to Himself. Jesus Christ breaks the bread and multiplies it, and gives it to the disciples to divide among the multitude. Many a man becomes empty handed because he does not know the art of distribution. He has his hands full and cries out, "Where shall I bestow my goods? My hands are full and I would keep it for myself and my family." My brother, wave it among your neighbors, lift it up to God in solemn consecration, and then let it be laid upon God's altar, since for this purpose you were called to be a priest unto the Most High.

Last of all there followed a very pleasant part of the matter—they sat down and feasted. God had received His part in the burning of the victim on the altar, and now Aaron and his sons were to "eat those things wherewith the atonement was made." You cannot serve God without strength; you cannot have strength except you eat, and you must be careful what you take into your soul, for according to what your food is will your strength be. The Lord would have His people fed daily upon Christ, and fed in the holy place where they serve. Christ is delightful to God and is delightful to you, and you must feed on Him in communion with God, in the place of holy fellowship. There is no sustenance for our inner nature anywhere but in Jesus, but, blessed be His name, no other sustenance can be desired, for He fills us to the full, and gives us a strength which is equal to our day.

I know some good people who are very busy indeed in the service of God, and I am very delighted that they should be, but I would caution them against working and never eating. They give up attending the means of grace as hearers, because they have so much to do as workers. That is very well, and some strong men may be able to do it safely, but I do not think many of us can afford to do without the regular hearing of the Word. Whatever may be our zeal to work like Martha, we must also sit at Jesus' feet like Mary, or we shall become "cumbered with much serving." The priest is to offer sacrifice, but he must have time, also, to feed on the portion allotted to him. How sweet it is to enjoy the food of God, the flesh of Jesus, the bread of heaven. Aaron and his sons had the breast and the shoulder for their part—the love of Christ's heart and the power of Christ's arm. I am thankful, as one of God's priests, to have the shoulder and breast, for power and love are needful for my comfort and support. Eli's vile sons were wont to drive a three-pronged hook into the cauldron, and bring up what they thought the choicer portions, but my soul is more than content with what the rule of the house allots me, in fact, these are the best parts of the sacrifice.

In closing, I would call the attention of believers for a moment to the fact that Aaron and his sons received this consecration for life. You will find in the ninth verse the words, "The priests' office shall be theirs for a perpetual statute." "Once a priest, always a priest," is the rule in the priesthood to which we belong. We abide in Christ, and we also have an anointing which abideth in us, for we have been sealed with "that Holy Spirit of promise." Do not act at any time as if you were not priests. If you profess to be the Lord's do not lie about it, let it be truly so, and that every day, and all the day, and in all things, for He hath made us kings and priests unto God forever. Do not, I beseech you, dishonor your sacred character.

I shall ask two questions in closing. Do you and I offer sacrifice continually? Unto this we are called, according to the apostle, that we should offer the sacrifice of prayer and praise continually. To Him the cherubim continually cry, "Holy, holy, holy." Do we every day feel that our whole being is "Holiness unto the Lord?" In the workshop, in the home, at the fireside, in the field, as well as in the prayer meeting, the vows of God are upon us; we are a separated people, and belong unto God alone? O see ye to this!

What have you to offer now? Have you brought an offering now? What will you render unto God for all His benefits towards you? Is there nothing to be done for Christ this afternoon? No sick ones to be visited, no poor child to be instructed, no backslider to be reclaimed? Shall a single hour go by without a sacrifice? I charge you, brethren, continually bring of your substance, continually bring of your talent, continually bring of your influence. If God be God, and if you be His priests, serve Him. If you be not His ordained one, then you live unto yourselves, and it will be well to know it: anything is better than to be hypocrites: but if you be true men I beseech you by the mercies of God that ye present your bodies, your souls, your spirits unto God, which is but a reasonable service. When you have once for all made the consecration, may God grant you grace continually to stand to it, and He shall have the glory, forever and ever. Amen.

THE SIN OFFERING

SERMON NO. 739
DELIVERED ON LORD'S DAY MORNING, MARCH 10, 1867.
PORTIONS OF SCRIPTURE READ BEFORE SERMON—LEVITICUS 4:1–21;
HEBREWS 13:10–15.

If the priest that is anointed do sin according to the sin of the people; then let him bring for his sin, which he hath sinned, a young bullock without blemish, unto the LORD for a sin offering—Leviticus 4:3.

IN the previous chapters of the book of Leviticus you read of the burnt offering, the peace offering, and the meat offering—all types our Lord Jesus Christ, as seen from different points of view. Those three sacrifices were sweet savor offerings, and represent the Lord Jesus in His glorious Person and perfect righteousness as an offering of a sweet smell into God. The chapter before us, the whole of which we shall require as a text, describes the sin offering, which, although quite distinct from the sweet savor offerings, is not altogether to be separated from them, for the Lord Jesus Christ viewed in any light is very dear unto His Father; and even when beheld as a sin offering is elect and precious unto God, as we shall have to show you in the type before us; still, the sin offering does not set forth the acceptance of the substitute before the Lord, but rather brings out the abhorrence which God has towards sin, the putting away from His holy presence of everything upon which sin is laid. This morning, if God shall enable us, we hope to impress upon your minds, first of all, the great evil of sin; and secondly, the great and wonderful power of the blood of atonement by which sin is put away.

Without any further preface we shall invite you, in meditating upon the type before us, first, *to consider our Lord Jesus as made sin for us;* secondly, we shall *ask you to observe, carefully and prayerfully, His blood in its efficacy before the Lord;* and thirdly, *we shall bid you look at His substitution in the shame which it involved.*

I. First, brethren, let us by the aid of the Holy Spirit, VIEW OUR BLESSED LORD AS MADE SIN FOR US, as He is here typified in the bullock.

1. *His personal character* is set forth before us in the victim chosen, namely, a young bullock without blemish. It was a bullock, the most valuable of the sacrifices, an animal laborious in life and costly in death; it was a young bullock in the fullness of its strength and vigor; it was without blemish and the slightest fault disqualified

it from being laid upon the altar of God. Behold, O believer, your Lord Jesus, more precious far than ten thousands of the fat of fed beasts: a sacrifice not to be purchased with gold, or estimated in silver. Full of vigor, in the very prime of manhood, He offered up Himself for us. Even when He died, He died not through weakness; for that cry of His at His death, "with a loud voice," proved that His life was still firm within Him, and that when He gave up the ghost, His death was not one of compulsion, but a voluntary expiring of the soul. His glory is as the firstling of the bullock, full of vigor and of strength. How distinctly was our Lord proved to be without blemish! Naturally born without sin, practically He lived without fault. In Him there was neither deficiency nor excess. In no virtue did He come behind, and no fault could be found in Him. The prying eyes of the prince of this world could find nothing in Him, and the still more accurate search of the all-seeing God found no fault in Him. This spotlessness was necessary, for how could He have been made an offering for our sin, if it had not been true that personally "He knew no sin"? Shall one bankrupt stand in the debtor's court as a substitute for another? How shall one penniless wretch pay the debt of another who is about to be cast into prison? If the king require service of any man, how shall another from whom service is equally due, offer himself as a substitute for him? No, the savior of others must have no obligations of his own; he must owe no personal debts; there must be no claims on the part of justice against him, on his own account, or he cannot stand "the just for the unjust," to expiate the sins of men. Ye holy souls, feast your eyes upon the spotless Son of God. Ye pure in heart, delight your purified vision with a sight of His perfections. You shall one day be like Him—this will be your heaven; meanwhile, make it your rapture, your paradise on earth, to gaze upon the unrivaled beauties of the Altogether Lovely. "In him was no sin." In Him was all excellence. His body and soul are alike: white as the lily for holiness, though made by suffering red as the rose. Alabaster, and bright ivory overlaid with sapphires, are but dull and soiled types of His purity. Come, ye virgin souls, and let the eyes of your holy love survey Him, that ye may see how fit He was to suffer as "the just for the unjust, to bring us to God."

The act of transference of sin to the victim next calls for our attention. You will have noticed, in reading the chapter, that our Lord's being made sin is set forth to us by the very significant transfer of sin to the bullock, which was made by the priest, or by the elders of the people, as the case might be. We are expressly told, "He shall lay his hand upon the bullock's head," which act, our good Dr. Watts has interpreted in his well-known verse—

> My faith would lay her hand
> On that dear head of thine,
> While like a penitent I stand;
> And there confess my sin.

This laying of the hand does not appear to have been a mere touch of contact, but in some other places of Scripture has the meaning of leaning heavily, as in the expression, "Thy wrath lieth hard upon me" (Ps. 88:7).

Surely this is the very essence and nature of faith, which doth not only bring us into contact with the great Substitute, but teaches us to lean upon Him with all the burden of our guilt; so that if our sins be very weighty, yet we see Him as able to bear them all; and mark, the whole weight of our iniquity taken off from us, who must have been crushed to the lowest hell thereby, and laid on Him who took the weight and bore it all, and then buried it in His sepulcher forever. From of old it was decreed, "The Lord hath laid on him the iniquity of us all." Jehovah made to meet upon the head of the Substitute all the offenses of His covenant people; but each one of the chosen is brought personally to ratify this solemn covenant act of the great God, when by grace He is enabled by faith to put His hand upon the head of the "Lamb slain from before the foundation of the world." My fellow believers, do you remember that rapturous day? My soul recalls her day of deliverance with delight; laden with guilt and full of fears, I saw my Savior willing to be my Substitute, and I laid my hand, oh! how timidly at first, but courage grew and confidence was confirmed, I leaned my soul entirely upon Him; and now it is my unceasing joy to know that my sins are no longer imputed to me, but laid on Him, and like the debts of the poor wounded traveler, Jesus, like the good Samaritan, has said of all my future sinfulness, "Set that to my account." Oh! blessed discovery, sweet solace of a repenting heart.

> My numerous sins transferr'd to him,
>   Shall never more be found,
> Lost in his blood's atoning stream
>   Where every crime is drown'd!

We must now beg your notice of *the sins transferred.* In the case of the type, they were sins of ignorance. Alas! the Jew knew nothing about a sin offering for sins of presumption, but there is such a sin offering for us. Our presumptuous sins were laid on Christ; our willful sins; our sins of light and knowledge, are pardoned by His blood. The mention of sins of ignorance, suggests a very comfortable reflection, that if there are any sins which I know not, they were, notwithstanding my ignorance, laid on my Substitute and put away by His atonement. It is not sin as we see it which was laid on Christ, but sin as God sees it; not sin as our conscience feebly reveals it to us, but sin as God beholds it, in all its unmitigated malignity, and unconcealed loathsomeness. Sin in its exceeding sinfulness Jesus has put away. Not sham sin, but real sin; sin as before the Lord; sin as sin, Jesus has made an end of. Child of God, you will not misuse this truth and deny the need of repentance, for you well know that you cannot practically feel the power of this blood, except as your sin is known to you; this, indeed, is intimated in the type, for, according to verse fourteen, the bullock was only offered when the sin was known. It was to be laid by the elders upon the head of the bullock, when the sin was no longer hidden from the eyes of the congregation. Sin unknown, the sacrifice is unheeded. It is only as you know and perceive sin that you can consciously know and prize the atonement by which it is taken away. Mark, it is when you perceive sin that then you are to trust the blood; not when you perceive holiness in yourself, and goodness and virtue, but when you perceive sin, and iniquity, and defilement—it is then you are to lay your hand upon the head of the great

Atoning Sacrifice. Jesus is a *sinner's* Savior. "If any man sin, we have an advocate with the Father, Jesus Christ the righteous." It is not written, "If any man be holy, he has an advocate," but "if any man *sin*, we have an advocate"; so that in all our sin and iniquity, blackness, and defilement, when overwhelmed with our own vileness, we may still come to Christ, and believe that our most horrible and detestable sins were laid upon Him, and over and above that those sins which we do not feel, which may be even more detestable, even these, and what is more, the sinfulness of our nature itself—that black and polluted fount from which the streams of our trespasses take their rise; the guilt of all actual and original sin was laid upon Jesus, and by Him forever put away.

Passing on, still keeping to the same point, we would remark that the sin was laid upon the bullock most conspicuously "*before the Lord.*" Did you notice the frequent expressions: "shall bring him to the door of the congregation before the Lord"; "kill the bullock before the Lord"; "shall sprinkle the blood seven times before the Lord, and shall put some of it upon the horns of the altar of sweet incense before the Lord"? Clearly the most important part of the sacrifice was not before the people, but before the Lord. All that the onlookers outside could have seen was the bullock, when dead, carried by the priests without the camp. Some of them who came nearer might have seen the pouring of the blood at the bottom of the brazen altar, but they certainly never did and never could see the priest sprinkle the blood towards the veil, nor yet see him put it upon the horns of the golden altar, for the court of the priest was concealed from their view. We very much mistake if we think that the ceremonies of Jews were much seen by the people. They were mainly unseen except by the priests. The ritual of the old covenant must have been very little a matter of sight; for the Israelite, pure and simple, never penetrated beyond the first court; he stood before the brazen altar, but he never went further; and all that was done in the next court of the priests, and especially all that was done in the most holy place, must have been entirely a matter of faith to all the people. The fact was, the sacrifices were not so much for men to look at as for God Himself to gaze upon, and though this may seem to you a strange observation, there is no little value in it. You will hear men nowadays say that the purpose of atonement has reference to men, and not to God. Depend upon it there is a fatal error in this doctrine, and we must denounce it. Although its advocates take some few expressions of certain of our hymns, and pretend to believe that we teach that the blood placated an angry God, we never taught anything of the kind, and they know we never did; yet we are not to be frightened into denying or qualifying our assertion that the action of God towards man has been wondrously affected by the atonement of Christ. God the Judge would have condemned us to punishment had not Jesus suffered in our stead, so that, in justice, we might be permitted to go free. Not only is man made willing to love God by the manifestation of the love of God in Christ Jesus, but it has become possible for God to extend the hand of amity towards sinful man through the atonement; and this would not have been possible, consistently with the divine attributes, if it had not been for the atoning sacrifice. We must still stand to it, that the blood is not merely a comfort to the wounded conscience, but is really a satisfaction to divine justice; a covering, a pro-pitiation, a mercy-seat for the Most Holy God. That is a striking passage concerning the Passover and the destroying angel in Egypt. Thus spoke Jehovah, "When *I* see the blood, I will pass over you"; not, "When *you* see the blood." The spared ones did not see the blood at that moment; for, you will remember, that they were all inside the house feasting upon the lamb. The father of the family had put the blood outside upon the lintel and the side-posts, not for the inmates to see, but for God to see; and so, though a sight of the precious blood, thanks be to God, does bring us faith, and joy, and peace, yet the real work of our salvation is not the effect of the blood upon us, but the effect of the blood upon God Himself: not, it is true, a change produced in God, but a change which is thus produced in the action of divine justice. Apart from the blood, we are guilty, condemned: washed in blood, we are accepted and beloved. Without the atonement, we are aliens and strangers, heirs of wrath even as others; but, as seen in the eternal covenant purpose, through the precious blood of Jesus, we are accepted in the beloved. The great stress of the transaction lies in its being done "before the Lord."

Still, further, carefully observe that as soon as ever the sin was thus "before the Lord," laid upon the bullock, *the bullock was slain.* "He shall lay his hand upon the bullock's head, and kill the bullock before the Lord." So, in the fifteenth verse, "The elders of the congregation shall lay their hands upon the head of the bullock before the Lord, and the bullock shall be killed before the Lord." Ah! yes; as soon as the sin is transferred, the penalty is transferred too. Down fell the pole-axe the minute that the priestly hand had been laid on the bullock. Unsheathed was the bloody knife of sacrifice the moment that the elders had begun to lean upon the sacrificial head. So was it with our Savior; He must smart, He must die, for only as dying could He become our sin offering. Ah! brethren, those who would preach Christ, but not Christ crucified, miss the very soul and essence of our holy faith. "Let him come down from the cross, and we will believe in him," is the Unitarian cry. Anything but a crucified God. But there, indeed, lies the secret of that mystery, and the very core and kernel of our confidence. A reigning Savior I do rejoice in: the thought of the splendor yet to come makes glad our eyes; but after all, it is a bleeding Savior that is the sinner's hope. It is to the cross, the center of misery, that the sinner turns his eyes for comfort, rather than to the stars of Bethlehem, or to the blazing sun of the millennial kingdom. I remember one joining this church, who said, "Sir, I had faith once in Christ glorified, but it never gave me comfort: I have now come to a faith in Christ crucified, and I have peace." At Calvary there is the comfort, and there only. That Jesus lives is de-lightful; but the basis of the delight is, "He lives who once was slain." That He will reign forever is a most precious doctrine of our faith, but that the hand that wields the silver scepter, once was pierced, is the great secret of the joy. O beloved, abide not in any place from which your eye cannot behold the cross of Christ. When you are think-ing of the doctrines of the gospel, or the precepts of the Word, or studying the prophecies of Scripture, never let your mind relinquish the study of the cross. The cross was the place of your spiritual birth; it must ever be the spot for renewing your health, for it is the sanatorium of every sinsick soul. The blood is the true balm of Gilead; it is the only catholicon which heals every spiritual disease. Come, sin-sick soul, and breathe the air which was purified when the blood of the heart of Jesus fell from His wounds to the ground, for no spiritual disease can abide the presence of the healing blood. Hasten, ye weak ones, to Calvary, and partake in God-given strength and vigor. It is from Calvary that you shall see the Sun of Righteousness arising with healing beneath His wings. The beloved Physician meets His patients at the foot of the cross, and relieves them from all their ills.

I shall not ask you to dwell on any further details of the type, as they refer to the substitution, but I cannot leave the topic till I have asked each one this all-important question: "Is the Lord Jesus made a sin offering for you? It is written, "*He* hath made him to be sin for us"; and from this it appears that sin was laid upon Jesus by God Himself; but still it is true that each believer by faith lays his own sins there, and the hymn, "I lay my sins on Jesus," is quite scriptural. Have you, dear friend, seen your sins laid on Jesus? Has your faith laid its hand upon His head? My dear hearers, we shall soon, each one of us, have to pass through the vale of death; it may be but a very short time before some of us will know what are the solemnities of our last, departing hour. Are you ready?—quite ready? You have been a professor for years—are you ready now to die? Can you hope that if at this moment the summons were given, sitting where you are, you are so really and truly resting in the precious blood, that sin would not disturb your dying peace, because it is forgiven and put away! Search the ground of your hope, I pray you, and be not satisfied unless your faith be surely built upon the Rock of Ages. Get as much assurance as you can, my brethren, but beware of presumption. I have seen some of those fine Christians who will not say—

> Rock of Ages, cleft for me,
> Let me hide myself in thee!

And I think very little of them. It is their boast that no hymns will suit them but those which are full of assurance and conscious enjoyment. I admire their confidence, if it be the fruit of the Spirit; but I fear, in many cases, it is the offspring of proud, unhumbled self-conceit. I know that when shaking times, when I am sore vexed with bodily pain and mental distractions, I am glad enough to say—

> Let me hide myself in thee!
> Let the water and the blood,
> From thy riven side which flowed,
> Be of sin the double cure,
> Cleanse me from its guilt and power!

Without boasting, I can declare as much about strong faith in God as most men; and I can usually rejoice in the fullest confidence of my acceptance in the Beloved; but there are times with me of deeply awful depression of spirit, and horror of great darkness; and at such periods my joyous confidence takes the form of humbly pleading the blood once shed for sinner, and saying, with a broken heart—

> Nothing in my hand I bring:
> Simply to thy cross I cling.

It seems to me, that humbly resting upon Jesus is the best position for us; and I ask each of you, very affectionately, whether that is your position at this present moment? Does your heart rejoice in the Substitute? Do you rejoice in the language of these two precious verses?—

> When Satan tempts me to despair,
> And tells me of the guilt within,
> Upward I look, and see him there
> Who made an end of all my sin.

> Because the sinless Savior died,
> My sinful soul is counted free;
> For God, the Just, is satisfied
> To look on Him, and pardon me.

II. Let us turn to the second part of the subject. The chapter sets forth before us THE EFFICACY OF THE PRECIOUS BLOOD OF JESUS.

As soon as the bullock was slain, the priest carefully collected the blood. The bullock was slain in the court of the Israelites; see, there it lies at the foot of the brazen altar, with the blood in a basin. The priest passes into the court of the priests, passes by the golden altar of incense, which stood in the holy place, and proceeds to dip his finger in the basin, and to sprinkle the blood seven times towards the veil which concealed the Holy of Holies. Whether the blood fell on the veil or not we are not certain; but we have good reason to believe that it was cast upon the veil itself. The veil, of costliest tapestry, would thus become by degrees more and more like a vesture dipped in blood. Seven times towards the veil the blood of the sin offering was sprinkled by the priest. Why did he begin there? It was to show that *our communion with God* is by blood. The veil was not then, of course, rent. It showed that the way of access to God was not then revealed. The sprinkling of the blood showed that the only thing that could open the way of access to God was the blood; that the blood, when it should be perfectly offered, seven times sprinkled, would rend the veil. The blood of Jesus has to the letter fulfilled the type. When our Lord had sprinkled, if I may so say, seven times His own heart's blood upon the veil, He said, "It is finished," and "the veil of the temple was rent in twain from the top to the bottom." Beloved, through the perfect offering of the precious blood, we have access with boldness into this grace wherein we stand; and we who have faith in that blood have intimate communion with the living God, and come near to His mercy-seat to talk with Him, who dwelleth between the cherubim, as a man talketh with his friend. The priest began at the innermost point, because the first thing which a Christian loses through sin is communion with God, and free access to Him, and consequently the first thing to be restored to him must be this communion with his God. Suppose, my brother, you backslide, there are some things which you will not lose at once. You will still be able to pray in a feeble style; you will still have some sense of acceptance, but certainly your enjoyment and fellowship with God will be suspended so soon as you have fallen from your first estate. Therefore the blood is sprinkled upon the veil to show you that through the blood, and through the blood only, you can renew your access. You advanced Christians, you who have lived in the very heart of God, and have stood like Milton's angel in the sun; you who have been made to sit at the banqueting table, and to drink of the wines on the lees well refined; you who have been the King's favorites, and, like Mephibosheth, have always been made to sit at the King's own table, and to eat of the choice portions of His dainties, if you have lost your heavenly fellowship, it is through the blood, and through the blood alone, that you can again have access unto the heart of God.

The next act of the priest was to retire a little from the veil to the place where stood the golden altar of incense, adorned with four horns of gold, probably of a pyramidal shape, or fashioned like rams' horns, and the priest, dipping his finger in the basin, smeared this horn and the other, until the four horns glowed with crimson in the light of the golden candlestick. The horn is always, in the oriental usage, indicative of strength. What was the blood put upon the altar for, then? That incense altar was typical of prayer, and especially of the intercession of Christ; and the blood on the horn showed that the force and power of *all-prevailing intercession* lies in the blood. Why was this the second thing done? It seems to me that the second thing which a Christian loses is his prevalence in prayer. Whereas, first he loses communion with God when he backslides; the next thing he loses is his power in supplication. He begins to be feeble upon his knees; he cannot win of the Lord that which he desireth. How is he to get back his strength? Here the great Anointed Priest teaches us to look to the blood for renewed power, for see, He applies the blood to the horns of the altar, and the sweet perfume of frankincense ascends to heaven, and God accepts it. O beloved, think of this, Christ's intercessory power with God lies in His precious blood, and your power and mine with God in prayer must lie in that blood too. Oh! to see the horns of that altar smeared with blood! How can you ever prevail with God unless you plead the blood of Jesus? Believer, if thou wouldst overcome in prayer, tell the Lord of all the groans of His dear Son; never dream of arguing except with arguments fetched from Jesus' wounds: these are potent pleas with God—the bloody sweat, the flagellation, the nails, the spear, the vinegar, the cross—these must be the mighty reasons with which to overcome the Infinite One. Let the altar of your incense be smeared with blood.

This being finished, the priest goes backwards still further and enters the court of the Israelites. There stood the great altar of brass, whereon was consumed the burnt offerings; and now the priest, having his basin full of the blood of which only a small quantity had been used in sprinkling the veil and touching the horns of the golden altar, pours the whole of the remaining blood in a great stream at the foot of the altar of burnt offering. What does that typify? Did He not thus teach us that the only ground and basis (for mark, it is put at the foot of the altar), of the acceptance of our persons and of our thank offerings if found in the blood of Jesus? Did it never strike you how the whole tabernacle must have been smeared with blood everywhere? Blood was on every side. The priest himself, when at his work, with garments on which showed every stain, must have looked as though all besmeared with gore. You could not look at his hands or at his vestments without seeing everywhere blood: indeed, when consecrated, he had blood on his ear, blood on his foot, blood on his hand—he could not be made a priest without it. The apostle says, "Almost everything under the law was sprinkled with blood." It was blood, blood everywhere. Now, this could have been very far from a pleasant sight, except to the spiritual man who, as he looked at it, said, "What a holy God is the God of Israel! How He hates sin! See, He will only permit sinners to approach Him by the way of blood!" and then the inquiring mind would ask, "What blood is this which is here intended?" We know that the blood of bulls and of goats was but the visible symbol of the sufferings of Jesus, the great Sacrifice, whom God hath set forth to be a propitiation for our sins. All the blood-marks pointed to the "Lamb of God, which taketh away the sin of the world." Let us rejoice in the precious blood of Christ the Lamb without blemish and without spot, who was foreordained from the foundations of the world, but was manifest in these last days for us.

Will you now make a summary of what has been spoken? Come with me outside the Tabernacle. Let us begin at the opening in its curtains leading to the outer court. We have sinned, and desire acceptance with God; that must be the first blessing. The brazen altar of burnt offerings is standing before us, and we wish to offer our thank offering, may we do so? How can we be accepted? Look at the bottom of the altar! What see you there? A pool of blood all around it, as though the altar stood in blood! What means this? Surely the blood of Jesus is the basis of our acceptance before God, and here we stand as citizens of heaven, not accursed, but beloved; not rejected and abhorred, but elect and blessed through the blood which is the ground of our acceptance as believers and citizens of Zion. Now we have come so far, we remember that we are not only citizens of the new Jerusalem, but priests unto God, and as priests we desire to enter the court of the priests, and there is the golden altar, but where is our power to minister before the Lord? How shall we approach with the love of our hearts, our joyful thanks, and our fervent intercessions? Behold the answer to our inquiries! Observe with joy the blood-marks on the four horns! It is not our prayers that will be in themselves prevalent, nor our praises, nor our love; but the blood gives prevalence, acceptance, and power to all. Come hither, then, and let us lay our heart itself, all bleeding upon that altar, and let our prayers and praises rise to heaven, like pillars of smoke, accepted through the blood. But, beloved, this is not all, we are something more than priests, we are children of God, dear to His heart; let us, then, seek fellowship with our Father who is in heaven. How can we enter into the most holy place and commune with the God who hideth Himself? What is the mode of entrance, into that which is within the veil? We look, and lo, the veil is rent, but on the floor, right across where the veil was wont to hang, we see a line of blood, where, times without number, the blood had been sprinkled; and on the two pieces of the veil through which we pass, we can see many distinct traces of blood; yes, and when we come right up to the mercy-seat we can see the blood there too. What means this but that the blood is the means of access to God, and by no other means is He to be approached? When we shall be nearest to God and see Him face to face, and dwell with Him in heaven forever, it will be because Jesus Christ loved us and died for us, and sprinkled His blood for us, that we are permitted to have this close and wonderful communion with God, which even angels never had, for even they can only veil their faces with their wings, but must not dare to look upon God as we shall do, when our eyes shall see Him as our Father and our Friend.

Thus I have tried to set forth the threefold prevalence of the precious blood, but let it not be forgotten that the blood also put away sin; for you find at the end of the chapter, "His sin shall be forgiven." First forgiven, then accepted, then prevalent in prayer, and then admitted into access with boldness to God; what a chain of blessings! All, all through the blood of Jesus!

III. Thirdly, the most painful part of our sermon remains, while I beg you to view THE SHAME WHICH OUR LORD ENDURED.

While it is all so well for us, so sweet for us, I want you now to reflect how bitter, how shameful it was for our Lord! The offerer who brought the sin offering has been forgiven; he has been accepted at the brazen altar; his prayers have been heard at the golden altar; and the veil has been sprinkled on his behalf: but what of the Victim itself? Draw nigh and learn with holy wonder. In the first place, albeit that our Lord Jesus Christ was made sin for us, it is noteworthy that, though nearly all the bullock was burned without he camp, there was one portion left and reserved to be burnt upon the altar of burnt offering, that was the fat. Certain descriptions are given as to the fat which was to be consumed upon the altar, by which we believe it was intended to ensure that the richest part of the fat should be there consumed. As much as if God would say, "Though my dear Son must be made sin for this people, and consequently I must forsake Him, and He must die without the camp, yet still He is most dear and precious in my sight, and even while He is a sin offering, yet He is my beloved Son in whom in Himself I am still well pleased." Brethren, whenever we speak about our Lord as bearing our sins, we must carefully speak concerning Him—not as though God ever did despise or abhor the prayer of His afflicted Son, but only seemed to do so while He stood for us, representatively made sin for us, though He knew no sin. Oh! I delight to think that the Lord smelled a sweet savor unto God, even as a sin offering; the fat, the excellence of his heart, the consecration of His soul, were acceptable to God, and sweet in His esteem, even when He laid upon Him the iniquity of His people. Still, here is the shameful part of it: the priest then took the bullock, and gathering up all the innards, every part of it, the skin, the dung—all mentioned to teach us what a horrible thing sin is, and what the Surety was looked upon as being when He took our sin—he took it all up, and either himself personally, or assisted by others, took it away out of the camp. We are told that in the wilderness, so large was the camp, that it may have been the distance of four miles that this bullock had to be carried. I think I see the sad procession: the priest all smeared with blood, carrying the carcass of the bullock, taking it right away down the long line of tents, first through the abodes of one tribe and then of another, through the long streets of tents, while the people stood at their doors and saw the ghastly sight. It was killed at the altar of burnt offering. Why was it not burnt there? That altar was holy, and as soon as ever sin was laid upon the bullock, it ceased to be any longer looked upon as a holy thing; it could not, therefore, be burnt in the holy place, it must be taken right away. So the priest carried it away—a terrible load—till he reached the usual place where the ashes were kindled, and he put the bullock there, and heaped the hot ashes upon it till the whole smoked up to heaven, and was utterly consumed as a sin offering. My beloved, try if you can to grasp the idea of Jesus being put away from God. I cannot give you the thoughts, but if you could hear the air pierced with the dreadful cry, *"Eloi, Eloi, lama Sabachthani?"* "My God, my God, why hast thou forsaken me?" you would see Christ put away because He was made sin. It was not possible for God to look upon sin, even when it was in Christ, with anything like complacency. "It pleased the Father to bruise him; he hath put him to grief." If you have read the order of the burnt offering, you will have noticed that when the bullock of the burnt offering was offered, it was washed, to show the perfection of Christ as He is a sweet savor, all pure and clean; but in this case there is added that humiliating word, "with the dung." What a humiliating type of Christ! Ah! but what are your sins and mine that were laid upon Jesus? How could our iniquities and transgressions be better set forth than by that bleeding, mangled mass, which the high priest had to carry out away from the camp, as though it were a thing abhorred, which could not be endured in the camp any longer. It is your Savior made sin for you and put away on your behalf.

After the removal, they gathered the hot ashes, they kindled the fire, and burnt it all. See here a faint image of the fire which consumed the Savior upon Calvary! His bodily pains ought never to be forgotten, because there is so intimate an intercourse between physical suffering and mental grief, that it were hard to draw the line; but still the sufferings of His soul must have been the very soul of His sufferings; and can you tell what they were? Have you ever suffered from a raging fever? Have you felt at the same time the pangs of some painful disease? Has your mind refused to rest? Has your brain been tossed like the waves of a sea of fire within your head? Have you questioned whether you should lose your reason or not? Have you ever been near unto distraction? Have you ever been near unto the breaking of the cords of life? If so, you may guess feebly what He suffered when He said, "My soul is exceeding sorrowful, even unto death"; and when He "began to be sorrowful and to be very heavy." Those were the coals of juniper which were being heaped over the sin offering. As you see Jesus scourged by Herod and by Pilate, and afterwards bleeding on the accursed tree, you see the fire of divine wrath consuming the sin offering because our sin had been laid upon Him. I will not dwell longer on this, only ask the Holy Spirit to make you feel the shame that Christ suffered for you. Sometimes I cannot grasp the thought, when I have tried to think that He who made the heavens, to whom the whole blue arch is but as a span, and the depths of the seas as the hollow of His hand, should be made flesh! and suffer for such an insignificant worm as I am. That He should suffer, however, never amazes me so much as that He should bear my sin. Oh! marvelous! The angels say, "Holy! Holy! Holy! Lord God of Sabaoth!" What could they have said when He, whom they hymned as "glorious in holiness," bowed His head and gave up the ghost, because "made sin for us"? Blessed Son of God! where we cannot understand we will adore.

The Apostle Paul suggests to us the most practical conclusion of our sermon. He tells us that as our Savior, having given His blood to be sprinkled within the Tabernacle for us, was then taken without the camp, so it is our duty, aye, and our privilege, to go forth unto Him without the camp also, bearing His reproach. You have heard how He was reproached for you: are you unwilling to be reproached for Him! You have heard how He went without the camp in that shameful manner: are you unwilling to go without the camp for Him? Too many Christians try to be Christians in the camp, and it cannot be done. "Be not conformed to this world, but be ye transformed by the renewing of your minds." There is so much of worldly conformity among us; but the promise is not to worldly-minded Christians, but "Come ye out from among them; be ye separate; touch not the unclean thing; and I will receive you, and will be a Father unto you." How much we lose by affinities with the world! How much of distance there is between us and God, because of the nearness there is between us and the world! Come out, ye lovers of the Savior, and tread the separated way which your Savior trod before you!

And now, should there be any here who are unsaved, I should not wonder but what some of them will make the remark, the almost, nay, the quite profane remark, "Why, he spoke so much of blood!" Ah! sinner, and we need to speak much of it to you, for it is your only hope. God will either have *your* blood or *Christ's* blood, one of the two. If you reject Christ, you shall perish in your sin. "The blood is the life thereof," says the Word of God; and your life must be taken unless Christ's life shall avail for you. The very heart of Christ was broken to find out the way to save a sinner; and, sinner, there is no other; if you refuse the purple road, you shall never reach the pearly gate. Trust in the blood of Jesus. Dost thou doubt? How canst thou? Is there not efficacy enough in the blood of the Son of God to take away sin? Dost thou contradict God's declared truth? "The blood of Jesus Christ, his Son, cleanseth us from all sin." Oh! believe it, and cast thy soul upon it, and we will meet within the veil, one of these days, to sing, "To him that loved us, and washed us from our sins in his own blood . . . to him be glory forever and ever." Amen.

THE SIN-OFFERING FOR THE COMMON PEOPLE

Sermon No. 1,048
Delivered on Lord's day Morning, April 28, 1872.
Portion of Scripture read before Sermon—1 John 1 and 2.

> *And if any one of the common people sin through ignorance, while he doeth somewhat against any of the commandments of the LORD concerning things which ought not to be done, and be guilty; or if his sin, which he hath sinned, come to his knowledge: then he shall bring his offering, a kid of the goats, a female without blemish, for his sin which he hath sinned. And he shall lay his hand upon the head of the sin offering, and slay the sin offering in the place of the burnt offering. And the priest shall take of the blood thereof with his finger, and put it upon the horns of the altar of burnt offering, and shall pour out all the blood thereof at the bottom of the altar. And he shall take away all the fat thereof, as the fat is taken away from off the sacrifice of peace offerings; and the priest shall make an atonement for him, and it shall be forgiven him*—Leviticus 4:27–31.

Very much of interesting truth clusters around the sin-offering. The type is well worthy of the most careful consideration, and I regret that we shall not have time this morning to enter into all its details. The reader of the chapter will perceive that it gives us four forms of the same sacrifice. These may be regarded as four views of the same thing, probably views taken by four classes of believers, according to their standing in the divine life; for, although all men who are saved have the same Savior, they have not the same apprehensions of Him. We are all cleansed, if cleansed at all, by the same blood, but we have not all the same knowledge of the manner in which it is effectual for cleansing. The devout Hebrew had but one sin-offering, but that was set forth to him under varying symbols.

The following remarks may aid you in understanding the type before us. The chapter begins with the sin-offering for the anointed priest, and describes it with the fullest detail. It then proceeds, in the thirteenth verse and onwards, to give the sin-offering for the whole congregation, and it is most notable that the sin-offering for the anointed priest is almost in every circumstance identical with the sin-offering for the whole congregation. Is not this designed to show to us that when Christ, our anointed priest, took upon Him the sin of all the congregation of God's chosen as His own, there was demanded of Him the same expiation and atonement as would have been demanded of His people had they been reckoned within their own persons! His atonement for sins which were not His own, but which were laid upon Him by the Lord on our behalf, is equivalent to the penalty which would have been required of all the congregation of believers for whom His blood was especially shed. This is a memorable lesson, which ought not to be forgotten. We ought to see herein the inestimable value of the sacrifice of Christ, by which the many offenses of a number that no man can number are forever put away. There was given, in the death of our Lord, as full a recompense to justice as if all the redeemed had been sent into hell; nay, the truth goes far further than that, they could not have made a complete expiation, for even had they suffered for sin for thousands of years, the debt would "still be paying, never paid." Glory be to the name of our great Substitute, He by His sin offering hath perfected forever them that are set apart.

In the case of the sin-offering for the priest we have a fuller picture of the atonement than is offered by the two latter instances, and you will please to note that the sin-offering was a victim without blemish. In the first two cases a bullock was to be slain. Thus the most precious animal the Hebrew owned, the noblest, the strongest, the image of docility and labor, was to be presented to make atonement. Our Lord Jesus Christ is like the firstling of the bullock, the most precious thing in heaven, strong for service, docile in obedience, One who was willing and able to labor for our sakes; and He was brought as a perfect victim, without spot or blemish, to suffer in our stead. The priest slew the bullock, and its blood was poured forth; for without shedding of blood there is no remission. The vital point of the atonement of Christ lies in His death. However much His life may have contributed to it, and we are not among those who, in the matter of salvation, separate His life from His death by a hard and fast line, yet the great point of the putting away of human guilt was the Lord's obedience unto death, even the death of the cross. The victim was slain, and so the atonement was made. Returning to the passage before us, we find that the blood of this victim was taken into the holy place, which was immediately outside the sacred veil of the sanctuary; and there the priest dipped his finger in the blood, and sprinkled of the blood seven times before the Lord, before the veil of the sanctuary. So in making atonement for sin there is a perfect exhibition of the blood of Jesus before the Lord. That life has been given for life is openly proved where alone the proof is available. Before the offended Lord the vicarious death is thoroughly exhibited; for was it not written of old in the book of Exodus, "When I see the blood I will pass over you." Our sight of the blood of Christ gives us peace, but it does not make the satisfaction; it is God's sight of the blood which makes the atonement; and, therefore, seven times before the veil was this blood exhibited before the Lord, that a perfect atonement might be made.

The next thing the priest did was to go up to the golden altar of incense, which stood hard by the veil, and to put some of the blood upon each one of the horns, indicating that it is the blood of the atonement which gives power (for that is the meaning of the horns) to intercession. The sweet perfume of the altar of incense stands for the prayers and praises of the saints, and especially for the intercession of Christ Jesus; and, because the blood is there, therefore, Christ's intercession is heard; and, therefore, our prayers and praises come up with acceptance before the Lord.

Then the priest removed to the brazen altar of burnt sacrifice, and all the blood which remained he poured out at the bottom of the altar of the burnt offering which stood at the door of the tabernacle of the congregation. Full bowls of blood encrimsoned the base of the altar. Blood was seen on every side, on the veil, on the golden altar, and now upon the altar of brass. Within and without the holy place but one voice was heard, the voice of the blood of atonement crying to God for peace. The whole tabernacle must have been almost at all times so smeared with blood as to have been far from pleasant to the eye, and this was intended to teach to Israel, that God's anger against sin is terrible, and that the dishonored law will be satisfied with nothing less than the giving of life for life, if sinners are to be saved. The altar of burnt offerings was the altar of acceptance, it was the place where those sacrifices were presented in which there was no mention of sin, but which were brought as thanksgivings to God. Therefore, as much as to teach us that the very ground and foundation of the acceptance of the Christian, and his offering, lies in the precious blood of Jesus; full bowls of blood were poured upon the base of the altar. See what wonders the precious blood of Jesus Christ can do, it is the strength of intercession and the foundation of acceptance.

From the bullock which had been slain certain choice pieces were taken, and especially the inward fat, and there were laid upon the altar and consumed, to show us that even while the Lord Jesus was a sin-offering He was still accepted of God, and though His Father forsook Him so that He cried out, "Why hast thou forsaken me?" He was still a sweet savor unto the Lord in the obedience which He rendered.

But, the most significant part of the whole sacrifice remains to be described, and you will notice that it is only described in the first two forms of the sin-offering. The priest was not allowed to burn the bullock itself upon the altar, but he was commanded to take up the whole carcass, its skin, flesh, head, and everything, and carry the whole forth without the camp. It was a sin-offering, and therefore it was loathsome in God's sight, and the priest went right away from the door of the tabernacle, past all the tents of the children of Israel, bearing this ghastly burden upon him; went, I say, right away, till he came to the place where the ashes of the camp were poured out, and there, not upon an altar, but on wood which had been prepared, upon the bare ground; every single particle of the bullock was burned with fire. The distance the bullock was carried from camp is said to have been four miles. The teaching of which is just this, that when the Lord Jesus Christ took the sin of His people upon Himself, He could not, as a substitute, dwell any longer in the place of the divine favor, but had to be put into the place of separation, and made to cry, *"Eloi, Eloi, lama sabachthani?"* Paul in his epistle to the Hebrews puts the matter clearly, "For the bodies of those beasts, whose blood is brought into the sanctuary by the high priest for sin, are burned without the camp. Wherefore Jesus also, that he might sanctify the people with his own blood, suffered without the gate." Outside Jerusalem our Lord was led to the common place of doom for malefactors, for it is written (and oh, the power of those words, I dare not have uttered them if they had not been inspired). "He was made a curse for us, for it is written, cursed is every one that hangeth on a tree." The blessed Son of God was made a curse for us and put to an accursed death, by being gibbeted upon the cross, and all because sin anywhere is hateful to God, and He must treat it with indignation. The fire of divine justice fell upon our blessed sin offering until He was utterly consumed with anguish, and He said, "It is finished," and gave up the ghost. Now, this is the only way of the putting away of sin: it is laid upon another, that other is made to suffer as if the sin belonged to him, and then, since sin cannot be in two places at once, and cannot be laid upon another and rest upon the offerer too, the offerer becomes clear from all sin, he is pardoned and he is accepted because his substitute has been slain without the camp instead of him. I have thus introduced to you the first two forms of the sin-offering. It seemed necessary to begin there.

The third form of the sin-offering was for a ruler, a person of considerable standing in the camp. There is nothing very remarkable about that third form which need now detain us; we, therefore, come to the subject in hand. The sin offering for a common person.

I. And, here, we will begin our discourse upon the text itself by speaking of THE PERSON, *a common person.* It gives me unspeakable joy to read these words, "If any one of the common people sin," for which one of the common people does not sin? The text reminds me that, *if a common person sin his sins will ruin him;* he may not be able to do so much mischief by his sin as the ruler or a public officer, but his sin has all the essence of evil in it, and God will reckon with him for it. No matter how obscurely you may live, however poor and unlettered you may be, your sin will ruin you, if not pardoned and put away. If one of the common people sin through ignorance, his sin is a damning sin, he must have it put away, or it will put him away forever from the face of God. *A common person's sin can only be removed by an atonement of blood.* In this case you see the victim was not a bullock, it was a female of the goats or of the sheep, but still it had to be an offering of blood, for without shedding of blood there is no remission. However common-place your offenses may have been, however insignificant you may be yourself, nothing will cleanse you but the blood of Jesus Christ. That verse is quite correct—

> Could my zeal no respite know,
> Could my tears forever flow,
> All for sin could not atone:
> Christ must save, and Christ alone.

It is true the sins of great men cover a larger space, but yet there must be a bloody sacrifice for the smallest offenses. For the sins of a housewife or of a servant, of a peasant, or of a crossing-sweeper, there must be the same sacrifice as for the sins of the greatest and most influential. No other atonement will suffice, the sins of the common people will destroy them unless the blood of Jesus Christ shall cleanse them. But here is the point of joy, that *for the common people there was an atonement ordained of God.* Glory be to God I may be unknown to men, but I am not unthought of by Him. I may be merely one of the many, but still He has thought of me. As each blade of grass has its own drop of dew, so each guilty soul coming to Christ shall find an atonement for itself in Christ. Blessed be the name of the Lord, it is not written that there is a sacrifice for the great ones of the earth alone, but for the common people there is a sin-offering, so that each man coming to the Savior finds cleansing through His precious blood.

Observe with thankfulness that *the sacrifice appointed for the common people was as much accepted as that appointed for the ruler.* Of the ruler, it is said, "the priest shall make an atonement for him as concerning his sin, and it shall be forgiven him." The same thing is said of the common person. Christ is as much accepted for the poorest of His people as for the richest of them. He as much saves the unknown as He does the apostolic names of high renown. They need the sacrifice of blood, but they need nothing more, and the blood which pleads before the throne of God speaks as well for the least as it does for the chief of the flock.

Come hither, then, ye who belong to the common people, if any of you have sinned, come at once to Jesus the great sin-offering. Though ye are common in rank, know ye not that the common people heard Him gladly. Publicans and sinners pressed around Him to hear Him. Though ye are but commoners in your wealth, possessing little of this world's goods, yet, come, buy wine and milk without money and without price. Common in your talents and in your gifts, yet He bids you come, for these things are hid from the wise and prudent. It is not for those who think themselves distinguished that He has especially laid down His life, but "the poor have the gospel preached to them," and in their salvation He will be glorified.

Mark, it says, "If any one of the common people sin through ignorance, or if his sin which he hath sinned come to his knowledge, then he shall bring his offering." Has it suddenly come to the knowledge of any person here that he has sinned as he thought he had not sinned? Has some fresh light broken in upon you and revealed to you your darkness? Did you come to this house depressed in spirit because you have discovered that you are guilty and must perish, unless the mercy of God prevent you? Then, come ye common people who have discovered your sin, and bring your sacrifice. Nay, it is here already for you. Come and accept the sacrifice which God provides, and let your sin be forever put away.

I wish the words of the text could provoke the same feelings in every heart that they do in mine, for I could fain stand here and weep my soul away in joy that for the common people's sin there should be a sacrifice, for I can put my name down amongst them. I have sinned, I have come to the knowledge of my sin, and I thank God I need not ask myself any other question, be I who I may or what I am, though but one of the common people, there is a sin-offering for me.

II. Now, pass on from the person to THE SACRIFICE. "He shall bring his offering, a kid of the goats, a female without blemish, for his sin which he hath sinned."

Observe, first, my brethren, that there is a discrepancy between the type and the reality, for first *the sin-offering under the law was only for sins of ignorance.* But, we have a far better sacrifice for sin than that, for have we not read in your hearing this morning those precious words, "The blood of Jesus Christ, his Son, cleanseth us from *all* sin," not from sins of ignorance only, but from *all* sin. Oh, that blessed word "all." It includes sins of knowledge, sins against the light and love of God, sins wantonly perpetrated, sins against man and against God, sins of body and of soul, sins of thought and word and deed, sins of every rank and character, "sins immense as is the sea"— all, all are removed; no matter what they be, "the blood of Jesus Christ his Son cleanseth us from *all* sin." Yet do I bless God that the type deals with sins of ignorance, because we may get a gospel out of it. We have committed many sins which we know not of. They have never burdened our conscience because we have not yet discovered them; and, besides, we do not know them to be sins; but Christ takes those sins, too, and prays, "Father, forgive them, for they know not what they do." "Cleanse thou me," said David, "from secret faults," and that is just what Jesus does. It used to be a doctrine of the church of Rome that no man could have a sin forgiven which he did not confess. Truly, if it were so, there would be no salvation for any of us, since it is not possible for the memory to charge itself with the recollection of every sin, nor for the conscience to become so perfect as to take cognizance of every form of transgression. But, while we ought to confess to God all sins which we know; and, while we should confess them as much as can be in detail, yet, if through ignorance they remain unacknowledged, except in the gross and the bulk, Jesus Christ, the sin-offering, bears our sins of ignorance, sins which we knew not to be sins when we committed them, or which we still know not to be sins. He takes them away; it must be so, for He "cleanseth us from *all* sin"—sins of ignorance, as well as sins against light and knowledge. Now, what comfort there is here for all of you of the common people; be your sins what they may, there is a sin-offering which takes away all sin from you. However ye may have defiled yourselves, though ye be black as night and hideous as hell, yet is there power in the atoning blood of the incarnate God to make you white as newly-fallen snow. Washed once in the fountain opened for sin and for uncleanness, there shall remain upon you no trace of guilt.

Note another discrepancy, that *the sinner of the common people in this case had to bring his sacrifice*—"he shall *bring* his offering." But our sin-offering has been provided for us. You remember the question of Isaac to his father Abraham, as they went up Moriah; he said to him, "My father, behold the fire and the wood, but where is the lamb for the burnt-offering?" and Abraham said, "My son, God will provide himself a lamb." Isaac's inquiry might have been the eternal question of every troubled heart. "O God, where is the lamb for the burnt-offering?" Who will bear human sin? But JEHOVAH-JIREH. God hath provided Himself a lamb for burnt-offering and a sin-offering too, and now we have not to bring a sacrifice for sin, but have simply to take what God provided from before the foundations of the world.

Now, let us notice that in the type *the victim chosen for a sin-offering was un-blemished*; whether it was a goat or a sheep, it must be unblemished. How could Christ make an atonement for sins if He had had sins of His own. Had He been guilty, it would have required that He should suffer for His own guilt. But, being under no obligation whatever to the law of God, except such as He voluntarily undertook, when He had rendered obedience He had an obedience to give away, and He has graciously bestowed it upon us. When He suffered, His suffering not being due to God on account of anything that He had personally done, He had so much of suffering to spare, and He has transferred it to us. The immaculate Christ has died, the just for the unjust, that He might bring us to God. This is full of comfort, for if you will study, O seeking soul, the perfect character of your blessed Lord as God and as man, and see how fairer than the lilies is He in matchless purity, you will feel that if He suffered, there must be in such suffering a merit unspeakable, which being transferred to you, can save you from the wrath to come. In the dear Redeemer we have an unblemished sacrifice.

But, I do not understand, and, therefore, cannot explain why the victim was a female in this case, for most of the sacrifices were males of the first year, but this is peculiar in being a female. Is it because there is neither male nor female, bond nor free, but all are one in Christ Jesus? Or, am I wrong if I conjecture that this was intended to typify a view of Christ taken by one of the common people, and therefore it is purposely made incomplete? It is an incomplete view of Christ to have before you the female as the type, and the type is purposely made incomplete in order that this truth may be before us—that while a complete view of Christ is very comforting, instructive, and strengthening, yet even an imperfect view of Him will save us if accompanied by real faith. If we should make a mistake upon some point, yet, if we are clear upon the main truth of His substitution, it is well with us. On purpose, then, it seems to me, that a victim was introduced which did not with exactness set forth Christ, that the Lord might say to His people and to us, "You have not reached the perfect conception of my dear Son, but even an imperfect apprehension of Him will save you, if you believe in Him." Who among us knows much of Christ? Oh, brethren, we know enough to make our hearts love Him; we know enough of Him to make us feel that we owe all to Him, and we desire to live for His glory, but, He is far greater than our greatest thoughts. We have only skirted the shores and navigated the little bays and creeks of Christ; we have not sailed out into the main ocean, nor fathomed the great deeps as yet. Yet what little we know of Him has saved us, and for His dear sake we are forgiven and accepted in the Beloved. Does not the Lord seem to say to us, "Poor souls, you have misconceived my Son, and made many mistakes about Him, but you do trust Him, and I save you." A certain woman thought that there was power in the hem of Jesus' garment to make her whole. She was mistaken in imagining that there was a healing efficacy in His dress, but since it was a mistake of faith, and reflected honor upon Christ, the Lord made it true to her; He made virtue go out of Himself even into the skirts of His garments for her sake. And so, though we may err here and err there in reference to our Lord, yet, if our soul does but cling to Him like a child to its mother, knowing little of its mother except that its mother loves it, and that it is dependent upon her, that clinging will be saving.

But, the main point about the sacrifice was, it was *slain as a substitute*. There is nothing said about its being taken outside the camp—I do not think it was in this case: all that the offerer knew was, it was slain as a substitute. And, dear hearers, all and everything that is essential to know in order to be saved is to know that you are a sinner and that Christ is your substitute. I beseech the Lord to teach every one of us this, for though we should go to the University and learn all knowledge, though we should ransack all the stores of learning, unless we know this—"He loved me and gave Himself for me," we have not learned the very first principles of a true education for eternity. God gives us to know this this very day.

III. But, now thirdly, we pass on from the sacrifice to THE AFTER CEREMONIES; upon which only a word. In the case of one of the common people after the victim was slain, the blood was taken to the brazen altar, and the four horns of it were smeared, to show that the power of fellowship with God lies in the blood of substitution. There is no fellowship with God except through the blood, there is no acceptance with God for anyone of us except through Him who suffered in our stead.

But, then, secondly, the blood was thrown at the foot of this same brazen altar, as if to show that the atonement is the foundation as well as the power of fellowship. We get nearest to God when we feel most the power of the blood, aye, and we could not come to God at all except it were through that encrimsoned way.

After this, a part of the offering was put upon the altar, and it is said concerning it, what is not said in any other of the cases, "the priest shall burn it upon the altar for a sweet savor to the Lord." This common person had, in most respects, a dim view of Christ, compared with the others, for it does not say of the priest that what he offered was a sweet savor; but, for the comfort of this common person, that he might go his way having sweet consolation in his soul, he is told that the sin-offering he has brought is a sweet savor unto God. And oh, what a joy it is to think not only has Christ put away my sin if I believe in Him; but now for me He is a sweet savor to God, and I am for His sake accepted, for His sake beloved, for His sake delighted in, for His sake precious unto God. When God had destroyed the earth by a flood, and Noah came out of the ark, you will remember that he offered a sacrifice unto God, and it is said, "The Lord smelled a sweet savor," or a savor of rest, and then He said, "I will no more destroy the earth with a flood, and He entered into a covenant with Noah." Oh, happy is that soul that can see Christ his sin-offering, as being a savor of rest unto the Lord Most High, so that a covenant of grace is made with him, a covenant of sure mercies that shall never be removed.

But, I must pass on again.

IV. The fourth point is one to which I ask all your heart's attention. I have purposely omitted AN ESSENTIAL ACT in the sacrifice, in order to enlarge upon it now.

Please observe, that in all four cases there was one thing which was never left out, "He shall lay his hand upon the head of the sin-offering." It was no use killing the bullock, it was no use slaying the heifer, no use pouring out the blood, no use smearing the horns of the altar unless this was done. The guilty person must come, and must himself lay his hands upon the victim. Oh, that while I speak of this, some of you may lay your hands upon Christ Jesus, according to the verse of the poet—

> My faith doth lay her hand
>   On that dear head of thine,
> While like a penitent I stand,
>   And there confess my sin.

Now that act of laying on the hand signified confession. It meant just this: "Here I stand as a sinner, and confess that I deserve to die. This goat which is now to be slain represents in its sufferings what I deserve of God." O sinner, confess your sin now unto your great God, acknowledge that He would be just if He condemned you. Confession of sin is a part of the meaning of the laying on of the hand.

The next thing that was meant by it was *acceptance*. The person laying his hand said, "I accept this goat as standing for me. I agree that this victim shall stand instead of me." That is what faith does with Christ, it puts its hands upon the ever blessed Son of God, and says, "He stands for me, I take Him as my Substitute."

The next meaning of it was *transference*. The sinner standing there confessing, putting his hand on the victim and accepting it, did by that act, say, "I transfer, according to God's ordinance, all my sin which I here confess, from myself to this victim." By that act the transference was made. You know there is a blessed passage, which says, that "the Lord hath laid on Christ the iniquity of us all," from this expression an objection has been raised to that blessed hymn.

> I lay my sins on Jesus.

Yet, I think, the expression is quite correct. Cannot both utterances be true? God did lay sin in bulk upon Christ when He laid upon Him the iniquity of us all, but by an act of faith every individual in another sense lays his sins on Jesus, and it is absolutely needful that each man should so do, if he would participate in the substitution.

Now, do observe, I pray you, that this was *a personal act*. Nobody could lay his hand upon the bullock, or upon the goat, for another; each one had to put his own hand there. A godly mother could not say, "My graceless boy will not lay his hand upon the victim, but I will put my hand there for him." It could not be. He who laid his hand there had the blessing, but no one else, and had the godliest saint with holy but mistaken zeal said, "Rebellious man, wilt thou not put thy hand there, I will act as sponsor for thee," it had been of no avail; the offender must personally come. And so, dear hearer, must you have a personal faith in Christ for yourself. The word is sometime interpreted *to lean*, and some give it the meaning of leaning hard. What a blessed view of faith that gives us. Sometimes, according to the Rabbis, those who brought the victim leaned with all their might, and pressed upon it as if they seemed to say by the act, "I put the whole burden, weight, and force of my sin upon this unblemished victim." O my soul, lean hard on Christ, throw all the weight of thy sin upon Him, for He is able to bear it, and came on purpose to bear it, and He will be honored if thou wilt lean heavily on Him.

And, beloved, what *a simple act* it was. The man who would not be absolved from sin in this way deserved to perish—there was nothing but to lay his hand, nothing but to lean, how could he refuse. Faith in Christ is no mystery, no problem needed to be explained in long treatises—it is simply, trust Him, trust Him, trust Him, and you are saved. "There is life in a look at the crucified One." "Look unto him and be ye saved all the ends of the earth." Nothing can be plainer—nothing can be simpler—why is it that so many puzzle themselves where God has given us simplicities. It must be that God made man upright, but he hath found out many inventions with which to bewilder himself.

The laying on of the hand was *the act of a sinner*. He came there because he had sinned, and because his sin had come to his knowledge. Had he been sinless there would have been no meaning in his bringing a sin-offering. Innocence needs not a substitute or sacrifice for sin. The sin-offering is evidently for the man who has sin, and what if I say there is no soul here to whom Christ is so suitable as the soul that is most full of sin. Thou that art a great, big, black sinner, a thorough-paced sinner, a damnable sinner, thou art the very sinner to come to Christ and glorify His grace. He is a physician who did not come into this world to cure finger-aches, and pin-pricks, but to heal great diseases, loathsome leprosies, and burning fevers. Come, thou sinner of the common people, come thou and rest alone on Jesus! I wish I knew how to speak of this theme so as to move your souls. Within a few months or years at the longest, we shall all be before the bar of God; and what if some of us should be there with our sins upon us? I am afraid some of you will be there unforgiven. O you to whom I have so often spoken, will you be there unpardoned! I shall not be able to make excuse for you there, and say you did not know the way of salvation, for I have preached it with great plainness of speech. I have often cast aside language which commended itself to my taste, to use instead thereof more homely words, lest one of you should miss my meaning. God knoweth I have often forsaken tracks of thought which opened before me, and which might have interested many of my hearers, because I have felt while so many of you are unsaved, I must keep on plowing with simplicities, and sowing elementary truths, I am evermore telling over and over again the story of the substitutionary work of the Lord Jesus. What, do ye hate your souls so much that you will damn them to spite Christ? Is there such a hatred between you and yourself that you will reject God's own sacrifice for sin? You cannot say it is difficult for you to avail yourself of the death of Jesus. It is but to lay your hand of faith on that dear head. What enmity must there be in your hearts that you will not be reconciled to God even when He makes the reconciliation by the death of His own dear Son. To what a pitch hath man's rebellion against his Maker gone, when, sooner than be at peace with Him, he will reject eternal love, and will forever ruin his own soul? Oh, may God grant that some this morning may say, "I will stretch out my hand, I will trust in Jesus." You see that the hand to be stretched out is an empty one, and the heart which leans may be a fainting one. Weakness and sinfulness find strength and pardon by taking Jesus to be their All-in-all.

V. The last word I have to speak to you makes the fifth head, namely, THE AS-SURED BLESSING. Turn to your Bibles, at the 31st verse; let every soul here that is conscious of sin read those last lines: *"and it shall be forgiven him."* There is the sacrifice. The man must put his hand upon it. The sacrifice is slain, and "his sin shall be forgiven him." Was not that plain speaking? There were no ifs, no buts, no peradventures; but "it shall be forgiven him." Now, in those days it was only one sin, the sin confessed, that was forgiven, but now "all manner of sin and blasphemy shall be forgiven unto men." In those days the forgiveness did not give the conscience abiding peace, for the offerer had to come with another sacrifice by-and-by; but now the blood of Christ blots out all the sins of believers at once and forever, so that there is no need to bring a new sacrifice, or to come a second time with the blood of atonement in our hands. The sacrifice of the Jew had no intrinsic value. How could the blood of bulls and goats take away sin? It could only be useful as a type of the true sacrifice, the sin-offering of Christ. But in our Lord Jesus there is real efficacy, there is true atonement, there is real cleansing, and whosoever believeth in Him shall find actual pardon and complete forgiveness at this very moment. What a joy it is to know that—

> The moment a sinner believes,
> And trusts in his crucified God,
> His pardon at once he receives,
> Salvation in full through his blood.

I delight to believe that of Christ Jesus, Kent's verse is true—

> Here's pardon for transgressions past,
> It matters not how black their cast,
> And oh, my soul, with wonder view,
> For sins to come here's pardon too.

Our sins were all laid on Christ in one bulk, and were all put away at one time. Woe unto any man who should have to take his sins upon himself as they come, the blessing is that as our sins are committed they are still laid on Jesus, according to the words of the psalmist, "Blessed is the man whose transgression is forgiven, whose sin is covered. Blessed is the man unto whom the Lord imputeth not iniquity, and in whom there is no guile." The believer sins, but the Lord imputes not his sin to him, He lays it still upon the Scapegoat's head who bore our sins of old, even Christ Jesus our Savior.

The pith of all my discourse is this, if there be a child of God here who is in the dark and burdened with sin, dear brother, dear sister, do not stand controverting with the devil as to whether you are a child of God or not. Do not be going over your experience and saying, "I am afraid I am a hypocrite and I have been deceived." But, for the moment, suppose the worst. Let the devil take for granted all his accusations, and then reply to him in words like those of Martin Luther, "Thou sayest I am a great sinner and a law-breaker, and all this; to which I reply I will cut thy head off with thine own sword, for what if I be a sinner? It is written Jesus Christ came to save sinners, and I rest my soul as a sinner simply upon Him." I like beginning again. The best way to get back lost evidences is to leave the evidences alone, and go again to Jesus. Evidences are very like a sundial—you can tell what o'clock it is if the sun is shining, but not without; and truly a man of experience can tell the time of day without the sundial if he can but see the sun itself. Evidences are clearest when Jesus is near, and that is just the time when we do not need them. Here is God's direction for acting when under a cloud. "If any walk in darkness and see no light, let him"—what? Fret about his evidence? No, "let him trust," there is the end of it; "let him trust in the Lord and obey the voice of his servant," and the light will soon come to him. Come away, O burdened believer, to the sin-offering. "If any man sin we have an advocate with the Father." The fountain that was opened for sin and for uncleanness was not opened for the unregenerate only, but for the people of God, for it was opened "in the house of David," for the "inhabitants of Jerusalem," that is, for those who are God's people.

If there be a poor soul here who has never believed in Jesus, but is burdened with sin, I invite him, and I pray God the Holy Spirit to make the invitation effectual, to come now to Jesus Christ. I seem to think that when I was seeking the Savior if I had been in this congregation, and had heard Christ set forth as bearing sin as a substitute, and heard the plain talk you have listened to this morning, I should have found peace directly; instead of which I was months and months hunting after peace, because I did not know this, that I had nothing to do, for Christ had done it all; and all I had to do was to take what Christ had done, and simply trust in Him. Now, you know it, oh, may God add something to your knowledge! May He give you power to lay your hand on Jesus! Lean on Him, soul; lean on Him. If you cannot lean, fall back into His arms. Faint away upon the bosom of the Savior. Trust Him, rest in Him, it is all He asks you, and then faith shall justify you and cleanse you, and shall give you sanctification, and by-and-by perfection, and shall bring you into His eternal kingdom and glory. The Lord bless you, for Jesus' sake. Amen.

PUTTING THE HAND UPON THE HEAD OF THE SACRIFICE

SERMON NO. 1,771
DELIVERED ON LORD'S DAY MORNING, MARCH 16, 1884.
PORTIONS OF SCRIPTURE READ BEFORE SERMON—PSALM 51; LEVITICUS 1:1–9.
HYMNS FROM *Our Own Hymn Book*—395, 555, 51 (PART 2).

> *And he shall put his hand upon the head of the burnt offering; and
> it shall be accepted for him to make atonement for him. And he
> shall kill the bullock before the LORD*—Leviticus 1:4, 5.

No doubt there are clear distinctions in the teaching of the burnt offering, the meat offering, the peace offering, and the sin offering. In those various sacrifices we have views of our Lord's atoning work taken from different standpoints. On another occasion it will be profitable to note these delightful lessons and lay them to heart; but at this time I am not about to enter into such matters. These instructive distinctions are the special property of those who by reason of years have had their senses exercised, and therefore can discern not only the great work of our Lord, but the details of it. I am not sufficiently strong in mind at this time to bring forth "butter in a lordly dish" for men of robust constitution, but I must be content to serve the little ones with a cup of milk. I cannot carry the great cluster from Eshcol, and therefore I will bring you a few grapes in my trembling hand. I desire to preach this morning so that I may fulfill the prayer of a little boy who, one Saturday evening before he went to bed, said in his prayer, "Lord, grant that our minister may say something tomorrow that I may understand." I am very sorry that such a prayer should ever be necessary, but I am afraid it is not only needful for children, but sometimes for grown-up people to pray, "Lord, help our minister to say something that we can understand, and that is worth understanding." Some of my brethren appear to dwell on high Olympus among the clouds: it were better if they lived on Calvary. Little dew comes from the dark mountains of intellectual dreaminess; far more refreshing drops are found upon the Hermon of the gospel. I feel like Dr. Guthrie when he desired those around him to sing him a bairn's hymn; I would be a little child in preaching to you. Simple things are the most sublime, and to a sick man most sweet. I wish to be plain as a pikestaff in setting forth the way of expiation by the death of Jesus.

I have a reason also for preaching foundation truth today which to myself is powerful, though you may smile at it. It is this: If I have but few shots to fire, I should like each time to hit the center of the target; that is to say, if I may only speak to you once today, after having been laid aside for three weeks, I desire to speak only upon topics which touch the vitals of godliness. I would plunge into the heart of the matter, and deal with the essence and soul of true religion. There are some things that may be or may not be, and yet no great evil will come either way; but there are other things that must be, or all goes wrong; of these must-be's I would now speak. Some things are important for the *well*-being of Christians, but certain other things are absolutely essential to the very being of Christians; and it is upon these urgent necessaries that I shall now speak—namely, concerning the precious blood of the Lord Jesus Christ and our faith in it; for these two things are of the highest importance, and they cannot too often be brought before our minds.

Two matters were essential in the sacrifices of the ceremonial law; and you have them both in our text: "He shall put his hand upon the head of the burnt offering," and "He shall kill the bullock before the Lord." The appropriation by the offerer and the death of the offering are most fitly joined together, and must neither of them be overlooked.

For our immediate object there was no need to have taken our present text, for there are many others of like effect. Look at Leviticus 3:2: "And he shall lay his hand upon the head of his offering, and kill it at the door of the tabernacle." Glance at the eighth verse: "And he shall lay his hand upon the head of his offering, and kill it before the tabernacle." Turn to chapter 4, verse 4, the second clause of the verse: "He shall lay his hand upon the bullock's head, and kill the bullock before the Lord." As also at the fifteenth verse: "And the elders of the congregation shall lay their hands upon the head of the bullock before the Lord: and the bullock shall be killed before the Lord." To the same effect is the twenty-fourth verse: "And he shall lay his hand upon the head of the goat, and kill it in the place where they kill the burnt offering." All through the book of Leviticus the laying on of the hand and the killing of the victim are mentioned in immediate connection. These are each of them so important, and so full of meaning, that we must have a sermon upon each of them.

Let us on the present occasion look at THE LEADING ACT OF THE OFFERER: "*He shall lay his hand upon the head of the burnt offering.*" All that goes before is important, but this is the real sacrificial act so far as the offerer is concerned. Before he reached this point, the person who presented the offering had to make a selection of the animal to be brought before the Lord. It must be of a certain age, and it must be without blemish; and for this latter reason a careful examination had to be made; for the Lord would not accept a sacrifice that was lame, or broken, or bruised, or deficient in any of its parts or in any way blemished. He required an offering "without spot." Now I invite all those who seek reconciliation with God to look about them, and consider whether the Lord Jesus Christ be such an atoning sacrifice as they need and as God will accept. If you know of any other atonement for sin, examine it well, and

I am persuaded that you will find many a fault and flaw in it; but concerning the Lamb of God, I have no question; you may search, and test, and try, but you shall find no blemish in Him. If there were any fault in Him, either of excess or deficiency, you might well refuse Him; but since there is nothing of the kind, I pray you joyfully to accept Him at once. Come now and look at the Lord Jesus Christ, both at His God-head and His manhood, at His life and His death, His acts and His sufferings, and see if there be any iniquity in Him. He knew no sin: He had no acquaintance or dealing with it; "He was holy, harmless, undefiled." After you have well examined His blessed person and His spotless character, if you arrive at the conclusion that He is a fit and acceptable sacrifice for you to present before the Lord, then I long that you may take the much more practical step, and accept the Lord Jesus to be your representa-tive, your sin offering, your burnt offering, your substitute, and your sacrifice. I long that every unsaved person here may at once receive the Lord Jesus as his atone-ment, for this is the main part of that which the sinner must do in order to be cleansed from sin and accepted of God. Happily you have not to find a sacrifice as the Jew had to supply a bullock; God has provided Himself with a perfect sacrifice; that which you have to bring to God, God first brings to you. Happily, there is no need for you to repeat the examination through which the Lord Jesus passed both at the hands of men, and of devils, and of God, when He was tested and tried and examined, and even the prince of this world found nothing of his own in Him. You have to at-tend to this one thing, namely, the laying of your hands upon the sacrifice provided for you. To the Jew it was a sacrifice to be slain, to you it is a sacrifice already offered; and this you are to accept and recognize as your own. It is not a hard duty: you sang of it just now—

> My faith doth lay her hand
> > On that dear head of thine;
> While like a penitent I stand,
> > And there confess my sin.

If you have attended to this already, do so again this morning; if you have never done so, I pray from my inmost soul that you may immediately do that which was meant by laying the hand upon the victim's head.

I. To our work, then, at once. What did that mean? It meant four things, and the first was, CONFESSION. He that laid his hand upon the head of the offering made *con-fession of sin.* I do not care what offering it was that was brought by a believing Israelite, there was always a mention of sin in it, either implied or expressed. "But," says one, "the burnt offering was a sweet-savor offering, and how could there be any ref-erence to iniquity therein?" I know that the burnt offering was a sacrifice of sweet smell, and that it sets forth our Lord as accepted of the Father. But let me ask you, Why did the Israelite bring a sweet-savor offering? It was because he felt that in and of himself he was not a sweet savor unto God, for if had been so he would not have needed to have brought another sweet savor. When I accept the Lord Jesus to be my righteousness it is a confession sin, for I should not need His righteousness if I had one of my own. The very fact of presenting a sacrifice at all contains within it a confession of the need of a sacrifice, which is the confession of personal shortcomings, and a want of personal acceptableness. This is true of the burnt offering, but in other sacrifices, especially in the trespass offering, where the hands were laid upon the victim's head, the offerer was charged to "confess that he hath sinned in that thing" wherein he had trespassed. There was a detailed confession of sin joined with the laying on of hands in the case of the scapegoat. Let us read the passage in Leviticus 16:21: "And Aaron shall lay both his hands upon the head of the live goat, and confess over him all the iniquities of the children of Israel, and all their transgressions in all their sins, putting them upon the head of the goat, and shall send him away by the hand of a fit man into the wilderness."

See then that if you would have Him to be your atonement whom God has appointed to be His sacrifice, you must come to Him confessing your sin. Your touch of Jesus must be the touch of one who is consciously guilty. He belongs not to you unless you are a sinner.

Ah, Lord, confession of sin is no hard duty to some of us, for we can do no other than acknowledge and bemoan our guilt! Here we stand before thee self-condemned, and with aching hearts we each one cry, "Have mercy upon me, O God, according to thy lovingkindness." Do any of you refuse to make confession of guilt? Then, do not think it hard if, since according to your own proud notions you are not sinners, the Lord should provide for you no Savior! Should medicine be prepared for those who are not sick? Wherefore should the righteous be invited to partake of pardon? Why should a righteousness be provided for the innocent? You are the rich and you are sent empty away; the hungry shall be filled with good things. Go to; you that say, "I am clean; I am not defiled"; I tell you that you have no part in the great sacrifice for sin. For the blackest sinner out of hell that will confess his sin there is mercy; but there is none for you; your pride excludes you from pity: it bars the gate of hope against you. You sprinkle the blood of the lamb upon the threshold and trample on it in your arrogant self-conceit, by making yourself out to have no need of its cleansing power. O self-righteous man, you make out God to be a fool, since He gave His only-begotten Son to die, when according to you there was no necessity for His death. In your case at any rate there is no need of a sacrifice by blood, no need of an atonement through the Son of God laying down His life for men. By your refusal to trust in the Lord Jesus you charge God with folly; and therefore into His holy place, where His glory shines forth in its excellence, you can never come. Many of us come most readily at this time and lay our hand upon the head of the appointed sacrifice, even our Lord Jesus Christ, because we have sin to confess, and we feel that we need a Savior, even a Savior for the guilty. We are unworthy and undeserving. We dare say no otherwise. The stones of the street would cry out against us if we should say that we have no sin; the beams of every chamber in our house would upbraid us if we dared to assert that we are without transgression. Our true place is that of sinner: we plead guilty to the dread indictment of God's holy law, and therefore we are glad to lay our hand upon the head of the sinner's Savior and sacrifice.

In this act there was also a confession *of self-impotence*. The believer who brought the bullock did as good as say, "I cannot of myself keep the law of God, or make atonement for my past breaches of the commandments, neither can I hope through future obedience to become acceptable with God; therefore I bring this sacrifice because I myself cannot become acceptable without it." This is a truth which you and I must also confess if we would be partakers of Christ, and become "accepted in the beloved." Oh, brethren, what can we do without Christ?" I like what was said by a child in the Sunday-school when the teacher said, "You have been reading that Christ is precious: what does that mean?" The children stayed a little while, till at last one boy replied, "Father said the other day that mother was precious, for 'whatever should we do without her?' " His is a capital explanation of the word "precious." You and I can truly say of the Lord Jesus Christ that He is precious to us, for what should we do, what could we do without Him? We come and take Him now to be ours because if He be not ours we are utterly undone. I for one am lost forever if Jesus cannot save. There is in us no merit and no strength: but in the Lord Jesus Christ we find both righteousness and strength, and we accept Him this day for that reason. Because we are so deeply conscious of our own self-impotence we lean hard upon his all-sufficiency.

If you could read the text in the Hebrew you would find it runs thus: "He shall put his hand upon the head of the burnt offering, and it shall be accepted for him to make a cover for him"—to make atonement for him. The word is *copher* in the Hebrew—a cover. Why, then, do we hide behind the Lord Jesus? Because we feel our need of something to cover us, and to act as an interposition between us and the righteous Judge of all the earth. If the Holy One of Israel shall look upon us as we are He must be displeased; but when He sees us in Christ Jesus He is well pleased for His righteousness' sake. When the Lord looks this way we hide behind the veil, and the eyes of the Lord behold the exceeding glories of the veil, to wit the person of His own dear Son, and He is so pleased with the cover that He forbears to remember the defilement and deformity of those whom it covers. God will never strike a soul through the veil of His Son's sacrifice. He accepts us because He cannot but accept His Son, who has become our covering. With regard to God, when I am a conscious sinner I long to hide away from Him, and lo! the Lord Jesus is our shield and hiding-place, the cover, the sacred atonement within which we conceal ourselves from justice. Even the all-seeing eye of God sees no sin in a sinner that is hidden in Christ. Oh, what a blessing it is, dear friends, when our sense of self-impotence is so great that we have no desire to make a show of ourselves, but on the contrary long to be out of sight, and therefore we enter into Christ to be hidden in Him, covered in the Sacrifice which God has prepared. That is the second confession, and thus we have confession of sin and of need of covering.

There was a further confession of *the desert of punishment*. When a man brought his bullock, or his goat, or his lamb, he put his hand on it, and as he knew that the poor creature must die he thus acknowledged that he himself deserved death. The victim fell in the dust, struggling, bleeding, dying. The offerer confessed that this was what *he* deserved. He owned that death from the Almighty hand was due *to him*. And oh, when he speaks in anger, and clear when he judges and pronounces sentence in justice; when he confesses that he cannot deliver himself, but has so sinned as to deserve to be accursed of God, and adjudged to feel the horrors of the second death, then is he brought into a condition in which the great Sacrifice will be precious to him. Then will he lean hard upon Christ, and with broken heart acknowledge that the chastisement which fell upon Jesus was such as he deserved, and he will wonder that he has not been called upon to bear it. For my own part I deserve eternal damnation; but I trust in the Lord Jesus, and believe that he was punished in my stead. "The chastisement of our peace was upon him, and with his stripes we are healed." If you can thus confess sin, and bare your neck to punishment, and then lay hold upon the Lord Jesus, you are a saved man. Can your heart truly confess, "I am guilty; I cannot save myself; I deserve to be cast into the lowest hell; but I do now take Jesus to stand in my stead"? Then be of good cheer, "Thy faith hath saved thee: go in peace." May the Spirit of God bless this first point!

II. Secondly, the laying on of hands meant ACCEPTANCE. The offerer by laying his hand upon the victim's head signified that he acknowledged the offering to be for himself.

He accepted, first of all, *the principle and the plan*. Far too many kick against the idea of our being saved by substitution or representation. Why do they rebel against it? For my part, if God will but graciously save me in any way I will be far enough from raising any objection. Why should I complain of that which is to deliver me from destruction? If the Lord does not object to the way, why should I? Moreover, as to this salvation by the merit of another, I do remember that my first ruin did not come by myself. I am not speaking to excuse my personal sin, but yet it is true that I was ruined before I committed any actual sin by the disobedience of the first father of the race who was my representative. How this was just I do not know, but I am sure it must be right, or God would not so reveal it. In Adam we fell: "by one man's disobedience many were made sinners" (Rom. 5:19). If, then, the fall began by the sin of another, why should not our rising be caused by the righteousness and the atonement of another? What saith the Apostle? "For if through the offense of one many be dead, much more the grace of God, and the gift by grace, which is by one man, Jesus Christ, hath abounded unto many." At any rate, it is not for you and for me to raise objections against ourselves, but to feel that if God sees that this is a proper way of salvation, He knows best and we cheerfully accept what He approves. Who is there among you that will not do so? God grant that no one may hold out against a method of grace so simple, so sure, so available!

But, then, mind. After you have accepted the plan and the way, you must not stop there, but you must go on to accept *the sacred Person whom God provides*. It would have been a very foolish thing if the offerer had stood at the altar and said, "Good

Lord, I accept the plan of sacrifice; be it burnt offering or sin offering, I agree thereto." He did much more than that; he accepted the very bullock as his offering, and in token thereof placed his hand upon it. I pray you beware of resting satisfied with understanding and approving the plan of salvation. I heard of one who anxiously desired to be the means of the conversion of a young man, and one said to him, "You may go to him, and talk to him, but you will get him no further, for he is exceedingly well acquainted with the plan of salvation." When the friend began to speak with the young man, he received for an answer, "I am much obliged to you, but I do not know that you can tell me much, for I have long known and admired the plan of salvation by the substitutionary sacrifice of Christ." Alas, he was resting in the plan, but he had not believed in the Person. The plan of salvation is most blessed, but it can avail us nothing unless we believe. What is the comfort of a plan of a house if you do not enter the house itself? What is the good of a plan of clothing if you have not a rag to cover you? Have you never heard of the Arab chief at Cairo who was very ill and went to the missionary, and the missionary said he could give him a prescription? He did so; and a week after he found the Arab none the better. "Did you take my prescription?" he asked. "Yes; I ate every morsel of the paper." He dreamed that he was going to be cured by the plan of the medicine. He should have gone to the chemist's and had the prescription made up, and then it might have wrought him some good. So is it with salvation: it is not the plan, it is the carrying out of that plan by the Lord Jesus in His death on our behalf. The offerer laid his hands literally upon the bullock: he found something substantial there, something which he could handle and touch; even so do we lean upon the real and true work of Jesus, the most substantial thing under heaven. Brethren, we come to the Lord Jesus by faith, and say, "God has provided an atonement here, and I accept it; I believe it to be a fact accomplished on the cross that sin was put away by Christ, and I rest on Him." Yes; you must get beyond the acceptance of plans and doctrines to a resting in the divine person and finished work of the blessed Lord Jesus Christ, and a casting of yourself entirely upon Him.

III. But thirdly, this laying of the hand upon the sacrifice meant not only acceptance, but also TRANSFERENCE. The offerer had confessed his sin, and had accepted the victim then presented to be his sacrifice, and now he mentally realizes that his guilt is by divine appointment to pass over from himself to the sacrifice. Of course this was only done in type and figure at the door of the Tabernacle; but in our case the Lord Jesus Christ as a matter of literal fact has borne the sin of His people. "The Lord hath made to meet on him the iniquity of us all." "Who his own self bore our sins in his own body on the tree." "Christ was once offered to bear the sins of many."

But do we by faith pass our sins from ourselves to Christ? I answer, No: in some senses *no*. But by faith he that accepts Christ as his Savior *agrees with what the Lord did ages ago*, for we read in the book of Isaiah the prophet, "The Lord hath laid on him the iniquity of us all." That was Jehovah's own act in the ages past; and it was complete when Jesus stood as the great sin-bearer, and redeemed us from the curse of the law, being made a curse for us. All the transgressions of His people were laid on Him when He poured out His soul unto death, and "was numbered with the transgressors, and bore the sin of many." Then and there He expiated all the guilt of all His people; for He "finished transgression, made an end of sin, and brought in everlasting righteousness." By His death He cast the whole tremendous load of human guilt, which was laid upon Him, into the depth of the sea, never to be found again. When we believe in Him we agree to what the Lord has done, and so far we may sing—

> I lay my sins on Jesus,
>   The spotless Lamb of God;
> He bears them all and frees us
>   From the accursed load.

There are two ruling religions around us at this day, and they mainly differ in tense. The general religion of mankind is "Do," but the religion of a true Christian is "Done." "It is finished" is the believer's conquering word. Christ has made atonement, and we accept it as done. So in that respect we do lay our sins on Jesus, the holy Lamb of God, because we set our humble seal to that grand transaction which was the confirming of the covenant of old.

The laying of the hand upon the head of the sacrifice meant a transference of guilt to the victim, and, furthermore, *a confidence in the efficacy of the sacrifice* there and then presented. The believing Jew said, "This bullock represents to me the sacrifice which God has provided, and I rejoice in it because it is the symbol of a sacrifice which does in very deed take away sin." Brethren, there are a great number of people who believe in the Lord Jesus Christ after a fashion, but it is not in deed and in truth, for they do not believe in the actual pardon of their own sin: they hope that it may one day be forgiven, but they have no confidence that the Lord Jesus has already put away their sin by His death. "I am a great sinner," says one, "therefore, I cannot be saved." Man alive, did Christ die for those who are not sinners? What was the need of a Savior except for sinners? Has Jesus actually borne sin, or has He not? If He has borne our sin, it is gone; if He has not borne it, our sin will never depart. What does the Scripture say? "He hath made him to be sin for us, who knew no sin; that we might be made the righteousness of God in him." If, then, Christ did take the sinner's sin, it remains not upon the sinner that believeth. Assuredly, you my hearer, if you be a believer, cannot have sin if Jesus has taken it away. You are made clean in the sight of God because your uncleanness has been washed away in the blood of the great sacrifice. See you not this way of salvation? If you do see it, will you not accept it now? Do you not feel already a joy springing up within your soul that there should be such a blessed way of deliverance? At any rate, I tell you where I stand today: I stand guilty, and without a hope in anything I have ever done or ever hope to do; but I believe that the Lord Jesus Christ bore my sin in His own body on the tree, and I am at this moment putting my hands on Him in the sense in which the Hebrew has it, leaning with all my weight upon Him. If Jesus cannot save me I must be damned, for I cannot help Him, neither can I see anyone else who can do so much as a hand's turn in that direction. If there be not virtue enough in the blood of Jesus to cleanse me from all sin, then I must die in my sins: and if there be not sufficient merit in His righteousness to save me apart from any righteousness of my own, then I am a castaway, a spirit shipwrecked on the iron-bound coast of despair. But I have no fears, for I know whom I have believed, and I am persuaded that He is able to keep that which I have committed unto Him until that day. Now I pray you, dear people of God, to lean on Jesus, and keep on leaning there. Oh, that you who as yet do not know Jesus may be brought to touch Him by faith and to lean upon Him by full reliance. In times of sharp pain, or great depression of spirit, or in seasons when death is near, you are forced to look about you to see where your foundation is, and what it is; and, believe me, there is no groundwork that can bear the weight of a guilty conscience and a trembling, tortured body, except this foundation—"the precious blood of Christ cleanseth us from all sin." Jesus is the atonement: He is the covering: He is the refuge: in fine, He is our all and in all.

IV. Once more, this laying of the hand upon the head of the victim meant IDENTIFICATION. The worshiper who laid his hand on the bullock said, "Be pleased, O great Lord, to identify me with this bullock, and this bullock with me. There has been a transferring of my sin, now I beseech thee let me be judged as being in the victim, and represented thereby." Now consider that which happened to the sacrifice. The knife was unsheathed, and the victim was slain. He was not merely bound, but killed; and the man stood there and said, "That is me; that is the fate which I deserve." The poor creature struggled, it wallowed in the sand in its dying agonies, and if the worshiper was a right-minded person, and not a mere formalist, he stood with tears in his eyes, and felt in his heart, "That death is mine." I beseech you when you think of our blessed Lord to identify yourselves with Him. See the bloody sweat is trickling down His face; that is for you. He groans, He cries, for you. Your sins deserved that you should sweat great drops of blood, and Jesus sweats instead. The Lord is taken prisoner and scourged; see how the red streams of gore flow down those blessed shoulders! He bears the chastisement of our peace. He is nailed to the cross; and we are crucified with Him. By-and-by He dies, and we die in Him: "we thus judge that if one died for all, then all died." Believer, you died there in Christ. When your substitute rendered to the law of God the penalty which it demanded, you virtually rendered it. "The soul that sinneth, it shall die," and you have died, believer; you have paid the debt in the Person of the Lord Jesus Christ whom by the laying on of your hands you have accepted to be your substitute. You know that story—it is a capital one, well worth telling a thousand times. In the great French war a person was drawn for a conscript, but as he could not leave his family, he paid a very heavy sum for a substitute. That substitute went to the war and was killed. After a time Napoleon called out the rest of the conscription and the man was summoned because he had been formerly drawn; but he refused to serve. He said, "No, by my substitute I have served, and I am dead and buried: I cannot be made to serve again." It is said that the question was carried up to the highest court, and laid before the Emperor himself, and the Emperor decided that the man's claim of exemption was a just one. He had fulfilled the conscription by a substitute; that substitute had served for life, and could not be called upon to do more; and therefore the person for whom he was the substitute could not further be summoned under that conscription. This sets forth our joy and glory; we are identified with Christ, we are crucified with Him, buried with Him, and in Him raised to newness of life. "I am crucified with Christ, nevertheless I live." "Ye are dead, and your life is hid with Christ in God."

It ought to be remembered that we were identified with Christ in His passing under the wrath of God as a sin offering. If you read in this book you will find that the sin offering was burnt without the camp as an unclean thing; and so you and I were put without the camp long years ago as an unclean thing. That is over now, and we are at this hour no more cast out from the sight of God than Jesus is.

The burnt offering was consumed upon the altar as a sweet savor unto God; and in this also we are identified with Christ. We are now a sweet savor unto God in Christ Jesus our Lord. We are accepted in the Beloved. We are joined unto the Lord, and there is no separating our interests from His, nor His from ours. Who shall separate us from the Christ of God forever and ever? That is what the laying on of hands upon the beast meant. I trust, dear friends, you have known all this for years, and, if not, may you know it now.

If the Lord will enable me, I intend to enter into the second part of my text next Lord's day morning; and for this time it will suffice for me to drive this one nail home. Oh, that the Spirit of God would fasten it in a sure place in our hearts! My soul's yearning desire is that each one of you may come at once and lay your hands on Christ by confession, acceptance, transference, and identification. Nothing short of such an act will suffice to give you salvation.

Now, suppose that the Jew, who went up to the tabernacle and to the altar, when he came there had been content to *talk about* the sacrifice without personally placing his hand on it. To talk of it would be a very proper thing to do; but supposed that he had spent all his time in merely discoursing about the plan of a sacrifice, the providing of a substitute, the shedding of blood, the clearance of the sinner through sacrificial death; it would have been a delightful theme, but what would have come of it? Suppose he had talked on and on, and had gone away home without joining in the offering, he would have found no ease to his conscience; he would, in fact, have done nothing by going to the house of the Lord. I am afraid that this is what many of you have done hitherto. You are pleased to hear the gospel, you take pleasure in the doctrine of substitution, and you know true doctrine from the current falsehoods of the hour: for all which I am very glad; but yet you are not saved because you have not taken Christ to be your own Savior. You are like persons who should say, "We are hungry; but we admit that bread is a very proper food for men, besides which we know what sort of food makes bone, and what makes muscle, and what makes flesh." They keep on talking all day long about the various qualities of food: do they feel refreshed? No. Is their hunger gone? No. I should suppose that, if they are at all healthy, their appetite is increased, and the more they talk about food the more sharp set they become. Why, some of you here have been talking about the bread of heaven for years, and yet I am afraid you are no more hungry that you used to be. Do go beyond talking about Christ, and learn to feed upon Christ. Come, now, let us have done with talk, and come to deeds of faith. Lay hold on Jesus, who is set before you in the gospel: otherwise, dear friend, I fear you will perish in the midst of plenty, and die unpardoned, with mercy at your gate.

Suppose, again, that the Israelite instead of talking with his friends, had thought it wise to *consult with one of the priests*. "Might I speak with you, sir, a little? Have you a little room somewhere at the back where you could talk with me, and pray with me?" "Yes," says the priest, "what ails you?" "My sin lies heavy upon me." The priest replies. "You know that there is a sacrifice for sin; a sin offering lieth at the door, and God will accept it at your hands." But you say, "I beg you to explain this matter more fully to me." The priest answers, "I will explain it as well as I can; but the whole of my explanation will end in this one thing—bring a sacrifice, and over its head confess your sin, and let an atonement be made. The sin offering is what God has ordained, and therefore God will receive it. Attend to His ordinance and live: there is no other way. Fetch your offering; I will kill it for you, and lay it on the altar and present it to God." Do you say to him, "I will call again tomorrow, and have a little more talk with you?" Do you again and again cry, "Tomorrow?" Do you go again and again into the inquiry-room? O sir, what will become of you? You will perish in your sin; for God has not appointed salvation by inquiry-rooms and talks with ministers, but by your laying your own hand upon the Sacrifice which He has appointed. If you will have Christ, you shall be saved; if you will not have Him, you must perish; all the talking to you in the world cannot help you one jot if you refuse your Savior. Sitting in your pew this morning, without speaking to me or any living man or woman, I exhort you to believe in Jesus. Stretch out your withered hand, God helping you, and lay it on the head of Christ, and say, "I believe in the merit of His precious blood. I look to the Lamb of God that taketh away the sin of the world." Why, man, you are saved as sure as you are alive; for he that layeth the hand of faith upon this Sacrifice is saved thereby.

But I see another Israelite, and he stands by his offering, and begins *to weep* and groan, and bewail himself. I am not sorry to see him weep, for I trust he is sincerely confessing his guilt; but why does he not place his hand on the sacrifice? He cries and he sighs, for he is such a sinner; but he does not touch the offering. The victim is presented, and in order that it may avail for him, he must lay his hand upon it; but this vital act he neglects and even refuses to perform. "Ah," he says, "I am in such trouble, I am in such deep distress," and he begins starting a difficulty. You hunt that difficulty down, but there he stands, still groaning and moaning, and producing another difficulty, and yet another, world without end. The sacrifice is slain, but he has no part in it, for he has not laid his hand upon it, and he goes away with all the burden of his guilt upon him, though the sacrificial blood has reddened the ground on which he stood. This is what some of you do. You go about lamenting your sin, when your chief lament should be that you have not believed on the Son of God. If you looked to Jesus you might dry your eyes and bid all hopeless sorrows cease; for He gives remission of sins to all penitents. Your tears can never remove your sin; tears, though flowing like a river, can never wash away the stain of guilt. Your faith must lay her hand on the head of the Lord's sacrifice, for there and there only is there hope for the guilty.

"But surely," says one, "that cannot be everything." I tell you it is so much everything that

> Could your tears forever flow,
> Could your zeal no respite know,
> All for sin could not atone,
> Christ must save, and Christ alone.

Jesus will only save those who accept Him and desire to be identified with Him. I would to God that you would delay no longer, but come at once and freely accept what God has provided! I know the devil will tempt you to look for this and to look for that; but I pray you look at nothing but the Sacrifice that is before you. Lean on Jesus with all your weight.

Observe that the Israelite had to put his hand upon a victim which was not slain yet, but was killed afterwards. This was to remind him that the Messiah was not yet come; but you, beloved, have to trust in a Christ who has come, who has lived, who has died, who has finished the work of salvation, who has gone up into the glory, and who ever liveth to make intercession for transgressors. Will you trust Him or will you not? I cannot waste words; I must come to the point. John Bunyan says that one Sunday when he was playing the game of tip-cat on Elstow Green, as he was about to strike the cat with the stick, he seemed to hear a voice saying to him, "Wilt thou leave thy sins and go to heaven, or wilt thou keep thy sins and go to hell?" This morning the voice from heaven sounds forth this question, Will you trust in Christ and go to heaven, or will you keep apart from Him and go to hell? for thither you must go unless Jesus becomes your Mediator and your atoning sacrifice. Will you have Christ or no? I hear you say, "*But*"—O that I could thrust your "buts" aside. Will you have Christ or not? "*Oh, but*"—Nay, your "buts" ought to be thrown into limbo; I fear they will be your ruin. Will you trust Christ or not? If your answer is, "I trust Him with all my heart," then you are a saved man. I say not that you *shall be* saved; but you *are* saved. "He that believeth in him *hath* everlasting life." You know how our dear friend, Mr. Hill, put it the other night at the prayer-meeting. "He that believeth in him hath everlasting life." "H-A-T-H,"—that spells—"*Got it.*" Very good spelling too. If you believe in the Lord Jesus Christ you have eternal life in present possession; go your way and sing for joy of heart, because the Lord has loved you. Mind you keep on singing until you join the choristers before the eternal throne. The Lord save every person that shall hear or read this sermon, for Jesus' sake. Amen.

SLAYING THE SACRIFICE

SERMON NO. 1,772
DELIVERED ON LORD'S DAY MORNING, MARCH 23, 1884.
PORTION OF SCRIPTURE READ BEFORE SERMON—HEBREWS 9.
HYMNS FROM *Our Own Hymn Book*—427, 291, 428.

And he shall kill the bullock before the LORD—Leviticus 1:5.

YOU remember that last Sabbath day we spoke of two things vitally essential to a true sacrifice, and the first upon which we then enlarged was the laying on of the hands of the offerer upon the victim, by which he accepted it as his sacrifice, and made a typical transfer of his sin from himself to the victim.[†] Now, the second essential thing, of which we are to speak this morning, was this—that the victim thus bearing the guilt of the offerer must be killed: its blood must be shed before the Lord; nothing short of its death by violence would render it an atonement for the offerer: "He shall kill the bullock." You will find this order continually repeated whenever a sacrifice is spoken of.

As I said on the last occasion, I feel great satisfaction in this time of my weakness in being permitted to speak to you about essential things. It was always a stigma upon the character of Caligula that he gathered his warriors, and fitted out his ships; and, when the people of Rome looked for some great addition to the empire by the vast naval expedition, he simply anchored his vessels near the sea-beach, and bade his legions advance upon the shore and gather shells and pebbles, and carry them home as trophies of their undisputed conquest. He trifled where he should have struggled; spent time and labor upon matters of no importance, and neglected the weighty business of his kingdom. We shall not do so today: we have nothing to do with shells and stones, we have to do with matters worth more than gold or pearls, things essential to eternal life, and vital to the salvation of the souls of men.

Neither have I this morning a controversial topic upon which to debate before you. However important controversy may sometimes be, we are glad to be away from its strife, and to consider a doctrine around which true believers gather in hearty unity—a doctrine which must be taken for granted in the Christian church, which lies at the very root of truth, and in the very heart of true religion. Without controversy, great is this mystery of godliness, that Christ manifest in the flesh must die for sin, or oth-

---

[†] "Putting the Hand upon the Head of the Sacrifice," No. 1771, [p. 366].

erwise sin cannot be put away. You remember what the Greek said when he heard an old philosopher with hoary head and gray beard disputing upon how to live. "Goodness!" said he, "if at his age he is disputing upon that subject, when will he be able to practice his conclusions should he arrive at any?" Truly, I may say to you to whom I have so long ministered, if we are forever to be learning and never coming to a knowledge of the truth, what will become of us? If we are to have nothing but questionable matters laid before us, when shall the time come for the actual possession and enjoyment of the blessings of the gospel? At this hour my theme is such that I speak to you without diffidence or hesitation. In this case "we believe and are sure." Concerning our Lord Jesus Christ, the great sacrifice for sin, it was essential that He should die; for only through the blood which He shed on Calvary for human guilt can there be preached among men the remission of sins.

> What can wash away my stain?
>   Nothing but the blood of Jesus!
> What can make me whole again?
>   Nothing but the blood of Jesus!
>
> This is all my hope and peace—
>   Nothing but the blood of Jesus!
> This is all my righteousness—
>   Nothing but the blood of Jesus.

May the Holy Spirit lay home the blood of atonement to our consciences at this time to the glory of God and our own peace!

I. Concerning the killing and slaying of the offering, our first point is that it was ABSOLUTELY ESSENTIAL. The pouring out of the blood of the victim was of the very essence of the type. The death of Christ by blood-shedding was absolutely necessary to make Him an acceptable sacrifice for sin. "It behooved Christ to suffer." He could only enter into the presence of God with His own blood. He could not be the grain of wheat which bringeth forth much fruit unless He should die.

Remember that although there were important matters about the victim, yet nothing would have availed if it had not been slain. The Israelite brought an unblemished bullock, but the fact of its being unblemished did not make it an atonement for sin; no doubt, many faultless bullocks and lambs still fed in the plains of Sharon. If the most perfect animal had gone away from the altar alive it would have effected nothing whatever by way of atonement. It must be unblemished in order to be an offering at all; still, its perfections did not make it a sacrifice until it was killed. No matter what could be said of that bullock; it may have been the most laborious animal throughout all Israel; it may have dragged the plow to and fro, or even drawn the wagon loaded with the harvest; but that was nothing to make it a sacrifice for sin. It must die, and its blood must be sprinkled upon the altar, or else the offerer has brought no acceptable oblation. All its life and its labor would not satisfy.

Nor would it be enough to bring the bullock there and dedicate it to God. Some animals which had been dedicated to the divine service were used in the drawing of the wagons which carried the sacred furniture through the wilderness; but they were not sacrifices for all that, neither did they avail for the bearing away of sin. It was indispensably necessary that the bullock should be without blemish; it was necessary that it should be voluntarily dedicated to God; but if it had not been killed, there would have been no presentation of an offering according to the divine law, nor any easing of the conscience of the Israelite. Even so, Jesus must *die*: His perfect nature, His arduous labor, His blameless life, His perfect consecration, could avail us nothing without the shedding of His blood for many, for the remission of sin. So far from His death being a mere adjunct and conclusion of His life, it is the most important matter connected with Him; it stands in the foreground, it is the head and front of His redeeming work. We justly value Him for His example, and for His living intercession; but in the business of atonement it is beyond all things needful that we view Him as the Lamb slain.

Now notice that *this was expressly declared by God in the Jewish law-book in express words.* Kindly turn in this book of Leviticus to the seventeenth chapter, and there read in the eleventh verse, "For the life of the flesh is in the blood: and I have given it to you upon the altar to make an atonement for your souls; for it is the blood that maketh an atonement for the soul." It is not the burning of the victim, it is not the flaying of it, nor the washing of it, it is the shedding of its blood—that is to say, the taking of its life, which makes it an atonement for sin. I need not quote another Old Testament text, because this is so completely to the point, and so fully covers the whole of the ground. The atonement is not the animal itself, but the blood of the animal, which blood represents its life.

As to *the entire Scriptures*, they *teem with statements of this truth*. I will only call to our recollection a few prominent passages; to collect them all would be impossible. When a child doth gather flowers in the spring meadows when they are all golden with the kingcups, he fills his hand once, but he is almost persuaded to throw away what he has gathered that he may pluck yet more from the inexhaustible store around him; so do I feel that what I now bring before you might fitly be exchanged for another selection, aye, for many such, if time did not fail us.

In the Old Testament, one of the most instructive types of redemption ever given is that of the Passover lamb. When God was about to smite Egypt He promised to spare His people; and in order to their safety He bade each family take a lamb, and kill it, and sprinkle the blood upon the lintel and the two sideposts of their door. Then they were to keep within the house till the morning, and the destroying angel should not touch so much as one of them. What is expressly said by God Himself about this passing-over? Hear the words, and wonderingly drink in their teaching! "And when I see the blood, I will pass over you." There was never a fuller type of the redemption of Christ, I hardly think one so full, as that of the passing-over of Israel through the blood of the Paschal lamb; but the essence of that passing-over is displayed to us in this sentence—"When I see the blood, I will pass over you." God's eye resting upon the evidence of a life having been taken instead of the sinner's life, is the reason why He passes over the sinner, so that he does not die.

When Isaiah, the great evangelical prophet, spoke concerning Him upon whom the Lord laid our iniquity, he mentions His death as the main cause of His glorious reward. The last verse of the fifty-third chapter of Isaiah is the culminating point of the whole, and it runs thus: "Therefore will I divide him a portion with the great, and he shall divide the spoil with the strong; because he hath poured out his soul unto death." It is a wonderful expression: it shows that Christ must die, or else He could not achieve the victory for us, nor share the spoil thereof. He must pour out His soul, He must relinquish life, must pour it out lavishly, as though He possessed much of it: He must make it to flow like water gushing in a river from the smitten rock. This He must do voluntarily and without stint—"pouring out his soul unto death" till none remained, and the bottom of the vessel was reached in death. It is clear that if He had not done this, He had done nothing; for the victory comes to Him because of this; not because He kept His soul free from spot, not because He preached righteousness in the great congregation, not because of anything else which He did was He rewarded; but the victorious deed was that "He poured out his soul unto death." This is the verdict, not only of the Holy Ghost in the inspired prophecy, but also of all that dwell with God above, for they sing with sweet accord before the throne—"A new song, saying, Thou art worthy to take the book, and to open the seals thereof: for thou wast slain, and hast redeemed us to God by thy blood out of every kindred, and tongue, and people, and nation."

In the New Testament the passages abound which set forth the doctrine upon which we are now speaking. Look at that passage in Hebrews 9:12. There we are told expressly, "Without shedding of blood there is no remission." There is no remission by the life of Christ, no remission by the teaching of Christ, no remission by our repentance, no remission by our faith, apart from the shedding of the blood of Christ, by whom alone sin is put away. This is negative; but in this case the negative is as strong as the most positive statement could be; for if without shedding of blood there is no remission, then we see how all-important that blood-shedding becomes. If you desire a positive statement, a sentence rises to our lips at once—"The blood of Jesus Christ his Son cleanseth us from all sin." Observe, not the life, not the incarnation, not the resurrection, not the second coming of the Lord Jesus, but His blood, His death, the giving up of His life, is that which cleanseth us from all sin. This is that purging with hyssop whereof David speaks when he laments his sin, and yet looks to be made whiter than snow by the free pardon of his God.

This truth is the subject of all true gospel preaching. Do you not know how Paul puts it—"The preaching of the cross is to them that perish foolishness; but unto us which are saved it is the power of God"; "for," He says, "the Jews require a sign, and the Greeks seek after wisdom: but we preach Christ crucified." It is not Christ in any other position, but Christ as crucified, Christ as made a curse for us upon the tree, that is the first and most prominent fact that we are called to preach among the sons of men. "In whom we have redemption though his blood, the forgiveness of sins, according to the riches of his grace." Take away this substitutionary death of our Lord, and you have taken all away: without the death of Jesus there remaineth nothing for us but death; forget the Crucified One, and you have forgotten the only name by which we can be saved. Oh, that all of you would trust in Him "whom God hath set forth to be a propitiation through faith in his blood, to declare his righteousness for the remission of sins that are past, through the forbearance of God."

My brethren, this is the cause of the saints being in heaven. In the first chapter of the Book of Revelation, verse 5, we have the doxology, which begins "Unto him that loved us, and washed us from our sins in his own blood." Thus say all the glorified. Further on we are told concerning the saints, "They have washed their robes, and made them white in the blood of the Lamb. Therefore are they before the throne of God, and serve him day and night in his temple: and he that sitteth on the throne shall dwell among them." This is the true reading of the fourteenth verse of the last chapter of the Book of Revelation: "Blessed are they that wash their robes, that they may have the right to the tree of life, and may enter in by the gates unto the city." Thus the passport to glory is the precious blood of Jesus. Access to God either on earth or in heaven is only by the blood of the Son of God.

Now and then we meet with some squeamish person who says, "I cannot bear the mention of the word *blood*." Such individuals will be horrified this morning: and it is intended that they should be. Sin is such a horrible thing that God has appointed blood to wash it away, that the very horror which the thought of it causes may give you some notion of the terrible nature of sin as God judges it. It is not without a dreadful blood-shedding that your dreadful guilt could by any possibility be cleansed. Sin-bearing, and suffering for sin, can never be pleasant things; neither should the type which sets it forth be pleasing to the observer. On great days of sacrifice the courts of the tabernacle must have seemed like a shambles, and fitly so, that all might be struck with the deadly nature of sin.

If it be so, that the blood of Jesus is mentioned in the songs of heaven, let it not be forgotten in the hymns of earth.

> To him that loved the souls of men,
> And wash'd us in his blood,
> To royal honors raised our head,
> And made us priests to God;
>
> To him let every tongue be praise,
> And every heart be love!
> All grateful honors paid on earth,
> And nobler songs above!

The church militant is called upon continually to commemorate the blood-shedding. So often as we gather to the Communion Table we may ask the question, "The cup of blessing which we bless, is it not the communion of the blood of Christ?" At the sacred table we show the death of our Lord until He come. He says to us in express words, "This is my blood of the new testament, which is shed for many for the remission of sins." He bids you remember the blood as you drink of the fruit of the vine, saying, "This cup is the new testament in my blood." Take the blood away, and the communion of the Lord's Supper has gone; there remains nothing but the Popish mass which is so blasphemously called an unbloody sacrifice for the quick and dead.

Forget not that every person gathering to that table of communion is, if he be what he professes to be, a consecrated man, and how comes he to be so but for this reason—"Ye are not your own, for ye are bought with a price"? We are redeemed unto God by the blood of Jesus. "Ye were not redeemed with corruptible things, as silver and gold; but with the precious blood of Christ, as of a lamb without blemish and without spot." It is the blood that makes you what you are, and the blood that permits you to enjoy what God has prepared for you; so that every way you see the absolute essentiality of the death of the great Sacrifice.

Here let us further consider that *death is the result and penalty of sin*—"The soul that sinneth it shall die." "Sin, when it is finished, bringeth forth death." "The wages of sin is death." It was meet that the Substitute should bear a similar chastisement to that which should have fallen upon the sinner. Our Savior did not endure annihilation, for that is not the meaning of death: neither the first nor the second death should be so explained. Jesus was not annihilated, but He bore the pain, the loss, the ruin, the separation, the overwhelming which is intended by death. He was even forsaken of God, so that He cried out, "My God, my God, why hast thou forsaken me?" The penalty was death, and therefore Jesus was exceeding sorrowful even unto death; He laid down His life for us, and became obedient to death, even the death of the cross. The law demanded death, and death has fallen upon our great Covenant Head. "In due time Christ died for the ungodly."

There is great comfort to my soul in this; for if the Lord Jesus has paid the capital sentence nothing remains unpaid. "He that is dead is freed from sin"; that is to say, if the law has killed the man it can ask no more of him, he must be free from further charge of guilt. When the criminal has died he has suffered the last sentence of the law, and is now beyond its jurisdiction. Our Lord Jesus has died the just for the unjust, and as that which He has borne is nothing less than death, it must cover all that is due to sin.

> He bore on the tree the sentence for me,
> And now both the Surety and sinner are free.

Since Jesus has died unto sin once, He dieth no more, death hath no more dominion over Him; He has borne the last and most far-reaching penalty of the law, and there can be nothing left upon the score. His atonement was a complete redemption. If you were in debt, and were bound to pay so much every month, you would be very grateful to a friend who should step in and pay several installments for you; but if one of more liberal spirit discharged the whole amount your gratitude would be deep and overflowing. Let us rejoice that the Lord Jesus Christ has evidently by his substitutionary sacrifice put away, not a part and a portion of our sin, but the whole of it. By bearing death itself He has removed all our legal obligations, and has placed us beyond the reach of further demands. "Christ hath redeemed us from the curse of the law, being made a curse for us." Now we may sing unto Him who has removed our transgressions from us as far as the east is from the west.

This death of Christ was absolutely necessary also for the clearing of the troubled conscience. An awakened conscience will never be quieted with anything less than the blood of the Lamb: it rests at the sight of the great Sacrifice, but nowhere else. A conscience smarting under a sense of sin is an unequaled fountain of misery. Let conscience once begin to scourge the sinner, and he will find it to be the most terrible tormentor out of hell. I do not know whether the prophet Isaiah was really sawn asunder by Manasseh, but we know that some of the saints suffered that torture; yet surely a saw that should gradually cut a man in halves from head to foot is a faint picture of what conscience can do when it begins to operate upon the mind with all its cutting force. What a divine atonement, that must be which calms the storms of an accusing conscience and gives the soul a lasting peace. Some may trifle with their consciences, but where God is at work men dare not attempt it. The most important thing in the world to a sensible man is the condition of his own conscience: if that be restless he is in an evil case. Thomas Fuller in his quaint way tells us that he one day asked a neighboring minister to preach for him, when he called upon a short visit. "No," said the other, "I cannot, for I am not prepared." "But," said Fuller, "though you are unprepared, I am sure you will preach well enough to satisfy my people." His friend answered, "That may be true, but I could not preach well enough to satisfy my own conscience." There's the rub with a true man. We cannot live well enough to satisfy our conscience, and we cannot pray well enough to satisfy our conscience. A really tender conscience is as greedy as the horse-leech which crieth "Give! Give!"—perfection it asks, and as we cannot render it by reason of sin, conscience will never cease its outcries till it is quieted with the precious blood of Jesus Christ. Once let us see Jesus offered up upon the cross for sin, and our heart feels that it is enough. When God is well pleased we may well be satisfied, and go our way enjoying peace with God henceforth and forever.

Thus much, then, upon our first point: for many reasons it was absolutely essential that our great Sacrifice should die.

II. Secondly, we will with great delight mediate upon the fact that the death of Christ is EFFECTUALLY PREVALENT. Other offerings, though duly slain, did nothing thoroughly, did nothing lastingly, did nothing really, by way of expiation; for the Scripture saith, "It is not possible that the blood of bulls and of goats should take away sins": the true purification is alone found in the death of the Son of God. When our Lord was fastened to the tree, and cried, "It is finished," and gave up the ghost, He had finished transgression, made an end of sin, and brought in everlasting righteousness. By offering one sacrifice for sins forever the work was done, the accusing record was altogether blotted out. Why was there such cleansing power in the Redeemer's blood? I answer, for several reasons.

First, because of *the glory of His person.* Only think who He was! He was none other than the "Light of light, very God of very God." He counted it not robbery to be equal with God, yet He took upon Himself our nature, and was born of a virgin. His holy soul dwelt in a perfectly pure body, and to this the Godhead was united: "For in him dwelleth all the fullness of the Godhead bodily." Now for this glorious, this sinless, this divine person, to die is an amazing thing. For the Lord of angels, Creator of all things, sustaining all things by the power of His Word—for Him, I say, to bow His head to death as a vindication of the law is an inconceivably majestic recompense to the honor of eternal justice. Never could justice be more gloriously exalted in the presence of intelligent beings than by the Lord of all submitting Himself to its requirements. There must be an infinite merit about His death: a desert unutterable, immeasurable. Methinks if there had been a million worlds to redeem, their redemption could not have needed more than this "sacrifice of Himself." If the whole universe, teeming with worlds as many as the sands on the seashore, had required to be ransomed, that one giving up of the ghost might have sufficed as a full price for them all. However gross the insults which sin may have rendered to the law, they must be all forgotten, since Jesus magnified the law so abundantly, and made it so honorable by His death. I believe in the special design of our Lord's atoning death, but I will yield to no one in my belief in the absolutely infinite value of the offering which our Lord Jesus has presented; the glory of His person renders the idea of limitation an insult.

Next, consider *the perfection of our Lord's character*. In Him was no sin, nor tendency to sin. He was "holy, harmless, undefiled, and separate from sinners." In His character we see very virtue at its best; He is incomparable. If He therefore died, "the just for the unjust," what must be the merit of such a death? His righteousness has such sweetness in it that all the ill-savor of our transgression is put away thereby: it is no wonder that by the obedience of such an one as this second Adam many are made righteous.

Think next, dear friends, of *the nature of the death of Christ*, and you will be helped to see how effectual it must be. It was not a death by disease, or old age, but a death of violence, well symbolized by the killing of the victim at the altar. He did not die in His bed, sleeping Himself out of the world; but He was taken by wicked hands, and scourged, and spit upon, and then fastened up to die a felon's death. His was a cruel doom; human malice could scarcely have invented any method of execution more sure to create pain and anguish than death by hanging on a tree, fastened by nails driven through hands and feet. In addition to His physical pain, our Lord was sore vexed in spirit. His soul sufferings were the soul of His sufferings: "He was exceeding sorrowful even unto death." Heaven refused its smile: His mind was left in darkness. To be frowned upon of God was part of the punishment of our sin, and He was not spared that direst and bitterest woe. God Himself turned away His face from Him, and left Him in the dark. He died a dishonorable death, yea, a cursed death—"As it is written, cursed is every one that hangeth on a tree." Now, for the Son of God to die, and die in such a manner, was a marvel. Never martyr died crying that he was forsaken of his God: that desertion was the lowest depth of the Savior's grief, and since He died thus I can well understand that He has thereby made an ample atonement for the sins of all who believe in Him. Oh, great atonement of my blessed Lord, my sins are swallowed up in thee! Looking to the cross and to the pierced heart of Jesus my Lord, I am assured that if I am washed in His blood I shall be whiter than snow.

And then think of *the spirit in which our Lord and Savior bore all this*. Martyrs who have died for the faith have only paid the debt of nature a little before its time, for they must have died sooner or later; but our Lord needed not to have died at all. He said of His life, "No man taketh it from me, but I lay it down of myself." The pouring out of His soul unto death was not in the power of man until the Lord was pleased to yield himself a sacrifice. "He gave Himself for me." He laid down His life for His sheep. Out of love to God and man He willingly drank of the appointed cup: the only compulsion which He knew was His own desire to bless His chosen. "For the joy that was set before him he endured the cross, despising the shame." Oh, it was splendidly lived, that life of our Lord; the spirit which guided it lights it up with an unrivaled brightness! Oh, it was splendidly died, that death of our Lord, for He went up to the cross with such a willing submission that it became His throne! The thorn crown was such a diadem as emperor never wore, it was made of the ended sorrows of His people—sorrows ended by their encircling His own majestic head. On the cross He routed His enemies and made a show of them openly, triumphing over them in it. In the act of death He nailed the handwriting of ordinance that was against us to His cross, and so destroyed the condemning power of the law. O glorious Christ, there must be infinite merit in such a death as thine, endured in such a style!

And then I bid you to remember once more *the covenant character which Christ sustained*: for when He was crucified we thus judge that one died for all, and in Him all died. He was not slain as a private individual, but He was put to death as a representative man. God had entered into covenant with Christ, and He was the Surety of that covenant; therefore His blood is called "the blood of the everlasting covenant." Remember the expression of the apostle where he speaks of "the blood of the covenant wherewith we are sanctified." Neither the first nor the second covenant was dedicated without blood; but the new covenant was established by no blood of beasts, but by the blood of our Lord Jesus Christ, that great Shepherd of the sheep. When He offered Himself He was accepted in that character and capacity in which God had regarded Him from before the foundations of the world; so that what He did He did as the Covenant-head of His people. It was meet that He should die for us, seeing He had assumed the position of the second Adam, being constituted our federal Head and Representative. The chastisement of our peace was upon Him because He condescended to be one flesh with us; and with His stripes we are healed because there is a covenant union between us. Thus much upon the effectual prevalence of that great Sacrifice: a theme so vast that one might enlarge upon it throughout all time.

III. Beloved friends, it seems to me that no one will now forbid my saying, thirdly, that the fact of the necessity for the death of the Lord Jesus is INTENSELY INSTRUCTIVE. Listen while I repeat the lessons very briefly: you can enlarge upon them when you go hence to meditate in solitude.

Must the victims die? Must Jesus bleed? Then let us *see what is claimed by our righteous God.* He claims our life: He claimed of the offering its blood, which is the life thereof: He justly requires of each of us our whole life. We must not dream of satisfying God with formal prayers, or occasional alms-deeds, our outward ceremonies, or a half-hearted reverence. He must have our heart, and soul, and mind and strength —all that makes our true self, the life of our being. Dead works are worthless before the living God. He claims our life, and He will have it one way or another; either by its being perfectly spent in His service, or else by its being smitten down in death as the righteous punishment of rebellion. Nor is the demand unjust. Did He not make us, and does He not preserve us? Should He not receive homage from the creatures of His hand?

Next, must the sacrifice die? Then *see the evil of sin.* It is not such a trifle as certain men imagine. It is a deadly evil, a killing poison. God Himself in human form took human guilt upon Him: the sin was none of His, it was only imputed to Him, but when He was made sin for us, and bore our iniquities, there was not help for it, He must die! Even He must die! It was not possible that the cup should pass from Him. A voice was heard from the throne—"Awake, O Sword, against my Shepherd, and against the man that is my fellow, saith the Lord of hosts: smite the Shepherd!" So unflinching is divine justice that it will not, cannot spare sin, let it be where it may: nay, not even when that guilt is not the person's own, but is only taken up by Him as a substitute. Sin wherever it is must be smitten with the sword of death: this is a law fixed and unalterable. Who, then, will take pleasure in transgression? Will not every man who loves his own life arouse himself to fight against iniquity? Sinner, shake off your sin, as Paul shook off the viper into the fire. It is a horrible and grievous thing, and God saith to you "Oh, do not this abominable thing which I hate." God help you to flee from all iniquity.

Next *learn the love of God.* Behold how He loved you and me! He must punish sin, but He must save *us*, and so He gives His Son to die in our stead. I shall not go too far if I say that in giving His Son the Lord God gave Himself, for Jesus is one with the Father. We cannot divide the Substance though we distinguish the Persons: thus God Himself made atonement for sin committed against Himself. The church is "the flock of God which he hath purchased with his own blood." Wonder of wonders! Truly love is strong as death as we see it in the heart of God! "Scarcely for a righteous man will one die: yet peradventure for a good man some would even dare to die. But God commendeth his love toward us, in that, while we were yet sinners, Christ died for us." This is a heaped-up marvel. Behold what manner of love the Father hath bestowed upon us!

Next *learn how Christ has made an end of sin.* Sin is laid on Him and He dies; then sin is dead and buried; if it be sought for it cannot be found. Speak of finality, this is the truest and surest finality that ever was, or shall be. "If a man die, shall he live again?" Not as before. If Christ died, what is there after death? Nothing but the judgment, and lo, He comes to that judgment: "being raised from the dead he dieth no more, death hath no more dominion over him." This is our joy because neither sin nor death can have dominion over us for whom Christ died, and who died in Him. Christ has made an end of sin. His one offering has perfected forever the set-apart ones.

These are but a few of the great lessons which we may learn from the necessity that the Sacrifice should be slain. I pray you learn them well. May they be engraven on your hearts by the Holy Ghost.

IV. And so I shall close by saying that this blessed subject is not only full of instruction, but it is ENERGETICALLY INSPIRING.

First, this inspires us with *the spirit of consecration*. When I think that I could not be saved except by the death of Jesus, then I feel that I am not my own, but bought with a price. I remember reading of Charles Simeon, the famous evangelical clergyman of Cambridge, that he was one day thrown from his horse, and was fearful that he had sustained serious injury. When he had recovered from the force of the fall, he stretched out his right arm, felt it, and finding that there was not a bone broken, he consecrated that arm anew to the living God, who had so graciously preserved it. Then he examined his left arm and found it all right, and so held that up, and dedicated it anew unto the divine service. He did the same with his head, his legs, and his whole body. As I was thinking over this subject I felt as if I must go over my body, soul, and spirit, and dedicate all to that dear Savior by whose blood I am altogether redeemed from death and hell. "Bless the Lord, O my soul: and all that is within me, bless his holy name." As I am not cast away from God, as I am not destroyed, as I am not in torment, not in hell, I dedicate to God my blood-bought spirit, soul, and body from henceforth to be the Lord's as long as ever I live. Brothers and sisters, do you not feel the same? I pray God the Holy Spirit to make you do so in a very practical manner. This doctrine of the death of Christ ought to inspire you till you sing—

> Jesus, spotless Lamb of God,
> Thou hast bought me with thy blood,
> I would value naught beside
> Jesus—Jesus crucified.
>
> I am thine, and thine alone,
> This I gladly, fully own;
> And, in all my works and ways,
> Only now would seek thy praise.

Next, this truth should create in us *a longing after the greatest holiness*, for we should say, "Did sin kill my Savior? Then I will kill sin! Could I not be saved from sin except by His precious blood? Then, O sin, I will be revenged upon thee! I will drive thee out by the help of God's Spirit. I will not endure thee, nor harbor thee. I will make no provision for the flesh. As sin was the death of Christ for me, so Christ shall be the death of sin in me."

Does not this inspire you with *great love for the Lord Jesus*? Can you look at His dear wounds, and not be wounded with love for Him? Are not His wounds as mouths which plead with you to yield Him all your hearts? Can you gaze upon His face bedewed with bloody sweat, and then go away and be ensnared with the world's painted beauties? Heard you ever of a wooer dressed in such robes of love as those which Jesus wore? Did ever love use such sacred means to win the beloved heart as Christ hath done? What can any one of us do but answer Him thus—

> Here, Lord, I give myself away,
> 'Tis all that I can do?

Do you not think that this solemn truth should inspire us with *great zeal for the salvation of others*? As Christ laid down His life for us, should we not lay ourselves out for perishing souls, and, if necessary, lay down our lives for the brethren? Should we not practice self-denial in our labors to bring men to Jesus? Should we not joyfully toil, and cheerfully bear reproach, if by any means we may save some?

Methinks if this subject should go home to our hearts it would be beneficial to us in a thousand ways, and make us better soldiers of the cross, closer followers of the Lamb. I pray that God the Holy Ghost may place it in the center of our souls, and keep it there. It will bring with it peace and rest. Why should we be troubled, since Jesus died? It will fill our mouths with praises. Hallelujah to the Lamb that was slain, who has redeemed us by His blood! It will draw us into closer communion with Him. If He loved us and died for us, we must live with Him, and in Him, and to Him. Surely it will also make us long to behold Him! Oh, for the vision of the Crucified! When shall we see the face that was so marred for us? When shall we behold the hands and feet which bear the nail-marks still, and look into the wounded side bejeweled with the spear-wound? Oh, when shall we up and away from all our sins and griefs, forever to behold Him shine and see Him still before us? Oh, when shall we be—

> Far from a world of grief and sin,
> With God eternally shut in?

Till then our hope, our solace, our glory, our victory, are all found in the blood of the Lamb, to whom be glory forever and ever. Amen.

THE SPRINKLING OF THE BLOOD OF THE SACRIFICE

SERMON NO. 1,780
DELIVERED ON LORD'S DAY MORNING, MAY 11, 1884.
PORTIONS OF SCRIPTURE READ BEFORE SERMON—LEVITICUS 4:1–21; ISAIAH 53.
HYMNS FROM *Our Own Hymn Book*—429, 285, 282.

> *And the priest shall dip his finger in the blood, and sprinkle of the blood seven times before the LORD, before the veil of the sanctuary. And the priest shall put some of the blood upon the horns of the altar of sweet incense before the LORD, which is in the tabernacle of the congregation; and shall pour all the blood of the bullock at the bottom of the altar of the burnt offering, which is at the door of the tabernacle of the congregation*—Leviticus 4:6, 7.

I HAVE aforetime preached to you upon the types of our Lord's sacrifice: the subject is as large as it is important. We began with the laying of the hands upon the offering, and we went on to the all-important matter of the slaying of the victim.[†] Now we come to the use which was made of the blood of the sacrifice after it had been slain. In thinking upon this subject, I seem to hear a voice saying to me, "Put off thy shoes from off thy feet, for the place whereon thou standest is holy ground." This is the central mystery of our religion, it becomes us to be reverent in heart as we approach it. The doctrine of substitution is the heart of the whole matter, our whole heart needs to be aroused while we speak upon it. The Son of God Himself, assuming human nature, and in that nature bleeding and dying in our place and stead, is the Revelation of revelation, the Wonder of wonders, the Glory of the glorious God. Solemnity and awe may well fill us while we meditate on such a theme. Oh, that the Spirit of God may rest upon us now! May His melting power be over this vast assembly! May the speaker feel it, may the hearer experience it, so that we may with one consent, in spirit, and in truth, look to Him who, by the Eternal Spirit, offered Himself without spot unto God!

[†] See sermon nos. 1,771 and 1,772: "Putting the Hand upon the Head of the Sacrifice," and "Slaying the Sacrifice," [pp. 366 and 378].

The sacrifices under the law were varied according to the uppermost thoughts in the offerers' minds and their peculiar conditions before God. A burnt-offering, a peace-offering, or a sin-offering might be brought, according as men wished to give unto the Lord, to have fellowship with Him, or to confess their sin to Him. There was a sacrifice specially arranged for the anointed priest, another for all the congregation, another for a ruler, and yet another for one of the common people: in truth the typical sacrifices all pointed to the one great sacrifice, but they indicated various marks and characteristics of the undivided Lamb of God. The victims varied from a bullock or a lamb down to a pair of turtledoves or two young pigeons. We take different views of the sacrifice of Christ according to our capacity to see it; and yet all these views may be quite in accordance with truth, for the atonement is many-sided, and operates in many directions. The Levitical types represent the different views which believing minds take of our Lord Jesus Christ: they set forth but one Christ, but that one Christ from various standpoints. The mercy is that the sacrifice of our Lord Jesus is suitable to you, and equally suitable to me, and to all that come to Him by faith. The rich, the poor, the brave, the timid, the amiable, and the immoral, all find in Jesus that which fits the individual case. You may be a person of great mind and profound thought, but you shall find in Jesus all that your high intelligence can desire. I may be a person of slender education and of narrow powers of thought, but I shall find the Lord Jesus humbling Himself to my limited capacity. The manna is said by the rabbis to have pleased every man's taste, and even so the Christ of God is every man's Christ, so that no man who comes to Him shall be disappointed, but each shall find his need supplied. Each man shall find his case perfectly met by the Savior's atonement, as much so as if Jesus were prepared for that man only, as if that man were the only sinner under heaven, or Jesus a Redeemer sent to him alone of all the family of man. Oh, the depth of the wisdom and of the grace of God in the person and work of our Lord Jesus Christ!

Note particularly, with great interest, that there were sacrifices provided for sins of ignorance under the law: therefore we safely conclude that a sin of ignorance is a sin. There is not that intensity of evil in a sin of ignorance which is to be seen in willful, deliberate transgression; but still there is sin in it: for no law can allow ignorance to be an excuse for trespass, since it is the duty of the subject to know the law. Even if I do that which is wrong with a sincere wish to do right, still my wrong act has a measure of sin in it. No amount of sincerity can turn injustice into righteousness, or transform falsehood into truth. You can illustrate this by the stern facts of nature. Certain inventors have thought that they could fly, and they have in perfectly honest faith leaped from a lofty crag; but their honest belief has not saved them from the result of violating the law of gravitation: they have fallen to the ground, and have been dashed in pieces just as surely and terribly as if they had felt no real belief in their powers of flight. If a man partakes of a deadly poison believing it to be a health-giving medicine, his sincerity will not hinder the natural course of nature: he will die in his error. It is precisely so in the moral and spiritual world. Sins committed in ignorance must be still sins in the sight of the Lord, or else no expiation would have been provided for them. Without shedding of blood there is no remission even for sins of ignorance. Paul persecuted the saints ignorantly, but he thereby incurred sins which required to be washed away; so Ananias told him, and so he felt, for he called himself the chief of sinners because he persecuted the church of God. When the people sinned through ignorance, and the thing was hid from the eyes of the assembly, they were to bring an offering as soon as the sin was known. If you have transgressed ignorantly, my brother, the time may come when you will find out that you were sinning, and it will then rejoice your heart to find that the Lord Jesus has made atonement for your sins before you knew them to be sins.

I am greatly rejoiced to think there should be such a sacrifice provided, since it may yet turn out that the larger number of our sins are sins of which we have not been aware, because the hardness of our heart has prevented our discovering our error. You may have sinned and have no conscience of that sin at this present, aye, and you never may have a conscience of that particular offense, in this world, yet will it be sin all the same. Many good men have lived in an evil habit, and remained in it unto death, and yet have known it to be evil. Now, if the precious blood of Jesus only put away the sin which we perceived in detail, its efficacy would be limited by the enlightenment of our conscience, and therefore some grievous sin might be overlooked and prove our ruin: but inasmuch as this blood puts away all sins, it removes those which we do not discover as well as those over which we mourn. "Cleanse thou me from secret faults" is a prayer to which the expiation of Christ is a full answer. The atonement acts according to God's sight of sin and not according to our sight of it, for we only see it in part, but God sees it all and blots it all out. When we discover our iniquity it is ours to weep over it with true and deep repentance; but if there be some sins which in detail we have not discerned, and consequently have not by a specific act of repentance confessed them separately, yet, for all that, the Lord doth put away our sin; for it is written, "The blood of Jesus Christ his Son cleanseth us from *all* sin." Those unknown sufferings of Christ which the Greek Liturgy mentions so wisely, have put away from us those unknown sins which we cannot confess in detail because we have not yet perceived them. Blessed be God for a sacrifice which cleanses away forever not only our glaring faults, but those offenses which the most minute self-examination has not yet uncovered.

After the blood had been spilt by the killing of the sacrifice, and thus atonement had been made, three several acts were to be performed by the priest: we have them described in our text; and if you will kindly look you will see that very much the same words follow in the seventeenth and eighteenth verses, so also in the twenty-fifth verse, and in the thirty-fourth verse, where with somewhat less of detail much the same act is set forth. "And the priest shall dip his finger in the blood, and sprinkle of the blood seven times before the Lord, before the veil of the sanctuary. And the priest shall put some of the blood of the bullock at the bottom of the altar of the burnt offering, which is at the door of the tabernacle of the congregation." All this is symbolic of the work of the Lord Jesus and the manifold effects of His blood.

There were three things: first, "the priest shall dip his finger in the blood, and sprinkle of the blood seven times before the Lord, before the veil of the sanctuary": this represents *the atoning sacrifice in its reference to God*. Next, "The priest shall put some of the blood upon the horns of the altar of sweet incense before the Lord": this sets forth *the influence of the blood upon the offering of intercessory prayer*. Thirdly, we read, "he shall pour all [the rest] of the blood of the bullock at the bottom of the altar of the burnt offering": this displays *the influence of the blood of Christ on all our service for the Lord*. Oh, for the Spirit's power to us to show the things of Christ!

I. We begin with THE SACRIFICE OF CHRIST IN ITS RELATION TO THE LORD GOD OF ISRAEL.

In the type before us *the prominent thing before God is the blood of atonement*. No mention is made of a meat-offering, or a drink-offering, or even of sweet spices upon the golden altar; the one conspicuous object is blood. This was sprinkled before the Lord before the veil of the Most Holy place. I am well aware that some persons cry out, "The preacher continually talks about blood, and this morning from the first hymn to the last he has brought before us constant allusions to blood. We are horrified by it!" I wish you to be horrified; for, indeed, sin is a thing to shudder at, and the death of Jesus is not a matter to be treated lightly. It was God's intent to awaken in man a great disgust of sin, by making him see that it could only be put away by suffering and death. In the tabernacle in the wilderness almost everything was sanctified by blood. The purple drops fell even on the book, and all the people. The blood was to be seen everywhere. As soon as you entered the outer court you saw the great brazen altar; and at the base of it bowls of blood were constantly being poured out. When you passed the first veil and entered the Holy Place, if you saw a priest he was bespattered from head to foot with blood, his snow-white robes bringing the crimson spots most vividly before the eye. If you looked around, you saw the horns of the golden altar of incense smeared with blood and the gorgeous veil which hid the innermost sanctuary was bedewed with a frequent sprinkling of the same. The holy tent was by no means a place for sentimentalists; its emblematic teachings dealt with terrible realities, in a boldly impressive manner; its ritual was not constructed to gratify the taste, but to impress the mind. It was not a place for dainty gentlemen, but for broken-hearted sinners. Everywhere the ignorant eye would see somewhat to displease; but the troubled conscience would read lessons of peace and pardon. Oh, that any words of mine could cause triflers with sin to be shocked at the abominable thing! I would have them filled with horror of that detestable thing which cannot be put away except by that which is infinitely more calculated to shock the instructed mind than rivers of the blood of bulls and of goats—I mean the sacrifice of God's own Son, whose soul was made an offering for sin.

The blood of the sacrifice was sprinkled before the veil seven times, signifying this—first, that *the atonement made by the blood of Jesus is perfect in its reference to God*. All though the Scriptures, as you well know, seven is the number of perfection, and in this place it is doubtless used with that intent. The seven times is the same as once for all: it conveys the same meaning as when we read, "For Christ also hath once suffered for sins," and again, "We are sanctified through the offering of the body of Jesus Christ once." It is a complete act. In this text we understand that the Lord Jesus offered unto the justice of God an absolutely complete and satisfactory atonement by His vicarious suffering and death for guilty men. There is no need of further offering for sin. "It is finished." He hath by Himself purged our sins. In old time, before the coming of our Lord, the veil hung darkly between the place of God's glorious presence and His worshiping people: it was only lifted for a moment once a year, and then that one only of all living men might enter into the Holy of Holies for a brief space, the way into the Holiest not being yet made manifest; but still the blood was sprinkled towards the place where the glory of God was pleased to dwell; indicating that access to Him could only be by the way of the blood. Albeit that modern thought will contradict me, I shall not cease to assert perpetually that the greatest result of the death of the Lord Jesus was God-ward. Not only does He reconcile us unto God by His death, and turn our enmity into love, but He has borne the chastisement of our peace, and thus magnified the law and made it honorable. God, the Judge of all, is enabled without the violation of His justice to pass by transgression, iniquity, and sin. The blood of the sin-offering was sprinkled before the Lord because the sin was before the Lord. David says—"Against thee, thee only, have I sinned," and the prodigal cries, "I have sinned against heaven and before thee." The sacrifice of Christ is so mainly a propitiation before God, so thoroughly a vindication of divine righteousness, that this one view of the atonement is sufficient for any man, even if he obtains no other; but let him beware of trusting to a faith which does not look to the great propitiation. This is the soul-saving view; the idea which pacifies conscience and wins the heart: we believe in Jesus as the propitiation for sin. The lights which stream from the cross are very varied; but as all the colored rays are found in the white light of day, so all the varied teachings of Calvary meet in the fact that Jesus suffered for sin, the just for the unjust. Do not your hearts feel glad to think that the Lord Jesus Christ has offered a perfect atonement, covering all, removing every obstacle to the mercy of God, making a clear way for the Lord most justly to justify the guilty? No man need bring anything more, or anything of his own, wherewith to turn away the anger of God; but he may come just as he is, guilty and defiled, and plead this precious blood which has made effectual atonement for him. O my soul, endorse the doctrine, feel the sweet experiences that flow from it, and stand thou now in the presence of God without fear: for seven times has the blood spoken for thee unto God.

Note next, that not only is the atonement itself perfect, but that *the presentation of that atonement is perfect, too.* The sevenfold sprinkling was typical of Christ as a Priest presenting unto the Father Himself as a sacrifice for sin. This has been fully done. Jesus has in due order carried the propitiation into the sanctuary, and appeared in the presence of God on our behalf. Here are the apostle's own words, "by his own blood he entered in once into the holy place, having obtained eternal redemption for us." It is not our presenting of the blood, but Christ's presenting of the blood, which has made the atonement; even as it is not *our* sight of the blood, but Jehovah's sight of it which causes us to escape; as it was written concerning the Passover, "When I see the blood, I will pass over you." Jesus at this moment sets His atonement within view of a righteous God, and therefore is the Judge of all the earth, able to look on the guilty with eyes of mercy. Let us rest perfectly satisfied that all we require to bring us near to God has been done for us, and we may now come boldly unto the throne of the heavenly grace.

No longer far from God: but now
By precious blood made nigh,
Accepted in the well-beloved
Near to his heart we lie.

We now pass on to a few thoughts about ourselves in relation to this type. This sevenfold sprinkling of the blood upon the veil meant that *the way of our access to God is only by virtue of the precious blood of Christ.* Do you ever feel a veil hanging between you and God? In very truth, there is none; for Jesus has taken it away through His flesh. In the day when His blessed body was offered up, the veil of the temple was rent in twain from the top to the bottom, showing that there is nothing now to divide the believer from his God; but still, if you think there is such a separating veil, if you feel as if the Lord had hidden Himself, if you are so despondent that you are afraid you never can draw near to the mercy-seat, then sprinkle the blood *towards* the throne of grace, cast it on the very veil which appears to conceal your God from you. Let your heart go towards God even if you cannot reach Him, and let this blood go before you; for rest assured nothing can dissolve obstacles and furnish you with an open access to God save the blood of Jesus Christ the Son of God. Rest assured that you are already come unto God if boldly, aye, even if timidly with trembling finger, you do but sprinkle the blood in the direction which your faith longs to take. If you cannot present the atonement of Christ yourself by the firm hand of an undaunted faith; yet, remember, Christ's own hand has presented the propitiation long before, and therefore the work will not fail because of your feebleness. O that by a simple confidence in the Lord, your Redeemer, you may this day imitate the example of the priest under the law, for Jesus makes you a priest by the gospel. You may now look towards the Lord and plead that all-prevailing blood which makes us near who were once afar off. I have often admired that blessed gospel precept, "Look unto me, and be ye saved, all the ends of the earth"; for suppose I cannot see, yet if I look I have the promise of being saved. If there should be a mist and a cloud between me and the brazen serpent, yet if I look that way I shall be healed. If I cannot clearly discern all the glories of my Lord and Savior, yet if I look with the glance of trust He saveth me. Turn, then, your half-opened eyes, which only at one corner admit light, turn them I say, God-ward and Christ-ward, and know that by reason of the atoning blood you are saved. The blood-bespattered way is the only one which a sinner's feet can traverse if he would come to God. It is easy, plain and open. See, the priest had the gospel at his fingers' ends; at every motion of his hand he preached it, and the effect of such preaching remained wherever the drops found a resting-place.

I further think that the blood was sprinkled on the veil seven times *to show that a deliberate contemplation of the death of Christ is greatly for our benefit.* Whatever else you treat slightly, let the sacrifice of Calvary be seriously considered again and again; even unto seven times let it be meditated on! Read the story of our Lord's death in the four Evangelists and ponder every detail till you are familiar with His griefs. I would have you know the story by heart, for nothing will do your heart so much good. Read over the twenty-second Psalm and the fifty-third of Isaiah every day if you are in any kind of trouble of heart about sin, and pray to God for enlightenment that you may see the exceeding greatness of His grace to us in Christ Jesus. Oh, that you may with all your heart believe in the Lamb of God! Angels desire to look into these things, therefore, I pray you, do not neglect so great salvation. Think lovingly of the atoning sacrifice; earnestly consider it a second time, do it a third time, do it a fourth time, do it a fifth time, do it a sixth time, do it a seventh time!

Remember, too, that *this sets out how great our guilt has been,* since the blood must be sprinkled seven times ere the work of atonement is fully seen by you. Our guilt has a sevenfold blackness about it, and there must be a sevenfold cleansing. If you plead the blood of Jesus once and you do not obtain peace thereby, plead it again; and if still the burden lies upon your heart, still go on pleading with the Lord the one prevailing argument that Jesus bled. If for the present you do not gain peace through the blood of the cross, do not conclude that your sin is too great for pardon, for that is not the fact, since "all manner of sin and blasphemy shall be forgiven unto men." A fuller acquaintance with Him who has made peace by His blood will calm the tempest of your mind. Christ is a great Savior for great sinners, and His precious blood can remove the blackest spots of iniquity. See it sprinkled seven times for a seven times polluted sinner, and rest your soul on Him though seven devils should have entered into you. God, who bids us forgive unto seventy times seven, sets no bound to His own forgiveness.

Do reflect that *if your case seems to yourself to be very difficult, it is provided for by this sevenfold sprinkling of the blood.* If you say, "My heart is so hard! I cannot make it feel"; or if you say, "I am so frivolous and foolish I seem to forget what once I knew"; then continue still to look to the blood of Jesus, and draw hope from it even to seven times. Do not go away from *that,* I charge you—where else can you go? The devil's desire will be to keep you from thinking upon Christ; but do remember that thoughts about anything else will do you very little good. Your hope lies in thinking upon Jesus, not upon yourself. Masticate and digest such a text as this every morning—"He is able to save them to the uttermost that come unto God by him." Go to bed at night with this verse upon your tongue, "The blood of Jesus Christ his Son cleanseth us from all sin." Or this, "Him that cometh unto me I will in no wise cast out." That dear man of God, Mr. Moody Stuart, somewhere tells us that he once talked with a woman who was in great trouble about her sins. She was a well-instructed person, and knew the Bible thoroughly, so that he was in a little difficulty what to say to her, as she was so accustomed to all-saving truth. At last he urged upon her very strongly that passage,

"This is a faithful saying, and worthy of all acceptation, that Jesus Christ came into the world to save sinners," and he noticed that she seemed to find a quiet relief in a gentle flow of tears. He prayed with her, and when she rose from her knees she seemed much comforted. Meeting her the next day, and seeing her smiling face, and finding her full of rest in the Lord, he asked, "What was it wrought your deliverance?" "Oh," she said, "it was that text, 'Jesus Christ came to save sinners.' " "Did you not know that before?" said Mr. Stuart. Yes, she knew the words before, but she found that in her heart of hearts she had believed that Jesus came to save *saints*, and not sinners. Do not many awakened persons abide in the same error? Well, I want you, poor troubled heart, aye, and you also who are of a joyful spirit, to keep on with this sevenfold presentation of the sacrifice of Christ unto God; and even if a veil should hang between you and the Lord, I beg you to continue to sprinkle the veil with blood until before the eyes of your faith the veil rends in twain, and you stand in the presence of your reconciled God, rejoicing in Christ Jesus.

II. Our second head is this—THE BLOOD IN ITS INFLUENCE UPON PRAYER. "The priest shall put some of the blood upon the horns of the altar of sweet incense before the Lord." The priest in this case goes from the inside of the holy place towards the outer court; having dealt with the veil of the Holy of Holies, he turns around and finds close at his side the altar of incense made of gold, and surmounted with a golden crown; to this he goes deliberately, and places a portion of the blood upon each of its horns. Horns signify power, and the explanation of the symbol is that there is no power in intercessory prayer apart from the blood of expiation.

Remember, first, that *the intercession of Christ* Himself *is based upon His atonement*. He is daily pleading before the throne of God, and His great argument is that He offered Himself without spot unto God. It seems to me most clear and blessed that our Lord Jesus makes this the main plea with the Father on our behalf—"I have finished the work which thou gavest me to do." He has suffered in our stead, and every day He pleads these sufferings for us: His blood speaketh better things than that of Abel. He seeks no new plea, but always urges this old one—His blood shed for man for the remission of sins. "It pleased the Father to bruise him," and now it pleases the Father to hear Him. The bruised spices of His passion are an incense of sweet smell, and derive a double acceptance from the blood-smeared altar upon which they are presented.

And now take the type to yourselves. You and I are to offer incense upon this golden altar by our daily intercession for others, but *our plea must always be the atoning blood of Jesus*. I pray you, dear friends, to urge this much more than you have been accustomed to do in your prayers. We are to cry to God for sinners, and we are to cry to God for saints, but the sacrifice of Jesus must be our strength in petitioning. Intercession is one of the most excellent duties in which a Christian man can be engaged: it has about it the honor both of priesthood and kingship. The incense-altar ought to be continually smoking before the Lord God of Israel, not only in our public prayer-meetings, but in our private supplications. We should be continually pleading for our children, for our friends, for our neighbors, for those who are hopeful, and those who seem hopeless; but the great plea must always be, "By thine agony and bloody sweat; by thy cross and passion." Offer sweet spices of love, and faith, and hope, and lay on the burning coals of strong desire, but on the horn of your altar smear the blood.

> Blood has a voice to pierce the skies,
> "*Revenge*" the blood of Abel cries;
> But the rich blood of Jesus slain
> Speaks "*peace*" as loud from every vein.

Take care you never advance another plea, or if another let it be very subsidiary to this master reason. We may say, "O Lord, save men; because their immortal souls are precious; save them that they may escape from endless misery, and that they may display the power of thy grace; save them also that thy word may not return unto Thee void, and that thy church may be built up by their means"; but we must never be content with these pleas; we must go on to plead the name of Jesus, for whatsoever we ask in that name we shall receive. He who once poured out His soul unto death, and now maketh intercession for the transgressors, will see to it that our pleadings shall not be rejected. In all our intercessions we must remember Calvary; the incense altar for us must on the horn of its strength be always sprinkled with the blood.

And, dearly beloved, as this must be the plea of our intercession, so it must be *our impulse in making intercession*. When we pray we come, as it were, to this golden altar, and we look thereon: what is that we see? Stains of blood! We look again, and again see crimson spots, while all the four horns are red with blood. Did my Lord pour out His soul unto death for men, and shall not I pour out my soul in living earnest when I pray? Can you now bow your knee to plead with God and not feel your heart set upon the good of men, when you see that your Lord has laid down His life that they may be saved? Cold prayers and dull pleadings would vanish if we would but remember how Jesus loved; how being in an agony He sweat as it were great drops of blood. Brethren, we are sadly blameworthy for neglect of intercessory prayer. I cannot tell you how much of a blessing is being withheld, because we do not pray importunately for our fellow men. May the Lord arouse us! May He never permit us to neglect the precious use of the mercy seat! When the late Dr. Bacchus was ill, and near to die, a surgeon visited him, and as he went out of the door, he was observed to speak to the servant. The good old divine begged the attendant to tell him what the surgeon said. After some pause he said, "Dear Sir, he told me not to leave you, for you could not live more than another half-hour." "Then," said the saint, "help me out of bed, let me get upon my knees and spend my last half hour on earth in praying for the church of God, and for the salvation of men." What a blessed way of spending one's last half-hour; let me rather say—what a blessed way of spending half-an-hour at any time! Try it this afternoon! I do not know any method of benefiting our friends which is more constantly open to us all than that of intercessory prayer; and I cannot give you a better argument why you should use it than this, that your Lord has sprinkled the golden altar of intercession with His own blood. Where He poured out His blood, will not you pour out your tears? He has given His bleeding heart for men, will not you give your pleading lips?

I think, too, I must say that this smearing of the horns of the altar with blood is meant to *give us very great encouragement and assurance whenever we come to God in prayer.* Never give anybody up, however bad he may be. If you know a man that is as much like the devil as two peas are like each other, still have hope for him, because when you come to the golden altar to offer your prayers on his behalf what do you see? Why, there is the blood of Christ. What sin is there which it cannot remove? "Oh," you say, "did Jesus die for sinners like this man, and shall I despair of him, and therefore refuse to pray for him?" This is logical argument. We are slow to labor for men because we are slow of heart in expecting their salvation, and this arises out of our narrow views of our Lord Jesus. I pray you enlarge your ideas of God's mercy and of Christ's power to cleanse. Pray not with a phantom hope, but with solid confidence, and say, "Lord, I do but follow with my tears where thou hast been with thy blood. I am pleading this man's pardon, and Thou art also making intercession for trans-gressors. I am pleading for those whom Thou hast bought with thy blood, and therefore I am confident that my desire is in consonance with thy will, and that I shall be heard in heaven, thy dwelling-place." When we pray, let us with vehement desire plead the blood of Jesus Christ. Perhaps fewer petitions, and more urging of the merit of Christ, would make better prayers. If we were shorter in what we ask for, but longer in pleading the reason why we should obtain, we might prevail more easily. I suggest that we use fewer nails; but take care that those nails are driven in with Calvary's blood-stained hammer, and clenched with this argument, "For Jesus' sake." May this sort of prayer be used by us all in private and in public, and then we must and shall prevail.

III. Time flies too quickly this morning, and therefore I must pass over many things I had thought to dwell upon. The last point is, THE BLOOD IN ITS INFLUENCE UPON ALL OUR SERVICE. You see we have been coming outwards from the veil to the golden altar, and now we pass outside the holy place into the outer court, and there in the open air stands the great brazen altar—the first object that the Israelite saw when he entered the sacred precincts. As soon as ever he entered into the first enclosure his eye lighted upon the great altar of brass upon which burnt-offerings were burned, and oblations were presented unto the Lord. It was at the foot of this brazen altar that the bowls of blood were poured out continually, so that the altar was encrimsoned with it, and the soil around was soaked with the sanguine flood.

That altar represents a great many things, and among the rest our Lord Jesus pre-senting Himself to God as an acceptable sacrifice. Whenever you think of our Lord as being an offering of a sweet smell unto God, never disassociate that fact in your mind from His being slain for sin, for all our Lord's service is tinged by His atoning death. It is a great mistake when you are trying to explain any one of the Levitical sac-rifices to run entirely upon one line, for there is a blessed union of all of them in

Christ. The offerings of a sweet savor were all of them in a sense sin-offerings: there are clear indications of this. At the same time the sin-offering for the fat, as we have seen in our reading, was presented upon the altar. What God hath joined together let no man put asunder. You may look at your Lord under various headings, and separately think of His life and of His death; but never stereotype even that division, for His death was the climax of His life, and His life was necessary to His death. Always think of Jesus in all your meditations upon Him as presenting Himself to God and pouring out His soul unto death by way of atonement. When I see that great brazen altar I do not forget how our Lord was accepted of God, but when I see the floods of blood at the foot of the altar I am reminded of the fact that "He his own self bore our sins in his own body on the tree."

Viewing the type in reference to ourselves, let us learn that *whenever we come to offer any sacrifice unto the Lord we must take care that we present it by virtue of the precious blood of Christ*. The worship of this morning—God knows our hearts, He knows how many have really adored Him, and He knows out of those who do worship, how many of us have presented our sacrifice, thinking only of the merit of Jesus as the reason why it should be received. When you rise from your knees after your morning prayer, have you really pleaded the precious blood? Your petitions will not else be acceptable to God. When you are praying at eventide, and speaking with your heavenly Father, have you your eye upon Christ? If not, your devotion will be rejected. As it is with worship in the form of prayer, so is it with worship in the form of praise. Sweet sounds are very delightful when we sing the praises of God, but unless the altar be blood-stained upon which we lay our psalms and hymns, they will not be accepted for all their music. We also bring to God our gifts as He prospers us; I trust we are all ready to give Him a portion of our substance; but do we present it upon the altar which sanctifieth the giver and the gift? Do we see the blood of Christ upon it, and present our gold and silver through that which is more precious far? If not, we might as well retain our money in our purse. When you go this afternoon to your Sunday-school classes, or go out into the streets to preach, or go round with your tracts, will you present your holy labor to God through the precious blood? There is but one altar on which He will accept your services, that altar is the person of His dear Son, and in this matter Jesus must be viewed as pouring out His blood for us. We must view the atonement as connected with every holy thing. I believe that our testimonies for God will be blessed of God in proportion as we keep the sacrifice of Christ to the forefront. Somebody asked our brother, Mr. Moody, how it was that he was so successful, and he is said to have replied, "Well, if I must tell you, it is I believe because we come out fair and square upon the doctrine of substitution." In that remark he hit the nail on the head. That is the saving doctrine; keep that before your own mind, keep it before the minds of those whom you would benefit. Let the Lord see that you are always thinking of His dear Son.

And, beloved, do you not think that this pouring of the blood at the foot of this brazen altar indicates to us *how much we ought to bring there*? If Jesus has brought His life there, and laid Himself thereon, ought we not to bring all that we are and all that we have, and consecrate all to God? Let us not offer a lean, scraggy sacrifice, or one that is half dead, or broken, or diseased; but let us bring our best at its best, and cheerfully present it unto the Most High through the precious blood. One said of a young man who had lately joined the church, "Is he O and O?" and another answered, "What do you mean by that?" "Why," said the first, "I mean—Is he out and out for Christ? Does he give himself spirit, soul, and body to Jesus?" Surely, when we see the altar with Christ Himself upon it, and His blood poured out there, we must acknowledge that if we could spend our whole life in zealous labor, and then die a martyr's death, we should not have rendered even half what such amazing love deserves. Let us be stimulated and quickened by the sight of the blood upon the brazen altar!

Lastly, you notice the blood was poured out *at the bottom of the altar.* What could that mean but this—that *the altar of thank-offering stood upon and grew out of a basis of blood.* So all our deeds for God, our sacrifices for His cause, must spring out of the love which He has manifested in the death of His dear Son. We love Him because—you know the "because"—because He first loved us. And how do we know that He loves us? Behold the death of Jesus as the surest proof. I long to put my whole being upon that altar, and I should feel as I did so that I was not giving my God anything, but only rendering to Him what His dear Son has bought a million times over by once shedding His lifeblood. When we have done all, we shall be unprofitable servants, and we shall say so. All that we have given to God has been presented out of gratitude for the fact that God so loved us that He gave His only begotten Son to die for us that we might live through Him. Load the altar! Heap it high! Let hecatombs smoke thereon, for it is built upon God's unspeakable gift. When sin is removed, service is accepted—"then shall they offer bullocks upon thine altar." Attempt no offering of your own works till then, for unpardoned sinners bring unaccepted offerings. First, let the blood be recognized, and let the full atonement be rejoiced in. Service rendered to God with a desire for personal merit is abominable in His sight; but when our merit is all found in the divine person of His Son, then will He accept us and our offering too in Christ Jesus. God grant unto you, dear hearers, to be accepted in the Beloved. Amen.

EATING THE SACRIFICE

SERMON NO. 2,528

INTENDED FOR READING ON LORD'S DAY MORNING, AUGUST 1, 1897;
DELIVERED ON LORD'S DAY EVENING, MARCH 30, 1884.

*And they shall eat those things wherewith the atonement was made,
to consecrate and to sanctify them: but a stranger shall not eat thereof,
because they are holy*—Exodus 29:33.

ON two following Sabbath mornings, I have spoken concerning the sacrifices under
the law. Our first subject was, "Putting the Hand upon the Head of the Sacrifice" (Sermon No. 1,771 [p. 366]), and the next was "Slaying the Sacrifice" (No. 1,772 [p.
378]). Now we are to make an advance and to speak about the eating of the sacrifice,
for in certain cases the offerer ate a portion of that which had been presented to God.
It has been said by some people, who are very particular in drawing nice distinctions,
that there was no eating of a sacrifice in which there was any connection with sin. I
beg to differ from that opinion, and I have showed you that every sacrifice had something to do with sin, since no sacrifice would have been needed if the man bringing it
had not been a sinner; and here, in this case, I might have selected many texts to teach
the truth I want to bring out just now, but I have specially chosen this one because it
says, "They shall eat those things wherewith the atonement was made." You all know
that a covering is only needed for those who are naked, or who have something that
requires to be hidden; so, the atonement, or the covering, is evidently intended for the
guilty, and has something to do with sin; yet of the things wherewith the atonement
was made Aaron's sons were to eat, so that there is to be an eating, a joyous reception
into ourselves even of those things which have a connection with the putting away of
sin.

The first thing that an offerer did with his victim when he brought it was to appropriate it to himself by laying his hands upon it. So, when a sinner come to Christ,
his first act is to lay his hands upon Christ, that Christ may be shown to belong to the
sinner, and that the sinner's guilt may be transferred to Christ, and borne by Him as
the sinner's Substitute. In afterlife, we are continually to look to Christ, and by faith
to lay our hand upon Him; but we are to advance to a yet more lively and more intensely spiritual way of appropriating Him to ourselves. This is indicated in the text
by eating.

There is life for a look at the Crucified One;

but, after you have begun to live, the substance of that life comes through feeding upon the sacrifice. The first appropriation—the laying on of the hands—is an outward act; but the after appropriation—feeding upon the sacrifice, taking it into yourself—is altogether an inward matter. You who are not yet saved have not at present anything to do with this eating of the sacrifice; your first business is to look to Jesus—not so much spiritually to enjoy Him as, by faith, to look to Him as outside of you, to be regarded by the eye of faith while you, a poor guilty sinner, simply look to Him, and find salvation in Him. It is afterwards, when you shall have made some advance in the divine life, when you shall have clearly seen the Victim sacrificed, and His blood making an atonement for your sins, that you shall come and feed upon Jesus Christ. At the time of the Passover, the Jew must first take the lamb, and kill it, and sprinkle the blood on the lintel and the two sideposts of his house; and after that he must go inside, and when the door is shut, feed upon that lamb whose blood is sprinkled outside. He must eat the Passover supper that he may be refreshed before starting on his journey through the wilderness. Let not this distinction be forgotten; the eating of the sacrifice is not intended to give life, for no dead man can eat, but to sustain the life which is there already. A believing look at Christ makes you live, but spiritual life must be fed and sustained, and the feeding of that life is explained by our Savior in the words I read to you just now, "Except ye eat the flesh of the Son of man, and drink his blood, ye have no life in you. Whoso eateth my flesh, and drinketh my blood, hath eternal life; and I will raise him up at the last day. For my flesh is meat indeed, and my blood is drink indeed," spiritual meat and spiritual drink to support the spiritual life which God has given. Hence it was ordained, even under the law, that after the atonement was made, to consecrate and to sanctify the priests, they were to come, and sit down, and "eat those things wherewith the atonement was made."

I. The first thing about which I have to speak to you at this time is THE PARTICIPATION—the eating of the sacrifice.

So, first, I will *describe it*. We are to "eat those things wherewith the atonement was made," to participate in Christ, to take Him into ourselves. The act of eating is very common but a very expressive method of setting forth participation, for it is entirely personal. Nobody can eat for you, or drink for you; it is personally for yourself that you partake of bread, and the bread goes into yourself, to build up yourself, to be assimilated by yourself into yourself as to become part of yourself; and, dear friend, the Lord Jesus Christ must thus be received into your heart and soul by yourself, for yourself, and must remain within yourself, you exercising upon Him continually a blessed act of faith by which you have communion and fellowship with Him. This cannot be done by any sponsor, or any proxy, or through any means; it must be done personally, directly, and distinctly, by yourself. God help you to receive Christ unto yourself! That point, surely, is plain enough; as a man himself receives food into himself, to become part of himself, so must you and I receive the Lord Jesus into ourselves for ourselves, to be interwoven with ourselves, so that we twain shall be one.

This participation is not only personal, but it is distinctly inward. There is no receiving Christ by any exercise of the flesh, by aught that we can do externally; it is within that we are to receive Christ, with our heart, with our spirit. We are not to regard Him alone as yonder on the cross, but as formed in us the hope of glory, as coming into us to sit as King upon His throne, and to reign within us; for it is into our innermost nature that we are to receive the blessed truth concerning Christ and His atonement.

And it is an active reception, too. A man can receive some things into himself passively. Oil may penetrate into his flesh; certain drugs may be injected beneath the skin, and so may permeate the blood; but eating is an active exercise, a thing done by a man, not in his sleep, but with the full intent that he may receive unto himself that which he eats. So must you receive the Lord Jesus Christ, feeding upon Him willingly, actively taking Him into yourself with the full consent and power of your whole being.

You know, also, that eating arises from a sense of need, and it leads to a sense of satisfaction. The most of people eat because they are hungry, though I suppose there are some who eat simply because the time has come, whether they need food or not. I have heard that the best time for a poor man to have his dinner is when he can get it, and that the best time for a rich man to have his dinner is when he wants it; and I think there is something in the saying. In this spiritual feeding, if you will feed on Christ when you can get Him, you may begin at once. What is wanted in most cases is an appetite; but when a man has an appetite for Christ, when he says, "I must have pardon, for I am a sinner; I must have a renewed heart, for I have an evil one; I must have spiritual life, for I am in a state of spiritual death," then he has the appetite which only Christ can satisfy. Then, when he receives Christ into his heart, there follows a sense of satisfaction, as you have sometimes seen in the case of a person who has enjoyed a good meal. He wants no more; he lies down, and is perfectly content. Oh, but what a satisfaction Christ brings to the soul that feeds upon Him! When you have fed on Him, dear friends, how full you have become—not to repletion, for the more you receive of Him the more He will enlarge your capacity—but you have received Him to the fullness of satisfaction. Mind you not that Psalm where David says, "My soul shall be satisfied as with marrow and fatness; and my mouth shall praise thee with joyful lips?" Oh, yes! and it is so with us when we receive Christ into our heart, then are we filled to the full; and this is the kind of participation which is meant in our text. We are to "eat those things wherewith the atonement was made," we are to receive Christ personally, inwardly, actively, because of our soul's hunger, and that our feeding upon Him may lead to an intense satisfaction with Him. Do you want another Savior, you who have received Christ Jesus into your souls? I know that you do not. Is there something, after all, that you desire to add to the blessed Lord and His divine work? I know that there is not, for, "ye are complete in him,"—perfectly satisfied with Christ Jesus, filled up to the brim with all spiritual blessings.

Thus I have tried to describe this participation, now I want you to *practice it*. Notice that the text says, "They shall eat those things wherewith the atonement was made." Among "those things" there was flesh, there was bread in the basket, and so forth; and they were to eat of all those things. I gather from this injunction that you and I must endeavor to feed upon all that makes up the atonement, and all that is connected with the atonement. For instance, let us feed upon the Father's love that gave the Lord Jesus Christ to bleed and die. Then let us feed on the fact of the divine person of the Lord Jesus. Oh, what a blessed loaf that is! What is the use of a Savior to me if He is not divine? I am sure that nothing short of Deity can ever save such a soul as mine from the sin in which it is found; but Christ is "very God of very God," so I feed upon that glorious truth. Will you not do the same, dear friends? Then feed upon the fact of his perfect humanity, bone of our bone and flesh of our flesh, of a human mother born, as certainly man as we are. Oh, there is many a satisfying meal in the blessed doctrine of the true and indisputable humanity of our Lord Jesus Christ!

Then, when you have fed upon Christ's deity and humanity, feed upon the willingness with which He came to save us. Long before He was born into this world, His delights were with the sons of men, and He looked forward with joy to the time of His appearing. "Lo I come": said He, "in the volume of the book it is written of me, I delight to do thy will, O my God." In the fullness of time He came, leaping over the mountains, skipping over the hills, that He might save His people. It is no unwilling Savior who has come to save you and me, beloved. Feed on that sweet truth. Think of the love that did lie at the back of it all, the love He had to His church and people, which moved Him to lay aside all His glory, and take upon Himself all our shame, to surrender the ineffable splendor of His throne to be nailed up to the shameful cross. O brethren, there is a great feast for the soul in the love of Christ! This is "butter in a lordly dish." There was never such wine, even at a king's marriage, as that which Christ Himself made, and we can truly say to Him, "Thou hast kept the best wine until now."

Aye, but I believe that there is food for us at every stage of the Redeemer's passion. There are sweet fruits to be gathered even in dark Gethsemane; there are precious clusters of the vine to be found at Gabbatha, the pavement where the cruel scourges made the sacred drops to roll. What food there is for our souls upon Calvary! Every item of our Lord's death is sacred; we would not omit any of the details of His suffering, for some strike one mind, and some strike another; but could we go through the whole history of our Savior, from the agony in Gethsemane till He said, "It is finished," we should find all the way full of food for our souls. Where are there such pastures as those that grow on Calvary? Sharon, thou art altogether outdone! O plains that fed the flocks of old, ye are barren compared with this little hill whereon the Savior poured out His soul unto death! Try, dear Christian friends, to feed on all these things. I cannot keep you to do it now, but at such times as you can get an hour, or even a few minutes, say to yourself, "This is all spiritual food for me. I am to feed on 'those things wherewith the atonement was made.' "

Before I pass to the second division, I want to tell you one thing more about this participation which, I think, *ennobles it*, and lifts it altogether out of the commonplace, namely, that this feeding of the priests—or, if you turn to the peace offering, the feeding of the offerer himself—upon the sacrifice, was in fellowship with God. When the sacrifice was offered, a part of it was burnt on the altar; that was God's portion. The altar represented God, and the Lord received the portion that was consumed by the fire. In the text before us, we see that the priest was also to take his share; it was part of the same sacrifice, so both God and the priest fed upon it. You and I, beloved, are to feed with God on Christ. That is a blessed sentence in the parable of the prodigal son where the father said, "Let us eat, and be merry." The father feeds, and the family feed with him: "Let *us* eat, and be merry." Oh, it is indeed joyful for us to remember that the Father finds satisfaction in the work and merit, the life and death of the Only-begotten! God is well pleased with Jesus, for He has magnified the law, and made it honorable; and that which satisfies the heart of God is passed on to satisfy you and me. Oh, to think of our being entertained in such a fashion as this! You remember that it is said of the elders, who went up with Moses and Aaron into the mount, that "they saw God, and did eat and drink"; and surely, we are as favored as they were, for now in Christ Jesus we behold the reconciled God, and we do eat and drink with Him; and while the Father smiles because the work of atonement is finished, we sit down, and we rejoice, too. Even we poor weeping sinners wipe our tears away, and sing,—

> Bless'd be the Father, and his love,
> To whose celestial source we owe
> Rivers of endless joy above,
> And rills of comfort here below.

If God is content, so are we. If the Judge of all the earth says, "It is enough," we also say, "It is enough." Our conscience echoes to the verdict of the Eternal. Christ has finished the transgression, and made an end of sins, and brought in everlasting righteousness, and therefore we enjoy the sweetest imaginable rest in Him. The Father's delight is in Him, and so is ours. Oh, who among us that knows the Lord Jesus, will stand back for a moment from this blessed eating with God? "They shall eat those things wherewith the atonement was made, to consecrate and to sanctify them."

II. This brings me to my second point, which is an advance upon the former one, namely, THE OFFICIAL CHARACTER OF THIS PARTICIPATION. In this particular form, the participation was for the priests only.

Now mark this. The child of God, when he is first converted, does not know much about being a priest, he does not know much about doing anything for Christ. I heard of a good Scotch woman, whose style of speech I cannot imitate, but I like the sense of it. Someone said to her, "How long have you been a servant of the Lord?" She said, "Nay, nay, but He has been a servant to me, for does He not say, 'I am among you as he that serveth'?" "Ah!" replied the other, "that is true; but, still, you have served the Lord." "Yes," answered she, "but it is such poor work I have ever done that I do not like to think of having done anything at all for Him; and I would rather talk of how long He has been doing something for me, than how long I have been doing anything for Him." That is quite true; yet, inasmuch as the Lord Jesus Christ died for us, we reckon that we all died, and that He died for us that we henceforth should live, not unto ourselves, but unto Him; and so we do. If the Lord has really blessed us with His love, we have begun to be priests, and we have begun to serve Him.

Now the priest, because he is a priest, is the man who must take care that he feeds upon the sacrifice. But how are we priests? I am not now talking about the ministers, I am talking about all of you who love the Lord. Christ has made all of us, who believe in Him, to be kings and priests unto God; there is no priesthood in the world that is of God save the high-priesthood of our Lord Jesus Christ, and, next to that, the priesthood which is common to all believers; and the idea of there being any priesthood on earth above and beyond the priesthood of all believers, is a false one, and there is no Scripture whatever to vindicate it, to justify it, or even to apologize for it, it is one of the lies of old Rome. All believers are priests, but they do not all fully recognize that great truth. It is a pity they do not realize that glorious fact, and so join in the apostle John's doxology, "Unto him that loved us, and washed us from our sins in his own blood, and hath made us kings and priests unto God and his Father; to him be glory and dominion forever and ever. Amen."

Being priests, they are, first of all, *to offer themselves*. What says the apostle? "I beseech you, therefore, brethren, by the mercies of God, that ye present your bodies a living sacrifice, holy, acceptable unto God, which is your reasonable service." Now, you will never do this unless you feed upon Christ. I shall never be myself a sacrifice to God unless my soul is nourished upon the true and living sacrifice, Christ Jesus my Lord. To attempt sanctification apart from justification, is to attempt an impossibility; and to endeavor to lead a holy life apart from the work of Christ, is an idle dream. You priests who offer yourselves unto God must take care that it is all done through Christ who is in you.

Next, as priests, we are *to intercede for others*. A priest was chosen to offer prayer for others, and every Christian ought to pray for those who are round about him; but you will never be men of prayer unless you feed on Christ, I am sure of that. If Christ be not in your heart, intercessory prayer will not be in your mouths. You will never be true pleaders with God for men unless you are yourselves true feeders upon the atoning sacrifice of Christ.

A true priest is, next, *to be a teacher*. The prophet Micah said, "The priest's lips should keep knowledge"; and so should it be with all Christians. They are to teach others. But you cannot teach others what you do not know yourselves; and unless you are first partakers of the fruits, you will never be able to sow the seed. You must feed upon Christ in your inmost soul, or else you will never speak of Him with any power to others.

Priests, again, were chosen from among men *to have compassion on the ignorant*, and on such as were out of the way. That is your duty, too, as Christians, to look after the weak ones and the wandering ones, and to have compassion upon them; but, unless you live by faith upon the compassionate Savior, you will never keep up the life of compassion in your own soul. If Christ be not in you, neither will you be in the Spirit of Christ, full of love to such as need your help; but coming fresh from communion with the Father, and with His Son Jesus Christ, your words of consolation will sweetly drop into afflicted hearts, and will comfort them. You will have the tongue of an instructed one, and be able to speak words seasonable and sweet to such as are weary. Take care, then, that you do feed upon Christ.

I believe, also, that a Christian man is to act as a priest for a dumb world, and *to express the worship of creation*. It is he who is to chant creation's hymn; it is his voice that must lift up the hallelujahs of the universe. The world lacks a tongue. Yon sea, with all its rolling billows, yet speaks not a word articulately; and yonder stars, with all their brilliance, cannot tell out the glory of God in human language, or, indeed, in any language at all. "There is no speech, nor language; their voice is not heard." Nor can the sweet flowers, nor even the birds, in actual language tell of Him who made them, and express their gratitude to Him; but you and I have a tongue, which is the glory of our frame, and with that tongue we are to open our mouths for the dumb, and speak the praises of God for all creation. Take care that you do it; before you lies the world, like a great organ, all ready to sound forth the sweetest music, but it cannot play itself. Those little hands of yours, if they are instinct with heavenly life, are to be laid among the keys, and you are to fetch forth strains of mighty hallelujahs unto Him who has made all things, and sustains all things by the power of His hand. Feed on Christ, and you will be able to do this, for He speaks to reveal God, and He becomes the tongue of men unto the Father. Live on Him, and you shall learn the art of speaking for creation unto the Creator.

III. Now I have done when I have very solemnly noticed, in the third place, THE ABSOLUTE PROHIBITION: "They shall eat those things wherewith the atonement was made; . . . but"—"*but* a stranger shall not eat thereof, because they are holy."

Who was a "stranger" in such a case as this? Everybody was a stranger, in the matter of the priests, but such as belonged to the priests; and strangers might not partake of the sacrifices with the priests. The prohibition is clearly given in the 22nd chapter of Leviticus, at the 10th verse: "There shall no stranger eat of the holy thing: a sojourner of the priest,"—that is, a mere guest—"or an hired servant, shall not eat of the holy thing." Listen: you who only come into the house of God just to look on, you who do not belong to the family, but are only sojourners—welcome as sojourners—you may not eat of the holy thing. You cannot enjoy Christ, you cannot feed upon the precious truth connected with Him, for you are only a sojourner. I am very sorry, on the first Sabbath night in the month, and I think that some of you must feel very sorry and sad, too. There is to be the communion, the Lord's Supper; you have been hearing the sermon, but you have to go away from the table, or else to take your place among the spectators. You are only sojourners, you do not belong to the family, and dare not profess that you do; you are only a sojourner, or a stranger.

And it was the same in the case of a hired servant, he might not eat of the holy thing; and he who only follows Christ for what he can get out of Him, he who works for Christ with the idea of meriting salvation, hoping that he may earn enough to save himself by his works, is only like a priest's hired servant. He says, "I do my best, and I believe that I shall go to heaven." Yes, just so; you are a hired servant, even though heaven seems to be the wage you are expecting; and you may not eat of the holy thing.

Now notice what is written in Leviticus 22:11: "But if the priest buy any soul with his money, he shall eat of it." Is not that a blessing? *If the Lord Jesus Christ has bought you with His precious blood*, and you by faith recognize yourself as not your own, but bought with a price, then you may eat of the sacrifice. "If the priest buy any soul with his money,"—it may be a very queer person, somebody for whom you and I would not give twopence—but if the great High Priest has bought any soul with His money, "He shall eat of it."

"And he that is born in his house, shall eat of his meat." There is the doctrine of regeneration, as the former part of the verse spoke of redemption. *If you have been born again*, and are no more in the house of Satan, but in the house of the great High Priest, you may come and eat of this spiritual meat. If you have the blood-mark, having been bought by Christ, and if you have the life-mark, having been quickened by the Spirit, and born into the family of Christ, then come along with you. Though least and weakest of them all, come and welcome.

Listen to this next verse: "If the priest's daughter also be married unto a stranger, she may not eat of an offering of the holy things." She is the priest's daughter, mark you; nobody denies that, and shall not the child partake with the father? No, not if she is married to a stranger; she bears her husband's characteristics now, she has given herself up to him; she is no longer her father's, she belongs to her husband. Oh, is there anybody here who once made a profession of religion, but who has gone aside? Have you got married to the world? Have you got married to amusements and Sabbath-breaking? Have you got married right away from the Priest, your Father—right away from the church of Christ—right away from the people of God? Then you cannot eat of the holy thing.

Yet listen to one other verse: "But if the priest's daughter be a widow, or divorced, and have no child, and is returned unto her father's house, as in her youth, she shall eat of her father's meat; but there shall no stranger eat thereof." Perhaps there is someone here who says, "I am a widow." I do not mean that your natural husband is dead, but that the world has become dead to you. You went and married into the world for wealth, and you have lost it; you are poor now, riches are dead to you. You used to be such a fine woman, but now your face has lost its comeliness, your beauty is dead. Everybody used to admire your talent; but you have not any talent now, and they all give you the cold shoulder. Ah, well, I am not sorry that the world has cast you out, and cast you off! Perhaps the men of the world have said concerning you, "We will have no more to do with him." You are divorced, you see. Long ago, I was divorced from the world; I got a bill of divorcement pretty quickly when I began to preach the gospel in London. If it were worthwhile, I could publish some of the cruel and false things that men said; according to them, I was the biggest charlatan and the greatest hypocrite and deceiver who ever lived. That was my bill of divorcement; the world said, "We have done with you," and I replied, "I have done with you"; and so we parted. There were not many words on my part, but there were a great many on theirs. Well, if it is so with you, if you feel that the world has done with you, and you have done with the world, and you are willing to come back to your Father's house, just as in the days of your youth, come along with you; come in, and eat of His dainties, feed upon Christ on earth by faith, and then go up and feed on Him even to the full in glory everlasting. But you must get away from your stranger-husband, for if you cleave to him, you will have to be counted with that which your heart lusts after. What you love shall label you. Where your delight is, where your treasure is, there your heart is, and there your portion is; but if the Lord will help you now to escape right away from the clutches of error and sin, then it shall be with you as it was with the priest's daughter: "If she is returned unto her father's house, as in her youth, she shall eat of her father's meat."

"But there shall no stranger eat thereof." If you will not believe on the Lord Jesus Christ, you are a stranger to the commonwealth of Israel; and there is no way of your being made nigh but by the blood of the cross. If you believe in Him, you are "no more strangers and foreigners, but fellow-citizens with the saints, and of the household of God." But if you are not bought with His money, or born in His house, then you must remain strangers, and there is no blessing for you, no comfort for you. The other day, one who had been attending a religious service, and mocking and jesting at everything sacred said, when he was talked to about it, "Oh, but I am a Christian! Jesus died for me." It was a lie; he had neither part nor lot in the matter, or else he could not have acted profanely as he did; and there are others who talk as he did, but I tell you, sirs, whatever you say, this is what God says, "A stranger shall not eat thereof." If you have not been born again, you cannot feed upon Christ; but, oh, if you will look to Him who died for the sinner, then you shall feed upon Him who lives for the saint. God bless you in both these respects, for Jesus Christ's sake! Amen.

THE LAMB OF GOD IN SCRIPTURE

Sermon No. 2,329
Intended for Reading on Lord's day Morning, October 8, 1893;
Delivered on Lord's day Evening, August 25, 1889.

*Again the next day after John stood, and two of his disciples; and
looking upon Jesus as he walked, he saith, Behold the Lamb of
God.*—John 1:35, 36.

You all know the old, old story. The world was lost; God must punish sin; He sent
His Son to take our sin upon Him that He might honor the law of God, and establish
God's government by being obedient to the law, and yielding Himself up to the death-
penalty. He whom Jehovah loves beyond all else came to earth, became a man, and,
as a man, was obedient unto death, even the death of the cross. It is He who is called
in our text "the Lamb of God," the one Sacrifice for man's sin. There is no putting
away of sin without sacrifice; there is only one Sacrifice that can put away sin, and that
is, Jesus Christ the righteous. He is divine, yet human; Son of God, yet son of
Mary. He yielded up His life, "the Just for the unjust," the Sinless for the sinful, "that
He might bring us to God," and reconcile us to the great Father. That is the story, and
whosoever believeth in Him shall live. Any man, the world over, who will trust
himself to Christ, God's great Sacrifice, shall be saved, for this is our continual witness, "He that believeth on the Son hath everlasting life." "For God so loved the world,
that he gave his only-begotten Son, that whosoever believeth in him should not perish but have everlasting life."

Tonight I do not intend so much to preach a sermon as to urge those who have
seen the Lamb of God to look at Him more intently, to study Him more, and especially to plead for the power of the Holy Ghost to reveal Him to them. I want to
entreat men, who have looked elsewhere, now to turn their eyes away from the
fruitless search after peace and life, and to come and "Behold the Lamb of God, which
taketh away the sin of the world." May the Spirit of God open their eyes, and incline
their hearts, that tonight, even tonight, they may look unto Him and live!

When John saw Jesus Christ on that memorable day, he, first of all, beheld Him
himself, and then he said to others, "Behold the Lamb of God." "Looking upon Jesus
as He walked," steadfastly beholding Him, watching Him, gazing with humble admiration at Him, he said, "Behold the Lamb of God!" Brethren, we cannot preach

what we have not practiced. If these eyes have never looked to Jesus, how can I bid your eyes look at Him? Beholding Him, I found peace to my soul; I, who was disposed even to despair, rose from the depths of anguish to the heights of joy by looking unto Him; and I therefore dare to say to you, "Behold the Lamb of God!" Oh, that each one of you might believe our testimony concerning Jesus and look to Him and live!

What did John mean by saying, "Behold the Lamb of God?" Behold, in the Latin, *ecce*, is a note of admiration, of wonderment, of exclamation. "Behold the Lamb of God!" There was nothing of greater wonder ever seen than that God Himself should provide the Lamb for the burnt offering, that He should provide His only Son out of His very bosom, that He should give the delight of His heart to die for us. Well may we behold this great wonder. Angels admire and marvel at this mystery of godliness, God manifest in the flesh; they have never left off wondering and adoring the grace of God that gave Jesus to be the Sacrifice for guilty men. Behold and wonder, never leave off wondering; tell it as a wonder, think of it as a wonder, sing of it as a wonder; even in heaven you will not cease to wonder at this glorious Lamb of God.

I think that John also meant his disciples to consider when he said to them, "Behold the Lamb of God!" So we say to you, "Think of Him, study Him, know all that you can about Him, look Him up and down. He is God; do you understand that He stood in the sinner's stead? He is man; do you know how near akin He is to you, how sympathetic He is, a brother born for your adversity?" The person of Christ is a great marvel; how God and man can be in one person, it is impossible for us to tell. We believe what we cannot comprehend; and we rejoice in what we cannot understand. He whom God has provided to be your Savior is both God and man; He can lay His hand upon both parties, He can touch your manhood in its weakness, and touch the Godhead in its all-sufficiency. Study Christ; the most excellent of all the sciences in the knowledge of a crucified Savior. He is most learned in the university of heaven who knows most of Christ. He who hath known most of Him still says that His love surpasseth knowledge. Behold Him, then, with wonder, and behold Him with thankfulness.

But when John says, "Behold the Lamb of God!" he means more than wondering or considering. "Looking" is used in Scripture for faith: "Look unto me, and be ye saved." Therefore we sing—

> There is life for a look at the crucified One,
> There is life at this moment for thee!

Beholding is a steady kind of looking. Believe then, in Christ with a solid, abiding confidence. Come, ye sinners, come, and trust your Savior, not for tonight only, but forever. Believe that He is able and willing to save you, and trust Him to do so.

> Venture on him, venture wholly,
> Let no other trust intrude.

Take your eyes off everything else, and behold the Lamb of God! You need not see anything else, nothing else is worth seeing; but behold Him. See how He takes your guilt, see how He bears it, see how He sinks under it, and yet rises from it, crying, "It is finished." He gives up the ghost, He is buried, He rises again from the dead because He is accepted of God, and His redeeming work is done. Trust Him, trust Him, trust Him. "Look and live," is now our message; not "do and live," but "live and do." If you ask how you are to live, our answer is look, trust, believe, confide, rest in Christ, and the moment you do so, you are saved.

But once more, when John said to his disciples, "Behold the Lamb of God!" it was a hint that they should leave off looking at John, and turn their attention wholly to Jesus, and follow Him. Hence we find that John's two disciples left him, and became the disciples of Christ. Beloved, we who preach long to have your attention, but when you give your attention to us, our longing then is to pass it on to Christ our Lord. Look on Him, and follow Him, not us. What can we do, poor creatures that we are? Look unto Him, mark His footsteps, tread in them. Do as He bids you, take Him for your Lord, become His disciples, His servants. Behold the Lamb of God, and always behold Him. Look to Him, look up to Him, and follow where He leads the way.

Thus I have put the text before you pretty simply. Now, I want to talk to you a little about beholding this Lamb of God, taking a hasty run through various Scripture references to the lamb; and I will ask you, first, to *Behold the Lamb of God in His connections with men,* and secondly, to *Behold the Lamb of God in His benedictions to men.*

I. Let us, first, BEHOLD THE LAMB OF GOD IN HIS CONNECTIONS WITH MEN.

How was the Lamb of God first seen in the world? It was the case of *the lamb for one man,* brought by one man for himself, and on his own behalf. You all know that I refer to Abel, who was a shepherd, and brought of the firstlings of his flock, that is, a lamb, and he brought this lamb for himself, and on his own account, that he might be accepted of God, and that he might present to God an offering well-pleasing in His sight. Cain brought of the fruit of the ground as an offering to God. I think that there was a difference in the sacrifice, as well as in the man bringing it, for the Holy Ghost says little about the difference of the man, but He says, "By faith Abel offered unto God a more excellent sacrifice than Cain," and he was accepted because he brought a more excellent sacrifice. The one sacrifice was bloodless, the fruit of the ground, the other was typical of Christ, the Lamb of God, and was therefore accepted: "and the Lord had respect unto Abel, and to his offering."

Now, beloved, our first view of Christ usually is here, to know Him for ourselves. I am a sinner, and I want to have communion with my God; how shall I obtain it? I am guilty, I am sinful; how shall I draw near to the holy God? Here is the answer. Take the Lord Jesus Christ to be yours by faith, and bring Him to God; you must be accepted if you bring Christ with you. The Father never repelled the Son, nor one who was clothed with the Son's righteousness, or who pleaded the Son's merit.

Come you, as Abel came, not with fruits of your own growing, but with the sacrifice of blood, with Christ the holy Victim, the spotless Lamb of God, and so coming, whoever you may be, you shall be acceptable before God by faith. Now, behold Him, each one of you for yourself!

I know what someone will say, "I hope to do that by-and-by." I hope you do not so deceive yourself. I have heard that there was once a great meeting in the den of the arch-enemy, and he was stirring up his myrmidons to seek the destruction of men. One of the them said, "I have gone forth, and I have told men that there is no God, and no hereafter, and no difference between sin and righteousness, and that they may live as they like"; and there was considerable approbation among the evil spirits. But Satan himself said, "Thou hast done small service, for man has a conscience, and his conscience teaches him better; he knows that there is a God, he knows that there is a difference between sin and righteousness, he knows that there must be future punishment; you have done but little." Then another stood up, and said, "I have done better, I think, most mighty chieftain, for I have told them that the Bible is a worn-out book, that it was a fable at the first, and that they need not believe it." There was a round of cheers, for they said that he had done splendid service for the cause of darkness; but Satan said, "It is in vain that you meddle with the old Book, it has taken care of itself, and it can still do so. There is no shaking, it is like a rock. Thou hast done service for a time, but it will soon pass away." And scarcely did anyone of the fallen spirits venture to bring forward his boasting in the presence of the terrible master who sat in the midst of them; but, at last, one said, "I have told men that they have souls, and that there is a God, and that the Bible is true. I have left them to believe as they will, but I have whispered in their ear that there is plenty of time to consider all this." Then there was a hush, and the great master of demons said, "Thou hast done best of all. This is my great net in which I take more souls than with any other, this net of procrastination or delay." Therefore say I to you, my hearers, disappoint the fiend. Fly to Jesus. Fly to Jesus at once. Behold, not tomorrow, but tonight, behold the Lamb of God, each man for himself.

Now turn over the pages of this grand old Book, and you will find the Lamb in another connection. Israel was in Egypt, and there they had *the lamb for the family*; "In the tenth day of this month they shall take to them every man a lamb, according to the house of their fathers, a lamb for an house." Oh, I wish that you would all go on to behold the Lamb of God for your households! "Believe on the Lord Jesus Christ, and thou shalt be saved." Why do you stop before you finish the verse? What said the apostle to the trembling jailer? Not merely all that I have quoted, but more: "Believe on the Lord Jesus Christ, and thou shalt be saved, *and thy house*." Are there not many believers who do not believe for their house? Come, now, and believe in this provision of the Lamb for the house. Trust the grace of God for that little girl, the last born, and for that boy who is still at school, who does not think much of these things as yet; and for that son of yours who has left home, and gone out as an apprentice. Oh, that the Lamb of God might be for him! Pray for him, tonight; and you older parents, pray for your sons who are married, and your daughters who have taken to themselves husbands, and are away from you. The Lamb is for the house, pray for the whole household tonight; take in your grandchildren, all you old folks, all of them who are in your house. Pray that the Lamb may be for the house. I do bless God that I can look upon all my household, and rejoice that they are converted to Christ. My father has this joy, too; and my grandfather also had that joy. Oh, it is a great bliss to have families, generation after generation, all brought to Christ without exception! Why should it not be so? Let us cry for it; surely we may expect the same blessing that God gave to His chosen people under the law, and expect it more largely. Grace does not run in the blood, but grace often runs side by side with it, so that Abraham is loved, and Isaac, and Jacob, and Joseph, and Ephraim, and Manasseh. Thus the covenant blessing goes on from one to another. Plead with God, tonight, that all in your house may be beneath the sprinkled blood of the Lamb, and be saved from the destroying angel, and that all with you may go out of Egypt to have a possession in the land of the promise.

A little further on, following the Scripture, and asking you still to behold the Lamb, in the twenty-ninth chapter of that famous Book of Exodus, at the thirty-eighth and thirty-ninth verses, we come across God's command for *the lamb for the people*: "Now this is that which thou shalt offer upon the altar; two lambs of the first year day by day continually. The one lamb thou shalt offer in the morning; and the other lamb thou shalt offer at even." Here is the lamb for all the chosen people, the lamb for Israel. It began with the unit, it went on to the family; and here the Lord, who "loveth the gates of Zion more than all the dwellings of Jacob," makes His tabernacle to be the central place where a lamb shall be offered for the whole nation. Think of it with delight, tonight, that Christ died for all His chosen people. He hath redeemed them from among men. Though they be as many as the stars for number, or as the sand on the sea-shore innumerable, yet that one Sacrifice has redeemed them all. Glory be to God for the blood of the Lamb, by which the whole of Christ's people are redeemed!

Then let your mind take wing right out of the Old Testament into the New, for I have not time to trace all the successive steps. Come now to John, saying, in the twenty-ninth verse of this chapter, "Behold the Lamb of God, which taketh away the sin of the world." Now you have gone beyond the bounds of Israel, and have come to *the Lamb for the world*. You have come to the Lamb of God, who dies for Gentiles as well as for Jews, for men in the isles of the sea, for men in the wilds of Africa, for men of every color, and every race, and every time, and every clime. Oh, glory be to God, wherever there are men, we may go and tell them of Christ! Wherever there are men born of Adam's race, we may tell them of the second Adam, to whom looking, they who look shall live, and in Him they shall find eternal life. I love to think of the breaking down of the bounds that shut in the flow of grace to one nation. Behold, it flows over all Asia Minor, at first, and then over all Greece, and then to Rome, and Paul talks of going to Spain, and the gospel is borne across the sea to England, and from this country it has gone out unto the utmost ends of the earth.

Well, now, take your flight, if you can get beyond that, away to heaven itself, and there you will see *the Lamb for all heaven*. Look at Revelation, the seventh chapter, and the fourteenth verse; no, you need not look it out, you know it. All the saints in heaven are standing in their glittering ranks, white-robed, pure as the driven snow. They sing and praise one glorious name; when one of the elders first asked the question, "What are these which are arrayed in white robes, and whence came they?" he himself gave the answer, "These are they which came out of the great tribulation, and have washed their robes, and made them white in the blood of the Lamb."

'Round the altar priests confess,
If their robes are white as snow,
'Twas the Savior's righteousness,
And his blood that made them so.

The blood of the lamb has whitened all the saints who are in heaven; they sing of Him who loved them, and saved them from their own sins in His own blood. I have often wondered why that second word was not brought into our translation, for it so beautifully fits the language of the beloved Apostle John: "Unto him that loved us, and saved us from our sins in his own blood, and hath made us kings and priests unto God and his Father; to him be glory and dominion forever and ever. Amen." There is no whiteness in heaven but what the Lamb has wrought, no brightness there but what the Lamb has bought; everything there shows the wondrous power and surpassing merit of the Lamb of God.

If it be possible to think of something more glorious than I have already described, I think you will find it in the fifth chapter of Revelation, at the thirteenth verse: "And every creature which is in heaven, and on the earth, and under the earth, and such as are in the sea, and all that are in them, heard I saying, Blessing, and honor, and glory, and power, be unto him that sitteth upon the throne, and unto the Lamb forever and ever." The day shall come when, from every place that God has made, there shall be heard the voice of praise unto the Lamb; there shall be found everywhere men and women redeemed by blood, angels and glorious spirits, rejoicing to adore Him who was, and is, and is to come, the Almighty Lamb of God.

I think I have given you something to consider if you turn over the pages of Scripture, and follow the track of the bleeding Lamb.

II. But now, taking you again over the same road a little, I want you, in the second place, TO BEHOLD THE LAMB OF GOD IN HIS BENEDICTIONS TO MEN.

The first blessing of all is that of Abel. *He was accepted of God*; he offered a more acceptable sacrifice than Cain. Well now, let anybody here, who does not know it, try to learn this lesson tonight. You can only be "accepted in the Beloved." God loves His Son with such an overflowing love that He has love enough for you, love enough for me, if we are in Christ Jesus. He is the great conduit or channel of God's love, and that love flows through all the pipes to every soul that believes in Jesus. Hide behind your Lord, and you are safe. Trust His name, living and dying, and nothing can harm you. How many dear hearts, when passing through the valley of death-shade, when grim thoughts have clustered about them, have been cheered, and comforted by the thought of Christ! Remember the monk who, as he died, put away the priest, and the crucifix, and everything else, and cried, *"Tua vulnera, Jesu! Tua vulnera, Jesu!"* "Thy wounds, Jesus! Thy wounds, Jesus!" I am not saved by what I can do, but by what He has done; not by what I have suffered, but by what He has endured. There hangs our everlasting hope; we trust to Christ in life and in death, and we are accepted for His sake. Come, every sinner, bring the Lamb of God; put Him on the altar, and you shall be accepted at once, and you may at once begin to praise the name of the Lord.

But then, as we go on, we find this Lamb of God useful, not only for acceptance, but also for *rescue and deliverance*. It is a dark and dreadful night; Egypt shivers, and stands aghast; and just at twelve at night forth flies an angel, armed with the sword of death. In every house of Egypt there is heard a wail, for the firstborn is dead, from the firstborn of Pharaoh to the firstborn of the woman who turns the mill to grind the daily corn. Death is in every house; nay, stay; there are houses wherein there is no death. What has secured those habitations? The father took a lamb, shed its blood, dipped the bunch of hyssop in it, and smeared the lintel and the two side posts; and then all sat down and feasted on the lamb undisturbed, and calm, and happy. They rejoiced to have for food that lamb whose blood was the ensign of their safety. There was no crying there, no dying there; death could not touch the inhabitants of the house that was marked with the blood of the Paschal lamb. Beloved, you and I are perfectly safe if we are sheltered beneath the blood of the Lamb of God; nothing can harm us, everything must bless us; and we may go to our beds tonight singing—

> Sprinkled afresh with pardoning blood,
> I lay me down to rest,
> As in the embraces of my God,
> Or on my Savior's breast.

We may rise tomorrow morning, if we are spared, and go into this busy world without any fear. The broad arrow of the King is set upon us in the blood-mark of the atoning sacrifice, and we are safe, and safe forever. Glory be to the name of the Lord for this!

Nor was that all. As I have told you, the blood of the Paschal lamb was not only sprinkled for the protection of the house, but its flesh was the *food* of the inmates. Oh, brethren, we do not at first know what it is to feed on Christ! We are satisfied to be sprinkled with His blood; but the believer afterwards finds that Christ is the food of his soul. His blood is drink, indeed, and His flesh is meat, indeed. Oh, what a festival have we kept over the person of our Lord! Sometimes, when faint and hungry, we have begun to think of the Incarnate God, the bleeding Lamb, the full atonement paid, and we have said, "My soul is full, satisfied with favor, full of the blessing of the Lord." I do not know what there is in the gospel if you take away the atoning sacrifice; it seems to me that there would be nothing left but chaff, which might suit asses and horses, but would not be fit for men. Look to Jesus Christ dying in our stead, and here is something for the soul to feed upon, aye, and to be satisfied with, as with marrow and fatness!

I pointed you a little further on, to the lamb in the wilderness, the lamb offered up every day; that brings us to another point in our Lord's work. We have had Christ for acceptance, Christ for safety, and Christ for food, now we have Christ for *perpetual resort*. The Lamb of God in the morning! Oh, blessed be God for a Savior in the morning! If the night has gathered aught of evil, He doth then disperse it, as the sun dispels the darkness. But oh, what a precious thing also to have the Lamb of God in the evening! If in the day we have soiled our feet in traversing this busy world, here we come to the fountain, and we are made clean through the blood of the Lamb. Perpetual merit, perpetual intercession, perpetual life-giving, perpetual salvation, flow from Jesus Christ the Lamb of God. He is not slain twice; His one wonderful offering has finished transgression, and made an end of sin; but its efficacy continues as though He were sacrificed often, ever supplying us with merit, so that, in effect, His wounds continually do bleed. He is always a new Savior for me every morning, always a new Savior every night, and yet always the same Savior, the same Christ. There is no getting weary of Him, there is nothing "stale" in Him. They may talk about "a new view of the atonement." I have no view of the atonement but this, "Who loved me, and gave himself for me"; "Who his own self bore our sins in his own body on the tree"; and that old view of the atonement is ever fresh and ever new to the heart and conscience.

Well now, beloved, when we come to John again, following our former run of thought, we find the Lamb of God useful for *guidance*, for when John said, "Behold the Lamb of God," the two disciples followed Jesus; and we read of some, "These are they which follow the Lamb whithersoever he goeth." The Lamb is our Guide. The Lord is a Shepherd as well as a Lamb, and the flock following in His footsteps is safely led. My soul, when thou wantest to know which way to go, behold the Lamb of God! Ask, "What would Jesus do?" Then do thou what Jesus would have done in such a case, and thou canst not do amiss.

Further on we find such a passage as this, telling us of *victory* through the Lamb of God: "They overcame him by the blood of the Lamb." The Lamb is a great Warrior; there is none like Him. Is He not the Lion of the tribe of Judah? Though He be gentle as a lamb, yet against sin and iniquity He is fiercer than a young lion when it roareth on its prey. If we follow Him, hold fast His truth, believe in His atonement, and perpetually proclaim His gospel, we shall overcome all error, and all sin, and all evil.

Well now, this blessed Lamb—it is not easy to leave off talking about Him when one once begins—is so blessed that you may well behold Him, for all *happiness* comes through Him. In heaven you will see nothing without Him. "Nothing?" say you. No, nothing; here is a proof of my words. "The city had no need of the sun, neither of the moon, to shine in it: for the glory of God did lighten it, and the Lamb is the light thereof." All the light, the knowledge, the joy, the bliss of heaven, come through the atoning sacrifice of Christ. Not Jesus only, but Jesus slain, Jesus the Lamb of God, is the very light of heaven.

And what, think you, is the joy-day of heaven, the time for the highest *exultation*? Why, the joyous day when all the golden bells shall peal out their glorious melodies, and all the silver trumpets shall ring out their jubilant notes, will be the day of the marriage of the Lamb. It is the heaven of heaven, the climax of ineffable delight; and the voice of the great multitude, as the voice of many waters, and as the voice of mighty thunderings, sings, "Alleluia: for the Lord God omnipotent reigneth. Let us be glad and rejoice, and give honor to him: for the marriage of the Lamb is come, and his wife hath made herself ready." So that, at the topmost round of the ladder of eternal bliss, there do you find the Lamb. You cannot get beyond Him. He gives you all He has, even Himself. Behold Him, then, and go on beholding Him throughout the countless ages of eternity.

I would to God that you had all beheld Him, and I pray you to behold Him tonight. It is but a little while, and the death-film will gather about your eyes; and if you have not seen the Lamb while yet you have mortal eyes, you will see Him, you will certainly see Him, but your vision will be like that of Balaam, "I shall see Him, but not now: I shall behold Him, but not nigh." If it is with you "not now," it may be "not nigh." It will be an awful thing to see the Lamb with a gulf between yourself and Him, for there is a great impassable gulf fixed in the next world; and when you see Him across that gulf, how will you feel? Then shall you cry to the mountains and rocks, "Fall on us, and hide us from the face of him that sitteth on the throne, and from the wrath of the Lamb!" Jesus will still be a Lamb, even to the lost; it is "the wrath of the Lamb" that they will dread. The Lamb is always conspicuous; He may be neglected, rejected, refused tonight, but He will be beheld in eternity, and beheld to your everlasting confusion and unutterable dismay if you refuse to behold Him now. Let it not be so with any of you.

> Ye sinners, seek his face,
>   Whose wrath ye cannot bear;
> Fly to the shelter of his cross,
>   And find salvation there.

Amen.

THE ANNUAL ATONEMENT

SERMON NO. 1,923
DELIVERED ON LORD'S DAY MORNING, OCTOBER 3, 1886.
PORTION OF SCRIPTURE READ BEFORE SERMON—LEVITICUS 16.
HYMNS FROM *Our Own Hymn Book*—240, 291, 564.

*For on that day shall the priest make an atonement for you, to cleanse you, that ye may be clean from all your sins before the LORD—*Leviticus 16:30.

BEFORE Adam transgressed he lived in communion with God; but after he had broken the covenant, and grieved God's Spirit, he could have no more familiar fellowship with God. Under the Mosaic dispensation, in which God was pleased in His grace to dwell among His people and walk with them in the wilderness, it was still under a reserve: there was a holy place wherein the symbol of God's presence was hidden away from mortal gaze. No man might come near to it except in one only way, and then only once in the year, "The Holy Ghost this signifying, that the way into the holiest of all was not yet made manifest, while as the first tabernacle was yet standing." Our subject today illustrates the appointed way of access to God. This chapter shows that the way of access to God is by atonement, and by no other method. We cannot draw near unto the Most High except along the blood-besprinkled way of sacrifice. Our Lord Jesus said, "No man cometh unto the Father, but by me"; and this is true in many senses, and in this among them, that our way to God lies only through the sacrifice of His Son.

The reason of this is that sin lieth at the door. Brethren, a pure and holy God cannot endure sin: he cannot have fellowship with it, or with those who are rendered unclean by it, for it would be inconsistent with His nature so to do. On the other hand, sinful men cannot have fellowship with God: their evil nature could not endure the fire of His holiness. Who among us shall dwell with the devouring fire? Who among us shall dwell with everlasting burnings? What is that devouring fire, and what are those everlasting burnings, but the justice and holiness of God? The apostle saith, "Even our God is a consuming fire." A guilty soul would perish if it were possible for it to draw near to God apart from the Mediator and His atonement. The fire of God's nature must consume the stubble of our nature so long as there is sin in us or about us. Hence the difficulty of access, a difficulty which only a divine method can remove.

God cannot commune with sinful men, for He is holy. Sinful men cannot commune with a holy God, because He must destroy them, even as He destroyed Nadab and Abihu when they intruded into His holy place. That terrible judgment is mentioned in the opening verses of the chapter before us as the reason why the ordinances herein contained were first of all made.

How, then, shall men come to God? Only in God's own way. He Himself devised the way, and He has taught it to us by a parable in this chapter. It would be very wrong to prefer any one passage of Scripture beyond another, for all Scripture is given by inspiration; but if we might do so, we should set this chapter in a very eminent and prominent place for its fullness of instruction, and its clear yet deep doctrinal teaching. It treats upon a matter which is of the very highest importance to all of us. We are here taught the way by which the sin that blocks the door may be taken away, so that a seeking soul may be introduced into the presence of God and stand in His holy place, and yet live. Here we learn how we may say, with the astonished prophet, "I have seen God, and my life is preserved." Oh that we might today so learn the lesson that we may enter into the fullest fellowship with the Father, and with His Son Jesus Christ, in that safe way, that only way, which God has appointed for us. Oh for the power and guidance of the Holy Spirit, that we may know and use "the new and living way!"

Before I proceed to enlarge upon this chapter, I want to notice that, of course, this was only a type. This great day of atonement did not see an actual atonement made, nor sin really put away; but it was the figure of heavenly things—the shadow of good things to come. The substance is of Christ. If this day of atonement had been real and satisfactory, as touching God and the conscience of men, there would never have been another; for the worshipers once purged would have had no more conscience of sin. If they had lived fifty or a hundred years, they would never had needed another day of atonement; but because this was, in its nature, imperfect and shadowy, being only typical, therefore every year, on the seventh month, on the tenth day of the month, a fast was proclaimed, sin was confessed, victims were slain, and atonement was again presented. In the Jewish year, so often as it came round, on one special day they were commanded to afflict their souls, even though it was a Sabbath of rest. In very deed a remembrance of sin was made every year, a painful remembrance for them, although sweetened by a new exhibition of the plan by which sin is cleansed. The Lord said, "This shall be an everlasting statute unto you"; it lasted as long as the Mosaic economy in the letter, and its spirit and substance last on forever. They had that day to remember that their sin was not put away once for all and forever, by all their types and ceremonies, and therefore they had again to humble themselves and come before God with sacrifices which could never truly put away sin. This Israel had to do constantly until Jesus, the true High Priest appeared, and now they have no sacrificing priest, nor altar, nor Holy of Holies. By Jesus Christ's one offering of Himself, sin was put away, once for all, effectually and finally, so that believers are really clean before God. Now if I should seem to run the type into the substance you will just dissever them in your own minds. It is not easy so to speak as to keep shadow and substance quite clear of each other. We are apt to say, "This is so and so," when we mean, "this represents so and so"; and we have our Lord's example for so doing, for He said, "This is my body and my blood," when He meant that the bread and wine represented His body and blood. We are not speaking to fools, nor to those who will wrench the letter from its obvious spiritual sense. I shall trust to your intelligence and the guidance of the Holy Spirit that you will in this discourse discern between the symbol and the substance. May the divine Spirit help men and help you to a right understanding of this sacred type!

I. Now, then, let us come to the text, and note, first, WHAT WAS DONE on that particular day. The text tells us what was done symbolically—"On that day shall the priest make an atonement for you, to cleanse you, that ye may be clean from all your sins before the Lord."

The persons themselves were cleansed. If any of them had become unclean so as to be denied communion with God and His people, they were made clean, so that they might go up to the tabernacle, and mingle with the congregation. All the host were that morning regarded as unclean, and all had to bow their heads in penitent sorrow because of their uncleanness. After the sacrifice and the sending away of the scapegoat the whole congregation was clean and in a condition to rejoice. If it happened to be the year of jubilee, the joyful trumpets rang out as soon as the atonement was complete. Every year, within four days after the Day of Atonement, the people were so clean that they kept the joyful Feast of Tabernacles. Jewish Rabbis were wont to say that no man had ever seen sorrow who had not seen the Day of Atonement, and that no man had ever seen gladness who had not witnessed the hilarity and delight of the people during the Feast of Tabernacles.

The people themselves were made to be a clean people; and I lay great stress on this, because unless you yourself are purged, everything that you do is defiled in the sight of God. When a man was unclean, if he went into a tent and sat upon anything it was unclean; if a friend touched his garments, he was rendered unclean. The man himself first needed to be delivered from impurity, and it is precisely the same in your case and mine. I have need to cry, "Purge *me* with hyssop, and *I* shall be clean; wash *me*, and *I* shall be whiter than snow." Your very person by nature is defiled, and obnoxious to the justice of God. In body, soul, and spirit you are by nature altogether as an unclean thing, and all your righteousness are as filthy rags: you yourself need to be washed and renewed. It is a far simpler thing to remove outward stains than it is to purge the very substance and nature of man; yet this is what was done on the day of atonement typically, and this is what our redeeming Lord actually does for us. We are outlaws, and His atonement purges us of outlawry, and makes us citizens; we are lepers, and by His stripes we are so healed as to be received among the clean. By nature we are only fit to be flung into those fires which burn up corrupt and offensive things; but His sacrifice makes us so precious in the sight of the Lord that all the forces of heaven stand sentinel about us. Once black as night, we are so purged that we shall walk with Him in white, for we are worthy.

Their persons being made clean, *they were also purged of all the sins confessed.* I called attention, in the reading of the chapter, to its many "alls." I think there are seven or eight of them. The work which was done on that day was comprehensive: a clean sweep was made of sin. I begin with that which was confessed, for it was that for which cleansing would be most desired. It is said that "Aaron shall lay both his hands upon the head of the live goat, and confess over him *all* the iniquities of the children of Israel." All sin that was confessed over the scapegoat was carried away into a land not inhabited. Sin that is confessed is evidently real sin, and not a mere dream of a morbid conscience. There is a certain mythical cloud of sin which people talk about, and affect to deplore, and yet they have no sense of the solid weight and heinousness of their actual iniquity. Certain grievous sins are comparable to cauldrons of foaming filth: no man will willingly own to them, however clearly they may be his; but when he does own to them before God, let him recollect that it is this real sin, this foul and essentially abominable transgression, which is put away by the atonement of Christ. Sin confessed with tears, sin which causes the very heart to bleed—killing sin, damning sin—this is the kind of sin for which Jesus died. Sham sinners may be content with a sham Savior; but our Lord Jesus is the real Savior, who did really die, and died for real sin. Oh, how this ought to comfort you, you that are sadly bearing the pressing burden of an execrable life; you, too, who are crushed into the mire of despondency beneath the load of your guilt! Brethren, sin which you are bound to own to as most assuredly committed is the sort of pollution from which Jesus cleanses all believers. Sin which you dare not confess to man, but acknowledge only as you lay your hand upon the divine sacrifice—such sin the Lord removes from you.

The passage is very particular to mention "all sins." "The goat shall bear upon him *all* their iniquities." This includes every form of sin, of thought, of word, of deed, of pride, of falsehood, of lust, of malice, of blasphemy. This comprehends crimes against man, and offenses against God, of peculiar blackness; and it does not exclude sins of inadvertence, or carelessness, or of omission. Transgressions of the body, the intellect, the affections are all blotted out. The outrageous scandals which I dare not mention are yet pardonable; yea, such have been pardoned. There is not the like degree of virus in all sins; but whether or not, the atonement is for all transgressions. The Lord Jesus Christ did not pour out His heart's blood to remove one set of stains and leave the rest; but every spot and trace of sin He takes away from the soul that puts its trust in Him. "Wash me," said David, "and I shall be whiter than snow." He looked for the extreme of cleanness: and such the Savior brings to the soul for whom He has made effectual atonement. I desire to be so plain and broad that the chief of sinners may gather hope from my words. I speak in very simple language, but the theme is full of sublimity, especially to you that feel your need of it. The atonement removed *all* sin. I must give you the exact expression. He says, "*all* the iniquities of the children of Israel, and *all* their transgressions in *all* their sins."

It seems that the divine atonement *puts away the sin of sin*—the essence and heart of sin. Sin has its core, its kernel, its mortal spot. Within a fruit there is a central stone, or pip; this may serve as the likeness of sin. Within each iniquity there seems to lie a something more essentially evil than the act itself: this is the kernel of intent, the core of obstinacy, the inner hate of the mind. Whatever may be the sin of the soul, or the soul of the sin, atonement has been made for it all. Most sins are a conglomerate of sins. A sin may be compared to a honeycomb: there are as many sins within one sin as there are cells within a piece of comb. Sin is a swarming, hiving, teeming thing. You can ever estimate its full vileness, nor perceive all its evil bearings. All sorts of sins may hide away in one sin. It would puzzle all the theologians in the world to tell what sin was absent from Adam's first offense. I could take any point you choose, and show that Adam sinned in that direction. All sin was within that first sin. Sin is a multitudinous evil, an aggregate of all manner of filthiness, a chain with a thousand deadly links. A sinner is like a man possessed with a devil who cries, "My name is Legion: for we are many": it is one in evil, and yet countless in forms. The atonement is more than equal to sin: it takes away all our transgressions in all our sins. It is the fullest purgation that could be imagined. The Lord Jesus has not left upon those for whom He has made atonement a single spot, or wrinkle, or any such thing, so far as their justification is concerned. He has not left an iniquity for which they can be condemned before the bar of judgment. "Ye are clean every whit" is His sure verdict, and none can contradict it.

It appears from this chapter, too, that another thing was done. Not only were all the sins that they had committed put away, but also *all their holy things were purged.* There stood the altar upon which only holy things were offered; but because imperfect men ministered there it needed to be sprinkled with blood before it could be clean. There was the holy place of the tabernacle, which was dedicated solely to God's service, wherein the holiest rites of God's ordaining were celebrated; but because the priests that served there were fallible, and unholy thoughts might cross their minds even when they handled the holy vessels, therefore the blood was sprinkled seven times within the holy place. Inside, within the veil, the sanctuary was called the "Holy of Holies." Yes, but standing, as it did at first, in the midst of the camp of an erring people, and afterwards near to it, it needed to be purged. It is written, "the priest shall make an atonement for the holy place, because of the uncleanness of the children of Israel." Even the mercy-seat, and the ground whereon it rested, were sprinkled with the blood of the sacrifice seven times. O brothers and sisters, I do feel so glad that our Lord has atoned for the sins of our holy things. I rejoice that Jesus forgives the sins of my sermons. I have preached my very soul out among you with purity of motive, seeking to win men for Christ; but I dare not hope to have them accepted in and of themselves, for I perceive that they are defiled with sin. I feel so glad that Jesus has purified our prayers. Many saints spend much time in hearty, earnest cries to God; but even on your knees you sin; and herein is our comfort, that the precious blood has made atonement for the shortcomings of our supplications. Sometimes when we get together, beloved, we sing to the praise of our Lord with heart and will. I have felt in this place as if you and I and all of us were so many burning coals, all blazing within a censer, and thus letting loose the odors of the sweet incense of our Lord's praise. How often has a pillar of fragrant smoke risen from this house to heaven! Yes, but even then there was sin in our praises, and iniquity in our doxologies. We need pardon for our psalms, and cleansing for our hymns. Blessed be God, atonement is made for all our faults, excesses, and shortcomings. Jesus puts away, not only our unholy things, but the sins of our holy things also.

Once more, on that day *all the people were cleansed*. All the congregation of the house of Israel were typically cleansed from all sin by the day of atonement: not the priests only, but all the people: not the princes only, but the poorest servants in the camp. The aged woman and the little child, the gray beard and the youth, were alike purified. Men of business inclined to covetousness, they were cleansed; and young men and maidens in their gaiety, too apt to descend into wantonness—they were all made clean that day. This gives great comfort to those of us who love the souls of the multitude. All who believe are justified from all things. It is written, "The blood of Jesus Christ his Son cleanseth us from all sin." I have often heard the text quoted with the "us" left out; permit me to put it in at this moment—"cleanseth *us* from all sin." Now put yourself into the "us." Dare to believe that grace admits you there. By an act of faith let all of us all round the galleries and in this great area say, "The blood of Jesus Christ his Son cleanseth us." If you pull "us" to pieces it is made up of a great many "*me's*." A thousand thousand times "*me*" will all pack away into a single "*us*." Let each one say—" The blood of Jesus Christ His Son cleanseth *me*, and cleanseth *me* from *all* sin." Be glad and rejoice forever because of this gracious truth. This was done on the day of atonement in the symbol, and it has been really done by the Lord Jesus through His atoning sacrifice.

II. Now we notice, in the second place, HOW IT WAS DONE. We have seen what was done, and this is most cheering; but now we will see how it was done. I shall have to be brief in this description. The atonement was made first of all *by sacrifice*. I see a bullock for a sin-offering, a ram for a burnt-offering, and again a goat for a sin-offering. Many victims were offered that day, and thus the people were reminded of the instrumental cause of atonement, namely, the blood of sacrifice. We know that the blood of bulls and of goats could never take away sin; but very distinctly do these point to the sufferings of our dear Redeemer. The woes He bore are the expiation for our guilt. "He was wounded for our transgressions, he was bruised for our iniquities: the chastisement of our peace was upon him; and with his stripes we are healed." If you want to know by what means sin is put away, think of Messiah's life of grief and shame and arduous service; think of His agony and bloody sweat in the garden; think of the betrayal and denial, the scourging and the spitting. Think of the false accusations and the reproaches and the jeers; think of the cross, the nailed hands and feet, the bruised soul, and the broken spirit. Fierce were the fires which consumed our sacrifice. "My God, my God, why hast thou forsaken me?" is the quintessence of agony; and this came from the heart which was crushed for our sins. Atonement was made for your sins and mine by the shedding of blood—that is to say, by our Lord's suffering, and especially by His laying down His life on our behalf. Jesus died: by that death He purged our sins. He who only hath immortality gave up the ghost; in the cold embrace of death the Lord of glory slept. They wrapped Him in spices and linen clothes and laid Him in the tomb of Joseph of Arimathea. In that death lay the essential deed by which sin dies and grace reigns through righteousness unto eternal life.

Notice, next, that the atonement was made not only by the blood of sacrifice, but *by the presentation of the blood within the veil*. With the smoke of incense and a bowl filled with blood Aaron passed into the most holy place. Let us never forget that our Lord has gone into the heavenly places with better sacrifices than Aaron could present. His merits are the sweet incense which burns before the throne of the heavenly grace. His death supplies that blood of sprinkling which we find even in heaven. "For Christ is not entered into the holy places made with hands, which are the figures of the true; but into heaven itself, now to appear in the presence of God for us." "Neither by the blood of goats and calves, but by his own blood he entered in once into the holy place, having obtained eternal redemption for us." The presenting of the blood before God affects the atonement. The material of the atonement is in the blood and merits of Jesus, but a main part of the atoning act lies in the presentation of these in the heavenly places by Jesus Christ Himself.

Furthermore, *atonement was made effectual by its application to the thing or person cleansed*. The atonement was made for the holy place: it was sprinkled seven times with blood. The same was done to the altar; the horns thereof were smeared seven times. So to make the atonement effectual between you and God the blood of Jesus must be sprinkled upon you by a lively faith. Though this does not so plainly appear in the type before us as to the people on this occasion, yet it comes out in other types: the cleansing blood was ever the blood of sprinkling. Before the blood of the Paschal lamb could cause the avenger to pass over the house, it must be marked with the crimson sign. This is that scarlet thread in the window which delivers Rahab in the day of the Lord's destruction. Before any man can receive reconciliation with God the atonement must be applied to his own heart and conscience. Faith is that bunch of hyssop which we dip into the blood, and with it sprinkle the lintel and two sideposts of the house wherein we dwell, and so we are saved from destruction.

Further, my dear brethren and sisters, inasmuch as no one type was sufficient, *the Lord set forth the method of the removal of sin, as far as we are concerned, by the scapegoat*. One of two goats was chosen to live. It stood before the Lord, and Aaron confessed all the sins of Israel upon its head. A fit man, selected for the purpose, led this goat away into a land not inhabited. What became of it? Why do you ask the question? It is not to edification. You may have seen the famous picture of the scapegoat, representing it as expiring in misery in a desert place. That is all very pretty, and I do not wonder that imagination should picture the poor devoted scapegoat as a sort of cursed thing, left to perish amid accumulated horrors. But please observe that this is all fancy—mere groundless fancy. The Scripture is entirely silent as to anything of the kind, and purposely so. All that the type teaches is this: in symbol the scapegoat has all the sin of the people laid upon it, and when it is led away into the solitary of wilderness, it has gone, and the sin with it. We may not follow the scapegoat even in imagination. It is gone where it can never be found, for there is nobody to find it; it is gone into a land not inhabited—into "no man's land" in fact. Stop where the Scripture stops: to go beyond what is written is unwise, if not presumptuous. Sin is carried away into the silent land, the unknown wilderness. By nature sin is everywhere, but to believers in the sacrifice of Christ sin is nowhere. The sins of God's people have gone beyond recall. Where to? Do not ask anything about that. If they were sought out for they could not be found; they are so gone that they are blotted out. Into oblivion our sins have gone, even as the scapegoat went out of track of mortal man. The death of the scapegoat does not come into the type; in fact, it would mar the type to think of it. Of Melchizedek, we read that he was without father, without mother, without descent, and so on, because these things are not mentioned in Scripture, and the omission is part of the teaching; so in this case, the fate of the scapegoat is not spoken of, and the silence is a part of the instruction. The scapegoat is gone we know not where; and so our sin has vanished quite away; nobody will ever find the scapegoat, and nobody will ever find the believer's sins.

"Where are my sins? Oh where?" Echo answers, "Where?" Gone to the land of nobody, where Satan himself could not find them. Yea, where God Himself cannot find them. He says He has cast our sin behind His back, where He cannot see. What part of the creation must that be which lies behind God's back, whereas He is everywhere present, beholding all things both by night and by day? There is no such place as "behind His back"; and there is no place for our sins. They have gone into the nowhere. "As far as the east is from the west, so far hath he removed our transgressions from us." He has cast them into the depths of the sea—and even that is not so good a figure as the scapegoat, for things that are at the bottom of the sea are still there, but the scapegoat soon passed away altogether, and, as far as Israel was concerned, it ceased to be. The sins of God's people are absolutely and irrevocably forgiven. Never, never, never can they be laid to our charge; they are extinct, buried, blotted out, forgotten. "Who shall lay anything to the charge of God's elect?"

Yet, dear friends, the ceremony was not quite finished; for now *everybody who had had a hand in it must needs be washed, so that everybody might be clean*. There is Aaron, he takes off his garments, and washes himself scrupulously clean; yea, he does it a second time. Here is the man who took the scapegoat away, and he washes himself. Here is a third person, who carried away the skin and the flesh of the sin-offering, and burnt them without the camp; he also washes himself. Everybody becomes purged; the whole camp is clean right through. So, when Jesus completes His sacrifice, we sing:

Now both the sinner and surety are free.

No sin remains upon Him on whom the Lord once laid the iniquities of us all. The great atonement is made, and everything is cleansed, from beginning to end. Christ hath put it all away forever by the water and the blood which flowed from His riven side. All is purified, and the Lord looks down on a clean camp; and soon he will have them rejoicing before Him, each man in his tabernacle, feasting to the full. I am so glad: my joy overflows. O Lord, who is a pardoning God like Thee? Where can such forgiveness be found as Thou dost freely give to sinners through Jesus, thy Son?

III. In the third place, I ask your attention, for a brief interval, to this special point—WHO DID IT? The answer is, Aaron did it all. Aaron was quite alone in the work of that day. It was heavy, and even exhausting work, but he had no assistant. Aaron performed the work of priest and Levite that day, and no one helped him; for it is written, "There shall be no man in the tabernacle of the congregation when he goeth in to make an atonement for himself, and for his household, and for all the congregation of Israel." The tabernacle seemed lonely that day. Aaron went into its courts and chambers, and saw no sign of man. Of course there were lamps to be lighted, but Aaron had to light them himself: the shewbread had to be changed—Aaron had to change it. All the offices of the tabernacle were left to his sole care for the day. When it came to killing the victims, priests and Levites were there on other days, but now the high-priest must do it all. He must kill, and receive the blood, and himself sprinkle it. He must kindle the sacrificial fire, and lay the burning coals upon the incense. Both the incense and the basin of blood he must carry into the holy place with his own hands. Methinks I see him looking around in the solitude. He says, "I looked, and there was no man." Of the people there was none with him. In the holy place there stood no priest to minister before the Lord save himself alone. It must have been with trembling that he lifted up the curtain and passed into the secret place of the Most High with the censer smoking in his hand. There he stood in that awful presence quite alone with the Eternal: no man was with him when he sprinkled the blood again and again till the seven-fold rite was finished. Three times he goes in and out, and never a soul is there, so much as to smile upon him. The tension of mind and heart which he endured alone that day must have been trying indeed. All that livelong day he must have been conscious of a burden of responsibility and a weight of reference enough to bow him to the dust, and yet no one was present to cheer him. Now fix your eye on the great antitype of Aaron. There was none with our Lord: He trod the winepress alone. He His own self bore our sins in His own body on the tree. He alone went in where the thick darkness covered the throne of God, and none stood by to comfort Him, and even died with Him; but no one died with Jesus except thieves, and nobody could suspect that thieves aided Him in His sacrifice: they showed the need of the sacrifice, but they could do no more. Worship our Lord as working salvation by His own single arm. Do not tolerate those who would share His work. Do not believe in priests of any church who pretend to offer sacrifice for the quick and the dead. They cannot help you, and you do not need their help. Do not put your own merits, works, prayers, or anything else side by side with your one lone High Priest, who in His white garments of holy service performed the whole work of expiation, and then came forth in His garments of glory and of beauty to gladden the eyes of His chosen. I say no more. Let that truth abide in your hearts—our High Priest alone has made reconciliation.

IV. Lastly, WHAT WERE THE PEOPLE TO DO for whom this atonement was made? There were two things they had to do that day, only I must add that one of them was doing nothing. For the first thing, they had *to afflict their souls* that day. Brethren, does it seem to you a strange thing that on a day of rest they were to afflict their souls? Think of it a little, and you will see that there was cause for it. We most rightly sing—

> Here let our hearts begin to melt,
>   While we his death record,
> And, with our joy for pardon'd guilt
>   Mourn that we pierced the Lord.

It was a day of confession of sin. And should not confession be made with sorrowful repentance? A dry-eyed confession is a hypocritical confession. To acknowledge sin without grieving over it is to aggravate sin. We cannot think of our sin without grieving, and the more sure we are that it is forgiven, the more sorry we are that ever it was committed. Sin seems all the greater because it was committed against a sin-forgiving God. If you do wrong to a person, and he grows angry, you may be wicked enough to persist in the wrong; but if, instead of growing angry, he forgives, and does you good in return, then you will deeply regret that ever you had an unkind thought towards him. The Lord's pardoning love makes us feel truly sorry to have offended Him.

Not only was it a day of confession, but it was a day of sacrifice. No tender-hearted Israelite could think of that bullock, and ram, and goat dying for him, without saying, "This is what I deserve." If he heard the moans of the dying creature he would say, "My own heart groans and bleeds." When we think of our dying Lord our emotions are mingled: we feel a pleasing grief and a mournful joy, as we stand at Calvary. Thus it is we sing—

> Alas! and did my Savior bleed?
>   And did my Sovereign die?
> Could he devote that sacred head
>   For such a worm as I?
>
> Was it for crimes that I have done
>   He died upon the tree?
> Amazing pity, grace unknown,
>   And love beyond degree.
>
> Well might the sun in darkness hide,
>   And shut his glories in,
> When God the mighty Maker died
>   For man, the creature's sin!
>
> Well might I hide my blushing face
>   When his dear Cross appears,
> Dissolve my heart in thankfulness,
>   And melt my eyes to tears.

It was a day of sacrifice, and hence a day of affliction of their souls, and herein we are in sympathy with them.

Once more, it was a day of perfect cleansing, and hence, by a strange logic, a day of the affliction of the soul; for, oh! when sin is forgiven, when we know it is forgiven, when by divine assurance we know that God has blotted out our sins like a cloud, then it is we mourn over our iniquities. "They shall look upon me whom they have pierced"—that look gives life: "and they shall mourn for Him as one mourneth for his only son, and shall be in bitterness for Him, as one that is in bitterness for his first-born"—this bitterness is one of the truest signs of life. They were to afflict their souls. Brethren, we cannot talk of the cross of Christ except in subdued tones. If you think you can laugh and sport yourself because your sin is forgiven, you know nothing of the matter. Sin has been pardoned at such a price that we cannot henceforth trifle with it. The sacrifice was so august that we must ever speak of it with holy trembling. I always feel a suspicion of those converts who get up and glibly boast that once they were drunkards, thieves, blasphemers, and so forth. Brother, if you do tell the story of your sin, blush scarlet to think it should be true. I am ashamed to hear a man talk of his sins as an old Greenwich pensioner might talk of his sea-fights. I hate to hear a man exhibiting his old lusts as if they were scars of honor. Friend, these things are disgraceful to you, however much the putting of them away may be to the honor and glory of God; and they are to be spoken of by you with shame and confusion of face. Afflict your soul when you remember what you once were.

On the day of atonement they were to afflict their souls, and yet they were to *rest*. Can these things come together—mourning and resting? Oh yes, you and I know how they meet in one bosom. I never am so truly happy as when a sober sadness tinges my joy. When I am fullest of joy I could weep my life away at Jesus' feet. Nothing is more really sweet than the bitterness of repentance. Nothing is more healthful than self-ab-horrence, mixed with the grateful love which hides itself in the wounds of Jesus. The purified people were to rest; they were to rest from all *servile* work. I will never do a hand's turn to save myself by my own merits, works, or feelings. I have done forever with all interference with my Lord's sole work. Salvation as to its meritorious cause is complete; we will not think of beginning it over again; for that would be an insult to the Savior. "It is finished," saith our Lord Jesus, as He bowed His dear tri-umphant head and gave up the ghost; and if it is finished we will not dream of adding to it. It is finished; we have no work to do with the view of self-salvation. But you say to me—"Have we not to work out our own salvation?" Certainly we have. We are to work out our own salvation because God works it in us. It is our own salvation, and we show it forth in our lives: we work it out from within; we develop it from day to day, and let men see what the Lord has done for us. It must first be worked for us, and then in us, or we can never work it out.

They were assuredly to cease from all *sinful* work. How can the pardoned man continue in sin? We have done with toiling for the devil now. We will no more waste our lives in his service. Many men are worn to rottenness in the service of their lusts, but the servant of God has been set free from that yoke of bondage. We are slaves no longer: we quit the hard bondage of Egypt and rest in the Lord.

We have also done with *selfish* work; we now seek first the kingdom of heaven, and look that all other things shall be added unto us by the goodness of our heavenly Father. Henceforth we find rest by bearing the easy yoke of Christ. We joy to spend and be spent in His beloved service. He hath made us free, and therefore we are under bonds to His love forever. O Lord, I am thy servant, I am thy servant, Thou hast loosed my bonds; henceforth I am bound to Thee. God grant that this may be a high day to You, because You gladly realize the grand truths which are shadowed forth in these delightful types. Amen.

THE RED HEIFER

SERMON NO. 1,481
DELIVERED ON LORD'S DAY MORNING, JUNE 29, 1879.
PORTION OF SCRIPTURE READ BEFORE SERMON—NUMBERS 19.
HYMNS FROM *Our Own Hymn Book*—395, 561, 303.

> *For if the blood of bulls and of goats, and the ashes of an heifer sprinkling the unclean, sanctifieth to the purifying of the flesh: how much more shall the blood of Christ, who through the eternal Spirit offered himself without spot to God, purge your conscience from dead works to serve the living God?*—Hebrews 9:13, 14.

BELOVED brethren in Christ, you dwell in great nearness to God. He calls you "a people near unto Him." His grace has made you His sons and daughters, and He is a Father unto you. In you is His word fulfilled, "I will dwell in them and walk in them, and I will be their God, and they shall be my people." Remember that your favored position as children of God has placed you under a peculiar discipline, for now God dealeth with you as with sons, and sons are under household law. The Lord will be sanctified in them that come near unto Him. Special favor involves special rule. There were no strict laws made as to the behavior of the Amalekites, Amorites, and Egyptians, because they were far off from God, and the times of their ignorance He winked at; but the Lord set Israel apart to be His people, and He came and dwelt in the midst of the congregation; the sacred tent wherein He displayed His presence was pitched in the center of the camp, and there the great King uplifted His banner of fire and cloud; hence, as the Lord brought the people so near to Himself, He put them under special laws, such as belong to His palace rather than to the outskirts of His dominion. They were bound to keep themselves very pure, for they bore the vessels of the Lord, and were a nation of priests before Him. They ought to have been holy spiritually, but being in their childhood they were taught this by laws referring to external cleanliness. Read the laws laid down in Leviticus and see what care was required of the favored nation, and how jealously they were to keep themselves from defilement.

Just as the children of Israel in the wilderness were put under stringent regulations so do those who live near to God come under a holy discipline in the house of the Lord. "Even our God is a consuming fire." We are not now speaking of our salvation, or of our justification as sinners, but of the Lord's dealings towards us as saints. In that respect we must walk carefully with Him, and watch our steps, that we offend not. Our earnest desire is so to behave ourselves in His house that He may always permit us to have access with boldness to His presence, and may never be compelled to reject our prayers because we have been falling into sin. Our heart's desire and inward longing is that we may never lose our Father's smile. If we have lost fellowship with Him, even for an hour, our cry is, "Oh that I knew where I might find Him, that I might come even to His seat"; for when we are in fellowship with God we are happy, we are strong, we are full of heavenly aspirations and emotions. Beneath the sky there is no joy like that of communion with God; it is incomparable and inexpressible, and therefore when we lose the presence of God, even for a little, we are like a dove bereaved of its mate, which ceases not to grieve. Our heart and our flesh cry out for God, for the living God. When shall we come and appear before God?

Now, beloved, in order that we may learn how to renew our fellowship with God whenever we lose it by a sense of sin, I have selected the subject of this morning. If the Holy Spirit will graciously enlighten us, we shall see how the conscience can be kept clean, that so the heart may be able to dwell with God. We shall see our danger of defilement and the way by which our uncleanness can be put away; may we have grace given to avoid the pollutions which would hinder fellowship, and grace to seek the purification by which uncleanness is removed and fellowship restored. I shall first endeavor to *describe the type* which is alluded to by the apostle in the words, "The ashes of an heifer sprinkling the unclean," and then secondly, we shall *magnify the Antitype*, dwelling upon the words, "How much more shall the blood of Christ, who through the eternal Spirit offered Himself without spot to God, purge your conscience from dead works to serve the living God?"

I. LET US DESCRIBE THE TYPE. In the nineteenth chapter of Numbers you will find the type; be so good as to open your Bibles, and refresh your memories.

First, the type mentions ceremonial defilements, which were the symbols of the uncleanness caused by sin. The Israelites could very readily render themselves unclean, so as to be unfit to go up to the tabernacle of God. There were uncleannesses connected both with birth and with death, with meats and with drinks, with garments and with houses. The rules were very minute and all-pervading, so that a man could scarcely move abroad, or even remain within his own tent, without incurring uncleanness in one way or another, and becoming unfit to enter the courts of the Lord or to be an accepted member of the congregation. In the passage in Numbers which is now before us, the one source of defilement dealt with is death. "Whosoever toucheth one that is slain with a sword in the open fields, or a dead body, or a bone of a man, or a grave, shall be unclean seven days." Now, death is peculiarly the symbol of sin, as well as the fruit of sin. Sin, like death, defaces the image of God in man. As soon as death grasps the body of a man it destroys the bloom of beauty and the dignity of strength, and drives forth from the human form divine that mysterious something which is the token of life within. However comely a corpse may appear for a time, yet it is defaced; the excellence of life has departed, and alas, in a few hours, or at longest in a few days, the image of God begins utterly to pass away; corruption and the worm commence their desolating work, and horror follows in their train. Abraham, however much he may love his Sarah, soon becomes anxious to bury his beloved dead out of his sight. Now, what death does for the "human face divine," that sin does for the spiritual image of God upon us. It utterly defaces it. Human nature in perfection is a coin of the realm of God, minted by the great King; but by sin it is battered and defaced, to the great dishonor of the King whose image and superscription it bears. Hence sin is most obnoxious to God, and death is obnoxious as the type of sin.

The defilements which came to the Israelite by death must have been very frequent. As a whole generation died in the wilderness, most of the inhabitants must again and again have come under the law of uncleanness on account of the death of parents or friends. In the field a man might dig up human remains, or plow over a grave, or find a body slain by accident, and he was at once unclean. How frequent therefore, were the occasions of defilement! But ah, my brethren, not so frequent as the occasions of pollution to our consciences in such a world as this, for in a thousand ways we err and transgress.

> Oh for a lodge in some vast wilderness,
> Some boundless contiguity of shade,

where never sin might reach my soul again! But it is in vain to sigh in this fashion, even if we could escape from the throng of men we should not thereby escape from sin. The Israelite might meet with defilement even in his tent. I have already reminded you that these statutes about the dead present to us only a part of the occasions of defilement which surrounded the people of Israel: they were much more numerous than this. A man might become unclean even in his sleep; so closely did the law track him into his most secret places, and surround his most unguarded hours. Even thus doth sin beset us. Like a dog at one's heels, it is always with us! Like our shadow, it follows us, go where we may. Yea, and when the sun shines not, and shadows are gone, sin is still there. Whither shall we flee from its presence, and where shall we hide from its power? When we would do good, evil is present with us. How humbled we ought to be at the recollection of this!

The Israelite became unclean even in the act of doing good; for assuredly it was a good deed to bury the dead. A man would be defiled if out of charity he helped to inter the poor, or the slain, or the poor relics of mortality which might lie exposed upon the plain, and yet this was a praiseworthy action. Alas, there is sin even in our holy things. A morality so pure that no human eye can detect a flaw may yet be faulty to the eye of God. Brethren, sin stains our piety and pollutes our devotion. We do not even pray without needing to ask God to forgive the prayer. Our acts of faith have a measure of unbelief in them, for the faith is never so strong as it ought to be. Our penitential tears have some grit of impenitence in them, and our heavenly aspirations have a measure of carnality to degrade them. The evil of our nature clingeth to all that we do. Who shall bring a clean thing out of an unclean? Not one. One way or another defilement will come upon us. We have been once washed in the blood of Jesus, and we are clean before the bar of God, and yet in the divine family we need that our feet be washed after walking awhile in this dusty world, and there is not one disciple who is above the need of this washing. To one and all our Lord saith, "If I wash thee not, thou hast no part in me."

The touching of the dead not only made the man unclean, but he became a fountain of defilement. "And whatsoever the unclean person toucheth shall be unclean; and the soul that toucheth it shall be unclean until even." While a man was unclean he might not go up to the worship of God, and he was in danger of being cut off from among the congregation, "because," saith the law, "he hath defiled the sanctuary of the Lord." Pollution went forth from the polluted. Do you and I sufficiently remember how much of evil we are spreading when we are out of communion with God? Every ungenerous temper creates the like in others. We never cast a proud look without exciting resentment and bad feelings in others. Somebody or other will follow our example if we be slothful; and thus we may be doing great mischief even when we are doing nothing. You cannot even bury your talent in a napkin without setting an example to others to do the like, and were that example followed by all how dreadful would be the consequences! Observe that I am not now speaking of outside sinners, but of the saints of God. As the ordinances in the chapter before us were for Israel, so these things are spoken to those in whom the Spirit of the Lord is. My soul's longing is, that we may walk worthy of the Lord unto all well pleasing, and may not become unfit for communion with Him.

This uncleanness prevented the man from going up to the worship of God, and it separated him from that great, permanent congregation which was called to dwell in God's house by residing all around the holy place. He was, so to speak, excommunicated, suspended, at any rate in his communion: he could bring no offering, he could not stand among the multitude and view the solemn worship, he was unclean and must regard himself so. Do children of God ever get here? Ah, dear friends, so far as our consciences are concerned we too often come among the unclean. We are not polluted as the heathen, nor condemned with the world, but as children of God we feel that we have erred, and our conscience smites us. Sin is already put away from us, as we are criminals tried before a judge, but it comes upon the conscience even as a child's faults cause him to grieve. It is from the conscience that this uncleanness is to be purged, and our whole sermon is upon that matter. I speak not of the actual taking away of sin before God, but the removal of its defilement from the conscience, so that communion with God may be possible. Remember the word of the Lord, "Your iniquities have separated between you and you God, and your sins have hid his face from you that he will not hear." When sin is on your conscience it wants no law to prevent your communion with God; for you cannot approach Him, you are afraid to do so, and you have a distaste for it. Until the pardoning blood speaks peace within your spirit, you cannot draw near unto God. The apostle saith, "Let us draw near with a true heart in full assurance of faith, having our hearts sprinkled from an evil conscience, and our bodies washed with pure water." It is the washing which enables us to draw near. We shrink, we tremble, we find communion impossible until we are made clean.

This much about the defilements described in the chapter; now concerning the cleansing which it mentions.

The defilement was frequent, but the cleansing was always ready. At a certain time all the people of Israel brought a red heifer to be used in the expiation. It was not at the expense of one person, or tribe, but the whole congregation brought the red cow to be slain. It was to be their sacrifice, and it was brought for them all. It was not led, however, up to the holy place for sacrifice, but it was brought forth without the camp, and there it was slaughtered in the presence of the priest, and wholly burnt with fire, not as a sacrifice upon the altar, but as a polluted thing which was to be made an end of outside the camp. It was not a regular sacrifice or we should have found it described in Leviticus; it was an ordinance entirely by itself, as setting forth quite another side of truth.

To return to the chapter; the red heifer was killed, before the uncleanness was committed, just as our Lord Jesus Christ was made a curse for sin long, long ago. Before you and I had lived to commit the uncleanness there was a sacrifice provided for us. For the easing of our conscience we shall be wise to view this sacrifice as that of a substitute for sin, and consider the results of that expiation. Sin on the conscience needs for its remedy the result of the Redeemer's substitution.

The red heifer was slain: the victim fell beneath the butcher's axe. It was then taken up—skin, flesh, blood, dung, everything—no trace of it must be left, and it was all burnt with fire, together with cedar wood, and hyssop, and scarlet wool, which I suppose had been used in the previous sprinkling of the heifer's blood, and so must be consumed with it. The whole was destroyed outside the camp! Even as our Lord, thought in Himself without spot, was made sin for us, and suffered without the camp, feeling the withdrawings of God, while He cried, "My God my God, why hast thou forsaken me?" Ah, what it cost our Lord to come into our place and to bear the iniquities of men!

Then the ashes were collected and laid in a clean place accessible to the camp. Everybody knew where the ashes were, and whenever there was any uncleanness they went to this ash-heap and took away a small portion. Whenever the ashes were spent they brought another red heifer, and did the same as they had done before, that always there might be this purification for the unclean.

But while this red cow was slaughtered for all, and the blood was sprinkled towards the holy place for all, no one derived any personal benefit from it in reference to his own uncleanness unless he made a personal use of it. When a man became unclean he procured a clean person to go on his behalf to take a little of the ashes, and to put them in a cup with running water, and then to sprinkle this water of purification upon him, upon his tent, and all the vessels therein. By that sprinkling, at the end of seven days, the unclean person was purified. There was no other method of purification from his uncleanness but this. It is so with us. Today the living water of the divine Spirit's sacred influences must take up the result of our Lord's substitution, and this must be applied to our consciences. That which remaineth of Christ after the fire hath passed upon Him, even the eternal merits, the enduring virtue of our great sacrifice, must be sprinkled upon us through the Spirit of God. Then are we clean in conscience, but not till then. We have two degrees of purification by this means, as in the type. Our Lord rose again on the third day, and blessed are they who receive the third day justification by the resurrection of the Lord. Thus is sin removed from the conscience; but yet as long as we are here in this body there will be some tremblings, some measure of unrest, because of sin within; but blessed be God there is a seventh day purification coming, which will complete the cleansing. When the eternal Sabbath breaks, then shall be the last sprinkling with the hyssop, and we shall be clean, and we shall enter into the rest which remaineth for the people of God, clean every whit. We shall come before God at last without spot or wrinkle, or any such thing, and be as able to commune with Him as if we had never transgressed, being presented faultless before His presence with exceeding great joy.

Thus much concerning the type, with which we have already mingled some degree of exposition.

II. LET US MAGNIFY THE GREAT ANTI-TYPE. "For if the blood of bulls and of goats, and the ashes of an heifer sprinkling the unclean, sanctifieth to the purification of the flesh: how much more shall the blood of Christ?" How much more? He doth not give us the measure, but leaves it with a note of interrogation. We shall never be able to tell how much more, for the difference between the ashes of a red cow and the eternal merits of the Lord Jesus, must be infinite. Let us help your judgments while we set forth the exceeding greatness of our mighty Expiator, by whom we are reconciled to God.

First, then, *our defilement is much greater*, for the defilement spoken of in the text is on the conscience. Now, I can believe that the Israelite when he was rendered unclean by touching a corpse by necessity, or a piece of a bone by accident, felt nothing on his conscience, for there was no sin in the matter; he was only ceremonially unclean, and that was all. His ceremonial disability troubled him, for he would be glad to go up to the tabernacle of the Lord and hold fellowship with the hosts of Israel, but there was nothing on his conscience. If there had been, the blood of bulls and goats could not have helped him. Beloved, you and I know what it is at times to have defilement upon the conscience, and to go mourning because we have erred from the Lord's commands. The ungodly do not thus sorrow: their conscience by fits and starts accuses them, but they never listen to its accusations so as to feel their inability to draw nigh to God. Nay, they will even go with a guilty conscience to their knees, and pretend to offer to God the sacrifice of prayer and of praise, while still they are unforgiven, alienated, rebellious. You and I, if we are indeed the Lord's people, cannot do this. Guilt on our conscience is to us a horrible thing. There are no pains of body, there are no tortures inflicted by the Inquisition which are at all comparable to the whips of burning wire which lash the guilty conscience. You hear persons speak about the horrible figure of medieval ages with regard to hell, and the strong metaphors sometimes used by the orthodox to this day; let them remember that they are only figures, and then let any man who has felt the agonies of a guilty conscience judge whether the figures can possibly be overdrawn. It is an awful thing to feel yourself guilty, and the better man you are, the more will it grieve you to be consciously in a wrong state. I ask any truly regenerate man here, who at the bottom has an assurance that his sin is already forgiven before God, whether he can do wrong without smarting? Whenever you have transgressed, and you are conscious of it, though you do not doubt the love of God to you, are you not like one who has all his bones broken? I know you are, and the better man you are the more intense will have been the terror of your spirit while guilt has been upon your conscience in any degree. Well, now, that which can take guilt off the conscience must be infinitely greater than that which can merely put away a ceremonial defilement.

Brethren, guilt on the conscience is a most effectual bar to drawing near to God. The Lord bids His people come near to Him, and there is a way of access always open; but as long as you are conscious of sin you cannot use that way of access. We can come to God as sinners to seek pardon, but we cannot come before the Lord as dear children while there is any quarrel between us and our great Father. No, we must be clean, or we cannot approach our God. See how the priests washed their feet at the laver before they offered incense unto the Lord. We cannot have fellowship with God while there is a sense of unconfessed and unforgiven sin upon us. "Be ye reconciled to God" is a test for saints as well as for sinners: children may quarrel with a father as well as rebels with a king. There must be oneness of heart with God, or there is an end to communion, and therefore must the conscience be purged.

The man who was unclean *could* have come up to the tabernacle if there had been no law to prevent it, and it is possible that he could have worshiped God in spirit, notwithstanding his ceremonial disqualification. The defilement was no barrier in itself except so far as it was typical; but sin on the conscience is a natural wall between God and the soul. You cannot get into loving communion until the conscience is at ease; therefore, I charge you, fly at once to Jesus for peace.

Beloved, if our consciences were more fully developed than they are we should have as great a sense of the frequency of our uncleanness as ever the thoughtful Israelite had of his danger of ceremonial uncleanness. I tell you solemnly that the talk which we have heard lately about perfection in the flesh cometh of ignorance of the law and of self. When I have read expressions which seem to claim that the utterers were free from sin in thought, and word, and deed, I have been sorry for the deluded victims of self-conceit, and shuddered at their spirit. The sooner this boasting is purged out of the church of God the better. God's true people have the spirit of truth within them, convincing them of sin, and not the proud and lying spirit which leads men to say they have no sin. True saints abide in the place of penitence and constant faith in the atoning blood, and dare not exalt themselves as the Pharisee who cried,

"God, I thank thee that I am not as other men are." "There is not a just man upon earth, that doeth good, and sinneth not." (Eccl. 7:20). Why, beloved, according to my own experience, we are constantly being defiled by being in this polluted world, and going up and down in it. As a man could not take a walk without stumbling over a grave, nor could he shut himself up in his house without the danger of death entering there, so are we everywhere liable to sin. It seems all but inevitable so long as we are in this body and in this sinful world that we should come into contact with sin in some form or other, and any contact with sin is defiling. Our Lord could live among sinners and remain undefiled, because there was no evil in his heart; but in our case sin without awakes the echoes from within, and so causes a measure of consent and defilement. The will more or less yields to the temptation, and when the will does not yield, the imagination plays the traitor, and the affections parley, and so betray the soul. Although it may be accompanied with a resolve not to fall into evil, the very thought of evil is sin. Sin does not cross over the sensitive plate of our soul as it is exposed in its daily care without leaving, even if we do not see it ourselves, some trace and stain which God sees. Our fellowmen are a terrible source of defilement to us. Did you not notice in the chapter which we read (Num. 19) that he who touched the dead body of a man was unclean seven days? Now, if you look in Leviticus 11:22 you will see that whosoever toucheth the carcass of an unclean beast was only unclean until the evening. Thus a dead man was seven times more defiling than a dead beast. Such is God's estimate of fallen, unregenerate man, and it is a just one, for wicked men do many things which brute beasts never do. All ungodly men defile us, and I am not sure that I may end there, the truth is wider still: I do not care how you pick your company, and you ought to pick it with great choiceness, but even if you associate with none but saints they will be an occasion of sin to you at some time or other: there will be something about them, aye, even about their holiness, which may raise your idolatry of them, or your envy of them, and in some way or other cause you to sin. You cannot, as you are a man of unclean lips, and dwell among a people of unclean lips, be altogether without uncleanness, and therefore you will always have need to use the way of cleansing which the Lord has prepared and revealed.

Remember that in the type the least touch defiled: if they only picked up a bone the Israelites were unclean; if they only walked over a grave they were unclean. My brethren, the best of you can hardly read in the newspaper an account of a crime without some taint clinging to you. You cannot see sin in another without standing in fearful jeopardy of being in some degree infected thereby. Sin is of so subtle and penetrating a nature that long before we are aware it tarnishes our brightness and eats into our spirit. The pure and holy God alone is undefiled; but as for the best of his saints they need to veil their faces in His presence and cry, "Unclean, unclean."

Under the old law men might be unclean who did not know it. A man might have touched a bone and not be aware of it, yet the law operated just as much: he might walk across a grave and not know it, but he was unclean. I fear that our proud sense of what we think to be our inward cleanness is simply the stupidity of our conscience. If our conscience were more sensitive and tender, it would perceive sin where now we congratulate ourselves that everything is pure. My brethren, this teaching of mine puts us into a very lowly place, but the lowlier our position the better and the safer for us, and the more shall we be able to prize the expiation by which we draw near to God.

Since the stain is upon the conscience, its removal is a far greater work than is the removal of a mere ritual uncleanness.

Secondly upon this head, *our sacrifice is greater in itself.* I will not dwell upon each point of its greatness lest I weary you, but just notice that in the slaughter of the heifer blood was presented and sprinkled towards the holy place seven times, though it came not actually into it; so in the atonement through which we find peace of conscience there is blood, for "without shedding of blood there is no remission of sin." That is a settled decree of the Eternal Government, and the conscience will never get peace till it understands the mystery of the blood. We need not only the sufferings of Christ, but the death of Christ, which is set forth by His blood. The substitute must die. Death was our doom, and death for death did Christ render unto the eternal God. It is by a sense of our Lord's substitutionary death that the conscience becomes purged from dead works.

Furthermore, the heifer itself was offered. After the blood was sprinkled towards the tabernacle by the priestly hand, the victim itself was utterly consumed. Read now our text: "Christ, who through the eternal Spirit offered up himself without spot unto God." Our Lord Jesus Christ gave not merely His death, but His whole person, with all that appertained unto it, to be our substitutionary sacrifice. He offered Himself, His person, His glory, His holiness, His life, His very self, in our stead. But, brethren, if a poor heifer when it was offered and consumed made the unclean man clean, how much more shall we be cleansed by Jesus, since He gave Himself, His glorious self, in whom dwelt the fullness of the Godhead bodily? Oh what a sacrifice is this!

It is added that our Lord did this "by the Eternal Spirit." The heifer was not a spiritual but a carnal offering. The creature knew nothing of what was being done, it was the involuntary victim; but Christ was under the impulses of the Holy Ghost, which was poured upon Him, and He was moved by Him to render up Himself a sacrifice for sin. Hence somewhat of the greater efficacy of his death, for the willingness of the sacrifice greatly enhanced its value. To give you another, and probably a better, interpretation of the words, there was an eternal spirit linked with the manhood of Christ our Lord, and by it He gave Himself unto God. He was God as well as man, and that eternal Godhead of His lent an infinite value to the sufferings of His human frame, so that He offered Himself as a whole Christ, in the energy of His eternal power and Godhead. Oh, what a sacrifice is that on Calvary! It is by the blood of the man Christ that you are saved, and yet it is written, "The church of God which he"—that is God—"hath redeemed with his own blood." One who is both God and man has given Himself as a sacrifice for us. Is not the sacrifice inconceivably greater in the fact than it is in the type? Ought it not most effectually to purge our conscience?

After they had burnt the heifer they swept up the ashes. All that could be burnt had been consumed. Our Lord was made a sacrifice for sin, what remains of Him? Not a few ashes, but the whole Christ, which still remaineth, to die no more, but to abide forever unchanged. He came uninjured through the fires, and now he ever liveth to make intercession for us. It is the application of His eternal merit which makes us clean, and is not that eternal merit inconceivably greater than the ashes of an heifer ever can be?

Now, my brethren, I want you for a moment to recollect that our Lord Himself was spotless, pure and perfect, and yet—speak it with bated breath—God "hath made him to be sin for us," even Him who knew no sin. Whisper it with greater awe still, "He was made a curse for us,"—yes, a curse, as it is written, "Cursed is everyone that hangeth on a tree." That red heifer, though without spot and never having borne a yoke, was regarded as a polluted thing. Take it out of the camp. It must not live; kill it. It is a polluted thing; burn it right up; for God cannot endure it. Behold, and wonder that God's own ever blessed, adorable Son in inconceivable condescension of unutterable love, took the place of sin, the place of the sinner, and was numbered with the transgressors. He must die, hang Him up on a cross; He must be forsaken of men, and even deserted of God. "It pleased the Father to bruise him; he hath put him to grief; he shall make his soul an offering for sin." "All we like sheep have gone astray; we have turned everyone to his own way, and the Lord hath laid on him the iniquity of us all,"—not the punishment merely, but the iniquity, the very sin itself was laid upon the Ever Blessed. The wise men of our age say it is impossible that sin should be lawfully imputed to the innocent; that is what the philosophers say, but God declares that it was done: "He hath made him to be sin who knew no sin." Therefore, it was possible; yea, it is done; it is finished. The sacrifice then is much greater. "How much more," we may cry exultingly as we think of it, "shall the blood of Christ, who through the eternal Spirit offered himself without spot to God, purge our conscience from dead works to serve the living God?"

Now we will take a step further. As the defilement and the sacrifice were greater, so *the purging is much greater*. The purifying power of the blood of Christ must be much greater than the purging power of the water mixed with the ashes of the heifer. For, first, that could not purge conscience from sin, but the application of the atonement can do it, and does do it. I am not going to speak this morning about doctrine at all, but about fact. Did you ever feel the atonement of Christ applied by the Holy Ghost to your conscience? Then I am certain of it that the change upon your mind had been as sudden and glorious as if the darkness of midnight had glowed into the brightness of noonday. I remember well its effects upon my soul at the first, how it broke my bonds and made my heart to dance with delight. But I have found it equally powerful since then, for when I am examining myself before God it sometimes comes to pass that I fix my eye upon some one evil which I have done, and I turn it over until the memory of it eats into my very soul like a caustic acid, or like a gnaw-ing worm, or like coals of fire. I have tried to argue that the fault was excusable in me, or that there were certain circumstances which rendered it almost impossible that I could do otherwise, but I have never succeeded in quieting my conscience in that fashion; yet I am soon at rest when I come before the Lord, and cry, "Lord, though I am thine own dear child, I am unclean by reason of this sin: apply, again, the merit of my Lord's atoning sacrifice, for hast thou not said—If any man sin we have an ad-vocate with the Father, Jesus Christ the righteous? Lord, hear His advocacy, and pardon my offenses." My brethren, the peace which thus comes is very sweet. You can-not pray acceptably before that peace, and you may thank God that you cannot pray, for it is a dreadful thing to be able to go on with your devotions as well under a sense of guilt as when the conscience is at rest. It is an ill child that can be happy while its father is displeased; a true child can do nothing till he is forgiven.

Now, the sprinkling of the ashes of the heifer upon the unclean was not com-prehensible as to its effect by anybody who received it. I mean that there was no ob-vious connection between the cause and the effect. Supposing an Israelite had been unclean, and had been sprinkled with this water; he might now go up to the house of the Lord, but would he see any reason for the change? He would say, "I have re-ceived the water of separation and I am clean, but I do not know why the sprinkling of those ashes should make me clean except that God has so appointed." Brethren, you and I do know how it is that God has made us clean, for we know that Christ has suffered in our stead. Substitution explains the mystery, and hence it has much more effect upon the conscience than an outward, ritualistic form which could not be explained. Conscience is the understanding exercised upon moral subjects, and that which convinces the understanding that all is right soon gives peace to the conscience.

Time presses, and therefore I will only just say, that as the ashes of the heifer were for all the camp so are Christ's merits for all His people. As they were put where they were accessible, so may you always come and partake of the cleansing power of Christ's precious atonement. As a mere sprinkling made the unclean clean, even so may you come and be cleansed even though your faith be but little, and you seem to get but little of Christ. O brethren, the Lord God of His infinite mercy give you to know the power of the great sacrifice to work peace in you, not after three or seven days, but at once; and peace not merely for a time, but forever.

One riddle I must explain to you. Solomon, according to the Jewish tradition, declared that he did not understand why the ashes of the heifer made everybody un-clean except those who were unclean already. You saw in the reading that the priest, the man who killed the red cow, the person who swept up the ashes, and he who mixed the ashes with water and sprinkled them, were all rendered unclean by those acts, and yet the ashes purified the unclean. Is not this analogous to the riddle of the brazen serpent? It was by a serpent that the people were bitten, and it was by a ser-pent of brass that they were healed. It is by Christ's being regarded as unclean that we become clean, and the operation of his sacrifice is just like that of the ashes, for it both reveals uncleanness and removes it. If you are clean, and you think of Christ's death, what a sense of sin it brings upon you! You judge of the sin by the atonement. If you are unclean, drawing near to Christ takes that sin away.

> Thus while his death my sin displays
> In all its blackest hue,
> Such is the mystery of grace,
> It seals my pardon too.

If we think we are unclean, a sight of the atoning blood makes us see how unclean we are; and if we judge ourselves unclean, then the application of the atoning sacrifice gives our conscience rest.

Now, what is all this business about? This slain heifer,—I understand that, for it admitted the unclean Israelites to the courts of the Lord;—but this Christ of God offering Himself without spot by the eternal Spirit,—what is that for? The object of it is *a service far higher:* it is that we may be purged from dead works to serve the living God. The dead works are gone, God absolves you, you are clean, and you feel it. What then? Will you not abhor dead works for the future? Sin is death. Labor to keep from it. Inasmuch as you are delivered from the yoke of sin, go forth and serve God. Since He is the living God, and evidently hates death, and makes it to be an uncleanness to Him, get you to living things. Offer to God living prayers, and living tears, love Him with living love, trust Him with living faith, serve Him with living obedience.

Be all alive with His life; not only have life, but have it more abundantly. He has purged you from the defilement of death, now live in the beauty and glory and excellency of the divine life, and pray the Holy Ghost to quicken you that you may abide in full fellowship with God. If an unclean person had been made clean, and had then said, "I will not worship the Lord, neither will I serve Him," we should account him a wretched being! And if any person here were to say, "My sin is forgiven and I know it, but I will do nothing for God," we might well cry, "Ah, wretched man!" What a hypocrite and a deceiver such a person must be. Where pardon is received at the hand of the Lord the soul is sure to feel a love to God rising within itself. He who has had much forgiven is certain to love much, and to do much for Him by whom that forgiveness has been obtained.

The Lord bless you for Jesus' sake. Amen.

THE BLOOD OF SPRINKLING

SERMON NO. 1,888

DELIVERED ON LORD'S DAY MORNING, FEBRUARY 28, 1886.

PORTIONS OF SCRIPTURE READ BEFORE SERMON—EXODUS 20:1–21; 24:1–8.

HYMNS FROM *Our Own Hymn Book*—236, 279, 291.

> *And to Jesus the mediator of the new covenant, and to the blood of sprinkling, that speaketh better things than that of Abel. See that ye refuse not him that speaketh. For if they escaped not who refused him that spoke on earth, much more shall not we escape, if we turn away from him that speaketh from heaven*—Hebrews 12:24, 25.

WE are joyfully reminded by the apostle that we are *not* come to Mount Sinai and its overwhelming manifestations. After Israel had kept the feast of the Passover, God was pleased to give His people a sort of Pentecost, and more fully to manifest Himself and His law to them at Sinai. They were in the wilderness, with the solemn peaks of a desolate mountain as their center; and from the top thereof, in the midst of fire, and blackness, and darkness, and tempest, and with the sound of a trumpet, God spoke with them. "The earth shook, the heavens also dropped at the presence of God: even Sinai itself was moved at the presence of God, the God of Israel." We are not come to the dread and terror of the old covenant, of which our apostle saith in another place, "The covenant from the Mount Sinai engendereth unto bondage" (Gal. 4:24). Upon the believer's spirit there rests not the slavish fear, the abject terror, the fainting alarm, which swayed the tribes of Israel; for the manifestation of God which he beholds, though not less majestic, is far more full of hope and joy. Over us there rests not the impenetrable cloud of apprehension; we are not buried in a present darkness of despair; we are not tossed about with a tempest of horror; and, therefore, we do not exceedingly fear and quake. How thankful we should be for this! Israel was privileged even in receiving a fiery law from the right hand of Jehovah; but we are far more favored, since we receive "the glorious gospel of the blessed God."

Our apostle next tells us what we are come to. I suppose he speaks of all the saints after the death and resurrection of our Lord and the descent of the Holy Ghost. He refers to the whole church, in the midst of which the Holy Spirit now dwells. We are come to a more joyous sight than Sinai, and the mountain burning with fire. The Hebrew worshiper, apart from his sacrifices, lived continually beneath the shadow of the darkness of a broken law; he was startled often by the tremendous note of the trumpet, which threatened judgment for that broken law; and thus he lived ever in a condition of bondage. To what else could the law bring him? To convince of sin and to condemn the sinner is its utmost power. The believer in the Lord Jesus Christ lives in quite another atmosphere. He has not come to a barren crag, but to an inhabited city, Jerusalem above, the metropolis of God. He has quitted the wilderness for the land which floweth with milk and honey, and the material mount which might be touched for the spiritual and heavenly Jerusalem. He has entered into fellowship with an innumerable company of angels, who are to him, not cherubim with flaming swords to keep men back from the tree of life, but ministering spirits sent forth to minister to the heirs of salvation. He is come to the joyous assembly of all pure intelligences who have met, not in trembling, but in joyous liberty, to keep the feast with their great Lord and King. He thinks of all who love God throughout all worlds, and he feels that he is one of them; for he has come to "the general assembly and church of the first-born, which are written in heaven." Moreover, he has come "to God the Judge of all," the umpire and rewarder of all the chosen citizens who are enrolled by His command, the ruler and judge of all their enemies. God is not to them a dreadful person who speaks from a distance; but He is their Father and their Friend, in whom they delight themselves, in whose presence there is fullness of joy for them. Brethren, our fellowship is with the Father, our God. To Him we have come through our Lord Jesus Christ. Moreover, in the power of the Spirit of God we realize the oneness of the church both in heaven and earth, and the spirits of just men made perfect are in union with us. No gulf divides the militant from the triumphant; we are one army of the living God. We sometimes speak of the holy *dead*; but there are none such: they live unto God; they are perfected as to their spirits even now, and they are waiting for the moment when their bodies also shall be raised from the tomb to be again inhabited by their immortal souls. We no longer shudder at the sepulcher, but sing of resurrection. Our condition of heart, from day to day, is that of men who are in fellowship with God, fellowship with angels, fellowship with perfect spirits.

We have also come to Jesus, our Savior, who is all and in all. In Him we live; we are joined unto Him in one spirit; He is the Bridegroom of our souls, the delight of our hearts. We are come to Him as the Mediator of the new covenant. What a blessed thing it is to know that covenant of which He is the Mediator! Some in these days despise the covenant; but saints delight in it. To them the everlasting covenant, "ordered in all things, and sure," is all their salvation and all their desire. We are covenanted ones through our Lord Jesus. God has pledged Himself to bless us. By two immutable things wherein it is impossible for Him to lie, he has given us strong consolation, and good hope through grace, even to all of us who have fled for refuge to the Lord Jesus. We are happy to live under the covenant of grace, the covenant of promise, the covenant symbolized by Jerusalem above, which is free, and the mother of us all.

Then comes the last thing of all, mentioned last, as I shall have to show you, for a purpose. We have come *"to the blood of sprinkling."* On that first day at Sinai no blood of sprinkling was presented; but afterwards it was used by divine order to ratify the national covenant which the tribes made with Jehovah at the foot of the hill. Of that covenant the Lord says, "which my covenant they broke, although I was an husband unto them." *He* never broke His covenant, but *they* broke it; for they failed to keep that condition of obedience without which a covenant founded upon works falls to the ground. We have come to the covenant of grace, to Jesus the Mediator of it, and to His blood, which is the seal of it. Of this last we are going to speak at this time—"The blood of sprinkling which speaketh better things than that of Abel."

I shall need this morning to occupy all the time with what I regard as only the first head of my discourse. *What is it?* "The blood of sprinkling." It will be our duty afterwards to consider *where we are*—"we are come unto this blood"; and thirdly, to remember *what then?* "See that ye refuse not him that speaketh."

I. FIRST, WHAT IS IT? What is the "blood of sprinkling"? In a few words, "the blood of sprinkling" represents the pains, the sufferings, the humiliation, and the death of the Lord Jesus Christ, which He endured on the behalf of guilty man. When we speak of the blood, we wish not to be understood as referring solely or mainly to the literal material blood which flowed from the wounds of Jesus. We believe in the literal fact of His shedding His blood; but when we speak of His cross and blood we mean those sufferings and that death of our Lord Jesus Christ by which He magnified the law of God; we mean what Isaiah intended when he said, "He shall make his soul an offering for sin"; we mean all the griefs which Jesus vicariously endured on our behalf at Gethsemane, and Gabbatha, and Golgotha, and especially His yielding up His life upon the tree of scorn and doom. "The chastisement of our peace was upon him, and with his stripes we are healed." "Without shedding of blood there is no remission"; and the shedding of blood intended is the death of Jesus, the Son of God.

Remember that His sufferings and death were not apparent only, but true and real; and that they involved an incalculable degree of pain and anguish. To redeem our souls cost our Lord an exceeding sorrowfulness "even unto death"; it cost Him the bloody sweat, the heart broken with reproach, and especially the agony of being forsaken of His Father, till He cried, "My God, my God, why hast thou forsaken me?" Our mediator endured death under the worst possible aspects, bereft of those supports which are in all other cases of godly men afforded by the goodness and faithfulness of God. His was not merely a natural death, but a death aggravated by supernatural circumstance, which infinitely intensified its woe. This is what we mean by the blood of Christ, His sufferings, and His death.

These were voluntarily undertaken by Himself out of pure love to us, and in order that we might thereby be justly saved from deserved punishment. There was no natural reason on His own account why He should suffer, bleed, and die. Far from it,—"He only hath immortality." But out of supreme love to us, that man might be forgiven without the violation of divine rectitude, the Son of God assumed human flesh, and became in very deed a man, in order that He might be able to offer in man's place a full vindication to the righteous and unchangeable law of God. Being God, He thus showed forth the wondrous love of God to man by being willing to suffer personally rather than the redeemed should die as the just result of their sin. The matchless majesty of His divine person lent supreme efficacy to His sufferings. It was a man that died, but He was also God, and the death of incarnate God reflects more glory upon law than the deaths of myriads of condemned creatures could have done. See the yearning of the great God for perfect righteousness: He had sooner die than stain His justice even to indulge His mercy. Jesus the Lord, out of love to the Father and to men, undertook willingly and cheerfully for our sakes to magnify the law, and bring in perfect righteousness. This work was so carried out to the utmost, that not a jot of the suffering was mitigated, nor a particle of the obedience foregone: "He became obedient unto death, even the death of the cross." Now He hath finished transgression, made an end of sin, and brought in everlasting righteousness: for He has offered such an expiation that God is just, and the justifier of him that believeth. God is at once the righteous Judge, and the infinitely loving Father, through what Jesus hath suffered.

Brethren, though I have said that there was no reason why the Son of God should bleed and die on His own account, yet towards us there was a reason. Our Lord from of old in the eternal covenant was constituted the head and representative of all who were in Him; and so, when the time came, He took the place, bore the sin, and suffered the penalty of those whom the Father gave Him from before the foundations of the world. He is as much the representative man as the first Adam was the representative man; and as in Adam the sin was committed which ruined us, so in the second Adam the atonement was made which saves us. "As in Adam all die, even so in Christ shall all be made alive." There was no other person so fit to undertake the enterprise of our redemption as this second man, who is the Lord from heaven. He properly, but yet most generously and spontaneously, came and shed His precious blood, in the room and place and stead of sinners, to bring the guilty near to God.

But the text does not merely speak of the blood *shed*, which I have explained to you, but of "the blood of *sprinkling*." This is the atonement applied for divine purposes, and especially applied to our own hearts and consciences by faith. For the explanation of this sprinkling we must look to the types of the Old Testament. In the Old Testament the blood of sprinkling meant a great many things; in fact, I cannot just now tell you all that is signified. We meet with it in the Book of Exodus, at the time when the Lord smote all the first-born of Egypt Then the blood of sprinkling meant *preservation*. The basin filled with blood was taken, and a bunch of hyssop was dipped into it, and the lintel and the two sideposts of every house tenanted by Israelites were smeared with the blood; and when God saw the blood upon the house of the Israelite, He bade the destroyer pass that family by, and leave their first-born unharmed. The sprinkled blood meant preservation: it was Israel's passover and safeguard.

The sprinkled blood very frequently signified the confirmation of a covenant. So it is used in Exodus 24, which I read to you just now. The blood was sprinkled upon the book of the covenant, and also upon the people, to show that the covenant was, as far as it could be, confirmed by the people who promised, "All that the Lord hath said will we do." The blood of bulls and of goats in that case was but a type of the sacrificial blood of the Lord Jesus Christ. The lesson which we learn from Exodus 24 is that the blood of sprinkling means the blood of ratification or confirmation of the covenant, which God had been pleased to make with men in the person of our Lord Jesus Christ. Since Jesus died, the promises are Yea and Amen to all believers, and must assuredly be fulfilled. The covenant of grace had but one condition, and that condition Jesus has fulfilled by His death, so that it has now become a covenant of pure and unconditional promise to all the seed.

In many cases the sprinkling of the blood meant *purification*. If a person had been defiled, he could not come into the sanctuary of God without being sprinkled with blood. There were the ashes of a red heifer laid up, and these were mixed with blood and water; and by their being sprinkled on the unclean, his ceremonial defilement was removed. There were matters incident to domestic life, and accidents of outdoor life, which engendered impurity, and this impurity was put away by the sprinkling of blood. This sprinkling was used in the case of recovery from infectious disease, such as leprosy; before such persons could mingle in the solemn assemblies, they were sprinkled with the blood, and thus were made ceremonially pure. In a higher sense this is the work of the blood of Christ. It preserves us, it ratifies the covenant, and wherever it is applied it makes us pure; for "the blood of Jesus Christ his Son cleanseth us from all sin." We have our hearts sprinkled from an evil conscience; for we have come unto the obedience and sprinkling of the blood of Jesus Christ.

The sprinkling of the blood meant, also, *sanctification*. Before a man entered upon the priesthood the blood was put upon his right ear, and on the great toe of his right foot, and on the thumb of his right hand, signifying that all his powers were thus consecrated to God. The ordination ceremony included the sprinkling of blood upon the altar round about. Even thus hath the Lord Jesus redeemed us unto God by his death, and the sprinkling of his blood hath made us kings and priests unto God forever. He is made of God unto us sanctification, and all else that is needed for the divine service.

One other signification of the blood of the sacrifice was *acceptance and access*. When the high priest went into the most holy place once a year, it was not without blood, which he sprinkled upon the ark of the covenant, and upon the mercy-seat, which was on the top thereof. All approaches to God were made by blood. There was no hope of a man drawing near to God, even in symbol, apart from the sprinkling of the blood. And now today our only way to God is by the precious sacrifice of Christ; the only hope for the success of our prayers, the acceptance of our praises, or the reception of our holy works, is through the ever-abiding merit of the atoning sacrifice of our Lord Jesus Christ. The Holy Ghost bids us enter into the holiest by the blood of Jesus; there is no other way.

There were other uses besides these, but it may suffice to put down the sprinkling of the blood as having these effects, namely that of preservation, satisfaction, purification, sanctification, and access to God. This was all typified in the blood of bulls and of goats, but actually fulfilled in the great sacrifice of Christ.

With this as an explanation, I desire to come still closer to the text, and view it with great care; for to my mind it is singularly full of teaching. May the Holy Spirit lead us into the truth which lies herein like treasure hid in a field!

First. *The blood of sprinkling is the center of the divine manifestation under the gospel.* Observe its innermost place in the passage before us.[†] You are privileged by almighty grace to come first to Mount Zion, to climb its steeps, to stand upon its holy summit, and to enter the city of the living God, the heavenly Jerusalem. In those golden streets, surrounding the hallowed shrine, you behold an innumerable company of angels. What a vision of glory! But you must not rest here; for the great general assembly, the festal gathering, the solemn convocation of the enrolled in heaven is being held, and all are there in glad attire, surrounding their God and Lord. Press onward to the throne itself, where sits the Judge of all, surrounded by those holy spirits who have washed their robes, and, therefore, stand before the throne of God in perfection.

Have you not come a long way? Are you not admitted into the very center of the whole revelation? Not yet. A step further lands you where stands your Savior, the Mediator, with the new covenant. Now is your joy complete; but you have a further object to behold. What is in that innermost shrine? What is that which is hidden away in the holy of holies? What is that which is the most precious and costly thing of all, the last, the ultimatum. God's grandest revelation? The precious blood of Christ, as of a lamb without blemish and without spot—the blood of sprinkling. This comes last; it is the innermost truth of the dispensation of grace under which we live. Brethren, when we climb to heaven itself, and pass the gate of pearl, to the throne of God, and see the spirits of the just made perfect, and hear their holy hymn, we shall not have gone beyond the influence of the blood of sprinkling; nay, we shall see it there more truly present than in any other place beside. "What!" say you, "the blood of Jesus in heaven?" Yes. The earthly sanctuary, we are told, was purified with the blood of bulls and of goats, "but the heavenly things themselves with better sacrifices than these" (Heb. 9:23). When Jesus entered once for all into the holy place, He entered by His own blood, having obtained eternal redemption for us: so saith the apostle in the ninth chapter of this epistle. Let those who talk lightly of the precious blood correct their view before they be guilty of blasphemy; for the revelation of God knows no lower deep, this is the heart and center of all. The manifestation of Jesus under the gospel is not only the revelation of the Mediator, but especially of His sacrifice. The

---

[†] For this line of thought I am much indebted to a chapter in an admirable book, entitled *Every-day Life*, by C. H. Waller, M.A. Shaw and Co.

appearance of God the Judge of all, the vision of hosts of angels and perfect spirits, do but lead up to that sacrifice which is the source and focus of all true fellowship between God and His creatures. This is the character which Jesus wears in the innermost shrine where He reveals Himself most clearly to those who are nearest to Him. He looks like a lamb that has been slain. There is no sight of Him which is more full, more glorious, more complete than the vision of Him as the great sacrifice for sin. The atonement of Jesus is the concentration of the divine glory; all other revelations of God are completed and intensified here. You have not come to the central sun of the great spiritual system of grace till you have come to the blood of sprinkling—to those sufferings of Messiah which are not for Himself, but are intended to bear upon others, even as drops when they are sprinkled exert their influence where they fall. Unless you have learned to rejoice in that blood which taketh away sin, you have not yet caught the key-note of the gospel dispensation. The blood of Christ is the life of the gospel. Apart from atonement you may know the skin, the rind, the husk of the gospel; but its inner kernel you have not discovered.

I next ask you to look at the text and observe that *this sprinkling of the blood*, as mentioned by the Holy Ghost in this passage, *is absolutely identical with Jesus Himself.* Read it. "To Jesus the mediator of the new covenant, and to the blood of sprinkling, that speaketh better things than that of Abel. See that ye refuse not *him* that speaketh." He saith it is the blood that speaketh; and then he proceeds to say, "See that ye refuse not *him* that speaketh." This is a very unexpected turn, which can only be explained upon the supposition that Jesus and the blood are identical in the writer's view. By what we may call a singularity in grammar, in putting *him* for *it*, the Spirit of God intentionally sets forth the striking truth, that the sacrifice is identical with the Savior. "We are come to the Savior, the mediator of the new covenant, and to the blood of sprinkling that speaketh; see that ye refuse not *him*." Beloved friends, there is no Jesus if there is no blood of sprinkling; there is no Savior if there is no sacrifice. I put this strongly, because the attempt is being made nowadays to set forth Jesus apart from His cross and atonement. He is held up as a great ethical teacher, a self-sacrificing spirit, who is to lead the way in a grand moral reformation, and by His influence to set up a kingdom of moral influence in the world. It is even hinted that this kingdom has never had prominence enough given to it because it has been overshadowed by his cross. But where is Jesus apart from His sacrifice? He is not here if you have left out the blood of sprinkling, which is the blood of sacrifice. Without the atonement, no man is a Christian, and Christ is not Jesus. If you have torn away the sacrificial blood, you have drawn the heart out of the gospel of Jesus Christ, and robbed it of its life. If you have trampled on the blood of sprinkling, and counted it a common thing, instead of putting it above you upon the lintel of the door, and all around you upon the two sideposts, you have fearfully transgressed. As for me, God forbid that I should glory save in the cross of our Lord Jesus Christ, since to me that cross is identical with Jesus Himself. I know no Jesus but He who died the just for the unjust. You can separate Jesus and the blood materially; for by the spear-thrust, and all His other wounds, the blood was drawn away from the body of our Lord; but spiritually this "blood of sprinkling" and the Jesus by whom we live, are inseparable. In fact, they are one and indivisible, the selfsame thing, and you cannot truly know Jesus, or preach Jesus, unless you preach Him as slain for sin; you cannot trust Jesus except you trust Him as making peace by the blood of His cross. If you have done with the blood of sprinkling, you have done with Jesus altogether; He will never part with His mediatorial glory as our sacrifice, neither can we come to Him if we ignore that character. Is it not clear in the text that Jesus and the blood of sprinkling are one? What God hath joined together, let no man put asunder. Note this right carefully.

Thirdly, observe that *this "blood of sprinkling" is put in close contact with "the new covenant."* I do not wonder that those who are lax in their views of the atonement have nothing honorable to say concerning the covenants, old or new. The doctrine of the covenants is the marrow of divinity; but these vain-glorious spirits affect to despise it. This is natural, since they speak slightingly of atonement. What covenant is there without blood? If it be not ratified, if there be no sacrifice to make it sure, then is it no covenant in the sight of God or of enlightened men. But, O beloved, ye who know your Lord, and follow on to know Him yet better, to you the covenant of promise is a heritage of joy, and His atonement is most precious as the confirmation of it. To us the sacrificial death of our Lord is not *a* doctrine, but *the* doctrine, not an outgrowth of Christian teaching, but the essence and marrow of it. To us Jesus in His atonement is Alpha and Omega, in Him the covenant begins and ends. You see how it was confirmed by blood. If it be a man's covenant, if it be confirmed, it standeth; but this is God's covenant, confirmed with promises, oaths and blood, and its stands fast forever and ever. Every believer is as much interested in that covenant as was Abraham the father of believers; for the covenant was made with Abraham and his spiritual seed; and in Christ it is confirmed to all that seed forever by His most precious blood. That, also, is evident enough in the text: fail not to consider it well.

But, fourthly, I want you to notice that according to the text *the blood is the voice of the new dispensation.* Observe that on Sinai there was "the sound of a trumpet, and the voice of words; which voice they that heard entreated that the word should not be spoken to them any more." You look, therefore, under the new dispensation, for a voice, and you do not come to any till you reach the last object in the list, and there see "the blood of sprinkling that speaketh." Here, then is the voice of the gospel; it is not the sound of a trumpet, nor the voice of words spoken in terrible majesty; but the blood speaks, and assuredly there is no sound more piercing, more potent, more prevailing. God heard the voice of Abel's blood and visited Cain with condign punishment for killing his brother; and the precious blood of Jesus Christ, the Son of God, cries in the ears of God with a voice which is ever heard. How can it be imagined that the Lord God should be deaf to the cry of His Son's sacrifice? Lo, these many ages the blood has cried—"Forgive them! Forgive them! Accept them! Deliver them from going down into the pit, for I have found a ransom!"

The blood of sprinkling has a voice of instruction to us even as it has a voice of intercession with God. It cries to us, "See the evil of sin! See how God loveth righteousness! See how He loveth men! See how impossible it is for you to escape from the punishment of sin except by this great sacrifice in which the love and the justice of God equally appear! See how Jehovah spared not His own Son, but freely delivered Him up for us all."

What a voice there is in the atonement!—a voice which pleads for holiness and love, for justice and grace, for truth and mercy. "See that ye refuse not him that speaketh."

Do you not hear it? If you take away the blood of sprinkling from the gospel, you have silenced it. It has no voice if this be gone. "Oh," they say, "the gospel has lost its power!" What wonder when they have made it a dumb gospel! How can it have power when they take away that which is its life and speech? Unless the preacher is evermore preaching this blood, and sprinkling it by the doctrine of faith, his teaching has no voice either to rouse the careless or to cheer the anxious. If ever there should come a wretched day when all our pulpits shall be full of modern thought, and the old doctrine of a substitutionary sacrifice shall be exploded, then will there remain no word of comfort for the guilty or hope for the despairing. Hushed will be forever those silver notes which now console the living, and cheer the dying; a dumb spirit will possess this sullen world, and no voice of joy will break the blank silence of despair. The gospel speaks through the propitiation for sin, and if that be denied, it speaketh no more. Those who preach not the atonement exhibit a dumb and dummy gospel; a mouth it hath, but speaketh not; they that make it are like unto their idol.

Let me draw you nearer still to the text. Observe, that *this voice is identical with the voice of the Lord Jesus*; for it is put so. "The blood of sprinkling that speaketh. See that ye refuse not *him* that speaketh." Whatever the doctrine of the sacrifice of Jesus may be, it is the main teaching of Jesus Himself. It is well to notice that the voice which spoke from Sinai was also the voice of Christ. It was Jesus who delivered that law the penalty of which He was Himself to endure. He that read it out amidst the tempest was Jesus. Notice the declaration—"Whose voice then shook the earth." Whenever you hear the gospel, the voice of the precious blood is the voice of Jesus Himself, the voice of Him that shook the earth at Sinai. This same voice shall by-and-by shake, not the earth only, but also heaven. What a voice there is in the blood of sprinkling, since indeed it is the voice of the eternal Son of God, who both makes and destroys! Would you have me silence the doctrine of the blood of sprinkling? Would any one of you attempt so horrible a deed? Shall we be censured if we continually proclaim the heaven-sent message of the blood of Jesus? Shall we speak with bated breath because some affected person shudders at the sound of the word "*blood*"? or some "cultured" individual rebels at the old-fashioned thought of sacrifice? Nay, verily, we will sooner have our tongue cut out than cease to speak of the precious blood of Jesus Christ. For me there is nothing worth thinking of or preaching about but this grand truth, which is the beginning and the end of the whole Christian system, namely, that God gave His Son to die that sinners might live. This is not the voice of the blood only, but the voice of our Lord Jesus Christ Himself. So saith the text, and who can contradict it?

Further, my brethren, from the text I learn another truth, namely, that *this blood is always speaking*. The text saith not "the blood of sprinkling that spoke," but "that speaketh." It is always speaking, it always remaineth a plea with God and a testimony to men. I never will be silenced, either one way or the other. In the intercession of our risen and ascended Lord His sacrifice ever speaketh to the Most High. By the teaching of the Holy Ghost the atonement will always speak in edification to believers yet upon the earth. It is the blood that speaketh. According to our text, this is the only speech which this dispensation yields us. Shall that speech ever be still? Shall we decline to hear it? Shall we refuse to echo it? God forbid. By day, by night, the great sacrifice continues to cry to the sons of men, "Turn ye from your sins, for they cost your Savior dear. The times of your ignorance God winked at, but now commandeth all men everywhere to repent, since He is able to forgive and yet be just. Your offended God has Himself provided a sacrifice; come and be sprinkled with its blood, and be reconciled once for all." The voice of this blood speaks wherever there is a guilty conscience, wherever there is a believing mind. It speaketh with sweet, familiar, tender, inviting voice. There is no music like it to the sinner's ear: it charms away his fears. It shall never cease its speaking so long as there is a sinner yet out of Christ; nay, so long as there is one on earth who still needs its cleansing power because of fresh backslidings. Oh, hear ye its voice! Incline you ear and receive its blessed accents: it says, "Come now, and let us reason together, saith the Lord; though your sins be as scarlet, they shall be as white as snow; though they be red like crimson, they shall be as wool." This part of my discourse will not be complete unless I bid you notice that we are expressly told that *this precious blood speaks "better things than that of Abel."* I do not think that the whole meaning of the passage is exhausted if we say that Abel's blood cries for vengeance, and that Christ's blood speaks for pardon. Dr. Watts puts it:—

> Blood has a voice to pierce the skies:
> "Revenge!" the blood of Abel cries;
> But the dear stream when Christ was slain
> Speaks peace as loud from ev'ry vein.

That is quite true; but I conceive that it is not all the sense, and perhaps not even *the* sense here intended. Revenge is scarcely a good thing; yet Abel's blood spoke good things, or we should hardly read that Christ's blood speaks "better things." What does the blood of Abel speak? The blood of Abel speaks to a complete and believing obedience to God. It shows us a man who believes God, and, notwithstanding the enmity of his brother, brings to God the appointed sacrifice of faith, strictly following up, even to the bitter end, his holy obedience to the Most High. That is what the blood of Abel says to me; and the blood of Jesus says the same thing most emphatically. The death of Jesus Christ was the crown and close of a perfect life; it was a fit completion of a course of holiness. In obedience to the Great Father, Jesus even laid down His life. But if this be all the blood of Jesus speaks, as some say that it is, then it does not speak better things than the blood of Abel; for it only says the same things in a louder voice. The martyrdom of any saint has a voice for obedience to God as truly as the martyrdom of Jesus; but the death of our Lord says far more, infinitely more, than this: it not only witnesses to complete obedience, but it provides the way by which the disobedient may be forgiven and helped to obedience and holiness. The cross has a greater, deeper, gladder gospel for fallen men than that of a perfect example which they are unable to follow.

The blood of Abel said this, too—that he was not ashamed of his faith, but witnessed a good confession concerning his God, even to the death; he put his life in his hand, and was not ashamed to stand at the altar of God, and avow his faith by obediently offering the ordained sacrifice. Now I grant you that the blood of Jesus also declares that He was a faithful and true witness, who willingly sealed His witness with His blood. He proved by shedding His blood that He could not be turned aside from truth and righteousness, even though death stood in His way; but if that is all that the blood of sprinkling speaketh, it saith no better things than the blood of Abel. "Be faithful unto death," is the voice of Abel as well as of Jesus. Jesus must have said more than this by His blood-shedding.

The blood of Abel said good things; that is implied in the fact that the blood of Jesus Christ says better things; and no doubt the blood of Abel rises to the dignity of teaching self-sacrifice. Here was a man, a keeper of sheep, who by his mode of life laid out his life for the good of those committed to his charge; and at the last, in obedience to God, he yielded himself up to die by a brother's hand. It was the first draft of a picture of self-sacrifice. Our Lord Jesus Christ also made a complete self-sacrifice. All His life long He gave Himself to men. He lived never for Himself. The glory of God and the good of men were united in one passion which filled His whole soul. He could say, "The zeal of thine house hath eaten me up." His death was the completion of His perfect self-sacrifice. But if that were all, the blood of Jesus saith no better thing than Abel's death saith, though it may say it more emphatically.

Our Lord's blood saith "better things than that of Abel"; and what doth it say? It saith, "There is redemption through his blood, the forgiveness of sins according to the riches of his grace." "He his own self bore our sins on his own body on the tree, that we being dead to sins should live unto righteousness: by whose stripes we were healed." "He hath made him to be sin for us, who knew no sin; that we might be made the righteousness of God in him." The voice of the blood is this, "For I will be merciful to their unrighteousness, and their sins and their iniquities will I remember no more." "The blood of Jesus Christ his Son cleanseth us from all sin." Now, my brethren, these are better things than Abel's blood could say, and they are what the blood of Jesus speaks to every one upon whom it is sprinkled by faith. It must be applied to each one of us by faith, or it says nothing to us. But when it falls on each believing individual, it saith to him words of blessing which pacify his conscience and delight his soul.

The apostle says that "Ye are come to the blood of sprinkling." Is it so? Has that blood of sprinkling ever been applied to you? Do you feel it? Are you preserved? Are you cleansed? Are you brought nigh to God? Are you sanctified unto God's service by the atoning sacrifice? If so, then go you out, and in firm confidence that never can be shaken, make your glory in the blood of sprinkling. Tell every sinner whom you meet that if the Lord Jesus wash him he shall be whiter than snow. Preach the atoning sacrifice of the Lamb of God, and then sing of it. Recollect that wondrous threefold song in the fifth chapter of Revelation, where, first of all, the elders and living creatures round about the throne, sing a new song, saying, "Thou wast slain, and hast redeemed us to God by thy blood out of every kindred, and tongue, and people, and nation." Then ten thousand times ten thousand, and thousands of thousands of angels take up the strain and cry, "Worthy is the Lamb that was slain." Nor is this all; for the apostle tells us, "Every creature which is in heaven, and on the earth, and under the earth, and such as are in the sea, and all that are in them, heard I saying, Blessing, and honor, and glory, and power, be unto him that sitteth upon the throne, and unto the Lamb forever and ever." See you not that they all extol the Lord Jesus in His sacrificial character as the Lamb slain? I have scant patience with those who dare to put this great truth into the background, and even sneer at it or misrepresent it of set purpose. Sirs, if you would be saved you must have the blood of Jesus sprinkled upon you. He that believeth not in Christ Jesus, in Jesus the atoning sacrifice, must perish. The eternal God must repulse with infinite disgust the man who refuses the loving sacrifice of Jesus. Inasmuch as he counted himself unworthy of this wondrous sacrifice, this marvelous expiation, there remaineth no other sacrifice for sin, and nothing for Him but that eternal blackness and darkness and thunder which were foreshadowed at Sinai. Those who refuse the atonement which wisdom devised, which love provided, and which justice has accepted, have signed their own death-warrant, and none can wonder that they perish. The Lord lead us to glory in Christ crucified. Amen.

PROCLAMATION OF ACCEPTANCE
AND VENGEANCE

Sermon No. 1,369
Delivered on Lord's day Morning, August 12, 1877.
Portions of Scripture read before Sermon—Leviticus 16:29–34; 25:1–24, 39–43.
Hymns from *Our Own Hymn Book*—289, 271, 299.

To proclaim the acceptable year of the LORD, and the day of
vengeance of our God; to comfort all that mourn—Isaiah 61:2.

WE know that this Scripture speaks concerning the Lord Jesus Christ. We say not this as if we relied upon our own opinion, we know it of a surety from the Lord's own lips, for, reading this passage in the synagogue at Nazareth, He said, "This day is this Scripture fulfilled in your ears." It is Jesus of Nazareth whom the Lord hath anointed to preach deliverance to the captives and recovering of sight to the blind, and our text tells us that He was also sent to make a proclamation which should usher in the year of acceptance and the day of vengeance.

Notice well the expression, *to proclaim*, because a proclamation is the message of a king, and where the word of a king is there is power. The Lord Jesus Christ came into the world to announce the will of the King of kings. He saith, "I am come in my Father's name," and again, "My doctrine is not mine, but his that sent me." Every word of the gospel is backed by the authority of "the King eternal, immortal, invisible," and he who rejects it is guilty of treason against Jehovah, God of all. The gospel is not of the nature of a commonplace invitation or human exhortation, which may be accepted or refused at will without involving guilt; but it is a divine proclamation, issued from the throne of the Eternal, which none can reject without becoming thereby rebels against the Infinite Majesty. Now if it be so, let us give the divine edict our most earnest attention, and take heed what we hear. When a proclamation is issued by the head of a state, all good citizens gather around to read what has been said to them, and to know what the supreme law may be: and so, when God proclaims His will, all right-hearted men desire to know what it is, and what bearing it has upon them, what the Lord demandeth or what the Lord promiseth and what is their share therein. Beloved hearers, listening to the gospel should always be very solemn work, since it is listening to the Word of God. Though the voice is that of man yet the truth is of God; I pray you do not trifle with it.

456

Nor let it be forgotten that a proclamation must be treated with profound respect, not merely by receiving attention to its contents, but by gaining obedience to its demands. God does not speak to us by His Son that we may be gratified by hearing the sound of His voice, but that we may yield to His will. We are not to be hearers only, but doers of the Word. We should be quick in obedience to the command of the proclamation, swift in acceptance of its promise, and cheerful in submission to its demand. Who shall resist the proclamations of Jehovah? Is He not our Creator and King? Who is stubborn enough to refuse obedience? Or who hath brazen face enough to dispute His sway? Shall not He who made heaven and earth, and shaketh them when He pleaseth, and will destroy them at His pleasure, be regarded with reverential awe by the creatures of His hand? O Son of God, since it is a divine proclamation which Thou dost publish, send forth thy Holy Spirit that we may receive it with deepest reverence and lowliest obedience, lest, through our neglect, we do despite to Thee as well as to thy Father. When a proclamation is not made by an ordinary herald, but when the Prince Himself comes forth to declare His Father's will, then should all hearts be moved to sevenfold attention. It is the Son of God, anointed by the Spirit of God, who acts as herald unto us, and so by each person of the divine Trinity we are called upon to bow a listening ear and an obedient heart to what the Lord proclaims. Attention, then! The Messenger of the Covenant makes proclamation! Attention for the King of kings!

With this as a preface, let me notice, that there are three points in the proclamation worthy of our best attention: the first is *the acceptable year*; the next, *the vengeance day*; and the third, *the comfort derived from both*—"to comfort all that mourn."

I. Jesus, in the first place, proclaims THE ACCEPTABLE YEAR OF THE LORD. Take the expression to pieces and it comes to this—the year of the Lord, and the year of acceptance.

Now, what was *the year of the Lord?* There can be, I think, very little question that this relates to the jubilee year. Every seventh year was the Lord's year, and it was to be a sabbath of rest to the land; but the year after that seventh seventh year, the fiftieth year, which the Lord reserved unto Himself, was in a very marked and especial sense the year of the Lord. Now, our Lord Jesus has come to proclaim a period of jubilee to the true seed of Israel. The seed of Abraham now are not the seed according to the law, but those who are born after the promise. There are privileges reserved for Israel after the flesh, which they will yet receive in the day when they shall acknowledge Christ to be the Messiah; but every great blessing which was promised to Abraham's seed after the flesh is now virtually promised to Israel after the Spirit, to those who by faith are the children of believing Abraham.

Now, beloved, to all who believe, our Lord Jesus proclaims a year of jubilee. Let us dwell upon the four privileges of the jubilee, and accept with delight the proclamation which our Lord has made.

In the year of jubilee, as we read in the twenty-fifth chapter of Leviticus, there was *a release of all persons* who had sold themselves for servants. Pinched by great poverty, and unable to meet their debts, it sometimes happened that men were compelled to say to their creditor, "Take us and our wives and children, and accept our services instead of money. We have no goods or chattels, and our land has been mortgaged long ago, but here we are; we cannot pay in any other way—give us food and raiment and lodging, and we will put ourselves under apprenticeship to you." The law of Moses ordained that such persons were not to be treated harshly, nor regarded as slaves, but as hired servants, but still it must have been an unpleasant condition of servitude for a freeborn Israelite. How happy then was the morning when the jubilee trumpet sounded, and the generous law came into operation which said, "He shall serve thee unto the year of jubilee, but then shall he depart from thee, both he and his children with him." From that moment he owed no more service, however great his debt might have been; he looked upon his wife and children and rejoiced that they were all his own and all free from the yoke, so that they could at once return to the possession of their fathers, all live in the cottage in which they formerly dwelt, and enjoy the piece of land which they formerly called their own. Liberty, that gladsome sound, liberty had come to them; no matter that they had long been under obligations to the creditor, those obligations ceased on the sound of the sacred trumpet. Beloved souls now present, proclamation is made to you in the Lord's name that if you are under bondage to sin and to sinful habits, there is liberty for you; faith in Jesus will set you free. If you are in bondage under justice and the broken law there is deliverance. If you are under bondage through fear of death, or from the rage of Satan, our divine Lord and Master has come into the world on purpose to break these bonds in sunder, and to proclaim liberty to the captives. Ye need be bound no longer; if ye believe in Jesus ye *are* bound no longer, but ye are set free from all the bondage of the law, from the slavery of Satan and from the dread of death. Take the liberty which the great Lord freely presents to you, and be no longer slaves. Jesus has brought in redemption and finished atonement, and believers are free; come and rejoice therein.

The next jubilee blessing was *the redemption of alienated possessions.* Every man had his own plot of ground in the Holy Land, but through the pressure of the times it sometimes happened that a man alienated his property: he was in need of ready money, his children wanted bread to eat, and he, therefore, parted with his land. It was gone: the vines and the fig trees, the corn and the oil, passed over to another; but it was not gone forever, he had no power to sell beyond the year of jubilee. When this joyful morning dawned he went back to his family estate; it was all his own again, clear of all encumbrances; the little homestead, and the farmyard, and the fields, and the garden, all had come back to him, and none could dispute his right. Just so my Lord and Master declares to all who believe in Him that the estate which Adam forfeited is restored to all for whom the Second Adam died. The alienated heritage is our own again. The great Father's love, and favor, and care, yea, all things, whether things present or things to come, or life or death, all are ours, and we are Christ's and Christ is God's. If we are believers, and we are of the true seed of Israel, this day the

Lord Jesus proclaims to us a restoration of all the lost privileges and blessings which originally belonged to manhood. Behold, believers, all covenant blessings are yours, rejoice in them! Partake of heavenly blessings freely. Let your soul rejoice in its portion, and delight itself in fatness.

It followed, also, as a third blessing of the year of the Lord that *all debts were discharged*. The man who had sold himself had, as it were, made a composition of his debts by the sale of himself, and this implied a full and final discharge at the jubilee. The person also who had mortgaged his land up to the jubilee year had discharged his debts thereby, and when the man received back himself and his property, no further liability rested upon him, he was cleared of all charges. The jubilee did not give the man back himself and his land under a reserve, but unreservedly. If debt had still been due the release would have been a mere farce, since he would have had to mortgage his land and sell himself again directly to meet the demand. No, there was a full discharge, a canceling of all debts, a removal of all encumbrances upon the man and upon his estate, and he was free. What a joy this must have been! He who is in debt is in danger; a honest man sleeps on a hard bed till he has paid what he owes. He who is immersed in debt is plunged in misery, driven to his wits' end, not knowing what to do. Happy is he that is delivered from debt once for all. Now behold, O believers in Jesus, your debts before the Lord are all discharged, the handwriting that was against you is nailed to the cross, receipted in the crimson lines of Jesus' precious blood. Being justified by faith ye are clear before the sight of the Eternal; none can lay anything to your charge. What joyful notes are these! Jesus makes the proclamation, who will not believe it and be glad?

A fourth blessing of the jubilee trumpet was *rest*. They had their lands, but they were not to till them for a year. No more the spade and the plow, the sickle and the flail—they were to put away instruments of labor, and rest for twelve months. Think of a whole year of perfect repose, wherein they might worship and adore God all the week round, make every day a holy festival, and the whole year a Sabbath of Sabbaths unto the Most High. Brethren, the Israelites had no small privileges under the ceremonial covenant, if they had lived up to it, but they failed to do so, for it has sometimes been questioned whether they ever kept a jubilee at all, and whether the Sabbatic year was ever once observed. If they had obeyed the Lord they would have been favored indeed: for in the matter of holidays and quiet resting times they were favored above all people. Think of one year in seven of absolute cessation from toil. What repose for them! And then they had also the year after the seventh seven, so that every man who reached the fiftieth year enjoyed two consecutive years of absolute rest from all labor, and yet knew no want, for the ground brought forth plentifully, and every man helped himself. Those who had land had a good store to last them through three years, and those who had none were fed by the spontaneous produce of the soil. We live not under such laws, and if we did I am afraid we should not have the faith to trust in the Lord and avail ourselves of the divinely appointed holiday. But, beloved, we rest spiritually. He that believes in the Lord Jesus Christ has entered into rest. Now no more does he strive to work out a righteousness of his own, for he has already a divine one, and needs no other. It is his pleasure to worship God, but he no longer trembles beneath His wrath; it is his delight to do His command-ments, but he toils and frets no longer as a slave under the law; he has become a free man, and a beloved child, and the peace of God which passeth all understanding keeps his heart and mind. Being justified by faith he has peace with God, and enjoys his in-fluences of the divine Comforter whose indwelling gives rest to the soul.

The jubilee year, according to our text, was called "the year of the Lord"; and the reason for all the four jubilee blessings was found in the Lord. First, the servants were set free because God said, "they are my servants, which I brought forth out of the land of Egypt" (Lev. 25:42). Ah, poor burdened soul, if thou believest in Christ thou shalt go free, for thou art the Lord's own—His chosen, His redeemed, and therefore He claims thee, and will suffer no other lord to have dominion over thee. The devil seeks to lay an embargo upon thee, and hold thee a slave, but Jesus saith, "Let go my captives, for I have redeemed them with my blood." Jesus claims you, O penitent souls; He cries to sin as once the Lord said to Pharaoh, "Thus saith the Lord, let my people go." Jesus says of each repenting soul, "Loose him and let him go, for he is mine. My Father gave him to me—he is my chosen, my beloved. Neither sin nor Satan, nor death nor hell, shall hold him, for he is mine."

The land also was set free for this same reason, for concerning it the Lord said, "The land is Mine" (Lev. 25:23). The freehold of the land was vested in Jehovah Him-self, consequently He ordained that no man should hold any portion of it by right of purchase beyond the fiftieth year, for the land was entailed and must go back to those for whom He had appointed it at the jubilee year. So the blessings of the everlasting covenant are God's and therefore He appoints them unto you poor be-lieving sinners, and you shall have them, for the divine decree shall not be frustrated. As surely as He appointed Christ to reign, and placed Him on the throne, so does He appoint you to reign with Him, and you shall sit upon His throne though all the devils in hell should say you nay.

So, too, the debts were all discharged, because on the day before the jubilee the great atonement had swept away all transgression and indebtedness towards God, and He would have His people forgive all the debts of their fellow men. All things are the Lord's and He exercised His crown rights on the day of jubilee so far as to declare all debts discharged. "The earth is the Lord's and the fullness thereof" was the motto of the jubilee, and sufficient reason for the canceling of obligations between man and man.

As for rest, that came also, because it was God's year, and was hallowed unto the Lord. "A jubilee shall the fiftieth year be unto you: ye shall not sow, neither reap that which groweth of itself in it, nor gather the grapes in it of thy vine undressed. For it is the jubilee; it shall be holy unto you: ye shall eat the increase thereof out of the field." During man's years the earth brings forth thorns and thistles, and man must earn his bread, with the sweat of his face; but when God's year comes then the wilder-ness and the solitary place are glad, and the desert rejoices and blossoms as the rose.

When the Lord's own kingdom cometh then shall the earth yield her increase as she has never done before. My beloved, I trust you know the blessedness of living in God's year, for you live by faith upon His providence, casting all your care upon Him, for He careth for you. This is the Sabbath of the soul, the counterpart of heaven. You behold the work of atonement fully accomplished on your behalf, and know yourselves to be delivered from all your liabilities to the law, and therefore your heart leaps within you. You are clean, delivered, set free, washed in the blood of the Lamb, and therefore do you come to Zion with songs and everlasting joy upon your heads.

But the text speaks also of the *"acceptable year of the LORD."* Now, our Lord Jesus Christ has come to proclaim to sinners the Lord's acceptance of guilty men through His great sacrifice. Apart from the work of our Lord Jesus, men as sinners are unacceptable to God. Some of you know the misery of being in that condition; it is horrible to feel that the Lord is weary of you and your vain oblations. Since you have come in your own name and righteousness, God has not accepted you, neither has He heard your prayers nor listened to your cries, nor had respect unto your religious observances, for He saith, "Yea, when ye make many prayers, I will not hear." If the Spirit of God has convinced you of your natural unacceptableness with God, you must have been brought into a very sad state indeed; for not to be accepted of God, and to be aware of it, is cause for intense sorrow. But now be sure, thou that believest in Jesus, that thou art accepted of God: notwithstanding thine infirmities and sins thou art "accepted in the Beloved," by Him who hath said, "I will accept you with your sweet savor." And now, being thus accepted as to your persons, your petitions shall come up with acceptance before the Lord. As for your prayers, God heareth them; as for your tears, He putteth them into His bottle; as for your works, He counteth them to be fruits of His Spirit and accepts them. Yea, now that thou art accepted in Christ, all that thou art and all that thou hast, and all thou dost—the whole of thee is acceptable to God through Jesus Christ our Lord.

Thrice happy am I to have to talk upon such a subject as this. Come ye who are willing now to believe in Jesus, this is the acceptable year of the Lord; God is reconciled, man is favored, blessings abound. Now is the accepted time, now is the day of salvation. Let sin be confessed and the confession shall be accepted, and you shall find forgiveness. Let transgression be repented of, the repentance shall be accepted, and you shall hear a voice saying, "Go and sin no more; thy sins, which are many, are forgiven thee." Hail! thou that art graciously accepted, blessed art thou among women! And thou too, my brother, remember the words of Solomon, "Go thy way, eat thy bread with joy, and drink thy wine with a merry heart; for God now accepteth thy works" (Eccl. 9:7). Come to Jesus by faith, for though you come with a limping walk, and your hearts and sorrowing spirits, come ye that are downcast and dare not look up, this is no common time, the Lord Jesus has made it a red letter year for you; for He proclaims a year of grace and acceptance. Behold in this *anno Domini*, or year of our Lord, we have a choice year of grace set apart for us. Who will not come to our gracious Prince, accept His mercy, and live?

Thus you see we get a double meaning from the text—the year of jubilee with all its accumulated privileges of free grace, and the year of acceptance in which whosoever will may come, and God will accept him if he cometh in the name of Jesus, trusting alone in the atoning blood.

II. May the Lord help us while we speak upon the second part of the text: the "day of vengeance of our God." Does not the sound of vengeance grate upon your ear? Does it not seem discordant to the sweet tenor of the passage? Vengeance! Shall that happen side by side with acceptance? Yes, beloved, this is the mystery of the gospel; the system of redemption marries justice and mercy; the method of surety-ship unites severity and grace; the economy of substitution blends acceptance and vengeance. This gospel mystery is to be published to every creature under heaven, for it is the power of God unto salvation to every one that believeth. We sweetly sang just now:

> Here I behold his innermost heart,
> Where grace and vengeance strangely join,
> Piercing his Son with sharpest smart,
> To make the purchased pleasure mine.

Now behold in this text you have the heart of God laid bare, for you have the year of acceptance coupled with the day of vengeance. Let us explain this strange commingling, and at the same time expound the text.

In the first place, whenever there is a day of mercy to those who believe, it is always a day of responsibility to those who reject it, and if they continue in that state *it is a day of increased wrath to unbelievers.* It is not possible for the gospel to be without some effect. If it be a savor of life unto life to those who receive it, it must of necessity from its own intrinsic vigor be a savor of death unto death to those who reject it. To this sword there are two edges—one will kill our fears, or the other will surely kill our pride and destroy our vain hopes if we yield not to Christ. You may, perhaps, have noticed that when our Lord read this passage at Nazareth, He stopped short, He did not read it all; He read as far down as, "to proclaim the acceptable year of the Lord," and then He closed the book and gave it to the minister and sat down. I suppose that at the commencement of His ministry, before He had been rejected by the nation, and before He had suffered for sin, He wisely chose to allude to the gentler topics rather than to those more stern and terrible ones; but He did not conclude His ministry without referring to the stern words which followed those which He had read. If you will turn to Luke's twenty-first chapter you will find Him saying in the twenty-first and twenty-second verses, "Then let them which are in Judea flee to the mountains; and let them which are in the midst of it depart out; and let not them that are in the countries enter thereinto. For these be the days of vengeance, that all things which are written may be fulfilled." You know the story of the siege of Jerusalem, the most harrowing of all narratives, for the anger of God was concentrated upon that wicked city beyond all precedent. It was because they rejected Christ that vengeance came upon them. They filled up the measure of their iniquity when at last they disowned their king and cried out, "Away with him, away with him, let him be crucified." Mark you then, dear hearer, that if you have heard the gospel and rejected it, you have incurred great guilt, and you can never sin so cheaply as you did before; for you there will be a day of vengeance above the men of Sodom and Gomorrha, because you have perpetrated a crime which they were not capable of committing—you have rejected the Christ of God. The year of acceptance to believers will be a day of vengeance to those who obey not His gospel.

Another meaning of the text comes out in the fact that *there is appointed a day of vengeance for all the enemies of Christ*, and this will happen in that bright future day for which we are looking. Not merely for rejecters of His gospel will there be vengeance, but for all men and fallen spirits who dare to oppose His sway. Behold He comes a second time; every winged hour hastens His advent, and when He comes it will be a great and a dreadful day to His foes. It will be to His saints the day of their revelation, manifestation, and acceptance, but to the ungodly "the day of vengeance of our God." "Enoch, the seventh from Adam, prophesied of these, saying, Behold, the Lord cometh with ten thousands of his saints, to execute judgment upon all, and to convince all that are ungodly among them of all their ungodly deeds which they have ungodly committed, and of all their hard speeches which ungodly sinners have spoken against him." Paul also bears witness the Lord Jesus shall be revealed from heaven with His mighty angels, "In flaming fire taking vengeance on them that know not God, and that obey not the gospel of our Lord Jesus Christ: who shall be punished with everlasting destruction from the presence of the Lord, and from the glory of his power; when he shall come to be glorified in his saints, and to be admired in all them that believe." Note the vengeance and the grace combined. The prophet Isaiah saw our great champion returning from his last fight, and thus spoke concerning him: "Who is this that cometh from Edom, with dyed garments from Bozrah? this that is glorious in his apparel, traveling in the greatness of his strength? I that speak in righteousness, mighty to save. Wherefore art thou red in thine apparel, and thy garments like him that treadeth in the wine vat? I have trodden the winepress alone; and of the people there was none with me: for I will tread them in mine anger, and trample them in my fury; and their blood shall be sprinkled upon my garments, and I will stain all my raiment. For the day of vengeance is in mine heart, and the year of my redeemed is come." Observe, again, the connection between the day of vengeance and the year of the redeemed. At the second advent Christ will come to be glorified in His saints, and they shall be manifested in the fullness of their acceptance, but it will be an overwhelming day of vengeance for all those who have hardened their hearts and continued in their sins. "Behold, the day cometh, that shall burn as an oven; and all the proud, yea, and all that do wickedly, shall be stubble: and the day that cometh shall burn them up, saith the Lord of hosts, that it shall leave them neither root nor branch."

However, I consider that the chief meaning of the text lies in this—that "*the day of vengeance of our God" was that day when He made all the transgressions of His people to meet upon the head of our great Surety.* Sin with many streams had been flowing down the hills of time and forming by their dread accumulation one vast and fathomless lake. Into this the sinner's substitute must be plunged. He had a baptism to be baptized with and He must endure it, or all His chosen must perish forever. That was a day of vengeance when all the waves and billows of divine wrath went over His innocent head.

> Came at length the dreadful night;
>   Vengeance with its iron rod
> Stood, and with collected might
>   Bruised the harmless Lamb of God.
> See, my soul, thy Savior see,
>   Prostrate in Gethsemane!

From His blessed person there distilled a bloody sweat, for His soul was exceedingly sorrowful even unto death. All through the night with scourgings and buffetings and spittings of cruel men, He was tortured and abused; He was rejected, despised, maltreated, and pierced in His inmost soul by man's scorn and cruelty. Then in the morning He was taken out to be crucified, for nothing could suffice short of His death. The outward sorrows of crucifixion ye know, but the inward griefs ye do not know, for what our Lord endured was beyond what any mortal man could have borne. The infinity of the Godhead aided the manhood, and I doubt not Hart was right in saying that He

> Bore all Incarnate God could bear
> With strength enough but none to spare.

It was an awful "day of vengeance of our God," for the voice cried aloud, "Awake, O sword, against my shepherd, against the man that is my fellow, saith the Lord of hosts." The doctrine that justice was executed upon our great Substitute is the most important that was ever propounded in the hearing of men; it is the sum and substance of the whole gospel, and I fear that the church which rejects it is no longer a church of Christ. Substitution is as much a standing or falling article in the church as the doctrine of justification by faith itself. My brethren and sisters, there would never have been an acceptable year if there had not been a day of vengeance. Be ye sure of this.

And now let us look at the instructive type by which this truth was taught to Israel of old. The year of jubilee began with the day of atonement. "Then shalt thou cause the trumpet of the jubilee to sound on the tenth day of the seventh month, in the day of atonement shall ye make the trumpet sound throughout all your land." What did the high priest do on that day? Read for yourselves the sixteenth chapter of Leviticus. On that day he washed himself and came forth before the people, not wearing his breastplate, nor his garments of glory and beauty, of blue and scarlet and fine linen; but the high priest wore the ordinary linen garments of a common priest. Even thus the Lord, who counted it not robbery to be equal with God, laid aside all His glory, and was found in fashion as a man. Then the priest took a bullock and, having offered it, went within the veil with the censer full of burning coals of fire, and sweet incense beaten small, with which he filled the inner court with perfumed smoke. After this he took the blood of the bullock and sprinkled it before the mercy-seat seven times. Thus our Lord entered within the veil with His own blood and with the sweet incense of His own merits, to make atonement for us. Of the two goats, one was killed as a sin-offering, and his blood was sprinkled within the veil, and the other was used for a scapegoat. Upon the head of the scapegoat Aaron laid both his hands, and confessed all the iniquities of the children of Israel, "putting them upon the head of the goat," which was then taken into the wilderness as the type of the carrying away of sin into oblivion. Do you not see your Lord and Master bearing your sin away? "As far as the east is from the west, so far that he removed our transgressions from us." Is there any wonder that a jubilee of peace should follow such a taking away of iniquity as our great High-priest has accomplished? Jesus is entered into the heavens for us, can we doubt of our acceptance with God?

The bodies of the beasts whose blood was brought into the sanctuary for sin on the day of atonement were not suffered to remain in the holy place, but were carried forth without the camp to be utterly consumed with fire, in token that sin is loathsome in the sight of God, and must be put away from His presence. Even thus did our Lord suffer without the gate and cry, "My God, my God, why hast thou forsaken me?" "Christ also hath once suffered for sins, the Just for the unjust, that He might bring us to God." All this was absolutely needful to a jubilee. Without atonement, no rejoicing. Before there can be acceptance for a single sinner, sin must be laid on Jesus and carried away. The blood of Jesus must be shed, and must be presented within the veil, for "without shedding of blood there is no remission of sin"; for no man living under heaven can there be pardon or acceptance with God in any way but by the bloody sacrifice which our Redeemer offered when He bowed His head and gave up the ghost on Calvary. This great truth we must never becloud, nor ever cease to publish so long as we have a tongue to move.

The day of vengeance then is intimately connected with the year of acceptance; and mark, beloved, *they must be so connected experimentally in the heart of all God's people by the teaching of the Holy Ghost,* for whenever Christ comes to make us live, the law comes first to kill us. There is no healing without previous wounding. Depend upon it, there never will be a sense of acceptance in any man until first he has had a sense of the just and righteous vengeance of God against his sin. Have you noticed that remarkable parallel to our text in the thirty-fifth chapter of Isaiah, where salvation and vengeance are so closely joined? There we read in the third verse and onward, "Strengthen ye the weak hands, and confirm the feeble knees. Say to them that are of a fearful heart, be strong, fear not: behold, your God will come with vengeance, even God with a recompense; he will come and save you. Then the eyes of the blind shall be opened, and the ears of the deaf shall be unstopped. Then shall the lame man leap as an hart, and the tongue of the dumb sing: for in the wilderness shall waters break out, and streams in the desert." O poor trembling convinced sinner, God has come with vengeance to you, but His intent is to save you. Every soul that is saved must feel that wrath is deserved and that the death punishment is due on account of sin, and when this is known and felt acceptance by faith will follow. There must be a death blow struck at all self-sufficiency and self-righteousness, and the man must be laid as dead at the feet of Christ before ever he will look up and find life and healing in the great atoning sacrifice. When our Lord puts on the helmet of salvation, He also girds about Him the garments of vengeance, and we must see Him in all His array. (See Is. 59:17). The day of vengeance is a needful companion to the year of acceptance; have they gone together in your experience?

III. I wish time would occasionally stay his rapid flight, or at least allow us to pluck a feather from his wing while we contemplate such a subject as this. But I must close with the third head, namely THE COMFORT FOR MOURNERS DERIVABLE FROM BOTH THESE THINGS. "*To comfort all that mourn.*"

Now, I have no hope of interesting, much less of doing any good to, any in this house of prayer who do not come under the description of mourners. The sower's duty is to sow the seed everywhere, but he knows within himself that it will take no root anywhere except where the plow has been first at work. If the Lord has made thee a mourner then the blessed subject of this morning will comfort thee; but the Lord never comforts those who do not want comfort. If you can save yourself, go and do it: if you are righteous, "he that is righteous let him be righteous still." I say it in sarcasm, as you perceive, for you cannot save yourself, nor are you righteous; but if you think so, go your way and try it—vainly try it, for surely when you have fanned your best works into a flame, and have walked by the light of the sparks of the fire which you have kindled, you shall have this at the Lord's hands—you shall lie down in sorrow and be astonished that you were ever so mad as to dream of self-salvation or of justification by your own works.

But oh, ye mourners, what joy is here, joy because this is the year of acceptance, and in the year of acceptance, or jubilee, men were set free and their lands were restored without money. No man ever paid a penny of redemption money on the jubilee morning: every man was free *simply because jubilee was proclaimed*: no merit was demanded, no demur was offered, no delay allowed, no dispute permitted. Jubilee came, and the bondman was free. And now, today, whosoever believeth in Jesus is saved, pardoned, freed, without money, without merit, without preparation, simply because he believeth, and God declareth that he that believeth is justified from all things from which he could not be justified by the law of Moses. Dost thou believe? Then art thou of the house of Israel, and thou hast God's warrant for it, thou art free. Rejoice in thy liberty! Surely this is sweet comfort for all that mourn. Look not for any marks and evidences, signs and tokens, look not for any merits or attainments, look not for any progress in grace or advancement in piety as a ground of salvation; listen only to the proclamation of the gospel, and accept the divine decree which ordains a jubilee. Art thou but of the chosen seed, dost thou believe in Jesus, then for thee it is an accepted year. Come, bring hither thy griefs and sorrows, and leave them at the cross, for the Lord accepts thee, and who shall say thee nay?

An equal joy-note however rings out from the other sentence concerning the day of vengeance. If the day of vengeance took place when our Lord died, then it is over. The day of vengeance was past and gone eighteen hundred years ago and more.

> Now no more His wrath we dread,
> Vengeance smote our Surety's head;
> Legal claims are fully met,
> Jesus paid the dreadful debt.

My heart, dost thou bleed for sin and mourn because of it? Be it so; but it has ceased to be, for Christ made an end of it when He took it up to His cross and bore it there in His own body on the tree. O believer, art thou bowed down and troubled on account of past sin? It is right thou shouldst repent, but still remember thy past sin exists no more, the pen is drawn through it and it is canceled, for the day of vengeance is over. God will not twice take vengeance for the same sin. Either the atonement which Jesus offered was enough, or it was not; if it was not, then woe be to us, for we shall die; but if it was sufficient—if "It is finished" was not a lie but a truth, then He hath "finished transgression and made an end of sin." The sin of the believer is annihilated and abolished, and can never be laid to his charge. Let us rejoice that the day of vengeance is over, and the year of acceptance has begun.

In another sense, however, it may be that some are mourning because of the temptations of Satan. Here, too, they may be comforted, for Jesus has come to take vengeance on the evil one, and the God of peace shall bruise Satan under your feet shortly. Are you afraid of death? Behold Christ has taken revenge on death, for He bids you cry, because of His resurrection, "O death, where is thy sting? O grave, where is thy victory?"

Are we mourning today because our dear ones are not converted? It is a good thing to mourn on that account, but let us take comfort, for this is an acceptable year; let us pray for them, and the Lord will save them. Are we mourning because sin is rampant in the wide world? Let us rejoice, for our Lord has broken the dragon's head, and the day of vengeance must come when the Lord will overthrow the powers of darkness. Have we been looking with mournful spirit upon old Rome, and the Mohammedan imposture, and the power of Buddhism and Brahminism and other the sway of ancient idolatries? Let us be glad. Behold the Avenger cometh! He comes a second time, and comes conquering and to conquer. Then shall the day of His vengeance be in His heart, and the year of His redeemed shall come. From the seven hills the deceiver shall be torn, no more to curse the sons of men with his pretensions to be the vicar of God. In blackest night shall set forever the crescent of Mohammed, which already wanes; its baleful light shall no more afflict unhappy nations. Then shall fall the gods of the Hindus and the Chinese, broken like potters' vessels by the rod of iron which Jesus wields. At His appearing the whole earth shall acknowledge that He who was "despised and rejected of men" is "King of kings and Lord of lords." Behold, the day cometh on apace, let all that mourn be comforted. The day of vengeance, the full year of the millennial glory, the day of the overthrow of error, the year of the acceptance of creation in all her former beauty, the age when God shall be all in all, is near at hand. Hasten it, O Lord. Amen.

III. PROPHETICAL

FOOTSTEPS OF MERCY

SERMON NO. 905

If there be a messenger with him, an interpreter, one among a thousand, to show unto man his uprightness: then he is gracious unto him, and saith, Deliver him from going down to the pit: I have found a ransom—Job 33:23, 24.

WHEN God has distinct and definite purposes of mercy towards an individual, he often begins with stern discipline, and brings him low by affliction and sorrow. As the good husbandman cuts down the trees and makes a clearance of the soil before he sows the grain and prepares for a harvest, so does our God cut down all our goodly cedars, our pleasures, and our pride, in order that the heart may be afterwards plowed, broken, harrowed, and made ready to receive the good seed of the Word. Elihu describes this preparatory breaking-up process as being brought about by sickness. It is often so: I doubt not, that a sickbed is one of God's best orators to the sons of men. But God is by no means restricted to any uniform method; nor is the experience of the redeemed precisely similar in its details, though notwithstanding all its diversities, it leads to one and the same result. Sometimes a storm at sea has brought men to their senses, and aroused their conscience, and so they have cried to the Lord in their trouble. At other times, serious losses in business have brought men into such distress of mind, that they have been driven to seek riches more enduring than silver and gold; a competence more to be relied on than the profits of trade or the stability of banks; and comfort more genuine and lasting than wealth, though it be the accumulation of years, can afford. Yea, and without either of these, the Holy Ghost has not infrequently been pleased to convince men of their sin, and reduce them to utter self-despondency and abject self-abhorrence. This He has effected in such a way as neither sickness nor poverty could have done of themselves. He has brought the man very low, even to the gates of hell. In his own apprehension the man has been lost, and then it is that mercy has commenced her work, her blessed work that shall open to him the gates of righteousness, and bring the soul up to heaven itself.

Now, I hope there are some here present whom God has been preparing for His grace—to such there will be good tidings in the sermon. I shall not delay you, but proceed at once to deal with the text in the natural order it suggests, as the welcome facts are marshaled before us. Does it not tell of *a messenger—a message—a gracious disposition—a great deliverance—and an amazing ransom*?

I. When God has thus, in the way of providence, prepared any human heart for a work of grace, one of the first means of blessing the chosen man is TO SEND HIM A MESSENGER.

I suppose the passage before us may be primarily referred to Christian ministers, who become, through God the Holy Ghost, interpreters to men's souls. They should be men of a thousand, well taught; they should have high moral and spiritual qualifications; in fact, they should be the pick and cull of mankind. When God sends a faithful gospel-messenger to a man, it is a sign of great love to that man's soul. I ask no honor for ministers as men, but this I do ask, that when they preach to you the gospel of Jesus Christ, they shall be accepted as God's messengers, and that their message at least shall be treated with the respect which God's word demands.

But I prefer to believe, with many expositors, that the full meaning of these words will never be found in ministers of mortal race; we must rather refer it to the Great Messenger of the covenant, the Great Interpreter between God and man, whose presence to the sin-sick soul is a sure prophecy of mercy. Where God the Father sends His beloved Son to a man, where Christ comes to the man's conscience and talks with him, showing the credentials of a Savior, and constraining the faith of the sinner, there it is that salvation is obviously intended by the Lord, and will be effectually perfected in that man unto everlasting life. With this view I proceed, regarding our Lord Jesus Christ as the herald of mercy. Mark well the titles, a messenger, an interpreter, one among a thousand. Is there any other than Jesus to whom they so fitly belong? Let us contemplate Him as a messenger. That is just what Jesus Christ is. Now, a messenger cometh not in his own name, he must be sent, and it is a great comfort to know that Jesus Christ did not come to save men merely on His own account, but He came commissioned by the Father, He was sent of God. God has appointed Christ to be the Savior. Those who accept Christ, and trust in Him, accept the very Person God Himself has ordained. Christ is no amateur Savior, who comes without a commission. In His Hands He bears the royal stamp of the divine authority. O trembling sinner, trust Him whom God has trusted. Lay hold of Him whom God has appointed.

Another description that belongs to Him, as I believe, is an interpreter. Jesus Christ is indeed a blessed interpreter. An interpreter must understand two languages. Our Lord Jesus understands the language of God. Whatever are the great truths of divine intelligence and infinite wisdom, too high and mysterious for us to comprehend or even to discern, Christ fully understands them all. He knows how to speak with God as the fellow of God, coequal and coeternal with Him. His prayers are in God's language. He speaks to God's heart. He can make out the sighs, and cries, and tears of a poor sinner, and He can take up the meaning, and interpret them all to God. He understands the divine language, and thus He can communicate with God. Moreover, Jesus understands our language, for He is a man like ourselves, touched with a feeling of our infirmities, and smarting under our sicknesses. He can read whatever is in the heart of man, and so He can tell to God the language of man, and speak to man in the language of man what God would say to him. How happy we ought to be that there is so blessed a Daysman to put His hand upon us both, that He can be equal with God, and yet can be brother with poor simple men! The best of it is that our Lord is such an interpreter that He can not only interpret to the ear but also to the heart, and this is a great point. I, perhaps, might be enabled to interpret a Scripture to your ears, but, O beloved, when you have heard the letter you may miss the right, heavenly, and spiritual meaning. But our Lord can bring the Word home to your soul. He can tell you of God's mercy, not in words only, but with a sweet sense of mercy shed abroad in your heart. He can make the sinner feel the way of salvation, as well as know it; He can make him rejoice in it as well as listen to it; He can lead him to accept it as well as to understand it. Oh, blessed Interpreter! Mighty with God, so that the heart of God is affected with the woes and griefs of men; mighty with men so that the great love of God, which is an ocean without a bottom or a shore, is made intelligible to us, and even our poor stony hearts are softened, and the adamant is made to run like wax, while the divine Interpreter talks to our inmost souls.

This messenger, then, this interpreter, is He not *"one among a thousand"*? O peerless Jesus! who among the sons of the mighty can be compared with Thee? Elihu may well be supposed to use a definite number when an indefinite is intended. What is one of a thousand, or one of ten thousand, when surely there is never the like of Christ between heaven and hell? All the range of the universe cannot find His equal, His equal as a Savior, as a Messenger, as an Interpreter. Oh! but those who know Him will tell you that no words can ever set forth His worth. Disciples of Jesus who have followed Him and held communion with Him for the space of 20 years and more, will tell you that His preciousness grows upon them by acquaintance. Whereas they thought Him sweet at first, they think Him sweetest and best of all now, the loveliest of all the lovely, the fairest of all the fair, the chief among ten thousand, yea, and altogether lovely. I tell you that if there were a thousand saviors, I would have none but Christ. If the gods of the heathen, and the saints of the papists could help them, if the ceremonies of our modern papists could deliver their souls instead of enthralling them, yet would we repudiate them, we would have nothing to do with them in whole or in part; but we would still cling to Him who is the one Mediator between God and men, for He is the chief among ten thousand to our souls. He is such a Savior that there is no other can vie with Him: all rivalry must prove abortive, seeing that other foundation can no man lay. He is the door of heaven, all the rest is hard wall, and there is no passing through—a light from God, and all other lights are darkness—very God come down to us in our flesh to save us, and where shall you find the match of this? O cherubim and seraphim, what Savior could ye devise that should emulate the only-begotten Son of God? O ye angels, fairest among the goodly throng that salute Jehovah day and night with your ceaseless music, whom will ye laud and magnify but Jesus in your jubilant, worshipful songs? As ye survey the glorious company of the apostles, the noble army of the martyrs, and the radiant fellowship of the church redeemed, will ye chant any other name? Is He not in your esteem the chief among a thousand, the sole inheritor of all blessing and praise? Accept Him, sinner; receive Him joyfully into thy spirit, for such a one will never woo thee as this precious One, the chosen of God. Who, save Jesus, then, should be chosen and precious to thy soul?

It is a great sign of mercy whenever Christ comes to any sinner. But how, say you, can He come to a sinner? I will tell you. He has come to you now, to every one of you. Jesus comes in the preaching of the gospel. There is never a gospel sermon preached but it is, in fact, Jesus coming with open arms of love to receive the sinner. He comes to you in these Bibles and New Testaments of yours. Every one of those volumes that lies in your house is a standing token of Christ's mission, whispering to him that hath ears to hear that He is still ready to receive the sinner. And I trust He comes to some of you now, in the motions of the Holy Ghost upon your heart, saying to you, "Close in with Him; reject Him no longer, bow down thine ear and listen to Him, lift up thine eyes and look to Him," concerning whom we sang so truly just now:—

> There is life for a look at the Crucified One,
> There is life at this moment for thee.

This is the first stage.

II. Now, secondly, wherever this divine messenger comes, according to the text, HE REVEALS GOD'S UPRIGHTNESS.

A lesson, let me assure you, of deep interest and paramount importance; the occasion on which it is taught is peculiarly impressive. You remember Elihu has been describing a man greatly afflicted, chastened with pain, wasted with disease, reduced to a skeleton, and brought nigh to death. We have shown you that before the Lord Jesus Christ comes in mercy to deal with a soul, such tribulation is dealt out by God to break up the fallow ground of the heart. No marvel that the sufferer is appalled with tokens of judgment. What message, then, can the divine messenger bring more suitable or more refreshing than that which reveals to man the uprightness of God in having afflicted him? You think, perhaps, that God has been very hard with you. In your distraction you say, "How long I have been ill! How long I have been out of work! How long my wife has been afflicted! How many of my dear children have died! What strokes God has laid upon me without intermission!" Now shall new views spring up, and comfortable thoughts arise. But who shall bridge the interval? When Christ comes to you as an interpreter He will make you discern the wisdom, and the love, and cause you to feel the pity and the tenderness of Him, who as a father rebukes you, not in anger but in His dear covenant love. Instead of kicking against the pricks, you will say, "Ah! Lord, it is of thy mercy I am not consumed; I can see there is a hand of love in this; God would not let me go on in sin, and wander into endless woe; He is blocking up my road, He is putting massive chains across the broad way to stop me; He is digging pits in my path that I may come to a pause, and so I will turn back from this." Depend upon it, there is nothing more dreadful in the conclusion than a life that is happy in the commission of sin. If you have prosperity, and all that heart can wish, while pursuing an evil course, tremble, for it is likely enough that God will give you up; you are having your portion in this life. O ye unconverted! Are any of you tried and troubled, vexed and disquieted? While I am sorry for your troubles, I hope God has designs of love towards you; if you look to Christ He will explain to you the heavenly moral of these earthly trials, and show you the uprightness of God in dealing thus severely with His rebellious child.

Further than this, the gospel of Christ explains to the sinner the uprightness of God in the doom of the impenitent, *even if He send him down to hell.* Oh! A man may find fault with hell, and say, "Will God consign men to the devouring fire? Will He destroy their souls? Will He damn men for their offenses?" but if once the Great Interpreter comes to you, you will wonder, not that God should destroy men for sin, but that He has not destroyed you long ago. Oh! I could have argued with a bold front against eternal punishment till I knew what sin meant, and then I gave in at once, and I wish that some of my brethren who seem to speak dubiously about the wrath of God, could feel, as some of us have felt, the horror of great darkness that sin brings across a soul when it is made to feel the righteous ire that encompasses and impends it; there is no caviling then, the only cry is, "O my God, deliver me, for I deserve all thy wrath can bring upon me, and if Thou shouldst smite me to destruction Thou wilt be justified when Thou judgest, and clear when Thou condemnest." Mark you, it is a blessed thing when Christ brings a sinner to plead guilty, when he is quite willing to plead guilty, and when, instead of railing at the justice of the sentence, he stands dumb with silence, feeling that God is upright, and would not be upright even if He did not thus condemn. There is hope, there is more than hope, there is confidence in our heart towards any sinner who is convinced of the uprightness of God in his present affliction or in any other that God may please to send upon him, either in this life or in the life to come. Ah! but this is learning to some profit for a man to see the uprightness of God in everything, and then by contrast to bewail his own ignorance and foolishness. Mercy is surely come to you when you can think of God's holiness with reverence, and upbraid yourself with bitter reproach for what an unholy creature you have been. It is a rough wind, that north wind, but, O my brethren, what a healthy wind it is! It sweeps away the fevers of our pride, and drives away the mists of our self-righteousness. Self-righteous, indeed! Such wretches as we are, such offenders against God and truth as we have been, for us to talk of goodness when we are altogether vile, for us to boast of something hopeful in us when the whole head is sick, and the whole heart faint—this is sheer insanity. When the blessed Interpreter comes and deals graciously with the spirit, we confess that God is upright, but as for ourselves we have gone astray like lost sheep; we have done the things which we ought not to have done, we have left undone the things which we ought to have done, and there is no health in us. Oh, those visions of God, how humiliating they are! So Job himself made confession, "I have heard of thee by the hearing of thee: but now mine eye seeth thee. Wherefore I abhor myself, and repent in dust and ashes." This supplies us with the second stage in the experience of divine mercy—Christ is recognized, the uprightness of God is revealed and understood.

III. The third stage is this—"THEN HE IS GRACIOUS UNTO HIM."

God deals with convinced sinners in a way of grace. Every word here is weighty. "Then He is gracious unto him." *Mark the time—then!* God is gracious to a man *when*, Christ having come to him as a Messenger and an Interpreter, he is led to discern his own sin and God's uprightness. When he is humble, then God shows Himself to be gracious. No debts are pronounced forgiven by the Great Master of all till they are owned, and no release from the pains of bankruptcy are granted until we feel that we have naught with which to pay. When a soul pleads total insolvency and is truly penniless, then there is free forgiveness. When men admit the justice of God if He should punish them, *then*, not till then, mercy comes in and the punishment is put away. It is not consistent with the holiness of God to pardon a sinner while he denies his guilt, or invents excuses to palliate his crimes; nor is it reasonable for a sinner to expect remission while he vaunts his self-righteousness. How shall the hardness of a man's heart move the compassion of his Judge? Come, poor soul, fall on thy knees, confess that God is upright, and then He will be gracious to thee.

The *way* as well as the time demands your notice. It is through the Messenger that God is gracious. *Then*—that is when the Messenger comes. When Jesus interposes then God is gracious. You shall never taste of grace except out of the golden cup of Christ's atonement. It is into that golden cup that God has poured the infinity of His grace. Drink of it, sinner, by simply trusting in Christ. Drink of it in any other way thou never canst. Narrowly observe what the text says, "Then *he is gracious* unto him." All salvation comes by way of grace. The word "grace" as used by us in its Latin form explains its own meaning. We speak of "gratis"—a thing free from cost; like the prescription of a physician if given without fee; or the medicine supplied at the dispensary without charge. All God's mercy to a sinner is gratis. He never sells, He always gives. He asks no payment. He acts from no motives raised or suggested by anything in us, but because He will have mercy on whom He will have mercy, and He will have compassion on whom He will have compassion. Dear heart, it is a blessing for thee when thou canst see that nothing but Christ can serve thy turn, when thou hast done with appealing to justice, and all thy knocks are at mercy's door. O sinner, you cannot be saved except by grace in the beginning, grace in the middle, and grace in the end. What but grace can pardon sins such as yours and mine? What but grace could take such as we are and make us God's children? What but grace could snatch us from hell, and lift us up to heaven? When the man is humbled, and Christ is revealed to him, then it is that God deals graciously with the man, and then it is that he knows he has found grace in the eyes of the Lord. And I like the thought, that it does not say God ever leaves off being gracious to that man. Where we do not read that God ceases, we may believe that He continues. Does He once deal graciously with a sinner? He will always be gracious to that sinner. Never will He change. That sinner once blessed, shall be blessed through life, and blessed in death, and blessed in eternity, through the sovereign, overflowing, immutable grace which is in Jesus Christ our Lord.

Well, we have come a long way. We have found the sinner sick and near to die; the interpreter has come; he has shown him the uprightness of God and given him an assurance of God's gracious disposition—now the sinner knows that Christ alone can save him.

IV. Let us proceed to the next stage—GOD DELIVERS THE SINNER. "He saith, Deliver him from going down into the pit." What shall we understand by this? Does it refer to "*the grave*" which is dug like a pit? Well, such an interpretation may harmonize with Elihu's discourse as he describes the man whose soul draweth near to the grave and his life to the destroyers; but when delivered from going down into the pit, his flesh shall be fresher than a child's, he shall return to the days of his youth. So when the psalmist celebrates the lovingkindness of the Lord—"O Lord, thou has brought up my soul from the grave; thou hast kept me that I should not go down into the pit." What more shall we understand by the pit from which the soul is delivered? The pit is often used in Scripture as the emblem of great distress and misery. Captives in the East were frequently shut up in pits all night. So Isaiah says, "They shall be gathered together as prisoners are gathered in the pit, and shall be shut up in the prison" (Is. 24:22). And again in another place, "The captive exile hasteneth that he may be loosed, and that he should not die in the pit, nor that his bread should fail" (Is. 51:14). There is a bondage of soul, which involves depression of spirits, and failing of heart that may well be likened to confinement in a pit from which there appears no way of escape. But may we not understand still more by the pit? Alas! Then, dear friends, we sometimes read of the pit, when the word is pregnant with deeper meaning, even of the pit that is bottomless, that place of torment prepared for devils and lost souls. Oh, if there were time, what a picture we have before us! The pit, the bottomless pit—an awful representation, a horrible vision of the future wrath of God! The pit, black, dark, descending, down which the soul slips and slides, and falls headlong! Going down into the pit—what a dreadful expression! Not going down as miners do to seek for ore, but being hurled by the strong hand of the avenging angel downwards into the abyss! There on the verge of the precipice you are; though not falling down that abyss yet, your feet have almost gone, your steps have well nigh slipped. At such a crisis the mercy of God comes to the sinner's aid, and cries in thrilling tones, "Deliver him!" It is not a mere shout of warning, it is a voice that hath power in it, it is the clear silvery note of rescue, and the man is delivered just as he is about to sink to rise no more. Kings and emperors, when they have condemned men to die, can exercise the prerogative of mercy. Let the royal mandate issue concerning a prisoner, "Deliver him," for the prison doors are opened, for the king's pardon has been given. Just such a thing doth God with condemned sinners, when they bow down before Him and confess the righteousness of the sentence. Through Jesus Christ, the heavenly Messenger, He saith, "Deliver him! Deliver him!" There is a legal pardon. The man is set free from the bonds of the jailer, instead of being given over to the hands of the executioner. Henceforth he shall live in peace and joy. "Deliver him!" Perhaps the three significations of the pit I have alluded to may be combined in one dark picture. Sickness brings the sinner to the immediate prospect, not of death only, but of his endless doom. The sorrows and remorse of his soul produce, as it were, a foretaste of that anguish which knows no abatement. And anon! Hell doth yawn at his feet "a universe of death"—"worse than fables yet have feigned, or fear conceived."

How many witnesses we might call to speak to the truth of all this! Why, Elihu said, "Lo, all these things worketh God oftentimes with man." The anguish is real, and the joy of rescue is real likewise. Did not Hezekiah feel them both? The message came to him, "Thus saith the Lord, set thine house in order, for thou shalt die and not live." Then he prayed vehemently, and he wept sore. Afterwards the Word of the Lord came to him that his prayer was heard, that his tears were seen, and that his life should be spared. And this is what he said: "Behold, for peace I had great bitterness; but thou hast in love to my soul *delivered it from the pit of corruption*; for thou hast cast all my sins behind thy back." What a shout of joy is that of David when he says, "He brought me up out of a horrible pit, out of the miry clay, and set my feet upon a rock, and established my goings!" In like manner Jonah speaks, "Thou hast brought up my life from the pit, O Lord my God." Very memorable too is the sweet promise of God to the daughter of Zion, by the mouth of the prophet Zechariah, "As for thee also, by the blood of thy covenant I have sent forth thy prisoners out of the pit wherein is no water." Yes, my dear friends, and I feel bound to say for myself, to the praise of my God—

> Thy love was great, thy mercy free,
> Which from the pit delivered me.

Well do I remember when the sentence went forth to my soul, "Deliver him!" The time did indeed seem long first. I was years and years upon the brink of hell—I mean in my own feeling. I was unhappy, I was desponding, I was despairing. I dreamed of hell, my life was full of sorrow and wretchedness, believing that I was lost. But oh! The blessed gospel of the God of grace came to me at length with that soft voice, "Look unto Me, and be ye saved, all ye ends of the earth!" With it came a sovereign word, "Deliver him!" and I who was but a minute before as wretched as a soul could be, could have danced for merriment of heart, and as the snow fell on my road home from the little house of prayer I thought every snowflake talked with me, and told of the pardon I had found; for I was white as the driven snow through the grace of God. Oh! That word, "Deliver him!" It so restrains the temptations of Satan, and quells the strivings of conscience, that the poor soul has instantaneous liberty, and rejoices with joy unspeakable. Mark you, my dear friend, if ever you should look to Christ by simple faith, and God should say, "Deliver him"; that "Deliver him" will last you forever. God does not play fast and loose with sinners. If He pardons today He will not condemn tomorrow. He does not loose and then bind again. He openeth, and no man shutteth. Once He says, "Deliver him," you may walk through all the earth, and who shall lay anything to your charge: for who is he that can arrest you and cast you into prison against this, "Deliver him!"? There may have come into this place some great offender. It is impossible for me to discriminate among you, or single out any one of these thousands, but there may be here some one of the very blackest class of sinners. To you Christ's gospel has come. I hope you have been led to feel that you are guilty, to confess your sins, and to own that you can only be saved through God's grace and mercy. Well now, if you will but trust my Savior, the Lord Jesus who once died on Calvary's cross, and now lives enthroned in glory; if you will but trust Him now, the sentence shall come from the throne, "Deliver him," or "Deliver her, from going down into the pit." Oh! There have been many outcasts in these very aisles, who have found grace and obtained remission of their sins. The harlot has heard the word, "Deliver her from going down into the pit." The thief and the drunkard too, though in their own conscience on the very brink of hell, and all but sliding in, have heard it, and they are here among the happy worshipers that praise God. Some of us who never fell into those fouler vices, though depraved in our hearts as they, have heard that blessed sound, and we are here to express our soul's desire that you all knew it. O that you all trusted Christ. O that you were all saved by that blessed mandate, "Deliver him from going down into the pit."

V. The last thing is that GOD EXPLAINS TO THE SINNER WHOM HE DELIVERS THE REASON OF HIS DELIVERANCE. "Deliver him from going down in the pit; I have found a ransom."

"I have found a ransom"—a covering. Catch the thought. There are your sins like a fetid slough, reeking with corruption, they are black; like a huge pool of blood, they are scarlet. It is abhorrent to the pure eyes of God to look upon the heart that is a very reservoir of pollution. He must smite you if He look at it. Listen—"I have found a covering." Christ comes in and covers it all. "Blessed is that man whose transgression is forgiven, whose sin is covered." As the mercy-seat covered the law, and was called a covering, so does the atonement of Christ cover the perfect law of God, and it puts out of God's sight every sin of all those who trust in Christ.

But take the word as we get it in the English version—a ransom, that means a price. When a man was in debt, he used to be, according to the old law, put into prison. Well, how did he get his discharge? He came out if the debt was paid, of course, at once. So God saith, "Deliver him; I have found a price, I have found a recompense, I have found a substitute, I have found a ransom." The Lord Jesus Christ has suffered for us what God's wrath demanded of us.

> He bore that we might never bear,
> His Father's righteous ire.

Christ stood in our stead that we might go free. I have told you this grand old tale so many times in this house, that sometimes as I am coming here I think to myself—

"I can find no new metaphor to illustrate it, and no new words to rouse the languid attention; they will tell me that I am always harping on the same string." Still, still, I must continue to expound and enforce this substitutionary suffering of Christ. I cannot help it. It is as much as my soul is worth to keep it back, for I am persuaded that it is the very essence of the gospel—the vicarious sufferings of Christ. At any rate, I have no gospel to preach to you but this, that God has punished Christ instead of you that will believe on Christ, and therefore He cannot punish you; you are clear. Christ has paid your debts; the receipt is given; you are liberated. God has no claims upon you from His justice now; they are all discharged. Christ has discharged all your liabilities. "By Him all that believe are justified from all things, from which ye could not be justified by the law of Moses."

Never listen, I entreat you, my dear hearers, to the derisive sneer of the scorner, as he attempts to cast discredit upon the righteousness of God in the imputation of our sins to the great Redeemer. I know that it is not in the power of skeptic, rationalist, socinian, or infidel to bring forth one argument that can refute the plain testimony which abounds in the Scriptures. But they can and they do ask if our moral sense of rectitude is not shocked at inflicting punishment on the innocent, and bestowing rewards as well as pardon on the guilty. Do they object to you that it were unjust on the part of God to make one man suffer personally for another man's sin? Tell them, if they better understood the doctrine, they would see that instead of outraging the morality of men, it manifests the righteousness of God. Tell them, as one of our most famous Puritans did, that the Redeemer and redeemed have such an intimate relation, that what one doeth or suffereth, the other may be accounted to do or suffer; it is no unrighteousness, if the hand offend for the head to be smitten; Christ is our head, and we are His members. Tell them that He who suffered, the Just for the unjust, had power to lay down His life and power to take it again: His submission therefore was voluntary. Tell them that He who His own self bore our sins in His own body on the tree, agreed and stipulated to bear our iniquities; the whole matter was settled in covenant between the Father and the Son. Tell them once more that our Lord Jesus Christ counted the cost and estimated the recompense, when He for the joy that was set before Him endured the cross; he shall see of the travail of His soul and shall be satisfied; with honor and glory shall he be crowned. Because He humbled Himself, therefore God also hath highly exalted Him: and because He made Himself of no reputation, to Him is given a name which is above every name. Tell them His mediatorial glory surpasseth thought. Bid them cease their pitiless clamor and leave us to our joys. It is the sweetest music out of heaven, and it is the source of the music of heaven. "I have found a ransom." Christ's ransom for enslaved sinners is the world's good news. Tell it, then, and as you hear it, let your hearts rejoice.

You notice these words, "I have found a ransom." You do not find it for yourselves. You could not ever have discovered it, much less have brought it into the world. But God found it out. The infinite wisdom of God was needed to find out the way of salvation by a substitute. "I have found a ransom." Now, since God has found it, and God is satisfied with it, let me, chief of sinners though I be, find rest in this divine satisfaction. Conscience says to me, "Well, but how can your sins be forgiven?" Again conscience thunders, "Recollect such a day, such a night, such an act, such a blasphemy. Dost thou think Christ can wash such a devil as thou art?" I answer, "Well, if God is satisfied, I am sure I will be." If you owe a debt, and your creditor takes the money of another, and he is quite easy about it, wist, man, do not you be uneasy about it; if he is satisfied you may be, and if God is content with Christ, so, poor sinner, let you and I be satisfied, and let us begin to sing—

> I will praise thee every day!
> Now thine anger's turn'd away,
> Comfortable thoughts arise
> From the bleeding sacrifice.
> Jesus is become at length
> My salvation and my strength
> And his praises shall prolong
> While I live, my pleasant song.

O bless the dear name of Him who suffered in your stead. O take His ransom-price; look at it; turn over every sacred drop of it in your memory and your gratitude. Be satisfied, and more than satisfied; rejoice and be exceeding glad to be delivered from going down into the pit. God has found an all-sufficient and a most blessed ransom for your souls, and therefore you are delivered.

What more can I say of you, my dear hearers? I have told you the way of mercy, and I have described to you the footsteps of mercy in the experience of those who have proved its saving efficacy; but I cannot bring Christ to your souls, or when Christ comes nigh unto you, as He doth now in the ministry of His gospel, I cannot make you open the doors of your hearts to receive Him. O ye who do not believe and are yet in your sins, what more can I do for you than thus to cry aloud in your ears, and proclaim to you the path of life? This one thing I can do: I can stand here and break my heart to think that you refuse Him. But no; I cannot take leave of you thus. I must again beseech, and entreat, and implore you as you love your souls, turn not away from the divine Messenger, from Jesus Christ the Friend of sinners. He asks no great thing of you; He bids you not pass through ceremonies that will take you days and months, but now, one believing glance at yonder cross, one glance at Him who died there for sinners, and it is done. Christ is honored; God is satisfied; you are saved. Go your way and tell your friends what great things He has done for you, and God bless you. Amen.

I KNOW THAT MY REDEEMER LIVETH

SERMON NO. 504
DELIVERED ON LORD'S DAY MORNING, APRIL 12, 1863.

*For I know that my redeemer liveth, and that he shall stand at the latter day upon the earth: and though after my skin worms destroy this body, yet in my flesh shall I see God: whom I shall see for myself, and mine eyes shall behold, and not another; though my reins be consumed within me—*Job 19:25–27.

THE hand of God has been upon us heavily this week. An aged deacon, who has been for more than 50 years a member of this church, has been removed from our midst; and a sister, the beloved wife of another of our church officers, a member for nearly the same term of years, has fallen asleep. It is not often that a church is called to sorrow over the departure of two such venerable members—let not our ears be deaf to such a double admonition to prepare to meet our God. That they were preserved so long, and upheld so mercifully for so many years, was not only a reason of gratitude to them, but to us also. I am, however, so averse to the preaching of what are called funeral sermons, that I forbear, lest I appear to eulogize the creature, when my only aim should be to magnify the grace of God.

Our text deserves our profound attention; its preface would hardly have been written had not the matter been of the utmost importance in the judgment of the patriarch who uttered it. Listen to Job's remarkable desire: "Oh that my words were now written! Oh that they were printed in a book! That they were graven with an iron pen and lead in the rock forever!" Perhaps, hardly aware of the full meaning of the words he was uttering, yet his holy soul was impressed with a sense of some weighty revelation concealed within his words; he therefore desired that it might be recorded in a book; he has had his desire—the Book of books embalms the words of Job. He wished to have them graven on a rock; cut deep into it with an iron pen, and then the lines inlaid with lead; or he would have them engraven, according to the custom of the ancients, upon a sheet of metal, so that time might not be able to eat out the inscription. He has not had his desire in that respect, save only that upon many and many a sepulcher those words of Job stand recorded, "I know that my redeemer liveth." It is the opinion of some commentators that Job, in speaking of the rock here, intended his own rock-hewn sepulcher, and desired that this might be his epitaph; that it might be cut deep, so that ages should not wear it out; that when any asked, "Where does Job sleep?" as soon as they saw the sepulcher of the patriarch of Uz, they might learn that he died in hope of resurrection, resting upon a living Redeemer. Whether such a sentence adorned the portals of Job's last sleeping-place we know not; but certainly no words could have been more fitly chosen. Should not the man of patience, the mirror of endurance, the pattern of trust, bear as his memorial this golden line, which is as full of all the patience of hope, and hope of patience, as mortal language can be? Who among us could select a more glorious motto for his last escutcheon? I am sorry to say that few of those who have written upon this passage cannot see Christ or the resurrection in it at all. Albert Barnes, among the rest, expresses his intense sorrow that he cannot find the resurrection here, and for my part I am sorry for him. If it had been Job's desire to foretell the advent of Christ and his own sure resurrection, I cannot see what better words he could have used; and if those truths are not here taught, then language must have lost its original object, and must have been employed to mystify and not to explain; to conceal and not to reveal. What I ask, does the patriarch mean, if not that he shall rise again when the Redeemer stands upon the earth? Brethren, no unsophisticated mind can fail to find here what almost all believers have here discovered. I feel safe in keeping to the old sense, and we shall this morning seek no new interpretation, but adhere to the common one, with or without the consent of our critics.

In discoursing upon them I shall speak upon three things. First, *let us, with the patriarch, descend into the grave and behold the ravages of death.* Then, with him, *let us look up on high for present consolation.* And, still, in his admirable company, let us, in the third place, *anticipate future delights.*

I. First of all then, with the patriarch of Uz, LET US DESCEND INTO THE SEPULCHER.

The body has just been divorced from the soul. Friends who loved most tenderly have said—"Bury my dead out of my sight." The body is borne upon the bier and consigned to the silent earth; it is surrounded by the earthworks of death. Death has a host of troops. If the locusts and the caterpillars be God's army, the worms are the army of death. These hungry warriors begin to attack the city of man. They commence with the outworks; they storm the munition, and overturn the walls. The skin, the city wall of manhood, is utterly broken down, and the towers of its glory covered with confusion. How speedily the cruel invaders deface all beauty. The face gathers blackness; the countenance is defiled with corruption. Those cheeks once fair with youth, and ruddy with health, have fallen in, even as a bowing wall and a tottering fence; those eyes, the windows of the mind whence joy and sorrow looked forth by turns, are now filled up with the dust of death; those lips, the doors of the soul, the gates of Mansoul, are carried away, and the bars thereof are broken. Alas, ye windows, of agates and gates of carbuncle, where are ye now? How shall I mourn for thee, O thou captive city, for the mighty men have utterly spoiled thee! Thy neck, once like a tower of ivory, has become as a fallen column; thy nose, so lately comparable to "the tower of Lebanon, which looketh toward Damascus," is as a ruined hovel; and thy head, which towered like Carmel, lies low as the clods of the valley. Where is beauty now? The most lovely cannot be known from the most deformed. The vessel so daintily wrought upon the potter's wheel, is cast away upon the dunghill with the vilest potsherds. Cruel have ye been, ye warriors of death, for though ye wield no axes and bear no hammers, yet have ye broken down the carved work; and though ye speak not with tongues, yet have ye said in your hearts, "We have swallowed her up, certainly this is the day that we have looked for; we have found, we have seen it." The skin is gone. The troops have entered into the town of Mansoul. And now they pursue their work of devastation; the pitiless marauders all upon the body itself. There are those noble aqueducts, the veins through which the streams of life were wont to flow, these, instead of being rivers of life, have become blocked up with the soil and wastes of death, and now they must be pulled to pieces; not a single relic of them shall be spared. Mark the muscles and sinews, like great highways that penetrating the metropolis, carry the strength and wealth of manhood along—their curious pavement must be pulled up, and they that do traffic thereon must be consumed; each tunneled bone, and curious arch, and knotted bond must be snapped and broken. Fair fabrics, glorious storehouses, costly engines, wonderful machines—all, all must be pulled down, and not one stone left upon another. Those nerves, which like telegraphic wires connected all parts of the city together, to carry thought and feeling and intelligence— these are cut. No matter how artistic the work might be—and certainly we are fearfully and wonderfully made, and the anatomist stands still and marvels to see the skill which the eternal God has manifested in the formation of the body—but these ruthless worms pull everything to pieces, till like a city sacked and spoiled that has been given up for days to pillage and to flame, everything lies in a heap of ruin—ashes to ashes, dust to dust. But these invaders stop not here. Job says that next they consume his reins. We are wont to speak of the heart as the great citadel of life, the inner keep and dungeon, where the captain of the guard holdeth out to the last. The Hebrews do not regard the heart, but the lower viscera, the reins, as the seat of the passions and of mental power. The worms spare not; they enter the secret places of the tabernacle of life, and the standard is plucked from the tower. Having died, the heart cannot preserve itself, and falls like the rest of the frame—a prey to worms. It is gone, it is all gone! The skin, the body, the vitals, all, all has departed. There is naught left. In a few years ye shall turn up the sod and say, "Here slept so-and-so, and where is he now?" and ye may search and hunt and dig, but ye shall find no relic. Mother Earth has devoured her own offspring.

Dear friends, why should we wish to have it otherwise? Why should we desire to preserve the body when the soul has gone? What vain attempts men have made with coffins of lead, and wrappings of myrrh and frankincense. The embalming of the Egyptians, those master robbers of the worm, what has it done? It has served to keep some poor shriveled lumps of mortality above ground to be sold for curiosities, to be dragged away to foreign climes, and stared upon by thoughtless eyes. No, let the dust go, the sooner it dissolves the better. And what matters it how it goes! If it be devoured of beasts, if it be swallowed up in the sea and become food for fishes! What, if plants with their roots suck up the particles! What, if the fabric passes into the animal, and from the animal into the earth, and from the earth into the plants, and from the plant into the animal again! What, if the winds blow it along the highway! What, if the rivers carry it to the waves of ocean! It is ordained that somehow or other it must be all separated—"dust to dust, ashes to ashes." It is part of the decree that it should all perish. The worms or some other agents of destruction must destroy this body. Do not seek to avoid what God has purposed; do not look upon it as a gloomy thing. Regard it as a necessity; nay more, view it as the platform of a miracle, the lofty stage of resurrection, since Jesus shall surely raise again from the dead the particles of this body, however divided from one another. We have heard of miracles, but what a miracle is the resurrection! All the miracles of Scripture, yea even those wrought by Christ, are small compared with this. The philosopher says, "How is it possible that God shall hunt out every particle of the human frame?" He can do it: He has but to speak the word, and every single atom, though it may have traveled thousands of leagues, though it may have been blown as dust across the desert, and anon have fallen upon the bosom of the sea, and then have descended into the depths thereof to be cast up on a desolate shore, sucked up by plants, fed on again by beasts, or passed into the fabric of another man—I say that individual atom shall find its fellows, and the whole company of particles at the trump of the archangel shall travel to their appointed place, and the body, the very body which was laid in the ground, shall rise again.

I am afraid I have been somewhat uninteresting while tarrying upon the exposition of the words of Job, but I think very much of the pith of Job's faith lay in this, that he had a clear view that the worms would after his skin destroy his body, and yet that in his flesh he should see God. You know we might regard it as a small miracle if we could preserve the bodies of the departed. If, by some process, with spices and gums we could preserve the particles, for the Lord to make those dry bones live, and to quicken that skin and flesh, were a miracle certainly, but not palpably and plainly so great a marvel as when the worms have destroyed the body. When the fabric has been absolutely broken up, the tenement all pulled down, ground to pieces, and flung in handfuls to the wind, so that no relic of it is left, and yet when Christ stands in the latter days upon the earth, all the structure shall be brought together, bone to his bone—then shall the might of Omnipotence be seen. This is the doctrine of the resurrection, and happy is he who finds no difficulty here, who looks at it as being an impossibility with man but a possibility with God, and lays hold upon the omnipotence of the Most High and says, "Thou sayest it, and it shall be done!" I comprehend Thee not great God; I marvel at thy purpose to raise my moldering bones; but I know that Thou doest great wonders, and I am not surprised that Thou shouldst conclude the great drama of thy creating works here on earth by re-creating the human frame by the same power by which Thou didst bring from the dead the body of thy Son Jesus Christ, and by that same divine energy which has regenerated human souls in thine own image.

II. Now, having thus descended into the grave, and seen nothing there but what is loathsome, LET US LOOK UP WITH THE PATRIARCH AND BEHOLD A SUN SHINING WITH PRESENT COMFORT.

"I know," said he, "that my Redeemer liveth." The word "Redeemer" here used, is in the original "goel"—kinsman. The duty of the kinsman, or goel, was this: suppose an Israelite had alienated his estate, as in the case of Naomi and Ruth; suppose a patrimony which had belonged to a family, had passed away through poverty, it was the goel's business, the redeemer's business to pay the price as the next of kin, and to buy back the heritage. Boaz stood in that relation to Ruth. Now, the body may be looked upon as the heritage of the soul—the soul's small farm, that little plot of earth in which the soul has been wont to walk and delight, as a man walketh in his garden or dwelleth in his house. Now, that becomes alienated. Death, like Ahab, takes away the vineyard from us who are as Naboth; we lose our patrimonial estate; Death sends his troops to take our vineyard and to spoil the vines thereof and ruin it. But we turn round to Death and say, "I know that my Goel liveth, and he will redeem this heritage; I have lost it; thou takest it from me lawfully, O Death, because my sin hath forfeited my right; I have lost my heritage through my own offense, and through that of my first parent Adam; but there lives one who will buy this back." Brethren, Job could say this of Christ long before He had descended upon earth, "I know that he liveth"; and now that He has ascended up on high, and led captivity captive, surely we may with double emphasis say, "I know that my Goel, my Kinsman liveth, and that He hath paid the price, that I should have back my patrimony, so that in my flesh I shall see God." Yes, my hands, ye are redeemed with blood; bought not with corruptible things, as with silver and gold, but with the precious blood of Christ. Yes, heaving lungs and palpitating heart, ye have been redeemed! He that redeemed the soul to be His altar has also redeemed the body, that it may be a temple for the Holy Ghost. Not even the bones of Joseph can remain in the house of bondage. No smell of the fire of death may pass upon the garments which His holy children have worn in the furnace.

Remember, too, that it was always considered to be the duty of the goel, not merely to redeem by price, but where that failed, to redeem by power. Hence, when Lot was carried away captive by the four kings, Abraham summoned his own hired servants, and the servants of all his friends, and went out against the kings of the East, and brought back Lot and the captives of Sodom. Now, our Lord Jesus Christ, who once has played the kinsman's part by paying the price for us, liveth, and He will redeem us by power. O Death, thou tremblest at this name! Thou knowest the might of our Kinsman! Against His arm thou canst not stand! Thou didst once meet Him foot to foot in stern battle, and O Death, thou didst indeed tread upon

His heel. He voluntarily submitted to this, or else, O Death, thou hadst no power against him. But He slew thee, Death, He slew thee! He rifled all thy caskets, took from thee the key of thy castle, burst open the door of thy dungeon; and now, thou knowest, Death, thou hast no power to hold my body; thou mayst set thy slaves to devour it, but thou shalt give it up, and all their spoil must be restored. Insatiable Death, from thy greedy maw yet shall return the multitudes whom thou has devoured. Thou shalt be compelled by the Savior to restore thy captives to the light of day. I think I see Jesus coming with His Father's servants. The chariots of the Lord are twenty thousand, even thousands of angels. Blow ye the trumpet! Blow ye the trumpet! Immanuel rides to battle! The Most Mighty in majesty girds on His sword. He comes! He comes to snatch by power, His people's lands from those who have invaded their portion. Oh, how glorious the victory! No battle shall there be. He comes, he sees, he conquers. The sound of the trumpet shall be enough; Death shall fly affrighted; and at once from beds of dust and silent clay, to realms of everlasting day the righteous shall arise.

To linger here for a moment, there was yet, very conspicuously in the Old Testament, we are informed, a third duty of the goel, which was to avenge the death of his friend. If a person had been slain, the Goel was the avenger of blood; snatching up his sword, he at once pursued the person who had been guilty of bloodshed. So now, let us picture ourselves as being smitten by Death. His arrow has just pierced us to the heart, but in the act of expiring, our lips are able to boast of vengeance, and in the face of the monster we cry, "I know that my Goel liveth." Thou mayst fly, O Death, as rapidly as thou wilt, but no city of refuge can hide thee from him; he will overtake thee; he will lay hold upon thee, O thou skeleton monarch, and he will avenge my blood on thee. I would that I had powers of eloquence to work out this magnificent thought. Chrysostom, or Christmas Evans could picture the flight of the King of Terrors, the pursuit by the Redeemer, the overtaking of the foe, and the slaying of the destroyer. Christ shall certainly avenge Himself on Death for all the injury which Death hath done to His beloved kinsmen. Comfort thyself then, O Christian; thou hast ever living, even when thou diest, One who avenges thee, One who has paid the price for thee, and One whose strong arms shall yet set thee free.

Passing on in our text to notice the next word, it seems that Job found consolation not only in the fact that he had a Goel, a Redeemer, but that this Redeemer liveth. He does not say, "I know that my Goel *shall live*, but that he *lives*"—having a clear view of the self-existence of the Lord Jesus Christ, the same yesterday, today, and forever. And you and I looking back do not say, "I know that He *did live*, but He *lives* today." This very day you that mourn and sorrow for venerated friends, your prop and pillar in years gone by, you may go to Christ with confidence, because He not only lives, but He is the source of life; and you therefore believe that He can give forth out of Himself life to those whom you have committed to the tomb. He is the Lord and Giver of life originally, and He shall be specially declared to be the resurrection and the life, when the legions of His redeemed shall be glorified with Him.

If I saw no fountain from which life could stream to the dead, I would yet believe the promise when God said that the dead shall live; but when I see the fountain provided, and know that it is full to the brim and that it runneth over, I can rejoice without trembling. Since there is one who can say, "I am the resurrection and the life," it is a blessed thing to see the means already before us in the Person of our Lord Jesus Christ. Let us look up to our Goel then who liveth at this very time.

Still the marrow of Job's comfort it seems to me lay in that little word "My." "I know that my Redeemer liveth." Oh, to get hold of Christ! I know that in His offices He is precious. But, dear friends, we must get a property in Him before we can really enjoy Him. What is honey in the wood to me, if like the fainting Israelites, I dare not eat. It is honey in my hand, honey on my lip, which enlightens mine eyes like those of Jonathan. What is gold in the mine to me? Men are beggars in Peru, and beg their bread in California. It is gold in my purse which will satisfy my necessities, purchasing the bread I need. So, what is a kinsman if he be not a kinsman to me? A Redeemer that does not redeem me, an avenger who will never stand up for my blood, of what avail were such? But Job's faith was strong and firm in the conviction that the Redeemer was his. Dear friends, dear friends, can all of you say, "I know that *my* Redeemer liveth"? The question is simple and simply put; but oh, what solemn things hang upon your answer, "Is it my Redeemer?" I charge you rest not, be not content until by faith you can say, "Yes, I cast myself upon Him; I am His, and therefore He is mine." I know that full many of you, while you look upon all else that you have as not being yours, yet can say, "*My* Redeemer is mine." He is the only piece of property which is really ours. We borrow all else, the house, the children; nay, our very body we must return to the Great Lender. But Jesus, we can never leave, for even when we are absent from the body we are present with the Lord, and I know that even death cannot separate us from Him, so that body and soul are with Jesus truly even in the dark hours of death, in the long night of the sepulcher, and in the separate state of spiritual existence. Beloved, have you Christ? It may be you hold Him with a feeble hand, you half think it is presumption to say, "He is my Redeemer"; yet remember, if you have but faith as a grain of mustard seed, that little faith entitles you to say, and say now, "I know that my Redeemer liveth."

There is another word in this consoling sentence which no doubt served to give a zest to the comfort of Job. It was that he could say, "I know"—"I know that my Redeemer liveth." To say, "I hope so, I trust so," is comfortable; and there are thousands in the fold of Jesus who hardly ever get much further. But to reach the marrow of consolation you *must* say, "I know." Ifs, buts, and perhapses, are sure murderers of peace and comfort. Doubts are dreary things in times of sorrow. Like wasps they sting the soul! If I have any suspicion that Christ is not mine, then there is vinegar mingled with the gall of death. But if I know that Jesus is mine, then darkness is not dark; even the night is light about me. Out of the lion cometh honey; out of the eater cometh forth sweetness. "I know that my Redeemer liveth." This is a brightly-burning lamp cheering the damps of the sepulchral vault, but a feeble hope is like a flickering smoking flax, just making darkness visible, but nothing more. I would not like to die with a mere hope mingled with suspicion. I might be safe with this but hardly happy; but oh, to go down into the river knowing that all is well, confident that as a guilty, weak, and helpless worm I have fallen into the arms of Jesus, and believing that He is able to keep that which I have committed to Him. I would have you, dear Christian friends, never look upon the full assurance of faith as a thing impossible to you. Say not "It is too high; I cannot attain unto it." I have known one or two saints of God who have rarely doubted their interest at all. There are many of us who do not often enjoy any ravishing ecstasies, but on the other hand we generally maintain the even tenor of our way, simply hanging upon Christ, feeling that His promise is true, that His merits are sufficient, and that we are safe. Assurance is a jewel for worth but not for rarity. It is the common privilege of all the saints if they have but the grace to attain unto it, and this grace the Holy Spirit gives freely. Surely if Job in Arabia, in those dark misty ages when there was only the morning star and not the sun, when they saw but little, when life and immortality had not been brought to light—if Job before the coming and advent still could say, "*I know*," you and I should not speak less positively. God forbid that our positiveness should be presumption. Let us try ourselves, and see that our marks and evidences are right, lest we form an ungrounded hope; for nothing can be more destructive than to say, "Peace, peace, where there is no peace." But oh, let us build for eternity, and build solidly. Let us not be satisfied with the mere foundation, for it is from the upper rooms that we get the widest prospect. Let us pray the Lord to help us to pile stone on stone, until we are able to say as we look at it, "Yes, I *know*, I KNOW that my Redeemer liveth." This, then, for present comfort today in the prospect of departure.

III. And now, in the third and last place, as THE ANTICIPATION OF FUTURE DELIGHT, let me call to our remembrance the other part of the text. Job not only knew that the Redeemer lived, but he anticipated the time when He should *stand in the latter day upon the earth*. No doubt Job referred here to our Savior's first advent, to the time when Jesus Christ, "the Goel," the Kinsman, should stand upon the earth to pay in the blood of His veins the ransom price, which had, indeed, in bond and stipulation been paid before the foundation of the world in promise. But I cannot think that Job's vision stayed there; he was looking forward to the second advent of Christ as being the period of the resurrection. We cannot endorse the theory that Job arose from the dead when our Lord died, although certain Jewish believers held this idea very firmly at one time. We are persuaded that "the latter day" refers to the advent of glory rather than to that of shame. Our hope is that the Lord shall come to reign in glory where He once died in agony. The bright and hallowed doctrine of the second advent has been greatly revived in our churches in these latter days, and I look for the best results in consequence. There is always a danger lest it be perverted and turned by fanatical minds, by prophetic speculations, into an abuse; but the doctrine in itself is one of the most consoling, and, at the same time, one of the most practical, tending to keep the Christian awake, because the bridegroom cometh at such an hour as we think not. Beloved, we believe that the same Jesus who ascended from Olivet shall so come in like manner as He ascended up into heaven. We believe in His personal advent and reign. We believe and expect that when both wise and foolish virgins shall slumber; in the night when sleep is heavy upon the saints; when men shall be eating and drinking as in the days of Noah, that suddenly as the lightning flasheth from heaven, so Christ shall descend with a shout, and the dead in Christ shall rise and reign with Him. We are looking forward to the literal, personal, and actual standing of Christ upon earth as the time when creation's groans shall be silenced forever, and the earnest expectation of the creature shall be fulfilled.

Mark, that Job describes Christ as *standing*. Some interpreters have read the passage, "He shall stand in the latter days against the earth"; that as the earth has covered up the slain, as the earth has become the charnel-house of the dead, Jesus shall arise to the contest and say, "Earth, I am against thee; give up thy dead! Ye clods of the valley cease to be custodians of my people's bodies! Silent deeps, and you, ye caverns of the earth, deliver, once for all, those whom ye have imprisoned!" Machpelah shall give up its precious treasure, cemeteries and graveyards shall release their captives, and all the deep places of the earth shall resign the bodies of the faithful. Well, whether that be so or no, the posture of Christ, in standing upon the earth, is significant. It shows His triumph. He has triumphed over sin, which once like a serpent in its coils had bound the earth. He has defeated Satan. On the very spot where Satan gained his power Christ has gained the victory. Earth, which was a scene of defeated goodness, whence mercy once was all but driven, where virtue died, where everything heavenly and pure, like flowers blasted by pestilential winds, hung down their heads, withered and blighted—on this very earth everything that is glorious shall blow and blossom in perfection; and Christ Himself, once despised and rejected of men, fairest of all the sons of men, shall come in the midst of a crowd of courtiers, while kings and princes shall do Him homage, and all the nations shall call Him blessed. "He shall stand in the latter day upon the earth."

Then, at that auspicious hour, says Job, "In my flesh I shall see God." Oh, blessed anticipation—"I shall see God." He does not say, "I shall see the saints"—doubtless we shall see them all in heaven—but, "I shall see *God*." Note he does not say, "I shall see the pearly gates, I shall see the walls of jasper, I shall see the crowns of gold and the harps of harmony," but "I shall see God"; as if that were the sum and substance of heaven. "In my flesh shall I see *God*." The pure in heart shall see God. It was their delight to see Him in the ordinances by faith. They delighted to behold Him in communion and in prayer. There in heaven they shall have a vision of another sort. We shall see God in heaven, and be made completely like Him; the divine character shall be stamped upon us; and being made like to Him we shall be perfectly satisfied and content. Likeness to God, what can we wish for more? And a sight of God, what can we desire better? We shall see God, and so there shall be perfect contentment to the soul and a satisfaction of all the faculties. Some read the passage, "Yet, I shall see God in my flesh," and hence think that there is here an allusion to

Christ, our Lord Jesus Christ, as the word made flesh. Well, be it so, or be it not so, it is certain that we shall see Christ, and He, as the divine Redeemer, shall be the subject of our eternal vision. Nor shall we ever want any joy beyond simply that of seeing Him. Think not, dear friend, that this will be a narrow sphere for your mind to dwell in. It is but one source of delight, "I shall see God," but that source is infinite. His wisdom, His love, His power, all His attributes shall be subjects for your eternal contemplation, and as He is infinite under each aspect, there is no fear of exhaustion. His works, His purposes, His gifts, His love to you, and His glory in all His purposes, and in all His deeds of love—why, these shall make a theme that never can be exhausted. You may see with divine delight anticipate the time when in your flesh you shall see God.

But I must have you observe how Job has expressly made us note that it is in the same body. "Yet, *in my flesh* shall I see God"; and then he says again, "Whom I shall see for myself, and mine eye shall behold and not another." Yes, it is true that I, the very man standing here, though I must go down to die, yet I shall as the same man most certainly arise and shall behold my God. Not part of myself, though the soul alone shall have some view of God, but the whole of myself, my flesh, my soul, my body, my spirit shall gaze on God. We shall not enter heaven, dear friends, as a dismasted vessel is tugged into harbor; we shall not get to glory some on boards, and some on broken pieces of the ship, but the whole ship shall be floated safely into the haven, body and soul both being safe. Christ shall be able to say, "*All* that the Father giveth to me shall come to me," not only all the persons, but all of the persons—each man in his perfection. There shall not be found in heaven one imperfect saint. There shall not be a saint without an eye, much less a saint without a body. No member of the body shall have perished; nor shall the body have lost any of its natural beauty. All the saints shall be all there, and all of all; the same persons precisely, only that they shall have risen from a state of grace to a state of glory. They shall be ripened; they shall be no more the green blades, but the full corn in the ear; no more buds but flowers; not babes but men.

Please to notice, and then I shall conclude, how the patriarch puts it as being a real personal enjoyment. "Whom mine eye shall behold, and not another." They shall not bring me a report as they did the Queen of Sheba, but I shall see Solomon the King for myself. I shall be able to say, as they did who spoke to the woman of Samaria, "Now I believe, not because of thy word who did bring me a report, but I have seen Him for myself." There shall be personal intercourse with God: not through the Book, which is but as a glass; not through the ordinances; but directly, in the Person of our Lord Jesus Christ, we shall·be able to commune with the Deity as a man talketh with his friend. "Not another." If I could be a changeling and could be altered, that would mar my comfort. Or if my heaven must be enjoyed by proxy, if drafts of bliss must be drunk for me, where were the hope? Oh, no; for myself, and not through another, shall I see God. Have we not told you a hundred times that nothing but personal religion will do, and is not this another argument for it, because resurrection and glory are personal things? "Not another." If you could have sponsors to repent for you, then, depend upon it, you would have sponsors to be glorified for you. But as there is not another to see God for you, so you must yourself see and yourself find an interest in the Lord Jesus Christ.

In closing let me observe how foolish have you and I been when we have looked forward to death with shudders, with doubts, with loathings. After all, what is it? Worms! Do ye tremble at those base crawling things? Scattered particles! Shall we be alarmed at these? To meet the worms we have the angels; and to gather the scattered particles we have the voice of God. I am sure the gloom of death is altogether gone now that the lamp of resurrection burns. Disrobing is nothing now that better garments await us. We may long for evening to undress, that we may rise with God. I am sure my venerable friends now present, in coming so near as they do now to the time of the departure, must have some visions of the glory on the other side the stream. Bunyan was not wrong, my dear brethren, when he put the land Beulah at the close of the pilgrimage. Is not my text a telescope which will enable you to see across the Jordan; may it not be as hands of angels to bring you bundles of myrrh and frankincense? You can say, "I know that my Redeemer liveth." You cannot want more; you were not satisfied with less in your youth, you will not be content with less now. Those of us who are young, are comforted by the thought that we may soon depart. I say comforted, not alarmed by it; and we almost envy those whose race is nearly run, because we fear—and yet we must not speak thus, for the Lord's will be done—I was about to say, we fear that our battle may last long, and that perhaps our feet may slip; only He that keepeth Israel does not slumber nor sleep. So since we know that our Redeemer liveth, this shall be our comfort in life, that though we fall we shall not be utterly cast down; and since our Redeemer liveth, this shall be our comfort in death, that though worms destroy this body, yet in our flesh we shall see God.

May the Lord add His blessing on the feeble words of this morning and to Him be glory forever. Amen.

> Grave, the guardian of our dust!
> Grave, the treasury of the skies!
> Every atom of thy trust
> Rests in hope again to rise.
> Hark! the judgment trumpet calls;
> Soul, rebuild thy house of clay,
> Immortality thy walls,
> And Eternity thy day.

"LO, I COME": EXPOSITION

SERMON NO. 2,202
DELIVERED ON LORD'S DAY MORNING, APRIL 26, 1891.
PORTION OF SCRIPTURE READ BEFORE SERMON—PSALM 40.
HYMNS FROM *Our Own Hymn Book*—383, 271, 229.

Sacrifice and offering thou didst not desire; mine ears hast thou opened: burnt offering and sin offering hast thou not required. Then said I, Lo, I come: in the volume of the book it is written of me, I delight to do thy will, O my God: yea, thy law is within my heart— Psalm 40:6–8.

Explained to us by the Apostle Paul in Hebrews 10:5–7:

Wherefore when he cometh into the world, he saith, Sacrifice and offering thou wouldest not, but a body hast thou prepared me: In burnt offerings and sacrifices for sin thou hast had no pleasure. Then said I, Lo, I come (in the volume of the book it is written of me,) to do thy will, O God.

WE have, in the use made of the passage by the inspired apostle, sufficient authority for applying the quotation from the fortieth psalm to our divine Lord and Savior Jesus Christ. With such a commentary, we are sure of our way and our whereabouts. We might have been perplexed as to its meaning had it not been for this; although, I think, even without the guidance of the New Testament passage, those who are familiar with Holy Writ would have felt that the words could not be fulfilled in David, but must belong to a greater than he, even to the divine Messiah, who in the fullness of time would come into the world. We rejoice that the Lord Jesus Himself here speaks of Himself. Who but He can declare His own generation? Here He is both the subject of the words and the speaker also. The word is from Himself and of Himself, and so we have double reason for devout attention. He tells us what He said long ago. He declares, "Then I said, Lo, I come." Because He has come to us, we gladly come to Him; and now we reverently wait upon Him to hear what our Lord shall speak; for, doubtless, He will speak peace to us, and will cause us to learn, through His Spirit, the meaning of His words. O Savior, say to each of our hearts, "Lo, I come!"

I. Without further preface, I call upon you to notice, first, THE SWEEPING AWAY OF THE SHADOW. "Sacrifice and offering thou didst not desire . . . : burnt offering and sin offering hast thou not required."

When the Son of God is born into the world, there is an end of all types by which He was formerly prefigured. The symbols end when the truth itself is made fully manifest. The sacrifices of the law had their times and place, their teaching and their influence. Blessed were those in Israel whose spiritual minds saw beneath the outward sign, and discerned the inward truth! To them the sacrifices of the holy place were a standing means of fellowship with God. Day after day they saw the Great Propitiation as they beheld the morning and the evening lamb: so often as they looked upon a sacrifice, they beheld the Lamb of God which taketh away the sin of the world. In the Paschal supper they were instructed by the slaying of the unblemished victim, the roasting with fire, the sprinkling of the blood upon the door without, and the feasting upon the sacrifice within. Spiritual men could have found in the rites and ceremonies of the old law a very library of gospel literature; but, alas! the people were carnal, sensual, and unbelieving, and therefore they often forgot even to celebrate the appointed sacrifices: the Passover itself ceased for long periods, and when the festivals were maintained, there was no life or reality in them. After they had been chastened for their neglect, and made to wander in exile because of the wandering of their hearts after their idols, they were restored from captivity, and were led to keep the ceremonial law; but they did it as a heartless, meaningless formality, and thus missed all spiritual benefit: with the unlighted candle in their hand they blindly groped in the dark. They slew the sacrifices, and presented their peace-offerings; but the soul had gone out of the service, and at last their God grew weary of their formal worship, and said, "Bring no more vain oblations; incense is an abomination unto me." We read, "To what purpose is the multitude of your sacrifices unto me? saith the Lord: I am full of the burnt offerings of rams, and the fat of fed beasts; and I delight not in the blood of bullocks, or of lambs, or of he goats. When ye come to appear before me, who hath required this at your hand, to tread my courts?" When once the life is gone out of the best symbolism, the Lord abhors the carcass; and even a divinely ordained ritual becomes a species of idolatry. When the heart is gone out of the externals of worship, they are as shells without the kernel. Habitations without living tenants soon become desolations, and so do forms and ceremonies without their spiritual meaning. Toward the time of our Lord's coming, the outward worship of Judaism became more and more dead: it was time that it was buried. It had decayed and waxed old, and was ready to vanish away, and vanish away it did; for our Lord set aside the first, or old, that He might establish the second, or new. The stars were no longer seen with their twinklings, for the sun had arisen.

The removal of these things was wholesale. We have four sorts of sacrifice mentioned here, but I need not go into details. Sacrifices in which blood was shed were abolished when the Son of God offered Himself without spot unto God. Bloodless offerings, such as fine flour, and wine, and oil, and sweet cane bought with money, and precious incense—which were tokens of gratitude and consecration—these also were no longer laid upon the altar. Sacrifice and offering both were not desired; and burnt-offerings, which signified the delight of God in the great Sacrifice, were ended by the Lord's actual acceptance of that Sacrifice itself. Even the sin-offering, which was burned without the camp as a thing accursed, altogether ceased. It represented sin laid upon the victim, and the victim's being made a curse on that account. It might have seemed always useful as a reminder, for they were always sinning, and always needing a sin-offering; but even this was not required. Nothing of the old ceremonial law was spared. Now we have no ark of the covenant, with its shekinah light between the wings of the cherubim. Now we have no brazen laver, no table of shewbread, no brazen altar, and no sacred veil: the holy of holies itself is gone. Tabernacle and temple are both removed. "Neither in this mountain, nor yet at Jerusalem, shall men worship the Father"; but the time is come when "they that worship him must worship him in spirit and in truth." A clean sweep has been made of all the ancient rites, from circumcision up to the garment with its fringe of blue. These were for the childhood of the church, the pictures of her first school-books; but we are no longer minors, and we have grace given us to read with opened eyes that everlasting classic of "the glory of God in the face of Jesus Christ." Now hath the brightness of the former dispensation been quite eclipsed by the glory which excelleth.

As these outward things vanish, they go away with God's mark of non-esteem upon them: *they are such things as he did not desire.* "Sacrifice and offering thou didst not desire." The Lord God had no desire for matters so trivial and unsatisfactory. They were good for the people, to instruct them, if they had been willing to learn; but they fulfilled no desire of the heart of God. He says, "Will I eat the flesh of bulls, or drink the blood of goats?" By the prophet Micah He asks, "Will the Lord be pleased with thousands of rams, or with ten thousands of rivers of oil?" These furnish no delight for the great Spirit, and give no pleasure to the thrice holy Jehovah. The formal worshiper supposed that his offerings were, in and of themselves, pleasing to God, and therefore brought his "burnt offerings with calves of a year old." So far as they believingly understood the meaning of a sacrifice, and presented it in faith, their offerings were acceptable; but in themselves considered these were far from being what the Lord desired. He that filleth heaven and earth saith, "I will not reprove thee for thy sacrifices or thy burnt offerings, to have been continually before me. I will take no bullock out of thy house, nor he goats out of thy folds. For every beast of the forest is mine, and the cattle upon a thousand hills. I know all the fowls of the mountains: and the wild beasts of the field are mine. If I were hungry, I would not tell thee: for the world is mine, and the fullness thereof." The spiritual, the infinite, the almighty Jehovah could not desire merely outward ritual, however it might appear glorious to men. The sweetest music is not for His ear, nor the most splendid robes of priests for His eye. He desired something infinitely more precious than these, and He puts them away with this note of dissatisfaction.

And more, these sacrifices passed away with the mark upon them that *they were not what God required.* "Burnt offering and sin offering hast thou not required." What did God require of man? Obedience. He said by Samuel, "To obey is better than sacrifice, and to hearken than the fat of rams." He saith in another place, "He hath showed thee, O man, what is good; and what doth the Lord require of thee, but to do justly, and to love mercy, and to walk humbly with thy God?" The requirement of the law was love to God and love to men. This has always been God's great requirement. He seeks spiritual worship, obedient thought, holy living, grateful praise, devout prayer—these are the requirements of the Creator and Benefactor of men. Ritualistic matters were so far required as they might minister to the good of the people, and while thy stood they could not neglect them without loss; but they were not the grand requirement of a just and holy God, and therefore men might fulfill these without stint or omission, and yet God would not have of them what he required. Yea, He asks, "Who hath required this at your hand, to tread my courts?" To see His law magnified, His justice vindicated, His sovereignty acknowledged, and His holiness imitated, is more to His mind. Absolute conformity to the standard of moral and spiritual rectitude which He has set up is His demand, and He can be content with nothing less. These things are not found in sacrifice and offering, neither do they always go therewith, and therefore the outward sacrifice was not what God required.

They were so to be put away as never to be followed by the same kind of things. Shadows are not replaced by other shadows. The ceremonials of Aaron are not to be followed by another set of carnal ordinances. There are some who seem to think that they are so to be. Instead of Aaron, whom God ordained, we have a so-called priesthood among us at this day, claiming an apostolic succession, which is impossible if they are priests, since no apostle was a priest. Instead of rites which God has ordained we have rites of man's invention. The blessed ordinances of our Lord Jesus Christ, such as baptism and the Lord's Supper, have been prostituted from their instructive and memorial intent into a kind of witchcraft; so that by what is called baptism children are said to be born again, and made members of Christ and children of God, while in the second, or what they call Holy Communion, the sacrifice of Christ is profanely said to be repeated or continued, even in the unbloody sacrifice of the mass. Ah, friends! Our Lord did not put away that grand, magnificent system of Mosaic rites to introduce the masquerade in which Rome delights, which certain Anglicans would set up among us. No, no; we have done with the symbolic system, and have now but the two outward ordinances of baptism and the Lord's Supper, which are meant only for believers who know what it is to be buried with Christ, and to feed on Him. You have no right to bring in your own forms and ceremonies, and place them in the church of Christ. Beyond what God has ordained we may not dare to go; and even in those things we may not rest as though there were anything in them of their own operation, apart from their sacred teaching. These are instructive to you if you have a mind to be instructed, and if you know the truths which they set forth; but do not imagine that men have come under another system of ritualism and rubric, for it is not so. The rites appropriate to priests are abolished with the Aaronic priest-hood, and can never be restored: "He that taketh away the first, that he may establish the second." When he cometh into the world, these carnal ordinances must go out of the world. Sacrifice and offering, burnt offering and sin offering, and all other patterns of heavenly things, are swept away when the heavenly things themselves appear.

II. Thus much upon the shadows being swept away; and now, secondly, let us view THE REVELATION OF THE SUBSTANCE. We find the Son of God Himself appearing. We read here, and we hear Him say—"Mine ears hast thou opened." The Lord Himself comes, even He who is all that these things foreshadowed.

When He comes He has a prepared ear. The margin hath it, "Mine ears hast thou digged." Our ears often need digging; for they are blocked up by sin. The passage to the heart seems to be sealed in the case of fallen man. But when the Savior came, His ear was not as ours, but was attentive to the divine voice. He says, "He wakeneth mine ear to hear as they that are taught. The Lord God hath opened mine ear, and I was not rebellious." Our Lord was quick of understanding in the fear of the Lord: He knew what the will of the Lord was, and He could say, "I do always the thing that pleases Him." As man, He had a divine instinct of holiness, which made Him to know and love the Father's will, and caused Him always to translate that will into His own life. You see He came with an opened ear, and some think that here we have an allusion to the boring of the ear in the case of the servant who had a right to liberty, but refused to quit his servitude, because he loved his master, and wished to remain with him forever. It is not certain that there is any such reference; but it is certain that our Lord was bound forever to the service which He had undertaken for His Father, and that He would not go back from it. He pledged Himself to redeem us, and He set His face like a flint to do it. He loved His Father, and He loved His chosen so much that He vowed to execute the Father's work, even to what I might call "the bitter end," if I did not know that it was a sweet and blessed end to Him. His ear was prepared for His service.

But *our Lord came also with a prepared body*: hence, the Apostle Paul, when he quoted this passage, probably taking the words from the Septuagint translation, writes, "A body hast thou prepared me." You will wonder how, in one passage, it should speak of the ear, and the next should speak of the body; and yet there is small difference in the sense. We do not think of an ear without a body—that would be a sorry business. The reading in the Hebrews is involved in the text as it stands in the Psalm. If the ear is there, a body is there; you cannot even dream of an ear hearing if separate from the rest of the body. The Apostle gives us the sense of the text rather than the words; and, at the same time, dealing as he was with the Jews by whom the Septuagint was prized, he quoted from the version which they would be sure to acknowledge—and very properly and wisely so—because that version was perfectly accurate as to the meaning of the Hebrew. Anyway, he was inspired to read it—"A body hast thou prepared me." There was fashioned by the Holy Ghost, in the womb of the blessed Virgin, a body fitted to embody the Son of God. Wrought mysteriously, by means into which we must not inquire—for what God hath veiled must remain covered—that body was suited to set forth the great mystery, "God manifest in the flesh."

The whole body of Christ was prepared for Him and for His great work. To begin with, it was a sinless body, without taint of original sin, else God could not have dwelt therein. It was a body made highly vital and sensitive, probably far beyond what ours are; for sin has a blunting and hardening effect even upon flesh, and His flesh, though it was in the "likeness of sinful flesh," was not sinful flesh, but flesh which yielded prompt obedience to His spirit, even as His whole human nature was obedient unto death, even the death of the cross. His body was capable of great endurance, so as to know the griefs and agonies and unspeakable sorrows of a delicate, holy, and tender kind which it was necessary for Him to bear. "A body hast thou prepared me." In the fullness of time He came into that body, which was admirably adapted to enshrine the Godhead. Wondrous mystery, that the infant of Bethlehem should be linked with the Infinite; and that the weary man by the shores of Galilee should be very God of very God, revealed in a body prepared for Him! "A body hast thou prepared me": He had a prepared ear and a prepared body.

He who assumed that body was existent before that body was prepared. He says, "A body hast thou prepared me. Lo, I come." He from old eternity dwelt with God: the Word was in the beginning with God, and the Word was God. We could not any one of us have said that a body was prepared for us, and therefore we could come to it; for we had had no existence before our bodies were fashioned. From everlasting to everlasting our Lord is God, and He comes out of eternity into time—the Father bringing Him into the world. He was before all worlds, and was before He came into the world to dwell in His prepared body.

Beloved, *the human nature of Christ was taken on Him in order that He might be able to do for us that which God desired and required.* God desired to see an obedient man, a man who would keep His law to the full; and He sees Him in Christ. God desired to see One who would vindicate the eternal justice, and show that sin is no trifle; and behold our Lord, the eternal Son of God, entering into that prepared body, was ready to do all this mighty work by rendering to the law a full recompense for our dishonor of it! An absolutely perfect righteousness He renders unto God: as the second Adam, He presents it for all whom He represents. He bows His head a victim beneath Jehovah's sword, that the truth, and justice, and honor of God might suffer no detriment. His body was prepared to this end. Incarnation is a means to atonement. Only a man could vindicate the law, and therefore the Son of God became a man. This is a wonderful Being, this God in our nature. "Emmanuel" is a glorious word. Surely for the incarnation and the atonement the world was made from the first. Was this the reason why the morning stars sang together when they saw the cornerstone of the world, because they had an inkling that here God would be manifest as nowhere else beside, and the Creator would be wedded to the creature? That God might be manifested in the Christ, it may even be that sin was permitted. Assuredly, there could have been no sacrifice on Calvary if there had not first of all been sin in Eden. The whole scheme, the whole of God's decrees and acts, worked up to an atoning Savior. Of the pyramid of creation and of providence Christ is the apex: He is the flower of all that God hath made. His divine nature in strange union with humanity constitutes a peerless Personage, such as never was before, and can never be again. God is in our nature one Being, and yet wearing two natures, is altogether unique. He saith, "A body hast thou prepared for me. Lo, I come." Think of this: it is a truth fitter for meditation than for sermonizing. The Lord give us to know it well by faith!

III. But now, thirdly, I call your attention to THE DECLARATION OF THE CHRIST, made in the text: "Sacrifice and offering thou didst not desire. Then said I, Lo, I come." Observe *when* He says this. *It is in the time of failure.* All the sacrifices had failed. The candle flickered, and was dying out, and then the great light arose, even the eternal light, and like a trumpet the words rung out, "Lo, I come." All this has been of no avail: now I come. It is in the time of failure that Christ always does appear. The last of man is the first of God; and when we have come to the end of all our power and hope, then the eternal power and Godhead appears with its "Lo, I come."

When our Lord comes, *it is with the view of filling up the vacuum* which had now been sorrowfully seen. God does not desire these things; God does not require these things; but He does desire and He does require something better: and lo, the Christ has come to bring that something. That awful gap which was seen in human hope when Moses had passed away, and the Aaronic priesthood, and all the ordinances of it were gone, Christ was born to fill. It looked as if the light of ages had been quenched, and God's glorious revelation had been forever withdrawn; and then, in the dark hour, Jesus cries, "Lo, I come!" He fills the blank abyss: He gives to man in reality what he had lost in the shadow.

When He appears, it is as the personal Lord. Lay the stress upon the pronoun, "Lo, I come." The infinite *Ego* appears. "Lo, *I* come." No mere man could talk thus, and be sane. No servant or prophet of God would ever say, "Lo, I come." Saintly men talk not so. God's prophets and apostles have a modest sense of their true position: they never magnify themselves, though they magnify their office. It is for God to say, "Lo, I come." He who says it takes the body prepared for Him, and comes in His own proper personality as the I AM. "In him dwelleth all the fullness of the Godhead bodily." He comes forth from the ivory palaces to inhabit the tents of manhood. He takes upon Himself the body prepared for Him of the Lord God, and He stands forth in His matchless personality ready to do the will of God. "It pleased the Father that in him should all fullness dwell." Everything is stored up in His blessed Person, and we are complete in Him.

Observe the joyful avowal that He makes—"Lo, I come." This is no dirge: I think I hear a silver trumpet ring out—"Lo, I come." Here is a joyful alacrity and intense eagerness. The coming of the Savior was to Him a thing of exceeding willingness. "For the joy that was set before Him He endured the cross, despising the shame."

He comes with a word calling attention to it; for He is not ashamed to be made partaker of our flesh. "Lo," saith He, "I come. Behold, behold, I come." This is no clandestine union; He bids heaven behold Him come into our nature. Earth is bidden to gaze upon it. O ye sinners, listen to his inviting "Lo!" Others have cried to you, "Lo, here! and Lo, there"; but Jesus looks on you, and cries, "Lo, I come." Look hither: turn all your thoughts this way, and behold your God in your nature ready to save you. Verily, the incarnate God is a subject meet for the loftiest thought of sages, and for the lowliest thoughts of children. Blessed are the children of grace who can sit at the feet of the incarnate God and look up, forgetting all the wisdom of the Greeks, and all the sign-seeking of the Jews in the satisfaction which they find in Jesus.

I think, too, *I heard in this declaration of the coming One a note of finality.* He takes away the sacrifice from Aaron's altar; but He says, "Lo, I come." There is an end of it. "Lo, I come." Is there anything after this? Can anything supersede this—"Lo, I come." "Lo, I come" has been in the perpetual music of the ages. Read it, "Lo, I am come"; for it is in the present tense, and how sweet the sound! Christ is come, and joy with Him. Read it as well in the future, if you will, "Lo, I come," for He comes "the second time without sin unto salvation"; here is our chief hope! "Lo, I come." He Himself is the last word of God. "In the beginning was the Word"; and so He was God's first word. But He is the end as well as the beginning: God's last word to man; Christ is God's ultimatum. Look for no new revelation—"Lo, I am come," shines on forever. Do not ask, "Art thou He that should come, or do we look for another?" He has come; look for no other. Behold, He came to give what God desires, what God requires; what would you more? Let Him be all your salvation and all your desire. Let Him be "the desire of all nations." He is the fulfillment of all the requirements of the human race, as well as the full amount of what God requires.

IV. Next, I beg you to note THE REFERENCE TO PRECEDING WRITINGS. He says, "Lo, I come: in the volume of the book it is written of me." If I preached from the passage in the Epistle to the Hebrews, I might fairly declare that in *the whole volume of Holy Scripture* much is written of our Lord and prescribed for Him as Messiah. The page of inspiration is fragrant with the name of Jesus. He is the top line of the entire volume, and in the Greek word I see a half allusion to this. He is the headline of contents to every chapter of Scripture. He is of all Scripture the sum. "In the beginning was the Word." Everything speaks of Him. The Pentateuch, and the books of the prophets, and the Psalms, and the gospels, and the epistles all speak of Him. "In the volume of the book it is written of me."

Preaching as I am from the Psalms, I cannot take so long a range. I must look back and find what was written in David's day, and within *the Pentateuch certainly*; and where do I find it written concerning His coming? The Pentateuch drips with prophecies of Christ as a honeycomb overflowing with its honey. Chiefly is He to be found in the head and front of the book: so early as the opening chapters of the Book of Genesis, when Adam and Eve had sinned, and we were lost, behold He is spoken of in the volume of the book in these terms: "The seed of the woman shall bruise the serpent's head." So early was it written that the Redeemer would be born in our nature to vanquish our foe.

But I confess I do not feel shut out from another interpretation. I conceive that our Lord here refers to another book, *the book of the divine purposes*, the volume of the eternal covenant. There was a time before all time, when there was no day but the Ancient of Days, when all that existed was the Lord, who is all in all: then the sacred Three entered into covenant, in mutual agreement, for a sublime end. Man sinning, the Son of God shall be the surety. Christ shall bear the result of man's offense; He shall vindicate the law of God, and make Jehovah's name more glorious than ever it has been. The second Person of the divine Unity was pledged to come, and take up the nature of men, and so become the firstborn among many brethren to lift up a fallen race, and to save a number that no man can number, elect of God the Father, and given to the Son to be His heritage, His portion, His bride. Then did the Well-beloved strike hands with the eternal God, and enter into covenant engagements on our behalf: "In the volume of the book it is written." That sealed book upon whose secrets no angel's eye has looked, a book written by the finger of God long before He wrote the book of the law upon tables of stone, that book of God may be spoken of in the Psalm, "And in thy book all my members were written, which in continuance were fashioned, when as yet there was none of them." Our Lord came to carry out all His suretyship engagements: His work is the exact fulfillment of His engagements recorded in the eternal covenant, "ordered in all things and sure." He acts out every mysterious line and syllable, even to the full. Then He said, "A body hast thou prepared for me. Lo, I come: in the volume of the book it is written of me." It is ever a pleasing study to see our Lord, both in the written Word, and in the eternal covenant of grace.

V. I must close with the fifth point, THE DELIGHT OF HIM THAT COMETH. He said, "Lo, I come." As I have already told you, there is wonderful delight in that exclamation—"Lo, I come"; but lest we should mistake our Lord, He adds, "I delight to do thy will, O my God; yea, thy law is within my heart." There can be no denial of His joy in His service.

Note well, that *He came in complete subserviency to His Father, God.* "I delight to do"—what? "Thy will." His own will was absorbed in the divine will. His pleasure it was to say, "Not as I will, but as thou wilt." It was His meat and His drink to do the will of Him that sent Him, and to finish His work. Though He was Lord and God, He became a lowly servant for our sakes. Though high as the Highest, He stooped low as the lowest. The King of kings was the Servant of servants, that He might save His people. He took upon Him the form of a servant, and girded Himself, and stood obediently at His Father's call.

He had a prospective delight as to His work. Before He came, He delighted in the thoughts of His incarnation. The Supreme Wisdom saith, "My delights were with the sons of men." Happy in His Father's courts, He yet looked forward to an access of happiness in becoming man. "Can that be?" saith one. Could the Son of God be happier than He was? As God, He was infinitely blessed; but He knew nothing by experience of the life of man, and into that sphere He desired to enter. To the Godhead there can be no enlargement, for it is infinite; but still there can be an addition; our Lord was to add the nature of man to that of God. He would live as man, suffer as man, and triumph as man, and yet remain God: and to this He looked forward with a strange delight, inexplicable except upon the knowledge of the great love He bore to us. He had given His heart so entirely to His dear bride, whom He saw in the glass of predestination, that for her He would endure all things.

> Yea, saith the Lord, for her I'll go
> Through all the depths of care and woe,
> And on the cross will even dare
> The bitter pangs of death to bear.

It was wondrous love. Our Lord's love surpasses all language and even thought. I am talking prodigies and miracles at every word I utter. It was delightful to our Lord to come hither.

"What did He delight in?" saith one. Evidently He delighted in God's *law*. "Thy law is within my heart." He resolved that the beauties of the law of the Lord should be displayed by being embodied in His own life, and that its claims should be vindicated by His own death. To achieve this, He delighted to come and keep it and honor it by an obedience both active and passive. He delighted in God's *will* also, and that is somewhat more; for law is the expression of will, and this may be altered; but the will of the great King never changes. Our Lord delighted to carry out all the purposes and desires of the Most High God. He so delighted in the will of God that He came to do it, and to bear it, "by the which will we are sanctified through the offering of the body of Jesus Christ once for all."

He delighted also in *God*. He took an intense delight in glorifying the Father. He came to reveal the Father, and make Him to be beloved of men. He did all things to please God. Moreover, He took a delight in *us;* and here, though the object of His love is less, the love itself is heightened by the conspicuous condescension. The Lord Jesus took a deep delight in His people, whose names were written on His heart, and graven on the palms of His hands. His heart was fixed on their redemption, and therefore He would present Himself as a sacrifice on their behalf. The people whom the Father gave Him from before the foundation of the world lay on His very soul; for them He had a baptism to be baptized with, and He was straitened till it was accomplished. He gave Himself no rest till He had left both joy and rest to ransom His own.

May I go a step further and say that *He had an actual delight in His coming among men*? "I delight to do thy will, O my God"—not merely to think of doing it. When our Lord was here, He was the most blessed of men. Do you start? Do you remind me that He was "a man of sorrows"? I grant you that none was more afflicted; but I still stand to it, that within Him dwelt a joy of the highest order. To Him it was joy

to be in sorrow, and honor to be put to shame. Do you think that lightens our estimate of His self-denial and disinterestedness? Nay, it adds weight to it. Some people
fancy that there is no credit in doing a thing unless you are miserable in doing it. Nay,
brethren, that is the very reverse. Obedience which is unwillingly offered and causes
no joy in the world, is not acceptable. We must serve God with our heart, or we do
not serve Him. Obedience rendered without delight in rendering it is only half
obedience. You shall say what you will about the greatness of my Lord's agonies. You
shall never go too far in your estimate of His unfathomable griefs; but going with you
to the full in it all, I shall take liberty still to say that He had within Himself a fountain of joy, which enabled Him to endure the cross, and even to despise the shame.
Blessed among men was He, even when He was made a curse for us! What a delight
He gave Himself for us, and made a cheerful surrender of Himself, that He might be
the ransom for many. The text is express upon that fact.

And all this because *our Lord came with such intense heartiness*. He says, "Yea, thy
law is within my heart." Our Lord is most thorough in all that He does. His work is
never slovenly, nor in a half-hearted way. He does not even sit on the well and talk to
a poor woman, but what His heart is there. He does not go into a fisherman's hut, but
what His heart is there, and He heals the sick one. He does not sit down to supper
with His followers, but what His heart is there, and He reveals His love. I wish we were
always at home when the Lord calls for us! Sometimes we are all abroad, and our heart
is away from the service of our Father; but He loved the Lord with all His heart, and
mind, and strength. For us He gave His whole being, rejoicing to redeem us. He was
always intense. Whether He preached or practiced, Jesus was all there and always
there. Hence His delight; for what a man does with his heart he delights to do. These
two sentences are melodious of joy to my ear. "I delight to do thy will, O my God:
yea, thy law is within my heart."

Hear this one other word. It is all done now. Jesus has fulfilled the Father's will
in the salvation in the midst of His ransomed ones. And shall I tell you, need I tell
you, what must be the delight, *the heavenly joy of our Lord, now that the work is finished?* He is now the Focus, the Center, the Source of bliss. What must be His
own delight! We often say of the angels that they rejoice over one sinner that repenteth. I doubt not that they do, but the Bible does not say so. The Bible says,
"There is joy in the presence of the angels of God over one sinner that repenteth."
What means the presence of the angels? Why, that the angels see the joy of Christ
when sinners repent. Hear them say to one another, "Behold the Father's face!
How He rejoices! Gaze on the countenance of the Son! What a heaven of delight
shines in those eyes of His! Jesus wept for these sinners, but now He rejoices over
them. How resplendent are the nail-prints today, for the redeemed of the Lord's death
are believing and repenting! That blessed countenance which is always as a sun,
shineth in the fullness of its strength, now that He sees of the travail of His soul." He
who suffered feels a joy unsearchable,

> The first-born sons of light
> > Desire in vain its depths to see:
> They cannot read the mystery—
> > The length, the breadth, the height.

Oh, the joy of triumphant love! The joy of the crucified, whose prepared body is the body of His glory as once it was the body of His humiliation! In that manhood He still rejoices, and delights to do the will of the Father.

My time has fled, and yet I am expected to say something about missions. What shall I say? My brothers, sisters, all of you, do you know anything about the truths I have spoken? Then go and tell the heathen that the Lord is come. Here is a message worth the telling. Mary Magdalene and the other Marys, haste to tell the disciples that the Lord had risen; will you not go and tell them that He has come down to save? "Lo, I come," saith He. Will you not take up His words, and go to the people who have never heard of Him, and say, "Lo, He has come." Tell the Ethiopians, the Chinese, the Hindus, and all the islands of the sea, that God has come hither to save men, and has taken a prepared body, that He might give to God all He required, and all that He desired, that sinful men might be accepted in the Beloved, with whom God the Father is well pleased. Go, and take to the heathen this sacred Book. "In the volume of the book it is written of him." Do not begin to doubt the Book yourself. Why should you send missionaries to teach them about a book in which you do not yourself believe? Tell the nations that "In the volume of the book it is written of Him." Believe this Book, and spread it. Help Bible societies, and all such efforts; and aid missionary societies, which carry the Book and proclaim the Savior. The men of the Book of God are the men of God, such as the world needs. Bid such men go and open the Book of God, and teach the nations its blessed news. Go, dear friends, and assure the heathen that there is happiness in obedience to God. So the Savior found it. He delighted in God's will, even to the death, and they will also know delight as in their measures they bow before the authority of the Word and the will of the one living and true God, the God of Abraham, of Isaac, and of Jacob. Jehovah, the I AM, must be worshiped, for beside Him there is none else. Give glory unto God, whom our Lord Jesus has come to glorify. Amen.

"LO, I COME": APPLICATION

SERMON NO. 2,203

DELIVERED ON LORD'S DAY MORNING, MAY 3, 1891.

Then said I, Lo, I come—Psalm 40:7.

To my great sorrow, last Sunday night I was unable to preach. I had prepared a sermon upon this text, with much hope of its usefulness; for I intended it to be a supplement to the morning sermon, which was a doctrinal exposition. The evening sermon was intended to be practical, and to commend the whole subject to the attention of inquiring sinners. I came here feeling quite fit to preach, when an overpowering nervousness oppressed me, and I lost all self-control, and left the pulpit in anguish. I come hither this morning with the same subject. I have been turning it over, and wondering why it was so. Peradventure, this sermon was not to be preached on that occasion, because God would teach the preacher more of his own feebleness, and cast him more fully upon the divine strength. That has certainly been the effect upon my own heart. Perhaps, also, there are some here this morning who were not here last Lord's day evening, whom God intends to bless by the sermon. The people were not here, peradventure, for whom the eternal decree of God had designed the message, and they may be here now. You that are fresh to this place, should consider the strange circumstance, which never happened to me before in the forty years of my ministry; and you may be led to whether my bow was then unstrung that the arrow might find its ordained target in your heart. The two sermons will now go forth together from the press; and perhaps, going together, they may prove like two hands of love wherewith to embrace lost souls, and draw them to the Savior, who herein saith, "Lo, I come." God grant it may be so!

The times when our Lord says, "Lo, I come," have all a family likeness. There are certain crystals which assume a regular shape, and if you break them, each fragment will show the same conformation; if you were to dash them to shivers, every particle of the crystal would be still of the same form. Now the goings forth of Christ which were of old, and His coming at Calvary, and that great advent when He shall come a second time to judge the earth in righteousness, all these have a likeness the one to the other. But there is a coming of what I may call a lesser sort, when Jesus cries, "Lo, I come" to each individual sinner, and brings a revelation of pardon and salvation; and this has about it much which is similar to the great ones. My one desire this morning is to set forth the Lord Jesus as saying to you, as once He did to me, "Lo, I come." Still He cries to the weak, destitute, forlorn, hopeless sinner, "Lo, I come." I shall talk about that coming, and hope that you will experience it now, and thus be able to follow me in what I say. I speak to the unconverted mainly; but while I do so I shall hope to be refreshing the grateful memories of those already saved; but this will all depend upon the working of the Spirit of God. To Him, then, lift up your hearts in prayer.

I. I will commence with this observation: THE LORD CHRIST HAS TIMES OF HIS FIRST COMINGS TO MEN: "*Then* said I, Lo, I come."

What are these times? Perhaps some here present have reached this season, and this very day is the time of blessing when the text shall be fulfilled: "Then said I, Lo, I come." Go with me to the first record in the volume of the Book, when it was said that He should come. You will find it in the early chapters of Genesis.

Jesus said, "Lo, I come" *when man's probation was a failure.* Man in the Garden of Eden had every advantage for obedience and life. He had a perfect nature, created without bias towards evil, and he was surrounded with every inducement to continue loyal to his Maker. He was placed under no burdensome law. The precept was simple and plain: "Of every tree of the garden thou mayest freely eat: but of the tree of the knowledge of good and evil, thou shalt not eat of it: for in the day that thou eatest thereof thou shalt surely die." Only one tree was reserved: all the rest were given up to be freely enjoyed. In a very short time—some think it was on the first day, but that we do not know—our mother Eve ate of the fruit, and father Adam followed her, and thus human probation ended in total failure. They were weighed in the balances, and found wanting: "Adam being in honor continued not." At that point we read in the volume of the Book that the Seed of the woman should bruise the serpent's head. *Then* our Redeemer said, "Lo, I come." Hearken to me, my friend: you also have had your probation, as you have thought it to be. You quitted your father's roof with every hope, your mother judged you to be of a most amiable character, and your friends expected to see in you one whose life would honor the family. You thought so yourself. Your probation has reversed that hope: you have turned out far other than you should have been; and looking back upon the whole of your life to this moment, you ought to be ashamed. It has been a terrible breaking down for you, and for all who know you; and you are sitting in this place feeling, "Yes, it is so; the tests have proved me to be as a broken reed. I am under condemnation by reason of my transgressions against God." How rejoiced I am to tell you that, at such a time when you are conscious that your are a dead failure, Jesus says, "Lo, I come!" If you had not been a failure you would not have wanted Him, and He never comes as a superfluity; but now in your complete breakdown you must have Him or perish, and in infinite pity He cries, "Lo, I come." Is not this good news for you? Believe it and live.

That also was *a time when man's clever dealing with the devil had turned out a great failure.* The serpent came and said, "God doth know that in the day ye eat thereof, then your eyes shall be opened, and ye shall be as gods, knowing good and evil." How craftily he put it! How cunningly he insinuated that God was jealous of what man might become, and was keeping him back from a nobler destiny! He even dared to say, "Ye shall not surely die," thus giving the Lord the lie direct. He seemed to say— His threat is a mere bugbear, a thing to scare you from a great advance in knowledge and position. "Ye shall not surely die." Eve, in her supposed wisdom, was not able to cope with the serpent's subtlety. "And when the woman saw that the tree was good for food, and that it was pleasant to the eyes, and a tree to be desired to make one wise, she took of the fruit thereof, and did eat, and gave also unto her husband with her; and he did eat." The devil had played his cards so well that man was left bankrupt of virtue, bankrupt of happiness, bankrupt of hope. *Then*, in the volume of the Book, it was written, "I said, Lo, I come." Yes, in the hour when hellish falsehood had robbed man of everything. No man hath yet dealt with the devil without being a loser. The arch-deceiver promises very fairly; but he lies from beginning to end. I know he promised you pleasure unbounded, and liberty unrestrained. Now, the pleasure is burnt out, and the ashes of that which once blazed and crackled, are terrible to look upon. As for liberty, where is it? You have become the bond-slave of sin. You were to enjoy life, and lo, you are plunged in death! It may be, there are in this house persons who bear in their bodies the marks, not of the Lord Jesus, but of the devil's temptations. He has made you so to sin that your bones are filled with the sins of your youth; and you know it. He needs a long spoon who eats out of the same dish as the devil, and your spoon has not been long enough. Sin has overreached and betrayed you; and you stand trembling before God as the result of having listened to the falsehoods of hell, and having rejected the commands of heaven. Supposing such a person to be present—and I feel sure he is—I pray that he may hear my text as from the Lord Jesus Himself. "Then said I, Lo, I come." The devil has trodden you down, but Jesus comes to raise you up. Your paradise is lost, and by Him it is to be restored. Jesus has come to give repentance and remission of sins. That crafty head which deceived you, the Lord Jesus has broken; He came for this purpose. If you had not been betrayed, you would not have needed a deliverer; but your misery has made room for His mercy. Not while Adam is perfect in paradise is there any news of the Seed of the woman bruising the serpent's head; but after the serpent has done his deceitful work, and has ruined the race, then we hear that ancient gospel of God, and see the sole hope of fallen man. Here is good cheer for you who look with shame upon your foolish yielding to Satan's deceits. You are caught as silly birds in a snare; you have been as foolish as the fish of the sea which are taken in a net; but when you are captives, Christ comes to be your Liberator, and God commends His love towards you in that while you are yet sinners Christ died for the ungodly.

Further than this, when we find the first promise of our Lord's coming, "in this volume of the Book," we find that *man's covering was a failure*. The guilty pair had gathered the leaves of the fig-tree, and had made themselves aprons, for they knew that they were naked. This was the first fruit of that boasted tree of knowledge, and it is the principal one to this day. Their scant coverlet contented them for a little while;

but when the voice of the Lord God was heard in the garden they confessed that their aprons were good for nothing; for Adam owned that he was afraid because he was naked, and that therefore he had hidden himself in the thick groves of the garden. It is easy to make a covering which pleases us for a season; but self-righteousness, presumption, pretended infidelity, and fancied natural excellence—all these things are like green fig-leaves which shrivel up before long, lose their freshness, and are rather an exposure than a covering. It may be that my hearer has found his imaginary virtues failing him. It was when our first parents knew that they were naked that the Savior said, "Lo, I come." My downcast hearer, if you are no longer in your own esteem as good as you used to be; if you can no longer hide the fact that you have broken God's law, and deserve His wrath; if you no longer believe the devil's lie that you shall suffer no penalty, but may even be the better for sin, then the Lord the Savior says to you, "Lo, I come." To you, O naked sinner, shivering in your own shame, blushing scarlet with conviction—to you He comes. When you have nothing left of your own, He comes to be your robe of righteousness, wherein you may stand accepted with God.

That first news of the coming Champion came at a time *when all man's pleas were failures*. Adam had thrown the blame on Eve—"The woman whom thou gavest to be with me, she gave me of the tree, and I did eat." Eve had also thrown the blame on the serpent; but the Lord God had silenced all such excuses, and driven them from their refuges. He had made them feel their guilt, and had pronounced upon them the inevitable sentence; and then it was that He spoke of the "Seed of the woman." Here was man's first, and last, and best hope. So too, my friend, why you dare no longer plead your innocence, nor mention extenuations and excuses, then Jesus comes in. If conscience oppresses you so sorely that you cannot escape from it; if it be so that all you can say is "Guilty, Willfully Guilty," then Jesus comes. If you neither blame your surroundings, nor your companions, nor the providence of God, nor your physical weakness, nor anything else, but just take all the blame to yourself because you cannot help doing so, then Jesus comes in. Verily you have sinned against God, against your parents, against your fellowmen, against light, against knowledge, against conscience, and against the Holy Ghost; no wonder, therefore, that you stand speechless, unable to offer any plea by way of self-justification. It is in that moment of shame and confusion that the Savior says, "Lo, I come." For such as you are He is an Advocate. When a sinner cannot plead for Himself, Christ pleads for him; when his excuses have come to an end, then will the Lord put away his sin, through His own great sacrifice. Is not this a precious gospel word?

When our Lord did actually arrive, fulfilling the text by being born of a woman, it was *when man's religion had proved a failure*. Sacrifices and offerings had ceased to be of any value: God had put them away as a weariness to Him. The scribes and the Pharisees, with all their phylacteries and wide-bordered garments, were a mere sham. There seemed to be no true religion left upon the earth. Then said Christ, "Lo, I come." There was never a darker thirty years than when Herod slew the innocents, and the chief priests and scribes pursued the Son of God, and at last nailed Him to the tree. It was *then* that Jesus came to us to redeem us by His death. Do I speak to any man here whose religion has broken down? You have observed a host of rites and ceremonies: you were christened in your infancy, you were duly confirmed, you have taken what you call "the blessed sacrament"; or it may be that you have sat always in the most plain of meeting-houses, and listened to the most orthodox of preachers, and you have been amongst the most religious of religious people; but now, at length, the Spirit of God has shown you that all these performances and attendances are worthless cobwebs which avail you nothing. You see now that—

> Not all the outward forms on earth,
> Nor rites that God has given,
> Nor will of man, nor blood, nor birth,
> Can raise a soul to heaven.

You are just now driven to despair, because the palace of your imaginary excellence has vanished like the baseless fabric of a vision. If I had told you that your religiousness was of no value, you would have been very angry with me, and perhaps you would have said, "That is a bigoted remark, and you ought to be ashamed of making it." But now the Spirit of God has told it you, and you feel its force: He is great at convincing of sin. When the Spirit of truth comes to deal with the religiousness of the flesh, He withers it in a moment. All religion which is not spiritual is worthless. All religion which is not the supernatural product of the Holy Ghost is a fiction. One breath from the Spirit of God withers all the beauty of our pride, and destroys the comeliness of our conceit; and *then*, when our own religion is dashed to shivers, the Lord Jesus comes in, saying, "Lo, I come." He delights to come in His glorious personality, when the Pharisee can no longer say, "God, I thank thee, that I am not as other men"; and when the once bold fisherman is crying, "Lord, save, or I perish." If you feel that you need something infinitely better than Churchianity, or Dissenterism, or Methodism—in fact, that you need Christ Himself to be formed in you—*then* to you, even to you, Jesus says, "Lo, I come." When man is at his worst, Christ is seen at His best. The Lord walks to us on the sea in the middle watch of the night. He draws nigh to those souls which draw nigh to death. When you part with self you meet with Christ. When no shred of hope remains, then Jesus says, "Lo, I come."

Once more. The Lord Jesus is to come a second time; and when will He come? He will come *when man's hope is a failure.* He will come when iniquity abounds, and the love of many hath waxed cold. He will come when dreams of a golden age shall be turned into the dread reality of abounding evil. Do not dream that the world will go on improving and improving, and that the improvement will naturally culminate in the millennium. No such thing. It may grow better for a while, better under certain aspects; but, afterwards the power of the better element will ebb out like the sea, even though each wave should look like an advance. That day shall not come except there be a falling away first. Even the wise virgins will sleep, and the men of the world will be, as in the day of Noah, eating and drinking, marrying and being given in marriage. On a sudden, the Lord will come as thief in the night. The deluge of fire will find men as unprepared as did the deluge of water. He will come taking vengeance on His adversaries. When things wax worse and worse we see the tokens of His speedy coming. He will shortly appear, for the sky is darkening. When every hope will seem blotted out, and nothing but grim ages of anarchy and ungodliness are to be expected, then our Deliverer will come. When the tale of bricks was doubled in Egypt, Moses came; and when the world attains to its utmost unbelief and iniquity, Jesus will come. So at this moment my hearer may be saying, "I cannot be worse than I am; if I am not actually in hell already, yet I feel a fire within which tortures my soul. The sword of vengeance hangs over my head suspended by a single hair. I tremble to live, and I fear to die. Lost! Lost! Lost! I am past hope!" This is the time for my text: "*Then* said I, Lo, I come." He who is able to save to the uttermost appears to the soul when every other hope disappears. In your deep distress I see a token for good. You are now reduced to spiritual death, and now I trust the eternal life will visit you.

Now all this I put before you in simple language, believing what I say, and trusting that if I describe your case, you will know that I mean it for you. I have heard of a preacher who was so fearful lest he should be thought personal, that he said to his congregation, "Lest any of you should think that what I have said was meant for you, I would observe that the sermon I am preaching was prepared for a congregation in Massachusetts." I can plead nothing of the sort. I refer to you, my hearer, in the most pointed manner. I will attend to Massachusetts, if ever the Lord sends me there; but just now *I mean you*. Oh, that you may have the grace to take home these thoughts to yourselves; for if you do so, they will by the Spirit's power bring the light of hope into your souls!

II. Secondly, I would remark that CHRIST COMES TO SINNERS IN THE GLORY OF HIS PERSON: "Then said I, Lo, I come." Note that glorious *I!* Have you not seen people engaged in urgent work who did not understand their business? Apprentices, and other unskillful people, are muddling time away. They are making bad worse, and running great risk. Perhaps a great calamity will occur if the work is not done well and quickly. A first-rate worker is sent for. See, the man has come who understands the business. He cries, "Let me come! Stand out of my way! You are on the wrong tack: let me do it myself!" You have not blamed him for egotism, for the thing needed to be done, and *he* could do it, and the others could not. Everybody recognized the master workman, and gave place to him. The announcement of his coming was the end of the muddle, and the signal of hope. Even so Jesus comes to you sinners, and His presence is your salvation. He says, "Lo, I come." What does He mean?

He means, *the setting of all else on one side*. There is the priest—he has not helped you much; he may go, for Jesus says, "Lo, I come." There are your own efforts and doings; there are your feelings and thinkings; there are your ceremonies and austerities; there are your prayers and tears; there are your hearings and readings—

all these must be laid aside as grounds of confidence, and Jesus alone must be your trust. He can do for you what none of these can. You are trying to work yourself up to repentance and faith, and you cannot succeed. Let Him come, and He will bring every good thing with Him. It is glorious to see our Lord throwing down all our bowing walls and tottering fences, and to hear Him cry, "Behold, I lay in Zion for a foundation." Everything else vanishes before His perfect salvation.

Before Him there is *a setting of self aside*. You have been your own confidence. What you could feel, or do, or think, or resolve, had become the ground of your confidence; but now Jesus puts self down, and He is Himself exalted. By working yourself to death, you cannot effect your own salvation. Lo, Jesus comes to save you. You cannot weave yourself a garment. Lo, He comes to clothe you from head to foot with His own seamless robe of righteousness. He annihilates self that He may fill all things.

Here is a glorious *setting of Himself at our side and in our place*. Mr. Moody tells a story, which I would fain hope may be true; for one would like to hear something good about a Czar of Russia, and especially about our once enemy, the Emperor Nicholas. The story concerns a soldier in the barracks who was much distressed by his heavy debts. He was in despair, for he owed a great deal of money, and could not tell where to get it. He took a piece of paper, and made a list of his debts, and underneath the list he wrote, "Who will pay these debts?" He then lay down on the barrack bed, and fell asleep, with the paper before him. The Emperor of Russia passed by, and, taking up the paper, read it, and being in a gracious mood signed at the bottom, "Nicholas." Was not that a splendid answer to the question? When the soldier woke up and read it, he could scarcely believe his own eyes. "Who will pay these debts?" was the despairing question. "Nicholas" was the all-sufficient answer. So are we answered, Who will bear our sins? The grand reply is "Jesus." He puts His own name to our liabilities, and in effect, that He may meet them, He says, "Lo, I come." Your debt of sin is discharged when you believe in Christ Jesus. "Without shedding of blood is no remission"; but the blood of Jesus Christ, God's dear Son, cleanseth us from all sin. You are not now to bear your own sins. Behold the scapegoat, who carries them away into the wilderness! Yea, Jesus says, "Lo, I come!" He takes our sins upon Himself, He bears their penalty, and we go free. Blessed word— "Lo, I come": I come to take your weight of sin, your burden of punishment. I come to be made a curse for you, that you may be made the righteousness of God in me. Sinner, stand out of the way, and let Jesus appear for you, and fill your place! He sets you on one side, and then He sets Himself where you have been. Jesus is now the one pillar on which to lean, the one foundation on which to build, the one and only rest of our weary souls.

He sets Himself where we can see Him; for He cries, "*Lo, I have come*"; that is to say, "See Me come." He comes openly, that we may see Him clearly. How I wish the Lord would reveal Himself at this moment to each one of those who are weary of earth, of self, of sin, and possibly even weary of life itself! Oh, if you could but see

Jesus standing in your room and stead, you would have faith to stand in His place, and so become "accepted in the Beloved!" O Lord, hear my prayer, and cause poor hearts to see Thee descending from the skies, to uplift sinners from the dark abyss! Holy Spirit, touch that young man's eyes with heavenly salve, that he may see where salvation lies. Deal with that poor woman's dim eyes also, that she may perceive the Lord Christ, and find peace in Him. Jesus cries, "Lo, I come! Look unto me, and be ye saved, all the ends of the earth."

> There is life for a look at the Crucified One;
> There is life at this moment for thee.
> Then look, sinner—look unto him, and be saved—
> Unto him who was nail'd to the tree.

Should you even lie in all the despair and desolation which I described, I would persuade you to believe in Jesus. Trust Him, and you shall find Him all that you want.

Our Lord sets Himself to be permanently our all in all. When He came on earth, He did not leave His work till He had finished it. Even when He rose to glory, He continued His service for His chosen, living to intercede for them. Jesus was a Savior 1900 years ago, and He is a Savior still; and He will be a Savior until all the chosen race shall have been gathered home. He tells us, "I said, Lo, I come"; but He does not say, "I said, I will go away, and quit the work." Our Lord's ear is bored, and He goes out no more from the service of salvation. It is not written of any penitent souls, "Ye shall seek me, but shall not find me"; but it is written, "If thou seek him, he will be found of thee." O my hearer, you are now in the place where the gospel is preached to you—yes, to you, for we are sent to preach the gospel to every creature; and though you should be the worst, and most benighted, and most guilty of all the creatures out of hell, yet you are a creature, and we preach Christ to you. O poor heart, may the Lord Jesus say to you, "Lo, I come!" for He comes to stay—to stay until He has worked salvation *in* you as He has worked out salvation *for* you. He will not leave a believer till He has presented him spotless before the throne of God with exceeding joy. I wish I could make all this most clear and plain. You are altogether ruined by your own fault, and you cannot undo the evil. You have done all you can, and it has come to nothing. You are steeped in sin up to your throat; yea the filth has gone over your head: you are as one drowned in black waters. Despairing one, cast not your eyes around to seek for a friend, for you will look in vain to men. No arm can rescue you, save one; and that is the arm of Jesus, who now cries, "Lo, I come." Set everything else on one side, and trust yourself with the Savior, Christ the Lord.

III. Oh, that many may be comforted while I dwell on a third head! CHRIST IN HIS COMING IS HIS OWN INTRODUCTION.

Here our Lord is His own herald. "Lo, I come." He does not wait for an eloquent preacher to act as master of the ceremonies to Him: He introduces Himself. Therefore even I, the simplest talker on earth, may prove quite sufficient for my Lord's purpose if He will graciously condescend to bless these plain words of mine. It is not I that says that Jesus comes, but in the text our Lord Himself declares, "Then said I,

Lo, I come." You need not do anything to draw Christ's attention to you; it is Christ who draws your attention to Himself. Do you see this? You are the blind bat; and He is all eye towards you, and bids you look on Him. I hear you cry, "Lord, remember me," and I hear Him answer, "Soul, remember Me." He bids you look on Him when you beseech Him to look on you.

He comes when quite unsought, or sought for in a wrong way. To many men and women Christ has come though they had not even desired Him. Yea, He has come even to those who hated Him. Saul of Tarsus was on his way to worry the saints at Damascus, but Jesus said, "Lo, I come"; and when He looked out of heaven He turned Saul, the persecutor, into Paul, the Apostle. The promise is fulfilled, "I was found of them that sought me not, I was made manifest unto them that asked not after me." Herein is the glorious sovereignty of His love fully exercised, and grace reigns supreme. "Lo, I come," is the announcement of majestic grace which waiteth not for man, neither tarrieth for the sons of men.

Our Lord Jesus is the way to Himself. Did you ever notice that? He comes Himself to us, and so He is the way by which we meet Him. He is our rest, and the way to our rest; He says, "I am the way." You want to know how to get to Christ? You have not to get to Christ, for He has come to you. It is well for you to come to Christ; but that is only possible because Christ has come to you. Jesus is near you: near you *now*. Backslider, He comes to you! Wandering soul, roving to the very brink of perdition, the good Shepherd cries, "Lo, I come." He is the way to Himself.

Remember, also, that *He is the blessing which He brings.* Jesus not only gives life and resurrection, but He says, "I am the resurrection and the life." Christ is salvation, and everything needful to salvation is in Him. If He comes, all good comes *with* Him, or rather *in* Him. An inquirer once said to a minister, "The next step for me is to get a deeper conviction of sin." The minister said, "No such thing, my friend: the next step is to trust in Jesus, for He says, 'Come unto me.' " To come to Jesus, or rather to receive Jesus who has come to us, is the one essential step into eternal salvation. Though our Lord does say, "Come unto me," He has preceded it with this other word, "Lo, I come." Poor cripple, if you cannot come to Jesus, ask Him to come to you; and He will. Here you lie, and you have been for years in this case; you have no man to put you into the pool, and it would do you no good if he did; but Jesus can make you whole, and He is here. You cannot stir hand or foot because of spiritual paralysis; but your case is not hopeless. Listen to my Lord in the text, "Then said I, Lo, I come." He has no paralysis. He can come, leaping over the mountains of division. I know my Lord came to me, or I should never have come to Him: why should He not come to you? I came to Him because He came to me.

> He drew me, and I followed on,
> Charmed to confess the voice divine.

Why should He not draw us also? Is He not doing so? Yield to the pressure of His love.

"Then said I, Lo, I come." You see *our Lord is His own spokesman.* He says to me, "Go and tell those people about my coming"; and I gladly do so; but you will forget *my* words, and refuse to accept the Coming One. Your consciences will be un-awakened, your hearts unmoved: I fear it will be so. But if this text be fulfilled concerning our Lord this day—"Then said I, Lo, I come"—you will hear HIM. If He speaks He is Himself the Almighty Word, and His voice will reach your hearts, and accomplish His purpose. Dear Christian people, join with me in this prayer: Lord speak to thy chosen ones that lie here in their death-like despair, far off from Thee, and say to each one of them, "Lo, I come." O downcast soul, this is your morning: this is the set time to favor you: this day is salvation come to your house and to your heart. Make haste and come down from the tree of your frivolity or your self-right-eousness. Receive the Lord Jesus, for today He must abide in your house and in your heart: the hour for the imperial "*must*" of the eternal purpose has arrived. God grant it may be so! May this be an hour of which Jesus shall declare—"Then said I, Lo, I come!"

IV. Our next point is this—CHRIST, TO CHEER US, REVEALS HIS REASONS FOR COMING. Only a few words on this. Note the rest of the verse: "Lo, I come: in the vol-ume of the book it is written of me." When we were yet without strength, in due time Christ died for the ungodly, because it was the due time *according to covenant pur-poses*. Christ comes to a guilty sinner, just as He once came to a manger and a stable, because so it was appointed. There is nothing for Him to get, but everything for Him to give; but He comes because so it is written in the volume of the divine de-crees—

> Thus the eternal counsel ran—
> Almighty grace, arrest that man!

THEREFORE, IN LOVE THE SAVIOR APPEARS TO THE SINNER, AND BY GRACE ARRESTS HIM IN HIS MAD CAREER.

It is His Father's will. Christ's coming to save a soul is with His Father's full con-sent and aid. The Father wills that you who believe in Him, lost though you be, should now be saved, and Jesus comes to do the will of the Father.

He comes because His heart is set on you. He loves you, and so He hastens to your rescue. Your salvation is His delight. Though your soul is sunk in a sea of need, and you are in despair because of that need, Jesus loves you, and comes to meet your case. The best of all is that Jesus loves you. One asked an old man of ninety, "Do you love Jesus?" and the old man answered with a smile, "I do, indeed; but I can tell you some-thing better than that." His friend said, "Something better than loving Jesus! What is that?" The old disciple replied, "*He loves me.*" O soul, I wish you could see this fact, which is indeed better than your love to Jesus, namely His love to you! Because He loved His redeemed from before the foundation of the world, therefore in due time He says, "Lo, I come."

The fact is, *you have need, and He has love, and so He comes*. There is no hope for you unless He does come, and that is why He comes. If you had a penny of your own, He would not give you His purse; if you had a rag of your own, He would not give you His robe; if you had a breath of your own, He would not give you His life. But now you are naked, and poor, and miserable, and lost, and dead, Jesus reveals Himself, and you read concerning Him, "Then said I, Lo, I come." He gives you His reasons—reasons not in yourself, but all in *His* grace. There is no good in you; there is no reason in you why the Lord should save you; but because of His free, spontaneous, rich, sovereign, almighty grace, He leaps out of heaven, He descends to earth, He plunges into the grave to pluck His beloved from destruction.

V. Here is my last word: CHRIST'S COMING IS THE BEST PLEA FOR OUR RECEIVING HIM, and receiving Him now. O sirs, remember you have not to raise the question whether He will come or not. He is come. You have not to say, How can I come to Him? He comes to you. You do want a Mediator between your soul and God; but you do *not* want any mediator between yourself and Jesus; for He says, "Lo, I come." To you in all your filthiness, in all your condemnation, in all your hopelessness, He comes. Wait not for anybody to introduce you to Him, or Him to you; He has introduced Himself, and here is His card—"Then I said, Lo, I come." No pleas are needed to persuade Him to come to you, for He says, "Lo, I come." Though you cannot think of a single argument why He should appear to you in mercy, He does so appear. It is written, "I will have mercy upon her that had not obtained mercy; and I will say to them which were not my people, thou art my people; and they shall say, thou art my God." O words of wondrous grace! Our gracious Lord does not wait for our entreaties; but of His own accord He says, "Lo, I come." Without asking you, and without your asking Him, He puts in an appearance in the sovereignty of His grace.

No search is needed to find the Lord, for He comes in manifested grace, and calls upon us to see Him. "I have long been searching for Christ" murmurs one. What! Seeking for the sun at noonday? Jesus is not lost. It is you that are lost, and He is searching for you. He says, "Lo, I come": it is *you* that will not come. Still one declares that he has been seeking the Lord Jesus for many a day. This is sadly strange, for Jesus is near. "Say not in thine heart, Who shall ascend into heaven? or, Who shall descend into the deep? The word is nigh thee, even in thy mouth, and in thy heart, that if thou wilt confess with thy mouth the Lord Jesus, and shalt believe in thy heart that God hath raised him from the dead, thou shalt be saved." If thou believest in the Lord Jesus Christ, thou shalt be saved. Searching after Christ? Nay, verily He saith, "Lo, I come."

Moreover, no waiting is needed, and no preparation is to be made by you. Why do you wait? HE does not wait, but cries, "Lo, I come!" "I will get ready for Christ," say you; but it is too late to talk so, when He cries, "Lo, I am come." Receive Him! If you are in yourself sadly unready, yet He Himself will make everything ready for Himself. Only open wide the door and let Him in. Do you say, "But I am shamed?" Be ashamed. He bids you be ashamed, and be confounded, while He declares, "I do not this for your sakes." Yet be not so ashamed as to commit another shameful deed by shutting the door in your Redeemer's face. Shut not out your own mercy. A pastor in Edinburgh, in going round his district, knocked at the door of a poor woman, for whom he had brought some needed help; but he received no answer.

When next he met her, he said to her, "I called on Tuesday at your house." She asked, "At what time?" "About eleven o'clock; I knocked, and you did not answer. I was disappointed, for I called to give you help." "Ah, sir!" said she, "I am very sorry. I thought it was the man coming for the rent, and I could not pay it, and therefore I did not dare to go to the door." Many a troubled soul thinks that Jesus is one who comes to ask of us what we cannot give; but indeed He comes to give us all things. His errand is not to condemn, but to forgive. Miss not the charity of God through unbelief. Run to the door, and say to your loving Redeemer, "Lord, I am not worthy that Thou shouldest come under my roof; but as Thou hast come to me, I welcome Thee with all my heart."

No assistance is wanted by Christ on your part. He does not come with half a salvation, and look to you to complete it. He does not come to bring you a robe half woven, which you are to finish. How could you finish it? Could the best saint in the world add anything to Christ's righteousness? No good man would even dream of adding his homespun to that raiment which is of wrought gold. What! Are *you* to make up the deficient ransom price? Is it deficient? Would you bring your clods of mud into the royal treasury, and lay them down side by side with sapphires? Would you help Christ? Go, yoke a mouse with an elephant! Go harness a fly side by side with an archangel. But dream not of yoking yourself with Christ.

He says, "Lo, I come," and I trust you will reply, "My Lord, if Thou art come, all is come, and I am complete in Thee."

> Thou, O Christ, art all I want,
> More than all in thee I find.

Receive Him: receive Him at once. Dear children of God, and sinners that have begun to feel after Him, say with one accord, "Even so, come quickly, Lord Jesus." If He says, "Lo, I come," and the Spirit and the bride say, Come; and he that heareth says, Come, and he that is athirst comes, and whosoever will is bidden to come and take the water of life freely; then let us join the chorus of comers, and come to Christ ourselves. "Behold the Bridegroom cometh; go ye out to meet him!" Ye who most of all need Him, be among the first and gladdest, as you hear Him, say, "Lo, I come."

All that I have said will be good for nothing as to saving results unless the Holy Ghost shall apply it with power to your hearts. Join with me in prayer that many may see Jesus just now, and may at once behold and accept the present salvation which is in Him.

BROUGHT UP FROM THE
HORRIBLE PIT

SERMON NO. 1,674
DELIVERED ON LORD'S DAY MORNING, AUGUST 13, 1882.
PORTION OF SCRIPTURE READ BEFORE SERMON—PSALM 40.
HYMNS FROM *Our Own Hymn Book*—196, 40, 332.

I waited patiently for the LORD: and he inclined unto me, and heard my cry. He brought me up also out of an horrible pit, out of the miry clay, and set my feet upon a rock, and established my goings. And he hath put a new song in my mouth, even praise unto our God: many shall see it, and fear, and shall trust in the LORD—Psalm 40:1–3.

THIS passage has been used with great frequency as the expression of the experience of the people of God, and I think it has been very rightly so used. It is a very accurate picture of the way in which sinners are raised up from despair to hope and salvation, and of the way in which saints are brought out of deep troubles, and made to sing of divine love and power. Yet I am not certain that the first verse could be truthfully uttered by all of us; I question, indeed, whether any of us could thus speak. Could we say—"I waited patiently for the Lord." Think ye, brethren, might it not read—"I waited impatiently for the Lord," in the case of most of us? All the rest may stand true, but this would need to be modified. We could hardly speak in our own commendation if we considered our conduct in the matter of patience, for that is, alas, still a scarce virtue upon the face of the earth. If we read the psalm through we shall see that it was not written exclusively to describe the experience of God's people. Secondarily we may regard it as David's language, but in the first instance a greater than David is here. The first Person who uttered these words was the Messiah, and that is quite clear if you read the psalm through; for we fall upon such language as this: "Sacrifice and offering Thou didst not desire; mine ears hast Thou opened: burnt offering and sin offering hast Thou not required. Then said I, Lo, I come: in the volume of the book it is written of Me, I delight to do thy will, O my God: yea, thy law is within my heart." We need not say with the Ethiopian, "Of whom speaketh the prophet this? Of himself or of some other?" For we are led at once by the plainest indications to see that He is not speaking of Himself, but of our Lord;

and if we needed confirmation of this we get it in Hebrews 10, where Paul expressly quotes this passage as referring to the Lord Jesus. To Him, indeed, alone of all men can it with accuracy be applied. So this morning I shall have to show that this text of ours is most fit to be the language of the Lord, our representative and covenant Head. When I have shown this, you will then see how we can use the self-same expressions, because we are in Him. Each believer becomes a mirror in which is reflected the experience of our Lord; but it would be ill for us to be so taken up with the mere reflection as to forget the express image by which this experience is formed in us.

I shall ask you, then, at this time, to observe our divine Lord when in His greatest trouble. Notice, first, *our Lord's behavior*—"I waited patiently for the Lord; and he inclined unto me, and heard my cry": then consider, secondly, *our Lord's deliverance*, expressed by the phrase, "He brought me up also out of a horrible pit, out of the miry clay," and so forth: then let us think, thirdly of *the Lord's reward* for it— "many shall see it, and fear, and trust in the Lord":—that is His great end and object, and in it He sees of the travail of His soul and is satisfied. We shall close, fourthly, by perceiving *the Lord's likeness* in all His saved ones; for they also are brought up from the pit of destruction, and a new song is put into their mouths. He is not shamed to call them brethren, since in each one of them his own experience is repeated though upon a smaller scale.

I. First, let us think of OUR LORD'S BEHAVIOR. "I waited patiently for the Lord." Here we greatly need the teaching of the Holy Ghost; may it be given us abundantly. First, our Lord's conduct when He was under the smarting rod was that of *waiting*. He waited upon the Lord all His life, and this waiting became more conspicuous in His passion and death. He went down into Gethsemane, and there He prayed earnestly; but with sweet submission; for He said, "Nevertheless, not as I will, but as thou wilt." Complete submission was the essential spirit of His prayer. He rose up from prayer all crimson with His bloody sweat, and He went to meet His foes, delivering Himself up voluntarily to be led as a sheep to the slaughter. He did not unsheathe the sword as Peter did; much less did He flee, like His disciples, but He waited upon the will of the Most High, enduring all things till the Father should give Him deliverance. When they took Him before Annas and Caiaphas, and Pilate and Herod, hurrying Him from bar to bar, how patiently He kept silence, though false witnesses appeared against Him. Like a sheep before her shearers He was dumb, submitting Himself without a struggle. In the omnipotence of patience He held His peace even from good, because it was so written of Him. When they led Him away to crucifixion through the streets of Jerusalem He did not even encourage the lamentations of the sympathizing women who surrounded him; but in His wondrous patience He said, "Daughters of Jerusalem, weep not for me." He did not refuse to bear His cross, or to let the cross bear Him. He did not complain of contempt and contumely, since these were appointed Him. When they nailed Him to the tree, and there He hung in the burning sun, tortured, fevered, agonizing, the words that escaped Him were not those of murmuring and repining, but those of pity, pain, patience, and submission. Till He bowed His head, and gave up the ghost, He bowed His whole being to His Father's will, waiting His time and pleasure. He steadily took a long draft at the appointed cup, and drained it to the bitter end. His eyes were unto the Lord as the eyes of servants are to the hands of their masters; He waited in service, in hope, in resignation, and in confidence. He knew that God would help Him and deliver Him, He knew that His head would be raised on high above the sons of men; but still He waited for the Father's time, and meanwhile made Himself of no reputation, and took upon Himself the form of a servant, and as a servant yielded all His strength to the work which was given Him to do. He was willing in the hour of His passion to be treated as the scum and scorn of all mankind, nor did He hurry the hour when all the shame and scorn should blossom into glory and honor. He went down in His waiting even to the utmost of self-denial, and truly proved that He came not to do His own will, but the will of Him that sent Him. Never man served and waited like this man.

Our text adds to this word "waited" the word "patiently." "I waited *patiently.*" If you would see patience, look not at Job on the dunghill, but look at Jesus on the cross. Job, the most patient of men, was assuredly impatient at the same time; but this blessed Lord of ours gave Himself up completely, and showed not the slightest sign of repining. Not a speck of impatience can be detected in the crystal stream of our Lord's submission. His soul was all melted, and it all flowed into the mold of the Father's will: no dross was in or about Him, nothing which refused to melt and to run into the mold. One would have supposed that He would have spoken an angry word to Judas, who betrayed Him; instead of which He gently asked of Him, "Friend, wherefore art thou come?" It would not have seemed wonderful if He had upbraided the Jews who so falsely accused Him, or the rulers who so unjustly treated Him; but here is the patience of the saintly One, He was perfect master of His own Spirit. His answer to His murderers was the prayer, "Father, forgive them, for they know not what they do." So meek and lowly in heart was He that to men He gave no sharp replies: His answers were all steeped in gentleness; take for example His word to the high priest: "If I have spoken evil, bear witness of the evil; but if well, why smitest thou me?" They sat down around the cross and mocked Him, jeered at Him, insulted over Him, and made mirth even of His cries and prayers; but He did not utter a single word of rebuke, much less did He leap from the cross to dash His mockers in pieces, and prove by their destruction that He was indeed the mighty Son of God. "I waited patiently," saith He. No thought or word or deed of impatience can be charged upon Him; waiting, He waited, and waited still. We are in such a hurry when we are in trouble; we hasten to escape from it at once; every minute seems an hour, and every day an age. "Help me speedily, O my God!" is the natural cry of the child of God under the rod; but our Savior was in no ill haste to get from the chastisement which came upon Him for our sakes: He was at leisure in His woe. So thoroughly was He resolved to do His Father's will that even on the morning of His resurrection He arose with deliberation, and quitted the grave in order, folding

His graveclothes and laying the napkin by itself. He steadily persevered in all His work of holiness and sorrow of sacrifice, never accepting deliverance till His work was done. Patiently He endured to have His ear bored to the doorpost, to have His head encircled with thorns, His cheeks disdained with spittle, His back furrowed with the lash, His hands and feet nailed to the wood, and His heart pierced with the spear. In His body on the tree patience was written out in crimson characters.

Now, this was needful for the completeness of His atonement. No expiation could have been made by an impatient Savior. Only a perfect obedience could satisfy the law; only an unblemished sacrifice could put away our sins. There must not, therefore, be about our Substitute a trace of resistance to the Father's will, nor as a sacrifice must He struggle against the cords, or turn His head away from the sacrificial knife. In truth, His was a willing, patient doing and suffering of the divine will. "He *gave* His back to the smiters and His cheeks to them that plucked off the hair: He hid not His face from shame and spitting." "I waited patiently for the Lord," saith He; and you know, brethren, how true was the declaration.

But while the Savior thus waited, and waited patiently, we must not forget that He waited *prayerfully*; for the text speaks of a cry which He lifted up, and of God's inclining Himself to it. That patience which does not pray is obstinacy. A soul silent to God is apt to be sullen rather than submissive. A stoical patience hardens itself against grief, and asks no deliverance; but that is not the patience which God loves, it is not the patience of Christ. He used strong crying and tears unto Him that was able to save Him from death. Let Gethsemane tell of that wrestling which infinitely excelled the wrestling of Jacob: Jabbok is outdone by Kedron. His was a wrestling, not to sweat alone, but unto sweat of blood: he sweats who works for bread, the staff of life; but He sweats blood who works for life itself. What prayers those must have been under such a fearful physical, mental, and spiritual agony which were so fervent that they brought an angel from the throne, and yet so submissive that they are the model of resignation. He agonized as earnestly as if He sought His own will, and yet He wholly resigned Himself to the Father, saying, "Lo, I come: in the volume of the book it is written of me, I delight to do thy will, O my God." Our Lord was always praying: there never was a moment in His life in which He was not in full communion with God, unless we except the period when He cried, "Why hast thou forsaken me?" He did often go aside to pray a more special prayer, but yet even when He spoke to the people, even when He faced His foes, His soul was still in constant fellowship with His Father. But ah, when He came between the upper and the nether millstones, when this good olive was ground in the olive press, and all the oil of His life was extracted from Him, then it was that His strong crying and tears came up before the Lord His God, and He was heard in that He feared.

Now, brothers and sisters, look at your pattern, and see how far short you have come of it. At least, I will remember with regret how far short I have come of it. Have we waited? Have we not been in too great a hurry? Has it not been too much our desire that the Lord might make His will like our will rather than make our will like His? Have you not had a will of your own sometimes, and a strong will too? Have you not been as the bullock unaccustomed to the yoke? Have you not kicked against the pricks? You have not waited, but you have worried. Can we say that we waited patiently? Oh, that patience! Every man thinks he has it until he needs it, but only let his tender point be touched, and you will see how little patience he possesses. It is the fire which tires our supposed resignation, and under that process much of our palace of patience burns like wood, hay, and stubble. Old crosses fit the shoulder, but let a new cross be laid upon us and we writhe under it. Suffering is the vocation of a Christian, but most of us come short of our high calling. Our Lord Jesus has joined together reigning and suffering, for we read of "the kingdom and patience of Jesus Christ"; He was the royal example of patience, but what are we? Remember, again, that Jesus prayed importunately while He waited: "being in an agony, he prayed more earnestly." Have we not at time restrained prayer? Have we not pleaded as an excuse for our feeble petitions the very facts which ought to have been a spur to our earnestness? "I felt too ill to pray." Couldst thou not pray for health with all the more fervency? "I felt too burdened to pray." Shouldst thou not pray for help to bear thy burden? Can we ever safely say to ourselves, "I may be excused from supplication now, for my sorrow is great." Talk not so. Here is thy balm and benediction, thy comfort and thy cordial: here is thy strength and succor, thy constancy and confidence. Even in the midnight of the soul let us arise and pour out our hearts like water before the Lord. O tried believer, get thee to thy knees, and from above the mercy-seat the glory of the Lord shall shine forth upon thee. Pray even as Jesus did, and as all His saints have done, so shall you in patience possess your soul. In due time the Lord inclined to the afflicted suppliant, listening to his moaning from the bottom of the pit; of this it is high time for us to speak. Yet let us not leave this first point till we learn from the example of our Lord that patience is seen in waiting as well as in suffering. To bear a great weight for an hour or two is nothing compared with carrying a load for many a day. Patience knows its letters, but waiting reads the page, and praying rehearses it in the ears of God. Let us add to our patience waiting, and to waiting prayer.

II. We come, secondly, to consider OUR LORD'S DELIVERANCE. In due time, when patience had had her perfect work, and prayer had at last prevailed, our suffering Lord was brought up again from the deeps of sorrow. His deliverance is set forth under two images.

First, it is represented as *a bringing up out of a horrible pit*. It is a terribly suggestive metaphor. I have been in the dungeon in Rome in which, according to tradition, Peter and Paul were confined (though, probably, they were never there at all). It was indeed a horrible pit, for originally it had no entrance but a round hole in the rock above; and when that round hole at the top was blocked with a stone, not a ray of light nor a particle of fresh air could possibly enter. The prisoners were let down into the cavern, and there they were left. When once the opening was closed they were cut off from all communication with their fellow men. No being has ever been so cruel to man as man. Man is the worst of monsters to his kind, and his cruel inventions are many. He has not been content to leave his fellows their natural liberty, but he built prisons and digged pits in which to shut up his victims. At first they would place a man in a dry well merely for custody and confinement, or they would drop him into some hollow cavern in the earth in which corn or treasure had been concealed; but afterwards with greater ingenuity of malice they covered over the top of these pits so that the prisoners could not be partakers of God's bountiful air, or the merciful light of the sun, or the silver sheen of the moon. Covered all over and shut in, the captives were buried alive. Even in modern times we have seen what they call *oubliettes*, or dungeons in which prisoners were immured, to be forgotten as dead men out of mind, buried so as never to come forth again. Such unfortunates as were doomed to enter these tombs of living men bade farewell to hope. They were inhabitants of oblivion, dwellers in the land of deathshade, to remain apart from their kind, cut off from memory. These worst of dungeons may illustrate our text—"He brought me up also out of an horrible pit."

In the original we get the idea of a crash, as when some mailed warrior in the midst of the battle stumbles into a pit, and there he lies bruised and broken: and there is the thought of the fall of waters rushing strangely, furiously, mysteriously. The Hebrew hath it, "The pit of noises," or as some render it, "the pit of destruction." Such was the condition of our dear Redeemer when He was bearing our sin and suffering in our stead.

Just notice, first, that our Lord was like a man put into a pit, and so made to be *quite alone*. Imagine yourself now confined in one of those caverns, with the big stone rolled over the mouth of it. There would be neither hearing nor answering. Now will you know the dread solemnity of silence. You may speak, but no gentle whisper of sympathy will reach your ears in return; you may cry again and again and make the dungeon's dome echo to your voice, but you are speaking as to brass—no man cares for your soul. You are alone; alone in a fearful solitude. Thus it happened to our Savior. All His disciples forsook Him and fled, and what was infinitely worse, His God forsook Him too. He cried, "My God, my God, why hast thou forsaken me?" Can any man tell me all that was meant by that infinite lament?

Of course, a prisoner in such a pit as that was *in total darkness*. He could not see the walls which enclosed him, nor so much as his own hand. No beam of sunlight ever wandered into that stagnant air; the captive would have to grope for the pitcher of water and the morsel of bread which a cruel mercy would allot to him. Our Lord was in the dark; midnight brooded over His spirit. He said—"Now is my soul troubled." "My soul is exceeding sorrowful even unto death." His was a pit of gloom, the region of the shadow of death, a land of darkness as darkness itself.

When a man is shut up in a pit he is, of course, *full of distress*. If you were, any of you, to go into one of the solitary cells of our own jails, I warrant you a short sojourn in it would be quite enough. These cells some years ago were thought to be wonderful cures for all sort of evil dispositions in men, but probably they have oftener destroyed reason than conquered depravity. Go in, if you dare. Ask the warder to shut to the door, and leave you in the dark all alone, that you may try the solitary system for yourself. No, I should not advise you to try it even for five minutes, for you might even in that short pace inflict such an injury upon your nervous system as you would never recover. I believe that many of the gentler ones here would be quite unable to bear total darkness and solitude even for the shortest space. In the grim gloom the soul is haunted with phantom fears, while horror peoples the place which is empty of human beings; the heart is worried with evil imaginations, and pierced with arrows of distress; grief takes hold of the spirit, and alarm conquers hope. In our Lord's case, the grief and sorrow which He felt can never be described, nor need it be conceived. It was something tantamount to the miseries of damned souls. The holy Jesus could not feel the exact misery which takes hold on abandoned rebels, but He did suffer what was tantamount to that at the judgment seat of God. He gave a *quid pro quo*, a something which in God's esteem, reckoning the dignity of His mighty person, stood instead of the sinner's eternal suffering. He felt woe upon woe, night blackening night. Do not try to realize His agony; He wills that you should note, for He has trodden the winepress alone, and of the people there were none with Him, as if to show that none could understand His sorrows, and that we can do no more than speak of His "unknown sufferings."

But I must add, to complete the figure, that shut up in such a pit there might be a great tumult above, like to the tramping of armed hosts, or there might be a rush of waters underneath the captive deep in earth's bowels. He could not tell what the noise was, nor whence it came; and hence he would often be in terrible fear while he sat alone in the thick darkness. Our Lord had His fears, for we read that He was heard in that He feared. Torrents of sin rushed near Him; floods of wrath were heard around Him, and cataracts of grief fell upon Him. Besides, there was a mystery about this anguish which intensified it—a mystery not to be written or explained. Our Redeemer's spirit was cast down within Him far beyond anything that is common to men; in that horrible pit, that pit of destruction, He lay with none to pity or sustain.

But, oh, change the strain, and sing unto the Lord awhile, as we read the verse, "He brought me up out of a horrible pit." The Lord Jesus Christ was lifted up from all sorrow of spirit at that moment when He said so bravely, "It is finished," and though He died yet was He lifted up from death, as it is written, "Thou wilt not leave my soul in hell; neither wilt thou suffer thine Holy One to see corruption." His Spirit ascended to God, and by-and-by, when the third day had blushed with morning light, His body rose from the tomb, to ascend in due time to glory. He came up out of the pit of the grave, delivered from all fear of corruption, pain, or defeat. Now His sorrow is ended, and His brow is clear from care. His visage is marred no more: He bears the scars which do but illumine His hands and feet with splendor, but

> No more the bloody spear,
> The cross and nails no more,
> For hell itself shakes at his name,
> And all the heavens adore.

Sing ye unto the Lord, ye saints of His, as ye behold your Master brought up again from among the sorrowful, the despised, the deserted, the dead.

A second figure is, however, used here to express our Lord's grief and deliverance from it—"*Out of the miry clay.*" Travelers tell us that wherever pits are still used as dungeons, they are damp, foul, and utterly loathsome; for they are never cleansed, however long the prisoner may have been there, or however great the number of victims shut up within them. You know what the prisons of Europe were in Howard's days, they were even worse in the East in periods further back. The imprisoned wretch often found himself sinking in more; he found no rest, no hope of comfort, and when extricated he needed a hand to drag him out of the thick clay. Our blessed Lord and Master found Himself when He was suffering for us where everything appeared to give way beneath Him; His spirits sank, His friends failed Him, and His heart melted like wax. Every comfort was taken from Him. His blessed manhood found nothing upon this earth upon which it could stay itself, for He had been made sin for us, made a curse for us, and so every foundation of comfort departed from Him. He was deprived of visible support, and reduced to a sad condition. As a man who has fallen into a slough cannot stir so as to recover himself, so was it with our Redeemer, who says in the Psalms—"I sink in deep mire, where there is no standing." Some morasses are so destructive that, if a man should once fall into them, he might give up his life for lost unless some one came that way to drag him out. So did the Savior sink in the miry clay of our sin and misery until the Lord Almighty lifted Him out. The clay of sorrow clung to Him; it held to Him while He was performing the great work of our redemption. But the Lord brought Him up out of it. There is no mire upon His garments now: his feet no longer sink, He is not held by the bands of death, He slides not into the grave again. He was dragged down, as it were, by bearing our sin, but that is over, and He hath ascended on high: He hath led captivity captive, and received gifts from men. All honor be unto Him, and to His Father who delivered Him.

As we read our text we pursue this story of our Master's deliverance, and we are told that *He was brought up* out of the lowest deeps. Say the words or sing them as you choose—"He brought me up." God upraised His obedient Son from the depths into which He had descended on our account. He was brought up, like Jonah who went to the bottom of the mountains, and yet was landed safely on the shore. He was brought up like Joseph, who rose from a pit to a palace; like David, who was led up from the sheepfold to the kingdom. "The king shall joy in thy strength, O Lord; and in thy salvation how greatly shall he rejoice! His glory is great in thy salvation: honor and majesty hast thou laid upon him. For thou hast made him most blessed forever: Thou hast made him exceeding glad with thy countenance."

Then we are told *He was set on a rock*, and oh, the glory of our blessed Lord in this matter, for now He stands on a firm foundation in all that He does for us. Judgment and truth confirm His ways, and the Judge of all the earth approves His doings. Christ has no sandy foundation for His work of mercy or His word of comfort. When He saves He has a right to save: when He puts away sin He does it on indisputable grounds: when He helps and delivers His people He does it according to law, according to the will of the Highest. As Justifier, Preserver, and Perfecter of His people, He stands upon a rock. This day I delight to think of my Lord as settling His church with Himself upon the immutable foundations of the covenant, on the decree of God, on the purpose of the Father, on His own work, and on the promise of God that He would reward Him in that work. Well may we say that His feet are upon a rock, for He is Himself, by another figure, the Rock of ages, the Rock of our salvation.

And now *the goings of our glorious Christ are established.* When He goes out to save a sinner, He knows that He can do it, and has a right to do it. When He goes up to His Father's throne to make intercession for sinners, His goings are established, and the desire of His heart is given Him. When He comes in among His church, or marches forth with his people to the ends of the earth, His goings are established. "For the king trusteth in the Lord, and through the mercy of the most High he shall not be moved." He shall surely come a second time without sin unto salvation, for so has the Father decreed: His glorious goings are as surely established as were those of His labor and suffering. We shall never be without a Savior: we shall never have a fallen or a vanquished Savior; for His goings are established for continuance, certainty, and victory. Such honor have all His saints; for "the steps of a good man are ordered of the Lord"; and again, "none of his steps shall slide."

Best of all, there is *a new song in the mouth of our Well-beloved.* It is grand to think of Jesus singing. Read the twenty-second Psalm, and you will find Him doing it, as also in the Hebrews: "In the midst of the church will I sing praise unto thee." Toward the end of His earthly career you hear Him bursting into song. Was not that a grand occasion just before His passion, when He was going out to die; we read that "after supper they sang a hymn." If we had been bound to die that night, as He was, we should rather have wept or prayed than sang. Not so our Lord. I do not know what psalm they sang: probably a part of the great Hallel, usually sung after the Passover, which consists of those Psalms at the end of the book which are so full of praise. I believe the Savior Himself pitched the tune and led the strain. Think of Him singing when near His hour of agony! Going to scorn and mockery, singing! Going to the thorn-crown and the scourge, singing! Going to death, even the death of the cross, singing! For the joy that was set before Him He endured the cross, despising the shame! But now, what must that new song be which He leads in heaven? "They sang, as it were, a new song before the throne"; but it is He that leads the heavenly orchestra. How greatly He excels Miriam, the sister of Moses, when she took her timbrel and led forth the women in their dances, saying, "Sing unto the Lord, for he hath triumphed gloriously: the horse and his rider hath he thrown into the sea." This is called "the song of Moses, the servant of God and of the Lamb"; so I gather that the Lamb's new song is after the same triumphant fashion: it is the substance of that which Moses' song foreshadowed. In Christ Jesus the Lord our God has led captivity captive. Let us praise Him on the high sounding cymbals. Sing unto the Lord, for He hath triumphed gloriously. The powers of darkness are destroyed; sin, death, and hell are drowned in the atoning blood: the depths have covered them: there is not one of them left. Oh, "sing unto the Lord, for he hath triumphed gloriously." "Ascribe ye greatness unto our God."

III. Such is the exalted condition of our Lord at this hour; let us turn and look upon THE LORD'S REWARD. The Lord's reward for having gone down into the horrible pit, and having sunk in the miry clay for us, is this—that "many shall see, and fear, and trust in the Lord. "*Many!*" Not all mankind, but "many" shall look to Jesus and live. Alas! Vast numbers continue in unbelief; but "many" shall believe and live; and the Lord's "many" means very many. As I was thinking over my text, I thought, "I hope there will be some at the Tabernacle this morning that belong to the 'many' who shall see and fear and trust in the Lord." "Many *shall*," for the Lord hath promised it. But, Lord, they will not. "But they shall," says God. Oh, but many refuse. "But they shall," says God and He hath the key of men's hearts, and power over their judgments and their wills. "Many shall." Do you, oh ye unbelievers, think that Jesus shall die in vain? Oh, sinners, if you will not have Christ, others will. You may despise Him, but He will be none the less glorious. You may reject His salvation but He shall be none the less mighty to save. He is a king, and ye cannot pluck a single jewel from His crown. If you are so foolish as to provoke His iron rod so that He shall break you in shivers with it, yet He will be glorious in the sight of God, and He will save His own. Notwithstanding your hardness of heart, be this known unto you, oh House of Israel, that "many shall see, and fear, and trust in the Lord."

What shall the many do? They shall "*see*." Their eyes shall be opened, and they shall see their Lord in the horrible pit, and in the miry clay; and as they look they shall see that He was there for them. What joy this will create in their spirits! If they do not see the Lord Jesus as their Substitute they shall, at any rate, be made to see the exceeding sinfulness of sin. If when Jesus only takes imputed sin, and has no sin of His own, yet He must be cast into the horrible pit and sink in the miry clay; then what will become of men who have their owns sins about them, provoking the fierce anger of the Lord? If God thus smites His well-beloved, oh sinner, how will He smite you! Beware, ye that forget Him, lest He tear you in pieces, and there be none to deliver you. By the suffering Surety all covered with His own gore, I do beseech you, provoke not God; for if His Only-Begotten must suffer so, you must suffer yet more if you break His law, and next reject His gospel.

"Many shall see." Do you wonder that it is added, "and shall *fear*?" It makes men fear to see a bleeding Christ, and to know that they crucified Him. It makes men fear, however, with a sweet filial fear that is akin to hope, when they see that Jesus died for sinners, the Just for the unjust, to bring them to God. Oh, when they see the Lord of love acting as a scapegoat, and bearing their sins away into the wilderness of forgetfulness, they begin to hate their evil ways, and to have a reverent fear of God; for so saith the Scripture, "there is forgiveness with thee that thou mayest be feared."

But best of all—and this is the chief point—they come to "*trust* in the Lord." They build their hope of salvation upon the righteousness of God as manifested in Christ Jesus. Oh, I would to God that some of you would trust Him at once. Beloved friend, are you trying to be saved by your own works? That is a delusion. Are you hoping to be saved by your own feelings? That is a lie. But you can be saved, you shall be saved: if you will trust yourself with that blessed One who was alone in the dark pit of noises for the sake of sinners, and slipped in the miry clay for the ungodly, you shall assuredly be saved from wrath through Him. Trust Him, and as surely as He liveth you shall be saved; for he that trusteth in Him cannot perish. God's truthfulness were gone if the believer could be lost. Hath He not said, "He that believeth and is baptized shall be saved." The throne of God must rock and reel before the cross of Christ shall lose its power to save those that believe.

IV. Fourthly, let us see THE LORD'S LIKENESS in His people. This whole passage, as I said in the beginning, has often been used by individual believers as a description of their own deliverance. It is a true picture, because we are made like unto our Head, and all the brethren are partakers of that which the Head has endured. Do I speak to any of my Master's servants in sore trouble? Dear friends, are you made to wait, though your trial is sharp and severe? Is it so that your prayer has not yet been answered? Then remember the waiter's place was once occupied by the Lord Jesus, for He says, "I waited patiently." If the Lord keeps you waiting for a certain blessing year after year do not despair. He will give it at length if it be truly for your good, for He hath said, "no good thing will I withhold from them that walk uprightly." He kept His Son waiting, and He may very well keep you in like posture, for how long did you delay, and cause the Lord of grace to wait on you! "Blessed are they that wait for Him." I have seen people very uppish when they have called on a public man and have had to wait a little; they feel that they ought not to be kept in the lobby; but suppose some young man said to them, "I am his own son, and yet I have been waiting an hour." Then they are more patient. So when God keeps you waiting do not be proud, and say, "Wherefore should I wait for the Lord any longer?" but remember "It is good for a man both to hope and quietly wait for the salvation of God." Jesus waited—"waited patiently." Seek to be like Him, and in patience possess your soul. "I cannot see how I am to be delivered." Wait. "Ah, this is such a heavy burden." Wait. "But I am ready to die under this terrible load." Wait! Wait on! Though He tarry, wait for Him: He is worth waiting for. "Wait" is a short word, but it takes a deal of grace to spell out its full meaning, and still more grace to put it in practice. Wait: wait. "Oh, but I have been unfortunate." Wait. "But I have believed a promise, and it has not been fulfilled." Wait; for you wait in blessed company: you may hear Jesus saying, "I waited patiently." Blessed be His name, He is teaching us to do the same by His gracious Spirit.

Next, the Lord may send you, His dear child, a very heavy sorrow: you may fall into the horrible pit, and see no light, no comfort, and no one may be able to cheer you or help you. Some that have a touch of despondency in their nature have been brought so low as almost to despair of life. They have sat in darkness and seen no light: they have felt the walls of their prison and have not discovered a crack or cranny through which escape was possible: they have looked up, and even then they have seen nothing to console them. Ah, well, here is a word I commend to you—the Savior says it: "He brought me up." The Lord God can and will bring up

His troubled ones. You will have to write in your diary one of these days, "He brought me up." I was in the dark, I was in the dungeon, but "He brought me up." I can personally say this with gladsome gratitude, for "He hath brought me up," again and again. My heart is glad as I reflect upon my past deliverances. I have often wondered why I so often shut up in prison, and bound as with fetters of steel; but I cease to wonder when I think of the many among you who are called to wear the like bonds. This is my portion, that I may be a witness-bearer for my God, and that I may be able to speak to the experiences of God's tempted people, and tell how graciously the Lord delivers His servants who trust in Him. Faith shall never be shamed or confounded, world without end. God can and will hasten to the rescue of the faithful. I set to my seal also that "He brought me up"; and, beloved brother in tribulation, He will bring *you* up; only rest in the Lord, and wait patiently for Him.

"Ah," say you, "But I do not know how to stand, for I sink as in miry clay, through faintness of heart: I cannot find the slightest foothold for my hope." No, you are sinking in the miry clay like your Master; but in answer to prayer the Lord will bring you up out of your hopeless state, and He will set your feet upon a rock and establish your goings, and give you joy, and peace, and delight. Wherefore see, and fear, and trust in God, and give glory to His blessed name.

Lastly, do I address any seeking one who finds no rest for the sole of his foot? Dear friend, are you sinking in the deep mire of your guilt? The Lord can pardon you, for "the blood of Jesus Christ, his Son, cleanseth us from all sin." Are you shut up by conscience in the prison-house under a just sense of deserved wrath? Jesus will give you immediate rest if you come to Him. Do you feel as if you cannot kneel to pray, for your very knees slip in the mire of doubt? Remember, Jesus makes intercession for the transgressors. Do you seem as if, every time you move, you are burying your hope, and slipping deeper and deeper into ruin? The Lord hath plenteous redemption. Do not despair. You cannot deliver yourself, but God can deliver you: you cannot stand of yourself, but God can make you to stand. You cannot go to Him nor go abroad among your fellow-men with comfort, but the Lord can make you to run in His ways. You shall yet go forth with joy and be led forth with peace; the mountains and the hills shall break forth before you into singing, and all the trees of the field shall clap their hands. Only see Christ, and fear and trust your God, and you too shall sing unto Jehovah your deliverer, and this shall be your song:—

> He raised me from a horrid pit,
>   Where mourning long I lay,
> And from my bonds released my feet,
>   Deep bonds of miry clay.
>
> Firm on a rock he made me stand,
>   And taught my cheerful tongue
> To praise the wonders of his hand
>   In a new thankful song.

OUR LORD'S TRIUMPHANT ASCENSION

Sermon No. 2,142
Intended for Reading on Lord's day Morning, May 11, 1890;
Delivered on Lord's day Morning, April 27, 1890.
Portions of Scripture read before Sermon—Psalm 68; Ephesians 4:1–13.
Hymns from *Our Own Hymn Book*—322, 317, 449.

*Thou hast ascended on high, thou hast led captivity captive: thou
has received gifts for men; yea, for the rebellious also, that the Lord
God might dwell among them—Psalm 68:18.*

The hill of Zion had been taken out of the hand of the Jebusites. They had held it
long after the rest of the country had been subdued; but David at last had taken it
from them. This was the mountain ordained of Jehovah of old to be the place of the
Temple. David, therefore, with songs and shouts of rejoicing, brought up the ark from
the abode of Obed-edom to the place where it should remain. That is the literal fact
upon which the figure of the text is based. We are at no loss for the spiritual interpretation, for we turn to Ephesians 4:8, where, quoting rather the sense of the passage than the exact words, Paul says, "When he ascended up on high, he led captivity
captive, and gave gifts unto men." The same sense is found in Colossians 2:15:
"And having spoiled principalities and powers, he made a show of them openly, triumphing over them in it." Not misled by the will-o'-the-wisp of fancy, but guided by
the clear light of the infallible Word, we see our way to expound our text. In the words
of David we have an address to our Lord Jesus Christ, concerning His ascent to His
glory. "Thou hast ascended on high, thou hast led captivity captive: thou has received
gifts for men; yea, for the rebellious also, that the Lord God might dwell among
them."

Our Savior *descended* when He came to the manger of Bethlehem, a babe; and
further descended when He became "a man of sorrows, and acquainted with grief."
He descended lower still when He was obedient to death, even the death of the cross;
and further yet when His dead body was laid in the grave. Well saith our apostle,
"Now that He ascended, what is it but that He also descended first into the lower parts
of the earth?" Long and dark was the descent: there were no depths of humiliation,

temptation, and affliction which He did not fathom. Seeing He stood in their place and stead, He went as low as justice required that sinners should go who had dared to violate the law of God. The utmost abyss of desertion heard Him cry, "My God, my God, why hast thou forsaken me?" Low in the grave He lay, but He had His face upward, for He could not see corruption.

On the third day He quitted the couch of the dead, and rose to the light of the living. He had commenced His glorious ascent. To prove how real was His resurrection, He stayed on earth some forty days, and showed Himself to many witnesses. Magdalene and James saw Him alone; the eleven beheld Him in their midst; the two on the road conversed with Him; five hundred brethren at once beheld Him. He gave infallible proofs that He was really risen from the dead, and these remain with us unto this day as historic facts. He ate a piece of a broiled fish and of a honeycomb, to prove that He was no phantom. He said to the apostles, "Handle me, and see that it is I myself; for a spirit hath not flesh and bones, as ye see me have." One laid his finger in the print of the nails, and even thrust his hand into His side. Their very doubts were used to make the evidence clearer. The fact that Jesus died was put beyond question by the spear-thrust; and the fact that He was alive, in a material form, was equally well established by the touch of Thomas. Beyond a doubt, Christ Jesus has risen from the dead, and become the firstfruits of them that slept.

This being settled beyond question, the time came for our Lord to continue His homeward, upward journey, and return unto the glory from which He had come down. From "the mount called Olivet," while His disciples surrounded Him, "He was taken up; and a cloud received him out of their sight." The rest of His upward progress we cannot describe. Imagination and faith step in, and conceive of Him as rising beyond all regions known to us, far above all imaginable height. He draws near to the suburbs of heaven; and surely the poet is not wrong when he says of the angels—

> They brought his chariot from on high
> To bear him to his throne;
> Clapp'd their triumphant wings, and cried,
> "The glorious work is done."

"Lift up your heads, O ye gates, and be ye lift up, ye everlasting doors, that the King of glory may come in." How high He ascended after He passed the pearly portal Paul cannot tell us, save that he says "he ascended up far above all heavens," and describes Him as "set at God's right hand in the heavenly places, far above all principality, and power, and might, and dominion"; and as "dwelling in the light which no man can approach unto." The man Christ Jesus has gone back to the place from whence His Godhead came. Thou art the King of glory, O Christ! Thou art the eternal Son of the Father! Thou sittest ever in the highest heaven, enthroned with all glory, clothed with all power, King of kings and Lord of lords. Unto thy name we humbly present our hallelujahs, both now and forever.

I. Now, concerning the text itself, which speaks of the ascent of our ever blessed Lord, we shall say, first, that OUR LORD'S TRIUMPH WAS SET FORTH BY HIS ASCENSION.

He came here to fight the foes of God and man. It was a tremendous battle, not against flesh and blood, but against spiritual wickednesses and evil powers. Our Lord fought against sin, and death, and hell, and hate of God, and love of falsehood. He came to earth to be our champion. For you and for me, beloved, He entered the lists, and wrestled till He sweat great drops of blood: yea, "He poured out his soul unto death." When He had ended the struggle He declared His victory by ascending to the Father's throne.

Now His descent is ended. There was no need for Him to remain amid the men who despised Him. The shame, and suffering, and blasphemy, and rebuke are far beneath Him now. The sun has risen, and the darkness of night has fled. He has gone up beyond the reach of sneering Sadducees and accusing Pharisees. The traitor cannot again kiss Him, Pilate cannot scourge Him, Herod cannot mock Him. He is far above the reach of priestly taunt and vulgar jest.

> No more the cruel spear,
> The cross and nails no more;
> For hell itself shakes at his frown,
> And all the heavens adore.

Now, also our Lord's work was done. We are sure that the purpose of His love is secure, or He would not have returned to His rest. The love that brought Him here would have kept Him here if all things necessary for our salvation had not been finished. Our Lord Jesus is no sudden enthusiast, who rashly commences an enterprise of which He wearies before it is accomplished. He does not give up a work which He has once undertaken. Because He said, "I have finished the work which thou gavest me to do," and then ascended to the Father, I feel safe in asserting that all that was required of the Lord Christ for the overthrow of the powers of darkness is performed and endured: all that is needed for the salvation of His redeemed is fully done. Whatever was the design of Christ's death, it will be accomplished to the full; for had He not secured its accomplishment He would not have gone back. I do not believe in a defeated and disappointed Savior, nor in a divine sacrifice which fails to effect its purpose. I do not believe in an atonement which is admirably wide but fatally ineffectual. I rejoice to hear my Lord say, "All that the Father giveth me shall come to me." Whatever was the purpose of the Christ of God in the great transaction of the cross, it must be fully effected: to conceive a failure, even of a partial kind, is scarcely reverent. Jesus has seen to it that in no point shall His work be frustrated. Nothing is left undone of all His covenanted engagements. "It is finished" is a description of every item of the divine labor; and, therefore, has He ascended on high. There are no dropped stitches in the robe of Christ. I say again, the love that brought our Lord here would have kept Him here if He had not been absolutely sure that all His work and warfare for our salvation had been accomplished to the full.

Further, as we see here the ending of our Lord's descent and the accomplishment of His work, remember that *His ascent to the Father is representative.* Every believer rose with Him, and grasped the inheritance. When He uprose, ascending high,

He taught our feet the way. At the last His people shall be caught up together with the Lord in the air, and so shall they be forever with the Lord. He has made a stairway for His saints to climb to their felicity, and He has trodden it Himself to assure us that the new and living way is available for us. In His ascension, He bore all His people with Him. As Levi was in the loins of Abraham, when Melchizedek met Him, so were all the saints in the loins of Christ when He ascended up on high. Not one of the number shall fail to come where the head has entered, else were Jesus the Head of an imperfect and mutilated body. Though you have no other means of getting to glory but faith in Jesus, that way will bring you there without fail. Not only will He not be in glory and leave us behind, but He cannot be so, since we are one with Him; and where He is His people must be. We are in the highest glory in Jesus as our Representative, and by faith we are raised up together, and made to sit together in the heavenlies, even in Him.

Our Lord's ascent is to the highest heaven. I have noticed this already; but let me remind you of it again, lest you miss an essential point. Our Lord Jesus is in no inferior place in the glory land. He was a servant here, but He is not so there. I know that He intercedes, and thus carries on a form of service on our behalf; but no strivings, and cryings, and tears are mingled with His present pleadings. With authority He pleads. He is a priest upon His throne, blending with His plea the authority of His personal merit. He saith, "All power is given unto me in heaven and in earth"; and therefore He is glorious in His prayers for us. He is Lord of every place, and of everything; He guides the wheel of providence, and directs the flight of angels; His kingdom ruleth over all. He is exalted above every name that is named, and all things are put under Him. Oh, what a Christ we have to trust in and to love!

And on this account *we are called upon in the text to think much of His blessed Person.* When we speak of what Christ has done, we must think much of the doing, but still more of the Doer. We must not forget the Benefactor in the benefits which come to us through Him. Note well how David puts it. To him the Lord is first and most prominent. He sees Him, he speaks to Him. "*Thou* has ascended on high. *Thou* hast led captivity captive. *Thou* hast received gifts for men." Three times he addresses Him by that personal pronoun "Thou." Dwell on the fact that He, the Son of David, who for our sakes came down on earth and lay in the manger, and hung upon a woman's breast, has gone up on high, into the glory infinite. He that trod the weary ways of Palestine now reigns as a King in His palace. He that sighed, and hungered, and wept, and bled, and died, is now above all heavens. Behold your Lord upon the cross—mark the five ghastly wounds, and all the shameful scourging and spitting which men have wrought upon Him! See how that blessed body, prepared of the Holy Ghost for the indwelling of the Second Person of the adorable Trinity, was evil entreated! But there is an end to all this. "*Thou* has ascended on high." He that was earth's scorn is now heaven's wonder. I saw Thee laid in the tomb, wrapped about with cerements, and embalmed in spices; but Thou has ascended on high, where death cannot touch

Thee. The Christ that was buried here is now upon the throne. The heart which was broken here is palpitating in His bosom now, as full of love and condescension as when He dwelt among men. He has not forgotten us, for He has not forgotten Himself, and we are part and parcel of Himself. He is still mindful of Calvary and Gethsemane. Even when you are dazzled by the superlative splendor of His exalted state, still believe that He is a Brother born for adversity.

Let us rejoice in the ascent of Christ as being the ensign of His victory, and the symbol thereof. He has accomplished His work. If Thou hadst not led captivity captive, O Christ, Thou hadst never ascended on high; and if Thou hadst not won gifts of salvation for the sins of men, Thou hadst been here still suffering! Thou wouldst never have relinquished thy chosen task if Thou hadst not perfected it. Thou art so set on the salvation of men, that for the joy that was set before Thee, Thou didst endure the cross, despising the shame; and we know that all must have been achieved, or Thou wouldst still be working out thy gracious enterprise. The voice of the ascension is—CONSUMMATUM EST: "It is finished."

II. Having led your thoughts that way, I would, secondly, remind you that THE LORD'S TRIUMPHAL ASCENT DEMONSTRATED THE DEFEAT OF ALL OUR FOES. "Thou has led captivity captive" is as certain as "Thou has ascended on high."

Brethren, *we were captives once*—captives to tyrants, who wrought us woe, and would soon have wrought us death. We were captives to sin, captives to Satan, and therefore captives under spiritual death. We were captives under diverse lusts and imaginations of our own hearts: captives to error, captives to deceit. But the Lord Jesus Christ has led captivity captive. There is our comfort. Yet, forget not that we were hopeless captives to all these: they were too strong for us, and we could not escape from their cruel bondage.

The Lord Jesus, by His glorious victory here below, has subdued all our adversaries, and in His going up on high He has triumphed over them all, exhibiting them as trophies. The imagery may be illustrated by the triumph of Roman conquerors. They were wont to pass along the Via Sacra, and climb up to the Capitol, dragging at their chariot wheels the vanquished princes with their hands bound behind their backs. All those powers which held you captive have been vanquished by Christ. Whatever form your spiritual slavery took, you are clean delivered from it; for the Lord Christ has made captives those whose captives you were. "Sin shall not have dominion over you." Concerning Satan, our Lord has bruised his head beneath His heel. Death also is overcome, and his sting is taken away. Death is no more the king of dread: "The sting of death is sin; and the strength of sin is the law. But thanks be to God, which giveth us the victory through our Lord Jesus Christ." Whatever there was or is, which can oppress our soul, and hold it in bondage, the Lord Jesus has subdued and made it captive to Himself.

What then? Why, *henceforth the power of all our adversaries is broken*. Courage, Christians! You can fight your way to heaven, for the foes who dispute your passage have been already worsted in the field. They bear upon them the proofs of the valor of your leader. True, the flock of the Lord is too feeble to force its way; but listen, "The Breaker is come up before them, and the King at the head of them." Easily may the sheep follow where the Shepherd breaks the way. We have but to follow those heavenly feet, which once were pierced, and none of our steps shall slide. Move on, O soldiers of Jesus, for your Captain cries, "Follow me!" Would He lead you into evil? Has He not said, "Thou shalt tread upon the lion and adder: the young lion and the dragon shalt thou trample under feet." Your Lord has set His foot on the necks of your enemies: you wage war with vanquished foes. What encouragement this glorious ascension of Christ should give to every tried believer!

Remember, again, that *the victory of our Lord Christ is the victory of all who are in Him.* "The seed of the woman shall bruise the serpent's head." Now, the seed of the woman is, first of all, the Lord Jesus; but also, it is all who are in union with Him. There are still two seeds in the world—the seed of the serpent, and these cannot enter into this rest; and the seed of the woman, who are born, not of blood, nor of the will of man, nor of the will of the flesh, but of God: in these last is the living and incorruptible seed, which liveth and abideth forever. Jesus, our Lord, represents them in all that He does—they died in Him, were buried in Him, are raised in Him, and in the day when He triumphed, they led captivity captive in Him. Looking at the great battle now raging in the world, I gaze with joyful confidence. We are fighting now with Popery, with Mohammedanism, with idolatry in the foulest forms; but the battle is in effect won. We are struggling with the terrible infidelity which has fixed itself like a cancer upon the church of God, and our spirit sinks as we survey the horrors of this almost civil war. How often we groan because the battle does not go as we would desire it! Yet there is no reason for dismay. God is in no hurry as we are. He dwells in the leisure of eternity, and is not the prey of fear, as we are. We read concerning the multitude, when they needed to be fed, that Jesus asked Philip a question; but yet it is added, "howbeit Jesus knew what he would do." So today the Lord may put many questions to His valiant ones, and "For the divisions of Reuben there may be great searchings of heart"; but He knows what He is going to do, and we may lay our heads upon His bosom and rest quiet. If He does not tell us how He will effect His purpose, yet assuredly He will not fail. His cause is sure to win the victory, for how can the Lord be defeated? A vanquished Christ! We have not yet learned to blaspheme, and so we put the notion far from us. No, brethren, by those bleeding hands and feet He has secured the struggle. By that side opened down to His heart we feel that His heart is fixed in our cause. Especially by His resurrection, and by His climbing to the throne of God, He has made the victory of His truth, the victory of His church, the victory of Himself most sure and certain.

III. Let us notice, thirdly, that OUR LORD'S TRIUMPHANT ASCENSION WAS CELEBRATED BY GIFTS. The custom of bestowing gifts after victory was practiced among the Easterns, according to the song of Deborah. Those to whom a triumph was decreed in old Rome scattered money among the populace. Sometimes it seemed as if every man in the city was made rich by his share of the spoils of vanquished princes.

Thus our Lord, when He ascended on high, received gifts for men, and scattered largess all around.

The psalm says: "Thou has *received* gifts for men." The Hebrew hath it, "Thou has received gifts in Adam"—that is, in human nature. Our Lord Christ had everything as Lord; but as the man, the Mediator, He has received gifts from the Father. "The King eternal, immortal, invisible," has bestowed upon His triumphant General a portion with the great, and He has ordained that He shall divide the spoil with the strong. This our Lord values, for He speaks of all that the Father has given Him with the resolve that He will possess it.

When Paul quotes the passage, he says, "He *gave* gifts to men." Did Paul quote incorrectly? I think not. He quoted, no doubt, from the Greek version. Is the Greek version therefore compatible with the Hebrew? Assuredly; for Dr. Owen says that the word rendered "received" may be read "gave." And if not, for Christ to receive for men is the same thing as to give to men, for He never receives for Himself, but at once gives it to those who are in Him. Paul looks to the central meaning of the passage, and gives us the heart and soul of its sense. He is not intending to quote it verbatim, but to give in brief its innermost teaching. Our Lord Jesus Christ has nothing which He does not give to His church. He gave Himself *for* us, and He continues still to give Himself *to* us. He receives the gift, but He only acts as the conduit-pipe, through which the grace of God flows to us. It pleased the Father that in Him should all fullness dwell; and of His fullness have all we received.

What are these great ascension gifts? I answer that *the sum of them is the Holy Spirit.* I invite your adoring attention to the sacred Trinity herein manifested to us. How delightful it is to see the Trinity working out in unity the salvation of men! "Thou hast ascended on high": there is Christ Jesus. "Thou has received gifts for men": there is the Father, bestowing those gifts. The gift itself is the Holy Spirit. This is the great largess of Christ's ascension, which He bestowed on His church at Pentecost. Thus you have Father, Son, and Holy Spirit blessedly co-working for the benediction of men, the conquest of evil, the establishment of righteousness. O my soul, delight thyself in Father, Son, and Holy Spirit. One of the sins of modern theology is keeping these divine Persons in the background, so that they are scarcely mentioned in their several workings and offices. The theology which can feed your souls must be full of Godhead, and yield to Father, Son and Holy Spirit perpetual praise.

Beloved, the gifts here spoken of are those brought by the Holy Spirit. "The water that I shall give him," said Christ, "shall be in him a well of water springing up into everlasting life." He said again, "If any man thirst, let him come unto me, and drink." We read that He "spoke of the Spirit, which they that believed on him should receive." "If ye then, being evil, know how to give good gifts unto your children: how much more shall your heavenly Father give the Holy Spirit to them that ask him?" To conquer the world for Christ we need nothing but the Holy Spirit, and in the hour of His personal victory He secured us this boon. If the Holy Spirit be but given we have in Him all the weapons of our holy war.

But observe, according to Paul, these gifts which our Lord gave are *embodied in men*; for the Holy Spirit comes upon men whom He has chosen, and works through them according to His good pleasure. Hence He gave some, apostles, some, evangelists, and some, pastors and teachers. No one may be judged to be given of God to the church in any of these offices unless as the Spirit dwells upon him. All are given of God upon whom the Holy Spirit rests, whatever their office may be. It is ours to accept with great joy the men who are chosen and anointed to speak in the name of the Lord, be they what they may. Paul, Apollos, Cephas, they are all the gifts of the risen Christ to His redeemed ones, for their edifying and perfecting. The Holy Spirit, in proportion as He abides in these servants of God, makes them to be precious benisons of heaven to His people, and they become the champions by whom the world is subdued to the Lord Jesus Christ.

These gifts, given in the form of men, *are given for men*. Churches do not exist for preachers; but preachers for churches. We have sometimes feared that certain brethren thought that the assemblies of believers were formed to provide situations for clerical persons; but, indeed, it is no so. My brethren in the church, we who are your pastors are your servants for Christ's sake. Our rule is not that of lordship, but of love. Every God-sent minister, if he discharges his duty aright, waits upon the bride of Christ with loving diligence, and delights greatly to hear the Bridegroom's voice. I wish that you who talk of my Lord's servants as if they were rival performers would cease thus to profane the gifts of the ascended King. The varying abilities of those by whom the Lord builds up His church are all arranged by infinite wisdom, and it should be ours to make the most we can of them. Comparing and contrasting the Lord's gifts is unprofitable work. It is better to drink of the well of Elim than to grow hot and feverish in disputing as to whether it is better or worse than Beersheba or Sychar. One minister may be better for you than another; but another may be better for somebody else than the one you prefer. The least gifted may be essential to a certain class of mind; therefore, despise no one. When God gives gifts, shall you turn them over contemptuously, and say, "I like this well; but the other I like not?" Did the Father bestow these gifts upon His Son, and has the Holy Spirit put them into different earthen vessels that the excellency of the power might be of God; and will you begin judging them? No, Beloved, the Lord hath sent me to preach His gospel, and I rejoice to feel that I am sent for your sake. I entreat you to profit as much as you can by me by frequent hearing, by abounding faith, by practical obedience to the Word. Use all God's servants as you are able to profit by them. Hear them prayerfully, not for the indulgence of your curiosity, nor for the pleasing of your ear with rhetoric, but that you, through the Word of God, may feel His Spirit working in our hearts all the purpose of His will. Our conversion, sanctification, comfort, instruction, and usefulness, all come to us by the Holy Spirit, and that Spirit sends His powerful messages by the men whom He has given to be His mouths to men. See how wonderful was that ascension of our Lord, in which He scattered down mercies so rich and appropriate among the sons of men. From His glorious elevation above all heavens, He sends forth pastors, and preachers, and evangelists, through whom the Holy Spirit works mightily in them that believe. By them He gathers the redeemed together, and builds them up a church to His glory.

IV. I want the attention of all who are unconverted, for I have glorious tidings for them. To them I speak under my fourth head, OUR LORD'S TRIUMPH HAS A VERY SPECIAL BEARING.

"Thou has received gifts *for men*," not for angels, not for devils, but for men—poor fallen men. I read not that it is said, "for bishops or ministers," but "for men"; and yet there is a special character mentioned. Does the text particularly mention "saints," or those that have not defiled their garments? No, I do not read of them here. What a strange sovereignty there is about the grace of God! Truly He will have mercy on whom He will have mercy; for in this instance He selects for special mention those that you and I would have passed over without a word. "*Yes, for the rebellious also.*" I must pause to brush my tears away. Where are you, ye rebels? Where are those who have lived in rebellion against God all their lives? Alas! You have been in open revolt against Him: you have raged against Him in your hearts, and spoken against Him with your tongues. Some have sinned as drunkards, others have broken the laws of purity, truth, honesty. Many rebel against the light, violate conscience, and disobey the Word—these also are among the rebellious. So are the proud, the wrathful, the slothful, the profane, the unbelieving, the unjust. Hear, all of you, these words, and carry them home; and if they do not break your hearts with tender gratitude you are hard indeed. "Yea, for the rebellious also." When our Lord rode home in triumph He had a pitying heart towards the rebellious. When He entered the highest place to which He could ascend, He was still the sinner's friend. When all His pains and griefs were being rewarded with endless horror, He turned His eye upon those who had crucified Him, and bestowed gifts upon them.

This description includes those who have rebelled against God, though once they professed to be His loyal subjects. Perhaps I am addressing some who have so far backslidden that they have thrown up all religion and have gone back into the world and its sins: these are apostates from the profession which once they made. To these I would give a word of encouragement, if they will turn to the Lord. Once upon a time, John Bunyan was under great temptation from the devil. This trial he records in his *Grace Abounding*. He thought that God had given him up, and that he was cast away forever; and yet he found hope in this text. I have copied out a little bit which refers to it: "I feared also that this was the mark that the Lord did set on Cain, even continual fear and trembling under the heavy load of guilt that he had charged upon him for the blood of his brother Abel. Then did I wind and twine and shrink under the burden that was upon me, which burden did also so oppress me that I could neither stand, nor go, nor lie, either at rest or quiet. Yet that saying would sometimes come into my mind, 'He hath received gifts for the rebellious.' Rebellious, thought I, why surely they are such as once were under subjection to their Prince, even those who, after they had sworn subjection to His government, have taken up arms against Him;

and this, thought I, is my very condition. Once I loved Him, feared Him, served Him; but now I am a rebel, and I have sold Him. I said, Let Him go if He will, but yet He has gifts for rebels; *and then why not for me?*"

Oh, that I could cause every despairing heart to reason in this way! Oh, that the Holy Spirit would put this argument into every troubled mind at this moment: "*And then why not for me?*" Come home, dear brother, come home, for there are gifts for the rebellious; *and why not for you?* I know you deserted the Lord's Table, but the Lord of the Table has not deserted you. I know you have, as far as you could, forsworn the name of Christ, and even wished you could be unbaptized: but that could not be, nor can the Lord leave you to perish. I know you have done evil with both hands eagerly; and perhaps now you are living in a known sin, and when you go home today you will see it before your eyes. Nevertheless, I charge you, return unto the Lord at once. Come to your Lord and Savior, who still prays, "Father, forgive them; for they know not what they do." Behold how in His glory He "hath received gifts for men; yea, for the rebellious also." O my soul, I charge thee, on thine own account, hang on to this most precious declaration, for thou, too, hast been a rebel. Would God that all my brothers and sisters would be cheered by this dear word, and take it home to themselves with a believing repentance and a holy hatred of sin! I would print the words in stars across the brow of night. "*Yea, for the rebellious also.*"

V. I have done when I have handled the fifth point, which is this: OUR LORD'S TRIUMPHANT ASCENSION SECURES THE CONSUMMATION OF HIS WHOLE WORK. What doth it say? "That the Lord God might dwell among them." When our Lord Christ came here at the first He was willing enough to "dwell" among us; but it could not be. "The Word was made flesh and tabernacled among us," like a Bedouin in his tent, but not as a dweller at home. He could not "dwell" here on that occasion. He was but a visitor, and badly treated at that. "There was no room for him in the inn," where everybody else was freely welcome. "He came unto his own"—surely they will lodge Him, "but his own received him not." There was no room for Him in the temple—there He had to use the scourge. There was room for Him in the open streets, for they took up stones to stone Him. Out of the synagogue they hurried Him, to cast Him down headlong from the brow of the hill. "Away with him! Away with him!" was the cry of the ribald crowd. This dear visitor, who came here all unarmed, without sword or bow, they treated as though He had been a spy or an assassin, who had stolen among them to do them ill. And so they ran upon Him with a spear, and He, quitting these inhospitable realms which knew Him not, took home with Him the marks of man's discourtesy. O earth, earth, how couldst thou drive away thy dearest Friend, and compel Him to be as a wayfaring man, that tarrieth but for a night; nay, worse, as a man astonished, who meets with wounding in the house of His friends?

After He had risen again, He went home, that from this throne He might direct a work by which earth should become a place where God could abide. Again is the temple of God to be with men, and He shall dwell among them. This world of ours has been sprinkled with the precious blood of the Lamb of God, and it is no longer as an unclean thing. Jesus is the Lamb of God who so taketh away the sin of the world that God can treat with men on terms of grace, and publish free salvation. The Lord God Himself had long been a stranger in the land. Did not the holy man of old say, "I am a stranger with thee, and a sojourner, as all my fathers were?" But Jesus, the ascended One, is pouring down such gifts upon this sin-smitten world, that it will yet become a new earth, wherein dwelleth righteousness and the God of righteousness.

This promise is partly fulfilled before your own eyes this day; for the Holy Spirit came at Pentecost, and He has never returned. Jesus said, "He shall abide with you forever." The Holy Dove has often been greatly grieved, but He has never spread His wings to depart. This is still the dispensation of the Spirit. You hardly need to pray to have the Spirit poured out; for that has been done. What you need is a baptism of the Holy Spirit; namely, to go down personally into that glorious flood which has been poured forth. Oh, to be immersed into the Holy Ghost and into fire: covered with His holy influence, "plunged in the Godhead's deepest sea, and lost in His immensity!" Here is our life and power, for thus the Lord God doth dwell among us. Ever since the ascension the Holy Ghost has remained among men, though He has not been, at all seasons, equally active. All through the night of Romanism, and the schoolmen, He still tarried: there were humble hearts which rejoiced to be His temples even in those doleful days. Today He is still with His regenerated ones. In spite of impudent strivings against the divine inspiration of His Holy Scripture, and, notwithstanding the follies of ecclesiastical amusements, He is with His chosen. Lord, what is man that thy Spirit should dwell with him? But so it is; and this is why our Lord went up to Heaven and received divine gifts that by Him the Lord God might dwell among us.

But there cometh a day when this shall be carried out to the letter. Methinks I hear the angels say, "Ye men of Galilee, why stand ye gazing up into heaven? This same Jesus, which is taken up from you into heaven, shall so come in like manner as ye have seen Him go into heaven." Now, "in like manner" must mean in Person. In Person our Lord was taken up into heaven, and in Person He will come again; and when He cometh, the Lord God will, indeed, dwell among us. Oh, that the day would come! We wait and watch for His glorious appearing; for then will He dwell among men in a perfect fashion. What happy days shall we have when Jesus is here! What a millennium His presence will bring; there can be no such auspicious era without it, any more than there can be summer without the sun. He must come first, and then will the golden age begin. The central glory of that period shall be that the Lord is here. "The Lord God shall dwell among them." Then shall be heard the song which will never end, earth's homage to the Lord, who renewed the heavens and the earth, and has taken up His dwelling in them. "They shall hunger no more, neither thirst any more; neither shall the sun light on them, nor any heart; for he that sitteth on the throne shall dwell among them." Up till now this work has been going on; but as yet it is incomplete. "Every prospect pleases, and only man is vile," is still most sadly true. The rankness of sin destroys the sweet odors of this world, so that the pure and holy God cannot abide in it; but since the Lord Jesus hath sweetened it with His sacred merits, and the Spirit is purifying it by His residence in men, the Lord smelleth a savor of rest, and He will not give up this poor fallen planet. Even now His angels come and go in heavenly traffic with the chosen. Soon the little boat of this globe shall be drawn nearer to the great ship, and earth shall lie alongside heaven. Then shall men praise God day and night in His temple. Heaven shall find her choristers among the ransomed from among men. The whole world shall be as a censer filled with incense for the Lord of hosts. All this will be because of those gifts received and bestowed by our Lord Jesus in the day when He returned to His glory, leading captivity captive. O Lord, hasten thy coming! We are sure that thine abiding presence and glorious reign will come in due season. Thy coming down secured thy going up: thy going up secures thy coming down again. Wherefore, we bless and magnify Thee, O ascended Lord, with all our hearts, and rise after Thee as Thou dost draw us upward from groveling things. So be it! Amen.

CHRIST'S UNIVERSAL KINGDOM, AND HOW IT COMETH

SERMON NO. 1,535

DELIVERED ON LORD'S DAY MORNING, APRIL 25, 1880.

Ask of me, and I shall give thee the heathen for thine inheritance, and the uttermost parts of the earth for thy possession. Thou shalt break them with a rod of iron; thou shalt dash them in pieces like a potter's vessel—Psalm 2:8, 9.

OBSERVE, dear friends, the wonderful contrast between the violent excitement of the enemies of the Lord, and the sublime serenity of God Himself. He is not disturbed though the heathen so furiously rage, and their kings and mighty ones set themselves in battle array. He smiles at them: He hath them in derision. You and I are often downcast and depressed, and our forebodings are dark and dismal, but God sits in His eternal peacefulness, and serenely overrules tumult and rebellion. The Lord reigneth, and His throne is not moved, nor His rest broken, whatever may be the noise and turmoil down below.

Notice the sublimity of this divine calm. While the heathen and their princes are plotting and planning how to break His bands asunder, and cast His cords from them, He has already defeated their devices, and He says to them, "Yet have I set my king upon my holy hill of Zion." "You will not have my Son to reign over you, but nevertheless He reigns. While you have been raging I have crowned Him. Your imaginations are indeed vain, for I have forestalled you, and established Him upon His throne. Hear Him as he proclaims my decree, and asserts His filial sovereignty." God is ever beforehand with His adversaries: they find their scheming frustrated, and their craft baffled, even before they have begun to execute their plans. By God's decree the ever blessed Son of the Highest is placed in power, and exalted to His throne. The rulers cannot snatch from His hand the scepter, nor dash from His head the crown: Jesus reigns and must reign till all enemies are put under His feet. God has set Him firmly upon Zion's sacred hill, and raging nations cannot cast Him down: the very idea of their so doing excites the derision of Jehovah, He disturbs not His great soul because of their blustering. As if it were a banquet rather than a conflict, the Lord God, as Himself a King, speaks to the King's Son, even to His Anointed on His right hand,

and having owned His royal rank, confers upon Him the highest honors. At great feasts many a monarch has been known to say to his favorite, "Ask what I shall give thee, and nothing shall be denied thee this day." Even thus doth the great Father say to His glorious Son the Prince of peace, "Ask of me, and I will give thee the heathen, thine inheritance, and the uttermost parts of the earth, thy possession." He bids Him open His mouth wide, and request a boundless dominion. He will give Him distant nations, yea, and the whole round earth to be His kingdom. There is an air of regal festivity and peaceful joy about all this which strangely contrasts with the uproar of the adversaries. Brethren, I wish we could enter in some measure into this sublime quiet. We may well be confident since God is so. If the Captain be assured of victory it behooves the common soldier to be bravely hopeful. The battle is the Lord's and since He is the Lord God omnipotent, fear about the issue of the conflict is foolish and wicked. All events are in His hand—His hand who can dash whole worlds to dust, or make them when it pleases Him. What can stand against the almighty will? Who shall say unto Jehovah, "What doest Thou?" In this eternal all-sufficiency is our rest, and we may therefore cease from anxiety. Stand thou still, my weary brother, and see the salvation of God. Put not forth thy timorous hand to stay the trembling ark, but know that Jehovah can protect His own. Lay thy Martha cares aside: sit at thy Savior's feet, and listen to His voice. He will tell thee that God reigneth yet, and that His anointed shall reign also. Things are not as they seem: all is well when all looks ill. If the heavens are clouded the sun is not put out: if the evening hath darkened, even to midnight, yet the morning cometh: to the moment shall it break, nor can all the powers of darkness hinder the dawning day. Jehovah's fixed decrees remain engraved as in eternal brass, nor can the craft of hell efface a single line nor stay the execution of a single purpose. Despite all opposition the sacred purpose will blossom into the actual providence, and the providence will ripen into salvation. God's plan will be carried out without failure in any point, and there is no cause for alarm.

If we were more calm and restful we should do our work better, for do we not gather both wisdom and courage when we abide in quietness and confidence? The joy of the Lord is the strength of His saints. The assurance of faith, if we were filled with it, would make us go forth "fair as the moon, clear as the sun, and terrible as an army with banners." Alas, our short-sighted fretfulness, our anxious mistrust, and our timorous suspicion cause us needless distress, weaken us for service, and expose us to the assaults of our adversaries. Without the preparation of the gospel of peace our feet are unshod, and we are unfit for the heavenly pilgrimage. Groveling here below among the troubles of the hour, the most of Christians are a timorous folk, and act like the tribe of Reuben in the day of Barak's battle, to whom Deborah cried, "Why abodest thou among the sheep-folds, to hear the bleatings of the flocks?" O ye who lie among the pots, and do servile work in abject fear, arise to a braver spirit. Up ye to the everlasting hills and breathe a purer air: gird yourselves with the belt of confidence in God, and you shall be "strong in the Lord and in the power of his might."

May God grant that the subject of this morning may help us out of the depressing influences which surround us, and raise us into fellowship with the calm in which Jehovah sits smiling, and out of which He saith, "Yet have I set my king upon my holy hill of Zion."

Our text suggests to us this morning, first, that *the kingdoms of the earth, and the earth itself, are Christ's inheritance*—"I will give thee the heathen for thine inheritance." Leave out those little words which the translators have inserted, for they but feebly help the sense. "I will give the heathen, thine inheritance, and the uttermost parts of the earth, thy possession." When we have dwelt upon that we shall then notice *that this is to be had for the asking*: "Ask of me, and I shall give." Thirdly, we shall note that *the power by which the dominion shall be gained is altogether of God*: "I shall give." And fourthly, we shall remark that in order to complete the conquest of the world *all existing and all future confederacies against the Lord, and against His Christ, shall be utterly destroyed*: "Thou shalt break them with a rod of iron; thou shalt dash them in pieces like a potter's vessel."

I. For our comfort let us notice the teaching of the text that THE LORD WILL GIVE TO CHRIST THE HEATHEN AS HIS INHERITANCE AND THE UTTERMOST PARTS OF THE EARTH AS HIS POSSESSION. This I take to refer to our Lord as man. Already as God the kingdom of the divine Son ruleth over all. There never was a limit to the reign of Jesus as God, not even when He was hanging on the cross; He was the everlasting Father even when He was "the child born, the Son given."

It is in His wondrous nature as God-Man Mediator that these words may be understood, for so the Apostle Paul evidently interpreted them. The mysterious sentence, "Thou art my Son; this day have I begotten thee," may refer to the deep and secret truth of the eternal foliation of our Lord, whatever that may be; but Paul quotes it in the thirteenth Acts as referring to His resurrection. Here are his words, "And we declare unto you glad tidings, how that the promise which was made unto the fathers, God hath fulfilled the same unto us their children, in that he hath raised up Jesus again; as it is also written in the second psalm, thou art my Son, this day have I begotten thee." It is in resurrection power that Christ comes forth, and God gives to Him to have dominion over the earth and all that is upon it. Because He liveth and was dead He hath the keys of hell and of death. By virtue of His humiliation He reigns. For the suffering of death He is crowned with glory and honor. The heavenly host proclaim His worthiness to take the book and open its seven seals, singing, "For thou was slain, and has redeemed us to God by thy blood." He descended that He might ascend above all things and fill all things; He laid aside His glory that He might be crowned with this new glory and honor, and might have all things put under His feet as the Son of man. We speak therefore of Jesus Christ the risen One, who once died, but has not risen from the tomb, and quitted this earth for the splendors of the New Jerusalem.

Our conviction is that this same Jesus is to reign over the whole world. I shall not enter into the question whether this will be accomplished before His second advent, or will be result of His glorious appearing. I should not like to assert that this consummation will be reached before His advent, for that might seem to militate against our duty to watch for His coming, which may be at any moment: on the other hand, I would not venture to assert that the gospel cannot be universally victorious before His coming, because I perceive that this opinion is a pillow for many an idle head, and is ruinous to the hopeful spirit of missionary enterprise. It is enough for me that a wide dominion will be given to our Lord at some time or other, and that assuredly His kingdom shall embrace all the nations of mankind. The whole earth shall yet be filled with His glory; the seed of the woman shall bruise the serpent's head and clear the world of his slimy trail.

For the next few minutes you will be good as to keep your Bibles going, for the appeal must be to God's own Word. I gather that the kingdom of Christ is to be so extensive as to comprehend all mankind, first, because, of the exceeding breadth of the prophecy of it which was made to Abraham in Genesis 12:3. That is an old covenant promise which refers to Abraham as the father of the faithful, and to His one great seed, even Jesus, the promised Messiah. Here are the far-reaching words—"In thee shall all families of the earth be blessed." Assuredly they are not as yet all blessed in Him to such an extent as to exhaust the divine meaning. When God in covenant promises a blessing it is no light thing, and therefore I am sure that this grand covenant blessing of the nations is something more than a name. Though I doubt not that the whole earth is to some extent the better because of the coming of Christ, and His peace-making death, and the spread of His pure faith, yet I cannot believe that multitudes who live and die in the thick darkness of ignorance and idolatry are really blessed in Christ in such a sense as to make it a covenant blessing. How much are Tartary, China, and Tibet blessed by the gospel? There must be something better yet for all the families of the earth shall yet know that the promised seed hath lived and died for them, and some of every kindred and tongue shall find salvation in Him.

Jacob, too, when he spoke concerning the Shiloh in Genesis 49:10, said, "Unto him shall the gathering of the people be." By the people is not meant the seed of Israel, but the nations, or the Gentiles; so the Septuagint and the Syriac understand it, and so indeed it is. Jesus, our great Shiloh, sets up the standard, and His chosen rally round in ever growing numbers till the dispersed of Babel shall find in Him a new center, and a pure language shall be given to them in Him. The words mean not "gathering" only, but a willing obedience, the fruit of faith and the expression of piety. To this is parallel the word of Paul in Romans 15:12: "And again, Esaias saith, There shall be a root of Jesse, and he that shall rise to reign over the Gentiles; in him shall the Gentiles trust." It is evident, then, that the nations shall come to trust in the Messiah, and thus shall they find life eternal.

Moses, too, in Deuteronomy 32:21, to which passage Paul in the Romans so especially refers, speaks of the heathen nations when he says, "I will move them to jealousy with those who are not a people; I will provoke them to anger with a foolish nation." Truly this is fulfilled in these days when the gospel line hath gone out throughout all the earth, and its words unto the ends of the earth; and this our own foolish nation, this once barbarous people which seemed shut out from God, worshiping idols with all the cruel rites of the Druids, has been brought into covenant with God and made to rejoice in Him. Degraded heathen in all lands have become believers, and so shall all nations be brought believingly to Jesus' feet, that Israel may be angered and provoked to jealousy until her time shall come, when she shall look on Him whom she hath pierced, and shall mourn for Him, and turn to Him with full purpose of heart.

When we reach the Psalms we come into the clear light of prophecy concerning the kingdom of our blessed Master. Our text stands first, and is sufficient in itself: the heathen are to be His inheritance, and the utmost bounds of the world are to be His possession. Turn to that famous passion psalm, the twenty-second. Its pathos with regard to the griefs of the crucified One is deep and touching. You see Him hanging on the tree, a gazing-stock to scoffers, with His tongue cleaving to His jaws, and His heart melting like wax in the midst of His bowels; and yet ere the psalm closes the plaintive gives place to the triumphant, and the dying One cries, "All the ends of the world shall remember and turn unto the Lord: and all the kindreds of the nations shall worship before thee. For the kingdom is the Lord's: and he is the governor among the nations. All they that be fat upon earth shall eat and worship: all they that go down to the dust shall bow before him: and none can keep alive his own soul." On the cross this prospect cheered our dying Master's heart, that the kingdom should be the Lord's and that all the kindreds of the nations should come and worship before Him; let it cheer us also. Do you think that the crucified Lord will be disappointed of the end for which He died? Will you venture to assert that a single drop of His blood was shed for naught? Rest assured that He shall see of the travail of His soul, till even His great loving heart shall be content. God hath said it, "I will divide him a portion with the great, and he shall divide the spoil with the strong, because he hath poured out his soul unto death"; and be ye calmly confident that the Word of the Lord will stand.

Turn your Bibles over till you reach Psalm 66, and the fourth verse, and there you come upon another word of comfort: "All the earth shall worship thee, and shall sing unto thee; they shall sing to thy name." This sentence is not merely the passionate hope of an enthusiastic worshiper, but a voice inspired of the Holy Spirit, plainly declaring that all peoples shall adore their Maker with hearty praise and joyful song.

How glowing is the language of Psalm 72. Can we expect too great things for our King when we remember the gracious words beginning at the eighth verse: "He shall have dominion also from sea to sea, and from the river unto the ends of the earth. They that dwell in the wilderness shall bow before him; and his enemies shall lick the dust. The kings of Tarshish and of the isles shall bring presents: the kings of Sheba and Seba shall offer gifts. Yea, all kings shall fall down before him: all nations shall serve him." Read on at verse seventeen: "His name shall endure forever: his name shall be continued as long as the sun: and men shall be blessed in him: all nations shall call him blessed." These terms include the most barbarous tribes that exist, and they especially mention nations which boast that they were never conquered: such as the un-tamed rovers of the wilderness, who centuries ago laughed at the Roman power. The legions which subdued all other peoples could not conquer the sons of Ishmael; fleet of foot as a hart, swift as a young roe, they fled over the desert sands, out of reach of the pursuer; yet these shall bow before our Lord, and joyfully pay Him homage. He will sway His scepter where scepter was never owned before; He shall set up a throne where all other authority has been laughed to scorn.

You will not be wearied if I ask you to look at Psalm 86, verse 9. There you will find it written, "All nations whom thou hast made shall come and worship before thee, O Lord; and shall glorify thy name." It is not to be mere outside worship that shall be paid, for the nations are to glorify His name, which is a high form of praise. All nations are to glorify the Lord, and this they have not done as yet.

We expected to find, and we are not disappointed in our expectation, that Isaiah would be sure to speak concerning these things. I would rather you heard the Word of God by far than my word, and therefore we will keep to our reading. It will bring you encouragement and heart-cheer to know what prophets said in the olden time, when only Israel had the light. They did not think the light would be confined to the one peculiar people, but they expected that on the nations which sat in darkness light would break, and they also would seek the Lord. Turn to Isaiah and read. See what he says in his second chapter.

> It shall come to pass in the last days, that the mountain of the Lord's house shall be established in the top of the mountains, and shall be exalted above the hills; and all nations shall flow unto it. And many people shall go and say, Come ye, and let us go up to the mountain of the Lord, to the house of the God of Jacob; and he will teach us of his ways, and we will walk in his paths: for out of Zion shall go forth the law, and the Word of the Lord from Jerusalem. And he shall judge among the nations, and shall rebuke many people: and they shall beat their swords into plowshares, and their spears into pruning hooks: nation shall not lift up sword against nation, neither shall they learn war any more.

I can but give samples. The passages abound all through Isaiah in which there is the intimation of the general spread of the Redeemer's kingdom. Turn to Isaiah 49:6–7:

> It is a light thing that thou shouldest be my servant to raise up the tribes of Jacob, and to restore the preserved of Israel: I will also give thee for a light to the Gentiles, that thou mayest be my salvation unto the end of the earth. Thus saith the Lord, the Redeemer of Israel, and His Holy One, to him whom man despiseth, to him whom the nation abhorreth, to a servant of rulers, Kings shall see and arise, princes also shall worship, because of the Lord that is faithful, and the Holy One of Israel, and he shall choose thee.

Now read verses 12 and 18:

> Behold, these shall come from far: and, lo, these from the north and from the west; and these from the land of Sinim. Lift up thine eyes round about, and behold: all these gather themselves together, and come to thee.

Nor is Isaiah alone in such prophecies as these. I cannot detain you by reading what Ezekiel saith concerning the ever deepening waters which shall carry life to all lands; and I will only mention one word of Jeremiah, because it so peculiarly proves that the homage paid by heathen nations to our Lord will be that of their hearts; and that the reign of Christ, whatever it may be else, will certainly be a spiritual reign. Jeremiah 3:17: "They shall call Jerusalem the throne of the Lord; and all the nations shall be gathered unto it, to the name of the Lord, to Jerusalem: neither shall they walk any more after the imagination of their evil heart." Christ will work a heart-change when He shall win the nations to allegiance, and this shall lead to a manifest change of life—"neither shall they walk any more after the imagination of their evil heart."

Daniel, that John of the Old Testament, of course saw more clearly than any the coming kingdom of the Anointed One. What doth he say in chapter 7:18? "But the saints of the Most High shall take the kingdom, and possess the kingdom forever, even for ever and ever. Until the Ancient of days came, and judgment was given to the saints of the Most High; and the time came that the saints possessed the kingdom. And the kingdom and dominion, and the greatness of the kingdom under the whole heaven, shall be given to the people of the saints of the Most High, whose kingdom is an everlasting kingdom, and all dominions shall serve and obey him." Can anything be more positive than this last word?

Look how the idols are to be destroyed according to the prophet Zephaniah (2:11): "The Lord will be terrible unto them: for he will famish all the gods of the earth; and men shall worship him, every one from his place, even all the isles of the heathen." Zechariah says to the same effect (9:10): "He shall speak peace unto the heathen, and his dominion shall be from sea even to sea, and from the river even to the ends of the earth." (14:2) "And the Lord shall be King over all the earth: in that day there shall be one Lord, and his name one."

Lest I should weary you, I forbear to quote any more. To me it is evident beyond all contradiction that according to the whole run of Scripture the kingdom of Christ is to extend over all parts of the earth, and over all races and conditions of men, and therefore I charge you never despair for the grand old cause. An infidel notion is abroad that these different religions have sprung up at different times as developments of the religious instinct, and that they may all profitably exist side by side with ours. It is admitted that the religion of Christ is excellent, and that it deserves a huge following, but still other religions have their advantages and must not be despised: nay, something better than the gospel of Christ may yet be discovered. This is the current talk in certain circles, and we would at once express our horror at it. Jesus is not to share a divided throne. Cast ye with abhorrence from your souls every such blasphemous thought. Jesus must reign till all enemies are put under His feet, and to Him all rivals are enemies. If Jesus be King He is the only Potentate. Christians are enlisted under a banner which does not brook another standard side by side with it, they serve a Prince who will not share dominion with others, who will not submit that even a province shall be rent away from His government. He shall reign forever and ever, King of kings, and Lord of lords. Hallelujah! Like a burst of thunder let all hearts that love Him say, Amen.

II. It appears from our text that THIS UNIVERSAL DOMINION IS TO BE ASKED FOR. Thus saith the Father to His glorious Son, "Ask of me, and I will give thee." Beloved, Jesus fails not to ask. We do not doubt that He responds to the Father's invitation, and asks for His inheritance. This is the way in which the psalm before us touches upon the priestly character of Christ as combined with His Kingly office. He ever liveth to intercede, and a part of His daily intercession is to ask that the heathen may be His inheritance. Now, beloved, this is a lesson to us. We belong to Christ; we are members of that body of which He is the mystical Head, and it is ours to act with Him in His life-work: as He asks, we are to ask with Him. As Jesus suffers in His people, so He pleads in them. Let us cry day and night unto God for the coming and kingdom of our Lord. Let the throne of the Highest be surrounded by our perpetual prayers. Let us urge for the Lord Jesus His suit in the courts above, that the heathen may be His inheritance, and the uttermost parts of the earth His possession. We are so truly one with Him that His sympathies and hopes are ours; His glory is our glory, His victory our victory, and therefore our supplications should naturally and spontaneously arise for Him every day of our lives. Our union with Him has given us a kingdom, the same kingdom as that which He claims. He Himself has said it: "It is your Father's good pleasure to give you the kingdom." As surely as He sets His Son upon His holy hill of Zion, so surely will the Lord bring us all there. Our prayers therefore should daily rise together with the pleadings of the great Intercessor Himself. O Lord, thine is the kingdom, and the power, and the glory; let thy will be done in earth as it is in heaven.

This prayer is one which is commanded by God Himself. About its fitness we can, therefore, have no doubt. Your Savior taught you to say, "Thy kingdom come." In this text we find it prescribed as a prayer to the Well-beloved—"Ask of me"; and therefore it is certainly a proper prayer for us, and we may use it without question. We are highly honored in being permitted to present such a petition: to be allowed to pray for myself is mercy, to be permitted to pray for my fellowman is favor, but to be suffered to pray for Jesus is honor. It is written, "Prayer also shall be made for him continually," and thus there is a special honor put upon those who intercede. My Lord's prayer for me saves me; but when He bids me pray for Him, He dignifies me, and I say with David, "Thy gentleness hath made me great." Whatever else we forget, never from our private intercessions let us omit the prayer that the heathen may come to glorify Christ.

It is a joy to know that this prayer will be effectual to the full. It is no vain desire, no dream of a fevered brain: the infinite wisdom of God Himself suggests it, for He says, "Ask, and I shall give thee." This union of precept and promise is found attached to every covenant blessing, but here it is conspicuously and distinctly stated in so many words—"Ask, and I shall give thee." Concerning this thing the promise of God is definite, we may therefore pray with full assurance. Let us avail ourselves of this plain direction every hour of our lives. O church of God, ask on Christ's behalf, and the Lord God will give Him the kingdom. Heir of heaven, ask on behalf of the Elder Brother, for the Elder Brother pleads in thee, and God will hear both thee and Him, and He will grant the united request. My heart is full of confidence when pleading upon this subject: what surer warrant do we want than "Ask, and I shall give thee"?

Let our prayer be wide and far-reaching. Let our desires embrace the world. Pray not for your own country only, though it needs it, and God alone knows how much; but pray for the colonies, the continent, and the far off lands. Ask that all heathens may become Christians. Plead that the whole round earth may be the Lord's: that the uttermost parts of the earth may resound with songs in His praise. On this earth His blood has fallen; the precious drops could not be gathered up again, and so this globe remains blood-marked—the one star upon which the Son of God poured out His life. It must be the Lord's: the sacrifice of Calvary has made it sacred to the Son of God. As our Government marks with the broad arrow those stores which belong to it, so did Christ upon the tree, when the blood fell from His hands, and feet, and side, mark, as it were, with something more full of meaning than the broad arrow, this round earth on which He bled, and it must be forever and ever His by right of purchase and ransom. It was made subject to vanity for a little season, but it is to be redeemed from it; and when it shall be purified and beautified in the day of the manifestation of the sons of God, you will not know it: for it will come forth as "a new heavens and new earth, wherein dwelleth righteousness." Its sister stars have long wondered at its silence, or its discord, but at the sight of its restoration to the choirs of holiness they will sing in deep delight, and chant a new song unto the Lord. With what admiration will they perceive, rising up from this once beclouded orb, a flame of unquenchable praise with pillars of perfumed smoke, the incense of eternal gratitude. Sweeter the offer of this once fallen world than that of any other sphere, for it has been redeemed, and upon it have been seen marvels of free grace and dying love such as no other world has known. Oh, may this soon come to pass; may the prayer be heard; and God be praised; but it can only be accomplished through His own appointed method, the asking of Christ, the pleading of the church. Oh, rouse thee, church, to ask. Awake thee from thine unholy lethargy, and cry day and night unto God. Cease not, but with anguish, like a woman in travail, cry aloud and spare not, until He give the risen Lord the heathen for His inheritance, and make His throne higher than the kings of the earth.

III. Thirdly, THIS DOMINION IS TO BE GAINED BY THE POWER OF GOD. Notice the text, for it is very explicit: "Ask of me, and *I shall give thee.*" The power and grace of God will be conspicuously seen in the subjugation of this world to Christ: every heart shall know that it was wrought by the power of God in answer to the prayer of Christ and His church. I believe, brethren, that the length of time spent in the accomplishment of the divine plan has much of it been occupied with getting rid of those many forms of human power which have intruded into the place of the Spirit. If you and I had been about in our Lord's day, and could have had everything managed to our hand, we should have converted Caesar straight away by argument or by oratory; we should then have converted all his legions by every means within our reach; and, I warrant you, with Caesar and his legions at our back we would have Christianized the world in no time: would we not? Yes, but that is not God's way at all, nor the right and effectual way to set up a spiritual kingdom. Bribes and threats are alike unlawful, eloquence and carnal reasoning are out of court, the power of divine love is the one weapon for this campaign. Long ago the prophet wrote, "Not by might, nor by power, but by my Spirit, saith the Lord." The fact is that such conversions as could be brought about by physical force, or by mere mental energy, or by the prestige of rank and pomp, are not conversions at all. The kingdom of Christ is not a kingdom of this world, else would His servants fight; it rests on a spiritual basis, and is to be advanced by spiritual means. Yet Christ's servants gradually slipped down into the notion that His kingdom was of this world, and could be upheld by human power. A Roman emperor professed to be converted, using a deep policy to settle himself upon the throne; then Christianity became the State-patronized religion: it seemed that the world was Christianized, whereas, indeed, the church was heathenized. Hence sprang the monster of a State-church, a conjunction ill-assorted, and fraught with untold ills. This incongruous thing is half human, half divine; as a theory it fascinates, as a fact it betrays; it promises to advance the truth, and is itself a negation of it. Under its influences a system of religion was fashioned, which beyond all false religions and beyond even Atheism itself, is the greatest hindrance to the true gospel of Jesus Christ. Under its influence dark ages lowered over the world; men were not permitted to think; a Bible could scarcely be found, and a preacher of the gospel, if found, was put to death. That was the result of human power coming in with the sword in one hand and the gospel in the other, and developing its pride of ecclesiastical power into a triple crown, an Inquisition, and an infallible Pope. This parasite, this canker, this incubus of the church will be removed by the grace of God, and by His providence in due season. The kings of the earth who have loved this unchaste system will grow weary of it and destroy it. Read Revelation 17:16, and see how terrible her end will be. The death of the system will come from those who gave it life: the powers of earth created the system, and they will in due time destroy it.

Frequently do we meet with the idea that the world is to be converted to Christ by the spread of civilization. Now, civilization always follows the gospel, and is in a great measure the product of it; but many people put the cart before the horse, and make civilization the first cause. According to their opinion trade is to regenerate the nations, the arts are to ennoble them, and education is to purify them. Peace Societies are formed, against which I have not a word to say, but much in their favor; still, I believe the only efficient peace society is the church of God, and the best peace teaching is the love of God in Christ Jesus. The grace of God is the great instrument for uplifting the world from the depths of its ruin, and covering it with happiness and holiness. Christ's cross is the Pharos of this tempestuous sea, like the

Eddystone lighthouse flinging its beams through the midnight of ignorance over the raging waters of human sin, preserving men from rock and shipwreck, piloting them into the port of peace. Tell it out among the heathen that the Lord reigneth from the tree; and as ye tell it out believe that the power to make the peoples believe it is with God the Father, and the power to bow them before Christ is in God the Holy Ghost. Saving energy lies not in learning, nor in wit, nor in eloquence, nor in anything save in the right arm of God, who will be exalted among the heathen, for He hath sworn that surely all flesh shall see the salvation of God. The might of the Omnipotent One shall work out His purposes of grace, and as for us, we will use the simple processes of prayer and faith. "Ask of me, and I shall give thee." Oh, that we could keep in perpetual motion the machinery of prayer. Pray, pray, pray, and God will give, give, give, abundantly, and supernaturally, above all that we ask, or even think. He must do all things in the conquering work of the Lord Jesus. We cannot convert a single child, nor bring to Christ the humblest peasant, nor lead to peace the most hopeful youth; all must be done by the Spirit of God alone, and if ever nations are to be born in a day, and crowds are to come humbly to Jesus' feet, it is thine, Eternal Spirit, thine to do it. God must give the dominion, or the rebels will remain unsubdued.

IV. Thus the power of God worketh to bring about the kingdom of Christ; and THIS INVOLVES THE BREAKING UP OF ALL THE CONFEDERACIES WHICH NOW EXIST OR EVER SHALL EXIST FOR THE HINDRANCE OF THE REDEEMER'S KINGDOM.

Our text employs a figure which is very full of meaning. "He shall break them with a rod of iron." He breaks not the subject nations, nor the inherited heathen, but the kings of the earth who stood up and took counsel together against the Lord, and against His Anointed. Against these He will lift up His iron rod of stern justice and irresistible power. Over His own inheritance He will sway a silver scepter of love; over His own possession He shall reign with gentleness and grace; but as for His adversaries, He will deal with them in severity, and display His power in them. How shall they stand out against Him? They have formed their confederacy with great care and skill: as when men prepare clay and make it plastic for the potter's use, so have they made all things ready; they have set their design upon the wheel, and caused it to revolve in their thoughts, and with great skill they have fashioned it. Lo, there it stands finished, and fair to look upon. Yet at its very best it is nothing more than a potter's vessel. It may be of the purest clay, and of such exquisite workmanship that it shall enchant every man of taste, but it attaineth to be nothing more than an earthen vessel, and therefore woe unto it when the rod of iron falls upon it. Woe to all human societies and brotherhoods which are framed to resist the Lord. Mark the conflict and its end! It is brief enough. A stroke! Where is the hope of the Lord's adversary? Gone, gone, utterly gone; only a few potsherds remain. Oh for such a smiting of the apostasy of Rome! Oh for one touch of the iron rod upon the imposture of Mohammed! Oh, for a blow at Buddhism, and a back stroke at the superstition of Brahminism, and at all the idols of the heathen! Woe unto the gods of the land of Sinim in that day; a single stroke shall set the potsherds flying. Wherefore, then, should we fear, although they plot and plan; although a solemn conclave of cardinals be held, though the Pope fulminate his bulls, though the Sultan ordain that every convert to Christianity shall be put to death, though still the scoffers revile at Christianity, and say that it spreads not as once it did? A speedy answer shall confound them, or if not speedy yet the stroke shall be sure. Our King waits a while. He hath leisure. Haste belongs to weakness; His strength moves calmly. Only let Him be aroused and you shall see how quick are His paces. He redeemed the world in a few short hours upon the tree, and I warrant you that when He getteth that iron rod once fairly to work He will not need many days to ease Him of His adversaries, and make a clean sweep of all that set themselves against Him. If you want to see how it will be done, read, I pray you, Daniel 2:31:—"Thou, O king, sawest, and behold a great image. This great image, whose brightness was excellent, stood before thee; and the form thereof was terrible. This image's head was of fine gold, his breast and his arms of silver, his belly and his thighs of brass, his legs of iron, his feet part of iron and part of clay." It was a strange conglomeration: all the metallic empires are set forth as combined in one image; which image is the embodied idea of monarchical power, which has fascinated men even to this day. The prophet goes on to say, "Thou sawest still that a stone was cut out without hands, which smote the image upon his feet that were of iron and clay, and broke them to pieces. Then was the iron, the clay, the brass, the silver, and gold, broken to pieces together, and became like the chaff of the summer threshingfloors; and the wind carried them away, that no place was found for them: and the stone that smote the image became a great mountain, and filled the whole earth." And so it is to be: the vision is being each day fulfilled. The gospel stone, which owes nothing to human strength or wisdom, is breaking the image, and scattering all opposing powers. No system, society, confederacy, or cabinet can stand which is opposed to truth and righteousness. I, even I, that am but of yesterday, and know nothing, have seen one of the mightiest of empires of modern times melt away on a sudden as the rime of the morning in the heat of the sun. I have seen monarchs driven out of their tyrannies by the powers of a single man, and a free nation born as in an hour. I have seen states which fought to hold African Americans in perpetual captivity subdued by those whom they despised, while the slave has been set free. I have seen nations chastened under evil governments, and revived when the yoke has been broken, and they have returned to the way of righteousness and peace. He who lives longest shall see most of this. Evil is short-lived. Truth shall yet rise above all. The Lord saith, overturn, overturn till He shall come whose right it is, and God shall give it to Him. Woe unto those that stand against the Lord and His anointed, for they shall not prosper. "Be wise now therefore, O ye kings: be instructed, ye judges of the earth. Kiss the Son, lest he be angry, and ye perish from the way, when his wrath is kindled but a little. Blessed are all they that put their trust in him."

CHRIST'S WORK NO FAILURE

SERMON No. 1,945
DELIVERED ON LORD'S DAY MORNING, JANUARY 30, 1887.
PORTION OF SCRIPTURE READ BEFORE SERMON—ISAIAH 41:28, 29; 42:1–16.
HYMNS FROM *Our Own Hymn Book*—72 (SONG I), 339, 953.

He shall not fail nor be discouraged, till he have set judgment in the earth: and the isles shall wait for his law—Isaiah 42:4.

PREVIOUS verses at the close of the forty-first chapter indicate the utter failure of the hope of man from man. God Himself looked, and behold "there was no man; even among them, and there was no counselor, that, when I asked of them, could answer a word." How often it is so in human history: man fails to find leadership and help in man! Great men are raised up now and then, and the tendency is to make idols of them, and so to trust in an arm of flesh. These die, and then their fellows look out in the church, and in the world, for other men upon whom they may dote after the same manner; but it sometimes happens that they look in vain; none arise whom they can elect for leaders. Just now I think it is so in more departments than one. Look where you may, where will you see the man who is equal to the crisis? Somehow or other, in the providence of God, every hour has, in due time, had its man; but if our hopes are fixed in men, we must feel at this time sorely pressed.

In expounding the one verse which I have selected for a text, I shall need to open up the whole passage. Follow me, therefore, with opened Bibles, and obey the first word of the chapter, which is, *Behold*.

We are commanded at all times *to behold the Son of God*. There is never a season in which He is not a fit subject for contemplation and expectation. "Behold the Lamb of God" is the standing rule from generation to generation, from the first of January to the last of December. But especially in cloudy and dark days ought we to behold Him. When after having looked, and looked long, you see no man and no counselor, then this precept has an emphatic force about it, "Behold my servant, whom I uphold; mine elect, in whom my soul delighteth." When all other saviors fail, look to *the* Savior whom God has set up. The darker all things else become, the more eagerly look for His appearing, whose coming is as a morning without clouds. When the lower lights are burning dim, behold the lamp above.

553

Our great comfort is that *the Lord Jesus Christ is always to be beheld*. He lives ever and ever works for His people. We must view Him not merely as one who appeared upon the scene years ago, but as still living. He died in the heat of the battle, but He rose again to secure the victory. We do not found our hopes of a brighter future upon a dead Savior; our hopes for the future of the world, and for the accomplishment of God's gracious purposes hang upon One who ever liveth, and is at this time in the place of vantage, carrying on His great work and warfare at the right hand of God. My text saith, "Behold my servant"; and that matchless Servant of God is to be beheld—not with the eye of sense, that were little worth, for men saw Him in that way, and crucified Him; but He is to be beheld with the eye of faith, and this is a noble sight; for those who look to Him in that manner are lightened, and their faces are not ashamed. At the commencement of my discourse, I beseech you, dear brethren, to look to Jesus Christ the ever-living Worker. If you have been troubled and fretted by peering into these gloomy times and perceiving nothing that can raise your spirits, I pray you look about you no longer, but look up! There *He* sits at the right hand of God, even the Father, the appointed man, the glorious, chosen Deliverer. Behold Him, and your fears and sorrows will fly away.

The text declares concerning our Lord that "He shall not fail nor be discouraged." This leads us to consider what is the work which Jesus Christ has undertaken, in which He will not fail nor be discouraged. Our text directs us in this matter, for it tells us that He has come to "set judgments in the earth," and that "the isles shall wait for his law." The earth is to be delivered from misrule and sin, and men are to be submissive to His instruction and direction. There are some who doubt it, but I still believe in that verse which we sang just now—

> Jesus shall reign where'er the sun
> Does his successive journeys run;
> His kingdom stretch from shore to shore,
> Till moons shall wax and wane no more.

Our Lord has come to save His own elect, and He will save every one of them. No soul for whom He stood as Surety and Substitute shall ever be cast away. The sheep shall pass again under the hand of Him that telleth them, and they shall all be there. "He shall not fail nor be discouraged"; but He shall see of the travail of His soul, and shall be satisfied.

As for the Lord's second coming, we know not when it shall be. Shall the world grow darker and darker till He comes? It may be so. There are passages of Scripture and signs of the times which may be taken to indicate it. On the other hand, shall the age grow brighter and brighter till He appears to bring the perfect day? Through the preaching of the gospel shall there yet be periods in which multitudes shall be converted, and whole nations shall be saved? I do not know: there are texts that seem to look that way, and many a brave worker hopes as much. There are brethren who can map out unfulfilled prophecy with great distinctness; but I confess my inability to do so. They get a shilling box of mathematical instruments. They stick down one leg of the compasses and describe a circle here and a circle there, and they draw two or three lines, and there it is. Can you not see it, as plain as a pikestaff? I am sick of diagrams; I have seen enough of them to make another volume of Euclid. My impression is that very little is to be learned from the major part of these interpretations or speculations. I do not think that anybody can map out the future so as to be absolutely sure of anything definite except certain great, clearly-stated facts. It is certain that the Lord will come, that He will come in such an hour as the most of men look not for Him; and that His coming will be a surprise even to many of His own church. He may come at this moment while yet I am speaking to you, and He may delay His coming, if so it pleaseth Him, through many a century yet. It may sound strange for me to say so, but if our Lord were not to come for ages, we should not be justified in saying, "My Lord delayeth His coming," nor would any prophecy of Scripture be broken. Furthermore, it seems to me pretty clear that truth and righteousness are to win the day upon the earth; the idols are to be abolished, war is to cease, and the great Jehovah is to be called "the God of the whole earth." Either before or after His second advent—I am not going into that question this morning—this polluted earth is to be cleansed, and this round planet of ours, which today is darkened by sin, shall yet shine out, like a newborn sun, in all the pristine light which beamed from it when first it came from its Maker's hands. The Lord shall reign over all mankind, and a period of peace, and rest, and holiness shall be the fruit of His blessed sway. The Lord Jesus will not rest till He has subdued all things unto Himself, and put down all the spiritual wickednesses which now tyrannize over the world.

I do not think it necessary for me to go further into detail as to all that our Lord is resolved to do. What I have to say is this, *whatever He has undertaken, He will perform*: whatever commission He has received He will fulfill. "He shall not fail nor be discouraged" till all His work is done. Brethren, we get doubting sometimes. We ask, Is it all right? Are matters moving on? Behold Him who is at the head of all affairs, the Director of the high politics of heaven, the great One upon whose shoulders rests the business of God in the salvation of men! Behold Him, and be comforted. You and I may fail; shame on us if we do! We may be discouraged; it will be our sin if we are: but *He* shall not fail nor be discouraged till He shall have wrought out every point of the promise of grace, and shall have accomplished every iota of the eternal purpose of love.

I believe in the final perseverance of the Lord Jesus Christ. I believe in the final perseverance of every saint as an individual. Furthermore, I believe in the final perseverance of the saints as a body: the church of God shall live, and continue her work till she has accomplished it. "The gates of hell shall not prevail against her." But far diviner is the thought to me of the final perseverance of the Christ of God. If *He* were to lay down the task and say it is impossible, woe worth the day to us! If He were to turn His back upon His high enterprise, and say, "I will save no more of these rebellious beings; I will attempt no more to shed light into the darkness which comprehendeth it not; I will give up the task in which men so madly oppose me"; then were hope blotted out of the language of men. But while this text stands true the door of hope is open. *We* need not fail or be discouraged, since *He* will not.

This morning I shall speak to you in the hope that the Spirit of God may fire you with new courage for the holy war. First, *let this truth be considered and believed*; and then, secondly, *let this truth be believed and enjoyed*.

I. First, then LET THIS TRUTH BE CONSIDERED AND BELIEVED.

Will you now thoughtfully turn it over in your minds? It is certainly a very marvelous enterprise which our Lord Jesus Christ has undertaken. The salvation of a single soul involves a miracle. The salvation of myriads upon myriads of the human race: what shall I call it but a mountain of marvels? The removal of the darkness which has settled over mankind in tenfold night—what a divine labor! The ending of the enmity which exists between man and God, the reconciling of man unto his Maker—what a design! The redeeming of this world from the bondage of corruption, the setting up of a kingdom of truth and holiness—what an enterprise! Such wonders has Jesus undertaken, and such wonders He will achieve. He died to lay the foundation of His all-conquering kingdom, and He still lives that this kingdom may be established in its supremacy, and all nations may flow to it. Beloved, I fail to conceive, much more to express, the vastness of the task which He has undertaken. Those of you who love your fellowmen often mourn your powerlessness with a single individual. What hard work it is to deal with our own countrymen! How are we baffled by their poverty, their ignorance, their misery, their sin! You have only to battle with a single vice, drunkenness, to wit, to feel what a monster is to be overcome. Only think for a moment of the social impurity of this city, and you are sick at heart as you remember it. Now, the Lord Jesus Christ has come to cleanse this Augean stable; and He will cleanse it. The stream of the river of life shall run through the foulest parts of the earth till even those horrible regions which are comparable to the Dead Sea shall be reclaimed.

The problem staggers us. The systems of evil are colossal. The hold of evil on the race is terrible. Man is inveterately a sinner. You cannot cure him of rebellion: he is desperately set on mischief. Even when the consequences of his sin wound and afflict him he still returns to it. If you prove to him to a demonstration that a thing is right and profitable, he does not therefore love it; if you prove it to be injurious, he therefore chooses it. By the use of an accursed logic he puts darkness for light and light for darkness, and thus stultifies his conscience, and hardens his heart. If, perchance, you convince his judgment, you have not won his affection, you have not carried his will, you have not subdued his mind. Nothing but Omnipotence itself can save a single soul. What must be that mighty power which shall cause nations to run unto the Lord? They that dwell in the wilderness are to bow before Him, and His enemies are to lick the dust. What a conquest this! How shall Ethiopia be made to stretch out her hands to Him? Look how black are the hearts of her inhabitants, as well as their faces! How shall China and Hindustan, beclouded by their false philosophies, be led to own the truth? Look you, sirs, look at this great mountain, and do not underestimate its mass; and then remember that before our Zerubbabel it must and shall become a plain. The stone mentioned by Daniel, cut out of the mountain without hands, smote the monstrous image and broke it, and in due time filled the whole earth. In the night visions the same prophet saw the Son of Man having dominion, and glory, and a kingdom, that all people should serve Him. So must it be. But how great a thing it is!

The task is rendered the more severe because our Lord Jesus at this present works largely by a church, which is a poor and faulty instrument for the accomplishment of His purpose. I sometimes think there are more difficulties connected with the church than with the world; for the church is often worldly, faithless, lethargic, and I was about to add, inhuman. Might I not almost say as much, for she seems at times well nigh destitute of tender sympathy for the lost and perishing? The church at one hour receives the light and reflects it like a full moon, so that you have hope of her enlightening men; but soon she wanes into a mere ring of light, and becomes obscured. She declines from the truth, she forgets the glorious gospel entrusted to her, and she seeks after the rotten philosophies of men. How many times since Pentecost has the church started aside after the wisdom of men, and after a while has painfully returned to her first faith? At the present moment there is just that kind of wandering going on; and this hinders the work of the Lord. If a man has to do a work, he says to himself, "Give me good tools, at any rate. If I have to strike a heavy blow, do not trouble me with a broken hammer. If I have to write, give me a pen that will not hinder my hand." But alas! the church is too often false to her Master's purpose, and traitorous to His truth. Yet, brethren, the Lord will largely do His work and accomplish His good pleasure by such means as these. He will not fail nor be discouraged. If all Christians should become lukewarm, till the whole church became nauseous, as the church of Laodicea, yet still the Lord Jesus will not fail nor be discouraged. The disciple may sleep, but the great Savior agonizes over men. Let this battalion and the other waver as it may, He who holds the banner in the very center of the fight will never be moved: He will hold the field against all comers; for the Altogether Lovely One is the Standard-bearer among ten thousand. Though you mourn over the disciples, rejoice over their Master. They faint or fly, but "he shall not fail nor be discouraged."

To help you to believe this great truth, I beg you to notice who He is that hath undertaken all this: kindly read at the commencement of the chapter: "Behold my servant, whom I uphold, mine elect, in whom my soul delighteth." I am sure that He who is thus spoken of will not fail nor be discouraged; for, first, *He is God's own special Servant.* God has many servants, but the Christ is above all others called of God "my servant." He is a Son far excelling all other sons, and in the same sense He is a Servant far exceeding all other servants. He took upon Himself the form of a servant, and was made in the likeness of sinful flesh. He is a servant as none of us can ever hope to be in so high and wonderful a sense: He performs all the will of the Father. If He that was Lord of all became a servant, do you think He will not accomplish His service? If He that made the heavens and the earth laid aside His splendor and veiled Himself in our inferior clay, do you think He will fail in the purpose for which He did this? Can the incarnation of God be a failure? Can the life of the Son of God among men end in defeat? Your heart gives immediate answer—God's own servant will fulfill His service.

Then the great God says of Him, *"My servant whom I uphold."* If God upholds Him, how can He fail? Though God upholds all His people, yet beyond all others He is upholding His own chosen Son and Servant: how, then, can He fail? Is it possible with the divine power perpetually streaming into Him and abiding in Him, that he should fail, or be discouraged? The text may be read, "Behold my servant upon whom I lean," and the picture of a great Oriental monarch who comes forth leaning upon a favorite lord, whom he honors by placing him in that position, indicating thereby that he trusts his affairs with him, and regards him as his right-hand man, a very pillar of the State. Yes, we say it with reverence, God the Father leans on Jesus the Christ. He rests His honor and glory with the Person of the incarnate God: and now He comes before us as God in Christ Jesus, revealing His glory through the Mediator, putting His own sovereign power into the keeping of His Son, whom He hath appointed heir of all things. Can that Glorified One fail? Has the Father trusted His kingdom of grace with One who will be overcome? How can He fail whom the Father upholds, and upon whom the Father leans all the dignity and glory of His moral government? "He shall not fail nor be discouraged."

Then the Scripture adds this very significant word, *"Mine elect in whom my soul delighteth."* The chosen of God, the most choice One that God knows, shall He prove a failure? Not only does God delight in Him, but it is put more strongly still: "In whom my soul delighteth." Do you taste the marrow of the expression? It seems to me to be exceeding full. The chief delight of God is in His Son, as Mediator. God said of the world, that it was very good; but we read not that His soul delighted in it: but, see, the very soul of the Godhead is moved and filled with delight because of the Savior, commissioned to redeem. Blessed Father, we do not wonder that Thou art taken up with delight in Jesus; for even we ourselves, when we get a sight of Him, are ravished with His charms. There is none like Him. He is thine Only Begotten, the Son of thy heart; well mayest Thou be well pleased with Him. How, then, is it possible that One whom the Lord loves so well, in whom His soul delighteth, should be put upon a work in which He can fail, or should be left in that work to be discouraged? It is impossible. The connection of Jesus of Nazareth with Jehovah, God of all, makes it absolutely certain that the divine enterprise to which He has pledged Himself shall assuredly succeed. "He shall not fail nor be discouraged."

Furthermore, *our Lord is in the abiding place of the Holy Spirit.* The text says, "I have put my spirit upon him"—the Holy Ghost, to whom be glory and honor forever, the Holy Spirit, very God of very God, dwells in Christ. Upon us He comes in measure. We sometimes receive a large portion of His power, but still we are not capable of receiving all the fullness of the Holy Ghost. But Christ has the residue of the Spirit abiding in Him. The Holy Spirit descended like a dove, and rested upon Him, and it does rest upon Him still. My brethren, do you dream that He on whom the Holy Ghost always rests can fail or be discouraged? Do you believe that the Gospel system is to die out? Is it going to be throttled by philosophy? Strangled by modern thought? Trampled down beneath the hoof of anarchy? Nay, while the Holy Ghost abideth upon the great Servant of Jehovah we cannot know a fear. The anointing on the head will descend to the skirts of the garments; and as *He* cannot fail nor be discouraged, neither shall we be dismayed. He who is owned, honored, trusted, sustained, loved, and anointed of God cannot but be successful. Jesus must persevere successfully to the end.

Notice yet further, that *the success of Jesus is guaranteed by the decree of God.* It is written, "He shall bring forth judgment to the Gentiles." Oh, those blessed "shalls" and "wills!" Some people make little of them, but I make everything of them. Here my heart rests; if God says "shall," then it certainly shall be. "The Lord said unto my Lord, Sit thou at my right hand, until I make thine enemies thy footstool." Think you He spoke in vain? Turn to the second Psalm, and read: "I will declare the decree: the Lord hath said unto me, thou art my Son; this day have I begotten thee. Ask of me, and I shall give thee the heathen for thine inheritance, and the uttermost parts of the earth for thy possession. Thou shalt break them with a rod of iron; thou shalt dash them in pieces like a potter's vessel." Shall this solemn proclamation of Jehovah be mere waste paper? My brethren, the sun may forget to shine, the eye of the world may be darkened; yon mighty ocean may cease to ebb and flow, and the heart of the earth may die; all nature may be driven on the rock of fate in general wreckage and confusion; but no Word of God shall fall to the ground; for that Word is essential life and power. If Jehovah hath spoken, it is done. If He declares it, it shall be. Therefore the Christ must and shall succeed, for His work is the subject of a divine decree.

Yet, brethren, it may be that at times we fear that the gospel is not prospering nor fulfilling the purpose for which God hath sent it. Looking back on past history, and looking out upon the present state of affairs, we are afraid that things are not going well. Possibly this may arise out of *our Lord's way of working*, which is so different from what our minds would choose. It is written in the second verse, "He shall not cry, nor lift up, nor cause his voice to be heard in the street." You are in an awful hurry, are you not? But He is never in haste. You would make a great stir and noise, I know, but Jesus will not thus spread the gospel. You would go out and fight all the enemies of truth, and set clamor against clamor, cry against cry, but "He shall not strive." You would shout, and rage, and rave; but He shall not cause His voice to be heard in the street. When Mohammed commenced his enterprise he announced that Paradise was to be found beneath the shadow of words, and numbers of brave men rushed to the battle; they swept everything before them, and stained continents with blood: they carried the name of Allah and Mohammed over Asia and Northern Africa, and seemed intent on conquering Europe: and yet the work done will not endure. The prophet and his caliphs did indeed strive, and cry, and cause their voices to be heard in the street: but Christ's system is the very reverse of that: His weapons are not carnal. Behold His battle-axe and weapons of war! Truth divinely strong, with no human force at the back of it but that of holiness and love; a gospel full of gentleness and mercy to men, proclaimed not by the silver trumpets of kings, but by the plain voices of lowly men. The gospel seeks neither prestige nor patronage from the State; nor does it ask to be advocated by scholastic sophistry, or human eloquence. It does not even aim at becoming predominant by force of the learning or talent of its teachers. It has neither pomp to commend it, nor arms to enforce it. It finds its strength rather in feebleness than in power. The kingdom comes by the Holy Spirit dropping like dew on human hearts, and fertilizing them with a divine life. Christ's kingdom comes not with observation, but in the stillness of the soul. All that is really the work of God is wrought in the silence of the heart by that wind which bloweth where it listeth. Sweetly the Holy Spirit constraineth all things by His own power; but the day of His power is not with roar of tempest, but with the noiseless fall of the dew. You ardent spirit that you are, are all in a hurry; you are going to push the church before you, and drag the world after you. Go and do it! But if the Lord works not after your fashion, be not greatly surprised; for it is written, "He shall not cry, nor lift up, nor cause his voice to be heard in the street."

His purpose shall stand, and He will do all His pleasure. He will do His work all the more surely because He sets about it quietly. I always delight in a man who can afford to go about his life-work without fuss, bluster, or loud announcement. See how a master-workman lays down his tools! He arranges his plan, sketches his ideal, and then begins as he means to go on. He will do the thing in that way, depend upon it. Another fellow flings his tools about, rushes at the work without system, makes the dust fly, litters the place with chips, spoils the work and leaves it in disgust. Our Savior works not so: He calmly, deliberately, resolutely pursues His mighty plan; and He will perform it. "He shall not fail nor be discouraged."

Note well the spirit in which He works. He is gentleness itself, and that always: "A bruised reed shall he not break, and the smoking flax shall he not quench." You cannot work in hot haste in this spirit. Gentleness makes good and sure speed, but it cannot endure rashness and heat. We know reformers who, if they had the power, would be like bulls in a china-shop; they would do a great deal in a very short time. But the world's best Friend is not given to quench and bruise. Here is a bruised reed, and it is of no use to anybody: you cannot even get music out of it, much less lean upon it; yet He does not break it. Here is a smoking flax, a wick with an offensive smell, containing very little heat, and no light; yet He does not put it out. This oft quoted text is used, as you know, in the New Testament, in reference to the Pharisees: they thought themselves strong pillars, but the Lord knew that they were only bruised reeds; they thought themselves great lights, but he knew that they were only as smoking flax; and yet He did not go out of His way to snuff them out. Even to them, though often righteously indignant, He was yet gentle, and only assailed them when they put themselves in His way, and forced a verdict from Him. The Lord Jesus was too good and great to be irritated by Pharisees. Lions do not hunt for "rats and mice, and such small deer." Great principles are laid down, which in due time destroy the meannesses which it is not worthwhile to attack in detail. The smoking flaxes of error, and the bruised reeds of pretense go in due season, but the gentle Lord is not in hot haste to put them out of the way. Hence we grow discouraged. But He will not fail nor be discouraged any the more because of His gentleness. Nay, let me tell you, brethren, it is the quiet man, the meek man, who is always hard to be turned aside from his purpose. When a man is passionate, and easily excited, you have only to wait a while, and he will cool down; perhaps chill down below zero. These fiery fellows will be easily managed by the devil, or somebody else, after the flame is over. Give me a man who deliberately makes up his mind, calmly sets to work, and patiently bears all rebuffs, and I know that what he sets himself to do will be done. He will work in God's way, and will not put forth his hand to snatch a premature success at the expense of principle. He is quiet because he is sure, patient because he is strong, gentle because he is firm. The man who cannot be provoked is the man who cannot be turned aside. You cannot discourage him: he will go through with his work, even to the end; be you sure of that. As you look at our blessed Master, patient and immovable amidst all the battle and the strife, you may assure yourself that He will not fail nor be discouraged. I do not admire Napoleon, except in the matter of his cool courage, but for that he was noteworthy. They always represent him in the midst of the battle with folded arms. His eagle eye is on the conflict, but he is motionless as a statue. Every soldier in the imperial army felt that victory was sure, for the captain was so self-possessed. If he had been hurrying to and fro, rushing here, there, and everywhere, and making a great fuss about everything, they would have inferred that defeat was impending. But see him yonder! All is well. He knows what he is at. It is all right, for he dost not strive, nor cry, nor cause his voice to be heard; he is calm, for he can see that all is well. There stands the Crucified this day, upon the vantage ground, at the right hand of God, and He surveys the battlefield in calm expectancy until His enemies are made His footstool. Tender towards the weakest of the weak, and kind even to the unthankful and the evil, we may see in all this mercifulness the pledge of His success. "He shall not fail nor be discouraged, till he has set judgment in the earth: and the isles shall wait for his law."

Consideration of the statement leads us to believe it firmly.

II. I want you to give me a few minutes while I say, LET THIS TRUTH BE BELIEVED AND ENJOYED. I want you to enjoy the fruit of this truth, and to be made glad by it.

First, enjoy it by recollecting that *Jesus has finished the work for His people*; that first work wherein He brought in everlasting righteousness, and bore the penalty of human guilt, and laid the foundation whereupon should be built the temple of God. Jesus has done all things well. He persevered in His life labor till He could say, "It is finished." From the hour when as a child He said, "Wist ye not that I must be about my Father's business?" all through the contradiction of sinners, and the weakness, and the poverty, and the shame in which His life was spent, you never see about our Divine Master any indication of failing or of being discouraged. We sorrowfully cry,

"I am almost ready to give up"; but He never spoke in that fashion, or even thought it. He had reckoned upon all the toil and the grief. He had foreseen it all: He had taken it into His calculations, and therefore He was not surprised and downcast. He determined to go, for our sakes, to death and the grave, and to bear the shame of our sin and the curse of our guilt, and even to be put by the Father into darkness on our account. He set His face like a flint; and like a flint His face remained to the bitter end. He never turned aside. Let us bless Him this day for His persevering love. It is not a half-finished salvation that we behold on yonder bloody tree: it is not an incomplete redemption that we see in that rising again of Jesus from the dead. When we look up to Him in His glory we know and feel that through all the agony and death He did not fail, and was not discouraged, and that He has set up a kingdom which cannot be removed forever. There let us rest with peaceful confidence.

The next reflection I want you to enjoy is this—*He will finish the work in His believing people.* He will not fail nor be discouraged until He has completely saved you and me. If I had been my own savior I should have given up the work long ago. We meet now and then with supposed perfect people, but the most of us dare not whisper the word perfection. When I have overcome a whole body of sin, and have risen to be somewhat like my Lord, it seems to me as if a new body of death were formed about me. I kill one dragon, and lo, his boy yields a crop of monsters. My evil nature seems to have coats like an onion, and when I have taken off one of them, it only lays bare another quite as offensive. Will it not be so to the end of the chapter? You may be growing better; I hope you are, but I shall be all the more hopeful that you are so if you fear that you are growing worse. If you think less and less of yourselves, it is probably true that you are growing in grace; but if you think more and more of yourselves, it is highly probable that you are growing in pride. There is a great difference between being puffed up and being built up. I can clearly see that I shall fail and be discouraged if salvation rests with me; but here is my comfort— *He* will not fail nor be discouraged. If my Lord begins with me, He will never be beaten off from His purpose. What bad stuff is our humanity! What wretched raw material for sainthood! It must be hard, treading and pounding such gritty clay; and I wonder not that both the hands and the feet of the great Worker were sorely wounded, since He had such clay to deal with. When He fashions us on the wheel, and we begin to assume somewhat of the form which He intends for us, yet we crack and spoil when we come to the oven, and all His work upon us seems lost. He has to grind us down again, to a powder, and begin with us again *de novo*, and fashion us once more. It would have been an easier work to have created new beings altogether than to take us poor fallen ones and lift us up to become sons of God. The Almighty Lord had only to have said, "Let a church be!" and a church most fair and spotless would have leaped into being; but instead thereof, He works upon us sinful ones, and undertakes to make us perfectly pure, and present us to Himself without spot, or wrinkle, or any such thing. What a marvel of grace! He will do it, brother. He will do it, sister. He has not grown weary of the work, neither is He discouraged by all our ill behavior. Before He began He knew all about it. Had He not been a far-see-ing Christ, able to foresee all our shortcomings and backslidings, He might have been surprised into weariness; but He says, "I knew that thou art obstinate"; and again, "I knew that thou wouldest deal very treacherously." He foreknew all our ingratitude, backsliding, unbelief, and unworthiness, and therefore He will not fail nor be dis-couraged till His work in us is done, and we are fit for heaven.

Again, dear friends, *He will finish His work by His people.* Whatever the work is that is to be done by the church, He will not fail nor be discouraged until it is per-formed. I do not know whether any of you have noticed in my text a very singular thing. If you have the Revised Version, the margin will give you some rather singular information. The text might be read thus: "A bruised reed shall he not break, and the smoking flax shall he not quench: yet he shall not burn dimly nor be bruised." Though He deals with bruised reeds and smoking flaxes, yet He Himself is not crushed, nor does His light become a mere glimmer. To my mind, this is a deeply in-teresting use of words, and should not be allowed to slip. Christianity just now, they say, is a mere smoke, the old-fashioned doctrine especially burns very dim. Do not you believe it: the light of Jesus shall not darken or grow less. Those souls that can see His light will tell you that His face shines still like the sun. There is a glory about Him that is undiminished and undiminishable. He does not glimmer, and He is not crushed. He is no reed; His enemies will one day find that he carrieth a rod of iron. He is a pillar of the house of our God: He beareth up all things, for He is strong and mighty, and He cannot fail. I want you to eject at the back door every suggestion that enters your house as to the defeat of the Christ and the failure of the gospel; it is not possible, it cannot be. *You* may smoke like the flax, *you* may be broken like the reed; but He will never glimmer nor be a crushed reed, even to the end: wherefore com-fort one another with these words.

And to conclude, I should not have treated the text properly if I did not say that it has in it great comfort to those of you who are as yet outside of the church of God, and are not numbered with His people. Will you kindly read the sixth and seventh verses?—"He shall not fail nor be discouraged," till He has done, what?—the Divine will, and this is a part of it: "*To open the blind eyes, to bring out the prisoners from the prison, and them that sit in darkness out of the prison house.*" Oh, say you, I cannot see Christ! He has come on purpose to make you see. Turn your sightless eyeballs this way. Breathe this prayer, "Thou Son of David, have mercy on me." And if he saith: "What wilt thou that I should do unto thee?" answer, "Lord, that I might receive my sight." In one single moment, aye, while the clock is ticking, Jesus Christ can take the scales from a blind man's eyes and let in such a flood of daylight that he shall see heaven itself. Lord, do it this morning. O dear hearts, will you not each one cry, Lord, do it to me? Are you saying that, my friend? He will do it. He loves to hear a blind man's cry. Do you not remember in the New Testament how often He stood still when He heard a blind man's cry. Poor blind soul! Cry to Him now. He shall not fail nor be discouraged, He will come to you and save you.

"Ah!" saith one, "but I am worse than that, I am shut up in prison." Kindly read the seventh verse again—"To bring out the prisoners from the prison." You are miserable, without hope, shut up in an iron cage. He has come who will not fail nor be discouraged; He has come on purpose to fetch you out of the cage. Ask Him to break the bars in sunder. I see Him lay His pierced hand to that iron bar. You have filed it a long while, and it has broken the teeth of your file; you have tried to shake it in its place, but you could not stir it in the least. See what He does! He plucks bar after bar out of its place, as if they had been so many reeds, and you are free. Arise and take your liberty! The Son of God has made you free. If thou hast trusted Him, He has broken the gates of brass, and cut the bars of iron in sunder; thou art free, enjoy thy liberty.

"Oh, but," saith one, "in my case it is blindness and slavery united." Listen, then. He has come to "bring them that sit in darkness out of the prison-house." You cannot see the bars that shut you in, nor even mark the limits of your narrow cell; but He has come who will give eyes to you, and light to those eyes, and liberty to your enlightened sight. Only trust Him. All things are possible to Him that believeth when Christ is near. Thou knowest now, thou who are now at the bottom of the sea, how high He can lift thee in an instant? Out of the belly of hell, if thou wilt cry, He can lift thee in a moment, to the very heights of heaven. I say no more of my Lord than He deserves to have said of Him; nay, nor yet half as much. Try Him, and see if He will fail. Try Him now, thou in the worst and lowest of circumstances, thou devil-bound and devil-tortured spirit. Dare to believe that Jesus can do all things for thee. Leave thyself with Him. Go thy way, for as thou hast believed so shall it be unto thee. To the name of Him that will not fail nor be discouraged be glory forever and ever! Amen.

THE SHAME AND SPITTING

SERMON No. 1,486
DELIVERED ON LORD'S DAY MORNING, JULY 27, 1879.
PORTIONS OF SCRIPTURE READ BEFORE SERMON—ISAIAH 50; 53:1–7; MATTHEW
26:62–68; 27:27–30; LUKE 23:8–11.
HYMNS FROM *Our Own Hymn Book*—327, 937, 268.

I gave my back to the smiters, and my cheeks to them that plucked off the hair: I hid not my face from shame and spitting—Isaiah 50:6.

OF whom speaketh the prophet this? Of himself or of some other? We cannot doubt but what Isaiah here wrote concerning the Lord Jesus Christ. Is not this one of the prophecies to which our Lord Himself referred in the incident recorded in the eighteenth chapter of Luke's gospel at the thirty-first verse? "Then he took unto him the twelve, and said unto them, Behold, we go up to Jerusalem, and all things that are written by the prophets concerning the Son of man shall be accomplished. For he shall be delivered unto the Gentiles, and shall be mocked, and spitefully entreated, and spitted on: and they shall scourge him and put him to death." Such a remarkable prophecy of scourging and spitting as this which is now before us must surely refer to the Lord Jesus; its highest fulfillment is assuredly found in Him alone.

Of whom else, let me ask, could you conceive the prophet to have spoken if you read the whole chapter? Of whom else could he say in the same breath, "I clothe the heavens with blackness and I make sackcloth their covering. I gave my back to the smiters, and my cheeks to them that plucked off the hair" (vv. 3, 6). What a descent from the omnipotence which veils the heavens with clouds to the gracious condescension which does not veil its own face, but permits it to be spat upon! No other could thus have spoken of Himself but He who is both God and man. He must be divine: how else could He say, "Behold, at my rebuke I dry up the sea, I make the rivers a wilderness" (v. 2)? And yet he must at the same time be a "man of sorrows and acquainted with grief," for there is a strange depth of pathos in the words, "I gave my back to the smiters, and my cheeks to them that plucked off the hair: I hid not my face from shame and spitting." Whatever others may say, we believe that the speaker in this verse is Jesus of Nazareth, the King of the Jews, the Son of God and the Son of man, our Redeemer. It is the Judge of Israel whom they have smitten with a rod upon the cheek who here plaintively declares the griefs which He has undergone. We have before us the language of prophecy, but it is as accurate as though it had been written at the moment of the event. Isaiah might have been one of the Evangelists, so exactly does he describe what our Savior endured.

I have already laid before you in the reading of the Scriptures some of the passages of the New Testament wherein the scourging and the shame of our Lord Jesus are described. We saw Him first at the tribunal of His own countrymen in Matthew 26, and we read, "Then did they spit in his face, and buffeted him: and others smote him with the palms of their hands." It was in the hall of the high priest, among His own countrymen, that first of all the shameful deeds of scorn were wrought upon Him. "He came unto his own, and his own received him not." His worst foes were they of His own household; they despised and abhorred Him, and would have none of Him. His own Father's husbandmen said among themselves— "This is the heir; let us kill him, and let us seize on his inheritance." This was His treatment at the hand of the house of Israel.

The same treatment, or the like thereto, was accorded Him in Herod's palace, where the lingering shade of a Jewish royalty still existed. There what I might venture to call a pattern mixture of Jew and Gentile power held court, but our Lord fared no better in the united company. By the two combined the Lord was treated with equal derision. "Herod with his men of war set him at naught, and mocked him, and arrayed him in a gorgeous robe" (Luke 23:11).

Speedily came His third trial, and He was delivered altogether to the Gentiles. Then Pilate, the governor, gave Him up to the cruel process of scourging. Scourging as it has been practiced in the English army is atrocious, a barbarism which ought to make us blush for the past, and resolve to end it for the future. How is it that such a horror has been tolerated so long in a country where we are not all savages? But the lash is nothing among us compared with what it was among the Romans. I have heard that it was made of the sinews of oxen, and that in it were twisted the hucklebones of sheep, with slivers of bone, in order that every stroke might more effectually tear its way into the poor quivering flesh, which was mangled by its awful strokes. Scourging was such a punishment that it was generally regarded as worse than death itself, and indeed, many perished while enduring it, or soon afterwards. Our blessed Redeemer gave His back to the smiters, and the plowers made deep furrows there. O spectacle of misery! How can we bear to look thereon? Nor was that all, for Pilate's soldiers, calling all the band together, as if there were not enough for mockery unless all were mustered, put Him to derision by a mock enthronement and a mimic coronation; and when they had thus done they again buffeted and smote Him, and spat in His face. There was no kind of cruelty which their heartlessness could just then invent which they did not exercise upon His blessed Person: their brutal sport had full indulgence, for their innocent victim offered neither resistance nor remonstrance. This is His own record of His patient endurance. "I gave my back to the smiters, and my cheeks to them that plucked off the hair: I hid not my face from shame and spitting."

Behold your King! I bring Him forth to you this morning in spirit and cry, "Behold the Man!" Turn hither all your eyes and hearts and look upon the despised and rejected of men! Gaze reverently and lovingly, with awe for His sufferings and love for His Person. The sight demands adoration. I would remind you of that which Moses did when he saw the bush that burned and was not consumed—fit emblem of our Lord on fire with griefs and yet not destroyed; I bid you turn aside and see this great sight, but first attend to the mandate—"Put off thy shoes from off thy feet, for the place whereon thou standest is holy ground." All round the cross the soil is sacred. Our suffering Lord has consecrated every place whereon He stood, and therefore our hearts must be filled with reverence while we linger under the shadow of His passion.

May the Holy Spirit help you to see Jesus in four lights at this time. In each view He is worthy of devout attention. Let us view Him first as *the Representative of God*; secondly, as *the Substitute of His people*; thirdly, as *the Servant of Jehovah*; and fourthly, as *the Comforter of His redeemed*.

I. First, I invite you to gaze upon your despised and rejected Lord as THE REPRESENTATIVE OF GOD. In the Person of Christ Jesus, God Himself came into the world, making a special visitation to Jerusalem and the Jewish people, but at the same time coming very near to all mankind. The Lord called to the people whom He had favored so long and whom He was intent to favor still. He says, in the second verse, "I came" and "I called." God did in very deed come down into the midst of mankind.

Be it noted, that when our Lord came into this world as the Representative of God, He came with all His divine power about Him. The chapter before us says, "Is my hand shortened at all, that it cannot redeem? or have I no power to deliver? behold, at my rebuke I dry up the sea, I make the rivers a wilderness." The Son of God, when He was here, did not perform those exact miracles, because He was bent upon marvels of beneficence rather than of judgment. He did not repeat the plagues of Egypt, for He did not come to smite, but to save; but He did greater wonders and wrought miracles which ought far more powerfully to have won men's confidence in Him because they were full of goodness and mercy. He fed the hungry, He healed the sick, He raised the dead, and He cast out devils. He did equal marvels to those which were wrought in Egypt when the arm of the Lord was made bare in the eyes of all the people. It is true He did not change water into blood, but He turned water into wine. It is true He did not make their fish to stink, but by His word He caused the net to be filled even to bursting with great fishes. He did not break the whole staff of bread as He did in Egypt, but He multiplied loaves and fishes so that thousands of men and women and children were fed from His bounteous hand. He did not slay their first-born, but He restored the dead. I grant you that the glory of the Godhead was somewhat hidden in the Person of Jesus of Nazareth, but it was still there, even as the glory was upon the face of Moses when he covered it with a veil. No essential attribute of God was absent in Christ, and every one might have been seen in Him if the people had not been willfully blind. He did the works of His Father, and those works bore witness of Him that He was come in His Father's name. Yes, God was personally in the world when Jesus walked the blessed fields of the Holy Land, now, alas, laid under the curse for rejecting Him.

But when God thus came among men He was unacknowledged. What saith the prophet? "Wherefore when I came was there no man? when I called was there none to answer?" A few, taught by the Spirit of God, discerned Him and rejoiced; but they were so very few that we may say of the whole generation that they knew Him not. Those who had some dim idea of His excellence and majesty yet rejected Him. Herod, because he feared that He was a King, sought to slay Him. The kings of the earth set themselves, and the rulers took counsel together, against the Lord, and against His anointed. He was emphatically and beyond all others "despised and rejected of men." Though, as I have said, the Godhead in Him was but scantily veiled, and gleams of its glory burst forth ever and anon, yet still the people would have none of it, and the cry, "Away with him, away with him, let him be crucified," was the verdict of the age upon which He descended. He called and there was none to answer; He spread out His hands all the day long unto a rebellious people who utterly rejected Him.

Yet our Lord when He came into the world was admirably adapted to be the Representative of God, not only because He was God Himself, but because as man His whole human nature was consecrated to the work, and in Him was neither flaw nor spot. He was untouched by any motive other than the one desire of manifesting the Father and blessing the sons of men. Oh, beloved, there was never One who had His ear so near the mouth of God as Jesus had. His Father had no need to speak to Him in dreams and visions of the night, for when all His faculties were wide awake there was nothing in them to hinder His understanding the mind of God; and therefore every morning when His Father wakened Him He spoke into His ear. Jesus sat as a scholar at the Father's feet that He might learn first, and then teach. The things which He heard of the Father He made known unto men. He says that He spoke not His own words but the words of Him that sent Him, and He did not His own deeds, but "my Father," saith He, "that dwelleth in me, he doeth the work." Now, a man thus entirely agreeable to the mind and will of the great God was fitted to be the Representative of God. Both the alliance of His manhood with the Godhead and its perfect character qualified it to be the fittest dwelling of God among men. Yes, dear friends, our Savior came in a way which should at once have commanded the reverent homage of all men. Even His great Father said, "They will reverence my Son." Enough of the Godhead was manifested to impress and no more, lest it should alarm. With a soul of gentlest mold and a body like our own He was altogether adapted to be the Representative of God. His errand, too, was all gentleness and love, for He came to speak words in season to the weary, and to comfort those that were cast down: surely such an errand should have secured Him a welcome. His course and conduct were most conciliatory, for He went among the people, and ate with publicans and sinners; so gentle was He that He took little children in His arms, and blessed them; for this, if for nothing else, they ought to have welcomed Him right heartily and rejoiced at the sight of Him. Our text tells us how contrary was their conduct towards Him to that which He deserved: instead of being welcomed He was scourged, and instead of being honored He was scorned. Cruelty smote His back and plucked off the hair from His face, while derision jeered at Him and cast its spittle upon Him. Shame and contempt were poured upon Him, though He was God Himself. That spectacle of Christ spat upon, and scourged, represents what man virtually does to his God, what he would do to the Most High if he could. Hart well puts it—

> See how the patient Jesus stands,
> Insulted in his lowest case!
> Sinners have bound the Almighty hands,
> And spit in their Creator's face.

When our parents broke the command of their Maker, obeying the advice of the devil rather than the Word of God, and preferring a poor apple to the divine favor, they did as it were spit into the face of God; and every sin committed since has been a repetition of the same contempt of the Eternal One. When a man will have his pleasure, even though it displeases God, he as good as declares that he despises God, prefers himself, and defies the wrath of the Most High. When a man acts contrary to the command of God he does as good as say to God, "This is better for me to do than what Thou bidst me do. Either Thou art mistaken, in thy prohibitions, or else Thou dost willfully deny me the highest pleasure, and I, being a better judge of my own interests than Thou art, snatch at the pleasure which Thou dost refuse me. I judge Thee either to be unwise or unkind." Every act of sin does despite to the sovereignty of God: it denies Him to be supreme and refuses Him obedience. Every act of sin does dishonor to the love and wisdom of God, for it seems to say that it would have been greater love to have permitted us to do evil than to have commanded us to abstain from it. All sin is in many ways an insult to the majesty of the thrice Holy God, and He regards it as such.

Dear friends, this is especially the sin of those who have heard the gospel and yet reject the Savior, for in their case the Lord has come to them in the most gracious form, and yet they have refused Him. The Lord might well say, "I have come to you to save you, and you will not regard me. I have come saying to you, 'Look unto me and be ye saved all the ends of the earth,' and you close your eyes in unbelief. I have come saying, 'Let us reason together: though your sins be as crimson, they shall be as wool,' but you will not be cleansed from your iniquity. I have come with the promise, 'All manner of sin and iniquity shall be forgiven unto men.' What is your reply?" In the case of many the answer is, "We prefer our own righteousness to the righteousness of God." If that is not casting spittle into the face of God I know not what is, for our righteousnesses are well described as "filthy rags," and we have the impudence to say that these are better than the righteousness of God in Christ Jesus. Or if we do not say this when we reject the Savior we tell Him that we do not want Him, for we do not need a Savior: this is as good as to say that God has played the fool with the life and death of His own Son. What greater derision can be cast upon God than to consider the blood of atonement to be a superfluity? He who chooses sin sooner than repentance prefers to suffer the wrath of God rather than be holy and dwell in heaven forever. For the sake of a few paltry pleasures men forego the love of God, and are ready to run the risk of an eternity of divine wrath. They think so little of God that He is of no account with them at all. All this is in reality a scorning and despising of the Lord God, and is well set forth by the insults which were poured upon the Lord Jesus.

Woe's me that it should ever be so. My God! My God! To what a sinful race do I belong. Alas, that it should treat thine infinite goodness so despitefully! That Thou shouldst be rejected at all, but especially that Thou shouldest be rejected when dressed in robes of love and arrayed in gentleness and pity is horrible to think upon. Do you mean it, O men? Can you really mean it? Can you deride the Lord Jesus who died for men? For which of His works do ye stone Him, when He lived only to do good? For which of His griefs do you refuse Him, when He died only that He might save? "He saved others, himself he cannot save," for He had so much love that He could spare Himself. I can understand your resisting the thunder of Jehovah's power, for I know your insanity; but can you resist the tenderness of Jehovah's love? If you do I must charge you with brutality, but therein I wrong the brutes, to whom such crimes are impossible. I may not even call this cruel scorning *diabolical,* for it is a sin which devils never did commit, perhaps would not have committed had it been possible to them. They have never trifled with a Redeemer, nor rejected the blood of the seed of Abraham. Shall the favored race spit upon its friend? God grant we may be brought to a better mind. But there is the picture before you. God Himself set at naught, despised, rejected, put to shame, perpetually dishonored in the Person of His dear Son. The sight should breed repentance in us. We should look to Him whom we have scourged, and mourn for Him. O Holy Spirit, work this tender grace in all our hearts.

II. And now, secondly, I want to set the Lord Jesus before you in another light, or rather beseech Him to shine in His own light before your eyes—AS THE SUBSTI-TUTE FOR HIS PEOPLE. Recollect when our Lord Jesus Christ suffered thus it was not on His own account nor purely for the sake of His Father, but He "was wounded for our transgressions, he was bruised for our iniquities: the chastisement of our peace was upon him; and with his stripes we are healed." There has risen up a modern idea which I cannot too much reprobate, that Christ made no atonement for our sin except upon the cross: whereas in this passage of Isaiah we are taught as plainly as possible that by His bruising and His stripes, as well as by His death, we are healed. Never divide between the life and the death of Christ. How could He have died if He had not lived? How could He suffer except while He lived? Death is not suffering, but the end of it. Guard also against the evil notion that you have nothing to do with the righteousness of Christ, for He could not have made an atonement by His blood if

He had not been perfect in His life. He could not have been acceptable if He had not first been proven to be holy, harmless, and undefiled. The victim must be spotless, or it cannot be presented for sacrifice. Draw no nice lines and raise no quibbling questions, but look at your Lord as He is and bow before Him.

Understand, my dear brothers and sisters, that Jesus took upon Himself our sin, and being found bearing that sin He had to be treated as sin should be treated. Now, of all the things that ever existed sin is the most shameful thing that can be. It deserves to be scourged, it deserves to be spit upon, it deserves to be crucified; and because our Lord had taken upon Himself our sin, therefore must He be put to shame, therefore must He be scourged. If you want to see what God thinks of sin, see His only Son spat upon by the soldiers when He was made sin for us. In God's sight sin is a shameful, horrible, loathsome, abominable thing, and when Jesus takes it He must be forsaken and given up to scorn. This sight will be the more wonderful to you when you recollect who it was that was spat upon, for if you and I, being sinners, were scourged, and smitten, and despised, there would be no wonder in it; but He who took our sin was God, before whom angels bow with reverent awe, and yet, seeing the sin was upon Him, He was made subject to the most intense degree of shame. Seeing that Jesus stood in our stead, it is written of the eternal Father that "He spared not his own Son." "It pleased the Father to bruise him: he hath put him to grief"; He made His soul an offering for sin. Yes, beloved, sin is condemned in the flesh and made to appear exceeding shameful when you recollect that, even though it was only laid on our blessed Lord by imputation, yet it threw Him into the very depths of shame and woe ere it could be removed.

Reflect, also, upon the voluntariness of all this. He willingly submitted to the endurance of suffering and scorn. It is said in the text, "He *gave* his back to the smiters." They did not seize and compel Him, or, if they did, yet they could not have done it without His consent. He gave His back to the smiters. He gave His cheek to those that plucked off the hair. He did not hide His face from shame and spitting: He did not seek in any way to escape from insults. It was the voluntariness of His grief which constituted in great measure the merit of it. That Christ should stand in our stead by force were a little thing, even had it been possible; but that He should stand there of His own free will, and that being there He should willingly be treated with derision, this is grace indeed. The Son of God was willingly made a curse for us, and at His own desire was made subject to shame on our account. I do not know how you feel in listening to me, but while I am speaking I feel as if language ought scarcely to touch such a theme as this: it is too feeble for its task. I want you to get beyond my words if you can, and for yourselves meditate upon the fact that He who covers the heavens with blackness, yet did not cover His own face, and He who binds up the universe with the girdle which holds it in one, yet was bound and blindfolded by the men He had Himself made; He whose face is as the brightness of the sun that shineth in its strength was once spit upon. Surely we shall need faith in heaven to believe this wondrous fact. Can it have been true, that the glorious Son of God was jeered and jested at? I have often heard that there is no faith wanted in heaven, but

I rather judge that we shall want as much faith to believe that these things were ever done as the patriarchs had to believe that they would be done. How shall I sit down and gaze upon *Him* and think that His dear face was once profaned with spittle? When all heaven shall lie prostrate at His feet in awful silence of adoration will it seem possible that once He was mocked? When angels and principalities, and powers shall all be roused to rapture of harmonious music in His praise, will it seem possible that once the most abject of men plucked out the hair? Will it not appear incredible that those sacred hands, which are "as gold rings set with the beryl," were once nailed to a gibbet, and that those cheeks which are "as a bed of spices, as sweet flowers," should have been battered and bruised? We shall be quite certain of the fact, and yet we shall never cease to wonder, that His side was gashed, and His face was spit upon? The sin of man in this instance will always amaze us. How could you commit this crime? Oh, ye sons of men, how could ye treat such an One with cruel scorn? O thou brazen thing called sin, thou hast, indeed, as the prophet saith, "a whore's forehead"; thou hast a demon's heart, hell burns within thee. Why couldst thou not spit upon earthly splendors? Why must heaven be thy scorn? Or if heaven, why not spit on angels! Was there no place for thy spittle but *His* face? *His* face! Woe is me! His face! Should such loveliness receive such shame as this? I could wish that man had never been created, or that being created, he had been swept into nothingness rather than have lived to commit such horror.

Yet, here is matter for our faith to rest upon. Beloved, trust yourselves in the hands of your great Substitute. Did He bear all this shame? Then there must be more than enough merit and efficacy in this, which was the prelude of His precious death —and especially in His death itself—there must be merit sufficient to put away all transgression, iniquity, and sin. Our shame is ended, for He has borne it! Our punishment is removed: He has endured it all. Double for all our sins has our Redeemer paid. Return unto thy rest, O my soul, and let peace take full possession of thy weeping heart.

III. But time fails us, and therefore we will mention, next, the third light in which it is our desire to see the Savior. Beloved, we desire to see the Lord Jesus Christ AS THE SERVANT OF GOD. He took upon Himself the form of a servant when He was made in the likeness of man. Observe how He performed this service right thoroughly, and remember we are to look upon this third picture as our copy, which is to be the guide of our life. I know that many of you are glad to call yourselves the servants of God; take not the name in vain. As Jesus was, so are you also in this world, and you are to seek to be like Him.

First, as a servant, Christ was personally prepared for service. He was thirty years and more here below, learning obedience in His Father's house, and the after years were spent in learning obedience by the things which He suffered. What a servant He was, for He never went about His own errands nor went by His own will, but He waited always upon His Father. He was in constant communication with heaven, both by day and by night. He says, "He wakeneth morning by morning, he wakeneth mine ear to hear as the learned." The blessed Lord or ever the day broke heard that gentle voice which called Him, and at its whisper He arose before the sunrise, and there the dawning found Him, on the mountain side, waiting upon God in wrestling prayer, taking His message from the Father that He might go and deliver it to the children of men. He loved man much, but He loved His Father more, and He never came to tell out the love of God without having as man received it fresh from the divine heart. He knew that His Father heard Him always, and He lived in the spirit of conscious acceptance. Have you ever noticed that sometimes a passage will begin, "At that time Jesus answered and said," and yet there is no notice that He had been speaking to anybody before, or that anybody had been speaking to Him? What He said was an answer to a voice which no ear heard but His own, for He was always standing with opened ear, listening to the eternal voice. Such service did Jesus render, and you must render the same. You cannot do your Lord's will except you live near to Him. It is of no use trying to preach with power unless we get our message from our heavenly Father's own Self. I am sure you as hearers know the difference between a dead word which comes from a man's own brain and lip, and a living word which the preacher delivers fresh as the manna which fell from heaven. The word should come from the minister like bread hot from the oven, or better still, like a seed with life in it; not as a parched grain with the germ dead and killed, but as a living seed which roots itself in your souls, and springs up to a harvest. This made our Lord such a good servant that He listened to His Father's voice and yielded Himself to the Father's will to perfection.

Our text assures us that this service knew no reserve in its consecration. We generally draw back somewhere. I am ashamed to say it, but I mourn that I have done so. Many of us could give to Christ all our health and strength, and all the money we have, very heartily and cheerfully; but when it comes to a point of reputation we feel the pinch. To be slandered, to have some filthy thing said of you; this is too much for flesh and blood. You seem to say, "I cannot be made a fool of, I cannot bear to be regarded as a mere impostor"; but a true servant of Christ must make himself of no reputation when he takes upon himself the work of his Lord. Our blessed Master was willing to be scoffed at by the lewdest and lowest of men. The abjects jeered at Him; the reproach of them that reproached God fell upon Him. He became the song of the drunkard, and when the rough soldiery detained Him in the guard-room they heaped up their ridicule, as though He were not worthy of the name of man.

> They bow their knees to me, and cry, "Hail, King":
> Whatever scoffs or scornfulness can bring,
> I am the floor, the sink, where they it fling:
> > *Was ever grief like mine?*
>
> The soldiers also spit upon that face
> Which angels did desire to have the grace
> And prophets once to see, but found no place:
> > *Was ever grief like mine?*

Herod and Pilate were the very dross of men, and yet He permitted them to judge

Him. Their servants were vile fellows, and yet He resigned Himself to them. If He had breathed upon them with angry breath, He might have flashed devouring fire upon them, and burned them up as stubble; but His omnipotent patience restrained His indignation, and He remained as a sheep before her shearers. He allowed His own creatures to pluck His hair and spit in His face. Such patience should be yours as servants of God. We are to be willing to be made nothing of, and even to be counted as the offscouring of all things. It is pitiful for the Christian to refuse to suffer, and to become a fighting man, crying, "We must stand up for our rights." Did you ever see Jesus in that posture? There is a propensity in us to say, "I will have it out." Yes, but you cannot picture Jesus in that attitude. I defy a painter to depict Him so: it is somebody else, and not Christ. No! He said, "I gave my back to the smiters, and my cheeks to them that plucked off the hair: I hid not my face from shame and spitting."

There is something more here than perfect consecration in the mere form of it, for its heart and essence are manifest in an obedient delight in the will of the Father. The words seem to me to express alacrity. It is not said that He reluctantly permitted His enemies to pluck His hair, or smite His back, but it is written, "I *gave* my back to the smiters, and my cheeks to them that plucked off the hair." He could not delight in it; how could He delight in suffering and shame? These things were even more repugnant to His sensitive nature than they can be to us; and yet, "For the joy that was set before him he endured the cross, despising the shame." He was ready for this dreadful treatment, for He said, "I have a baptism to be baptized with, and how am I straitened until it be accomplished!" He was ready for the cup of gall, and willing to drink it to its dregs, though it was bitterness itself to Him. He gave His back to the smiters.

All this while—now follow me in this next point—there was no flinching in Him. They spat in His face, but what says He in the seventh verse. "I have set my face like a flint." If they are about to defile His face He is resolved to bear it; He girds up His loins and makes Himself more determined. Oh, the bravery of our Master's silence! Cruelty and shame could not make Him speak. Have not your lips sometimes longed to speak out a denial and a defense? Have you not felt it wise to be quiet, but then the charge has been so excessively cruel, and it has stung you so terribly that you hungered to resent it. Base falsehoods aroused your indignation, and you felt you must speak and probably you did speak, though you tried to keep your lips as with a bridle while the wicked were before you. But our own beloved Lord in the omnipotence of His patience and love would not utter a word, but like a lamb at the slaughter He opened not His mouth. He witnessed a good confession by His matchless silence. Oh, how mighty—how gloriously mighty was His patience! We must copy it if we are to be His disciples. We, too, must set our faces like flints, to move or to sit still, according to the Father's will, to be silent or to speak, as most shall honor Him. "I have set my face like a flint," saith He, even though in another place He cries, "My heart is like wax, it is melted in the midst of my bowels."

And do you notice all the while the confidence and quiet of His spirit? He almost seems to say, "You may spit upon Me, but you cannot find fault with Me. You may pluck my hair, but you cannot impugn my integrity; you may lash my shoulders, but you cannot impute a fault to Me. Your false witnesses dare not look Me in the face: let Me know who is mine adversary, let him come near to Me. Behold, Adonai Jehovah will keep Me, who is he that shall condemn me! Lo, they all shall wax old as a garment, the moth shall eat them up." Be calm then, O true servant of God! In patience possess your soul. Serve God steadily and steadfastly though all men should belie you. Go to the bottom of the service, dive even to the very depth, and be content even to lie in Christ's grave, for you shall share in Christ's resurrection. Do not dream that the path to heaven is up the hill of honor, it winds down into the valley of humiliation. Imagine not that you can grow great eternally by being great here. You must become less, and less, and less, even though you should be despised and rejected of men, for this is the path to everlasting glory.

I have not time to expound the last two verses of the chapter, but they read you a noble lesson. "He gave his back to the smiters"; if, then, any of you walk in darkness and have no light, this is no new thing for a servant of God. The chief of all servants persevered, though men despised Him. Follow Him, then. Stay yourselves upon God as He did, and look for a bright ending of your trials. He came out into the light ultimately, and there He sits in inconceivable splendor at His Father's right hand, and so shall all the faithful come out of the cloud and shine forth as the sun in the kingdom of their Father. Only bear on with resolute patience, and glory shall be *your* reward, even as it is His.

IV. Lastly, I am to set Him forth in His fourth character, as THE COMFORTER OF HIS PEOPLE; but I must ask *you* to do this, while I just, as it were, make a charcoal sketch of the picture I would have painted.

Remember, first, our blessed Lord is well qualified to speak a word in season to him that is weary, because He Himself is lowly, and meek, and so accessible to us. When men are in low spirits they feel as if they could not take comfort from persons who are harsh and proud. The Comforter must come as a sufferer; He must come in a lowly broken spirit, if He would cheer the afflicted. You must not put on your best dress to go and visit the daughter of poverty, or go with your jewels about you to show how much better off you are than she. Sit down by the side of the downcast man and let him know that you are meek and lowly of heart. Your Master "gave his back to the smiters, and his cheek to them that plucked off the hair," and therefore He is the Comforter you want.

Remark not only His lowliness, but His sympathy. Are you full of aches and pains this morning? Jesus knows all about them, for He "gave his back to the smiters." Do you suffer from what is worse than pain, from scandal and slander? "He hid not his face from shame and spitting." Have you been ridiculed of late? Have the graceless made fun of your godliness? Jesus can sympathize with you, for you know what unholy mirth they made out of Him. In every pang that rends your heart your Lord has borne His share. Go and tell Him. Many will not understand you. You are a speckled bird, differing from all the rest, and they will all peck at you; but Jesus Christ knows this, for He was a speckled bird, too. He was "holy, harmless, undefiled, and separate from sinners," but not separate from such as you. Get you to Him and He will sympathize with you.

In addition to His gentle spirit and His power to sympathize, there is this to help to comfort us—namely, His example, for He can argue thus with you, "I gave my back to the smiters. Cannot you do the like? Shall the disciple be above his Master?" If I can but get on the doorstep of heaven and sit down in the meanest place there I shall feel I have an infinitely better position than I deserve, and shall I think of my dear, blessed Lord and Master giving His face to be spit upon, and then give myself airs, and say, "I cannot bear this scorn, I cannot bear this pain!" What, does the King pass over the brook Kedron, and must there be no brook Kedron for you? Does the Master bear the cross, and must your shoulders never be galled? Did they call the Master of the house "Beelzebub," and must they call you "Reverend Sir"? Did they laugh at Him, and scoff at Him, and must you be honored? Are you to be "gentleman" and "lady" where Christ was "that fellow"? For His birth they loaned Him a stable, and for His burial He borrowed a grave. O friends, let pride disappear, and let us count it our highest honor to be permitted to stoop as low as ever we can.

And, then, His example further comforts us by the fact that He was calm amid it all. Oh, the deep rest of the Savior's heart! They set Him up upon that mock throne, but He did not answer with an angry word; they put a reed into His hand, but He did not change it to an iron rod, and break them like potters' vessels, as He might have done. There was no wincing and no pleading for mercy. Sighs of pain were forced from Him, and He said, "I thirst," for He was not a stoic; but there was no fear of man, or timorous shrinking of heart.

The King of Martyrs well deserves to wear the martyr's crown, for right royally did He endure: there was never a patience like to His. That is your copy, brother, that is your copy, sister—you must write very carefully to write as well as that. You had need your Master held your hand; in fact, whenever children in Christ's school do write according to His copy, it is always because He holds their hand by His Spirit.

Last of all, our Savior's triumph is meant to be a stimulus and encouragement to us. He stands before us this morning as the Comforter of His people. Consider Him that endured such contradiction of sinners against Himself lest ye be weary and faint in your minds; for though He was once abased and despised, yet now He sitteth at the right hand of God, and reigns over all things; and the day is coming when every knee shall bow before Him, and every tongue confess that Jesus Christ is Lord, to the glory of God the Father. They that spat upon Him will rue the day. Come hither, ye that derided Him! He has raised you from the dead, come hither and spit upon Him now! Ye that scourged Him, bring your rods, see what ye can do in this day of His glory! See, they fly before Him, they invoke the hills to shelter them, they ask the rocks to open and conceal them. Yet it is nothing but His face, that selfsame face they spat upon, which is making earth and heaven to flee away. Yea, all things flee before the majesty of His frown who once gave His back to the smiters, and His cheeks to them that plucked off the hair. Be like Him, then, ye who bear His name; trust Him, and live for Him, and you shall reign with Him in glory forever and ever. Amen.

THE SURE TRIUMPH OF THE CRUCIFIED ONE

SERMON NO. 1,231
DELIVERED ON LORD'S DAY MORNING, APRIL 25, 1875.
PORTION OF SCRIPTURE READ BEFORE SERMON—ISAIAH 52.
HYMNS FROM *Our Own Hymn Book*—72, 418, 352.

Behold, my servant shall deal prudently, he shall be exalted and extolled, and be very high. As many were astonished at thee; his visage was so marred more than any man, and his form more than the sons of men: So shall he sprinkle many nations; the kings shall shut their mouths at him: for that which had not been told them shall they see; and that which they had not heard shall they consider—Isaiah 52:13-15.

Modern Jewish writers refuse to see the Messiah in this passage, but their predecessors were not so blind. The Targum and the ancient Rabbins interpreted it of the Messiah, and indeed all attempts to explain it apart from Him are palpable failures. Christian commentators in all ages have seen the Lord Jesus here. How could they do otherwise? To whom else could the prophet have referred? If the Man of Nazareth, the Son of God, be not right visible in these three verses, they are dark as midnight itself. We do not hesitate for a moment in applying every word to our Lord Jesus Christ.

Dear brethren, when our Lord ascended on high He gave us this commission: "Go ye into all the world and preach the gospel to every creature." Our duty is to obey that command, whether men will hear or whether they will forbear; the commission is unconditional, and is not dependent upon our success. If up to this date, 1875, there had never been a solitary convert through Christian ministry, if the whole of the church of God had hitherto labored in vain, and the succession of saints had only been kept up by miracle, it would not affect our duty one iota. Our business is to preach the gospel, even to those who are aroused to persecution thereby. We are to sow, whether a harvest follow or not. Success is with God; service belongs to us. I believe, therefore, that true faith, when it is in a healthy condition, will enable us to go plodding on, carefully scattering the seed, even by the wayside and on stony places; yet there is flesh about us all, and faith is not always unalloyed with sight, and consequently we occasionally flag and almost faint if we do not see some present usefulness.

This passage may cheer us if we fear that we have spent our strength for naught, for such certainly was the condition of the church of God at the time when this passage was addressed to it. There is a break made in our version between the 52nd and 53rd chapters, but no such break should have been made, and if we read straight on we shall see that these consoling words are meant for mourning workers. We hear even prophets saying, "Who hath believed our report, and to whom is the arm of the Lord revealed?" Even the bravest of the prophets lamented that the offense of the cross hindered men from seeing the comeliness of the Messiah. All glorious as He was to the prophets when they beheld His substitutionary griefs, He was not understood by the multitudes who only saw in Him a man smitten of God and afflicted, having no beauty that they should desire Him. To support them under circumstances so dispiriting there comes in this comfortable word of our text, in which the marred visage and disfigured form of the great servant of the Lord are fully recognized, and yet the voice of the Lord declares that the shame and contempt caused thereby will be temporary, and the ultimate result will be sure; the issue of the great scheme of redemption is by no means uncertain, His cause must prosper, His throne must be established, and the will of the Lord must be done. Let us brace ourselves up this morning with the delightful prospect of the predestinated triumph of the kingdom of our Lord and of His Christ.

In handling our text we shall note, first, that, directing us to the Lord Jesus Christ, it dwells upon *the character of His dealings*—"My servant shall deal prudently, he shall be exalted and extolled, and be very high." Then, secondly, it mentions *the stumblingblock which lies in his way*, the great hindrance to the progress of his work: "Many were astonished at thee; his visage was so marred more than any man, and his form more than the sons of men." Thirdly, we see in the verses before us *the certainty of the removal of this hindrance*: "He shall sprinkle many nations; the kings shall shut their mouths at him." And, fourthly *the manner of its accomplishment*, namely, by instruction in the gospel: "For that which had not been told them they shall see; and that which they had not heard shall they consider."

1. THE CHARACTER OF OUR LORD'S DEALINGS. He is called in the text, "*My servant*," a title as honorable as it is condescending. The Lord Jesus has undertaken in infinite love to become the servant of the Father for our sakes, and He is a servant like unto Moses, who was set over the Lord's house to manage the affairs of the dispensation. Jesus, though a Son and therefore Lord, has deigned to become the great servant of God under the present economy; He conducts the affairs of the household of God, and it is said in the text, and it is to that we have to draw attention, that *He deals prudently*. He who took upon Him the form of a servant acts as a wise servant in everything; and indeed it could not be otherwise, for "in him are hid all the treasures of wisdom and knowledge." This prudence was manifest in the days of His flesh, from His childhood among the doctors in the temple on to His confession before Pontius Pilate. Our Lord was enthusiastic: there was a fire burning within Him which nothing could quench, He found His meat and drink in doing His Father's will; but that

enthusiasm never carried Him into rashness, or forgetfulness of sound reason; He was as wise and prudent as the most cold-hearted calculator could have been. Our Savior was full of love, and that love made Him frank and open-hearted; no frigid reserve kept Him at a distance from the people, or shrouded Him in a cloud of mystery, He was a man among men, transparent, childlike, "the holy child Jesus"; but for all that He was ever prudent, and "committed Himself unto no man, for he knew what was in man." Too many who aspire to be leaders of the people study policy, craft, and diplomacy, and think it needful to use language as much for the concealment as for the declaration of their thoughts; such men watch their own words till their very soul seems withered within them. The Friend of sinners had not a fraction of that thing about Him; and yet He was wiser and more prudent than if diplomacy had been His study from His youth up. You see His wisdom when He baffles His adversaries; they think to entangle Him in His speech, but He breaks their snares asunder as with a wave of our hand we sweep cobwebs from our path. You see His wisdom when He deals with His friends: He has many things to say unto them, but He perceives that they cannot bear them; He, therefore, does not overload their intellects, lest undigested truth should breed mischief in their souls. Little by little, like the increasing brightness of the dawn, He lets light into their souls, lest their eyes should utterly fail before the brilliance thereof. He does not send them upon difficult errands at first; He reserves for their riper years and stronger days the sterner tasks and more heroic deeds of daring. As we see His career in the light of the four evangelists, it is distinguished for His prudence, and in that respect "never man spoke like this man."

He who on earth became obedient unto death has now gone *into the glory*, but He is still over the house of God, conducting its affairs. *He deals prudently still.* Our fears lead us to judge that the affairs of Christ's kingdom are going amiss, but we may rest assured that all is well, for the Lord hath put all things under the feet of Jesus, and made Him to be head over all things to His church. The pleasure of the Lord shall prosper in the hand of Jesus still. *We* err, but *He* does not. Nay, the very points wherein we err are overruled by Him for the display of His unerring wisdom and consummate skill. The storms and tempests which surround the church serve only to illustrate the wisdom and power of our great Pilot; He has ultimate designs which are not apparent upon the surface, and these He never fails to accomplish.

Brethren, all along through the history of the church the dealings of the Lord Jesus with His people have been very remarkable. The wisdom in them is often deep, and only discoverable by those who seek it out, and yet frequently it sparkles upon the surface like gold in certain lands across the sea. Note how the Lord has made His church learn truth by degrees, and purified her first of one error and then of another. The church has fallen first into one folly and then into another, but her Lord has borne with her and delivered her. Full often He has allowed her to work her folly out, so as to see its result, and by this process He has stamped out the error effectually, so that it will never gain power again. At the present time the gross folly of uniting with the

State is being practically proved before the eyes of all men, and when it has come to its fullness it will end, never to be revived again. We wonder sometimes why He allows this or that error to exist, and we ask how it can be that the church should be so despoiled of her purity and weakened in her strength. We wonder that our Lord does not judge the evil and punish it at once, or that He does not raise up some strong voice to protest against it, and, sending His Holy Spirit therewith, destroy the evil at once. I think He might, but there is prudence in the withholding of His power. The wise physician tolerates disease until it shall have reached the point at which he can grapple with it, so as to eradicate it from the system, so has the good Lord allowed some ills to fester in the midst of His church, that He may ultimately exterminate them. We wish to see great success following all forms of ministry, we would see our missionary societies prosperous to such a degree that a nation should be born in a day; but the Lord withholds success in a great measure, and herein He is dealing prudently. He keeps us back from prosperity, till we have learned that it does not after all arise out of our plans, and schemes, and resources, and energies: He would strip us of pride; He would put us in such a condition that it would be safe to us to give us success, and would be glorious to Himself also. Often has a church, like Israel of old, to suffer defeat till it finds out and destroys the Achan who troubles the camp. The church has been foiled and humbled till at last in sheer despair she has fallen upon her face in prayer, and lifted up her heart to the strong for strength, and then her strength has returned, and victory has waited on her banners. As rivers filter and purify in their running, so does the church in her course become pure through the manifold wisdom of her Lord.

Study the pages of ecclesiastical history, and you will see how Jesus Christ has dealt wisely in the raising up of fitting men for all times. I could not suppose a better man for Luther's age than Luther, yet Luther alone would have been very incomplete for the full service needed had it not been for Calvin, whose calm intellect was the complement of Luther's fiery soul. You shall not find a better age for Wycliffe to have been born in than the time in which he shone forth as the morning star of the Reformation. God fits the man for the place, and the place for the man; there is an hour for the voice, and a voice for the hour.

Our Lord has done all things well even unto this day, but now, perhaps, we are getting a little tired; it is near two thousand years since He died, and there has been a long talk about its being the end of the six thousand years since creation's day, and we murmur to each other that the great Sabbath must surely be very near. I am not much in love with this chronological theory, for I think we cannot be very certain that we have not long ago passed beyond the seventh thousand years. It is very questionable to me whether we do not altogether misunderstand the chronology of the Old Testament; certainly nothing is more perplexing than the ancient Hebrew numbering. Still, so the many will have it, and possibly so it is. A portion of the church not only expects the Lord's second advent, but gets into a state of feverishness about the matter. Surely, say they, His delays have been very great: why are His chariots so long in coming? Ah, brethren, the Master knows best. It may please Him to finish up the present dispensation today; if so, He will doubtless deal prudently in so doing: but it may be that myriads of years are yet to elapse before His appearing, and if so there will be wisdom in the delay. Let us leave the matter alone, for while the general fact that He will come is clearly revealed in order to quicken our diligence, the details are veiled in mystery, since they would only gratify our curiosity. If I knew that our Lord would come this evening, I should preach just as I mean to preach; and if I knew He would come during this sermon, I would go on preaching until He did. Christian people ought not be standing with their mouths open, gazing up into heaven and wondering what is going to happen; but they should abide with loins girt and lamps burning, ready for His appearing, whenever it may be. Go straight ahead upon the business your Lord has appointed you, and you need be under no apprehension of being taken by surprise. On one occasion I called to see one of our friends, and I found her whitening the front steps. When she saw me she jumped up and blushingly said, "Oh dear, sir, I am sorry you caught me like this; I wish I had known you were coming." "My dear sister," I said, "I hope that is how the Lord will find me at His coming—doing my duty." I should like to be found whitening the steps when the Lord comes, if that were my duty. Steady perseverance in appointed service is far better than prophetical speculation, especially if such speculation leads us to self-conceit and idleness. We may rest assured that the future is safe, for Jesus will deal wisely and come at the right time; therefore we may leave all matters in His hands. If the times are dark, it is right they should be; if the times are bright, it is right they should be; I at least cannot change the times, and therefore my duty is to do the work God has given me to do, whether the times be dark or bright. For all practical purposes it is enough for us that infinite wisdom is at the helm of affairs; "My servant shall deal prudently."

Another translation of the passage is "my servant shall have prosperous success." Let us append that meaning to the other. *Prosperity will grow out of our Lord's prudent dealings.* The pleasure of the Lord prospers in the hands of Jesus. The gospel will prosper in the thing whereto God has sent it. The decrees of God will be accomplished; His eternal purposes will be fulfilled. We may desire this or that, and our wish may or may not be granted, but whatsoever the Lord has appointed in His infinite wisdom to be done will come to pass to the last jot and tittle. The blood of Jesus Christ will not miss of its foreseen result in reference to any individual under heaven, and no end that was designed in the eternal plan of redemption shall be left unaccomplished. All along the line the Captain of our salvation will be victorious, and in every point and detail of the entire business the will of the Lord shall be done, and all heaven and earth shall be filled with praise as they see that it is so.

In consequence of this the text tells us the Lord shall be exalted and extolled. How well he deserves to be exalted and extolled for His matchless prudence! Too highly He cannot be esteemed. At the present time you will say the name of Christ is not honored; but wait awhile, and He shall be very high. His name is even now more honored than in former days, when it was the jest of the nations. The prudent plans which the Lord has adopted are surely working out the growth of His kingdom, and will certainly result in bringing to the front His name, and person and teaching. Perhaps you think that certain doctrines are hindrances to the success of the gospel: you know not what you say. In the end it shall be seen that every part of His teachings, and procedure, and every act of His life, and all His government in providence were so wisely ordered, that as a whole they secured in the best and speediest manner the exalting and extolling of His holy name. The star of Jesus rises higher every hour; the twilight of Calvary brightens towards millennial day. He was despised and rejected of men, but now tens of thousands adore Him; and, according to the omnipotent promise of the Father, to Him every knee shall bow and every tongue confess that He is Lord. The Spirit of God is at work glorifying Jesus, and providence is bending all its forces to the same end. In heaven Jesus is exalted and extolled; in His church He is very high; and even in the world itself His name is a word of power already, and destined to be supreme in ages to come. Thus much, then, upon the character of Messiah's dealings.

II. Now let us view THE STUMBLINGBLOCK IN THE WAY OF OUR LORD. It is His cross, which to Jew and Greek is ever a hindrance. As if the prophet saw Him in a vision, he cries out, "As many were astonished at thee; his visage was so marred more than any man, and His form more than the sons of men." When He was here, His personal position and condition and appearance were very much against the spread of His kingdom. He was the son of a carpenter, He wore the smock-frock of a peasant, He associated with publicans and sinners. Is He the Son of David? We looked for a great prince; we hoped for another Solomon. Is this He? Therefore the Jews rejected the meek and lowly prince of the house of David, and, alas, they persist in their rejection of His claims.

Today He has risen from the grave and gone into His glory, but the offense of the cross has not ceased, for upon His gospel there remains the image of His marred visage, and therefore men despise it. The preaching of the cross is foolishness to many. The main doctrine of the gospel concerns Jesus crucified—Jesus, the Son of God, put to an ignominious death, because for our sakes He was numbered with the transgressors, and bore the sin of many. Men will tell you they could believe Christianity if it were not for the atonement; that is to say, if Jesus will come down from the cross, modern scoffers will believe in Him, just as the ancient ones tauntingly promised to do; but of the gospel we may say that atoning blood is the pledge thereof, and if you leave out the substitutionary work of Christ from it, there is no gospel left. It is a body without a soul. This, then, seems to be the impediment to the spread of the Redeemer's kingdom:—He Himself with His marred visage, and His gospel with a visage equally uncomely in the eyes of carnal men.

The practical part of the gospel is equally a stumbling-block to ungodly men, for when men inquire what they must do to be saved, they are told that they must receive the gospel as little children, that they must repent of sin, and believe in the

Lord Jesus Christ. Very humbling precepts for human self-sufficiency! And after they are saved, if they inquire what they should do, the precepts are not those which commend themselves to proud, hectoring human nature—for they are such as these—"Be kindly affectioned one to another," "forgiving one another and forbearing one another even as God for Christ's sake has forgiven you." To the world, which loves conquerors, and blasts of trumpets, and chaplets of laurel, this kind of teaching has a marred visage, and an uncomely form.

Then, what seems even more humbling, the Lord Jesus Christ in His prudent dealing not only brings before us a gospel offensive, because of the doctrine of atonement, and offensive in its practical precepts, but He sends this gospel among us by men who are neither great nor noble, nor even among the wise of this world. The proud say, "We would submit ourselves to men of master-minds, but we cannot endure these foolish ones. Send us philosophers and orators combined, let men overcome us by cogent arguments, let them master us by words whose splendor shall dazzle our intellects." Instead of which the Lord sends a man who talks humbly, plainly, and perhaps even coarsely. Very simple is what he says: "Believe and live; Christ in your stead suffered for you, trust Him": He says this and little more. Is not this the fool's gospel? Is it not worthy to be called the foolishness of preaching? Men do not like this, it is an offense to their dignity. They would hear Caesar if he would officiate in his purple, but they cannot endure Peter preaching in his fisherman's coat. They will hear a pope in his sumptuous array, or a cardinal in his red hat, and they would not object to listen to a well-trained dialectician of the schools, or an orator from the forum; but they are indignant at the man who disdains the excellency of speech, and styles the wisdom of this world folly. How can the gospel spread by such means? How, indeed, unless the Lord be with it, using human weakness to display the power of His grace?

Worse still, if worse can be, the people who become converted and follow the Savior are generally of the poorer sort, and lightly esteemed. "Have any of the rulers believed?" is still the question. With what scorn do your literary men speak of professed Christians! Have you ever seen the sneer upon the face of your "advanced thought" gentleman, and of the far-gone school of infidels, when they speak of the old women and the semi-idiots who listen to the pious platitudes of evangelical doctrines? They know how to despise us if they know nothing else! But is such scorn worthy of men? It is only another version of the old sneer of the Pharisees when they said, "Hearest thou what these say?" and pointed to the boys and the rabble, who shouted, "Hosanna, blessed is he that cometh in the name of the Lord." Contempt has always followed at the heels of Jesus, and it always will till the day of His glory. If the great ones of the earth despise the Lord Jesus, on their own heads be their blood; to Him it is a glory rather than a shame that "the poor have the gospel preached to them." He is the people's Christ of whom it was written of old—"I have exalted one chosen out of the people." He rejoices to be called a leader and commander of the people, and He is glad that "the common people hear him gladly." But here stands the head and front of the difficulty—the cross, which is the soul of Christianity, is also its stumblingblock.

If any here are offended with Christ because of His cross, I beg them to dismiss the prejudice. Should it lead any man to doubt the Savior or withhold his heart from Him because He comes with a visage marred with sorrow? If He came to teach us to be unhappy and to prescribe to us rules for increasing misery, we might be excused if we shunned His teaching; but if He comes bearing the grief Himself that we may not bear it, and if those lines of agony were wrought in His countenance because He carried our griefs and our sorrows, they ought to be to us the most attractive of all beauties. I reckon that the scar across the warrior's face, which he gained in defending his country, is no disfigurement to him; it is a beauty spot. If my brother had in saving my life lost an arm or received a hideous wound, he would be all the more beautiful in my esteem; certainly I could not shun him on that account. The wounds of Jesus are precious jewels which should charm our eyes, eloquent mouths which should win our hearts. Be attracted by Him, all of you! Hide not your faces from Him! Look on Him and live and love. That crown of thorns has far more true glory about it than any crown of gold; those hands pierced and nailed it should be your delight to kiss; before that once sorrowing Person you should bow with joyful alacrity. Jesus, Thou marred One, thy cross, instead of being a stumbling-block to us is the glory of our faith.

That the gospel is spoken very plainly and that God blesses very simple people ought not to offend anybody. Ought it not rather to make us hopeful for the conversion of men because God may so largely bless commonplace instruments. Ought the conversion of the poor and the illiterate to be any offense to us? It shows a want of humanity; it looks as if pride had dried up the milk of human kindness in us, if we can grudge to those who have so little of this present world the priceless boons of another.

III. THE CERTAINTY OF THE REMOVAL OF THIS STUMBLINGBLOCK and the spread of Christ's kingdom. As His face was marred, so surely "shall he sprinkle many nations"; by which we understand, first, that the doctrines of the gospel are to fall in a copious shower over all lands. Jesus shall by His speech which drops as the dew and distills as the rain, sprinkle not the Jews only, but the Gentile nations everywhere. Thy brethren abhorred Thee, O Immanuel! They despised Thee, O Man of Nazareth! But all lands shall hear of Thee, and feel Thee coming down like showers upon the mown grass. The dusky tribes afar off, and the dwellers in the land of the setting sun shall hear thy doctrine, and shall drink it in as the fleece of wool sucks up dew. Thou shalt sprinkle many nations with thy gracious Word.

This sprinkling we must interpret according to the Mosaic ceremonies, and you know there was a sprinkling with blood, to set forth pardon of sin, and a sprinkling with water to set forth purification from the power of sin. Jesus Christ with

> The water and the blood
> From his riven side which flowed,

has sprinkled not only many men but many nations, and the day will come when all nations shall feel the blessed drops which are scattered from His hands, and know them to be "of sin the double cure," cleansing transgressors both from its guilt and power.

Dr. Kitto explains the passage by an Oriental custom. He says that kings when they invited their subjects to great festivals would employ persons to sprinkle with perfume all who arrived, as they passed the palace gate. I scarcely think that that is the meaning of the text, but at any rate it supplies an illustration of it. Jesus invites men of all nations to come to the gospel feast, and as they enter He casts upon them the sweet perfumes of His love and grace, so that they are fragrant before the Lord. There were no perfumes for Thee, O Jesus, upon Calvary! Vinegar and gall were all they could afford Thee; but now, since Thou has gone to heaven Thou dost provide perfumes for multitudes of the sons of men, and nations north and south and east and west are refreshed with the delicious showers of fragrance which through the gospel fall upon them.

The text, then, claims for Jesus Christ that the influence of His grace and the power of His work shall be extended over many nations, and shall have power not over the common people only, but over their leaders and rulers. "The kings shall shut their mouths at him"; they shall have no word to say against Him; they shall be so subdued by the majesty of His power that they shall silently pay Him reverence, and prostrate themselves before His throne. Kings, mark you. I am always glad to hear of noblemen being converted, though I am by no means inclined to flatter the great, or to think more of one man's soul than of another's. I am glad, however, to hear of the salvation of peers and princes, for it indicates the wide spread of the gospel when all classes are affected by it, and when those who usually stand aloof yield themselves to its power. "Kings shall shut their mouths at him." This promise has not been fulfilled yet. There are those who think that the Biblical prophecies are pretty nearly accomplished, and that we are passing into a new dispensation. Well, I dare not dogmatize, but I dare question most of the talk I hear nowadays about the future. Scores of prophecies are not yet fulfilled. Kings have not shut their mouths at Him yet: they have mostly opened their mouths wide against Him, and reviled and blasphemed Him and persecuted His saints. There must be brighter days to come for this poor world yet, when even princes shall humbly obey our Lord. The more I study the Bible, the more sure I am of two things which I cannot reconcile; first, that Christ will come at such an hour as men look not for Him, and may come now; and secondly, that the gospel is to be preached in all nations, and that "all the ends of the earth shall remember and turn unto the Lord." I do not know which of the two things I am surest of; neither do I know how to reconcile them; but they are both in the Word, and in due time they will be reconciled by history itself. Assuredly the day will come when the mightiest prince shall count it his highest honor to have his name enrolled as a member of the church of Christ. "Yea, all kings shall fall down before him; all nations shall serve him." The little handful of corn in the earth upon the top of the mountains is yet to increase till the fruit thereof shall shake like Lebanon. "They shall not teach every man his neighbor, and every man his brother, saying, Know the Lord; for all shall know him from the least to the greatest."

We look for this, and come it will. O thorn-crowned King of Calvary, kings shall be thy courtiers yet!

IV. Let us consider THE MANNER OF ITS ACCOMPLISHMENT. How will it come to pass? Will there be a new machinery? Will the world be converted, and the kings be made to shut their mouths by some new mode of operation? I do not think so. Will the saints take the sword one day? Will it be accomplished by that wonderful implement of civilization, a gun-boat? Shall we convert the Hottentots by gunpowder? We have had a little trial of these carnal weapons, and some admire the success, but they may live to lament it. The Prince of Peace bids us put the sword into the scabbard; His weapons, like His kingdom, are not carnal. No, the way which has been from the beginning of the dispensation will last to its close. I believe that this battle is to be fought out on the line upon which it began. It pleases God by the foolishness of preaching to save them that believe. To conceive that our Lord will end the present mode of warfare, as though it were admitted that evil could not be conquered by the use of instrumentality, is to my mind to do Him great dishonor. To me it is plain that, as He has chosen to magnify His power by using feeble instruments, He will continue to do so till the victory is won. He has never yet relinquished His work so as to give the enemy an opportunity of claiming a victory. To change weapons is to lay one's self open to the charge of being unable to conquer with those first used; but it is not so with our Lord. The very same grain of mustard which is now so small is yet to become a tree with far-spreading branches, the leaven is yet to leaven the whole lump. The last harvest will be the result of sowing by men and not by some miraculous agency. The dividing of the people at last will be made from the contents of one and the same gospel dragnet, which we are bound to use till the heavens be no more.

According to this passage, these kings and nations are first of all to hear. "Faith coming by hearing." They are to hear something new. Well, brethren, if they are to hear, we must preach and teach, so that our clear line of duty is to go on spreading the gospel. Jesus Christ would have His servants preach and teach the gospel. Are you doing it? Go on doing it, brother, in the power of the Holy Ghost, whatever comes. Have you not done it? Begin to do so now, as one of Christ's servants, and pray for divine help. Do you say you cannot do it? You can. You are hiding your talent in a napkin; take it out, thou unfaithful servant, lest thy Lord come and judge thee! But you cannot teach many? Who said you could? Teach one. Oh, but you cannot preach? Who said preach? Teach; teach somehow. Cause the people to know the story of the cross. But you cannot teach kings you say. Why need you? Teach servants and children; only do spread the gospel. The world is to be won to Christ, if it be ever won at all, by hearing the glad tidings of a dying Savior's love, and how can they hear without a preacher, and how can they preach except they be sent? Christ sends you, for He says, "Let him that heareth say 'Come.'" In the power of that commission say at once,

Now will I tell to sinners round
What a dear Savior I have found,
Point them to his redeeming blood
And say, Behold the way to God.

These people appear not only to have heard, but have *seen*. "That which had not been told them shall they see." This seeing is not with their bodily eyes but by the perceptions of their minds. Faith comes by the soul perceiving what the gospel means. We cannot believe in that which we do not perceive. Therefore we must go on telling people the gospel till they see what the gospel is. Many men will never know the gospel till they have been told it a thousand times, and you must keep on telling it to them till you get to that thousandth time. "What do you mean by that?" say you. I mean this, that it must be line upon line and precept upon precept, almost to the exhaustion of patience, a mother's prayers, a teacher's anxieties, providences, sicknesses, twitches of conscience, ministries of all sorts, and many pleadings, and it is only at the last stroke that the Word will be achieved, though all the other efforts will have contributed towards it. Go on, dear brother, go on, and teach Jesus Christ till the people see Him. That sight will come upon a sudden. How many times have I heard the young convert say, "I knew all about this before, sir; I have heard it many times, but I could not see it; now I do see it." Oh, how it makes a man shut his mouth at Christ in humble silence, when he perceives at last that His marred visage and suffering form were tokens of divine love, and that by such sorrows sin is purged away. Would to God you all saw Him now.

After they had seen, it appears from the text that they *considered*. "That which they had not heard shall they consider." This is how men are saved: they hear the gospel, they catch the meaning of it, and then they consider it. Let us pray, dear friends, that God would set unconverted people considering. If we can but get them to think, we have great hopes of them. If any of you here have never yielded to Jesus Christ, I would ask you to hear or read about Him; spend this afternoon in carefully reading one of the gospels; turn to Matthew, or Mark, or Luke, or John, and read the story of His passion, and ask God to let you see what it all means; and when you do see it, turn it all over in your minds. Think of it. Think how wonderful it is that God should become man to suffer in your stead. See if it be reasonable to disbelieve it or right to refuse to love the Savior. There are a thousand reasons why you should rush into His arms and say, "Incarnate Deity, how can I resist Thee? Bleeding Omnipotence, how dare I doubt Thee? Immortal love, crucified for my sins, I yield myself to Thee! I would be thy servant forever."

It is clear that those people, when they had seen and considered silently, accepted the Lord as their Lord, for they shut their mouths at Him; they ceased from all opposition; they quietly resigned their wills, and paid allegiance to the great King of kings. Brothers and sisters, we want to see this done for Christ now by hundreds here. There is a great religious stir just now, and we desire that this church, and all the churches abroad, should use the favorable breeze. You know how in harvest time the farmer gets all the men he can to work, and they toil on through long hours. I have seen them working briskly beneath the bright moonlight to get in the wheat. This is our harvest time, and we must get our sheaves in. The Lord has much corn, and it needs to be garnered; I pray you make long hours and work hard for Jesus, and let the subject expounded this morning inspirit you therein. The success of the gospel is in no jeopardy whatever. Jesus must reign till He hath put all enemies under His feet. If the devil can persuade you that Christ is going to give up the war, or is going to fight it out on another line, and dispense with your efforts, you will soon grow idle. You will find an excuse for laziness in some supposed conversion of the world by miracle, or some other wonderful affair. You will say the Lord is coming, and the war will all be over at once, and there is no need of your fighting it out now. Do not believe it. Our Commander is able to fight it through on this line; in the name of Jesus of Nazareth, by the power of the Eternal Spirit, we are bound to keep right on till this world yields before God. You remember the American general, who, when the nation was eager for speedy victory, said he did not know when that would come, but that he would keep on pegging away. That is what we are bound to do; to keep on "pegging away." No gunner may leave his gun, no subaltern may disperse his band, no officer may suggest a retreat. Brethren, Popery must fall, Mohammedanism must come down, and all the idol gods must be broken, and cast to the moles and to the bats. It looks a task too, gigantic, but the bare arm of God—only think of that—His sleeve rolled up, omnipotence itself made bare—what cannot it accomplish? Stand back, devils! When God's bare arm comes into the fight, you will all run like dogs, for you know your Master. Stand back, heresies and schisms, evils and delusions; you will all disappear, for the Christ of God is mightier than you. Oh believe it. Do not be downhearted and dispirited, do not run to new schemes and fancies and interpretations of prophecy. Go and preach Jesus Christ unto all the nations. Go and spread abroad the Savior's blessed name, for He is the world's only hope. The cross is the banner of our victory. God help us to look to it ourselves, and then to hold it up before the eyes of others, till our Lord shall come upon His throne. Amen.

A SIMPLE REMEDY

SERMON NO. 1,068
DELIVERED ON LORD'S DAY MORNING, SEPTEMBER 1, 1872.
PORTIONS OF SCRIPTURE READ BEFORE SERMON—MARK 15:1–39; ISAIAH 53.

With his stripes we are healed—Isaiah 53:5.

EVER since the fall, healing has been the chief necessity of manhood. There was no physician in paradise, but outside that blissful enclosure professors of the healing art have been precious as the gold of Ophir. Even in Eden itself there grew the herbs which should in after days yield medicine for the body of man. Before sin came into the world, and disease, which is the consequence of it, God had created plants of potent efficacy to soothe pain, and wrestle with disease. Blessed be His name, while thus mindful of the body, He had not forgotten the direr sickness of the soul; but He has raised up for us a plant of renown, yielding a balm far more effectual than that of Gilead. This He had done before the plague of sin had yet infected us. Christ Jesus, the true medicine of the sons of men, was ordained of old to heal the sickness of His people.

Everywhere, at this present hour, we meet with some form or other of sickness; no place, however healthful, is free from cases of disease, it is all around us, and we are thankful to add that the remedy is everywhere within reach. The beloved physician has prepared a healing medicine which can be reached by all classes, which is available in every climate, at every hour, under every circumstance, and effectual in every case where it is received. Of that medicine we shall speak this morning, praying that we have God's help in so doing.

It is a great mercy for us who have to preach, as well as for you who have to hear, that the gospel healing is so very simple; our text describes it—"With his stripes we are healed." These six words contain the marrow of the gospel, and yet scarcely one of them contains a second syllable. They are words for plain people, and in them there is no affectation of mystery or straining after the profound. I looked the other day into old Culpepper's Herbal. It contains a marvelous collection of wonderful remedies. Had this old herbalist's prescriptions been universally followed, there would not long have been any left to prescribe for; the astrological herbalist would soon have extirpated both sickness and mankind. Many of his receipts contain from twelve to twenty different drugs, each one needing to be prepared in a peculiar manner; I think

I once counted forty different ingredients in one single draught. Very different are these receipts, with their elaboration of preparation, from the Biblical prescriptions which effectually healed the sick—such as these: "Take a lump of figs, and lay it for a plaster upon the boil," or that other one: "Go and wash in Jordan seven times"; or that other: "Take up thy bed and walk." One cannot but admire the simplicity of truth, while falsehood conceals her deformities with a thousand trickeries. If you would see Culpepper's Herbal carried out in spiritual things, go and buy a Directory for the carrying on of the Ritualistic services of the Church of England, or the Church of Rome. You shall find there innumerable rules as to when you shall bow, and to what quarter of the heavens you shall look: when you shall stand up, and when you shall kneel: when you shall dress in black, in white, in blue, or in violet: how you shall pray, and what you shall pray, a collect being appointed for today, and another for tomorrow. On the other hand, if you would know the true way of having your souls healed, go to the Word of God, and study such a text as this: "With his stripes we are healed." In the one case all is mysterious, in the other all is simple and clear. Quackery cannot live without mystery, show, ceremony, and pretense. But the truth is as plain as a pikestaff, legible as though it were written on the broad heavens, and so simple that a babe may comprehend it. "With his stripes we are healed." I saw in Paris, years ago, a public vendor of quack medicines, and an extraordinary personage he was. He came riding in to the market-place with a fine chariot drawn by horses, richly comparisoned, while a trumpet was sounded before him. This mighty healer of all diseases made his appearance clothed in a coat of as many colors as that of Joseph, and on his head was a helmet adorned with variegated plumes. He delivered himself of a jargon which might be French, which might also be Latin, or might be nonsense, for no one in the crowd could understand it. With a little persuasion the natives bought his medicines, persuaded that so great and wise a man could surely cure them. Truly, this is one reason why there is an adoption in the Romish Church of the Latin tongue, and why in many other churches there is an affectation of a theological jargon which nobody can comprehend, and which would not be of any use to them if they did comprehend it; the whole is designed to delude the multitude. To what purpose are fine speeches in the gospel ministry? Sicknesses are not healed by eloquence. It was an ill day in which rhetoric crept into the church of God, and man attempted to make the gospel a subject for oratory. The gospel wants no human eloquence to recommend it. It stands most securely when without a buttress. Like beauty, it is most adorned when unadorned the most. The native charms of the gospel suffice to commend it to those who have spiritual eyes, and those who are blind will not admire it, deck it as we may. I shall, therefore, content myself this morning with declaring the gospel to you in the plainest possible language, without any attempts at excellency of speech. I know it to be the gospel of God; I know it will save you if you receive it; it has saved me; it has saved thousands more. I shall put it before you in plain, unvarnished language. I beseech you to receive it; and I pray that God's Holy Spirit may lead you so to do.

Coming at once to our text, we observe, first, *that these are sad words*: "With his stripes we are healed"; we remark, secondly, that *these are glad words*; and, then, we shall notice, thirdly, that *these are very suggestive words*.

I. THESE ARE SAD WORDS. They are part of a mournful piece of music, which might be called "the Requiem of the Messiah." Hear ye its solemn notes: "Surely he hath borne our griefs, and carried our sorrows: yet we did esteem him stricken, smitten of God, and afflicted. But he was wounded for our transgressions, he was bruised for our iniquities: the chastisement of our peace was upon him; and with his stripes we are healed." Do you not feel that the song so softly plaintive has touched your heart to pity, and moistened your eye with tears. "With his stripes we are healed." This is not the brine of woe, but yet it is salt with sorrow. The sun is not eclipsed, but it shines through a cloud. No one reads the inner sense of these words without feeling grief of soul. This is caused by the fact, that the words imply the existence of disease, and speak of great suffering connected with the remedy.

I say these are sad words, because *they imply disease*. "With his stripes we are healed." This "we," comprehends within itself all the saints, and hence it is clear that all the saints needed healing. Those who are today before the throne of God, without spot, or wrinkle, or any such thing, were once defiled as the lepers who were shut out of the camp of Israel. Enoch, Noah, Abraham, Jacob, David, Elijah, Hezekiah, Daniel—all these were once sick of the accursed malady of sin. All the excellent of the earth among us now, who have been saved by sovereign grace, were once heirs of wrath even as others; as surely shaped in iniquity and conceived in sin as the rest of mankind. There is a confession here, by implication, of all who are washed in the blood of Jesus, that they needed washing; of all who are healed by His stripes, that they were sore sick with sin. This confession is true, every child of God will join in it, and he that knows himself best will make it with greatest emphasis. We were so diseased, that nothing could have restored us but the precious blood of our dear Lord and Savior Jesus Christ. It is a dread fact that sin has infected the entire family of man. We are all sinful, sinful through and through, corrupt with evil passions and depraved desires. Our fathers were fallen men, and so are we, and so will our children be. The putting of bitter for sweet, and of sweet for bitter, of darkness for light, and light for darkness, is engendered in us all. "Every one of them is gone back; they are altogether become filthy, there is none that doeth good, no not one."

Oh, mournful, miserable fact—in a fair world, "where every prospect pleases," beneath a glorious sky where stars peer down upon us like the eyes of God, man lives a rebel to his God, a traitor to the truth, an enemy of good, a slave of evil. He who was made to rule the world rules not himself. Fashioned for wisdom, he drivels like a fool ordained for immortality, he labors for the wage of sin, which is death. Sin has dimmed his eye, hardened his heart, uncrowned his head, weakened his strength, filled him with putrefying sores, and left him naked to his shame.

The disease of sin is of the most loathsome character. Supposing it possible for every man to have had the leprosy, and yet for no man to have had sin, that would have been no calamity at all compared with that of our becoming sinful. If it could so have happened that we could have been deprived of our most useful faculties, and yet had remained innocent, that would have been a small catastrophe compared with this depraving of our nature by sin. To inoculate the parent stock with evil was the great design of Satan, for he knew that this would work the worst conceivable ill to God's creatures. Hell itself is not more horrible than sin. No vision ghastly and grim can ever be so terrible to the spiritual eye as the hideous, loathsome thing called sin. Remember that this dread evil is in us all. We are at this day, every one of us, by nature only fit to be burned up with the abominations of the universe. If we think we are better than that we do not know ourselves. It is a part of the infatuation of evil that its victims pride themselves upon their excellence. Our infernal pride makes us cover our leprous foreheads with the silver veil of self-deception. Like a foul bog covered over with greenest moss, our nature hides its rottenness beneath a film of suppositious righteousness.

And, brethren, while sin is loathsome before God at the present time, it will lead to the most deadly result in due season. There is not a man, or woman among us that can escape the damnation of hell apart from the healing virtue of the Savior's atoning sacrifice. No, not one. Yon lovely little girl is defiled in heart, albeit that as yet nothing worse than childish folly is discoverable; leave but that little mind to its own devices, and the fair child will become an arch-transgressor. Yonder most amiable youth, although no blasphemous word has ever blackened his lip, and no lustful thought has yet inflamed his eye, must yet be born again, or he may wander into foulest ways; and yonder most moral tradesman, though he has as yet done justice to his fellowmen, will perish if he be not saved by the grace of God through Christ Jesus. Sin dwelleth in us, and will be deadly in the case of every one among us, without a solitary exception, unless we accept the remedy which God has provided.

Ah, dear friends, this disease is none the better because we do not feel it. It is all the worse. It is one of the worst symptoms in some diseases, when men become incapable of feeling. It is dreadful when the delirious sick man cries out, "I am well enough; I will leave this bed; I will go to my business." Hear how he raves; must we not put him under restraint? The louder his boasts of health the more sad the delirious patient's condition. When ignorance is known and felt it is not dense, but he who knows nothing, and yet fancies that he knows everything, is ignorant indeed.

Sin is also a very painful disease when it is known and felt. When the Spirit of God leads a man to see the sin which is really in himself, then how he changes his note. Oh, children of God, have you forgotten how acutely sin made you smart? Those black days of conviction!—my soul hath them still in remembrance, remembering the wormwood and the gall. The period of my conviction of sin is burnt into my memory as with a red-hot iron: its wounds are cured, but the scars remain. As Habakkuk has well put it, "When I heard, my belly trembled, my lips quivered at the voice, rottenness entered into my bones, and I trembled in myself." Oh, 'tis a burden, this load of sin, a burden which might crush an angel down to hell.

There I stood, and seemed like another staggering Atlas, bearing up a world of sin upon these shoulders, and fearing every moment lest I should be crushed into the abyss and justly lost forever. Only let a man once feel sin for half-an-hour, really feel its tortures, and I warrant you he would prefer to dwell in a pit of snakes than to live with his sins. Remember that cry of David, "My sin is ever before me"; he speaks as though it haunted him. He shut his eyes but he still saw its hideous shape; he sought his bed, but like a nightmare it weighed upon his breast; he rose, and it rose with him; he tried to shake it off among the haunts of men, in business and in pleasure, but like a blood-sucking vampire it clung to him. Sin was ever before him, as though it were painted on his eyeballs, the glass of his soul's window was stained with it. He sought his closet but could not shut it out, he sat alone but it sat with him; he slept, but it cursed his dreams. His memory it burdened, his imagination it lit up with lurid flame, his judgment it armed with a ten-thonged whip, his expectations it shrouded in midnight gloom. A man needs no worse hell than his own sin, and an awakened conscience. Let this be instead of racks and whips of burning wire. Conscience once aroused will find in sin the worm undying, the unquenchable fire, and the bottomless pit. Though God Himself will punish sin, yet it is a wolf which tears its own flesh, a viper which turns its envenomed fang upon itself. Peradventure many of you may reply, "But we do not feel this!" True, because you have contrived for the present to give sedatives to conscience. I pity you because you are not aware of the truth. I see how it is with you. You think your money making, or spending your days pleasantly, or your performance of your daily labor, is all you need consider; but if you were not deceived by sin you would know better; you would understand that you are God's creatures and that God did not make you to live for yourselves. Which among you builds a house and does not intend either to live in it or gain something by the letting of it? And do you think God made you without designing to glorify Himself in you? Oh, men and women, did your Creator make you that you might live only for yourselves, and make your bellies your gods? Do you dream that you may miss the end of your being, and not have it required at your hands? Will He suffer you to rob Him of your service, and wink at your rebellion, and treat it as if it were nothing? It shall not be so, as ye will find to your cost. Oh, may you be taught now the evil of sin. Spirit of God, it is thine office to convince the world of sin, of righteousness, and of judgment; do thine office now, for none will apply for healing till they feel the smart, none will look to the stripes of Jesus till they feel the wounds of sin. When sin is bitter, Christ is sweet; but only then. When death threatens, then do men fly to Christ for life. No man ever loves Christ till he loathes himself; no man ever cares for Jesus till he comes to see that out of Jesus he is a lost, ruined, and undone soul. Oh, may God grant you that the sorrowful part of these words may ring in your ears till you mourn your grievous sin.

But there is a second sorrow in the verse, and that is sorrow for the *suffering by which we are healed.* "With his stripes we are healed." I find that the word here used is in the singular, and not as the translation would lead you to suppose. I hardly know how to translate the word fully. It is read by some as "weal," "bruise," or "wound," meaning the mark or print of blows on the skin; but Alexander says the word denotes the tumor raised in flesh by scourging. It is elsewhere translated "blueness," "hurt," and "spots," and evidently refers to the black and blue marks of the scourge. The use of a singular noun may have been intended to set forth that our Lord was as it were reduced to a mass of bruising, and was made one great bruise. By the suffering which that condition indicated we are saved.

Our text alludes partly to the sufferings of His body, but much more to the agonies of His soul. The body of our Lord and Savior was bruised. Scourging under the Jewish law was always moderate; there was a pause made at a point which mercy had appointed. Thirty-nine stripes were all that could be given. But our Lord was not beaten according to the Jewish law; He was scourged by Pilate, and the scourging of the Romans was peculiarly brutal. They stopped not at the forty stripes save one, they smote at random, according to their own will. The Savior endured a scourging which was intended to be a substitute for death—"I will scourge him and release him," said Pilate—but instead of its being a substitute for death it became a prelude to it. Probably most men would prefer to die rather than to be scourged after the Roman fashion, and might be wise in making such a choice. Sinews of oxen were intertwisted with knuckle bones of sheep, and these were armed with small slivers of bone, so that every stroke gashed the flesh deeply, and caused fearful wounds and tearings; as saith the prophet, "the plowers made deep furrows." Our Savior's back was plowed and furrowed deeply in the day of His scourging. Now you may look at the Person of Jesus, your Substitute and Sacrifice, covered with livid bruises by human cruelty, and say, "With his stripes we are healed."

But you must not stop there and think that flesh wounds were all His stripes, for our Lord bore more terrible stripes in His soul. He was smitten in His heart every day of His life. He had to suffer the ills of providence. Being a man he had sympathy with us in all those stripes which are the inheritance of Adam's sons; He felt the stripes of poverty, stripes of weariness, stripes of sickness, stripes of heaviness, stripes of bereavement; above all others, he was a "man of sorrows and acquainted with grief." Moreover, He had to run the gauntlet of all mankind. Stripes fell upon our Savior from all sorts of men, for every man's sin laid a stroke upon His shoulder. When He was here on earth, if He saw men sin, that smote Him; if He heard them speak a wrong word, that smote Him; having sinned, we have been hardened by sin; but He was pure and perfect, and it was a bruise to Him to come into contact with sin. You know how His adversaries called Him a drunken man and a winebibber; how they said He had a devil, and was mad. Thus they were all striking Him; each man laying on his blow with all his might. Worse than all, He was wounded in the house of His friends. Was any blow equal to that which Judas lay upon those shoulders? And next to that, could anything surpass in pain the blows which Peter gave when he said, "I know not the man!" There was a cruel process in the English navy, in which men were made to run the gauntlet all along the ship, with sailors on each side, each man being bound to give a stroke to the poor victim as he ran along. Our Savior's life was a running of the gauntlet between His enemies and His friends, who all struck Him, one here and another there. By those sorrowful and shameful stripes we this day are healed.

Satan, too, struck Him. I think I see the Arch-fiend ascend from the pit with haste, and, lifting himself upon his dragon wings, come forward to strike the Savior, daring to inflict upon His soul the accursed temptations of hell. He smote Him in the desert, and in the garden, till beneath that smiting great drops of blood crimsoned His face. But this was nothing, compared with the fact that He was smitten of God. Oh, what a word is that! If God were to lay His finger on any one of us this morning, only His finger, we should be struck with sickness, paralysis, aye, and death. Then think of God smiting! God must smite sin wherever He sees it; it is just that He should do so; it is as much an essential part of God's nature that He should crush sin, as that He should love, for, indeed, it is only love in another form that makes Him hate that which is evil. So when He saw our sin laid upon His Son, He smote Him with the blows of a cruel One, till beneath that smiting His Son cried out, "My God, my God, why hast thou forsaken me?" He was bearing in that moment all the crushing blows of that great sword of vengeance, of which we read in the prophets—"Awake, O sword, against my shepherd, and against the man that is my fellow, saith the Lord."

Put these things all together as best you can, for I lack words with which fitly to describe these bruises from the ills of life; bruises from friends and foes, stripes from Satan, and smiting from God, and surely it is the most sorrowful story that ever was told.

> O king of grief! (a title strange, yet true;
> To thee, of all kings, only due).
> O king of wounds! how shall I grieve for thee
> Who in all grief outrunnest me?
> Shall I weep blood? why, thou has wept such store,
> That all thy body was one sore.
> Shall I be scourged, flouted, boxèd, sold?
> 'Tis but to tell the tale is told;
> My God, my God, who dost thou part from me,
> Was such a grief as cannot be.

One needs to be a Niobe, a dripping well of tears, to mourn the chief among ten thousand made the chief of sufferers. That the ever blessed One should suffer! That the Lord of life should bleed! The angels worship Him, and yet Jehovah smote Him! He is so fair, that nothing else is beautiful to any eye that has once gazed upon Him, and yet they spit in His face and mar His lovely countenance with cruel blows of fatal fists! He is all tenderness, but they are all cruelty! He is harmless as a lamb, He never thought nor spoke a thing of wrong to mortal man, but yet they strike Him as though He were a fierce beast of prey, fit only to be bruised to death. He is all love, and, when they smite Him worst, He doth but pray for them, yet smite they still! No curses drop from those dear lips, but words of pity only, and of sweet intercession, follow each blow, yet still they wound and buffet, and blaspheme! Oh, grief, far deeper than the sea! Oh, woe immeasurable! They smite Him for whom they ought to have gladly died, Him for whom the noble army of martyrs counted it all joy to render up their lives. They despitefully entreat Him who came on errands of pure mercy and disinterested grace. Oh, cruel whips and cruel hands, and yet more cruel hearts, of wicked men! Surely we should never read such words as these without feeling that they call for sorrow—sorrow, which if mingled with spiritual repentance, will be a fit anointing for His burial, or, at least, a bath in which to wash away the bloodstains from His dear and most pure flesh.

II. Next—and may the Spirit of God help us with fresh power—THESE ARE GLAD WORDS. "With his stripes we are healed." They are glad words, first, because *they speak of healing*. "We are healed." Understand these words, Oh, beloved, of that virtual healing which was given you in the day when Jesus Christ died upon the Cross. In the moment when Christ yielded up the ghost, all His elect might have said, and said with truth, "We are healed"; for, from that moment their sins were put away; a full atonement was made for all the chosen. Christ had laid down His life for His sheep; He had redeemed His saints from among men; the ransom price was fully paid; for sin a complete expiation was made; the redeemed were clear. Let us this morning walk up and down with perfect peace and confidence, for from the day that Jesus died we were perfectly clear before the judgment seat of God. "With his stripes we are healed," or rather "we were healed," for the words are in the past in the original Hebrew. "With his stripes we were healed." My sins, they ceased to be, centuries ago; my debts, my Savior paid them before I was born, and nailed up the receipted bill to His Cross, and I can see it there. The handwriting of ordinances that was contrary to us, He took it away and nailed it to His Cross. I can see it. And while I read the long list of my sins—oh, how long, what a roll it wanted to contain them—yet I see at the bottom, "The blood of Jesus Christ His Son cleanseth us from all sin." It matters not how long that roll was; the debt is all discharged. I am acquitted before God, and so is every believer in Jesus. Every soul that rests in Jesus was at the time when Jesus died, there and then absolved before the sacred judgment seat. "Who shall lay anything to the charge of God's elect?" is a fit challenge to ring forth from the Cross where atonement was finished.

But, dear friends, there is an actual application of the great expiation to us when by faith we receive it individually, and it is that also which is intended here. To as many as have believed in Jesus, His stripes have given the healing of forgiveness of sin, and, moreover, it has conquered the deadly power of sin. Sin no longer hath dominion over them, for they are not under the law but under grace. Nothing ever delivers a man from the power of sin like a sight of the suffering Savior. I have heard of a man who had lived a dissolute life, who could never be reclaimed from it by any means, but at last, when he saw his mother sicken and die from grief at his ways, the thought that she had died because of his sins touched his heart, and made him repent of his ungodliness. If there was such efficacy to cause repentance in that form of suffering, much more is there when we come to see Jesus die in our stead. Then our heart melts with love to Him; then hatred of sin takes possession of the soul; and the reigning power of evil is therefore destroyed. Christ's stripes have healed us of all love of sin. Faith in the Crucified One has healed our eyes; once they were blind, for "when we saw him, there was no beauty that we should desire him." Now, since we have seen His stripes, we see all beauties unite in His adorable Person. I know, beloved, if you have put your trust in the sufferings of Jesus you think Him to be the most precious of beings, you see a loveliness in Him which all heaven's angels could not rival. The stripes of Immanuel have also healed our hearts. "We hid, as it were, our faces from him; he was despised, and we esteemed him not," but now our hearts delight in Him, and we turn our faces towards Him as the flowers look to the sun. We only wish that we could see Him face to face. And He has healed our feet, too, for they were prone to evil; note the verse that follows our text, "All we like sheep have gone astray; we have turned every one to his own way." A sight of His stripes has brought us back; and, charmed by the disinterested love which suffered in our stead, we follow the great bishop and shepherd of our souls, and desire never again to wander from His commands. From head to foot His stripes have bound up our wounds, and mollified them with ointment. He forgiveth all our iniquities, He healeth all our diseases. Beloved, if you would be cured of any sin, however spreading its infection, fly to Jesus' wounds. This is the only way to be rid of the palsy of fear, the fever of lust, the sore blains of remorse, or the leprosy of iniquity; His stripes are the only specific for transgression.

Men have tried to overcome their passions by the contemplation of death, but they have failed to bury sin in the grave; they have striven to subdue the rage of lust within their nature by meditating upon hell, but that has only rendered the heart hard and callous to love's appeals. He who once believingly beholds the mystery of Christ suffering for him, shakes of the viper of sin into the fire which consumed the great sacrifice. Where falls the blood of the atonement, sin's hand is palsied, its grasp is relaxed, its scepter falls, it vacates the throne of the heart; and the spirit of grace, and truth, and love, and righteousness occupies the royal seat.

I may be addressing some this morning who despair of being saved. Behold Christ smarting in your stead, and you will never despair again. If Jesus bore the transgressors' punishment there is every room for hope. Peradventure your disease is love of the world and a fear of man; You dare not become a Christian because men would laugh at you. If you could hear the scourges fall upon the Savior's back, you would henceforth say, "Did He suffer thus for me? I will never be shamed of Him again," and instead of shunning the fight you would seek out the thick of the fray. "With his stripes we are healed." It is a universal medicine. There is no disease by which your soul can be afflicted, but an application of the blue bruises of your Lord will take out the deadly virus from your soul. Are you ambitious? This will bring you down. Are you desponding? This will lift you up. Are you hot with passion? This will cool you.

Are you chill with indolence? This will stimulate you. The Cross! The Cross! The Cross of Christ! What power dwells in it! Full sure if even for Satan that Cross had been set up on earth, it would have lifted him from hell to heaven! But it is not for him; it is, however, for the vilest of the sons of men; and there are no sons of men so corrupt that the Cross of Christ cannot purge them of all evil. Bear ye this gospel into Africa, where superstitious sorcery holds men's minds in thralldom, it will uplift before all eyes the charter of Africa's liberty; Ethiopia shall stretch out her hands, liberated from her chains, when she shall see a Crucified Savior. Bear ye the Cross amongst the Brahmins or among the Soodras of Hindostan, preach the Cross amongst a race of men who boast their wisdom; and they shall become ignorant in their own esteem but truly wise before the Lord, when they shall see the light that streams from Immanuel's wounds. Even Oriental cunning and lasciviousness are thus healed.

Do not tell me that we ought mainly to preach Christ exalted. I will preach my Lord upon the throne and delight therein, but the great remedy for ruined manhood is not Christ in glory, but Christ in shame and death. We know some who select Christ's Second Advent as their one great theme, and we would not silence them; yet do they err. The second coming is a glorious hope for saints, but there is no cure in it for sinners; to them the coming of the Lord is darkness and not light; but Christ smitten for our sins, there is the star which breaks the sinner's midnight. I know if I preached Christ on the throne many proud hearts would have Him; but, Oh, sirs, ye must have Christ on the Cross before ye can know Him on the throne. Ye must bow before the Crucified, ye must trust a dying Savior, or else if ye pretend to honor Him by the glories which are to come, ye do but belie Him, and ye know Him not. To the Cross, to the Cross, to the Cross! Write that upon the signposts of the road to the city of refuge! Fly there, ye guilty ones, as to the only sanctuary for the sinful, for "with his stripes we are healed." There is joy in this.

There is another joy in the text—*joy in the honor which it brings to Christ.* The stripes, let us lament them; the healing, let us rejoice therein; and then, the physician, let us honor Him. "With his stripes we are healed." Jesus Christ works real cures. We are healed, effectually healed. We were healed when we first believed, we are healed still. Abiding cure we have, for still to His wounds we fly. An eternal cure have we, for never man was healed by Christ and then relapsed and died. "With his stripes we are healed," by nothing else; by no mixture of something else with those stripes; not by priestcraft, not by sacraments, not by our own prayers, not by our own good works. "With his stripes we are healed"—healed of all sin of every kind, of sins past, of sins present, and sins to come; we are healed, completely healed of all, and that in a moment; not through long years of waiting and of gradually growing better, but "With his stripes we are healed," completely healed, even now. Blessed be His name. Now, child of God, if thou wouldst give glory to God, declare that thou art healed this morning. Be not always saying, "I hope I am saved." The man who says he hopes he is cured does not greatly recommend the physician; but the man who knows he is, he is the man who brings him honor. Let us speak positively: we can do so. Let us speak out in the face of all mankind, and not be ashamed. Let us say, "As surely as we were diseased, so surely are we healed through the stripes of our Lord Jesus Christ." Let us give Jesus all glory, let us magnify Him to the utmost.

I see now in vision a company of men gathering herbs along the slopes of the Seven Hills of Rome; with mystic rites they cull those ancient plants, whose noxious influence once drugged our fathers into deadly slumbers. They are compounding again the cup of Rome's ancient sorcery, and saying: "Here is the universal medicine! The great catholic remedy." I see them pouring their Belladonna, Monkshood, and deadly Henbane, into the great pot forever simmering on the Papal hearth. Think you the nations are to be healed by this accursed amalgam? Will not the end be as in the days of the prophets, when one gathered wild gourds, and they cried out, "there is death in the pot?" Aye, indeed, so it will be, even though Oxford and Canterbury set their seal upon the patent medicine. Come, ye brave sons of protesting fathers! Come and overturn this witches' caldron, and spill it back into the hell for which alone it is fit. Pity that even old Tiber's tawny flood should be poisoned with it, or bear its deadly mixture to that sea across which once sailed the apostolic bark. The wine of Rome's abominations is now imported into this island, and distributed in a thousand towns and villages by your own national clergy, and all classes and conditions of men are being made drunk therewith. Ye lovers of your race, and of your God, stop the traffic, and proclaim around the Popish caldron, "There is no healing there." No healing plants ever grew upon the Seven Hills of Rome, or are the roots improved in virtue if transplanted to Canterbury, or the city on the Isis. There is one divine remedy, and only one. It is no mixture. Receive ye it and live—"With his stripes we are healed." No sprinkling can wash out sin, no confirmation can confer grace, no masses can propitiate God. Your hope must be in Jesus, Jesus smitten, Jesus bruised, Jesus slain, Jesus the Substitute for sinners. Whosoever believes in Him is healed, but all other hopes are a lie from top to bottom. Of sacramentarianism, I will say that its Alpha is a lie, and its Omega is a lie, it is false as the devil who devised it; but Christ, and only Christ, is the true Physician of souls, and His stripes the only remedy. Oh, for a trumpet to sound this through every town of England! Through every city of Europe! Oh, to preach this in the Colosseum! or better still from the pulpit of St. Peter's!— "With his stripes we are healed." Away, away ye deceivers, with your mixtures and compounds: away ye proud sons of men with your boastings of what ye feel, and think, and do, and what ye intend and vow. "With his stripes we are healed." A crucified Savior is the sole and only hope of a sinful world.

III. Now, I said this is a VERY SUGGESTIVE text, but I shall not give you the suggestions, for time has failed me, except to say that whenever a man is healed through the stripes of Jesus, the instincts of his nature should make him say, "I will spend the strength I have, as a healed man, for Him who healed me." Every stripe on the back of Christ cries to me, "Thou art not thine own; thou art bought with a price." What say you to this—you who profess to be healed? Will you live to Him? Will you not say, "For me to live is Christ. I desire now, having been healed through His precious blood, to spend and be spent in His service." Oh, if you all were brought to this it would be a grand day for London—if we had a thousand men who would preach nothing but Christ, and live nothing but Christ, what would the world see? A thousand? Nay, give us but a dozen men on fire with the love of Jesus, and if they would preach Christ out and out, and through and through, and nothing else, the world would know a change before long. We should hear again the cry, "The men that turn the world upside down have come hither also." Nothing beneath the sun is so mighty as the gospel. Believe me, there is nothing so wise as Christ, and nothing so potent over human hearts as the Cross. Vain are the dreams of intellect, and the boasts of culture. Give me the Cross and keep your fineries.

You will know this when you come to die, beloved. You will find nothing able to cheer your departing moments but the Savior on the bloody tree. When the man is panting for existence, and the breath is hard to fetch, and the spirit faces eternity, you want no priest, no dead creed, no gaudy oratory, no sacraments, no dreams; you will demand certainties, verities, divine realities; and where find you them but in the divine Substitute? Here is a rock to put your foot on, here are the rod and the staff of God Himself to comfort you. Then nothing will seem more admirable than the simple truth that God became man and suffered in man's stead, and that God has promised that whosoever believeth in His Son shall not perish, but have everlasting life.

Beloved, if you know that Jesus has healed you, serve Him, by telling others about the healing medicine. Whisper it in the ear of one; tell it in your houses to the twos; preach it, if you can, to the hundreds and thousands; print it in the papers; write it with your pen; spread it through every nook and corner of the land. Tell it to your children; tell it to your servants; leave none around you ignorant of it. Hang it up everywhere in letters of boldest type. "With his stripes we are healed." Oh, sound it! Sound it! Sound it loud as the trump of doom! Make men's ears to hear it, whether they will or no! The Lord bless you with this healing. Amen.

INDIVIDUAL SIN LAID ON JESUS

SERMON NO. 925

DELIVERED ON LORD'S DAY MORNING, APRIL 10, 1870.

PORTION OF SCRIPTURE READ BEFORE SERMON—ISAIAH 53.

All we like sheep have gone astray; we have turned every one to his own way; and the LORD hath laid on him the iniquity of us all —
Isaiah 53:6.

I THINK I addressed you from this text four years ago,† but I feel quite safe in returning to it, for we shall never exhaust it; it is a verse so wealthy in meaning, that if I had during the whole four years dilated upon it every Sabbath, it would be my fault if the theme were stale. On this occasion I desire mainly to draw attention to a part of the text upon which little was said on the former occasion. The vine is the same, but we shall gather clusters from a bough ungleaned before. The jewels are the same, but we will place them in another light and view them from another angle. May God grant that some who derived no comfort from our former word may be led to find peace and salvation in Christ this morning. The Lord in His infinite mercy grant it may be so.

I shall first *give a general exposition of the text*; then in the second place, shall *dwell upon the special doctrine which I wish to teach*; and then, thirdly, we shall *draw from that special doctrine a special lesson*.

I. First, we will GIVE A GENERAL EXPOSITION OF THE TEXT. "All we like sheep have gone astray; we have turned every one to his own way; and the Lord hath laid on him the iniquity of us all."

The text naturally breaks itself up into these three heads—is *a confession general to all penitents*, "All we like sheep have gone astray"; *a personal confession peculiar to each one*, "We have turned every one to his own way"; and then, *the august doctrine of substitution*, which the very soul and spirit of the entire gospel, "The Lord hath laid on him the iniquity of us all."

Our exposition, then, begins with *the confession which is universal to all penitents*— it is acknowledged here by the person speaking, who call themselves "all *we*"— that they all had, like sheep, broken the hedge of God's law, forsaken their good and

---

† "Sin Laid on Jesus," No. 694, Metropolitan Tabernacle Pulpit.

ever blessed Shepherd, and wandered into paths perilous and pernicious. A comparison is here used, and its use shows that the confession was a thoughtful one, and not a matter of careless form. Man is here compared to a beast, for sin brings out the animal part of us, and while holiness allies us to angels, sin degrades us to brutes. We are not likened to one of the more noble and intelligent animals, but to a silly sheep. All sin is folly, all sinners are fools. Sheep are dishonored by the comparison here used, for with all their silliness they have never been known to rush into the fire after having felt the flame. You will observe that the creature selected for comparison is one that cannot live without care and attention. There is no such thing as a wild sheep. There could not long be sheep unless they were tended and cared for by a shepherd. The creature's happiness, its safety, and very existence, all depend upon its being under a nurture and care far above its own. Yet for all that, the sheep strays from the shepherd. Man's happiness lies in being under the direction of the Lord, in being obedient to God, in being in communion with God, and departure from God is death to all his highest interests, destruction to all his best prospects; yet for all that, as the sheep goeth astray, even so doth man.

The sheep is a creature exceedingly quick-witted upon the one matter of going astray. If there be but one gap in the hedge the sheep will find it out. If there be but one possibility out of five hundred that by any means the flock shall wander, one of the flock will be quite certain to discover that possibility, and all its companions will avail themselves of it. So is it with man. He is quick of understanding for evil things. God made man upright, but he hath sought out many inventions, the inventions being all to destroy his own uprightness, and to do despite to the law of God. But that very creature which is so quick-witted to wander is the least likely of all animals to return. The ox knoweth its owner, and the ass knows its master's crib; even the swine that will wander by day will return to the trough by night, and the dog will scent out his master over many a league, but no so the sheep. Sharp as it is to discover opportunities for going astray, it seems to be bereft of all wit or will to come back to the fold. And such is man—wise to do evil, but foolish towards that which is good. With a hundred eyes, like Argus, he searches out opportunities for sinning; but, like Bartimaeus, he is stone blind as to repentance and return to God.

The sheep goes astray, it is said, all the more frequently when it is most dangerous for it to do so; propensities to stray seem to be developed in the very proportion in which they ought to be subdued. Whereas in our own land a sheep might wander with some safety, it wanders less than it will do in the Oriental plains, where for it to go astray is to run risks from leopards and wolves. Those very men who ought to be most careful, and who are placed in positions where it is best for them to be scrupulous, are those who are most prone to follow after evil, and with heedless carelessness to leave the way of truth.

The sheep goes astray ungratefully. It owes everything to the shepherd, and yet forsakes the hand that feeds it and heals its diseases. The sheep goes astray repeatedly. If restored today it may not stray today if it cannot, but it will tomorrow if it can. The sheep wanders further and further, from bad to worse. It is not content with the distance it has reached, it will go yet greater lengths; there is no limit to its wandering except its weakness. See ye not your own selves, my brethren, as in a mirror? From Him that has blessed you have gone astray; to Him you owe your all, and yet from Him you continually depart. Your sins are not occasional, they are constant, and your wanderings are not slight, but you wander further and further, and were it not for restraining grace which has prevented your footsteps you would have wandered even now to the utmost extremities of guilt, and utterly destroyed your souls.

"All we like sheep have gone astray." What, is there not one faithful soul? Alas! No! "There is none that doeth good, no not one." Search the ranks of the blessed in heaven, and there is not one saint before the throne who will boast that when on earth he never sinned. Search the church of God below, and there is not one, however closely he walks with God, but must confess that he has erred and strayed from God's ways like a lost sheep. Vain is the man who refuses to confess this, for his hypocrisy or his pride, whichever may be the cause of such a nonconfession, proves that he is not one of God's chosen, for the chosen of God unanimously, mournfully, but heartily take up this cry, "All we like sheep have gone astray." A general confession, then, is uttered in our text.

This confession by the mass is backed up by *a personal acknowledgement from each one*, "We have turned every one to his own way." Sin is general but yet special; all are sinners, but each one is a sinner with an emphasis. No man has of himself turned to God's way, but in every case each one has chosen "his own way." The very gist of sin lies in our setting up our own way in opposition to the way and will of God. We have all done so, we have all aspired to be our own masters, we have all desired to follow our own inclinations, and have not submitted ourselves to the will of God. The text implies that each man has his own peculiarity and speciality of sin; all diseased, but not all precisely with the same form of disease. It is well, my brethren, if each of us in examining himself has found out what is his own peculiar transgression, for it is well to know what evil weeds flourish most readily in the soil of our heart, what wild beast that is most native to the forests of our soul. Many have felt that their peculiar sin was so remarkably evil and so surpassingly vile, that it separated them altogether from the common rank of sinners. They felt that their iniquities were unique, and like lone peaks lifted themselves defiantly towards the pure heavens of God, provoking the fiercest thunderbolts of wrath. Such persons have almost been driven to despair under the belief that they were peculiarly great sinners, as Paul puts it, the very chief of sinners. I should not wonder if this feeling which each one imagines to be peculiar to himself may have come over very many of us, for it is no unusual thing for an awakened conscience to feel its own sinfulness to be above measure and parallel, the worst that has ever defiled mankind.

As this speciality of sin happens to be the point to which I desire to call your attention, as I wish to show that the atoning sacrifice of Christ not only applies to sin in the general, since "all we like sheep have gone astray," but applies to sin in the special, for "we have turned every one to his own way"—I pass it over slightly now, and introduce you further in the exposition of the text, to what I called *the august doctrine of the substitution of Christ,* "The Lord hath laid on him the iniquity of us all."

We have seen the confession of sin made by the mass, we lightly touched the peculiar confession made by each awakened individual, put all these together and you see a mass of sin—did I say you see it? It is a mass of sin too great to be beheld by the human understanding, an enormous load of iniquity against God. What is to be done with the offenders? The only thing that can be done with them, in the ordinary rule of justice, is to punish them for their offenses; and that punishment must be such as was threatened, indignation, wrath, destruction, death. That God should punish sin is not a matter of caprice with Him; it was not with Him an alternative as to whether He might or might not punish sin. We speak always with holy awe when we speak of anything concerning Him, but with reverence we say it was not possible that God should wink at the iniquity of man; it was not possible that He should treat it with indifference. His attribute of justice, which is as undoubtedly a part of His glory as His attribute of love, required that sin should be punished. Moreover, as God had been pleased to make a moral universe to be governed by laws, there would be an end of all government if the breaking of law involved no penalty whatever. If, after the great King of all the earth had promulgated a law, with certain penalties annexed to the branch of it, He did not cause those penalties to be exacted, there would be an end to the whole system of His government, the foundations would be removed; and if the foundations be removed what shall the righteous do? It is infinitely benevolent of God, I will venture to say, to cast evil men into hell. If that be thought to be a hard and strange statement, I reply that inasmuch as there is sin in the world, it is no benevolence to tolerate so great an evil; it is the highest benevolence to do all that can be done to restrain the horrible pest. It would be far from benevolent for our government to throw wide the doors of all the jails, to abolish the office of the judge, to suffer every thief and every offender of every kind to go unpunished; instead of mercy it would be cruelty; it might be mercy to the offending, but it would be intolerable injustice towards the upright and inoffensive. God's very benevolence demands that the detestable rebellion of sin against His supreme authority should be put down with a firm hand, that men may not flatter themselves that they can do evil and yet go unpunished. The necessities of moral government require that sin must be punished. The effeminate and sentimental talkers of this boastful age represent God as though He had no attribute but that of gentleness, no virtue but that of indifference to evil; but the God of the Bible is glorious in holiness, He will by no means spare the guilty, at His bar every transgression is meted out its just recompense of reward. Even in the New Testament, wherein stands that golden sentence, "God is love," His other attributes are by no means cast into the shade. Read the burning words of Peter, or James, or Jude, and see how the God of Sabaoth abhorreth evil! As the God who must do right, the Lord cannot shut His eyes to the iniquities of man; He must visit transgression with its punishment. He had done it, has done it terribly, and He will do it; even to all eternity He will show Himself the God that hateth iniquity and sin.

What, then, is to become of man? "All we like sheep have gone astray"; sin must be punished; what, then, can become of us? Infinite love has devised the expedient of representation and substitution. I call it an expedient, for we can only use the language of men. You remember, brethren, that you and I fell originally from our first estate by no act of our own, we all of us fell in the first Adam's transgression. Now, had we fallen individually and personally, in the first place, apart from another, it may be that our fall would have been hopeless, like the fall of the apostate angels, who having sinned one by one and not representatively, are reserved in chains of darkness forever under the condemnation and wrath of God; but inasmuch as the first fountain of evil came to us through our parent, Adam, there remained for God a loophole through which His divine love might enter without violation of justice. The principle of representation wrecked us, the principle of representation rescues us. Jesus Christ the Son of God becomes a man and re-heads the race, becomes the second Adam, obeys the law of God, bears the penalty of sin, and now stands as the Head of all those who are in Him: and who are these but such as repent of sin and put their trust in Him? These get out of the old headship of the first Adam wherein they fell, and through the atoning sacrifice are cleansed from all personal guilt, brought into union with the second Adam, and stand again in Him, abiding forever in acceptance and felicity. See, then, how it is that God has been pleased to deliver His people. It has been through carrying out a principle with which the very system of the universe commenced, namely, that of representation. I repeat it, had we been always and altogether separate units, there might have been no possibility of our salvation; but though every man sins separately, and the second clause of our text confesses that fact, yet we all sin in connection with others. For instance, who shall deny that each man receives propensities to sin from his parents, and that we transmit peculiarities of sin to our own children? We stand in connection with race, and there are sins of races peculiar to races and to nationalities. We are never put on a probation of entire separation; we always stand in connection with others, and God has availed Himself of this which I called a loophole to bring in salvation for us, by virtue of our union with another man, who is also more than man, the Son of God and yet the son of Mary, the Infinite who once became an infant, the Eternal who lived, and bled, and died as the Representative of all who put their trust in Him.

Now you will say, perhaps, that still, albeit this might have been at the bottom of the whole system of moral government, you do not quite see the justice of it. The reply to that remark is this, if God sees the justice of it you ought to be content with it. He it was against whom every sin was aimed, and if He pleased to gather up the whole bundle of the sin of His people, and say to His beloved Son, "I will visit thee for all these," and if Jesus our Representative joyously consented to bear our sins as our Representative, who are you and who am I that we should enter any caveat against what God the infinitely just One consents to accept? The text does not say that our sins were laid on Christ Jesus by accident, but "*the Lord* hath laid on him the iniquity of us all." We sing sometimes, "I lay my sins on Jesus"; that is a very sweet act of faith, but at the bottom of it there is another laying, namely, that act in which it pleased the Lord to lay our sins on Jesus, for apart from the Lord's doing it our sins could never have been transferred to the Redeemer. The Lord is so just, that we dare not think of examining His verdicts, so infinitely pure and holy, that what He does we accept as being necessarily right; and inasmuch as we derive such blessed results from the divine plan of substitution, far be it from us to raise any question concerning it. Jesus was accepted as the natural substitute and representative of all those who trust Him, and all the sin of these was laid on Him, so that they were freed from guilt. Jesus was regarded as if all these sins were His sins, was punished as if these were His sins, was put to shame, forsaken of God, and delivered to death as if He had been a sinner; and thus through divine grace those who actually committed the sins are permitted to go free. They have satisfied justice through the sufferings of their substitute. Beloved brethren, the most fit person to be a substitute for us was Christ Jesus; and why? Because He had been pleased to take up His people into union with Himself. If He was our Head, and He had made us to be members of His body, who more fit to suffer for the body than the Head? If He had, and Scripture tells us so, entered into a mysterious conjugal union with us, who more fit to suffer for the spouse than her Husband? Christ is man, hence His fitness and adaptation to be a substitute for man. The creature that sins must be the creature that suffers; man breaks God's law, and man must honor it. As by man came death, by man also must come the resurrection from the dead, and Jesus Christ was undoubtedly man of the substance of His mother. He was fit to be our substitute because He was a pure man. He had no offense in Him; neither Satan, nor the more searching eye of God could find any evil in Him; He was under no obligation to the law except as He put Himself under the law; He owed nothing to the great moral Governor until He voluntarily became a subject of His moral government on our behalf. Hence, being without obligation Himself, having no debts of His own, He was fit to take upon Himself our liabilities; and as He was under no obligations for Himself, He was a fitting One to become under obligations for us. Moreover, He did all this voluntarily, and His fitness much lies here. If a substitute should be dragged to death for us unwillingly, if such could be the case, an injustice would be perpetrated in the very act, but Jesus Christ taking up His cross, and going forth willingly to suffer for us, proved His fitness to redeem us. Once more, His being God as well as man, gave Him the strength to suffer, gave Him the power to stoop. If He had not been so lofty as to be fellow with the eternal God, He would not have stooped so low as to redeem us, but—

> From the highest throne in glory
> To the cross of deepest woe,

was such a descent that there was an infinite merit in it; when He stooped, even to the grave itself, there was an infinite merit by which justice was satisfied, the law was vindicated, and those for whom He died were effectually saved.

I do not want to proceed to the other point until every one here has got the thought, and grasped it, and received it; we have gone astray, but the strayings of many of us as believe were laid on Christ; we have each chosen our own way of sin, but those sins are not ours now, they are laid on our great Substitute if we are trusting in Him; He has paid to the utmost farthing all the debt of those sins, has borne the fullness of divine wrath, and there is no wrath against us. Just as the bullock was laid on the altar to be burnt, God's wrath came like consuming fire and burnt the bullock, and there was no fire left; so when the wrath of God fell on Christ, it consumed Him, and there was no fire left, no wrath left, it spent itself. God has no anger against a soul that believes in Jesus, neither has that soul any sin, for its sin has been laid on Christ, and it cannot be in two places at once: Christ has carried it, and the sin has ceased to be—and the believing soul though in itself as black as hell, is now as bright as Christ Himself when He was transfigured, for Christ has finished transgression, made an end of sin, and brought in everlasting righteousness. Thus we conclude our general exposition of the verse.

II. I now desire for a short time, but with all the earnestness of my soul, to dwell on THE SPECIAL DOCTRINE taught in the central clause of the text—"We have turned every one to his own way; and the Lord hath laid on him the iniquity of us all."

Each man and each woman, from a natural difference of constitution, from the variations in education, and from the diversities of circumstances, has sinned somewhat differently from every other. Two brothers educated by the same parents will yet display diversities of transgression. No man treads exactly in the same footsteps as another, and some take roads which, though equally wrong, are diametrically opposite. One turns to the right hand, and another to the left, both equally renouncing the onward path. Now, the glory of the text that I want to bring out is this, that if thou believest in Jesus Christ, this special sin of thine was laid on Him, as well as all those thine other sins, in which thou standest on an equality with thy fellowmen. There was a publican, he had been a common, gross offender, rough and harsh to his brother Jews, in demanding an inordinate tax; he was a man of low habits, indulging in drunkenness, unchastity, and other defilements, yet when that publican went up to the house of God and said, "God be merciful to me a sinner," the atonement just met the publican's iniquity, and exactly took away the publican's transgression. But, on the other hand, there was a Pharisee, the opposite of the publican, proud and self-righteous, not submitting himself to the righteousness of God, but considering himself to be in all things better than other men, yet you will remember that when he fell from off his horse as he was riding to Damascus, and heard a voice that said, "Why persecutest thou me?" that very same Pharisee said, "God forbid that I should glory save in the cross of our Lord Jesus Christ," for there was in Christ precisely that which met the Pharisee's sin. In our Lord's day there were Sadducees, too—that is, men who said there is neither angel nor spirit, infidels, skeptics, free-thinkers, your Broad Church sinners. Now, these men neither went into coarse transgression with the publican nor into superstition with the Pharisee, but they had their direct antagonism to the truth of God, and I doubt not cases occurred to prove that in the pardoning blood of Christ the Sadducee's case was met. No matter in what peculiar direction any one of the Lord's sheep has gone astray, the Lord has laid that particular straying upon the Savior. I want to speak now so as to fetch forth some individuals here this morning. It may be that one here today is saying, "I sinned against an early Christian training; no one ever had a better mother or a tenderer father; I knew the Word of God, like Timothy, from my youth; but I did despite to all this teaching, and sinned, with what aggravation of infamy I sinned against the clearest light!" Brother, thy sin is very great, but the Lord hath laid on Jesus thine iniquity. Look thou to the cross, and see it laid there. "Aye," saith another, "but I have had the strivings of God's Spirit; in addition to an early Christian education, I have sat under an earnest gospel ministry; I have often been impressed; I have been driven to my chamber to pray, but I have quenched the holy emotions, and have continued in sin." O guilty one, the Lord has laid on His dear Son thine iniquity. Canst thou look to Jesus now and trust Christ, "The Lamb of God which taketh away the sin of the world?" Then this offense of thine against the Holy Ghost is put away. "But," saith another, "I am conscious of having had naturally a remarkable tenderness of spirit; from my early childhood I knew right from wrong, and when I sinned it cost me much trouble to sin; I have had to wound my conscience before I could speak an ill word, or commit an evil action." Ah! my brethren, that is a very condemning thing to sin against a tender conscience. It is a great boon, and in this age a very unusual boon, to have much sensitiveness and delicacy of moral constitution, and if you have violated it, it is certainly a great transgression, but though "we have turned every one to his own way, the Lord hath laid on him the iniquity of us all." Let no despairing thought come upon thee as though this sin were unpardonable. "The blood of Jesus Christ, His Son, cleanseth us from all sin." Look thou, now, by faith to Jesus, and thou shalt find that thy sin is blotted out.

There may be one in this place who says, "Sir, I committed a sin under certain remarkable circumstances which I would not, could not, mention, but the remembrance of that one sin rankles in my soul at this hour; if I had not deliberately and with malice aforethought, not having the fear of God before mine yes, chosen that sin, there might have been hope, but that sin like a millstone is about my neck and will sink me forever and ever." Hark thee, soul, canst thou see Christ on the cross? Wilt thou now confide in Him? If so, though thy sin be as scarlet it shall be as wool, though it be red like crimson, it shall be as snow. I know not what thy sin may have been, but if it were murder itself, if thou wouldst now trust the Son of God, thy sin should vanish quite away from thee, and thou shouldst be clean, clean every whit, before the all-seeing eye of eternal justice. O that thou wouldst believe, and this should be true to thee. "Nay," cries another, "but mine has been a life of peculiarly gross sin; I would not have my character unmasked before this congregation on any account." Consider then, my friend, what it will be to have it published before a greater congregation, before the entire universe? "Ah," sayest thou, "I fear my condemnation is certain, for my transgressions have not been those of thought merely, but of act; the members of my body have been the instruments of uncleanness." Listen, I pray thee, "All manner of sin and of iniquity shall be forgiven unto men." There is no sin so black, save only one, but it may find forgiveness; aye, and without exception, there is no sin that is possible to man but what it shall be forgiven to any man who comes to Christ, and with simple trust doth cast himself on Him. Thine extreme evil was laid on Christ; though thou hast turned unto thine own way, yet this too was laid on Him.

Do I not hear here and there in the congregation hearts sighing out. "He does not strike my case yet; mine has not been gross sin, but I have hardened my heart; I used to feel at one time; I had great drawings towards the Lord Jesus, but I gave Him up; I have backslidden, I have from time to time rejected gospel invitations, until now at last the Lord has sworn in His wrath that I shall not enter into His rest; my transgressions have gone over my head like overflowing waters, I sink in them as in deep mire where there is no standing." Aye, but soul, I must bring thee back to the text. Thou has turned to this iniquity also; if thou will trust Him, thy hardenings of heart shall now be forgiven thee. Thou art not too late, the gate of mercy still stands open wide; if thou trustest in Jesus this iniquity shall be blotted out. "Alas!" saith another, "but I have been a hypocrite; I have come to the Lord's table, and yet I have never had an interest in Christ; I have been baptized, but yet I never had true faith." Well, now, I will say this to end all matters—if thou has perpetrated all the sins that ever were committed by men or devils, if thou hast defiled thyself with all the blackness that could be raked out of the lowermost kennels of hell, if thou hast spoken the most damnable blasphemies and followed the most outrageous vices, yet Jesus Christ is an infinite Savior, and nothing can exceed the merit of His precious blood. "The blood of Jesus Christ, God's dear Son, cleanseth us from all sin." Canst thou believe this? Canst thou do Christ the honor to believe this, and come and crouch at the feet that once were pierced? Ah! man, thou shalt find mercy now, and thou shalt clap thine hands and say, "He hath blotted out my sins like a cloud, and like a thick cloud mine iniquities."

I am afraid I do not convey to you the pleasure of my own soul in turning over this thought, but it has charmed me beyond measure. Here were Lot's sins, scandalous sins, I cannot mention them, they were very different from David's sins. Black sins, scarlet sins, were those of David, but David's sins are not at all this those of Manasseh; the sins of Manasseh were not the same as those of Peter—Peter sinned in quite a different track; and the woman that was a sinner, you could not liken her to Peter, neither if you look to her character could you set her side by side with Lydia; nor if you think of Lydia, can you see her without discovering a great divergence between her and the Philippian jailer. They are all alike, they have all gone astray, but they are all different, they have turned every one to his own way; but here is the blessed gathering up of them all, the Lord hath made to meet on the Redeemer, as in a common focus, the iniquity of all these; and up yonder Magdalena's song joins sweetly with that of the woman who was a sinner, and Lydia, chaste, but yet needing pardon, sings side by side with Bathsheba and Rahab; while David takes up the strain with Samson and Gideon, and these with Abraham and with Isaac, all differently sinners, but the atonement meeting every case. We always think that man a quack who advertises a medicine as healing every disease, but when you come to the great gospel medicine, the precious blood of Jesus Christ, you have there in very deed what the old doctors used to call a *catholicon*, a universal medicine which meets every case in its distinctness,

and puts away sin in all its separateness of guilt as if it were made for that sin, and
for that sin alone.

III. My time has gone, and therefore I must close with this, A SPECIAL DUTY ARIS-
ING OUT OF THE SPECIAL DOCTRINE.

My dear brother, if in my discourse I have at all described you, or if not having
described you, I have yet from that very reason indicated you as an indescribable, look
thou to Christ and find mercy, and then ever afterwards make it a rule with thy soul,
that as thou hast been a special sinner thou wilt have special love and special gratitude, and do thy Lord special service. Oh! if it takes twenty times the grace to save
me that it does another, then I will render to my Savior twenty times the love and
twenty times the service. If I am an out-of-the-way straying sheep, peculiarly and specially black, defiled and disgraced, then if He loves me I will go upon this rule, that
having had much forgiven I will love much.

Brethren and sisters, I wish you did feel, more and more the peculiarity of the
weight of our personal sin, for I am sure it is the way to drive us into manliness of
Christian service. If you perform homage to Christ as one of a crowd, you do but little, and that little badly. For eminent service you need to get away from the crowd,
and serve the Lord personally by yourself, and as an individual. Get alone, I mean in
a sense of obligation, separate yourself, as if you were a marked man, and must
serve Jesus Christ in a marked way. The separation of pride is detestable, but individuality of service is admirable. Those who stand steadily in the rank and file do well,
but those who step forward to lead the forlorn do better. O for more Davids to
come forth and say, "Who is this uncircumcised Philistine that he should defy the
armies of the living God?" O that the Christian church had more self-sacrificing men,
like old Curtius, who, when there is a chasm to fill up, leap into it, and feel it an honor
to be swallowed up for Christ's sake and the truth's sake. O for many a Christian
Scaevola, who, like the Roman hero, will hold his hand in the fire if need be, and flinch
not, feeling that all suffering were little to bear for One who bled for us. We want more
consecrated men. May God raise them up; and He will if you who feel your special
sinnership find special mercy, and then render to God special returns.

It has struck me that we want more and more in the pulpit, and in the pew, individuality in our Christian experience and service. You see we are all individuals in
sinning, we have turned every one to his own way, and yet many Christian people want
to have their experience modeled after the example of someone else. They do not like
to grow like God's trees in the forest, with their gnarled roots and twisted boughs; they
want to be clipped like Dutch trees into one uniform stiffness. Why, you lose the
beauty of Christianity when you lose the individuality of Christians. In preaching and
Sunday school teaching, and everything else, the tendency is to go too much in ruts
and grooves; one might fancy that men and women were made by machinery like pens
at Birmingham, all of a sort. We would have every man in grace as individual as he
was in sin. We need the originality of saintly life as well as of sinnership. It were well
if a Christian man would step out of the beaten track and carry out his individuality,
and be what God especially meant him to be. Brethren, there is a part of this world

which can never get a blessing except through you. Christ has power over all flesh, and He has given His servants power over their little portions of that great mass. All the ministers that ever lived cannot bring to Christ those souls whom God has ordained that I shall be the means of turning to Christ; and neither I nor my brethren, preach as we may, can bring to Christ the man whom God has ordained to save through yonder obscure village local preacher who is now standing on a log on the village green, or holding forth in a wooden shed in the backwoods of America. There is a place for every man, and the way for every man to find that out is to be himself and nobody else; as he used to be himself when he was a sinner, so let him be himself now he has become a saint, and follow out, under God's guidance, the movements of his own individualities, the singularities of his own nature. Tush, about planing off your angles and getting rid of the points God has made in you distinct from other men. It will never do. You lose of Christianity the very beauty and excellence if you do this. Your fine critics would have Rowland Hill preach like Thomas Chalmers; Rowland Hill must never utter a witticism in the pulpit, yet he could not be Rowland Hill if he did not; he must, therefore, be transmogrified into someone else, for these superfine gentlemen will not allow that Rowland Hill as Rowland Hill can honor God. Wisdom will be justified of all her children. Whether you speak of the learning of Apollos, or with the eloquence of a Paul, or with the blunt homeliness of a Cephas, the Lord will get to Himself honor, if you speak sincerely; and it is not for Paul to mimic Cephas, nor for Cephas to ape Apollos. As we have turned every one to his own way, and our peculiar sin has been laid on Christ, so let each believer now in his own way, under the direction of Christ, seek to serve his Lord and Master.

My great practical lesson from it is this. You are always seeing new inventions in the world, men are evermore bringing out some new system or scheme; we tunnel the earth, we split the clouds, we speak by lightning, we ride on the wings of the wind, but in the Christian church how few inventors we have! Robert Raikes invented the Sunday School, John Pounds invented Ragged Schools; have we come to the end of gracious ingenuity? Oh, if we loved Christ better, every man would invent something, he would have a mode of action growing out of his own peculiar capacities; he would feel that God meant to meet a case by him that would never be met by anybody else. Men are all alive about this world, and all asleep about the world to come. I would urge you each to have a mission, to espouse a work, to obtain a calling. Ask God not to put you into the Sunday School as a matter of mere providence, but as a matter of special ordination; and if you are ordained to be a Sunday-school teacher, ask Him to put you into some particular class, not as by an accident, but as a special sphere for your special character and taste, and mode of thought, and manner of action. Follow out as God the Holy Spirit shall help you, the promptings of the divine life that God has put within you, and as you served Satan with all your individuality, even so serve Him upon whom the Lord of old did lay your iniquity. The Lord bless you for Christ's sake.

THE SHEEP BEFORE THE SHEARERS

SERMON NO. 1,543
PORTION OF SCRIPTURE READ BEFORE SERMON—ISAIAH 53.
HYMNS FROM *Our Own Hymn Book*—758, 752, 703.

As a sheep before her shearers is dumb, so he openeth not his mouth—Isaiah 53:7.

IT is very suggestive of the way in which our Lord Jesus took the sinner's place that we are here in the context compared to sheep: "All we like sheep have gone astray," and then He who comes to take our place is compared to a sheep also—"As a sheep before her shearers is dumb." It is wonderful how complete was the interchange of positions between Christ and His people, so that what they were that He became, in order that what He is they may become. See how closely He became like His brethren? I can very well understand how we should be like to the sheep and He to the shepherd; but I should never have dared to coin the comparison which likens *Him* to a sheep. I dare try to explain, but I should never have dared to utter it if I had not found it here. To like the Son of the Highest to a sheep would have been unpardonable presumption had not His own Spirit employed the condescending figure.

Though the emblem is very gracious, it is by no means novel, for our Lord had been long before Isaiah's day typified in the lamb of the Passover. To call Him "the Lamb of God which taketh away the sin of the world," is a very frequent mode of explaining to us how He made expiation for our transgressions: and indeed even in His glory He is the Lamb in the midst of the throne, before whom angels and the redeemed are bowing. I delight to bring before your minds the singular communion between yourselves and Jesus: you "like sheep," and He "as a sheep"; you like sheep in your wanderings, He like a sheep in His patience; you most like sheep—I mean myself and you—most like sheep for foolishness, but He only like a sheep for the sweet submissiveness of His Spirit, so that beneath the shearer's hand "He openeth not his mouth."

I. I will not keep you with any preface, but invite you to consider, first, OUR SAVIOR'S PATIENCE, under the figure of a sheep before her shearers. Let us view our Lord's patience by the help of the Holy Spirit.

I do not think I will preach to you, but I will set before you as open a window as I can, and ask you to look in, and behold the Lamb of God. Our Lord was brought to the slaughter, and brought in another sense by another figure to the shearers: to the slaughter that He might die; to the shearers that He might be shorn of His comfort, and of His honors, shorn even of His good name, and shorn at last of life itself. While He was before the slaughtermen He was quiet as a lamb that is led: when He was under the shearers He was as silent as a sheep that lieth to be shorn. You know the story of how patient He was before Pilate, and Herod, and Caiaphas, and on the cross. You have no record of His groaning, or of His uttering any exclamation as though impatient of the pain and shame which He received at the hands of wicked men; you have not one bitter word, one hard speech. Pilate cries, "Answerest thou nothing? Behold how many things they witness against thee"; and Herod is bitterly disappointed, for he expected to see some miracle wrought by Him. All that He does say is like the bleating of a sheep, only so infinitely more full of meaning. He utters sentences likes these: "For this purpose was I born, and came into the world, that I might bear witness to the truth," and, "Father, forgive them, for they know not what they do." He is all patience and silence.

Now remember, first, that our Lord was dumb and opened not His mouth *against His adversaries*, and did not accuse one of them of cruelty or injustice. They slandered Him, but He replied not; false witnesses arose, but He answered them not. He did not say, like Paul, "God shall smite thee, thou white wall." I am not going to condemn Paul, but I certainly am not going to commend him. In contrast with the Master how differently he behaves! Jesus lets not fall a word against anybody, though they are doing everything that malice can invent against Him. For Pilate He even makes a half apology, "He that delivered me unto thee hath the greater sin." One would have thought He must have spoken when they spat in His face. Might He not have said, "Friend, why doest thou this? For which of all my works dost thou insult Me?" But the time for such expostulations was over. When they smote Him on the face with the palms of their hands, it would not have been wonderful if He had said, "Wherefore do you smite me so?" But no; He speaketh not. He brings no accusation to His Father. He had only to have lifted His eye to heaven, or to have felt a wrathful wish, and legions of angels would have chased out the ribald soldiery; one flash of a seraph's wing and Herod had been eaten by worms, and Pilate had died the death he well deserved as an unjust judge. The hill of the cross might have become a volcano's mouth to swallow up the whole multitude who stood there jesting and jeering at Him: but no, nothing of the kind, there was no display of power, or rather there was so great a display of power over Himself that He did not use His might against His bitterest foes; He restrained Omnipotence itself with a strength which can never be measured, for His mighty love availed even to restrain divine wrath. He kept back the natural indignation which must have come over His spirit against the injustice, the falsehood, the shameful malice of His foes; He held it all back, and was patient, meek, silent to the end.

Again, as He did not utter a word against His adversaries, so He did not say a word *against any one of us*. You remember how Zipporah said to Moses, "Surely a bloody husband art thou to me," as she saw her child bleeding; and surely Jesus might have said to His church, "Thou art a costly spouse to Me, to bring Me all this shame and bloodshedding." But He giveth liberally, He openeth the very fountain of His heart, and He upbraideth not. He had reckoned on the uttermost expenditure, and endured the cross, despising the shame.

> This was compassion like a God,
> That when the Savior knew
> The price of pardon was his blood,
> His pity ne'er withdrew."

No doubt He looked across the ages; for that eye of His was not dim, even when bloodshot on the tree, and He might have looked at your indifference and mine, at our coldness of heart, and unfaithfulness, and He might have left on record some such words as these: "I am suffering for those who are utterly unworthy of my regard; their love will be a very poor return for mine. Though I give my whole heart for them, how lukewarm is their love to Me! I am sick of them, I am weary of them, and it is woe to Me that I should be laying down My heart's blood for such a worthless race as these my people are." But there is not a hint of such a feeling, not a trace of it. He is dumb before the shearers. They shear away everything from Him, they strip Him to the last rag, till, as He hangs upon the tree, He says, "I can tell all my bones, they look and stare upon Me," and yet He murmurs not against our cruel sins. He was stripped because we were naked, that He might cover our nakedness, and yet He makes no complaint against us, nor utters a single syllable by way of regret that He had entered upon so severe an enterprise, and that He was paying so heavy a price. No. "For the joy that was set before him he endured the cross, despising the shame," and not a syllable is uttered that looks like murmuring, or wishing that He had not commenced the work.

And again, as there was not a word against His adversaries, nor a word against you nor me, so there was not a word *against His Father or of repining at the severity of the punishment of our sin*. You know how Cain said, "My punishment is greater than I can bear," and yet to me he seems to have been treated with strange leniency, that first red-handed man. Sometimes you and I have cried, when under a comparatively light grief, "Surely my grief cannot be weighed in the scales, nor measured in the balances." We have thought ourselves hardly done by. We have dared to cry out against God, "My face is foul with weeping, and on my eyelids is the shadow of death; not for any injustice in mine hands: also my prayer is pure." But not so the Savior; in His mouth were no complaints. Yet it is quite impossible for us to conceive how the Father pressed and bruised Him. How often did that olive press revolve; how was the screw tightened again and again and again, to bring the stones together, to bruise out of Him His very life! "It pleased the Lord to bruise him; he hath put him to grief." He alone of all mankind could truly say, "All thy waves and thy billows have gone over me"; yet there is not a complaint, for "My God, my God, why hast thou forsaken me?" is a cry of grief, but it is not a cry of repining. It shows manhood in its weakness, but not manhood in revolt. There is the cry of grief, but there is not the voice of rebellion there, nor even of despair. We have the Lamentations of Jeremiah, but where are the lamentations of Jesus? Jesus wept, and Jesus sweated great drops of blood, but He never murmured nor felt rebellion in His heart.

Beloved, I feel as if I could not preach upon this, but ask you just to look in there, within the open door, and see Jesus like the lamb waiting in the shambles: not struggling, when the knife is at His throat, but waiting there to die, and dying with His own consent; laying down His life willingly for our sakes. Look again, and see your Lord and Savior lying down stretched out in passive resignation beneath the shearers, as they take away everything that is dear to Him, and yet He openeth not His mouth. I see in this, in Christ our Lord, *complete submission*. He gives Himself up; there is no reserve about it. The sacrifice did not need binding with cords to the horns of the altar. How different from your case and mine? He stands there willing to suffer, to be spit upon, to be shamefully entreated, and to die, for in Him there was a complete surrender. There was no reserve about His body, soul, or spirit. He was wholly given up to do the Father's will, and work out our redemption. There was a complete self-conquest, too. In Him no faculty arose to plead for liberty, and ask to be exempted from the general strain; no limb of the body, no portion of the mind, no faculty of the spirit started, but all submitted: a whole Christ giving up His whole being unto God, that He might perfectly offer Himself without spot for our redemption.

There was not only self-conquest, but there was *a complete absorption in His work*. The sheep, lying there, thinks no more of the pastures, it just gives itself up to the shearer. And Christ forsook His Father that He might be one flesh with us; that was at the very first, and therefore He came here and was joined unto us at Bethlehem. He kept up the union to the end, and hence He was one with us in death. The zeal of God's house did eat Him up in Pilate's hall as well as everywhere else, for there He witnessed a good confession. No thought had He but for the clearing of the divine honor, and the salvation of God's elect. His powers were concentrated into one desire, and the passion of love to men made His heart hot within Him till it melted and ran out in a stream of love and blood. Oh, brethren, I wish we could ever get to this, to submit our whole spirit to God, to resign ourselves completely, to learn self-conquest, and then the delivering up of conquered self entirely to God: the absorption of it all in one desire, the burning up of the sacrifice till it should be like Elijah's sacrifice on Carmel, when the fire came down from heaven, and consumed not only the bullock, but the wood and the stones of the altar, and licked up the water that was in the trenches, and the whole sacrifice went up in one vast cloud of fire and smoke to heaven, a whole burnt offering to the living God. This is just what one could wish might happen unto us, even as it happened unto the Lord's Christ on that day.

The wonderful serenity and submissiveness of our Lord are still better set forth by our text, if it be indeed true that sheep in the east are even more docile than with us. Those who have seen the noise and roughness of many of our washings and shearings will hardly believe the testimony of that ancient writer Philo-Judaeus when he affirms that the sheep came voluntarily to be shorn. He says: "Wooly rams laden with thick fleeces put themselves into his hands [the shepherd's] to have their wool shorn, being thus accustomed to pay their yearly tribute to man, their king by nature. The sheep stands in a silent inclining posture, unconstrained under the hand of the shearer. These things may appear strange to those who do not know the docility of the sheep, but they are true."

II. Thus I have very feebly indeed set before you, dear friends, the patience of our beloved Master. Now I want you to follow me, in the second place, to VIEW OUR OWN CASE UNDER THE SAME METAPHOR AS THAT WHICH IS USED IN REFERENCE TO OUR LORD.

Did not I begin by saying that because we were sheep He deigns to compare Himself to a sheep? Now, just go back again. Our Lord was a sheep under the shearers, and as He is so are we also in this world. Though we shall never be offered up like a lamb in the temple by way of expiation, yet the saints for ages were the flock of slaughter, as it is written, "For thy sake we are killed all the day long, we are accounted as sheep for the slaughter!" Jesus sends us forth as sheep in the midst of wolves, and we are to regard ourselves as living sacrifices, ready to be offered up. I dwell, however, more particularly upon the second symbol: we can go, and do go, as sheep under the shearers' hands. I want to speak to you a little tonight about this figure, as I have no doubt it has been wrought out in the lives of many here present, and may perhaps be wrought out at this present time, and in future days in the rest of you.

Just as a sheep is taken by the shearer, and its wool is all cut off, so doth the Lord take His people and shear them, taking away all their comforts at times, all their earthly comforts, and leaving them bare as shorn sheep. I wish when it came to our turn to undergo this shearing operation it could be said of us as of our Lord, "As a sheep before her shearers, so he openeth not his mouth." I fear that we open our mouths a great deal, and make no end of complaint. But now to the figure. We need to be reconciled to the shearing process, and to that end I shall speak at this time.

First, remember that *a sheep rewards its owner for all his care and trouble by being shorn*. There is nothing else that I know of that a sheep can do. It yields food when it is killed, but while it is alive the one payment that the sheep can make to the shepherd is to yield its fleece in due season. And so, dear friends, a sheep, if it were intelligent, might well be reconciled to be shorn because it would say, "The shepherd deserves to be rewarded for his pains, and so I am content to go down to the shearing house, to yield my fleece that he may be repaid." Some of God's people can give to Christ a tribute of gratitude by active service, and they should do so gladly every day of their lives; but many others cannot do much in active service, and about the only reward they can give to their Lord is to give up their fleece by suffering when He calls upon them to suffer; submissively yielding to be shorn of their personal comfort when the time comes for patient endurance. And mark you, those who serve

Christ actively ought to feel that what they do in that way is all too little, and if they can supplement it by passive service, by yielding themselves to be shorn as others are, they ought to rejoice that in this way they can show forth to Christ the more abundant gratitude for what He has done for them.

Here comes the shearer; He takes the sheep and begins to cut, cut, cut, cut, taking away the wool by wholesale. Affliction is often used as the big shears. The husband is taken away, or perhaps the wife, little children are taken away, property is taken away, health is taken away. Sometimes the shears even cut off your good name; slander comes, everything seems to come and remove your consolations, till all comforts vanish. Well, this is your shearing time, and it may be that you are not able to glorify God to any very large extent except by undergoing this process; and if this be the fact, do you not think that you and I, like good sheep of Christ, should surrender cheerfully and say, "I lay myself down with this intent, that thou shouldst take from me anything and everything, and do what thou wilt with me; for I am not mine own, I am bought with a price, and so I would cheerfully yield to anything by which Thou mayest get some honor out of me. Thou great Shepherd of the sheep, clip and shear me as Thou wilt so long as Thou seest some sort of return for all thy tender care and bitter woe."

Notice that the sheep is itself *benefited by the operation of shearing*. Before they begin to shear the sheep the wool is long and old, and every bush that catches it, every thistle with which it gets entangled, every briar that it passes by, tears off a bit of the wool, and the sheep looks ragged and forlorn. If the wool were left on it when the heat of summer came it would not able to bear itself, it would be so overloaded with clothing that it would be as we ourselves are when we have kept on our borrowed wool, our flannels and broadcloths, too late. After the heat of summer has come we have to throw off our thick clothes: we cannot bear them; so the sheep is the better for losing its wool, it would become a hindrance to it and not a comfort if it could retain it. So brethren, when the Lord shears us, we do not like the operation any more than the sheep do; but first, it is for *His glory*, and secondly, it really is for *our benefit*, and therefore we are bound most willingly to submit. There are many things which we should have liked to have kept which, if we had kept them, would not have proved blessings, but curses. Remember, a stale blessing is a curse. The brazen serpent preserved as a relic became a snare to the people till it was broken up and called Nehushtan, a piece of brass. The manna, though it came from heaven, was only good so long as God's command made it a blessing, but when they kept it over its due time it bred worms and stank, and then it was no blessing. I do believe that many persons if they could would keep their blessings stinking in the house till they filled their cupboards with worms. But God will not have it so. Up to a certain point for you to be wealthy was a blessing; it would not have been a blessing any longer, and so the Lord took your riches away. Up to that point your child was a boon, but it would have been no longer so, and therefore it fell sick and died. You may not be able to see it, but it must certainly be, that God, when He withdraws a blessing from His people, takes it away because it would not be a blessing any longer. Remember this text, "No good thing will I withhold from them that walk uprightly," and if that be true, then this is true, "No really good thing will I take away from them that walk uprightly," for that is something more than withholding.

When the wool goes, it is because the sheep does not really want it, it is better without it. Mr. Jouatt, who has written upon sheep, tells us, "As the spring advances the old wool is no longer needed to defend the animal from the cold, and it becomes, from its weight and its warmth, a nuisance rather than a comfort." When the Lord Jesus Christ sends affliction and trial to shear us, while we hope to glorify Him in the process, it is also good for us that we should have it cut away. Though we do not like it at the time, it is working our lasting good.

You who know something about sheep will remember that before sheep are shorn *they are always washed*. Were you ever present at the scene when they drive them down to the brook, to the place where they have dammed up the stream to make a pool for washing? There the men stand in rows, while the shepherd stands in the water breast high. The sheep are driven down, and the men seize them, throw them into the water, keeping their faces above water, and swill them round and round and round to wash the wool before they clip it off. You see them come out on the other side frightened to death, poor things, wondering whatever is coming, no doubt under the impression that they are going to be drowned, and when they escape they stand bleating on the other shore as one by one they finish their swim. I want to suggest to you, brethren, that whenever a trial threatens to overtake you, before it actually arrives you should ask the Lord to sanctify you. If He is going to clip the wool, ask Him to wash it before He takes it off; ask to be cleansed in spirit, soul, and body. That is a very good custom Christian people have of asking a blessing on their meals before they eat bread. Do you not think it is even more necessary to ask a blessing on our troubles before we get into them? Here is your dear child likely to die; will you not, dear parents, meet together and ask God to bless the death of that child, if it is to happen. Here are things going badly in trade: would it not be a good thing to hold a special meeting in the family, and ask God to bless your declining business to you? There is a bad crop; the harvest fails; would it not be well to say, "Lord, sanctify this poverty, this loss, this year's bad harvest: cause it to be a means of grace to us. The evil is coming, and ere it comes we would ask a blessing on it." Why not ask a blessing on the cup of bitterness as well as upon the cup of thanksgiving? Ask to be washed before you are shorn, and if the shearing must come, let that be your chief concern. "Lord, if Thou art coming to take my wool, make it clean before Thou takest it: wash what Thou takest, and wash me also, and I shall be clean; yea, wash me, and I shall be whiter than snow."

After the washing, and the sheep has dried, the sheep actually *loses what was its comfort*. It is thrown down, and you see the shearers; you wonder at them and pity the poor sheep. The sheep is losing what was its comfort. It will happen to you that you shall lose what is your comfort. Will you recollect this? Because the next time you receive a fresh comfort you must say, this is a loan. Oh sheep, there is no wool on your back but what will come off; child of God, there is no comfort in your possession but what will either leave you, or you will leave it. Nothing is our own except our God. "Why," says one, "not our sin?" That was our own, I own that, but Jesus has taken that upon Himself, and we call it no more our own. There is nothing our own but our God, and there is no blessing that we have but what, when the Lord sends it to us, it is on the agreement that we shall have it only for a time. It is held on lease, terminable at the will of the Lord. We foolishly consider that our mercies belong to us, and when the Lord takes them away we half grumble. If you borrow anything of a neighbor, you ought not to send it back with tears, or say, "I am sorry you recall it." A loan, they say, should go laughing home, and so should what God loans us. We should rejoice. He gives, and blessed be His name, He takes but what He gave; He does not take to Himself anything of ours, He takes to Himself what He lent us. All our possessions are but favors borrowed here to be returned anon. So as the sheep yields up its wool and loses its comfort, so must we yield up all our comforts one by one; or if they remain with us till we die, we shall part with them, then, we shall not take so much as one of them across the stream of death. Our spiritual riches are of another kind, and they are laid up already in heaven, but of all things here below we shall take not a thread with us.

The shearers when they are taking the wool off the sheep, *take care not to hurt the sheep*; they clip as close as they can, but they do not cut the skin. If possible they will not make a gash or a wound, or draw blood, even in the smallest degree. When they do make a gash, it is because the sheep does not lie still; but a careful shearer has bloodless shears. Of this Thomson sings in his Seasons, and the passage is so good an illustration of the whole subject that I will adorn my discourse with it:

> How meek, how patient, the mild creature lies!
> What softness in its melancholy face,
> What dumb complaining innocence appears!
> Fear not, ye gentle tribes! 'tis not the knife
> Of horrid slaughter that is o'er you waved;
> No, 'tis the tender swain's well guided shears,
> Who having now, to pay his annual care,
> Borrow'd your fleece, to you a cumbrous load,
> Will send you bounding to your hills again.

Be sure that when the Lord is clipping and shearing us He will not hurt us; He will take our comforts away, but He will not really injure us, or cause a wound to our spirits. Hath He not said, "In the world ye shall have tribulation, but in me ye shall have peace?" If ever the shears do make us bleed, it is because we kick, because we struggle. If we were patient as the sheep, we should just lie still, and the process would cost us very little pain. What pain there was would become delightful, seeing we had submitted ourselves entirely to the divine will. Pain grows into pleasure when you come to feel that God wills it; you are glad to suffer because He ordains you should. It is the kicking and the struggling that make the shearing work at all hard, but if we are dumb before the shearers no hurt can come. The Lord may clip wonderfully close: I have known Him clip some very close, who did not seem to have a bit of wool left, for they were stripped entirely, just as Job was when he cried, "Naked came I out of my mother's womb, and naked shall I return thither," but still he was able to add, "The Lord gave, and the Lord hath taken away, and blessed be the name of the Lord."

You will notice about sheepshearing that the shearers always *shear at a suitable time*. It would be a very wicked, cruel, and unwise thing to begin sheepshearing in winter time. There is a proverb which talks about God "tempering the wind to the shorn lamb." It may be so, but it is a very wicked practice to shear lambs while winds need tempering. Sheep are shorn when it is warm, genial weather, when they can afford to lose their fleeces, and are all the better for being relieved of them. As the summer comes on sheepshearing time comes. Have you ever noticed that whenever the Lord afflicts us He selects the best possible time? There is a prayer that He puts into His disciples' mouths, "Pray that your flight be not in the winter": the spirit of that prayer may be seen in the seasonableness of our sorrows. He will not send us our worst troubles at our worst times. I have frequently noticed, and I have treasured it up with gratitude, that when I have had strong inclinations to sin, the opportunity has not come; that if ever I have had opportunities of sinning temptingly put before me, then I have had no inward longing towards the sin. When the inward desire and the opportunity meet, that is a very dangerous case indeed, but the Lord keeps His people from that. So if you notice, if your soul is depressed the Lord does not send you a very heavy burden; but reserves such a load for times when you have had joy in the Lord, and that joy has been your strength. It has got to be a kind of feeling with us that when we have much delight a trial is near, but when sorrow thickens deliverance is approaching. The Lord dost not send us two burdens at a time, or if He does He sends double strength. It is an observation which I suppose no one would make but an Irishman, and I am not one, that you never knew the west wind blow when the east wind is troubling you. You never knew the wind blow from the north when it was blowing from the south. As a rule, except it be in a tornado or a cyclone, the wind blows from some one quarter. "He stayeth his rough wind in the day of the east wind." He knows how to prevent our suffering more tribulation than we can bear. He shears us, but not to injure us; He clips away the wool, but sends the genial temperature so that we may be able to flourish under our loss. Let that be noted, and let God be thanked for it.

There is another thing to remember. When God takes away our mercies He is ready to supply us with more. It is with us as with the sheep, *there is new wool coming*. Whenever the Lord takes away our earthly comforts with one hand, one, two, three, He restores with the other hand, six, twelve, scores, a hundred; He takes away by spoonfuls, and He gives by carloads: we are crying and whining about the little loss, and yet it is necessary in order that we may be able to receive the great mercy. Yes, it will be so, we shall yet have cause for rejoicing, "joy cometh in the morning." There is always as good fish in the sea as ever came out of it, and when one set of favors is taken away there are more mercies to come. The great sea of divine love has bigger fish in it than ever we have taken out of it. If we have lost one position, there is another position for us; if we have been driven out of one place, there is yet a refuge for us. God opens a second door when He shuts the first. If He takes away the manna, as He did from His people Israel, it is because there is the corn of Canaan for them to live upon. If the water of the rock did not follow the tribes any longer, it was because they could drink of the Jordan, and of the brooks that flowed in that land of hills and valleys. Yes, there is new wool coming; do not therefore fret at the shearing. I have given these thoughts in brief, that we may come to this last word.

III. Let us, in the third place, endeavor to IMITATE THE EXAMPLE OF OUR BLESSED LORD WHEN OUR TURN COMES TO BE SHORN. Let us be dumb before the shearers, submissive, quiescent, even as He was.

I have been giving, in everything I have said, a reason for so doing. I have shown that it glorifies God, rewards the Shepherd, and benefits ourselves. I have shown that He measures and tempers our affliction, and sends the trial at the right time. I have shown you in many ways that we are wise to submit ourselves as the sheep does to the shearer, and the more completely we do so the better. Oh, brethren, we shall be happy when we have done with self: it will be all well with us whatever we may have gone through, when we learn that verse of Toplady's:

> Sweet to lie passive in Thy hand,
> And know no will but thine.

I know we struggle a good deal, and we make excuses for struggling. Sometimes we say, "Oh, this is so painful, I cannot be patient! I could have borne anything else; but not this." When a father is going to correct his child does he select something that is pleasant? Oh dear no. The painfulness of the chastisement is the essence of it, and even so the bitterness of your sorrow will be a blessing to you. By the blueness of the wound the heart will be made better. Do not rebel because your trial seems strange. It is as good as saying, "If I have it all my own way I will not rebel, but if everything does not please me I will not endure it." Sometimes we complain because of our great weakness. "Lord, were I stronger I would not mind this heavy loss; I am like a sore leaf driven of the tempest." But who is to be the judge of the suitability of your trial? You or God? Since the Lord judges this trial to be suitable to your weakness, depend upon it, it is so. Lie still, lie still, lie quite still! "Alas," you say, "my grief comes from the most cruel quarter; this trouble did not arise directly from God, it came through my cousin or my brother, who ought to have treated me with gratitude. I could have borne it if it had not come in that way; it was not an enemy, then I could have borne it." Then let me tell you it is not a traitor after all. God is at the bottom of all your tribulation—look through the second causes to the great First Cause. It is a great mistake when we fret over the human instrument which smites us, and forget the hand which uses the rod. If I strike a dog with a stick, he bites my stick—that is because he is stupid; if he thought a little he would bite me, or else take the blow and bow in obedience. Now, you must not begin biting the stick. After all, it is God that uses that staff, though it be of ebony or of blackthorn. It is well to have done with all this picking and choosing, and to leave the whole matter in the hand of infinite wisdom. A sweet singer has put this matter very prettily, let me quote the lines:—

> But when my Lord did ask me on what side
> I were content,
> The grief whereby I must be purified,
> To me was sent,
>
> As each imagined anguish did appear,
> Each withering bliss
> Before my soul, I cried, "Oh! spare me here,
> Oh, no, not this!"
>
> Like one that having need of, deep within,
> The surgeon's knife,
> Would hardly bear that it should graze the skin,
> Though for his life.
>
> Nay, then, but He, who best doth understand
> Both what we need,
> And what can bear, did take my case in hand,
> Nor crying heed.

This is the pith of my sermon: oh sheep, yield thyself, yield thyself! Oh believer, yield thyself, lie passive, lie passive, struggle not! There is no use in struggling, for our great Shearer, if He means to shear, will do it; if He means to send us trials and troubles He will not spare for our crying, He will not mind our whining, He will do His will and carry out His purpose. What is the good, therefore, of rebellion? Did not I say just now that the sheep, by struggling, might be cut by the shears! So you and I, if we struggle against God, we shall get two troubles instead of one, and after all there is not half so much trouble in a trouble as there is in our kicking against the trouble. The eastern plowman when he plows has a goad, and pricks the ox to make it move along; he does not hurt it much, but suppose the ox flings out the moment it touches him, he drives the goad into himself, and bleeds. So is it with us, if we kick out against divine providences we shall get a sore wound, much more than was ever needful; we shall endure much more pain than would have come if we had yielded to the divine will. What is the use of kicking and struggling then, you fretful ones? You cannot make one hair white or black. You that are troubled, rest with us, for you cannot make shower or shine, rain or fine weather, with all your groaning. Did you ever bring a penny into the till by fretting, or put a loaf on the table by complaint, or get a shilling in your pocket by murmuring? Murmuring is wasted breath, and fretting is wasted time. I wish myself that I could be more quiet, calm, and self-possessed, but an active mind is apt to turn upon itself to its own wounding, when all the cares of a church and a great work press heavily. I long to cry habitually, "Lord, do what Thou wilt, when Thou wilt, as Thou wilt with me, thy servant: appoint me honor or dishonor, wealth or poverty, sickness or health, exhilaration or depression, and I will take all right gladly from thy hand." A man is not far from the gates of heaven when he is fully submissive to the Lord's will. Though heaven is uphill the road to it is downhill, and when a man has gone down so much that he is dead to self, he is not far from entering into that eternal life where God shall be all in all, in bliss forever and ever. You that have been shorn have, I hope, received a word of comfort tonight through the ever blessed Spirit of God. May God bless it to you. Oh that the sinner, too, would submit himself to God, yield himself up, and rebel no longer! Submit yourselves unto God, let every thought be brought into captivity to Him, and the Lord send His blessing, for Christ's sake. Amen.

OUR EXPECTATION

SERMON NO. 2,186
PORTION OF SCRIPTURE READ BEFORE SERMON—JOHN 12:20–45.
HYMNS FROM *Our Own Hymn Book*—325, 332, 302.

He shall see his seed—Isaiah 53:10.

THE first thought suggested by this text is, that Jesus is still alive; for to see anything is the act of a living person. *Our Lord Jesus died.* We know that He died. We are glad that there is overwhelming evidence that, not in appearance, but in fact, He died. His side was pierced; He was given up by the Roman authorities for burial; the imperial authorities were sure of His death. The soldier had made assurance doubly sure by piercing His side. His disciples buried Him. They would not have left Him in the cave if they had felt any doubt about His death. They went in the morning after the Sabbath to embalm Him. They were all persuaded that He had really died. Blessed be the dying Christ! Here our living hopes take their foundation. If He had not died, we must have died forever. The more assured we are of His death, the more assured we feel of the life of all who are in Him.

But, my brothers, He is not dead. Some years ago, someone, wishing to mock our holy faith, brought out a handbill, which was plastered everywhere—"Can you trust in a dead man?" Our answer would have been, "No; nobody can trust in a man who is dead." But it was known by those who printed the bill that they were misrepresenting our faith. Jesus is no longer dead. He rose again the third day. We have sure and infallible proofs of it. It is a historical fact, better proved than almost any other which is commonly received as historical, that He did really rise again from the grave. He arose no more to die. He has gone out of the land of tears and death. He has gone into the region of immortality. He sits at the right hand of God, even the Father, and He reigns there forever. We love Him that died, but we rejoice that He who died is not dead, but ever liveth to make intercession for us.

Dear children of God, do not be afraid that Christ's work will break down because He is dead. *He lives to carry it on.* That which He purchased for us by His death, He lives to secure for us by His life. Do not let your faith be a sort of dead faith dealing with a dead man; let it be instinct with life, with warm blood in its veins. Go to your own Christ, your living Christ; make Him your familiar Friend, the Acquaintance of your solitude, the Companion of your pilgrimage. Do not think that there is a great gulf between you, a living man, and Him. The shades of death do not divide you from Him. He lives, He feels, He sympathizes, He looks on, He is ready to help, He will help you even now. You have come into the place where prayer is wont to be made, burdened and troubled, and you seek relief; let the thought that your Lord is a living Friend ease you of your burden. He is still ready to be your strong Helper, and to do for you what He did for needy ones in the days of His sojourn here below. I want even you, who do not know Him, to remember that He lives, that you may seek Him tonight—that ere another sun shall rise you may find Him, and, finding Him, may yourselves be found, and saved. Do not try to live without the living, loving Friend of sinners. Seek His healing hand; then beg for His company; get it; keep it; and you shall find that it makes life below like heaven above. When you live with the living Christ, you will live indeed. In Him is light, and the light is the life of men.

And now to the text itself, with brevity. I have to observe upon it, first, that *Christ's death produced a posterity.* "When thou shalt make his soul an offering for sin, he shall see his seed." Evidently the death of Christ was fruitful of a seed for Him. Secondly, *that posterity remains.* Our Lord Jesus Christ does not look today on emptiness: He is not bereaved of His household, but still He sees His seed. And, thirdly and lastly, *that posterity is under His immediate eye at all times,* for "*He shall see* his seed."

I. Well, first of all, THE DEATH OF CHRIST HAS PRODUCED A POSTERITY. We do not read here that the Lord Christ has followers. That would be true; but the text prefers to say He has a seed. We read just now that the Lord Jesus has disciples. That would be distinctly true; but the text does not so read. It says, "He shall see *his seed.*" Why His seed? Why, because everyone, who is a true follower or disciple of Christ, has been born by a new birth from Him into the position of disciple. There is no knowing Christ except through the new birth. We are naturally sold under sin, and we cannot discern the spiritual and real Christ until we have a spirit created within us by the new birth, of which He said, "Ye must be born again." This is the gate of entrance into discipleship. None can be written in the roll of followers of Christ unless they are also written in the register of the family of God—"this and that man was born there." Other men can get disciples for themselves by the means that are usual for such ends; but all the disciples of Christ are produced by miracle. They are all discipled by being newly-created. Jesus, as He looks upon them all, can say, "Behold, I make all things new." They all come into the world, of which He is King, by being born into it. There is no other way into the first world but by birth: and there is no other way into the second world, wherein dwelleth righteousness, but by birth, and that birth is strictly connected with the pangs of the Savior's passion, "when thou shalt make his soul an offering for sin, he shall see his seed." See, then, the reason why we have here the remarkable expression—"his seed."

Learn from this that all who truly follow Christ, and are saved by Him, *have His life in them.* The parent's life is in the child. From the parent that life has been received. It is Christ's life that is in every true believer—"For ye are dead, and your life is hid with Christ in God; when Christ, who is our life, shall appear, then shall ye also appear with him in glory." We have our natural life, and this makes us men: we have our spiritual life, and this makes us Christians. We take life from our parents, this links us with the first Adam: we have taken life from Christ, and this joins us to the second Adam. Do no mistake me; that same life which abides in Christ, at the right hand of God, is that everlasting life which He has bestowed upon all those who put their trust in Him. That water springing up into everlasting life He gave us. He made it to be in us a well of water springing up. The first drops of that living spring, the whole outcome of the spring, and the spring itself, came from Him.

Let me put it to you, beloved hearers. Do you know anything about this new birth? Do you know anything about this divine life? There are multitudes of religious people, very religious people; but they are as dead as doornails. Multitudes of religious persons are like waxworks, well-proportioned, and you might mistake them by candlelight for life; but in the light of God you would soon discover that there is a mighty difference, for the best that human skill can do is a poor imitation of real life. You, dear hearer, dressed in the garments of family religion, and adorned with the jewels of moral virtue, may be nothing beyond "a child of nature finely dressed, but not the living child." God's living children may not seem to be quite so handsome, nor so charmingly arrayed as you are, and in their own esteem they may not be worthy to consort with you; but there is a solemn difference between the living child and the dead child, however you may try to conceal it. Righteous men know themselves to be sinners: sinners believe themselves to be righteous men. There is more truth in the fear of the first than there can be in the faith of the second; for the faith of the second is founded on a falsehood. Beloved, we become, I say again, the followers of Christ by being made partakers of His life, and unless His life be in us, we may say what we will about Christ, and profess what we like about following Him; but we are not in the secret. We are out of the spiritual world altogether—that world of which He is the Head, the Creator, the Lord. You see why the word "seed" is used. We come to Him by birth: we are partakers of His life.

Furthermore, believers in our Lord are said to be His seed because *they are like Him*. I wish that I could say this with less need to qualify it; but the man who really believes in Jesus, and in whom the divine life is strong and powerful, is like to Jesus, and especially like to Jesus in this—that, as the Christ consecrated Himself wholly to God's service and glory, so has this believer done; and as the Christ founded His successes on being dead and buried, surrendering honor, and comfort, and life itself, for His work, so should the true believer be willing to give up anything and everything, that He may achieve His life-purpose, and bring glory to God. "As he is, so are we in this world"—that is, we are bent upon the glory of God; filled with love to men, and anxious for their salvation, that God may be glorified thereby. You know best, brothers and sisters, whether this is true of you; but if we have not the Spirit of Christ, we are none of His. If we are not like Christ, it is not possible that we are His seed, for the seed is like the parent. Surely, children are like their father—

not all to the same degree; but still there is the evidence of their sonship in their like-ness to Him from whom they came. Our Lord's true people are like Him, or they could not be styled "his seed." Alas, the old nature blots and blurs the resem-blance! The stamp of the first Adam is not altogether removed; but it ought to grow fainter and fainter, while the lines of the divine portrait should grow stronger and clearer. Is this the experience of our life in Christ? I pray that it may be so. It should cause us great searching of heart if there is not in us an increasing likeness to our Lord.

There is this to be said also for those who are called His seed—that *they prose-cute the same ends, and expect to receive the same reward*. We are towards Christ, His seed, and thus we are heirs to all that He has—heirs to His business on earth, heirs to His estate in heaven. We are to be witnesses to the truth as Jesus was, and to go about doing good as He did, and to seek and save the lost after His example. This we must inherit, as a son follows his father's business. All that Christ has belongs to His seed. As a man hands down to his posterity his possessions, Christ Jesus has made over to His people all that He is, and all that He has, and all that He ever will be, that they may be with Him, and behold His glory, and shine with Him as the stars forever and ever. We are His seed in this respect—that He has taken us into His family, and given us the family patrimony, and made us partakers of all things in Himself.

Now, beloved, this is all through His death. We are made His seed through His death. Why through His death principally? Why, because it was by reason of His death for us that the Father could come and deal with us, and the Spirit could breathe upon us, and new-create us. There was no dealing with us by a just God until the atoning Sacrifice had rolled away the stone that blocked the way, namely, the necessity that sin should be punished. Christ having died for us, we came into another relation to justice, and it became possible for us to be regenerated, and brought into the house-hold of God. Beloved, I think that you know, in your own experience, that it was His death that really operated most upon you in the matter of your conversion. I hear a great talk about the example of Christ having great effect upon ungodly men; but I do not believe it, and certainly have never seen it. It has great effect upon men when they are born again, and are saved from the wrath to come, and are full of grat-itude on this account; but before that happens, we have known men admire the con-duct of Christ, and even write books about the beauty of His character, while, at the same time, they have denied His Godhead. Thus they have rejected Him in His es-sential character, and there has been no effect produced upon their conduct by their cold admiration of His life. But when a man comes to see that He is pardoned and saved through the death of Jesus, he is moved to gratitude, and then to love. "We love him because he first loved us." That love which He displayed in His death has touched the mainspring of our being, and moved us with a passion to which we were strangers before; and, because of this, we hate the sins that once were sweet, and turn with all our hearts to the obedience that once was so unpleasant. There is more effect in faith in the blood of Christ to change the human character than in every other consideration. The cross once seen, sin is crucified: the passion of the Master once apprehended as being endured for us, we then feel that we are not our own, but are bought with a price. This perception of redeeming love, in the death of our Lord Jesus, makes all the difference: this prepares us for a higher and a better life than we have ever known before. It is His death that does it.

And now, beloved, if by His death we have become His seed (and I think I speak at this time to many who can truly say they hope that it is so with them), then let us consider the fact for a minute. We are His seed. They speak of the seed royal. What shall I say of the seed of Christ? Believer, you may be a poor person, living in an obscure lane, but you are of the imperial house. You are ignorant and unlettered, it may be, and your name will never shine in the roll of science, but He who is the divine Wisdom owns you as one of His seed. It may be that you are sick: even now your head is aching, your heart is faint; you feel that by-and-by you will die. Ah, well! But you are of the seed of Him "who only hath immortality." You may put away your crowns, ye kings and emperors—earth, yellow earth, hammered, and decorated, with other sparkling bits of soil—you may put them all away, as altogether outdone in value! We have crowns infinitely more precious, and we belong to a royal house transcendently more glorious than any of yours.

But then it follows, if we are thus of a seed, that we ought to be united, and love each other more and more. Christian people, you ought to have a clannish feeling! "Oh," says one, "you mean that the Baptists ought to get together!" I do not mean anything of the kind. I mean that the seed of Christ should be of one heart; and we ought to recognize that, wherever the life and love of Jesus are to be found, there our love goes out. It is very delightful, at Christmas time, or perhaps at some other time in the year, for all the family to meet; and though your name be "Smith" or "Brown," yet you feel there is some importance in your name, when all your clan have met together. It may be a name that is very common, or very obscure; but, somehow, you feel quite great on that day when all the members of the family have joined to keep united holiday. Your love to one another gathers warmth, as the glowing coals are drawn together. So may it be in your heart towards all those that belong to Christ! You are of the blood royal of heaven. You are neither a Guelph or a Hohenzollern, but you are a Christian; and that is a greater name than all. HE has a seed—even He whom, unseen, we this night adore. My inmost soul glories in the Head of my clan—in Him of the pierced hands, and the nailed feet, who wears for His princely star the lance-mark in His side! Oh, how blessedly bright is He! How transcendently glorious are the nail-prints! We adore Him in the infinite majesty of His unutterable love. We are of His seed, and so we are near akin to Him. Do not think that I am too familiar. I go not beyond the limit which this Word allows me; nay, I have scarcely come up to the edge of it. We are truly of the seed of Jesus, even as the Jews are of the seed of Israel—not born after the flesh, for He had none born to Him in that way; but born after the Spirit, wherein His seed is as the stars of heaven. We rejoice with exultation as we read the text, "He shall see his seed."

Thus much on our first point.

II. Now, my second point is, THAT POSTERITY OF HIS REMAINS. Our Lord always has a seed. That seems to me to be clear from the indefiniteness of the text. It does not say that He shall see His seed for so long, and then no longer; but it stands as a prophecy fulfilled, always fulfilling, and always to be fulfilled:—"He shall see his seed." Christ will always have seed to see. His church, then, will never die out while the world standeth; and throughout eternity that seed must still exist in the endless state; for world without end our Lord Jesus shall see His seed.

I notice that the word is in the plural—"He shall see his *seeds*," as though some were truly His seed, and yet for a time, at least, differed from the rest. Our Lord said of those not yet converted, "Other sheep I have, which are not of this fold: them also I must bring"; and again, "Neither pray I for these alone, but for them also which shall believe on me through their word." Christ will see generation after generation of those redeemed by His blood who shall be born into His family, and shall call Him blessed. Instead of the fathers shall be the children, whom He will make princes in all the earth. The Septuagint reads it, "He shall see a long-lived seed." Though I do not think that the version is correct, it shows that still it was thought and believed that the Messiah would have a perpetual seed. Certainly it is so. Beloved, if it had been possible to destroy the church of God on earth, it would have been destroyed long ago. The malice of hell has done all that it could do to destroy the seed of Christ— the seed that sprang from His death. Standing in the Colosseum in Rome, I could not, as I looked around on the ruins of that vast house of sin, but praise God that the church of God existed, though the Colosseum is in ruins. Anyone standing there, when the thousands upon thousands gloated their eyes with the sufferings of Christians, would have said, "Christianity will die out; but the Colosseum, so firmly built, will stand to the end of time"; but lo, the Colosseum is a ruin, and the church of God more firm, more strong, more glorious than ever! Only read the story of the persecutions under Nero, and under Diocletian, in the olden times, and you will wonder that Christianity survived the cruel blows. Every form of torture which devils could invent was inflicted upon Christian men and women. Not here and there, but everywhere, they were hunted down and persecuted. It makes one thrill with horror as he reads of women tossed on the horns of bulls, or set in red-hot iron chairs; and men smeared with honey to be stung to death by wasps, or dragged at the heels of wild horses, or exposed to savage beasts in the amphitheater. But I will say no more about it. The gallant vessel of the church plowed the red waves of a crimson sea, her prow scarlet with gore, but the ship itself was the better for its washing, and sailed all the more gallantly because of boisterous winds. As to our own country, read the story of persecutions here. You will have enough if you only read Foxe's "Book of Martyrs." Well do I recollect, as a child, how many hours, how many days, I spent looking at the pictures in an old-fashioned "Book of Martyrs," and wondering how the men of God suffered, as they did, so bravely. I recollect how I used to turn to that boy of Brentford, who was first beaten with rods, and afterwards tied to the stake, cheerfully to burn for Christ's sake. I am reminded, by the effect which it had upon my mind, of what was said of a certain ancient church in this city of London, which was greatly persecuted. Many, many years ago, a number of persons were noticed to be going towards Smithfield, early one morning, and somebody said, "Whither are you going?" "We are going to Smithfield." "What for?" "To see our pastor burnt." "Well, but what, in the name of goodness, do you want to see him burnt for? What can be the good of it?" They answered, "We go to see him burn that we may learn the way." Oh, but that was grand! "To learn the way!" Then the rank and file of the followers of Jesus learned the way to suffer and die as the leaders of the church set the example. Yet the church in England was not destroyed by persecution, but it became more mighty than ever because of the opposition of its foes.

Since then there have been laborious attempts to destroy the church of Christ by error. One hundred years ago or so, throughout the most of our Dissenting churches, a sort of Unitarianism was triumphant. The essential doctrines of the gospel were omitted, the pith of it was taken away, the marrow was torn out of its bones. The Church of England was asleep, too; and everywhere it seemed as if there was a kind of orthodox heterodoxy that did not believe anything in particular, and did not hold that there was a doctrine worth anybody's living or dying for, but that all religious teaching should be like a nose of wax, that you might shape whichever way you liked. It looked as if the living church of God would be extinguished altogether; but it was not so, for God did but stamp His foot, and, from all parts of the country, men like Mr. Wesley and Mr. Whitefield, came to the front, and hundreds of others, mighty men of valor, proclaimed the gospel with unusual power, and away went the bats and the owls back to their proper dwelling-place. The same mischievous experiment is being tried now, and there will be the same result; for the living Christ is still to the front. The King is not off the ground yet: the battle will be won by His armies. Jehovah has declared His decree, "Yet have I set my king upon my holy hill of Zion." Our Lord shall see His seed on the conquering hand yet.

Worldliness has gone a long way to destroy the church of God. I judge it to be the worst cankerworm that assails us. Persons come into the church with a profession which they never carry out. Have we not all around us persons who say that they are Christians, and are not, but do lie. And many who, we hope, are Christians, are but very poverty-stricken specimens of the race, with little love, little zeal (indeed, they are afraid to be too zealous), little searching of the Word, little prayer, little consecration, little communion with God. They are enough to kill all hope of better things. The Lord have mercy upon His poor church when she comes to be neither cold nor hot, so that He is ready to spew her out of His mouth! Yet, still the lukewarm can be heated: the cause is not dead. "He shall see his seed." Take it as a standing miracle that there are any godly people on the face of the earth; for there would not be one were it not for the exertion of miraculous power. Christianity is not a natural growth: it is constantly a divine creation. Christian life needs to have daily the baptism of the Holy Ghost. The church must perpetually receive fresh light and life from above, or else it would die; but still stands the promise, "He shall see his seed." While sun and moon endure, there shall be a people who follow the Lamb; and even though they be so few that Elijah might say, "I, only I, am left, and they seek my life to take it away," God will reserve to Himself thousands that have not bowed the knee to Baal.

III. And now I am to wind up with this third thought:—THIS POSTERITY IS ALWAYS UNDER THE IMMEDIATE EYE OF CHRIST. "He shall see his seed." Oh, I like this, "He shall *see* his seed!" He sees them when they are first born anew. I keep looking out from this pulpit for that small portion of them that may be born in this place; and there are many watchful brethren and sisters here, who try to speak to all that come into the place in whom there are movings of the Spirit. If there is an anxious soul, they seek to find him out. *We* cannot see them all; but HE shall see His seed. Sometimes it is a question whether they are His seed or not—a very great question with themselves, but none with Him: He sees His seed. Some are seeking; they have hardly found; they are longing; they have scarcely realized the way of faith. Ah, well! He sees your first desires, your humble breathings, your lowly hopes, your trembling approaches. He sees you. There is not a child of His, born in any out-of-the-way place, but what He perceives him at once. The first living cry, the first living tear, He observes. "He shall see his seed." What a mercy to have such a Watcher! We poor earthly pastors are of small use; but this great Shepherd and Bishop of souls, with an eye that never misses a single newborn lamb of grace—what a mercy to have such a Shepherd to look after the whole flock! "He shall see his seed."

Yes, and ever afterward, wherever His seed may wander, He still sees them. Some of you, perhaps, have lived long in England, but you are contemplating going far away—to Australia or America. You wonder whether you will meet with any friend who will help you spiritually. Do not fear. "He shall see his seed." "Rivers unknown to song, are not unknown to God." And if you should have to dwell quite alone in the bush, and have no Christian acquaintance, still go direct to the Son of God, for "He shall see his seed." The eye of Christ is never off from the eye of faith. If you look to Him, rest you well assured that He looks to you.

The beauty of it is, that this look of Christ, whereby He sees His seed, is one of intense delight. I cannot preach upon that most precious topic, but I wish you to think it over: it is a divine pleasure to the Lord Jesus to look at you: it is promised Him as a reward for His death. Mother, you know yourself what a pleasure it has been for you to look at your daughter, and to see her grow up. You would not like to tell her all you have thought of her: you have looked at her with intense delight. Now, the Lord Jesus Christ looks at you in just the same way. Love is blind, they say. Jesus is not blind; but He does see in His people much more than they ever will see in themselves. He sees their hopes, their desires, their aspirations; and He often takes the will for the deed, and marks that for a beauty which now may be half-developed, and therefore not all we could wish it to be. It is, at present, the caricature of a virtue; but it is well meant, and will come right, and the Lord sees it as it will be, and He rejoices in it. Oh, what blessed eyes those are of His that can spy out beauties which only He can see! Since He has created them, and put them there Himself, He sees them. "He shall see his seed." He suffered so much for our redemption, that He must love us. We cost Him so much, that He must delight in us.

> The Son with joy looks down, and sees
> The purchase of his agonies.

"He shall see his seed."

Brethren, our Savior will always behold His redeemed ones. He will see all His seed to the last. When they come to the river which divides them from the celestial country, "He shall see his seed." It may possibly be gloomy with some of you; but it is not often dark at death-time. Many of the Lord's children have a fine candle to go to bed with. Even if they go to bed in the dark, they fall asleep the sooner; but in either case, their Lord will see *them* if they cannot see *Him*. When you can see nothing, and the brain begins to reel, and thought and memory flee, He sees His seed.

But what a seed He will have to see in the morning! I am not yet an old man, as some suppose from the many years of my ministry, but I am often looking forward to that blessed morning, when all the sacred seed shall meet around the throne. I believe the Christ will come in to see all His beloved purchased ones; and He will search to see whether we are all there. Then shall the sheep pass again under the hand of Him that telleth them, and He will count them, for He knows whom He bought with His blood, and He will see that they are there in full tale. I think that I hear the reading of the register, the muster-roll. Will you be there to answer to your name? Dear friends, all the Lord's seed will be there—all that were born into His house with a new birth. They shall answer, "Aye, aye, aye, we are here; we are here!" Oh, but the joy we shall have in being there—the delight in beholding His face, yet, if all our joys are put together, they will not equal the joy that He will have when He finds them all there for whom He shed His blood—all whom he Father gave Him—all who gave themselves to Him—all who were born as His seed—not one lost! "Of all whom thou hast given me, I have lost none." Oh, the joy, the delight, of our Well-beloved in that day! Then shall He see His seed!

And I believe that it will be part of His heaven for Him to look upon His redeemed. He is the Bridegroom, they make up the bride; and the bridegroom's joy is not in seeing his bride for once on the wedding-day, but he takes delight in her as long as they both live. A true husband and a true spouse are always lovers: they are always linked together by strong ties of affection; and it is so with that model Husband, the Lord Christ, and His perfect church above. He loves His people no less, and He could not love them any more, than when He died for them, and so forever "He shall see his seed."

Thus have I talked with you in a very poor and feeble way, as far as my speech is concerned: but the doctrine is not feeble, the gospel is not poor. O you that are the seed of Christ, go out and magnify Him by your lives! Be worthy of your high calling. Show the nobility of your pedigree by the magnanimity of your lives. And, you that are not among His seed, see where you are! What can you do? All that you can do will bring you no further: you must be born again; and this is the work of the Spirit of God. The Spirit of God works the new birth in His own way, but He works according to the gospel. What is the gospel? "He that believeth and is baptized shall be saved." I give you the gospel without mutilating it, just as I get it in the gospel by Mark, "He that believeth and is baptized shall be saved." Obey the precept, and the promise is yours. God help you to believe in the Lord Jesus, and so to have eternal life! The moment you believe in Jesus Christ you are born again. May He, by His Holy Spirit, seal the message with His blessing to everyone in this house, for His own name's sake! Amen.

JESUS INTERCEDING FOR TRANSGRESSORS

SERMON NO. 1,385
DELIVERED ON LORD'S DAY MORNING, NOVEMBER 18, 1877.
PORTION OF SCRIPTURE READ BEFORE SERMON—ISAIAH 53.
HYMNS FROM *Our Own Hymn Book*—327, 412, 329.

And made intercession for the transgressors—Isaiah 53:12.

OUR blessed Lord made intercession for transgressors in so many words while He was being crucified, for He was heard to say, "Father, forgive them; for they know not what they do." It is generally thought that He uttered this prayer at the moment when the nails were piercing His hands and feet, and the Roman soldiers were roughly performing their duty as executioners. At the very commencement of His passion He begins to bless His enemies with His prayers. As soon as the rock of our salvation was smitten there flowed forth from it a blessed stream of intercession.

Our Lord fixed His eye upon that point in the character of His persecutors which was most favorable to them, namely, that they knew not what they did. He could not plead their innocence, and therefore He pleaded their ignorance. Ignorance could not excuse their deed, but it did lighten their guilt, and therefore our Lord was quick to mention it as in some measure an extenuating circumstance. The Roman soldiers, of course, knew nothing of His higher mission; they were the mere tools of those who were in power, and though they "mocked him, coming to him, and offering him vinegar," they did so because they misunderstood His claims and regarded Him as a foolish rival of Caesar, only worthy to be ridiculed. No doubt the Savior included these rough Gentiles in His supplication, and perhaps their centurion who "glorified God, saying, Certainly this was a righteous man," was converted in answer to our Lord's prayer. As for the Jews, though they had some measure of light, yet they also acted in the dark. Peter, who would not have flattered any man, yet said, "And now, brethren, I know that through ignorance ye did it, as did also your rulers." It is doubtless true that, had they known, they would not have crucified the Lord of glory, though it is equally clear that they ought to have known Him, for His credentials were clear as noon day. Our Redeemer, in that dying prayer of His, shows how quick He is to see anything which is in any degree favorable to the poor clients whose cause

634

He has undertaken. He spied out in a moment the only fact upon which compassion could find foothold, and He secretly breathed out His loving heart in the cry. "Father, forgive them; for they know not what they do." Our great Advocate will be sure to plead wisely and efficiently on our behalf; He will urge every argument which can be discovered, for His eye, quickened by love, will suffer nothing to pass which may tell in our favor.

The prophet, however, does not, I suppose, intend to confine our thoughts to the one incident which is recorded by the evangelists, for the intercession of Christ was an essential part of His entire life-work. The mountain's side often heard Him, beneath the chilly night, pouring out His heart in supplications. He might as fitly be called the man of prayers as "the man of sorrows." He was always praying, even when His lips moved not. While He was teaching and working miracles by day He was silently communing with God, and making supplication for men; and His nights, instead of being spent in seeking restoration from His exhausting labors, were frequently occupied with intercession. Indeed, our Lord's whole life is a prayer. His career on earth was intercession wrought out in actions. Since "He prayeth best who loveth best," He was a mass of prayer, for He is altogether love. He is not only the channel and the example of prayer, but He is the life and force of prayer. The greatest plea with God is Christ Himself. The argument which always prevails with God is Christ incarnate, Christ fulfilling the law, and Christ bearing the penalty. Jesus Himself is the reasoning and logic of prayer, and He Himself is an ever living prayer unto the Most High.

It was part of our Lord's official work to make intercession for the transgressors. He is a Priest, and as such He brings His offering, and presents prayer on the behalf of the people. Our Lord is the Great High Priest of our profession, and in fulfilling this office we read that He offered up prayers and supplications with strong crying and tears; and we know that He is now offering up prayers for the souls of men. This, indeed, is the great work which He is carrying on today. We rejoice in His finished work, and rest in it, but that relates to His atoning sacrifice; His intercession springs out of His atonement, and it will never cease while the blood of His sacrifice retains its power. The blood of sprinkling continues to speak better things than that of Abel. Jesus is pleading now, and will be pleading till the heavens shall be no more. For all that come to God by Him He still presents His merits to the Father, and pleads the causes of their souls. He urges the grand argument derived from His life and death, and so obtains innumerable blessings for the rebellious sons of men.

I. I have to direct your attention this morning to our ever-living Lord making intercession for the transgressors; and as I do so I shall pray God, in the first place, that all of us may be roused to ADMIRATION FOR HIS GRACE. Come, brethren, gather up your scattered thoughts and meditate upon Him who alone was found fit to stand in the gap and turn away wrath by His pleading. If you will consider His intercession for transgressors I think you will be struck with the love, and tenderness, and graciousness of His heart, when you recollect that *He offered intercession verbally while He was standing in the midst of their sin.* Sin heard of and sin seen are two very different things. We read of crimes in the newspapers, but we are not at all so horrified as if we had seen them for ourselves. Our Lord actually saw human sin, saw it unfettered and unrestrained, saw it at its worst. Transgressors surrounded His person, and by their sins darted ten thousand arrows into His sacred heart, and yet while they pierced Him He prayed for them. The mob compassed Him round about, yelling, "Crucify him, crucify him," and His answer was "Father, forgive them": He knew their cruelty and ingratitude, and felt them most keenly, but answered them only with a prayer. The great ones of the earth were there, too, sneering and jesting—Pharisee and Sadducee and Herodian—He saw their selfishness, conceit, falsehood, and bloodthirstiness, and yet He prayed. Strong bulls of Bashan had beset Him round, and dogs had compassed Him, yet He interceded for men. Man's sin had stirred up all its strength to slay God's love, and therefore sin had arrived at its worst point, and yet mercy kept pace with malice, and outran it, for He sought forgiveness for His tormentors. After killing prophets and other messengers, the wicked murderers were now saying, "This is the heir; come, let us kill him, that the inheritance may be ours." And yet that heir of all things, who might have called fire from heaven upon them, died crying, "Father, forgive them." He knew that what they did was sin, or He would not have prayed "forgive them," but yet He set their deed in the least unfavorable light, and said, "they know not what they do." He set His own Sonship to work on their behalf, and appealed to His Father's love to pardon them for His sake. Never was virtue set in so fair a frame before, never goodness came so adorned with abundant love as in the person of the Lord Jesus, and yet they hated Him all the more for His loveliness, and gathered around Him with the deeper spite because of His infinite goodness. He saw it all, and felt the sin as you and I cannot feel it, for His heart was purer, and therefore tenderer than ours: He saw that the tendency of sin was to put Him to death, and all like Him, yea and to slay God Himself if it could achieve its purpose, for man had become a Deicide and must needs crucify His God—and yet, though His holy soul saw and loathed all this tendency and atrocity of transgression, He still made intercession for the transgressors. I do not know whether I convey my own idea, but to me it seems beyond measure wonderful that He should know sin so thoroughly, understand its heinousness, and see the drift of it, and feel it so wantonly assailing Himself when He was doing nothing but deeds of kindness; and yet with all that vivid sense of the vileness of sin upon Him, even there and then He made intercession for the transgressors, saying, "Father, forgive them; for they know not what they do."

Another point of His graciousness was also clear on that occasion, namely, that He should *thus intercede while in agony*. It is marvelous that He should be able to call His mind away from His own pains to consider their transgressions. You and I, if we are subject to great pains of body, do not find it easy to command our minds, and especially to collect our thoughts and restrain them, so as to forgive the person inflicting the pain, and even to invoke blessings on his head. Remember that your Lord was suffering while He made intercession, beginning to suffer the pangs of death, suffering in soul as well as in body, for He had freshly come from the garden, where His soul was exceeding sorrowful, even unto death. Yet in the midst of that depression of spirit, which might well have made Him forgetful of the wretched beings who were putting Him to death, He forgets Himself, and He only thinks of them, and pleads for them. I am sure that we should have been taken up with our pains even if we had not been moved to some measure of resentment against our tormentors; but we hear no complaints from our Lord, no accusations lodged with God, no angry replies to them such as Paul once gave—"God shall smite thee, thou whited wall"; not even a word of mourning or of complaining concerning the indignities which He endured, but His dear heart all ascended to heaven in that one blessed petition for His enemies, which there and then He presented to His Father.

But I will not confine your thoughts to that incident, because, as I have already said, the prophet's words had a wider range. To me it is marvelous *that He, being pure, should plead for transgressors at all:* for you and for me amongst them—let the wonder begin there. Sinners by nature, sinners by practice, willful sinners, sinners who cling to sin with a terrible tenacity, sinners who come back to sin after we have smarted for it; and yet the Just One has espoused our cause, and has become a suitor for our pardon. We are sinners who omit duties when they are pleasures, and who follow after sins which are known to involve sorrow: sinners, therefore, of the most foolish kind, wanton, willful sinners, and yet He who hates all sin has deigned to take our part, and plead the causes of our souls. Our Lord's hatred of sin is as great as His love to sinners; His indignation against everything impure is as great as that of the thrice holy God who revengeth and is furious when He comes into contact with evil; and yet this divine Prince, of whom we sing, "Thou lovest righteousness and hatest wickedness," espouses the cause of transgressors, and pleads for them. Oh, matchless grace! Surely angels wonder at this stretch of condescending love. Brethren, words fail me to speak of it. I ask you to adore!

Further, it is to me a very wonderful fact that *in His glory He should still be pleading for sinners.* There are some men who when they have reached to high positions forget their former associates. They knew the poor and needy friend once, for, as the proverb hath it, poverty brings us strange bedfellows, but when they have risen out of such conditions they are ashamed of the people whom once they knew. Our Lord is not thus forgetful of the degraded clients whose cause He espoused in the days of His humiliation. Yet though I know His constancy I marvel and admire. The Son of man on earth pleading for sinners is very gracious, but I am overwhelmed when I think of His interceding for sinners now that He reigns yonder, where harps unnumbered tune His praise and cherubim and seraphim count it their glory to be less than nothing at His feet, where all the glory of His Father is resplendent in Himself, and He sitteth at the right hand of God in divine favor and majesty unspeakable. How can we hear without amazement that the King of kings and Lord of lords occupies Himself with caring for transgressors—caring indeed for you and me. It is condescension that he should commune with the bloodwashed before His throne, and allow the perfect spirits to be His companions, but that His heart should steal away from all heaven's felicities to remember such poor creatures as we are and make incessant prayer on our behalf, this is like His own loving Self—it is Christlike, Godlike. Methinks I see at this moment our great high Priest pleading before the throne, wearing His jeweled breastplate and His garments of glory and beauty, wearing our names upon His breast and His shoulders in the most holy place. What a vision of incomparable love! It is a fact, and no mere dream. He is within the Holy of Holies, presenting the one sacrifice. His prayers are always heard, and heard for us, but the marvel is that the Son of God should condescend to exercise such an office and make intercession for transgressors. This matchless grace well nigh seals my lips, but it opens the floodgates of my soul, and I would fain pause to worship Him whom my words fail to set forth.

Again, it is gloriously gracious *that our Lord should continue to do this;* for lo, these eighteen hundred years and more He has gone into His glory, yet hath He never ceased to make intercession for transgressors. Never on heaven's most joyous holiday when all His armies are marshaled, and in their glittering squadrons pass in review before the King of kings, has He forgotten His redeemed ones. The splendors of heaven have not made Him indifferent to the sorrows of earth. Never, though, for aught we know, He may have created myriads of worlds, and though assuredly He has been ruling the courses of the entire universe, never once, I say, has He suspended His incessant pleading for the transgressors. Nor will He, for the Holy Scriptures lead us to believe that as long as He lives as Mediator He will intercede: "He is able to save them to the uttermost that come unto God by Him, seeing He ever liveth to make intercession for them." He lived and lives to intercede, as if this were the express object of His living. Beloved, as long as the great Redeemer lives and there is a sinner still to come to Him, He will still continue to intercede. Oh, my Master, how shall I praise thee! Hadst Thou undertaken such an office now and then, and hadst Thou gone into the royal presence once in a while to intercede for some special cases, it would have been divinely gracious on thy part, but that Thou shouldst always be a Suppliant, and never cease to intercede, surpasses all our praise. Wonderful are His words as written in prophecy by Isaiah—"For Zion's sake will I not hold my peace, and for Jerusalem's sake I will not rest until the righteousness thereof go forth as brightness, and the salvation thereof as a lamp that burneth." As the lamp in the temple went not out, so neither hath our Advocate ceased to plead day nor night. Unwearied in His labor of love, without a pause, He has urged our suit before the Father's face. Beloved, I will not enlarge, I cannot, for adoration of such love quite masters me; but let your hearts be enlarged with abounding love to such an intercessor as this, who made, who does make, and who always will make intercession for the transgressors. I have said, *"will make,"* and indeed this is no bare assertion of mine, for my text may be read in the future, as well as in the past: indeed, as you will perceive upon a little thought, it must have been meant to be understood in the future, since the prophecy was written some 700 years before our Lord had breathed His intercessory prayer at the cross: although the prophet, in order to make his language pictorial and vivid, puts it in the past tense, it was actually in the future to him, and therefore we cannot err in reading it in the future, as I have done—"he *shall* make intercession for the transgressors." Constant love puts up a ceaseless plan. Endless compassion breathes its endless prayer. Till the last of the redeemed has been gathered home that interceding breath shall never stay, nor cease to prevail.

II. Thus have I called you to feel admiration for His grace; and now, secondly, I do earnestly pray that we may be led of the Holy Ghost so to view His intercession for transgressors as to put our CONFIDENCE IN HIMSELF. There is ground for a sinner's confidence in Christ, and there is abundant argument for the believer's complete reliance in Him, from the fact of His perpetual intercession.

Let me show you this first, because, beloved, *His intercession succeeds*. God heareth Him, of that we do not doubt; but what is the basis of this intercession? For whatever that is, seeing it makes the intercession to be successful, we may safely rest on it. Read carefully the verse: "Because he hath poured out his soul unto death: and he was numbered with the transgressors; and he bore the sin of many." See, then, the success of His plea arises out of His substitution. He pleads and prevails because He has borne the sin of those for whom He intercedes. The main stay and strength of His prevalence in His intercession lies in the completeness of the sacrifice which He offered when He bore the sin of many. Come, then, my soul, if Christ's prayer prevails because of this, so will thy faith. Resting on the same foundation, thy faith will be equally secure of acceptance. Come, my heart, rest thou on that truth—"He bore the sin of many." Throw thyself with all thy sin upon His substitution and feel that this is a safe resting-place for thy believing, because it is a solid basis for thy Lord's intercession. The perfect sacrifice will bear all the strain which can possibly come upon it; test it by the strongest faith and see for thyself; plead it with the boldest requests and learn its boundless prevalence. Thou mayest urge the plea of the precious blood with the Father, seeing the Lord Jesus has urged it, and has never failed.

Now, again, *there is reason for transgressors to come and trust in Jesus Christ, seeing He pleads for them*. You never need be afraid that Christ will cast you out when you can hear Him pleading for you. If a son had been disobedient and had left his father's house, and were to come back again, if he had any fear about his father's receiving him, it would all disappear if he stood listening at the door and heard his father praying for him. "Oh," saith he, "my coming back is an answer to my father's prayer, he will gladly enough receive me." Whenever a soul comes to Christ it need have no hesitancy, seeing Christ has already prayed for it that it might be saved. I tell you transgressors, Christ prays for you when you *do not* pray for yourselves. Did He not say of His believing people, "Neither pray I for these alone, but for them also which shall believe on me through their word?" Before His elect become believers they have a place in His supplications. Before you know yourselves to be transgressors and have any desire for pardon, while as yet you are lying dead in sin, His intercession has gone up even for such as you are. "Father, forgive them" was a prayer for those who had never sought forgiveness for themselves. And when you *dare not* pray for yourselves He is still praying for you: when under a sense of sin you dare not lift so much as your eyes toward heaven, when you think "Surely it would be in vain for me to seek my heavenly Father's face," He is pleading for you. Aye, and when you *cannot* plead, when through deep distress of mind you feel choked in the very attempt to pray, when the language of supplication seems to blister your lip because you feel yourself to be so unworthy, when you cannot force even a holy groan from your despairing heart, He still pleads for you. Oh, what encouragement this ought to give you. If *you* cannot pray *He* can, and if you feel as if your prayers must be shut out, yet His intercession cannot be denied. Come and trust Him! Come and trust Him! He who pleads for you will not reject you: do not entertain so unkind a thought, but come and cast yourself upon Him. Hath He not said, "Him that cometh to me I will in no wise cast out"? Venture upon the assured truth of that word, and you will be received into the abode of His love.

I am sure too that if Jesus Christ pleads for transgressors as transgressors, while as yet they have not begun to pray for themselves, *He will be sure to hear them when they are at last led to pray.* When the transgressor becomes a penitent, when he weeps because he has gone astray, let us be quite sure that the Lord of mercy who went after him in his sin will come to meet him now that he returns. There can be no doubt about that. I have known what it is to catch at this text when I have been heavy in heart. I have seen my sinfulness, and I have been filled with distress, but I have blessed the Lord Jesus Christ that He makes intercession *for the transgressors*, for then I may venture to believe that He intercedes for me, since I am a transgressor beyond all doubt. Then again, when my spirit has revived, and I have said, "But yet I am a child of God, and I know I am born from above," then I have drawn a further inference—if He makes intercession for transgressors then depend upon it He is even more intent upon pleading for His own people. If He is heard for those who are out of the way, assuredly He will be heard for those who have returned unto the shepherd and bishop of their souls. For them above all others He will be sure to plead, for He lives to intercede for all who come unto God by Him.

In order that our confidence may be increased, *consider the effect of our Lord's intercession for transgressors.* Remember, first, that many of the worst of transgressors have been *preserved in life* in answer to Christ's prayer. Had it not been for His pleading they would have been dead long ago. You know the parable of the fig tree that cumbered the ground, bearing no fruit, and impoverishing the soil? The master of the vineyard said, "Cut it down," but the vinedresser said, "Let it alone this year also, till I shall dig about it, and dung it: and if it bear fruit, well." Need I say who he is that stays the axe which else had long ago been laid at the root of the barren tree? I tell you ungodly men and women that you owe your very lives to my Lord's interference on your behalf. You did not hear the intercession, but the great owner of the vineyard heard it, and in answer to the gracious entreaties of His Son He has let you live a little longer. Still are you where the gospel can come at you, and where the Holy Spirit can renew you? Is there no ground for faith in this gracious fact? Can you not trust in Him through whose instrumentality you are yet alive? Say to your heavenly Father,

> Lord, and am I yet alive,
> Not in torments, not in hell!
> Still doth thy good Spirit strive—
> With the chief of sinners dwell?

And then believe in Him to whose pleading you owe the fact that you are within reach of mercy. Well doth it become you to confide in Him who has already been your preserver from death and hell. May the divine Spirit teach you the reasonableness of my argument, and lead you at once to humble faith in Jesus.

Remember next, that *the gift of the Holy Spirit* which is needful for the quickening of transgressors was the result of Christ's intercession. Our poet was right when he said:—

> 'Tis by thine interceding breath
> The Spirit dwells with men.

I do not doubt but that between the prayer of Christ for His murderers and the outpouring of the Holy Ghost at Pentecost there was an intimate connection. As the prayer of Stephen brought Saul into the church and made him an apostle, so the prayer of Christ brought in three thousand at Pentecost to become His disciples. The Spirit of God was given "to the rebellious also" in answer to the pleadings of our Lord. Now, it is a great blessing thus to have the Spirit of God given to the sons of men, and if this comes through Jesus' prayers, let us trust in Him, for what will not come if we rely upon His power? Upon sinners He will still display His power; they will be pricked in their hearts, and will believe in Him whom they have pierced.

It is through Christ's intercession that *our poor prayers are accepted with God.* John, in Revelation, saw another angel standing at the altar, having a golden censer, to whom there was given much incense, that he should offer it with the prayers of all saints upon the golden altar which was before the throne. Whence comes the much incense? What is it but Jesus' merits? Our prayers are only accepted because of His prayers. If, then, the intercession of Christ for transgressors has made the prayers of transgressors to be accepted, let us without wavering put our trust in Him, and let us show it by offering our supplications with a full assurance of faith, and an unstaggering confidence in the promise of our covenant God. Are not all the promises yea and amen in Christ Jesus? Let us remember Him, and ask in faith, nothing wavering.

It is through the prayers of Christ, too, that we are *kept in the hour of temptation.* Remember what He said to Peter, "I have prayed for thee, that thy faith fail not," when Satan desired to have him and sift him as wheat. "Father, keep them from the evil" is a part of our Lord's supplication, and His Father hears Him always. Well, if we are kept in the midst of temptation from being destroyed because Christ pleads for us, let us never fear to trust ourselves in His kind, careful hands, He can keep us, for He has kept us. If His prayers have delivered us out of the hand of Satan, His eternal power can bring us safely home, though death lies in the way.

Indeed, it is because He pleads *that we are saved* at all. He is "able also to save them to the uttermost that come unto God by him, seeing he ever liveth to make intercession for them." This, also, is one grand reason why we are able to challenge all the accusations of the world and of the devil, for "Who is he that condemneth? It is Christ that died, yea, rather, that is risen again, who is even at the right hand of God, who also maketh intercession for us." Satan's charges are all answered by our Advocate. He defends us at the judgment seat when we stand there like Joshua in filthy garments, accused of the devil; and therefore the verdict is always given in our favor—"Take away his filthy garments from him." Oh, ye that would bring slanderous accusations against the saints of God, they will not damage us in the court of the great King, for "if any man sin, we have an Advocate with the Father, Jesus Christ the righteous." Think, my dear brethren and sisters, of what the intercession of Jesus has done, and you will clearly perceive great inducements to place your sole reliance in your Lord. You who have never trusted Him, will you not this very morning begin to do so? Come, weary heart, take the Lord Jesus to be your confidence—what more do you want? Can you desire a better friend than He is, a more prevalent advocate before the throne? Come, leave all other trusts, and yield yourselves to Him this morning. I pray you accept this advice of love. And you, ye saints, if you are foolish enough to have doubts and fears, come, see how Jesus pleads for you. Give Him your burden to bear, leave with Him your anxieties at this moment that He may care for you. He will carry on your suit before the eternal throne, and carry it through to success. He who engages a solicitor to manage his legal business among men leaves his affairs in his hands, and he who has such a pleader before God as Christ Jesus, the Wonderful, Counselor, has no need to torment himself with anxieties. Rather let him rest in Jesus, and wait the result with patience.

> Give him, my soul, thy cause to plead,
> Nor doubt the Father's grace.

So much, then, for the duty of exercising confidence in Him. May the Holy Ghost fill you with faith and peace.

III. And now, in the third place, I pray that our text may inspire us with the spirit of OBEDIENCE TO HIS EXAMPLE. I say obedience to His example, for I take the example of Christ to be an embodied precept as much binding upon us as His written commands. The life of Christ is a precept to those who profess to be His disciples. Now, brethren in Christ, may I put a few practical matters before you, and will you endeavor by the help of God's Spirit to carry them out?

First, then, your Lord makes intercession for the transgressors, therefore *imitate Him by forgiving all transgressions against yourself.* Have any offended you? Let the very recollection of the offense as far as possible pass from your minds, for none have ever injured you as men injured Him; let me say, as you yourself have injured Him. They have not nailed you to a cross, nor pierced your hands, and feet, and side; yet if *He* said "Father, forgive them," well may you say the same. Ten thousand talents did you owe? Yet He forgave you all that debt, not without a grievous outlay to Himself: your brother owes you but a hundred pence, will you take him by the throat? Will you not rather freely forgive him even to seventy times seven? Can you not forgive him? If you find it to be impossible I will not speak to you any longer as a Christian, because I must doubt if you are a believer at all. The Lord cannot accept you while your are unforgiving, since He Himself says, "Therefore if thou bring thy gift to the altar, and there rememberest that thy brother hath ought against thee; leave there thy gift before the altar, and go thy way; first be reconciled to thy brother, and then come and offer thy gift." If peace be not made thou wilt not be accepted. God hears not those in whose hearts malice and enmity find a lodging. Yet I would speak to thee in tones of love rather than with words of threatening: as a follower of the gentle Christ I beseech thee imitate Him in this, and thou shalt find rest and comfort to thine own soul. From the day in which Christ forgiveth thee rise to that nobility of character which finds a pleasure in forgiving all offenses fully and frankly for Christ's sake. Surely, the atonement which He offered, if it satisfied God, may well satisfy thee, and make amends for the sin of thy brother against *thee* as well as against the Lord. Jesus took upon Himself the transgressions of the second table of the law, as well as of the first, and wilt thou bring a suit against thy brother for the sin which Jesus bore? Brethren, ye must forgive, for the blood has blotted the record! Let these words of Scripture drop upon your hearts like gentle dew from heaven—"Be ye kind one to another, tender-hearted, forgiving one another, even as God for Christ's sake hath forgiven you."

Next, imitate Christ, dear friends, *in pleading for yourselves*. Since you are transgressors, and you see that Jesus intercedes for transgressors, make bold to say, "If He pleads for such as I am, I will put in my humble petition and hope to be heard through Him. Since I hear Him cry, 'Father, forgive them,' I will humbly weep at His feet, and try to mingle my faint and trembling plea with His all-prevalent supplication." When Jesus says, "Father, forgive them," it will be your wisdom to cry, "Father, forgive *me*." Dear hearer, that is the way to be saved. Let thy prayers hang, like the golden bells, upon the skirts of the great High Priest; He will carry them within the veil, and make them ring out sweetly there. As music borne on the breeze is heard afar, so shall thy prayers have a listener in heaven because Jesus wafts them there. Since thy prayers are feeble, yoke them to the omnipotence of His intercession: let His merits be as wings on which they may soar, and His power as hands with which they may grasp the priceless boons. What shall I say to those who refuse to pray when they have such an encouragement as the aid of Jesus? Tones of tenderness are suitable when addressing the ungodly, when we would persuade them to pray; but if they refuse the intercession of Jesus Christ Himself, then must we add our solemn warnings. If you perish, your blood be on your own heads: we must say Amen to your condemnation, and bear witness that you deserve to be doubly punished. Rejecters of great mercy must expect great wrath. The intercession of your Savior, when refused, will be visited upon you most terribly in the day when He becomes your judge.

Let us imitate your Lord in a third point, dear friends: namely, if we have been forgiven our transgressions, *let us now intercede for transgressors*, since Jesus does so. He is the great example of all His disciples, and, if He makes it His constant business to supplicate for sinners, should not His people unite with Him? Therefore would I stir up your pure minds by way of remembrance, to come together in your hundreds, and in your thousands, to pray. Never let our prayer meetings decline. Let us, as a church, make intercession for transgressors, and never rest from seeking the conversion of all around us. I trust that every day, so often as you bow the knee for yourselves, you will make intercession for the transgressors. Poor things, many of them are sinning against their own souls, but they know not what they do. They think to find pleasure in sin: in this also they know not what they do. They break the Sabbath, they despise the sanctuary, they reject Christ, they go downward to hell with mirth, singing merry glees as if they were going to a wedding feast: they know not what they do. But you do know what they are doing. By your humanity—scarcely shall I need to urge a stronger motive—I say, by mere humanity, I beseech you, do all you can for these poor souls, and especially pray for them. It is not much you are asked to do; you are not pointed to the cross and bidden to bleed there for sinners, you are but asked to make intercession. Intercession is an honorable service; it is an ennobling thing that a sinner like yourself should be allowed to entreat the King for others. If you could have permission to frequent the Queen's courts you would not think it a hardship to be asked to present a petition for another; it would be to you a delight to be enjoyed, a privilege to be snatched at eagerly, that you should be permitted to present requests for others. Oh, stand where Abraham stood and plead for sinners: Sodom could scarce be worse than many portions of the world at this hour. Plead, then, with all your hearts. Plead again and again, and again with the Lord, though ye be but dust and ashes, and cease not till the Lord say, "I have heard the petition, I will bless the city, I will save the millions, and my Son shall be glorified."

I have not quite done, for I have a further duty to speak of, and it is this; let us take care, dear friends, that if we do plead for others *we mix with it the doing of good to them*, because it is not recorded that He made intercession for transgressors until it is first written, "He bore the sin of many." For us to pray for sinners without instructing them, without exerting ourselves to arouse them, or making any sacrifice for their conversion, without using any likely means for their impression and conviction, would be a piece of mere formality on our part. According to our ability we must prove the sincerity of our petitions by our actions. Prayer without effort is falsehood, and that cannot be pleasing to God. Yield up yourselves to seek the good of others, and then may you intercede with honest hearts.

Lastly, *if Christ appears in heaven for us, let us be glad to appear on earth for Him.* He owns us before God and the holy angels, let us not be ashamed to confess *Him* before men and devils. If Christ pleads with God for men, let us not be backward to plead with men for God. If He by His intercession saves us to the uttermost, let us haste to serve Him to the uttermost. If He spends eternity in intercession for us, let us spend our time in intercession for His cause. If He thinks of us, we ought also to think of His people, and especially supplicate for His afflicted. If He watches our cases, and adapts His prayers to our necessities, let us observe the needs of His people, and plead for them with understanding. Alas, how soon do men weary of pleading for our Lord. If a whole day is set apart for prayer and the meeting is not carefully managed it readily becomes a weariness of the flesh. Prayer-meetings very easily lose their flame and burn low. Shame on these laggard spirits and this heavy flesh of ours, which needs to be pampered with liveliness and brevity, or we go to sleep at our devotions. "Forever" is not too long for *Him* to plead, and yet an hour tries us here. On, and on, and on through all the ages, still His intercession rises to the throne, and yet we flag and our prayers are half dead in a short season. See, Moses lets his hands hang down, and Amalek is defeating Joshua in the plain! Can we endure to be thus losing victories and causing the enemy to triumph? If your ministers are unsuccessful, if your laborers for Christ in foreign lands make little headway, if the work of Christ drags, is it not because in the secret place of intercession we have but little strength? The restraining of prayer is the weakening of the church. If we aroused ourselves to lay hold upon the covenant angel and resolutely cried, "I will not let thee go, except thou bless me," we should enrich ourselves and our age. If we used more of the strong reasons which make up the weapon of all-prayer, our victories would not be so few and far between. Our interceding Lord is hindered for lack of an interceding church; the kingdom comes not because so little use is made of the throne of grace. Get ye to your knees, my brethren, for on your knees ye conquer. Go to the mercy-seat and remain there. What better argument can I use with you than this—Jesus is there, and if you desire His company you must oftimes resort thither. If you want to taste His dearest, sweetest love, do what He is doing: union of work will create a new communion of heart. Let us never be absent when praying men meet together. Let us make a point of frequenting assemblies gathered for prayer, even if we give up other occupations. While we live let us be above all things men of prayer, and when we die, if nothing else can be said of us, may men give us this epitaph, which is also our Lord's memorial—"He made intercession for the transgressors." Amen.

WHO IS THIS?

SERMON NO. 1,947

DELIVERED ON LORD'S DAY MORNING, FEBRUARY 13, 1887.

PORTIONS OF SCRIPTURE READ BEFORE SERMON—ISAIAH 62; 63:1–14.

HYMNS FROM *Our Own Hymn Book*—317, 315, 563.

Behold, the LORD hath proclaimed unto the end of the world, Say ye to the daughter of Zion, Behold, thy salvation cometh; behold, his reward is with him, and his work before him. And they shall call them, The holy people, The redeemed of the LORD: and thou shalt be called, Sought out, A city not forsaken. Who is this that cometh from Edom, with dyed garments from Bozrah? this that is glorious in his apparel, traveling in the greatness of his strength? I that speak in righteousness, mighty to save—Isaiah 62:11—63:1.

ISRAEL was often in great trouble, frequently oppressed by neighboring nations. It would not have been so if they had been faithful to Jehovah; but as a chastisement for their idolatry they were given over into the hands of adversaries. One nation, near akin to them, was very jealous of them. The Edomites, the seed of Esau, were always watching against Israel, and whenever the nation fell on evil times, and powerful kingdoms invaded them, Edom was ever in alliance with the enemy, ready to profit by Israel's sorrows. Hence Edom was the typical adversary of Israel, and is in that manner mentioned here with Bozrah, its capital city.

The Lord God of Israel often interposed to rescue His people. I need not go over the history; but any one of these appearances for the overthrow of Israel's enemies may be represented in the language now before us, in the commencement of the sixty-third chapter. God coming forth in the glory of His strength overthrows Israel's enemies, and is seen in vision returning from their slaughter. I take the text as a representation of those marvelous victories which the Lord wrought for His chosen people when He put forth His power on their behalf. The first verse represents the astonishment of the prophet and of the people, as they beheld the Lord glorious in power, when He had vindicated the cause of His oppressed people, and had crushed the power of their adversaries.

As in God's immediate dealings with men we usually see the Son of God most manifest, this passage may fitly represent the glorious appearings of our Lord Jesus

Christ whenever He has come forth to vindicate the cause of His people and to over-throw their enemies. This vision will be astoundingly fulfilled in the second coming of our Lord Jesus Christ. The fourteenth and nineteenth chapters of the Book of Revelation give us parallel passages to this. What astonishment there will be among the sons of men when He shall appear in His vesture dipped in blood, smiting the nations with His iron rod—yea, dashing them in pieces as potters' vessels! In those last tremendous times, when the day of vengeance shall have arrived, then shall the winepress be trodden without the city, even the great winepress of the wrath of God. No tongue can fully tell the terrors of that day when our Lord shall say, "Ah, I will ease me of mine adversaries." While He shall give victory to the cause of peace, and purity, and truth, and righteousness, and shall save all those who believe in Him, He shall bruise Satan under His feet, and crush the powers of darkness. Then shall these words of the prophet be more fully understood: "Who is this that cometh from Edom, with dyed garments from Bozrah? This that is glorious in his apparel, traveling in the greatness of his strength?"

The commentators and expositors almost universally deny that this text may be used as referring to our Lord's passion. They tell us that to do so would be to wrest the Scripture from its obvious meaning; at any rate, at the best, it would be a mere accommodation of the passage. Now, I take up the gage of battle, and deny the assertion. The church by a holy instinct has referred the passage to our Lord's first as well as His second coming, and she has not been in error. The very first reference of this test is to the Lord's passion in its spiritual aspect as a battle against the enemies of our souls. I grant you that the text does not speak of our Lord as trampled upon and crushed in the winepress, and the blood which stains His garments is not said to be His own blood, but that of His foes. Such a representation might have been expected had it been the prophet's design to describe the sufferings of our Lord; he does not describe the sufferings themselves, but he does most clearly depict their grand result. If we take a deeply spiritual sight of our Lord's passion, such as a prophet would be likely to have before Him in vision, we see upon His garments, as the result of His sufferings, not so much His own blood as the blood of the enemies whom in death He overthrew.

The passage is poetical: the battle is a spiritual one; the conflict is with sin and with the powers of darkness; and the conqueror returns from the fight having utterly destroyed His foes, of which His blood-dyed garments are the surest evidence. Our Lord's passion was the battle of all battles, upon which the whole campaign of His life turned; and had He not there and then vanquished all our adversaries, and had He not at the resurrection come back as One who had trampled down all His foes, then there had been no glorious appearing in the latter days. That first combat is the cause of the ultimate triumph. I look upon this sixty-third of Isaiah as the prophetic statement of the event described by Paul in Colossians 2:15:—"And having spoiled principalities and powers, he made a show of them openly, triumphing over them in it." On the resurrection morning it would have been correct poetically to have used the language of our text. Unseen spirits, viewing our Lord after a spiritual manner, might have exclaimed as they beheld the risen Savior—

> Who is this that comes from Edom,
>   All his raiment stain'd with blood;
> To the slave proclaiming freedom;
>   Bringing and bestowing good:
> Glorious in the garb he wears,
> Glorious in the spoils he bears?

I mean so to use the passage this morning, with a consciousness that I am not accommodating it, nor taking it from its natural sense at all; but rather placing it in the light of its first great fulfillment. I have not concealed from you its relation to the Second Advent, when the Lord Jesus shall appear in victory "clothed with a vesture dipped in blood"; but at the same time this is a picture of salvation rather than destruction, and its hero appears as "mighty to save," in fulfillment of a divine proclamation: "Behold, thy salvation cometh." The scene before us describes an interposition of the Messiah; the return of the divinely appointed champion from the defeat of His enemies. As it is evidently a picture of salvation rather than of damnation; as the main feature in it is that He is mighty to save; as the great and chief element of the whole thing is that the year of His redeemed is come, and that the warrior's own arm has brought salvation to His people; I cannot for a moment question that this text is applicable to the first coming of Christ. Then He did battle with the hosts of sin and death and hell, and so vanquished them that in His resurrection He returned with the keys of death and of hell at His girdle. Then was He seen as "mighty to save." Now lend me your hearts as well as your ears, while I proceed to the great subject before us, and may the Holy Spirit grant us His gracious aid!

I. First, in my text there is A PROCLAMATION: "Behold, the Lord hath proclaimed unto the end of the world, Say ye to the daughter of Zion, Behold, thy salvation cometh; behold, his reward is with him, and his work before him. And they shall call them, The holy people, The redeemed of the Lord: and thou shalt be called, Sought out, A city not forsaken." The commentators as a whole can see no connection between the sixty-third chapter and the preceding part of the Book of Isaiah; but surely that connection is plain enough to the common reader. In these verses the coming of the Savior is proclaimed, and in the next chapter that coming is seen in vision, and the evangelical prophet beholds the Savior so vividly that he is startled, and inquires, "Who is this?"

Let us consider this proclamation broadly; for we have no time to dwell upon its details. I desire to apply its spiritual lessons as I go on, aiming chiefly at the comfort of those who are in soul trouble. Are any of you oppressed with a sense of sin? Do you see sin to be an enemy too powerful for you to overcome? Are you unable to escape out of the hand of the enemy? Here is a proclamation. God, the ever-gracious One, demands you attention while, as a King, He proclaims His word of mercy to the daughter of Zion: "Behold, thy salvation cometh."

This great announcement tells you that *there is a salvation from without*. Within your heart there is nothing that can save you: all within you is carnal, sold under sin. Out of bondage only bondage can arise. The proclamation is, "Behold, thy salvation cometh." It comes to you from a source beyond yourself; it does not arise from within you, for it could not do so. Salvation comes from God Himself. What a blessing, that when there was no salvation in you, nor the possibility of its coming from within, it came from above! Salvation comes not from man's will, or merit, or efforts. "Salvation is of the Lord." "It is not of him that willeth, nor of him that runneth, but of God that showeth mercy." O soul, if the Lord God comes to save you, Edom and Bozrah, sin and hell, will soon be broken in pieces! The power of your sins, and the tyranny of your sinful habits, the cords of your companionships, the bondage of Satan himself, must speedily yield when salvation comes from the eternal throne, and the mighty One of Israel hastens to the rescue.

It is a salvation which comes through a person. "Thy salvation cometh; behold, his reward is with him, and his work before him." The great salvation which we have to proclaim is salvation by Jesus Christ, the Son of God. Jesus of Nazareth, who died on the cross, is also the Son of the Highest. Him hath God set forth to be the propitiation for sin, to be the deliverer of mankind from the bondage of evil. Behold Him, the Lamb of God which taketh away the sin of the world! Behold Him, the beloved of the Father! Power to save unto the uttermost is laid upon Him; He is a Savior, and a great one. Remember this, and do not look to rites and ceremonies, or to creeds and doctrines, but to the person of Jesus who is God and man. Simeon said, when he beheld our Lord as a babe, "Mine eyes have seen thy salvation": truly we may say the same with emphasis when we see Him in His resurrection.

This salvation leads to holiness; for the test says of those who receive the Savior, "They shall call them, The holy people." If, dear friend, you are to be saved, you are also to be sanctified; indeed, that sanctification is the essence of salvation. This will give you great joy, I know; for no man really desires salvation, rightly understanding what he desires, without meaning by it that he may be saved from the power of sin, and may no longer be in servitude to his own lusts, or to the wicked customs of the world. Sinners, rejoice; the great Jehovah proclaims to you a salvation which shall so purify you that you shall be saved from your sins, and shall be called "The holy people." Is not that the best news you have ever heard?

Further, *it is salvation by redemption*; for it is written that they shall be called "The redeemed of the Lord." In the sacred Scriptures there is no salvation for men except by redemption. You have enslaved yourselves, and your heritage is under bond; and therefore you and it must be ransomed. Behold, your Redeemer pays your ransom. His own heart's blood Messiah pours forth, that men who have been enslaved may be set free. Redemption by substitution is the gospel. Christ stands in your stead, a sufferer because of your sins: you are set in Christ's stead, rewarded because of His righteousness, accepted because of His acceptableness with God. This is a sure and satisfactory salvation; a salvation which satisfies the conscience of man as well as the justice of God. This salvation is to you without money and without price; but it cost the Redeemer, nothing less than Himself. Behold in Him the ransom paid in full, so that He bids you go free. He saith, "Fear not: for I have redeemed thee." Tell it out among the heathen, tell it out among the fallen, that there is salvation, salvation by a great redemption, full and free. All that lost ones have to do is joyfully to accept the purchased freedom, and go forth in joy and peace.

This salvation is complete. "Thou shalt be called, Sought out, A city not forsaken." See the beginning of it: "Thou shalt be called, Sought out." See the end of it: thou shalt be called, "Not forsaken." You will not begin with God, but God will begin with you. You shall be sought out, and then you will seek Him. He seeks you even now. You shall be known as one that was sought out, a sheep that wandered, a piece of money that fell into the dust; but, behold, you are sought out till the Savior says, "Rejoice with me; for I have found my sheep which was lost." This is the gracious beginning of salvation. But suppose the Lord found you, and then left you; you would perish after all. But it shall not be so; for the same Lord who calls you "Sought out" also calls you "Not forsaken." You shall never be forsaken of the grace of God, nor of the God of grace. Whatever you may be, notwithstanding your weakness and your waywardness, you shall be known in heaven by these two names—first, that you were "sought out," and next, that you were "not forsaken." It makes my eyes sparkle with delight to think how fully those two names describe myself. I delight to sing—

> Jesus sought me when a stranger,
> > Wandering from the fold of God;
> He, to rescue me from danger,
> > Interposed his precious blood.

Equally true is that other word, "not forsaken." Notwithstanding all my provocations and rebellions, I believe in Him who hath said, "I will never leave thee, nor forsake thee." I shall not die but live, because He is with me.

This salvation which we have to proclaim to you, then, is one that comes to you who lie despairing at hell's dark door. You shall be sought out according to the sovereign grace of God. Jesus comes to you when you are afraid to come to Him. You fear that if you were to commence the march to heaven you would faint by the way; but He who travels in the greatness of His strength is come that you may lean on Him. You that are smitten with faintness of heart because you know your own weakness and changeableness, you shall be helped and sustained to the end. He that begins the good work of grace in the heart is no changeling, but He will carry it on and carry it out to the praise of the glory of His grace. Oh, this is worth proclaiming! Oh, for a silver trumpet with which to blow a blast that might awaken all who slumber! There is salvation; salvation by a glorious Person; salvation unto holiness; salvation by redemption; a salvation so perfect that those who receive it shall never be forsaken. O dear hearer, do you not wish to have this salvation? Do you not desire to obtain it at once? If you do, I beg you to follow me now, while I direct you to Him who is the salvation of His people. While we fix our eyes upon the glorious Person raised up and upheld by God, by whom this salvation is brought to the sons of men, I pray that you may believe in Him unto eternal life.

II. To introduce this Person, I now come to consider THE QUESTION "Who is this that cometh from Edom?" The prophet beholds in vision the Captain of salvation, returning from battle, arrayed like the warriors of whom we read, "the valiant men are in scarlet." He beholds the majestic march of this mighty Conqueror, and he cries, "Who is this?" Now when a soul first hears the proclamation of God's salvation, and then sees Jesus coming to him, he says, "Who is this?" *The question in part arises from anxiety*, as if he said, "Who is this that espouses my cause? Is He able to save? Has He really conquered my enemies?" The heart inquires, "You preach to me a Savior, but what sort of a Savior is He? Is He able? Is He willing? Is He tender? Is He strong?" What *you* are, dear friend, is easily told, for you are lost and ruined; but the great question you need to consider, is—Who is *He* that comes to save you? And you may well with anxiety put the question, because it concerns your own personal welfare—"Is He such a Savior as will be able to save me?"

The question arose from anxiety, but *it also indicates ignorance*. We do not any of us know our Lord Jesus to the full yet. "Who is this?" is a question we may still put to the sacred oracle. Paul, after he had known Christ fifteen years, yet desired that he might know Him; for His love passeth knowledge. If this passage refers to our resurrection, it is a remarkable truth that even His disciples did not know Him when He had arisen. Launcelot Andrewes, in a famous sermon on this text, enlarges on this point, and I am content to borrow from Him. Magdalene, of all the women in the world, ought to have known Him, but she supposed Him to be the gardener. The two disciples that walked with Him to Emmaus were with Him long enough to have spied Him out, and yet in all that long walk they did not know Him. Do you wonder that they did not discern their Lord? Would it have been a marvel had they said, "Who is this? Behold Him traveling in the greatness of His strength, and yet a few hours ago we saw Him dead, and helped to lay His lifeless body in Joseph's tomb! Who is this? We saw Him stripped! They took His garments from Him on the cross, and now He is 'glorious in His apparel.' Who is this? His enemies made nothing of Him, they spat in His face, they nailed Him to the tree; but, lo, His garments are dyed with the blood of His foes, and He comes back more than conqueror! Who is this?" I do not wonder that when the Person of Christ first flashes on the sinner's eye, he thinks to himself: He was once a babe at Bethlehem, a weary man before His foes, scourged, spat upon; is this the Savior? And does He come to me and propose that I should put my trust in Him as having overthrown all my adversaries? "Who is this?"

As the sinner looks, and looks again, he cries, "Who is this?" *in delighted amazement.* Is it indeed the Son of God? Does He intervene to save me? The God whom I offended, does He stoop to fight and rout my sins? He without whom was not anything made, heaven's darling, and the delight of angels, can it be He? The soul is astonished, and scarce believes for joy. Yet, beloved, it is even He. This same Jesus is both Lord and God. When He ascended upon high He led captivity captive, and made an open show of His vanquished foes. He nailed the handwriting of ordinances that was against us to His cross; He broke the head of the serpent, and destroyed him that had the power of death, that is, the devil. How could He be less than God? It is He, and none other than He, God over all, blessed forever, who took upon Himself the form of a servant, and was made in the likeness of men, and became obedient to death, even the death of the cross. It is He whom God hath highly exalted, and given Him a name that is above every name, that at the name of Jesus every knee should bow. No wonder that the soul inquires, "Who is this?"

I think *the question is asked, also, by way of adoration.* Such a question is elsewhere so used. Here is an instance—"Who is a God like unto thee, that pardoneth iniquity, and passeth by the transgression of the remnant of his heritage?" So that, as the soul begins to see Jesus, its anxiety is removed by knowledge, and is replaced by an astonishment which ripens into worship. Adoringly the spirit cries, "Who is this?" What a Savior I have! How could it have come about that He should die for me? What a Savior is He in His death! What a Savior in His rising again! What a Savior in His ascension up to heaven! What a Savior in His enthronement! What a Savior in His glorious advent, when He shall come to gather together His own! Who is this? We are lost in wonder as we bow before the infinite majesty of the Son of God, and adore Him as God, our Savior, forever and ever.

It appears from the question that the person asking it knows whence the Conqueror came; for it is written, "Who is this that cometh from Edom, with dyed garments from Bozrah?" Yes, our Redeemer has returned from death, as said the Psalmist, "Thou wilt not leave any soul in hell, neither wilt thou suffer thine Holy One to see corruption." He came again from the land of the enemy. He died and descended into the regions of the dead; but He loosed the bands of death, for He could not be holden of them. He went forth to fight with all the adversaries of our souls, even with all the powers of darkness. It was a terrible battle. How thick and fast the shafts flew at the commencement of the fight! Our hero soon knew the garments rolled in blood, for He became covered with a bloody sweat. He flinched not from the horrible conflict, although His body had become one bleeding wound. How sharp were the swords that wounded Him, when His friends proved cowards, and one of them betrayed Him! How terrible were the blades that sheathed themselves in His body and mind! They pierced His hands and His feet: they laid open His very heart. His head was bleeding with the thorns, and His back with the knotted scourges; but He ceased not to grapple with the evil powers. He said, "This is your hour," and full well He found it so. He had in the midst of the fight to groan as well as sweat; that cry was forced from Him, "My God, my God, why hast thou forsaken me?" But quickly followed the victorious shout of "It is finished," and there and then He hurled His tremendous adversary headlong, crushed His head, and left Him fallen, no more to rise!

> "'Tis finished," said his dying breath,
> And shook the gates of hell.

As on this Resurrection day we see our Lord come back to us, we perceive His garments sprinkled with the blood of all who strove against us. I beseech you to lay hold of this, and trust my blessed Lord; for He has fought with all the enemies of our souls, and He has returned from the enemy's country, leading captivity captive. We may look at Him this day right trustfully, for His fight is over, and His enemies are crushed, as grapes in the wine vat. We not only trust our Lord, but we worship Him this day as King of kings and Lord of lords.

> Bruisèd is the serpent's head,
> Hell is vanquish'd, death is dead
> And to Christ gone up on high,
> Captive is captivity.   Alleluia!

Next notice that *the prophet in vision observes the color of the Conqueror's garments:* "Who is this that cometh from Edom, with dyed garments from Bozrah?" Red is not Christ's color; hence the question arises, "Wherefore art thou red in thine apparel?" Our Beloved's garments are whiter than any fuller can make them. The glory of His purity is such that we say to ourselves, "Red, why, that is the color of Edom, the adversary! Red, that is the color of the earth of our manhood! Red is the color of our scarlet sins." Why is He red? Brethren, although the text treats of the blood of His adversaries, yet I would have you devoutly think of our Lord literally as shedding His own blood, for his victory was thus accomplished. The text sets forth the result of that blood-shedding in the overthrow of His enemies and ours; but we cannot separate the effect from the cause. As a matter of fact, when our Lord's own blood was shed, sin and death and hell were trodden down and destroyed as grapes in the winepress. When He was suffering He was then smiting down His enemies. By the shedding of His own blood He was shedding the blood of His foes. The life of the powers of darkness was taken away by His death. When I see Jesus coming back literally covered with His own blood, I discern Him spiritually as encrimsoned with the slaughter of evil and its abettors. Glory be to His name! I shall never cease to look upon my Lord in the red colors as in the prime of His beauty. The blood-red colors are the colors of victory. He never looks so lovely as when He appears as "a Lamb that has been slain." I remember how Rutherford seems to glow and burn when in his prose poetry he talks of "the bonnie red man." That crimson vest is His most royal garment. He hath taken away all our transgressions and iniquities, and covered all our scarlet sins, and we see the blood of them in His blood. Glory be to the bleeding Christ, I say! If there be one hallelujah louder than any other, let it be unto Him who wears the vesture dipped in blood. His own blood is the token and proof that the blood of all His spiritual foes has been shed. Our warfare is accomplished and our sin is pardoned. Behold the colors of atonement, for they are the ensigns of eternal victory.

> Why that blood his raiment staining?
> 'Tis the blood of many slain;
> Of his foes there's none remaining,
> None the contest to maintain:
> Fallen they are no more to rise,
> All their glory prostrate lies.

But yet the question comes from one who perceives that the Conqueror is royally arrayed. "This that is glorious in his apparel." O dear hearers, the Jesus we have to preach to you is no mean Savior; He is clothed with glory and honor because of the suffering of death. He wears today a greater splendor than adorned the sons of Aaron; our great High Priest hath put on all His jewels. He wears also the majesty of His Kingship: "On his head are many crowns." He is this day arrayed in light and glory. His majesty is too bright for mortal eyes to gaze upon. When the beloved John beheld Him he fell at His feet as dead. He is "glorious in his apparel."

The question ends with "traveling in the greatness of his strength." He did not come back from slaughtering our enemies feeble and wounded, but He returned in majestic march, like a victor who would have all men know that His force is irresistible. The earth shook beneath our Lord's feet on the resurrection morning, for "there was a great earthquake." The Roman guards became as dead men at His appearing. Beloved, the Lord Jesus Christ is no petty, puny Savior. He is traveling to meet poor sinners; but He is traveling in the greatness of His strength. "All power is given unto me in heaven and in earth," said He. As He travels through the nations it is as a strong man against whom none can stand, mighty to rescue every soul that puts its trust in Him.

There is the question. I leave it with you, praying that every soul here that is oppressed by the powers of hell, may ask the question, "Who is this that cometh from Edom?"

III. Thirdly, let us consider THE ANSWER. Upon this I must be brief.

No one can answer for Jesus: *He must speak for Himself.* Like the sun, He can only be seen by His own light. He is His own interpreter. Not even the angels could explain the Savior: they get no further than desiring to look into the things which are in Him. He Himself answers the question, "Who is this?" His personality comes out: "I, the Lord Jesus. It is none other than myself who has come forth to overthrow the adversary." The speaker was too modest to ask the mighty Savior who He was; but that Savior was not too lofty to give Him the information which was desired. O poor heart! Jesus will show Himself to you if you desire to know Him. In His own light you will see Him, and if you are bewildered and befogged, but yet truly anxious, He will manifest Himself to you in His great love, and say to you, "It is I; be not afraid."

The answer which our Lord gives is twofold. He described Himself first as a *speaker*: "I that speak in righteousness." Is He not the Word? Every word that Christ speaks is true: He speaks not in falsehood, but in righteousness. The gospel which He proclaims is a just and righteous one, meeting both the claims of God and the demands of conscience. O soul, if thou wilt hearken to Jesus thou shalt hear that from Him which thou couldst never hear from any other lip! "Never man spoke like this man." He will speak of God's holiness, and yet He will speak to thy comfort. He will reveal God's justice, and yet God's love to thee. Oh, hear thou what the Christ has to say, and believe every word of it without a cavil, for therein lies salvation. "Hear, and your soul shall live."

Our Lord also describes Himself as *a Savior*: "I that speak in righteousness, mighty to save." Now, observe that the word "mighty" is joined with His saving, and not with His destroying. Although He can crush His foes as easily as a man can crush with His feet the berries of the grape, the prophet does not speak of Him as "mighty to tread down his enemies." He will prove Himself thus mighty in that day of vengeance which is in His heart; but just now He reveals Himself in the year of His redeemed as "mighty to save." Rejoice in this, O my hearers! The Lord Jesus Christ is a Savior, and He is grand in that capacity. Nothing is beyond His power in the line of salvation. He saith, "Him that cometh to me I will in no wise cast out." There is no manner of sin which He cannot forgive; there is no sort of hardness of heart which He cannot remove; there are no spiritual difficulties which He cannot surmount. "His reward is with him, and his work before him." "He shall not fail, nor be discouraged." Oh that He stood here this morning instead of me! I do but prattle concerning Him, and yet it is the best that I can do. If you use the eyes of faith, my Lord, who hath overcome the foes of His redeemed, stands before you today; and if you ask who He is, He proclaims Himself, for He would have you know Himself. To know Jesus is the first, the chief, the highest piece of human knowledge. He is your teacher, and this is your lesson. He answers the question of the prophetic catechism, and when it is asked, "Who is this?" He replies, "I that speak in righteousness, mighty to save." Fall at His feet, and love and adore Him this day, and then your heaven shall begin below.

Thus have we gone through the text in a very poor and hurried way; for I want just a few minutes to make practical use of the subject ere I send you away.

May the Holy Ghost, now apply the truth with power! Poor troubled one! Thy sins are many, and they grievously oppress thee. Thou seest no hope of escape from the justice of God, or from the power of evil within thy nature. Hearken to the proclamation, as I dwell upon it again. "Behold, thy salvation cometh." Jesus can save you, for He is "mighty to save!"

He can save *you*; for He has saved others like you. He has these many years kept His hand at this work. Your case will not perplex Him; He is at home at the business of saving sinners. The chief of sinners was saved long ago; and if the chief, then, you, although you may be the next greatest, can be saved. Jesus has never been put to a nonplus yet. He that conquered Edom and Bozrah, He that led captivity captive and vanquished all the hosts of hell shall never be defeated. Do not tell me that His arm is shortened, that He cannot save. He can save *you*, you who now desire to be made holy. You with the hard heart, who desire to have it softened, He can do the mighty deed. He can raise the spiritually dead and even restore those who have become corrupt. He can do it, though nobody else can.

He can overthrow all your enemies. Satan has you now in his grasp, and you are not able to war with him. One evil passion or another binds you. You seem watched like Peter in prison, and bound even as he was; but He who loosed Peter can release you. Jesus can say to the prisoners, "Go forth," and forth they shall go. There is no temptation, no sin, no infernal influence from which He cannot rescue His chosen. He is so mighty to save that He can deliver every soul that trusts in Him, however great its extremity. Leave your enemies to Jesus; they baffle you, but He can rout them. His garment is already dyed with their blood, wherefore be not afraid!

He can do this alone. If you trust Jesus, and none but Jesus, you have an all-sufficient salvation. "I have trodden the winepress alone, and of the people there was none with me." "I looked, and there was none to help; and I wondered that there was none to uphold: therefore mine own arm brought salvation unto me." Poor sinner! Hang on to Jesus and His one salvation. If you have no other sort of hope, if thou canst see no good thing in thyself, if thy prayers die on thy lips, if thou canst not weep, if thou canst not feel, if thou hast not even so much as jot of anything that is commendable about thee, still cling thou to Jesus, to Jesus only. The great battle of salvation He fought single-handed; and He can save thee single-handed. He is exalted to be a Prince and a Savior, and He will not stain His princedom by failing in salvation. I fear I have never done more in my own salvation than rather to hinder than help my Lord, and yet I know that though I believe not, He abideth faithful. He will stand to His office, even though I fail in my pledges. When He saves, He does truly save. He is master of the business. He put Himself apprentice to it when He was here below, and set to work to heal all manner of sickness, and He never failed even then; but now that He has gone through death and hell for us, and made Himself perfect through suffering, He is a master workman, and He can save in the teeth of all opposition. Do but trust Him, and thou shalt find it so.

Let me add to this, dear troubled friend, that He is able to save you *now*. Do you notice that verse, "The day of vengeance is in mine heart, and the year of my redeemed is come?" I leaped with joy at those words as I studied them. Yes, I thought,

I will tell these sinners that the day of vengeance is in God's heart, and I will warn them that if they do not turn to Him He will destroy them. Ah! But that vengeance is as yet in His heart; He lets it lie there in His long-suffering patience. But *the year of His redeemed is come:* it is present, it is now. It is not, "Today will I destroy you"; but, "Today, if ye will hear his voice, harden not your hearts, as in the provocation." Today is the day of salvation: "the year of my redeemed is come." We speak of our dates as "*Anno Domini,*" and so they are: these days are in the year of our Lord. We live in the years of our Redeemer, years of His redeemed, years of pardoning love. Oh, that *you* would come now that your year is come! Jesus is able to save you at this hour. This morning in February, this cold and bitter morning, when the east wind searches you to the very marrow, the Lord Jesus Christ can warm your hearts with a summertide of love. It was such a morning as this when I first found my Lord: when the snowflakes fell so abundantly, each one seemed to say that Jesus had made me whiter than snow. Even this cruel east wind will breathe comfort to you if you will look to my Lord dressed in His vesture dipped in blood. Behold the glorious apparel of His love and righteousness. He comes back from death and hell triumphant, so that you may never come under their yoke. He proclaims life to you because your foes are dead. He washes your garments white because His are dyed with blood. You shall live forever because He died, and you shall triumph because He has won the battle on your behalf. You shall go forth conquering and to conquer because He conquers.

Jesus has done the work already. There is nothing to be endured by Him in order to save you from your sins: the expiation is made, the redemption is paid, the righteousness is wrought out. Of this salvation our Lord said, at the moment when He won the victory, "It is finished"; and finished it is forever. Without seam, and woven from the top throughout, was the garb the Savior's body wore, and now He presents a garment like to it to every naked sinner who trusts Him, and He says, "Put it on." It is freely given though it was dearly wrought. It cost our Lord His life to weave it, His blood to dye it; but to the sinner it is a free gift, and if he will but have it, he also shall be glorious in his apparel, and Jesus will strengthen him till he also shall travel in the greatness of His strength. Oh that you would believe in Jesus Christ this morning!

It is a sad wonder that men do not believe in Jesus. It is a mournful wonder that you, who have been hearing the gospel for so many years, do not believe in Him. What are you at? Why, if somebody were to preach to you any other gospel than what I have delivered, you would grow angry, you would not hear it. Why is it that you delight to hear the gospel, and yet will not accept it to your own salvation? Many of you have a great admiration of my Lord, after a fashion, and you love to hear me praise Him; but what is it to you? What can He be to you unless you trust Him? "Oh, but I don't feel my sins." Have I not told you many times that salvation does not lie in your feelings? "Oh, but I am not—" Have I not told you over and over again that it is not what *you* are, but what Jesus is? Hearken unto me. Cease from self, and come to Jesus just as you are. Let us finish by each one of us singing this verse from the heart, and all of us together with our tongues:—

> A guilty, weak, and helpless worm,
>   On Christ's kind arms I fall:
> He is my strength and righteousness,
>   My Jesus and my all.

SHUTTING, SEALING, AND COVERING; *OR,* MESSIAH'S GLORIOUS WORK

SERMON NO. 1,681

DELIVERED ON LORD'S DAY MORNING, SEPTEMBER 24, 1882.

Seventy weeks are determined upon thy people and upon thy holy city, to finish the transgression, and to make an end of sins, and to make reconciliation for iniquity, and to bring in everlasting righteousness, and to seal up the vision and prophecy, and to anoint the most Holy—Daniel 9:24.

THE Lord God appointed a set time for the coming of His Son into the world; nothing was left to chance. Infinite wisdom dictated the hour at which the Messiah should be born, and the moment at which He should be cut off. His advent and His work are the highest point of the purpose of God, the hinge of history, the center of providence, the crowning of the edifice of grace, and therefore peculiar care watched over every detail. Once in the end of the world hath the Son of God appeared to put away sin by the sacrifice of Himself, and this is the event before which all other events must bow. The studious mind will be delighted to search out the reasons why the Messiah came not before, and why He did not tarry till yet later ages. Prophecies declared the date; but long before infallible wisdom had settled it for profoundest reasons. It was well that the Redeemer came: it was well that He came in what Scripture calls the fullness of time, even in these last days.

Note, again, that the Lord told His people somewhat darkly, but still with a fair measure of clearness, when the Christ would come. Thus He cheered them when the heavy clouds of woe hung over their path. This prophecy shone like a star in the midst of the sorrow of Israel: so bright was it that at the period when Christ came there was a general expectation of Him. Holy men and women, diligent in the study of the Scriptures, were waiting for Him: Simeon was waiting for the consolation of Israel, and Anna looked for redemption in Jerusalem with others of like mind. Not only the Jews, but the Samaritans expected Him, for the woman at the well exclaimed, "I know that Messias cometh, which is called Christ." Even in heathen lands there was remarkable

659

cessation from stir and battle; an unusual peace reigned over all the nations, and the hush of expectation ruled the hour—

> No war, or battle's sound,
> Was heard the world around:
>   The idle spear and shield were high uphung;
> The hooked chariot stood
> Unstained with hostile blood;
>   The trumpet spoke not to the armèd throng;
> And kings sat still with awful eye,
> As if they surely knew their sovran Lord was by.

Men were looking out for the coming One; for the corn of earth was ripe for the reaper. Men were on the tiptoe of expectation, and wondered when the promised Prince would arrive. Alas, they knew Him not when He appeared. After this fashion are things at the present moment with regard to the Second Advent of our Lord Jesus Christ. "Of that day and of that hour knoweth no man"; but it is known unto God, and fixed in the roll of His eternal purposes. "Known unto God are all his works from the creation of the world," and especially those grand works which concern the person of our adorable Lord Jesus. He shall come as God hath appointed: the vision of His glory shall not tarry. He has given us suggestive hints as to that glorious appearing; and He has plainly taught us to be looking for and listening unto the day of the Lord. Among His last words are these, "Surely I come quickly": these are words of consolation as well of warning. He bids us watch constantly for the coming of the Lord, that it overtake us not as a thief in the night; and He assures us that He will descend from heaven with a shout, with the voice of the archangel, and the trump of God: wherefore comfort one another with the glad tidings, and whenever your hearts sicken because of abounding sin, hear ye with the ear of faith the voice of promise crying, "Behold, the Bridegroom cometh." Rest assured that He cometh who will in the fullest and most manifest sense finish transgression, and make an end of sin, and bring in everlasting righteousness. The advent of the Well-beloved is the consolation of His mourning saints. Both at His first and second appearings the Lord not only cometh to drive away the wicked as chaff, but also to comfort and exalt His elect: it is a day that shall burn as an oven, and yet to the redeemed it will be the gladdest day that ever dawned.

The first advent of our Lord is spoken of in our text as ordained to be ere the seventy weeks were finished, and the city should be destroyed; and so it was even as the prophet had spoken. I shall not occupy your time by attempting to fix the beginning and the end of the period intended by the seventy weeks, and the seven weeks and three-score and two weeks. That is a deep study, requiring much research and learning, and I conceive that the discussion of such a subject would be of no great practical use to us this Sabbath morning. You will be better nourished upon the Lord Himself than upon times and seasons. Suffice it to believe that Jesus Christ our Lord, the Messiah, came exactly as it was prophesied, and remained on earth as it was foretold He should do: in the middle of the predestined week He was cut off, when He had completed three years and a half of saving ministry, and within another period of like length the gospel was preached throughout all nations, and Messiah's peculiar relation to Israel was cut off. At another time it may afford you profitable contemplation if you consider the four hundred and ninety years from the decree of the king for rebuilding to the overthrow of Jerusalem.

We will at this present hour survey the work of the *Messiah*—that is His Hebrew name, or of *Christ*, which is the Greek interpretation thereof. *Let us survey the work of the Anointed.* Secondly, *let us inquire as to our participation in it;* and then, thirdly, *let us contemplate the consequences which follow upon us being sharers in it, or upon our not being participants in it.* Oh for a measure of the anointing, that we may fitly meditate upon our great theme. Come, Holy Spirit and rest upon us.

I. First, Let us survey the Messiah's work. According to my text it divides itself into two grand works, which two works subdivide themselves in each case into three particulars.

The first work of our Lord Jesus Christ is the overthrow of evil, and it is thus described,—"To finish the transgression, and to make an end of sins, and to make reconciliation for iniquity." But our Lord's labor is not all spent upon down-pulling work; He comes to build up, and His second work is the setting up of righteousness in the world, described again by three sentences: "To bring in everlasting righteousness, and to seal up the vision and prophecy, and to anoint the Most Holy."

The first work of the Messiah is the overthrow of evil. This overthrow of evil is described by three words. If I were to give you a literal translation from the Hebrew I might read the passage thus: "To shut up the transgression, to seal up sin, and to cover up iniquity." According to learned men, those are the words which are here used, and the three put together are a singularly complete description of the putting away of sin. First, it is *shut up:* it is, as it were, taken prisoner, and confined in a cell; the door is fastened, and it is held in durance: it is out of sight; held to a narrow range; unable to exercise the power it once possessed. In a word, it is "restrained"—so the margin of our Bibles reads it. The Hebrew word signifies to hold back, to hold in, to arrest, to keep in prison, to shut in or shut up. Its dominion is finished, for sin itself is bound. Christ has led captivity captive.

But it is not enough to shut up the vanquished tyrant, unless he be shut up forever; and therefore, lest there should be any possibility of his breaking loose again, the next sentence is, "*To seal up.*" The uses of the seal are many, but here it is employed for certainty of custody. Just as when Daniel was thrown into the lions' den the king sealed the stone with his own signet and with the signet of his lords; or, better still, as when our divine Master was laid in the grave, they rolled the stone to the mouth of the sepulcher, and His enemies set a seal and a watch, lest His body should be stolen by His disciples. In His case,

> Vain the stone, the watch, the seal,
> Christ has burst the gates of hell.

But sin cannot thus arise. It is imprisoned in the sepulcher of Jesus, and never can it come forth; for the seal royal of the immutable God is set upon the door. Thus is sin placed doubly out of sight: it is shut up and sealed up, as a document put into a case and then sealed down. "Finished" and "made an end of" are the two words used in our authorized version, and they give the essence of the meaning. To borrow a figure from current events,—Arabi, the Egyptian rebel, is shut up as our prisoner, and his defeat is sealed, therefore his rebellion is finished and an end made of it. Even thus is it with transgression: our Lord has vanquished evil, and certified the same under the hand and seal of the Omnipotent, and therefore we may with rapture hear Him say, "It is finished," and also behold Him rise from the dead to seal our justification.

Yet, as if this might not suffice, the next term in the Hebrew is *to cover up;* for the word to make reconciliation or expiation is usually in the Hebrew to cover over. "Blessed is the man whose transgression is forgiven, whose sin is covered." Christ has come to cover sin, to atone for it, and so to hide it. His glorious merits and substitutionary sufferings and death put away sin so completely that God Himself beholds it no more. He has blotted it out, cast it into the sea, and removed it from us as far as the east is from the west. The two former sentences speak of finishing transgression and making an end of sin, and these expressions are full and complete, while this third one explains the means by which the work is done, namely, by an expiation which covers up every trace of sin. Thus in the three together we have a picture of the utter extinction of sin both as to its guilt and its power, aye, and its very existence: it is put into the dungeon and the door is shut upon it; after this the door is sealed and then it is covered up, so that the place of sin's sepulchre cannot be seen anymore forever. Sin was aforetime in God's sight, but through Christ Jesus we read, "Thou hast forgiven the iniquity of thy people; thou hast covered all their sin; thou hast taken away all thy wrath." Sin was in God's way till Christ shut it up, and now it pushes itself no more into the sight of the Lord. Sin was always breaking loose till Jesus sealed it up, and now it cannot come forth to lay any accusation against the justified.

The three words might be put into one word by saying Christ has made a clean sweep of sin of every kind. Whatever may be its special development, whether it be transgression, which means the breaking of bounds, or sin, which is any want of conformity to the law, or iniquity—that is to say, in-equity, or the want of equity, a default in righteousness; in all forms in which it can be described Christ has shut it up, sealed it up, and covered it up by His atoning sacrifice once for all. The depths have covered it; if it be searched for, it cannot be found; our blessed Scapegoat has carried it away into the land of forgetfulness; it shall not be mentioned against us anymore forever. Those three words contain infinitely more of meaning than I have either space or ability to set forth.

Observe, dear friends, that the terms for sin are left in an absolute form. It is said, "to finish transgression," "to make an end of sins," "to make reconciliation for iniquity." Whose transgression is this? Whose sins are these? Whose iniquity is it? It is not said. There is no word employed to set out the persons for whom atonement is made, as is done in verses like these—"Christ loved the church and gave himself for it"; "I lay down my life for the sheep." The mass of evil is left unlabeled, that any penitent sinner may look to the Messiah and find in Him the remover of sin. What transgression is finished? Transgression of every kind. But what sins are made an end of? Sins of every sort—against law and against gospel, against God and against men, sins past, sins present, sins to come. And what iniquity is expiated? Every form of iniquity, whatever falls short by omission, whatever goes beyond by commission. Christ in this passage is spoken of in general terms as removing sins, transgressions, and iniquities in the mass. In other places we read of the objects of His substitution but here all is left indefinite to encourage all. He gives us no catalogue of offenses; for where should He write it? The very heavens could not hold the enumeration; but He just takes the whole, unformed, horrible, black, disgusting mass, and this is what He does with it— He encloses it, fastens it up, and buries it forever. In the words of our version He finishes it, makes an end of it, and makes expiation for it. The Messiah came to wipe out and utterly destroy sin, and this is, and will be, the effect of His work. Put all the three sentences into one and this is the sum of them.

Indulge me for a few minutes while I take the sentences separately and press each cluster by itself. And first notice that it is said he came *to finish the transgression.* As some understand it, our Lord came that in His death transgression might reach its highest development, and sign its own condemnation. Sin reached its finish, its ultimatum, its climax, in the murder of the Son of God. It could not proceed further: the course of malice could no further go. They had stoned the prophets and killed everyone that was sent unto them; but now He came, and God said, "They will reverence my Son," but they did not; on the other hand, they cried, "This is the heir; let us kill him, and the inheritance shall be ours." Sin finished itself when it brought forth the death of the Son of God. It could produce no riper fruit, for no supposable crime can exceed the putting to death of Jesus our Lord. Now hath sin finished itself, and now hath Jesus come to finish it. "Thus far," saith He, "thou shalt go, but no further: here in my wounds and death shall thy proud waves be stayed." Sin virtually committed suicide when it slew the Savior, for His death became its death. The kingdom of sin was overthrown in that day when it smote the Prince of Peace: then was a period put to the dominion of evil; and, to come back to the Hebrew, the Lord restrained transgression, and Satan was bound with a great chain. "The times of this ignorance God winked at; but now commandeth all men everywhere to repent." Sin may no longer range unchecked. Sin is now arrested and held under warrant, restrained under the bonds of law; and from the day of our Lord by the preaching of the gospel sin has become more and more shut up as to its reigning power. Some men have been altogether delivered from the rule of evil, and other men who remain its slaves yet go not to such a pitch of outward riot as they would have done had not Christ appeared. Sin is being besieged; it skulks behind its earthworks; its sorties are becoming fewer and less forcible; and though it is still powerful, the hour of its pride is passed, its head has received a deadly wound: the age has come in which the victory of truth and righteousness is guaranteed by the death of Jesus Christ our Lord. Thy finis is written, O transgression! Written by the pierced hand! Thy huge volume has in it writing long enough and grievous enough, full enough of blasphemy against God and of evil towards men; but now the Lord Jesus takes the pen from thee, and thou shalt write no more, as thou hast done. The huge leviathan of evil has met its match, and is placed under the power of the Avenger. Thus saith the Lord, "Behold, I will put my hook in thy nose and my bridle in thy lips, and I will turn thee by the way by which thou camest." The Lord hath set bounds to the transgression which aforetime broke all bounds. Where sin abounded, grace doth much more abound. Sin is shut up that grace may have liberty. This is one part of our Lord's great work: all glory be unto His name, He has accomplished it with power, and the power of the enemy is broken.

Now take the second sentence, which in our version is, "*To make an end of sin.*" Messiah has come to proclaim so free, so rich, so gracious a pardon to the sons of men that when they receive it sin virtually ceases to be: it is made an end of. The man that is in Christ, and hath Christ for his covenant Head, is this day so delivered from all sin whatsoever, that he may boldly ask the question, "Who shall lay anything to the charge of God's elect?" If Christ has made an end of sin there is an end of it: the matter is ended, and no more is to be said. Down among the dead men let sin lie, forever buried by the right hand of the conquering Savior.

But the Hebrew has it "to seal up sins." Now I take it to mean just this. There are certain handwritings which are against us, and they would be produced against us in court but by order of the judge all these handwritings are sealed up, and regarded as out of sight: no man dare break the seal, and no man can read them unless the seal be broken; therefore they will never be brought against us. They have become virtually null and void. Everything that can be brought as an accusation against God's people is now sealed up and put out of the way once for all, never to be opened and laid to their charge before the living God. Or, if you regard sin as a captive prisoner, you must now see that by Christ's death the prison wherein sin lies is so sealed that the enemy can never come forth again in its ancient power. Sin could once sit on the highest mountain, and look over the world and say, "All this is mine"; and the embodiment of sin could come to Christ and say of all the kingdoms of the world, "All these will I give thee," as though he claimed them all for his own. But it is not so today. The mountain of the Lord's house is this day exalted upon the top of the hills, and though as yet all nations do not flow unto it, yet a glorious company comes streaming up to the temple of the living God, and that company shall increase from day to day. As when a brooklet groweth to a stream, and the streamlet rises to a river, and the river swells till it rolls in fullest force into the shoreless main, so is it yet to be with the ever-growing church of Jesus Christ, which ere long shall carry all before it, and cover the earth with blessing. Evil, thou canst not reign! Jesus has come and overcome thee Himself, and taught man to vanquish thee! Thou canst not come again to the crown thou once hadst, for the seed of the woman hath broken thy head: He shall reign forever and ever, and thou shalt die! Hallelujah! The coffin of sin is both shut up and fastened down with the seal of Christ's victory.

But now, the last expression is in English, He hath come *"to make reconciliation for iniquity"*; that is, to end the strife between God and man by a glorious reconciliation, a making again of peace between these twain; so that God loveth man, and, as a consequence, man loveth God. In the blessed atonement of Christ, God and man meet at a chosen meeting-place. Christ is Jehovah's darling and our delight. A slain Savior is well pleasing to God, and oh, how pleasing He is to a sinner who is deeply under a sense of sin! Here, here is that mercy seat sprinkled with blood where man may speak to God without fear, and where God doth speak to man without wrath. Here righteousness and peace have met together; mercy and truth have kissed each other. Oh, glorious reconciliation which Christ has made by honoring the law in His life and in His death.

Now, take the Hebrew for it, and read the sentence thus,—to cover iniquity. Oh, what bliss this is: to think, dear friends, that sin is now once for all covered! Not as though it lay rankling there beneath some coverlet through which fire might burn, or lightning strike; but Christ's covering is such that, if you could heap hell over sin, it were not so hidden; and if you could pile worlds upon it, were not so concealed; and if all heaven bowed to overlay it, it were not so out of sight as when Jesus buried it deeper than the lowest depths, where no memory can remember it, or mind perceive it.

> Our guilt shall vanish quite away,
>   Though black as hell before,
> Shall be dissolved beneath the sea,
>   And shall be found no more.

This is what is to be done with the whole kingdom of evil, as well with the power of it as with the guilt of it. Dagon is to fall and to be broken, and the very stump of him is to be demolished. As when the darkness flies before the sun, not a trace of its blackness is left, so is sin to be destroyed utterly from the redeemed of the Lord. It is not merely the guilt of sin that is shut up and sealed and covered, but sin itself, its power, its dominion, its habit, its defilement, the dread that comes of it, and the fear and the burning of heart which it engenders. All the foul birds of sin's filthy cage must fly away, never to return, chased away by the glorious work of Him who shall save His people from their sins. For this the Messiah was cut off, and this by His death is achieved.

> O love! thou bottomless abyss!
>   My sins are swallow'd up in thee;
> Cover'd is my unrighteousness,
>   Nor spot of guilt remains on me.
> While Jesus' blood, through earth and skies,
> Mercy, free, boundless mercy cries!

I fail to describe this triumphant overthrow of sin and Satan. I have neither wisdom nor language answerable to such a theme. I invite you now for a few minutes to consider the second work, namely, *the setting up of righteousness*. This is set before us in three expressions: first, in the words "to bring in everlasting righteousness." And what is that? Why, His own righteousness which is from everlasting to everlasting, and will never be taken way from those who have it, and will never cease to be their beauty and their glorious Jesus. The work of Christ in His life and death is by God imputed to His people: indeed, it is theirs because they are one with Christ. He is the Lord their righteousness, and they are the righteousness of God in Him. Saints are so righteous in Jesus Christ that they are more righteous than Adam was before he fell, for he had but a creature righteousness, and they have the righteousness of the Creator: he had a righteousness which he lost, but believers have a righteousness which they can never lose, an everlasting righteousness. Nor is that all the meaning of our text: those to whom God imputes righteousness, to them also He imparts righteousness. He makes them pure in heart, He changes their desires, He makes them love that which is right and just and good, and so He gives them grace to lead godly, sober, honest, and holy lives. This righteousness shall not be crushed out of them, for the work of the Spirit shall continue until they shall become perfect, and be meet to dwell with God in light. Happy are those spirits to whom Christ gives an everlasting righteousness, for theirs is the kingdom and in it they shall shine forth as the sun. They are right and they shall be right; they are true and they shall never degenerate into falsehood; they are God's own children and they shall go on to develop the image of Christ, their elder brother, till they shall be without spot or wrinkle or any such thing. This Christ came to do: He imputes and imparts righteousness, and thus brings in everlasting righteousness as the foundation of His kingdom.

Next, in order to the setting up of a kingdom of righteousness He is come that He may "seal up vision and prophecy." That is, by fulfilling all the visions and the prophecies of the Old Testament in Himself, He ends both prophecy and vision. He seals up visions and prophecies so that they shall no more be seen or spoken; they are closed, and no man can add to them; and therefore—and that is the point to note— the gospel is forever settled, to remain eternally the same. Christ has set up a kingdom that shall never be moved. His truth can never be changed by any novel revelation. If any man come to you and say, "I am a prophet!" bid him go and find believers among the foolish for to you Jesus has sealed up prophecy and vision, and there is to be no more of it. There is no need of it, because in Christ God has spoken all He means to say concerning the way of salvation. Until such time as Christ Himself shall come the canon is complete; and though there be many voices crying, "Lo, here!" and "Lo, there!" and some so fascinating that they might deceive, if it were possible, the very elect, yet those whom Christ has chosen know the Shepherd's voice, and "a stranger will they not follow, for they know not the voice of strangers." Brethren, there always was something better yet to come in all times till Christ arrived; but after the best there cometh none. A certain philosopher taught *this*; the next philosopher taught *that*, and the next one contradicted this and that, and taught another thing;

while another master arose and contradicted all who went before. So man groped as in the dark for the wall; but now the day has dawned, and the true light shineth, for Christ hath appeared. This, then, is an essential part of the setting up of that which is good—namely, to settle truth on a fixed basis, whereon we may stand steadfast, immovable. The candles are snuffed out because the day itself looks out from the windows of heaven. Rejoice in this, beloved. God makes you righteous in Christ and with Christ, and in order that you shall never be perplexed with change, He sets aside all other teachers, that Christ may be your all in all.

Then, as if this were not enough, and truly it would not be enough, He is also come *to anoint the Most Holy,* or the Holy of Holies, as you may read it. And what means this? Nothing material, for the Holy of Holies, the place into which the High Priest went of old is demolished, and the veil is rent. The most holy place is now the person of the Lord Jesus Christ; He was anointed that God might dwell in Him. Together with Christ the Holy of Holies is now His church, and that church was anointed or dedicated when the Holy Ghost fell at Pentecost, to be with us, and to abide in us forever. That was a noble part of the setting up of the great kingdom of righteousness, when tongues of fire descended and sat upon each of the disciples, and they began to speak with other tongues as the Spirit gave them utterance. This is Christ's work, for which He came, and for which He ascended on high, to set up the truth, to set up righteousness, and to make it everlasting by the dwelling of the Holy Ghost in the church of God in the midst of the sons of men.

Thus you see, in six ways, which condense themselves into two, our Lord set about His lordly enterprise. Heaven rings with the praises of the Messiah who came to destroy the work of sin, and to set up the kingdom of righteousness in the midst of the world.

II. LET US NOW INQUIRE AS TO OUR PARTICIPATION IN THESE TWO WORKS. I will put a few questions as briefly as I can, and I pray God, the Holy Ghost, that every one of us may honestly answer them.

First, dear brethren, Christ has come into the world to do all this good work, but has He done it for us? "God so loved the world, that he gave his only begotten Son." What for? "That whosoever believeth in him might not perish." There is a general aspect to the atonement, but there is quite as surely a special object in it. God loved the world, and therefore He gave His Son. But to what end did He give His Son? Here is the answer, "That whosoever believeth in him might not perish, but have everlasting life." There was a special eye to believers. Come, then, have you believed? The first question that is to help you to answer that inquiry is this—Is your sin shut up as to its power? "Sin shall not have dominion over you" if Christ is in you. How is it between your soul and evil? Is there war or peace? Once you loved sin; you could not have enough of it. Is it so now? Do you still delight in evil? For if you do, the love of God is not in you. Can you still put forth your hand to iniquity as you once did? Then do not pretend that Christ has done anything for you. If you are a believer, your sin may not be absolutely dead, but it is shut up for dead: it is fast held in the condemned cell. It may still breathe, but it is crucified with Christ. How it tugs to get its hands loose from the nails! How it struggles to get its feet down from the tree! But it cannot, for He that nailed it there knew how to drive nails, and how to fasten the offender to the tree. Do you begin to grow weary of iniquity? Is it distasteful and unpleasant to you? And when looking over the day you perceive where you have spoken unadvisedly or acted hastily, or in any other way soiled your character, do you feel as if you would fain wash out every spot with tears? If it be so, Christ has begun with you: He has come to shut up your sin, and to end its reign: it shall no more have dominion over you. It may be in you, but it shall not be on the throne: it may threaten you, but it shall not command you: it may grieve you, but it shall not destroy you. You are under another Master: you serve the Lord Christ. Judge you how this matter fares with you.

The next question arising out of the text is, Is your sin sealed up as to its condemning power? Have you ever felt the power of the Holy Spirit in your soul, saying to you, "Go in peace; thy sins which are many, are all forgiven thee"? Have you clutched that promise, "He that believeth in him is not condemned"? Have you believed in Jesus? Has that blessed word, "There is therefore now no condemnation," breathed a deep calm over your spirit? Some of you do not know what I mean; but others of you do. Oh, what bliss, what a heaven it is to know, "I am washed in the blood of the Lamb—I am delivered, clean delivered from every sin, past, present, and to come, as to any possibility of its being laid to my charge. Christ has put my sins into a bag, sealed them up, hurled that bag into the sea, and flung them out of existence, and they are gone, never to be found again any more." He has made an end of sin. Come, dear hearer, do you know anything about this? If you do not, it is the one thing you want to know, and until you know it you will never have any rest to your spirit, but you will be tossed to and fro as upon a raging sea. "There is no peace, saith my God, to the wicked." There is no peace to any of us till Christ hath made an end of our sin. How is it with your hearts?

And next, is your sin covered as to its appearance before God? Has the Lord Jesus Christ made such an expiation for your sin that it no longer glares in the presence of the Most High, but you can come unto God without dread? Can you hopefully say, "Lord God, thou seest no sin in me, for Thou has covered me with the righteousness of Christ, and washed me in His blood"? Did you ever feel the sweetness of that? It is rapture! I can recollect times when I have been driven to doubt whether it could be true, it seemed too good; and then again, when my faith has revived I have said, "Good as it is, it is true, for it is like God to do these great marvels, and to put away the sins of His people and cover them once for all." Oh then there has been a joy within my spirit not at all like the joy of harvest, or the joy of marriage, or the joy of a firstborn child in the house. No; it is a joy like the bliss of angels, deep, unspeakable, mysterious, divine. Have you ever felt it? You will feel constantly if Christ comes to dwell with you: you will then be assured in your heart that He has made an end of your sin.

Further, let me question you about the next point. Has the Lord Jesus Christ made you righteous? Do you glory in His blood and righteousness, and do you now seek after that which is pure and holy? "Be not deceived; God is not mocked: for whatsoever a man soweth, that shall he also reap." If we continue in sin we shall perish in sin. He is saved who comes out from evil and seeks to live honestly, righteously, soberly, after the manner of the godly and the saintly. Is it so with you? Is there a great and deep change in your spirit, so that you now love those good things which once you despised and ridiculed in others? Oh, if you cannot answer my poor questions, how will you stand before the judgment seat of God when He shall test you as with fire?

Furthermore, are the prophecies and visions sealed up as to you? Are they fulfilled in you? When God declares that He will wash us and make us whiter than snow, is it so with you? When He declares that He will cleanse our blood, which has not yet been cleansed, is it so with you? When He says, "A new heart also will I give them, and a right spirit will I put within them: and I will write my law upon their hearts"; is it so with you? Are you fishing about after empty dreams and fancies, or have you laid hold upon the old prophecies and the ancient visions, and discovered the substance of them to be deeply wrought in your very heart?

Nor is this all: are you anointed to be most holy to the Lord? Are you set apart that you may serve Him? Has the Holy Spirit come upon you, giving you a desire to do good? Have you a wish to rescue the perishing, a longing to bring the wandering sheep back to the great Shepherd's fold? Is the Spirit of God so upon you today that you can truly say, "I am not my own; I am bought with a price?" Jesus, the Messiah, came to do all these things, and if He has not done them to you, then He has not come to you; you are still a stranger, still far off from Him. Oh, may the Lord make you desperately unhappy till you come to Jesus: may you never know what quiet means till you find it at the pierced feet! From this hour may you breathe sighs, and may every pulse be a new agony of spirit, till at last you can say, "Yes, the Messiah was cut off, and cut off for me, and all that He came to do He did for me, and I am a sharer and a partaker in it all."

III. Lastly, we have but a brief interval in which to speak of THE RESULTS OF PARTICIPATING IN ALL THIS. The results! I want a week to speak of them in. They are, first of all, *security.* How can that man be lost whose transgression is finished, and whose sin has ceased to be? What is there for him to dread on earth, in heaven, or in hell? If Christ has put away my sin, I cannot die; if Christ has washed away my guilt, I cannot be condemned; I am safe, and may triumphantly sing—

> More happy, but not more secure,
> The glorified spirits in heaven.

Wherefore, rejoice in this.

And now, inasmuch as you are secure, you are also *reconciled to* God, and made to delight in Him. God is your friend and you are one of the friends of God. Rejoice in that hallowed friendship, and live in the assurance of it. Now you have the anointing, do not doubt it. Christ has made it yours by His death. The Spirit of the Lord resteth upon you; you are fit for service; set about it without further question. The anointing is upon you; you are most holy to the Lord; so let your life be wholly consecrated. Your heart ought to be, and shall be by the Spirit's power, as holy as that innermost shrine into which no unauthorized foot ever intruded, into which only once in the year the high priest went, and then not without blood. God dwelleth in you, and you in God. Oh, blessed consequences—you shall soon dwell with Him forever!

But now suppose when I put the question you had to shake your head and say, "No, it is not so with me." Then hear these few sentences. If the Messiah has not done this for you, then your sin will be finished in another way—sin, when it is finished, bringeth forth death. An awful death awaits you—death unto God, and purity and joy. Woe, woe, to you. Death on the pale horse pursues you, and will overtake you soon. Then will one woe be past, but another will follow it. If Christ has never made an end of your sin, then mark this, your sin will soon make an end of you, and all your hopes, your pleasure, your boasting, your peace will perish. Oh, terrible end of all that is hopeful within you. You shall be a desolation forever and forever. Has not Christ reconciled you? Then mark this, your enmity will increase. There is no peace between God and you now, but soon will the war begin in which He must conquer, and you, never yielding, will continue forever more to hate God, and to find in that hate your utmost torment, your fiercest hell. Have you never had the righteousness of Christ brought in? Then mark this, your unrighteousness will last forever. One of these days God will say, "He that is unholy, let him be unholy still: he that is filthy, let him be filthy still." That will be the most awful thing that can ever happen to you. You have heard of the fable of Medusa's head: whoever looked upon it when it was held up was turned to stone, and one day, sinner, you shall look at death, and it will petrify your character so that it shall be forever what it is when death came to you. Where death finds you, there judgment shall find you, and there eternity shall leave you. Oh, wretched soul, to have nothing to do with the everlasting righteousness of Christ!

Are not the prophecies fulfilled in you, the prophecies of mercy? Then listen. The prophecies of woe will be written large across your history. "The wicked shall be turned into hell, with all the nations that forget God." Beware, ye that forget God, lest He tear you in pieces, and there be none to deliver. I will not detain you with many such words of terror, but through the Old Testament they roll like peals of thunder, nor is the New Testament less stern towards him that goeth on in his iniquity and will not turn unto the Christ.

Lastly, will you never be anointed to be most holy? Then remember, holiness and you will stand at a distance forever, and to be far off from holiness must necessarily be to be far off from heaven and happiness. Sin is misery; in it lies both the root and the fruit of eternal woe. Purity is paradise: to be right with God is to be right with yourself and all created things; but if ye will not be holy, then must ye by force of your own choice be forever tossed about upon the restless sea of wretchedness. God save you, brothers and sisters; God save you for Christ's sake. Amen.

THE KING-PRIEST

SERMON NO. 1,495

DELIVERED ON LORD'S DAY MORNING, SEPTEMBER 21, 1879.

PORTIONS OF SCRIPTURE READ BEFORE SERMON—PSALM 110; ZECHARIAH 6:9–15;

EPHESIANS 2:11–22.

HYMNS FROM *Our Own Hymn Book*—154, 419, 395.

He shall sit and rule upon his throne; and he shall be a priest upon his throne: and the counsel of peace shall be between them both—Zechariah 6:13.

LET us first look at the historical setting of this passage. It would seem that three Jews of the captivity had come from Babylon with a contribution towards the building of the temple at Jerusalem under Zerubbabel and Joshua. Their names are given in the tenth verse of the chapter before us. Now, the Jews at Jerusalem had become exceedingly exclusive, and in some measure rightly so. They would not accept help for the building of the temple from the Samaritans because they were a mixed race, but they said to them "Ye have nothing to do with us to build a house unto our God, but we ourselves together will build unto the Lord God of Israel." Possibly they had begun to feel some coolness with reference to the captivity at Babylon that inasmuch as they did not come back to their own land their descent must be proved before they acknowledged them. If they would not quit the ease and comfort of the towns in which they were settled, and come up to Jerusalem to work with their brethren, could they be sure that they were really Israelites? At any rate there would need to be some inquiry into their pedigree that they might not be receiving help from Samaritan pretenders. There was, however, no difficulty about the acceptance of the offerings in this case, for the prophet Zechariah was bidden to hasten down that same day and meet the three worthy Jews from Babylon. He was to accept for the Lord the tribute which they had brought, and make of it crowns of silver and gold. He was then to go with these brethren and Josiah, the son of Zephaniah, their host, down to the temple, call for the high priest, Joshua, or Jesus, the son of Josedech, and place these coronets of silver and gold upon his head. This was to be done, not as an honor to the individual, but as a prophetic token that there would in due time arise one who would be a priest crowned with many crowns. This illustrious personage, who is called "the Branch," was to spring out of the decayed house of David, like a shoot from a tree which has been cut down even to the stump: according to the prophecy of Isaiah, "and there shall come forth a rod out of the stem of Jesse, and a Branch shall grow out of his roots" (Is. 11:1). He was to be both a priest and a king, even as David had prophesied in the hundred and tenth Psalm—"The Lord hath sworn, and will not repent, thou art a priest forever after the order of Melchizedek." Now Melchizedek combined the king and the priest in one person, as also doth our Lord Jesus of whom Zechariah spoke. This royal priest was to build the real temple of God, which the temple at Jerusalem could never be, for the Most High dwelleth not in temples made with hands. It was also intimated by the prophet that as at that particular time men had come from afar, and had brought offerings to the temple, so in the days of this great priest-king many should come from the uttermost ends of the earth, and should themselves be built into the temple of the Lord God. This is the historical setting of our text: now we have to learn its spiritual lesson. May the Holy Spirit be our instructor.

Last Sabbath morning we spoke of the foundation of the temple of God. We saw how

> The church's one foundation
> Is Jesus Christ, our Lord.

We may not forget that He who is the Foundation is also the Builder of the spiritual house: "He shall build the temple of the Lord; and he shall bear the glory." There is but One who is the true Architect and Master-builder of the church of God, even Jesus Christ. His hands have laid the foundation of the house, His hands shall also finish it. So great is the fullness of our Lord Jesus that no figures can exhaust His character; He is not only foundation and builder, but He is the "head stone of the corner"; the pinnacle as well as the basement, the Omega as well as the Alpha, the finisher as well as the beginner. He begins, He carries on, and He completes the divine structure of the church, and when all this is done, it is He that establishes the structure, provisions and furnishes it, keeps and preserves it, and, best of all, it is He that is the glory in the midst, dwelling in the church, as a monarch in His own halls, and making it to be a palace as well as a temple. It is the Lord Jesus who walks among the golden candlesticks of the church, who loads her table with bread and wine, and sends forth His rod of power from her midst. As a King as well as a Priest He dwells in His palace-temple. As the Shekinah was the glory of the tabernacle of God among men in days of old, so is the presence of Jesus the glory of the church at this hour. "Lo, I am ever with you; even unto the end of the world" is our pillar of cloud and of fire, our glory and our defense.

Our text tells us that the promised Builder of the spiritual temple will inhabit and build it in His double character as Priest and King. The church is built up by none other than by this Melchisedek, and it is built by Him in virtue of both His offices as King and Priest. As King He puts forth power, and as Priest He displays holiness; as a King He uprears the walls, and as a Priest He sanctifies them unto the Lord. At this moment it will be well for our faith to open her eyes and look up into heaven itself and see our great Priest-King sitting at the right hand of God exalted, and yet at the same time working by His Spirit among men for the perfecting of His church below. Our Solomon is both reigning and building. Of His throne we may well say "there was not the like in any kingdom," and of His temple we may also add that it is "exceeding magnifical, of fame and glory throughout all countries."

I shall try this morning to set our Lord Jesus before you, as far as I can, in that double glory which is peculiar to Himself: in the majesty of His royalty and the holiness of His priesthood. Such lights meet not in any other star. To no one else belongeth the royal priesthood, save only that He reflects His own brightness upon His brethren, whom He hath made to be priests and kings.

The subject will run thus: first let us consider *the glorious combination of offices in the person of Christ*; secondly, let us notice *the happy result of it*—"the counsel of peace shall be between them both"; and then, thirdly, let us suggest *the action on our part which is harmonious thereto*—make crowns and set them upon the head of Jesus.

I. First, then, I want you to consider at this time THE GLORIOUS COMBINATION which is found in the person of Jesus Christ our Lord.

Note, first that He is *King*, and of Him as King it is written, "He shall sit and rule upon His throne." One has the idea of ease suggested by the expression. Few kings have been able to sit and rule, but they have been forced to rise and rush hither and thither to defend their sovereignty. No other seat in the world is so uneasy as a throne. We have seen monarchs elevated by their soldiery, or borne aloft by the fickle throng; bayonets or ballot boxes have been the frail supports of their thrones. The later centuries have been a sorry time for kings. As once men feared to be thought prophets, so might men in revolutionary times have cried out each one, "I am not a king nor the son of a king." But our Lord Jesus sits upon a throne which knows no trouble; once for all has He bled and died, but now He has gone into His glory never to be disturbed again. The Lord who hath set Him on the throne by an unalterable decree hath His enemies in derision, and Jesus waits in perfect rest until His foes shall be made His footstool. Publicly recognized as King of kings by the divine enthronement which His Father has given Him, He is not a king warring for a disputed crown, nor battling to drive invaders from His realm, but He sits and rules upon His throne.

Sitting is the posture of abiding as well as resting. Jesus reigns on, and will reign on so long as the moon endureth. "Thy throne, O God, is forever and ever." Even we, who are yet young, have seen dynasties come and go, and we have seen the kingdoms of the earth moved and tossed to and fro as the waves of the sea, yet the throne of Jesus has not been shaken, for it is written, "The Lord sitteth upon the flood; yea, the Lord sitteth King forever." "The Lord is great in Zion, and he is high above all the people." "The Lord shall reign forever and ever." Hallelujah.

As a King, He is described as sitting *upon His own throne*. He has not usurped the throne of another, but His right to sovereignty is indisputable. He has well deserved to be King of men since He is their Redeemer. His Father hath given Him a crown as the reward of the travail of His soul, even as He promised "Therefore will I divide him a portion with the great, and he shall divide the spoil with the strong, because he hath poured out his soul unto death." He sits upon a throne which He has won by conquest, for He has vanquished the powers of darkness, and led captivity captive. His right to His throne can never be disputed, for it is accorded to Him by the enthusiastic suffrages of all His people. Do we not sing, "Bring forth the royal diadem, And crown him Lord of all"? There is no monarch so secure as He. He is really and truly King by right divine. He is King by descent, for He is Son and Heir of the Highest. He is King by His own intrinsic excellence, for there is none to be compared to Him. And He is King by His own native might and majesty, for He Himself holds the throne against all comers, and shall hold it till all enemies shall be under His feet. Thus is He spoken of as King.

A hint or two is given as to His position as *Priest*, namely that He is first Priest before He is King, for so was the type in the text. Jesus the son of Josedech was already high priest, and then he was crowned with the gold and silver crowns. Now, the kingdom of which we speak today is not that of Christ's essential royalty as by nature divine, and therefore Lord of all, but that which His Father hath given Him, because, "Being found in fashion as a man, he humbled himself, and became obedient unto death, even the death of the cross. Wherefore God also hath highly exalted him, and given him a name above every name: that at the name of Jesus every knee should bow, of things in heaven, and things in earth, and things under the earth; and that every tongue should confess that Jesus Christ is Lord, to the glory of God the Father." Jesus reigns because He died. For the suffering of death He is crowned with glory and honor. The saints in heaven sing, "Thou art worthy to take the book and to open the seals thereof, for thou wast slain, and hast redeemed us to God by thy blood."

We note, too, with regard to our Lord's priesthood that He is said to sit, for if He sits as King it is implied that He sits as priest: indeed, it is expressly said, "He shall be a priest upon his throne." Now, of no other priest is it said that he sitteth, for the apostle saith, "Every priest standeth daily ministering and offering oftentimes the same sacrifices, which can never take away sins." There was no seat provided within the holy place for Aaron, or for any of the priests; they were servants of God, and they stood daily ministering. "But this man, after he had offered one sacrifice for sins forever, sat down on the right hand of God; from henceforth expecting till his enemies be made his footstool. For by one offering he hath perfected forever them that are sanctified." Jesus sitteth still forevermore in quiet expectancy, for all His work is done: no merit to be wrought out to complete His righteousness, no sufferings to be endured to perfect His atonement. "It is finished," He said as He gave up the ghost, and it is finished; and in token thereof Jehovah saith unto Him, "Sit thou at my right hand until I make thine enemies thy footstool." So far, then, we have a glimpse of the King sitting on His throne, and of the Priest, crowned, and resting from His labors.

Thus far we have seen each office, now we are to see the two combined in the Lord Jesus: and to make the combination clear we shall notice, first, that as a Priest He is royal; and then, secondly, that as a King He is priestly. Consider, now, that *as a Priest our Lord is royal.* He was a Priest when He honored the law by His own death: He was a Priest when He took upon Himself our sin, and bore it, offering His own soul as the victim upon the altar of His body: He was to the full a priest when He presented His one sacrifice for sin, but never let it be forgotten that even then, in His nature, He was a King. The sword of vengeance awoke against the man who was Jehovah's fellow even when He bled. The laws which He vindicated had been ordained by Himself; and it adds a special glory to His priestly work of atonement that it was wrought by the royal Lawgiver Himself. The subject broke the law, but it was the King who bore the penalty. He that is under law offendeth, but He that made the law came under the law that He might make amends to the injured honor of His own justice. This was a notable deed of love and of justice combined. Let us confide the more surely upon the sacrifice of our great High Priest, because of the dignity of His nature, and the supremacy of His rank, even when He made Himself of no reputation and took upon Himself the form of a servant.

Our Lord stooped to the lowest service for our sakes when He was acting a priest among us in these lower realms. He presented Himself as an offering for sin, and men scourged Him, and spat upon Him; and hung Him up like a felon, and in all this shame and suffering we look to Him as our Savior. Thus He made expiation for sin. But though we are to look to Him in that capacity for the pardon of sin, as men sought cleansing of a priest, we must never forget that now He expects homage from us, and we must come to Him for government as men pay obedience to a king. Think of Him as the crucified One as much as you will, for as such He is your atoning sacrifice, but remember that this same Jesus which was crucified God hath proclaimed to be both Lord and King. Trust in the man of the thorn-crown must foster and nourish reverence for the Lord who weareth many crowns. We must not only trust but worship. We must never dissever from that shame and spitting the fact that the four living creatures and the elders prostrate themselves before the Lamb, and sing unto His praise, "Thou art worthy to take the book, and to open the seals thereof: for thou wast slain, and has redeemed us to God by thy blood."

> Salvation to God, who sits on the throne,
> Let all cry aloud, and honor the Son;
> The praises of Jesus the angels proclaim,
> Fall down on their faces and worship the Lamb.

O you that come to Him today laden with guilt and full of fears, to wash yourselves in the fountain which He filled from His own veins, you must also come to obey Him, and to walk in His statutes. You may not come to Him merely that you may get your sins forgiven, you must come to be cleansed from the power of evil, and to yield yourselves unto God. Jesus was given that He might be a leader and a commander to the people, as well as their deliverer and Savior. A true disciple looks to his Master for ruling as well as for teaching, and he expects to render obedience as well as to receive instruction. There may be no separation between these two points:—our priest to save must ever be regarded as our king to rule. He puts away sin, but He expects to reign over the forgiven spirit; He washes our feet, but He looks that we also practice His precepts and example of love, for He says—"Ye also ought to wash one another's feet."

At this moment in heaven, if your eyes of faith can see the Lord Jesus, you perceive that He is pleading for His people as a Priest. It is a priest's duty to offer intercession for those over whom he is appointed; and this Jesus does continually. Hath He not said, "For Zion's sake will I not hold my peace, and for Jerusalem's sake I will not rest?" He ever liveth to make intercession for them that come to God by Him. But do not forget that our Lord does not make intercession otherwise than royally. There is no prostration now amidst the olives of the gloomy garden, no bloody sweat, no strong crying and tears. He saith not, "Not as I will, but as thou wilt," but He urges His suit in another fashion. The interceding Priest has laid aside His blood-stained garments and put on His robes of holiness for glory and for beauty. Jeweled breastplate; ephod of gold and blue, and purple and scarlet; miter and fine linen and gold; and girdle of needlework the high priest wore on favored days; all typical of the glory of the Lord Jesus now that He has gone within the veil. With authority He pleads with God from the throne of His power. He asks and He has; He speaks and it is done; for the intercessor of the saints before the throne of God is now the King immortal, eternal, invisible, the only wise God, our Savior. Oh, what prevalence there is in His plea, and when we give Him our cause to plead, how confident we may feel that the blessing will come to us.

As a priest our Redeemer not only pleads with God, but He blesses the people. It was the work of the high priest to pronounce the benediction over the house of Israel. Jesus does that, but He does it royally; I mean He does it with the power of a king as well as with the commission of a priest. He does not merely wish us good, but He works us good. There is omnipotent sovereignty at the back of the priestly benediction. He that speaks and declares His people to be justified, accepted, preserved, and blessed is He who can make good His words. The benediction of Jesus the Priest is the benediction of Jesus the King. Let us rejoice and be glad in this.

And now, beloved, it is as priest that Jesus sends out His gospel to the ends of the earth. In that gospel He invites men to come to Him that He may purge them from their uncleanness. Today He speaks by us, His ministers, and bids men come to the great Priest that He may heal them of their leprosy, and deliver them from all manner of defilement; but, mark you, it is an invitation from a King as well as from a Priest, and he that rejects it shall be counted guilty of disloyalty and high treason. "He that believeth not shall be damned." It is not, O sons of men, that Jesus offers you salvation, and leaves it to you whether you will have it or not; but if you reject it your rejection will be required at your hands. Beware, ye despisers, and wonder and perish. The invitation to the wedding of the great King is made freely, of His voluntary bounty, but if any who are bidden shall refuse to come the King will be wroth, and send forth His armies against those who thus proclaim their enmity. Jesus is not only Priest, asking you to come to Him and receive of His forgiving love, but He is a King as well, who will break with a rod of iron all that dare to trample on His blood, and slight His priestly grace.

Thus I have put forward the combination in one form, and testified that Jesus as a Priest is right kingly in all that He doth. Let us now turn the other side of the truth towards the light, and see that *as a King He always retains His priestly charac-ter*, and in the deeds of His sovereignty He acts not otherwise than as the High-Priest of His people.

The Lord Jesus Christ is King over all at this very moment. He reigns over the whole world, and, notwithstanding all this hurly-burly of affairs, this perpetual clamor of wars and rumors of wars, His kingdom ruleth over all. Our Lord is Mas-ter of the game, and He shall surely win at the end. "The government shall be upon his shoulders." But, blessed be His name, our Lord's kingly majesty is ever softened and sweetened by His priestly tenderness, else He would have crushed this world out of existence long ago. If rule had been all, and mercy had not claimed her share, jus-tice would have swept away this rebellious race. If Jesus were not Priest as well as King He would say to His angels, "Go and smite that nation which refuses my gospel. De-stroy antichrist that lifts his triple crown against my sole sovereignty. Go and scourge that favored nation which, having the gospel of peace, yet chooses war, and with high looks and lofty words provokes bloodshed." He does not destroy, because His office is to forgive and save. A priest must show longsuffering, gentleness, and compassion, for to that end is he taken from among men and ordained for men in the things of God. Such is our Lord: "He is not slack concerning his promise, but he is longsuffering to usward, not willing that any should perish, but that all should come to repentance." This longsuffering of the King leadeth to repentance: its intent is man's salvation. We, who are short of patience, cry eagerly to Him, "Come, O King. Come, O King"; but He answers, "I tarry yet a while in mercy that still more may be gathered to my name, and wash themselves in my atoning blood." Think of this, my brethren. Do not lower Christ's sovereignty, but at the same time learn to see it shining with gentler beams through the medium of His priestly character.

And, now, today, among His servants Jesus alone is King, and as a King He com-mands us. He lays certain laws upon His servants, and He bids us teach all men to ob-serve His statutes; but, oh, it is so sweet to think that our King in Zion is also a faithful and merciful high priest, touched with a feeling of our infirmities, ready to help us, and prompt to forgive us. My brother, though Jesus commands thee, yet He pities thy weakness, and helps thee to obey. He had given thee a law, but He knows thy fee-bleness, and so He gives thee grace to keep it; aye, and when thou dost not keep it He hath pity upon the ignorant, and upon them that are out of the way, and thy sins of ignorance and of transgression He continues still to put away. When His servants were about Him here on earth, He not only gave His commands to them, but He prayed for them that they might be kept from disobeying in the hour of trial, and He restored them when they had fallen. He not only ruled His little band of followers, but He kept them in the name of the Lord. He was their King, and their Priest too. Read the commands of Jesus with becoming reverence, for He is your king; but let them not distress you, for He knows your weakness and will help you to do what of yourself you are incapable of doing. He is a King, but the priestly garment is always over the kingly vesture: whatever the ornaments of His imperial splendor, He is still clothed with a garment down to the foot. The priesthood covers all, and removes all cause of dread from every believing mind.

The same is true of our great King when He goes out to war. He is the Lord mighty in battle; in righteousness He doth judge and make war. The psalmist crieth, "Gird thy sword upon thy thigh, O most mighty, with thy glory and thy majesty. And in thy majesty ride prosperously because of truth and meekness and righteousness; and thy right hand shall teach thee terrible things. Thine arrows are sharp in the heart of the king's enemies; whereby the people fall under thee." But the wars of Christ are not like the wars of earthly monarchs. His sword is not in His hand, but it goeth out of His mouth, and with this He smites and rules the nations. He is clothed in a vesture dipped in blood, but it is His own blood. Every battle of the warrior is with confused noise, for he wrestles not with men, but with their sins; not with princes and armies, but with falsehood and iniquity. His victories are not those of mighty men who return from the fray, amidst the groans of widows and the cries of orphans; but His bloodless triumphs make glad the poor and the oppressed, and only crush down principalities and powers and spiritual wickednesses in high places, bringing good to all who seek His face. He is a King, but evermore the patron and true Priest of men.

Among ourselves at this day, beloved, we who know Him delight to own Him as our King. O Lord Jesus, thou greater Joseph, the shepherd and stone of Israel; all our sheaves pay obedience unto thy sheaf, and all thy father's children bow down before Thee. Thou more glorious Judah, Thou art He whom thy brethren shall praise, unto Thee shall the gathering of the people be. The chief among ten thousand and the altogether lovely art Thou. Yes, beloved, this glorious One is our brother, and delights to be regarded as priest taken from among men, being one of ourselves, able to sympathize with our infirmities. Our Lord is higher than the highest, and yet He stoops as low as the lowest. He is kingly even to deity, and yet so truly a priest that in all our afflictions He is afflicted. He is not ashamed to call us brethren. Ruler of our race, He is yet partaker of our flesh and blood, and He is acquainted with all its sorrows. True King, and yet true Priest.

Thus I would have you blend the idea in both ways, and see Jesus as a royal priest and a priestly king.

> Jesus, the King of glory, reigns
> On Sion's heavenly hill;
> Looks like a lamb that has been slain,
> And wears his priesthood still.

Such is your Lord. May your view of Him be clear, your faith in Him be firm, your love to Him be fervent, your joy in Him be overflowing, and your obedience to Him be constant. Trust the Priest and serve the King, and ever pay your vows unto Him who is "a priest upon his throne."

II. Secondly, and very briefly, we shall now meditate upon THE HAPPY RESULT of all this. The text says, "The counsel of peace shall be between them both." I confess myself unable dogmatically to interpret this passage, for there are no less than three possible meanings. I must give you them all, and leave you to judge for yourselves. The most natural reading, to my mind, is this—that when we shall see in the person of Christ the King and the Priest combined, the counsel of peace shall be between them both. These offices, the King and the Priest, being combined in one, shall make a deep and lasting peace for us, a peace arranged by the deep thought and counsel of God, and therefore full of wisdom, truth, and certainty. When we see the Lawgiver Himself making atonement for our transgressions we have peace indeed: when Ruler and Savior meet in one Person the rest is sure and profound. Beloved, if this be not the meaning of the passage, it is at least a precious truth. If we want peace we can only obtain it by knowing Christ as Priest and King—the counselor peace must lie between these two. Oh, do you know Christ, my dear hearers, as your priest? Have you seen Him offering sacrifice for your sin? Does He stand instead of you before God? Do you present your prayers and your praises to God through Him? Well, then, you have begun to know what peace is, for peace comes through the blood of Jesus the Priest—peace by His righteousness, peace by His sacrifice. But if, knowing this, you are still in trouble of heart, remember that you need to know Him also as your King. When He subdues your iniquities, when the power of sin is taken away as well as the guilt of it, then you shall know the perfection of peace. "Take my yoke upon you," saith He, "and learn of me, and ye shall find rest unto your souls." It is not in a mere belief in Christ as your Savior that you will ever get perfect peace, it is by yielding up yourself unto Him that He may rule and reign over you completely. This man shall be the peace when He is Lord as well as priest. As long as your will rebels against your Redeemer's rule you cannot have unbroken rest. It is idle for you to talk about trusting in the blood of Jesus unless you submit to His scepter. The cross itself cannot save you if you divorce it from the crown. Your Savior must be a Priest upon His throne to you; His blood must be on your conscience, and His yoke must be upon your neck. There is no counsel of peace until it is between both these: the kingly Priest, the priestly King, alone can make and maintain the peace of God within you. That is a great and deep truth: may we learn it well.

But it is thought by some wise men that the text means the counsel of peace shall be between Jehovah the Father, and the Son. I am not sure that such a meaning would suggest itself to every reader, and as the most obvious meaning is generally to be preferred, I will not contend for this second meaning. However, as an interpretation it is certainly not too far-fetched, and, even if it cannot be sustained, it is certainly a very great truth. It is between God, the Eternal Father, and Jesus Christ, our Melchizedek, or King-Priest, that the counsel of peace has been established on our behalf. You never know God so as to have peace with Him till you know God in human flesh. Only the incarnate God can end the trouble of your spirit. Aye, and it must be that incarnate God, bleeding, suffering, dying, making expiation for sin, and then rising to the throne and ruling over all, that must be seen before you can perceive how the infinitely glorious Jehovah can be at peace with you. God in covenant is God at peace with man. There was a counsel between the Trinity at the making of man, "Let us make man"; and so also there was a counsel between the divine Persons at the redemption of man—the counsel of peace is between them both. It is a joy for us to know that between Jesus our Priest-King and the everlasting God peace has been established for us, peace which never can be broken. Our first covenant-head broke the treaty, and left us at war with God, but the second Adam has fulfilled and established the covenant of grace, and believing in His name we have peace with God.

But there is a third meaning, and although I am not sure of it as the sense here, it is assuredly a blessed truth, and appears to me to be congruous with the connection. Let me go back to the historical circumstances. Here were these three men that had come from Babylon. The prophet is to take them to the house of a Jew resident in Jerusalem. There might be some little differences between these men and the Jerusalem Jews. These Babylonian Jews had not come up to dwell in Jerusalem: but Josiah the son of Zephaniah was a resident there, and he might have demurred, and have said, "We cannot take your present to the temple because you do not bring yourselves and come to abide with your own people." No, but they were to go up, together, bearing the gold and silver crowns, and put them upon the head of the priest. They were to go up in unity and love, and they were to furnish in their own persons types of other far-off ones who should come to the great crowned Priest whose coming the prophet had foretold. Thus said the prophet, "They that are far off shall come and build in the temple of the Lord, and ye shall know that the Lord of hosts hath sent me unto you." Now, certainly, it is in Jesus Christ the Priest and King that the Jews who were nigh, and the Gentiles who were afar off, are brought together, and made one. In Him the middle wall of partition is broken down, and the counsel of peace is between us both. The day shall come when our glorious Lord shall be more clearly manifested than now in the glory of His second advent, and when the Jews shall behold Him as the priestly King, and bow before Him; then shall the fullness of the Gentiles also be gathered in, and the Lord Jesus Christ shall reign over the whole earth. May that day speedily dawn! We have reason to expect it; therefore, let us pray for it and strive for its on-bringing. Jesus the Priest and King is the uniter of the divided nations. Jew and Gentile are, after all, of one blood, and one God is the Father of all; why should they not become one? "One touch of nature makes the whole world kin"; but one touch of Jesus Christ shall do it infinitely better, shall do it once for all.

III. I close with the third point which was this, THE ACTION WHICH IS HARMONIOUS WITH THESE TRUTHS. The connection of our text suggests to us to do exactly what the prophet Zechariah advised the Babylonian Jews and Josiah to do. I will read you what he said: "Take silver and gold and make crowns and set them upon the head of Joshua" or Jesus. This is what is to be done.

First, "*take*." "Take silver and gold." That is, bring the choicest things you have. If Jesus Christ be a Priest, should you not bring your offerings to Him? If Jesus Christ be King, should you not bring tribute to your King? If you have gold and silver, bring them, for to Him shall be given the gold of Ophir. If you have talent, which is much more valuable than gold and silver, bring ability, tact, genius; bring all the acquisitions of learning, all the acquirements of experience, and all your natural gifts, and consecrate them all to Him. Whether you have these or not, bring your heart, which is more precious by far, the very essence of your being; make this a crown for Jesus. Come, bring your soul, your life, your all. Has He redeemed you? Then be His forever. Is He your King? Do not mock Him with a half-hearted service; be loyal to such a sovereign, and serve Him with spirit, soul, and body. Take silver and gold and bring them unto Him. Bring your whole being to Him.

What next? "Take"; then "make": "make crowns." Come, my brethren, I invite you to this occupation. You say, "We are neither goldsmiths nor silversmiths." Nevertheless, make crowns. Try your hands this morning, and make crowns for Jesus with such material as ye have. Fashion the crown of memory. Think of what He has done for you from the first day until now. Interweave and intertwist the recollections of the past: hammer out the gold of gratitude, set in it the gems of love, and make a coronet for His dear head. Make crowns by holy contemplation and thought. Think how great your Lord is, and how great He deserves to be—how blessed, how ever-blessed. Then make crowns of purposes of what you hope to be and do. Plot and plan within your spirit something you have not yet done, which you are able to do before you go home to heaven. Look out some child you may teach, some sinner you may woo and win, some treasure you may spend for Jesus, some precious promise you may whisper in the ear of the distressed, some holy enterprise you may suggest to earnest youth. Make crowns!

It seems to me so sweet that it should be said, "Set them upon the head of Jesus." Brethren and sister, let us crown Him ourselves. We hope to do so in heaven: let us do it here. Our love shall be the gold, our praise shall find the gems, our thanksgivings and our humble labors shall furnish the silver, and then we will set the golden chaplets about His brow, which once was rent with thorns for us. Coronets for Jesus! Coronets for Jesus! Crowns for our priestly King! Let us make and bring them.

I return to that blessed precept, "Set them upon the head of Jesus." Whenever we have made a crown let us take care to put it on His head ourselves. Have you never, when you have been doing something for Him, or giving something to His cause, wished that you could present it to Him personally. Well, you may do so in spirit, and that is as much a matter of fact as if you did it bodily. With your shoe from off your foot, let your spirit draw near to Jesus, and in thought offer to His own self the deed which you have wrought. Speak to Him, and tell Him that this is done for Him alone.

I do not know a greater pleasure upon earth than to think of something you can do for Jesus, and then to do it for Him, and to tell Him so—"Jesus, I did it all for Thee. I thought not of my brethren's praise, nor do I think of it now, but I did this deed unto Thee alone. Here is the best crown I can make, and I put it on thy head." The love of Jesus will suggest and produce many a deed which else had never been done. If you have a beautiful alabaster box it is not pleasant to break it, and if you have choice ointment it is not according to nature to pour it out upon another. No, but when you are before *His* feet, the feet of Jesus your Lord, then is it a delight to break the alabaster box and to pour out its fragrant contents for *Him*. The utmost waste is economy when it is done for Him, and to sacrifice strength, soul, health, life, is to save it all, when it is spent for Him. Where should it go? Where should my all go? For what should my bodily frame be consumed? Where should my soul be poured out but for His honor? Do you not feel it so? You will if you distinctly recognize that He is King and Priest. You will bring crowns and put them on His head if you know who and what He is.

And what is said last? It is said that this should be a memorial to those three men and to the brother who had entertained them. I suppose these crowns of silver and gold were hung up in the temple, and when anybody said, "What are those crowns yonder?" it would be answered, "Those are coronets which were made by order of the prophet Zechariah, by Heldai and Tobijah and Jedaiah, who came from Babylon, and they are in memorial of those men, and in memorial of the hospitality of Josiah the son of Zephaniah, who entertained them at his house when they came. They are hung up in the temple of honor of the coming priestly King, and in memorial of those four men who presented an offering to the Lord." It seems very wonderful that God should allow in His house memorials of His servants, but He does so; and our great priestly King allows memorials of his people in his temple now. We shall never forget, shall we, while the world standeth the sacrifice of Paul, and how he made crowns and set them on the head of Jesus? Never while the earth lasts shall we forget the sacrifice of John, and Peter, and James. Nay, the church will not forget the sacrifices of Luther, and Calvin, and Zwingle, and Wycliffe, and the holy lives and ardent ministries of Whitefield and Wesley shall not be forgotten in the church, because they made crowns and set them on the head of Jesus. "Oh," say you, "but we must not remember *men*." "Nay," say I, "but we may remember men, and women, too, for our Lord has set us the example. 'Wheresoever this gospel is preached there shall this which this woman hath done be mentioned for a memorial of her.' " My Master thinks much of His people, and in the plenitude of His great goodness the little things which they do for Him are had in remembrance. Did He not say of Cornelius, "Thy prayers and thine alms have come up as a memorial of thee." This is sweet to think upon. While our King-Priest shall have the crowns, and wear them, yet we, if we bring love-tokens and honorable spoils to Him, shall be remembered, too, in that day when He shall award the praise to His people, saying, "Well done, good and faithful servants." The Lord whom we serve will immortalize our service by uniting it with His service. We shall rest from our labors, but our works shall follow us. The righteous shall be had in everlasting remembrance, they shall shine forth as the sun when their Lord's glory shall be revealed. Their Priest shall make them priests, their King shall make them kings, and they shall forever be filled with the vision of the Priest upon His throne. So may it be with us. Amen.

THE LOWLY KING

SERMON No. 1,861
DELIVERED ON THURSDAY EVENING, JUNE 25, 1885.
PORTION OF SCRIPTURE READ BEFORE SERMON—MATTHEW 11.
HYMNS FROM *Our Own Hymn Book*—878, 765, 384.

Rejoice greatly, O daughter of Zion; shout, O daughter of Jerusalem;
behold, thy King cometh unto thee: he is just, and having salvation;
lowly, and riding upon an ass, and upon a colt the foal of an ass—
Zechariah 9:9.

I DO not intend to expound the whole text at any length, but simply to dwell upon *the lowliness of Jesus*. Yet this much I may say: whenever God would have His people especially glad, it is always in Himself. If it be written, "Rejoice greatly," then the reason is, "Behold, thy King cometh unto thee!" Our chief source of rejoicing is the presence of King Jesus in the midst of us. Whether it be His first or His second advent, His very shadow is delight. His footfall is music to our ear.

That delight springs much from the fact that He is ours. "Rejoice greatly, O daughter of Zion: . . . behold, *thy* King cometh unto thee." Whatever He may be to others, He is thy King, and to whomsoever He may or may not come, He cometh *unto thee*. He comes for thy deliverance, thine honor, thy consummated bliss. He keeps thy company: He makes thy house His palace, thy love His solace, thy nature His home. He who is thy King by hereditary right, by His choice of thee, by His redemption of thee, and by thy willing choice of Him, is coming to thee; therefore do thou shout for joy.

The verse goes on to show why the Lord our King is such a source of gladness: "He is just, and having salvation." He blends righteousness and mercy; justice to the ungodly, and favor to His saints. He has worked out the stern problem—how can God be just, and yet save the sinful? He is just in His own personal character, just as having borne the penalty of sin, and just as cleared from the sin which He voluntarily took upon Him. Having endured the terrible ordeal, He is saved, and His people are saved in Him. He is to be saluted with hosannas, which signify, "Save Lord"; for where He comes He brings victory and consequent salvation with Him. He routs the enemies of His people, breaks for them the serpent's head, and leads their captivity captive. We admire the justice which marks His reign, and the salvation which attends His sway; and in both respects we cry, "Blessed is he that cometh in the name of the Lord!"

Moreover, it is written of Him that He is lowly, which cannot be said of many kings and princes of the earth; nor would they care to have it said of them. Thy King, O daughter of Jerusalem, loves to have His lowliness published by thee with exceeding joy. His outward state betokens the humility and gentleness of His character. He appears to be what He really is: He conceals nothing from His chosen. In the height of His grandeur He is not like the proud monarchs of earth. The patient ass He prefers to the noble charger; and He is more at home with the common people than with the great. In His grandest pageant, in His capital city, He was still consistent with His meek and lowly character, for He came "riding upon an ass." He rode through Jerusalem in state; but what lowliness marked the spectacle! It was an extemporized procession, which owed nothing to Garter-king-at-arms, but everything to the spontaneous love of friends. An ass was brought, and its foal, and His disciples sat Him thereon. Instead of courtiers in their robes, He was surrounded by common peasants and fishermen, and children of the streets of Jerusalem: the humblest of men and the youngest of the race shouted His praises. Boughs of trees and garments of friends strewed the road, instead of choice flowers and costly tapestries: it was the pomp of spontaneous love, not the stereotyped pageantry which power exacts of fear. With half an eye every one can see that this King is of another sort from common princes, and His dignity of another kind from that which tramples on the poor. According to the narrative, as well as the prophecy, there would seem to have been two beasts in the procession. I conceive that our Lord rode on the foal, for it was essential that he should mount a beast which had never been used before. God is not a sharer with men; that which is consecrated to His peculiar service must not have been aforetime devoted to lower uses. Jesus rides a colt whereon never a man sat. But why was the mother there? Did not Jesus say of both ass and foal, "Loose them, and bring them unto me?" This appears to be to be a token of His tenderness: he would not needlessly sever the mother from her foal. I like to see a farmer's kindness when he allows the foal to follow when the mare is plowing or laboring; and I admire the same thoughtfulness in our Lord. He careth for cattle, yea, even for an ass and her foal. He would not even cause a poor beast a needless pang by taking away its young; and so in that procession the beast of the field took its part joyfully, in token of a better age in which all creatures shall be delivered from bondage, and shall share the blessings of His unsuffering reign. Our Lord herein taught His disciples to cultivate delicacy, not only towards each other, but towards the whole creation. I like to see in Christian people a reverence towards life, a tenderness towards all God's creatures. There is much of deep truth in those lines of "The Ancient Mariner":

> He prayeth best who loveth best
> All things both great and small.

Under the old law this tenderness was inculcated by those precepts which forbade the taking of the mother-bird with her young, and the seething of a kid in its mother's milk. Why were these things forbidden? There would seem to be no harm in either of these practices, but God would have His people tenderhearted, sensitive, and delicate in their handling of all things. A Christian should have nothing of the savage about him; but everything that is considerate and kind. Our Lord rode through the streets of Jerusalem with an ass, and a colt the foal of an ass; for He is lowly in heart, and gentle to all. His is no mission of crushing power, and selfish aggrandizement; He comes to bless all things that be, and to make the world once more a Paradise, wherein none shall be oppressed. Blessed Savior, when we think of the sufferings of thy creatures, both men and beasts, we pray thee to hasten thy second advent, and begin thy gentle reign!

Now, this riding of Christ upon an ass is remarkable, if you remember that no pretender to be a prophet, or a divine messenger, has imitated it. Ask the Jew whether he expects the Messiah to ride thus through the streets of Jerusalem. He will probably answer "No." If he does not, you may ask him the further question, whether there has appeared in his nation anyone who, professing to be the Messiah, has, at any time, come to the daughter of Jerusalem "riding upon an ass, and upon a colt the foal of an ass." It is rather singular that no false Messiah has copied this lowly style of the Son of David. When Sapor, the great Persian, jested with a Jew about his Messiah riding upon an ass, he said to him, "I will send him one of my horses": to which the Rabbi replied, "You cannot send Him a horse that will be good enough, for that ass is to be of a hundred colors." By that idle tradition the Rabbi showed that he had not caught the idea of the prophet at all, since he could not believe in Messiah's lowliness displayed by His riding upon a common ass. The rabbinical mind must needs make simplicity mysterious, and turn lowliness into another form of pomp. The very pith of the matter is that our Lord gave Himself no grand airs, but was natural, unaffected, and free from all vainglory. His greatest pomp went no further than riding through Jerusalem upon a colt the foal of an ass. The Mohammedan turns round with a sneer, and says to the Christian, "Your Master was the rider on an ass; our Mohammed was the rider on a camel; and the camel is by far the superior beast." Just so; and that is where the Mohammedan fails to grasp the prophetic thought: he looks for strength and honor, but Jesus triumphs by weakness and lowliness. How little real glory is to be found in the grandeur and display which princes of this world affect! There is far more true glory in condescension than in display. Our Lord's riding on an ass and its foal was meant to show us how lowly our Savior is, and what tenderness there is in that lowliness. When He is proclaimed King in His great father's capital, and rides in triumph through the streets, He sits upon no prancing charger, such as warriors choose for their triumphs, but he sits upon a borrowed ass, whose mother walks by its side. His poverty was seen, for of all the cattle on a thousand hills He owned not one; and yet we see His more than royal wealth, for He did but say, "The Lord hath need of them," and straightway their owner yielded them up. No forced contributions supply the revenue of this Prince; but His people are willing in the day of His power. He is thy King, O Zion! Shout, to think that thou hast such a Lord!

Where the scepter is love, and the crown is lowliness, the homage should be peculiarly bright with rejoicing. None shall groan beneath such a sway; but the people shall willingly offer themselves; they shall find their liberty in His service, their rest in obedience to Him, their honor in His glory.

Now, my brethren, you may forget the hosannas of that day of Palms, for I beg you to confine your thoughts to the consideration of the lowliness of our divine Lord and Master. "Behold, thy King cometh unto thee . . . lowly, and riding upon an ass."

Let us think for a few minutes upon *the displays of the lowliness* of our Lord Jesus Christ; then upon *the causes of that lowliness*; and thirdly, upon *certain lessons to be learnt from that lowliness*.

I. First, then, let us think of THE DISPLAYS OF LOWLINESS MADE BY OUR LORD JESUS CHRIST. You do not need me to remind you how devoutly we worship Him as God over all, blessed forever. Yet while on earth He veiled His Godhead, and laid bare His lowliness. His sojourn here below was full of the truest greatness; but it was a grandeur, not of loftiness, but of lowliness; not of glory, but of humiliation. Our Lord was never more glorious in the deepest sense than in His humiliation: because of it "He shall be exalted, and extolled, and shall be very high."

First, think of the lowliness of Christ in even *undertaking the salvation of guilty men*. Man without sin, as God first made Him, is certainly a noble creature. It is written, "Thou has made him a little lower than the angels." But, as a sinner, man is a base and dishonorable being, only worthy to be destroyed. In that character He has no claims to be regarded of God at all. If it had pleased the divine supremacy to blot this rebel race from existence, God might readily have repaired the loss by the creation of superior beings; and it was lowliness of the tenderest kind which led our Lord, who took not up angels when they fell, to take up the seed of Abraham. If it were possible for some tall archangel to espouse the cause of ants upon their hill in yonder forest, it would be a wondrous stoop; yet it would be nothing compared with the condescension of the eternal God in bowing from His lofty throne to redeem and sanctify the sons of men. We are frail creatures at the best; born yesterday, we die today; we are as green leaves in the forest for a while, and then our autumn comes, we fade, and the wind carries us away. For such ephemera the Lord of glory came to this sin-shadowed globe. Were He not of a lowly mind, He had never found His delights with the sons of men, nor would He have thought upon the woes of poor and needy ones.

Herein, in the next place, He showed His lowliness—that *He actually assumed our nature*. I cannot tell that story, it is too wonderful. A free spirit voluntarily encases itself in human clay: a pure spirit willingly becomes a partaker of flesh and blood! This is marvelous lowliness. The strong is compassed with infirmity; the happy assumes capacity for suffering; the infinitely holy becomes one of a race notorious for its iniquity! This is a triumph of lowliness. The great God, the Infinite of ages, unites Himself with a human body; He is born into our infancy, He grows up into our youth, He toils through our manhood; He accomplishes a life like our own! This is a miracle of lowliness. Methinks the angels still gaze into these things, and wonder at the Word made flesh. It is particularly said of our incarnate Lord that he was "seen of angels"; and that leads us to believe that angels watched Him with intense curiosity, and ever-growing interest, wondering what it all could mean, that He, who made and ruled the heavens should be born of a woman, and made under the law. They wondered that He should eat, and drink, and sleep, and sigh, and suffer, like the creatures of His hand; and should, indeed, be such as they were! Surely they talk of it now with hushed voices and astonished hearts, and will so talk of it throughout the ages. Made lower than His angels are, His angels must feel a solemn awe at such a divine descent of love. This lowliness was such as only God could display: let us worship in the Person of our Lord a condescending love as unique as the Person who exhibited it.

Furthermore, when our Lord found Himself below, in the fashion of a man, He manifested His true lowliness by *carrying out to the full the part of a servant*. He had taken upon Himself the form of a servant by becoming man, but it was no matter of form with Him. He became actually obedient; having put on the livery of service, He executed the lowest office. Never scullion in a king's kitchen did menial work so thoroughly as He. In His great house there are vessels to honor and to dishonor, and He selected to be used for the lowest offices; He made Himself of no reputation; He became a servant of servants; all they that saw Him laughed Him to scorn; "He was despised, and we esteemed him not." If anybody was wanted to talk with a fallen woman, He was soon seen sitting on the well; if anyone was needed to win a publican, He was speedily at the house of Zaccheus. If any man must needs be slandered as having a devil and being mad, He is ready to bear the worst reproach. He could truthfully say, "Ye call me Master, and Lord: and ye say well; for so I am"; yet He, their Master and Lord, had washed their feet, and therein proved that He was meek, and lowly of heart. Brothers, it is a wonderful thing that the Lord of all should have become the servant of all; it is so wonderful that many have lost their way in thinking of it; they have been unable to grasp the idea of Godhead combined with servitude, majesty united with obedience. Indeed, it is only by faith that we can realize that He that built all things yet became so poor a thing as Mary's Son, so sad a being as the Man of sorrows, so lowly a personage as the "despised and rejected of men." Yet so it was; and herein He showed the truth of His own statement, "I am meek and lowly in heart." He wore the yoke Himself, and therefore can experimentally say, "Take my yoke upon you, and learn of me . . . and ye shall find rest unto your souls." This is He who breaks not the bruised reed, and quenches not the smoking flax. This is He who "endured such contradiction of sinners against himself." His life was one long proof of meekness and lowliness, and in nothing did He fail: He exhorts us to conquer by the same persevering methods; for He has proved that gentleness and meekness will prevail.

Still, let me keep you thinking upon the lowliness of your Lord when I bid you remember *his lifelong poverty*. He does not advise His disciples voluntarily to espouse poverty, unless it be for His sake, and then they do well. Times have been, and may be again, when believers must forsake all things for His cause; but in His day some of His disciples ministered to Him of their substance, and therefore had substance. He did not command these to renounce that substance, and become poor, though I doubt not that, when persecution came, many of them gladly did so for His sake. Not to all did He put the test, "Sell all that thou hast"; but it was needful to His own personal work that he should become poor, that His people might be made rich; and this He cheerfully endured. He was laid in a borrowed cradle in the stable wherein He was born; He dwelt in His work-life in borrowed houses, and lived upon the charity of His followers; and when He rested, it was in a borrowed bed; for though the foxes had holes, He had not where to lay His head. He preached from a borrowed boat; and when He fell asleep, and died, He was buried in a borrowed tomb, for He had no foot of land for a possession. He endured poverty as if He were to the manner born; for He was quite at home among the poor and lowly, receiving sinners and eating with them. Truly, a dignity surrounded Him far more real than that which has been conceived to hedge a king; and yet in His poverty He never seemed uneasy, and the society of the poor and unlearned never grieved Him. He was with the poorest as one of them; and they knew it, and therefore they loved to gather about Him. He was so sweetly and tenderly their associate that the common people heard Him gladly.

Remember, that He might have quitted that poverty at any moment, He that could turn water into wine, might have quaffed full many a delicious draught had He so willed; He that could multiply bread and fish needed never to have hungered. A word from Him might have created palaces more wonderful than the dreams of Aladdin, and wealth greater than the abundance of Solomon, for nothing was impossible to Him. If He had willed to make Himself the object of His own life, He could have surrounded Himself with every luxury; but, instead thereof, "though he was rich, for your sakes he became poor, that ye through his poverty might be rich." In this He magnified His lowliness.

But I think I see more of His lowliness at times in *His associates* than in anything else; because men may be very poor, and yet they may be very proud. I think I have seen it sadly so. I have known men without a penny wherewith to bless themselves as full of caste feeling as the wealthiest peer. They are workingmen, it may be, but they think themselves superior persons, or remarkable gifts, and eminent respectability. We are a little overdone with superior persons just now. Almost everywhere I come across them, in this department and in that, and, of course, I look up to them with such respect as I can; but sometimes a little more reverence is asked of us than we can conveniently bestow. In this age we have to be careful not to trench upon the dignity of certain persons; and yet He who was in all respects superior to us all, never played the superior person once in all His life. He sat on a well, and talked to a woman; and His disciples, we read, marveled that He spoke to *a woman*. It is not to "*the* women," as we get in our Authorized Version, but the Revised Version puts it more correctly, "they marveled that he was speaking with a woman." They thought that such a one as He should not speak to any woman; for they were tinctured with the exclusiveness of the period. I do not suppose that it occurred to our Lord that He was doing anything remarkable in speaking to a woman; for He was born of woman, and He never disowned the tender ties which come of such a birth. To some men it would be a great come-down to speak familiarly to any one if he did not keep a carriage. Even in our churches the silly caste feeling will intrude, and brethren in Christ hardly think a poor saint to be their equal. Our Lord had no pride of manner about Him, for His lowliness was in His heart. We read that the *publicans and sinners* gathered round Him: even women of ill-fame listened with tearful eyes to His teaching. Oh, no, *we* never mention them, of course! We call them "outcasts," and treat them as offcasts: yet Jesus had a kind word for them. What a congregation He often had, of those whom Pharisees abhorred! Yet He never said to one of them, "Begone!" His rule was to welcome all, saying, "Him that cometh to me I will in no wise cast out." Those publicans were certainly very mean characters; they collected a hateful tax for the foreigner, and squeezed out an extra portion for themselves: but yet the Savior never said to a single publican "Begone!" Quite the contrary, He gave the publican an honorable place in His parable; He made one of them an apostle, and He went to abide in the house of another, who received Him joyfully. He did not merely speak a good word to these degraded persons, but He actually sat at the table with them as a friend. "Horrible, was it not?" So the Pharisees thought. "Glorious," say we, as we reverence that divine humility which scorned nothing that lived, and especially nothing in the form of man or woman. "This man receiveth sinners," was said in disdain: let it be thundered out in a hymn as glorious as the song of the seraphim, who continually do cry, "Holy, holy, holy!" Never was purity more pure than when its incarnation bowed to become "a friend of publicans and sinners."

He did what was more singular still: He received *little children.* Now, I can see some reason for talking with grown-up men and women, even if they be debased and depraved; but as for those boys and girls, what can be done with them? When they heard the children crying "Hosanna" in the temple, the Pharisees demanded of Him, "Hearest thou what *these* say?" As much as to say, "These boys! Are these thine admirers? Dost thou find thy followers among children?" He had a lowly answer for them; but it was one which silenced them. These hosannas came of our blessed Lord having said, "Suffer the little children to come unto me, and forbid them not: for of such is the kingdom of God." He accepted children as the pattern of the kind of people who enter His kingdom; He Himself was called God's holy child Jesus; and He was at home with children because of His perfect guilelessness and gentleness. Proud men seldom care for children, nor children for them; but our Lord, in His true lowliness of heart loved children, and they loved Him.

I wish we had a longer time in which to set out all the lovely lowliness of our adorable Christ; but I must only gather a few ears where I would have preferred to have reaped sheaves. Our Lord's *patient bearing under accusations* that were so foul and false, was another proof of His lowliness. "I hear," says a man, "that a calumny has been whispered against me, and I will drag it to light. I will have it out, let it cost what it may. Who dares breathe upon my character? He shall feel the law, and know that he cannot defame me with impunity." Some professing Christians appear to lose their balance when misrepresented: the lamb roars like a lion, and the ox eats flesh like the leopard. Churches have been rent, and families ruined, to avenge a hasty word. Is not that spirit the opposite of the mind of our blessed Master? They said He was a drunken man and a winebibber: the charge must have grieved Him, but He did not become angry, and threaten His accusers. It was most important that His character should be cleared; He smiled to Himself as He thought, "I will not contradict the accusation, for everybody knows that it is not true." They said that He had a devil, and He did condescend to answer *that*, and confounded all His accusers by making them see the absurdity of the charge; for if the devil was in Jesus fighting against the devil, then the devil must have become divided against himself, and his kingdom would soon come to an end. Towards the end of our Lord's life, His enemies gathered up their charges, and flung them in set form before Pilate's judgment seat, but He answered them never a word: "He was led as a sheep to the slaughter; and like a lamb dumb before her shearer, so opened he not his mouth." In silence He maintained His lowliness. Oh, if He had spoken who could speak as never man spoke; if He had defended Himself with His own irresistible oratory, with such a subject as Himself to speak upon, He might have made them all go out of the judgment hall, as once He had scattered them when His client was a woman taken in adultery. He might have turned the crowd against their rulers, had He chosen; or divided their counsels by setting Pharisees against Sadducees, but He sought not Himself. He had been content to ask, "Which of you convinceth me of sin?" "For which of those works do ye stone me?" And when He came to His end He had no harder word for them than "Father, forgive them!"

To crown all, you know how our Well-beloved *died*. He laid down His life for us—dearest pledge of lowliness! The decease which He accomplished at Jerusalem was no famous death in battle, amid the roar of victory. His was no death amid the tears of a nation who prepare for their beloved prince a more than royal mourning. No, He dies with malefactors; He dies at the common gallows; He dies amid a crowd of scoffers, where felons cast contempt upon Him as He hangs between them. Hear how the ribald throng challenge His divine Sonship, and say, "If thou be the Son of God, come down from the cross!" The bearing of such obloquy, the endurance of such scorn, was the utmost proof of a lowliness of spirit which we humbly admire, and feebly imitate, but which we can never equal.

II. I shall but occupy you one or two minutes while I try to explain THE CAUSE OF THIS LOWLINESS.

His supreme lowliness of character grew out of *the actual lowliness of His heart*. He never aimed at humility, nor labored after it: it was natural to Him. Of all sickening things, the pride that apes humility is the most loathsome: not a particle of that nauseous vice was found in our Lord. He never puts on an air, nor strikes an attitude, nor plays the humble part; but He *is* meek and lowly, and all can see it. He is never other than He seems to be, and He always is and seems to be the meekest of mankind. His inmost heart was seen, and seen to be all lowliness.

Why was He so? I conceive that He was so lowly because *He was so great*. A little man feels the necessity of magnifying himself, and therefore becomes proud. Pride is essentially meanness. It is the little man that cannot afford to belittle himself. Some of us are too low to be lowly, too mean to be meek. True greatness is ever unconscious, and never seeks to make a display. It magnifies a man when he can sink himself for the good of others. No one knew how to descend so gracefully as our Lord, for His great mind knew well the ways of self-denial. A man who is greatly rich is not ashamed to be seen in well-worn clothes in those same places where the pretentious bankrupt would not venture except in his newest attire. He who has a small estate puts a diamond ring upon his finger, and holds it so that it sparkles in the light, to let all people see that he is a man worth something; but your eminent men of wealth scorn such display. Truly great men are humble. I have often heard it said of men of large substance, "He is singularly unassuming; you would never dream that he is a man of property." So, too, of men of genius have we heard it said, "he gave himself no airs, he was as modest and friendly as the least of us." Just so; and that very much accounts for his high standing. He that is somebody to others is nobody to himself. He who was more than all, even our Lord Jesus Christ, was, therefore, for that very reason, lowly of heart.

He was lowly, next, because *He was so loving*. Mothers are frequently proud *of* their children, but, I think, they are seldom, if ever, proud *to* their children. No, if they love them, they do not think that it is any condescension to kiss them, or wash them, or carry them in their bosom. I never heard of a father who thought that he was very humble-minded because he allowed his boy to clamber upon his knee, and hold on with his arms about his neck. Those whom we love we elevate to an equality with ourselves; or, rather, we go down to them. Love is a charming leveler. Jesus had so much love that He could not be anything but lowly towards His little ones. You never yet heard even a blasphemer impute pride to God. Though our blood has chilled when we have heard the High and Mighty One arraigned for this and that by arrogant tongues; yet we have not known profanity to run in that line. It would be too absurd to impute pride either to God, or to His ever-blessed Son, Jesus Christ. The reason for this evident freedom from pride is the fact that "God is love." The fullness of divine love blinds the eye which looks askance upon it. God is patient, for He is loving: Christ is lowly of heart, because His heart is made of love.

Moreover, once more, our blessed Master was *so absorbed in His great object* that He was necessarily lowly. The man who is driving at a great object has no time for the affectations of self-adulation. He has no time in which to think of how he appears to others. He does not stand at the glass to arrange his beauties; the idea would be too absurd. He cannot be too particular about how he puts that poetic word, or how he mouths that polished sentence; his sole desire is to deliver his message and to impress men with the matter at hand. Earnestness carries the speaker beyond the orator's rules of self-display; his rhetoric is melted down by his enthusiasm. A great orator can readily be made to appear ridiculous by the comic critic, who coolly looks down from the gallery upon him; but what cares he? His theme so absorbs him that he has forgotten all elegance of attitude and gesture, and only cares to carry his point. He would make himself a fool, ten thousand times deep, if he could but win his suit, and bless his country thereby. He cares for nothing but his subject and his aim. So is it preeminently with our Lord: He pursues His course careless of man's esteem. He burns His way, His zeal eats Him up, He is straitened till His work is accomplished, and therefore He has no thought about the maintaining of His dignity. His greatness and His intense devotion forbid anything approximating to pride, and by force of nature He is meek and lowly in heart. Because He has a great object to achieve, and that object has absorbed His whole self, He must walk in all lowliness of mind. Blessed Master, teach us this way of lowliness! Fire us with an ambition for thy glory which shall shut out every thought of pride!

III. What are the LESSONS TO BE LEARNED FROM THIS LOWLINESS OF OUR LORD?

The lessons are first, brethren, *let us be lowly.* Did I hear one say, "Well, I will try to be lowly?" You cannot do it in that way. We must not try to act the lowly part; we must *be* lowly, and then we shall naturally act in a humble manner. It is astonishing how much of pride there is in the most modest. Of course I do not mean in those who say that they are perfect. No, I leave them to their own vainglory; but in us poor, imperfect creatures, what a deal of pride there is! How we condemn pride! We feel that it would be well if all were as humble as we are. We boast that we detest boasting. We flatter ourselves that we hate flattery. When we are told that we are singularly free from pride, we feel as proud as Lucifer himself at the consciousness that the compliment is right well deserved. We are so experienced, so solid, so discerning, so free from self-confidence, that we are the first to be caught in the net of self-satisfaction. Brethren, we must pray God to make us humble. If we become lowliest of the lowly it will not be much of a condescension on our part; we shall only come down to the point which we ought never to have left. Down in the dust is the fit place for such poor mortals as we are. What right have we to be anything else but meek and lowly?

Alas! We can be very proud in many ways: let me give you a case or two in point. Yonder is one that is called to suffer, and he rebels against it. Hear his complaint: "Why should I be called to endure such great trials? What have I done that I am thus tried?" Do you not at once detect the great "I?" Very different is this from the lowly prayer, "Nevertheless, not as I will, but as thou wilt."

"But, then, persons have spoken evil of me. I do not deserve to be treated thus." Clearly it is especially wrong for any one to speak amiss of such an excellent being as you are. There lies the grievance. Because you are so good, it is horrible wickedness to reduce you. You reply, "But really, it was so malicious, and the charge was so absurd and unreasonable." Just so. People ought to be peculiarly careful not to hurt your feelings, for you are so deserving and praiseworthy. Is not self-esteem the spring of half our sorrow? We are so wonderfully good in our own judgment that we claim the box seat of the coach, and the chief seat in the synagogue. If we were really lowly of heart, we should say, "I have been treated very badly, but when I think of how my Lord was treated, I cannot dream of complaining. This severe critic cannot see my excellences; but I do not wonder, for I cannot see them myself. He has been finding fault with me, and his charges were not true; but, if he had known me better, he might have found more fault with me, and have been nearer the truth. If I do not deserve censure in this way, I do in another; and so I will cheerfully bear what is measured out to me. Yea, if it be in no sense my due, I will give my back to the smiters, as my Master did." Oh, that the Lord would make us meek and lowly in heart, and we should submit to wrong rather than resist evil!

"But surely," cries one, "you do not want me to associate with sinners!" No, dear friend, I do not want such a good person as you are to go near them at all; I could not so degrade your honorable self. Moreover, if you did go near them, you would aggravate them by your self-opinionated goodness. If your perfections are not quite so fullblown as usual, I would, however, suggest that you might do sinners good by kindly speaking to them; and that to gather up your skirts in fear and trembling, lest you should be defiled by their presence is not the most excellent way. When you are afraid lest the wind should blow from a sinful person towards your nobility, you act the fool, if not the hypocrite, perhaps both. Why, you would have been in hell yourself if it had not been for sovereign grace! You, fine ladies and prime gentlefolk, you would have been as surely cast away as the vilest of mankind, if it had not been for infinite compassion! It ill becomes us to boast, since we have enough sins of our own to plunge us in despair, were it not for the love of the lowly Savior, who His own Self bore our sins in His own body on the tree. O Lord, stamp out our pride, and make us lowly in heart!

Lastly, *let us learn to say to the despondent and timorous words of cheer*. Since the Lord Jesus Christ is so meek and lowly, poor, trembling, guilty one, you may come to Him! You may come to Him now! I was sitting the other night, amongst some excellent friends, who, I suppose, were none of them rich, and some of them poor. I am sure it never entered into my head to think how much money they owned, for I felt myself very much at home with them, until one of them remarked, "You do not mind mixing with us poor folk?" Then I felt quite ashamed for myself that they should think it necessary to make such a remark. I was so much one with them that I felt honored by having fellowship with them in the things of God, and it troubled me that they should think I was doing anything remarkable in conversing with them. Dear friends, do not think hardly of any of us who are ministers of Christ; and you will think hardly of us if you conceive that we think it a coming-down to associate with any of you! We are in heart and soul your brothers, bone of your bone, your truest friends whether you are rich or poor. We desire you good, for we are your servants for Christ's sake. Above all, do not think hardly of our Lord and Master by supposing that it will be a strange thing for Him to come to your house, or to your heart. It is His habit to forgive the guilty, and renew the sinful. Come to Him at once, and He will accept you now. Jesus is exceedingly approachable. He is not hedged about with guards to keep off the poor or the sinful. Your room may be very humble; what cares He for that? He will come, and hear your prayer. Many a time Jesus has had no room to pray in, but,

> Cold mountains, and the midnight air,
> Witnessed the fervor of his prayer.

Do you complain that you cannot arrange your words correctly? What is that to Him? He looks more at the sincerity of your heart than at the grammar of your language. Let your heart talk to Him without words, and He will understand you.

Do you complain with shamed face that you are such a sinner? You are not the first sinner that Jesus has met with, nor will you be the last. You are heavy-laden with sin; but He knows more about the weight of sin than you do. That terrible load of guilt wearies you; but it pressed Him down even more terribly when it brought Him into the dust of death. It makes you weep to think of sin; but it caused Him to sweat great drops of blood. You feel that you cannot live under so crushing a burden; and He did not live under it, but gave up the ghost in agony. Do not crucify your Lord afresh by suspecting that He is proud, and will therefore pass you by. Do not insult Him by dreaming that He will reject you for your insignificance or unworthiness. Come, and welcome, to Him who will delight to bless you. Come to Him at once, without further question or hesitation. Come just as you are, fall at His pierced feet, and trust the merit of His blood, and the good Lord will accept you on the spot, for He has said, "Him that cometh to me I will in no wise cast out."

God bless you, by leading you all to love this lowly and loving Lord! Even at this present moment I pray that you may take that step which will secure our meeting in heaven to adore eternally our King, so meek and lowly, who will then dwell in the midst of us, and lead us to living fountains of water!

HOW HEARTS ARE SOFTENED

SERMON NO. 1,983
DELIVERED ON LORD'S DAY MORNING, SEPTEMBER 18, 1887.
PORTION OF SCRIPTURE READ BEFORE SERMON—ZECHARIAH 11:3; 12.
HYMNS FROM OUR OWN HYMN BOOK—296, 284, 290.

*And I will pour upon the house of David, and upon the inhabitants
of Jerusalem, the spirit of grace and of supplications: and they shall look
upon me whom they have pierced, and they shall mourn for him, as
one mourneth for his only son, and shall be in bitterness for him, as
one that is in bitterness for his firstborn. In that day shall there be a
great mourning in Jerusalem, as the mourning of Hadad-rimmon in
the valley of Megiddon*—Zechariah 12:10, 11.

HARDNESS of heart is a great and grievous evil. It exists not only in the outside world,
but in many who frequent the courts of the Lord's house. Beneath the robes of religion
many carry a heart of stone. It is more than possible to come to baptism and the sacred supper, to come constantly to the hearing of the Word, and even, as a matter of
form, to attend to private religious duties, and yet still to have an unrenewed heart, a
heart within which no spiritual life palpitates, and no spiritual feeling exists. Nothing
good can come out of a stony heart; it is barren as a rock. To be unfeeling is to be un-
fruitful. Prayer without desire, praise without emotion, preaching without earnestness—
what are all these? Like the marble images of life, they are cold and dead. Insensibility
is a deadly sign. Frequently it is the next stage to destruction. Pharaoh's hard heart was
a prophecy that his pride would meet a terrible overthrow. The hammer of vengeance
is not far off when the heart becomes harder than an adamant stone.

Many and great are the advantages connected with softness of spirit. Tenderness
of heart is one of the marks of a gracious person. Spiritual sensibility puts life and feeling into all Christian duties. He that prays feelingly, prays indeed; he that praises God
with humble gratitude, praises Him most acceptably, and he that preaches with a loving heart has the essentials of true eloquence. An inward, living tenderness, which trembles at God's Word, is of great price in the sight of God.

You are in this matter agreed with me: at least, I know that some of you are thoroughly thus minded; for you are longing to be made tender and contrite. Certain
of you who are truly softened by divine grace are very prone to accuse yourselves of

being stony-hearted. We are poor judges of our own condition, and in this matter many make mistakes. Mark this: the man who grieves because he does not grieve is often the man who grieves most. He that feels that he does not feel is probably the most feeling man of us all; I suspect that hardness is almost gone when it is mourned over. He who can feel his insensibility is not insensible. Those who mourn that their heart is a heart of stone, if they were to look calmly at the matter might perceive that it is not all stone, or else there would not be a mourning because of hardness. But, whether this be so or not, I address myself to all of you whose prayer is for godly sorrow for sin. It is written in the covenant of grace, "I will take away the stony heart out of your flesh, and I will give you a heart of flesh." I pray that this may be fulfilled in you even now. The object of this sermon is to show how this tenderness is to be obtained, and how an evangelical sorrow for sin can be produced in the heart, and maintained there. I would set forth the simple method by which the inward nature can be made living, feeling, and tender, full of warm emotions, fervent breathings, and intense affections towards the Lord Jesus Christ. While I speak I beseech you to pray: Create in me a tender heart, O Lord, and renew within me a contrite spirit.

It will be instructive to keep to the words of the text. This passage is peculiarly suited to our purpose, and it will add authority to that which we teach. Observe that holy tenderness *arises out of a divine operation*. "I will pour upon the house of David, and upon the inhabitants of Jerusalem, the spirit of grace and of supplications." Secondly, *it is actually wrought by the look of faith*: "And they shall look upon me whom they have pierced, and they shall mourn for him." And, thirdly, the tenderness which comes in this way *leads to mourning for sin of an intense kind*: "They shall mourn for him, as one mourneth for his only son, and shall be in bitterness for him, as one that is in bitterness for his firstborn. In that day shall there be a great mourning in Jerusalem, as the mourning of Hadad-rimmon in the valley of Megiddon."

I. First, note that THE HOLY TENDERNESS WHICH MAKES MEN MOURN FOR SIN ARISES OUT OF A DIVINE OPERATION. It is not in fallen man to renew his own heart. Can the adamant turn itself to wax, or the granite soften itself to clay? Only He that stretcheth out the heavens and layeth the foundation of the earth can form and re-form the spirit of man within him. The power to make the rock of our nature flow with rivers of repentance is not in the rock itself.

The power lies in the omnipotent Spirit of God, and it is an omen for good that He delights to exercise this power. The Spirit of God is prompt to give life and feeling. He moved of old upon the face of the waters, and by His power order came out of confusion. That same Spirit at this time broods over our souls, and reduces the chaos of our natural state to light and life and obedience. There lies the hope of our ruined nature. Jehovah who made us can make us over again. Our case is not beyond His power. Is anything too hard for the Lord? Is the Spirit of the Lord straitened? He can change the nether millstone into a mass of feeling, and dissolve the northern iron and the steel into a flood of tears. When He deals with the human mind by His secret and mysterious operations, He fills it with new life, perception, and emotion. "God maketh my heart soft," said Job, and in the best sense this is true. The Holy Spirit makes us like wax, and we become impressible to His sacred seal. Remember, you that are hard of heart, that your hope lies this way; God Himself, who melts the icebergs of the northern sea, must make your soul to yield up its hardness in the presence of His love. Nothing short of the work of God within you can effect this. "Ye must be born again," and that new birth must be from above. The Spirit of God must work regeneration in you. He is able of these stones to raise up children unto Abraham; but until He works you are dead and insensible. Even now I perceive the goings forth of His power: He is moving you to desire His divine working, and in that gracious desire the work has already begun.

Note next, that as this tenderness comes of the Spirit of God, so *it also comes by His working in full co-operation with the Father and with the Son.* In our text we have all the three Persons of the divine Trinity. We hear the Father say, "I will pour upon the house of David the spirit of grace," and that Spirit when poured out leads men to look to Him whom they pierced, even to the incarnate Son of God. Thus the Holy Ghost proceeding from the Father and the Son, fulfills the purpose of the Father by revealing the Son, and thus the heart of man is reached. The divine Father sends forth the Holy Ghost, and He bears witness to the Son of God, and so men come to mourn for sin. We believe in the three Persons of the blessed God, and yet we are equally clear that God is one. We see the diverse operations of these three divine Persons, but we perceive that they are all of one, and work to the selfsame end, namely, that grace may reign by delivering us from our natural impenitence, and by causing us to sorrow because we have sinned. The Holy Spirit worketh not without the Father and the Son, but proves Himself to be in full union with both by His operations upon the soul of man. Do not think, therefore, when thou feelest the Holy Ghost melting thee, that the Father will refuse thee: it is He that sent the Holy Spirit to deal with thee. Imagine not that thou canst feel repentance for sin and bow in sorrow at the Savior's feet, and that Jesus will reject thee; for it is He who sent the Spirit of grace to bring thee to repentance, and make thee mourn because of the ill which thou has done. The glorious one God, who made the heavens and the earth, is dealing with thy heart if the Holy Ghost is now working in thee as "the spirit of grace and of supplications."

This operation is an unseen secret work. Thou canst not perceive the work of the Spirit by the senses of the flesh; it is spiritually discerned. When the Spirit of God was poured out at Pentecost, there were diverse signs attendant thereupon, such as rushing mighty wind, and cloven tongues as it were fire; but these were outward signs only, the Spirit Himself is inward and secret. The Spirit is as the wind, invisible save by its effects. The Holy Ghost cometh as the dew which in soft silence refreshes the tender herb. Not with sound of trumpet or observation of man doth the Spirit perform His gracious deeds. His working is one of the secrets and mysteries which no man can explain to his fellow. He that feels the movement of the Holy Spirit, knows what a singular work is going on within him, but what it is, or who it is that worketh it, he knoweth not. Do not, therefore, expect to be informed when the Spirit is upon thee.

Marvel not if it should so happen that He is dealing with thee now, though thou knowest it not, "For God speaketh once, yea twice, yet man perceiveth it not." The operations of the Holy Ghost are consciously perceived by the human heart, but they are not always attributed to their right cause. Many a man, to use the words of our hymn,

> Wonders to feel his own hardness depart.

He does not know how his new tenderness has been produced. He finds himself anxious to hear and understand the gospel, and he feels that the gospel affects him as it never did before, but he does not perceive those "invisible" cords of love which are drawing him towards his Savior. Before long he will cry, "This is the finger of God"; but as yet he perceives not the divine cause. It is well set forth by Mr. Bunyan in his parable of the fire which burned though a man tried to quench it. There was one behind the wall who secretly poured oil upon the fire. He himself was unperceived, but the fire burned because of what he poured on it. You can see the flame, but you cannot see the hidden One who ministers the fuel. The Spirit of God may work in you, my dear hearer, this morning, but it will not be with special token of marvel, or voice, or vision. Not with earthquake, nor wind, nor fire will He come, but with "a still small voice." He may deal with many of you at once, and yet none may see it in his fellow. I expect that He will work upon many at this time, for much prayer has been put up that the Lord Jesus may be glorified in our midst.

But the secret operation of the Spirit is known by its effects, for *it is sweetly productive.* We read in the text of "the spirit of grace and of supplications," which must mean that the Spirit produces graciousness and prayerfulness in the soul upon which He works. The man is now willing to receive the grace or free favor of God; he ceases to be proud, and becomes gracious. He is put into a condition in which God's grace can deal with him. As long as you are self-righteous, God cannot deal with you in the way of favor; you are upon wrong ground, for you are making claims which He cannot possibly allow. Mercy and merit can no more blend than fire and water. You must be willing to receive as a free favor what God will never give you if you claim it by right. When thou art made conscious of sin, then forgiveness can be granted. When thou art malleable under the hammer of God's Word, then will He work His work of love upon thee. When thou dost lay thine own righteousness aside, and take up the cry, "God be merciful to me a sinner," then shalt thou go to thy house justified. It needs the Spirit of grace to give us grace to receive grace. We are so graceless that we will not even accept grace till God gives us "grace for grace"—grace to accept grace. Blessed is the hour when the Spirit of God comes to us as the Spirit of grace, and works in us that graciousness which makes us value and seek after the free grace of God in its further forms. Grace itself clears out a space in the heart for grace to enter and carry on its work.

It is also said that the Lord will pour out "the spirit of supplications." This is the creation of desires and longings which express themselves in prayer. When the Holy

Ghost works savingly upon the heart, then the man begins to approach the mercy-seat with frequent and fervent supplications. The words may be broken and confused; but what are words? Sighs, tears, heavings of the breast, and upward glancings of the eye—these are true prayers, and are very prevalent with God. Brethren, we poor preachers cannot make men pray. We can produce a Book of Common Prayer, and read it to them, and get them to utter the responses; but we cannot make them pray by this means: the Spirit of God is still needed. The child may be taught a form of prayer at its mother's knee, and he may repeat it daily till he is old, and yet he may never have prayed in all those years. Only the Spirit of God can produce the smallest atom of prayer. I tell you, there was never a prayer on earth that God could accept, but what first came down from heaven by the operation of the Spirit of God upon the soul. But here is the point: have you this "spirit of supplications" this morning? Are you groaning, crying, sighing—"Lord, save, or I perish; give me Christ, or else I die?" Well then, I trust you have come under the sacred outpouring promised in the text—"I will pour upon the house of David, and upon the inhabitants of Jerusalem, the spirit of grace and of supplications."

All this leads on towards the tenderness which begets mourning for sin. Again, I say, this is the point from which help must come for the sinner. You that have been striving to feel, and yet cannot feel, and do not feel—you should look to the strong for strength, and to the living for life. He who in the day of His creation breathed into the nostrils of man the breath of life, so that he became a living soul, can infuse the new life into you, and give you with it all the feeling which is natural thereto. Think much of the Holy Spirit, for He can make thee live in the truest sense. It is God's to give thee a tender heart, not think to create it within thyself. Do not attempt first to renew thy heart, and then to come to Christ for salvation; for this renewal of heart is salvation. Come thou as thou art, confessing all thy hardness, thy wicked, willful obduracy and obstinacy, confess it all; and then put thyself into the hands of the Spirit, who can remove thy hardness at the same time that grace removes thy guilt. The Holy Spirit can make thy heart as tender as the apple of the eye, and cause thy conscience to be as sensitive as a raw wound, which feels the slightest touch. God grant us grace to deal with Him about these things, and not to be looking to ourselves. As well hope to extract juice from the stones of the sea-beach, as spiritual feeling from the carnal mind. He who can make the dry bones live, and He alone, can make the hardened mourn over sin.

II. But now I come to the core and center of our subject: THIS TENDERNESS OF HEART AND MOURNING FOR SIN IS ACTUALLY WROUGHT BY A FAITH-LOOK AT THE PIERCED SON OF GOD. True sorrow for sin comes not without the Spirit of God; but even the Spirit of God Himself does not work it except by leading us to look to Jesus the crucified. There is no true mourning for sin until the eye has seen Christ. It is a beautiful remark of an old divine, that eyes are made for two things at least; first, to look with, and next, to weep with. The eye which looks to the pierced One is the eye which weeps for Him. O soul, when thou comest to look where all eyes should look, even to Him who was pierced, then thine eye begins to weep for that for which all eyes should weep, even the sin which slew thy Savior! There is no saving repentance except within sight of the cross. That repentance of sin which omits Christ, is a repentance which will have to be repented of. If such sorrow may be called repentance at all, it is only as wild grapes are yet called grapes, though they have in them none of the qualities and virtues of the clusters of the true vine. Evangelical repentance is acceptable repentance, and that only; and the essence of evangelical repentance is that it looks to Him whom it pierced by its sin. Sorrow for sin without faith in Christ is the hard bone without the marrow: it kills, but never blesses. It is a tempest of the soul with thunder and lightning, but no rain. God save us from remorse! It worketh death.

Mark you, *wherever the Holy Spirit does really come, it always leads the soul to look to Christ.* Never yet did a man receive the Spirit of God unto salvation, unless he received it to the bringing of him to look to Christ and mourn for sin. Faith and repentance are born together, live together, and thrive together. Let no man put asunder what God hath joined together. No man can repent of sin without believing in Jesus, nor believe in Jesus without repenting of sin. Look, then, lovingly to Him that bled upon the cross for thee, for in that look thou shalt find pardon, and receive softening. How wonderful that all our evils should be remedied by that one sole prescription, "Look unto me and be ye saved, all the ends of the earth!" Yet none will look until the Spirit of God inclines them so to do; and He works on none to their salvation unless they yield to His influences and turn their eyes to Jesus.

Note well that *this look to the pierced One is peculiarly dear to God.* Observe the change of the pronoun in the middle of the verse: "They shall look upon *me* whom they have pierced, and they shall mourn for *him.*" The *me* and the *him* refer to the same person. I lay no special stress upon this, and I do not attempt to *prove* any doctrine from it; but certainly it is remarkable that when we read this verse with defined views as to the oneness of Christ with God, and the union of God and man in one person in the Lord Jesus, we find the pronouns perfectly correct, and understand why there should be "*me*" in one case, and "*him*" in another. If you adopt any other theory, then the passage would seem to be a jumble of words. It is instructive to note that the Lord, instead of saying, "They shall look upon him whom they have pierced," cannot keep Himself in the third person, but bursts upon the scene in His own individuality. Either you have here the Father regarding Himself as pierced in His Son, or the Lord Jesus Christ Himself speaking in the spirit of prophecy of Himself, and personally noting those looks of faith and penitence which are fixed upon His sacred Person. He has such a delight in those looks of believing sorrow, that He mentions them as having personally beheld them: "They shall look upon *me* whom they have pierced." Nothing pleases Jesus more than the faith-looks of His people. In every stage of their history the glances of believers' eyes are very precious to Him. "Thou hast ravished my heart, my sister, my spouse; thou has ravished my heart with one of thine eyes," saith the Bridegroom in the heavenly canticle. Surely the first glance of a tearful, penitent eye to Christ is very dear to Him. He saith, "I have seen Him and observed Him."

Nobody sees our look of faith but Himself, and it is not needful that anyone else should see it: is it not a matter between our own soul and our Lord? He foresaw that look and in this verse uttered a prophecy concerning it; and He looks back upon it with pleasure, keeping it before His mind as a part of His satisfaction for the travail of His soul. The looks of faith and the tears of repentance are precious jewels to our Lord Jesus. He rejoices so much when one sinner repenteth that the angels see His joy. O dear hearts, if this morning, in those pews, you look to Christ believingly, accepting Him as God's salvation, then is the promise fulfilled before the eyes of Him who spoke it, and said, "They shall look on me whom they have pierced." He will be glad of your faith: He invites it, He accepts it, He rewards it. "They looked unto him and were lightened: and their faces were not shamed." Looking unto Jesus we receive joy, and we give Him joy. As He delighteth in mercy, so He delights in those who come to Him and accept His mercy. He was lifted on a cross to be looked at, He was nailed there that he might be a perpetual spectacle, and His heart was pierced that we might see the blood and water, which are our double cure.

The look which blesses us so as to produce tenderness of heart, is a look to Jesus as the pierced One. On this I want to dwell for a season. It is not looking to Jesus as God only which affects the heart, but looking to this same Lord and God as crucified for us. We see the Lord pierced, and then the piercing of our own heart begins. When the Lord reveals Jesus to us, we begin to have our sins revealed. We see who it was that was pierced, and this deeply stirs our sorrow. Come, dear souls, let us go together to the cross for a little while, and *note who it was* that there received the spear-thrust of the Roman soldier. Look at His side, and mark that fearful gash which has broached His heart, and set the double flood in motion. The centurion said, "Truly this was the Son of God." He who by nature is God over all, "without whom was not anything made that was made," took upon Himself our nature, and became a man like ourselves, save that He was without taint of sin. Being found in fashion as a man, He became obedient unto death, even the death of the cross. It is He that died! He who only hath immortality condescended to die! He was all glory and power; and yet He died! He was all tenderness and grace; and yet He died! Infinite goodness was hanged upon a tree! Boundless bounty was pierced with a spear! This tragedy exceeds all others! However dark man's ingratitude may seem in other cases, it is blackest here! However horrible his spite against virtue, that spite is cruelest here! Here hell has outdone all its former villanies, crying, "This is the heir; let us kill him." God dwelt among us, and man would have none of Him. So far as man could pierce his God, and slay his God, he went about to commit the hideous crime; for man slew the Lord Christ, and pierced Him with a spear, and therein showed what he would do with the Eternal Himself, if he could come at Him. Man is, at heart, a deicide. He would be glad if there were no God: he says in his heart, "No God"; and, if his hand could go as far as his heart, God would not exist another hour. This it is which invests the piercing of our Lord with such intensity of sin; it meant the experiencing of God. But why? Why and wherefore is the good God thus persecuted? By the lovingkindness of the

Lord Jesus, by the glory of His person, and by the perfection of His character, I beseech you be amazed and shamed that He should be pierced. This is no common death! This murder is no ordinary crime. O man, He that was pierced with the spear was thy God! On the cross behold thy Maker, thy Benefactor, thy best Friend!

> Alas! and did my Savior bleed?
> And did my Savior die?
> Would he devote that sacred head
> For such a worm as I?

Look steadily at the pierced One, and *note the suffering* which is covered by the word "pierced." Our Lord suffered greatly and grievously. I cannot in one discourse rehearse the story of His sorrows; the griefs of His life of poverty and persecution; the griefs of Gethsemane, and the bloody sweat; the griefs of His desertion, denial, and betrayal; the griefs of Pilate's hall and the scourging, and the spitting, and the mockery; the griefs of the cross, with its dishonor and agony. The sufferings of our Lord's body were only the body of His sufferings.

> 'Twas not the insulting voice of scorn
> So deeply wrong his heart;
> The piercing nail, the pointed thorn,
> Caused not the saddest smart:
>
> But every struggling sigh betray'd
> A heavier grief within,
> How on His burden'd soul was laid
> The weight of human sin.

Our Lord was made a curse for us. The penalty for sin, or that which was equivalent thereto, He endured. "He his own self bore our sins in his own body on the tree." "The chastisement of our peace was upon him; and with his stripes we are healed." Brethren, the sufferings of Jesus ought to melt our hearts. I mourn this morning that I do not mourn as I should. I accuse myself of that hardness of heart which I condemn, since I can tell you this story without breaking down. My Lord's griefs are untellable. Behold and see if there was ever sorrow like unto His sorrow! Here we lean over a dread abyss and look down into fathomless gulfs. Now we are upon great waters, where deep calleth unto deep. If you will steadfastly consider Jesus pierced for our sins, and all that is meant thereby, your hearts must relent. Sooner or later the cross will bring out all the feeling of which your are capable, and give you capacity for more. When the Holy Spirit puts the cross into the heart, the heart is dissolved in tenderness. *Crux in corde*, as the old preachers used to say, this is the source of godly sorrow. The hardness of the heart dies when we see Jesus die in woe so great.

It behooves us further to *note who it was that pierced Him*—"*They* shall look on me whom *they* have pierced"; the "they," in each case, relates to the same persons. We slew the Savior, even we, who look to Him and live. If a man were condemned and put to death, you might inquire who it was that slew him; and you might be told that it was the judge who condemned him; but that would not be all the truth. Another might blame the jury who brought in the verdict of guilty, or the executioner who actually hanged him; but when you go to the root of the matter, you would find that it was the man's crime which was the real blameworthy cause of His death. In the Savior's case sin was the cause of His death. Transgression pierced Him. But whose transgression? Whose? It was not His own, for He knew no sin, neither was guile found in His lips. Pilate said, "I find no fault in this man." Brethren, the Messiah was cut off, but not for Himself. *Our* sins slew the Savior. He suffered because there was no other way of vindicating the justice of God and allowing us to escape. The sword which else had smitten us was awakened against the Lord's Shepherd, against the man that was Jehovah's fellow. Truly may we sing—

> 'Twas for my sins my dearest Lord
> Hung on the cursèd tree,
> And groan'd away a dying life
> For thee, my soul, for thee.

> Oh, how I hate those lusts of mine
> That crucified my God;
> Those sins that pierced and nail'd his flesh
> Fast to the fatal wood!

> Oh, if my soul were form'd for woe,
> How would I vent my sighs!
> Repentance should like rivers flow
> From both my streaming eyes.

If this does not break and melt our hearts, let us *note why He came into a position in which He could be pierced by our sins*. It was love, mighty love, nothing else but love which led Him to the cross. No other charge can ever be laid at His door but this, that He was "found guilty of excess of love." He put Himself in the way of piercing because He was resolved to save us. He loved us better than He loved Himself. And shall we hear of this, and think of this, and consider this, and remain unmoved? Are we worse than brute? Has all that is human quitted our humanity? If God the Holy Ghost is now at work, a sight of Christ will surely melt our heart of stone.

Furthermore, notice that *looking to the pierced One causes mourning in every case*. All hearts yield to this. Under the power of the Holy Ghost *this works efficaciously of itself*. Nothing else is needed. "They shall look upon me," and "they shall mourn." Faith in Christ is sufficient for the production of acceptable and deep repentance; this, and this only, without mortifications and penances.

Let me also say to you, beloved, that *the more you look at Jesus crucified, the more you will mourn for sin*. Growing thought will bring growing tenderness. I would have you look much at the pierced One, that you may hate sin much. Books which set forth the passion of our Lord, and hymns which sing of His cross, have ever been most dear to saintly minds because of their holy influence upon the heart and conscience. Live at Calvary, beloved; for there you will live at your best. Live at Calvary, and love at Calvary, till live and love become the same thing. I would say, look to the pierced One till your own heart is pierced. An old divine saith, "Look at the cross until all that is on the cross is in your heart." He further says: Look at Jesus until He looks at you. Steadily view His suffering Person until He seems to turn His head and look at you, as He did at Peter when he went out and wept bitterly. See Jesus till you see yourself: mourn for Him till you mourn for your sin.

The whole of this subject leads me to observe that the conversion of the Jews will come from a sight of the crucified Messiah. I conclude from this text that Israel will be brought to know the Lord, not by a vision of Christ in His glory, but by a sight of Christ in His humiliation. "They shall look upon me whom they have pierced, and shall mourn for him." But I also conclude that this holds good of all mankind. By the preaching of Christ crucified will their hearts be broken. The cross is God's hammer of love, wherewith He smites the hearts of men with irresistible blows. Men tell us we should preach Christ as an example. We do preach Him as an example, and rejoice to do so; but we can never allow that view of our Lord to overshadow our preaching of Him as a sacrifice for sin. He suffered in the room, and place, and stead, of guilty men, and this is the gospel. Whatever others may preach, "we preach Christ crucified." We will ever bear the cross in the forefront. The substitution of Christ for the sinner is the essence of the gospel. We do not keep back the doctrine of the Second Advent; but, first and foremost, we preach the pierced One; for this it is that shall lead to evangelical repentance, when the Spirit of grace is poured out. O brethren, whatever else you preach, or do not preach, preach Christ crucified! Jesus Christ my Lord as crucified is my main topic, and shall be till I die. I trust you feel a pleasure in thinking of the Lord Jesus in any character in which He is revealed, but yet the cross is that whereon He is most lifted up, and this is the chief attraction for sinful men. Though it be to the Jews a stumblingblock and to the Greeks foolishness, it is still the power of God unto salvation to every one that believeth.

III. My time is nearly over, and therefore I must only for a minute touch upon the surface of my third subject: THE SIGHT OF CHRIST CRUCIFIED WILL PRODUCE A MOURNING FOR SIN OF A VERY THOROUGH CHARACTER. It will be *immediate*. If the Spirit of God grants us an inward sight of Christ, we shall bleed inwardly at once. The sentences are fast joined together: "They shall look upon me whom they have pierced, and they shall mourn." How rapidly the Spirit of God often works! "His word runneth very swiftly." With a single blow of grace the bars of iron are broken. Saul of Tarsus was foaming at the mouth with rage against Jesus of Nazareth and His disciples, but a flash and a word changed him. "Why persecutest thou me?' showed him the pierced Lord, and "Lord, what wilt thou have me to do?" was his speedy answer. One glimpse at Christ will make yonder stubborn sinner bow the knee. Look on him, Lord!

This mourning, according to our text, is *refined and pure*. They shall mourn *for Him*, they shall be in bitterness *for Him*. For Jesus they sorrow rather than for themselves. Sin is not mentioned in these verses, and yet the sorrow is all concerning sin. The grief for sin itself is overborne and compassed about by the greater grief occasioned by the sad results of sin upon the person of the pierced One. Sin is grieved over as it is against the Lord: even as David cries, "Against thee, thee only, have I sinned." The mounting of a penitent is not because of hell: if there were no hell he would mourn just as much. His grief is not for what sin might cost himself, but for what it has cost the Substitute. He bemoans himself thus: "Oh, how could I have pierced Him? How could I have wounded the Beloved? Lover of my soul, how could I have pierced Thee?" True penitents smite upon their breasts as they behold their Savior bleeding on the tree. This is the sense of sin which is the mark of God's electing love, the token of the effectual calling of His grace.

In this mourning there is a *touching tenderness*: "They shall be in bitterness for him, as one that is in bitterness for his firstborn." It is not a son lamenting for a father, for there the grief might be as much for the loss of the father's care and help as for the father's self; but in the case of a father mourning his young son, the father is not supposed to lose anything but his boy; his grief is for the child himself. Mourning for a son is caused by a peculiarly pure and unmixed love. Somewhat that is of the earth earthy may enter into the mourning for a wife; but for his son a father laments with a love which none may question. For an only son the mourning is bitter indeed, and for a firstborn it is as gall and wormwood. The Israelite was especially sensitive concerning the death of his offspring. To lose his firstborn was as when a nation loses its prince. To lose his only son was to quench the light of the house. The old man mourns, "I am as good as dead. I am blotted out of the blood of the living, for I have no son to bear my name. The lamp has gone out in my tent, for my son, my only son, my firstborn, has gone down to the gates of the grave!" The case was hopeless for the future; none remained to continue his family among those who sit in the gate, and the old man rent his clothes and wept sore. It is a bitter mourning which we have when we see Jesus slain by our sins. Were it not for the consequences which grace has caused to flow therefrom, our sorrow would be hopeless and helpless; for we feel that in killing Jesus we have destroyed our best, our only hope, our one and only joy. His death was the hiding of the sun, and the shaking of the earth, and we feel it to be so within our own souls. All that is worth having is gone when Jesus is gone. When God's only Son, His firstborn, dies, we sympathize with the great Father, and feel ourselves bereaved of our chief joy, our hope, our delight.

This sorrow is *intense*. The word "bitterness" is used twice. Sorrow at the crossfoot is sorrow indeed, sorrow upon sorrow, grief upon grief. Then we have bitterness and bitterness, bitterness upon bitterness, the bitterness of bitterness. Thank God, it is a healthy tonic: he that hath tasted this bitterness may say, "Surely the bitterness of death is past."

And this kind of mourning is *very extraordinary*. The prophet could not recollect any mourning which he had ever heard of that was like it, except the lamentation of the people for the death of Josiah. Then all Judah mourned, and Jeremiah wrote sad dirges, and other prophets and poets poured forth their lamentations. Everywhere throughout the land there went up an exceeding great and bitter cry, for the good king had fallen, and there were no princes of like mind to follow him. Alas, poor nation! It was thy last bright hour which saw him ride to the battle; in his death thy star has set! In the valley of Hadad-rimmon the mourning began, but it spread through all the land. The fatal fight of Megiddon was wailed by every woman in Jerusalem. Bravely had Josiah kept his word, and sought to repel the Egyptian invader; but the hour of Judah's punishment was come, and Josiah died. A mourning as sincere and deep comes to us when we perceive that Jesus died for us. Blessed be His name; the joy that comes of it when we see sin put away by His death, turns all the sorrow into joy.

This mourning is *personal grief*; every man repents apart, and every woman apart. It is a private, personal grief; it is not produced by the contagion of example, but by the conviction of the individual conscience. Such sorrow is only to be assuaged by Jesus Christ Himself when He is revealed as the salvation of God.

Brethren, I am conscious that I have not preached as I ought to have preached this morning. I have been mastered by my subject. I could sit down alone and picture my divine Master on the cross. I delight to do so. It is my comfort to meditate on Him. I see Him hanging on the tree, and carefully survey Him, from His head encircled with the thorns, down to His blessed feet, made by the nails to be fountains of crimson blood. I have wept behind the cross at the marks of the dread scourging which He bore; and then coming to the front I have gazed upon His pierced hands, and lingered long before that opened side. Then I feel as if I could die of a pleasing grief and mournful joy. Oh, how I then love and adore! But here before this crowd I am a mere lisper of words—words which fall far below the height of this great argument. Ah me! Ah me! Who among the sons of men could fitly tell you of His unknown agonies, His piercing anguish, His distraction and heartbreak? Who can fully interpret that awful cry of "*Eloi, Eloi, lama sabachthani?* My God, my God, why hast thou forsaken me?" Alone I can hide my face and bow my head; but here what can I do? O Lord, what can thy servant do?

> Words are but air, and tongues but clay,
> And thy compassions are divine.

I cannot tell of love's bleeding, love's agony, love's death! If the Holy Ghost will graciously come at this time, and put me and my words altogether aside, and set my Lord before you, evidently crucified among you, then shall I be content, and you will go home thoughtful, tender, hating sin, and therefore more deeply happy, more serenely glad than ever before. The Lord grant it for His name's sake! Amen.